AF842904

Eleventh Five Year Plan (2007–2012)

Inclusive Growth

Volume I

सत्यमेव जयते

Planning Commission
Government of India

OXFORD
UNIVERSITY PRESS

YMCA Library Building, Jai Singh Road, New Delhi 110 001

Oxford University Press is a department of the University of Oxford. It furthers the University's objective of excellence in research, scholarship, and education by publishing worldwide in

Oxford New York
Auckland Cape Town Dar es Salaam Hong Kong Karachi Kuala Lumpur Madrid Melbourne Mexico City Nairobi New Delhi Shanghai Taipei Toronto

With offices in
Argentina Austria Brazil Chile Czech Republic France Greece Guatemala Hungary Italy Japan Poland Portugal Singapore South Korea Switzerland Thailand Turkey Ukraine Vietnam

Oxford is a registered trademark of Oxford University Press in the UK and in certain other countries

Published in India
By Oxford University Press, New Delhi

© Planning Commission (Government of India) 2008

The moral rights of the authors have been asserted

First published 2008

All rights reserved. No part of this publication may be reproduced or transmitted, in any form or by any means, electronic or mechanical, including photocopying, recording or by any information storage and retrieval system, without permission in writing from Planning Commission, Government of India

ISBN-13: 978-0-19-569650-9
ISBN-10: 0-19-569650-6

Typeset in Minion in 11/13
by Eleven Arts, Keshav Puram, Delhi 110 035
Printed by Tara Art Printers Pvt. Ltd., Noida
Published by Oxford University Press
YMCA Library Building, Jai Singh Road, New Delhi 110 001
On behalf of Planning Commission, Government of India, Yojna Bhawan,
Sansad Marg, New Delhi 110 001

सत्यमेव जयते
प्रधानमंत्री
Prime Minister

Foreword

India's commitment to planned economic development is a reflection of our society's determination to improve the economic conditions of our people and an affirmation of the role of the government in bringing about this outcome through a variety of social, economic, and institutional means. The Eleventh Five Year Plan, which was approved by the National Development Council on 19 December 2007 reaffirms this commitment. It provides a comprehensive strategy for inclusive development, building on the growing strength of the economy, while also addressing weaknesses that have surfaced.

The strength of the economy is evident from the remarkable transition to a high growth path, which has been achieved in recent years. The Tenth Plan period (2002–03 to 2006–07) began modestly, but then saw the economy accelerating steadily to achieve an average growth rate of 7.7%, for the Plan period as a whole, which is the highest ever achieved in any Plan period. In the last four years the growth rate has averaged 8.9% making India one of the fastest growing economies in the world.

The transition to high growth is an impressive achievement, but we must not forget that growth is not the only measure of development. Our ultimate objective is to achieve broad based improvement in the living standards of all our people. Rapid growth is essential for this outcome because it provides the basis for expanding incomes and employment and also provides the resources needed to finance programmes for social uplift. However, it is not by itself sufficient. We also need to ensure that growth is widely spread so that its benefits, in terms of income and employment, are adequately shared by the poor and weaker sections of our society, especially the Scheduled Castes (SCs) and the Scheduled Tribes (STs), Other Backward Classes (OBCs) and minorities. For this to happen, the growth must be inclusive in the broadest sense. It must occur not just in our major cities but also in our villages and small towns. It must be spread across all states and not just limited to some. It must generate sufficient volumes of high quality employment to provide the means for uplift of large numbers of our population from the low income low quality occupations in which too many of them have been traditionally locked.

The Eleventh Plan addresses itself to the challenge of making growth both faster and more inclusive. The rapid growth achieved in the past several years demonstrates that we have learnt how to bring about growth, but we have yet to achieve comparable success in inclusiveness. Poverty, whether we look at it narrowly in terms of the population below consumption based poverty line or more broadly in terms of population without access to essential services, is definitely declining but the pace of decline is slower than it should be. Our people have a right to expect that the evidently increased economic capabilities of our economy are translated into accelerating progress in these dimensions also. The Eleventh Plan aims at achieving a radical transformation in this aspect of our development. It sets a target for 9% growth in the five year period 2007–08 to 2011–12 with acceleration during the period to reach 10% by the end of the Plan. It also identifies 26 other measurable indices of performance relating to poverty, education, health, women and children, infrastructure, and environment and sets monitorable targets in each of these.

Planning in a market economy which is becoming increasingly integrated with the world is bound to be different from what it used to be in earlier years. Much of what used to be done by governments, including especially the establishment of production units producing manufactured goods and commercial services, is now being done by the private sector. India is blessed in having a long tradition of private entrepreneurship and the private sector has responded magnificently to the new opportunities opened up by economic reforms. However, this does not mean that the role of the government must shrink. On the contrary, the government must play a much larger role in some areas even while shifting out of others.

The Eleventh Plan outlines the new priorities for the public sector. These relate to reviving dynamism in agriculture and building the necessary supportive infrastructure in rural areas, expanding access to health and education, especially in rural areas, undertaking programmes for improving living conditions for the weaker sections and for improving their access to economic opportunity. It also includes a major thrust for infrastructure development in general, which is a critical constraint on our development.

Improved performance in agriculture is necessary if our growth is to be inclusive. The Eleventh Plan adopts a multi-pronged approach towards this end. It provides for a major expansion in the programmes for irrigation and water management. The Rashtriya Krishi Vikas Yojana (RKVY) has been launched to assist the States in development and implementation of district level agricultural plans, based on local agro-climatic conditions. As a step towards food security, which has assumed special relevance in view of recent international developments, the National Food Security Mission aims at increasing cereal and pulses production by 20 million tons over a five year period.

There is a massive thrust in the Eleventh Plan on access to education and health, which are critical to social and economic empowerment of the people. In education, the Plan will spend more than double of what was spent in the Tenth Plan, as a proportion of the total budgetary support to Central Ministries. We have made good progress in providing access to primary education but there are quality issues that need to be addressed. We must also expand access to secondary education in the Eleventh Plan. In higher education, the Plan will work towards increasing enrolment rates from 11 to 21 percent over a ten year period. This will require a massive expansion in our university system. There will also be emphasis on creating competitive, world class institutions of higher learning. The National Skill Development Mission will help in meeting the demands for skills in our growing economy as well as in generating high quality employment. Both in higher education and skill development, the private sector will be encouraged to augment the government's efforts appropriately. Given the special focus on education in the Eleventh Plan, I have no hesitation in calling this Plan a 'National Education Plan'.

In health, the Plan aims at providing improved broad based health care in rural areas through the National Rural Health Mission. The Rashtriya Swasthya Bima Yojana will provide the much needed insurance cover against illness to the population below the poverty line. Our initiatives in implementing a nationwide mid-day meals scheme in schools and improving the implementation of the ICDS will also improve the health and nutrition status of our children.

Availability of affordable energy is critical for our growth. With international oil prices rising sharply over the last couple of years, and coal prices more recently, our efforts towards energy security have acquired urgency. The Eleventh Plan will work towards policies for various energy sectors that are consistent with the optimal use of the different sources of energy. The Plan emphasizes the need for energy conservation, increasing energy efficiency, and development of renewable sources of energy. Rational pricing of energy is necessary for a number of reasons and this requires transmission of permanent changes in prices to consumers while at the same time protecting the vulnerable sections of the society through appropriate interventions. These are challenges that we will have to overcome for achieving the targets and objectives of the Plan.

The very first year of the Eleventh Plan has seen a resurgence of inflation in the last quarter mainly due to the steep rise in international prices of oil and food-grains. Though these supply side factors are largely beyond our control, we have launched a determined effort to moderate the inflationary trend while simultaneously insulating the poor to the extent possible through targeted food and energy subsidies. These efforts will continue and I am confident that we can bring inflation under control in a manner which does not hurt the longer term growth prospects of the economy. This poses a major challenge for short term macroeconomic policies in the coming months.

An important aspect of the Eleventh Plan is that most of the public sector programmes are in areas that are normally in the domain of State Governments and where implementation depends upon the active involvement of local level bodies including the Panchayati Raj Institutions. More than any other Plan, the Eleventh Plan places a much greater reliance upon the involvement of the Panchayati Raj Institutions.

The higher rate of growth that we have set out for ourselves, coupled with our thrust on the growth process being inclusive, should ensure that the struggle for the removal of chronic poverty, ignorance, and disease will register major gains in the Eleventh Plan. I am confident that the Eleventh Plan will achieve its targets and objectives despite the challenges we face. This would be a major step in realizing our vision of a prosperous, inclusive, happy, and caring India where all citizens reap the benefits of economic development and feel empowered.

I congratulate the Deputy Chairman, Planning Commission and his team for putting together an excellent Plan. I also thank all those from whose advice we have benefitted in the formulation of the Plan.

Manmohan Singh

New Delhi
25 June 2008

(Manmohan Singh)

Preface

The Eleventh Plan began in very favourable circumstances with the economy having grown at the rate of 7.7% per year in the Tenth Plan period. However, far too many of our people still lack the basic requirements for a decent living in terms of nutrition standards, access to education and basic health, and also to other public services such as water supply and sewerage. Disadvantaged groups, especially the Scheduled Castes and Scheduled Tribes and the minorities have benefited less than they should have. Regional imbalances have emerged across and even within states.

The Eleventh Plan seeks to remedy these deficiencies by seeking to accelerate the pace of growth while also making it more inclusive. The growth objective is to achieve an average growth rate of 9% per annum for the Plan period. The objective of inclusiveness is reflected in the adoption of 26 other monitorable targets at the national level relating to (i) income and poverty, (ii) education, (iii) health, (iv) women and children, (v) infrastructure, and (vi) environment. Some of these national targets have also been disaggregated into 13 state level targets and it is expected that the state governments design policies and programmes to achieve them.

THE MACROECONOMIC PERSPECTIVE

The macroeconomic requirements for 9% growth are challenging but not impossible. The average investment rate must rise from 32% in the Tenth Plan to around 37% in the Eleventh Plan period, reaching 39% at the end of the period. This increase is entirely feasible. Private investment, which has been buoyant in the Tenth Plan, is expected to provide the bulk of the increased investment accounting for 78% of the total, about the same as in the Tenth Plan. The share of public investment in total investment has been declining over successive Plan periods from 34.7% in the Eighth Plan to 29% in the Ninth Plan and 22% in the Tenth Plan. In the Eleventh Plan its share is expected to stabilize at the level in the Tenth Plan implying that the volume of public investment must increase in line with private investment. This is necessary if we are to achieve the expansion in social sector investment and in infrastructure which is necessary for ensuring faster and more inclusive growth.

These rates of investment will be supported by a buoyant domestic savings rate of 34.8% and a relatively manageable current account deficit of around 2% of GDP. The household sector is the main contributor to the domestic savings, but the public sector is also expected to contribute positively to savings reflecting a significant turnaround compared with past experience. The projected current account deficit could easily be higher because of the likely continuance of high oil prices but even so, it should remain sustainable given the likely availability of foreign inflows.

The strategy for achieving faster growth with greater inclusiveness involves several interrelated components. These are: (i) a continuation of the policies of economic reform which have created a buoyant and competitive private sector capable of benefiting from the opportunities provided by greater integration with the world, (ii) a revival in agricultural growth which is the most important single factor affecting rural prosperity, (iii) improved access to essential services in health and education (including skill development) especially for the poor, which is essential to ensure inclusiveness and also to support rapid growth, (iv) a special thrust on infrastructure development which is a critical area for accelerating growth, (v) environmental sustainability which is becoming increasingly important, (vi) special attention to the needs of disadvantaged groups, and (vii) good governance at all levels, Central, state, and local.

As in most market economies, the dominant impulse for growth will come from the private sector. India is fortunate in having a strong private sector capability ranging from agriculture, which is entirely dependent on private farmers, most of whom have modest land holdings, through small and medium entrepreneurs in industry and services to larger domestic corporate entities, many of which benefit from FDI to varying degrees. The Eleventh Plan must ensure a policy environment that is supportive of this vibrant and globalized private sector which has an important contribution to make in India's future development.

Emphasizing the importance of the private sector is not to downplay the role of the government. On the contrary, apart from the usual role of government in providing a stable macroeconomic policy, the Eleventh Plan envisages a very large role for public policy in a number of sectors.

Agriculture and Rural Development

One of the most disappointing features of the Ninth Plan was the deceleration in agricultural growth which set in after the mid 1990s with GDP in agriculture growing at only around 2% per annum after growing at 3.6% per annum between 1980 and 1996. Reversing this deceleration to achieve a growth target of 4% per annum in agricultural GDP is a key element of the Eleventh Plan strategy for inclusive growth.

In the medium term, the focus has to be on improving yields with existing technology and there is considerable scope for doing so because yields obtained in the field in large parts of the country are much lower than what is achievable with existing technology, provided cultivation practices are improved and critical inputs made available. Timely availability of water is the most critical element in raising yields and the Plan therefore emphasizes expansion of irrigation where possible and also improvement of existing irrigation systems. Where irrigation is not possible—and this covers 60% of the land area—the solution lies in improving management of water resources through watershed development, covering rain water harvesting in farm ponds and tanks, and methods of ground water recharge. A major expansion in the Accelerated Irrigation Benefit Programme and a renewed thrust at watershed development has been planned. The National Rainfed Area Authority, which was established in 2006 and is now fully operational, is expected to help converge different programmes in rainfed areas to achieve better water management in rainfed areas.

On the output side, it is necessary to emphasize measures to ensure food security while also diversifying into non-foodgrain crops and promoting animal husbandry and fishery. The new National Food Security Mission, aims at increasing cereal and pulses production by 20 million tonnes by concentrating on those areas which have the greatest potential for increase in yields with given technology. The National Horticulture Mission which provides support for diversification has been expanded. A new Rashtriya Krishi Vikas Yojana (RKVY), has been introduced which provides additional financial resource to state governments to finance agriculture development programmes emerging from district level agricultural plans which take into account district specific agro-climatic constraints.

The strategy can be aided by the National Rural Employment Guarantee (NREG) Act which has put in place a historic rights-based employment guarantee which provides income support to the weaker sections of rural society. It can also serve the larger objective of enhancing agricultural productivity because the first priority under NREG is being given to projects aimed at water conservation. Effective convergence of resources available under NREG, with a large strategy for water management, will be crucial.

Education and Skill Development

An educated labour force is critical for achieving faster growth and education is also the key to ensuring greater inclusivity. The Eleventh Plan will build on ongoing efforts to strengthen elementary education. The infrastructure for primary schools has been almost completed under the Sarva Siksha Abhiyan and it is now necessary to focus our efforts on issues of quality and the expansion of infrastructure for secondary education. This involves upgradation of upper primary schools to secondary schools, expansion of intake capacity in existing secondary schools, and establishment of high quality model schools to serve as examples of excellence in secondary schooling. The quality of education in public schools suffers from a variety of problems including widespread teacher absenteeism, inadequate teacher training, outdated pedagogy, and insufficient accountability. These problems need to be addressed urgently by state governments and by the PRIs if we are to provide equality of opportunity for our weaker sections especially in the rural areas.

Higher education will be a key driver in an increasingly globalized and knowledge-driven world and we need to increase the enrolment rate in higher education from around 11% at present to 21% over a ten annum period. This will require a massive expansion in the university system which must be combined with efforts to create competitive world class institutions of higher education. Given the scarcity of resources, private sector initiatives in higher education and various forms of public–private partnerships (PPPs) must be encouraged.

Apart from formal education, there is need to expand the skill capabilities in the labour force as a precondition for embarking on a labour intensive growth process. At present, only 20% of those entering the workforce get some kind of formal training. This proportion must be greatly increased. The Plan proposes a National Skill Development Mission to expand and restructure the public sector skill development efforts and also to support private skill development initiatives in several high growth sectors of the economy.

Health and Nutrition

We have made progress in several areas related to health as evidenced by the success in eliminating or controlling diseases such as small pox, leprosy, polio, and TB, all of which is reflected in the steadily rising life expectancy of the population. However, there are other indicators which highlight serious problems in certain critical areas. High levels of malnutrition continue to affect a large part of our child population, limiting their learning capacity and influencing morbidity and mortality ratios in the country. Our maternal mortality rates and infant mortality rates are far too high. The incidence of anaemia among women and children is at unacceptable levels. Far too large a proportion of the population, especially in rural areas, lacks access to affordable health care.

These problems need to be addressed by multiple interventions, many of which range beyond curative health care. These include dietary improvement, nutrition supplementation for children, better child care practices, access to safe drinking water, improved sanitation, and immunization. However, these efforts must be accompanied by a much better system of affordable curative health care which is lacking at present. The National Rural Health Mission is an important step in providing broad based improvement in health care for the rural population. The Rashtriya Swasthya Bima Yojana is a new and important innovation providing the population below the poverty line with an insurance policy covering hospital treatment for a defined set of conditions with the government meeting the premium wit. The policy allows the patient to choose from multiple service suppliers including private hospitals who join the system.

Infrastructure Development

Poor quality of infrastructure seriously limits India's growth potential in the medium term and the Eleventh Plan outlines a comprehensive strategy for development of both rural and urban infrastructure, defined to include electric power, roads, railways, ports, airports, telecommunications, irrigation, drinking water, sanitation, storage, and warehousing. The total investment in these areas was around 5% of GDP in 2006–07 and the Plan aims at increasing this to about 9% of GDP by the terminal annum 2011–12.

Since various social sector and livelihood support programmes for the poor will have the first charge on public resources, the strategy for infrastructure development has been designed to rely as much as possible on private sector investment through various forms of PPPs. The Plan recognizes that the scope for private participation in infrastructure development in several areas is limited and the infrastructure requirement of these areas therefore, has to be met through public investment. However, it is therefore all the more necessary that the fullest possible use must be made of opportunities to attract private sector investment wherever this is feasible. Both the Centre and the states have seen varying degrees of success in attracting private investment in areas such as power generation, telecommunications, roads, railways, airports, and ports, though much more needs to be done.

The Central Government has sought to evolve policies for private sector participation which are transparent and where the responsibilities of the private concessionaire are clearly defined. Where the nature of the investment involves an element of monopoly rather than free entry by competing suppliers, the choice of concessionaire must be determined by an open competitive bidding process and standards of service should be clearly set and monitored by an independent regulatory authority. The key to successful PPP is that the public must perceive that PPP has added value in terms of the scale of services and also quality and cost.

Special attention is being paid to the Bharat Nirman programme which focuses on the provision of key elements of rural infrastructure such as irrigation, rural electrification, rural roads, rural drinking water supply and sanitation, housing for the poor, and rural connectivity via community IT service centres.

Urban Infrastructure

The rate of urbanization in India has been relatively slow so far, but faster growth is likely to change this in future leading to a faster pace of urbanization in the years ahead. Urbanization is a natural outcome of the process of development and we must gear up to the challenge to meet the need for providing infrastructure and utilities in the cities. It will be necessary to upgrade the quality of infrastructure in existing cities to provide improved municipal services and also to develop new cities and suburban townships in the vicinity of existing cities as satellites/counter magnets to redistribute the influx of population.

Urban infrastructure is expensive to construct and, the financial condition of most of our cities is such that they will not be able to finance the scale of investment for quite some time. Accordingly, the Jawaharlal Nehru National Urban Renewal Mission (JNNURM) seeks to provide Central assistance for urban infrastructure development linked to a process of reforms at the city and urban local body level which would make these bodies more financially viable, and ultimately capable of financing the investment we need in urban areas. The JNNURM has got off to a good start, but close monitoring will be necessary in the Eleventh Plan to ensure successful implementation of individual projects and also the larger reforms agenda.

Energy

As in other developing countries, our ability to sustain rapid growth will depend critically upon the availability or affordability of energy. The Eleventh Plan faces special challenges in this area since the start of the Plan coincides with a period of sharp increase in the world prices of petroleum products and a growing concern about the need to increase energy efficiency, both to economize on costs and also to reduce carbon emissions, as much as possible. These challenges must be met in a manner which does not come in the way of our objective of achieving faster and more inclusive growth. It will be essential to ensure efficient functioning of the major energy sectors to maximize domestic production of energy and also to import additional energy as needed. Energy pricing has a critical role to play in this context.

It will be necessary to evolve appropriate policies for the major energy producing sectors—electricity, coal, oil and gas, and various forms of renewable energy—which are consistent with optimal use of all these energy sources. The Eleventh Plan outlines a broad approach based on the Integrated Energy Policy formulated earlier by the Planning Commission. The sharp increase in international oil prices and also in coal prices poses a major challenge. While large price increases cannot be suddenly transmitted to the economy in one go, artificially suppressing energy prices cannot be a viable solution for an energy deficit economy. It comes in the way of expanding domestic supply, promoting energy conservation and demand management, and also encouraging growth of alternative energy sources. A gradual transmission of permanent changes in these prices is both possible and necessary and can be combined with protecting the most vulnerable sections of the community from sharp price changes.

The compulsions of moving to a rational energy policy are underlined by the emerging threat of climate change which presents special challenges over the longer term. The burden for reducing energy emissions must fall largely on the industrialized countries, which have contributed the most in creating the problem in the past and which today have much higher levels of per capita emissions than India. However, we also need to play our part in containing the growth of our per capita emissions to sustainable levels.

THE ROLE OF GOVERNMENT

As pointed out earlier, the strategy for delivering faster and more inclusive growth will require an expansion in the role of government in several areas. The Eleventh Plan envisages an expansion in the size of the Plan (Centre plus states) from 9.46% of GDP in the Tenth Plan to 13.54% of GDP in the Eleventh Plan. Part of this increase will come from expanded budgetary support from the Plan and the rest from the internal and extra budgetary reserves of the public sector at the Central Government and the state government levels.

The increase in budget resources depends critically upon the ability of both the Centre and the states to maintain the high growth in tax revenues observed in recent years. This will depend to some extent upon the pace of growth since rapid growth will produce buoyant revenues, but it will also depend significantly upon the continuation and deepening of tax reforms. The strategy of simplifying the tax structure and streamlining tax administration has generated better compliance in both the Centre and the states which is reflected in the rising share of taxes in GDP. This trend must be made to continue. Another important element in mobilizing resources for public investment is the ability to contain subsidies and use the resources thus saved to undertake much needed public investment. A comprehensive revision of subsidies in the system, including hidden subsidies of one type or another, with a view to rationalizing them to retain only those aimed at the truly vulnerable, is needed. The present subsidies on petroleum products are particularly relevant in this context.

A second aspect of the changed role of government in the Eleventh Plan is that the public sector will increasingly concentrate in areas that lie in the domain of the state governments, and within the states in the domain of panchayati raj institutions. This is especially true of elementary education, health, rural drinking water, rural sanitation, child nutrition, housing for the poor, the national employment guarantee, and schemes for watershed management. Programmes in these areas are implemented at the local level and often depend critically upon local level authorities and the system of governance and accountability should therefore be at the local level. The 93rd and 94th Amendments to the constitution were landmark steps in empowering the Panchayats and urban local bodies and to give full effect to these amendments it is necessary to transfer functions, functionaries, and funds to the PRIs. While the functions to be transferred have been clearly identified, the actual progress made in transferring the functionaries and funds remain limited. It is also necessary to build capacity at the local level. NGOs can play an important role in building capacity or in encouraging empowerment or participation or ways should be found of engaging the NGO community more actively in local level programmes.

THE EXTERNAL ENVIRONMENT

Work on the Eleventh Plan began in 2006 and the Plan was finally approved by the NDC in December 2007. During this period, there were significant developments in the world economy, the implications of which are not easy to quantify at this point. Oil prices increased very sharply in 2006 and this continued through 2007. Although there was uncertainty initially about whether they would return to more normal levels, the assessment today is that high oil prices are likely to continue, and indeed further increases cannot be ruled out. There has also been a massive increase in world prices of foodgrains and edible oils reflecting a variety of factors, some short term such as drought and low production in some of the major producing countries, and others long term such as the shift of land from foodgrains production to the production of biofuel crops, reflecting policies of industrialized countries on incentivizing such a shift. There has also been a sharp rise in prices of metals and mineral ores in world markets.

As price pressures have built up in world markets, the world economy also gives signs of entering a cyclical downturn led by a sharp slowdown in the United States. The extent and duration of this cyclical downturn remains uncertain, but it will clearly have some effect on the underlying growth potential of emerging market economies. The Indian economy is less dependent on global demand than many East Asian countries and therefore the impact of a global slowdown on India will be less than for others, but we are also much more integrated than in the past and we should therefore expect that just as we benefit from global prosperity in the upswing we will be affected by the downswing, although less than others.

These developments present formidable challenges as we implement the Eleventh Plan. The Plan is formulated on the assumption that it should be possible for the economy to meet these challenges while still achieving the medium term growth objective of 9% inclusive growth. The objective may have become more difficult, but it is still manageable, provided suitable policies, some of which are not easy to implement, are put in place.

The Tenth Plan marked a historic breakthrough on the aggregate GDP growth front. The challenge before the Eleventh Plan is to improve upon this growth performance and also ensure greater sustainability and inclusiveness so that the development process being unleashed has the widest possible spread of benefits. In the search for inclusion, the Plan pays special attention to the needs of the weaker sections including the Scheduled Castes, Scheduled Tribes, OBCs, and minorities. The objectives of the Plan cannot have meaning if they are not translated into a visible flow of benefits to these groups.

(Montek Singh Ahluwalia)
Deputy Chairman

New Delhi
25 June 2008

Contents

Tables

Figures

Boxes

Annexures

Acronyms

ACA	Additional Central Assistance
ADIP	Assistance to Disabled Persons for Purchase/Fitting of Aids/Appliances
AHWR	Advanced Heavy Water Reactor
AIBP	Accelerated Irrigation Benefit Programme
AICTE	All India Council for Technical Education
AICOPTAX	All India Coordinated Project on Taxonomy
APDRP	Accelerated Power Development and Reform Programme
APSARA	Assessment of Passive System Reliability
APTA	Asia-Pacific Trade Agreement
AR4	Fourth Assessment Report
ARC	Administrative Reforms Commission
ASHA	Accredited Social Health Activist
ATI	Advanced Training Institute
BADP	Border Areas Development Programme
BCR	Balance from Current Revenues
BOD	Biochemical Oxygen Demand
BPL	Below Poverty Line
BPO	Business Process Outsourcing
BRGF	Backward Regions Grants Fund
BSI	Botanical Survey of India
BTX	Benzene, Toluence, and Xylene
CAAPs	Clean Air Action Plans
CAD	Computer Aided Design
CADP	Command Area Development Programme
CAM	Computer Aided Manufacturing
CAPART	Council for Advancement of People's Action and Rural Technology
CBO	Community-based Organization
CBWTF	Common Bio-medical Waste Treatment Facilities
CCPD	Chief Commissioner for Persons with Disabilities
CDB	Core Database
CCI	Competition Commission of India
CDC	Consultancy Development Centre
CDM	Clean Development Mechanism
CDS	'Current Daily Status' Basis
CETP	Common Effluent Treatment Plant
CFC	Certified Filing Centre
CHC	Community Health Centre
CIN	Corporate Identity Number
CO_2	
COS	Committee of Secretaries
CPCB	Central Pollution Control Board
CPSE	Central Public Sector Enterprise
CPSU	Central Public Sector Units
CSC	Common Service Centre
CSIR	Council of Scientific and Industrial Research
CSO	Civil Society Organization
CSS	Centrally Sponsored Schemes
CSTC	Central Standing Tripartite Committee
CWS	Current Weekly Status
DAE	Department of Atomic Energy
DBT	Department of Biotechnology
DDP	District Domestic Product
DEM	Digital Elevation Map
DGCA	Director General Civil Aviation
DIN	Director Identification Number
DIT	Department of Information Technology

DLCP	Dal Lake Conservation Project
DMS	Data Management System
DO	Dissolved Oxygen
DoNER	(Ministry of) Development of North Eastern Region
DoS	Department of Space
DPC	District Planning Committees
DRM	Disaster Risk Mitigation
DSIR	Department of Scientific and Industrial Research
DST	Department of Science and Technology
EAP	Externally Aided Projects
EBR	Extra-Budgetary Resources
ECB	External Commercial Borrowing
EDI	Entrepreneurship Development Institutes
EIA	Environmental Impact Assessment
ENVIS	Environment Information System
FAIR	Facility for Antiproton and Ion Research
FDI	Foreign Direct Investment
FII	Foreign Institutional Investment
FIPB	Foreign Investment Promotion Board
FOB	Free on Board
FRBM	Fiscal Responsibility and Budget Management
FTA	Free Trade Agreement
GAP	Ganga Action Plan
GBPIHED	GB Pant Institute of Himalayan Environment and Development
GBS	Gross Budgetary Support
GCI	Global Competitive Index
GDP	Gross Domestic Product
GDP_{mp}	Gross Domestic Product at market prices
GEF	Global Environment Facility
GER	Gross Enrolment Ratio
GHG	Green House Gas
GIS	Geographical Information System
GMO	Genetically Modified Organism
GMP	Good Manufacturing Practices
GoI	Government of India
GSLV	Geosynchronous Launch Vehicle
GST	Goods and Service Tax
GSTP	Global System of Trade Preferences
HACCP	Hazard Analysis and Critical Control Points
HADP	Hill Area Development Programme
HBNC	Home Based Newborn Care
HDI	Human Development Index
HDR	Human Development Reports
HLC	High Level Committee
HPI	Human Poverty Index
HRD	Human Resources Development
IAY	Indira Awaas Yojana
ICAR	Indian Council of Agricultural Research
ICDS	Integrated Child Development Scheme
ICFRE	Indian Council of Forestry Research and Education
ICOR	Incremental Capital Output Ratio
IEBR	Internal and Extra Budgetary Resources
IIFCL	India Infrastructure Finance Company Ltd.
IITM	Indian Institute of Tropical Meteorology
IMD	India Meteorological Department
INO	Indian Neutrino Observatory
INSPIRE	Innovation in Science Pursuit for Inspired Research'
IPCC	Intergovernmental Panel on Climate Change
IT	Information Technology
ITES	IT enabled services
JFM	Joint Forest Management
JNNURM	Jawaharlal Nehru National Urban Renewal Mission
JRF	Junior Research Fellow
LGBRIMH	LGB Regional Institute of Mental Health, Tezpur
MCA	Model Concession Agreements
MFP	Minor Forest Produce
mg	Milligram
MLD	Million Litres per Day
MMA	Ministry of Minority Affairs
MMPs	Mission Mode Projects
MNRE	Ministry of New and Renewable Energy
MoEF	Ministry of Environment and Forests
MoES	Ministry of Earth Sciences
MSEs	Micro and Small Enterprises
MSMEs	Micro, Small and Medium Enterprises
MSP	Minimum Support Price
MW_e	Megawatt electrical
NBCFDC	National Backward Classes Finance and Development Corporation
NCA	Normal Central Assistance

NCCS	National Centre for Cell Science
NCEUS	National Commission for Employment in the Unorganized Sector
NCMP	National Common Minimum Programme
NCMRWF	National Centre for Medium Range Weather Forecasting
NCP	National Competition Policy
NDC	National Development Council
NDMA	National Disaster Management Authority
NDMP	National Disaster Mitigation Programme
NEC	North East Council
NEMP	National Environmental Monitoring Programme
NEPA	North East Police Academy
NFHS	National Family Health Survey
NHDP	National Highways Development Programme
NIC	National Informatics Centre
NITA	National Institute of Tribal Affairs
NISER	National Institute of Science Education and Research, Bhubaneswar
NLCP	National Lake Conservation Plan
NLCPR	Non-Lapsable Central Pool of Resources
NMITLI	New Millennium Indian Technology Leadership Initiative
NMNH	National Museum of Natural History
NPOP	National Policy on Older Persons
NPRE	Non-Plan Revenue Expenditure
NRCD	National River Conservation Directorate
NRCP	National River Conservation Plan
NREGA	National Rural Employment Guarantee Act
NREGP	National Rural Employment Guarantee Programme
NRHM	National Rural Health Mission
NRI	Non Resident Indian
NRM	Natural Resource Management
NSAP	National Social Assistance Programme
NSDP	Net State Domestic Product
NSFDC	National Scheduled Castes Finance and Development Corporation
NSSO	National Sample Survey Organization
NSTFDC	National Scheduled Tribes Finance and Development Corporation
NTFP	Non Timber Forest Produce
OBC	Other Backward Class
PAB	Project Approval Board
PAH	Polyaromatic hydrocarbons
PCB	Pollution Control Board
PESA	Panchayat (Extension to Scheduled Areas) Act
PFBR	Prototype Fast Breeder Reactor
PHC	Primary Health Centre
PHWR	Pressurized Heavy Water Reactor
PIM	Participatory Irrigation Management Act
PMGSY	Pradhan Mantri Gram Sadak Yojana
POL	Petroleum, Oil and Lubricants
PPP	Public–Private Partnership
PPPAC	Public–Private Partnership Appraisal Committee
PRI	Panchayati Raj Institution
PSE	Public Sector Enterprise
PSLV	Polar Satellite Launch Vehicle
PSU	Public Sector Undertaking
PTG	Primitive Tribal Group
QR	Quantitative Restriction
RCA	Revealed Comparative Advantage
RD	Rural Development
RFP	Request for Proposal Document
RGGVY	Rajiv Gandhi Grameen Vidyutikaran Yojana
RIMS	Regional Institute of Medical Sciences
RIPAN	Regional Institute of Para-medical and Nursing
RKVY	Rashtriya Krishi Vikas Yojana
RRB	Regional Rural Bank
RSPM	Respirable Suspended Particulate Matter
RTI	Right to Information Act
SAFTA	South Asian Free Trade Agreement
SARDP-NE	Special Accelerated Road Development Programme for the North East
SBBs	State Boards
SC	Scheduled Caste
SCA	Special Central Assistance
SCDC	Scheduled Castes Development Corporation
SCSP	Scheduled Caste Sub Plan
SDC	Skill Development Centre
SDH	Sub-Divisional Hospital
SERC	Science and Engineering Research Council
SFR	State of Forest Report
SGRY	Sampoorna Grameen Rozgar Yojana

SGSY	Swarnjayanti Gram Swarojgar Yojana
SHDR	State Human Development Reports
SHE	Scholarships for Higher Education
SHG	Self-Help Group
SJSRY	Swarna Jayanti Shahri Rozgar Yojana
SME	Small and medium scale enterprise
SO_2	Sulphur Dioxide
SoI	Survey of India
SSA	Sarva Siksha Abhiyan
ST	Scheduled Tribe
STP	Sewage Treatment Plant
SWAN	State-Wide Area Network
TAC	Tribes Advisory Council
TBA	Traditional Birth Attendant
TFC	Twelfth Finance Commission
TPDU	Technology Promotion, Development and Utilization Programme
TRIFED	Tribal Cooperative Marketing Development Federation of India Ltd.
TSC	Total Sanitation Campaign
TSDF	Transport, Storage and Disposal Facilities
TSP	Tribal Sub Plan
TTC	Technology Transfer Cell
UGC	University Grants Commission
UID	Unique ID
UIDSSMT	Urban Infrastructure Development Scheme for Small and Medium Towns
ULBs	Urban Local Bodies
UNCRPD	United Nations Convention on the Rights of People with Disabilities
UNESCO	United Nations Educational, Scientific and Cultural Organization
UNFCCC	United Nations Framework Convention on Climate Change
UNODC	United Nations Office on Drug and Crime
UPSS	Usual Principal and Subsidiary Status
us	Usual Status
USOF	Universal Service Obligation Fund
UT	Union Territory
VET	Vocational Education and Training
VGF	Viability Gap Funding
VO	Voluntary Organization
VOC	Volatile Organic Compound
VRC	Village Resource Centre
WGDP	Western Ghats Development Programme
WPR	Work Participation Rate
ZPs	Zilla Panchayat
ZSI	Zoological Survey of India

1

Inclusive Growth

Vision and Strategy

INTRODUCTION

1.1. India has entered the Eleventh Plan period with an impressive record of economic growth. After a lacklustre performance in the Ninth Plan period (1997–98 to 2001–02), when gross domestic product (GDP) grew at only 5.5% per annum, the economy accelerated in the Tenth Plan period (2002–03 to 2006–07) to record an average growth of 7.7%, the highest in any Plan period so far. Besides, there was acceleration even within the Tenth Plan period and the growth rate in the last four years of the Plan has averaged 8.7%, making India one of the fastest growing economies in the world.

1.2. It can be argued that there is an element of cyclicality in the high growth observed in the past four years since these were also years of a global upswing. However, India's growth performance goes beyond mere cyclicality. It is underpinned by a number of factors which are real sources of strength and will serve us well in the years ahead. Savings and investment rates have increased significantly. The industrial sector has responded well to economic reforms and has shown that it is capable of competing in the global economy. Perceptions about India among global investors are very favourable. These developments suggest that the economy is now at a point when it can achieve sustained economic expansion that has the potential to bring significant improvement in the lives of our people. If this momentum can be accelerated in the years ahead, it will put India on the path to becoming one of the key players in the world economy over the next two decades.

1.3. These positive factors notwithstanding, a major weakness in the economy is that the growth is not perceived as being sufficiently inclusive for many groups, especially Scheduled Castes (SCs), Scheduled Tribes (STs), and minorities. Gender inequality also remains a pervasive problem and some of the structural changes taking place have an adverse effect on women. The lack of inclusiveness is borne out by data on several dimensions of performance.

1.4. The percentage of the population below the official poverty line has come down from 36% in 1993–94 to 28% in 2004–05. However, not only is this still high, the rate of decline in poverty has not accelerated along with the growth in GDP, and the incidence of poverty among certain marginalized groups, for example the STs, has hardly declined at all. Because population has also grown, the absolute number of poor people has declined only marginally from 320 million in 1993–94 to 302 million in 2004–05. This performance is all the more disappointing since the poverty line on which the estimate of the poor is based is the same as it was in 1973–74 when per capita incomes were much lower. Other indicators of deprivation suggest that the proportion of the population deprived of a minimum level of living is much higher. For example, National Family Health Survey-3 (NFHS-3) shows that almost 46% of the children in the 0 to 3 years' age group suffered from malnutrition in 2005–06, and what is even more disturbing is that the estimate shows almost no decline from the level of 47% reported in 1998 by NFHS-2.

1.5. Indicators of human development such as literacy and education, and maternal and infant mortality rates, show steady improvement, but they also suggest that the progress is slow and we continue to lag behind several other Asian countries. While the literacy rate has gone up from 18.3% in 1951 to 64.8% in 2001, the number of illiterate persons still exceeds 304 million, making India the country with the highest number of illiterate persons in the world. Life expectancy at birth has increased from approximately 32 years for both males and females in 1951 to 63.9 years for males and 66.9 years for females in 2001–06. Yet this is well below the life expectancy of around 80 years in industrialized countries and 72 years in China. Although Indian women now have higher life expectancy than Indian men, as is the case in industrialized countries, India also has an adverse sex ratio with only 933 women per 1000 men. More disturbing, the child sex ratio (ages 0–6) has declined sharply from 962 in 1981 to 927 in 2001. India's maternal and infant mortality rates are much higher than those of countries in East Asia, showing poor access to essential health care services.

1.6. The composition of growth in recent years has also presented some problems. Agriculture has grown very slowly from the Ninth Plan onwards and this has widened the rural–urban divide and also contributed to the severe distress in rural areas in some regions. Although there is an upturn in agricultural growth after 2004, it is too early to be complacent. Total employment in the economy has improved in recent years, but the labour force has grown even faster, leading to an increase in the unemployment rate. Permanent employment in the organized sector has decreased, although organized sector firms may be increasing their informal employment. Also, economic growth across regions has not been balanced, with some of the most backward areas yet to experience any significant growth. The delivery of essential social services at the grass roots level is also poor and this is a major causative factor in unequal development. Much higher levels of human development can be achieved even with the given structure of the economy, if only the delivery system is improved.

1.7. These features suggest that while there are significant economic achievements that India can celebrate in its 60th year of Independence, it is still far from redeeming the pledge which Pandit Jawaharlal Nehru made on the eve of Independence: '[...] for ending of poverty, ignorance, disease and inequality of opportunity'. The Eleventh Plan provides an opportunity to act decisively to consolidate the gains that have been made in the Tenth Plan and also to correct the deficiencies that have been observed.

VISION FOR THE ELEVENTH PLAN

1.8. The central vision of the Eleventh Plan is to build on our strengths to trigger a development process which ensures broad-based improvement in the quality of life of the people, especially the poor, SCs/STs, other backward castes (OBCs), minorities and women. The National Development Council (NDC), in approving the Approach to the Eleventh Plan, endorsed a target of 9% GDP growth for the country as a whole. This growth is to be achieved in an environment in which the economy is much more integrated into the global economy, an integration that has yielded many benefits but also poses many challenges. If this is achieved, it would mean that per capita GDP would grow at about 7.6% per year to double in less than ten years. However the target is not just faster growth but also inclusive growth, that is, a growth process which yields broad-based benefits and ensures equality of opportunity for all.

1.9. This broad vision of the Eleventh Plan includes several inter-related components: rapid growth that reduces poverty and creates employment opportunities, access to essential services in health and education especially for the poor, equality of opportunity, empowerment through education and skill development, employment opportunities underpinned by the National Rural Employment Guarantee, environmental sustainability, recognition of women's agency and good governance.

RAPID GROWTH AND POVERTY REDUCTION

1.10. The persistence of poverty on the scale at which it still exists is not acceptable. A decisive reduction in poverty and an expansion in economic opportunities for all sections of the population should therefore be a crucial element of the vision for the Eleventh Plan. Rapid growth of the economy is an essential requirement to achieve this outcome since it is an instrument for achieving a steady increase in employment and incomes for large numbers of our people.

1.11. Growth in the Eleventh Plan should be better balanced to rapidly create jobs in the industrial and services sectors. This is necessary if a significant portion of the labour force is to shift out of agriculture, where it is currently engaged in low productivity employment, into a non-agricultural activity that can provide higher real incomes per head. This must be accompanied by efforts to improve the income-earning opportunities of those who remain in agriculture by raising land productivity. This process would also lead to higher farm incomes and a rise in real wages of agricultural labour whose bargaining power will improve as surplus labour is shifted out of this sector.

1.12. Rapid growth in the economy at large, and especially in the employment generating sectors such as medium and small industry and services, needs to be supplemented by targeted livelihood support programmes aimed at increasing productivity and incomes of the poor in several low income occupations which will continue as important sources of employment for quite some time. Special programmes aimed at target groups such as small and micro enterprises, weavers, artisans, craftsmen, etc. will therefore remain important in the Eleventh Plan period. Considerable experience has been gained over the years in the management of these programmes. This experience must be brought to bear in redesigning the programmes in the Eleventh Plan to make them more effective in achieving their stated objectives.

The Employment Challenge

1.13. The ability to generate an adequate number of productive employment opportunities will be a major factor on which the inclusiveness of growth will be judged. India is currently at a stage of 'demographic transition' where population growth is slowing down but the population of young people entering the labour force continues to expand. This means that a working person will have fewer dependents, children or parents. The dependency ratio (ratio of dependent to working age population) declined from 0.8 in 1991 to 0.73 in 2001 and is expected to decline further to 0.59 by 2011. If the workforce is gainfully employed, a lower dependency ratio means a higher rate of savings which, in turn, can raise the growth rate. This young demographic profile places India favourably in terms of manpower availability and could be a major advantage in an environment where investment is expanding in India and the industrial world is ageing.

1.14. It is, however, essential to produce a growth process in which employment would be available not only for new entrants to the labour force but also in the non-agricultural sector for workers leaving agriculture. Over 1999–2000 to 2004–05, urban employment has grown at a faster rate than population. However, since more urban women have joined the workforce, the unemployment rate has increased over these years.

1.15. Rapid growth focused on labour-intensive industries and small and middle enterprises will create employment opportunities in the manufacturing and services sectors. The ability to create jobs will be enhanced by greater labour flexibility which may require some changes in labour laws. This is a controversial issue on which it is difficult to reach a consensus but the weight of evidence suggests that while outright hire and fire approaches may not be desirable, there is room for creating greater flexibility, short of this position.

1.16. The ability to sustain a labour-intensive growth process depends crucially upon the expansion of skill capabilities in the labour force. Specific programmes for development of skills at all levels will be a part of the Eleventh Plan.

Access to Essential Services

1.17. A person is poor because her endowments of capital, land, labour and skills are meagre, and also because her access to public goods and services and natural resources is limited. Often, a poor person is trapped in the prison of illiteracy. Disease and ill-health prevent her from getting the most out of the one asset she has, her labour. Without training and skills she cannot aspire to do a better job. Without an all-weather road that connects her habitation to the nearest market, she cannot get a fair price for her produce. Without electricity and access to credit, her ability to increase productivity of land or of artisan activity is limited. Without the sewers and drains, water works and water mains that service her town; without the policing that should protect her life and limb, property (however meagre), person and dignity as an equal citizen of India; she cannot function effectively. Thus, while in the short run, access to basic facilities such as health, education, clean drinking water, etc. impacts directly on welfare, in the longer run, it determines economic opportunities for the future. Without access to these services one cannot be considered to have equality of opportunity.

1.18. Since access to these services for the majority of the population depends not only upon their income levels but upon the delivery of these services through publicly funded systems, the Eleventh Plan's vision of poverty reduction includes major expansion in the supply of these services. The resources needed to create the infrastructure necessary for delivering these services to the poor are large. Fortunately, the rapid growth being targeted for the Eleventh Plan will facilitate the ability to undertake these programmes, both by way of higher tax revenues resulting from higher growth and a larger borrowing capability even while adhering to fiscal deficit targets expressed as a percentage of GDP. These additional resources can be devoted to Plan expenditure aimed at ensuring effective delivery of essential services.

SOCIAL JUSTICE AND EMPOWERMENT

1.19. The vision of inclusiveness must go beyond the traditional objective of poverty alleviation to encompass equality of opportunity, as well as economic and social mobility for all sections of society, with affirmative action for SCs, STs, OBCs, minorities and women. There must be equality of opportunity to all with freedom and dignity, and without social or political obstacles. This must be accompanied by an improvement in the opportunities for economic and social advancement. In particular, individuals belonging to disadvantaged groups should be provided special opportunities to develop their skills and participate in the growth process.

1.20. This outcome can only be ensured if there is a degree of empowerment that creates a true feeling of participation so necessary in a democratic polity. Empowerment of disadvantaged and hitherto marginalized groups is therefore an essential part of any vision of inclusive growth. India's democratic polity, with the establishment of the third layer of democracy at the Panchayati Raj Institution (PRI) level, provides opportunities for empowerment and participation of all groups with reservations for SCs, STs, and women. These institutions should be made more effective through greater delegation of power and responsibility to the local level.

ENVIRONMENTAL SUSTAINABILITY

1.21. The vision of the Eleventh Plan must also include a clear commitment to pursue a development process which is environmentally sustainable. Natural resources such as water and land are limited and their per capita availability is actually diminishing because of rising population and also because of irrational exploitation of common pool resources. The Eleventh Plan must be based on a strategy that not only preserves and maintains natural resources, but also provides equitable access to those who do not have such access at present. Unless environment protection is brought to the centre stage of policy formulation, what is perceived as development may actually lead to a deteriorating quality of life. This seems to be happening all around, in the poor and generally worsening quality of air in cities and even villages; in the increasingly polluted waters of our lakes and rivers, which are not fit for even bathing, let alone drinking; in the loss of biodiversity, and in the shrinking habitats of wild animals. This degradation of natural resources reduces the well-being of people, and the poor and women suffer more, as they depend much more on natural common property resources for fuel and water, and also have fewer resources to take defensive actions.

1.22. The danger to environment is caused by activities worldwide. The growing evidence on climate change shows that Green House Gas (GHG) emissions, resulting from the cumulative action of all countries, will, if not effectively contained, produce changes in climate which would have very severe effects in the future. India will be seriously affected by such climate change in the form of receding Himalayan glaciers, a variably different hydrological cycle than at present, greater water scarcity and higher temperatures which would have an adverse impact on agricultural production with the presently known technologies. A rise in the sea level, leading to coastal submergence would cause large-scale displacement of people.

1.23. We must certainly begin to consider what steps we need to take to adapt to these changes and to mitigate the damage to climate. However, an effective strategy requires international co-operation to evolve forms of burden sharing for mitigation as well as adaptation that are fair and equitable across nations. We have to address these challenges in the years ahead.

GENDER EQUITY

1.24. For the first time in the history of Indian planning there is an attempt to move beyond empowerment and recognize women as agents of sustained socio-economic growth and change. The Eleventh Five Year Plan acknowledges women's agencies and tries to ensure that their needs, rights and contribution are reflected in every section of the Plan document. Gender is, therefore, a cross cutting theme; it is not confined to a single chapter on Women and Children. The vision is to develop an integrated approach which would eventually dispense the need for a separate chapter.

1.25. While endeavoring to guarantee the rights and entitlements of all women, the Eleventh Plan recognizes that women are not a homogenous category. Their situations, and consequently requirements, differ based on their locations within various castes, communities, religions, geographic and development zones and the effort during the Eleventh Plan is to cater to all these differential and specific requirements.

GOVERNANCE

1.26. Finally, the vision for the Eleventh Plan must include an improvement in governance. Over the years, the governments at the Centre and the States have launched a large number of initiatives at substantial public expense to achieve the objectives of growth with poverty alleviation and inclusiveness. Experience suggests that many of these initiatives have floundered because of poor design, insufficient accountability and also corruption at various levels. Increasingly, there is demand for effective implementation without which expanded government intervention will be infructuous.

1.27. The strategy for the Eleventh Plan must therefore aim at bringing about major improvements in governance which would make government-funded programmes in critical areas more effective and efficient. The best possible way of achieving this objective may be by involving communities in both the design and implementation of such programmes, although such involvement may vary from sector to sector. Experience shows that Civil Society Organizations (CSOs) can work with PRIs to improve the effectiveness of these programmes. For achieving the vision of the Eleventh Plan, it is extremely important to experiment with programme design to give more flexibility to decision making at the local level.

1.28. It is especially important to improve evaluation of the effectiveness of how government programmes work and to inject a commitment to change their designs in the light of the experience gained. Evaluation must be based on proper benchmarks and be scientifically designed to generate evidence-based assessment of different aspects of programme design. Along with greater transparency and feedback from community participation, this is particularly important in the case of programmes delivering services directly to the poor.

1.29. Accountability and transparency are critical elements of good governance. The Right to Information Act (RTI) enacted in 2005 empowers people to get information and constitutes a big step towards transparency and accountability.

The Role of the States

1.30. A notable feature of the Tenth Plan was the increase in the share of outlays for Centrally Sponsored Schemes (CSS) in the Gross Budgetary Support (GBS) for the Central Plan. This was done for two reasons; first, the Centre's own investment in industry was almost entirely funded by the Internal and Extra-Budgetary Resources (IEBR) of Public Sector Enterprises (PSEs); and, second, the enlarged role that the Centre has taken for itself in providing for social infrastructure, especially in the backward States, through programmes such as National Rural Employment Guarantee Programme (NREGP) Sarva Shiksha Abhiyan, Bharat Nirman, etc. The outlay on CSS, taken together with scheme-wise Central assistance provided to State Plans, amounts to over 55% of the Central GBS in 2007–08, the first year of the Eleventh Plan. This level will not go down during the Eleventh Plan period.

1.31. Many of the major CSS are in areas where the State Governments have traditionally borne the bulk of the expenditure. Even during the Eleventh Plan period, the non-Plan expenditure on these sectors by the State Governments will be considerable. The strategy for ensuring the best use of the available resources, therefore, requires that the Central Government engage more intensively with the States not only with regard to Plan expenditure but also in respect of what have traditionally been non-Plan expenditures. Separately, it is proposed to set up a high-level committee (HLC) to suggest how this planning for resources could be best accomplished. More than ever before, the success of the Eleventh Five Year Plan will depend upon the quality of service delivery by the State Governments.

STRATEGY FOR THE ELEVENTH PLAN: POLICIES FOR INCLUSIVE GROWTH

1.32. The strategy for inclusive growth in the Eleventh Plan is not just a conventional strategy for growth to which some elements aimed at inclusion have been added. On the contrary, it is a strategy which aims at achieving a particular type of growth process which will meet the objectives of inclusiveness and sustainability. This strategy must be based on sound macroeconomic policies which establish the macroeconomic preconditions for rapid growth and support key drivers of this growth. It must also include sector-specific policies which will ensure that the structure of growth that is generated, and the institutional environment in which it occurs, achieves the objective of inclusiveness in all its many dimensions.

1.33. The elements of the strategy proposed in the Eleventh Plan are discussed in detail in the individual chapters. The major components are summarized in the following sub-sections.

Macroeconomic Framework

1.34. The broad macroeconomic framework of the Plan is discussed in detail in Chapter 2. It envisages a continuation of the uptrend in domestic investment and savings observed in the Tenth Plan taking domestic investment from an estimated 35.9% of GDP in 2006–07 to an average of 36.7% of GDP in the Eleventh Plan period. This is expected to be supported by the domestic savings rate of 34.8% of GDP in the Eleventh Plan period. These investment rates are broadly consistent with achieving an average growth rate of 9% per year in the Eleventh Plan period. The Plan also implies a substantial increase in the total resources for the Central and State Plans from 9.46% of GDP in the Tenth Plan to 13.54% of GDP in the Eleventh Plan. This outcome depends upon government non-Plan expenditure, especially subsidies remaining under control and a significant improvement in the IEBR of the public sector in both the Centre and the States.

1.35. The macroeconomic projections involve a rise in the current account deficit from 1.1% of GDP in 2006–07 to an average of 1.9% of GDP in the Eleventh Plan period, based on oil prices at the average level of 2006–07. The recent hardening of oil prices, if it continues, will involve a further increase in the current account deficit by up to 1 percentage point of GDP. Even if this were to happen, it will be feasible to finance the increased deficit given India's export potential and the prospect of continuing inflows of foreign investment. The real challenge in the persistence of high oil prices lies in the need to pass on these prices to consumers which could moderate growth a little in the short run.

1.36. On balance, the Plan target of 9% per year appears achievable with some downside risks if oil prices harden further. The broad sectoral composition of growth associated with this projection involves doubling the growth rate of agriculture to 4% per year compared with a little over 2% per year in the Tenth Plan and raising the industrial growth rate from 9.2% in the Tenth Plan to between 10% and 11% in the Eleventh Plan. Further, manufacturing is targeted to grow at over 12% per year and this is expected to provide high-quality employment.

AGRICULTURE

1.37. The target of doubling the rate of growth of agriculture to 4% in the Eleventh Plan is critical for achieving greater inclusiveness. This calls for initiatives on several fronts.

1.38. The poor performance of agriculture in the past decade or so is partly due to the emergence of technology fatigue in the intensely irrigated crop production regions. This is reflected in the fact that the new varieties released do not seem to have produced significantly higher yields per hectare. The long-term response to this phenomenon is a comprehensive strengthening and restructuring of the Indian Council of Agricultural Research (ICAR) system to give greater focus to research in strategic areas which would help to evolve cropping systems suited to various agro-climatic zones. It is particularly important to focus research on raising the yield potential in rain-fed areas. There is also a need to increase the accountability of the State agricultural universities and to make their research more directly useful. Public expenditure on agricultural research, taking the Centre and the States together, needs to increase from 0.7% of agricultural GDP at present to at least 1% by the end of the Eleventh Plan.

1.39. In the short run, we must exploit the large scope for yield improvement which is reflected in the large gap that exists in most parts of the country between the yields that are actually being realized on the ground and yields that can be achieved with the existing varieties using best practices in farm conditions. This yield gap varies from 60 to 100%, depending on the crop and the region. The Eleventh Plan must focus on evolving suitable strategies for each agro-climatic zone to reduce the gap. This will require better assessment of location-specific potentials and constraints, and more effective extension. A new central assistance programme, the Rashtriya Krishi Vikas Yojana (RKVY) has been launched to incentivize State Governments to prepare district level agricultural plans that take account of local conditions. The programme will encourage effective convergence among various Central schemes which are currently implemented in districts as stand-alone schemes and will provide Central assistance to meet a part of the additional cost of the agricultural plans, above existing expenditure commitments. The preparation of district-specific agricultural plans is an important innovation and it is expected to sharpen the focus on local crop productivity constraints. Adequate funding will be provided to build capacity for such district planning and, simultaneously, there will be a very substantial increase in Central support to State extension systems.

1.40. Adoption of best practices typically involves additional investment. The most important area for investment in agriculture relates to the provision of water and its efficient use. There is definitely a need for more public investment to develop irrigation where it is feasible, including modernisation of the existing irrigation systems to improve efficiency. It is also necessary to undertake watershed management programmes in dryland areas. The specific initiatives needed in this regard are discussed later in the chapter.

1.41. Private investment by farmers is also needed in land development, pump sets and drip irrigation, agricultural machinery, etc. On-farm investments are limited by the availability of credit to farmers which needs priority attention. Commercial banks have extended credit to agriculture commendably in the later years of the Tenth Plan period, and this needs to continue. However, whereas overall credit has expanded, the number of loan accounts has declined, suggesting that small farmers are not receiving adequate credit. To correct this, the co-operative banking system must be revived along the lines recommended by the Vaidyanathan Committee. The Committee's recommendations have been accepted by many States, but implementation of follow-up action needs to be expedited.

1.42. Deteriorating soil health is a major constraint limiting productivity in agriculture. The present system of fertilizer subsidy which is based on subsidization of products rather than nutrients, contributes to the problem because there is excessive subsidy on nitrogen compared to potassium and phosphates, and no subsidy at all on micronutrients. The result is excessive use of nitrogenous fertilizer which depletes the soil of other micronutrients (sulphur, zinc, boron), reducing soil productivity over time. Most farmers do not have information on the soil health of their farms and the extent of micronutrient deficiency, which varies across areas. Increased awareness of this problem is extremely important. It is necessary to restructure the fertilizer subsidy to make it nutrient based and to enable production of composite fertilizers, including micronutrients, by giving producers the flexibility to charge higher prices which will cover the cost of adding micronutrients. There is also need to expand the network of soil testing laboratories in most States and also to extend soil testing to measure micronutrients, which are typically not covered at present.

1.43. Seed replacement is another major problem constraining crop productivity. Seed replacement rates in most parts of the country are much below recommended levels, partly because of lack of availability of certified seeds, but also because farmers do not trust the quality or truthfulness of labels of certified seeds available from public sector sources. A major effort is needed to increase the supply of certified seeds and also to achieve credibility in the quality of the seeds supplied. State governments must take steps to revamp seed production and distribution arrangements as quickly as possible. There may be a case in some States for State agricultural universities to take over management of public sector state seed corporations and the land under their control, to help improve seed production.

1.44. Growth of foodgrain production has fallen short of population growth during the last decade. More recently, foodgrain prices have flared up, reflecting both the rising trend of prices internationally, and more robust domestic demand. A strong effort in expanding foodgrain production is therefore needed. A National Food Security Mission has been launched in the first year of the Eleventh Plan which aims at increasing cereal production by 18 million tonnes and pulses production by 2 million tonnes. Nevertheless, it is unlikely that demand for foodgrains will expand by more than 2.5% per year. The target of 4% growth in agriculture will therefore require much faster growth in horticulture, floriculture, dairying, poultry, and fisheries. Agricultural strategies for each agro-climatic zone should pay attention to the scope for agricultural diversification along lines that are technically appropriate.

1.45. Agricultural diversification will pose special challenges in marketing because the high-value produce of diversified agriculture is much more perishable than foodgrains. Farmers need assured linkages to efficient markets with transparent pricing and also modern logistics and cold chains to ensure transportation with minimum spoilage. Several States have amended the Agricultural Produce Marketing Committee Acts to allow private markets to be set up in competition with the existing *mandis*. Modern markets, whether established by the private sector or by co-operatives, can improve marketing facilities by offering grading opportunities and cold storage facilities as well as more transparent price discovery through open auction. Contract farming, which is being encouraged by many States, also provides a mechanism for improving linkages between farmers and markets through the active involvement of the private sector, which can also serve as a supplier of key inputs and extension advice. An important issue in this context is the need to ensure that small and marginal farmers have adequate bargaining strength. An adequate dispute resolution mechanism is also necessary to encourage formation of farmers' groups, not only for contract farming but also to avail other economies of scale. Ways of incentivizing such group formation should be part of the agenda for agricultural policy in the Eleventh Plan.

1.46. There is also need for greater predictability in measures designed for price stability. Efforts to control sudden price rise of agricultural produce, such as bans on exports, have often been at the cost of farmers. Also, while the Minimum Support Price (MSP) policy has not reached most farmers at times when prices were low, inadequate procurement often leads to over-reaction. With international prices much more volatile than what Indian farmers are used to, a comprehensive view is required at the possibility of a predictable response both in terms of trade policy and proper regulation of India's new, but fast developing, futures markets in agricultural commodities so as to allow better transmission of price signals and management of risks.

1.47. More generally, market linkages can be improved by improving rural infrastructure, including especially, rural roads and rural electrification. The Pradhan Mantri Gram Sadak Yojana (PMGSY) has already done commendable work in extending rural connectivity and the programme will continue into the Eleventh Plan. The Rajiv Gandhi Grameen Vidyutikaran Yojana (RGGVY) also has ambitious plans to extend rural electrification to hitherto unserved rural areas. It is essential to ensure that RGGVY aims not only at household electrification but also at energization of pumpsets. This will make a big difference to the ability of farmers in the eastern States to utilize available ground water at more reasonable costs.

Irrigation and Watershed Development

1.48. The Bharat Nirman target is to more than double the pace of addition to the area under irrigation to 2.5 million hectares per year by 2008–09. If this momentum is maintained, we should be able to add 16 million hectares to the irrigated area during the Eleventh Plan.

1.49. There are, however, several problems in the irrigation sector which need to be addressed. A large number of projects have been under construction for a long time as resources have been spread too thin. This has increased costs and also delayed the creation of irrigation capacity. The Accelerated Irrigation Benefit Programme (AIBP) was started to incentivize States to complete projects in a time-bound manner, but progress in the programme has not been satisfactory. Several initiatives relating to irrigation were launched in the last years of the Tenth Plan, including conversion of loan assistance under AIBP to pure grant. The norms for approving projects under the programme were also relaxed to permit more projects to become eligible. States are being encouraged to change the system of contracting to a fixed cost, time-bound system. A system of monitoring projects through remote sensing has been introduced which will help to identify critical works needing attention and help reduce the large gap between the created and actually utilized irrigation potentials.

1.50. Repair, renovation and restoration of water bodies can expand irrigation capacity in a short period. States will be assisted to take up such projects provided they agree to hand over the water bodies to user groups after renovation so that future maintenance is assured. 25% of the project cost is eligible for grant assistance under AIBP and the rest could come from external assistance. Water-use efficiency in irrigation is quite low in the country. A larger area can be irrigated with the available water if sprinkler or drip irrigation is used to increase efficiency. This calls for additional investment. Assistance will also be extended to extension, renovation and modernization projects subject to the achievement of 'target irrigation efficiency' for water conservation.

1.51. To further reduce the gap between the potential and its utilization, the Command Area Development Programme (CADP) was modified in the Tenth Plan to include water management above the outlet for correcting system deficiencies. Beneficiary contribution of 10% was specified for the execution of Command Area Development works. A model Participatory Irrigation Management (PIM) Act was circulated to States to promote PIM, which is seen in many cases to improve irrigation water distribution to all farmers, including the tail-enders. During the Eleventh Plan, CADP will be made part of major and medium irrigation projects to accelerate utilization and focus on responsibility.

1.52. Groundwater, which is used for irrigating for nearly 60% of the irrigated area, also poses serious problems. Under the Easement Act of 1882, the ownership rights of groundwater rest with the owner of the land. This makes groundwater a common property resource with open access. As a result, groundwater was over exploited in nearly 15% of the blocks in 2004, compared to 4% in 1995 (though the classification scheme was different in the two surveys, they are roughly comparable). When the water table falls, some wells go dry and others have to spend more energy to lift water. It is therefore important to evolve a system of sustainable use of groundwater.

1.53. Under the Environment (Protection) Act, 1986, the Central Government can intervene where the water table falls. The Eleventh Plan will encourage co-operative management of groundwater by the community, as it is most likely to work. The objective would be to contain average groundwater extraction to average water recharge. For this, the local water user associations will have to be empowered with knowledge and information through monitoring of the water table and recharge by the Central and State Groundwater Boards.

1.54. While groundwater is being depleted in some parts of the country, large parts of eastern India have high water tables, reflecting large unexploited potential for expanding irrigation. This is not done for want of electricity as using diesel pumps is expensive and inconvenient. RGGVY aims at providing power to all villages, and this should facilitate rapid expansion of irrigation in eastern India.

1.55. Groundwater can be recharged through watershed development using check dams, contour bunding, etc. This not only increases availability of water, but also generally leads to its more equitable distribution. The Eleventh Plan will strengthen watershed development programmes and also increase the flow of resources to these programmes by their convergence with other schemes.

1.56. Though irrigation is by far the largest user of groundwater, in specific local situations, industrial use of groundwater can also stress the resource. Industry using water that falls within its land should be required to enhance recharge correspondingly. It is also vital to prevent groundwater contamination by enforcing strict effluent quality standards.

Industry and Minerals

1.57. The pace of industrial growth quickened during the Tenth Plan and manufacturing in particular showed considerable dynamism. It will be necessary to build on this momentum during the Eleventh Plan and, indeed, impart additional impetus to generate 10% growth in industry, and even higher growth in manufacturing. This will not only provide the additional job opportunities needed to absorb some of the surplus labour in the rural workforce but also generate employment for the new entrants that are expected to join the labour force both in rural and urban areas. For this, industries must not only grow, but grow in a manner that leads to the absorption of large numbers of workers.

1.58. Industries face a number of impediments in the country, which need urgent attention if industrial growth is to be sustained over a long period. Improvement of physical infrastructure must clearly come at the top of the agenda of action for achieving rapid industrialization. Continuous supply of good quality electrical power from the grid is critical for industries, but the situation in this regard is very unsatisfactory. Large-scale units can deal with this problem by setting up captive power plants, but this is not an economical option for small and medium units. Manufacturing also entails movement of large volumes of goods in order to compete in a globalized context and manufacturers need transport infrastructure which can ensure speedy and reliable movement. Deficiencies in the road infrastructure must be addressed urgently to increase the competitiveness of Indian manufacturing. Much the same is true of ports where insufficient port capacity and inadequate navigation aid facilities and cargo handling equipment lead to longer pre-berthing detention and turnaround time for ships. These problems are compounded by the fact that large vessels do not call on many Indian ports because of the lack of depth of the draft and poor connectivity with the hinterland. Without substantial improvement in all these aspects of the transport infrastructure, growth in manufacturing cannot be sustained.

1.59. A skill deficit has also emerged in virtually all areas of manufacturing as one of the major impediments to rapid industrial growth. The shortages are at all levels, from executives and designers at the top to base-level skilled worker such as tailors and machine operators. There is a huge gap in the vocational training capacity, which is less than one-fourth of the entrants to the work force per annum. There is an urgent need to attend to skill development and the Eleventh Plan strategy in this regard is discussed later in this chapter.

1.60. The perceived lack of flexibility in some of our labour laws, such as Chapter V-B of the Industrial Disputes Act, 1947 and the Contract Labour (Regulation and Abolition) Act, which focus on job protection, remains a psychological block for entrepreneurs against establishing new enterprises with a large workforce. Existing industrial units have learnt to live with Chapter V-B of the Industrial

Disputes Act, albeit at some cost, but newcomers are often deterred. The Contract Labour (Regulation and Abolition) Act also results in the industry letting go of the opportunities for seasonal supplies, particularly in international markets. In a globalized world where our manufacturers have to compete with others who enjoy greater flexibility, it is necessary to find practical solutions for the problems created by these laws.

1.61. The Micro and Small Enterprises (MSE) Sector accounts for the bulk of the employment in manufacturing and has been one of the sources of strength for manufacturing in the country. It has largely withstood the test of international competitiveness resulting from external economic liberalization since 1991–92. However, the ceiling on investment in plant and machinery, together with reservation of a large number of items for exclusive manufacture by small-scale industries, has in the past barred these units from undertaking efforts for upgrading technology, adopting modern manufacturing methods and achieving economies of scale. The loss of fiscal benefits by a small-scale unit graduating into a larger unit is an additional disincentive against expansion and leads to horizontal expansion and deliberate fragmentation. During the Tenth Plan period, major steps were taken to alleviate these problems: the number of reserved items was reduced from 675 to 114 and the ceiling on investment in plant and machinery was raised generally from Rs 3 crore to Rs 5 crore by the Micro, Small and Medium Enterprises Act, 2006. The Act also contains a number of provisions aimed at strengthening these enterprises and, in fact, seeks to integrate the three tiers—medium, small, and micro. This process must continue in the Eleventh Plan.

1.62. Small-scale and medium enterprises are the main beneficiaries of the investment incentives for modernization, upgradation, and additional capacity creation given in schemes such as the Technology Upgradation Fund Scheme for the textile sector. The schemes for establishment of industrial parks such as the Scheme for Integrated Textile Park in the same sector are also aimed at obtaining additional investment in small-scale and medium enterprises. These schemes will be continued and replicated in other areas during the Eleventh Plan.

1.63. Small-scale units are handicapped by insufficient flow of credit despite the measures taken to stimulate priority sector lending by Scheduled Commercial Banks and expansion of direct lending operations by the Small Industries Development Bank of India (SIDBI). During the Eleventh Plan, credit flows to these units will need to be monitored and improved.

1.64. The Central Public Sector Enterprises (CPSEs) on the whole have registered a strong performance during the Tenth Plan. The number of profit-making CPSEs has gone up and the number of loss-making ones has reduced. Granting of full autonomy to CPSEs remains an unfinished agenda before the government. A great deal of progress has been made in the revival of sick CPSEs, but close monitoring would be needed to implement their restructuring plans. Another issue of importance is the development of a mechanism to ensure optimum investment decisions by large profit-making enterprises.

1.65. A package of fiscal and other incentives has been in place since 1997 aimed at facilitating industrial development of the States of the North East Region (NER). During the Tenth Plan, similar schemes were notified for Jammu and Kashmir (J&K), Himachal Pradesh and Uttarakhand. While the response in the NER and the valley in J&K has not been significant, there is evidence that these incentives have stimulated industrial investment in Jammu, Himachal Pradesh, and Uttarakhand. However, there are complaints from other States, particularly the adjoining ones, of flight of capital induced by excise duty exemptions. Because of the distortions induced by excise duty exemptions in particular, consideration needs to be given to replacing the incentives, fully or partly, by an accelerated programme of infrastructure improvement.

Infrastructure Requirements of Inclusive Growth

1.66. Good quality infrastructure is the most critical physical requirement for attaining faster growth in a competitive world and also for ensuring investment in backward regions. This includes all-weather roads; round-the-clock availability of power at a stable voltage and frequency; water for irrigation; railways that are not overcrowded, which run on time and do not overcharge for freight; ports with low turnaround time to reduce costs of imports and exports; airports to handle the growing traffic; air services that provide connectivity to all parts of the country; and telecommunications and broadband connectivity to provide the benefits of the Internet to people all over the country.

1.67. The Eleventh Plan outlines a comprehensive programme for development of infrastructure, especially in rural areas, and in the remote and backward parts of the country, consistent with the requirements of inclusive growth at 9% per year. The total investment needed in infrastructure, defined to include electricity (including non-conventional energy), roads, bridges and railways (includes Mass Rapid Transit System, MRTS), ports, airports, telecommunications, irrigation (including watershed development), water supply and sanitation, storage and gas distribution will have to increase from an estimated 5.43% of GDP in 2006–07 to 9.34% by the terminal year of the Eleventh Plan. Though public investment has to be a large part of the solution, an increase of this magnitude cannot be achieved through public investment alone since there will be large demands on public sector resources from the health and education and agriculture sectors, and also from various programmes aimed at livelihood support for the poor. The Eleventh Plan therefore proposes a strategy for infrastructure development which involves a combined response—an increase in public sector investment in infrastructure as a percentage of GDP, and also an increase in private sector investment through some form of public–private partnership (PPP) or directly, where feasible.

1.68. The relative contributions of the public and private sectors in meeting the proposed investment targets are summarized in Table 1.1. It may be noted that the absolute increase in public investment is 2.22 percentage points of GDP, which is about 1.3 times the absolute increase in private investment of 1.69 percentage points. The proportional increase in private investment is much larger because of the initial low base but public investment will still constitute 70% of the total investment in infrastructure.

1.69. Public investment will have to give priority to meeting the infrastructure requirements in those sub-sectors and areas where private participation is unlikely to be forthcoming. These include irrigation and other general rural infrastructure (mainly rural roads, rural electrification, and water supply and sanitation), and also infrastructure development in the more backward areas and the remote parts of the country. In other areas where there is scope for private investment, the aim will be to attract private investment in a transparent manner in which the responsibilities of the private concessionaire are clearly defined and the choice of the concessionaire is determined by an open, competitive bidding process.

TABLE 1.1
Investment in Infrastructure

(Percentage of GDP)

	2006–07	2011–12
Public Sector (Centre + States)	4.23	6.45
Private Sector	1.20	2.89
Total	5.43	9.34

Source: Central Statistical Organization for 2006–07 and computations by the Planning Commission for 2011–12.

1.70. Attracting private investment on the scale envisaged presents formidable challenges. A good start has been made by the Central Government with PPP in many infrastructure sectors in the Tenth Plan, and many State Governments have also begun exploring this option. However, it must be recognized that it will not be easy to bring in private investment at the scale required. Much will depend on the overall investment climate as also the credibility and legitimacy of the processes, which, in turn, will be influenced by the transparency achieved in setting standards and allocating risks and the robustness of the competitive bidding process for awarding contracts. The major initiatives envisaged in each of the infrastructure sub-sectors are summarized below.

Railways

1.71. The Railways are an important part of our transport infrastructure and they have much higher fuel efficiency than trucks and cars in terms of fuel consumption per tonne kilometre or per passenger kilometre. For movement of bulk commodities, trucks cannot compete with the railways. With containerization, the railways can be competitive even for movement of other goods over long distances.

1.72. The rapid rise in international trade and domestic cargo has placed a great strain on the Delhi–Mumbai and Delhi–Kolkata rail tracks. The government has, therefore, decided to build dedicated freight corridors in the western and eastern high density routes involving construction of 7201 km of new rail tracks. This will help to decongest the two routes for freight movement and also increase the economic potential of the hinterland areas which will benefit from the reduced cost of transport. It will also provide spin-off benefits in terms of location of industrial clusters along the new corridors, thereby attracting potential investment in a number of States.

1.73. With increasing containerization of cargo, the demand for container movement by rail has grown rapidly. This was hitherto a monopoly of the Container Corporation of India, a public sector entity. In a major initiative in PPP, container movement has been thrown open to competition and 15 private sector entities have been licensed for running container trains on tracks owned by the Indian Railways. Private sector container trains have commenced operations and the operators would also be expanding investment into container handling facilities, such as Inland Container Depots, etc.

1.74. The Indian Railways also proposes to take the following steps in an effort to create world-class transport infrastructure:

- Strengthening of infrastructure and improvement in the design of wagons to facilitate movement of heavier freight trains.
- Redevelopment and modernization of important railway stations through PPP.
- A paradigm shift in the delivery of services to include quality passenger services at terminals, introduction of modern rolling stock and improvement in sanitation.
- On the Delhi-Agra route, a high speed train with a maximum speed of 150 km per hour has been introduced. Similar trains will be introduced in selected city pairs.
- Reduction in accidents per million train km; implementation of measures to reduce chances of passenger fatality as a result of train accidents; focus on development of manpower through major improvements in the working environment and training to reduce the accidents attributable to human failure.
- Introduction of a new accounting system in line with internationally accepted accounting principles. This will help to identify the unit cost of different services more accurately.

Roads

1.75. The Eleventh Plan envisages a major programme of road development covering the national highways, based on a combination of public investment and PPP and completion of rural road connectivity through the PMGSY.

1.76. PMGSY is a massive programme of expanding rural road connectivity and was begun in the Tenth Plan. This will continue into the Eleventh Plan to provide reliable road connectivity to all habitations with 1000+ population (500+ population in hilly regions) by 2009.

1.77. An expanded National Highways Development Programme (NHDP) is currently under way, involving a total investment of Rs 227258 crore. It includes four-laning of the Golden Quadrilateral and the North–South, East–West Corridors (NHDP I and II) covering 14488 km; four/six laning of 10000 km of national highways (the total length approved subsequently has gone up to 12109 km) connecting State capitals and places of tourist importance with the national network under NHDP III; widening of 20000 km of national highways to two lanes with paved shoulders under NHDP IV; six laning of 6500 km of selected national highways under NHDP V; development of 1000 km of expressways under NHDP VI and construction of ring roads around major towns and bypasses, flyovers, etc. on national highways under NHDP VII.

1.78. During the Eleventh Plan, a comprehensive Master Plan is proposed to be formulated for construction of 15600 km of Access Controlled Expressways. Action will also be taken for determining the alignments and acquiring land for about 6000 km of the total length. Establishment of an Expressways Authority of India for implementation of the Expressways Programme should be considered by the Ministry.

1.79. A balanced development of the highway network requires that apart from expeditious completion of the expanded NHDP involving augmentation of riding quality and capacity of 46000 km of national highways, out of the total present length of 66590 km, the non-NHDP section is also kept in reasonably good shape. In addition, the following qualitative improvements will be implemented:

- The NHAI, which is the implementing agency for NHDP, will be restructured and strengthened.
- High priority will be accorded to ensure integrated development of the entire road network, that is, national highways, State highways, major district roads, other district roads and village roads.
- Higher maintenance standards will be employed in order to reduce the frequency of reconstruction of capacity and to preserve road assets already created. The strategy will focus on optimum utilization of existing capacity rather than creating new capacities.

- Based on the lessons learnt, conditions conducive for private sector participation will be created in the States.
- In order to ensure safety along with free flow of traffic, various steps will be taken in the coming years, including strengthening the institutional mechanism by setting up of the National Road Safety and Traffic Management Board as an apex body. Appropriate design of roads with interchanges, segregation of slow moving traffic and adequate provision of underpasses and overpasses and, in some cases, service lanes, will be focused on.

1.80. A Special Accelerated Road Development Programme for the North East Region (SARDP-NE) is presently under implementation for providing road connectivity to all the State capitals and district headquarters in the NER.

Ports

1.81. Indian ports suffer from inefficiency and congestion as reflected in the high turnaround time of ships. New berths and better handling facilities are needed at the existing ports and new ports also need to be developed. The draft at some ports needs deepening to permit larger ships to berth. Rail connectivity to move goods from the ports is also inadequate. The Eleventh Plan envisages a major programme of expansion in port capacity based on PPP. Many State Governments are also taking initiatives to develop their ports through such partnerships and these initiatives will be encouraged.

Airports

1.82. Growth of air traffic in recent years has been very high—an average of 30% per year between 2003–04 and 2006–07. Increased competition in air services has lowered fares and contributed to this growth. However, development of airports and related facilities has not kept pace. The Eleventh Plan will accelerate the programme launched in the last two years of the Tenth Plan to upgrade airports and related facilities. Four major airports (Delhi, Mumbai, Hyderabad, and Bangalore) are being developed by private sector entities. Modernization of Kolkata and Chennai airports and 35 non-metro and 13 other airports is underway. Some new greenfield airports will also be constructed during the Eleventh Plan.

1.83. Civil aviation provides crucial transport infrastructure in hilly and inaccessible areas. It is therefore proposed to augment airport infrastructure in these areas during the Eleventh Plan. This will include: development of three greenfield airports and expansion/modification of six existing airports in the NER; and modernization and upgradation of Jammu, Dehradun, Agatti, and Port Blair airports under the scheme for modernization of 35 non-metro airports.

Telecommunications

1.84. The Eleventh Plan envisages continued progress towards developing a world-class telecommunications infrastructure with an emphasis on broadening access. It is an irony that the phenomenal growth in the telecom sector has also created a digital divide in terms of mobile and land line connections and Internet and broadband connections between urban and rural India. The Eleventh Plan will address this as an important issue. The targets for the Eleventh Plan period are to reach a telecom subscriber base of 600 million and a rural tele-density of 25%. Expanding rural telephony should be a priority area of the Plan.

1.85. Broadband connectivity plays an important role not only as a medium but also as a means of bringing knowledge and data though networking to the less fortunate institutions. To empower the nation, and to create a world-class ambience for education, science, technology and governance, the country should create a dynamically configurable national multi-gigabit backbone core network.

1.86. It should be our objective to connect 5000 institutions of education, science and technology to this core to enable collaborative research and development nationally and internationally. Campuses should be empowered technologically through campus-wide networks and by providing entry devices to the knowledge network in order to derive the full benefits of this effort.

1.87. India's prowess in software is world-renowned with an estimated share of 65% of global off-shore information technology (IT) and 46% of global business process outsourcing (BPO). The Indian IT and IT-enabled services (ITES)/BPO industry stands at US$ 31.3 billion in 2006–07. The addressable market for offshore BPO globally stands at US$ 300 billion, leaving enough headroom for further growth. The IT sector at present is estimated to employ over 3.08 million people and is expected to provide employment opportunity to over

8.73 million by 2012. The above mentioned figure indicate the direct employment in IT sector (both software and hardware). The indirect employment generated by the sector, is approximately three times of the direct employment. This throws up a great challenge for human resources (HR) development. There is an urgent need to augment the existing educational system by introducing special IT courses and establishing finishing schools to impart soft and other important skills.

1.88. With the weakening of the dollar against the Indian rupee, the ITES/BPO industry has come under pressure and it needs to be nurtured. Necessary policy interventions need to be put in place on a fast track mode. Extending the 10A and 10B benefits for the BPO industries beyond 2009 could be one such encouragement. Otherwise, this segment of the sector, which is a huge employment generator, could move to other countries which are more cost effective. The industry also needs to shift from Dollar to Rupee denominated contracts to combat the falling dollar.

Electric Power

1.89. Rapid economic growth cannot be realized if energy is not available at reasonable costs. Electricity is a crucial energy input in this context. Substantial progress was made in the Tenth Plan in certain dimensions. The Electricity Act, 2003 provides an excellent framework for restructuring of the power sector, and allows full scope for competition within a reasonable regulatory framework. However, while a good start has been made in setting up the regulatory framework and the institutional structure necessary for an efficient market for electricity generation and distribution, much more remains to be done. The performance in the Tenth Plan in adding capacity was disappointing. Against a target addition of 41110 MW, only 21080 MW were commissioned, out of which only 18000 MW were actually made fully operational. Investment in distribution has also been inadequate.

1.90. The most important problem in the power sector is the continued unviability of the distribution segment reflected in very high transmission and distribution losses, including pilferage and also uneconomic tariff for some categories of consumers. As a result, the financial position of the distribution companies, which are in the State sector, is severely strained and this is the cause of inadequate investment by the State sector, both in generation and in distribution. It also limits the appetite of private investors to invest in generation owing to problems anticipated about the capacity of the unviable public sector distribution companies to pay for power.

1.91. The Eleventh Plan must aim at making a radical break from past practice in the electricity sector. The main thrust should be on the following:

- The position at the start of the Eleventh Plan is better than at the start of the Tenth Plan because the volume of generation capacity under construction or ordered in the middle of the first year (September 2007) was 52000 MW compared with only 20500 MW at the start of the Tenth Plan. Further orders amounting to 23600 MW could be placed by the end of the first year of the Eleventh Plan. In view of the shorter pipeline, concerted attention on implementation and project management could ensure higher actual additions to capacity in the Eleventh Plan than in the Tenth Plan.
- While the regulatory structure consisting of the Central Electricity Regulatory Commission and State Electricity Regulatory Commissions have been established and have begun to operate, they have yet to stabilize and achieve credibility as independent regulators. Many of them suffer from serious staffing problems arising from an inability to attract the necessary technical expertise. Efforts must be made to strengthen the regulatory system by overcoming these constraints.
- Improvement in the efficiency of the distribution system is the most important factor for the health of the system. The Accelerated Power Development and Reform Programme (APDRP), initiated in the Tenth Plan, aimed at reducing aggregate technical and commercial losses from over 40% in 2002–03 to 15% by the end of the Plan. This target proved unachievable and excepting in a couple of States, the Aggregate, Technical and Commercial (ATC) losses were reduced by only 2 to 3 percentage points and are presently estimated at about 40%. The Eleventh Plan must aim to bring about at least a 15 percentage point reduction in these losses during the Plan period. For this purpose, the APDRP programme must be completely restructured and also expanded in scope.
- Rural electrification is an important instrument to bring about inclusive growth by making electricity available to farmers and in rural areas. The RGGVY

is an important initiative aimed at electrifying all un-electrified villages and providing access to 7.8 crore rural households. Efforts should be made to ensure that the rural electrification infrastructure thus created does not focus on households alone but is also capable of providing three phase supply which can be used to energize pump sets for agriculture.

- An important innovation of the Electricity Act, 2003 is the statutory provision for open access which allows generating stations to enter the market and sell directly to high tension consumers. They can do so through assured access to the grid to reach such consumers while paying the distribution company a reasonable wheeling charge and a surcharge in lieu of the cross subsidy element. Unfortunately, most regulators have fixed the surcharge at a very high level. It needs to be clarified that the surcharge is meant only to cover the legitimate loss of cross subsidy from high tariff paying consumers who may migrate to competing suppliers. It should not be set so high as to kill competition nor so low as to leave any uncovered cross subsidy burden on the distribution utilities. Credible steps to implement open access, with reasonable surcharge, will incentivize private investors to set up additional generation capacity while allowing the distribution system to collect the cross subsidy element.
- A major, new initiative for promoting competition and attracting private investment in the power sector launched in the last year of the Tenth Plan was the Ultra Mega Power Projects programme. Under this programme, the government would invite proposals on a competitive basis from the public and the private sector to set up nine large power projects of 4000 MW each. Three such projects have been successfully bid for and the remaining six are expected to be bid out in the first few years of the Eleventh Plan. Successful completion of this programme has the potential to add significantly to the total private sector generation capacity although the benefits would accrue mostly in the Twelfth Plan period.

Other Energy Sectors

1.92. Transport infrastructure is not of much use unless the fuel—petrol, diesel, and electricity—is available to run scooters, cars, trucks, and the railways. Thus, availability of energy at competitive prices is as important as infrastructure. One also wants clean and convenient cooking fuels to avoid indoor air pollution and the unnecessary burden of gathering and carrying head loads of wood. All households should be provided clean cooking fuel at reasonable prices. For those who cannot afford them, or need to supplement them, fuel-wood plantations within 1 km of habitations should be developed.

1.93. We are short of most energy resources. Even coal, which is our most abundant resource, may run out in 40–50 years. An integrated energy policy to stimulate efficient use and allocation of fuels is, therefore, important. A key requirement of such a policy is that relative prices of different fuels, their transportation charges, and taxes and subsidies have to be consistent so that they reflect true social costs. Such a pricing system should be established in the Eleventh Plan.

COAL

1.94. The bulk of electricity generated in the country is based on coal which is our main energy resource and will remain so in the foreseeable future. The coal industry was nationalized in 1973 and Coal India Ltd dominates in production of coal. Under the nationalization Act, only public sector units, and designated users are permitted to mine coal for their own use. There is need to bring in competition in the sector to increase efficiency and to inject new technology. The Eleventh Plan will carry forward the process initiated in the last year of the Tenth Plan of encouraging other public sector units and captive users in coal mining. At the same time, coal must be competitively priced. Sale of at least 20% of coal through e-auction, rail freight rationalization, imports without duty, and pricing of coal based on its gross calorific value will be promoted. Washing of coal to reduce its ash content and save on transport charges will also be encouraged.

OIL AND GAS

1.95. We are short on oil and gas resources and this is certain to continue. More than 70% of our oil needs are met by imports. The New Exploration Licensing Policy has met with some success in finding gas in the country and in offshore areas. The Eleventh Plan must continue to encourage national and international oil companies to come and explore for oil and gas in the country. New technology to extract more oil from known or depleted reserves will also be encouraged.

1.96. Oil and gas prices offered to producers have to be internationally competitive if we are to attract private firms and encourage efficient use of oil and gas products. Since the bulk of the oil is imported, crude oil should be priced at import parity price. And, since we have large refining capacities and export a large number of products, petroleum products should be priced at trade parity price, that is, products which are significantly exported should be priced at Free on Board (FOB) prices and products which are significantly imported, at CIF prices. This will be best accomplished by competitive pricing of oil products at the refinery gate and at the retail level. These prices, in turn, must be passed on to the consumer though there is some scope for cross subsidy.

1.97. The pricing policy for petroleum products will pose a major challenge in the Eleventh Plan, given the sharp increase in international oil prices which is yet to be passed on to the consumers. With the present domestic petroleum prices, the extent of under recovery in the petroleum sector is estimated at Rs 100000 crore. This situation is simply not sustainable. Consumer prices of petroleum products involve a significant burden of taxes. Either the taxes have to be reduced or consumer prices have to increase. Also, the subsidies on kerosene and LPG, which lead to substantial diversion, need to be reduced and also rationalized. The scope for disbursing subsidy through a smart card system while shifting to market prices needs to be explored.

1.98. Gas pricing is more complex as gas is not easily tradable. While the cost of imported Liquefied Natural Gas provides a ceiling on the domestic price of gas, the FOB price of gas less the cost of liquefaction and less the risk premium associated with exports constitutes long-term opportunity cost for producers. The price itself has to reflect its opportunity cost in its marginal use. Once we have adequate gas to meet the requirement of existing stranded assets, it will be possible to move to competitively determined gas pricing. In order that there is competition in the oil and gas sector, the distribution infrastructure of pipeline networks and associated facilities would have to be under open access regulated by regulators. While the oil and gas regulator has been put in place, there is no such regulator for coal. There is need to consider whether a coal regulator should also be established.

RENEWABLES

1.99. The importance of renewable energy in the country arises from a number of factors—it increases energy security, it provides energy at local levels, improving energy security at these levels and it involves little or no Green House Gas emissions. Appropriate policies will be pursued to encourage renewables by linking subsidies, wherever required, to outcomes rather than to outlays. The Eleventh Plan will follow an integrated energy policy to incentivize appropriate choice of fuels and technologies.

1.100. Most of the programmes for renewable energy development would continue to be promoted but with a maxim of providing subsidies or incentives which are linked to outcomes rather than capital expenditure. This is important to preserve incentives for not just setting up capacities, but also operating them and encouraging cost reduction and technology development.

1.101. Some of areas which would be pushed strongly are wind power, solar applications, biomass gasification, bio-fuels development and other clean technologies. The distributed generation based on wood gasification in rural areas, coupled with biogas plants, could provide village energy security, particularly in remote areas. Such plants can provide clean cooking energy and also electricity before the grid power reaches them and later can also feed into the grid. The programme for biodiesel and ethanol from feed-stocks that do not compete with food production will be encouraged by a well-designed policy to take care of the interests of all the stakeholders in the value chain.

ENERGY EFFICIENCY AND R&D

1.102. There is large scope for improving energy efficiency in the country and this must be pushed vigorously through a variety of measures. These include energy auditing of large energy consumers, benchmarking with more efficient units, labelling and rating energy consuming equipment, forcing higher efficiency standards in major energy consuming sectors such as automobiles, and promoting energy efficient buildings. While labelling can help consumers buy energy efficient products, changes will be made in procurement policies so that government departments buy equipment based on life cycle costs.

1.103. We need R&D in a number of areas to augment our energy resources and provide cleaner energy. Considering the threat of climate change and the need to find clean sources of energy, missions in the following areas should be mounted:

- Clean coal technologies of carbon capture and sequestration
- In-situ coal gasification
- Solar photo-voltaics and solar thermal electricity
- Cellulosic extraction of ethanol and butanol from agricultural waste and crop residues
- Improvement in the yield of Jatropha and other oilseeds for biodiesel.

1.104. Apart from these, a rigorous R&D programme will encourage development of new sources, more efficient utilization, and improvement in efficiency applications.

Education and Skill Development

1.105. Education and skill development will receive high priority in the Eleventh Plan, both to meet the needs of a growing economy and to promote social equality by empowering those currently excluded because of unequal access to education and skills to participate fully in the growth process. Public expenditure (Centre and States) on education is only around 3.6% of GDP. The National Common Minimum Programme (NCMP) had set a target of raising it to 6%.

1.106. Several steps were taken in the Tenth Plan to expand access to primary education, especially the expansion in the Sarva Shiksha Abhiyan (SSA) and the Mid-Day Meal Scheme. As a result, the number of out-of-school children declined from 32 to 7 million, indicating that SSA brought an additional 25 million children into the education system during the Tenth Plan period. The Gross Enrolment Ratio (GER) for elementary schools (Classes I–VIII) increased from 81.6% in 2001–02 to 94.9% in 2004–05. However, the drop out rate has remained high. It was as high as 48.71% at the elementary level at the end of the Tenth Plan, a decline of only 5.94 percentage points from 2001–02.

1.107. The quality of teaching in our elementary schools is also not what it should be. Teacher absenteeism is widespread, teachers are not adequately trained and the quality of pedagogy is poor. The Eleventh Plan aims to correct these deficiencies and focuses on improving the quality of education at the elementary level, especially in rural areas. It also begins the process of universalizing secondary education. The massive expansion required in secondary education calls for an expansion in both public schools as well as private aided and unaided schools. While private schools must be allowed to expand and even encouraged, it should be noted that a much larger proportion of the expansion in enrolment would come from the public schools.

1.108. The action proposed in the Eleventh Plan for secondary education includes the following:

- Rapid upgradation of 15000 Upper Primary Schools to Secondary Schools, and expansion of intake capacity in 44000 existing Secondary Schools;
- Establishment of 6000 high quality model schools at the block level to serve as benchmarks for excellence in secondary schooling. About 3500 of these will be public-funded schools while 2500 would be through PPP;
- Provision for laboratories/libraries and also strengthening of the existing facilities available;
- Continuous teacher training;
- Provision for hostels and residential schools for girls; and
- A more liberal approach on the part of State Governments on allowing private schools to be set up to meet the large unmet demand for quality education.

1.109. The Eleventh Plan must also focus on the pressing need to expand capacity in our institutions of higher education and technical and professional education (engineering, medicine, law, etc.). The GER for higher education (percentage of the 18–23 age group enrolled in a higher education institution) currently is around 11% whereas it is 25% for many other developing countries. China has increased its GER in higher education from 10% in 1998 to 21% in 2005. We must aim at increasing the GER to 15% by the end of the Plan and reach 21% by the end of the Twelfth Plan. This is necessary not only to meet the needs of a growing economy, but also to meet the aspirations of younger people who see education as an essential requirement for advancement. Along with expansion, it is also necessary to aim at improvement in quality. While the best of our institutions of higher education compare well internationally, a large number suffer from serious quality problems. A general improvement in the quality of existing universities is necessary, including upgrading of facilities and improved methods of teaching. There is also need for a special effort to set up world class higher educational institutions. The expansion should aim at a much larger provision for science teaching.

1.110. The following initiatives will be taken in the Eleventh Plan to attain these objectives in higher education.

- Establishment of 30 new Central universities, one in each of the 16 States which do not have a Central university at present, and 14 other Central universities in different parts of the country. Some of these universities will be targeted ab initio to achieve world class standards, which will involve coverage of a wider range of subjects, including, especially engineering and medicine.
- Establishment of eight IITs, seven IIMs and five Indian Institutes of Science Education and Research.
- Since the establishment of world class institutions involves considerable expenditure on creating facilities, the scope for public–private participation in setting up these universities will be carefully explored. The location of these institutions should take advantage of the co-location of other scientific and research institutions in certain places.
- The scope for setting up institutions of higher education in the private sector must also be explored. State governments would be well advised to adopt a supportive stance on this issue, including flexibility in charging higher fees.
- At present, fees vary across universities, but generally these have been kept very low, in many cases not even covering 5% of the operating cost. The Centre and State Governments must either be able to subsidize university education massively or try to mobilize a reasonable amount from those who can afford it by way of fees that cover a reasonable part of the running cost. Since most university students come from the top 10% of the population by income levels, they would be able to pay fees amounting to 20% of the operating cost of general university education. The fees for professional courses could be much higher. The fee levels should, therefore, be increased gradually in existing institutions but the new norms could be implemented in new institutions from the start.

Skill Development

1.111. In an economy growing at the rate of 9% plus, skill development poses major challenges and also opens up unprecedented doors of opportunity. The magnitude of the skill development challenge can be estimated by the fact that the NSS 61st Round results show that among persons of age 15–29 years, only about 2% are reported to have received formal vocational training and another 8% reported to have received non-formal vocational training, indicating that very few young persons actually enter the world of work with any kind of formal vocational training. This proportion of trained youth is one of the lowest in the world. Our Vocational Education and Training (VET) system needs to cover more trades. Qualitatively it suffers from disabilities such as poor infrastructure, ill-equipped classrooms/laboratories/workshops, below par faculty, absence of measurement of performance and outcomes, etc. Placements are not tracked, training institutions are not rated, and accreditation systems are archaic. End-of-the-training examinations and certification systems are either non-existent or flawed.

1.112. In addition to the existing basic problem with the skill development system in the country, the urgency of skill development is underscored by the demographic changes taking place. It is estimated that the ageing phenomenon globally will create a skilled manpower shortage of approximately 46 million by 2020 and if we can take effective action on skill development, we could have a skilled manpower surplus of approximately 47 million. In an increasingly connected world, where national frontiers are yielding to cross-border outsourcing, it is not inconceivable that within a decade we can become a global reservoir of skilled persons.

1.113. Taking cognizance of this challenge, the consequential endeavour to launch effective measures will require a paradigm change in our VET system and in other forms of skill development. It is, therefore, proposed to launch coordinated action for skill development which will be a major initiative for inclusive growth and development and will consist of an agglomeration of programmes and appropriate structures. The coordinated action would aim at creating a pool skilled personnel in appropriate numbers with adequate skills in line with the employment requirements across the entire economy with particular emphasis on the twenty-one high growth high employment sectors (10 in manufacturing and 11 in services).

1.114. The coordinated action will aim to initiate and guide policy dialogue to energize, re-orient, and sustain the development of skills through private and he public initiatives towards both self employment and wage employment at various levels. As a part of coordinated action, a National Skill Development Coordination Board will be set up which will act as an instrument of implementation and make appropriate and practical solutions and strategies to address regional imbalances in skill development infrastructure, the socio-economic (SC/ST/OBC, Minorities, BPL, etc.), rural–urban, gender divides and ensure that each sectoral plan have built-in long terms measures with a self-corrective mechanism.

1.115. Furthermore, it is proposed to create a 'Virtual Skill Development Resource Network', which can be accessed by trainees at 50000 Skill Development Centres, to provide web-based learning. It is also proposed to create a 'National Skills Inventory' and another database for 'Skills Deficiency Mapping' for facilitating tracking of careers and placement and for exchange of information between employers and employment seekers. The Eleventh Plan will also see repositioning of Employment Exchanges as outreach points for storing and providing information on employment and skill development, and to encourage them to function as career counselling centres.

Health and Nutrition

1.116. Good health is both an end in itself and also contributes to economic growth. Meeting the health needs of the population requires a comprehensive and sustained approach. Our health services should be affordable and of reasonable quality. The Eleventh Plan will try to strengthen all aspects of the health care system—preventive, promotive, curative, palliative and rehabilitative. This will be accompanied by emphasis on access to clean drinking water, sanitation, diet, hygiene and feeding practices, which will significantly affect the health status of the people. Public health spending will be raised to at least 2% of GDP during the Eleventh Plan period.

1.117. Both the Central and State Governments will have to augment resources devoted to health. This will be accompanied by building absorptive capacity for enhanced allocations and innovative health financing mechanisms, including health insurance for the poor, in which the premium for basic coverage will be borne by the Centre and the States. There is a strong case for experimenting with different systems of PPP and risk pooling. The Eleventh Plan aims to establish 60 medical colleges and 225 new nursing and other colleges in deficit States through PPP. Incentives linking payment to performance will also be introduced in the public health system.

1.118. The following targets have been set during the Eleventh Plan to ensure an efficient public health delivery system under the National Rural Health Mission (NRHM), which was launched in 2005.

- Over 5 lakh Accredited Social Health Activists (ASHAs), one for every 1000 population in 18 Special Focus States and in tribal pockets of all States by 2008.
- All sub-centres (nearly 1.75 lakh) functional with two Auxiliary Nurse Midwives by 2010.
- Primary Health Centres (PHCs) (nearly 30000) with three staff nurses to provide round the clock services by 2010.
- 6500 Community Health Centres (CHCs) strengthened or established with seven specialists and nine staff nurses by 2012.
- 1800 Taluka or Sub-Divisional Hospitals (SDHs) and 600 District Hospitals (DHs) to be strengthened to provide quality health services by 2012.
- Mobile Medical Units for each District by 2009.
- Functional Hospital Development Committees in all CHCs, SDHs, and District Hospitals by 2009.
- Untied grants and annual maintenance grants to every Sub-centre, PHC and CHC released regularly and utilized for local health action by 2008.
- All District Health Action Plans completed by 2008.

1.119. During the Eleventh Plan, special attention will be paid to various aspects of women's health, including maternal morbidity and mortality, and child sex ratio. Besides encouraging institutional deliveries under NRHM, Traditional Birth Attendants (TBAs) will be trained to upgrade them as Skilled Birth Attendants. Reducing travel time to two hours for emergency obstetric care will be a key social intervention.

1.120. For reducing infant mortality, focus will be on Home Based Newborn Care (HBNC) complemented by Integrated Management of Neonatal and Childhood Illnesses. HBNC will be provided by a trained Community Health Worker (such as ASHA) who will guide and support the mother, family and TBA in the care of the newborn, and attend to the newborn at home if she is sick. The strategy during the Plan is to introduce and make available high quality HBNC in all districts/areas with an infant mortality rate of more than 45 per 1000 live births.

1.121. Improving all district hospitals will be a key intermediate step in the health strategy, till health care through PHCs and CHCs is fully realized. During the Plan period, six AIIMS-like institutions will be set up and 13 medical institutes upgraded to that level.

1.122. For meeting the health needs of the urban poor, particularly slum dwellers, a health insurance based National Urban Health Mission will be launched.

1.123. The Eleventh Plan also focuses on developing human resources to not just meet the needs of the health care system, but also to increase employment opportunities and make India a hub for health tourism. This will involve reintroducing licentiate courses in medicine, and establishing medical, nursing, dental and paramedical colleges in the under-served areas.

1.124. Good governance, transparency and accountability in the delivery of health nutrition and related services will be ensured through involvement of local self governments, community and civil society groups. The Eleventh Plan aims to establish 60 medical colleges.

1.125. High levels of malnutrition continue to influence morbidity and mortality rates in the country. According to the NFHS-3 (2005–06), 38.4% of children under 3 years are stunted, 19.1% wasted and 45.9% underweight. These figures have not improved much since 1998–99 (NFHS-2); in fact the proportion of wasted children has increased. The Body Mass Index (BMI) of 33% of women and 28.1% of men is below normal. Prevalence of anaemia is very high among young children (6–35 months), ever married women (15–49 years) and pregnant women and has increased since 1998–99 in all the three groups.

1.126. A variety of interventions consisting of dietary diversification, nutrient supplementation and public health measures involving better hygiene, sanitation and deworming will be undertaken to tackle the problem of malnutrition. The Integrated Child Development Services (ICDS) scheme, the government's main programme for addressing the problem of malnutrition, will be universalized on a fully decentralized on-demand basis and restructured in the Eleventh Plan as described below. The implementation of ICDS will be improved by giving responsibility of execution to the community and PRIs. Besides, there will be wider coverage of hot cooked meals and extensive promotion of infant and young child feeding practices.

Women's Agency and Child Rights

1.127. Inclusive growth in the Eleventh Plan envisages respecting the differential needs of all women and children and providing them with equal access to opportunities. This can only happen when women are recognized as agents of socio-economic growth with autonomy of decision-making and the rights of children are respected.

1.128. The Eleventh Plan proposes a five-fold agenda for gender equity. This includes economic empowerment; social empowerment; political empowerment; strengthening mechanisms for effective implementation of women-related legislations; and augmenting delivery mechanisms for mainstreaming gender. For children, it adopts a rights framework based on the principles of protection, well-being, development and participation. Recognizing that women and children are not homogenous categories, the Eleventh Plan aims to have not just general programmes, but also special targeted interventions, catering to the differential needs of different groups. Thus during the plan period, specific pilots for girl children and Muslim women, will be taken up.

1.129. To ensure a gender responsive health care system, maternal health services will be improved and emergency and compulsory obstetrics care will be made available within a travel time of two hours. Targets for halving prevalence of anaemia and malnutrition among women and children have been set and the ICDS scheme is being restructured and reoriented towards this end. A new component of conditional maternity benefits is proposed to target foetal malnutrition, ensure better care for pregnant women and encourage breastfeeding. Universalization of Anganwadis will be carried out, and Panchayats and mothers' groups will be given resources to ensure effective implementation of the scheme. Need based, community-run crèches will also be introduced to tackle child malnutrition.

1.130. Departing from previous Plans, the Eleventh Plan views violence as a public health issue and calls for training of medical personnel at all levels of the health care system to recognize and report violence against women and children. The Eleventh Plan also introduces the Integrated Child Protection scheme and the Scheme for Relief and Rehabilitation of Victims of Sexual Assault. New and empowering bills like the Sexual Harassment at Workplace Bill and the Compulsory Registration of Marriages Bill are expected to become law during the Plan period.

Poverty, Livelihood Security, and Rural Development

1.131. Accelerating agriculture development with emphasis on watershed development in dryland areas and a special focus on small farmers will increase employment and help reduce poverty in rural areas. The Eleventh Plan also places emphasis on several other initiatives which will increase economic well-being and opportunities in rural areas. The NREGP provides income support for those in need of employment while also helping to create assets that will increase land productivity. The Bharat Nirman programme will provide electricity and drinking water to all habitations before the end of the Plan period. PMGSY will provide all-weather connectivity to all villages with a population of over 1000 or with a population of over 500 in hilly areas. SSA will provide eight years of education to all children. The other measures taken for improving education will help give opportunities to all children to fully develop their capabilities. The Rural Health Mission is directed to reach health services to all. The total sanitation campaign (TSC) should provide clean environment in villages.

1.132. When these programmes are effectively implemented, the benefits of growth would spread widely, especially in rural areas and backward regions. An important element of the Eleventh Plan strategy is to empower PRIs through special training as well as funds, supplemented by the Backward Regions Grants Fund (BRGF), to implement and oversee these programmes.

Urban Infrastructure and Urban Poverty Alleviation

1.133. India is relatively less urbanized (29.2% as on 1 October 2007 as per the projections made by the office of Registrar General of India) than other countries at the same level of development. However, since the scope for employment opportunities in rural areas is somewhat limited, accelerated growth as envisaged in the Eleventh Plan is expected to result in more rapid migration of rural populations to urban centres. To deal with the situation, a two-pronged action plan is necessary. First, the quality of infrastructure in existing cities will have to be upgraded to provide improved municipal services to larger numbers of people and, second, new suburban townships will have to be developed in the vicinity of existing cities as satellites/counter magnets to reduce/redistribute the influx of population.

1.134. Not only is India less urbanized, the state of urban infrastructure, especially the availability of water and sewage treatment facilities, is much lower than what it should be. Urban transport infrastructure also leaves much to be desired. The Jawaharlal Nehru National Urban Renewal Mission (JNNURM), which commenced in the Tenth Plan, will continue to be the main vehicle for raising the level of infrastructure and utilities in the existing cities. The aim of the Mission is to create economically productive, efficient, equitable and responsive cities and the focus is on: (i) improving and augmenting the economic and social infrastructure of cities; (ii) ensuring basic services to the urban poor, including security of tenure at affordable prices; (iii) initiating wide-ranging urban sector reforms whose primary aim will be to eliminate legal, institutional and financial constraints that have impeded investment in urban infrastructure and services; (iv) strengthening municipal governments and their functioning in accordance with the provisions of the Constitutional (Seventy-Fourth) Amendment Act, 1992.

1.135. The development of satellite townships can be left largely to the private sector. However, in order to facilitate and induce such development the State Governments will need to undertake provision of trunk level infrastructure. The National Capital Region Planning Board is tasked with planning the process of infrastructure development for the areas around Delhi. Similar boards can be set up to undertake coordinated development of townships around other large cities, learning from the Delhi experience to make the planning process more effective.

1.136. Urban poverty alleviation and slum development will continue to be an important component of the Eleventh Plan. Tenth Plan schemes under JNNURM for providing affordable shelter and decent living and working conditions to the poor and for helping them to develop self-employment enterprises will be continued. The Swarna Jayanti Shahri Rozgar Yojana (SJSRY), a CSS to provide gainful employment to the urban unemployed (below the poverty line) will be implemented in a revamped form during the Eleventh Plan period.

Science and Technology as a Driver of Growth

1.137. Science and Technology are important drivers of economic growth and development in the contemporary world. The present juncture is critical for Indian science and major positive steps in this area will help the country to achieve sustained and rapid growth in the future.

1.138. In order to enlarge the pool of scientific manpower in the country and to attract and foster talent in scientific research a programme for 'Innovations in Science Pursuit for Inspired Research' (INSPIRE) will be launched. This will involve innovation funding in schools, summer camp with Science Icons (for high performers), assured career opportunity scheme for proven talent, and retention of talent in publicly-funded research. In addition, the Oversight Committee recommendation regarding Scholarships for Higher Education (SHE) providing 10000 scholarships per year for attracting talented science students of BSc and MSc courses will also be effectively implemented. Further, discipline-specific education programmes would be launched particularly in strategic sectors like, Space Sciences and Nuclear Sciences to capture talent at 'plus two' level with a view to developing quality human resources in the country for these sectors.

1.139. Universities are the cradle for basic research. To promote basic research in the country, a two pronged strategy will be adopted, aiming at: (i) Expansion and strengthening of the S&T base in the universities, and (ii) providing support to established centres of advanced research on the basis of competitive research funding for undertaking major and internationally competitive research programmes.

1.140. An effort would also be made to ensure that the wide pool of excellence available in the publically funded research institutions also participate actively as adjunct faculty in the universities and newly created academic and research institutions.

1.141. Effective mechanisms for promoting scientific research in the country need to be established in the Eleventh Five Year Plan. The peer review system will be upgraded to make it more stringent. All matters relating to Science and Technology including scientific audit as well as performance measurement of scientists and scientific institutions would need to be dealt with holistically.

Environment and Sustainability

1.142. Translating the vision of environmental sustainability will require that environment concerns are given a very high priority in development planning at all levels in the Eleventh Plan. The responsibility of enforcing environmental laws will be defined and shared with the States to broad base the enforcement effort. Enforcement mechanisms for dealing with industrial and vehicular pollution will be strengthened on the principle of polluter pays concept.

1.143. Environmental management (including municipal solid waste and sewage management) is a crucial component of urban planning and has been sadly neglected. Sewage treatment must be given focused attention. Recycling of the treated water for appropriate purposes must be incentivized. Efforts will be made to integrate sewage treatment with water conservation. Local bodies will be provided with adequate financial support for the purpose.

1.144. The River Conservation Programme will be strengthened to ensure that river flows are adequate to provide water of at least bathing quality standards. A Comprehensive Action Plan for Yamuna and a manageable number of important rivers will be implemented urgently with a stiff penalty system for violators.

1.145. Participating systems will be strengthened for sustainable use of forests in keeping with the global consensus on the need for community involvement for management of natural resources. The livelihood potential of forests will be improved for enhancing the stake of the community in conservation. The scope of wildlife management principles will be extended beyond sanctuaries and national parks. Conservation efforts will include compatible human interface with forests. Scientific aspects of ecology and biodiversity will be the basis of conservation planning.

1.146. The prospect of climate change presents a serious threat to our development over the longer term horizon. Available scientific evidence suggests that India will be one of the countries that will be severely affected by climate change. The Himalayan glaciers are already receding and the trend could intensify. There is likely to be an increase in the mean temperatures which would have adverse effects on foodgrain production with the present level of technology. The monsoon would be affected with a greater frequency of extreme events. We have to evolve a positive stance toward adaptation and also engage constructively with the international community to reach a consensus on mitigation based on fair principles of burden sharing. Development and promotion of low carbon and high energy-efficient technologies with reasonable costs will be a priority. The Clean Development Mechanism (CDM) will be used as an incentive. A National Action plan on Climate Change is being prepared. The government's effort will be towards creating an enabling environment for encouraging energy and carbon efficiency in public and private sectors and towards internalizing climate change concerns in development planning.

Panchayati Raj Institutions (PRIs) as Delivery Mechanisms

1.147. The Eleventh Plan seeks to substantially empower and use PRIs as the primary means of delivery of the essential services that are critical to inclusive growth. The 73rd and 74th Amendments to the Constitution have led to the establishment of about 2.5 lakh elected institutions of local self-government. (about 2.38 lakh in rural areas and the rests in urban areas). As against about 540 directly elected Members of Parliament and about 4500 directly elected members of our State assemblies, we have about 3.2 million elected representatives in the PRIs of which as many as 1.2 million are women. There are more elected women in India alone than in the rest of the world put together. It is absolutely critical for the inclusiveness of our growth process that these large numbers of elected representatives in our PRIs are fully involved in planning, implementing and supervising the delivery of the essential public services.

1.148. The Eleventh Plan recognizes that there is a need to build in incentives that will encourage the States to devolve functions, funds and functionaries to the PRIs. In order to capture the extent to which this process and empowerment of PRIs has actually progressed in each State, a suitable Devolution Index will be developed and will be called PRI-Empowerment Index.

Monitorable Targets

1.149. A key feature of the inclusive growth strategy in the Eleventh Plan is that growth of GDP should not be treated as an end in itself, but only as a means to an end. This is best done by adopting monitor able targets which would reflect the multi-dimensional economic and social objectives of inclusive growth. Furthermore, to ensure efficient and timely implementation of the accompanying projects and programmes, these targets need to be disaggregated at the level of the States which implement many of the programmes.

1.150. Following this approach, 27 monitorable targets have been identified at the national level of which 13 can be disaggregated at the level of individual States. These targets are ambitious, but it is better to aim high and fail than to aim low. The Eleventh Plan lays great stress on attaining them.

The 27 National Targets

1.151. Twenty-seven targets at the national level fall in six major categories. The six categories are: (i) Income and Poverty; (ii) Education; (iii) Health; (iv) Women and Children; (v) Infrastructure; and (vi) Environment. The targets in each of these categories are given below.

(i) Income and Poverty

- Average GDP growth rate of 9% per year in the Eleventh Plan period.
- Agricultural GDP growth rate at 4% per year on the average.
- Generation of 58 million new work opportunities.
- Reduction of unemployment among the educated to less than 5%.
- 20% rise in the real wage rate of unskilled workers.
- Reduction in the head-count ratio of consumption poverty by 10 percentage points.

(ii) Education

- Reduction in the dropout rates of children at the elementary level from 52.2% in 2003–04 to 20% by 2011–12.
- Developing minimum standards of educational attainment in elementary schools, to ensure quality education.
- Increasing the literacy rate for persons of age 7 years or more to 85% by 2011–12.
- Reducing the gender gap in literacy to 10 percentage points by 2011–12.
- Increasing the percentage of each cohort going to higher education from the present 10% to 15% by 2011–12.

(iii) Health

- Infant mortality rate (IMR) to be reduced to 28 and maternal mortality ratio (MMR) to 1 per 1000 live births by the end of the Eleventh Plan.
- Total Fertility Rate to be reduced to 2.1 by the end of the Eleventh Plan.
- Clean drinking water to be available for all by 2009, ensuring that there are no slip-backs by the end of the Eleventh Plan.
- Malnutrition among children of age group 0–3 to be reduced to half its present level by the end of the Eleventh Plan.
- Anaemia among women and girls to be reduced to half its present level by the end of the Eleventh Plan.

(iv) Women and Children

- Sex ratio for age group 0–6 to be raised to 935 by 2011–12 and to 950 by 2016–17.
- Ensuring that at least 33% of the direct and indirect beneficiaries of all government schemes are women and girl children.
- Ensuring that all children enjoy a safe childhood, without any compulsion to work.

(v) Infrastructure

- To ensure electricity connection to all villages and BPL households by 2009 and reliable power by the end of the Plan.
- To ensure all-weather road connection to all habitations with population 1000 and above (500 and above in hilly and tribal areas) by 2009, and all significant habitations by 2015.
- To connect every village by telephone and provide broadband connectivity to all villages by 2012.
- To provide homestead sites to all by 2012 and step up the pace of house construction for rural poor to cover all the poor by 2016–17.

(iv) Environment

- To increase forest and tree cover by 5 percentage points.
- To attain WHO standards of air quality in all major cities by 2011–12.
- To treat all urban waste water by 2011–12 to clean river waters.
- To increase energy efficiency by 20% by 2016–17.

THE 13 STATE-SPECIFIC TARGETS

1.152. The Eleventh Plan has been formulated in a manner whereby 13 of the 27 monitorable national targets have been disaggregated into appropriate targets for individual States. These are

(i) GDP growth rate
(ii) Agricultural growth rate
(iii) New work opportunities
(iv) Poverty ratio
(v) Drop out rate in elementary schools
(vi) Literacy rate
(vii) Gender gap in literacy rate
(viii) Infant mortality rate (IMR)
(ix) Maternal mortality ratio (MMR)
(x) Total Fertility Rate (TFR)
(xi) Child malnutrition
(xii) Anaemia among women and girls
(xiii) Sex-ratio

1.153. Appropriate policies and programmes have to be identified both at the Central and State levels so as to ensure realization of these targets in the Eleventh Plan period.

SIZE OF THE ELEVENTH PLAN

1.154. The total public sector outlay in the Eleventh Plan (both Centre and States and including their PSEs) is estimated at Rs 3644718 crore. Of this total, the share of the Centre (including the plans of PSEs) will amount to Rs 2156571 crore, while that of the States and union territories (UTs) will be Rs 1488147 crore.

1.155. The proposed size of the Eleventh Plan is much larger than the projected outlay, as well as the actual realization, in the Tenth Plan. At comparable prices, the Eleventh Plan outlay will be 120% higher than the Tenth Plan realization. In relation to GDP, the projected Eleventh Plan public sector outlay will be an average of 13.54% compared to the average of 9.46% that was achieved in the Tenth Plan. It must be emphasized, however, that Plan expenditure is not the same as public investment. It includes revenue expenditure on items such as salaries, which is high precisely because the focus of the Plan has shifted to supporting the social sectors, especially health and education.

1.156. Mobilizing resources in the public sector to finance the proposed Eleventh Plan will call for a major effort at generating tax revenues and controlling non-Plan expenditure and also improving the resource generation capacity of the PSEs. These issues are examined in detail in Chapter 3.

2

Macroeconomic Framework

2.1. This chapter presents the basic macroeconomic projections underlying the Eleventh Plan consistent with achieving the target GDP growth rate of 9% on average over the Eleventh Plan period. These projections are not based on a single model of the economy, but on the results of several different models which have been used to explore feasible levels of growth and to derive a broadly consistent macroeconomic picture covering the broad sectoral composition of growth, savings and investment and projections of the balance of payments which are consistent with external viability of the strategy being proposed.

GROWTH POTENTIAL

2.2. The growth potential of the economy can be judged to some extent by the performance of the economy in the past, and especially the performance in recent years. Table 2.1 presents the growth rates achieved in each Plan period since the First Five Year Plan.

2.3. It shows that the economy grew at 6.5% per year in the Eighth Plan period (1992–1996) and then decelerated to 5.5% in the Ninth Plan period (1997–2001), but recovered sharply to achieve a growth rate of 7.7% during the Tenth Plan. The last four years of the Tenth Plan recorded an average of about 8.7% and this momentum has continued into 2007–08 which is the first year of the Eleventh Plan, and is likely to record a growth of around 8.5% or, perhaps, even a little higher.

2.4. In this background, the 9% growth target for the Eleventh Plan period (2007–2011) approved by the NDC, which involved accelerating gradually from around 8.5% in the first year of the Plan to 10% by the end of the Plan period, appears entirely feasible, provided supportive policies are put in place. China has achieved growth rates exceeding 9% for two to three decades and while circumstances in India are not identical, the Indian economy has many strengths and now looks well

TABLE 2.1
Growth Performance in the Five Year Plans

(% per annum)

Plan Period	Target	Realization	Plan Period	Target	Realization
1. First Plan (1951–55)	2.1	3.5	8. Sixth Plan (1980–84)	5.2	5.5
2. Second Plan (1956–60)	4.5	4.2	9. Seventh Plan (1985–89)	5.0	5.6
3. Third Plan (1960–65)	5.6	2.8	10. Annual Plan (1990–91)	–	3.4
4. Annual Plans (1966–68)	–	3.9	11. Eighth Plan (1992–96)	5.6	6.5
5. Fourth Plan (1969–73)	5.7	3.2	12. Ninth Plan (1997–2001)	6.5	5.5
6. Fifth Plan (1974–78)	4.4	4.7	13. Tenth Plan (2002–2006)	7.9	7.7
7. Annual Plan (1979–80)	–	–5.2			

Note: The growth targets for the first three Plans were set with respect to National Income. In the Fourth Plan it was Net Domestic Product. The actual growth rates are in terms of GDP at factor cost. Average growth rates over a short period can be misleading because of fluctuations in agricultural output due to variable monsoon.

positioned to achieve this goal. The economy has been accelerating gradually for the past fifteen years and the further acceleration needed to achieve the Eleventh Plan target is only modest. If this target is achieved, it would mean that per capita GDP would grow at around 7.6% per annum during the Eleventh Plan period. Per capita consumption growing by about 7% a year would double per capita consumption in about 10 years. Further, if growth is sufficiently inclusive, it will certainly provide an environment conducive to bringing about a broad-based improvement in living standards. Accelerated growth will also boost tax collections in both the Centre and the States, allowing the public sector to finance the special programmes needed to ensure inclusiveness.

2.5. The major macroeconomic parameters associated with achieving the average GDP growth of 9% during the Eleventh Plan are given in Table 2.2 with a comparative picture of the same parameters for the Tenth Plan. It may be noted that the higher growth target in the Eleventh Plan is premised upon a significant increase in the investment rate from an average of 32% of GDP in the Tenth Plan to an average of 36.7% of GDP in the Eleventh Plan. The Incremental Capital Output Ratio (ICOR) is expected to improve marginally. With the competition stimulated by openness and the expected improvement in infrastructure, ICOR can be expected to come down. Considering the acceleration in savings and investment rates in recent years, the projected growth may seem conservative. However, since private investment may fluctuate over a business cycle, a deliberately conservative target is set.

SECTORAL COMPOSITION OF GROWTH

2.6. Earlier, planning models placed heavy emphasis on estimating the sectoral composition of growth based on input-output balances established on the basis of detailed multi-sector models. Such detailed sectoral targets have little relevance in an open economy where necessary balances for all the tradable goods can be achieved through exports and imports. The only sectors where it is necessary to plan for a balance between domestic production and likely demands are the non-tradable sectors which are mainly in infrastructure, e.g. electric power, road transport, ports, airports, telecommunications, etc. The capacity requirements for these sectors have been worked out in detail and the policy implications and investment implications are discussed in Chapter 12 and also in the relevant chapters on individual sectors.

2.7. Although detailed sectoral targets are no longer relevant, it is possible to present a broad picture of sectoral growth prospects consistent with the target of 9% growth of the economy as a whole. Table 2.3 presents the sectoral composition of growth in the past three Plans together with indicative projections for the Eleventh Plan.

TABLE 2.2
Macroeconomic Parameters

(at 2006–07 prices)

	Tenth Plan	Eleventh Plan
1. Investment Rate (% of GDPmp)	32.4	36.7
2. Domestic Savings Rate (% of GDPmp)	30.9	34.8
3. Current Account Deficit (% of GDPmp)	1.5	1.9
4. ICOR	4.3	4.1
5. GDP Growth Rate (% per annum)	7.5	9.0

Note: GDPmp = GDP at market prices.

TABLE 2.3
Sectoral Growth in Recent Plans

(% per annum)

Sector	Eighth Plan (1992–96)	Ninth Plan (1997–2001)	Tenth Plan (2002–06)	Eleventh Plan (2007–11)
1. Agriculture	4.72	2.44	2.30	4.0
2. Industry	7.29	4.29	9.17	10–11
3. Services	7.28	7.87	9.30	9–11
4. Total	6.54	5.52	7.74	9.0

It may be seen that both agriculture and industry show a marked deceleration in the Ninth Plan compared to the Eighth Plan. The deceleration in industry was reversed in the Tenth Plan but the growth in agriculture continued to be slow. The services sector accelerated sharply in the Tenth Plan.

2.8. The deceleration in agriculture, which began in the Ninth Plan period and continued in the Tenth Plan period, has been a major area of concern from the point of view of inclusiveness. With half our population deriving the greater part of their income from agriculture, faster growth in agriculture is necessary to provide a boost to their incomes. Rising incomes in agriculture will also boost non-agricultural income in rural areas, thus helping redress the rural–urban imbalance. The Eleventh Plan has therefore set a sectoral target of doubling agricultural growth to 4% per year. In this context it may be noted that agricultural growth increased from less than 1% in the first three years of the Tenth Plan to average more than 4% in the last two years and, from early indications, this will be maintained in the first year of the Eleventh Plan also. Although no firm judgement is yet possible, this growth upturn in agriculture is a promising development and suggests that the target of 4% growth in agriculture for the Eleventh Plan is eminently achievable.

2.9. Industrial performance in the Tenth Plan period improved to a respectable 9.2% from the very low growth rate of 4.3% in the Ninth Plan. This revival of industrial growth is a major achievement of the policy in recent years. However, industrial performance needs to be improved further if high quality employment in the non-agricultural sector is to be generated. Within industry, the manufacturing sector, accounting for 77% of industrial output has shown significant growth acceleration in the last two years. This revival of dynamism in industry has to be sustained to reverse the unacceptable decline in the share of manufacturing in GDP that has happened since 1991. This will also help generate more employment opportunities for the burgeoning workforce. The Eleventh Plan aims at double digit growth both in manufacturing and in industry. At the same time, it will be critical to improve the performance of the core sector (steel, coal, cement, oil, fertilizers and refined petroleum) to ensure that their supply response is adequate to sustain double digit manufacturing and industrial growth. Accelerated growth in industry will help to provide faster growth in organized sector employment, which is typically of a higher quality.

2.10. The services sector has grown impressively in successive Plans with a sharp acceleration in the Tenth Plan period, reflecting the rapid growth in high-end services spurred by the IT revolution. This has opened up new and attractive employment opportunities for our educated youth. We can expect further improvement in performance in this sector with an acceleration of services growth to 10% in the Eleventh Plan. Rapid growth in IT related services and in tourism will contribute to this outcome as will the expected expansion in health and education which should provide additional jobs for teachers, doctors and medical attendants.

TABLE 2.4
Investment and Savings Rates

(% of GDP)

Year	Investment Rate	Savings Rate
Eighth Plan (1992–93 to 1996–97)	24.4	23.1
Ninth Plan (1997–98 to 2001–02)	24.3	23.6
2002–03	25.2	26.4
2003–04	28.2	29.8
2004–05	32.2	31.8
2005–06	35.5	34.3
2006–07	35.9	34.8
Tenth Plan (2002–03 to 2006–07)	32.1	31.9
Eleventh Plan Targets	36.7	34.8

Note: Ratios for Eleventh Plan are at constant 2006–07 price; Ratios for earlier years' Plans are at current price; 2005–06: Provisional Estimates; 2006–07: Quick Estimates.

AGGREGATE INVESTMENT

2.11. High levels of investment are critical for rapid growth and an important strength of the economy is that we are entering the Eleventh Plan after experiencing several years of a rising level of investment as a percentage of GDP. As shown in Table 2.4, the investment rate averaged 24.4% in the Eighth Plan period and was almost unchanged in the Ninth Plan period. Thereafter it rose to an average of 32.1% in the Tenth Plan with the last year of the Plan showing an acceleration to 35.9%. This rate of investment should normally be adequate to attain 9% growth, but in our circumstances, because of prolonged underinvestment in infrastructure and the consequent need to enhance investment in this area, the Eleventh Plan aims at a further increase in the rate of investment in succeeding years to reach 38% at the end of the Plan period, yielding an average of around 37% in the entire Plan period.

2.12. An important structural change in the investment behaviour of the economy in the recent past is the change in relative shares of public and private investment. As shown in Table 2.5, although the rate of total investment as a percentage of GDP was almost the same in the Eighth Plan as in the Ninth Plan, the composition shifted in favour of private investment. Public sector investment as a percentage of GDP declined from 8.5% in the Eighth Plan to 7% in the Ninth Plan. This meant that the share of public sector investment in total investment declined from 34.7% in the Eighth Plan to 29% in the Ninth Plan. This trend of a declining rate of public investment as a percentage of GDP continued in the first two years of the Tenth Plan but then began to be corrected in the rest of the Plan period. Private sector investment continued to be buoyant throughout the Tenth Plan period so the share of public investment in total investment in the Tenth Plan fell to 22%.

2.13. The rapid increase in private sector investment in the aggregate investment is in large part a reflection of the impact of the reforms initiated in the 1990s, which reduced restrictions on private investment and created a more favourable investment climate. It reflects the fact that the private sector has responded positively with an improvement in the investment climate. This is clearly a welcome development and should be encouraged in the Eleventh Plan. However, the declining trend in public investment as a percentage of GDP is a matter of concern. It reflects inadequate public investment in the Ninth Plan period in many critical areas such as agriculture and infrastructure. The reversal of the declining trend of public investment as a percentage of GDP in the Tenth Plan is a welcome development which needs to be continued in the Eleventh Plan. It must be emphasized that a higher share of public investment can be justified only if there is a demonstrable improvement in the efficiency of public investment. However, it can be argued that the infrastructure gaps are so large that an increase in public investment in infrastructure will actually crowd in private investment. These objectives are reflected in the projections for the Eleventh Plan, as shown in Table 2.5.

2.14. The private sector, which includes farming, micro, small and medium enterprises (MSMEs), and the larger

TABLE 2.5
Total and Public Investment in the Ninth and Tenth Plans

	Total Investment (% of GDPmp)	Private Investment (% of GDPmp)	Public Investment (% of GDPmp)	Public Investment (% of Total Investment)
Eighth Plan (1992–93 to 1996–97)	24.4	15.9	8.5	34.7
Ninth Plan (1997–98 to 2001–02)	24.3	17.3	7.0	29.0
2002–03	25.2	19.2	6.1	24.1
2003–04	28.2	21.8	6.3	22.5
2004–05	32.2	25.3	6.9	21.4
2005–06	35.5	27.9	7.6	21.4
2006–07	35.9	28.1	7.8	21.6
Tenth Plan (2002–03 to 2006–07)	32.1	25.1	7.1	22.0
Eleventh Plan	36.7	28.7	8.0	21.9

Note: Ratios for Eleventh Plan are at constant 2006–07 price; Ratios for earlier years' Plans are at current price; 2005–06: Provisional Estimates; 2006–07: Quick Estimates.

private corporate sector, accounts for over 77% of the total investment in the economy and an even larger share in employment and output. Expansion in this sector will have to play a critical role in achieving the objective of faster and more inclusive growth. The MSMEs, in particular, have a vital role to play in making the growth regionally balanced, and in generating widely dispersed off-farm employment, some of it in rural areas. The Eleventh Plan, therefore, aims at an increase in investment in the private sector to 28.7% from an average of 25.1% in the Tenth Plan. This is best done by creating an environment in which entrepreneurship can flourish at all levels. New entrepreneurs should be able to enter and expand. In order to compete with incumbents, there must be strong competitive pressures which promote efficiency, government policies must be investor friendly, transaction costs should be low and infrastructure services of good quality should be readily available, especially to small and medium enterprises. Many elements of this environment are already in place. Licensing controls and discretionary approvals have already been greatly reduced, but remnants of the control regime remain that still need drastic overhaul, if not elimination, especially at the State Government level. Quantitative controls, where they exist, should give way to fiscal measures and increased reliance on competitive markets, subject to effective and transparent regulation. The burden of multiple inspections by government agencies must be removed and tax regimes rationalized. Since MSMEs are expected to create the bulk of new employment, it is particularly important to make the financial system more efficient in meeting the needs of our expanding private sector, and to ensure financial inclusiveness.

2.15. While encouraging private investment, the Eleventh Plan also aims at a substantial increase in public investment in critical areas such as agriculture, irrigation and water management, and in social and economic infrastructure. Public investment in infrastructure is projected to increase from 4.1% in 2006–07 to 6.8% in 2011–12. Since this increase must be accommodated with the overall increase in public investment from 7.8% in 2006–07 to 8.6% in 2011–12, it implies that public investment will shift from the non-infrastructure to infrastructure sector.

AGGREGATE SAVINGS

2.16. The rise in investment projected in the Eleventh Plan is expected to be supported by a substantial increase in domestic savings. Table 2.6 presents the structure of savings since the Eighth Plan period. Private savings consist of household savings, including direct investment by households, and corporate sector savings. Public sector savings consist of the savings of the government departments (Centre and States) and public sector corporations. Both components of private savings (households and corporate sector) have risen as a per cent of GDP in the Ninth Plan and also in the Tenth Plan. Corporate savings have been especially buoyant in the Tenth Plan, reflecting the very strong output and financial performance of the private sector in recent years.

2.17. The behaviour of public savings displays a more varied pattern. There was a marked deterioration in public savings in the Ninth Plan period, reflecting the sharp deterioration in the performance of Departmental Savings mainly on account of the impact of the Fifth Pay Commission which led to an increase in government salaries. Departmental Savings deteriorated from –0.9% of GDP in the Eighth Plan to –4.1% of GDP in the Ninth Plan. There was a marginal improvement in the savings of public sector undertakings from 3% of GDP in the Eighth Plan to 3.3% in the Ninth Plan, but the deterioration in Departmental Savings in the Ninth Plan meant that total public sector savings deteriorated from 2.1% of GDP in the Eighth Plan to –0.8% of GDP, a turnaround of 3 percentage points.

2.18. As shown in Table 2.6, both components of public sector savings showed an improvement in the Tenth Plan. Reduction in the dis-savings of government administration has been due to three main reasons: first, the impact of the Fifth Pay Commission's recommendations worked itself out in the system; second the implementation of the Fiscal Responsibility and Budget Management (FRBM) Act, and the fiscal and revenue deficit targets for 2008–09 established thereby helped introduce an element of discipline; and third, the buoyancy in tax revenues arising out of the high growth rate recorded in the Tenth Plan combined with improvements in tax administration contributed to improved savings.

2.19. The projections for the Eleventh Plan assume that the private sector savings effort will continue to be strong with some further improvement and that this will be combined with a very strong improvement in public sector savings. The scale of the public sector effort can be seen from the fact that the Eleventh Plan projects a combined public sector savings rate of 4.5% of GDP compared with an achieved level of only 1.9% in the Tenth Plan. The projected turnaround of 2.6 percentage points of GDP in public sector savings requires a massive effort on the part of both the PSEs and the departments, mainly, the latter. It is important to note that this favourable outcome assumes that the award of the Sixth Pay Commission will not present severe difficulties. Hopefully, since the Fifth Pay Commission had indexed salaries fully to inflation, the pay increases should be only moderate. Pay revision should also increase private savings. If some of the subsidies financed by the government can be moderated, the savings target of public administration is realizable. It is also assumed that PSEs will maintain their savings performance of the Tenth Plan. One could expect it to increase. However, a slightly lower savings rate of 4% of GDP is conservatively projected to account for government policy on oil product price subsidies and its adverse impact on oil PSUs' balance sheets.

THE BALANCE OF PAYMENTS

2.20. A key aspect of macroeconomic consistency is the viability of the Plan targets in terms of their implications for managing the balance of payments.

2.21. During the Tenth Plan period, merchandise exports moved on to a new trajectory with an annual average growth rate of 23.2%. Similarly, with a buoyant economy, merchandise imports increased by 27.8% during this period. There has been a continuous shift of exports towards technology intensive high-value manufactures, including machinery and instruments and also petroleum products, gems and jewellery. Despite substantial growth in the export of petroleum products by an annual average of 54.3% in the Tenth Plan, net oil imports increased by 26.5% due to the steep rise in oil prices of the Indian basket. Services exports increased substantially in the Tenth Plan contributing to increase in net invisibles. This provided a cushion for financing a large part of the trade deficit on the merchandise account. The current account deficit in 2006–07 was US$ 9.6 billion, i.e. 1.1% of GDP.

2.22. Based on the Tenth Plan trends, projections for the Eleventh Plan have been made and are summarized in Table 2.7. These projections reflect a picture of a dynamic Indian economy taking full advantage of the opportunities provided by integration with the world economy.

2.23. Exports in the Eleventh Plan are projected to grow at about 20% per year in US$ terms, which is lower than

TABLE 2.6
Composition of Saving

(% of GDP)

Period/Years	Private Sector			Public Sector			
	Household Sector Sector	Private Corporate Sector	Total Private Sector	Government Administration	Public Sector Undertaking	Total Public Sector	Gross Domestic Savings
Eighth Plan (1992–93 to 1996–97)	17.0	4.0	21.0	(–) 0.9	3.0	2.1	23.1
Ninth Plan (1997–98 to 2001–02)	20.5	4.0	24.5	(–) 4.1	3.3	(–) 0.8	23.6
2002–03	23.2	3.9	27.0	(–) 4.7	4.0	(–) 0.6	26.4
2003–04	24.4	4.4	28.7	(–) 3.1	4.2	1.1	29.8
2004–05	23.0	6.6	29.6	(–) 2.0	4.2	2.2	31.8
2005–06	24.2	7.5	31.7	(–) 1.4	4.0	2.6	34.3
2006–07	23.8	7.8	31.6	(–) 0.8	4.0	3.2	34.8
Tenth Plan (2002–03 to 2006–07)	23.7	6.3	30.0	(–) 2.2	4.1	1.9	31.9
Eleventh Plan	23.0	7.3	30.3	0.5	4.0	4.5	34.8

Note: Ratios for Eleventh Plan are at constant 2006–07 price; Ratios for earlier years' Plans are at current price; 2005–06: Provisional Estimates; 2006–07: Quick Estimates.

the 23% rate at which they have been growing over the Tenth Plan reflecting somewhat the lower projections of growth in world trade. Even with this moderation in export growth, the projection implies that the share of exports to GDP in the Eleventh Plan period will rise from 13.9% in 2006–07 to 22.5% by the terminal year of the Eleventh Plan, reflecting the continued integration of the economy with the rest of the world. This also implies an increase in India's share of world exports since world trade is unlikely to grow by more than 6%.

2.24. Imports on the other hand are likely to continue increasing at an average rate of 23% over the Eleventh Plan. This will help address critical capacity constraints in the plant and equipment sectors, the demand for which is expected to remain strong due to rising investment. Petroleum, oil and lubricants (POL) imports, which currently accounts for nearly 30% of total imports, will be boosted by the higher oil prices and rising energy consumption levels.

2.25. As Table 2.7 shows, the trade deficit is expected to go up significantly to 16% of GDP by 2011–12. This appears high but is expected to be largely compensated by rising invisible account surplus on the back of accelerating services sector exports, tourist earnings and remittances. This surplus is projected to be as much as 13.5% of GDP and the current account deficit projected for the Eleventh Plan period therefore increases from 1.1% in 2006–07 to 2.4% of GDP in 2011–12. These projections are calibrated around an international crude oil price of US$ 80 per barrel. Financing a deficit of this order should not present a problem given the foreign capital inflows that are taking place and which can be expected to continue, barring an unexpectedly severe and prolonged downside shock to the world economy. In fact, the capital flows we have been experiencing in recent years have proved difficult to manage, leading to a sharp build-up in foreign exchange reserves and upward pressure on the exchange rate which has adverse consequences.

UNCERTAINTIES AND RISKS

2.26. The external environment facing the economy in the Eleventh Plan period presents some uncertainties and risks which could have an impact on performance. These include the following:

- A downturn in the global economy, given the current macro imbalances and uncertainties in the financial markets.
- Uncertainty about the price of oil in world markets.

TABLE 2.7
Balance of Payments

(at 2006–07 price)

Items	2006–07		2011–12		(2007–12)	
	US$ billion	% to GDP	US$ billion	% to GDP	US$ billion	CAGR
Current Account Balance						
Exports	127.1	13.9	316.2	22.5	1135	20.0
Imports	192.0	20.9	540.5	38.5	1864	23.0
Trade Balance	–64.9	–7.1	–224.3	–16.0	–729	–
Invisibles (net)	55.3	6.0	190.0	13.5	616	28.0
of which:						
Exports of Services	81.3	8.9	238.4	17.0	812	24.0
Imports of Services	48.6	5.3	217.9	15.5	653	35.0
Current Account Balance	–9.6	–1.1	–34.3	–2.4	–113.2	–1.9@
Capital Account						
Foreign Direct Investment (net)	8.4*	0.9	14.0	1.0	48.3	10.7
NRI Deposits	3.9	0.4	9.8	0.7	38.6	20.3
Portfolio (net)	7.1	0.8	11.2	0.8	43.3	9.7
Net Capital Flows	44.9	4.9	51.9	3.7	206.8	2.9

Note: *Foreign Direct Investment (net) includes US$ 20.41 billion inflows and US$ 11.97 billion outflows during 2006–07. @ indicates percentage to GDP.

- Capital flows and exchange rate risks. This risk is more likely to be an upside risk.
- Impact of increase in food prices in the world due to increasing use of foodgrains for ethanol production.
- Continued governance problems that prevent necessary efficiency improvements in public expenditure and public investments.

Slowdown in World Economy

2.27. The growth of the world economy affects our economy directly through exports and also through the impact of global growth prospects on Foreign Direct Investment (FDI). It is therefore relevant to evaluate the medium term prospects in this regard. Although unsettled financial conditions prevailing at the end of 2007, combined with the persistence of global imbalances, have raised the prospect of a slowdown in some of the major economies over the next 12 months; this is likely to be temporary and not a medium-term phenomenon. In any case, Indian exports have shown considerable resilience and have also diversified considerably so that the impact of a temporary slowdown in some of the major industrial economies may not be significant. India's share in global trade is still small and an aggressive policy drive for expanding exports may enable us to weather the impact of a temporary slowing down of the global economy. In effect, the constraints on our growth are primarily internal and it is reasonable to assume that uncertainties affecting the world economy are not such as to have an impact on India's growth potential over the Eleventh Plan period.

High Oil Prices

2.28. The impact of higher oil prices on our growth can be significant and will depend on the strategy we adopt to deal with the situation. A 25% increase in oil price from US$ 80 per barrel can be expected to increase our import bill by 5% and the current account deficit to GDP ratio by a little over one percentage point of GDP. Base year deficit at around 1.1% of GDP is projected to increase to 2.4% of GDP by the terminal year. With higher oil prices, the deficit is likely to increase further, but would still be financiable. In fact, it would enable us to deal with foreign inflows which, at present, appear excessive. The additional foreign exchange cost of oil imports therefore should not present a serious problem. The more important issue is how we deal with the need to pass on high oil prices to the consumer. The present policy of insulating consumers from the full impact of the rise in the global price of oil is not sustainable as the public sector oil majors bear a very large burden in terms of under-recoveries and there are also fiscal costs which run into constraints posed by the FRBM Act. It is always possible to undertake some subsidization for those who are really needy, but the bulk of the under-recoveries at present are not on account of such targeted subsidization. As and when the global price is passed on fully to the consumers, it would reduce the demand for oil, mitigating the impact on the balance of payments, and also raise the general level of prices somewhat. Given the low rate of inflation at present, this one-time adjustment could be absorbed in the system without too much disruption. A price adjustment would also moderate growth to some extent in the short run but it would not significantly affect growth in the medium term.

Volatility of Capital Flows

2.29. The volatility of capital flows in a globalized world is a major problem which affects many countries. Traditionally, we have been concerned with volatility in terms of possible outflows triggering a balance of payments crisis. However, recent experience has exposed us to a new phenomenon of managing a surge of inflows. From a low of US$1 billion in foreign exchange reserves in the middle of 1991, when the economy was plunged into a balance of payments crisis, our foreign exchange reserves have reached over US$ 290 billion which is generally regarded as more than necessary for managing any conceivable downside shock to external payments. The same phenomenon is evident in many Asian countries which have seen a build-up in foreign exchange reserves.

2.30. This build-up in foreign exchange reserves was facilitated by foreign capital inflows to emerging market countries which have been very buoyant. Some part of the build-up was justified as a measure of insurance against a possible adverse turn in the external climate in future. However it is clear that the accumulation in reserves in recent years is in excess of requirements and reflects the desire to manage capital inflows without allowing them to impact on the exchange rate.

2.31. The problem posed by having to manage large inflows has been discussed in Chapter 13. It arises because of the well known 'trilemma' that it is not possible to achieve three objectives simultaneously, i.e. free capital mobility, an independent monetary policy and a stable exchange rate. Attention should be given to measures to restrain these capital flows and enhance the absorptive capacity in the economy to avoid running into the classical 'Dutch Disease' situation where non-tradables become over-priced and erode the competitiveness of the economy in the tradable sector.

2.32. Faced with a surge of inflows as in the past year, we have to either protect the exchange rate by intervening in the forex market or allow the rupee to appreciate. Rupee appreciation has a negative effect on export, especially in the short run, and is therefore best avoided. However, the option of intervening to buy up foreign exchange and add to reserves also has adverse consequences. If the intervention is not sterilized it leads to a build-up of liquidity, which could lead to inflation. If it is sterilized, as has been done extensively in 2007–08, it involves a significant fiscal cost since the interest paid by the government on market stabilization bond is significantly higher than the interest earned on reserves. It may be noted that if the spread between the two rates is 5 percentage points then the cost of sterilization of US$100 billion of excess reserves is US$5 billion per year or Rs 20000 crore.

2.33. In practice, governments have rarely chosen pure strategies. Instead, efforts are made to respond in terms of a mixed strategy of allowing some appreciation in the currency, some unsterilized intervention and some effort to limit inflows at the margin. This is essentially the policy we have followed thus far, and it is on the whole well conceived.

2.34. The cautious approach to opening the capital account followed thus far as a conscious act of policy has given the government some leeway in limiting inflows of certain categories. In determining the categories of capital flows on which restrictions should be imposed, we have rightly followed the approach of exempting FDI flows completely from any restrictions associated with short-term compulsions. We have also kept the door open for genuine Foreign Institutional Investment (FII) flows, while introducing some regulation of flows through non-transparent mechanisms such as participatory notes. This leaves external commercial borrowing (ECB) (including non resident Indian [NRI] deposits) which is subject to control and should bear the brunt of short-term restrictions, if these become necessary.

RISING FOOD PRICES IN THE WORLD

2.35. Foodgrain prices in the world markets have increased significantly in the last year due to a combination of poor harvest and a shift towards bio-fuels. The latter tendency is bound to accelerate, which suggest that food prices may remain high in the near future. This will undoubtedly put pressure on Indian agricultural prices. It should be emphasized that farmers are likely to gain from higher prices and to the extent to which low profitability of agriculture have been a cause of low farm income and adequate investment, the favourable shift in prices could actually boost domestic production and rural incomes. However, it must also be noted that consumers are hurt by higher prices and since most of the poor in India are net purchasers of food, it would be necessary to protect them from any undue increases in food prices. How to balance these conflicting objectives will present a major problem especially in the short term.

CONCLUSION

2.36. On balance, the macroeconomic parameters facing the economy at the start of the Eleventh Plan are very positive reflecting strong fundamentals and the economy is well set to benefit from them. There are risks and uncertainties but these can be managed, especially over the medium term. On the whole, the growth target of 9% proposed for the Eleventh Plan is feasible provided necessary supportive policies are put in place to address domestic constraints. These are discussed in detail in the individual chapters of the Plan document.

3

Financing the Plan

Financial Resources: Centre and States

INTRODUCTION

3.1. This chapter presents projections of the likely availability of total savings in the economy and also of public sector resources in the Eleventh Plan period given the target GDP growth rate of 9%. The overall picture in terms of resources for the economy as a whole suggests that given recent trends, it will be possible to mobilize the savings needed to finance the gross domestic investment needed for 9% growth. As far as public sector resources is concerned, the estimates show resource availability for the Eleventh Plan of Rs 3644718 crore at 2006–07 price for the Centre and States taken together. At comparable prices, this amounts to an increase of 120.5% over the Tenth Plan realization.

3.2. These projections imply that public sector resources for the Plan will increase from 9.46% of GDP in the Tenth Plan to 13.54% in the Eleventh Plan. Thus outcome depends critically on achievement of buoyancy in tax revenue, effective control over consumption expenditure and subsidies, and an improvement in the resource mobilizing capacity of Public Sector Undertakings (PSUs) both at the Central and State levels.

PUBLIC SECTOR RESOURCES IN THE TENTH PLAN

3.3. This section presents an overview of the resources of the Centre and States in the Tenth Plan period.

CENTRE'S RESOURCES

3.4. The GBS to the Tenth Plan was projected at Rs 706000 crore at 2001–02 price. This included Rs 300265 crore of Central assistance (CA) to the States and UTs. With the Tenth Plan resources of Central Public Sector Units (CPSUs) projected at Rs 515556 crore, resources available for the Central Plan was fixed at Rs 921291 crore.

3.5. Table 3.1 shows the financing pattern of the Centre's Plan during the Tenth Plan. The realized GBS available for the Plan was 84.2% of the projected amount. Realized Central assistance to States and UTs at Rs 203117 crore was 67.6% of the projected level. As a percentage of GBS, this declined from 42.5% to 34.2%. This decline in the share of CA to States and UTs is partly a reflection of the disintermediation of the loan portion of CA following the Twelfth Finance Commission's (TFC) award in the middle of the Tenth Plan period, and partly also a result of the increasing resource transfers to States through CSS specially in health, education and rural development, which expanded well beyond what was originally projected. CPSUs achieved 71.5% of resources projected in the Plan.

3.6. The total resources available for the Central Plan, consisting of GBS for the Central Plan plus PSUs' resources, worked out to 82.5% of the projected level i.e. Rs 760327 crore at 2001–02 price.

3.7. The pattern of funding GBS in the Tenth Plan as actually realized reflects a significant deterioration of non-debt contribution compared with the Plan projections. The share of Balance from Current Revenues (BCR) in GBS was projected to be (–)0.9% but deteriorated sharply to (–)17.2%. The realized share of borrowings had to

TABLE 3.1
Projected vis-à-vis Realized Financing Pattern of the Plan Outlay of the Centre (including UTs)

(Rs crore at 2001–02 price)

	Sources of Funding	Tenth Plan		
		Projection	Realization	% Realization
1	BCR	–6385 (–0.9)	–102280 (–17.2)	–1601.9
2	Borrowings including net MCR	685185 (97.1)	683962 (115.0)	99.8
3	Net Flow from Abroad	27200 (3.9)	12966 (2.2)	47.7
4	Gross Budgetary Support for the Plan (1+2+3)	706000 (100.0)	594649 (100.0)	84.2
5	Central assistance to States and UTs	300265 (42.5)	203117 (34.2)	67.6
6	GBS for Central Plan (4–5)	405735 (57.5)	391532 (65.8)	96.5
7	Resources of PSEs	515556	368796	71.5
8	Resources for Central Plan (6+7)	921291	760327	82.5

Note: Figures in parentheses are percentages of Gross Budgetary Support to Plan (S. No. 4).
Source: Planning Commission.

increase to 115% as against the projected share of 97.1% to bridge the BCR gap.

3.8. The deterioration in BCR during the Tenth Plan as compared to the projections reflects a relatively poor performance in the earlier years of the Plan. The BCR improved continuously, however, during each of the successive years of the Plan and turned positive in 2006–07. A robust economic growth and improved performance of the manufacturing sector helped to ensure that revenue receipts, particularly tax revenues, were buoyant throughout the Tenth Five Year Plan. Gross tax revenue of the Central Government recorded an average annual growth of 20.5%. Net of the share of the States, the tax revenues of the Centre grew at 21.4%. However, growth in non-tax revenue in the same period was moderate at 4.0%. The average annual growth of revenue receipts of the Central Government during the Tenth Plan was 16.7%.

3.9. Revenue receipts of the Centre increased by 1.1 percentage points of GDP from 9.4% in 2002–03 to 10.5% in 2006–07. Between 2002–03 and 2006–07, gross tax revenue as a proportion of GDP increased by about 2.7 percentage points, of which 0.6 percentage points was the increase in the share of the States. The gross tax GDP ratio increased to 10.3% in 2005–06 and is expected to increase further to 11.5% in 2006–07. Tax revenues (net of States' shares) increased by about 2.1 percentage points from 6.4% in 2002–03 to 8.5% in 2006–07. However, non-tax revenue fell by about 0.9 percentage points from 2.9% of GDP in 2002–03 to 2.0% of GDP in 2006–07. The decline in non-tax revenue has been largely due to a steep decline in interest receipts by about one percentage point owing to debt swap, and debt consolidation and resetting of interest rates, and disintermediation in borrowings arising from the award of the TFC.

3.10. The Non-Plan Revenue Expenditure (NPRE) declined by about 1.86 percentage points from 10.87% of GDP in 2002–03 to 9.01% of GDP in 2006–07 (refer to Table 3.2). This was mainly because of a sharp decline in interest payments of about 1.17% of GDP. Subsidies actually reflected in the Central budget declined by about 0.49% of GDP between 2002–03 and 2006–07. However, this ignores the fact that there was substantial under-provisioning in the budget for fertilizer subsidy. It also does not account for the under-recovery by petroleum companies because of the inadequate adjustment in prices to compensate for oil price increases.

TABLE 3.2
Non-Plan Revenue Expenditure (NPRE) and its Components

(Rs crore)

		2002–03 Actual	2006–07 Provisional
1	Interest	117804 (4.79)	149553 (3.62)
2	Pension	14496 (0.59)	21984 (0.53)
3	Salary*	18253 (0.74)	23232 (0.56)
4	Subsidies	43533 (1.77)	52935 (1.28)
5	Other NPRE	73058 (2.97)	123940 (3.00)
6	(Total) NPRE	267144 (10.87)	371644 (9.01)

Note: *2006–07 is BE. Figures in parentheses are percentages of GDP.
Source: Planning Commission.

TABLE 3.3
Gross Fiscal Deficit

(as % of GDP)

Year	Centre	States	Combined
2002–03	5.9	4.2	9.6
2003–04	4.5	4.5	8.5
2004–05	4.0	3.5	7.5
2005–06	4.1	2.5	6.7
2006–07 (RE)	3.7*	2.8	6.4
2007–08 (BE)	3.3	2.4	5.6
Tenth Plan (2002–07)	4.4	3.5	7.7

Note: *3.5 (2006–07 Provisional). BE stands for Budget Estimates.
Source: Macroeconomic and Monetary Developments Mid-Term Review 2007–08, 30 October 2007, RBI.

3.11. During the Tenth Plan, expenditure on subsidies increased by 22.8% from Rs 43533 crore in 2002–03 to Rs 52935 crore in 2006–07. The main factor behind the increase was fertilizer subsidy, which more than doubled. While food subsidy remained stable and other subsidies increased by 29%, petroleum subsidies reflected in the budget declined in nominal terms. The apparent decline in petroleum subsidies, however, does not reflect the quasi-fiscal subsidization of oil prices through the issue of oil bonds. Subsidy rationalization, including targeting of the poor, has been an announced policy objective of the government for over a decade. However, success in this area has been rather limited.

3.12. Because of buoyant revenue receipts and some control over expenditure following the enactment of the fiscal responsibility legislation (see Box 3.1), the borrowings of the Central Government have been contained within the projected level in absolute terms. The percentage of interest payments to revenue receipts declined from 51% in 2002–03 to 34.5% in 2006–07 implying improved sustainability of the Centre's debt burden. The debt burden of the Centre has declined by almost 3.1 percentage points from 63.4% in 2002–03 to 60.3% of GDP as per 2006–07 BE.

3.13. The gross fiscal deficit of the Centre, as a percent of GDP, declined from 5.9% in 2002–03 to 4.1% in 2005–06 and further to 3.5% in 2006–07. The gross fiscal deficit of the States, as a percent of GDP, also declined from 4.2% in 2002–03 to 2.8% in 2006–07 revised estimates (RE). As a result, the combined fiscal deficit of the Centre and States came down from 9.6% in 2002–03 to 6.4% in 2006–07 (RE). The average fiscal deficit for the Tenth Plan, as a percent of GDP, was 4.4% for the Centre, 3.5% for the States and 7.7% for the Centre and States combined. The year-wise figures of fiscal deficit are provided in Table 3.3.

3.14. The net inflow from abroad on government account, which is deployed for funding externally aided projects, was projected to contribute 3.9% of GBS in the Tenth Plan. However, actual realization was less than half of the projected level, thereby reducing its realized share in Plan resources to 2.2% of GBS. The fall in net inflow from abroad is due to the repayment of costlier debt in the initial years of the Tenth Plan.

3.15. The IEBR of the CPSUs was projected to provide Rs 515556 crore but the actual realization was only Rs 368796 crore or 71.5% of the projected amount. As a result the realized share of IEBR in the Central Plan resources was only 48.5%, substantially lower than the projected share of 56%.

3.16. The investment by CPSUs is financed through budgetary support provided by the Central Government, which is a part of total plan outlay and GBS, and IEBR raised by CPSUs on their own. IEBR comprises of Internal Resources, and Extra-Budgetary Resources (EBR). Internal Resources comprise retained profits—net of dividend paid to government, depreciation provision, and carried forward reserves and surpluses. EBR consist of receipts from the issue of bonds, debentures, ECB, suppliers' credit, deposit receipts, and term loans from financial institutions.

3.17. IEBR contributed 83% of the Plan outlay of CPSUs during the Tenth Plan. Of this, Internal Resources contributed 47% and Extra-Budgetary Resources, 36%. In the original projections, Internal Resources (IR) were to contribute 79% and EBR were to contribute only about 21%. However, over the Tenth Plan, realization of IR has been about half the projection. The shortfall in IR has led to increased borrowings by the CPSUs. Consequently, EBR have exceeded the Tenth Plan target by about 51%.

RESOURCES OF STATES AND UNION TERRITORIES (UTs)

3.18. The Tenth Plan resources of the States and UTs were projected at Rs 590948 crore at 2001–02 price. The realization at 2001–02 prices is placed at Rs 569233 crore or 96.3% of the projected level. The realized pattern of funding, however, shows a divergence from the projected levels (as shown in Table 3.4). BCR has deteriorated by about 67 percentage points over the projected

Box 3.1
FRBMA, 2003 and Fiscal Consolidation

The Fiscal Reforms and Budget Management Act (FRBMA) enacted in 2003, is an important institutional mechanism to ensure fiscal prudence and support for macro economic balance. According to the Rules framed under the Act, revenue deficit is to be eliminated by 31 March 2009, and fiscal deficit is to be reduced to no more than 3% of estimated GDP by March 2009. The process of fiscal consolidation under FRBMA has been continuous. It has yielded rich dividends in terms of creating fiscal space for increased spending on infrastructure and social sectors. The traditional annual budgeting has moved to a more meaningful medium-term fiscal planning framework. FRBMA provides the basic structure around which many fiscal measures have been implemented. Some of the important among these include: reducing peak rates of customs duties, rectifying anomalies like inverted duty structure, rationalizing excise duties, relying on voluntary tax compliance, introduction of State-level VAT, increasing productivity of expenditure through an outcome budget framework, and innovative financing mechanisms like creation of special purpose vehicles for infrastructure projects. The success in fiscal consolidation in the Tenth Plan has provided a good foundation to build the Eleventh Plan.

TABLE 3.4
Core Tenth Plan Resources of States and UTs

(Rs crore at 2001–02 price)

	Sources of Funding	Projection	Realization	% realization
1	Balance from Current Revenues	–15295 (–2.6)	–25514 (–4.5)	–166.8
2	Resources of PSEs	82684 (14.0)	95714 (16.8)	115.8
	i) Internal resources	–7760 (–1.3)	9653 (1.7)	224.4
	ii) Extra-Budgetary resources	90444	86061	95.2
3	Borrowings	264802 (44.8)	299022 (52.5)	112.9
4	State's Own Resources (1+2+3)	332191 (56.2)	369222 (64.9)	111.1
5	Central assistance	258757 (43.8)	200011 (35.1)	77.3
6	Aggregate Plan Resources (4+5)	590948	569233	96.3
7	GBS to Plan (6–2)	508264	473519	93.2
8	GBS as percentage of GDP	3.6	3.4	

Note: Figures in parentheses are percentages of Aggregate Plan Resources.
Source: Planning Commission.

level. However, with resources of the PSEs being 16% higher and borrowings 13% higher, the States' own resources have improved by 11 percentage points over the projected level.

3.19. Performance of the States can be analysed, broadly, in terms of three components, viz, the BCR reflecting non-debt resources, States' borrowings reflecting debt based funding, and Central assistance, which is now all grant.

3.20. The BCR of the States was expected to be (–)Rs 15295 crore but the actual situation has been much worse, with a negative BCR of Rs 25514 crore. The States' own tax revenues have increased due to improvements made possible through the introduction of value-added tax (VAT). The share of Central taxes devolved to the States has also improved owing to buoyant resources of the Centre. However, compression of non-Plan expenditure has not been as expected.

3.21. Against a projected contribution of 44.8% of the Plan resources, borrowings in the Tenth Plan reached 52.5%. The higher share of borrowings is partly due to the deterioration in BCR. Central assistance to States and UTs in the Tenth Plan was 77.3% of the projected level, and its contribution to Plan resources however, has been only 35% as against the projection of about 44%. This has been a consequence of disintermediation of Plan loans to States and UTs in the wake of recommendations of the TFC and increased resource transfers through CSS.

PUBLIC SECTOR RESOURCES IN THE ELEVENTH PLAN

CENTRE'S RESOURCES

3.22. There have been several important developments during the Tenth Plan that have implications for financing of the Eleventh Plan. FRBMA, 2003 is in force and the TFC award for 2005–10 is being implemented. Service tax has emerged as a very promising source of revenue. An announcement has also been made that efforts will be made to introduce an unified goods and service tax (GST) by 1 April 2010. The Sixth Central Pay Commission was constituted in October 2006 and is scheduled to submit its recommendations in 2008–09.

Effect of FRBMA

3.23. FRBMA, 2003 and the associated rules notified on 5 July 2004, enjoined the Central Government to reduce the fiscal deficit by no less than 0.3% of GDP every year and to bring it down to no more than 3% of GDP by 2008–09. The imposition of a ceiling on the fiscal deficit constrains the scope for enhancing GBS by resorting to more borrowings. While in the short to medium run this appears to constrain the government from making productive investments, it is necessary to take a more long-term view of the implications of FRBMA. Borrowings increase resource availability in the short run but they also increase the outstanding debt, and hence the interest burden of the Centre. This increases NPRE and hence reduces GBS in the future. High fiscal deficits also generate other undesirable consequences such as uncertainty about macro fundamentals which can affect investor confidence and make the climate unsuitable for private investment with adverse effects upon growth.

3.24. The projections assume that FRBMA will effectively constrain the fiscal deficit to the levels indicated, leading to a reduction in debt financing for funding of GBS for the Eleventh Plan. Accordingly, the Centre's net borrowings, which stood at 3.47% of GDP in 2006–07, are projected to decline to 3% in 2008–09 and remain at this level during the Eleventh Plan. Eleventh Plan projections on borrowings do not distinguish between external and domestic debt.

3.25. FRBMA not only prescribes the required reduction in fiscal deficit, but also a reduction in revenue deficit by no less than 0.5% of GDP every year and the elimination of such deficit by 2008–09. The imposition of a zero revenue deficit condition has an impact on total revenue expenditure given revenue receipts. This, in turn, has implications for the composition of Plan expenditure in terms of the revenue component of the Plan. The Centre's GBS deployment now involves a substantial component of revenue expenditure exceeding 80%, reflecting the large grants to States under the CSS which show up as revenue expenditure in the Centre's budget. The imposition of a revenue deficit ceiling, in addition to a fiscal deficit ceiling, makes it vitally important to control non-Plan expenditure to ensure that the total of Plan and NPRE does not exceed the permitted ceiling.

Effect of TFC

3.26. The Twelth Finance Commission's recommendations have essentially two critical implications for Plan financing. First, the TFC award increased the devolution to the States and thus improved their financial position and hence their capacity to finance the Plan. This increased capacity must be kept in mind when determining the necessary Plan transfers from the Centre to the States in the form of Normal Central Assistance (NCA). Second, implementation of the TFC's award has also led to a problem of straightforward comparison of GBS in the pre- and post-TFC period. For example, in 2004–05, GBS for the fourth year of the Tenth Plan of Rs 132292 crore included Rs 24806 crore of State Plan loans intermediated by the Centre. A straightforward comparison with GBS of Rs 140638 crore in 2005–06 gives an increase of only 6.3%. However, a proper comparison, after deducting what would have been dis-intermediated in 2004–05 under the TFC award, shows an increase of 30.8% in 2005–06 over the previous year.

3.27. The TFC's recommendations cover the period up to 2009–10, which includes the first three years of the Eleventh Plan. The projections of resources for the Eleventh Plan have been made assuming that the same proportions of resource transfers as under the TFC award will continue in 2010–11 and 2011–12. The assumption may not prove valid, as it is not possible to anticipate the nature of the Thirteenth Finance Commission's recommendations. The only possible basis on which projection can be made is to assume continuation of the existing proportions.

Effect of Service Tax

3.28. The introduction of service tax has provided a promising source of revenue, but there are some caveats which have to be kept in mind before making projections for the Eleventh Plan. First, the scope for expanding the service tax net to more and more services gets narrower as the net is widened. The contribution of the expanding net will, therefore, reduce over time. Second, the preponderance of small service providers below the taxable limit of turnover constrains the scope of revenue mobilization beyond a certain level. Third, service tax was introduced under the residuary entry No. 97 in List I in the Seventh Schedule of the Constitution and, as such, is not subject to sharing with the States. There are already strong demands for a sharing of the tax base between the Centre and the States, particularly in the context of phasing out of Central Sales Tax. Any sharing of the tax base with the States will diminish the Centre's available resources to finance the Plan. Fourth, with the declared goal of introducing a unified GST by 1 April 2010, there is considerable uncertainty about the rates, base, and mechanism for setting off (i.e. input tax credit), all of which have implications for future revenue collections.

3.29. Keeping in mind the implication of the FRBM and also the prospects for service tax, an assessment has been made of the likely GBS of the Centre, assuming that the growth rate of GDP will average 9% per annum in the Eleventh Plan, reaching 10% growth in the final year. The resource projection made by the Working Group on the Centre's resources yields a projection of GBS of the Centre which indicates that it will grow from 2.99% of GDP in 2006–07 to 5.38% of GDP in 2011–12. The average GBS for the Central Plan in the Eleventh Plan period stands at 3.97% of GDP as against 2.77% of GDP realized in the Tenth Plan.

3.30. The tax revenue (net of States' share) increases from 8.5% of GDP in 2006–07 to 10.26% of GDP in 2011–12, averaging 9.28% during the Eleventh Plan. Collection of direct tax is projected to exceed indirect tax collection, for the first time in history, from 2008–09 onwards. Corporate tax collection averages 63% of direct tax collection during the Eleventh Plan. It increases from 3.5% of GDP in 2006–07 to 5.31% of GDP in 2011–12 averaging 4.28% of GDP, that is, 1.66 percentage points increase over the average Tenth Plan realization. It may be mentioned that the projection regarding corporate taxes by the Working Group is based on the assumption of a corporate tax elasticity of 2.27. This is the weighted average of the estimated elasticity over the period 1995–96 to 2005–06 and the buoyancy estimated by the Task Force on the implementation of the FRBM Act, 2003.

3.31. Subsidies in the first year of the Eleventh Plan have been taken as per 2007–08 BE. As a proportion of GDP at current market prices, the projection assumes that the total subsidies will decline from 1.17% in 2007–08 BE to 0.93% in 2011–12. This, however, ignores the under recoveries on petroleum items because of the failure to fully pass on the effects of world oil prices and also underpayment on fertilizer subsidy. Inability to pass on increases in global oil prices to the consumers would have a substantial impact on resources for the Plan if this situation is not addressed urgently.

3.32. Table 3.5 presents the resources of the Centre and its funding in the Eleventh Plan. The GBS available for the Plan is estimated at Rs 1421711 crore at 2006–07 price. Central assistance to the States' and UTs' Plan works out to be Rs 324851 crore. IEBR of CPSUs is estimated at Rs 1059711 crore. The total resources available for the Central Plan are projected at Rs 2156571 crore.

TABLE 3.5
Projection of the Eleventh Plan Resources of the Centre

(Rs crore at 2006–07 price)

	Sources of Funding	Projection
1	Balance from Current Revenues	653989 (46.0)
2	Borrowings including net MCR	767722 (54.0)
3	Gross Budgetary Support to Plan (1 + 2)	1421711 (100)
4	Central assistance to States & UTs	324851 (22.8)
5	Total GBS for Central Plan (3–4)	1096860 (77.2)
6	Resources of PSEs including borrowed resource	1059711 (74.5)
7	Total Resources for Central Plan (5+6)	2156571

Note: Figures in parentheses are percentages of GBS to Plan (S. No. 3).
Source: Planning Commission.

3.33. Table 3.6 compares the funding pattern in the Eleventh Plan with the Tenth Plan realization as percentages of GDP. The imposition of the fiscal deficit ceiling ensures that borrowings, including net miscellaneous capital receipts, decline from 5.03% of GDP to 2.86% in the Eleventh Plan.

STATES' RESOURCES

3.34. The FRBM legislations in the States prescribe that they should achieve a fiscal deficit of 3% of GDP by the end of 2008–09. Therefore, the gross fiscal deficit of all the States, which stood at 3.73% of GDP in 2006–07 has been projected to decline to 3% by 2008–09 and to remain at this level in the remaining years of the Eleventh Plan. This inevitably limits the scope for mobilizing borrowed resources and the States, therefore, have to look at improving revenue realization and controlling non-Plan expenditure.

3.35. The core aggregate Plan resources of the States and UTs have been projected to be Rs 1488147 crore at 2006–07 price (see Table 3.7). This comprises of Rs 1163296 crore of own resources (including borrowings) and Rs 324851 crore of Central assistance. UTs account for 3.8% of the combined aggregate Plan resources of the States and UTs.

3.36. As a proportion of GDP, aggregate Plan resources of the States and UTs are projected at 5.55% of GDP, registering an increase of 1.47 percentage points over the Tenth Plan realization (refer to Table 3.8). The BCR, which was negative in the Tenth Plan, is projected to improve to a large positive figure of Rs 385050 crore. This represents an improvement of 1.59 percentage points of GDP per

TABLE 3.6
Tenth Plan Realization and Eleventh Plan Projection of Resources of the Centre

(as % of GDP)

	Sources of Funding	Tenth Plan Realization	Eleventh Plan Projections	Increases (+)/ Decreases (–)
1	Balance from Current Revenues	–0.84	2.31	3.15
2	Borrowings including net MCR	5.03	2.86	–2.17
3	Net Flow from Abroad	0.06	–	–
4	Gross Budgetary Support to Plan (1 to 3)	4.25	5.17	0.92
5	Central assistance to States & UTs	1.48*	1.20	–0.28
6	GBS for Central Plan (4–5)	2.77	3.97	1.20
7	Resources of PSEs	2.61	4.02	1.41
8	Resources for Central Plan (6+7)	5.38	7.99	2.61

Note: * If Plan loans intermediated to States and UTs are excluded, this reduces to 0.99% of GDP, which is the relevant figure for comparison.
Source: Planning Commission.

year over the Tenth Plan. However, projections of resources of PSEs and Central assistance to the States show a decline of 0.19 percentage points and 0.23 percentage points, respectively as compared with the Tenth Plan.

3.37. Mobilization of resources of such a magnitude for the Eleventh Plan is contingent upon significant improvement in the States' own resources, mainly through improved BCR. The States will have to step up efforts to increase their own tax and non-tax revenue collections through better tax administration, plugging the scope for leakages and recovery of cost based user charges.

3.38. As shown in Table 3.8, the Central assistance being transferred to the States in the Eleventh Plan amounts to 1.2% of GDP as against 1.43% in the Tenth Plan. However, as noted in the footnote of Table 3.8, if the Tenth Plan figure is adjusted to remove loans intermediated through

TABLE 3.7
Eleventh Plan Resources of States and UTs

(Rs crore at 2006–07 price)

	Sources of Funding	Projection		
		State	UTs	Total
1	Balance from Current Revenues	341202 (23.8)	43848 (77.2)	385050 (25.9)
2	Resources of PSEs	128824 (9.0)	–	128824 (8.7)
	i) Internal resources	5692 (0.4)		5692 (0.4)
	ii) Extra-Budgetary resources	123132 (8.6)		123132 (8.3)
3	Borrowings	636459 (44.5)	12964 (22.8)	649423 (43.6)
4	State's Own Resources (1 to 3)	1106485 (77.3)	56811 (100.0)	1163296 (78.2)
5	Central assistance	324851 (22.7)	–	324851 (21.8)
6	Aggregate Plan Resources	1431336 (100.0)	56811 (100.0)	1488147 (100.0)

Note: Figures in parentheses are percentages of aggregate Plan resources.
Source: Planning Commission.

TABLE 3.8
Core Tenth Plan Realization and Eleventh Plan Projection of Resources of States and UTs

(% of GDP)

	Sources of Funding	Tenth Plan Realization	Eleventh Plan Projections	Increases (+)/ Decreases (–)
1	Balance from Current Revenues	–0.18	1.41	1.59
2	Resources of PSEs	0.69	0.49	–0.19
3	Borrowings	2.14	2.45	0.30
4	States' Own Resources (1 to 3)	2.65	4.35	1.70
5	Central assistance	1.43*	1.20	–0.23
6	Aggregate Plan Resources (4+5)	4.08	5.55	1.47

Note: *This is based on the figures reported by the States. Hence, it is slightly different from the figure of Central assistance to States and UTs in Table 3.5. If Plan loans intermediated to States and UTs are excluded, this reduces to 0.99% of GDP which is the relevant figure for comparison.
Source: Planning Commission.

the Centre, the Tenth Plan figure is lower at 0.99%. Besides, Central assistance is not the only means of Plan transfer. Large transfers take place through the CSS which have been greatly expanded in the Eleventh Plan. Accordingly, the States will receive larger transfer of Central resources to them.

OVERALL FINANCING PATTERN

3.39. Table 3.9 compares the structure of financing projected in the Eleventh Plan for the Centre and States, combined with that actually realized in the Tenth Plan. The most notable feature is that the Eleventh Plan projections show relatively modest dependence on borrowings amounting to 38.9% of the total Plan resources compared with 73.9% in the Tenth Plan realization. This outcome is the consequence of tighter fiscal discipline imposed by the fiscal responsibility framework, both at the Centre and the States, and an optimistic revenue outlook driven by the buoyancies in revenue collections during the last three years of the Tenth Plan reflecting the robust performance of the economy. This is reflected in the projected massive improvement in BCR which was negative in the Tenth Plan and is projected as a large positive figure for both the Centre and the States.

3.40. The financing plan outlined above will pose major challenges. As shown in Table 3.10, the total resources for the Central and State Plans taken together have to increase from an average of 9.46% of GDP in the Tenth Plan to an average of 13.54% of GDP in the Eleventh Plan. It may be noted that while the total size of the Plan is projected at 13.54% of GDP, the total public investment in the economy is projected to be lower at 8.6% (see Chapter 1). This difference reflects the fact that a great deal of Plan expenditure finances current expenditure on various items of public service delivery which are not counted as investment. The increase of 4.08% of GDP in total resources for the Plan has to be achieved while keeping borrowing within the FRBM requirement of reducing the fiscal deficit of the Centre and States to 3% on each account. Taking account of the resources mobilized by the public sector, the combined BCR of the Centre and the States has to increase by more than the projected increase in Plan resources.

3.41. The Centre's BCR, realized in the Tenth Plan, averaged (–)0.84% of GDP. It is projected to average 2.31% of GDP over the Eleventh Plan, that is, an improvement of 3.15 percentage points of GDP. Similarly, the BCR of

TABLE 3.9
Comparison of Tenth Plan Realization with Eleventh Plan Projection of Resources

(Rs crore at 2006–07 price)

		Tenth Plan Realization			Eleventh Plan Projection		
	Sources of Funding	Centre	States & UTs	Total	Centre	States & UTs	Total
1	Balance from Current Revenues	–127166 (–13.4)	–31722 (–4.5)	–158888 (–9.6)	653989 (30.3)	385050 (25.9)	1039039 (28.5)
2	Borrowings including net MCR	850382 (89.9)	371779 (52.5)	1222161 (73.9)	767722 (35.6)	649423 (43.6)	1417145 (38.9)
3	Net Inflow from Abroad	16121 (1.7)	–	16121 (1.0)	–	–	–
4	Centre's GBS (1+2+3)	739337 (78.2)	–	739337 (44.7)	1421711 (65.9)	– –	1421711 (39.0)
5	Resources of PSEs	458530 (48.5)	119003 (16.8)	577533 (34.9)	1059711 (49.1)	128824 (8.7)	1188535 (32.6)
6	State's Own Resources (1+2+5)		459060 (64.9)	459060 (27.8)	– –	1163296 (78.2)	1163296 (31.9)
7	Central assistance to States & UTs	–252539 (–26.7)	248677 (35.1)	–3862 (–0.2)	–324851 (–15.1)	324851 (21.8)	– –
8	Resources of the Public Sector Plan (1+2+3+5+7)	945328	707737	1653065	2156571	1488147	3644718

Note: Figures in parentheses are percentages of Resources of the Public Sector Plan.
Source: Planning Commission.

TABLE 3.10
Plan Resources as Per Cent of GDP

Aggregate Plan Resources	Tenth Plan	Eleventh Plan	Increase over Tenth Plan
Centre	5.38	7.99	2.61
States	4.08	5.55	1.47
Centre and States	9.46	13.54	4.08
Balance from Current Revenues			
Centre	–0.84	2.31	3.15
States	–0.18	1.41	1.59
Centre and States	–1.02	3.72	4.74

Source: Planning Commission.

the States is also expected to improve substantially from (–) 0.18% of GDP as realized in the Tenth Plan to 1.41% of GDP in the Eleventh Plan. As can be seen from Table 3.10, the projected improvement required in the combined BCR of the Centre and States taken together is therefore 4.74 percentage points of GDP. It must be emphasized that achievement of these BCR targets is a key element in the financing of the Plan.

3.42. Underlying the projected BCR is a projection that tax revenues (net to Centre) would grow from 8.5% of GDP in 2006–07 to 10.26% of GDP in 2011–12. NPRE is expected to decline from 9.01% of GDP in 2006–07 to 6.91% in 2011–12. Thus the projected improvement of 3.15% of GDP in BCR of the Centre is expected to come slightly more from contraction in NPRE than growth in taxes.

3.43. The assumption of strong growth in tax revenues of the Centre and the States built into the projections is not unreasonable. Tax revenues recorded in the recent past has shown high buoyancy facilitated by tax reforms and also significant improvements in the efficiency of tax administration. These efforts will continue in the Eleventh Plan period and should contribute to achieving the targeted tax-to-GDP ratios. However, the BCR projections are equally dependent upon the ability to moderate the growth in NPRE and this aspect of the projections deserves focused attention.

3.44. There are several factors which could make it difficult to contain expenditures to the projected level. There are inevitable uncertainties associated with the impact of the Sixth Pay Commission's recommendations. Equally, if not, more important is the upward pressure of subsidies, particularly on fertilizer and petroleum, and also on food. Petroleum subsidies have not so far been factored into the plan resources calculations since they have been financed by the issue of bonds not included in fiscal deficit accounting, and some portion being borne by the oil companies themselves. However, this practice cannot be sustained indefinitely. Reform of the subsidy regime has to be urgently taken up to keep the total subsidy, including the present off-budget subsidy, to within the ceiling of 0.93% of GDP in 2011–12 that the resources projections have built in.

ALLOCATION OF PUBLIC SECTOR RESOURCES: CENTRE AND STATES

3.45. The projection of the overall resources for the Eleventh Plan has been presented in the preceding section. This section focuses on the allocation of Public Sector Resources for the Eleventh Plan between the Centre and the States/UTs and the proposed sectoral distribution of the resources in keeping with the objective of achieving faster and more inclusive growth.

3.46. The projected assessment of resources of the public sector for the Eleventh Plan at Rs 3644718 crore at 2006–07 prices comprises of the Centre's share at Rs 2156571 crore and the States/UTs share at Rs 1488147 crore. The resources for the Central Plan includes the GBS component of Rs 1096860 crore and the IEBR component of Rs 1059711 crore at 2006–07 prices. Resource allocation in the Central sector according to different Heads of Development is indicated in Annexure 3.1 and the ministry/department-wise details of budgetary support and IEBR are indicated in Annexure 3.2.

3.47. The Eleventh Plan resources of the States and UTs are projected at Rs 1488147 crore at 2006–07 prices, out of which States' own resources are Rs 1163296 crore and the Central assistance to States and UTs is Rs 324851 crore at 2006–07 prices. Head of Development-wise allocation for the States/UTs is indicated in Annexeure 3.1 with States/UTs-wise core plan details furnished in Annexure 3.3. These allocations would be finalized in consultation with the States. Table 3.11 indicates the resources and allocation of public sector resources for the Eleventh Plan.

TABLE 3.11
Public Sector Allocation for Eleventh Plan

(Rs crore at 2006–07 prices)

	Centre	
	Sources of Funding	Allocation
1	Budgetary Support	1096860
2	IEBR	1059711
3	Total Centre(1+2)	2156571
	States and UTs	
	Sources of Funding	Allocation
4	State Own Resources	1163296
5	Central assistance to State/UT Plan	324851
6	Total States & UTs (4+5)	1488147
	Total Public Sector Outlay	
7	Grand Total (3+6)	3644718

Source: Planning Commission.

TABLE 3.12
GBS Allocation in Tenth and Eleventh Plans

(Rs crore at 2006–07 prices)

	Tenth Plan Realization		Eleventh Plan Projections		
	Amount	% share in Total GBS	Amount	% share in Total GBS	% increase over Tenth Plan
Central Sector	486798	73.6	1096860	77.2	125.3
Support to State Plan*	175021	26.4	324851	22.8	85.6
Total	661819	100	1421711	100	114.8

Note: *Grant component only.
Source: Planning Commission.

3.48. A comparison of the distribution of the total GBS in the Tenth and the Eleventh Plan has been shown in Table 3.12. In comparison to the Tenth Plan realization, there is an increase of 125% in the projected GBS for the Centre for the Eleventh Plan. Central assistance to State/UT Plans for State sector programmes is about 85.6% higher than the grant component realized during the Tenth Plan. The share of the projected grant component of the Central assistance to States/UTs plan in the total GBS for Eleventh Plan has decreased slightly from what has been realized in the Tenth Plan (from 26.4% to 22.8%) primarily because a much higher allocation has been made to the CSS. The allocation to CSS has increased from 1.40% of GDP for the Tenth Plan to 2.35% of GDP in the Eleventh Plan.

3.49. The projection of GBS allocation to different sectors, Ministries/Departments and the support to the State/UT Plan has been made in tune with the approach adopted for the Eleventh Plan for 'faster, more broad-based and inclusive growth'. The Eleventh Plan aims at putting the economy on a sustainable growth trajectory with a growth rate of 10% by the end of the Plan period by targeting robust growth in agriculture at 4% per year and by creating productive employment at a faster pace than before. The Eleventh Plan focuses on poverty reduction, ensuring access to basic physical infrastructure, health and education facilities to all while giving importance to bridging the regional/social/gender disparities and attending to the marginalized and the weaker social groups. Accordingly, a major structural shift

TABLE 3.13
Sectoral Allocation—Tenth Plan and Eleventh Plan

(Rs crore at 2006–07 prices)

S. No.	Sectors	Tenth Plan		Eleventh Plan	
		BE#	% to Total	Projected Allocation	% to Total
1	Education	62461	7.68	274228	19.29
2	Rural Development Land resources and Panchayati Raj	87041	10.70	190330	13.39
3	Health Family Welfare and Ayush	45771	5.62	123900	8.71
4	Agriculture and Irrigation	50639	6.22	121556	8.55
5	Social Justice	36381	4.47	90273	6.35
6	Physical Infrastructure	89021	10.94	128160	9.01
7	Scientific Departments	29823	3.66	66580	4.68
8	Energy	47266*	5.81	57409	4.04
	Total Priority Sector	448403	55.10	1052436	74.03
9	Others	365375	44.90	369275	25.97
	Total	813778	100.00	1421711	100.00

Note: #Tenth Plan BE represents the actual allocation during the five years and not the original Tenth Plan projections; *Includes APDRP grant component only.

across sectors has been proposed by allocating more resources to the priority areas identified for ensuring inclusiveness. A broad picture of the structural change in terms of sectoral allocation of resources has been shown in the Table 3.13.

3.50. About 74% of the total central allocation for the Eleventh Plan has been put aside for the priority sectors listed in Table 3.13, whereas, their share was only 55% in the Tenth Plan. It may be noted that the share of infrastructure and energy in the GBS allocation has fallen despite their being in the priority list. This is not a reflection of lack of priority but a reflection of a conscious policy to shift from public sector funding in these sectors to a strategy of increased IEBR and Public-Private Partnership.

3.51. As pointed out in Chapter 1, the objective of the Eleventh Plan is to increase investment in infrastructure (including irrigation) from 5% of GDP in 2006–07 to 9% by 2011–12.

3.52. The sector-wise thrust areas identified for Eleventh Plan are given in Box 3.2.

3.53. To mobilize resources for allocation to the priority sectors and to realize a sustainable growth of 10% by the end of the Plan period, there is a need to substantially enhance the resources for infrastructure development, skill development and industrial growth, as well. This will contribute to raising the income levels through employment generation and will also provide impetus to the other programmes. In addition to the identified priority sectors, investment in the private sector including farming, MSMEs has a vital role in achieving regionally balanced and more inclusive growth and also the potential to generate off-farm employment. Steps are proposed to be taken to provide a comfortable and competitive environment for the MSMEs to grow and some structural and regulatory changes have also been proposed to attract private and foreign investors. Keeping in mind the socio-economic diversity in the country, decentralized planning complemented with greater transparency and accountability is desirable for the overall development of the country. Also, our development strategy should be well complemented by policies for environmental protection and sustainability.

3.54. The Eleventh Plan proposes to provide Rs 324851 crore at 2006–07 prices as CA to State/UT Plans. Table 3.14 indicates the details of sector-wise CA component of the resources of the States/UTs. Out of the total CA to States/UTs of Rs 324851 crore at 2006–07 prices, 37% (i.e., Rs 122852 crore) has been earmarked for the Gadgil Formula driven NCA, Special Plan Assistance (SPA) for Special Category States and Special Central

Box 3.2
Thrust Areas of the Eleventh Plan

Sectors	Thrust Areas
Education	Quality upgradation in Primary Education, Expansion of Secondary Education, major emphasis on upgradation of Higher Education including Technical Education, ICT throughout education system.
Health, Nutrition, Drinking Water, and Sanitation	Major upgradation of rural health infrastructure, Medical education, Nutritional support to children and pregnant and lactating women through ICDS, health insurance based urban health facilities, Health care for elderly, achieving sustainability, improvement in service levels and moving towards universal access to safe and clean drinking water.
Agriculture and Irrigation	Ensuring Food Security, Supporting State-specific agriculture strategy and programmes, Better seed production, Focused agricultural research, Extension, Development of modern markets.
Rural Development, Land Resources and Panchayati Raj	Universalization and improvement in programme delivery of NREGP, Integrated Watershed management including management of underground water level.
Social Justice and Empowerment	Special attention to the needs of SCs, STs and minorities and other excluded groups through pre and post-metric scholarship, Hostels for boys/girls, Income and employment generation opportunities, Multi-sectoral development programmes for minorities in minority concentration districts.
Physical Infrastructure	Emphasis on the public–private partnership in investment, Initiate policies to ensure time-bound creation of world-class infrastructure, especially in remote and inaccessible rural areas and NE, Hinterland connectivity through improved rail and road infrastructure.
Energy	Electrification of all villages and extending free household connections to all 2.3 crore BPL households through RGGVY, Nuclear power development.
Scientific Departments	Development of satellite launch capabilities to GSLV-Mk-III, Development of new energy systems, viz. advance heavy water reactor and nanotechnology.

TABLE 3.14
Projected Central Assistance to States/UTs for Eleventh Plan

(Rs crore at 2006–07 price)

Sectors	Programme	Allocation
State Development Plan	Normal Central assistance	94720
Special Category States	Special Plan Assistance	13238
	Central Pool for North East and Sikkim	3095
Agriculture	Rashtriya Krishi Vikas Yojana	22104
	Shifting Cultivation	212
SCA	Border Area Development Programme/Hill Area Development Programme/North Eastern Council	14894
Irrigation	Accelerated Irrigation Benefit Programme	41568
Power	Accelerated Power Development & Reform Programme	12820
Urban/Local Area Development	Jawaharlal Nehru Urban Renewal Mission	41490
	Brihan Mumbai Storm Water Drain Project, Mumbai	113
	MPs' Local Area Development Programme	6985
Balanced Regional Development	Backward Region Grant Fund	25711
Elderly and Weaker Section	National Social Assistance Programme	15691
Adolescent Girls	National Programme for Adolescent Girls	886
Roads and Bridges		7972
Externally Aided Projects	Various EAPs	14273
Disaster Management	Tsunami Rehabilitation Programme	2985
Sports	Commonwealth Games, 2010	2133
E-governance	National e-Governance Action Plan	2942
Total		324851

Assistance (SCA) for the Border Areas Development Programme (BADP)/Hill Area Development Programme (HADP)/North East Council (NEC), etc. The remaining 63% of Central assistance to the States is assigned to Additional Central Assistance (ACA) for various flagship programmes in accordance with the priority set for the Eleventh Plan, such as the AIBP, National Social Assistance Programme (NSAP), APDRP, BRGF, and JNNURM. A new programme, the RKVY, has been introduced to incentivize the States to accord a much higher priority to the agriculture sector in their investment planning by supplementing area specific agricultural strategies and programmes.

3.55. The overall plan outlay of all the States and UTs is projected to increase from Rs 673132 crore in the Tenth Plan to Rs 1488147 crore in the Eleventh Plan (both at the same 2006–07 price levels), an increase of 21.1% on a comparable basis. The aggregate picture indicates that the States would be allocating more than proportionate increase to social services (40.1%), transport (38.7%) and agriculture and allied activities (37.8%). The States would also be actively pursuing PPP models for infrastructure development wherever possible. The aggregate picture, it must be noted, conceals wide inter-State variations in terms of Plan sizes relative to GSDP, per capita plan expenditure and percentage sectoral outlays.

ISSUES IN PLAN FINANCING

3.56. Several conceptual issues arise from the present structure of the Plan financing. Important among these are classification of expenditure—which has a bearing on the overall expenditure management, the Central Plan transfers mechanism, the treatment of investment of PSUs financed by IEBR under the Plan, and the role of SPVs/PPPs and other innovative methods of raising additional resources for investment.

CLASSIFICATION OF EXPENDITURE

3.57. There has been much debate about the utility or otherwise of the classification of expenditure into Plan and Non-Plan. It has been argued that this distinction is illogical and, what is more, even dysfunctional. The argument against continuing with this distinction is that the focus on new schemes/new projects/new extensions to currently running schemes, etc., which alone qualify for being included in the Plan, results in neglect of maintenance of the existing capacity and service levels. Thus, while strenuous efforts are made by both the Centre and the states to achieve a large increase in Plan size, its impact is often negated by a running down of service delivery capacity already created. The problem arises from a framework that creates a distinction between Plan and non-Plan expenditure within each sector, motivated solely by the need to identify and highlight provision of incremental service.

3.58. Other perceptions that have developed around this distinction, namely, that Non-Plan expenditure is inherently wasteful and has to be minimized, that Non-Plan expenditure is different in kind from Plan expenditure, etc., are patently incorrect assessments that have nevertheless taken deep root in the process of government expenditure planning. This dichotomy also results in a fragmented view of resource allocations to various sectors. The problem has become particularly acute as government's emphasis has shifted to the social sectors where salary costs are high. Routine bans on recruitment for Non-Plan posts, ostensibly imposed to conserve expenditure, cause serious problem for service delivery in health, education, extension systems, etc. The case against the use of these categories, both on grounds of illogicality and dysfunctionality, is therefore indisputable.

3.59. At the same time, it is necessary to understand that this classification of expenditures has been used essentially as a convenient shortcut for the performance of functions that are inherent in public expenditure management. It is perhaps in the manner in which the Plan and Non-Plan distinction has been denuded of its substance over the years, rather than in any inherent conceptual inadequacy, that the causes of the present state of affairs need to be found.

3.60. The basic functions of government expenditure management, as applied to an annual budgeting process, are the following:

(i) Assessing the amount of committed expenditure, that is, expenditure whose level cannot be altered during the Budget period by any decision that might be taken (though the areas where these expenditures can be applied may still be open to alteration, and, in any case, the levels of expenditures themselves would be capable of being altered over a longer time horizon);

(ii) The amount of headroom available within the resource envelope after the committed expenditures are provided for;
(iii) The sectors in which this 'discretionary' expenditure is to be applied; and
(iv) The process of monitoring and evaluating the efficiency and effectiveness with which the expenditures are made.

3.61. These functions would have to be performed irrespective of whether we continue to have the two categories of Plan and Non-Plan expenditures or not. These two categories, which were initially designed to enable the fulfilment of the above functions, have now acquired connotations that lead to dysfunctionality. The solution, therefore, would be to do away with these categories and, instead, devise other mechanisms that will perform the requisite functions in a rational and effective manner. We need to draw up protocols that will specify who is to perform what part of the above functions and how the entire activity will be coordinated. In this effort, there would be a need to redefine organizational mandates. This activity will be taken up during the Eleventh Plan period.

3.62. The Revenue–Capital categorization of expenditure has acquired renewed significance in the post-FRBM scenario. The FRBM law has stipulated the elimination of revenue deficit in a context where more than three-fourths of Plan expenditure is revenue expenditure. Strict adherence to the FRBM stipulation would have a bearing on the ability of the Centre to formulate Plan schemes directed at national priorities and also at equalizing the availability and provision of services across States. In effect, we may be in a position where the total resources that can be mobilized within the fiscal deficit ceiling cannot be deployed into schemes which have a high revenue component.

3.63. The problem is further complicated by the fact that the categorization of expenditure into revenue and capital that has evolved over the years, does not appear to be strictly in conformity with the constitutional position on this issue. The Constitution distinguishes only between 'expenditure on revenue account' and 'other expenditure'. Over the years, 'expenditure on revenue account' has been construed to mean revenue expenditure. This could be an incorrect interpretation as expenditure met out of revenues of the Government of India (GoI) has been interpreted earlier (as is clear from reports of Finance Commissions) as expenditure that is not self financing, that is, both revenue expenditure and those capital expenditures that are not self liquidating (in the sense of not providing financial returns to the government that could be used for servicing debt). In this view, the present category of Defence Capital Expenditure, for instance, would have to be treated as 'expenditure on revenue account' only. This is in keeping with the economic classification in the national accounts where Defence capital expenditure is treated as consumption and not as investment.

3.64. It is also relevant to note that capital expenditure as currently defined is not always and invariably tantamount to investment. For example, recapitalization of PSEs, though classified as capital expenditure, is not, in most cases, investment. In fact a loss-making PSU may receive injections of equity to fund losses, in which case what is conceptually a subsidy will be classified as a capital expenditure.

3.65. Some argue that the Revenue–Capital classification is also dysfunctional from an economic management perspective as it militates against the principle of sound and efficient management of the entire expenditure in an integrated manner. Over the years, essential maintenance expenditure has become a casualty of the revenue–capital distinction.

3.66. There are other inconsistencies also with our current system of classification. For example, fertilizer and food subsidies are not counted as Plan expenditure but subsidy to socially desirable insurance schemes, and several other subsidies are also included. Exclusion of large subsidy items from Plan expenditure has the effect of avoiding any resource prioritization in the matter of determining the appropriate balance between subsidy levels and other expenditure to promote common developmental objectives.

3.67. Against the above backdrop, it would be appropriate to set up a HLC that could look into the entire gamut of issues arising from the present classification of expenditure and suggest measures for efficient management of public expenditure.

CENTRAL PLAN TRANSFERS

3.68. The last two decades have seen a massive increase in both the number of CSS as well as funds available under individual schemes. These schemes provide CA for Plan expenditure in particular sectors which are normally in the domain of the States. However, unlike normal CA which is not tied to specific programmes, funds available under CSS are tied to schemes in particular sectors and are subject to centrally prescribed guidelines. The share of normal Central Plan assistance to the States has declined as a proportion to total Plan transfers. The role of CSS has often been discussed and a view frequently expressed is that CSS should be abolished and the funds flowing through these schemes should simply be transferred to the States directly, presumably as NCA. There are two arguments against this approach. First, there is merit in using Central resources to tackle the specific obstacles that would prevent the achievement of inclusive growth and this is best done by effectively earmarking resources to support State expenditure in particular areas such as rural development, health, education, agriculture and irrigation. Unless this is done, it will be difficult to give a special impetus to these critical areas. Second, the mechanism of CSS enables the Centre to address problems as they exist in different States without being constrained by the Gadgil Formula, which would otherwise guide the transfer of untied funds.

3.69. A large proportion of the fund transfers to the States under CSS are also being routed to State and district level bodies directly by the Central Government, bypassing the State Governments. This practice is motivated by a desire to avoid delays in administrative approvals and to prevent diversion of CSS funds by the States for supporting their ways and means position. Concerns about what this does to accountability mechanisms have been expressed. In view of the growing volume of such transfers, suitable mechanisms would have to be devised to ensure there is no dilution of accountability.

MONITORING OF PLAN EXPENDITURE

3.70. The existing system of accounting for Plan schemes, both for the Centre and the States, does not adequately support informed planning, budgeting, effective monitoring and decision making regarding these schemes. The current accounting system does not capture transaction-oriented information. It also does not distinguish between transfers to States, final expenditure and advance payments against which accounts have to be rendered. The extant accounting framework is also not structured to generate State-wise and scheme-wise releases of funds by the Central Government to States and other recipients, and also the actual utilization for the intended purpose. Hence, there is a great need to design and implement a Plan scheme that would thoroughly reform this process. This Plan scheme would, inter-alia, modify the existing Code of Accounts so as to fully capture the entire range of Plan schemes operated by the GoI and the States. The Code of Accounts needs to be restructured to provide information relating to each implementing agency. While there have been stand-alone efforts by various Ministries and programmes, there is no consolidated financial information system based on the accounting structure. A comprehensive Decision Support System (DSS) and Management Information System (MIS) for effective monitoring of Plan schemes would need to be set up. This will work through a core accounting solution on a central data centre. The scheme will be implemented by the Controller General of Accounts (CGA). The details of the scheme would be finalized during the Eleventh Plan.

SCOPE OF THE PUBLIC SECTOR PLAN

3.71. The administrative machinery through which the public sector plan is implemented has been continuously changing over the years. The setting up of PRIs, the establishment of special purpose societies and agencies and companies that have been mandated to perform special functions, are all elements of the plan implementation machinery that did not exist earlier. At the same time, some organizations that were earlier part of the public sector may have moved out of the public sector due to privatization as in the case with a few enterprises—both in the Centre and in the States. The focus on public–private partnership also creates new categories where public sector resources are made available to projects owned and managed by the private sector. In this context, the definition of the organizational boundaries of the public sector plan assumes importance, both for reasons of analytical clarity as well as inter-temporal comparability. This was a specific issue on which the Working Groups that were set up for estimation of Central and State resources were specifically required to comment.

3.72. While the Centre has consistently followed the practice of including the investment plans of a large number of PSEs in the public sector plan, the States have not adopted any uniform policy in this regard. Even in the case of the Centre, the PSEs that are included in the Plan from year to year show minor variations. Even among those PSEs that are included in the Plan, the resources estimates do not capture the entire quantum of resources available, and a portion of the available resources is treated as being outside the Plan.

3.73. As far as the States are concerned, there is no uniform practice across all States. While requesting the States to estimate resources for the Eleventh Five Year Plan, they were advised that the public sector plan of the States would have to be defined as the sum total of investments made in a State by the State Government, taken as a composite economic entity. It was explained that this economic entity would be comprised of more than one legal entity, and would include, apart from the State Government itself, other legal entities such as the State PSEs, and all urban and rural local bodies. As far as the PSEs themselves are concerned, the guidelines provided that PSEs which are separate from the government only as legal entities (through share-holding or other form of capital being wholly or substantially held by the State Government) and which make materially significant investments (i.e., other than small investments that are only incidental to or supportive of routine activities) in a direct manner (i.e., who are not financial intermediaries whose activities consist of providing either loan or equity capital to other entities who in turn make investments) should be included in the scope of the public sector plan. Unfortunately, the States have not uniformly rationalized their definitions of the public sector plan on these principles. Consequently, the resources estimates have proceeded on the same basis as in earlier plans and, to that extent, comparability across States is not what it should be.

3.74. One of the new innovations that is likely to gain importance in the Eleventh Plan period is the concept of investment in infrastructure through PPPs, which is promoted through means such as Viability Gap Funding (VGF). In such a case, the extent to which the investment was eventually made should be reflected as part of the public sector is an issue on which there is lack of clarity. If the expenditure from the public sector is viewed as a grant, then it is a revenue expenditure on the part of the government which finances investment in the private sector, the grant being a source of financing for the private investor.

3.75. The HLC referred to above (paragraph 3.67) would perhaps have to be entrusted the task of laying down clearly the definition of the public sector plan.

REVENUE DEFICIT CONSTRAINT

3.76. Under the FRBM Act, all the States as well as the Centre are committed to reducing the revenue deficit to zero by 2008–09. This would mean that there would be no net dis-saving on account of government administration. In fact, given the relationship between the revenue deficit and savings of the government, a zero revenue deficit would probably, in fact, result in a small positive saving from government administration. One of the problems with achieving a zero revenue deficit is that the Plan outlays of both the Centre and the States have, in recent years, had an increasing share of revenue expenditure. In the Central budget, in particular, the grant component of transfers to the States is revenue expenditure. As a result, the revenue expenditure component of the Centre's GBS for the Plan has risen to more than 80% in recent years. While the actuals of 2005–06 show that 79.5% of GBS was revenue expenditure, this increased to 83.7% in the revised estimates for 2006–07, and 85% in the budget estimates for 2007–08.

3.77. If the revenue deficit is to be reduced to zero from 2008–09 onwards, this would mean that the revenue expenditure component of GBS cannot exceed the BCR. In recent years, the Central Government has been achieving a positive BCR. However, going by the present projections, the BCR would reach only around 70% of GBS by the end of the Plan period if the gross fiscal deficit were to be taken at the ceiling of 3% of GDP. In other words, leaving the revenue expenditure share in GBS at the same levels at present would effectively mean that the total GBS would have to be reduced to a level below what would be permissible under a 3% gross fiscal deficit constraint.

3.78. The resources estimates now prepared make it very clear that the constraint of maintaining the revenue deficit at zero from 2008–09 onwards will have the inevitable consequence of very substantially limiting the overall GBS for the Plan. The overall pattern of revenue and capital expenditure in the GBS is the result of the core strategy of the Plan which seeks to substantially improve the supply of social services in the relatively backward States through increased Central funding, while at the same time providing an incentive framework for physical infrastructure to be created under PPP models. Given this strategy, and the consequent high revenue expenditure to GBS percentage, one option would be to insist on the binding nature of only the GFD to GDP constraint while accepting the inevitability of high revenue expenditure in view of the Plan strategy. The other option would be to try and identify components of what is booked as revenue expenditure in the accounts of the Central Government that lead to capital asset creation in the economy and to suitably reflect this asset creation in the accounting for the purposes of the FRBM Act. On a balance of advantage, it would appear that the former course would be preferable.

ANNEXURE 3.1

Sectoral Allocation for Public Sector's Resources—Tenth Plan (2002–07) Realizations and Eleventh Plan (2007–12) Projections

(Rs crore at 2006–07 prices)

	Centre									States and UTs			Centre, States, and UTs		
	Budgetary Support			IEBR			Total Outlay						Total Outlay		
Head of Development	Tenth Plan Realization	Eleventh Plan Projection	% increase	Tenth Plan Realization	Eleventh Plan Projection	% increase	Tenth Plan Realization	Eleventh Plan Projection	% increase	Tenth Plan Realization	Eleventh Plan Projection	% increase	Tenth Plan Realization	Eleventh Plan Projection	% increase
1. Agriculture and Allied Activities	26108	50924	95.0				26108	50924	95.0	34594	85458	147	60702	136381	124.7
2. Rural Development	79291	190330	140.0				79291	190330	140.0	58419	110739	89.6	137710	301069	118.6
3. Special Area Programmes										16423	26329	60.3	16423	26329	60.3
4. Irrigation & Flood Control	1716	6747	293.3				1716	6747	293.3	110699	203579	83.9	112415	210326	87.1
5. Energy	27262	36912	35.4	238957	591826	147.7	266220	628739	136.2	97415	225385	116.1	363635	854,123	134.9
6. Industry & Minerals	24146	54382	125.2	25108	67196	167.6	49254	121579	146.8	15401	32021	107.9	64655	153600	137.6
7. Transport	97711	120188	23.0	85405	266118	211.6	183116	386306	111.0	80818	186137	130.3	263934	572443	116.9
8. Communications	5312	16133	203.7	77109	79204	2.7	82422	95337	15.7	523	43	-91.8	82945	95380	15
9. Science, Technology & Environment	26667	75421	182.8		25		26667	75446	182.9	2006	12487	522.4	28673	87933	206.7
10. General Economic Services	9972	13920	39.6	456	891	95.3	10428	14811	42.0	19921	47712	139.5	30349	62523	106.0
11. Social Services	183725	524414	185.4	31494	54450	72.9	215219	578864	169.0	221310	523463	136.5	436529	1102327	152.5
12. General Services	4887	7489	53.2				4887	7489	53.2	15602	34794	123	20489	42283	106.4
Total	486798	1096860	125.3	458530	1059711	131.1	945328	2156571	128.1	673132#	1488147	121.1	1618460	3644718	125.2

Note: # Based on the sectoral outlay reported by the States. Totals may not tally due to rounding errors.

ANNEXURE 3.2

Budget Support, IEBR, and Outlay for Central Ministry/Department—Tenth Plan (2002–07) Realizations and Eleventh Plan (2007–12) Projections

(Rs crore at 2006–07 prices)

	Ministry/Department	Budgetary Support			IEBR			Total Outlay		
		Tenth Plan Realization	Eleventh Plan Projection	% increase	Tenth Plan Realization	Eleventh Plan Projection	% increase	Tenth Plan Realization	Eleventh Plan Projection	% increase
1.	Agriculture And Cooperation	16025	36549	128.07				16025	36549	128.07
2.	Agricultural Research and Education	4956	11131	124.60				4956	11131	124.60
3.	Animal Husbandry Dairying and Fisheries	2520	7121	182.58				2520	7121	182.58
4.	Micro, Small, and Medium Enterprises	5786	10168	158.33	339.58	261.71	–22.93	6126	10430	141.16
	(i) Agro And Rural Industries	3914	6631	69.43				3914	6631	69.43
	(ii) Small-Scale Industries	1872	3537	88.90	340	262	–23	2212	3798	71.73
5.	Atomic Energy	16435	20318	23.63	9093	28699	216	25528	49017	92.01
6.	Chemicals and Petrochemicals	612	1733	183.32	58	303	421	670	2036	203.99
7.	Fertilizers	714	1320	84.84	3210	16919	427	3924	18239	364.76
8.	Civil Aviation	588	1680	185.93	9947	41880	321	10535	43560	313.49
9.	Coal	1019	1326	30.07	15563	61826	297	16582	63152	280.84
10.	Commerce	5062	8767	73.19	53			5115	8767	71.39
11.	Industrial Policy and Promotion	1941	3698	90.47				1941	3698	90.47
12.	Posts	3845	3536	–8.03				3845	3536	–8.03
13.	Telecommunications	906	1549	70.98	76338	79204	4	77244	80753	4.54
14.	Information Technology	1902	11048	480.77	771			2674	11048	313.23
15.	Corporate Affairs	1	187					1	187	
16.	Consumer Affairs	284	958	237.04				284	958	237.04
17.	Food and Public Distribution	268	614	128.96	456	891	95	725	1505	107.75
18.	Culture	1643	3116	89.63				1643	3116	89.63
19.	Defence									
20.	Development of North Eastern Region	169	447	164.91				169	447	164.91
21.	Earth Sciences	1060	6193	484.45				1060	6193	484.45
22.	Environment and Forests	5600	8841	57.86				5600	8841	57.86
23.	External Affairs	3463	2201	–36.44				3463	2201	–36.44
24.	Economic Affairs*	2893	3946	36.42				2893	3946	36.42
25.	Expenditure	2	5	189.35				2	5	189.35
26.	Food Processing Industries	531	3564	570.78				531	3564	570.78
27.	Health and Family Welfare	38344	120375	213.93		504		38344	120879	215.24
28.	AYUSH	1112	3526	217.13				1112	3526	217.13

(Annexure 3.2 contd.)

(Rs crore at 2006–07 prices)

	Ministry/Department	Budgetary Support			IEBR			Total Outlay		
		Tenth Plan Realization	Eleventh Plan Projection	% increase	Tenth Plan Realization	Eleventh Plan Projection	% increase	Tenth Plan Realization	Eleventh Plan Projection	% increase
29.	Heavy Industry	1409	3619	156.82	2074	6373	207	3483	9992	186.88
30.	Public Enterprises	101	48	–52.68				101	48	–52.68
31.	Home Affairs	1438	6189	330.31				1438	6189	330.31
32.	School Education and Literacy	50112	163506	226.28				50112	163506	226.28
33.	Higher Education	13112	75102	472.76				13112	75102	472.76
34.	Information and Broadcasting	1611	4809	198.50	1371	127	–91	2982	4936	65.51
35.	Labour and Employment	904	2210	144.48				904	2210	144.48
36.	Law and Justice	519	1300	150.35				519	1300	150.35
37.	Mines	1118	1043	–6.70	2293	6387	179	3411	7430	117.83
38.	Minority Affairs	120	6189					120	6189	5078.13
39.	Non-Conventional Energy Sources	1808	3537	95.65	2367	6246	164	4175	9783	134.31
40.	Panchayati Raj	136	775	471.57				136	775	471.57
41.	Parliamentary Affairs									
42.	Personnel, Public Grievances and Pensions	188	491	161.43				188	491	161.43
43.	Petroleum and Natural Gas	370	174	–52.88	148532	244973	65	148902	245148	64.64
44.	Planning **	207	22799	10919.26				207	22799	
45.	Power	14444	26924	86.41	72495	278781	285	86938	305705	251.63
46.	Railways	40119	40513	0.98	51431	150000	192	91551	190513	108.10
47.	Revenue									
48.	Rural Development	98432	172350	75.10				98432	172350	75.10
49.	Land Resources	6224	17205	176.42				6224	17205	176.42
50.	Drinking Water Supply	19893	41825	110.25				19893	41825	110.25
51.	Science and Technology	4407	9750	121.23				4407	9750	121.23
52.	Scientific and Industrial Research	3256	7957	144.36		25		3256	7982	145.12
53.	Biotechnology	1795	5649	214.74				1795	5649	214.74
54.	Shipping	1450	4465	207.86	8704	39409	353	10154	43874	332.09
55.	Road Transport and Highways	40294	73530	82.48	15323	34829	127	55617	108359	94.83
56.	Social Justice and Empowerment	7691	11532	49.95				7691	11532	49.95
57.	Space	11945	27305	128.59				11945	27305	128.59
58.	Statistics and Programme Implementation	314	530	68.59				314	530	68.59

(Rs crore at 2006–07 prices)

Ministry/Department		Budgetary Support			IEBR			Total Outlay		
		Tenth Plan Realization	Eleventh Plan Projection	% increase	Tenth Plan Realization	Eleventh Plan Projection	% increase	Tenth Plan Realization	Eleventh Plan Projection	% increase
59.	Steel	113	192	69.84	7979	8254	3	8092	8447	4.39
60.	Textiles	4909	12378	152.13	8			4918	12378	151.70
61.	Tourism	2849	4558	59.96				2849	4558	59.96
62.	Tribal Affairs	1481	3633	145.22				1481	3633	145.22
63.	Urban Development	12805	11001	–14.09	5066	13599	168	17871	24600	37.65
64.	Urban Employment and Poverty Alleviation	2850	3260	14.37	25057	40220	61	27907	43480	55.80
65.	Water Resources	2435	2870	17.88				2435	2870	17.88
66.	Women and Child Development	16307	48420	196.92				16307	48420	196.92
67.	Youth Affairs And Sports	1949	5305	172.26				1949	5305	172.26
68.	**Grand Total**	486798	1096860	125.32	458530	1059711	131	945328	2156571	128.13

Note: Totals may not tally due to rounding errors. * The allocation also includes funds for Central Road Fund. ** Includes allocation for Energy (R&D) and Skill Development Mission.

ANNEXURE 3.3
Proposed Sectoral Allocations for States and Union Territories in the Eleventh Plan

(Rs crore at 2006–07 price)

S. No.	Major Heads of Development	Andhra Pradesh	%-age to total	Arunachal Pradesh	%-age to total	Assam	%-age to total	Bihar	%-age to total	Chhattisgarh	%-age to total	Goa	%-age to total
1	2	3	4	5	6	7	8	9	10	11	12	13	14
I.	Agriculture and Allied Activities	7377.69	5.01	752.00	9.52	517.94	2.16	1697.71	2.80	1482.96	2.76	211.76	2.50
II.	Rural Development	14520.28	9.85	258.22	3.27	1878.69	7.84	7848.78	12.95	3234.57	6.02	234.98	2.77
III.	Special Area Programmes	3552.61	2.41	423.38	5.36	97.41	0.41	646.43	1.07	198.80	0.37	23.10	0.27
IV.	Irrigation and Flood Control	34292.18	23.27	516.95	6.54	2862.96	11.95	7876.15	12.99	5550.35	10.33	579.74	6.83
V.	Energy	22582.35	15.32	1280.19	16.20	2601.67	10.86	4717.84	7.78	13991.40	26.04	830.08	9.78
VI.	Industry and Minerals	5233.51	3.55	195.49	2.47	360.08	1.50	1982.43	3.27	924.16	1.72	117.73	1.39
VII.	Transport	12629.76	8.57	1589.50	20.12	3173.47	13.25	14726.26	24.29	6007.06	11.18	716.84	8.45
VIII.	Communications	0.00	0.00	0.00	0.00	0.00	0.00	0.00	0.00	0.00	0.00	0.00	0.00
IX.	Science and Technology	35.41	0.02	44.94	0.57	213.74	0.89	311.32	0.51	2772.49	5.16	315.33	3.72
X.	General Economic Services	2544.80	1.73	442.88	5.61	575.66	2.40	2797.37	4.61	1015.51	1.89	181.19	2.14
XI.	Social Services	43111.28	29.25	2237.91	28.32	11152.75	46.56	17480.06	28.83	18316.70	34.09	3977.70	46.88
	Education	6061.14	4.11	1131.59	14.32	3306.90	13.81	5385.65	8.88	4217.84	7.85	1568.60	18.49
	Medical and Public Health	4206.26	2.85	287.62	3.64	848.06	3.54	872.54	1.44	1665.64	3.10	254.69	3.00
	Water Supply and Sanitation	5778.65	3.92	278.63	3.53	426.25	1.78	1587.39	2.62	5625.58	10.47	883.74	10.42
	Housing	5895.80	4.00	189.36	2.40	5.86	0.02	1429.28	2.36	182.68	0.34	94.68	1.12
	Urban Development	5332.86	3.62	230.99	2.92	5948.67	24.83	3666.88	6.05	4411.27	8.21	437.99	5.16
	Others Social Services	15836.57	10.74	119.72	1.52	617.01	2.58	4538.32	7.49	650.14	1.21	738.00	8.70
XII.	General Services	1515.12	1.03	159.54	2.02	519.65	2.17	546.66	0.90	236.41	0.44	1296.55	15.28
	Grand Total	147395.00	100.00	7901.00	100.00	23954.00	100.00	60631.00	100.00	53730.43	100.00	8485.00	100.00

(Annexure 3.3 contd.)

S. No.	Major Heads of Development	Gujarat	%-age to total	Haryana	%-age to total	Himachal Pradesh	%-age to total	Jammu & Kashmir	%-age to total	Jharkhand	%-age to total	Karnataka
1	2	15	16	17	18	19	20	21	22	23	24	25
I.	Agriculture and Allied Activities	5639.37	5.27	1636.27	4.90	1470.08	10.67	1818.21	7.04	2517.75	6.26	4317.30
II.	Rural Development	3154.80	2.95	1536.29	4.60	355.62	2.58	615.61	2.38	5500.57	13.67	4822.5
III.	Special Area Programmes	83.61	0.08	173.54	0.52	20.47	0.15	1419.76	5.50	1855.78	4.61	683.35
IV.	Irrigation and Flood Control	29196.49	27.31	3975.82	11.91	1220.62	8.86	735.02	2.85	3379.37	8.40	26033.78
V.	Energy	3767.21	3.52	3901.64	11.69	1122.14	8.14	8196.95	31.73	5634.62	14.00	12876.51
VI.	Industry and Minerals	3203.92	3.00	410.08	1.23	177.68	1.29	550.88	2.13	871.34	2.17	1259.31
VII.	Transport	9368.75	8.76	4625.88	13.86	2142.28	15.55	2660.81	10.30	4712.74	11.71	12599.10
VIII.	Communications	0.00	0.00	0.00	0.00	0.05	0.00	42.34	0.16	0.00	0.00	0.00
IX.	Science and Technology	793.82	0.74	27.08	0.08	2.92	0.02	23.70	0.09	911.55	2.27	1370.23
X.	General Economic Services	2057.60	1.92	1136.00	3.40	798.59	5.80	2740.98	10.61	647.65	1.61	2461.42
XI.	Social Services	49586.47	46.38	15610.80	46.78	6060.29	43.99	6501.40	25.17	13261.34	32.96	33977.03
	Education	*		3113.30	9.33	1679.87	12.19	2160.37	8.36	4468.63	11.10	5842.5
	Medical and Public Health	*		676.31	2.03	1445.19	10.49	1353.15	5.24	1809.37	4.50	1963.01
	Water Supply and Sanitation	*		4879.76	14.62	1443.93	10.48	1406.28	5.44	1225.51	3.05	5328.05
	Housing	*		406.75	1.22	553.76	4.02	9.90	0.04	17.51	0.04	3931.04
	Urban Development	*		817.66	2.45	127.54	0.93	788.39	3.05	1721.55	4.28	9510.28
	Others Social Services	*		5717.02	17.13	810.00	5.88	783.31	3.03	4018.77	9.99	7402.11
XII.	General Services	65.97	0.06	340.59	1.02	407.25	2.96	528.32	2.05	947.30	2.35	1263.46
Grand Total		106918.00	100.00	33374.00	100.00	13778.00	100.00	25834.00	100.00	40240.00	100.00	101664.00

(Annexure 3.3 contd.)

(Annexure 3.3 contd.)

S. No.	Major Heads of Development	%-age to total	Kerala	%-age to total	Madhya Pradesh	%-age to total	Maharashtra	%-age to total	Manipur	%-age to total	Meghalaya	%-age to total
1	2	26	27	28	29	30	31	32	33	34	35	36
I.	Agriculture and Allied Activities	4.25	2418.65	5.77	3751.24	5.33	10203.04	8.00	439.23	5.39	735.22	8.00
II.	Rural Development	4.74	1926.64	4.59	10739.26	15.27	13391.49	10.50	271.14	3.33	802.30	8.73
III.	Special Area Programmes	0.67	344.88	0.82	887.60	1.26	765.23	0.60	231.43	2.84	189.09	2.06
IV.	Irrigation and Flood Control	25.61	2343.41	5.59	14934.79	21.24	26782.98	21.00	772.38	9.47	219.72	2.39
V.	Energy	12.67	5547.94	13.23	9416.25	13.39	19130.70	15.00	1498.71	18.38	1084.88	11.81
VI.	Industry and Minerals	1.24	1180.84	2.82	591.12	0.84	1913.07	1.50	656.14	8.05	290.50	3.16
VII.	Transport	12.39	2524.56	6.02	8006.72	11.38	8927.66	7.00	403.16	4.94	1623.62	17.68
VIII.	Communications	0.00	0.00	0.00	0.00	0.00	0.00	0.00	0.00	0.00	0.00	0.00
IX.	Science and Technology	1.35	1094.17	2.61	161.05	0.23	127.54	0.10	127.63	1.57	245.07	2.67
X.	General Economic Services	2.42	2197.05	5.24	1564.95	2.23	5101.52	4.00	157.98	1.94	253.00	2.75
XI.	Social Services	33.42	10056.12	23.98	20159.98	28.67	38261.40	30.00	3273.20	40.14	3481.74	37.91
	Education	5.75	687.38	1.64	8684.21	12.35	7652.28	6.00	748.44	9.18	1336.29	14.55
	Medical and Public Health	1.93	423.74	1.01	1318.37	1.87	2550.76	2.00	103.05	1.26	633.81	6.90
	Water Supply and Sanitation	5.24	1202.52	2.87	1558.92	2.22	14870.93	11.66	1135.14	13.92	580.99	6.33
	Housing	3.87	367.29	0.88	6.49	0.01	1836.55	1.44	309.20	3.79	121.48	1.32
	Urban Development	9.35	204.92	0.49	4606.36	6.55	5917.76	4.64	237.63	2.91	321.66	3.50
	Others Social Services	7.28	7170.26	17.10	3985.64	5.67	5433.12	4.26	739.74	9.07	487.51	5.31
XII.	General Services	1.24	12305.74	29.34	116.04	0.16	2933.37	2.30	322.98	3.96	259.86	2.83
	Grand Total	**100.00**	**41940.00**	**100.00**	**70329.00**	**100.00**	**127538.00**	**100.00**	**8154.00**	**100.00**	**9185.00**	**100.00**

(Annexure 3.3 contd.)

S. No.	Major Heads of Development	Mizoram	%-age to total	Nagaland	%-age to total	Orissa	%-age to total	Punjab	%-age to total	Rajasthan	%-age to total	Sikkim	%-age to total
1	2	37	38	39	40	41	42	43	44	45	46	47	48
I.	Agriculture and Allied Activities	469.58	8.49	494.95	8.28	708.20	2.20	302.76	1.05	1330.46	1.85	276.01	5.85
II.	Rural Development	197.70	3.57	311.81	5.22	1864.71	5.79	2544.37	8.80	4244.11	5.92	510.30	10.81
III.	Special Area Programmes	57.12	1.03	578.93	9.68	4888.23	15.17	0.00	0.00	817.55	1.14	104.70	2.22
IV.	Irrigation and Flood Control	199.06	3.60	151.23	2.53	6518.18	20.23	1404.76	4.86	7655.29	10.67	84.76	1.80
V.	Energy	691.41	12.49	646.94	10.82	3431.93	10.65	8075.08	27.92	26441.82	36.86	511.54	10.84
VI.	Industry and Minerals	196.86	3.56	375.70	6.28	132.66	0.41	363.28	1.26	1005.02	1.40	233.90	4.9
VII.	Transport	886.58	16.02	821.90	13.75	3033.34	9.41	4290.29	14.83	4831.93	6.74	546.84	11.59
VIII.	Communications	0.00	0.00	0.00	0.00	0.00	0.00	0.00	0.00	0.00	0.00	0.00	0.00
IX.	Science and Technology	88.13	1.59	55.39	0.93	1176.94	3.65	8.48	0.03	31.14	0.04	147.60	3.13
X.	General Economic Services	345.91	6.25	341.06	5.71	1670.47	5.18	2080.37	7.19	754.00	1.05	158.78	3.36
XI.	Social Services	2305.82	41.67	1854.19	31.02	8473.99	26.30	9469.55	32.74	20031.68	27.93	1882.32	39.88
	Education	755.94	13.66	505.03	8.45	2426.52	7.53	1898.92	6.57	3654.31	5.09	799.29	16.93
	Medical and Public Health	495.92	8.96	252.64	4.23	515.55	1.60	406.21	1.40	1549.10	2.16	368.95	7.82
	Water Supply and Sanitation	480.18	8.68	260.05	4.35	1726.24	5.36	2129.89	7.36	5331.95	7.43	255.27	5.41
	Housing	318.64	5.76	302.66	5.06	305.54	0.95	349.14	1.21	847.09	1.18	141.20	2.99
	Urban Development	131.73	2.38	396.43	6.63	579.53	1.80	417.30	1.44	5274.33	7.35	122.05	2.59
	Others Social Services	123.41	2.23	137.37	2.30	2920.61	9.06	4268.10	14.76	3374.90	4.70	195.55	4.14
XII.	General Services	95.82	1.73	345.90	5.79	326.34	1.01	384.05	1.33	4588.99	6.40	263.24	5.58
	Grand Total	5534.00	100.00	5978.00	100.00	32225.00	100.00	28923.00	100.00	71732.00	100.00	4720.00	100.00

(Annexure 3.3 contd.)

(Annexure 3.3 contd.)

S. No.	Major Heads of Development	Tamil Nadu	%-age to total	Tripura	%-age to total	Uttar Pradesh	%-age to total	Uttara-khand	%-age to total	West Bengal	%-age to total	Total (States)	%-age to total
1	2	49	50	51	52	53	54	55	56	57	58	59	60
I.	Agriculture and Allied Activities	7831.57	9.18	694.35	7.84	19146.37	10.57	4564.47	10.67	1122.01	1.76	83927.15	5.94
II.	Rural Development	10241.28	12.00	906.40	10.24	7658.00	4.23	2483.90	5.80	7289.65	11.43	109344.00	7.74
III.	Special Area Programmes	0.0	0.0	497.22	5.62	4534.39	2.50	61.12	0.14	3193.28	5.01	26329.03	1.86
IV.	Irrigation and Flood Control	3313.36	3.88	520.78	5.88	16338.22	9.02	2661.10	6.22	2626.76	4.12	202746.20	14.36
V.	Energy	10743.30	12.59	636.44	7.19	26371.03	14.56	4966.05	11.60	17630.11	27.64	218326.74	15.46
VI.	Industry and Minerals	3715.98	4.35	278.62	3.15	2347.10	1.30	324.25	0.76	1920.67	3.01	30812.34	2.18
VII.	Transport	11646.95	13.65	1024.39	11.57	27328.64	15.09	8376.33	19.57	4601.60	7.21	163826.95	11.60
VIII.	Communications	0.0	0.0	0.37	0.00	0.00	0.00	0.00	0.00	0.00	0.00	42.76	0.00
IX.	Science and Technology	146.59	0.17	43.74	0.49	303.93	0.17	590.13	1.38	592.91	0.93	11762.96	0.83
X.	General Economic Services	284.15	0.33	255.46	2.89	11798.77	6.52	1567.35	3.66	310.26	0.49	46240.73	3.27
XI.	Social Services	36732.06	43.04	3827.30	43.24	64820.85	35.79	16547.89	38.67	23780.29	37.29	486232.14	34.43
	Education	3649.61	4.28	1068.39	12.07	18850.83	10.41	4323.85	10.10	5955.41	9.34	101933.15	7.22
	Medical and Public Health	2730.00	3.20	638.28	7.21	13194.05	7.29	2189.01	5.11	3532.80	5.54	46284.08	3.28
	Water Supply & Sanitation	7555.35	8.85	482.39	5.45	5367.34	2.96	2582.72	6.03	2013.62	3.16	76397.29	5.41
	Housing	2045.24	2.40	490.63	5.54	2824.06	1.56	417.34	0.98	698.09	1.09	24097.25	1.71
	Urban Development	6110.63	7.16	239.56	2.71	10913.17	6.03	3502.72	8.18	6331.72	9.93	78301.58	5.55
	Others Social Services	14641.22	17.16	908.04	10.26	13671.40	7.55	3532.25	8.25	5248.66	8.23	108068.75	7.65
XII.	General Services	688.78	0.81	166.93	1.89	446.70	0.25	655.41	1.53	711.45	1.12	32438.42	2.30
	Grand Total	85344.00	100.00	8852.00	100.00	181094.00	100.00	42798.00	100.00	63779.00	100.00	1412029.43	100.00

(Annexure 3.3 contd.)

S. No.	Major Heads of Development	Andaman & Nicoabar Islands	%-age to total	Chandigarh	%-age to total	Dadra & Nagar Haveli	%-age to total	Daman & Diu	%-age to total	Delhi	%-age to total
1	2	61	62	63	64	65	66	67	68	69	70
I.	Agriculture and Allied Activities	107.50	2.62	4.34	0.20	29.61	2.28	21.63	2.40	163.79	0.30
II.	Rural Development	221.63	5.41	19.24	0.90	35.36	2.72	15.59	1.73	712.69	1.30
III.	Special Area Programmes	0.00	0.00	0.00	0.00	0.00	0.00	0.00	0.00	0.00	0.00
IV.	Irrigation and Flood Control	52.94	1.29	3.19	0.15	52.41	4.03	27.89	3.10	333.67	0.61
V.	Energy	183.96	4.49	305.19	14.31	235.14	18.09	138.07	15.34	5488.68	10.02
VI.	Industry and Minerals	27.40	0.67	4.14	0.19	45.37	3.49	35.07	3.90	547.99	1.00
VII.	Transport	1843.63	44.97	189.61	8.89	136.81	10.52	179.71	19.97	18572.89	33.89
VIII.	Communications	0.00	0.00	0.00	0.00	0.00	0.00	0.00	0.00	0.00	0.00
IX.	Science and Technology	93.43	2.28	151.10	7.09	117.59	9.05	12.32	1.37	81.89	0.15
X.	General Economic Services	73.21	1.79	15.82	0.74	70.96	5.46	61.51	6.83	173.53	0.32
XI.	Social Services	1237.39	30.18	1418.24	66.52	527.22	40.56	370.59	41.18	27434.52	50.06
	Education	351.65	8.58	282.09	13.23	180.55	13.89	108.59	12.07	4464.55	8.15
	Medical and Public Health	161.25	3.93	472.97	22.18	165.03	12.69	82.93	9.21	5309.43	9.69
	Water Supply and Sanitation	237.78	5.80	55.97	2.63	72.66	5.59	53.55	5.95	9125.89	16.65
	Housing	185.33	4.52	53.49	2.51	17.86	1.37	35.51	3.95	729.44	1.33
	Urban Development	139.06	3.39	484.12	22.71	69.35	5.33	50.96	5.66	5879.34	10.73
	Others Social Services	162.30	3.96	69.59	3.26	21.77	1.67	39.05	4.34	1925.89	3.51
XII.	General Services	258.92	6.32	21.12	0.99	49.52	3.81	37.61	4.18	1289.48	2.35
	Grand Total	4100.00	100.00	2132.00	100.00	1300.00	100.00	900.00	100.00	54799.15	100.00

(Annexure 3.3 contd.)

(Annexure 3.3 contd.)

S. No.	Major Heads of Development	Lakshadweep	%-age to total	Puducherry	%-age to total	Total (UTs)	%-age to total	Total (States & UTs)	%-age to total
1	2	71	72	73	74	75	76	77	78
I.	Agriculture and Allied Activities	185.30	8.82	1018.20	9.44	1530.37	2.01	85457.53	5.74
II.	Rural Development	12.25	0.58	378.25	3.51	1395.02	1.83	110739.02	7.44
III.	Special Area Programmes	0.00	0.00	0.00	0.00	0.00	0.00	26329.03	1.77
IV.	Irrigation and Flood Control	47.55	2.26	314.98	2.92	832.63	1.09	203578.84	13.68
V.	Energy	165.30	7.87	541.58	5.02	7057.94	9.27	225384.68	15.15
VI.	Industry and Minerals	9.12	0.43	539.35	5.00	1208.45	1.59	32020.79	2.15
VII.	Transport	564.91	26.90	822.51	7.63	22310.08	29.31	186137.03	12.51
VIII.	Communications	0.15	0.01	0.00	0.00	0.15	0.00	42.91	0.00
IX.	Science and Technology	81.85	3.90	186.25	1.73	724.43	0.95	12487.39	0.84
X.	General Economic Services	638.43	30.40	438.17	4.06	1471.63	1.93	47712.35	3.21
XI.	Social Services	297.12	14.15	5946.89	55.13	37231.97	48.91	523463.11	35.18
	Education	60.97	2.90	1348.27	12.50	6796.67	8.93	108729.83	7.31
	Medical and Public Health	34.53	1.64	1386.85	12.86	7613.01	10.00	53897.09	3.62
	Water Supply and Sanitation	37.26	1.77	466.33	4.32	10049.44	13.20	86446.74	5.81
	Housing	61.42	2.92	827.18	7.67	1910.23	2.51	26007.48	1.75
	Urban Development	23.51	1.12	582.17	5.40	7228.51	9.50	85530.10	5.75
	Others Social Services	79.42	3.78	1336.09	12.39	3634.10	4.77	162852.88	10.94
XII.	General Services	98.02	4.67	600.82	5.57	2355.49	3.09	34793.91	2.34
	Grand Total	**2100.00**	**100.00**	**10787.00**	**100.00**	**76118.15**	**100.00**	**1488147.48**	**100.00**

4

Employment Perspective and Labour Policy

4.1. The generation of productive and gainful employment, with decent working conditions, on a sufficient scale to absorb our growing labour force must form a critical element in the strategy for achieving inclusive growth. Past record in this respect is definitely inadequate and the problem is heightened by the fact that the relatively higher rate of growth achieved during the last decade or so is not seen to generate a sufficient volume of good quality employment.

4.2. The Eleventh Plan provides an opportunity to focus on and diagnose the reasons for past failings observed in the employment situation and to reverse at least some of the adverse employment outcomes associated with the pattern of economic growth in the recent past.

WEAKNESSES IN PAST PERFORMANCE

4.3. The basic weakness in our employment performance is the failure of the Indian economy to create a sufficient volume of additional high quality employment to absorb the new entrants into the labour force while also facilitating the absorption of surplus labour that currently exists in the agricultural sector, into higher wage, non-agricultural employment. A successful transition to inclusive growth requires migration of such surplus workers to other areas for productive and gainful employment in the organized or unorganized sector. Women agricultural workers in families where the male head has migrated, also require special attention given the need for credit and other inputs if they are self-employed in agriculture or for wage employment if they do not have land.

4.4. The approach to the Eleventh Plan had identified the following specific weaknesses on the employment front which illustrate the general failing just discussed.

- The rate of unemployment has increased from 6.1% in 1993–94 to 7.3% in 1999–2000, and further to 8.3% in 2004–05.[1,2]
- Unemployment among agricultural labour households has risen from 9.5% in 1993–94 to 15.3% in 2004–05.
- Under-employment appears to be on the rise, as evident from a widening of the gap between the usual status (us) and the current daily status measures of creation of incremental employment opportunities between the periods 1994 to 2000 and 2000 to 2005 (Annexure 4.1).
- While non-agricultural employment expanded at a robust annual rate of 4.7% during the period 1999–2000 to 2004–05, this growth was largely in the unorganized sector.
- Despite fairly healthy GDP growth, employment in the organized sector actually declined, leading to frustration among the educated youth who have rising expectations.
- Although real wages of casual labour in agriculture continue to rise during 2000–2005, growth has decelerated strongly, as compared to the previous

[1]Unless otherwise stated, the employment and unemployment estimates are on 'Current Daily Status' (CDS) basis. See Box 4.1 for other measures of employment which are also relevant.

[2]Three kinds of estimates for the unemployed are obtained following the three different approaches. See Box 4.1.

quinquennium (1994–2000), almost certainly reflecting poor performance in agriculture. However, over the longer periods 1983 to 1993–94 (period I) and 1993–94 to 2004–05 (Period II), the decline is moderate for rural male agricultural casual labour, from 2.75% to 2.18% per annum.

- Growth of average real wage rates in non-agriculture employment in the period 1999–2000 to 2004–05 has been negligible. Seen over the longer period of two decades (Period I and Period II), the wages have steadily increased at over 2% per annum.
- In respect of entire rural male casual labour, the growth in real wages accelerated from 2.55% (Period I) to 2.78% per annum (Period II) (Annexure 4.6).
- Real wages stagnated or declined even for workers in the organized industry although managerial and technical staff did secure large increase.
- Wage share in the organized industrial sector has halved after the 1980s and is now among the lowest in the world.

4.5. It is only through a massive effort at employment creation, of the right quality, and decent conditions of work for all sections of population and at all locations that a fair redistribution of benefits from growth can be achieved. This indeed is a stupendous task. Alternative policy measures focusing on different sectors and occupations, and the specific requirements of different target groups are needed to create employment on a sustainable basis.

Recent Experience Revisited

4.6. The Tenth Plan was framed against the backdrop of concerns that were posed by the employment and unemployment survey in 1999–2000 (NSS 55th Round), which showed very low growth of employment compared with 1993–94. Jobless growth therefore became a key concern and the Plan set a target of creating 50 million new employment opportunities on a current daily status basis. (For a brief description of different concepts of employment see Box 4.1.)

4.7. The results of the most recent 61st Round of NSS for 2004–05 reveal a somewhat better picture of employment growth in the Tenth Plan period than in the previous period. During 1999–2000 to 2004–05, about 47 million work opportunities were created as compared to only 24 million in the previous period 1993–94 to 1999–2000. Further, employment growth accelerated from 1.25% per annum during the period 1993–94 to 1999–2000 to 2.62% per annum during the period 1999–2000 to 2004–05. The annual increase in work opportunities increased from 4.0 million per year in the first period to 9.3 million per annum in the second period (Table 4.1).

Box 4.1
The Three Kinds of Estimates of the Unemployed[1]

Unemployment rate is defined as the number of persons unemployed per 1000 persons in the labour force. Three kinds of estimates for the unemployed are obtained following the three different approaches. These are:

(i) number of persons usually unemployed based on 'usual status' approach,
(ii) number of persons unemployed on an average in a week based on the 'weekly status' and
(iii) number of person-days unemployed on an average during the reference period of seven days preceding the survey.

The first estimate indicates the magnitude of persons unemployed for a relatively longer period during a reference period of 365 days and approximates to an estimate of chronically unemployed. Some of the unemployed on the basis of this criterion might be working in a subsidiary capacity during the reference period. The former is called as the usually unemployed according to the principal status and the latter, the usually unemployed excluding the subsidiary status workers (us adjusted) which admittedly will be lower than the former. The second estimate based on the weekly status gives the average weekly picture during the survey year and includes both chronic unemployment and also the intermittent unemployment, of those categorized as usually unemployed, caused by seasonal fluctuations in the labour market. The third estimate based on the daily status concept gives average level of unemployment on a day during the survey year. It is the most inclusive rate of 'unemployment' capturing the unemployed days of the chronically unemployed, the unemployed days of the usually employed who become intermittently unemployed during the reference week, and the unemployed days of those classified as employed according to the priority criterion of current weekly status.

[1]NSSO Report No. 409: Employment and Unemployment in India 1993–94: NSS 50th Round; Chapter 7.

4.8. Despite these positive features, it must also be noted that the labour force also grew faster in the second period. However, the pace of growth in labour force in the second period at 2.84% per annum exceeded the growth in the workforce (employment) of 2.62% per annum, so that the unemployment rate increased from 7.3% in 1999–2000 to 8.3% in 2004–05.

LONG-TERM TRENDS IN EMPLOYMENT SITUATION: 1983 THROUGH 2005

4.9. Some analysts have viewed the 1999–2000 survey as an 'outlier' because of the relatively depressed employment situation in that year, and have commented that 1999–2000 was a case of low statistical base, which shows up as high growth of employment in the next period 2000–05. On this view, a better assessment of trends emerges if we compare developments over two relatively longer periods, that is, 1983 to 1993–94 (period I–10.5 years) and 1993–94 to 2004–05 (period II–11 years).

4.10. Table 4.1 presents a comparison of the trends in employment and labour force over a longer period. It is evident that population growth decelerated in Period II as compared with Period I and this led to a deceleration in labour force growth also. However, the growth of the workforce, that is, total employment, also decelerated in Period II. Employment grew more slowly than the labour force in Period II which raised the unemployment rate from 6.1% in 1993–94 to 8.3% in 2004–05. Measured in absolute terms, the average annual increase in employment opportunities during Period II was 6.45 million, which is lower than the annual increase of 7.09 million in Period I.

4.11. The inadequate increase in aggregate employment in Period II is associated with a sharp drop in the pace of creation of work opportunities in agriculture. Agriculture should not be expected to create additional employment but, rather, to reduce the extent of under-employment and thereby increase incomes and wages

TABLE 4.1
Past and Present Scenario on Employment and Unemployment

(current daily status basis)

	1983	1993–94	1999–2000	2004–05	1993–94 to 1999–2000	1999–2000 to 2004–05	1983 to 1993–94	1993–94 to 2004–05
	('000 person years)				(% per annum)			
All India								
Population	718101	893676	1005046	1092830	1.98	1.69	2.11	1.85
Labour Force	263824	334197	364878	419647	1.47	2.84	2.28	2.09
Workforce	239489	313931	338194	384909	1.25	2.62	2.61	1.87
Unemployment Rate (%)	9.22	6.06	7.31	8.28				
No. of Unemployed	24335	20266	26684	34738	4.69	5.42	-1.73	5.02
Rural								
Population	546642	658771	728069	779821	1.68	1.38	1.79	1.55
Labour Force	206152	252955	270606	303172	1.13	2.3	1.97	1.66
Workforce	187899	238752	251222	278076	0.85	2.05	2.31	1.40
Unemployment Rate (%)	8.85	5.61	7.16	8.28				
No. of Unemployed	18253	14203	19383	25097	5.32	5.3	-2.36	5.31
Urban								
Population	171459	234905	276977	313009	2.78	2.48	3.04	2.64
Labour Force	57672	81242	94272	116474	2.51	4.32	3.32	3.33
Workforce	51590	75179	86972	106833	2.46	4.2	3.65	3.25
Unemployment Rate (%)	10.55	7.46	7.74	8.28				
No. of Unemployed	6082	6063	7300	9641	3.14	5.72	-0.03	4.31

Note: Estimates both on UPSS basis and CDS basis are given in Annexure 4.1.

of those employed in agriculture while surplus labour shifts to the non-agriculture sector. However, the increase in employment in the non-agricultural sectors was disappointing.

4.12. As shown in Table 4.2, the dependence of the work-force on agriculture and allied sectors declined from 61% in 1993–94 to 52% in 2004–05, that is, a decline of 9 percentage points as compared with a decline of only 4 percentage points in the period 1983 to 1993–94. Thus, work opportunities diversified away from agriculture at a faster pace during the latter period 1993–94 to 2004–05.

4.13. Table 4.3 shows the annual increase in the work-force by category of employment in Period I compared with Period II. There has been a sustained increase in employment opportunities since 1993–94, although at a slower rate than in the earlier period. A notable feature is the sharp increase in the number of jobs created at regular salaried wage—from 0.98 million per year in Period I to 1.68 million per year in Period II. This is a direct consequence of the step-up in the expansion of the manufacturing and services sectors, as already discussed. However, the pace of opening up of employment opportunities for casual wage labour getting released from the agriculture sector has slowed down sharply in Period II. The annual increase in this category was 2.40 million in Period I but which declined to 0.54 million in Period II (Table 4.3), mainly reflecting the lower absorption in agriculture which was not offset by an expansion in other sectors.

TABLE 4.2
Sector-wise Share of Employment by Current Daily Status

(CDS basis) (%)

Industry	1983	1993–94	1999–2000	2004–05	2006–07
Agriculture	65.42	61.03	56.64	52.06	50.19
Mining and Quarrying	0.66	0.78	0.67	0.63	0.61
Manufacturing	11.27	11.10	12.13	12.90	13.33
Electricity, water, etc.	0.34	0.41	0.34	0.35	0.33
Construction	2.56	3.63	4.44	5.57	6.10
Trade, hotel, and restaurant	6.98	8.26	11.20	12.62	13.18
Transport, storage, and comm.	2.88	3.22	4.06	4.61	5.06
Financial, insurance, real estate, and business services	0.78	1.08	1.36	2.00	2.22
Community, social, and personal services	9.10	10.50	9.16	9.24	8.97
Total	**100.00**	**100.00**	**100.00**	**100.00**	**100.00**

Note: *Projected.

TABLE 4.3
Annual Increase in Workforce by Category of Employment

(CDS basis) (million)

Category of Employment	1983 to 1993–94	1993–94 to 2004–05
Self-employed	3.71 (52.39)	4.23 (65.57)
Salaried wage	0.98 (13.83)	1.68 (26.02)
Casual wage	2.40 (33.78)	0.54 (8.41)
Workforce	7.09 (100.00)	6.45 (100.00)

Note: Figures in parentheses are percentages.
Source: Derived from data in Annexure 4.3(C).

SECTOR-WISE EMPLOYMENT GENERATION ACHIEVED IN THE TENTH PLAN

4.14. Though the aggregate employment generation of 47 million work opportunities in the period 1999–2000 to 2004–05 was fairly close to the target of 50 million employment opportunities for the Tenth Plan, the performance across sectors has varied (see Table 4.4).

4.15. The achievement with respect to employment creation was short of the Tenth Plan target in the agriculture sector by 0.6 million persons (8.84 million increase against a target of 9.47 million). The increase in the manufacturing sector was short by 3 million persons (8.64 million increase against a target of 11.62 million); in trade, hotel, and restaurants by 0.53 million (10.70 million against a target

TABLE 4.4
Sector-wise Performance and Targets of Employment

(CDS basis)

Sector	Incremental Employment (million)			
	Target (2002–07) (5 years)	Achievement (2000–05) (5 years)	Achievement (1994–2005) (11 years)	Projected (2007–12) (5 years)
Agriculture	9.47	8.84	8.82	0.00
Mining and Quarrying	–0.2	0.17	0.00	0.00
Manufacturing	11.62	8.64	14.84	11.94
Electricity, water, etc.	–0.21	0.18	0.00	0.02
Construction	6.3	6.44	10.05	11.92
Trade, hotel, and restaurant	11.23	10.70	22.67	17.40
Transport, storage, and comm.	5.51	4.04	7.64	9.02
Financial, insurance., real estate, and business services	1.93	3.12	4.31	3.43
Community, social, and personal services	0.49	4.59	2.62	4.34
Total	49.00 {(a)(b)}	46.72	70.98	58.07

Notes: [a] Including 2.87 million contribution from special employment programmes.
[b] To create 50 million opportunities, the Tenth Plan envisaged a contribution of 20 million from selective innovative programmes and policies leading to a changed pattern of growth in favour of the labour intensive sectors, over and above 30 million through normal buoyancy from growth.

of 11.23 million); and in transport and communication by 1.47 million (4.04 million against a target of 5.51 million). In contrast, the construction, financial services, and community, social and personal services sectors exceeded the Tenth plan target of employment. In proportional terms, the largest shortfall in employment generation has been in manufacturing.

INFORMALIZATION OF EMPLOYMENT

4.16. A critical issue in assessing employment behaviour of the economy is the growth of employment in the organized sector vis-à-vis the unorganized sector. Public debate on this issue is usually conducted on the basis that unorganized sector employment is generally of low quality while organized sector employment is of high quality, and the focus of attention is on whether employment has increased in the organized sector. The inadequacy of growth in the organized sector has traditionally been illustrated using data on employment by units registered with the Directorate General of Employment and Training, which are typically large units in the organized sector. These data are presented in Table 4.5 below and they clearly show that whereas organized sector employment increased at the annual rate of 1.2% per year in the period 1983–1994, it actually declined at 0.3% per year in the period after 1994.

TABLE 4.5
Growth in Organized Employment

(% per annum)

Sector	1983–1994	1994–2005
Public Sector	1.53	–0.70
Private Sector	0.44	0.58
Total Organized	1.20	–0.31

This decline is shown to occur primarily on account of a decline in employment in public sector units. Employment growth in the private sector units has accelerated in the second period but the acceleration is clearly insufficient to offset the decline in public sector employment.

4.17. This issue can be explored further on the basis of data from the NSS employment surveys in 1999–2000 and 2004–05 which distinguish individuals according to type of establishment and also type of labour conditions. Data for the 61st Round[3] is presented in Annexures 4.4

[3]Wage workers among the household members who answered NSSO questions in the 61st Round (2004–05) were asked as to whether the employers provide the following types of benefits to them, and also the method of receiving payment:

and 4.5. The design of enquiry in the two rounds was not identical, and in the 55th Round it was restricted only to the receipt of PF benefits by employees.[4]

4.18. Using this data it is possible to obtain a broad picture of employment growth in three categories of establishments, that is, private establishments hiring less than 10 workers, private establishments hiring 10 workers or more, and public sector establishments. Within each category, one can distinguish between regular employees, casual employees, and self-employed. Table 4.6 presents data for the set of employees other than those engaged in crop agriculture.

TABLE 4.6
Non-Agricultural Workers by Size and by Ownership of Establishment (Usual Principal Status Basis)

Employment Status by Ownership and by Workers' Size of Enterprise	1999–2000	2004–05	Increase/Decrease (absolute)	Increase/Decrease (%)
	(thousands)			
I. Regular Employees				
Private < 10	24171	27446	3275	13.55
Private > 10	11225	15650	4425	39.42
Public	19760	22042	2283	11.55
Subtotal I–Regular Employees	55155	65138	9983	18.10
II. Casual Employees				
Private < 10	26197	28497	2300	8.78
Private > 10	5083	8075	2992	58.86
Public	943	1102	159	16.86
Subtotal II–Casual Employees	32223	37674	5451	16.92
III Self-Employed				
Private < 10	65514	81535	16021	24.45
Private > 10	1330	1998	668	50.23
Public	145	250	105	72.41
Subtotal III–Self Employed	66989	83783	16794	25.07
All Enterprises and All Employment Status				
Private < 10	115882	137478	21596	18.64
Private > 10	17637	25722	8085	45.84
Public	20848	23394	2547	12.22
Total I–III	**154367**	**186595**	**32228**	**20.88**

Note: Derived from unit level data of NSS 55th round and 61st round

4.19. The picture that emerges is the following:

- Total employment in public sector establishments has increased by 12.2% in the period 1999–2000 to 2004–05.
- Total employment in private sector establishments hiring less than 10 workers has increased by 18.6% in the same period.

---

[4]In the 55th Round (1999–2000), all the usual status workers (note here '*all*' includes self-employed workers, too) were asked whether they had the benefit of:

1. GPF
2. PPF
3. CPF
4. A combination of the above
5. None of the above

No question was asked on the method of payment to wage workers.

(i) Benefits eligible for:
1. Only PF/pension (that is, GPF, CPF, PPF, pension, etc.)
2. Only gratuity
3. Only health care and maternity benefits
4. Only PF/pension and gratuity
5. Only PF/pension and health care and maternity benefits
6. Only gratuity and health care and maternity benefits
7. PF/pension, gratuity, health care, and maternity benefits
8. Not eligible for any of above social security benefits

(ii) Method of payment received by the wage workers:
1. Regular monthly salary
2. Regular weekly payment
3. Daily payment
4. Piece rate payment
5. Others

- Total employment in private sector establishments hiring more than 10 workers has increased by as much as 45.8%!

4.20. If we treat employment in establishments hiring more than 10 workers as a measure of organized sector employment, the increase in organized sector employment in the private sector is more than the increase in the private unorganized sector.

4.21. If we limit our focus on regular employees in the larger private sector units, this category shows growth of 39.42%. However, the growth of casual employees in the larger private sector units was even faster at 58.9%.

4.22. The above conclusions emerge from unit level data of the NSS surveys focusing on the distinction between regular and casual employees. However some so-called regular employees do not have the benefits of social security. It is also possible to define organized employment more tightly to limit it to employees who receive provident fund and social security benefits. This has been done by the National Commission for Employment in the Unorganized Sector (NCEUS). As per NCEUS estimates, 20.46 million of the 54.12 million employees working in the organized sector in 1999–2000, were unorganized workers, and the remaining 33.67 million were organized. During the next five-year period, that is, 2000–05, while the number of organized workers by this definition remained constant, the number of unorganized workers in organized enterprises increased by 8.68 million to 29.14 million (Table 4.7).

4.23. The NCEUS data does not correspond with those in Table 4.6 since they include all of agriculture workers in the unorganized sector. Of the total increase in employment of 61 million on a Usual Principal and Subsidiary Status (UPSS) basis, the increase in the unorganized sector is 52 million and the increase in the organized sector is 9 million. However, while total employment in the organized sector has increased over the period, the increase is entirely on account of what is classified as informal employment in the organized sector, that is, workers who do not have the benefit of provident fund and social security. Whereas employment of this category expanded by over 42%, employment categorized as formal was more or less stagnant.

4.24. To summarize, the recent experience with employment growth presents a mixed picture. If we focus on the most recent period, 1999–2000 to 2004–05, there appears to be an acceleration in employment growth compared with the preceding period which is consistent with expectations, given the acceleration in GDP growth. However, looking at longer term trends, this acceleration in employment growth disappears and in any case the rate of unemployment has increased throughout. Concerns about the quality of employment appear valid although different sources of data are not easily reconciled. However, it does appear that total employment provided by the organized sector has expanded in the period 1999–2000 to 2004–05 and this is entirely because of the growth of informal employment in the organized sector.

4.25. These trends highlight the major challenges of employment in the Eleventh Plan which can be summarized as follows:

- How to ensure faster growth in employment than in the labour force so as to reduce unemployment.

TABLE 4.7
Distribution of Workers by Type of Employment and Sector

(million)

Sector	1999–2000			2004–2005		
	Informal	Formal	Total	Informal	Formal	Total
Unorganized Sector	341.28	1.36	342.64	393.47	1.43	394.90
	(99.60)	(0.40)	(100)	(99.64)	(0.36)	(100)
Organized Sector	20.46	33.67	54.12	29.14	33.42	62.57
	(37.80)	(62.20)	(100)	(46.58)	(53.42)	(100)
Total:	361.74	35.02	396.76	422.61	34.85	457.46
	(91.17)	(8.83)	(100)	(92.38)	(7.46)	(100)

Notes: 1. UPSS basis.
2. Figures in bracket indicate percentages.

Source: Estimates by NCEUS.

- How to ensure faster growth in the organized sector than the unorganized sector so that the share of organized sector employment increases.
- How to ensure growth in formal employment in the organized sector and not just the informal employment.

UNEMPLOYMENT AMONG THE YOUNG AND EDUCATED

4.26. Unemployment is typically higher among the youth and the educated who look for better quality of jobs, and this phenomenon is illustrated in Tables 4.8 and 4.9. Table 4.8 shows that unemployment among the age group 15–29 years for both males and females and in urban and rural areas is significantly higher than the average level of unemployment of all persons.

TABLE 4.8
Unemployment Rate among Youth (Age Group 15–29 Years)

(%) (CDS basis)

Year	Rural Areas		Urban Areas	
	Male	Female	Male	Female
1993–94	9.0	7.6	13.7	21.2
1999–2000	11.1	10.6	14.7	19.1
2004–05	12.0	12.7	13.7	21.5

Source: NSSO Report No. 515(61/10/1)

TABLE 4.9
Unemployment Rates for Persons of Age 15 Years and above by Level of Education on Current Weekly Status (CWS) Basis

(%)

General Level of Education	Rural male			Rural female			Urban male			Urban female		
	1993–94	1999–2000	2004–05	1993–94	1999–2000	2004–05	1993–94	1999–2000	2004–05	1993–94	1999–2000	2004–05
Not literate	1.8	3.0	2.7	2.2	2.7	2.5	2.2	3.1	2.8	2.2	2.0	2.5
Literate and up to primary	1.9	3.0	3.0	2.6	2.6	3.1	3.5	4.1	3.7	4.8	3.6	4.0
Secondary and above	8.3	7.3	6.5	19.8	16.9	18.2	7.0	6.9	6.2	19.6	15.8	17.9
ALL	3.1	3.9	3.8	2.9	3.7	4.2	5.2	5.6	5.2	7.9	7.3	9.0

Source: NSSO Report No. 515(61/10/1).

4.27. CDS measure has been used for analysis of trends in workforce, in keeping with the practice followed in the Tenth Five Year Plan. However this, being a person days measure (that is, a time-based measure), is not amenable, straightaway, to study of person-specific characteristics of the workers. Current weekly and the us measures study the activity status of a person over the reference period (week or the year) (CWS, UPSS, and UPS) and are therefore amenable to study of person-specific characteristics. Hence, in presenting the person-specific features of employed or unemployed persons Current Weekly Status (CWS) or the UPSS measures have been used.

THE EMPLOYMENT SITUATION AMONG THE VULNERABLE GROUPS

4.28. It is useful to distinguish between several different groups who face special difficulties in employment.

(i) Agricultural Labour Households and Casual Labour in Rural Areas

4.29. Out of 460 million workers (UPSS), 94 million earn so little that they are below the poverty line. And if that is the lot of employed workers, the lot of the poor who are unemployed in the labour force must be worse, which is a cause of concern to the planning process.

4.30. The proportion of poor among the workers in the rural areas decreased from 25.2% in 1999–2000 to 20.3% in 2004–05. In urban areas, the incidence of poverty among the workers decreased from 22.29% to 21.22%. Though there is a net decrease by 3.5 million in the number of poor workers during 2000–05, the magnitude of poor workers at 94.3 million in 2004–05 remains very high. The incidence of poverty among the regular wage/salaried workers is much lower (around 11%) as compared to the casual labour (32%) and the self-employed workers (17%). This suggests that all efforts should be made to increase the regular wage/salaried jobs. (Annexure 4.7).

TABLE 4.10
Incidence of Unemployment among Rural Agricultural Households

(CDS basis)

Year	Unemployment Rate (%)
1983	7.73
1993–94	9.50
1999–2000	12.29
2004–05	15.26

4.31. Unemployment among the rural agriculture labour households, which is the single largest segment of the poor labour households, is now 15.3% (Table 4.10). It is possible to infer that the magnitude of poverty among them may have remained the same or even increased.

4.32. There has been a slight deceleration in the growth in wages of rural male casual agricultural labour from 2.75% per annum during 1983–94 to 2.18% per annum during 1994–2005. The fall in the case of females is more steep, from 3.07% per annum to 2.10% per annum (Annexure 4.6).

(ii) Weaker Social Groups: The Scheduled Castes (SCs) and Scheduled Tribes (STs)

4.33. Table 4.11 gives the unemployment rates among SCs vis-à-vis others (excluding SC, ST and OBC) from National Sample Surveys from 1983 (38th Round) to 2004–05 (61st Round). It is pertinent to mention here that for 1983 (38th Round) and 1993–94 (50th Round), there was no separate category of OBC and therefore the category 'others' included OBC also in these two rounds. It may be seen that between 1999–2000 and 2004–05, the unemployment rates for females, SCs as well as others, in both rural and urban areas have increased; by 0.8 percentage point in rural areas and 1.5 percentage point in urban areas. For urban males, unemployment among SCs increased by 0.4 percentage point, whereas among others it declined by 0.8 percentage point during 1999–2000 to 2004–05.

4.34. Table 4.12 presents a comparative picture of unemployment among STs and Others; so far as rural males are concerned, there is no change in unemployment rates between 1999–2000 and 2004–05 for SCs; but for others, the unemployment rate has declined slightly. On the other hand, during the same periods, the unemployment rate for females in rural areas has declined for SCs, and for Others it has increased by 0.8

TABLE 4.11
Unemployment Rate according to Usual Status (ps+ss)[1,2,3] for Scheduled Castes during 1983 to 2004–05

(%)

	1983	1993–94	1999–2000	2004–05
Rural Areas				
Male	1.2 (1.4)	1.2 (1.4)	1.8 (1.8)	1.7 (1.6
Female	0.5 (0.7)	0.4 (0.8)	0.6 (1.0)	1.4 (1.8)
Urban Areas				
Male	5.1 (0.7)	4.6 (4.0)	5.1 (4.6)	5.5 (3.8)
Female	2.9 (4.9)	4.4 (6.2)	3.1 (5.4)	4.6 (6.9)

Note: [1]CDS measure has been used for analysis of trends in the work-force, in keeping with the practice followed in the Tenth Five Year Plan. However, this, being a person days measure (that is, a time based measure), is not amenable, straightaway, to the study of person-specific characteristics of the workers. Current weekly and the us measures study the activity status of a person over the reference period (week or the year) (CWS, UPSS, and UPS) and are therefore amenable to the study of person-specific characteristics. Hence, in presenting the person-specific features of employed or unemployed persons, CWS or the UPSS measures have been used.

[2]CDS estimates are not available from NSS reports. Therefore, UPSS estimates are given in this Table. However it should be noted that these are under-estimates of unemployment because CDS measure is the most comprehensive measure of unemployment and CDS estimates are significantly higher than UPSS estimates.

[3]Figures in parentheses are the corresponding unemployment rates for others (excluding SC, ST, and OBC).

Source: Report No. 516 (61/10/2), *Employment and Unemployment Situation among Social Groups in India, 2004–05.*

TABLE 4.12
Unemployment Rate according to Usual Status (ps+ss)[1,2,3] for Scheduled Tribes during 1983 to 2004–05

(%)

	1983	1993–94	1999–2000	2004–05
Rural Areas				
Male	0.5 (1.4)	0.8 (1.4)	1.1 (1.8)	1.1 (1.6)
Female	0.1 (0.7)	0.3 (0.8)	0.5 (1.0)	0.4 (1.8)
Urban Areas				
Male	4.3 (0.7)	4.7 (4.0)	4.4 (4.6)	2.9 (3.8)
Female	1.5 (4.9)	1.7 (6.2)	2.8 (5.4)	3.4 (6.9)

Note: [1]CDS measure has been used for analysis of trends in the work-force, in keeping with the practice followed in the Tenth Five Year Plan. However, this, being a person days measure (that is, a time based measure), is not amenable, straightaway, to the study of person-specific characteristics of the workers. Current weekly and the us measures study the activity status of a person over the reference period (week or the year) (CWS, UPSS, and UPS) and are therefore amenable to the study of person-specific characteristics. Hence, in presenting the person-specific features of employed or unemployed persons, CWS or the UPSS measures have been used.

[2]CDS estimates are not available from NSS reports. Therefore, UPSS estimates are given in this Table. However it should be noted that these are under-estimates of unemployment because CDS measure is the most comprehensive measure of unemployment and CDS estimates are significantly higher than UPSS estimates.

[3]Figures in parentheses are the corresponding unemployment rates for others (excluding SC, ST, and OBC).

Source: Report No. 516 (61/10/2), *Employment and Unemployment Situation among Social Groups in India, 2004–05.*

percentage point. In urban areas, the unemployment rate for males in both categories, namely SCs and Others has declined, but for females it has increased.

(iii) The Children at Work

4.35. Estimates from the 61st Round reveal that 5.82 million children (age 5–14 years) work; 1.136 million in urban areas and 4.682 million in rural areas (Table 4.13).

TABLE 4.13
Estimated Number of Children (5–14 Years) in the Labour Force, Workforce, and Unemployed—All India (CDS Basis)

('000)

Heads	1993–94		1999–2000		2004–05	
	Rural	Urban	Rural	Urban	Rural	Urban
Labour Force	9919	1552	7792	1447	5182	1292
Workforce	9441	1442	7203	1320	4682	1136
Unemployed	479	110	589	127	501	156
Unemployment Rate (%)	4.83	7.08	7.56	8.78	9.66	12.08

4.36. The Child Labour (Prohibition and Regulation) Act, 1986 prohibits employment of children below 14 years in hazardous occupations and processes and regulates the working conditions in other employments. Compliance with the provisions of this Act is the responsibility of Labour Sector of the Plan (Ministry of Labour and Employment). At present, the laws do not prohibit employment of children in non-hazardous occupations but children so employed must have access to education. Against this background, the Eleventh Plan Working Group on Child Labour has estimated that 3.643 million children (5–14 years) were working in the non-agricultural sector, out of which 1.219 million children were engaged in hazardous occupations. Chapter 6 (Volume II) Towards Women's Agency and Child Rights gives the comprehensive approach to deal with the problem of children at work and exposed to other risks.

4.37. The education sector has a pre-eminent role in ensuring that all children in the age group 9–14 years are at school. To the extent this goal of SSA can be ensured (now that there is a fourfold increase, at constant price, in the Eleventh Plan over the Tenth Plan, duly backed by scheme-tied revenue through a Cess), the tendency to utilize child labour at a cheap cost to increase profits from making children work, can be curbed. The Integrated Child Development Scheme (ICDS), also, has a responsibility with regard to the development of adolescent girls and thus keeping them away from wage employment.

4.38. The focus of efforts to eradicate child labour has to be location specific, confined to those pockets where employers are prone to be exploitative in accessing the cheapest cost labour. High per-capita income locations (metro towns, in particular), destinations of migrant worker families and 'industrial belts', where informal work relationships for labour-intensive occupations thrive, have therefore to be closely monitored through innovative mechanisms that provide intelligence to the enforcement agencies.

4.39. Any expansion of the Child Labour Eradication Plan has to be made only after a careful evaluation of the existing scheme with regard to:

- Its effectiveness in dovetailing SSA and ICDS;
- The ability to involve State administrations which implement the CSS pertaining to the development, education, nutrition, and protection of children;
- A purely Central Plan funded effort should be in the nature of an emergent action over a limited duration at the location, where the local administration are, by ignorance or by design, seem to be aiding the use of cheap child labour for serving the profit motive of the citizens at that location.
- A suitable form of penalization should be imposed in such local and State Governments that seem to be paying only 'lip service' to curb the problem of the use of 'cheap cost child labour'.

(iv) Women Workers

4.40. Women comprise 48.3% of the population but have only 26.1% share in the persons employed. This is presently because their share is in the labour force is only 26.4% (Table 4.14). The female labour force participation rates (LFPR) across all age groups are 25 to 30% of the male LFPR in urban areas, and 35 to 40% of male LFPR in the rural areas.

4.41. Along with lower participation rates, women face a higher incidence of unemployment than men. This is especially so for higher levels of education. While the unemployment rates between men and women

TABLE 4.14
Past and Present Macro Scenario on Employment and Unemployment—Male and Female

(CDS basis)

	1983	1993–94	1999–2000	2004–05	1993–94 to 1999–2000	1999–2000 to 2004–05	1983 to 1993–94	1993–94 to 2004–05
	('000 person years)				(% per annum)			
All India								
Population	718101	893676	1005046	1092830	1.98	1.69	2.11	1.85
Labour Force	263824	334197	364878	419647	1.47	2.84	2.28	2.09
Workforce	239489	313931	338194	384909	1.25	2.62	2.61	1.87
Unemployment Rate (%)	9.22	6.06	7.31	8.28				
No. of Unemployed	24335	20266	26684	34738	4.69	5.42	–1.73	5.02
Female								
Population	346546	430188	484837	527355	2.01	1.70	2.08	1.87
Labour Force	68011	86728	92859	110886	1.14	3.61	2.34	2.26
Workforce	61218	81151	85952	100491	0.96	3.18	2.72	1.96
Unemployment Rate (%)	9.99	6.43	7.44	9.37				
No. of Unemployed	6793	5578	6907	10395	3.63	8.52	–1.86	5.82
Male								
Population	371556	463488	520209	565475	1.94	1.68	2.13	1.82
Labour Force	195813	247468	272019	308761	1.59	2.57	2.25	2.03
Workforce	178270	232780	252242	284417	1.35	2.43	2.57	1.84
Unemployment Rate (%)	8.96	5.94	7.27	7.88				
No. of Unemployed	17542	14688	19777	24343	5.08	4.24	–1.68	4.70

do not differ much up to the primary level of schooling, unemployment among women educated up to the secondary and higher levels is much higher than among men. In the urban areas, unemployment among young women in the 15–29 years age group is much higher than for men, and is highest among young urban women in the 20–24 years age group where one among every four girls seeking work cannot find it. They are in a especially vulnerable position when they seek entry into the regular wage jobs in the unorganized or even in the private organized sector, in urban areas. This has many implications for our labour policy, particularly the gender sensitive regulations, the social policies and programmes that are designed to promote 'equality' at work.

4.42. A measure of 'underemployment' is the change in activity status of the persons employed, when the reference period for the study of time disposition is reduced from one year (the us measure) to an average day of the past week (CDS measure). Only 66% of rural women who are counted as employed on the US measure, are seen as employed on the CDS measure, whereas the corresponding proportion for men is higher at 89% (NSS Report No. 515 (61/10/1) (Part I) (September 2006) (Statement 7.2.1). The deceleration in wage rates of casual labour in agriculture between the periods 1994–2000 and 2000–05 has been higher for women (2.93% per annum to 0.93% per annum) than for men (2.79% to 1.21%). Participation in education by girls (15–19 years) in rural areas is only 33% (as compared to 47% for men), and the gender disparity increases sharply in the next age group, that is, 20–24 years. Only 1.3% of young women (15–29 years) in rural areas received formal vocational training. Such features of the labour market for women are reflected in the fact that as much as 21.7% of employed women have consumption levels below poverty line in 2004–05, that is, they are employed yet still poor. This proportion is lower among men—19.9%. (Annexure 4.7).

4.43. The principal reasons for low participation by women in the labour force are:

- Wage rates of women are lower than of male for comparable occupations.
- Women are denied access to certain occupations, though they may be capable of doing that work as well as the men.
- Skill development of women is not uniform across all trades; participation by them remains confined to a few labour-intensive occupations such as stitching, teachers training, etc., which forces a majority of the women to enter the labour market as unskilled labour.

4.44. Whenever equal opportunity has been given to women in recruitments, equality in wage with the men has been ensured, and an equal exposure in training has been given, the participation by women in work has improved. This is illustrated in ample measure in the IT and enabled services sectors and in various other professional services—legal, financial, commercial, education and health.

4.45. In order to promote gender equity, steps have to be taken to increase women's participation in the labour force. This has to be pursued through skill development, labour policies and also the social security framework. Significant outcomes can be expected only if the gender issue is addressed through the planning initiatives across all the 'heads of development' in the Plan, with requisite lead from the 'Women and Child Development' Head. Gender-budgeting has not, so far, received due attention.

4.46. The Eleventh Plan must seek to reduce the gender differentials by pursuing (i) target shares for women beneficiaries in the programmes for 'Skill Development initiatives', 'New initiatives at Social Security', implementation of regulations such as the Apprentices Act, 1961, the Factories Act, the Building and Construction Workers (Conditions of Service) Act, and better implementation of The Maternity Benefit Act, 1976 and The Equal Remuneration Act, 2000, and for guarding against sexual harassment at the work place.

(v) Migrant Workers

4.47. Inter-State population migration rates for the inter-census period (1991–2001) are given in Annexure 4.8. The net out-migrant and in-migrant States are presented in this Annexure. Large absorbers of migrants are the States of Punjab, Haryana, Delhi, Gujarat, Maharashtra, Karnataka and Goa. The large net out-migrant States are Rajasthan, Uttar Pradesh, Bihar, Assam, West Bengal, Jharkhand, Orissa, Chhattisgarh, Andhra Pradesh, Kerala, and Tamil Nadu. Implicit in these population movements is an origin-destination migration matrix of workers. The numbers shown in the Annexure are inter-decadal and are presumably much smaller than the shorter period movements of migrant workers.

4.48. Migration itself is not an abnormal phenomenon and is common all over the world since growth centres which generate demand for labour often tend to concentrate in certain areas. However, migrant workers are the most vulnerable and exploited among the informal sector workers, and have not received any attention in the labour policy. In the States which are sources (origin) of supply of migrant workers—and most of them migrate to take up some labour-intensive, low-wage occupation—an effective and large-scale effort for vocational training in the labour intensive occupations is required. And such a programme should be amenable to the special needs of the entrants to informal labour markets. In the destination States, the focus of public policy (including Labour Policy) should be to improve the conditions under which the bulk of these in-migrants live and work. And in so far as the destination locations fail to provide certain basic minimum conditions to the new in-migrants, it would be better to restrain economic growth at such locations. In the labour and employment sector, better implementation of certain legislations pertaining to unorganized workers can protect the interests of most of the migrant workers; for example, the Building and Other Construction Workers (Regulation of Employment and Conditions of Service) Act, 1976; the Building and Other Construction Workers (Cess) Act, 1976; the Workmen's Compensation Act, 1923 and the Minimum Wages Act, 1948. An initiative has been taken recently by the government (in September 2007) with the introduction of 'The Unorganized Workers' Social Security Bill, 2007' in the Rajya Sabha.

(vi) The Self-employed and Casual Wage Employed

4.49. The self-employed and casual wage employed account for 83% of the workforce. About 20–25 million enter the labour force each year. Thus 17–21 million will enter the labour market in the non-regular wage employed category. The only strength of the self and the casual employed is their occupational skill, and the entrepreneurial skill to negotiate the price of labour put in by them. At present, a majority of the new entrants in this category have little or no education, not to speak of any vocational training. And many of them migrate to new locations, and to new occupations other than their traditional ones. The skill development set up of the government(s) has practically no space for them, at present. The National Skills Mission, discussed in the Chapter 5 on Skill Development and Training could make a major difference by upgrading the skills of new entrants to the informal sector.

EMPLOYMENT PROJECTIONS FOR THE ELEVENTH AND TWELFTH PLANS

4.50. The Approach Paper for the Eleventh Plan had projected an addition of 52 million to labour force in the Plan period and had called for the creation of 70 million employment opportunities. However, the projections of labour growth have been revisited in view of the latest population projections made available by the National Commission on Population and work done by the Eleventh Plan Working Group on Labour Force and Employment Projections. The projected increase in labour force during the Eleventh Plan period is now estimated at 45 million.

4.51. The employment prospects in the Eleventh Plan period have also been revised and the results are presented in Tables 4.15(A) and (B) with projections of labour force and employment over a longer period, 2006–07 to 2016–17, encompassing both the Eleventh and the Twelfth Plans.

4.52. As shown in Table 4.15(B), population growth is expected to decelerate through this period with a corresponding deceleration in labour force growth to 1.6% per year. However, although the labour force growth is projected to decelerate, the absolute increase in the labour force is very large. In fact, India's demographic profile is

TABLE 4.15(A)
Population, Labour Force, Employment Projections

('000)

	Basis	1993–94*	2004–05*	2006–07	2011–12	2016–17
Population (age 0+)		893676	1092830	1128313	1207971	1283242
Population (age 15–59)		501760	652940	687120	760110	820570
Labour Force	UPSS	378650	471250	492660	541840	586440
Labour Force	CDS	334197	419647	438948	483659	524057
Employment Opportunities	CDS	313931	384909	402238	460310	51820
Unemployed ('000)	CDS	20266	34738	36710	23348	5853
Unemployment Rate (%)	CDS	6.06	8.28	8.36	4.83	1.12

Note: * Actual estimates derived from NSS.

TABLE 4.15(B)
Projected Population, Labour Force, and Employment in Different Periods

Growth rates (% per annum) and absolute increase ('000)

	Basis	1993–94 to 2004–05*	2004–05 to 2006–07	2006–07 to 2011–12	2011–12 to 2016–17
Growth Rate in Population (age 0+)		1.85	1.43	1.37	1.22
Growth Rate in Population (age 15–59)		2.42	2.29	2.04	1.54
Growth Rate in Labour Force	UPSS	2.01	1.99	1.92	1.59
Growth Rate in Labour Force	CDS	2.09	2.02	1.96	1.62
Growth Rate in Employment Opportunities	CDS	1.87	1.98	2.73	2.40
Addition to Population ('000)	UPSS	199154	35483	79658	75271
Addition to Labour Force ('000)	UPSS	92600	21410	49180	44600
Addition to Labour Force ('000)	CDS	85450	19301	44711	40398
Addition to Employment Opportunities ('000)	CDS	70978	17330	58072	57893

Note: * Actual estimates derived from NSS.

such that the expansion in the labour force in India will be larger than in the industrialized countries, and even China. As discussed in Chapter 5, the demographic dividend could be a source of global competitive advantage if it is combined with successful efforts at skill upgradation and at expansion of employment opportunities.

4.53. The growth of total employment over the period has been estimated on the basis of employment projections for individual sectors which are then aggregated. These sectoral employment projections are based on sectoral GDP growth rates combined with assumptions about employment elasticity moderated by the implicit growth of productivity (see Annexure 4.2). The resulting projections indicate that 58 million job opportunities will be created in the Eleventh Plan period which exceeds the projected addition to the labour force, leading to a reduction in the unemployment rate to below 5%.

4.54. Over the longer period up to 2016–17, spanning the Eleventh and Twelfth Plan periods, the additional employment opportunities created are estimated at 116 million as compared to 71 million during the 11-year period from 1993–94 to 2004–05 (Table 4.16). Since the labour force will increase by 85 million in this period, a substantial part of the surplus of labour force that exists at the commencement of the Eleventh Plan could get absorbed into gainful employment by the end of the period. The unemployment rate at the end of the Twelfth Plan period is projected to fall to a little over 1%.

4.55. There are important qualifications to these projections which must be kept in mind, arising from the limitation of employment elasticity as a projection tool. The concept of employment elasticity is at best a mechanical device to project employment on the basis of projected growth of output and past relationships between employment and output. These relationships can change as a result of changing technology and change in real wages. The labour force participation rate is also subject to changes, especially because of possible changes in female participation rates in urban areas associated with advances in women's education. For all these reasons, the projected decline in the unemployment rate must be treated with caution. It could well be that the projected increase in labour demand induces greater labour supply through an increase in participation rates and also higher wages which moderate demand. However, the overall picture of an acceleration in the rate of creation of job opportunities and a reduction in unemployment rates is relatively robust, if GDP growth takes place as projected.

SECTORAL EMPLOYMENT PROJECTIONS

4.56. The projected growth of employment in the Eleventh Plan and beyond is decomposed into its sectoral components in Table 4.16.

AGRICULTURE EMPLOYMENT

4.57. The agriculture sector has long been known to be characterized by underemployment, which means that with the same number of workers it is possible to generate

TABLE 4.16
Projected Increase in Number of Workers by Sector, 2007–12 and 2007–17

(CDS) ('000)

Industry	Estimated		Projected	
	1983 to 1993–94 ($10^1/_2$ Years)	1993–94 to 2004–05 (11 Years)	2006–07 to 2011–12 (5 Years)	2006–07 to 2016–17 (10 Years)
Agriculture	34900	8816	0	–3967
Mining and Quarrying	855	3	1	3
Manufacturing	7850	14834	11937	24516
Electricity, water, etc.	487	30	17	36
Construction	5260	10052	11922	26370
Trade, hotel, and restaurant	9190	22667	17397	34402
Transport, storage, and communication	3213	7639	9025	18764
Finance, insurance, real estate, and business services	1524	4312	3428	7472
Community, social, and personal services	11163	2624	4344	8369
Total	74442	70978	58072	115965

more output. The projection for the Eleventh Plan assumes that the projected doubling of the rate of agricultural growth during the Eleventh Plan will be possible without any increase in agricultural employment. Whereas agriculture contributed 8.8 million job opportunities in the 11-year period from 1993–94 to 2004–05, it is projected to contribute no increase in the Eleventh Plan and a net decrease of 4 million agricultural workers over the Twelfth Plan period (2006–07 to 2016–17). This is a reasonable projection considering that the number of main workers in agriculture declined by about 1.8 crore between 1991 and 2001 and there has been a large increase in marginal workers in agriculture during 1991–2001. Rising wage differentials between the agriculture and non-agriculture sectors are also very likely to shift labour out of agriculture, and the continued growth into the Twelfth Plan period would provide sufficient pull factor from non-agriculture to encourage such a shift.

4.58. An alternative projection of agricultural employment has also been made, applying the actual employment elasticity (0.15) observed during 1993–94 to 2004–05 to the projected growth of output over the perspective period (2007–2017). This gives an estimate of employment in agriculture for 2011–12, that is, about 9 million more than in Table 4.16. In this projection there is positive growth of employment in agriculture at 0.6% per year and productivity growth is correspondingly lower at 3.4% per annum. In this scenario, employment increase would be 9 million more, with unemployment correspondingly less at only 14 million in 2011–12. However, this would be at the cost of lower productivity growth and, therefore, wages and incomes in agriculture and a larger proportion of low quality jobs.

4.59. During the 11-year period 1994–2005, the pace of increase in per worker GDP in agriculture was only 2.24% per annum as compared to 4.35% per annum growth in aggregate GDP per worker. (Annexure 4.2). During the Eleventh Plan, also, the pace of productivity increase being projected is lower for agriculture than for the aggregate economy, irrespective of the scenario regarding employment growth in agriculture. Since the main employment issue in the agriculture sector is the increase in farm labour income, and not the creation of a larger number of employed workers, it would be appropriate to work towards a strategy in which there is higher growth in non-services employment opportunities in rural areas which can provide additional income for the rural workforce by providing additional non-agricultural employment.

EMPLOYMENT IN MANUFACTURING, CONSTRUCTION, AND SERVICES

4.60. The Eleventh Plan should aim at significantly stepping up growth in employment in other sectors, countering the long-term trends observed in the past. Employment in manufacturing should grow at 4% per annum against the trend of growth in the preceding 11 years (1994–2005) of 3.3% per annum. Employment in construction should grow at 8.2% per annum against the trend of 5.9% growth, and in the transport and communication sector at 7.6% against the long-term trend of 5.3%.

4.61. These growth rates in employment in individual sectors are achievable provided they are supported by programmes for skill development, which will ensure availability of the relevant skills without which the growth of employment will probably choke. It is also necessary to ensure a wider provision of social security and welfare of unorganized workers, particularly in sectors such as construction and transport. Initiatives for these areas are elaborated in the Chapters on 'Skill Development and Training' and 'Nutrition and Social Safety Net'.

4.62. The sectors with prospects for high growth in output, creation of new establishments and for creation of new employment opportunities (direct as also indirect) are:

Services

- IT-enabled Services
- Telecom Services
- Tourism
- Transport Services
- Health Care
- Education and Training
- Real Estate and Ownership of Dwellings
- Banking and Financial Services
- Insurance
- Retail Services
- Media and Entertainment Services

Other Sectors and Sub-Sectors

- Energy-Production, Distribution and Consumption of Horticulture

- Floriculture
- Construction of Buildings
- Infrastructure Projects Construction

Industry Groups

- Automotive
- Food Products
- Chemical Products
- Basic Metals
- Non-Metallic Mineral Products
- Plastic and Plastic Processing Industry
- Leather
- Rubber and Rubber Products
- Wood and Bamboo Products
- Gems and Jewellery
- Handicrafts
- Handlooms
- Khadi and Village Industries

The Services Sector

4.63. The services sector is currently the fastest growing sector of the economy, and employment growth in the sector has remained more than 5% per annum since the 1990s as compared with the aggregate employment growth at less than 2%. This sector has the unique opportunity to grow due to its labour cost advantage, reflecting one of the lowest salary and wage levels in the world coupled with a rising share of working age population. However, two types of initiatives are required: (i) fostering the establishment of a viable size for delivery of services based on labour intensive occupations. Only in establishments of a reasonable size (in contrast to the average enterprise size of 1.2 workers, as it exists today), with a reasonable level of occupational specialization and corresponding productivity and wage levels, is this feasible; and (ii) a massive skill development effort, as discussed later, for vocational training of the new entrants to the labour force.

4.64. Planning initiatives in health, nutrition, care of children, care of the aged, education, skill development and expansion of social security services will create a large potential for employment for delivery of these services. Quantum jumps in the requirement of personnel, their skill and in their composition—by gender, by social group and by location in favour of the backward regions—will arise from:

- A massive increase in Central funding of education which is a four fold increase over the Tenth Plan in constant price;
- Emphasis on the next phase of SSA on improvement in the quality of education;
- Reaching these services to the districts having a concentration of SC, ST, and minorities;
- Rapid expansion in the mid-day meal (MDM) scheme to cover 60 million additional children at the upper primary level by 2008–09; and
- Enrolling one crore children in vocational education–skill development streams.

4.65. Already, a substantial increase in the number of teachers has been made, which will continue further. During the three-year period of 2002–03 to 2005–06, 0.285 million para teachers were recruited, of which 0.27 million are in the rural areas (NUEPA; *Progress Towards UEE—Analytical Report 2005–06*; Table E 20). And much of this expansion has occurred in the low per capita income States of Bihar, Madhya Pradesh, Chhattisgarh, Rajasthan, and Uttar Pradesh. Further, the expansion of mid-day meals programme, will require a substantial step up in the personnel required for delivery of such services.

4.66. The Central Government has recently announced an expansion in social security services such as: (i) Old age pension to all citizens, (ii) Life and disability cover against injury or death to either the head of, or to one earning member of each poor family; and (iii) Health insurance, so that the poor do not have to bear a high cost of medical care. These would require a commensurate expansion in the requirement of a variety of professionally trained and skilled personnel by the institutions that (i) cover risk; (ii) identify, issue and update the identity of the beneficiaries (smart cards); (iii) design specific schemes for the target groups and market the same; (iv) render medical services; or (v) reach out to the prospective beneficiaries. Most of the beneficiaries of the new Central initiatives would be the aged, the poor and the landless, and thus vulnerable to vagaries of the market. The institutional base that exists at present for delivery of the kinds of services, discussed here, is quite insensitive to the special needs of the prospective beneficiaries, and breeds 'exclusion'. While the beneficiaries could be (and should be) expected to make a contribution, howsoever small, to participate in the scheme, the personnel that are hired for rendering these services have to be trained to reach out to the prospective beneficiaries, in a manner that is responsible and transparent, and thus evokes her/his confidence to participate in the scheme. Moreover, some token contribution to become a member of the scheme is essential to empower these beneficiaries to lay a claim to the services that especially allocated funds by the Central Government for their benefit.

(i) EXPANSION OF IT SERVICES IN RURAL AREAS

4.67. Village kiosks will require expansion of IT personnel deployment across the rural areas of the country, in particular to facilitate the expansion of an IT enabled governance set-up. Such improvements are essential for keeping pace with the demand for public services that will guide the diversification of the economy away from agriculture and towards the secondary and tertiary sectors, duly supported by: (i) investments in industrial infrastructure, (ii) creation of institutional infrastructure in the rural areas, and (iii) for fostering integration of rural markets with the rest of the economy. These would require manifold expansion in a variety of matching services to be delivered by the local governments and by the village Panchayats, and that would be feasible only if the governance set-up at the local level is overhauled and handled in an IT-friendly mode.

(ii) PERSONAL SERVICES

4.68. The increase in the income of middle-class households in the high growth phase entails a spurt in consumption of personal services related to attire, appearance, baby care, health upkeep, personal drivers, security, care for the aged dependents, household governance and management, and so on. And such personal services have to be delivered by professionally trained, hired personnel of formal establishments, quite distinct from the earlier one-person operations. But in this area, a major effort at nurturing the right type of serving establishments at reasonable fees, training and certification of their personnel who can earn a reasonable income and thereby keep themselves above exploitation by the well off and informal employers, by way of access to the social security arrangements, is required. So far, services of a reasonable standard have by and large remained confined to the few who have a very high level of personal income, leaving the average urban consumer of such services to the vagaries of a market driven by 'short-life', one or two-person establishments, thriving on profits from cheap and untrained young in-migrants to high-income locations. The local administrations, including the labour administrations, have not handled the issue in a labour–employment–income perspective, and have generally ignored the problems arising due to the law and order enforcement agencies.

EMPLOYMENT AND LABOUR POLICY

4.69. The employment strategy for the Eleventh Plan must ensure rapid growth of employment while also ensuring an improvement in the quality of employment. While self employment will remain an important employment category in the foreseeable future—it accounted for 58% of all employment in 2004–05—there is need to increase the share of regular employees in total employment. As shown in Annexure 4.3(C), this category has increased from 17% of total employment in 1983 to 18% in 2004–05. It should be the focus of policy to achieve a substantial increase in the share of regular employment with a matching reduction in the share of casual employment which at present is as high as 23%.

4.70. The above analysis implies that the success of labour policy should be seen in terms of the number of regular wage employment opportunities based on some form of a written contract between the employer and the employee, that is, an increase in the number of 'formal' jobs. The potential for creation of formal employment can be fully utilized by making appropriate changes in rules and procedures. It is often said that one of the obstacles to growth of formal employment in the organized sector is the prevalence of excessively rigid labour laws which discourage such employment. Steps that should be taken for a greater flexibility in labour laws are discussed in the Chapter on Industry. Broadly, it is necessary to review existing laws and regulations with a view to making changes which would:

- encourage the corporate sector to move into more labour-intensive sectors
- facilitate the expansion of employment and output of the unorganized enterprises that operate in the labour-intensive sectors.

4.71. At present, the incentives and subsidies are so designed as to strongly penalize entrepreneurs for crossing a threshold size from a micro/small to a medium/

large unit. The excise and other taxation policies need to be reviewed in this perspective.

4.72. Changes in policies also need to be examined in regard to:

- Linking incentives with the outcomes measured in terms of employment. For example, incentives are given to a wide range of production activities primarily with the objective of promoting employment and income of workers engaged in such activities. However, such incentives are hardly ever calibrated against the benefits realized in terms of employment and wages.
- Regular wage employment, that is, formal employment, merits fiscal incentives. Such incentives already exist at a limited scale for the larger establishments, but are so designed as to make it difficult for medium and small establishments to benefit from these.

4.73. Changing labour laws is a sensitive issue and it is necessary to build a consensus. However, there are several changes short of hire and fire which should not present problems. These include:

- The locations and production activities that have a high potential for employment creation merit a differential treatment.
- Employment of women must be encouraged ensuring, inter alia, the special needs that they may have by virtue of change in working hours (night shifts, for example) or the requirements of the family, for example, child care.
- Contract labour in the domestic tariff area merits encouragement, provided commensurate steps are taken to increase social security
- Monitoring the implementation of labour laws, that is, the reporting system should be simplified and be permitted in an IT-friendly mode.

4.74. Even as steps are taken to increase the volume of formal or regular employment, it is also necessary to take steps to improve the quality of employment in the unorganized sector. NCEUS in its August 2007 Report has summarized, in the form of a 13-point Action Programme, the main recommendations for the workers of Enterprises in the Unorganized/Informal Sector. These are presented in Box 4.2.

4.75. Unorganized sector enterprises mostly hire most workers who get released, or relocated, from crop agriculture (due to the reasons discussed earlier), and seek wage employment in the manufacturing or services sector. Any significant improvement in their income, and quality of employment, is feasible only if the institutional environment in the labour market makes it feasible for the formal sector to reach out to such workers on a decentralized basis rather than through a centralized plan programme. The large coverage (in terms of absolute numbers) through Provident Fund (43 million), Employee State Insurance (33.0 million) a variety of welfare funds (5.0 million), for *beedi* workers, for example) has been possible because the institutional framework created through the various Acts[5] (P.F., E.S.I., Beedi Workers Welfare Fund, etc.) recognized a relationship of those employed on regular wage, with either the employer, or the specific formal commodity market that provides work to (that is, absorbs the output of labour put in by) the unorganized enterprises' workers.

4.76. As already argued, the creation of a formal relationship between the worker and the hiring establishment, in the regular wage employment mode, is a critical factor in improving the quality of employment of the workers hired by the unorganized enterprises. In this context, the work being done by NCEUS[6] on: (i) the 'employment strategy' to be pursued in respect of, and through the, unorganized enterprises, (ii) the regime of labour regulations to attract the unorganized enterprise to give a formal recognition to the multitudes of workers hired by them, and (iii) to enable them to gain access to 'social security', is of paramount importance.

[5]Of course, many of these organizations have to reorient their pattern of working to the new realities of the market for wage labour in which the role of public sector is diminishing and the average number of workers hired by the private enterprises is reducing consequent upon changes in technology leading to improvement in the productivity of labour.

[6]The relevant terms of reference of NCEUS are:

- Suggest elements of an employment strategy focusing on the informal sector;
- Review Indian labour laws, consistent with labour rights, and with the requirements of expanding growth of industry and services, particularly in the informal sector, and improving productivity and competitiveness; and
- Review the social security system available for labour in the informal sector, and make recommendations for expanding their coverage.

Box 4.2
A Thirteen Point Action Plan Suggested by the NCEUS for Employment in the Unorganized Sector

A. Protective Measures for Workers

1. *Ensuring Minimum Conditions of Work in the Non-agricultural and Agricultural Sectors:*
   Two bills, for agricultural workers and non-agricultural workers, that specify the minimum conditions of work, including a statutory national minimum wage for all workers
2. *Minimum Level of Social Security:*
   A universal national minimum social security scheme, as part of a comprehensive legislation covering life, health and disability, maternity and old age pension to protect the workers in the unorganized sectors.

B. Package of Measures for the Marginal and Small Farmers

3. *Special Programme for Marginal and Small Farmer:*
   Revival of the targeted programme focusing on small and minor farmers, with an initial thrust in the areas wherein the existing yield gap is also considered high. A special agency or a coordinating mechanism should be set up if required.
4. *Emphasis on Accelerated Land and Water Management:*
   Immediate priority to, and significant up-scaling of, programmes for land and water management.
   Revision of the priority sector landing policy to provide a quota for micro and small enterprises.
5. *Credit for Marginal/Small Farmers:*
   RBI to monitor, separately, credit to this segment, expansion in the outreach of credit institutions in rural areas and a credit guarantee fund to obviate the need for collateral by the marginal/small farmers in accessing the institutional credits. A 10% share for small and marginal farmers in the priority sector credit (Table below)
6. *Farmers' Debt Relief Commission*:
   The Central government to lay guidelines and provide 75:25 assistance for setting up State-level Farmers' Debt Relief Commissions, in the States experiencing agrarian distress—natural or market related.

C. Measures to Improve Growth of the Non-agricultural Sector

7. *Improve Credit Flow to the Non-agricultural Sector:*

Percent	Sector and Sub-Sector/Purpose
18	10% for small and marginal farmers; 8% for other farmers
10	4% for micro enterprises with capital investment (other than land and building) up to Rs 0.5 million and 6% for other micro and small enterprises
12	12% on loans up to Rs 0.5 million to the socio-economically weaker sections for housing, education, professions, and so on.
40	Total priority sectors lending

8. *Encouraging SHGs and MFIs for Livelihood Promotion:*
   Measures to encourage growth of micro finance and SHGs in poor States and in the backward areas
9. *Creation of a National Fund (NAFUS):*
   Rs 5000 crore initial corpus for an exclusive statutory agency to take care of requirements of micro and small enterprises in agriculture and non-agriculture sectors that are presently not reached by SIDBI and NABARD.
10. *Up-scaling Cluster Development through Growth Poles:*
    Twenty-five growth poles in the traditional industries clusters with incentives at par with SEZs

D. Measures to Expand Employment and Improve Employability

11. *Expand Employment through Strengthening Self-employment Programmes:*
    Rationalization and strengthening of the four major self-employment generation programmes with 5 million annual employment generation target.
12. *Universalize and Strengthen National Rural Employment Guarantee Act (NREGA)*:
    Extension of NREGA Programmes to all districts.
13. *Increase Employability through Skill Development:*
    On-job-training cum employment-assurance programme to provide incentive of Rs 5000 per person to any employer willing to provide one-year training on job skill enhancement.

ANNEXURE 4.1
Population, Labour Force, Employment, and Unemployment (1993–94 to 2016–17)

(million)

Status	Estimated			Projected		
	1993–94	1999–2000	2004–05	2006–07	2011–12	2016–17
Population						
Age 0+	893.68	1005.05	1092.83	1128.31	1207.97	1283.24
Age 15–59	501.76	572.23	652.94	687.12	760.11	820.57
Labour Force						
UPSS						
Age 0+	378.65	408.35	471.25	492.66	541.84	586.44
Age 15–59	337.71	369.22	431.95	451.70	496.65	535.20
CDS						
Age 0+	334.20	364.88	419.65	438.95	483.66	524.06
Age 15–59	298.95	330.78	385.87	403.75	444.72	479.70
Employment						
UPSS						
Age 0+	371.12	398.93	459.72			
Age 15–59	330.34	360.04	420.74			
CDS						
Age 0+	313.93	338.19	384.91	402.24	460.31	518.20
Age 15–59	279.88	305.70	352.92			
Unemployed						
UPSS						
Age 0+	7.53	9.41	11.53			
Age 15–59	7.37	9.17	11.21			
CDS						
Age 0+	20.27	26.69	34.74	36.71	23.35	5.86
Age 15–59	19.07	25.08	32.95			
Unemployment rate (%)						
UPSS						
Age 0+	1.99	2.30	2.45			
Age 15–59	2.18	2.48	2.60			
CDS						
Age 0+	6.06	7.31	8.28	8.36	4.83	1.12
Age 15–59	6.38	7.58	8.54			

ANNEXURE 4.2
Annual Growth Rate of GDP per Worker

(%)

	Industry	1983 to 1993–94	1993–94 to 2004–05	2006–07 to 2016–17
1.	Agriculture	1.03	2.24	4.57
2.	Minining and Quarrying	1.66	4.95	5.64
3.	Manufacturing	2.29	3.31	7.27
4.	Electricity, gas and water supply	3.70	5.46	7.51
5.	Construction	–1.43	1.45	5.56
6.	Trade, hotels and restaurants	1.06	2.69	5.68
7.	Transport, storage and communication	2.06	4.94	9.77
8.	Finance, insurance, real estate and business services	2.79	–0.40	4.26
9.	Community, social and personal services	1.57	5.90	6.11
	Total	2.29	4.35	7.82

ANNEXURE 4.3(A)
Percentage Distribution of Employed Persons by Category of Employment (CDS)—Rural India

('000)

Category	Male				Female				Persons			
	1983	1993–94	1999–2000	2004–05	1983	1993–94	1999–2000	2004–05	1983	1993–94	1999–2000	2004–05
Self-Employed	64.62	62.50	59.83	62.91	61.81	60.91	59.51	66.51	63.83	62.05	59.74	63.95
Regular Employees	11.50	9.52	10.25	10.25	4.45	4.55	4.88	5.12	9.52	8.10	8.72	8.76
Casual Labour	23.89	27.92	29.92	26.84	33.74	34.55	35.61	28.37	26.65	29.85	31.53	27.29
All	100.00	100.00	100.00	100.00	100.00	100.00	100.00	100.00	100.00	100.00	100.00	100.00
Estimated Number of Workers ('000)	135203	170677	179866	197391	52695	68075	71357	80685	187898	238752	251223	278076

Note: Derived from NSS reports on employment and unemployment situation in India.

ANNEXURE 4.3(B)
Percentage Distribution of Employed Persons by Category of Employment (CDS)—Urban India

('000)

Category	Male				Female				Persons			
	1983	1993–94	1999–2000	2004–05	1983	1993–94	1999–2000	2004–05	1983	1993–94	1999–2000	2004–05
Self-Employed	40.96	42.57	42.24	45.86	39.09	40.83	41.07	43.94	40.66	42.27	42.05	45.50
Regular Employees	46.68	43.78	43.47	42.39	35.72	36.67	40.18	43.18	44.87	42.54	42.92	42.54
Casual Labour	12.35	13.65	14.29	11.75	25.19	22.50	18.75	12.88	14.47	15.19	15.03	11.96
All	100.00	100.00	100.00	100.00	100.00	100.00	100.00	100.00	100.00	100.00	100.00	100.00
Estimated Number of Workers ('000)	43067	62103	72376	87027	8523	13076	14595	19806	51590	75179	86971	106833

Note: Derived from NSS reports on employment and unemployment situation in India.

ANNEXURE 4.3(C)
Percentage Distribution of Employed Persons by Category of Employment (CDS)—All India

('000)

Category	Male				Female				Persons			
	1983	1993–94	1999–2000	2004–05	1983	1993–94	1999–2000	2004–05	1983	1993–94	1999–2000	2004–05
Self-Employed	58.91	57.18	54.79	57.69	58.64	57.67	56.38	62.06	58.84	57.31	55.19	58.83
Regular Employees	20.00	18.66	19.78	20.08	8.81	9.72	10.87	12.62	17.14	16.35	17.52	18.13
Casual Labour	21.10	24.16	25.43	22.22	32.55	32.60	32.75	25.32	24.03	26.34	27.29	23.03
All	100.00	100.00	100.00	100.00	100.00	100.00	100.00	100.00	100.00	100.00	100.00	100.00
Estimated Number of Workers ('000)	178270	232780	252242	284418	61218	81151	85952	100491	239488	313931	338194	384909

Note: Derived from NSS reports on employment and unemployment situation in India.

ANNEXURE 4.4
Conditions of Employment of Regular Wage/Salaried Workers—2004–05

(per 1000) (UPSS basis)

Condition of Employment	Rural	Urban	All
No written job contract	592	592	592
Not eligible for Paid Leave	480	455	464
Neither written job contract nor eligible for paid leave	712	549	630
Not eligible for Social Security Benefit[1]	569	535	547
Paid a Monthly Salary	857	900	884
Non-existence of Union/Associations	513	541	531
Sample Workers	17033	26385	43418

Source: Derived from NSS 61st round (2004–05).

[1]Coverage under any of the Schemes-Provident Fund, PPF with employer contribution, Gratuity, Health care and Maternity benefits.

ANNEXURE 4.5
Distribution of Regular Wage/Salaried Workers by Type of Enterprise

Type of Enterprise	Distribution of Workers
Proprietory	378
Partnership	45
Employer household	49
Subtotal	472
Govt./Public sector	333
Public/Pvt.Ltd. Co.	127
Society/Trust	38
Subtotal	498
Others	18
N.R.	12
All	1000
Sample persons	43418

Source: Table 1, Appendix A, of NSS Report of 61st Round, No. 519.

ANNEXURE 4.6

Growth of Average Daily Wage Earnings in Rural India (at 1993–94 price)

(% per annum)

Category	Rural Male				Rural Female			
	1983 to 1993–94	1993–94 to 2004–05	1993–94 to 1999–2000	1999–2000 to 2004–2005	1983 to 1993–94	1993–94 to 2004–05	1993–94 to 1999–2000	1999–2000 to 2004–2005
Casual Labour in Public Works	2.28	3.81	3.83	3.15	4.10	3.83	5.03	2.01
Casual Labour in Agriculture	2.75	2.18	2.79	1.21	3.07	2.10	2.93	0.93
Casual Labour in Non Agriculture	2.38	2.34	3.69	0.62	4.08	3.47	5.06	1.32
Casual Labour in all Activities	2.55	2.78	3.59	1.51	3.13	2.40	3.19	1.21

ANNEXURE 4.7

The Working Poor in India by their Gender, Location, and Category of Employment, 1999–2000 and 2004–05

('000)

Population Segment	1999–2000				2004–05			
	Self Employed	Regular Wage/Salaried	Casual Labour	Total	Self Employed	Regular Wage/Salaried	Casual Labour	Total
Rural Persons	32762	2457	41466	76686	33139	2273	34125	69537
	(19.39)	(11.62)	(36.34)	(25.21)	(16.08)	(9.30)	(30.34)	(20.27)
Urban Persons	9387	4201	7531	21120	12141	5302	7321	24765
	(23.60)	(11.10)	(43.96)	(22.29)	(22.87)	(11.49)	(41.90)	(21.22)
All Males	27728	5545	31602	64875	29135	5863	27388	62386
	(19.68)	(11.18)	(36.77)	(23.47)	(17.17)	(10.24)	(31.85)	(19.94)
All Females	14421	1114	17396	32931	16145	1713	14058	31916
	(21.27)	(11.84)	(38.41)	(26.88)	(18.03)	(12.83)	(31.99)	(21.74)
All Persons	42150	6658	48998	97806	45280	7576	41446	94302
	(20.19)	(11.29)	(37.34)	(24.52)	(17.47)	(10.73)	(31.90)	(20.51)

Notes: 1. Figures in brackets are the proportion of Poor workers to total workers in that category.
2. UPSS basis.

ANNEXURE 4.8
Net Migrants Rate (1991–2001)

(%)

States/UTs	Male	Female	Person
1. Andhra Pradesh	–0.03	–0.03	–0.03
2. Assam	–0.06	–0.09	–0.07
3. Bihar	–0.39	–0.17	–0.28
4. Chhattisgarh	–0.06	–0.07	–0.06
5. Gujarat	0.22	0.09	0.16
6. Haryana	0.40	0.35	0.37
7. Himachal Pradesh	0.04	–0.06	–0.01
8. Jharkhand	–0.08	–0.02	–0.05
9. Karnataka	0.04	0.00	0.02
10. Kerala	–0.08	–0.08	–0.08
11. Madhya Pradesh	–0.01	0.00	–0.01
12. Maharashtra	0.37	0.21	0.29
13. Orissa	–0.10	–0.04	–0.07
14. Punjab	0.20	0.07	0.14
15. Rajasthan	–0.08	–0.05	–0.06
16. Tamil Nadu	–0.08	–0.07	–0.08
17. Uttranchal	–0.03	–0.06	–0.04
18. Uttar Pradesh	–0.25	–0.16	–0.21
19. West Bengal	–0.04	–0.04	–0.04
20. Delhi	1.93	1.57	1.77
21. Jammu and Kashmir	–0.04	–0.06	–0.05
22. Arunachal Pradesh	0.73	0.57	0.65
23. Manipur	–0.16	–0.13	–0.14
24. Meghalaya	0.09	0.04	0.07
25. Mizoram	–0.16	–0.35	–0.25
26. Nagaland	0.05	–0.41	–0.17
27. Sikkim	0.26	0.16	0.21
28. Tripura	0.02	0.02	0.02
29. Andaman and Nicobar	0.80	0.66	0.74
30. Chandigarh	2.15	1.78	1.98
31. Dadra and Nagar Haveli	4.29	1.90	3.12
32. Daman and Diu	6.15	1.88	4.05
33. Lakshadweep	1.04	0.20	0.63
34. Pondicherry	0.74	0.94	0.84
35. Goa	0.83	0.59	0.71
36. NE States	0.07	–0.03	0.02

5

Skill Development and Training

INTRODUCTION

5.1. Skills and knowledge are the driving forces of economic growth and social development of any country. They have become even more important given the increasing pace of globalization and technological changes provide both challenges that is taking place in the world. Countries with higher and better levels of skills adjust more effectively to the challenges and opportunities of globalization.

5.2. As India moves progressively towards becoming a 'Knowledge economy' it becomes increasingly important that the Eleventh Plan should focus on advancement of skills and these skills have to be relevant to the emerging economic environment. In old economy, skill development largely meant development of shop floor or manual skills. Even in this area there are major deficiencies in our work-force which need to be rectified. In new or knowledge economy the skill sets can range from professional, conceptual, managerial, operational behavioural to inter-personal skills and inter-domain skills. In the 21st century as science progresses towards a better understanding of the miniscule, that is, genes, nano-particles, bits and bytes and neurons, knowledge domains and skill domains also multiply and become more and more complex. To cope with this level of complexity the Eleventh Plan has given a very high priority to Higher Education (See Volume II, Chapter 1). Initiatives such as establishing 30 new Central universities, 5 new IISERs, 8 IITs, 7 IIMs, 20 IIITs, etc. are aimed at meeting that part of the challenge of skill development. In this Chapter, however, it is proposed to focus on mass-scale skill development in different trades through specially developed training modules delivered by ITIs, Polytechnics, vocational schools, etc. The Eleventh Plan aims at launching a National Skill Development Mission which will bring about a paradigm change in handling of 'Skill Development' programmes and initiatives.

5.3. The NSS 61st Round results show that among persons of age 15–29 years, only about 2% are reported to have received formal vocational training and another 8% reported to have received non-formal vocational training indicating that very few young persons actually enter the world of work with any kind of formal vocational training. This proportion of trained youth is one of the lowest in the world. The corresponding figures for industrialized countries are much higher, varying between 60% and 96% of the youth in the age group of 20–24 years. One reason for this poor performance is the near exclusive reliance upon a few training courses with long duration (2 to 3 years) covering around 100 skills. In China, for example, there exist about 4000 short duration modular courses which provide skills more closely tailored to employment requirement.

REVIEW OF THE EXISTING VOCATIONAL TRAINING SYSTEM

5.4. In India, skill acquisition takes place through two basic structural streams—a small formal one and a large informal one. The formal structure includes: (i) higher technical education imparted through professional colleges, (ii) vocational education in schools at the post-secondary stage, (iii) technical training in specialized institutions, and (iv) apprenticeship training. A number of agencies impart vocational education/training a various levels. Higher professional and technical education, primarily in the areas of agriculture, education, engineering and technology, and medicine, is imparted through various professional institutions.

5.5. There are seventeen ministries and departments of GoI which are imparting vocational training to about 3.1 million persons every year. Most of these are national-level efforts and individually they are able to reach a very small part of the new entrants to the labour force. Even collectively, they provide training to about 20% of the number of annual additions to the labour force. Each ministry/department in charge of subject sets up training establishments in its field of specialization. The attempt to meet training needs through multiple authorities—labour, handlooms, handicrafts, small industry, education, health, women and child development, social welfare, tourism, etc. leads to redundancy at some locations. While each of the training initiatives has a definite area of specialization, there is need for coordination amongst these ministries/departments.

5.6. Vocational training being a concurrent subject, Central Government and the State Governments share responsibilities. At the national level, Director General of Employment & Training (DGE&T), Ministry of Labour is the nodal department for formulating policies, laying down standards, conducting trade testing and certification, etc. in the field of vocational training. At the State level, the State Government departments are responsible for vocational training programmes.

5.7. There are 1244 polytechnics under the aegis of the Ministry of Human Resource Development with a capacity of over 2.95 lakh offering three-year diploma courses in various branches of engineering with an entry qualification of 10th pass. Besides, there are 415 institutions for diploma in pharmacy, 63 for hotel management, and 25 for architecture.

5.8. There are about 5114 Industrial Training Institutes (ITIs) imparting training in 57 engineering and 50 non-engineering trades. Of these, 1896 are State Government-run ITIs while 3218 are private. The total seating capacity in these ITIs is 7.42 lakh (4 lakh seats in government ITIs and the remaining 3.42 lakh in private ITIs). These courses are open to those who have passed either Class 8 or 10 depending on the trade and are of 1 or 2 years duration, which varies from course to course. In addition to ITIs, there are six Advanced Training Institutes (ATI) run by the Central Government which provide training for instructors in ATIs for electronics and process instrumentation, offering long and short courses for training of skilled personnel at technician level in the fields of industrial, medical, and consumer electronics and process instrumentation.

5.9. In order to provide sufficient autonomy in academics, administration, finance, management, improved physical infrastructure (building, equipments) etc., the government launched a scheme for upgradation of 100 ITIs into Centres of Excellence, with effect from the year 2004–2005.

5.10. The Apprentices Act, 1961, as amended from time to time, regulates the training of apprentices. The Act serves a dual purpose—first, it regulates the programme of training apprentices in industry so as to conform to the prescribed syllabi, period of training, etc. prescribed by the Central Apprenticeship Council and second, to utilize fully the facilities available in industry for workers. As on 30.06.2006, over 20800 public/private sector establishments were covered under the Act and number of seats allocated were 2.30 lakh, out of which about 1.72 lakh seats were utilized.

5.11. Skill building activity was also initiated under the 10+2 level of school education. A scheme of pre-vocational education at lower secondary level was started from 1993–94 to impart training in simple marketable skills and to develop vocational interests. There are now about 9583 schools offering about 150 educational courses of two years duration in the broad areas of agriculture, business and commerce, engineering and technology, health and paramedical, home science and science and technology at +2 stage covering about one million students. Under the aegis of the Ministry of Rural Development, banks and Non-Governmental Organizations, through 2500 Rural Development and Self-Employment Training Institutes (RUDSETI), have undertaken entrepreneurship and skill building of the rural youth for self-employment in areas with a pre-existing market for the goods/services produced, with a reported success rate of 70%. The Entrepreneurship Development Initiative (EDI) and other programmes of the Ministry of Micro, Small and Medium Enterprises train about one lakh persons a year.

5.12. The unorganized sector which constitutes about 93% of the workforce is not supported by any structural system of acquiring or upgrading skills. By and large, skill formation takes place through informal channels like family occupations, on the job training under master craftsmen with no linkages to the formal education training and certification. Training needs in this sector are highly diverse and multi skill-oriented. Many efforts for imparting training through Swarnjayanti Gram Swarojgar Yojana (SGSY), PMRY, KVIC, Krishi Vigyan Kendra (KVK) and Jan Shiksha Sansthan (JSS) are in place but the outcome is not encouraging.

5.13. The quantitative dimension of the Skill Development challenge can be estimated by the following:

- 80% of new entrants to workforce have no opportunity for skill training. Against 12.8 million per annum new entrants to the workforce the existing training capacity is 3.1 million per annum.
- about 2% of existing workforce has skill training against 96% in Korea, 75% in Germany, 80% in Japan, and 68% in the United Kingdom.

The Quantitative Aspect of the Skill Shortage

5.14. The NSS 61st Round Survey on Employment and Unemployment indicates (Annexures 5.1.1. to 5.1.4) that educational institutions attendance rates (5–14 years) drop by nearly half in the age group 15–19 years and by 86% after the age 15 years. Labour force participation rates rise sharply after the age of 14 years and reach close to 100% at the age of 25–29 years. The said results also reflect that 38.8% of the Indian labour force is illiterate, 24.9% of the labour force has had schooling up to the primary level and the balance 36.3% has had schooling up to the middle and higher level. They also reveal that about 80% of the workforce in rural and urban areas do not possess any identifiable marketable skills.

The Qualitative Aspect of Deficiencies

5.15. A basic problem with the skill development system is that the system is non-responsive to labour market, due to a demand—supply mismatch on several counts: numbers, quality and skill types. It is also seen that the inflexibilities in the course/curriculum set-up, lead to over supply in some trades and shortages in others. Of the trained candidates, the labour market outcomes as seen from placement/ absorption rates are reportedly very low. The institutional spread in the VET system shows acute regional disparity with over half of the ITIs/ITCs located in the southern States, both in terms of number of institutions as well as the number of seats.

5.16. The quality of the training system is also a matter of concern, as the infrastructural facilities, tool/kits, faculty, curriculum are reportedly substandard. The existing institutions also lack financial and administrative autonomy. The testing, certification and accreditation system is reportedly weak, and since the deliverables are not precisely defined, there is no effort at evaluating outcomes and tracking placements. The problem is further complicated with lack of industry–faculty interaction on course curricula and other factors.

5.17. The training system for capital-intensive sectors and hi-tech areas has always received a highly preferential treatment in contrast to those working in the informal sector. Further there is no certification system for a large chunk of workers, who do not have any formal education but have acquired proficiency on their own or through family tradition/long experience. In the absence of a proper certificate, these classes of workers in the informal sector are subjected to exploitation and they do not get any avenues for better employment in the market and their mobility is very restricted.

5.18. The private sector-run Industrial Training Centres (ITCs) do not seem to be any better than the ITIs, and the low-paying capacity of learners and consequently low fee structure and absence of quality consciousness are said to be major reasons for the current state of affairs.

5.19. The Planning Commission held extensive consultations with the industry, various Central ministries running training programmes, State Governments. The discussions have revealed that the present system of skill formation has certain critical gaps in that the curricula are inflexible and outmoded. There is an inadequate fitness-testing mechanism of the institutions with a mismatched fee structure and admission criteria. The capacities of the trainers are also not in consonance with the current requirement of various sectors due to various restrictions of the affiliating agencies.

5.20. The private sector does undertake in-house training programmes and to a very limited extent, trains 'outsiders'. However, such programmes are limited to catering to their own felt needs, in the nature of captive skill development. Low-paying capacity of learners and reluctance of industries to train workers for fear of losing them to competition has resulted in chronic deficiency in private investment in this area. All these deficiencies mentioned in the above five paras will need to be rectified during the Eleventh Plan.

SKILL DEVELOPMENT AND SELF-EMPLOYMENT

5.21. NSSO 61st Round data also reveals that the proportion of persons (15–29 years) who received formal vocational training was around 3% for the employed, 11% for the unemployed and 2% for persons not in the labour force. In order to link skills developed into actual productive use thereof including self-employment, steps will be taken in the Eleventh Five Year Plan by providing adequate incentives, not necessarily monetary but in terms of skill and entrepreneurship development and forward and backward linkages to finance, marketing and human resource management, to those who are or seek to be self-employed to enhance their productivity and value addition, making it an attractive option, rather than be an option *faute de mieux* as at present.

DEMOGRAPHIC DIVIDEND

5.22. The decline in the rate of growth of population in the past few decades implies that in the coming years fewer people will join the labour force than in preceding years and a working person would have fewer dependents, children or parents. Modernization and new social processes have also led to more women entering the work force further lowering the dependency ratio. This decline in the dependency ratio (ratio of dependent to working age population) from 0.8 in 1991 to 0.73 in 2001 is expected to further decline sharply to 0.59 by 2011 as per the Technical Group on Population Projections. This decline sharply contrasts with the demographic trend in the industrialized countries and also in China, where the dependency ratio is rising. Low dependency ratio gives India a comparative cost advantage and a progressively lowering dependency ratio will result in improving our competitiveness.

5.23. The unprecedented opportunity for Skill Development arises from a unique 25-year window of opportunity, called India's demographic dividend. The Demographic dividend consists of three elements of demographic trends fortuitously coinciding at a time when the economy is growing at 9% plus: (i) a declining birth rate means fewer people will be joining the workforce in coming years, than in previous years, (ii) a very slow improvement in life-expectancy around 63/64 years of age means an ageing population surviving fewer years after superannuation than in other countries, (iii) the baby-boomers generation having now crossed the age of 20, the demographic bulge is occurring at the age bracket of 15–29. All these trends combine to result in India having world's youngest workforce with a median age way below China and OECD countries. Figure 5.1 brings out this point very effectively. This would mean that dependency ratio, that is, the ratio of non-working population to working population will continue to be low, giving India

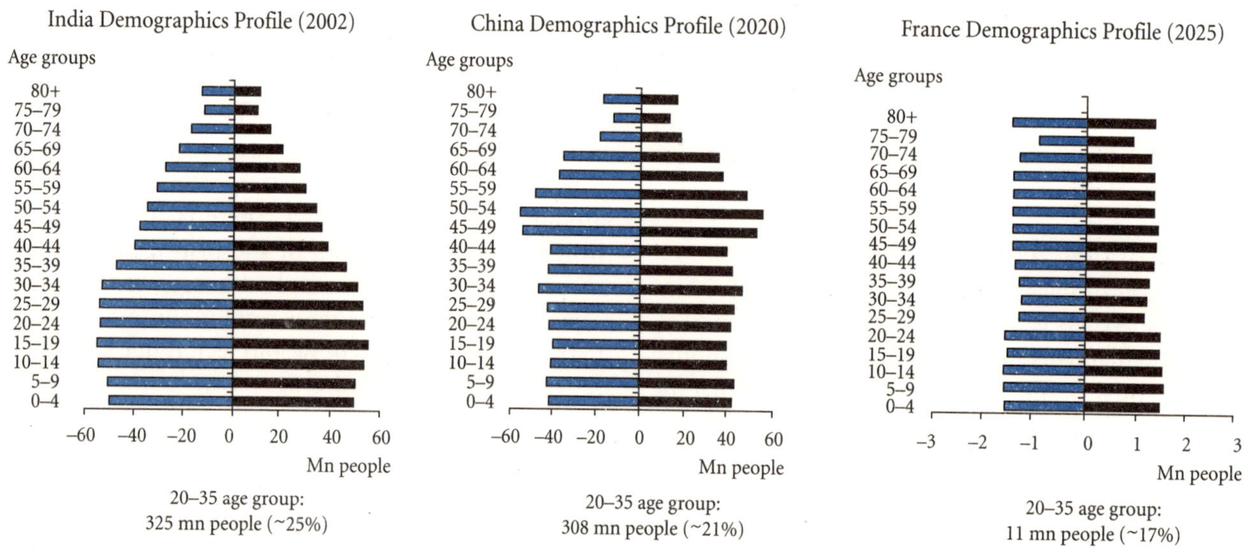

Source: CII Conference 2002 CSFB Report: UN Population Division: BCG.

FIGURE 5.1: Demographic Profile of Select Countries

a comparative cost advantage over others, for another 25–30 years. By that time the demographic bulge in India would be also reaching the age of superannuation, and India will also be joining the league of ageing economies.

5.24. It is expected that the ageing economy phenomenon will globally create a skilled manpower shortage of approximately 56.5 million by 2020 and if we can get our skill development act right, we could have a skilled manpower surplus of approximately 47 million (Annexure 5.2). In an increasingly connected world, where national frontiers are yielding to cross-border outsourcing, it is not inconceivable that within a decade we can become a global reservoir of skilled person power. As it is we account for 28% of graduate talent pool among 28 of the world's lowest cost economies. (Figure 5.2)

5.25. The criticality of Skill Development in our overall strategy is that if we get our skill development act right, we will be harnessing 'demographic dividend'; if we do not get there, we could be facing a 'demographic nightmare'. The Eleventh Plan takes cognizance of these and endeavours to take a slew of measures which will bring about a paradigm change in our Vocational Education System (VES).

5.26. India has the youngest population in the world; its median age in 2000 was less than 24 compared 38 for Europe and 41 for Japan. Even China had a median age of 30. It means that India has a unique opportunity to complement what an ageing rest of the world needs most. The demographic structure of India, in comparison with that of the competing nations, would work to the advantage to the extent our youth can acquire skills and seize the global employment opportunities in the future. This involves co-ordination, dialogue and discussions with the State Governments, private partners and other stakeholders, arriving at estimates of number of skilled personnel required across the sectors, aligning them with the career objectives of the youth drawing up different sector-specific modules of varying duration thereby.

Eleventh Plan Strategies

5.27. In the Eleventh Five Year Plan, the thrust will be on creating a pool of skilled personnel in appropriate numbers with adequate skills, in line with the requirements of the ultimate users such as the industry, trade, and service sectors. Such an effort is necessary to support the employment expansion envisaged as a result of inclusive growth, including in particular the shift of surplus labour from agriculture to non-agriculture. This can only take place if this part of the labour force is sufficiently skilled. During the Eleventh Plan it is proposed to launch a major 'Skill Development Mission' (SDM) with an outlay of Rs 22800 crores.

Skill Development Mission

5.28. In order to create a pool of skilled personnel in appropriate numbers with adequate skills in line with the employment requirements across the entire economy

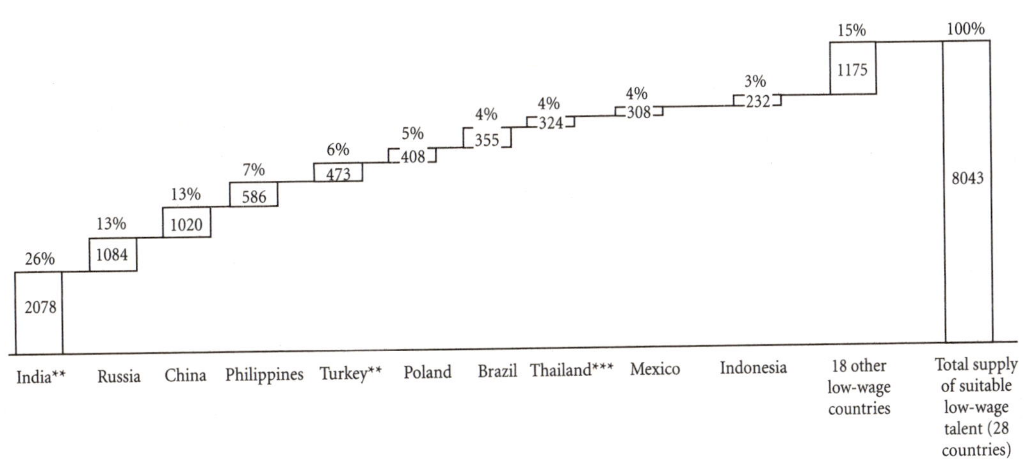

Note: * Graduate with skills for direct employment (does not consider willingness and accessibility of talent); ** Number derived via extrapolation; *** As of 2007.

Source: McKinsey Global Institute.

FIGURE 5.2: Aggregate Suitable* Graduate Talent Pool for Offshore IT and BPO Industries

with particular emphasis on the twenty high growth high employment sectors, the government will set up an SDM consisting of an agglomeration of programmes and appropriate structures aimed at enhancing training opportunities of new entrants to the labour force from the existing 2.5 million in the non-agricultural sector to 10 million per year.

MISSION GOAL

5.29. To provide within a five- to eight-year timeframe, a pool of trained and skilled workforce, sufficient to meet the domestic requirements of a rapidly growing economy, with surpluses to cater to the skill deficits in other ageing economies, thereby effectively leveraging India's competitive advantage and harnessing India's demographic dividend (On demographic dividend, see Annexure 5.2).

5.30. The Skill Development Mission (SDM) will have to ensure that our supply-side responses are perpetually in sync with the demand side impulses both from domestic as well as global economies. The mission will, therefore, have to involve both public and private sectors in a symbiotic relationship, with initiatives arising from both sides with reciprocal support. Thus public sector initiatives to repurpose, reorient and expand existing infrastructure, will need involvement of private sector for management and running of Skill Development Programmes, ending with placement of candidates. Similarly Private Sector Initiatives will need to be supplemented by government by one-time capital grants to private institutions and by stipends providing fee supplementation to SC/ST/OBC/Minorities/other BPL candidates. Thus the core strategy would consist of a two-track approach, of a public arm of amplified action through ministries and State Governments and a private arm of specific and focused actions for creating skills by the market through private sector-led action.

5.31. In case of government-led initiatives the concerned Ministries will conceptualize the initiatives for either expanding and improving existing institutions and providing them enlarged budgets and improved action plans or they will set up new generation institutions with budgetary support. For industry or service sector-specific private initiatives the entire strategic thinking and plan of action will emerge from industry associations and ministries will be involved in structuring government response and providing budgetary support. The SDM will oversee and facilitate entire process of collaborative action.

MISSION OBJECTIVES AND FUNCTIONS

5.32. Articulate a vision and framework to meet India's VET needs:

- Assess skill deficits sector wise and region wise and meet the gaps by planned action in a finite time frame.
- Orchestrate Public Sector/Private Sector Initiatives in a framework of a collaborative action.
- Realign and reposition existing public sector infrastructure ITIs, polytechnics and VET in school to get into PPP mode and to smoothen their transition into institutions managed and run by private enterprise or industry associations. Give them functional and governance autonomy.
- Establish a 'Credible accreditation system' and a 'guidance framework' for all accrediting agencies, set up by various ministries and or by industry associations. Get them to move progressively away from regulation to performance measurement and rating/ranking of institutions. Rate institutions on standardized outcomes, for example, percentage graduates placed, pre and post course wage differentials, dropout rates, etc.
- Encourage and support industry associations and other specialized bodies/councils and private enterprise to create their own sectoral skill development plans in 20 High Growth Sectors (Annexure 5.3.)
- Establish a 'National Skill Inventory' and another 'National Database for Skill Deficiency Mapping' on a national Web portal—for exchange of information between employers and employment seekers.
- Establish a Trainee Placement and Tracking System for effective evaluation and future policy planning.
- Reposition 'Employment Exchanges as Outreach points of the Mission' for storing and providing information on employment and skill development. Enable employment exchanges to function as career counseling centres.
- Enlarge the 50000 Skill Development Centres (SDCs) programme eventually into a 'Virtual Skill Development Resource Network' for Web-based learning.

MISSION STRATEGIES

5.33. The strategies of the Mission will be to bring about a paradigm change in the architecture of the existing VET System, by doing things differently.

- Encourage Ministries to expand existing Public Sector Skill Development infrastructure and its utilization by a factor of five. This will take the VET capacity from

3.1 million to 15 million. This will be sufficient to meet the Annual workforce accretion, which is of the order of 12.8 million. In fact, the surplus capacity could be used to train those in the existing labour force as only 2% thereof are skilled. This infrastructure should be shifted to private management over the next 2–3 years. States must be guided as incentivizer to manage this transition.

- Enlarge the coverage of skill spectrum from the existing level. Skill Development programmes should be delivered in modules of 6 weeks to 12 weeks; with an end of module examination/certification. For calibrating manual skills a 4–6 level certification system must be established based on increasing order of dexterity of the craftsman.
- Make a distinction between structural, interventional and last mile unemployability and correspondingly set up programmes for 24 months, 12 months and 6 months duration. Encourage 'Finishing Schools' to take care of last mile unemployability.
- Establish a National Qualifications Framework, which establishes equivalence and provides for horizontal mobility between various VET, Technical and Academic streams at more than one career points. Expand VET to cover more classes and move progressively from post matric to cover 9th class dropouts and then 7th class dropouts.
- Encourage 'Accreditation Agencies' in different domains to move away from regulation to performance measurement and rating and ranking of institutions.
- Encourage institutional autonomy coupled with self-regulation and stake-holder accountability. Institutions must have freedom of action in governance, as also on the financial management.
- For standard setting and curriculum setting, establish or notify at least one 'standard setting/quality audit institution' in each vertical domain.
- Move from a system of funding training institutes to funding the candidates. Institutional funding could be limited to an upfront capital grant. Recurring funding requirement could be met by appropriate disbursement to the institute at the end of successful certification. Candidates from SC/ST/ OBC/ Minorities/ BPL, etc. could be funded in two parts—
  - (i) Stipend (monthly) to be paid to trainee
  - (ii) Fee subsidization at the end of the programme to be given to the institute after placement.

5.34. The Mission will encompass the efforts of several ministries of the Central Government, State Governments and the activity of the private arm, supported by the following institutions: (i) Prime Minister's National Council on Skill Development, (ii) National Skill Development Coordination Board, and (iii) National Skill Development Corporation/Trust. The Central ministries which have skill development programmes will continue to be funded as at present. However the spectrum of skill development efforts will be reviewed periodically for policy directions by the Prime Minister's Council on Skill Development. The Council will be supported by a National Skill Development Coordination Board, which will be charged with the coordination and harmonization of the governments' initiatives for skill development spread across the seventeen Central ministries and State Governments with the initiatives of the National Skill Development Corporation/Trust. State governments will be encouraged to set up State-level Skill Development Missions. A non-profit National Skill Development Corporation may be set up as a Company under Section 25 of the Companies Act, and/or a National Skill Development Trust under the Societies Act may be set up, to encourage private sector arm of the Mission.

ACTION PLAN FOR COMPONENT—GOVERNMENT INITIATIVE IN PPP MODE

5.35. Over the years some 20 odd ministries have created an infrastructure for skill development. There are 1896 ITIs (under State Governments), 1244 Polytechnics, 669 Community Polytechnics, 9583 Secondary Schools with VET Stream and 3218 ITCs (in private sector). Besides Ministries of Rural Development (RD), MSME, Health, Tourism and several others have their own establishments. All these need to be restructured and repositioned in collaboration with private enterprises. Furthermore, new capacities are being created by the ministries. These need to be brought in PPP mode.

(i) Action Plan for ITIs

Action: Ministry of Labour and Employment

- Complete Upgradation of 500 ITIs by investing Rs 2.0–3.5 crore in each into institutions of excellence.
- Upgrade remaining 1396 ITIs in PPP mode by providing interest free loan up to Rs 2.5 crore each.
- Facilitate 1000 new ITIs in under-served regions –to be set up in PPP mode so that largely unskilled work-force of these backward areas could acquire skills and mainstream with workforce in progressive regions.

- Set up 500 new ITIs—in Industrial Clusters/SEZs on a demand-led basis—also in PPP mode.
- Quadruple ITI capacity by encouraging them to run two shifts or more. Introduce short term modules in 2nd Shift.
- Intensive Faculty Training Programme
- MoUs with States and ITIs defining outcomes and reforms and imposing obligation to transfer autonomy to the PPP.

(ii) Action Plan for Polytechnics

Action: Ministry of Human Resources Development (HRD)

- Upgrade 400 government polytechnics.
- Set up 125 new polytechnics in PPP mode in hitherto unserved districts.
- Run all polytechnics in two shifts to double the capacity utilization.
- Encourage much larger initiative in private sector since the demand for junior engineers is enormous and absorption and placements are nearly guaranteed.
- State governments may be encouraged to let their engineering colleges start polytechnics in evening shift to turnout junior engineers.

(iii) Action Plan for Vocational Education

Action: Ministry of HRD

- Expand VE from 9500 senior secondary schools to 20000 schools. Intake capacity to go up from 1.0 million to 2.5 million
- All VE schools must get into partnership with employers, for providing faculty/trainers, internship, advice on curriculum setting, in skill testing and certification, etc.
- Progressively move vocational education from an unviable 2–year stream, commencing after Class 10, to a stream that captures 9th Class dropouts and later on it should commence from Class 7, capturing 7th Class dropouts. Give emphasis to last mile employability related soft skills—viz., English language skills, quantitative skills, computer literacy, spreadsheet, word processing, computer graphics, presentation skills, behavioral and interpersonal skills, etc.

(IV) Action Plan For RUDSETIs

Action: Ministry of Rural Development

- Set up 600 RUDSETIS—one in each district
  - State governments to provide land
  - GoI to meet 75% of capital cost
  - Banks to meet 25% of capital cost plus provide the following handholding services:-
    1. Project consultancy and business counseling
    2. Incubation Assistance
    3. Marketing
    4. Sourcing of Credit and Raw Material Supply.
- Focus on Entrepreneurship Development Programmes.
- Link RUDSETIS to EDI of MSME.

(V) Action Plan for Setting Up a Virtual Skill Development Resource Network Linking 50000 Skill Development Centres (SDCs)

Action: DIT/ MSME/ MRD/ ARI/ Ministry of Textiles etc.

- It is proposed to set up 50000 SDCs to train approximately 200 persons per centre, i.e., 10 million people per year to take skill development to the doorstep of rural populations. Location could be chosen from the following:-
  - One lakh Common Service Centres (CSCs) set up by Ministry of Telecom and IT.
  - 108000 secondary schools being given IT support.
  - Over 147000 rural post offices or Panchayat offices per 6000 Block Headquarters.
- SDC to deliver training capsules of 8–12 week duration with an end of the course certification system. Instruction material to be provided on CD ROMS with 80–120 hours of computer time, 20% of which will be online, rest offline
- Training material will be created by participating ministries/enterprises/industry associations with help of NASSCOM.
- Mentor Groups for tutorial support in online interactive mode will be provided by service-providers engaged by industry associations.
- End of the programme toolkits will be provided by industry associations/State Governments.
- Employment *Melas* at the end of programmes to help unplaced trainees to get placed.

ACTION PLAN FOR COMPONENT II—PRIVATE SECTOR INITIATIVES

5.36. Twenty high growth sectors of industries and services have been identified which have the ability to provide expanded employment. The Mission, in its private arm, will encompass the efforts of industry associations of these sectors to identify and quantify skill deficiencies in their respective sectors and envision the sectoral plan to meet their growing skill needs. The corporation/trust will be a PPP on skill development conceived as a non-profit entity. It will make periodic as well as an annual report of its plans and activities and put them in the public domain. The National Skill Development Corporation or the National Skill Development Trust, as the case may be, will identify areas where support and supplementation will be required from the government. In respect of each of these, the respective industry association or group of industry leaders will articulate the sectoral vision for the sectoral Skill Development Initiative. The corporation/trust will refine and validate this vision and ensure complementarity between private initiative and government action, in the light of policy directives from the Prime Minister's Council and the operational guidelines of the Coordination Board.

5.37. The Mission will engage with ten high growths sectors on manufacturing side and an equal number on services side. The Mission's dialogue with private sector industry will be focused on—(i) automobile and auto components (ii) electronics hardware (iii) textiles and garments (iv) leather and leather goods (v) chemicals and pharmaceuticals (vi) gem and jewellery (vii) building and construction (viii) food processing (ix) handlooms and handicrafts (x) building hardware and home furnishings. The Apex Industry Association in each of these sectors will evolve the Skill Development Vision & Plan for their respective sector. The following are some examples of how sectr-specific initiatives might work:

- Society of Indian Automobile Manufacturers/Automobile Component Manufacturers Association of India will engage with the Mission to enable India's Automobile and Auto-components Industry to scale up by 2015–16 from current turnover of US$ 45 billion to US$ 145 billion and current employment of 10.5 million to target employment of 25.0 million. This industry is very skill-intensive (with 90% manpower as Skilled). They will require 6.25 million technical and managerial personnel and the training requirements of these will be in Manufacturing Management, SQC, TQM, 6-Sigma, Statistical Process Control, Kaizen practices, Lean Manufacturing & Breakthrough Management. The Skill-sets required will be at strategic and conceptual skills level and will, therefore, require retrofitting of special courses in IITs/IIMs and other Engineering and Management Institutes—courses like Infotronics/Mechatronics. For their shop-floor and other skilled personnel training modules imparting Computer Aided Design (CAD)/Computer Aided Manufacturing (CAM)/CNC Skills, skills relating to low cost automation and process improvement will be required. It may be necessary to set up one 'National Centre for Quality Management' in Automotive sector. It may be necessary to set up a network of institutes for motor mechanics. Another useful step could be two-way sabbaticals between Industry Personnel and Personnel of Training Institutes.
- Electronics Hardware Industry is growing at the rate of 25.30% and expects to scale up by 2015–16, from current turn over of US$ 30 bn to US$ 320 bn, with employment increasing from 1.5 million direct and 3.0 million indirect to 7.14 million direct and 14.00 million indirect. The industry requires 5% graduate engineers, 15% diploma-holders, 50% skilled workers and 30% semi skilled. The range of skills required will vary from chip manufacturer and VLSI design, to embedded software, to mere mechanical assembly line operations.
- Similarly Textile/Apparel and Garments Industry expects to scale up by 2015–16, from current turnover of US$ 47.0 billion to the targeted US$ 115.0 billion, raising the employment from current workforce level of 35 million to 41.5 million. Of the 6.5 million accretion is workforce only 20% will be unskilled, 50% will be semi skilled, 20% will have ITI certificates and 10% will be Management and Technical graduates. This industry alone could over next five years take over a very large number of ITIs.

5.38. The three examples described above illustrate how individual sectors may deal their specific requirements with strategies and plan of action which will be vastly different from each other. For this reason no generic template is being suggested and the vision/strategy and plan will have to be crafted within the overall policy framework.

5.39. On the services side ten High Growth Sectors have been identified separately, viz. (i) ITs or software services sector (ii) ITES—BPO services, (iii) tourism hospitality and travel trade (iv) transportation/logistics/warehousing and packaging (v) organized retail (vi) real estate services (vii) media, entertainment, broadcasting, content creation, animation (viii) healthcare services (ix) banking/insurance & finance (x) education/skill development services. Mission will engage with each of these sectors. Industry association and workout the appropriate Sectoral Skill Development Plans, strategies and deliverables.

5.40. The National Skill Development Mission's orchestration of private sector initiatives in concert with government action could give different results in different sectors, such as:

- Setting up of a domain-specific Apex Skill Development Institute for:
  - Domain specific Skill Development need assessment
  - Performance Rating of Institutions/Service Providers
  - Domain Standard setting and Quality benchmarking
  - Curriculum setting
  - Framework setting for end of programme testing and certification
  - Running special Skill Development Programmes in niche areas requiring superior skills
- Setting up of Regional Institutes/ Workshops/Tool-rooms and Online Mentoring Groups
- Retrofitting special courses in IITs/ IIMs/ NITs and other Engineering and Management Programmes or offering them as an elective
- Providing last mile employability training to engineering/management/ or other graduates from lesser known colleges.
- Establishing two-way Sabbatical Exchange Programme between Industry and Faculty of University/Colleges/ VET schools/ ITIs, etc.
- Collaborative action for faculty development
- Collaborative action for online 'Skill Development-content-creation'
- Private Management takeover of Public sector institutions viz. ITIs, polytechnics, vocational schools, etc.

PUBLIC–PRIVATE PARTNERSHIP (PPP)

5.41. PPP Mode will be the major vehicle for absorbing public expenditure in skill development in the Eleventh Five Year Plan. Apart from the financial contribution from the government, it is necessary to create an Enabling Environment for Private Investment in Skill Training. This requires the prescription of a National framework for domain specific standards and common principles such as (i) trainer not to be the examiner/certifier, (ii) certifier not to be the accreditation agency and (iii) a strict separation of all the three as the basic feature of the mechanism. The facilities for career tracking and placement—biometric smart card based ID, and a National database for location wise availability and shortage of skilled personnel will be established. The system should provide the options of multiple entry and exit points and total mobility between vocational, general and technical streams. In order to take on board the vulnerable sections, provision for fee vouchers for BPL/ SC/ST/OBC/Minority would also be made available. To overcome the regional disparities due to diverse socio-economic factors, VGF approach would be adopted to address regional imbalances through PPP.

MISSION STRUCTURE

5.42. The Skill Development Mission has to be conceived in a manner which recognizes that many Ministries are involved and also many separate Industry and service sectors. The Structure consists of Prime Minister's National Council on Skill Development for apex level policy directions, a National Skill Development Coordination Board, and a National Skill Development Corporation/Trust. The Central Ministries with Skill Development programmes will operate in a Mission mode and the State governments will gear their Departments/Agencies into a State Skill Development Mission. The private sector, especially the twenty high growth sectors will actively participate as the private arm of the Mission. The composition of the Prime Minister's Council on Skill Development and National Skill Development Coordination Board are as described below.

5.43. **Prime Minister's National Council on Skill Development:** The Council will comprise of Prime Minister as Chairman, Minister of Finance, HRD, Industries, Rural Developoment, Labour & Employment and Housing & Urban Poverty Alleviation, Deputy Chairman, Planning Commission, Chairperson, National Manufacturing Competitive Council, Chairperson of the National Skill Development Corporation, six experts in the area of Skill Development as Members and Pr. Secretary to Prime Minister as Member Secretary.

5.44. **National Skill Development Coordination Board:** This Committee will comprise of Deputy Chairman, Planning Commission as Chairman, Chairperson/Chief Executive Officer of the National Skill Development Corporation, Secretaries of Ministries of Finance, Human Resource Development, Labour and Employment, Rural Development, Housing and Employment, Rural Development, Housing & Urban Poverty Alleviation. Secretaries of Four States by rotation, for a period of two years, three Distinguished Academicians/Subject Area Specialists as Members and Secretary, Planning Commission as the Member Secretary.

Ministries of the Central Government having Skill Development Programmes

5.45. Line ministries/departments will continue to be responsible for the implementation of the skill development programmes, appropriately modifying them in line with the policies and strategies as decided by the Apex Committee into the Mission Mode.

5.46 Action by State Governments

- Transform Employment Exchanges to act as Career Counseling Centre
- Upgrade and strengthen State Council of Vocational Training
- Distance government and allow greater institutional autonomy. Maintain an arm's length relationship. Effectively delegate powers to local management of institutes
- Modernize the existing ITIs, etc. with better funding and enhancing the effectiveness of on-going programmes
- To cope with enhanced activities, existing vacancies in all training institutes must be filled
- Revamp the Institute Management Committee and ensure genuine PPP
- Draw up plan for strengthening existing infrastructure (short-term, medium-term and long-term)
- Personnel Policy to ensure accountability and outcomes.

State Skill Development Missions

5.47 The State Governments may establish State-level missions to gear skill development activities in the Mission mode, with appropriate structures. Departments of the State Governments having skill development programmes will be required to reorient their skill development strategies and programmes in line with the central objectives.

The Non-profit National Skill Development Corporation/Trust

5.48. The National Skill Development Corporation will be set up as a non-profit company under the Companies Act with appropriate governance structure (board of directors being drawn from the outstanding professionals/experts). The head of the corporation will be a person of eminence/reputed professional in the field of Skill Development. The Chairperson may also be the Chief Executive Officer of the Corporation, in which case S/he shall be known as the Chairperson-cum-Chief Executive Officer. The National Skill Development Corporation will be set up with as Government Equity with a view to obtaining about Rs 15000 crore as capital from governments, the public and private sector, and bilateral and multilateral sources for the promotion of skill development. The Corporation will be a public private partnership on skill development conceived as a non-profit Corporation. It will make periodic as well as an annual report of its plans and activities and put them in the public domain. There may also be a National Skill Development Trust which can receive funds to be managed by the National Skill Development Corporation. The corporation/trust will be a flexible institutional arrangement to be able to deliver on jobs required by the market, related to its skill deficit, through training programmes operated or partnered by it.

CONCLUSION

5.49. The initiatives described above involving both the States and the Centre, often with private partnership will lead to the establishment of a credible, trustworthy and reliable training, testing and certification edifice linked to global standards and responsive to the needs of the ultimate consumers of skill. With an estimated 58.6 million new jobs in the domestic economy and about 45 million jobs in the international economy inviting skilled personnel for quality jobs beckoning the Indian youth, the government and private sector will act in a concerted manner so that these opportunities materialize and operate as an employability guarantee.

ANNEXURE 5.1.1
Current Attendance Rates in Educational Institutions per 1000 Persons of Different Age Groups during 2004–05

Category of persons	Age groups					
	5–14	15–19	20–24	25–29	5–29	0–29
(1)	(2)	(3)	(4)	(5)	(6)	(7)
Rural						
Male	835	471	114	16	532	450
Female	767	333	45	11	436	370
Person	803	407	79	13	485	412
Urban						
Male	890	593	232	40	541	484
Female	879	571	164	21	519	465
Person	885	583	200	31	530	475
Rural + Urban						
Male	847	504	151	23	534	459
Female	792	396	77	14	456	393
Person	821	454	114	18	497	427

Source: NSS Report 517, Table 6.

ANNEXURE 5.1.2
Labour Force Participation Rates by Age, Area, and Sex, during 2004–05 (CDS)

Age Group	Rural Areas		Urban Areas	
	male	Female	male	female
(1)	(2)	(3)	(4)	(5)
5–9	2	2	3	2
10–14	58	52	50	28
15–19	486	231	370	116
20–24	853	295	755	216
25–29	950	365	944	221
30–34	959	413	979	256
35–39	963	467	975	288
40–44	954	457	973	266
45–49	949	459	962	229
50–54	928	405	926	225
55–59	890	376	802	190
60+	599	186	348	84
All age	531	237	561	150

Source: Report No. 515 (61/10/1)—NSS 61st Round (July 2004–June 2005).

ANNEXURE 5.1.3

Per 1000 Distribution of Persons in the Age Group 15–29 Years by Status of Vocational Training Received or being Received—2004–05

category of person	receiving formal vocational training	received vocational training: formal	received vocational training: Non-formal: hereditary	received vocational training: Non-formal: others	all (col. 3+4+5)	Received/ receiving training (col. 2+6)	no vocational training	n.r.	total
(1)	(2)	(3)	(4)	(5)	(6)	(7)	(8)	(9)	(10)
Rural									
Male	10	15	58	37	110	120	871	8	1000
Female	5	13	32	30	74	79	910	11	1000
Person	8	14	45	34	92	100	890	10	1000
Urban									
Male	33	52	31	61	144	178	817	5	1000
Female	19	45	17	32	12	113	881	6	1000
Person	27	49	25	48	121	148	847	6	1000
Rural + Urban									
Male	17	26	50	44	120	137	855	7	1000
Female	9	21	28	31	80	88	902	10	1000
Person	13	24	39	38	100	113	878	9	1000

Source: NSS Report 517, Table 10

ANNEXURE 5.1.4

Number per 1000 Persons of Different Age Groups who Received Formal Vocational Training—2004–05

Category of Persons	Age Group: 15–19	20–24	15–24	25–29	15–29
(1)	(2)	(3)	(4)	(5)	(6)
Rural					
Male	5	21	12	23	15
Female	7	15	11	16	13
Persons	6	18	11	19	14
Urban					
Male	19	72	45	69	52
Female	18	63	40	55	45
Persons	18	67	43	63	49
Rural + Urban					
Male	9	36	21	37	26
Female	10	28	19	26	21
Persons	9	32	20	32	24

Source: NSS Report 517, Table 10.

ANNEXURE 5.2
Potential Labour Surplus/Shortage in Working Age Group across the World (2020)

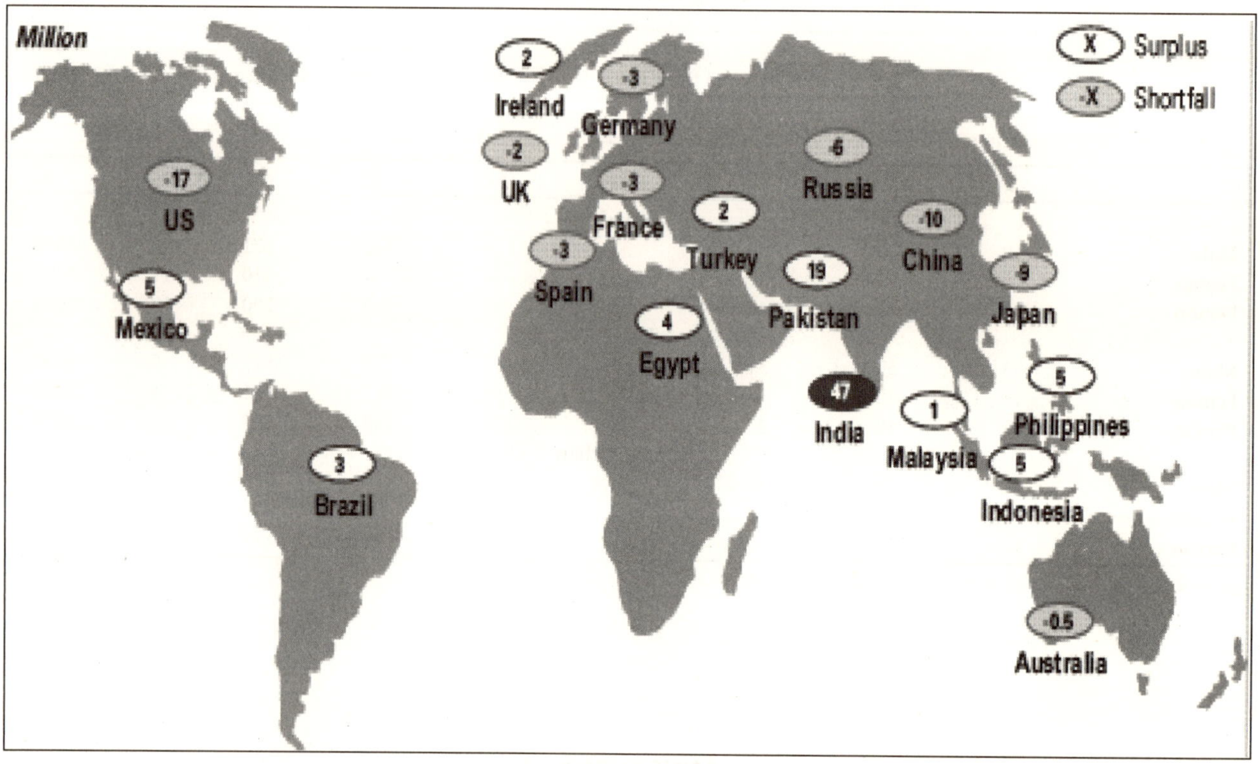

Note: Working population is defined at the 15–59 years age group. Ratio of working population to total population is assumed to be constant. Labor number are based on assumptions of no interventions by respective governments.
Source: US Census Bureau. BCG. 2002–2003.

ANNEXURE 5.3
List of Twenty High Growth Sectors

1. Automobile and Auto-components
2. Banking/Insurance and Finance Services
3. Building and Construction Industry
4. Chemicals and Pharmaceuticals
5. Construction Materials/Building Hardware etc.
6. Educational and Skill Development Services
7. Electronics Hardware
8. Food Processing/Cold Chain/Refrigeration
9. Furniture and Furnishings
10. Gem and Jewellery
11. Health Care Services
12. ITES or BPO
13. ITS or Software Services/Products
14. Leather and Leather goods
15. Media, Entertainment, Broadcasting, Content Creation and Animation
16. Organised Retail
17. Real Estate Services
18. Textiles, Apparel and Garments
19. Tourism, Hospitality and Travel Trade
20. Transportation Logistics, Warehousing and Packaging etc.

6

Social Justice

Scheduled Castes, Scheduled Tribes, Other Backward Classes, Minorities and Other Vulnerable Groups

INTRODUCTION

6.1. Inclusive growth demands that all social groups have equal access to the services provided by the State and equal opportunity for upward economic and social mobility. It is also necessary to ensure that there is no discrimination against any section of our society. In India, certain social groups such as the SCs, STs, OBCs and Minorities have historically been disadvantaged and vulnerable. Then there are certain other groups which may be discriminated against and which suffer from handicaps. These include persons with disabilities, older persons, street children, beggars and victims of substance abuse. Our Constitution contains various provisions for the development of such marginalized groups, for instance, Article 341 for SCs, Article 342 for STs, Article 340 for OBCs, Article 30 which provides the right to minorities to establish and administer educational institutions, and so on. Their individual and collective growth, however, cannot be ensured without improving their surroundings and providing clean drinking water, toilets and educational opportunities.

6.2. The present chapter deals with the efforts made for the socio-economic development of these groups and the new initiatives that will be taken during the Eleventh Plan.

SCHEDULED CASTES (SCs)

6.3. The SCs constitute 16.23% of India's population. In the past, they have been socially ostracized, economically exploited and denied human dignity and a sense of self-worth. The socio-economic development and protection of SCs from discrimination and exploitation has been a high priority from the very start of the planning process.

6.4. People belonging to SC communities are spread all over the country, with 80% of them living in the rural areas. They constitute more than a fifth of the population of Uttar Pradesh, Punjab, Himachal Pradesh and West Bengal. Punjab has the highest proportion of SCs to the State population. More than half of the SC population is concentrated in the five States of Uttar Pradesh (35.1 million), West Bengal (18.4 million), Tamil Nadu (11.8 million), Andhra Pradesh (12.3 million) and Bihar (13.0 million).

CONSTITUTIONAL SAFEGUARDS

6.5. The Constitution of India guarantees protection from social injustice and all forms of exploitation (Art. 46). It guarantees equality before law (Art. 14), and enjoins upon the State not to discriminate against any citizen on grounds of caste (Art. 15 (1)). Untouchability is abolished and its practice in any form is forbidden (Art. 17). The Constitution mandates that no citizen shall, on grounds only of caste or race, be subjected to any disability and restriction (Art. 15 (2)). It empowers the State to make provisions for reservation in educational institutions (Art. 15 (4) and (5)), and in appointments for posts in favour of SCs (Art. 16 (4), 16(4A), 16(4B) and Art. 335). Reservation of seats for SCs in the Lok Sabha is provided under Article 330, in the State Assemblies under Article 332 and in the Local Self-Governments bodies under

Articles 243D and 340T. In addition to the above, the Parliament has enacted the Untouchability (Offences) Act, 1955, renamed as Protection of Civil Rights Act, in 1976. To check and deter atrocities against SCs, the Scheduled Castes and the Scheduled Tribes (Prevention of Atrocities) Act, 1989 has also been enacted.

SCHEDULED CASTES DEVELOPMENT: AN OVERVIEW

6.6. The Tenth Five Year Plan (2002–07) adopted a multi-pronged approach for the socio-economic development of the SCs: social empowerment through educational development; economic empowerment through income and employment enhancing avenues; protection through effective implementation of protective legislations and eradication of occupations such as manual scavenging; and holistic development through earmarking of funds proportionate to the population. [Scheduled Caste Sub-Plan (SCSP) and Tribal Sub-Plan (TSP)].

Educational Development

6.7. With respect to the educational development of SCs, the Central Government has introduced major scholarship programmes and these are given in the Box 6.1

6.8. The other important schemes for the educational development of SCs: are (i) providing coaching facilities to students to prepare them for various competitive examinations being conducted by Union Public Service Comission (UPSC), State Public Service Commissions, banks, and so on; and (ii) hostel facilities to both boys and girls for pursuing education from middle level onwards.

Economic Development

6.9. The National Scheduled Castes Finance and Development Corporation (NSFDC) established in 1989, provides financial and other support to beneficiaries for taking up various income generating activities. An amount of Rs 388.80 crore was made available to the Corporation up to 31 March 2007 as equity share contribution against the authorized share capital of Rs 1000 crore. The number of SC persons who received assistance during the Tenth Five Year Plan (up to December 2006) is 257901.

6.10. The National Safai Karamcharis Finance and Development Corporation was established in 1997 to provide financial support to the *safai karamcharis* (scavengers) to take up various income-generating activities. During the Tenth Five Year Plan, the Corporation introduced the Micro Credit Finance Scheme and the Mahila Samridhi Yojana, benefitting 102187 persons. During 2006–07, it disbursed loans to 16545 beneficiaries (up to December 2006) for various income generating activities in 23 States and two UTs.

6.11. The scheme of grant-in aid to the Scheduled Castes Development Corporations (SCDCs) was introduced in 1978–79 as a CSS for participating in the equity share of the State corporations in a Centre–State ratio of 49:51. The SCDCs finance employment oriented schemes that cover: (i) agriculture and allied activities including minor irrigation; (ii) small-scale industry; (iii) transport; and (iv) trade and service sector. They also finance projects by dovetailing the loan component from NSFDC/Banks

Box 6.1
Major Scholarship Schemes under the Ministry of Social Justice and Empowerment

Post-Matric Scholarships (PMS) implemented since 1944–45 to promote higher education among SCs by extending scholarships to pursue studies beyond matriculation. In the Tenth Plan, an amount of Rs 1822.25 crore was utilized to reach the coverage of 29.59 lakh students in 2006–07.

Pre-Matric Scholarships are being awarded since 1977–78 with an objective to encourage children of scavengers and those engaged in menial works, to pursue education. 4.72 lakh children were awarded pre-matric scholarships for which Rs 56.41 crore was utilized in the Tenth Plan.

Upgradation of Merit for SC Students Scheme in operation since 1987–88 to extend remedial and special coaching offered to students to remove their deficiencies in school subjects (class IX to XII) into professional and technical courses. An expenditure of Rs 14.68 crore was incurred to benefit 10625 students.

Rajiv Gandhi National Fellowships launched in the Tenth Plan in 2005–06 as a special incentive to extend scholarships to SC students to pursue higher studies and research degrees such as M.Phil. and Ph.D. An amount of Rs 50.20 crore was earmarked for this scheme in the Tenth Plan to benefit 2666 SC students.

with margin money out of their own funds and subsidy out of the SCA.

Protective Measures

6.12. Two important protective legislations in operation for people belonging to SCs are the Protection of Civil Rights Act, 1955 and the Scheduled Castes and Scheduled Tribes (Prevention of Atrocities) Act, 1989. However, despite these Constitutional provisions, atrocities and crimes on members of SCs, especially the women, continue to occur in all parts of the country in varying degrees. As per the National Crime Records Bureau Report 2005, the crimes against SCs in the last few years were mainly atrocities followed by hurt and rape. Data for the last five years are reproduced in Table 6.1.

Implementation of the Scheduled Caste Sub-Plan (SCSP) and Tribal Sub-Plan (TSP)

6.13. In view of the persistent and wide-spread socio-economic backwardness of SCs and STs, a distinct need was felt for innovative policy intervention to enable these groups to share the benefits of growth in a more equitable manner. The government prepared a separate Development Plan called Tribal Sub Plan for STs in 1976. It was followed by the Special Component Plan for the SCs in 1978 (recently renamed the Scheduled Caste Sub Plan [SCSP]).

6.14. The SCSP and TSP aim at facilitating convergence and pooling of resources from all the other development sectors in proportion to the population of SCs and STs, respectively for their overall development.

6.15. At present, 27 States/UTs are implementing SCSP through different mechanisms. The State Governments generally divide their resources into 'divisible' and 'non-divisible' components and earmark funds for SCs only from the divisible pool. As a result, the actual funds flowing directly to SCSP from the total State Plan becomes much less than the proportion of SC population to the total population of the State.

6.16. The State Government of Maharashtra has pioneered a special mechanism to ensure effective operationalization of SCSP and TSP. Other States could explore replication of this mechanism.

6.17. The Prime Minister has reiterated the need for effective implementation of SCSP and TSP during the 51st and 52nd NDC meetings held on 27 June 2005 and 9 December 2006. He emphasized that the SCSP and TSP strategies should become an integral part of the Annual Plans as well as the Five Year Plans so that full inclusion of SCs and STs in socio-economic development is achieved within a period of 10 years.

6.18. All Central Ministries/Departments are also expected to formulate SCSP and ensure that the flow of funds to SCSP in their plans is at least in proportion with the SC population of the country. At present, 17 Central

TABLE 6.1
Comparative Incident of Crime against Scheduled Castes

S. No.	Crime-Head	Years					% Variation in
		2001	2002	2003	2004	2005	2005 over 2004
1.	Murder	763	739	581	654	669	2.3
2.	Rape	1316	1331	1089	1157	1172	1.3
3.	Kidnapping and Abduction	400	319	232	253	258	2.0
4.	Dacoity	41	29	24	26	26	0.0
5.	Robbery	133	105	70	72	80	11.1
6.	Arson	354	322	204	211	210	–0.5
7.	Hurt	4547	4491	3969	3824	3847	0.6
8.	Protection of Civil Rights Act	633	1018	634	364	291	–20.0
9.	SC/ST (Prevention of Atrocities) Act	13113	10770	8048	8891	8497	–4.4
10.	Others	12201	14383	11401	11435	11077	–3.1
	Total	33501	33507	26252	26887	26127	–2.8

Source: Crime in India-2005, National Crime Records Bureau, Ministry of Home Affairs.

Ministries/Departments have done so. These are the Ministries of Labour, Coal, Commerce and Industries, Textiles, Non-Conventional Energy Sources, Women and Child Development, Steel and Rural Development, and the Departments of Agriculture and Cooperation, Small-Scale Industries and Agro and Rural Industries, Biotechnology, Science and Technology, Health, Family Welfare, Elementary Education and Literacy and Secondary and Higher Education. Many Ministries/Departments maintain that they are unable to provide funds for SCSP because their funds are devoted expenditure on large projects and are not divisible.

6.19. The implementation of SCSP and TSP leaves much to be desired. This applies equally to the Central as well as State governments. Though there may be several reasons for this lacklustre implementation, lack of statutory or clear-cut administrative sanction is an important one.

6.20. To look into the issues related to TSP and SCSP, a Central Standing Tripartite Committee (CSTC) which includes representatives of the Planning Commission, National Commission for SCs and STs, the Ministries of Social Justice and Empowerment and States/UTs Ministries/Departments, was set up in May 1999. The CSTC was reconstituted in early 2006 to review the formulation, implementation and monitoring of SCSP and TSP and advise the Planning Commission and Prime Minister on measures which would serve the interests of the SCs and STs more effectively.

6.21. For effective implementation of SCSP and TSP, the Planning Commission also issued guidelines to all State Governments/UTs which have been revised from time to time, the last revision being on 31 December 2006. The main guidelines are given in Box 6.2.

Box 6.2
Main Guidelines for SCSP and TSP

- Earmarking of funds for SCSP and TSP from the total State Plan outlay should at least be proportionate to the SC and ST population of the State/UT.
- Making the Social Welfare/Tribal Welfare Department—which are concerned with the well-being and development of SCs and STs—the nodal department for formulation and implementation of SCSP and TSP.
- Placing the funds earmarked for SCSP and TSP at the disposal of the Principal Secretary/Secretary, Social Welfare/Tribal Welfare, who will work as Planning Secretary and have exclusive authority for the reallocation of funds to other line departments for of SC and ST development schemes.
- Placing the funds earmarked for SCSP and TSP under separate budget head/sub-head for each development department.
- Backing the SCSP and TSP earmarked funds by 100% budget provision, sanctions and timely release of funds to the line departments and implementing agencies.
- Including only those schemes under SCSP and TSP that ensure direct benefits to individuals or families belonging to SCs or STs.
- Preparing a detailed SCSP and TSP document with physical and financial targets against each Scheme with the objective of bridging the gap between the rest of the population and the SCs and STs within 10 years.
- Ensuring that the other line departments cooperate in the proper implementation of the SCSP and TSP schemes allocated to them and put up the schemes to the nodal departments for sanction and release of funds.
- To circumvent the problem of non-divisible nature of funds for certain sectors like major irrigation, power, roads, and so on, SCSP and TSP funds may be accounted only to the extent of about 5% or the actual area being covered or benefited by the SCs and STs by the projects and not the population percentage. The percentage of SC and ST beneficiaries and the area being covered/benefited is always less than the population percentage of the SC and ST population in the State/UT.
- Preventing the diversion and lapse of funds allocated to SCSP and TSP in the Annual Plans. SCSP and TSP should not be allowed to be changed at revised estimate (RE) stage by the Planning Commission.
- Carrying forward the lapsed/unutilized SCSP and TSP amount to the next Annual Plan of the State/UT as an additional fund for SCSP and TSP.
- All the CSS and SCA Schemes of the Centre necessarily should have a SCSP and TSP component in them as per the proportion of SCs and STs in the States/UTs.

(Box 6.2 contd.)

(Box 6.2 contd.)

Central Ministries/Departments

- Earmarking of funds by every Central Ministry/Department towards SCSP and TSP should be as per the proportion of SC and ST population in the country. Non-earmarking of SCSP and TSP funds by the Ministry/Department will result in non-approval of their Annual plan.
- SCSP and TSP funds should be non-divertible. Creation of separate budget heads and minor heads (789 for SCSP and 796 for TSP).
- A dedicated SCSP and TSP unit should be created for the formulation and implementation of SCSP and TSP schemes and programmes.
- Only those schemes/programmes should be implemented which accrue direct benefit to SCs and STs.
- All the other guidelines issued to Central Ministries/Departments should be followed strictly.

PRESENT STATUS OF THE SCHEDULED CASTES

Education

6.22. Although the literacy rate of SCs has increased considerably, from 10.3% in 1961 to 54.7% in 2001, till recently the gap between literacy rates of the general and SC population had not reduced. However, the Census in 2001 showed a distinct reduction in this literacy gap (see Table 6.2).

6.23. The school dropout rate is a crucial indicator of lack of educational development. The dropout rates for SC children are still very high –32.7% in Classes I to V; 55.2% in Classes I to VIII; and 69.1% in classes I to X in 2004–05 (see Table 6.3). The gap between the SC population and the general category increases at higher levels of schooling. However, an encouraging sign is the reduction in the gap between the dropout rates of the total population vis-à-vis the SCs at all levels.

6.24. In the area of higher education, also, there is a gap between the SCs and the general population. The gross enrolment ratio for the country as a whole in 2000 was about 10%. For the SCs, however, it was significantly lower at 6.4%.

TABLE 6.2
Literacy Rate of General Population and SC Population, 1961–2001

Year	General			SC		
	Male	Female	Total	Male	Female	Total
1961	34.44	12.95	24.02	16.96	3.29	10.27
1971	39.45	18.70	29.45	22.36	6.44	14.67
1981	46.89	24.82	36.23	31.12	10.93	21.38
1991	64.1	39.3	52.2	49.91	23.76	37.41
2001	75.3	53.7	64.8	66.64	41.90	54.69

Source: Census of India

TABLE 6.3
Dropout Rates, 2004–05—SC (Provisional)

Category	Classes I–V			Classes I–VIII			Classes I–X		
	All	Boys	Girls	All	Boys	Girls	All	Boys	Girls
General	31.47	33.74	28.57	52.32	51.85	52.92	62.69	60.98	64.92
SC	32.7	36.1	34.2	55.2	60.00	57.3	69.1	74.2	71.3

Source: Selected Educational Statistics 2004–05, Ministry of Human Resource Development.

Economic Development

OCCUPATIONAL CATEGORY

6.25. As can be seen in Table 6.4, 45.61% of SC workers at the all-India level and 52% at the rural level were agricultural labourers, compared to 26.55 and 33.05% among all workers at the national and rural levels, respectively. The position is reversed when we come to the share of SCs among cultivators, which is 19.99% and 23.47% for rural workers compared to 31.65 and 40.24%, respectively for all workers.

AVAILABILITY OF BASIC AMENITIES IN SC LOCALITIES

6.26. Another important dimension of discrimination is the wide gap between the SCs and the rest of the population with respect to the availability of basic civic amenities such as electricity, banking services, *pucca* houses, water supply, toilet facilities, drainage and telephone facilities.

6.27. In 2000, about two-thirds of rural SC households were landless and near landless, compared to one-third

TABLE 6.4
Percentage of Working and Non-working Population (Total and SCs), 2001

	Total Workers		Cultivators		Agricultural Labour		Household Industry		Other Workers		Non-Workers	
	All*	SC	All	SC	All	SC	All	SC	All	SC	All	SC
India	39.10	40.41	31.65	19.99	26.55	45.61	4.22	3.91	37.59	30.49	60.90	59.59
Rural	41.75	42.50	40.24	23.47	33.05	52.23	3.92	3.73	22.80	20.58	58.25	57.50
Urban	32.75	33.14	2.81	1.76	4.71	11.03	5.22	4.84	87.27	82.37	67.75	67.86

Note: * includes SCs.
Source: Census 2001.

among others. Less than one-third of SC households had acquired access to capital assets, compared to 60% among the others. About 60% of SC households still have to depend on wage labour, compared to one-fourth for the others. Employment rates and wage earnings among SCs have also tended to be low. Similar disparities exist in the status of health of SCs. The incidence of anaemia among women and mortality rate among children are higher than in other groups. Studies also show evidence of discrimination in various market and non-market transactions, including access to social services like education, health and housing, and in political participation.

6.28. The cumulative impact of all these disparities, therefore, is reflected in the high levels of poverty, about 36% among SCs as compared to only 21% among others.

ACCESS TO INCOME EARNING ASSETS—AGRICULTURAL LAND AND CAPITAL ASSETS

6.29. About 80% of the SCs live in rural areas. In 2000, only 16.8% of them pursued cultivation as an independent self-employed occupation, whereas among the non-SC/ST this percentage was more than double (41.11%). The percentage of those employed in some kind of non-farm self-employment activities (read business) was about 12% and 15%, respectively for SCs and others. In rural areas, about 28% of SC households had acquired some access to fixed capital assets compared to 56% for other households (non SC/ST). In urban areas, also, the access to capital assets for SCs was low (27%) as compared to other households (35.5%). In rural as well as urban areas, due to inadequate access to fixed capital assets, an exceptionally high percentage of all SC households, more than 62%, was dependent on wage employment.

UNEMPLOYMENT SITUATION

6.30. In 2000, the CDS employment rate in rural areas was 46% for SC male workers, compared with 48.40% for other male workers. Similarly, the CDS employment rate for SC workers in urban area was 45.8%, compared to 49.9% for other households. Disparities between the SC and others are also reflected in the unemployment rate. Unemployment rate based on CDS for SCs was about 5.0% as compared to about 3.5% for other workers in rural and urban areas. The NSSO data on wage earning revealed disparities in labour wages for SCs and others. For instance, in 1999–2000, the average weekly wage earning of an SC worker (at 1993–94 price) was Rs 174.50 compared to Rs 197.05 for other workers (estimate by Dubey 2003, Department for International Development [DFID] study).

ECONOMIC STATUS

6.31. Available empirical evidence suggests discrimination against SCs in employment, wages, credit, and so on. These factors have acted as constraints to their occupational mobility. In urban areas, too, there is prevalence of discrimination by caste; particularly discrimination in employment, which operates at least in part through traditional mechanisms; SCs are disproportionately represented in poorly paid, dead-end jobs. Further, there is a flawed, preconceived notion that they lack merit and are unsuitable for formal employment.

6.32. Due to the lack of access to fixed sources of income and high incidence of wage labour associated with high rate of under-employment and low wages, SC households are often faced with low incomes and high incidence of poverty. In 2004–05, about 36.80% of SC persons were BPL in rural areas as compared to only 28.30% for others (non-SC/ST). In urban areas the gap was slightly larger;

TABLE 6.5
Population Living Below Poverty Line—SC (1993–94 and 2004–05)

(in %)

Category	1993–94		2004–05		(% points) Decrease (1993–94 to 2004–2005)	
	Rural	Urban	Rural	Urban	Rural	Urban
All*	37.30	32.40	28.30	25.70	(–) 9.00	(–) 6.70
SCs	48.11	49.48	36.80	39.90	(–) 11.31	(–) 9.58
GAP	10.81	17.08	8.50	14.20	(–) 2.31	(–) 2.78

Note: *Include SC population. Source: Perspective Planning Division, Planning Commission, New Delhi.

39.20% of SC households were BPL compared to 25.70% among other households. The variation in poverty ratio across household types or occupational groups is striking. In 1993–94, the incidence of poverty was about 60% among agricultural labour followed by 41.44% among non-agricultural labour. The level was relatively low for persons engaged in self-employed activities in agriculture (37.71%) and in the non-agricultural sector (38.19%). In urban areas the incidence was astonishingly high among the casual labour (69.48%). Poverty was also high among the self-employed households (54%).

HUMAN DEVELOPMENT INDEX (HDI) AND HUMAN POVERTY INDEX (HPI) FOR SC VIS-À-VIS NON-SC/ST

6.33. According to the UNDP India Report (2007) on Human Poverty and Socially Disadvantaged Groups in India, the HDI at all India level for SCs is estimated to be 0.303, which is lower than the HDI for non-SC/ST at 0.393 for the period 1980–2000. The variation across States is very large, ranging from 0.661 for Kerala to 0.195 for Bihar. There are ten States with HDI value higher than the all-India average for SCs and six States with HDI value lower than this average.

6.34. HPI is a measure to assess the level of deprivation among a given social group with reference to Infant Mortality Rate, Illiteracy Rate, Poverty Ratio (Head Count Ratio), Health Status and Nutritional Status. The value of HPI was estimated at 33.63% for all social groups taken together at the all-India level. The HPI for SCs was estimated to be 41.47% for all India, which was much higher compared to non-SC/STs (31.34%). The HPI revealed significant variation across the States with values ranging from 18.62 to 59.36%. The level of deprivation was greatest in Bihar (59.36%) followed by Uttar Pradesh (50.03%), Orissa (47.66%), Rajasthan (43.78%) and Madhya Pradesh (43.68%), as compared to the all-India level (41.47%). In the remaining 11 States, the rate of deprivation was lower than the all-India value. Deprivation was found to be least in Kerala (18.62%).

REPRESENTATION IN GOVERNMENT SERVICES

6.35. Table 6.6 shows a marginal improvement in the percentage of overall SC representation in the Group A, B and C categories of Central Government services from 1994 to 2004, while there was a substantial decline in the Group D category.

APPROACH IN THE ELEVENTH FIVE YEAR PLAN: THE WAY AHEAD

6.36. The efforts made in the previous Five Year Plans have brought about some empowerment of SCs. However, gaps still exist in almost all social and economic dimensions between SCs and the general population. The Eleventh Plan provides an opportunity to restructure policies for faster, more broad-based and inclusive growth.

TABLE 6.6
SC Representation in Central Government Services in 1994, 1999, and 2004 (as on 1.1.2004)

Group	1994			1999			2004		
	Total	SCs	% Total	Total	SCs	% of total	Total	SCs	% of total
A	59016	6046	10.25	93520	10558	11.29	80011	9744	12.2
B	103198	12442	12.06	104963	13306	12.68	135409	19602	14.5
C	2381613	374758	15.73	2396426	378115	15.78	2040970	344865	16.9
D	1023285	209423	20.47	949353	189761	19.99	802116	147212	18.4
Total	3567112	602670	16.9	3544262	591740	16.7	3058506	521423	17.05

Source: Annual Reports, DOP&T, GoI.

In the following paragraphs, the steps that will be taken for the socio economic development of SCs are discussed.

Educational Development

6.37. With respect to elementary education, various incentives in the form of abolition of tuition fee, free supply of books, mid-day meals, scholarships, and so on, shall be provided to SC children. Among the SCs, children of scavengers are educationally the most backward. The existing Pre-Matric scholarship for them needs to be revised in its funding pattern from 50:50 to 100% so that more target families send their children to schools. Special attention needs be paid to retention in schools of SC students and the quality of teaching for them.

6.38. The scheme of Post-Matric Scholarships for SCs provides scholarships to SC students for pursuing higher education in various courses beyond matriculation. Under this scheme, States are required to bear the committed liability over and above the expenditure incurred in the last year of the Five Year Plan which becomes the committed liability of the States in the first year of the next Plan. The issue of the committed liability to be borne by the states always prevents the States from coming forward to access this Central assistance. Ultimately, it is the SC students who are deprived of higher education. This needs to be addressed. In order to maximize their capabilities, SC students should have the opportunity to study in quality institutions. Today, the high cost of private education turns them away. Thus, there is need for extending financial assistance so that they can access top class educational institutions, including those in the private sector.

6.39. SC students also need to be encouraged to prepare for various competitive examinations. Reputed institutions charge very high fees for coaching students for competitive examinations. The existing scheme of coaching for SCs does not cover the fees charged by such reputed coaching institutes. There is a need to modify the scheme to ensure such coverage.

6.40. Over the last few years, higher technical and professional education is increasingly being provided by private unaided institutions. In the absence of explicit government aid, they charge high fees which SC/ST students simply cannot afford to pay. Therefore, the government may reimburse the total fee charged by such institutions.

6.41. The Rajiv Gandhi National Fellowship for SC students was introduced in 2005–06 to provide fellowship to 1333 SC students for pursuing higher studies leading to M.Phil. and Ph.D. degrees. The response under this scheme has been very encouraging in the last two years and this will necessitate increasing the number of fellowships. Those who cannot continue their education after schooling, or who wish to diversify, should be provided with vocational training/skill training programmes in ITIs, polytechnics, or other institutes. These institutes should have adequate seats on population basis and should be located closer to the SC dominated communities. The stress should be not merely on subject learning but also on personality development and entrepreneurship skills.

Economic Development

6.42. In the Eleventh Plan, a Commission on Land Reforms will be set up which will specifically look into issues of: (i) continued possession and effective uses of land distributed earlier to SCs under various programmes/ legislative interventions; and (ii) availability of land for distribution to SCs/STs/landless families. In all these, care will be taken to ensure preferential/joint ownership by women.

6.43. The unemployment rate of SCs in rural and urban areas is about 5.5% as against 3.5% for others. Special programmes of employment are necessary to reduce this by increasing employment among SCs. Priority needs to be given to SCs in the Employment Guarantee Scheme with proper monitoring of coverage.

6.44. The National Sample Survey Organization (NSSO) on Employment and Unemployment Situation among Social Groups in India in its report (61st Round, July 2004–June 2005) brought out that the proportion of persons in the labour force was the highest among STs followed by SCs, OBCs and others. The labour force participation rate for these groups were 51%, 44% and 40%, respectively. Those belonging to the SC communities suffer from very high incidence of poverty and need to be provided with job-oriented training to enable them to have better opportunities. Such training will be provided under the Apprentice Act the (details of which can be read in the Chapter on Labour and Employment).

6.45. Large numbers of SCs and STs depend on agricultural wages to sustain themselves and the State

Governments thus needs to revise agricultural wages every five years.

6.46. Various financial institutions such as Public Sector Banks and National Finance and Development Corporations for SCs and safai karmcharis and State-level SCDCs providing credit to SCs have been facing the problem of low recovery rate of loans from the beneficiaries through SCAs. This puts a question mark on the economics of the schemes as well as on the capability of the loanees. There is a need to restructure the schemes so that they become more 'sustainable'. The corporations need to be thoroughly professionalized so that programmes financed by them help develop entrepreneurial skills of the loanees. Based upon the effective performance of the Finance and Development Corporations, the capital available at their disposal may be increased substantially to provide support to SC/ST businesses.

6.47. Among the SCs, persons engaged as manual scavengers need special attention to put an end to the degraded practice of manual scavenging. In the Eighth Five Year Plan, the National Scheme for Liberation of Scavengers was launched with the aim to train manual scavengers and rehabilitate them in alternative occupations. Despite commitments made to the eradication of the obnoxious and dehumanizing practice of handling night soil manually, it still continues. Only 19 States and all UTs have adopted the Employment of Manual Scavengers and Construction of Dry Latrines (Prohibition Act, 1993). Nine States are yet to adopt the Act. A new scheme, namely the, Self Employment Scheme for Rehabilitation of Manual Scavengers, has been formulated to rehabilitate the remaining 3.42 lakh of 7.73 lakh scavengers in a time-bound manner by March 2009 through training, and extension of loans and subsidies. This has to be done in a missionary mode with commitment and zeal.

PROTECTIVE MEASURES

6.48. There is a need to complement protective legislations, that is, the Protection of Civil Rights Act, 1955 and Scheduled Castes and Scheduled Tribes (Prevention of Atrocities) Act, 1989 with a promotive legislation which should cover the rights of SCs with respect to education, vocational training, higher education and employment. Such a legislation may be drafted along the lines of the Persons with Disabilities (Equal Opportunities, Protection of Rights and Full Participation) Act, 1995 which clearly spells out what is to be done, and who should do it. The implementation of the PCR Act, 1955 and SC and ST (POA) Act, 1989 has to be enforced in letter and spirit to bring about speedy justice to the aggrieved.

6.49. The Department of Justice in the GoI may establish a Special Law facility to deal with the legal issues of educating judicial officers, public prosecutors and police officials to carry out the necessary research for effective implementation of these two Acts. The Department should also review the judicial aspects and take appropriate steps towards sensitizing the Judiciary, especially at the level of lower courts, to ensure more and speedier convictions. It should also be ensured that Revenue, Health and other concerned Departments in the States become more sensitized on the issue so that procedural delays in the investigation of offences under the Act are reduced.

6.50. Elimination of caste-based discrimination and harassment in educational institutions should be ensured by institutions by establishing 'Equal Opportunity Offices'.

Reservation for SCs

6.51. The government is committed to providing reservations for SCs in education and employment. Action needs to be taken to clear the backlog in filling up SC reserved posts of various categories in the government. However, the government alone cannot accomplish the task of providing job opportunities to SCs. The private corporate sector will have to play a proactive role in providing sufficient job opportunities to the especially marginalized and discriminated sections of Indian society. The government shall explore all possibilities of introducing, in one form or the other, affirmative action including reservations, in the private sector.

6.52. Towards ensuring effective and meaningful implementation of SCSP and TSP and accomplishing SC- and ST-specific targets, efforts will be made to adopt the measures mentioned in Box 6.3 during the Eleventh Five Year Plan.

6.53. There is a need to monitor implementation of the programmes under the SCSP and Tribal Sub Plan. A Committee meant for this purpose will be set up which will ensure that each Ministry's allocation of SCSP is indicated well in advance. Further, if any particular Ministry is not able to utilize the earmarked allocation,

Box 6.3
SCSP and TSP—The Way Ahead

- Adoption and implementation of the Maharashtra Model of SCSP and TSP by all the States/UTs.
- Designing proper and appropriate developmental programmes/schemes/activities specifically relevant/useful for the overall development of SCs and STs both within the existing general programmes across sectors, and also conceiving new avenues/programmes for this purpose, if not there so far.
- Designing a special mechanism and making the same as the special agency responsible and accountable for formulation and implementation of SCSP and TSP effectively and meaningfully.
- Making actual budgetary provisions through allocation of funds under a special head designated for SCSP and TSP to avoid arbitrariness and ad hoc-ism.
- Ensuring timely release of SCSP and TSP funds for the purpose(s) they are meant for.
- The SCSP strategy needs to be evaluated at the end of the year in terms of financial allocations made and the expenditure incurred, and assessment of their impact through gauging physical achievements and ultimate outcomes.

action should be initiated to transfer the unused fund available to those Ministries/Departments which have implemented the SCSP/TSP more effectively.

THE SCHEDULED TRIBES

POPULATION PROFILE

6.54. The population of STs in India stood at 84.33 million as per the Census of 2001. STs constitute 8.2% of the total population of the country with 91.7% of them living in rural areas and 8.3% in urban areas. The sex-ratio of ST population in 2001 was 978, which was much higher than the national average of 933. The proportion of ST population to the total population had also increased from 6.9% in 1971 to 8.2% in 2001.

6.55. The proportion of STs to the total population in States/UT was highest in Mizoram (94.5%) and Lakshadweep (94.5%) followed by Nagaland (89.1%) and Meghalaya (85.9%). Within major States, Chhattisgarh (31.8%) had the highest percentage followed by Jharkhand (26.3%) and Orissa (22.1%). Of the total ST population in the country, Madhya Pradesh accounted for the highest proportion of ST population (14.5%) followed by Maharashtra (10.2%), Orissa (9.7%), Gujarat (8.9%), Rajasthan (8.4%), Jharkhand (8.4%) and Chhattisgarh (7.8%). In fact, 68% of the country's ST population lives in these seven States only.

CONSTITUTIONAL SAFEGUARDS

6.56. The Constitution of India has made several provisions to safeguard the interests of the STs in Articles 15(4), 16(4), 46, 243M, 243 ZC, 244, the first and second provisons to 275(1), Articles 334, 335, 338A, 339(1), and the Fifth and the Sixth Schedules. Besides these, several laws have been enacted by the Central Government like the Protection of Civil Rights Act, 1955; the Scheduled Castes and Scheduled Tribes (Prevention of Atrocities) Act, 1989; the Provisions of the Panchayats (Extension to Scheduled Areas) Act, 1996; the Scheduled Tribes and Other Traditional Forest Dwellers (Recognition of Forest Rights) Act, 2006 as well as by the State Governments (relating to the prevention of alienation and restoration of tribal land, money-lending, reservations, and so on). The Centre has been given the authority of giving directions to the State Governments (cf. Article 339(2), Para 3 of the Fifth Schedule) in the interest of tribal people. Further, a National Tribal Policy is on the Central anvil.

DEVELOPMENT OF SCHEDULED TRIBES: AN OVERVIEW

6.57. The Tenth Five Year Plan continued with the schemes and programmes directed at the socio-economic development of the tribal population through an area based approach. Initiatives to arrest the incidence of land alienation through legislative mechanisms were also explored during the Tenth Plan.

Educational Development

6.58. The Departments of Elementary Education and Literacy and of Higher Education in States have provided special incentives to ST students which include textbooks, uniform, abolition of tuition fee, and so on. Special focus is also accorded to ST students under the District Primary Education Programme, Kasturba Gandhi Balika Vidyalaya, Mid-day Meal Programme,

Navodaya Vidyalaya, National Talent Search Scheme, and the like.

6.59. The Post-Matric Scholarship scheme is in operation since 1944–45, and open to all ST students whose parents' annual income is up to Rs 1 lakh, to facilitate students to pursue professional courses. An amount of Rs 58.9 crore was utilized to benefit seven lakh ST students in the Tenth Plan. The scheme of establishing Ashram schools in TSP areas provides funds for construction of school buildings as well as hostels and staff quarters. Seventy-eight Ashram schools with a capacity of 9610 seats were supported at a cost of Rs 22.34 crore. The scheme of construction of hostels for ST boys and girls provides for the construction of new hostel buildings as well as extension of the existing hostel buildings. An amount of Rs 57.84 crore was utilized for the construction of 120 hostels for 9884 students. The scheme of setting up educational complexes is being implemented for promotion of education among tribal girls in 136 identified low literacy districts of the country. In the Tenth Plan, an amount of Rs 62 crore was allotted under the scheme to set up 76 complexes. A scheme for vocational training in tribal areas for developing the skills of tribal youth for a variety of jobs as well as self-employment, is also in operation.

6.60. However, the problem of adequacy of the school buildings, both in number and in facilities, still remains. The lack of education in the mother language or dialect in primary classes, ignorance of non-tribal teachers about tribal languages and ethos, delay in distribution of scholarships, textbooks and uniforms, continue to be sources of worry.

Economic Development

6.61. The National Scheduled Tribes Finance and Development Corporation (NSTFDC) was set up in 2001 with an authorized share capital of Rs 500 crore. The Corporation supports various income and employment generating activities though loans, marketing support, training, and so on. Special focus is accorded to ST women beneficiaries under programmes such as the Adivasi Mahila Shashaktikaran Yojana, which facilitate income generating activities through women's self-help groups (SHGs). Under NSTFDC, 14.53 lakh STs were benefited during the Tenth Plan. The State ST Development Corporations (STDCs) which function as channellizing agencies in identifying eligible beneficiaries and extending financial and other assistance to them, are also supported by NSTFDC. The STDCs were provided with funds to the tune of Rs 48.76 crore in the Tenth Plan. The Tribal Cooperative Marketing Development Federation of India Ltd (TRIFED) provides marketing assistance and remunerative prices to STs for collection of minor forest produce (MFP), and surplus agricultural produce to protect them from exploitative private traders and middlemen. In the Tenth Plan, States were provided SCA of Rs 2518.07 crore to strengthen their Tribal Sub Plans.

6.62. Though the majority of the tribals are settled cultivators, their farming activity is generally uneconomical and non-viable due to the lack of access to necessary agricultural inputs, specially assured irrigation. Therefore, a special provision of funds under grant-in-aid under Article 275 (1) of the Constitution has been made for financing minor irrigation works.

Restoration of Traditional Rights

6.63. The government took a major initiative in enacting the Scheduled Tribes and Other Traditional Forest Dwellers (Recognition of Forest Rights) Act, 2006 which was notified in the Gazette of India, extraordinarily, dated 2 January 2007. The Ministry has also framed the draft Rules for implementation of the provisions of the Act. The major rights that are granted under the Act inter alia are the right to cultivate forest land to the extent under occupation, (subject to a ceiling of 4 hectares); the right to own, collect, use and dispose of MFP; rights inside forests which are traditional and customary, for example, grazing.

Self Governance

6.64. Despite some protective measures and developmental efforts, the emerging tribal scenario characteristically continues to manifest:

- increasing tribal alienation on account of slipping economic resources like land, forest, common property resources;
- displacement and dispossession of life-support systems;
- general apathy of official machinery;
- escalating atrocities, at times related to assertion of rights;
- growing clout of market forces; and,
- meagre advancement through planned development efforts.

6.65. The scenario calls for a major shift towards entrusting, enabling and empowering the tribal people to look after their own welfare and address issues of development through their own initiative. The extant constitutional-cum-legal-cum-policy framework has been enormously strengthened by the enactment of the Provisions of the Panchayats (Extension to the Scheduled Areas) Act, 1996 (PESA), a charter of autonomous tribal governance, embodying rights in favour of tribal communities coupled with respect for their ethos.

Protective Measures

6.66. Despite protective legislation, incidents of atrocities on members of STs, including gang rape and murder, continue to take place in almost all parts of the country. During the period 2001 to 2005, the total recorded incidents of atrocities against STs were 30128.

6.67. Five States—Madhya Pradesh, Orissa, Rajasthan, Andhra Pradesh, and Chhattisgarh—contributed 72% of the total incidents of crimes against STs.

Primitive Tribal Groups (PTGs)

6.68. There are 75 identified Primitive Tribal Groups (PTGs) spread across 17 States/UTs living in utmost destitute conditions. Some of them, in dire straits, also face the threat of extinction. In order to provide focused attention to the survival, protection and development of these PTGs, a special scheme launched in 1998–99 was implemented during the Tenth Plan to provide tribe-specific services and support including, inter-alia, housing, land, agricultural inputs, cattle rearing, health, nutritional services and income generating programmes.

Tribal Sub Plan (TSP) and Special Central Assistance (SCA) to TSP

6.69. The TSP has been dealt with earlier in this chapter.

Displacement, Rehabilitation, and Resettlement

6.70. Ancestral land, villages, habitations and environs belonging to the tribal people have been made available for various development projects as tribal areas possess 60–70% of the natural resources of the country. In such cases, though primary displacement appears small due to low population density, secondary displacement has been extensive, encompassing common property resources that provided supplemental livelihoods, particularly to those with low or no dependence on farming. Estimates of STs displaced on account of acquisition over the past six decades vary between 8.5 and 10 million (roughly about 40% of all oustees). The widespread secondary displacement in the zone of influence has neither been measured nor was provided for, calling for an accurate verification of actual displacement both in terms of persons and resource loss. Cash compensation for land having been the practice as per the provisions of the Land Acquisition Act, 1894, oustees owning little land, such as wage-labour artisans, have hardly figured in the relief and rehabilitation packages. As a result, some groups have continued to suffer successive, multiple displacement.

6.71. Land (both owned by community and individuals) is the most important source of livelihood for the tribal people for agriculture (settled and shifting cultivation), horticulture, floriculture, forestry and animal husbandry. Several laws and regulations have been in place to prevent the alienation of tribal land and private grabbing of such land. A Report of the Ministry of Rural Development reveals in March 2005:

- 3.75 lakh cases of tribal land alienation have been registered covering 8.55 lakh acres of land;
- Out of the above, 1.62 lakh cases have been disposed of in favour of tribals covering a total area of 4.47 lakh acres;
- 1.55 lakh cases covering an area of 3.63 lakh acres have been rejected by the courts on various grounds; and
- 57521 cases involving 0.44 lakh acres of land are pending in various courts of the country.

6.72. Despite the fair rate of disposal, the other related issues are: (i) the time taken in disposal, (ii) the number of alienations for which STs found access to courts difficult, if not impossible and (iii) the physical possession of the land needs to be addressed comprehensibly.

PRESENT STATUS OF SCHEDULED TRIBES (STs)

Educational Status of STs

6.73. Between 1961 and 2001, the literacy rate of STs increased 5.32 times, while that of total population increased 2.69 times. However, the gap between the literacy rates of STs and of the general population continued during the three decades between 1971 and 2001 almost at the same level of 17.70% and above, but with marginal variations (see Table 6.7).

TABLE 6.7
Literacy Rate of General Population and ST Population during 1961–2001

Year	General			ST		
	Male	Female	Total	Male	Female	Total
1961	34.44	12.95	24.02	13.83	3.16	8.53
1971	39.45	18.70	29.45	17.63	4.85	11.30
1981	46.89	24.82	36.23	24.52	8.04	16.35
1991	64.1	39.3	52.2	40.65	18.19	29.60
2001	75.3	53.7	64.8	59.17	34.76	47.10

Source: Selected Educational Statistics 2004–05, Ministry of Human Resource Development.

TABLE 6.8
Dropout Rates, 2004–05—ST (Provisional)

Year	Sex	Classes I to V			Classes I to VIII			Classes I to X		
		All	ST	Gap	All	ST	Gap	All	ST	Gap
2004–05	Boys	31.8	42.6	(–)10.7	50.4	65.0	(–)14.6	60.4	77.8	(–)17.4
	Girls	25.4	42.0	(–)16.6	51.3	67.1	(–)15.8	63.9	80.7	(–)16.8
	Total	29.0	42.3	(–)13.3	50.8	65.9	(–)15.1	61.9	79.0	(–)17.1

Source: Selected Educational Statistics 2004–05 of India, Ministry of Human Resource Development.

TABLE 6.9
Percentage of Working and Non-working Population (Total and STs)

	Total Workers		Cultivators		Agricultural Labour		Household Industry		Other Workers		Non-Workers	
	All	ST	All	ST	All	ST	All	ST	All	ST	All	ST
India	39.10	49.06	31.65	44.71	26.55	36.85	4.22	2.13	37.59	16.31	60.90	50.94
Rural	41.75	50.37	40.24	47.07	33.05	38.37	3.92	2.08	22.80	12.48	58.25	49.63
Urban	32.75	34.56	2.81	6.55	4.71	12.38	5.22	2.87	87.27	78.20	67.75	65.44

Source: Census 2001, Registrar General of India.

6.74. The dropout rate is a critical indicator reflecting lack of educational development and inability of a given social group to complete a specific level of education. In the case of tribals, dropout rates are still very high –42.3% in Classes I to V; 65.9% in Classes I to VIII; and 79.0% in Classes I to X in 2004–05 (see Table 6.8).

6.75. About 4.34 lakh ST students were studying at different levels of higher education as on 30 September 2004.

Economic Status

OCCUPATIONAL CATEGORY

6.76. 81.56% of the total ST workers, both rural and urban taken together, are engaged in the primary sector, of whom 44.71% are cultivators and 36.85% are agricultural labourers. The corresponding figures for all workers are 31.65% (cultivators) and 26.55% (agricultural labourers). This indicates that STs are essentially dependent on agriculture. (Table 6.9).

AVAILABILITY OF BASIC AMENITIES AND INFRASTRUCTURE

6.77. Since most of the tribal habitations are located in isolated villages and hamlets in undulating plateau lands coinciding with forest areas, they have limited access to critical infrastructure facilities such as roads, communication, health, education, electricity, drinking water, and so on. This widens the gap between the quality of their life and the people in the country.

ACCESS TO INCOME EARNING ASSETS—AGRICULTURAL LAND AND CAPITAL ASSETS

6.78. The STs are mainly landless poor forest dwellers and shifting cultivators, small farmers and pastoral and nomadic herders. The livelihood strategy would thus have to take into account the land structure, level of skills, socio-economic conditions, low level of HDI along with the physical infrastructure and natural resource base in the tribal areas.

EXTENT OF POVERTY

6.79. The incidence of poverty amongst STs still continues to be very high at 47.30% in rural areas and 33.30% in urban areas, compared to 28.30% and 25.70%, respectively in respect of total population in 2004–05 (Table 6.10). A large number of STs who are living below the poverty line are landless, with no productive assets and with no access to sustainable employment and minimum wages. The women belonging to these groups suffer even more because of the added disadvantage of being denied equal and minimum wages.

HUMAN DEVELOPMENT INDEX (HDI) AND HUMAN POVERTY INDEX (HPI) FOR STS VIS-À-VIS NON-STS

6.80. As per the UNDP India Report 2007 on Human Poverty and Socially Disadvantaged Groups in India the HDI for STs at the all-India level is estimated at 0.270, which is lower than the HDI of SCs and non-SC/ST for the period 1980–2000. The HPI (explained earlier in this Chapter in the section on SCs) for STs is estimated at 47.79, which was higher than SCs and non-SC/ST for the period 1990–2000.

REPRESENTATION IN GENERAL SERVICES

6.81. Table 6.11 shows a marked improvement in the representation of STs in various categories of services during 1994 and 2004, though they are yet not adequately represented in any of the four categories. The situation

TABLE 6.10
Population Living Below Poverty Line—ST (1993–94 and 2004–05)

(%)

Category	1993–94		2004–05		Percentage Decrease (1993–94 to 2004–05)	
	Rural	Urban	Rural	Urban	Rural	Urban
All*	37.30	32.40	28.30	25.70	(–) 9.00	(–) 6.70
STs	51.94	41.14	47.30	33.30	(–) 4.64	(–) 7.84
GAP	14.64	9.76	19.00	7.60	(+) 4.36	(–) 2.16

Note: * includes ST population.
Source: Perspective Planning Division, Planning Commission, New Delhi.

TABLE 6.11
Percentage of ST Representation in Central Government Services in 1994, 1999, and 2004 (as on 1.1.2004)

Group	1994			1999			2004		
	All	STs	% All	All	STs	% of All	All	STs	% of All
A	59016	1727	2.92	93520	3172	3.39	80011	3311	4.1
B	103198	2902	2.81	104963	3512	2.35	135409	6,274	4.6
C	2381613	128228	5.38	2396426	145482	6.07	2040970	136630	6.7
D	1023285	62945	6.15	949353	66487	7.00	802116	53776	6.7
Total	3567112	195802	5.49	3544262	218653	6.17	3058506	199991	6.54

Source: Annual Reports, DoP&T, GoI.

is especially unsatisfactory with respect to the A and B categories.

Approach in Eleventh Plan: A Paradigm Shift

6.82. The Eleventh Plan will attempt a paradigm shift with respect to the overall empowerment of the tribal people, keeping the issues related to governance at the Centre. The operational imperatives of the Fifth Schedule, TSP 1976, PESA 1996, RFRA 2006; the desirability of a tribal-centric, tribal-participative and tribal-managed development process; and the need for a conscious departure from dependence on a largely under-effective official delivery system will be kept in view during this shift.

Self Governance

6.83. Article 243G of the constitution and PESA Act make it incumbent that State legislations endow power and authority on Panchayats in Scheduled Areas enabling them to function as institutions of self-governance, preparing and implementing schemes of economic development and social justice. The Act confers abundant powers on the four tiers—Gram Sabha, Gram Panchayat (extant since decades), Intermediate Panchayat (development block tier) and Zilla Panchayat (ZP, district tier)—which need to be given effect in real operational terms. The vision of self-governance should be made functional forthwith in keeping with the spirit of PESA.

6.84. The Gram Sabha and the three other hierarchical Panchayats would require infrastructure, personnel, and financial resources to carry out their tasks. Apart from other sources, the State Finance Commissions need to provide the necessary devolutions for Scheduled and Tribal Areas, as per Article 243(I) of the Constitution. The Ministry of Tribal Affairs should ensure direct flow of funds to the ZPs of the districts in these areas, which should apportion them on an equitable basis to the three lower Panchayat bodies for various programmes.

6.85. The Fifth Schedule needs to be urgently operationalized. The Tribes Advisory Council (TAC) needs to be made proactive, functioning as an advisory body to the State Government in matters relating to STs. Second, it should function as a tier in between the ZPs in Scheduled Areas and the State Government. Its jurisdiction should be expanded to cover all matters relating to tribes people, and not limited, as of now, to those which are referred to it by the Governor. The Ministry of Tribal Affairs is required to ensure regular and meaningful annual reports for the Governor as per para 3 of the Schedule. The Ministry should also examine the feasibility of insertion in the Fifth Schedule of a suitable provision to the effect that discretionary power may be exercised by the Governor on the advice of TAC. Lastly, the Scheduled Areas and Tribal Sub Plan areas should be made co-terminus, enabling protective and legal measures to be available in all TSP areas. To the extent possible, demarcation of Scheduled Areas should be notified down to the village level and other settlements.

Educational Development

6.86. The following measures should be taken to accelerate the educational progress among the tribal population during the Eleventh Plan:

- In the deficit areas, the requisite number of primary schools needs to be established. Specific norms for middle schools and high schools for tribal areas will be evolved and deficiencies made up. All schools should have proper school buildings, hostels, water, toilet facilities (particularly for the girls' schools).
- Residential high schools for ST boys and girls will be set up at suitable places. At the Gram Panchayat level, ensuring girls' hostels will be attached to the existing primary/elementary schools that do not have hostels, wherever it is feasible to do so.
- Textbooks in tribal languages, especially at the primary level, will be produced to enable better comprehension by ST students in classes up to III. Side by side, adequate attention will be paid to the regional language so that children do not feel handicapped in higher classes.
- Efforts will be made to set up Industrial Training Institutes (ITIs) in the TSP areas. Other training centres will include community polytechnics, and undertaking rural/community development activities in their proximity, through application of science and technology.
- Timely distribution of fellowships, scholarships, textbooks, uniforms and school bags to students.
- The ICDS/Anganwadi schemes for tribal areas will be evaluated and shortcomings eliminated.
- A larger number of special coaching classes will be organized and the concerned institutions will be

suitably aided to enable ST students to compete in entry-level competitive examinations for professional courses.

- Adult education will be paid adequate attention.
- Steps will be taken to promote tribal languages, culture and heritage through adaptation of pedagogical methods, community participation in school management, and so on.
- There is a need to constitute a special committee composed of eminent sociologists, anthropologists, educationists, administrators, representatives of ST communities, and so on, to comprehensively assess the problems of ST education and make recommendations for implementation.

Health

6.87. Efforts will be made to make available affordable and accountable primary health care facilities to STs and bridge the yawning gap in rural health care services through a cadre of ASHA and sectoral convergence of all the related sectors. Periodic reviews will be conducted on the delivery system and functioning of the health care institutions under three broad heads to optimize service in the tribal areas: (i) health infrastructure, (ii) manpower and (iii) facilities like medicines and equipment. Action will be taken to make up the shortfall in the different categories of health institutions, liberalization of norms, addressing infrastructural deficiencies, application of quality standards and revitalization of Health Care Systems, PHCs and CHCs (details are given in the chapter on Health).

Economic Sectors and Livelihood Opportunities

6.88. An overwhelming proportion of STs depend on MFP, cottage and small industries, and horticulture for their livelihood.

6.89. Towards making the existing tribal livelihoods more productive, intensive efforts will be mounted to restitute, vitalize and expand the agricultural sector. Use of irrigation in agriculture with a preference for organic farming, will be a major step. Training centres will be opened to impart skills for diverse occupations to the tribals. Efforts will be made to promote horticulture, animal husbandry, dairy farming, sericulture, sylviculture and cottage and small industry by extending the necessary technology and credit, marketing and entrepreneurial information, and training. TRIFED has to shoulder the task of marketing to ensure remunerative prices to STs.

6.90. Lending by agencies like the State Governments, NSTFDC and TRIFED will be streamlined by better coordination at higher levels and efficient delivery at the field level. Large-Scale Multi Purpose Corporate Societies and such like cooperative institutions in tribal areas will be revived to make them representative, autonomous and professional.

Tribal–Forest Interface

6.91. To enable the tribal primary producers, collectors and consumers to enter into transactions with primary cooperatives, the monopoly of corporations in certain items procured by them through contractors and middlemen will be replaced by alternative market mechanisms like minimum price support with institutional backing. It will be incumbent on the national-level organizations like TRIFED and NAFED to play their due role in marketing of the tribal MFP. Technological support for value addition will be extended to the corporations as well as other institutional and private processors. Skills like culling, barking, tapping of gums, storage of sal seeds and preparation of tamarind extracts, need to be upgraded through ITIs, TRIFED, NSTDFC and other training organizations.

6.92. As visualized under the National Forest Policy (NFP) Resolution (1988), tribal association with forestry will be maximized through tribal cooperatives and SHGs of tribal women. Specific schemes for quality improvement, higher productivity and regeneration of MFP species will be implemented to facilitate sustainability of this source of tribal livelihood. No outside labour will be engaged where tribal labour is available. Inter-disciplinary scientific studies to develop feasible agronomic strategies to make shifting cultivation ecologically compatible and economically viable will be undertaken. Special protection will be extended to Jhumias.

6.93. Rules under the Forest Rights Act, 2006 and PESA need to be framed expeditiously.

6.94. ST women will be recruited to the posts of forest guards, foresters and forest rangers, by suitably lowering the educational qualifications, if required. Such forest guards and foresters will ensure safety of the women venturing in the forest areas for their livelihood needs.

Tribal Sub-Plan and Tribal Policy

6.95. As has been explained in the earlier section on SCs, the TSP will be reformed to restore its dynamic character and make it an effective instrument for tribal development.

6.96. Once the National Tribal Policy is finalized, action will be taken to follow up on it.

Tribal Unrest and Socio-Political Movements

6.97. Lack of socio-economic development, physical and economic exploitation, land alienation and other problems have led to a situation in which 75 predominantly tribal districts are affected by violence. The situation could be remedied by taking the following steps.

- Prevention of exploitation of tribals through strict penal action against errant moneylenders, businessmen, traders, middlemen, government servants and other exploiters. Effective implementation of the SC and ST (Prevention of Atrocities) Act, 1989.
- The practice of employment of contractors and middlemen by public sector organizations should be replaced by tribes-benefitting procedures.
- Amendment of instruments the like Land Acquisition Act, 1894; Forest Act, 1927; Forest (Conservation) Act, 1980; Coal Bearing Areas (Acquisition and Development) Act, 1957; and National Mineral Policy, 1993 to eliminate iniquitous provisions ensuring protection of the interest of tribals.
- Displacement should be avoided in the first place. If inescapable, it should be the minimum possible; land for land will be the general rule. All those displaced need to be identified and rehabilitated suitably.
- Land reforms should be implemented stringently.
- The Scheduled Tribes and Other Traditional Forest Dwellers (Recognition of Forest Rights) Act, 2006 should be implemented by the States in letter and spirit.
- Rigorous implementation of the provisions of laws combating land alienation and simultaneous stringent steps to restore the alienated land back to the people.

Prevention of Land Alienation

6.98. Apart from rigorous implementation of laws for preventing alienation of tribal land and plugging loopholes in such laws, the following measures also need to be taken.

- Updating and computerization of land records in tribal areas
- Separate fast-track courts in the Scheduled Areas to deal with cases of tribal land alienation.
- Translation of anti-alienation laws into regional languages and, possibly, in tribal languages, for wide dissemination in tribal areas.
- A law for urban agglomerates in Scheduled Areas on the analogy of PESA Act, 1996 needs to be considered for enactment.

Rehabilitation and Resettlement

6.99. The government has recently approved the National Rehabilitation and Resettlement Policy 2007, with the following objectives:

- Minimize displacement and promote non-displacing or least-displacement alternatives
- Ensure adequate and expeditious rehabilitation with participation of the Project Affected Families (PAFs)—through an independent authority
- Create obligations on the State to protect the rights of weaker sections, particularly SCs and STs
- Provide a better standard of living with sustainable income
- Integrate rehabilitation concerns into development planning and implementation.

Effective follow-up action will be taken to operationalize the policy.

Infrastructure

6.100. Both the Fifth and Sixth Schedule Areas are considered backward, with poor infrastructure being a major handicap in improving the quality of life. The first proviso to Article 275(1) of the Constitution directs building infrastructure in such areas on par with that of the rest of the areas in the country by providing monies from the Consolidated Fund of India. Focused strategies for infrastructure development in sectors like education, drinking water, PDS, health, minor irrigation, roads, housing, tele-communications and electrification will be pursued.

Primitive Tribal Groups (PTGs)

6.101. The strategy will be different for the two distinct groups of PTGs. The approach for heritage groups will place emphasis on conservation of the eco-system, lifestyle and traditional skills along with an economic component. In the case of peripheral communities, the approach will be conservation of the eco-system, along with stress on economic programmes. For the purpose, the unique attributes of each group will determine specific treatment in planning and implementation.

6.102. A National Plan of Action for tribe-specific comprehensive conservation-cum-development needs to be formulated and executed.

6.103. Periodic reviews need to be conducted on the functioning of health care institutions in the tribal areas under three broad heads: (i) health infrastructure, (ii) manpower and (iii) facilities like medicines and equipment. The NRHM seeks to strengthen the public health delivery system at all levels.

6.104. The Department of Drinking Water Supply needs to cover all uncovered tribal areas before the end of the Plan period.

6.105. Urban tribal pockets and other tribal habitations need to be covered with sanitary latrines equipped with minimum basic facilities.

6.106. Many tribal areas receive adequate rainfall. Rain-water harvesting structures will be installed appropriately, particularly in schools and colleges.

6.107. TPDS will be revamped to ensure its outreach actually extends to tribal areas. The system should convey to them foodstuffs of their choice like coarse cereals, pulses, edible oils, and so on.

6.108. There is a need to ensure that the tribal villages are automatically electrified, taking recourse also to non-conventional sources of energy. Universal telecom voice coverage will be ensured in the tribal areas during the Plan period.

6.109. In 1975, guidelines to States/UTs were issued by the Centre for taking steps for discontinuation of commercial vending of liquor in tribal areas in pursuance of the Excise Policy, 1974. Although the States/UTs have accepted the guidelines, commercial vending of intoxicants continues in tribal areas and stringent measures are needed for its prevention.

Data-based Planning

6.110. The issues in tribal development are complex and often not understood very well. Each of the nearly 300 main tribal groups differ from each other in customs, practices, traditions, faith, and language. As such, uniformity in socio-economic development plans for all tribal groups and programmes is not appropriate. Vast quantities of data, generated at various geographical sites across the country, lie scattered, unanalysed and unused. They need to be processed and stored meaningfully in a tribal data bank. The programmes and schedules of the 18 State Tribal Research Institutes (TRIs) in the country demand coordination and synergy. The issues of scheduling and de-scheduling of communities have assumed national importance and need to be appraised rationally and dispassionately. All these point to the need at the Central level for a National Institute of Tribal Affairs (NITA) to deliberate on these matters as also on a whole range of other issues. NITA will serve as a think tank to the Ministry of Tribal Affairs. Expeditious steps will be taken to set up NITA.

OTHER BACKWARD CLASSES (OBCs)

POPULATION PROFILE

6.111. The Second Backward Classes Commission headed by B.P. Mandal (1980), basing its calculation on the Census of 1931, estimated that OBCs constituted 52% of the population. Recently, the NSSO 61st Round (July 2004 to June 2005) report on 'Employment and Unemployment Situation among Social Groups in India' gave an estimate of OBCs constituting 41% of the population. State-wise, OBC-wise data on population as well as vital and demographic variables are not available, which is the main hurdle in the formulation of policies and programmes for the development of the Other Backward Classes.

CONSTITUTIONAL SAFEGUARDS

6.112. Though the Constitution does not make specific provisions for OBCs, it empowers the State to make provisions for reservation in appointments or posts in favour of any backward class of citizens which, in the opinion of the State, is not adequately represented in the Services under the State [Article 16(4)]. It also empowers the State to appoint a commission to investigate into the conditions of socially and educationally backward classes (Article 340). In pursuance of the Supreme

Court judgment, *Indira Sawhney and Others* vs *Union of India* (1992), the National Commission for Backward Classes was set up on 14 August 1993 under the National Commission for Backward Classes Act, 1993. Thus, after 46 years of independence of the country, the backward classes or OBCs got recognition as a separate group of people for the purpose of 27% reservation in services in the GoI and public sector undertakings. The States/UTs were free to decide the quantum of reservation based on the OBC population in their State/UT. All State Governments/UT Administrations were also directed by the Supreme Court of India in the same case to set up a permanent body and to draw up their own list and decide the quantum of reservation as per their demography.

DEVELOPMENT OF OTHER BACKWARD CLASSES: AN OVERVIEW

6.113. Specific programmes for the development of OBCs were initiated from the Eighth Plan. The National Backward Classes Finance and Development Corporation (NBCFDC) was set up in 1992 with an authorized share capital of Rs 200 crore. This was augmented to Rs 700 crore in the Ninth Plan. The objective of NBCFDC is to promote self-employment projects among the OBCs living below the poverty line.

6.114. During the Ninth Five Year Plan period, programmes such as Pre-Matric and Post-Matric scholarship schemes, construction of hostels and pre-examination coaching centres for OBCs were introduced. The Pre-examination Coaching Scheme for OBCs was merged with the umbrella Coaching and Allied Scheme for Weaker Sections including SCs, OBCs, and minorities from September 2001.

TENTH PLAN ACHIEVEMENTS

Educational Development

6.115. The salient features of schemes for educational development of OBCs being implemented through State Governments/UT Administrations and voluntary organizations (VOs) are given in the Table 6.12

Economic Development

6.116. The NBCFDC provides financial assistance through SCAs nominated by the State Governments/ UTs. NBCFDC assists a wide range of income generating activities which include agricultural and allied activities, artisan and traditional occupations, technical trades, small-scale and tiny industry, small business, transport services. Entrepreneurs with annual income less than double the poverty line are eligible for concessional finance. The GoI has made available Rs 448.35 crore to the Corporation as paid-up capital towards the authorized share capital of Rs 700.00 crore. The Corporation has disbursed Rs 1150.89 crore, covering 750432 beneficiaries (up to December 2006).

Oversight Committee on Reservation in Higher Educational Institutions

6.117. In the last year of the Tenth Plan, the GoI decided on another way to introduce reservation for OBC students in institutes imparting higher education. The Oversight Committee under the Chairmanship of Veerapa Moily was constituted in 2006 to prepare a policy roadmap for implementation of reservation for OBCs in higher educational institutions. The matter, however, is sub-judice.

TABLE 6.12
Salient Features of Schemes for Other Backward Classes (OBCs)

S. No.	Name of the Scheme	Class	Parents annual income does not exceed (in Rs)	Funding pattern (%)	Tenth Plan	
					Financial achievement (Rs in crore)	Physical achievement
1.	Pre-Matric Scholarships	I to X	44500	50:50	96.60	56.53 lakh
2	Post-Matric Scholarships	XI onwards	44500	100	126.76	26.97 lakh
3.	Construction of hostels for Boys and Girls	–	–	50:50 to States, 100% to UTs	70.05	94606
4.	Assistance to VOs	–	–	90:10	25.35	760 NGOs

Source: Ministry of Social Justice and Empowerment.

Present Status of Target Groups

RESERVATION IN SERVICES

6.118. Despite 27% posts being reserved for OBCs from 1993, Table 6.13 shows that the overall representation of OBCs in government service is abysmally low, just 4.53%. Only 3.9, 2.3 and 5.2%, respectively of Group A, B, and C posts are occupied by OBC persons. This is indeed a matter of concern.

TABLE 6.13
Percentage of OBC Representation in Central Government Services (as on 1.1.2004)

Group	Total	OBCs	% of total
A	80011	3090	3.9
B	135409	3123	2.3
C	2040970	106309	5.2
D	802116	26158	3.3
Total	3058506	138680	4.53

Source: Annual Report, DoP&T, GoI, 2006–07.

ELEVENTH PLAN APPROACH: THE WAY AHEAD

6.119. The Eleventh Plan will address the issues for development of OBCs through a three-pronged strategy: of (i) educational development, (ii) economic development and (iii) social development.

EDUCATIONAL DEVELOPMENT

6.120. While the universalization of primary education through the SSA (dealt with in greater detail in the chapter on Education) is poised to take care of OBC children, their continued education through the secondary and higher education stages must be ensured. The Eleventh Five Year Plan shall give priority to designing and implementing of schemes to provide the necessary facilities to OBC students to get better education at all levels. Reservation for OBC students in all the Central and Centrally aided schools/colleges/professional institutes needs to be ensured.

6.121. Both Pre-Matric and Post-Matric Scholarship schemes should be revised by enhancing the income ceiling for eligibility and rate of scholarship and maintenance allowance, as these have not been revised since 1998.

6.122. The performance of the existing coaching scheme for SCs and OBCs is not good and the scheme needs to be revised to attract good, professionally reputed coaching institutions.

6.123. Hostels for OBC boys and girls are constructed by the State Governments and UT Administrations. However, where hostel facilities are not available for them, they should be provided facilities in general hostels by earmarking a certain percentage of seats for them.

6.124. National Overseas Scholarship Scheme for OBCs should also be formulated similar to those for SCs and STs so that OBC students can also go abroad for better educational and professional courses which are generally not available in the country

Economic Development

6.125. In economic and occupational terms, the backward classes comprise of peasants, landless labourers, artisanal communities such as handloom weavers, carpenters, metal workers, stone cutters and fishermen, and those who provide various traditional services. The plight of these categories of the backward classes has worsened in recent years due to extensive mechanization and market competition. There is a need to ensure upgradation of skills of such categories so that they can compete better in the market. Credit flow must be unhampered and easy to access, especially in occupations which have been the traditional forte of OBCs, for example, weaving, pottery, quarrying, cultivation of fruits and vegetable, and so on.

6.126. A suitable marketing strategy needs to be worked out on the lines of TRIFED to market the products manufactured by small artisans.

6.127. The strength and capability of NBCFDC should be augmented.

Social Development

6.128. Like SCs, STs, Minorities, and Persons with Disabilities, there is an imperative need to carry out a census of OBCs now or in the next census in 2011. In the absence of exact assessment of their population size; literacy rate; employment status in government, private and unorganized sectors; basic civic amenities; health status; poverty status; and human development and HPIs; it is very difficult to formulate realistic policies and programmes for the development of OBCs.

6.129. Since some backward class people are also working in occupations which are hazardous, the government should identify occupational diseases prevalent among them and take steps to prevent and treat such diseases. The *Report on Conditions of Work and Promotion of Livelihood in the Unorganized Sector* by Arjun K. Sengupta et al., National Commission of Enterprises in the Unorganized Sectors, New Delhi (August 2007) deals with the issue of workers in the unorganized sector. (This aspect has been discussed in detail in the chapter on Labour and Employment).

6.130. The income ceiling of Rs 2.5 lakh per annum for purposes of obtaining OBC certificates may be periodically reviewed to make it more realistic.

DE-NOTIFIED, NOMADIC, AND SEMI-NOMADIC TRIBES

6.131. De-notified, Nomadic and Semi-Nomadic Tribes and Banjara communities constitute the most vulnerable and disadvantaged sections of the Indian society. Some of these communities were identified as 'Criminal Tribes' (which included both castes as well as tribes) in pre-Independence India. Although the Criminal Tribes Act, 1871 was repealed soon after Independence, persons belonging to these communities are still viewed by society as habitual criminals.

6.132. After the repeal of the Criminal Tribes Act, 1924 in 1952, the government was keen to undertake schemes that would accelerate the process of integration of the de-notified tribes into mainstream society. A small beginning was made in the First Five Year Plan in this direction. In the Fifth Five Year Plan, all welfare schemes for de-notified tribes were transferred to the State Plans. Unfortunately, these groups still continued to be marginalized and their specific needs even today are neither adequately understood nor catered to. In order to acquire a comprehensive picture of the situation of these communities and to suggest action for their socio-economic development, a National Commission for De-notified Tribes, Nomadic Tribes and Semi-Nomadic Tribes was set up in 2005. In the Eleventh Plan, special attention will be accorded to the well-being of these groups through steps in pursuance of the recommendations of the Commission.

6.133. One particular area where attention must be paid is towards elementary education of the children of Nomadic, and Semi-Nomadic and De-notified tribes. Due to their family's mobility from one place to another, children in such tribes remain deprived educationally. Mobile schools of high quality should be set up to meet their specific needs.

6.134. Nomadic, Semi-Nomadic and De-notified tribes reside in secluded places. Arrangement should be made to extend the benefit of the flagship programmes to these areas on a priority basis.

MINORITIES

6.135. In pursuance of the Constitutional provisions, the government is committed to the well being of the minorities. Such measures are not limited to protecting and promoting their language, religion and culture, but also in making special efforts for their socio-economic development and mainstreaming. As per the provisions under the National Commission of Minorities Act, 1992, five religious communities including Muslims, Christians, Sikhs, Buddhists, and Zoroastrians (Parsis) have been notified as minorities. Among the minorities, Muslims, especially Muslim women, need special attention since relative to other communities they have remained socially, educationally and economically backward.

6.136. According to the Census of 2001, 18.4% of our population belongs to Minority communities. Muslims constitute 13.4%, Christians 2.3%, Sikhs 1.9%, Buddhists 0.8% and Parsis 0.07% of the country's total population. In absolute numbers, Muslims (nearly 140 million) account for 72.8% of the total minority population of 189.5 million.

6.137. The distribution of minority population indicates that Muslims are in majority in the Union Territory of Lakshadweep and in the State of Jammu and Kashmir. In six States the proportion of Muslims to total population is above the national percentage of 13.4%—Assam (30.9%), West Bengal (25.2%), Kerala (24.6%), Uttar Pradesh (18.55%), Bihar (16.5%) and Jharkhand (13.8%). In absolute numbers, Uttar Pradesh (30.7 million), West Bengal (20.2 million), Bihar (13.7 million), and Maharashtra (10.70 million) have the largest Muslim population. The highest percentages of Christians to total population are in Nagaland (90%), Mizoram (87%), and Meghalaya (70.03%). There are also substantial numbers of Christians in Kerala, Tamil Nadu, Andhra Pradesh, Jharkhand, Orissa, Maharashtra, and Karnataka. Sikhs constitute 60% of the population of Punjab. Buddhists are categorized into traditional and neo-Buddhists.

Traditional Buddhists are, by and large,from tribal communities inhabiting the hilly areas of Ladhakh, Himachal Pradesh, West Bengal, Sikkim, Assam and the North Eastern States. The highest percentage of Buddhists is in Sikkim (28.1%) followed by Arunachal Pradesh (13%). In absolute numbers, Maharashtra reported 58.38 lakh Buddhists, the highest in the country. Parsis number just 69000, and reside mostly in Maharashtra.

CONSTITUTIONAL SAFEGUARDS

6.138. Following are some of the special constitutional safeguards for minorities:

Box 6.4
Important Constitutional Provisions for Minorities

Article 15	Prohibition of discrimination on grounds of religion
Article 16	Equality of opportunity in matters of public employment
Article 25	Freedom of conscience and free profession, practice and propagation of religion.
Article 26	Freedom to manage religious affairs
Articles 29	Right to conserve language, script, and culture
Article 30	Right to establish and administer educational institutions
Article 347	Recognition of language
Article 350	Redressal of grievances to any authority in the government in any of the languages used in the States/ Union Territories
Article 350(A)	Instruction through mother tongue at the primary stage of education
Article 350(B)	Investigate all matters relating to linguistic minorities

DEVELOPMENT OF MINORITIES: AN OVERVIEW

6.139. As the well-being of minorities has been a deep concern of the government, a HLC to study their conditions was set up in 1980 under the chairmanship of Gopal Singh. The Committee, in its report, concluded that the poor among the Muslims could not avail opportunities in education, employment, and economic activities because of isolation and various historical factors. In view of this, in 1983, the Prime Minister's 15-Point Programme was launched to provide a sense of security to minority communities and ensure their rapid socio-economic development. This Programme was based on a three-pronged approach: (i) to tackle the situation arising out of communal riots; (ii) to ensure adequate representation of the minority communities in employment under the Central and State Governments as well as PSUs; and (iii) other measures, such as ensuring flow of benefits to the minority communities under various development programmes, maintenance and development of religious places, Wakf properties and redressal of grievances of the minorities.

6.140. Till the Seventh Five Year Plan, however, minorities continued to get the developmental benefits along with OBCs. In 1989, an autonomous, non-political, non-profit organization—the Maulana Azad Education Foundation (MAEF)—was set up to promote education among educationally backward Muslims in general, and Muslim girls in particular. With a corpus of Rs 100 crore, it undertook activities like establishing and expanding schools/residential schools/ colleges/hostels; purchasing laboratory equipment and furniture; setting up/strengthening vocational/technical training centre/ institutes; providing scholarships to meritorious girl students; opening Maulana Azad Sadbhawana Kendras; (since discontinued) and announcing Maulana Abul Kalam Azad Literacy Awards. In the final year of the Tenth Plan the corpus of Rs 100 crore with the Foundation was doubled. The interest accrued on the corpus was used for implementation of its educational schemes. It sanctioned a total grant-in-aid of Rs 91.81 crore to 702 NGOs/local bodies located in 20 States and two UTs for construction/expansion of schools/colleges/girls hostels/ polytechnics/ and purchase of equipments/machinery/ furniture up to December 2006. The Foundation also distributed scholarships amounting to Rs 6.98 crore to 6986 girl students in 29 States/UTs between 2003–04 and 2005–06.

6.141. During the Eighth Plan (1992–97), two exclusive schemes were introduced for their educational and economic development. In 1994, the National Minorities Development and Finance Corporation (NMDFC) was set up with an authorized share capital of Rs 500 crore. The Ninth Plan (1997–2002) saw a new Central Sector

Scheme for Pre-examination Coaching for Weaker Sections based on economic criteria. It assisted voluntary organizations to run coaching centres to prepare minorities for various competitive and professional examinations. As few organizations came forward, this scheme, along with the Pre-examination Coaching Scheme for OBCs, was merged with the existing Centrally Sponsored Coaching Scheme for Scheduled Castes in 2001. It was renamed Coaching and Allied Scheme for Weaker Sections including SCs, OBCs, and minorities. During the Tenth Five Year Plan, the authorized share capital for NMDFC was raised to Rs 650 crore. Of this, the share of the GoI is Rs 422.50 crore (65%) and that of the State Governments is Rs 169 crore (26%). The remaining Rs 58.50 crore (9%) is to be contributed by institutions/individuals interested in the well being and empowerment of minorities. The task of NMDFC is to extend loans at concessional rates to enable economically weak minorities to take up income generating activities. Since its inception, NMDFC has given financial assistance of Rs 827 crore to 2.16 lakh beneficiaries spread over 25 States and three UTs.

6.142. Despite these schemes, till the end of 2005–06, the Ministry of Social Justice and Empowerment continued to be the implementing agency for programmes for educational development and economic empowerment of minorities. Then, on 29 January 2006, a separate Ministry of Minority Affairs (MMA) was created. Meanwhile, the GoI also constituted a HLC under the Chairmanship of Justice (Retd.) Rajinder Sachar to prepare a report on the social, economic and educational status of the Muslim community. In its comprehensive Report, the Committee observed that Muslims have been left behind the growth and development process. It recommended setting up of an autonomous Assessment Monitoring Authority, creation of a National Data Bank and constitution of an Equal Opportunity Commission (EOC). It also suggested provision of hostel facilities at reasonable cost, inclusion of minority aspects in the general curriculum for teacher training, setting up and strengthening of State-run Urdu medium schools, linkage of madarsas to Higher Secondary Boards, recognition of degrees of madarsas for eligibility in competitive examinations, and provision of financial and other support to madarsas.

Prime Minister's New 15-Point Programme

6.143. The Prime Minister's New 15-Point Programme was launched in 2006 aimed at ensuring the well being, protection and development of minorities. While the 15-Point Programme of the 1983 centred on communal riots, representation of minorities in services and ensuring flow of benefits to individual beneficiaries, the

Box 6.5
Condition of Muslims as Reflected by the Sachar Committee Report

- Muslims have the highest rate of stunting and second-highest rate of underweight children.
- 25% Muslim children in the 6–14 years age group have either never attended school or have dropped out.
- Only one out of every 25 undergraduate and 50 postgraduate students in premier colleges is a Muslim.
- NCAER figures show that only about 4% of all Muslim students are enrolled in madarsas.
- Workforce participation rate among Muslim women is only 25%. In rural areas, 29% of Muslim women participate in the workforce as compared to 70% of Hindu women.
- 61% of the total Muslim workers are self-employed as against 55% of Hindu workers. 73% of Muslim women are self-employed as compared to 60% for Hindus.
- Only about 27% of the Muslim workers in urban areas are engaged in regular work as compared to 40% SC/ST, 36% OBC and 49% Hindu upper caste workers.
- Less than 24% of Muslim regular workers are employed in the public sector or in government jobs as compared to 39% regular SC/ST workers, 37% Hindu upper caste and 30% OBC workers.
- The share of Muslim male workers engaged in street vending (especially without any fixed location) is 12% as against the national average of less than 8%.
- The share of Muslims in Public Order and Safety Activities at the Central Government level is only about 6%. Hindu upper caste workers have a share of 42% and both SCs/STs and OBCs have 23% share each.
- The share of Muslims among defence workers is only 4%.
- Compared to other regular workers, a much larger proportion of Muslim regular workers have no written contract (73%, against 52% for Hindu upper caste and 63% each for Hindu-OBCs and SCs/STs) and no social security benefit (71% against the national average of 55%).

focus of the new Programme is to make certain that benefits of various schemes/programmes flow equitably to the minorities. For this, it quantifies a certain portion of development projects to be established in areas with a concentration of minorities. It stipulates that wherever possible, 15% of targets and outlays under various schemes will be earmarked for the minorities. All Central ministries/departments, State Governments/UT Administrations have been advised to implement this new Programme. Five Central Ministries—HRD, Labour and Employment, Housing and Poverty Alleviation, RD and Women and Child Development—have been given responsibilities in their respective areas. The procedure for monitoring the outcomes of these multiple initiatives is clearly laid out. It will be done on a half-yearly basis by the Committee of Secretaries (COS) and the Cabinet. MMA is the nodal Ministry for coordinating and monitoring the implementation. The key elements of the monitoring will be: (i) focus on meeting financial targets; (ii) target oriented monitoring based on a plan of achievable outcomes under each programme and Ministry; (iii) outcome targets to be staggered and time-bound, and monitored accordingly; (iv) regular evaluation studies conducted by both MMA and by external expert evaluators; (v) space for concurrent evaluation through existing, identified institutions in key target States; (vi) focus on regular and accurate information flow from District to State to Centre; (vii) focus onsmooth fiscal flow and regular identification of bottlenecks; and (viii) flexibility for review and revision of programme designs.

PRESENT STATUS OF MINORITIES

Education

6.144. Table 6.14 shows that literacy rates among Muslims, both men and women, have been the lowest among all the religious minorities.

TABLE 6.14
Literacy Rate among all Religious Communities in 2001

Communities	Male	Female	Total
All religious communities	75.38	53.7	64.8
Muslims	67.6	50.1	59.1
Christians	84.4	76.2	80.3
Sikhs	75.2	63.1	69.4
Buddhists	83.1	61.7	72.7

Source: The First Report on Religion data 'Census of India 2001', p.p. XXI, XIII.

6.145. The Sachar Committee Report found that enrolment of children aged 6–14 years at the all-India level was 85.3% for all communities. The enrolment figures for Muslims was lower (81.8%) than the national average as well as relative to 'All others' (89.9%), but higher than SCs/STs (79.3%). The gap between Muslims and other SRCs increases as the level of education advances.

6.146. The literacy rate for Muslim girls is particularly low. This can be attributed to a number of reasons. Many parents do not send their girls to school as they feel unsafe, especially in view of the growing communalism. Further, as the dependency ratio for the young is high among Muslims, older siblings often have to stay home and provide care. Given the high levels of poverty and self-employment, children also provide much needed labour.

6.147. While it is a misconception that most Muslim children go to madarsas, a large proportion of parents do want their children to receive some form of religious education in addition to the general curriculum. For this, it is vital to ensure that the school timings do not clash with those of madarsas and *maktabs*. Kerala has successfully managed to do this and hence has a high literacy rate among Muslims.

6.148. Finally, many Muslim girls and boys are first-generation learners. Like the children belonging to SC/ST communities, they need support and grooming. This, combined with the presence of women teachers who are non-partisan, will go a long way in checking dropout rates among Muslims.

TABLE 6.15
Children Currently Studying—Proportion of Population by Age Group, 2004–05

Age groups	Hindus			Muslims	Other
In Years	General	OBCs	SCs/STs		Minorities
6–13	19.1	36.1	25.7	14.00	5.1
	(17.3)	(35.5)	(27.4)	(15.1)	(4.8)
14–15	24.3	36.1	21.4	12.20	6.0
	(19.9)	(35.2)	(25.2)	(14.5)	(5.3)
16–17	28.9	33.7	20.2	10.70	6.3
	(21.1)	(35.0)	(24.7)	(14.0)	(5.1)
18–22	34.0	30.5	17.7	10.29	7.6
	(20.8)	(34.4)	(25.5)	(13.9)	(5.5)
23 & above	35.6	29.2	18.3	7.40	9.5
	(23.9)	(35.1)	(24.1)	(10.9)	(5.9)

Note: 1. Figures in parenthesis report the share of each socio-religious group in the total population of that age group.
Source: Estimated from NSSO (2004–05) 61st Round, Schedule 10.

Box 6.6

Prime Minister's New 15-Point Programme for the Welfare of Minorities

(A) Enhancing Opportunities for Education

- Equitable availability of ICDS services: A certain percentage of ICDS projects and Anganwadi Centres to be located in blocks/villages with a substantial population of minority communities; equitable availability of benefits to be ensured.
- Improving access to school education: A certain percentage of all schools under the Sarva Shiksha Abhiyan, the Kasturba Gandhi Balika Vidyalaya Scheme, and other similar government schemes will be located in villages/localities having a substantial minority population.
- Greater resources for teaching Urdu: Recruitment and posting of Urdu language teachers in primary and upper primary schools.
- Modernizing Madarsa Education: Strengthening the Central Plan Scheme of Area-Intensive and Madarsa Modernization Programme to provide basic educational infrastructure in areas of concentration of educationally backward minorities.
- Scholarships for meritorious students from minority communities: Formulation of schemes for pre-matric and post-matric scholarships for students from minority communities.
- Improving educational infrastructure through the Maulana Azad Education Foundation (MAEF): To expand the activities of MAEF more effectively.

(B) Equitable Share in Economic Activities and Employment

- Self-employment and wage employment for the poor: A certain percentage of the physical and financial targets under some schemes, for example, the SGSY, SJSRY, Sampurna Grameen Rozgar Yojana SGRY), will be earmarked for beneficiaries belonging to the minority communities and living below the poverty line in rural areas. Simultaneously, a certain percentage of the allocation will be earmarked for the creation of infrastructure in such villages which have a substantial population of minorities.
- Upgradation of skills through technical training: A certain proportion of all new ITIs will be located in areas predominantly inhabited by minority communities and a proportion of existing ITIs for upgradation to 'Centres of Excellence' will be selected on the same basis.
- Enhanced credit support for economic activities: To strengthen the National Minorities Development and Finance Corporation (NMDFC) by providing it greater equity support to enable it to fully achieve its objectives. An appropriate percentage of the priority sector lending in all categories to be targeted for the minority communities.
- Recruitment to State and Central services: In the recruitment of police personnel, Central and State Governments will be advised to give special consideration to minorities. The composition of selection should have Minorities' representation. Employment opportunities to be provided in the Railways, nationalized banks and PSEs. An exclusive scheme is to be launched to provide coaching to minority candidates.

(C) Improving the Conditions of Living of Minorities

- Equitable share in rural housing scheme: This is sought to be achieved through the Indira Awaas Yojana (IAY) for poor beneficiaries from minority communities in rural areas.
- Improvement in condition of slums inhabited by minority communities: Ensuring provision of physical amenities and basic services to be equitably extended under the schemes of the Integrated Housing and Slum Development Programme and JNNURM to the minority communities and to cities/slums with minority concentrations.

(D) Prevention and Control of Communal Riots

- Prevention of communal incidents
- Prosecution for communal offences
- Rehabilitation of victims of communal riots

Economic Development

WORK PARTICIPATION RATE (WPR)

6.149. The WPR for all religious communities was 39.1% in the Census of 2001. Buddhists had 40.6% WPR, Christians 39.7% and Muslims 31.3% (being the lowest) (Table 6.16).

TABLE 6.16
Work Participation Rate by Male and Female Population in Minority Communities

Communities	Male	Female	Total
All religious communities	51.7	25.6	39.1
Muslims	47.5	14.1	31.3
Christians	50.7	28.7	39.7
Sikhs	53.3	20.2	37.7
Buddhists	49.2	31.7	40.6

Sources: *Census of India 2001: The First Report on Religion Data.*

OCCUPATIONAL CATEGORY

6.150. Table 6.17 shows that Muslims and Buddhists both comprise 20% each of the cultivator category; Sikhs were highest at 32.4% followed by the Christians with 29.2%.

6.151. The Sachar Committee Report clearly shows that due to limited land ownership, most Muslims are engaged in non-agricultural occupations. They are usually merchants, shopkeepers, sales persons, shop assistants, tailors, dress makers, transport equipment operators, tobacco preparers, tobacco product makers, spinners, weavers, knitters, dyers, machinery fitters, assemblers and precision instrument makers. Being self-employed and often in the unorganized sector, they lack any kind of social security. Further, Muslims have traditionally been engaged in skilled occupations like weaving, spinning, artisanship and tailoring. A large proportion of them are also street vendors. As these are professions which have suffered maximum reversals due to globalization, more and more Muslim families are being left without a source of livelihood. The self-employed, especially entrepreneurs, are unable to get credit to expand and run their micro and small enterprises. This is leading to increasing frustration and discontent.

HEALTH

6.152. Census data indicates that Muslims have the highest sex-ratio of any social group in the country (950/1000).[1] However, among other minorities like the Sikhs and Jains, who incidentally have better female literacy figures, the sex-ratio is alarming (786 and 870 for Sikhs and Jains, respectively).

6.153. Muslims have the second lowest infant and under-5 mortality rate of any SRC in India. Infant mortality is lower for Muslims than Hindus—59 against 77 for every 1,000 births in 1998–99 (NFHS-2). Muslims are, however, worse off than most other groups in terms of child under-nutrition; for instance, Muslim children suffer from the highest rate of stunting and the second highest rate of under-weight children among all social groups.[2] This can be primarily attributed to lack of access to PHCs and ICDS centres.

6.154. Violence against minority communities is on the rise worldwide. India too has seen various instances of communal violence which has led to trauma and growing fear and suspicion in the minds of people. This—combined

TABLE 6.17
Distribution of Category of Workers

Category	All religious Communities	Muslims	Christians	Sikhs	Buddhists
Total	100.0	100.0	100.0	100.0	100.0
Cultivators	31.7	20.7	29.2	32.4	20.4
Agricultural labourers	26.5	22.0	15.3	16.8	37.6
Households Industry Workers	4.2	8.1	2.7	3.4	2.9
Other Workers	37.6	49.1	52.8	47.3	39.2

Sources: *Census of India 2001: The First Report on Religion Data.*

[1] *Census of India 2001: The First Report on Religion Data.*
[2] Sachar Committee, 2006

with economic and social backwardness—has resulted in the alienation of large segments of the population, many of whom belong to the minority communities. Provision of adequate social and physical infrastructure, economic opportunities, justice and counselling services are thus vital.

Eleventh Five Year Plan: A Way Ahead

6.155. Though previous Five Year Plans have attempted to focus on weaker sections of the society, they have failed to include many groups, especially Muslims, into the development net. The Eleventh Plan will therefore accord highest priority to the development of innovative programmes, expansion of existing schemes, implementation and monitoring of all initiatives for the minorities by making adequate budgetary allocations at every level of governance. The Eleventh Plan agenda for empowerment of the minorities will focus on:

- Access, retention and achievement in primary, elementary and higher education, with particular emphasis on the education of the minority, especially Muslim, girl child.
- Enhanced access to credit and subsidy for self-employment, export promotion of traditional crafts, upgradation of technical skills and provision of vocational training with forward linkages in terms of employment, that is, equal opportunity in public and private sector employment.
- Access to government schemes and programmes, including schemes aimed at poverty alleviation; provision of physical infrastructure such as housing; provision of civic amenities and health infrastructure in Muslim-dominated village clusters and urban neighbourhoods as envisaged under the PM's New 15-Point Programme Multi-sectoral Plan for Minority Concentration Districts and 338 towns with substantial Minority population.
- Create a national data bank to collect data on various aspects of socio-religious communities through comprehensive surveys on education, health, access to government, access to justice, situation of girls and women; conduct qualitative studies to understand the persisting bottlenecks in access to a wide range of government services and programmes, to understand patterns of discrimination and its socio-economic implications; to suggest long- and short-term remedies; and to understand regional variations in the condition of the minorities from the perspective of plan interventions.
- In-depth evaluation and performance reviews of a host of institutional mechanisms including the NMDFC and the MAEF to improve their efficacy and suggest other institutional innovations.
- Establish measurable, monitorable outcomes and set up national-level monitoring mechanisms for all aspects of plans, programmes and schemes intended to benefit the minorities, particularly poor Muslims.

6.156. In implementing this agenda, the Plan will recognize the heterogeneous nature of different minority groups and the need for common, as well as targeted, interventions based on differential situations.

Education and Social Security

6.157. The government is committed to mainstreaming minorities in the process of economic growth. The SSA will ensure universal coverage for the children of educationally backward sections, with special focus on Muslim girls. Specific SSA components like the centrally funded KBGVs will be set up for minority communities. At the same time, all State plans to access SSA funds will be reviewed to ensure that Minority children have equal space to participate in the State's school system. As SSA only covers children up to the elementary (Class VIII) level, measures will be undertaken to ensure that minority children have equal access to education up to senior secondary level (Class XII). The Eleventh Plan will also look at issues like recruitment of female teachers, provision of amenities and transportation to reach schools, and setting up of girls' hostels and girls' schools.

6.158. In pursuance of the guidelines issued under the Prime Minister's New 15-Point Programme, scholarship schemes, namely the Pre-Matric, Post-Matric, and Merit- and Means-based schemes for minority students will be formulated and implemented in the Eleventh Plan. The objective of Pre-Matric Scholarships will be to provide encouragement to students of the minority communities from Classes I to X for general and/or technical and vocational courses. Similarly, the Post-Matric Scholarship scheme will cover minority students studying in Classes XI and XII for general as well as technical and vocational courses. The major thrust will be on education of girls. Merit- and Means-based scholarship scheme will provide scholarships to meritorious students from poor families to pursue technical and professional courses. In order to ensure effective implementation of the New 15-Point Programme in letter and spirit, rigorous and continuous monitoring will be ensured. All State Governments will be required to submit half-yearly reports on their plans and achievements in reaching minority populations for elementary, secondary and senior secondary education. These reports will be made available in the public domain. Besides, periodic reviews will also be undertaken by the CoS and the Cabinet.

6.159. Concerted efforts will be made to ensure that universally available services under ICDS, NHRM, and so on, reach the localities where the minority communities live. Minority leaders will be roped in to communicate public health messages and dispel existing myths. As Muslims are mostly self-employed and work in professions such as weaving, spinning and dyeing, which lead to occupational ailments, appropriate health services will be made available. State governments will be required to report their achievements in terms of minority access to these services to the Planning Commission.

Employment and Skill Development

6.160. A majority of the Muslim workforce is self-employed and engages in artisanal work. These occupations have been under stress due to the radical changes in the economy. Developmental projects have also led to loss of livelihoods for street vendors, most of whom are Muslims. As a result, deskilling is taking place and artisans and vendors are being forced to move to unskilled, informal work. The Eleventh Plan recognizes the need to provide support to these artisanal groups not just for ensuring inclusive growth and development of the minorities, but for promotion of exports, employment and GDP as well. Consequently, schemes of the Ministries of Textiles; Micro, Small and Medium Enterprises; Agro and Rural Industries; and Food Processing Industries, among others, will be revised to accommodate the interests of minority community workers who are in distress. Provision of inputs including credit, design and marketing support will be undertaken. At the same time social security measures like health and life insurance will be provided.

6.161. Priority sector lending: Access of Muslims to bank credit, including priority sector advances, is low and inadequate. To empower Muslims economically it is necessary to support self-employed persons by ensuring smooth flow of credit to them. During the Eleventh Plan period, all public sector banks shall have targets for priority sector advances to members of the minorities, particularly Muslims. Steps shall be introduced to create awareness about various credit schemes, organize entrepreneurial development programmes, and bring transparency in reporting on credit availability.

New Scheme for Development of Minority Concentrated Areas

6.162. As many pockets with substantial minority populations continue to lack adequate physical and social infrastructure, the Eleventh Plan will adopt an area-based approach. According to the Census of 2001, 1228 community development blocks (out of a total of 6406 in the country), 338 Class I towns and 156 districts have minority populations of 25% and above. Both infrastructure development (physical, electricity, roads, that is, development of amenities) and beneficiary-oriented programmes will be launched in these areas.

6.163. To ensure comprehensive development through a multi-sectoral approach, 90 Minority Concentration Districts (MCDs) covering 34% of the minority population in the country, have been identified on the basis of either human development indicators or basic amenities indicators. The human indicators include: (i) literacy rate of minorities; (ii) female literacy rate; (iii) WPR; and (iv) female work participation. The basic amenities indicators include: (i) percentage of households with pucca walls; (ii) percentage of households with safe drinking water facilities; (iii) percentage of households with electricity; and (iv) percentage of households with W/C latrines. The identification of the MCDs was also based upon certain population norms:

- Districts where the minority population is at least 25% of the total population were identified in 29 States/UTs.
- Districts having a minority population exceeding five lakh where the percentage of minority population is between 20 and 25% were identified in 29 States/UTs.
- Six minority-concentrated States/UTs (Jammu and Kashmir, Meghalaya, Mizoram, Nagaland, Punjab, and Lakshadweep), and districts having 15% minority population other than the minorities (for example, other than Muslims in Jammu and Kashmir; other than Christians in Meghalaya, Mizoram, and Nagaland, Punjab, and Lakshadweep).

6.164. The preparation and implementation of area/problem-specific special developmental plans for these MCDs are already in progress. The effort is to improve the socio-economic conditions through provision of better infrastructure for education, health, sanitation, pucca housing, safe drinking water, promotion of income generating opportunities, skill development and marketing support.

6.165. Furthermore, about 35.7% Muslims live in urban areas and 36.92% of them are below the poverty line. During the Tenth Plan, an Inter-Ministerial Task Force was constituted under the chairmanship of Bhalachandra Mungekar to identify towns/cities that have substantial concentration of the minority population and require special attention, and to formulate the approach for a multi-sectoral plan for provision of basic civic amenities within those areas. The Task Force was also asked to suggest special schemes for funding specific projects which were not covered under existing schemes and programmes.

6.166. The Task Force reiterated the uneven distribution of minorities in the country and revealed that in six States/UTs—Jammu and Kashmir, Meghalaya, Mizoram, Nagaland, Punjab, and Lakshadweep—at least one of the minorities is in majority. Using socio-economic indicators similar to those used for MCDs, 338 towns/cities in which the minority communities constituted more than 25% of the population or more, were identified. Of these 338 towns/cities, 251 have emerged as being relatively backward and in need of urgent attention. Programmes for the provision and development of amenities and infrastructure should immediately be taken up in these towns and cities.

6.167. The endeavour in the Eleventh Plan will be to ensure the availability of all essential amenities in not just the identified MCDs and towns/cities, but in all the other minority localities as well. The area-based approach is not an attempt at ghettoization; it is a response to the existing ghettoization and location of the minorities. It is an attempt to provide each and every citizen of the country access to all amenities, irrespective of their religion or location.

Security and Freedom from Suspicion

6.168. In keeping with the Common Minimum Programme's (CMP) commitment of security and justice for minorities, efforts will be made to carry out interventions which ensure prevention of communal violence. A comprehensive communal violence legislation will be enacted and justice and reparations will be ensured for survivors of communal crimes. Minorities, especially Muslims, are under-represented in Public Security and Defence institutions. This will be remedied. Workshops will be carried out to sensitize law enforcers and ensure that youth are not harassed simply because they profess a certain faith. The government will partner with CSOs to spread the message of communal harmony and dispel suspicions, fears and biases. The government will, through the Ministry of Information and Broadcasting, ensure that no community is depicted in a manner that creates, propagates or nurtures biases and suspicions.

LINGUISTIC MINORITIES

6.169. Linguistic minorities living in relative social and economic backwardness and in need of preservation of their culture and language will be paid special attention. Protective and promotive measures will be undertaken to ensure their overall protection, well being and development in the Eleventh Plan.

MONITORING MECHANISMS

6.170. If the Eleventh Plan agenda for inclusive growth has to succeed, then monitoring of all existing and new interventions is imperative. One important activity of the MMA in the Eleventh Plan will be to ensure that the minorities get their due share in the developmental schemes of various ministries and departments at the Central as well as State level. The Ministry will have to advise other concerned Ministries and Departments and monitor the implementation of the PM's 15-Point Programme. This will entail collection of information at regular intervals, its analysis, preparation of various reports and providing suitable directions.To assist the Ministry, the government will examine the feasibility of a separate committee comprising of government as well as civil society representatives, to undertake a six-monthly review of all programmes deemed to be targeting the minorities. The idea of setting up a National Resource Group for Minority Affairs to strengthen specific components of the Plan based upon responses from the field and design special inputs, programmes or projects for particular social sub-groups will also be considered. Finally, efforts will be made to establish a Grievance Redressal Cell in the MMA as part of monitoring efforts to allow complaints of non-compliance, interference and non-implementation to be addressed.

OTHER VULNERABLE GROUPS

6.171. This section deals with certain other groups that suffer social and economic handicaps which must be addressed to ensure to them equality of economic opportunity and equal access to services by the State. Steps are also needed to prevent social discrimination against them. These groups include persons with disabilities (orthopaedic, visual, hearing, speech and mental disabilities), older persons, victims of substance and alcohol abuse, and so on.

EMPOWERING PERSONS WITH DISABILITIES

Statistics

6.172. The Census 2001 and NSSO 2002 figures for persons with disabilities are 2.13 and 1.8%, respectively but these figures could be an underestimation. According to the United Nations, the proportion of disabled people among the total population in the Asia-Pacific region varies from 0.7% (Cook Islands) to 20% (Australia and New Zealand). In our immediate neighbourhood, Bangladesh reports 5.6%; China 6.3%, whereas Sri Lanka reports 7%. The percentage of disabled people among the total population of any country would depend on the definition of 'disability' in that particular country as well as the enumeration methodology and its accuracy. In India, the definition of disability used in the Census is very different from that in the Persons with Disabilities Act, 1995. There is an urgent need for both a credible definition and a system of data collection relating to persons with disabilities. It can be reasonably assumed that persons with disabilities constitute anywhere between 5 to 6% of our total population.

Legal And Policy Framework

6.173. Article 14 of the Constitution guarantees that no person will be denied equality before the law. The State is directed to provide relief and help to the disabled and the unemployable, vide Entry 9 in List II of the Seventh Schedule. Article 41 states that the State shall, within the limits of its economic capacity and development, make effective provisions for securing the right to work, to education and to public assistance in cases of unemployment, old age, sickness and disablement. Additionally, there are four legislations specifically directed towards the protection, welfare, rehabilitation and development of people with disabilities—the Mental Health Act, 1987; Persons with Disabilities (Equal Opportunities, Protection of Rights and Full Participation) Act, 1995; the National Trust for Welfare of Persons with Autism, Cerebral Palsy, Mental Retardation and Multiple Disability Act, 1999 and the Rehabilitation Council of India Act, 1992. In addition to the legal framework, a comprehensive National Policy for Persons with Disabilities has been announced in February 2006.

Review of Policies and Programmes

6.174. From the Ninth Plan there was a slight shift from a welfare-based approach for the disabled to a rights-based approach. A comprehensive legislation, the Persons with Disabilities Act, was enacted in 1995. The government passed another landmark legislation in 1999, the National Trust for Welfare of Persons with Autism, Cerebral Palsy, Mental Retardation and Multiple Disability Act. Both these enabling legislations cover a wide range of activities, which include issuance of disability certificates and prevention and early detection of disabilities; promoting the integration of disabled students in mainstream schools and removal of architectural barriers from schools, colleges, and universities; providing incentives to private sector employers to ensure that persons with disabilities constitute at least 5% of their workforce; and framing a scheme for payment of an unemployment allowance to those disabled people who have been registered with a Special Employment Exchange for over two years but could not be placed in any gainful employment.

6.175. The Tenth Plan took serious note of the slow pace of implementation of the enabling legislations and advocated a multi-sectoral and multi-collaborative approach to make the provisions of the Persons with Disabilities Act more effective. This would be possible only through clear-cut delineation of responsibilities to the concerned Ministries/Departments. It was however recognized that the Ministry of Social Justice and Empowerment, being the nodal Ministry, should play a lead role in ensuring the objectives of the Act. The concerned Ministries/Departments were expected to formulate detailed rules and guidelines for effective implementation of the Act, besides monitoring/reporting the progress on a regular basis. To ensure adequate financial support to efforts to support the disabled, the Tenth Plan advocated the introduction of a 'Component Plan for the Disabled' in the budget of various Ministries/Departments.

6.176. As per the provisions of the Persons with Disabilities Act, 1995, 3% reservation in employment is being provided to the disabled people. For vocational training,

852 government-run and 105 privately run Industrial Training Institutes (ITIs) provide 3% reservation in seats for persons with disabilities. The SGSY, Indira Awaas Yojana (IAY), National Rural Employment Guarantee Act (NREGA) and Sampoorna Grameen Rozgar Yojana (SGRY) provide for 3% reservation/benefits to disabled people. The National Handicapped and Finance Development Corporation provide loans on concessional terms to self-employed persons with disabilities. Aids and appliances are provided to the disabled under the Scheme of Assistance to Disabled Persons for Purchase/Fitting of Aids/Appliances (ADIP). To enhance the economic potential of disabled people, by the end of the Tenth Plan, 128 District Disability Centres have been made operational. The National Trust for Welfare of Persons with Autism, Cerebral Palsy, Mental Retardation and Multiple Disability has, so far, registered 731 NGOs. Under the scheme to promote voluntary action for persons with disabilities during 2005–2006, 1533 VOs were supported financially for providing services to 1.8 lakh disabled persons. The government has been encouraging education among persons with disabilities. Five hundred scholarships were provided every year during the Tenth Plan for higher and professional courses. The Ministry of Health and Family Welfare has initiated a number of programmes for the prevention and reduction of the incidence of various disabilities.

6.177. The National Policy for Persons with Disabilities was adopted in 2006. It recognizes that disabled people are valuable human resources for the country. The policy focuses primarily on prevention of disability, early detection and appropriate interventions, physical and economic rehabilitation measures, inclusive education, employment in the public as well as private sector and self employment, creation of a barrier-free environment and development of rehabilitation professionals.

6.178. The United Nations Convention on the Rights of People with Disabilities (UNCRPD) was ratified by India in October 2007. It enjoins upon India to ensure that all the rights enshrined in the Constitution, the current legislations, as well as UNCRPD, are speedily and effectively operationalized.

Initiatives During the Eleventh Five Year Plan

6.179. India being a signatory of UNCRPD, it is now obligatory upon us to incorporate the essence of the convention in our planning, implementation, monitoring, and review processes. The eight basic principles of the Convention are: (i) respect for inherent dignity, individual autonomy including the freedom to make one's own choices, and independence of persons with disabilities; (ii) non-discrimination; (iii) full and effective participation and inclusion in society; (iv) respect for difference and acceptance of disabled people as part of human diversity and humanity; (v) equality of opportunity; (vi) accessibility; (vii) equality between men and women; and (viii) respect for the evolving capacities of children with disabilities and respect for their right to preserve their identities. There is an urgent need to review all the four disability legislations and to amend them suitably to bring them in consonance with UNCRPD.

6.180. In the Eleventh Plan, a firm four-pronged approach is necessary to: (i) delineate clear-cut responsibilities between the concerned ministries/departments; (ii) concerned ministries/departments to formulate detailed rules and guidelines within six months of approval of the Eleventh Plan; (iii) ensure that each concerned ministry/department shall reserve not less than 3% of their annual outlay for the benefit of disabled persons as enjoined in the Persons with Disabilities Act, 1995; (iv) set up monitoring mechanisms at various levels and develop a review system so that its progress can be monitored on a regular and continuing basis.

6.181. The 'Disability Division' of the Ministry of Social Justice and Empowerment will be strengthened by converting it into a separate department, so that it can liaise effectively with all the other concerned Ministries/Departments and fulfil its responsibilities towards the disabled.

6.182. Chapter XII of the Persons with Disabilities Act, 1995 mandates the appointment of a Chief Commissioner for Persons with Disabilities (CCPD) at the Central level and Commissioners at the State level to look into complaints of deprivation of rights of persons with disabilities and non-implementation of laws, rules, regulations and executive orders. The CCPD is also expected to coordinate the work of the Commissioners and monitor the utilization of funds. Thus, for the functioning of the CCPD and of the Commissioners leaves much to be desired. During the first year of the Eleventh Plan, steps will be taken to strengthen these offices with professional and budgetary support so that they can function meaningfully. The CCPD, as well as the Commissioners at the State level, will be granted more autonomy. Their recommendations should be made binding on the Centre as well as on State and local level authorities. They should ensure that various Ministries/Departments effectively perform their functions in relation to people with disabilities.

6.183. Since the National Institutes play a pivotal role in the empowerment of people with disabilities, it is essential that these Institutes be strengthened as Centres of Excellence on par with international standards for undertaking the following tasks: (i) training of professionals, (ii) capacity building and (iii) technology transfer and research. The director of the National Institute for the Hearing Handicapped (NIHH) should be well versed in sign language or should acquire this skill upon his posting so as to be able to make direct contact with deaf persons and establish rapport with them. To promote greater accessibility and a barrier-free environment to the disabled, a new National Institute of Universal Design will be set up in the Eleventh Plan. All National Institutes should undertake activities of community outreach to meet the needs of the neglected and disabled people in slums, tribal belts, semi-urban and rural areas.

6.184. To enhance the economic potential of persons with disabilities, 199 DDRCs for comprehensive service in community setting have been sanctioned, but only 128 were made operational by the end of the Tenth Plan. The Eleventh Plan will ensure that the remaining 71 centres are also operationalized. Also, a concerted effort will be made to extend the scheme to another 101 districts so that at least 300 districts are covered by the end of the Plan period. In the selection of the additional 101 districts, special care will be taken to cover backward areas where the prevalence of disability is higher and where services as well as facilities for them are inferior to those in other parts of the country.

6.185. The Scheme of ADIP, launched in 1981, was supposed to provide durable, sophisticated and scientifically manufactured, modern, standard aids and appliances to people with disabilities in order to promote their physical, social and psychological rehabilitation. However, due to the lack of awareness, very few disabled people are able to benefit from this Scheme. The Eleventh Plan will endeavour to create awareness about ADIP and other such schemes. This is one scheme which must be universalized. Any disabled person should be able to approach the district magistrate and derive benefit from her/him. The income ceiling for availing assistance will be raised to Rs 10000 per month. Moreover, the ceiling for purchase/fitting of aids and appliances should also be enhanced to Rs 25000 per month. For manufacturing these aids and appliances, there is need to enhance the production capacity and ALIMCO should not be a monopoly supplier. The approach should be to provide the best possible assistive devices by encouraging multiple manufacturers, and even through imports. The Eleventh Plan shall allocate adequate funds for strengthening ADIP.

6.186. The efforts of the Eleventh Plan will be to ensure that all Commercial Banks, Regional Rural Banks (RRBs) and Cooperatives should provide loans to disabled people on concessional terms for undertaking self-employment ventures. Such credit should be included in the Priority Sector and NABARD should ensure appropriate refinancing mechanisms.

6.187. The following innovative steps will also be taken during the Eleventh Plan:

- The Health Ministry will ensure that before the end of the Eleventh Plan, every disabled person possesses a disability certificate. This would help such a person to prove her/his identity as a person with disability for the purpose of availing the benefits for which he/she is eligible. A disabled person should be able to get his/her disability certificate within 30 days of making an application. The responsibility to ensure this will rest with the concerned district magistrate.
- The Eleventh Plan shall support the vigorous implementation of the Comprehensive Action Plan for the Inclusive Education of Children and Youth with Disabilities, as announced by the HRD Minister in 2005. A commitment has been given in Parliament that education would be made disabled friendly by 2020. If this commitment is to be fulfilled, certain urgent steps are necessary, including the setting up of disability units in the University Grants Commission (UGC), All India Council For Technical Education (AICTE), National Council of Educational Research and Training (NCERT), Kendriya Vidyalaya Sangathan (KVS), and all other apex education bodies. The scholarships provided by the Central Government and stipends for pre-matric education, mostly provided by the States, should be made equivalent to similar scholarships and

stipends given to students belonging to the SCs and STs. The scheme for postgraduate and professional education initiated in the Tenth Plan should be strengthened and expanded in the Eleventh Plan. Further, deserving persons with disabilities should be supported for training/education abroad, especially in studies relating to disability.

- Persons with disability can and should become productive contributors in the development process of the country. At present, the identification of jobs appropriate for them is done in an ad hoc and arbitrary manner. There is a need to have this task performed by a professional group with the involvement of Disabled Peoples' Organizations. The backlog of vacancies for persons with disability continues to be large, both at the Centre and in the States. This backlog should be cleared in a time-bound manner and in a campaign mode. Similarly, a suitable scheme to provide incentives to promote employment for disabled people in the private sector should be put in place as enjoined in Section 41 of The Persons with Disabilities (Equal Opportunities, Protection of Rights and Full Participation) Act, 1995.
- In the Eleventh Plan, a concerted effort should be made to make all public buildings and facilities such as schools, hospitals, public transport, and so on, compliant with the requirements of a barrier-free built environment. Towards this end, the building bye-laws, municipal and civic regulations, relevant codes for construction and design should incorporate the requirements of a barrier-free environment. Similarly, all shops/malls and similar places open to public, should be insisted upon to provide the facilities required for the disabled. In the Eleventh Plan, a National Centre to facilitate and support the development of universal design and barrier-free built environment will be established.
- Detection of mental disabilities and disorders is critical to addressing mental well being through both preventive and curative measures. It is vital to recognize that physical disabilities usually coexist with, and lead to, mental disturbance and ill health. The Eleventh Plan will emphasize and adopt a multi-pronged, cross-sectoral approach to identifying, preventing, managing, treating and rehabilitating persons with mental disabilities. There will be a focus on awareness drives, defining the various kinds of disabilities, generating valid census data, inclusion in all areas of development, and community based treatment and rehabilitation approaches. Efforts will be made to strengthen and develop trained human resource to address the growing magnitude of mental disabilities. There will be emphasis on research to generate relevant data and culturally valid rehabilitative measures.
- The needs of persons with hearing and/or speech impairment have been relatively neglected so far. In the Eleventh Plan, a determined effort will be made on mainstreaming this segment. The interventions planned will provide access to information in all its forms. A large number of sign language interpreters need to be developed for hearing impaired people to access health, employment and legal services. Sub-titling and captioning of all recorded information and similar support services is also essential. Therefore, during the Eleventh Plan period a Sign Language Research and Training Centre will be established which will be devoted to the development and promotion of sign language and training of teachers and interpreters. A National Captioning Centre will also be set up to provide sub-titling and captioning services. At least one residential special school up to Class XII and one Degree college for the deaf in every zone should be established to promote their educational development.

OLDER PERSONS AND OTHER SOCIAL DEFENCE GROUPS

OLDER PERSONS

6.188. India has the second largest population of older (60+) persons in the world. The number of older persons in the population is expected to increase from 71 million in 2001 to 173 million in 2026. A majority (80%) of the elderly population in India is in the rural areas, thus making service delivery to them a challenge, and there is a large number of 80+ persons in the country.

Initiatives for Older Persons during the Tenth Plan

6.189. As contemplated in the National Policy on Older Persons (NPOP), a National Council for Older Persons (reconstituted in 2005) has been set up to advise and aid the government on policies and programmes for older persons and to provide a feedback to the government on the implementation of NPOP.

6.190. The Maintenance and Welfare of Parents and Senior Citizens Bill, 2007 which has been presented to the Parliament, stipulates construction of at least one old age home in each district of the country to accommodate deserving and destitute senior citizens.

6.191. This intended Act will make the process for claiming maintenance simpler, speedier and less expensive. Further, the legislation would also ensure adequate medical facilities to older persons and protection of their life and property.

6.192. The programmes/schemes/incentives for older persons include income tax rebate, higher rates of interest in saving schemes, 30% concessions in all railway travel and 50% discount on basic fare for all domestic flights in the economy class in Indian Airlines, Jet Airways and others.

TABLE 6.18
Percentage of Elderly Persons to Total Population

Year	Total population (in million)	% of elderly persons
2001	70.69	6.90
2006	83.58	7.50
2011	98.47	8.30
2016	118.10	9.30
2021	143.24	10.70
2026	84.62	12.40

6.193. The Ministry of Social Justice and Empowerment implements an Integrated Programme for Older Persons through VOs. Under this scheme, VOs are given 90% grant for running old age homes, day care centres and mobile medical care units. Another scheme for construction of old age homes is being implemented through local SHGs, PRIs and VOs.

The Way Ahead

6.194. The Eleventh Plan proposes to further the right-based approach and also focus on bridging the gap between rural and urban areas.

6.195. A National Association for older persons, as per NPOP, will be set up. Protection of life and property by utilizing the services of Panchayats/Senior Citizens' Associations and other community-based groups and sensitizing and reorienting the law enforcement machinery to the vulnerability and special protection needs of older persons will be taken up in the Eleventh Plan.

6.196. The National Old Age Pension schemes will now be extended to all BPL persons above the age of 60 years. A pension of Rs 200 per month will be provided and States will be requested to add another Rs 200 to this scheme.

Other Social Defence Groups

6.197. The problems of substance (drug) and alcohol abuse have existed for a long time, although their nature and extent varies according to the prevailing social and economic conditions. There is, however, a dearth of reliable information to establish the exact magnitude of the problem and the size of the affected group. The National Survey on the Extent, Trends and Pattern of Drug Abuse in the Country, undertaken in collaboration with the United Nations Office on Drug and Crime (UNODC) and International Labour Organization (ILO), indicated that there are 732 lakh drug users and dependent users in the country. Going by estimation in India, there are approximately 625 lakh alcohol users, 87 lakh cannabis users and 20 lakh opiate users. In some parts, especially the north-east, drug addiction and incidence of HIV/AIDS have assumed alarming proportions.

6.198. A number of schemes for prevention, treatment and rehabilitation in respect of alcohol and drug abuse are being implemented in partnership with voluntary organizations. Eight Regional Resource and Training Centres have been established for training NGOs working for drug abuse prevention and also to undertake advocacy, research and monitoring of drug abuse programmes. Initiatives have been taken up jointly by the Ministry of Social Justice and Empowerment and National Aids Control Organization for the integration of HIV/AIDS prevention programmes with substance abuse prevention. Programmes are also being implemented through the UNODC prevention of spread of HIV.

The Way Ahead

6.199. In the Eleventh Plan, thrust will be given to the prevention of drug abuse by ensuring effective involvement of parents, community, schools and colleges. Efforts will also be made to involve the corporate sector, civil society and other institutions like religious and elected bodies, to prevent drug abuse.

6.200. Keeping in view the large number of drug users estimated (130 lakh) in the country, the available number of treatment centres is evidently inadequate. There is a need to have a National Policy on Drug Abuse Prevention and Rehabilitation, which will provide the basic framework for reduction of demand and supply of alcohol and drugs and prevention, treatment and rehabilitation of the addicts by involving all concerned agencies.

6.201. The National Institute of Social Defence (NISD) is the nodal training and research institute in the field of social defence. The ongoing programmes of the Institute such as collection of statistics, documentation research and programmes for training pertaining to prevention of drug abuse and care of older persons, will continue in the Eleventh Plan. The training programme should be organized both in-house as well as in collaboration with other organizations working in related areas.

BEGGARS

6.202. Beggars are found everywhere in the country, especially in urban centres, at religious places, traffic signals, and other places. They include several categories of persons such as homeless, abandoned, displaced, children, disabled, destitutes and eunuchs. Begging is a complex social problem and needs legislative, reformative and rehabilitative interventions. It is often organized and institutionalized as an economic activity. The States are responsible for taking the necessary preventive and rehabilitative steps. Neither is there any Central Act on prevention of begging and rehabilitation of beggars, nor a clear policy on how the problem is to be tackled. There is, therefore, a need to address the problem in a holistic manner at the national level.

6.203. The issues relating to juvenile and youth delinquents continue to be a matter of concern for the government. These groups need to be carefully reformed and mainstreamed through proper social rehabilitation. Similarly, certain categories of women such as Dalit women, widows and *devdasis* are especially disadvantaged and vulnerable, and require focused attention. They have been appropriately discussed in the chapter on Women's Agency and Child's Rights.

ROLE OF VOLUNTARY ORGANIZATIONS (VOs)

6.204. Recognizing the complementary and supplementary role played by VOs, the government has been extending financial and other support to them, especially to organizations which have an all-India base, to undertake activities aimed at socio-economic development and empowerment of the disadvantaged and the under-privileged sections such as SCs, STs, OBCs, minorities, disabled, older people and other social defence groups. Such VOs, especially those managed by the target group itself, will continue particularly in areas/regions which have not yet been covered.

6.205. Non-governmental organizations of repute should be invited to play the role of designated agents/informants and identify cases of untouchability, atrocities and other forms of discrimination based on caste, creed, religion, and so on. They need to be encouraged to assist the implementing agency in investigation and trial and also safeguarding against various pressures aimed at nullifying the impact of legal proceedings.

6.206. Voluntary action acquires greater significance in the tribal context in view of the virtual absence of tribes peoples' own VOs, that is, VOs as we understand the term, though they have their own traditional organizations. Their inability to negotiate with the formal administrative system, limited worldview and low level of awareness and literacy add to the need for bridges with the other worlds. Voluntary groups will be encouraged to train tribal peoples' own organizations to make them capable of articulating their own needs and advocating their rights.

6.207. While encouraging voluntary action, a system of accountability would have to be established for the NGOs so as to ensure effective delivery of services. The corporate sector and public sector undertakings could be encouraged for productive interventions for social welfare problems in their own industries.

RESEARCH, MONITORING, AND EVALUATION

6.208. Development programmes for the welfare of socially disadvantaged groups and marginalized sections of society have been in operation from the First Five Year Plan onwards. Whether the benefits of these programmes reach the targeted persons, needs to be monitored on a periodical basis at the district, State and national levels. Continuous monitoring and evaluation would justify the continuation of programmes. The Ministries of Social Justice and Empowerment, Tribal Affairs and Minorities have developed mechanisms of monitoring and evaluating their programmes. These Ministries also sponsor research studies by independent agencies such as university departments/reputed research bodies/VOs. Based on the findings of such studies, efforts are made to improve upon the strategy for implementation of schemes. During the

Eleventh Five Year Plan, particular stress will be laid on ensuring that such evaluation does not become routine, and results in actual improvements in the schemes.

NEED FOR DATABASE

6.209. The Census of India and NSSO are the two agencies which make available data on various aspects of social groups. Data on SCs, STs, Minorities and Persons with Disabilities have been made available by these agencies. Census data are not available for OBCs and persons who are victims of drug addiction and alcoholism. The Eleventh Plan will address the need for survey of such category of persons for proper formulation of policies and programmes towards their welfare and rehabilitation. The Eleventh Plan will also address the issue for adopting a uniform definition for identification of disabled persons by both the agencies.

AFFIRMATIVE LEGISLATION ACTION

6.210. The prevailing gaps in socio-economic status between SCs, STs and other disadvantaged groups vis-à-vis the rest of the population need to be speedily bridged by taking innovative measures. As a first step, there is a need to assess the gaps between SCs and other social groups with respect to various parameters of growth and development and construct an index of development/vulnerability/deprivation on the basis of which policy and programme interventions can be formulated and administered. State governments, Central ministries/departments and public authorities are to be made accountable for purposeful and affirmative action within their jurisdiction to bring about overall development of the people belonging to SCs/STs and to bridge the gaps between their and other social groups. The proposed legislation should cover assessing the gaps between SCs/STs and other social groups, constructing suitable indices and providing appropriate intervention in the areas of education, higher education including vocational training and employment for bridging the gaps on a lifetime capacity building basis. The legislation should also provide for appropriate penalty for non-performance of the obligations created by it. It should be adopted by all the States to implement it in its letter and spirit. Action may be taken on the lines of the Persons with Disabilities (Equal Opportunities, Protection of Rights and Full Participation) Act, 1995

PLAN OUTLAY

6.211. In the Eleventh Plan, a tentative outlay of Rs 13043 crore has been earmarked for the Ministry of Social Justice and Empowerment for the development of SCs, OBCs and other vulnerable groups. Similarly, tentative allocation of Rs 3709 crore and Rs 7000 crore have been made to the Ministry of Tribal Affairs and MMA, respectively for the welfare and development of STs and minorities. The allocation indicated for the Ministry of Tribal Affairs does not include SCA to TSP and grant-in-aid under Article 275(1) of the Constitution. In addition to this, social welfare programmes receive Plan financial support from the State sector also.

7

Spatial Development and Regional Imbalances

7.1 REGIONAL IMBALANCES

INTRODUCTION

7.1.1. As the Eleventh Plan commences, a widespread perception all over the country is that disparities among States, and regions within States, between urban and rural areas, and between various sections of the community, have been steadily increasing in the past few years and that the gains of the rapid growth witnessed in this period have not reached all parts of the country and all sections of the people in an equitable manner. That this perception is well founded is borne by available statistics on a number of indicators. Though there is some evidence to indicate a movement towards convergence on human development indicators across States, one of the reasons for this convergence could also be that most human development indicators have a value cap. However, widening income differentials between more developed and relatively poorer States is a matter of serious concern. The objective of the Eleventh Plan is 'faster and more inclusive growth' and each chapter has dealt with what the Plan proposes to do to achieve this objective, insofar as the sector dealt with by that chapter is concerned. In this chapter, the attempt is to look at broad aggregates in order to understand the dimensions of the issue and to highlight some of the methods by which the problem is being redressed.

STATE-WISE GROWTH RATES

7.1.2. The Tenth Plan was the first Plan that specified targets for the growth rate for each State, in consultation with the State Governments. Through the Eighth and Ninth Plan periods, the rate of growth in the better-off States (that is, States with per capita income above the national average) had been generally higher than those of the States with a lower than average per capita income. This had led to gradually increasing differences in per capita income among the States. The Tenth Five Year Plan targeted a growth rate of 8% per annum for the country as a whole; however, the Gross State Domestic Product (GSDP) growth rate targets for different States adopted by the Tenth Plan were both higher and lower than this average.

7.1.3. The latest available figures show the following growth rates as having been achieved by various States during the Tenth Plan period as compared to the targets. For obtaining a longer term perspective, growth rates achieved in the Eighth and Ninth Plans are also given in Table 7.1.1.

7.1.4. The Eleventh Plan has continued the Tenth Plan initiative of working out GSDP growth targets for States. Consistent with the country's overall GDP growth target

TABLE 7.1.1
Growth Rates in State Domestic Product in Different States

(% per annum)

S.No.	State/UT	Eighth Plan	Ninth Plan	Tenth Plan	
				Target	Actuals #
Non Special Category States					
1	Andhra Pradesh	5.4	4.6	6.8	6.7
2	Bihar	2.2	4.0	6.2	4.7
3	Goa	8.9	5.5	9.2	7.8
4	Gujarat	12.4	4.0	10.2	10.6
5	Haryana	5.2	4.1	7.9	7.6
6	Karnataka	6.2	7.2	10.1	7.0
7	Kerala	6.5	5.7	6.5	7.2
8	Madhya Pradesh	6.3	4.0	7.0	4.3
9	Maharashtra	8.9	4.7	7.4	7.9
10	Orissa	2.1	5.1	6.2	9.1
11	Punjab	4.7	4.4	6.4	4.5
12	Rajasthan	7.5	3.5	8.3	5.0
13	Tamil Nadu	7.0	6.3	8.0	6.6
14	Uttar Pradesh	4.9	4.0	7.6	4.6
15	West Bengal	6.3	6.9	8.8	6.1
16	Chhattisgarh	NA	NA	6.1	9.2
17	Jharkhand	NA	NA	6.9	11.1
Special Category States					
1	Arunachal Pradesh	5.1	4.4	8.0	5.8
2	Assam	2.8	2.1	6.2	6.1
3	Himachal Pradesh	6.5	5.9	8.9	7.3
4	Jammu & Kashmir	5.0	5.2	6.3	5.2
5	Manipur	4.6	6.4	6.5	11.6
6	Meghalaya	3.8	6.2	6.3	5.6
7	Mizoram	NA	NA	5.3	5.9
8	Nagaland	8.9	2.6	5.6	8.3
9	Sikkim	5.3	8.3	7.9	7.7
10	Tripura	6.6	7.4	7.3	8.7
11	Uttaranchal (now Uttarakhand)	NA	NA	6.8	8.8
	All India				

Note: # Average of 2002–03 to 2005–06 for all States except J&K, Mizoram, Nagaland (2002–03 to 2004–05) and Tripura (2002–03 to 2003–04).
Source: CSO (base 1999–2000 constant price) as on 31.8.2007.

of 9% per annum for the Eleventh Plan, the following growth targets for each State, broken up into targets for each sector, have been worked out (Table 7.1.2). For the agricultural sector, the State-wise projection has been made on the basis of a rigorous panel data regression model. The growth target for Industry and Services sectors has been made by linearly projecting the past contribution of each State to the overall growth performance of these two sectors at the national level.

7.1.5. The Eleventh Five Year Plan has attempted in a similar manner to break down the monitorable targets at the national level into State-level targets. These targets will help to focus attention on the extent to which progress has been achieved in the relatively backward States and districts.

7.1.6. Table 7.1.3 presents summary indicators of disparity in per capita income across States in India. This does not consider the intra-State distribution of income. The ratio of minimum to maximum per capita GSDP increased for three years from 21.56% in 2001–02 to 22.71% in 2003–04 and then decreased in 2004–05 to 20.11%. The weighted coefficient of variation also shows an increase over the years. The Gini Coefficient indicated in column

TABLE 7.1.2
State-wise Growth Target for the Eleventh Five Year Plan

(Annual Average in %)

	States/UTs	State-wise Growth Target			
		Agriculture	Industry	Services	GSDP Growth
	Non Special Category States				
1	Andhra Pradesh	4.0	12.0	10.4	9.5
2	Bihar	7.0	8.0	8.0	7.6
3	Chhattisgarh	1.7	12.0	8.0	8.6
4	Goa	7.7	15.7	9.0	12.1
5	Gujarat	5.5	14.0	10.5	11.2
6	Haryana	5.3	14.0	12.0	11.0
7	Jharkhand	6.3	12.0	8.0	9.8
8	Karnataka	5.4	12.5	12.0	11.2
9	Kerala	0.3	9.0	11.0	9.5
10	Madhya Pradesh	4.4	8.0	7.0	6.7
11	Maharashtra	4.4	8.0	10.2	9.1
12	Orissa	3.0	12.0	9.6	8.8
13	Punjab	2.4	8.0	7.4	5.9
14	Rajasthan	3.5	8.0	8.9	7.4
15	Tamil Nadu	4.7	8.0	9.4	8.5
16	Uttar Pradesh	3.0	8.0	7.1	6.1
17	West Bengal	4.0	11.0	11.0	9.7
	Special Category States				
1	Arunachal Pradesh	2.8	8.0	7.2	6.4
2	Assam	2.0	8.0	8.0	6.5
3	Himachal Pradesh	3.0	14.5	7.5	9.5
4	Jammu and Kashmir	4.3	9.8	6.4	6.4
5	Manipur	1.2	8.0	7.0	5.9
6	Meghalaya	4.7	8.0	7.9	7.3
7	Mizoram	1.6	8.0	8.0	7.1
8	Nagaland	8.4	8.0	10.0	9.3
9	Sikkim	3.3	8.0	7.2	6.7
10	Tripura	1.4	8.0	8.0	6.9
11	Uttarakhand	3.0	12.0	11.0	9.9

Source: Planning Commission.

(6) of Table 7.1.3 reflects the income inequality across the States, which increases from 0.2078 in 2001–02 to 0.2409 in 2004–05. In other words, the income inequality across States is worsening.

7.1.7. However, we also need to reckon with the fact that the slower growing States cannot catch up with the faster growing States within a short time period of five years. What this Plan seeks to do is to target the slower growing States, and the backward areas within these States, for higher levels of public investment that will enable the backlog in physical and social infrastructure to be addressed. This would, in turn, provide a platform for much more rapid growth in the Twelfth Plan period.

7.1.8. While differences in GSDP growth rates, and absolute levels of per capita GSDP, are summary economic indicators of disparities, there are wide variations between the States even on other health, education and infrastructure indicators. In the current scenario where high growth rates have led to a spiral of commercial and service sector activity in the already developed regions, the backward areas continue to lack even basic amenities such as education, health, housing, rural roads, drinking water and electricity. Livelihood options are also limited as agriculture does not give adequate returns and industry is virtually absent, leading to limited trade and services. People seeking employment in low skill, low paying jobs is a common

TABLE 7.1.3
Disparity in per capita GSDP

Year	State with lowest per capita GSDP	State with highest * per capita GSDP	Ratio of Minimum to Maximum per capita GSDP	Coefficient of variation	Gini Coefficient $
(1)	(2)	(3)	(4)	(5)	(6)
			(in %)	Weighted	
1993–94	Bihar	Punjab	30.527	34.549	0.1917
1996–97	Bihar	Maharashtra	27.586	36.781	0.2071
1999–2000	Bihar	Maharashtra	28.899	37.417	0.2173
2001–02	Bihar	Punjab	21.556	35.610	0.2078
2002–03	Bihar	Punjab	21.608	36.686	0.2771
2003–04	Bihar	Punjab	22.705	36.230	0.2290
2004–05	Bihar	Maharashtra	20.105	38.440	0.2409

Note: 1993–94, 1996–97 and 1999–2000 as per the TFC Report based on 1993–94 series; 2001–02 onwards. Comparable GSDP 1999–2000 Series: Current Prices; *excluding Goa; $ weighted by population; 1993–94, 1996–97 and 1999–2000 relates to 14 States (Assam and general category States excluding Goa) as per TwFC; and 2001–02 to 2004–05 relates to 27 States (excluding Goa).

Source: (i) TFC Report for the year 1993–94, 1996–97 and 1999–2000.
(ii) Central Statistical Organization for years 2001–02, 2002–03, 2003–04 and 2004–05.

manifestation of these constraints in many rural areas. Compounding these problems is the lack of manpower to man essential services such as educational institutions and health centres. A large part of the disparities are probably due to historical reasons, differences in initial conditions and natural resource endowments. However, there is no clear pattern that seems to be applicable to all cases.

7.1.9. While the above is the situation as between States, very much the same picture is seen among the different districts and regions within States. Even in highly developed States, there are regions and districts whose indicators are comparable to those of the poorest districts in the most backward States. While some level of intra-State and inter-State disparity is bound to exist even in the best possible situation, the effort of the planning process must be to enable backward regions to substantially overcome the disadvantages they labour under and to provide at least a certain minimum standard of services for their citizens.

INTER-STATE DISPARITIES AND THE ROLE OF THE CENTRE

7.1.10. Redressing regional imbalances has indeed been a vital objective of the planning process. However, despite the efforts made, regional disparities have continued to grow and the gaps have been accentuated as the benefits of economic growth have been largely confined to the better developed areas. Paradoxically, it is the natural resource-rich areas which continue to lag behind. This has in turn tightened the stranglehold of the Naxalite movement and demands for division of States in these areas. With the removal of controls and the opening up of the economy to external forces, the pressure of market forces may tend to exacerbate inter- and intra-State disparities. The role of the Centre in promoting equity among States and regions, therefore, has assumed added importance in the post liberalization era.

7.1.11. Redressing regional disparities is not only a goal in itself but is essential for maintaining the integrated social and economic fabric of the country without which the country may be faced with a situation of discontent , anarchy and breakdown of law and order.

7.1.12. There is probably no easy answer to the question of what really drives the growth process in the States. In the early years of planning, attempts were made to control a large part of the key drivers of growth and to make them fit into an overall consistency framework. This covered not only fiscal variables, but also other areas such as credit and financial markets, physical investments, locational decisions, and the like. However, this approach has now long since been given up for reasons that are not required to be discussed here. Over the past several years, the share of public investment in the overall investment made in the country has been steadily declining. In recent years, public investment has been a little over 20% in the aggregate. There is, therefore, a very great limitation on the influence that fiscal quantities, allocations and strategy can directly exert on growth rates, especially at the State level. States have, therefore, to focus on providing the necessary policy framework and supporting environment that makes economic activity possible and attractive enough for private sector investment. This would include the entire gamut of services provided by the State Governments, right from maintaining law and order, providing quick and effective dispute resolution through an efficient adjudication system, avoiding an extortionate and distortionary tax system to enabling and empowering the general mass of the population to take advantage of economic activity. Many of these factors are covered under the broad rubric of governance and have been discussed elsewhere in the Plan document. Here, we attempt to analyse the patterns of resource flows from the Centre to the States, and of government spending, in order to understand its implications for balanced development.

General Purpose Resource Transfers

7.1.13. In the system of division of powers between the Union and the States, the most productive sources of revenue have been assigned to the Union from the point of view of administrative convenience, uniformity and efficiency. At the same time, the major responsibility for the delivery of social services to the population has been vested with the States, and has now been devolved further downward to the PRIs. Given this situation, therefore, a very substantial responsibility falls on the Central Government to ensure that the overall flows of resources from the Centre to the States is such that the relatively backward States are enabled to achieve a level of service delivery at par with the more advanced States. This involves issues of the fiscal capacity available to States to raise revenues, the extent to which such capacity is actually being utilized and the specific difficulties that the States face which result in increased unit costs of service delivery.

7.1.14. Part of the Centre's responsibility in this regard is fulfilled through transfers under the Plan process. At the same time, an equally, if not more, significant volume of transfers takes place through the mechanism of the Finance Commissions. For a proper appreciation of the extent to which Central transfers help in mitigating inter-State disparities, it is necessary to look at transfers by the Finance Commissions also.

7.1.15. The TFC has used the following criteria and weights for transfers of Central taxes to the States. These have been applied uniformly across all States, both in the Special Category as well as others.

7.1.16. It is seen from Table 7.1.4 that the Income Distance criterion (which measures the extent to which the per capita income of a State is below that of the State with the highest per capita income) is given a weight of 50%. This has had the effect of making transfers of the share of Central taxes steeply progressive. The formula for inter se distribution of share of Central taxes is now generally more progressive than the formula used for the distribution of NCA among the States (Gadgil Mukherjee Formula). Under the NCA Gadgil Mukherjee Formula, the following criteria and weights are used.

7.1.17. The Gadgil Mukherjee formula applies only to States that are not in the Special Category. In the case of the Special Category States, 30% of the total NCA is

TABLE 7.1.4
Criteria and Weights

Criterion	Weight (%)
Population	25.0
Income Distance	50.0
Area	10.0
Tax Effort	7.5
Fiscal Discipline	7.5

Source: Report of the TFC.

TABLE 7.1.5
Criteria and Weights under Gadgil Mukherjee Formula

	Criterion	Weight (%)
1	Population (1971)	60
2	Per capita income	
	(i) For States with lower than National average	20
	(ii) For all States	5
3	Performance (Tax effort, fiscal management, national objectives)	7.5
4	Special Problems	7.5

Source: Planning Commission.

earmarked, and this amount has been apportioned among them in a constant ratio over the years.

7.1.18. Table 7.1.6 shows the share of each State as per the TFC in the share of Central taxes, share in NCA, the per capita income, and population share of a State in total population of the country. Since there is a difference in the manner in which NCA is provided to the Special Category States and the other States, these two groupings are taken separately.

7.1.19. While there could be different points of view about whether relative backwardness should be assigned as much weight as it has been under the TFC's award, or otherwise, it would also appear that there does not seem to be any reason any more for continuing with two different formulae for apportionment of share of Central taxes and NCA among the States. Elsewhere in the Plan, the need to do away with the distinction between Plan and non-Plan in expenditure has been emphasized. This would logically imply that the need for two different

TABLE 7.1.6
Inter-se Shares

S. No.	States	Per Capita GSDP 2004–05 (in Rupees)	Population (2001–census)	Share in NCA# (2007–08: BE)	Share % as per Twelfth Finance Commission
				Within Group (%)	
	Non-Special Category States				
1	Andhra Pradesh	26655	8.03	6.345	8.011
2	Bihar	7486	8.75	11.062	12.009
3	Chhattisgarh	20336	2.20	2.877	2.890
4	Goa	80392	0.14	0.495	0.282
5	Gujarat	34223	5.35	3.926	3.887
6	Haryana	35893	2.23	1.768	1.171
7	Jharkhand	19908	2.84	3.544	3.660
8	Karnataka	28774	5.57	4.417	4.856
9	Kerala	32818	3.36	3.259	2.902
10	Madhya Pradesh	16597	6.36	6.922	7.308
11	Maharashtra	37235	10.21	6.913	5.442
12	Orissa	18440	3.88	6.257	5.620
13	Punjab	36376	2.57	2.113	1.415
14	Rajasthan	18909	5.95	5.864	6.108
15	Tamil Nadu	31603	6.58	5.943	5.777
16	Uttar Pradesh	13842	17.52	19.481	20.978
17	West Bengal	23145	8.45	8.814	7.685
			(100.00)	(100.000)	(100.000)
	Special Category States				
1	Arunachal Pradesh	23326	1.75	7.928	3.525
2	Assam	18172	41.88	19.532	39.591
3	Himachal Pradesh	36785	9.55	9.656	6.388
4	Jammu and Kashmir	22430	15.92	19.148	15.873
5	Manipur	22457	3.34	5.840	4.430
6	Meghalaya	24978	3.66	4.849	4.540
7	Mizoram	27663	1.43	5.590	2.925
8	Nagaland	22021	3.18	5.908	3.219
9	Sikkim	28332	0.80	3.771	2.778
10	Tripura	26693	5.10	8.243	5.238
11	Uttaranchal (now Uttarakhand)	25276	13.38	9.535	11.492
			(100.00)	(100.000)	(100.000)

Note: # Calculated including a notional loan component.
Source: Planning Commission.

formulae for resource transfers would not exist any more. Two components of resource flows being distributed to the States on the basis of the same formula could continue. One portion, namely, the share of Central taxes, would be entirely untied; while the second could be earmarked for being spent on specific development sectors, with considerable flexibility to States about how exactly to spend the amounts. It needs to be remembered that, in fact, the significance of the NCA amount has got substantially reduced since 2005–06, the year from which the Central Government ceased to provide the loan component of NCA. This revised procedure would have the added advantage of providing for a fresh examination of the formula, criteria and weights by an impartial, professional body once every five years, unlike in the case of the Gadgil formula and its variants, where the process of adapting to change is very time consuming.

Transfers under Centrally Sponsored Schemes (CSSs) and Additional Central Assistance

7.1.20. Apart from the above, the Central Government also transfers substantial resources to the States in the form of CSS and ACA for State Plan schemes. These transfers have an in-built mechanism for progressiveness since they are directed at filling gaps in the provision of basic services in the most backward areas. The instruments being used by the Central Government to channellize funds into sectors and areas which need special attention include the Flagship Programmes, particularly Bharat Nirman, BRGF, and the NREGP.

7.1.21. Most of the schemes for rural development and poverty alleviation use poverty as a criterion for distribution of funds and therefore people and areas with low income benefit automatically. The NREGP is self targeting as it is expected that only the unemployed with no other source of income for that period would opt for a programme of wage employment. Also, NREGP provides an opportunity to States and districts to plan and execute programmes that provide employment and create rural assets that would support further economic activity. The availability of funds on demand distinguishes NREGP from other schemes. The SGSY is targeted at BPL families and has in-built safeguards for the weaker sections with 50% benefits reserved for SCs/STs.

7.1.22. Most of the flagship programmes also address backwardness in terms of the particular sector. Table 7.1.7 gives the State-wise allocation of funds under some of the major programmes in the budget estimates for 2007–08. The overwhelming shares of the relatively backward States clearly show that the flagship programmes are a major instrument to direct funds to areas which lack infrastructure.

7.1.23. Under the IAY, 75% weightage is given to housing shortage and 25% to poverty ratios. For district-level allocations, 75% weightage is given again to housing shortage and 25% to the SC/ST component of the population. In the Annual Plan 2007–08, Bihar has been allocated 26% of the total funds while Uttar Pradesh will get 12%.

7.1.24. Under the NRHM, 18 focus States which have weak public health indicators and/or weak infrastructure have been identified. These 18 States are Arunachal Pradesh, Assam, Bihar, Chhattisgarh, Himachal Pradesh, Jharkhand, Jammu and Kashmir, Manipur, Mizoram, Meghalaya, Madhya Pradesh, Nagaland, Orissa, Rajasthan, Sikkim, Tripura, Uttarakhand, and Uttar Pradesh. 30% of the funds in 2007–08 will flow to three States, namely, Uttar Pradesh (16%), Bihar, and Assam (7% each).

7.1.25. The SSA tackles backwardness in primary education through the formulation of district plans based on habitation level plans which are to be prepared on the basis of gaps in infrastructure for which norms have been laid down.

7.1.26. In the case of SSA, Uttar Pradesh alone receives nearly 17% of the allocation of the programme, while Bihar has been allocated 11%. In fact, seven States account for 64% of the total outlay.

7.1.27. The allocation under the PMGSY to the States is based on, inter-alia, a weightage of 75% for need (share of unconnected habitations in the total unconnected habitations of the country) and 25% on coverage (share of connected habitations in the total unconnected habitations in the country). Keeping the original inter-State allocations intact, the additional allocations on account of cess accruals are distributed to various States based on the target of road length to be connected under Bharat Nirman in each State. Madhya Pradesh, Chhattisgarh and Uttar Pradesh have been allocated one-third of the allocation under PMGSY in 2007–08.

TABLE 7.1.7
Allocation of Funds to States/UTs during 2007–08 under various Centrally Funded Schemes

(Rs in crore)

State	Population (2001)	PMGSY		NRHM		SSA		IAY		Supplementary Nutrition	
	% share	Allocation	%age	Allocation (Central Share)	%age	Allocation (Central Share)	%age	Allocation (Central Share)	%age	Allocation (Central Share)	%age
Andhra Pradesh	7.41	105.00	1.62	597.84	6.67	625.00	6.03	360.28	8.93	101.51	5.01
Arunachal Pradesh	0.11	77.00	1.18	43.39	0.48	57.04	0.55	13.95	0.35	5.32	0.26
Assam	2.59	456.00	7.02	642.28	7.16	498.34	4.81	308.54	7.65	76.71	3.78
Bihar	8.07	457.00	7.03	680.70	7.59	1154.46	11.13	1063.44	26.37	185.15	9.13
Chhattisgarh	2.03	690.00	10.62	225.23	2.51	390.25	3.76	55.71	1.38	59.02	2.91
Goa	0.13	5.00	0.08	13.38	0.15	10.18	0.10	2.22	0.05	1.54	0.08
Gujarat	4.93	65.00	1.00	380.58	4.24	190.97	1.84	176.69	4.38	58.69	2.89
Haryana	2.06	30.00	0.46	137.60	1.53	174.56	1.68	24.81	0.62	40.86	2.01
Himachal Pradesh	0.59	287.00	4.42	67.70	0.75	61.03	0.59	8.75	0.22	13.19	0.65
J & K	0.99	115.00	1.77	86.77	0.97	169.55	1.64	27.18	0.67	13.96	0.69
Jharkhand	2.62	225.00	3.46	262.92	2.93	668.99	6.45	94.85	2.35	59.58	2.94
Karnataka	5.14	110.00	1.69	395.95	4.41	348.62	3.36	138.80	3.44	108.63	5.36
Kerala	3.10	30.00	0.46	218.57	2.44	81.50	0.79	77.19	1.91	30.19	1.49
Madhya Pradesh	5.87	890.00	13.69	544.04	6.07	894.21	8.62	110.80	2.75	130.57	6.44
Maharashtra	9.42	145.00	2.23	671.14	7.48	509.11	4.91	217.27	5.39	145.29	7.17
Manipur	0.21	33.00	0.51	66.68	0.74	29.83	0.29	12.11	0.30	9.14	0.45
Meghalaya	0.23	45.00	0.69	62.27	0.69	43.77	0.42	21.09	0.52	8.02	0.39
Mizoram	0.09	52.00	0.80	36.70	0.41	22.03	0.21	4.50	0.11	4.89	0.24
Nagaland	0.19	30.00	0.46	56.19	0.63	29.67	0.29	13.96	0.35	11.69	0.58
Orissa	3.58	543.00	8.35	345.20	3.85	449.34	4.33	208.93	5.18	96.07	4.74
Punjab	2.37	35.00	0.54	161.97	1.81	111.32	1.07	30.68	0.76	36.02	1.78
Rajasthan	5.49	434.00	6.68	548.18	6.11	800.00	7.71	88.79	2.20	97.87	4.83
Sikkim	0.05	30.00	0.46	23.25	0.26	11.66	0.11	2.67	0.07	0.92	0.05
Tamil Nadu	6.07	90.00	1.38	433.16	4.83	345.50	3.33	144.25	3.58	36.59	1.80
Tripura	0.31	40.00	0.62	81.28	0.91	43.45	0.42	27.18	0.67	10.77	0.53
Uttar Pradesh	16.16	675.00	10.38	1459.42	16.27	1759.14	16.96	477.66	11.84	508.84	25.10
Uttarakhand	0.83	130.00	2.00	84.44	0.94	126.36	1.22	23.95	0.59	15.15	0.75
West Bengal	7.79	376.00	5.79	540.20	6.02	700.53	6.75	288.21	7.15	140.88	6.94
UTs	1.61	10.00	0.15	102.63	1.15	64.16	0.62	8.24	0.20	20.38	1.01
Others	–	290.00	4.46	0.00	0.00	0.00	0.00	0.00	0.00	0.00	0.00
Total	100.00	6500.00	100.00	8969.68	100.00	10370.57	100.00	4032.70	100.00	2027.44	100.00

Source: GoI Budget Estimates 2007–08.

BACKWARD REGIONS GRANT FUND (BRGF)

7.1.28. The development of backward regions has been a major concern of planners in India. However, prior to the Tenth Plan, the issue of development of backward areas was approached as primarily one of development of States through the formula for distribution of Central Assistance which was weighted in favour of less developed States and through Special Area Programmes such as Hill Area Development Programme, Border Area Development Programme, Drought Prone Area Programme, Tribal Sub-Plan, and so on. The emphasis was on backwardness in terms of economic performance, though the impact of historical and social factors in economic matters was also recognized. It was also observed that special development schemes should not be mere palliatives but the potential for growth present in most backward areas needs to be tapped if these schemes are to have an impact.

7.1.29. The Mid-Term Appraisal of the Ninth Plan showed that despite these efforts, one of the most serious problems facing the country was the wide disparity and regional imbalances between States, and within a State between districts. It was these pockets of high poverty, low growth and poor governance that were slowing down the growth and development of the country. In the Tenth Plan, it was decided to have a new approach to target these areas through a specific programme for Backward Areas, and the Rashtriya Sam Vikas Yojana (RSVY) was introduced in 2003–04.

7.1.30. The Rashtriya Sam Vikas Yojana covered 147 districts. Each district was to receive Rs 45 crore for schemes that would address the problems of low agricultural productivity, unemployment and fill critical gaps in infrastructure. Each district prepared a three-year Action Plan which showed the flow of funds from various schemes into the sector which was considered for additionality. An amount of Rs 4673 crore was released under RSVY during the Tenth Plan period. Thirty-three districts received the full allocation of Rs 45 crore during the Tenth Plan while others are in various stages of completion of the programme. Keeping in view the experience of the operation of the Programme in the first two years, it was decided that the process of implementation needed to be changed to provide a more participative and holistic approach and to involve PRIs. Thus, BRGF was initiated with two major changes, namely, the involvement of PRIs not only in the choice of schemes but also in their implementation and supervision, and the preparation of district plans which would ensure convergence and prevent duplication

7.1.31. The BRGF aims to help converge and add value to other programmes, like Bharat Nirman and NREGP, which are explicitly designed to meet rural infrastructural needs but which need supplementation to address critical gaps. It aims at catalysing development in backward areas by: (i) providing infrastructure; (ii) promoting good governance and agrarian reforms; (iii) converging, through supplementary infrastructure and capacity building, the substantial existing development inflows into these districts.

7.1.32. The Fund will accordingly provide financial resources for supplementing and converging existing development inflows into identified districts, so as to:

- Bridge critical gaps in local infrastructure and other development requirements that are not being adequately met through existing inflows;
- To this end strengthen Panchayat and Municipality level governance with more appropriate capacity building to facilitate participatory planning, decision making, implementation and monitoring and to reflect local felt needs;
- Provide professional support to local bodies for planning, implementation and monitoring their plans;
- Improve the performance and delivery of critical functions assigned to Panchayats, and counter possible efficiency and equity losses on account of inadequate local capacity.

7.1.33. A series of exercises have been undertaken to identify backward areas. Districts identified for coverage under RSVY used the criteria recommended by the 'Task Force on Identification of Districts for Wage and Self-Employment Programmes' (Planning Commission, 2003). The three criteria used were agricultural wage rate, value of output per agricultural worker and SC/ST population. However, the number of districts to be covered in a non-Special Category State was based on the proportion of poor in the State while in the case of Special Category States, population was the basis. The districts under BRGF include all the 200 districts covered under the first phase of NREGP which also used the same three criteria. Fifty districts (that were not covered under the list of 200 NREGP districts but were left out of the 170 districts identified by the Inter Ministry Task Group on Redressing Growing Regional Imbalances) were added to make a total of 250 districts for coverage under BRGF.

7.1.34. The BRGF will be anchored in a well conceived, participatory district plan by implementation of programmes selected through peoples' participation for which PRIs from the village up to the district level will be the authorities for planning and implementation. The dominant features include: (i) consolidation of sub-district plans by the District Planning Committees (DPC); (ii) convergence of all on-going Central Sector, Centrally Sponsored and State Plan Schemes operating at the sub district level; (iii) flexibility in the form of untied grants which may be used by Panchayats and Urban Local Bodies (ULBs) guided by transparent norms for filling critical gaps vital for development; (iv) capacity building grants for all stakeholders including professional support for preparation and consolidation of district plans; (v) empowerment of district-level local government institutions with adequate investments for social development such as education, health, food security, and so on; (vi) provision for specific social assistance programmes designed to deliver infrastructure and other financial support needed by them; (vii) concentration on pro-poor infrastructure with transparent norms for distribution of funds among various levels of rural and ULBs with focus on backward areas and disadvantaged people; and (viii) stress on development of assets and livelihood of the economically and socially weaker sections.

7.1.35. The scheme has two components, namely, (i) Districts Component covering 250 districts and (ii) Special Plans for Bihar and the Kalahandi–Bolangir–Koraput (KBK) districts of Orissa.

7.1.36. The Districts Component of BRGF covers 250 districts and has two funding windows, namely, (i) Capability Building Fund, and (ii) a substantially untied grant. The guidelines for BRGF already issued by the Ministry of Panchayati Raj in consultation with the Planning Commission contain detailed provisions for the processes of planning, capacity building, approvals and implementation of the district component.

7.1.37. In addition to the funding of the Districts Component of the programme, the Special Plans for Bihar and the KBK districts of Orissa, which were being funded under the erstwhile RSVY during the Tenth Plan, will also be funded under the BRGF during the Eleventh Five Year Plan.

7.1.38. The Special Plan for Bihar had been formulated, in consultation with the State Government of Bihar, to bring about improvement in sectors such as power, road connectivity, irrigation, forestry and watershed development. The prime emphasis has been laid on improvement of roads and power projects in the State under the Special Plan. An allocation of Rs 1000 crore per annum was being made for the Special Plan during the Tenth Five Year Plan period. The same allocation, that is, Rs 1000 crore per annum, will continue to be made during the Eleventh Five Year Plan period.

7.1.39. The KBK region comprises the undivided Kalahandi–Bolangir–Koraput districts situated in the southern and western parts of Orissa which have since been divided into eight districts, namely, Kalahandi, Nuapada, Bolangir, Sonepur, Koraput, Nabrangpur, Malkangiri, and Rayagada. A Revised Long-Term Action Plan was drawn up for these districts and the Planning Commission has been providing ACA to this region since 1998–99. To make the planning and implementation process more effective, the Central Government has been funding a Special Plan for these districts since 2002–03 using a project based approach and an innovative delivery and monitoring system. The Special Plan focus is on tackling the main problems of drought proofing, livelihood support, connectivity, health and education as per local priorities. In the Eleventh Plan, the total allocation for the KBK districts will be protected at Rs 250 crore per annum. These districts will be funded as per the BRGF district norms and the balance will be provided under the Special Plan.

7.1.40. It has been decided to provide Rs 5820 crore per annum during the Eleventh Five Year Plan for the two components, that is, the Districts Component and the Special Plans for Bihar and the KBK districts of Orissa. The total provision for BRGF during the Eleventh Five Year Plan would be Rs 29100 crore.

HILL AREA DEVELOPMENT PROGRAMME (HADP)/ WESTERN GHATS DEVELOPMENT PROGRAMME (WGDP)

7.1.41. The HADP/WGDP have been in operation since the Fifth Five Year Plan in designated hill areas. Under these programmes, SCA is given to designated hill areas in order to supplement the efforts of the State Governments in the development of these ecologically fragile areas.

7.1.42. Areas under HADP were identified in 1965 by a Committee of the NDC and areas to be covered by WGDP were recommended in 1972 by the HLC set up for the purpose. After the formation of Uttaranchal (now Uttarakhand) in 2001, the designated areas covered under HADP/WGDP include:

- Two hill districts of Assam—North Cachar and Karbi Anglong
- Major part of Darjeeling district of West Bengal
- Nilgiris district of Tamil Nadu
- 171 talukas of WGDP comprising the Western Ghats in Maharashtra (63 talukas), Karnataka (40 talukas), Kerala (32 talukas), Tamil Nadu (33 talukas), and Goa (3 talukas).

7.1.43. The main objectives of the programme have been eco-preservation and eco-restoration with emphasis on preservation of biodiversity and rejuvenation of the hill ecology. For the hill areas covered under HADP, the sub-plan approach has been adopted. The State Governments concerned prepare their total plan comprising of flow of funds from the State Plan, SCA made available under HADP and other sources. In the case of WGDP, the schematic approach was followed since the flow of funds from the State Plan to the taluka, which is the unit of demarcation, is difficult to quantify. Under WGDP, the States were advised to prepare their plans on watershed basis. Watershed-based development continued to be the basic thrust area of the programme. Allocation for the programme has remained almost static during the Tenth Plan period at Rs 160 crore. It was only during 2006–07 that the allocation was stepped up to Rs 250 crore.

7.1.44. Evaluation studies which have been carried out to assess the efficacy of these programmes have shown that while it is not possible to isolate the impact of the programme, the outcome of these programmes are visible in the form of increase in the level of the water table, preservation of forest area, increase in irrigated area, decrease in fallow land, increase in income, and so on.

7.1.45. The HADP and the WGDP will be continued in the Eleventh Plan with renewed vigour so that the natural resources of these fragile areas can be used in a sustainable manner based on environment-friendly technologies. These programmes need to be continued for the following reasons: first, most of the hill areas lack infrastructure facilities particularly roads, power, education and health facilities. Second, most of the hill areas lack political power and consequently adequate funding. Third, many of the programmes are not suitable to hill areas. For example, wages are often higher in the hill areas than the wages under wage employment programmes, and normally machines are required for earthwork as the rocky terrain is not suitable for manual labour. This also holds true for the norms set for some programmes as settlements are often small hamlets which do not qualify for coverage or are too expensive to cover. Hence, local solutions have to be found and encouraged.

7.1.46. The objectives would be two-fold—ecological balance and preservation as well as creation of sustainable livelihood opportunities.

7.1.47. Keeping in view the existing administrative and fund requirements of HADP areas, it could perhaps be more appropriate to have a different approach for HADP areas compared to WGDP areas. In the case of HADP areas, the district planning guidelines should be followed. District Plans should be prepared based on the vision for the district through a participative process starting from the grass roots level. This would involve articulation of a vision in each Planning unit right down to the village level. This vision would address the three basic aspects of development, namely, human development, infrastructure development and development of the productive sector. The Bill proposed to be introduced in Parliament to include the Darjeeling Gorkha Hill Council Area in the Sixth Schedule should be expeditiously considered.

7.1.48. In the case of the WGDP areas, the plan for these areas should be prepared as part of the district plan. While preparing the district plan, it should be ensured that WGDP areas receive priority and are brought at par with the best developed areas of the State. The ecological and biodiversity issues are to be dealt with on high priority. These areas should be given priority under other schemes, particularly the flagship schemes including Bharat Nirman, SSA, NRHM, and so on.

7.1.49. The State Governments need to allocate funds to the more fragile and backward pockets of the Western Ghats talukas. Keeping in view the increasing fragility of the hill areas, the allocation for the programme should be Rs 2500 crore for the Eleventh Plan.

BORDER AREA DEVELOPMENT PROGRAMME (BADP)

7.1.50. The BADP introduced during the Seventh Plan, aims at making special efforts for socio-economic development of the border areas and to promote a sense of security among the people living in these areas. The programme was revamped in the Eighth Plan and extended to the States adjoining the international border with Bangladesh and it was further extended during the Ninth Plan to the States which have borders with Myanmar, China, Bhutan, and Nepal.

7.1.51. The programme is a major intervention of the Central Government and is a part of the comprehensive approach to Border Management. The main aim has been to meet the special needs of people living in remote and inaccessible areas situated near international land borders.

7.1.52. On the basis of the report of the Task Force on BADP, it has been decided that the strategy for its implementation during the Eleventh Plan would be as follows:

- To accord high priority to the border areas (villages/blocks) in all the schemes of Bharat Nirman and other flagship programmes of the GoI and to saturate the border areas with full coverage of these schemes/programmes during the Eleventh Five Year Plan period, or earlier. To this end, appropriate modifications will be made in the relevant guidelines. The Planning Commission has comprehensively identified the border areas (villages/blocks/districts) and this data will be made available to all the ministries to facilitate early action.
- Ministries/Departments which do have programmes, schemes and projects focused on border areas, would initiate suitable programmes and activities.
- The Ministries of Power, Civil Aviation, IT, Telecom, Railways and Road Transport and Highways would prepare comprehensive proposals for infrastructure development in the border areas. These proposals, which would form part of the existing programmes and activities of the ministries, will then be collated with the overall infrastructure Plan for Border Areas. All incomplete large projects in border areas will receive priority for completion.
- Particular emphasis will be given to skill development and vocational education in the border areas. To this end, the Ministry of Labour and Employment and the Ministry of Human Resource Development would suitably re-orient their existing programmes, in consultation with the Planning Commission. Priority will be given to the border districts in the establishment of government sector polytechnics/ITIs/Skill Facilitation Centres.
- While modifying the guidelines, the relevant ministries will also revise the cost norms for border areas (villages/blocks/districts) and provide for necessary flexibility in order to accommodate accessibility issues.
- The Ministry of Finance will ensure by 31 March 2008 that all border blocks have at least one channel of Banking, be it a commercial bank, a cooperative institution or an RRB. The Ministry of Finance would also ensure that appropriate linkages with the overall plan for border development are developed in consultation with the National Bank for Agriculture and Rural Development (NABARD) and the Planning Commission.
- The planning process for the preparation of comprehensive perspective and annual plans for Gram Panchayats and Blocks on participatory basis should be significantly strengthened on the basis of guidelines issued by the Planning Commission and contained in the report of the Expert Group on the Planning at the Grassroot Level (Ministry of Panchayati Raj, 2006). These plans must show the convergence of the flow of funds for all ongoing Central and States programmes/schemes and identify the gaps in physical and social infrastructure and the livelihood options which should then be filled through funds available from BADP. Preparation of these plans and their use for all development activities, including BADP, should be insisted upon and arrangements for professional support and capacity development of PRIs, District Autonomous Councils, Traditional Village Bodies and DPC should be initiated.
- The Ministry of Home Affairs would augment the funds given to Para Military Forces guarding the border areas (namely, BSF, ITBP, Assam Rifles, and SSB) so that they too can undertake some civilian welfare activities in order to enhance their rapport with the civilian population in these areas.
- Since most of the border areas are remote and inaccessible, flexible financing through untied grants for attracting trained staff and participation of NGOs should be provided to strengthen the institutions and the personnel working in these areas.
- The Home Ministry would also undertake a special review of the infrastructure available at International Check Posts and Land Customs Stations. If required, additional funds would be earmarked under BADP for this purpose.

7.1.53. It is clear, therefore, that backward States and districts are being allocated a large proportion of the funds available under the flagship programmes. The effectiveness of these programmes will depend on the absorptive capacity of these States and regions. As administration in these areas tends to be weak and thin, this is an area which will require special attention. BRGF provides for strengthening of administrative machinery to deliver programmes more extensively. Similar provisions are also made in NREGP and other flagship programmes.

Local recruitment by PRIs can go a long way in ensuring attendance and availability of staff in remote areas. The State Governments also find it easier to invest in better developed areas as implementing agencies are available there. Backward areas also lack the voice and vote as they are often hilly, desert, forested, border or otherwise thinly populated areas. The other issue is the withdrawal of State Plan funds from these areas once Central funds become available. To circumvent this and ensure attention to these areas, district plans must be drawn up showing the availability of funds from all sources.

INTRA-STATE DISPARITIES AND DISTRICT PLANNING

Statistical Database

DISTRICT DOMESTIC PRODUCT (DDP) AND DISTRICT POVERTY ESTIMATES

7.1.54. That severe disparities exist between the districts and regions within States is well known, but statistics generated on the basis of a uniform methodology have yet to become easily available. Many States have been preparing estimates of the GDP of districts for quite some time now. However, these estimates are not comparable across States. It is only recently that the Central Statistical Organization (CSO) has come out with a uniform methodology for computation of DDP that will now be used throughout the country for these estimates. During the Eleventh Plan Period, therefore, the database for assessing the relative backwardness of districts would get substantially improved. Similarly, the poverty estimates prepared by the Planning Commission are available only at the State level and not for divisions below the State level. There are problems of sample size that do not permit the computation of poverty estimates at the district level at present. The Planning Commission has engaged the Indian Statistical Institute, Kolkata, to develop a methodology that will be capable of generating statistically valid estimates of poverty at district level from the existing NSSO sample data. Once this methodology is put in place, we should be able to obtain a better picture of the variation in poverty levels across districts within a State.

DISTRICT HEALTH PROFILE

7.1.55. During the Eleventh Plan period, it is proposed to start the preparation of District Health Profiles for all districts in the country based on an annual health survey undertaken through the Registrar General. The need for this has arisen because of the partial nature of coverage of the Civil Registration System.

STATE HUMAN DEVELOPMENT REPORTS (SHDR)

7.1.56. India today has the largest programme of any country in the world for the preparation of Human Development Reports (HDRs) at the sub-national (State and lower) level. As on date, 18 States have published State HDRs (SHDRs). Madhya Pradesh has already brought out three SHDRs, while Karnataka has published two. Several other States are also in the process of preparation of their second SHDR. Even with the problems at present regarding data, one of the major contributions of SHDR preparation has been the documenting and highlighting of inter se disparities among districts. The State HDRs have computed HDIs for each of the districts in the States. These reports are based on available summary indicators at the present time of the relative standing of districts on a development scale. The actual values of district HDIs are not comparable across the States because of differences in methodology, different data sources, the method of construction of indices, and so on. However, HDIs computed for districts within a State are comparable. The following table summarizes the range in HDIs among the districts within each State in comparison with the average for that State.

7.1.57. It is clear from Table 7.1.8 that in some States with high average level of development, there is a wide variation in the HDI of individual districts. For example, Maharashtra has calculated HDI of 1.00 for Mumbai city. However, considering this as an outlier, the next highest HDI in Maharashtra is 0.82 for Thane district. The lowest HDI for any district is only 0.210 (Gadchiroli). Even after removing the effect of the district with HDI of 1.0, the coefficient of variation for Maharashtra is 30.50% which remains the highest in the country. This shows the extent of intra-State disparity. On the contrary, all districts in Kerala lie between a range of 0.749 and 0.801, and with a coefficient of variation of only 2.37%, thereby denoting very limited intra-district disparity.

7.1.58. In States that have already published SHDRs, the emphasis now is on the preparation of District Human Development Reports (DHDRs), at least in a few selected districts to start with. As of date, DHDR preparation is

TABLE 7.1.8
Disparities in State HDI

S. No	State	No. of Districts in the State	State HDI	Highest HDI for a District in the State	Lowest HDI for a District in the State	Coefficient of Variation %
1.	Arunachal Pradesh	17	0.515	0.660	0.362	18.36
2.	Assam	23	0.407	0.650	0.214	27.99
3.	Chhattisgarh	16	0.471	0.625	0.264	21.16
4.	Gujarat	25	0.479	0.582	0.309	16.14
5.	Himachal Pradesh	12	0.433	0.534	0.390	11.14
6.	Karnataka	27	0.633	0.753	0.547	7.62
7.	Kerala	14	0.773	0.801	0.749	2.37*
8.	Madhya Pradesh	45	0.394	0.694	0.372	11.37
9.	Maharashtra	34	0.580	1.000	0.210	36.55
10.	Nagaland	8	0.620	0.733	0.450	15.89
11.	Orissa	30	0.404	0.736	0.389	16.94
12.	Punjab	17	0.537	0.761	0.633	4.93
13.	Rajasthan	32	0.424	0.656	0.456	8.88
14.	Sikkim	4	0.454	0.501	0.391	8.92
15.	Tamil Nadu	29	0.657	0.757	0.584	5.97
16.	Uttar Pradesh	70	0.532	0.710	0.366	11.59
17.	West Bengal	18	0.610	0.780	0.440	16.68

Source: SHDRs.

under way in over 45 districts all over the country. The process of preparation of DHDR is in itself as important as the final product. This is because the process is one of capacity building. Widespread participation among all the government departments dealing with Human Development, academic institutions, Civil Society organizations, NGOs, and so on, is the route adopted for preparation of DHDRs. This enables active dissemination of the findings and recommendations of SHDR on the one hand, and awareness building and sensitization among all key stake holders at the district and lower levels on the other. The process of preparation of DHDR is to be closely linked to the district planning process. During the Eleventh Plan period, all the districts in the country would need to be progressively covered. The DHDRs attempt to identify and quantify the status of Human Development in the administrative sub-divisions of the district. This process helps in assessing the development imbalance within the district and throws up possible solutions to these problems. Various districts have used innovative tools for this purpose, including extensive use of computerized (IT) NRDBMS. An advantage of the process of drilling down is that often, at the grass roots level, data problems are not as severe as at an intermediate aggregate level. In some States, a set of indicators that can be monitored at the Gram Panchayat level have been identified and efforts are on to vest the Gram Panchayats themselves with the responsibility of generating this information for their own use. One of the advantages of DHDRs has been stated to be the increased use of hard data in planning at the local level, and therefore of more rational decision making.

7.1.59. In the Eleventh Plan, the Planning Commission has issued detailed guidelines to the States reiterating the necessity of preparation of district plans through the DPC that are Constitutional bodies created for this purpose. In fact, in some of the new CSS and ACA Schemes, the preparation of the district plan has been insisted upon as a pre-requisite for accessing funds. Elsewhere in the Plan document, the details of these guidelines have been spelt out. This emphasis in the Planning process, it is hoped, will provide an institutional basis for the regular and systematic study of intra-State disparities as part of the Annual Plan and Five Year Plan processes.

INTERVENTIONS BY STATES

7.1.60. Simultaneously, many State Governments are also taking action to redress the problem of regional imbalances. In West Bengal, 4612 revenue villages have been identified for special attention. Female literacy and employment opportunity were used as variables to capture the extent of poverty. Thus villages in which over 60% of the population in the working age group are either non-workers or marginal workers and villages with female illiteracy over 70% have been identified for special attention. The services to be universalized in these villages are: (i) food security; (ii) social assistance; (iii) elementary education with emphasis on enrolment and retention of girl children; (iv) nutrition programmes; (v) employment generation; (vi) housing for the houseless; (vii) formation of SHGs and bank linkages to them; (viii) sustainable drinking water and strengthened public health services. As many of these villages are small hamlets hitherto excluded from proper connectivity and social infrastructure, they are to be given high priority now under all relevant schemes. The District Magistrates and other senior officials have been asked to visit these villages and ensure time-bound implementation of their activities. In addition to sensitizing the Panchayats at all levels about the priority to be given to these villages, all government departments have been instructed by the Chief Secretary to conduct special review of the implementation of their development programmes in these villages. The Government of West Bengal has been providing additional financial assistance since 2006–07 for meeting the critical gaps in these backward villages.

7.1.61. In Andhra Pradesh identified backward villages have been selected for saturation/universalization under eight schemes/activities under the 'Indiramma' Village Scheme. These schemes are: (i) Pension for all eligible old persons, persons with disability and widows; (ii) weaker section housing; (iii) sustainable drinking water; (iv) Power supply to every household; (v) sanitary latrines in every household; (vi) enrolment and drop out prevention in elementary education; (vii) Anganwadi with building and (viii) improvements in primary health with 100% immunization, 100% institutional delivery and 100% maternity benefit for eligible pregnant women.

7.1.62. The Government of Gujarat had set up a committee to study the backwardness of talukas in 2004. This Committee has now identified 30 talukas falling under least developed talukas in the State, based on 44 indicators. The Government of Gujarat has developed a strategy to raise the level of development of these talukas in a time-bound manner. The senior most officers of the rank of Secretary and above have been asked to voluntarily adopt one taluka each to prepare and implement development plans for these talukas in a time-bound programme.

7.1.63. Thus, it is seen that from a general area approach there is a move towards more vulnerable settlements. This approach of identifying settlements which need special attention will help to concentrate development efforts in laggard habitations which either because of their isolation or the social composition of their population, continue to depress the HDI and other development indicators of the district/State.

7.2 NORTH EASTERN REGION

7.2.1. The North Eastern Region (NER) of the country forms an area of low per capita income and major growth requirements. Growth in social infrastructure through national programmes must be complemented by development of physical and economic infrastructure. In this context, the development efforts of the States have to be supplemented in order to minimize certain distinct geo-physical and historical constraints.

BASIC FEATURES OF THE NORTH EASTERN REGION

7.2.2. The process of development had been slow in the NER for many reasons. Traditional system of self-governance and social customs of livelihood in NER remained virtually untouched during the British rule. The creation of a rail network for linking tea-growing areas for commercial interests was the only major economic activities taken up in the Region during this period. The partition of the country in 1947 further isolated the region. This has also disturbed the socio-economic equations in many parts of the Region resulting in the demand for autonomy by the relatively more backward areas. The late participation in planned development process by some of the North Eastern States (for example, Nagaland and Sikkim) has also deprived the region from the benefit of the strategies adopted for infrastructure improvement and creation of basic minimum services for some years after independence. While development efforts over the years have made some impact (as reflected in some of the HDIs which are comparable with the rest of the country), the region is deficit in physical infrastructure which has a multiplier effect on economic development. The basic development indicators of NER are provided in Annexure 7.2.1.

NER AS A SPECIAL CATEGORY FOR DEVELOPMENT EFFORTS

7.2.3. Recognizing the special requirements of the region and the need for significant levels of government investment, the North Eastern States have been categorized

TABLE 7.2.1
Central Assistance as Percentage of GSDP during the Tenth Plan

S. No.	Category	2002–03	2003–04	2004–05	2005–06	2006–07
1.	North Eastern States	9.07	9.18	10.67	10.55	10.60
2.	Special Category States	9.30	10.14	10.44	10.03	9.65
3.	Non-Special Category States	2.43	2.30	2.26	2.05	1.94
4.	All-India	2.83	2.75	2.72	2.49	2.35

as Special Category States and Central Plan assistance to these States is provided on liberal terms. For the Special Category States of NER, the per capita level of Central assistance is among the highest in the country. A statement indicating total Central assistance provided during Tenth Plan indicating per capita Central assistance is shown in Annexure 7.2.2(a). It may be observed that against the all-India average of Rs 683.94 the per capita Central assistance, in the NER was Rs 2574.98 in 2006–07. It may be observed that per capita Central assistance is the highest in the State of Sikkim. A statement indicating total Central assistance as a percentage of GSDP in the NE States, Special Category States and Non-Special Category States is given in Table 7.2.1.

7.2.4. It may be observed that Central Assistance as a percentage of GSDP of Special Category States had been considerably high as compared to Non-special Category States during the Tenth Plan period.

SPECIAL INITIATIVES (10% MANDATORY EARMARKING OF FUNDS FOR NER)

7.2.5. Special attention has been given to the economic development of the region from the Eighth Plan period onwards. In October 1996, the Central Government's announcement of 'New Initiatives for the North Eastern Region' included a number of measures for the development of the NER which covered policy changes, special area development and development projects in key sectors. In order to mobilize financial resources, a policy decision was taken to earmark at least 10% of the Plan Budget(s) of the Central ministries/departments for development of the North Eastern States.

NON-LAPSABLE CENTRAL POOL OF RESOURCES (NLCRP) AND SETTING UP OF MINISTRY OF DEVELOPMENT OF NORTH EASTERN REGION

7.2.6. The Non-Lapsable Central Pool of Resources (NLCPR) created in 1997–98 (operationalized in 1998–99) is the accrual of the unspent balance of the mandatory 10% budgetary allocation of the Ministries/Department. The broad objectives of the NLCPR Scheme is to ensure speedy development of infrastructure by way of filling the existing infrastructural gaps (economic and social) in the region by making funds available from the pool.

7.2.7. The Ministry of Development of North Eastern Region (DoNER) was set up in 2001 to coordinate and give impetus to the Centre's development efforts pertaining to socio-economic development of the region. NLCPR, which was initially handled by the Planning Commission, was transferred to DoNER after its creation. DoNER is responsible for coordination the planning, execution and monitoring of the developmental schemes and projects in NER; NEC; NEDFI; North Eastern Regional Agricultural Marketing Corporation Limited; NEHHDC, and so on. While DoNER is to coordinate with various Ministries/Departments primarily concerned with development and welfare activities in NER, the respective Ministries/Departments are responsible in respect of subjects allocated to them.

FLOW OF RESOURCES THROUGH SPECIAL INITIATIVES

7.2.8. A statement indicating year-wise expenditure by Central Ministries (other than exempted Ministries/Departments) in NER is given in Annexure 7.2.2(b). According to the assessment made by DoNER, the Central Ministries/Departments (except the exempted Ministries/Departments) invested Rs 35186.30 crore from 1998–99 to 2005–06 (2006–07 estimates are not available). The utilization of the 10% mandatory earmarked funds by the Central Ministries has gone up in recent years. An amount of Rs 10426.36 crore has accrued to NLCPR till the end March 2006. Out of this accrual, an amount of Rs 4660.46 crore has also been released to the States from NLCPR for specific projects. As on 31 May 2007, a total of 836 projects had been taken up (including four interstate/regional projects), out of which 389 projects have been completed.

Special Packages for NER

7.2.9. The Central Government has also been announcing special packages for socio-economic development of the NER from time to time. Priority funding (both in the Central plan and State Plan) are being arranged from time to time for expeditious implementation of these packages.

North Eastern Council (NEC)

7.2.10. The NEC was established under the NEC Act, 1971 to act as an advisory body in respect of socio-economic development and balanced development of the seven States of the NER. In 2002, Sikkim was included by an amendment and the Council has been designated the Regional Planning Body. The functions of NEC are to discuss matters of common interest in the field of economic and social planning of the region and advise the governments (Central and State) as to the action to be taken on such matters, formulate Regional Plans and recommend the manner in which the Regional Plan may be implemented. NEC is also to monitor the progress of project implementation and recommend to the Central Government the quantum of financial assistance to be given to the States. However, the absence of a well coordinated Regional Plan is being felt constantly.

7.2.11. Since its inception, NEC has invested Rs 7182.61 crore till the end of the Tenth Plan. Statement of sector-wise investment by NEC from 1973 to 2006–07 is given in Table 7.2.2.

TABLE 7.2.2
Sector-wise Investment by NEC from 1973 to 2006–07

Sectors	Rs crore
Agriculture and Allied Sectors	241.53
Water and Power	2586.27
Industry and Mining	110.36
Transport and Communication	3315.32
Manpower Development	393.15
Social and community services	472.85
General Services	48.07
Externally Aided Projects	15.06
Total	7182.61

7.2.12. The major investments had been in transport and communication followed by the water and power sector. Investments include construction of roads, upgradation/improvement of airports, survey and investigation of hydroelectric power projects, funding support for hydro and gas based power projects, transmission lines and transformation projects, and so on. Schemes taken up under the health sector are development of technical manpower (MBBS, postgraduate courses, para-medical and other specialists/super specialists' courses), improvement of health infrastructure/health centres, and so on. Important regional institutes funded by the NEC are the North East Police Academy (NEPA); Regional Institute of Medical Sciences (RIMS), Imphal; Regional Institute of Para-medical and Nursing (RIPAN), Aizawl; Regional College of Nursing, Guwahati; Regional Dental College (RDC), Guwahati; LGBRIMH, Tezpur; and Regional Institute of Pharmaceutical Science and Technology, Agartala. Based on the suggestion made by the Planning Commission, RIMS, Imphal; LGB Regional Institute of Mental Health (LGBRIMH), Tezpur; RIPAN, Aizawl; have been transferred to the Health Ministry and NEPA has been transferred to the Ministry of Home Affairs from the Annual Plan 2007–08.

7.2.13. Notwithstanding the volume of investments made by NEC, it is in the role definition and discharging of it that NEC requires a critical review. The function of NEC was to have been an effective regional planning body which will act as a bridge between the State's priorities and the regional perspectives and ensure well orchestrated investments of States and Central resources within a common regional perspective.

Total Flow of Plan Investment Resources in the Tenth Plan

7.2.14. As per the assessment made by DoNER, total Plan investment by the Centre and States of the NER had been approximately Rs 80000 crore during the Tenth Plan through various windows of funding (including Central assistance provided to the States under their plans) indicated above (Annexure 7.2.3). These include project-based assistance under the State Plan, NLCPR, NEC and the Central Ministries as well as CSSs.

7.2.15. It is often criticized that despite these huge investments the impact is not visible. Major projects in the transport and communication, irrigation and also in the power sectors are incomplete due to poor planning and execution. The need for a coordinated approach to investment is evident. Although it would be difficult to come to a definite conclusion on the impact of the investments made so far without any evaluation study, it is prudent to intensify closer monitoring and evaluation of outcomes from investment made as a self-improvement mechanism. It would be necessary to evaluate some of the programmes under DoNER (NEC, NLCPR).

7.2.16. The NEC's continued role as a Regional Planning Body is crucial for overall development of the region. Priorities for development, especially those which have a regional bearing, must not get diluted while selecting projects for sanction. The forward and backward linkages of developmental projects must be given due consideration. It is observed that major projects suffer immense time and cost overruns due to poor management and little accountability. NEC's role as a planning and coordinating body has to be considerably strengthened and its procedures streamlined, so that it may act as a mentor to the States in their quest to bring about greater inter-regional coordination. NLCPR funds are also sanctioned based on the priorities fixed by the States, at times without any regard to the regional thrust. DoNER's coordinating role for Central investments in the NER has become very effective in the Tenth Plan. It needs to be further strengthened. Some important decisions taken in this regard in the review meetings must be followed up. One of the important issue DoNER needs to stress is the monitoring of economic activity in terms of availability of credit.

Centrally Sponsored Schemes (CSS)

7.2.17. It is evident from the plan performance review that North Eastern States were unable to contribute the State's share as per the norms of various CSS due to fund constraints. As a result, North Eastern States are not availing of the programmes to the fullest extent. North Eastern States have been demanding an uniform funding pattern (90:10) for CSS for the NER. There is a need for a clear policy so that North Eastern States are able to take full advantage of all the CSS.

Financial Status of States

7.2.18. The States of the NER have a weak financial base and also limited scope to raise additional resources. While some States have made some efforts in controlling expenditure and have taken initiatives in fiscal reforms under the direction of the Ministry of Finance, other States in NER need to step up their efforts. Often, the full benefit which should be apparent from the total fund flow has been curtailed as the Central funds earmarked for development have been diverted towards meeting the non-plan revenue gap.

7.2.19. One of the critical developments having a major affect on the financial position of the States is the revision in the salaries of the State Government employees comparable to the Central pay pattern based on Fifth Central Pay Commission's recommendations. This has created a heavy burden, especially in the light of the States' inability to generate their own resources. Due to the sharp increase in the salary bill, States depend more on borrowing to finance their revenue expenditure.

7.2.20. Analysis of the States' plan resources during the Tenth Plan period shows that Sikkim, Nagaland, and Mizoram could achieve the projected SOR for the Tenth Plan. However, there had been deterioration in States Own Resources (SOR) of the remaining States. Additional Resource Mobilization (ARM) had been negligible in the North Eastern States. Funding of the Plan had mainly been through Central Assistance during the period.

Financial Institutions and Credit Availability

7.2.21. Availability of credit is one of the critical weaknesses in the development of economic activity. Various indicators for NER show that despite improvement in banking facilities the last five years, the level of financial outreach is low. Credit to Net State Domestic Product (NSDP) ratio of all the States ranging from nine in Nagaland to 41 in Meghalaya, is lower than the national average of 62. The ratio of current and savings accounts of scheduled commercial banks per 100 adult population as on 31 March 2005, ranged from 19.5 in Manipur to 40.9 in Meghalaya, with a regional average of 37.3, distinctly lower than the national average of 59.3 (Table 7.2.3).

7.2.22. The main impediments for banking and financial development are topography of the region, sparse population settlements, infrastructural bottlenecks, smaller size of the market, lack of entrepreneurship, law and order conditions in some parts of NER, land tenure system especially in hilly areas, development strategy based on grants rather than loans, low network of branches, lack of simple, customized and flexible financial products to suit the needs of the local population, poor loan recovery experience, lack of awareness of banking services and inadequate payment systems.

TABLE 7.2.3
Indicators of Banking Development in the North East

S. No.	States	APPBO		CD Ratio		Current and Savings Accounts per 100 adult		Credit Accounts per 100 Adult population		Per Capita Deposit (in Rs) Population		Per Capita Credit (in Rs)		Credit to NSDP Ratio
		2001	2005	2001	2005	2001	2005	2001	2005	2001	2005	2001	2005	Latest NSDP data
1	Arunachal Pradesh	15813	16211	15	22	45.9	37.8	6.8	6.2	5629	10869	786	2287	1
2	Assam	21008	20960	32	35	39.4	39.1	4.5	5.9	3701	6669	1155	2261	26
3	Manipur	28436	29791	40	42	20.1	19.5	3.2	4.0	1808	4289	717	1713	11
4	Meghalaya	12741	12658	17	44	44.3	40.9	6.9	8.3	7139	13087	1138	5281	41
5	Mizoram	11279	11278	24	48	25.8	29.0	5.4	7.7	4441	8741	1030	4028	NA
6	Nagaland	28009	27990	12	23	22.3	19.7	2.6	3.6	4513	6425	518	1356	9
7	Tripura	17438	17429	22	29	37.0	36.7	12.3	13.6	4905	8200	1015	2240	18
	NE Region	19894	19885	28	35	38.2	37.3	5.4	6.7	4003	7199	1068	2407	NA
	All India	15209	14949	57	66	55.0	59.3	9.7	13.3	9245	16700	4976	10474	62

Source: Report of the Committee on Financial Sector Plan for NER.

7.2.23. The penetration of banking in NER, particularly in the rural areas, has been very low. Though the annual growth rate of deposit for NER was more or less aligned with the national average, there is a wide variation among individual States. The CD ratio of NER as a whole, as also the individual States, was far below the national average, which is a matter of concern. The sectoral share of total credit shows significant divergence from the national pattern. The trend clearly shows the low level of commercialization of agriculture and low level of industrialization in NER. Poor recovery of loans, especially those under government-sponsored schemes, and default by borrowers act as a deterrent for granting fresh loans. Micro credit linkages of the banks with SHGs leave much scope for improvement. There is a need to upscale the operations through SHGs, especially for providing working capital and investment credit.

7.2.24. The land tenure system prevalent in most States of the region (except non-scheduled areas) restricting alienation of land from a tribal to a non-tribal, together with absence of personal ownership rights and commensurate land records, makes it difficult for the banks to lend in the region. Important suggestions have been given by committees set up for looking into the issues of credit supply in NER. Suggestions have been made for using social capital as alternative collateral and also devising an alternative to land documents for extending small credits. There are also other important suggestions for expanding credit supply for economic activity which need to be looked in to.

Task Force on Connectivity on Promotion of Trade and Investment in NER

7.2.25. The Planning Commission constituted a Task Force on Connectivity and Promotion of Trade and Investment in NER. The main recommendations of the Task Force are completion of modified Phase A of SARDP-NE, to take the Trans Arunachal Highway on priority; road links in Manipur; completion SARDP-NE Phase B selectively based on resources availability in the Eleventh Plan; construction of a bridge at Sadia-Dholaghat over the Brahmaputra River; completion of ongoing railway projects; priority funding for identified projects; construction of three greenfield airports at Pakyong in Sikkim, Itanagar in Arunachal Pradesh and Cheithu in Kohima; modernization of airports of NER and harnessing of the maximum potential of inland water as a mode of transport. Endeavour is on to look for possible funding arrangements for the priority projects during the Eleventh Plan.

Sectoral Summits

7.2.26. The North Eastern Council has been reviewing sectoral programmes of the respective ministries with regard to NER and has also suggested appropriate steps for expeditious implementation of important projects/programmes. Important suggestions have come out of these sectoral summits on Power, Health, Tourism and Hospitality, Roads, Irrigation and Flood Control and Education and Sports held during 2007.

7.2.27. NER has hydro-power potential of 63257 MW (42.54%), including Sikkim, against the all-India potential of 148701 MW. Arunachal Pradesh alone has the potential of 50328 MW which is 80% of the total hydro-power potential of the NER and 34% of the total potential of the country. Despite recognizing this potential, the desired thrust is not there as hydro power development requires huge investments. The sectoral summit on power suggested a two-pronged strategy for power generation with focus on small/localized hydel and thermal and NER power projects for local needs and high capacity hydel and thermal power projects with associated transmission lines for meeting the demands of the region and also supply to the rest of the country. Transmission, sub-transmission and distribution system improvements have been identified as one to the thrust areas for the Eleventh Plan. The summit also suggested preparation of a master plan for power development for NER, including an appropriate funding mechanism relevant to the Region.

Forest Resources and NER

7.2.28. The forests of NER face unrelenting pressures from increasing population and development resulting in degradation and deforestation. Over-exploitation due to the shortening cycle of shifting cultivation is assumed to be the core driver of this forest degradation and depletion, affecting the biodiversity of the region.

7.2.29. Forest cover statistics of NER reveals some contradictory trends. One set of data (forest survey) showed a steady reduction in forest cover at an annual rate of 0.15% during 1991–2001. However, State-level data provides a clear indication of increase in forest cover in almost all the States in 1997–2001. There is a popular perception that the biological potential for carbon finance in the forest sector of the NER is substantial. Afforestation and reforestation are being suggested for increasing forest cover in NER. However, this needs huge investment, which the States are unable to meet from their own resources. There is need for incentives to the States for increase in forest cover.

Natural Disasters and the NER

7.2.30. The NER is regularly struck by natural disasters in the form of floods and landslides, though other extreme events causing disaster are rare except the disastrous earthquake of 1950. Damages caused by the menace of floods, which assume an alarming proportion, especially in the Brahamputra and Barak Valleys of Assam, exert considerable strain on the economy not only of Assam but also other North Eastern States. Other than temporary measures like construction of embankments, long-term measures for construction of multi-purpose storage dams for moderating the effect of floods are lacking. Floods causing disruption in communication network and loss to human life and property have become almost an annual feature in Assam, Tripura, Arunachal Pradesh and other plains areas of North Eastern States. Considering the regular periodicity and gravity of such disasters, appropriate measures need to be adopted and continually refined for management and mitigation of the consequences.

Primary Sector Development

7.2.31. The pattern of agricultural growth has been uneven across the region. The NER is a category of its own kind. The Region, which is about 8% of the country's total geographical area, produces a very meagre proportion of food grains (1.5%). The enormous potential of the region in agriculture, horticulture, animal husbandry and fisheries is contrasted by the low levels of productivity in the region, which are generally below the national average.

7.2.32. To attain sustainable development of agriculture in the Region, the availability of the critical inputs like irrigation facilities, including field drainage to prevent water logging, fertilizers, high-yielding variety (HYV) seeds and institutional credit would have to be ensured. Large irrigation schemes may take their time. Modest but useful unexploited potential for groundwater, river lift and small diversions offer significant immediate possibilities by promoting the use of cost-effective means of irrigation. Agricultural growth can be stepped up by taking measures to improve cropping intensity. The problem of agricultural credit can be overcome by revitalizing the cooperative credit structure and availing of NABARD credit.

7.2.33. Taking into account the connectivity problem and the perishable nature of the primary produce, in the short run, greater emphasis needs to be given to food processing industries. Cultivation of vegetables, fruits and spices, and commercialization of agriculture needs to be encouraged by investing in marketing and storage facilities. Institutional reforms are needed to ensure equitable distribution of benefits from groundwater resources. The emphasis should be agricultural strategy and programmes for income enhancement of the farmer through provision of multiple livelihood opportunities.

Approach and Strategies for the Eleventh Five Year Plan (2007–12)

7.2.34. The NER, though rich in development potential in terms of human capital and natural resources, lacks in adequate physical infrastructure which is impeding its growth. While considerable progress has been made over the years, certain crucial gaps remain. The primary sector has remained largely stagnant; the secondary sector has been handicapped due to a variety of reasons. The planning exercise has resulted mainly in the expansion of the tertiary sector. Lack of employment opportunities, especially among the educated youth, gets reflected in social disturbances, further slowing down the developmental process.

7.2.35. The Approach document for the Eleventh Plan emphasizes inclusive growth as its aim. To this end, it is the collective endeavour of the Central and State Governments to formulate appropriate policies during the Eleventh Five Year Plan for NER. As stated earlier, significant levels of government investment had been made during the Tenth Plan. Both NEC and DoNER were strengthened. The mandatory earmarking of minimum 10% of Central ministries' budget as also setting up of NLCPR have accelerated the pace of development. These steps need to be continued during the Eleventh Five Year

Plan with strategy strengthening particularly in the area of regional planning.

7.2.36. The NEC has to convert itself into an effective planning body. The long awaited Vision 2020 document needs to be finalized at the earliest. The thrust of NEC has to be the preparation of a perspective plan for each of the major/critical sectors in consultation with the States and ensure that the forward and backward linkages are accorded priority as well as pledging of funds by the State Governments annually.

7.2.37. The Approach to the Eleventh Plan document has emphasized connectivity as the key area for the development of NER. The Eleventh Plan would have a special thrust on transport infrastructure under the identified programmes and areas identified by the Task Force which would necessitate a concerted and multi-pronged action, including resource mobilization, which may also comprise of VGF. Various road development programmes, including SARDP-NE would be taken up at an accelerated pace. High priority would be accorded for converting the Meter Gauge (MG) network to Broad Gauge (BG) in the region during the Eleventh Five Year Plan period. Efforts will be made to provide rail link to all State capitals of the NER. Construction of three greenfield airports at Pakyong in Sikkim, Itanagar in Arunachal Pradesh and Cheithu in Kohima would be taken up on priority. Important airports in the NER are proposed to be modernized. In order to harness the potential of inland water as a mode of transport, and the River Brahmaputra National Waterway 2, which provides trunk route connectivity to the Region, will be made fully functional.

7.2.38. 98% of the borders of the States of NER (excluding Sikkim) are with other countries—Bhutan and China in the north, Myanmar in the east, and Bangladesh in the south and west. Economic ties with the neighbouring countries have special significance for the States of the NER due to the long, common border with neighbouring countries and proximity to South-east Asian countries. There is wide scope of generating economic activity through interaction with these countries. A transit route through these countries could also provide larger integration of several States and bring considerable mutual economic advantage. The Look East Policy, hence, is important for bringing these areas out of isolation and gradually developing an economic identity and moving on a higher growth path. Land Customs Stations, which are the gateways for the transit of goods, services and people between neighbouring countries, need upgradation of infrastructure facilities. There are twelve Land Customs Stations in NER, which need to be strengthened on priority basis.

7.2.39. Agriculture, horticulture and related activities can be the engines of economic growth and should be the focus of development planning of the States as well as the Centre. For sustainable development of agriculture during the Eleventh Plan, the thrust would be to ensure availability of the critical inputs (irrigation, facilities of drainage, fertilizers, HYV seeds and institutional credit). Implementation of a region-specific strategy depends critically upon State-level agencies. The Central Government will provide them both technical and financial support.

7.2.40. Horticulture, including floriculture, is assuming great significance in NER. Apart from more predictable shortages of planting materials, marketing infrastructure is the weakest link in the value chain. The approach will be to substantially step up efforts in 'field to road' connectivity and also to strengthen the transportation network through dedicated road/rail/air cargo routes. There is need for greater research and training inputs for converting the horticulture produce to low volume, high value products having long shelf life. During the Eleventh Plan, the 'Technology Mission for Integrated Development of Horticulture' should address these issues. To realize the full potential of horticulture, all four stages between the producer and the consumer—production, procurement/transportation, processing and marketing/distribution—would be strengthened.

7.2.41. There is need for conscious effort in banking and financial sector development to ensure unhindered credit flow for supplementing the developmental efforts of the governments in NER. Periodic meetings between industry associations and banks would be of help in understanding the associated problems related to industries in the region. A dialogue with banking and financial institutions is necessary in order to review their existing norms and procedures and adapt suitably to respond to the special

Box 7.2.1
Critical Parameters for Growth of the North Eastern Region

- Two-pronged growth strategy: creation of critical infrastructure and creation of employment opportunities.
- Improvement in the security, law and order and governance.
- Capacity building of implementing machinery (government functionary); technical assistance programmes for capacity building.
- Thrust on major sectors of connectivity (road, rail, air, inland waterways, telecommunication) and power with major step-up in investment in these sectors.
- Thrust on major social infrastructure: Health, Education (upgradation of quality) and Tourism, clearly identifying gaps therein, and Skill Development.
- Emphasis on the primary sector of the economy to substantially step up productivity in food grains within a period of five years. Emphasis on agriculture extension services, irrigation.
- Farm-based economic activities: Horticulture, Animal Husbandry, Fisheries, Poultry, and so on.
- Post-harvest management and marketing infrastructure.
- Synergy and dovetailing of programmes/schemes between Central ministries and the State Governments for filling up gaps in infrastructure.
- Building capacity and bringing professionalism in NEC as a Regional Planning Body.
- Active involvement of Autonomous District Councils, Panchayati Raj and local Self Government institutions, communities and Self-Help Groups in various development welfare schemes.
- Making the region an attractive destination for private sector investment and PPP.
- State-specific approach for the creation of opportunities for employment generation.
- Development of the region linked to the Look East policy of the government and development of relationship with neighboring countries of the entire region.
- Development of LCS to make international trade attractive through the North East.
- Systematic approach to infrastructure development (road/rail/power/IWT/airports) in the Region. Resources requirement for development is huge. Many of these roads or airports cannot be justified on the basis of economic viability, but these are vital for opening up the region and better integration.
- Maintenance of roads is an important aspect and needs a separate financial arrangement.
- Setting up of an interdisciplinary body for overseeing the planning and timely execution of communication projects undertaken including, inter alia, the absorption capabilities and their augmentation.

land laws and other features prevailing in the NER with a view to augmenting the flow of credit to the Region during the Eleventh Plan.

7.2.42. There is an urgent need for intensive, effective, focused and time-bound drive for capacity building of State machinery wherever States feel that the existing capacity is inadequate. There is need to revisit the 'Capacity Building' scheme of DoNER. One critical area that requires immediate re-look is the States' capacity to mobilize their own resources. The desired Plan size will depend considerably upon the ability to mobilize resources. There is realization that it is through effective control on non-plan expenditure and generation of resources in all possible areas that sustainable growth is feasible. Capacity building of personnel in this area would have to be upgraded.

7.2.43. The development of human resources needs to be taken up on the highest priority. Upgrading of skills of the workforce, as are relevant to the area, need to be emphasized. Redesigning of the educational map for quality education in the NER should be a priority concern. A holistic planning of education and vocational skills are essential to provide enough opportunities for gainful employment to the youth of the Region. This would form an interfaced core point of the Plan.

7.2.44. Health and education requires an expanded role for the States of NER for achieving the 'monitorable targets' of the Eleventh Plan. Access to essential public services such as health, education, clean drinking water and sanitation calls for strong State intervention to ensure delivery of these services. The NRHM has been launched in order to improve the access and availability of quality health care and nutrition. However, due to the difficult terrain conditions, access to these basic services remains a concern for all. During the Eleventh Plan, the delivery mechanism will be strengthened and schematic flexibility of content as well as operationalization, and partnership with private/non-governmental organizations working in the area will be promoted.

7.2.45. Several areas of the region are sparsely inhabited or have special requirements (for example, the islands in the Brahamputra river) where development programmes, particularly basic services, like education and health have to be provided. State governments would be supported in all the schemes which aim at these.

7.2.46. While the above-mentioned issues are critical to the growth of the region, effective implementation and monitoring of the above programmes holds the key to any quantum jump in the growth of the region.

ANNEXURE 7.2.1
Socio-economic Indicator of North East and India

S. No.	Indicators	Name of the States								
		Arunachal	Assam	Manipur	Mizoram	Meghalaya	Nagaland	Sikkim	Tripura	All India
I.	General									
1.	Area(Sq. Km)—2001	83743.00	78438.00	22327.00	21081.00	22429.00	16579.00	7096.00	10486.00	3166414
2.	No. of Districts—2001	13	23	9	8	7	8	4	4	593
3.	No. of Blocks—2001	54	214	34	30	39	52	8	38	5550
4.	No. of Towns and Cities—2001	17	125	33	22	16	9	9	23	5161
5.	No. of Villages—2001	4065.00	26312.00	2391.00	817.00	6026.00	1317.00	452.00	870.00	638588
II.	Demography									
6.	Total population-2001	1091117	26638407	2388643	891058	2306069	1988636	540493	3191168	1027015247
	(i) Rural Poulation	868429	23248994	1818224	450018	1853457	1635815	480488	2648074	741660293
	(ii) Urban Population	222688	3389413	570410	441040	452612	352821	60005.00	543094	285354954
7.	Sex Ratio(female per 1000 male)	893	935	978	935	972	900	875	948	933
8.	SC/ST polulation									
	(i) SC	6188.00	1825949	60037.00	272.00	11139.00		27165.00	555724	1666635700
	(ii) ST	705158	3308570	741141	839310	1992862	1774026	111405	993426	84326240
9.	Population density(per sqkm)	13.11	339.83	97.05	42.15	103.38	236.37	76.22	305.07	324.85
10.	BPL (1999–2000)	33.47	36.09	28.54	33.87	19.47	32.67	36.55	34.44	26.02
	(i) Rural	40.04	40.04	40.04	40.04	40.04	40.04	40.04	40.04	27.01
	(ii) Urban	7.47	7.47	7.47	7.47	7.47	7.47	7.47	7.47	23.62
III.	Health									
11.	Crude Birth/Death rate									
	(i) Birth Rate	23.3	25.0	14.7	18.8	25.1	16.4	19.9	16.0	23.0
	(ii) Death Rate	5.0	8.7	4.1	5.1	7.5	3.8	5.1	5.7	7.6
12.	TFR	NA	2.9	NA	NA	NA	NA	NA	NA	NA
13.	IMR	37	68	13	20	49	18	30	31	58
14.	MMR	NA	301	NA	NA	NA	NA	NA	NA	301

(Annexure 7.2.1 contd.)

(Annexure 7.2.1 contd.)

		Name of the States								
S. No.	Indicators	Arunachal	Assam	Manipur	Mizoram	Meghalaya	Nagaland	Sikkim	Tripura	All India
IV.	Education									
15.	Literacy Rate(Total)	54.3	63.3	70.5	88.8	62.6	66.6	68.8	73.2	64.8
	(a) Male	63.8	71.3	80.3	90.7	65.4	71.2	76.0	81.0	75.3
	(b) Female	43.5	54.6	60.5	86.7	59.6	61.5	60.4	64.9	53.7
16.	Gross enrolment ratio (class I-VIII) 6–14 years-2001–02	98.82	99.54	91.65	105.21	94.26	89.72	97.72	89.83	82.35
17.	Drop out ratio (1–VIII)-2001–02	60.02	69.21	37.75	59.89	76.99	53.36	63.41	69.02	54.65
V.	Other Eco. Indicators									
18.	No. of Districts with access to Safe Drinking Water(2001)	13	23	9	8	7	8	4	4	593
	(a) 100% access	0	1	2	0	1	5	0	0	
	(b) 90% access	0	5	3	0	0	2	0	1	
	(c) 80% access	10	7	2	0	2	1	3	1	
	(d) less than 20%	3	10	1.00	0	4	0	0	2	
19.	Rail Density as on 31.03.2003 (Route Kms/1000 sq. Kms)	0.02	32.09	0.06	0.07		0.78		6.14	19.22
20.	Road per 100 Sq. Kms of area(Kms.)	21.80	109.04	51.20	23.00	40.70	122.70	26.10	148.40	76.80
21.	CDR (schedued Bank) March, 2002									
	(a) As per sanction	15.80	31.70	26.40	26.40	18.30	12.80	16.00	21.50	58.40
	(b) As per Utilisation	27.40	70.30	27.30	36.20	24.30	18.10	22.50	21.60	58.40

Note: Literacy Rate—percentage of literate to total population aged seven years. Per capita investment ratio is total investment (Public and Private divided by population 2001 Census).
Source: Census Website India—Demographic figures; Ministry of Health and Family Welfare—Health Sector.

ANNEXURE 7.2.2

(a) Central Assistance for State Plans during the Tenth Plan (2002–07)

(Rs crore)

S. No.	States	2002–03	Per Capita CA	2003–04	Per Capita CA	2004–05	Per Capita CA	2005–06	Per Capita CA	2006–07	Per Capita CA	Population
1.	Arunachal Pradesh	653.16	5937.82	695.49	6322.64	802.49	7295.35	859.31	7811.91	939.50	8540.91	0.11
2.	Assam	1962.99	737.97	2043.48	768.23	2720.99	1022.93	2907.45	1093.03	3008.02	1130.83	2.66
3.	Manipur	609.72	2540.50	668.79	2786.63	874.39	3643.28	1080.70	4502.92	1216.46	5068.58	0.24
4.	Meghalaya	452.59	1967.78	492.24	2140.17	611.36	2658.10	656.23	2853.17	695.78	3025.13	0.2
5.	Mizoram	471.24	5236.00	555.42	6171.33	675.72	7508.04	705.00	7833.33	717.25	7969.44	0.09
6.	Nagaland	497.36	2486.80	546.34	2731.70	662.06	3310.28	642.64	3213.20	721.97	3609.85	0.20
7.	Sikkim	320.02	6400.40	362.42	7248.40	437.19	8743.88	399.49	7989.80	464.92	9298.40	0.05
8.	Tripura	683.61	2142.31	754.93	2365.81	876.17	2745.76	860.98	2698.15	976.22	3059.29	0.32
9.	Total Northeast (1 To 8)	5650.69	1449.23	6119.11	1569.36	7660.38	1964.65	8111.80	2080.43	8740.12	2241.57	3.90
10.	Spcl. Cat. States	10349.82	1625.01	12294.28	1930.30	13880.23	2179.31	14559.74	2286.00	15310.33	2403.85	6.37
11.	Non-spcl. Cat. States	43829.92	455.75	46568.41	484.23	50343.89	523.49	51455.24	535.04	54820.41	570.04	96.17
12.	Grand Total (10+11)	54179.74	528.38	58862.69	574.05	64224.13	626.34	66014.98	643.80	70130.74	683.94	102.54

(b) Central Assistance to NE States, including NLCPR and NEC and per capita Assistance (eight States taken together)

(in Rs Crore)

	NLCPR	NEC	Central Assistance	Total	Per Capita Assistance
2002–03	550.00	450.00	5650.69	6650.69	1705.70
2003–04	550.00	500.00	6119.11	7169.11	1838.66
2004–05	650.00	500.00	7660.38	8810.38	2259.59
2005–06	679.17	461.5	8111.80	9252.47	2372.98
2006–07	700.00	600.00	8740.12	10040.12	2574.98

ANNEXURE 7.2.3
Year-wise Expenditure by Central Ministries in NER

Year	GBS	Expenditure in NER	%
	(In Rs Crore)		
1998–1999	32113.10	2128.28	6.63
1999–2000	3651.46	2228.57	6.25
2000–2001	42478.54	2920.49	6.88
2001–2002	52186.12	3802.93	7.29
2002–2003	*55297.08	5139.59	9.29
2003–2004	*58356.18	5237.31	8.97
2004–2005	*63030.75	6403.74	10.16
2005–2006	*87061.62	7325.39	8.41
2006–2007	*11279.57		

Note: *Excluding Externally Aided Projects (EAP)

ANNEXURE 7.2.4
Investment in NER during the Tenth Five Year Plan

Rs crore

Source of funding	2002–03 RE	2003–04 RE	2004–05 RE	2005–06 BE	2006–07 BE	Total
State Plan	5367	5702	6833	8274.00	9685.00	35861.00
Central Ministries/ Central Sector/CSS	5460	6776	6787	9150.14	11268.14	39441.28
NEC	450	500	500	461.50	600	2511.50
NLCPR	550	550	650	679.17	700	3129.17
Total	11827	13528	14770	18564.81	22253.14	80942.95

8

Innovation and Technology

INTRODUCTION

8.1. Since Independence, India has endeavoured to bring economic and social change through science and technology. The effort has been both on upgrading the traditional skills to make them relevant and competitive and developing advanced capabilities in frontier areas of science and technology. The visionaries who led the growth of science and technology (S&T) in India were convinced that S&T could play an important role in transforming India in to a modern, industrialized society. Experience and results show that this confidence was well placed. Science, technology, and innovation are even more relevant today. Scientific knowledge and expertise, innovation, high technology, industrial infrastructure and skilled workforce are the currencies of this new era.

8.2. The investments made in Research and Development (R&D) by the developed countries reveals that the comparative strength of India in knowledge sectors would be seriously disadvantaged in competition to other nations with similar or even smaller sizes of economy relative to India if adequate investments are not made in this domain. As per R&D statistics for 2004–05, India invests around 0.8% of GNP in R&D compared to more than 2% by the developed countries. India currently ranks 13th among the top 38 countries in terms of number of publications in SCI journals; China ranks ninth. On the other hand, India ranks second after China, among the top 23 developing countries. However, the productivity of Indian science as a measure of dollars spent per publication in Science Citation Index (SCI) journals is comparable with other countries.

ELEVENTH PLAN POLICY AND APPROACH

8.3. While India's economic growth in the recent years has been impressive, many challenges remain to be met to create a strong and vibrant innovation eco-system, which is the need of the day. This requires (i) an education system which nurtures creativity; (ii) an R&D culture and value system which supports both basic and applied research and technology development; (iii) an industry culture which is keen to interact with the academia; (iv) a bureaucracy which is supportive; (v) a policy framework which encourages young people to enter into scientific careers and (vi) an ability to scan scientific developments in the world and use technology foresight to select critical technologies in a national perspective. It is with this conviction that the Eleventh Five Year Plan approach to S&T has emphasized the following:

- Setting up a national-level mechanism for evolving policies and providing direction to basic research;
- Enlarging the pool of scientific manpower and strengthening the S&T infrastructure and attracting and retaining young people to careers in science;
- Implementing selected National Flagship Programmes which have direct bearing on the technological competitiveness of the country in a mission mode;
- Establishing globally competitive research facilities and centres of excellence;
- Kindling an innovative spirit among scientists to translate R&D leads into scalable technologies;
- Developing new models of PPPs in higher education, particularly for research in universities and high technology areas;

- Identifying ways and means of catalysing industry–academia collaborations; and,
- Promoting strong linkages with advanced countries, including participation in mega international science initiatives.

8.4. The Eleventh Five Year Plan will provide policy support for incentivizing greater accountability, administrative efficiency and flexibility and in some cases, systemic changes. The most important among these is the need for organizational and administrative changes in S&T departments/agencies/institutions to create a conducive environment for R&D and ensuring optimal/efficient use of pubic sector R&D resources. Manpower being critical for the successful implementation of research projects, approval of the scheme/project needs to be accompanied by approval of the scientific and technical manpower.

8.5. In addition there is a need to focus on policy issues relating to experiments on animals, women in science, cyber infrastructure for S&T, encouragement of S&T based entrepreneurs, mobility of scientists between organizations, multi-ministerial funding and implementation mechanisms for projects. The role of socio-economic ministries towards mainstreaming S&T in their programmes is also an important policy issue because many programmes/activities relating to S&T fall within the purview of these ministries. A substantial part of the activities that affect large sections of society are carried out at the State level using local infrastructure and resources. To derive maximum benefits from the application of science and technology, it is necessary that the State S&T departments and councils play a crucial role involving and using the facilities and expertise created within the State as well as by the Central agencies.

DOMAINS FOR FOCUSED ATTENTION FOR THE ELEVENTH PLAN

INNOVATION FOR FASTER AND MORE INCLUSIVE GROWTH

Innovation for Increasing Returns from Raw Materials

8.6. Innovation is linked to first application of concepts and the creation of value from an idea or concept. In the global market economy, the ability of nations to create, absorb and commercialize innovations determines their competitiveness. Innovation is closely linked to the creation of wealth in a modern knowledge economy. Value addition to raw materials in India through applications of technology has remained low compared to other nations such as Israel, Finland, Japan, and South Korea. Typically, innovation-led manufacturing provides 20–25% increase in value to raw material inputs. Increasing labour productivity through technology change and innovation is the main route for the creation of additional wealth to enterprises and better wages to employees.

Innovation as the Means for Sustained and Sustainable GDP Growth

8.7. There is a vast untapped potential in India for wealth creation by increasing the levels of innovation content in the entire economic development activities of the country. It is a tall call but an essential one, if the current levels of growth of GDP were to be maintained over the next two decades. There are several case histories of nations benefiting substantially from a flow of innovations. Innovation will also be a key for sustainability—the ability to meet developmental objectives while ensuring sustainable use of natural resources.

Institutional Elements of an Innovation Eco-system

8.8. The elements of an innovation ecology identified earlier fall into a number of institutional domains. An institutional representation of the innovation system is a useful tool for exploring the role of various actors in the innovation process and the way in which they may interact. Five categories of institutional participants can be identified:

(i) Governments, which play a key role in setting broad policy directions and a primary role in funding basic scientific research;
(ii) Private enterprises and their research institutes, which contribute to development and other activities that are closer to the market than governments are;
(iii) Universities and related institutions that provide key knowledge and skills;
(iv) Bridging institutions acting as intermediaries under such names as 'technology centre', 'technology brokers', or 'business innovation centres', which play an important role in closing the gaps among the other actors and have been important to the success of all types of research centres; and
(v) Other organizations, public and private, such as venture capital firms, federal laboratories, and training organizations.

8.9. The interaction and role of these stakeholders and institutions is defined and determined by four contextual factors sufficiently important to the operation of innovation systems to be able to make or break them: market conditions, physical infrastructure, education and training and regulatory conditions.

Role of Governments in the Innovation System—Global Experience

8.10. There is a wide spectrum with regard to the extent to which governments can influence the innovation system. To a large extent, the approaches adopted by various nations in the direction of innovation systems have varied depending on the overall national economic orientation. These approaches have ranged from a 'directed or coordinated' model such as the one selected by Japan, to a much more laissez faire model employed in the USA. Countries such as Canada and others in the European Union (EU) region have adopted models that fall in between those of Japan and the US, at least in terms of strategy and sector identification for leveraging innovations. Thus, from the standpoint of a national planning process, there are several approaches to directing and shaping the innovation-led development processes. Although there may be varying levels of the directed or coordinated functions of the governments in shaping the innovation infrastructure, most nations have recognized the similarity of needs for creating an innovation infrastructure.

Examples of Global Experiences

8.11. The economic rationale for government support and intervention in the innovation process described earlier provides the basis for most of the major innovation support programmes and mechanisms in different countries. Examples include the Small Business Innovation Research and the Advanced Technology Programme (ATP) in the US. An important part of the innovation system is courage on the part of the scientist to take risks and the support of risk-taking by the S&T system. The greater the innovation, the greater is the risk in converting it into a commercial product or process. Thus, the US Government provides between 20 to 25% of all funds for early stage technology development. This contribution is rendered more significant in segments of the innovation cycle that private investors often find too risky.

Intellectual Property Regime

8.12. As a result of global competition, it is becoming difficult for the Indian industry to compete on the basis of low cost alone without value creation through new technology. With the Indian Intellectual Property Regime (IPR) getting Trade Related Intellectual Property Rights (TRIPS) complaints since January 2005, many Indian companies have stepped up their R&D spending to keep generating new technology, particularly in the pharmaceutical and automobile sectors. Besides amendment of the Indian Patents Act, 1970, the country has also enacted intellectual property (IP) laws covering geographical indicators, biodiversity, plant varieties and farmers' rights and layout design of integrated circuits. The IP Acts covering designs, trademarks and copyrights have also been updated to be TRIPS compliant.

8.13. Due to increased patent awareness and changed circumstances, patent filing by Indians in the country has increased threefold from a stagnant figure of about 1000 in the pre-World Trade Organization (WTO) regime. Patent filing by foreigners in India has also increased substantially, which reflects increasing interest of foreigners in the Indian economy. Thus, the current patent filing by Indians and foreigners in India has reached a level of more than 17000. The Council of Scientific and Industrial Research (CSIR) alone is filing approximately 500 foreign patents and 400 Indian patent applications every year.

Creating an Innovation Infrastructure in India and the Need for a National Innovation Policy

8.14. Often missing within discussions of innovation in the developed countries is the role of innovation for directly improving the livelihood or quality of life of the poor. The general assumption is that the market mechanism will take care of this. However, innovation may also be important for the delivery of, and access to, services that are essential for a quality of life; whether it is clean water, modern energy or affordable health care. In terms of an innovation policy for India, this may be an important and distinguishing feature.

8.15. The forward plan of India is towards faster and more inclusive growth. Faster growth in a globally competitive market environment demands a national innovation infrastructure that connects knowledge systems to wealth creation efficiently and effectively. In the Indian social context, there is a need to ensure that innovative growth-linked processes do not bypass the poor and leave them out of developmental choices emanating from the benefits of globally competitive innovations. Therefore, the Indian model for innovation should be unique. The innovation infrastructure of India should aim to bridge the internal asymmetries and serve the dual purpose associated with global competitiveness and inclusive growth.

8.16. Both pro-poor and global competitiveness objectives should be embedded in the search for innovations. The number of grass-root innovators in the informal sector in India is large. However, grass-root innovations are not able to reap sufficient economic benefits for want of backing with adequate resources. The innovation infrastructure in the formal sector is thin. It requires deepening by referencing to global best practices and market demands. Such an innovation infrastructure would depend strongly upon a vibrant and gainful PPP in research and development as well as commercialization of innovations.

8.17. The prevailing asymmetry between inventors and investors is required to be bridged. Financing systems for backing up early-stage innovations with risk capital are required. Provisions for exiting from non-profitable innovations also need to be made. Innovations created at the expense of considerable investment of resources would demand a matching Intellectual Property Rights (IPR) regime. While the legal framework for protecting IPR is in place, infrastructure for capturing and protecting IPR is still evolving in India. Use of technology tools and capacity building in the area of IPR management require scaling up. New approaches and programmes are essential for unleashing India's innovation potential. Competitiveness innovation cluster has emerged as a successful global concept. Such innovation clusters in which academia, research and industry partner under viable and equitable PPP are the way forward.

8.18. The design and development of a sustainable innovation infrastructure should take into account global best practices, attraction, attachment, retention and renovation of talent within the research and development streams, PPPs, venture and angel financing and capacity building. The realization of Indian Vision 2025 to emerge as a major economic power in the global knowledge economy would call for a sustainable innovation infrastructure.

8.19. At the root of innovation is invention, which is an essential creative step that cannot really be directed or forced. However, there is much that can be done to facilitate this initial step and the many subsequent steps that will ultimately yield the value to society from the invention. These steps are not isolated or distinct from one another; therefore it is more appropriate to think of a comprehensive innovation policy, rather than a policy that is aimed at only one of the steps in the process or elements of the innovation system. Innovation policy needs to be placed within the broader social and economic context, informed by goals and aspirations of development and should reflect a fair and effective balance between public and private interests, social and economic goals and inclusiveness versus rapidity.

8.20. In order to unleash our full innovative potential, we need to put in place a National Innovation policy, which encourages competition among enterprises, greater diffusion of knowledge and increased support to early-stage technology development initiatives and grassroot-level innovators. We need to foster increased collaboration among R&D institutes, universities and private sector enterprises and leverage upon their cumulative strengths in designing and implementing various innovation programmes. There is also a need for an appropriate legislative framework for incentivizing the innovators and commercialization of public funded R&D, where the government, the recipient(s) of funds, the inventor, as well as the public benefit from the protection and commercialization of IP.

Science and Technology as a Career Option/ Choice for the Young

8.21. Attracting and retaining young meritorious students in science and technology is a major concern. The general perception among students and their parents about science as a career is that it is not an attractive enough option as it requires a long time to enter the job market, and that good employment opportunities do not exist for science degree holders, including those with doctorate degrees. The absence of colleges/universities with a brand value equivalent to that of the IITs for pursuing courses after Class XII also acts as negative factor.

8.22. In order to make science an attractive career option for the talented, scientists need encouragement. Peer-reviewed good performance should be given recognition through a suitable scheme of incentives. Assured career support for 15 years may induce meritorious students to opt for the science stream after the senior secondary ('Plus Two') stage. There is a need to multiply institutions like the Indian Institutes of Science Education and Research (IISER) at Pune, Kolkata, and Chandigarh, and discipline-specific institutions like the National Institute of Science

Education and Research (NISER) at Bhubaneswar and Indian Institute of Space Science and Technology (IISST) at Thiruvananthapuram, with a view to capture talent at senior secondary level for developing quality human resources in the country. There is also need to strengthen universities/colleges which already have accomplishments to their credit and who show promise for future growth. Such institutions should be identified and provided with the required infrastructure facilities. The focus should be on creating new integrated programmes to which bright students are attracted, rather than multiplying the existing conventional undergraduate (UG) and postgraduate (PG) programmes.

8.23. Unfortunately, mobility is conspicuously absent among college teachers. A strong and vibrant Visiting Teacher scheme should be launched through which teachers are able to go for six months, every five years, to reputed research institutions/university departments. Similar mobility is needed for PhD/PG/UG students working on their projects.

Promotion of Basic Sciences

8.24. Basic research in science, engineering, and medicine is essential for the overall growth of science and technology and it is a critical input for development. To promote basic science research in academic and research institutions, there is need of a well-defined and focused approach for building infrastructure of equipment, facilities in colleges/universities/institutions.

8.25. Apart from supply-side interventions through higher allocation of funds for S&T, there is also a need to increase efficiency of the delivery system so that the resources are made available to R&D groups in a much faster manner. The promotion of basic research in the different disciplines of science needs a mechanism which can be charged with the responsibility of formulating and implementing programmes, and playing a catalytic role for upgrading research infrastructure and attracting a new generation of students and faculty into the research system. This is essential since much of modern research in science and engineering requires development, acquisition and upgradation of sophisticated equipment facilities. The mechanism should act both as a creator of facilities and as a watchdog to ensure efficient operation. Most institutions have aged collectively with a consequent decline of their research profile. Vigorous and attractive recruitment policies for S&T personnel need to be introduced by the government and the corporate sector. Flexibility in salary support and start-up grants would facilitate to attract class scientists to work in India. There is also a need for improving inter-institutional linkages to quickly enhance scientific activities within the university system. Focus is also required on initiating programmes to promote establishment of technology business incubators in universities which support scientists to start commercial activities based on indigenous technologies developed at their institutions. This type of technology transfer can be very effective for implementation, particularly for low initial capital start-ups. Industries with active R&D divisions should be encouraged to recruit research students working in basic science areas related to new technology demands.

Mega Science Projects

8.26. The implementation of mega science projects in high technology areas will lead to direct technological gains for the country in terms of advanced technologies and equipment building, as well as development of expertise to take on similar projects in future. Mega science projects would involve multi-institutional teams, including possible international collaboration and linking projects to a broader academic framework would help in sustaining the research activities around these large facilities. Mega science projects would also create exciting opportunities for young students to actively involve them in cutting-edge research and attract them to science. India's successful participation in European Organization for Nuclear Research (CERN) has enabled it to participate in the International Thermonuclear Experimental Reactor (ITER) project as an equal partner. Some of the other mega science projects include: Nano-technologies, International Linear Collider and related programmes, India based Neutrino Observatory (INO), National Radioactive Ion Beam Facility, Facility for Antiproton and Ion Research (FAIR), astronomy based research, creation of National Hetero-structure Facility and the Square Kilometre Array (SKA). These programmes have a major component of international collaboration, and participation in them will allow the Indian scientific community to take its rightful place in the world scene.

Cross-Disciplinary Technology Areas

8.27. Modern technology development is increasingly becoming dependent on research inputs from a large number of disciplines. A seamless and multi-sectoral flow of technologies and inputs from scientists and engineers from various disciplines is essential for making a visible societal impact and create economic prosperity. Under the umbrella of cross-disciplinary technologies, efforts are needed to identify programmes cutting across the traditional divides of sciences, engineering, and medicine, where investments can pay rich dividends. Strong interfaces amongst academia, R&D laboratories and industries and special mechanisms need to be created for financing innovation in the early stage of technology development. Cross-disciplinary technology areas include: desalination and water purification technologies, nutrition, health care (medical diagnostics, medical devices, vaccines), advanced computing, advanced manufacturing, robotics and automation, combustion research, sensors and integrated systems, distributed sensors and networks, security technologies, and advanced functional materials. The list is not comprehensive and it represents a common denominator of cross-disciplinary areas where building core expertise and competence will have far-reaching consequences in the development of science-based technologies for societal benefits, economic competitiveness and national security.

STRENGTHENING ACADEMIA–INDUSTRY INTERFACE (INCLUDING PUBLIC–PRIVATE PARTNERSHIPS)

8.28. The relationship between the academia and industry should be of interactive, collaborative and participative nature, realizing and respecting each other's role and contribution. Efforts are needed to focus on PPP and creation of enabling environments. Effective academia–industry interaction will lead to: strengthening competitiveness, promoting innovation and new technology development on the one hand and ensuring development and supply of qualified S&T manpower. In order to strengthen the interface and tap the PPP potential effectively, the thrust should be on creation of new interface structures such as consortia, partnership research institutions for basic and applied R&D; enhancing mobility of S&T professionals; and promotion of technology transfer and new venture creation. Industrial houses may be encouraged to create corpus funds in academic institutions for promoting applied R&D relevant to their needs. Centres of Relevance and Excellence may also be set up in academic and R&D institutions in select areas of S&T, which are of direct relevance to industries. The student internship programme should also be made more meaningful, so that it benefits both the students and the industry.

8.29. The focus of consortia approach should be on pre-competitive partnerships involving academia to help the industries develop advanced technologies and upgrade their manufacturing competitiveness. While government participation could be in the form grant-in-aid to academia and/or conditional grant to innovative small companies, industry partners will bring with them inputs like domain knowledge, market research and facilities for testing and validation of prototypes. PPP can also comprise co-locating an industrial R&D Centre within the premises of a national laboratory or academic institution and co-sharing some of the laboratory's select facilities with industry. For enhancing the mobility of S&T professionals, the young faculty could be given an internship programme at an advanced level so that they can spend some time in industry. This would enable them to impart more practical knowledge to students, relevant to industry. Active programmes may be established for regular visits of experts from industry to address students, academic and scientific staff. Efforts are also needed to strengthen venture funding for an effective proliferation of knowledge-based entrepreneurship.

SCIENCE AND TECHNOLOGY FOR SMALL AND MEDIUM ENTERPRISES

8.30. Small and medium scale enterprises (SMEs) occupy an important and strategic place in economic growth and equitable development of the country and are the driving force behind a large number of innovations. The post-liberalization era has enhanced opportunities and challenges for this sector. For enabling the SMEs to tide over the problems of technological backwardness and to enhance their access to new technologies, it is essential to understand and assess the real needs of the SMEs and devise approaches accordingly. There is also a need to leverage on modern technologies through increased communication, cooperation and linkages both with in the enterprise as well as across enterprises and across knowledge-producing organizations.

EFFECTIVE DELIVERY AND PROPAGATION OF APPROPRIATE TECHNOLOGIES FOR RURAL DEVELOPMENT (INCLUDING PARTNERSHIP WITH VOLUNTARY ORGANIZATIONS)

8.31. The effective delivery of rural technologies is an important issue for the development and growth in the country. Technology transfer for rural areas is weak due to a lack of field-tested and validated models and inadequate institutional support both for technology development and transfer. The Council for Advancement of People's Action and Rural Technology (CAPART) is the nodal government agency for creation and delivery of rural development related technologies. The role of the Support Voluntary Organization (SVO) programme is to search out and link up the thousands of disparate, small but sincere, groups working in far-flung corners of the country and provide them the necessary wherewithal to implement watershed programmes in their areas and mobilize rural communities for this purpose. The SVOs should be linked to S&T institutions so that they can absorb and deliver the technology packages to grass-root NGOs/Community-based Organizations (CBOs). CAPART should become an effective link between the technology generation centres and the line Departments such as the Ministries of Rural Development (MoRD), Agro and Rural Industries, Welfare, Tribal Affairs and Human Resource Development, for dissemination and propagation of technology packages through schemes for income/employment generation and capacity building. The S&T interventions in all spheres of rural life, such as agriculture, sanitation, health, physical and social infrastructure, need to be strengthened. Efforts are also needed to develop cost-effective rural technologies for non-farm rural enterprises, since non-farm rural employment assumes increasing importance due to low employment elasticity in the farm sector.

8.32. The role of NGOs in rural technology delivery should relate to: field surveys for assessing feasibility; preparation of Detailed Project Report with inputs from potential users; networking, motivating and organizing rural poor producers, artisans, small farmers and other partners/beneficiaries. NGOs need to develop linkages with technology providers, development agencies, and financial institutions and provide support for location-specific technology adaptation and upgradation and assistance in marketing. The NGOs will also need to play an entrepreneurial role on behalf of pro-poor enterprises, especially in dealing with financial institutions, traders, and the like. The NGO efforts of disseminating technologies relating to rural development, however, need to be enhanced by establishing synergy with the efforts of other government agencies so as to strengthen the existing and nucleate new initiatives.

Leveraging International Collaboration Inputs

8.33. International S&T collaborations are essentially mechanisms of providing opportunities and platforms to various countries to work together, taking mutual advantage of complementary scientific & technological capabilities of each other. They provide first-hand acquaintance with scientific and technological developments and work cultures in other countries and access to sophisticated research facilities abroad. Interaction between scientific researchers helps in updating and refining their knowledge base for accelerating the pace of investigation as also to fill up information gaps. Science being location neutral, international collaboration affords the way forward for development of advanced technologies, high tech equipment/facilities and new-generation materials.

8.34. Technology-led growth of the economy is a proven global model of growth, more so of developed nations. This has brought technology-led diplomacy to the centre-stage in international cooperation, and India also needs to leverage such technology-led diplomacy. Several developed nations have been targeting the young population of India for catalysing the growth of their own science and technology systems. India cannot remain a supply system of talents alone. Our strategy for international cooperation needs to be based on mutual gain and complementary strength. There are nations from which India may stand to gain by teaming up in certain sectors of development. Overall growth in important sectors of the economy cannot be based on total self-reliance as that may prove too expensive and time consuming. Re-inventing and reverse engineering models of growth are also not sustainable for modern India. In such domains, India would need to develop strategic partnerships with other nations after appropriate cost benefit analysis. Energy-, water-, ecological and nutrition-security of India would call for large global models of S&T cooperation. Areas of research such as high energy physics, nuclear physics, accelerator physics and technology, are distinctly international in character. Suitable collaborative projects by mobilizing the national strengths in these areas would need to be evolved and funded in coordination with other agencies.

8.35. A mechanism will also need to be evolved for attracting the best talent from other parts of the world, particularly people of Indian origin settled abroad and excelling in their respective areas of S&T. There is need to attract them for building active research centres/schools in frontier areas of science, engineering and technology. Scientists and technologists of Indian origin, abroad, could contribute in developing capabilities of Indian institutions and S&T groups. International S&T collaboration inputs may also be leveraged effectively by undertaking joint

R&D projects of industrial interest/commercial value at the pre-commercial stage involving academic and R&D groups as well as industrial groups at both ends.

NUCLEAR RESEARCH

ELEVENTH PLAN OBJECTIVES/THRUST/FOCUS

8.36. The Department of Atomic Energy (DAE) has been pursuing research in high-tech areas and developing technologies to meet the technological requirements of the country and building self-reliant capabilities in all aspects of the nuclear fuel cycle. Even in the present era, when globalization and liberalization have become buzzwords, we have to retain and strengthen our capability in the nuclear field so that the country remains unaffected by technology denial regimes. That apart, India's nuclear power programme has to be in tune with our nuclear resource profile. Therefore, the R&D programmes have been designed keeping in view the modest uranium and vast thorium resources that we have. While the technologies for Pressurized Heavy Water Reactors (PHWR) developed indigenously are now in the commercial domain, the approach now is to push the fast breeder reactor and thorium technologies. The thrust would also be on expansion of human resource development activities and encouraging students to carry out research on the interface of science and engineering. To augment the installed nuclear power capacity, maximum possible thrust would be given to development of new techniques for exploration of uranium and deployment of known techniques extensively for quick results. For uranium resource sustainability, credible waste management, and eventual thorium utilization, focus would be on development of advanced fuels having short doubling time for use in fast breeder reactors. Major achievements of the DAE (R&D) sector during the Tenth Plan period are given in Box 8.1

ELEVENTH FIVE YEAR PLAN PROGRAMMES

8.37. During the Eleventh Plan, R&D support will continue to improve capacity utilization, environment and safety and economic competitiveness of PHWRs. Technology will be upgraded based on latest developments in the entire PHWR fuel cycle. R&D work on the development of 700 Megawatt electrical (MW_e) PHWR will also be taken up. Focus would also be on the development of new techniques for uranium exploration to increase installed capacity based on PHWRs. Since the nuclear power programme in the next few decades will have a large component of Fast Breeder Reactors (FBRs), major R&D programmes would be taken up for development of materials, equipment and processes for FBRs on a comprehensive basis.

8.38. R&D on advanced fuels for FBR, fuel reprocessing, study of fuel chemistry and other safety studies would also be carried out to be on a firm footing during the operation of Prototype FBR (PFBR) and planning of subsequent FBRs.

8.39. While the current generation nuclear energy systems have been very successful in terms of safety and economy, it is necessary to continue R&D for the development of advanced nuclear reactor systems. R&D towards the development of the thorium-fuelled Advanced Heavy Water Reactor (AHWR) would be continued. A demonstration unit of the Compact High Temperature Reactor would be built during the Eleventh Plan, which will serve as a platform for development and demonstration of very high temperature heat removal capabilities and other challenges associated with the operation of high temperature reactors. Work on the development of materials for high temperature reactors, including fusion reactor would also be taken up.

8.40. The International Thermonuclear Experimental Reactor (ITER) is a prestigious international project which will nearly complete the scientific and technological investigations required to build a prototype demonstration reactor, based on the magnetic confinement scheme of controlled thermonuclear fusion. India's contributions to ITER, worth nearly Rs 2500 crore in terms of equipment to the experiment, are largely based on the indigenous experience and the expertise available in Indian industry. India will also participate in the subsequent operation of ITER and the experiments thereon. R&D efforts on fusion and plasma science will continue to strengthen domestic technologies.

8.41. The research reactors, Assessment of Passive System Reliability (APSARA), CIRUS, DHRUVA, and KAMINI, which provide reactor based facilities for research in basic sciences, and other services like: production of radioisotopes, neutron radiography, neutron activation analyses, material irradiation testing, fuel testing, shielding studies, and so on, would be refurbished. It is also planned to set up a Multi-Purpose Research Reactor with high flux especially for basic research in frontier areas of science and for applied research related to development and testing of nuclear fuels and other

Box 8.1

Major Achievements of DAE (R&D Sector) during the Tenth Five Year Plan Period

- The DAE contributed significantly to international mega-science projects, particularly the CERN. This contribution has been recognized and lauded by the international scientific community.
- Some of the important deliverables under the Advanced Reactor Design and Technology Development Project include: polyurethane booting for rugged duty manipulators, special purpose water hydraulic valves, in-core flux mapping system, DNA micro arrayer, and so on. The technology for on-line vibration diagnostics of the steam turbine has now been offered to NTPC for their 500 MW_e thermal power plants. Using the tools developed by BARC, pre-service inspection was carried out on 20 coolant channels prior to criticality. BARC also developed a methodology, called Assessment of Passive System Reliability (APSARA), for evaluation of passive systems which would be useful in new reactors under development.
- A process for recovery of uranium from low grade Tummallapalle ore using the pressure alkali process has been successfully developed and a technology demonstration pilot plant was set up at Jaduguda. Processes have also been developed for bulk separation of trivalent actinides from high level waste (HLW). Removal of uranium from simulated HLW was also demonstrated on full scale. BARC has also established the 'Indian Environmental Radiation Monitoring Network' with 37 monitoring stations across the country.
- The emphasis of the nuclear power programme stage-II has been on development of materials, equipment and processes as well as development of advanced fuels for fast breeder reactors. The Mark-I fuel (uranium-plutonium mixed carbide fuel with 70% plutonium) for Fast Breeder Test Reactor (FBTR) has reached a burn-up of 154.3 GWd/t without any fuel pin failure in the core. Compact Reprocessing Facility for Advanced Fuels in Lead Cells, was commissioned successfully for reprocessing high Plutonium content mixed carbide fuel. Sodium resistant concrete has also been developed to protect the structural concrete of FBRs.
- As part of Reactor Engineering studies, towards developing robust steam generator for FBRs, a Steam Generator Test Facility has been commissioned. Scale model of reactor assembly was commissioned and several experiments were completed successfully for qualifying the PFBR design. Realization of a robust, safe and economic fuel cycle for fast reactors is the ultimate goal for achieving rapid growth of fast reactors in the country.
- Under the nuclear power programme stage-III, DAE has initiated work towards development of the thorium fuelled Advanced Heavy Water Reactor. One major deliverable under the project is the AHWR Fuelling Machine (prototype). Installation of passive valve test facility, development and demonstration of conductivity probe, procurement of high speed CCD camera, development of indirectly heated fuel rod simulator, and installation of the liquid metal loop have been completed. Under the Thorium Fuel Cycle Technology Development and U^{233} Clean up project, a new process based on coated agglomerate particles (CAP) for (Th-U^{233}) MOX fuels has been developed.
- Refurbishing the CIRUS Research Reactor and integration of a seawater desalination unit for demonstration of Low Temperature Vacuum Evaporation Process utilizing low-grade reactor waste heat from the CIRUS reactor has been completed. In the area of lasers, a facility for in-situ cutting operation using Nd:YAG lasers has been developed and deployed for en-mass coolant channel replacement at the Narora power plant. A facility for laser welding of automobile transmission gear assemblies using indigenously developed high power CO_2 laser was also set up. Substantial progress has also been made in the development of processes for ceramic materials synthesis and thin film processes for the solid oxide fuel cell components.
- Several new technologies have been developed for societal applications, which include: Sea water Reverse Osmosis plants for coastal areas, brackish water RO plant in villages for producing safe drinking water, Multistage Flash evaporator plant for seawater desalination using low grade steam, Low Temperature Evaporation plant using waste heat for seawater desalination, and waste water recycle and reuse plants for the effluent. In the field of nuclear agriculture, 26 elite Trombay varieties have been developed. In addition, a laser-based land levelling system was built at the behest of the Ministry of Agriculture, and this technology has been transferred to M/s OSAW Udyog of Ambala Cantonment for mass production.

materials. A radioisotope processing facility is also planned to be set up at Visakhapatnam.

8.42. Some of the other major programmes proposed to taken up include: setting up of the second campus of BARC at Visakhapatnam and R&D for Accelerator and Accelerator Driven Systems development; development of beam lines for Indus-2 and their utilization; and development of superconducting cavities and associated technologies for high energy accelerators. A proton therapy unit would be assembled and installed the Advanced Centre for Treatment, Research and Education in Cancer, Navi Mumbai, for clinical application in treatment of cancer. Medical cyclotron, which is under construction, would also be available during the Eleventh Five Year Plan period.

8.43. A programme on enhancement of the DAE Grid and Anunet facility will be taken up to improve the communication and computing power of the DAE units. It is also planned to have an INO in collaboration with the scientific community of the country. This would be open for international participation also. In addition, the project on energy conversion technologies for study of alternate energy conversion technologies will be strengthened.

8.44. Research–education linkages are the backbone for developing of scientific manpower for the country at large and within the DAE in particular. It is planned to have a separate training school for an Atomic Minerals Directorate for Exploration and Research in line with other training schools in the Department. The DAE has also initiated the process for establishment of the NISER at Bhubaneswar, at par with the IISER to undertake integrated five-year Masters' courses and integrated M.Sc–Ph.D. programme in core and emerging branches of science to provide world-class education to students.

8.45. The Eleventh Five Year Plan outlay of the DAE (R&D Sector) has been tentatively fixed at Rs 9726 crore at 2006–07 constant price and Rs 11000 crore at current price.

SPACE SCIENCE & TECHNOLOGY

ELEVENTH PLAN OBJECTIVES/THRUST/FOCUS

8.46. The major objectives of the Space Programme are to establish self-reliant operational space services in the areas of satellite communications, satellite-based information for management of natural resources and satellite meteorological applications. Over the years, India has established two operational space systems—the Indian National Satellite (INSAT) System providing services for telecommunications, TV broadcasting and meteorology including disaster warning support, and the Indian Remote Sensing Satellite (IRS) System for natural resource monitoring and management.

8.47. The focus of the INSAT programme will continue to provide a variety of services in telecommunications and television broadcasting, including meteorological observations, disaster communications, tele-education, tele-health services and village resource centres (VRCs). Under the IRS programme, the focus will be on vital applications of IRS data for identifying locations for ground water recharging, monitoring command areas, estimating crop areas and yields, assessing deforestation, mapping urban areas for planning purposes, delineating ocean areas with higher fish catch potential and monitoring of the environment. The emphasis of the space programmes will be on large-scale applications of space technology in the priority areas of national development. The already established space-based services for socio-economic development of the country will be sustained and strengthened. The future directions for the space programme will take into account the needs of the country in the context of emerging international environment and the potential that India holds for human development.

8.48. Technology advancement, which is essential to maintain competitive relevance, will be an important thrust area for space endeavours. Emphasis will be given to strengthening the ground segment to ensure and enhance effective utilization of the remote sensing data for programmes relating to the creation of a natural resource inventory and databases, food security, water security, disaster management support, infrastructure development, weather forecasting, ocean state forecasting, environment protection and climate variability and change. The emphasis in the area of satellite communications will be towards meeting the growing demand for transponders, ensuring continuity of quality services, protection of space systems, efficient spectrum management and continuous improvement in technology.

8.49. In the area of launch vehicle development, emphasis will be on the development of Geosynchronous Launch Vehicle (GSLV) Mk III capable of launching 4T class INSAT satellites. Polar Satellite Launch Vehicle (PSLV) and GSLV will continue to be workhorse vehicles for launching IRS and INSAT (2T class) satellites and their capabilities will be further improved. The objective of the Manned Mission programme would be to develop a fully autonomous manned space vehicle to carry two crew to 400 km Low Earth Orbit and safe return to earth. Major achievements of the Department of Space (DoS) during the Tenth Plan period are given in Box 8.2.

Box 8.2

Major Achievements of DoS during the Tenth Five Year Plan Period

- The Tenth plan witnessed significant progress in Indian space capabilities. Operationalization of GSLV, development and qualification of indigenous cryogenic engines, establishment of a state-of-the-art, second launch pad facility at Sriharikota, launch and operationalization of Kalpana (Metsat-1), Resourcesat-1, Cartosat-1/HAMSAT and Cartosat-2/SRE-1 by PSLV, augmentation of the INSAT system with INSAT-3A, 3E, GSAT-2, EDUSAT, INSAT-4A and 4B satellites are some of the important achievements of the period.
- GSLV Mk III has made good progress towards the establishment of S-200 facilities. With the successful initiation of stage hot tests, the GSLV flight with indigenous cryo stage will take place in 2008.
- The design, development, characterization and realization of the supersonic combustor module, required for future Reusable Launch Vehicles, were completed and the technology was successfully demonstrated through ground tests for 2.5 kg/s and 5 kg/s air flow rates.
- Yet another important technological achievement was the development and testing of an Electric Stationary Plasma Thruster (18 millinewton) for future inter-planetary missions. This will be flight tested onboard GSAT-4 spacecraft planned for launch during 2008. Planetary mission Chandrayaan-1, multi-wavelength astronomy mission ASTROSAT, Indo-French joint climatic mission Megha-Tropiques, microwave remote sensing mission RISAT and oceanography mission OCEANSAT-2 were other important initiatives during the Tenth Plan period. Work on the Indian Regional Navigational Satellite System (IRNSS) was initiated.
- Development of indigenous strategic capability in certain critical areas like ring rolling mill, alloy, Titanium sponge, hi-reliability electronic components and space materials were other important achievements. ANTRIX Corporation won contracts for two dedicated launches of PSLV and also supply of a sophisticated communication satellite in consortium with a leading European manufacturer M/s EADS ASTRIUM.
- India is now one among the six countries in the world to develop Geosynchronous Transfer Orbit (GTO) (36000 km high) launch capability. The technological capability to recover a satellite from orbit through a space capsule recovery experiment was demonstrated, thus laying the foundation for future reusable launch vehicle systems.
- India's first lunar mission, Chandrayaan-1 (scheduled for launch in 2008), and the multi-wavelength observatory satellite ASTROSAT are two important initiatives of the recent past in space science research. The end-to-end capability in space for vital applications in communications, broadcasting, meteorology and natural resource information, which are of direct relevance for national development, has secured India a unique place in the international community.

ELEVENTH FIVE YEAR PLAN PROGRAMMES

8.50. The major plans/programmes during the Eleventh Plan would be related to:

- Building capabilities in Space Communications and Navigation; development of high power Ka band satellites and ground systems for point-to-point connectivity; building navigational satellite systems and related services; R&D in satellite communications; institutionalization of tele-medicine, tele-education and VRCs; communications systems/support for disaster management; self sustenance of INSAT/GSAT system;
- Developing Leadership in Earth Observations: improved imaging capability and continuity of data/services; development of advanced microwave imaging capability; strengthening ground systems and State Natural Resources Management System; establishment of a national natural resource database; Data Management System (DMS) infrastructure and urban/rural development;
- Providing thrust in Space Transportation System: operationalization of GSLV Mk III; development of perfect payload recovery and re-entry technologies; reusable launch vehicle; and development of critical technologies for manned missions;
- Strengthening Space Science Enterprise: advanced space science endeavours, namely Chandrayaan, multi-wavelength X-ray astronomy, mission to Mars; establishing space science instrumentation facilities and an Indian Space Science Data Centre;
- Promoting spinoffs in the discipline of human resource development, space science and technology education, industry–academia interface and international

cooperation. The thirst for expanding knowledge about the universe, solar system and planet Earth would be the driving force of the programmes.

- Based on demand, the INSAT system capacity will be progressively augmented to about 500 transponders (currently 175). Development of a cost-effective 4T-12KW bus with capacity of more than 50 transponders and flexibility to accommodate a wide range of payloads, will also be undertaken.

8.51. Earth Observation (EO) Systems would be taken up primarily to ensure continuity and quality of EO data with a view to maintain global leadership in this area. The EO series of satellites, both in the IRS and INSAT/METSAT series, will address broadly the thematic applications in three streams—Resourcesat series, Cartosat series and Atmosphere series. The Radar Imaging Satellite (RISAT) would be launched to provide all-weather remote sensing capability critical for applications in agriculture and disaster management. The other thrust areas would include expansion of tele-education and tele-medicine networks and VRCs with the involvement of Central Government ministries/departments, State Governments and NGOs. Satellite navigation would be a vital component not only for civil aviation but in many other areas such as mobile telephony, surface transport, intelligent highway system, maritime transport, rail, oil and gas, precision agriculture, fisheries, survey and marine engineering, electricity networks, and so on. Besides the completion of GAGAN (Global Positioning System and Geo Augmented Navigation), focus will also be on the establishment of the IRNSS with a constellation of seven satellites. The realization of a national database for emergency management, impact mapping and monitoring support for disasters, satellite-based communication support for disaster management, strengthening of early warning systems and development of tools and techniques for decision support systems would be the major activities under the DMS programme.

8.52. Considering the need to provide an impetus to studies and research in the critical area of atmospheric research, an Atmospheric Science Programme has been planned with special emphasis on the use of satellites and advanced observation tools and techniques of modelling. A mechanism would be worked out for interactions with scientific departments and academia for initiating suitable projects, leading to operational end-user products in different domains. Human resource development, international cooperation, industry and academia interface, indigenous development of space materials and components and space commerce will continue to be priority areas. An important target during the Eleventh Plan period would be to set up an Indian Institute of Space Science and Technology with a view to capture the talent at the 'Plus Two' (senior secondary) level for creating quality human resources in the country for Indian Space Research Organization (ISRO). While efforts would be made to partner with Indian industries or outsource a majority of the production, fabrication, testing and software development activities, some of the routine production jobs, which requires capital intense infrastructure and involves strategic and security considerations, will be taken up in-house by creating a few production islands.

8.53. The Eleventh Five Year Plan outlay of the DoS has been tentatively fixed at Rs 27305 crore at 2006–07 constant price and Rs 30883 crore at current price.

BIOTECHNOLOGY RESEARCH

ELEVENTH PLAN OBJECTIVES/THRUST/FOCUS

8.54. The approach of the Department of Biotechnology (DBT) has been to create tools and technologies that address the problems of the largest section of the society and provide them with biotech products and services at affordable prices. The ultimate objective is to make India globally competitive in the emerging bio-economy by converting the country's diverse biological resources to useful products and processes. Developing a strong biotechnology industry and technology diffusion capacity is critical for fulfilling this objective. The advancement of biotechnology as a successful industry confronts many challenges related to research and development, creation of investment capital, technology transfer and technology absorption, patentability and intellectual property, affordability in pricing, regulatory issues and public confidence and tailor-made human resources related to all these aspects. The department has been working on cross-cutting issues such as human resource development, smarter re-entry for our scientists abroad, new and varied models of creating an innovation-friendly environment, R&D in small and medium size companies, newer ways of collaborating with large companies, establishing centres of excellence and translational research centres, remodeling life science departments in universities/institutions, establishment of technology management centres, promoting dynamic biotech regional clusters, establishment of biotechnology parks and incubators, and setting up of

Box 8.3
Major Achievements of DBT during the Tenth Five Year Plan Period

- In the area of Human Resource Development, the Department is implementing an Integrated Programme of Human Resource Development in Biotechnology to generate adequate and appropriately trained manpower required for overall development of Biotechnology in the country. The MSc/MTech teaching programme which was started in 1985–86 in five universities, has been gradually increased to 63 courses with a total intake of around 1000 students per annum. Of these, 22 courses were started during the Tenth Five Year Plan. The Junior Research Fellow (JRF) programme has also been started from 2004 to fill the gap between the PG teaching courses and the Post Doctoral Fellowship programme.
- 35 biotech facilities were established in the public sector for production and supply of biologicals, reagents, culture collection and experimental animals to scientists, industries and students at nominal costs and to conduct regular training progrmmes for capacity building. An International Depository Authority was established at Institute of Microbial Technology, Chandigarh, which is the first such facility in India, 7th in Asia and 34th in the World. The Department also initiated the Centres of Excellence programme during 2005–06 and supported five centres in the areas of cancer biology, industrially important non-conventional yeasts, drought tolerant crop varieties, genetics and genomics of silk moth, and tuberculosis.
- An extensive bioinformatics network, covering 65 institutions, spread geographically across the country, has been established. Scientists associated with this network have published more than 1200 bioinformatics research papers in peer reviewed journals and helped in publishing more than 3500 research papers in biology/biotechnology. Courses such as MSc/MTech/PhD in Bioinformatics have also been introduced.
- Technology for recombinant anthrax vaccine has been developed and transferred to M/s Panacea Biotech Ltd., New Delhi. Ovum pick up technology for production of a large number of embryos in cattle and buffalo has been standardized and ELISA/PCR based diagnostic kits for *Peste des petits ruminants* (PPR) virus and Buffalopox virus (BPV) have been developed.
- India has successfully decoded the genome information of the rice chromosome number 11. Some of the important achievements in the field of crop biotechnology include: transformation technologies for rice for salinity and drought tolerance; molecular marker for wheat quality traits; novel Bt-cotton technology; transgenic virus resistant tomato; Genetically Modified (GM) mustard with higher yields; and technology for double haploids in cereals. Four mass production technologies for bio-control agents/biopesticides have been developed and standardized and six patents have been filed.
- Development of newer technologies for affordable vaccines for malaria, tuberculosis, cholera, HIV, rabies and Japanese encephalitis, helicobactor, and filariasis has been undertaken. Efforts to develop a tetravalent dengue vaccine candidate are in progress. Two candidate vaccines on rotavirus developed under INDO-US Vaccine Action Programme, have been found to be safe in clinical settings. Limbal stem cells have been successfully used to repair cornea surface disorders and more than 220 patients have been treated. In the area of medicinal and aromatic plants, four technology transfer agreements have been made for further screening of compounds as potential anti-diabetic and immunomodulatory agents.
- In the area of environmental biotechnology, technologies for bioremediation of mine spoil dumps; ecological restoration of degraded ecosystems and wastelands; mangrove aforestation; biosensors for detection of organophosphorus pesticides; bioscrubber for removal of obnoxious odours from industrial emissions; and oilzapper technology for bioremediation of crude oil spills and treatment of oily sludge e ready for commercialization.
- Technologies have also been developed for the manufacture of nutrient supplements, health foods, fruit juice processing, production of natural food additives, oil and fat modification, ensuring food quality/safety, biodegradable food packaging and production of chitosan based packaging films. Out of 19 technologies developed, eight technologies were transferred to the industry. Diagnostic kits were developed for rapid detection of food-borne pathogens like E. coli, Listeria monocytogenes, Bacillus cereus, and so on.
- Four international patents and ten Indian patents were granted to the National Institute of Immunology (NII). A technology relating to novel molecules which inhibit tuberculosis bacteria with the potential to be developed as anti-mycobacterial drugs, is being explored under a memorandum of understanding with Astra Zeneca India, Bangalore, and Cadila, Ahmedabad. A technology developed for the high density culture of Vero cells of an Indian strain of Japanese encephalitis virus (JEV) has been transferred under a memorandum of agreement to International Panacea, New Delhi.
- The repository at the National Centre for Cell Science (NCCS) procured 34 new cell lines, raising the total culture collection to 1161. The Centre made a total of 155 publications and obtained six US and three Indian patents. Methodologies for cryo-preservation and revival of bone marrow and cord blood cells have been transferred to Armed Forces Medical College, Pune. A technology on use of selected amino acid–zinc complexes as anti-malarials has been transferred to Shreya Life Sciences, Mumbai.
- The Department supported the setting up of a biotechnology park at Lucknow, and five biotechnology incubation centres, one each at Hyderabad, Bangalore, Kochi, Chandigarh, and Solan. The Department has also launched the Small Business Innovation Research Initiative (SBIRI) to boost PPP efforts in the country. An agreement has been executed by the Department with Biotech Consortia India Ltd., New Delhi, which is acting as the Special Purpose Vehicle (SPV)/Fund Manager for smooth running of the scheme. So far, ten proposals have been recommended for support.

biotechnology regulatory mechanisms. For this purpose, the DBT will be formulating the 'National Biotechnology Development Strategy' during the Eleventh Five Year Plan in consultation with all the stakeholders. Major achievements of DBT during the Tenth Plan period are given in Box 8.3.

Eleventh Five Year Plan Programmes

8.55. The priority areas for the Eleventh Five Year Plan include the development of improved crops, functional foods, neutraceuticals, nutritional rich food for combating malnutrition, bioprocessing and scale up for production and manufacture of biologicals, R&D on bio-drugs, vaccines, biological reagents and adjutants, diagnostics, implants, devices, medical bioinformatics, clinical research, stem cell research and regenerated medicine. Nano-biotechnology applications for drug, delivery, biosensors, microbial prospecting for novel compounds, genes, bio-energy and bio-fuels, bioremediation, and so on, are other important thrust areas. International cooperation activities matching national needs and the above priorities, will also be accelerated.

8.56. A technology management network that is locally linked to stronger Central resources is an essential link. It is therefore proposed to create ten national/regional technology transfer cells (TTC) to provide high-calibre, specialized and comprehensive technology transfer services; evaluate technology and identify potential commercial uses; develop and execute commercialization and intellectual property protection strategies identifying appropriate potential licensees; negotiate a wide variety of licenses and monitor the licensing arrangements. Each TTC would service a cluster of institutions in a region. New Centres of Excellence (CoEs) would be established within existing universities and medical, agriculture and allied colleges, around innovative leaders.

8.57. Cutting-edge research in biotechnology requires creation of state-of-the-art infrastructure. Therefore, large animal house facilities with Good Manufacturing Practices (GMP) for testing candidate vaccines and biotherapeutics; DNA and stem cell banking facilities; depositories of biological materials; testing facilities for Genetically Modified Organism (GMO)/Living Modified Organism; and validated laboratory facilities to support major clinical trials would be set up. Upgradation/reengineering of existing life science departments of selected university departments and medical colleges by way of providing infrastructure support and faculty, and creating new research agenda would also be undertaken to develop world-class life science departments doing both education and research. Strengthening bioinformatics R&D and infrastructure in terms of higher super computing capabilities, expansion of biogrid, human resource development, linkages with industry, institutional mechanisms for software development and validation, development of an Indian portal site and bioinformatics parks and clusters through PPPs, would also be taken up.

8.58. In the areas of industrial biotechnology, priority would on biotransformation to make bioproducts cost effective; advanced manufacturing technologies for production of vaccines and other medical products; bio-separation technologies for recombinant DNA products; reactor engineering; and development of bioprocesses for high quality textiles, silk and paper industry. Some of the other important R&D areas would be genomics, proteomics, pharmaco-genomics, and in-silico drug design.

8.59. Interdisciplinary 'grand challenge' projects would be taken up in areas of national importance, where biotechnology interventions can bring about significant value addition, cost effectiveness and competitiveness in product and process development. These would be implemented through special management, administrative and organizational structures for time-bound results. Some of the areas identified for this purpose include: (i) food and nutrition security; (ii) molecular breeding of agricultural crops and silk worm; (iii) microbial prospecting for industrial, agricultural, environmental, medical and therapeutic purposes; (iv) new generation human and animal vaccines and delivery systems; (v) diagnostics for health care; (vi) integrated tuberculosis research; (vii) stem cell biology and regenerative medicine; and (viii) bioengineering for implants and medical devices.

8.60. With a view to focus on translational and innovation activities, the existing autonomous institutions would be remodelled. This would require expansion of the scope of the institutions by building centres of translation, innovations and services along with focused networking. The National Institute of Immunology, New Delhi, will establish translational research programmes for the development of anti-HIV microbicides, anti-viral vaccines and Cancer diagnostics and therapeutics. The NCCS,

Pune, will be initiating focused programmes on diabetes and an inter-institutional network programme on HIV and Tuberculosis, apart from establishing centres for cell and tissue engineering and immuno-therapeutics. The Centre for DNA Fingerprinting and Diagnostics, Hyderabad, will undertake new activities such as a national facility for training in DNA profiling; a Disaster Victim Identification Cell (DVIC); and creation of a national DNA database. The National Brain Research Centre, Manesar, will take up Neural Stem Cell research and set up a Clinical Research Centre for brain disorders and Brain Machine Interface. The Institute of Life Sciences, Bhubaneswar, will undertake translational activities for the development of DNA chip-based diagnostics and nano-medicine.

8.61. It is also proposed to establish new institutional structures, especially in the areas which have marginal strength and a critical mass of expertise. These include institutes for translational research in health science and technology; stem cell research and regenerative medicine; UNESCO regional centre for science, education and innovation; agri-food biotechnology and bioprocessing unit; animal biotechnology; marine biotechnology; seri and textile biotechnology and molecular medicine and medical genetics. Besides, three autonomous Translational Molecular Medicine Centres and one centre for plant sciences in existing institutions and taking over of the Rajiv Gandhi Institute of Biotechnology, Thiruvananthapuram, from the Government of Kerala, are also proposed.

8.62. The establishment of biotechnology parks and incubators as part of biotech clusters, essentially through PPPs would be supported. It is also proposed to promote the biotech cluster concept, and based on an analysis of opportunities and feasibility, creation of new clusters at Punjab, Delhi, Haryana, West Bengal, Gujarat, and Orissa would be considered. Major expansion of the SBIRI scheme has also been envisaged. A Special Purpose Vehicle (SPV) will be created for managing this scheme professionally. New models of partnership namely, the Biotechnology Industry Partnership Programme, would be worked out to pursue path-breaking technology initiatives and building greater flexibility in public institutes to enable them to work with industry. A Biotechnology Industry Research Assistance Council (BIRAC) would also be put in place for monitoring, supporting and nurturing R&D in small and medium biotechnology companies.

8.63. A scientific, rigorous, efficient, predictable and consistent regulatory regime for biosafety evaluation and release of protocols is essential. It is therefore proposed to create a 'National Biotechnology Regulatory Authority' to provide an effective, single window clearance mechanism for all biotechnology products.

8.64. The Eleventh Five Year Plan outlay of the DBT has been tentatively fixed at Rs 5649 crore at 2006–07 constant price and Rs 6389 crore at current price.

DEPARTMENT OF SCIENCE AND TECHNOLOGY (DST)

ELEVENTH PLAN OBJECTIVES/THRUST/FOCUS

8.65. It is envisaged that the S&T output indicators of India would register more than double growth rates during the Eleventh Plan period as a result of planned investments based on output directed development strategy. The thrust would be on developing processes and strategic alliances with other departments and State agencies for ensuring efficient delivery of the programmes.

8.66. The focus would be on strengthening R&D systems in order to shorten the waiting time for funds from the current 12–16 months on an average, to 4–6 months. The development of a measurement and assessment system suited to the S&T landscape of the country and an enhanced accountability of research and technology institutions are critical requirements. There is also a need for expanding and strengthening of the institutional framework of higher learning and research, which is showing signs of saturation and maturity. The accelerated growth processes desired by the country calls for development of new aggressive models and establishment of institutions without jeopardizing the existing S&T systems. Major achievements of the DST (R&D) sector during the Tenth Plan period are given in Box 8.4.

ELEVENTH FIVE YEAR PLAN PROGRAMMES

8.67. The low entry of talent into the S&T streams is one of the most serious challenges facing S&T systems in the country. Therefore, during the Eleventh Plan period and beyond, a new scheme under the title 'Innovation in

Box 8.4
Major Achievements of DST during the Tenth Five Year Plan Period

- The Science and Engineering Research Council (SERC) is the flagship programme of DST for Extra Mural Research (EMR) support to individual researchers in the country with a 40–44% share. The support provided by SERC has resulted in more than 500 research publications per year in Science Citation Index (SCI) journals with an average impact factor consistently in the range of 2.2 +/– 0.1.
- SERC has contributed significantly towards augmentation of R&D capabilities at academic institutions and national laboratories in terms of advanced research facilities, which include: National Facility for High Field Nuclear Magnetic Resonance (NMR) at Tata Institute of Fundamental Research; Non-Destructive Evaluation (NDE) facility at National Metallurgical Laboratory and IIT, Chennai; Low temperature High Magnetic field facility at University of Hyderabad; Centre for study of ultra fast processes at University of Madras; National Facility for protein sequencing at IIT, Mumbai; Superconducting Quantum Interference Device (SQUID) based Magneto Encephalography (MEG) system for non-invasive studies of human brain at Indira Gandhi Centre for Atomic Research (IGCAR); NMR facility for biological research at Indian Institute of Science (IISc), Bangalore; and Linear accelerator with conformal radiotherapy and intensity modulation radiotherapy facility at Sanjay Gandhi Post-Graduate Institute of Medical Sciences (SGPGIMS), Lucknow. Ten centres on nano science were also established for quality nano science research aimed at anchoring technology development programmes. SERC has also played a crucial role in strengthening S&T infrastructure in the Universities under the Fund for Improvement of S&T infrastructure (FIST) programme and has helped in rejuvenating to a great extent, R&D activities in the university system.
- The average output indicators per scientist per year of the autonomous institutions during the Tenth Plan period has been in the range of 2–6 publications with an aggregated average impact factor in the range of 2.3 per paper.
- Indian scientists were also assisted and supported in accessing/utilizing some of the major international research facilities like CERN (Geneva), ELETTRA (Italy), Sp Ring-8 (Japan), KEK Accelerator (Japan), National Laboratory for High Energy Physics (Japan), Synchrotron Radiation Sources Beam line facility (Novosibirsk, Russia), FAIR (Germany), Fermi Lab (United States), and Synchrotron Light Source (Singapore), for advanced training and conducting experiments in the fields of crystallography, condensed matter physics, high energy scattering, solid x-ray spectroscopy, nuclear resonance scattering, magnetic Compton studies, and so on.
- Under the Drug and Pharmaceutical Research programme, national facilities in the field of Regulatory toxicology, Proteomics, Pharmacokinetic Evaluation and Biosafety Facility at level 3 have been created. Collaborative R&D projects on diseases like AIDS, TB, diabetes, and leucoderma were supported in R&D and academic institutions with the participation of leading industries. R&D efforts have led to six product patents filed both in India and abroad, 13 process patents, and synthesis of over 250 New Chemical Entities (NCEs) resulting in around 25 lead molecules. Around 7000 molecules already existing in various national laboratories were screened for their efficacy. The programme has been able to bring in private contribution to the tune of Rs 150.00 crore for drugs and pharmaceutical research and has emerged as a good example of the PPP model in research and development.
- Inter-governmental agreements for cooperation in S&T were signed with 16 countries, which include Canada, China, Colombia, the EU, Islamic Republic of Iran, Iceland, Italy, Laos, Mozambique, South Korea, Serbia and Montenegro, Sudan, Sweden, Switzerland, Thailand and USA. Detailed protocols on IPR were also signed with Canada, Israel, USA and Switzerland. Eight joint centres were also set up with active cooperation of some of the bilateral partner countries, namely, Indo-French Centre on Organic Synthesis, IISc, Bangalore; Indo-French Laboratory for Solid State chemistry, IISc, Bangalore; Indo-Russian Centre for Ayurvedic Research, Moscow; Indo-Russian Centre for Gas Hydrate Studies, NIOT, Chennai; Indo-Russian Centre for Earthquake Research, Indian Meteorological Department (IMD), New Delhi; Indo-French Institute of Mathematics, Mumbai, and Indo-Russian Centre for Biotechnology, Allahabad. Several new programmes have also been launched during the Tenth Plan period, which include: Indo-Israel Industrial R&D Cooperation, Indo-Russian Technology Centre, Indo-UK Science and Innovation Council, Indo-Russian S&T Cooperation in cutting-edge areas, Indo-Canadian S&T Cooperation in cutting-edge areas, and establishment of Joint Bilateral Centres of Excellence in the areas of Non-ferrous Metallurgy, Biomedical Technology and Lasers and Accelerators.

Science Pursuit for Inspired Research' (INSPIRE) would be initiated to attract and foster talent in scientific research. The main features of the proposed scheme would be innovation funding in schools (one million young innovators); summer camp with Science Icons (for high performers); assured opportunity schemes for proven talent; and retention of talent in publicly-funded research through PPP. The Oversight Committee's recommendation regarding SHE providing 10000 scholarships of one lakh rupees each per year, for attracting talented science students to BSc and MSc courses, would also be subsumed in this scheme.

8.68. Research and development support mechanisms will be strengthened by launching a two-pronged strategy. While continuing its endeavour to widen and strengthen the base of basic research through appropriate HRD measures and building up of research capabilities of the academic sector, support would also be provided for undertaking major, internationally competitive and front-ranking projects through a Science and Engineering Research Board. For this purpose, the existing SERC mechanism would be restructured in to the National Science and Engineering Research Board. Necessary in-house infrastructure and suitable changes in procedural mechanisms will be undertaken to ensure both quality and speed in the delivery of resources. A special programme for rejuvenation of research in universities would be initiated.

8.69. The national mission on nano science and technology would be a major new programme, designed to enable India to become a significant player in the global race by tapping the potential applications of nano science and technology. The proposed Nano Science and Technology Mission would focus on basic research, infrastructure development for quality nano science and technology research, human resource development, forging international collaborations and most importantly, promoting PPP in the area of nano science and technology. The Drugs and Pharmaceutical Research Programme, which has emerged as a true PPP in the area of pharmaceutical research and development, will be another major programme to be pursued during the Eleventh Plan period.

8.70. Investment in autonomous institutions would be on the basis of performance and assistance will be provided to them to attain global best standards in science and engineering. A study of impact assessment of the Technology Information, Forecasting and Assessment Council (TIFAC) and National Accreditation Board for Testing and Calibration Laboratories (NABL) has also been planned. The proposed study will form a decision tool to shape the future structure and programmes of these two organizations. TIFAC will be developed into a policy body for developing technology foresight and strengthening the innovation infrastructure of the country. The Survey of India (SoI) enjoys brand equity in the area of geo-spatial products. In the wake of a new map policy of India, geo-spatial products have gained market value in the consumer market. Keeping this in view, SoI requires an urgent package for modernization of its physical, human, market and intellectual capitals. The modernization package of SoI will also bring about organic linkages in the programmes of the National Atlas and Thematic Mapping Organization. A few new autonomous S&T institutions would also be established in critical areas like glaciology, molecular materials, pre-competitive research institutes for computer sciences, and so on.

8.71. Several new initiatives like the Water Technology Initiative, setting up of innovation clusters, security technology initiative, and programmes for setting up mega facilities for basic research will also be taken up. The Water Technology Initiative would focus on the design and development of low-cost solutions for safe drinking water for domestic use. Innovation clusters are emerging on the global platform and numerous success stories of such innovation clusters benefitting both academic and industrial sectors have been reported. It is necessary for India to mount such an initiative under an effective PPP model in areas where the trade and advantages have already been established and the clustering processes are evident. A proposal for taking up a National Innovation Project has also been contemplated, which would be taken up after a dialogue with key stakeholders to identify the needs regarding the innovation system and possible interventions, with World Bank involvement. The Security Technology Initiative would address issues relating to internal security. DST, along with DAE, has also identified areas where an effective partnership of the two departments can bring about effective capacity building in the university and academic sector for building mega facilities for basic research both within and outside the country.

8.72. The Eleventh Five Year Plan outlay of DST has been tentatively fixed at Rs 9750 crore at 2006–07 constant price and Rs 11028 crore at current price. The existing allocation for schemes like INSPIRE, Security Technology Initiative and support to autonomous institutions may need to be enhanced during the course of the Plan, depending upon the actual progress.

SCIENTIFIC AND INDUSTRIAL RESEARCH

ELEVENTH PLAN OBJECTIVES/THRUST/FOCUS

8.73. The avowed objectives of the Department of Scientific and Industrial Research (DSIR) are to promote industrial research, technology development and transfer, and its utilization, with a view to making Indian industry globally competitive. During the Eleventh Plan, the focus would be on promoting creativity and innovation among individuals; promoting and supporting industry for development of new products, processes and technologies; attracting venture capital funding; developing the consultancy profession; promoting commercialization of technologies in India and abroad; and creating awareness about the latest IPR regime.

8.74. The focus of CSIR would be on finding holistic and optimal solutions to the pressing problems of the country by deploying technologies ranging from the simplest to the most sophisticated ones. Innovation in all spheres of activities, ranging from science, technology, management and financing, would be supported. The thrust would be on adoption of three-pronged approach to: (i) conceptualize, plan and work, in network mode, on R&D of relevance both nationally and globally and to align it with public, private, strategic or social needs as the case may be; (ii) forge viable, defined and scientifically challenging R&D projects in supra institutional mode to make each laboratory a cohesive and close-knit unit. This would help in aligning and reinforcing the core competency of the laboratory; and (iii) build within each laboratory, Centres of Sustainable Growth, a kind of magnet to attract scientists/technologists of Indian origin, industry (both national and foreign) and a large number of trainees. Such centres would aim to be creative think-tanks to look at the future with a clear vision. Major achievements of DSIR/CSIR during the Tenth Plan period are given in Box 8.5.

Box 8.5
Major Achievements of DSIR/CSIR during the Tenth Five Year Plan Period

- Major achievements under the Technology Promotion, Development and Utilization Programme (TPDU) programme include: Composite insulators for high power transmission; technologies for manufacture of digested organic supplement enriched with micronutrients, Tetrabromobisphenol-A; Liposomal Amphotericin-B, Pyrazinamide using the catalytic route; and processes for Hydrogen Sulphide removal and recovery of sulphur from sour gases; isolation of natural dyes from forest plants of Uttaranchal. A cotton seed delinting plant and an integrated pilot demonstration plant for spice processing have also been developed in collaboration with various industries.
- The two–seater, all composite trainer aircraft Hansa designed and built by National Aerospace Laboratories has been certified by Director General Civil Aviation (DGCA) for day and night flying. It is now being manufactured along with a private partner and a dozen of them are now flying successfully across the country. Saras, India's first indigenously developed, multi-role civilian aircraft, took its inaugural test flight on 22 August 2004, and till March 2007, the prototype-1 has made more than 110 test flights. Taxi trials for the second prototype have begun and it is expected that the prototype-2 test flight would commence soon. After successful completion of the test flights and DGCA license, the aircraft will go in for commercialization by Hindustan Aeronautics Limited.
- For the first time in India, an optical fibre amplifier for light wave telecommunication network has been developed using erbium-doped optical fibre (EDF) and power semiconductor pump laser source which has the potential for use in the propagation of 'Fibre-to–Home' technology. An alternative novel route for synthesis of 1, 1', 1"-Tris 4'-hydroxyphenyl ethane (THPE) was developed and transferred.
- CSIR operated a New Millennium Indian Technology Leadership Initiative (NMITLI) scheme in PPP mode through which 42 projects were developed involving 65 industrial partners and 222 research groups for capturing global technology leadership position. Some of the significant achievements were: development of a new pharmacophore for the treatment of tuberculosis where the molecule works through combination therapy (compatible with the present drugs), is less toxic, clears the total infection within two months and no recurrence has been observed; development of a novel drug delivery system based on dry powder inhalation of micro particles containing rifampicin/rifabutin and isoniazid; development of 'Bio Suite' and ' Geno Cluster' software, and also of two new varieties of *Mentha piperita* namely, 'CIM-Indus' (with the characteristic of high menthofuran and pulegone) and 'CIM-Madhuras' (with the characteristic of sweet smell).
- In the areas of drugs and pharmaceuticals, significant achievements were related to: isolation of a compound from the leaf of the betel plant (*piper betel*) that is able to induce death of cancer cells in chronic myeloid leukemia; crude extract prepared from a marine organism (mussel) by the enzyme-acid hydrolyzing process shows a potent anti-malarial activity when examined for *in-vitro* cultures of *Plasmodium falciparum* in human erythrocytes; isolation of a natural compound

from *Boswellia* species, and alternatively prepared its semi-synthetic compounds for cancer of colon, prostrate, liver, breast, central nervous system, leukemia and malignancy of other tissues, including ascites and solid tumors; herbal formulation from the plant extract of *Cedrus deodar* for the treatment of cancer, a process for high-level production of recombinant Staphylokinase which is produced intracellularly using a genetically engineered strain of *Escherichia coli*; developed a single plant base standardized hepatoprotective agent useful for the treatment of liver disorders such as alcoholic and viral cirrhosis; developed a herbal medicament which has shown promising anti-stroke activity along with antioxidant and anti-inflammatory properties on pre-treatment in rats; developed a process for the oral delivery of insulin and also of hepatitis B vaccine, this new invention is a boon to the diabetic population showing the reduction of blood glucose levels comparable to that of the injectable insulin; isolated the first biologically derived molecule ATB 1 that inhibits HIV-1 protease; developed gelatin micro spheres wherein SSD-loaded collagen membranes have been evaluated for wound healing; developed and commercialized two important formulations one as a brand name Regen-D™ –60 for skin graft and burn injuries, while the other, Regen-D™ –150, meant for diabetic foot ulcer.

- Some other important achievements include: development of synthetic peptide-based nanotubes; Thin Film Composite reverse osmosis high flux membrane suitable for treatment of tertiary treated sewage water; technology for arsenic and iron removal based on ceramic membrane technology for the production of safe drinking water from contaminated ground water; developed, demonstrated and transferred an Ultra Filtration (UF) membrane-based water purification technology which removes germs, cysts, spores, parasites, bacteria, cryptosporidium, endotoxin, Pseudomonas viruses of hepatitis A and E (the filtration unit requires no electricity and chemicals to filter water); and design and development of a 10HP small tractor. A Fog Forecast and Visibility model, which is a combination of high performance computing and new generation dynamical meso-scale models, advanced data analysis and informatics, was also developed and calibrated during this period.
- During the Tenth Plan, the research outputs of CSIR had been of a very high order. It has emerged among the top three entities from the developing world in terms of PCT filing. US patents granted are considered as one of the indices in measuring the technological achievement of a country. CSIR was granted 667 US patents during the Tenth Plan. 62% of the total US patents granted to Indians excluding, NRIs and foreign assignees, belonged to CSIR. As a result of researches carried out in the national laboratories, over 13000 basic research papers were published in internationally peer reviewed journals. The average impact factor per paper of nearly 2.01 has been achieved during 2005–06. The external cash flow from contract research was nearly Rs 1500 crore.
- HRD initiatives: During the Tenth Plan period, 5946 JRFs (NET qualified), 2228 Senior Research Fellows, 484 Research Associates, 375 Senior Research Associates (Under Scientist's Pool Scheme), and 35 Shyama Prasad Mukherjee Fellows were supported in different disciplines till 31 March 2007. 59 meritorious scientists were recognized with the prestigious Shanti Swarup Bhatnagar prizes for their outstanding research contributions done primarily in India, and 25 CSIR Scientists were given Young Scientist Awards to promote in-house excellence, during the same period.

ELEVENTH FIVE YEAR PLAN PROGRAMMES

8.75. During the Eleventh Five Year Plan, DSIR would continue the TPDU programme with increased emphasis on technopreneur promotion, technology development and demonstration, information facilitation, PPP with SMEs in SBIRI mode, and Funding for Accelerating Start-ups in Technology (FAST). These programmes will be supplemented by technology transfer and management assistance as well as incentives for research and development. Focus will be to create opportunities for starting new technology- and knowledge-based businesses by science entrepreneurs, encouraging small businesses to increase their R&D capabilities and capacities and stimulating technological innovation. The major objective of the FAST programme will be to prepare start-up companies to become eligible for venture capital funding. The IPR programme will aim at providing support for patent filing, creating information systems and facilities for patent searches by using modern software tools and commercialization of patented innovations. Efforts would also be made to operationalize an Indo-Australian Bi-national Industrial Research and Development Programme; undertake technology benchmarking and audit exercise; establish technology management national resource centres; and set up an S&T portal in a PPP mode. Central Electronics Limited has set a target to achieve solar photovoltaic production of 25 MW per annum and a production of 30000 to 40000 of phased control modules per year during the Eleventh Plan period. The focus of the National Research Development Corporation will be on incubation and venture capital funding, development of basic design engineering packages, development of rural clusters in dairy and sericulture industries and programmes for development of women entrepreneurship and the NER. The CDC will emphasize on consultancy services exports and implementation of the Technical Consultancy Development Programme for Asia and the Pacific.

8.76. CSIR laboratories will seek to leverage their unique scientific and technological capabilities through a series of:

- Supra-institutional project wherein the laboratory will have at least one flagship project in which a majority of the groups within the laboratory participate and synergize the in-house capabilities to optimize outputs;
- Inter-laboratory network mode projects started during the Tenth Plan which will be further strengthened with a sharp focus to develop products/processes and knowledge;
- Network mode with institutions/agencies outside CSIR to develop advanced technologies/products/prototypes/ knowledge base that require multi-disciplinary inputs and synergies; and
- Major national facilities which will be created in frontier areas to help in the generation of competitive knowledge capabilities at par with international standards of future relevance.

8.77. The Plan would be operationalized by undertaking projects which would create high value and large impact on socio-economic delivery. A few major projects are:

- Supra-institutional projects: technology development and R&D initiatives in aerospace; niche food processing technologies for cost effective, safe, hygienic, nutritious food for the targeted population; evolution of the Indian lithosphere—focus on major earth processes, natural resources and the geo-environment since the break-up of gondwana super content; science for the development of a forecasting system for the waters around India; development of know-how and technology for environmental friendly conversion and utilization of biomass to fuels, lubricants and additives; competencies in clean coal initiative and energy conservation technologies leading to development of Integrated Gasification Combined Cycle (IGCC) and Under Ground Coal Gasification (UGCG) in India; development of new drugs programmes for parasitic diseases and microbial infections.
- Networked projects: designing and developing a regional aircraft specially suited for developing economies; plasma proteomics health, environment and disease; exploitation of India's rich microbial diversity; pathway engineering and system biology approach towards homologous and heterologous expression of high-value phytoceuticals; multi-scale modelling platform including state-of–the-art multi tera flop high performance computing facility; uncertainty reduction, vulnerability impact assessment, mitigation policy intervention and capacity building for global change; programme on climate change; hydrogen energy initiative—overcoming materials challenges for the generation, storage and conversion of hydrogen using fuel cells; design and fabrication capabilities for very high power, high efficiency and very high frequency microwave tubes; fabrication of Light Emitting Diode devices and systems for solid state lighting applications; technology for assessment and refurbishment of engineering materials and components; development of advanced lightweight metallic materials for engineering applications; diabetes mellitus—new drug discovery R&D, molecular mechanisms and genetic factors; nano material and nano devices in health and disease; comparative genomics and biology of non-coding RNA in the human genome.
- Inter-agency projects: new insights in cancer biology—identification of novel targets and development of target based molecular medicine; development of cost effective mine water reclamation technology for providing safe drinking water; utilization of indigenous know-how to address drinking water needs in coastal/rural areas.
- National facilities: Advanced Centre for Flight Mechanics and Control; facilities for functional genomic research (i) cellomics facility, (ii) zebrafish facility, (iii) Liquid Chromatograph-Nuclear Magnetic Resonance Spectrometer facility; Advanced Centre for Protein Informatics, Science, Engineering and Technology; setting up a compact high energy light

source for the structural analysis of biomacromolecules; Centre of Excellence for lipid research; Bio-Safety Level-4 facility for infectious diseases research.

8.78. Recognizing the changing context of scientific enterprise and the present national needs, HRD programmes would be strengthened with a focus on fostering scientific research in universities and other academic, scientific and engineering institutions, and attract the brightest young persons to careers in science and technology. Under the Intellectual Property and Technology Management scheme, the major activities would be relating to: filing, capturing, prosecution and maintenance of IPR for CSIR R&D outputs; valuation and valorization of patent and IP portfolios; surveillance for infringement and enforcement of IPR; human resources in IP cells of CSIR laboratories; modernization of computing, communication and related facilities and infrastructure. Activities pertaining to Early-Stage Venture Fund; National Innovation Foundation; Human Resource Development Centre; R&D management and business development; international scientific collaboration; and science dissemination would be strengthened under the R&D Management Support scheme.

8.79. The New Millennium Indian Technology Leadership Initiative (NMITLI) scheme will be expanded with new approaches of innovation development and focus on funding with industry (50:50 Initiative); co-financing with venture capital funds; and acquisition of early stage relevant knowledge/IP for portfolio building. An Institute of Translational Research would be set up as a part of the new scheme for application of knowledge of modern biology into clinical care; systematic collection and analysis of large amounts of clinical data; development of specific stem cell populations to treat a variety of illnesses such as Parkinson's disease, Type I diabetes, retinal degeneration, spinal cord damage, multiple sclerosis; development of nano materials, and so on. Training programmes broadly in the areas of induction, orientation, refresher and skill upgradation, would be continued for different categories of CSIR staff in addition to the number of other programmes in specialized areas such as technology management, research methodology, development of management information system, e-procurement, and so on. The scope of the Human Resource Development Centre would be expanded to give impetus to produce specialized scientific human resource in selected frontier areas, to take up scientific industrial research as a career

8.80. The Eleventh Five Year Plan outlay of the DSIR, including CSIR, has been tentatively fixed at Rs 7957 crore at 2006–07 constant price and Rs 9000 crore at current price.

EARTH SCIENCES

ELEVENTH PLAN OBJECTIVES/THRUST/FOCUS

8.81. The Ministry of Earth Sciences (MoES) was created in July 2006, with the objective to reorganize national effort in atmospheric and ocean sciences and related services by integrating activities of related departments such as the Department of Ocean Development, India Meteorological Department (IMD), Indian Institute of Tropical Meteorology (IITM) and National Centre for Medium Range Weather Forecasting (NCMRWF). The focus will on the study of interdisciplinary links of phenomena relating to global climate change and to create a framework for understanding the complex interactions among key elements of the Earth system, namely ocean, atmosphere and the Earth, encompassing national programmes in ocean science, meteorology, climate, environment and seismology. The emphasis of activities in the area of ocean science would be towards the development of technology to harness ocean resources with the active participation and support of national R&D laboratories, educational institutions and industries. There will be a special thrust on the development of several cutting-edge technologies, including deep-sea mining technology; ocean information services; marine geophysical surveys; development of potential drugs from the sea; setting up of metallurgical plant for extraction of metals from polymetallic nodules; and to undertake front-ranking research in polar science and southern ocean studies. Major achievements of the MoES during the Tenth Plan period are given in Box 8.6.

ELEVENTH FIVE YEAR PLAN PROGRAMMES

8.82. India has made great strides both in polar sciences and related logistics, through a judicious and harmonious blend of multi-institutional expertise brought together under the umbrella of the MoES. This has paved the way

Box 8.6
Major Achievements of MoES during the Tenth Five Year Plan Period

- The major achievements in ocean science were related to:
  - Development and demonstration of desalination technology to cater to the requirement of fresh water in coastal States and island territories of India
  - Setting up an interim early tsunami and storm surge warning system
  - Strengthening of ocean observing network by deployment of state-of-the-art technology data buoys and Argo floats for operational weather forecast and climate variability studies
  - Indigenous development of data buoys and tide gauges to meet the requirement of ocean observations
  - Completion of geophysical surveys for delineation of the continental shelf
  - Close grid surveys for polymetallic nodules in the allotted area in the central Indian Ocean Basin
  - Establishment of an extractive metallurgical pilot plant to extract copper, nickel and cobalt from the nodules
  - Design, development and testing of soil sampler at 5000 m depth in the central Indian Ocean
  - Establishment of a Ferro-Silico pilot plant at NML
  - Design and development of Remotely Operable Vehicle capable of working up to 6000m depth
  - Development and testing of deep sea crawler at 500m depth
  - Completion of clinical trials of two potential drug molecules from marine organisms having anti-diabetic and anti-hyper lipedemic properties
  - Multi-disciplinary studies to assess the marine living resources of the Indian seas, and to understand the large-scale variation of fishery resources
  - Monitoring of coastal pollution to assess the health of the coastal seas of India;
  - Strengthening of basic research by setting up of a network of nine Ocean Science and Technology Cells in universities/ institutes and a chain of Marine Data Centres at National Institutions
- NIOT has developed and demonstrated commercial-scale Low Temperature Thermal Desalination Technology (LTTD) and a land based 0.1 million litre per day (MLD) plant was commissioned at Kavaratti, in May 2005. The technology was upgraded and a 1 MLD barge-mounted demonstration plant was commissioned in April 2006.
- Forecasting services for monsoons and other weather/climate parameters, ocean state, earthquakes, tsunamis and other phenomena related to earth systems were provided through well-integrated programmes. IMD acted as a national weather service provider by focusing its efforts on weather forecasting services for the government, public and weather-sensitive activities like agriculture, aviation, shipping, engineering industry, environment and hydrometeorology.
- IITM is an institution dedicated to atmospheric science, mesoscale processes, climate and paleo climate research. NCMRWF continued to develop expertise on numerical modelling and data assimilation. Capability to analyse the storm/cyclone structure using data received from Doppler Weather Radars installed at Chennai, Kolkata, Machhilipatnam, Vishakhapatnam and Sriharikota, helped in providing accurate cyclone and weather warning. About 100 Digital Cyclone Warning Dissemination centres were setup along the Andhra coast and the warnings were disseminated directly to the concerned agencies.
- The other major achievements in the areas of atmospheric sciences include: upgradation of meteorological capability at airports; establishment of a Mountain Meteorology Centre at Delhi to provide meteorological inputs to enable prediction of landslides, avalanches and flash floods; setting up of an Earthquake Risk Evaluation Centre at Delhi for seismic micro-zonation at a scale of 1: 50000; validation of crop-weather models for a variety of crops; preparation of atlases depicting the spatial and temporal variations in rainfall during 1813–2003 over India; and development of a state-of-the-art atmospheric chemistry model to study long-term trends in the atmosphere from the surface to 100 km

for the country to sustain its scientific endeavour in the icy continent on a year-round basis, from the Indian Permanent station, Maitri.

8.83. The major endeavours under polar science would include: launch of research expeditions to the Arctic, preferably through international cooperation; construction of a new Antarctic Research Station to enhance research activities; establishment of a dedicated satellite based communication and data transmission system between the Antarctic and India; undertake southern Indian oceanographic studies for assessment of living and non-living resources and acquisition of ice class vessels.

8.84. In the area of desalination technology, setting up of a 10 MLD capacity barge-mounted plant has been envisaged. In the next phase, this programme would be expanded with industry partnership, for taking up large-scale plants of 25–50 MLD capacity. The thrust of NIOT would be on the development of world-class ocean technology by strengthening its activities related to: design, development and demonstration of underwater technologies for deep sea mining; development of underwater materials and sensors; creation of seafront facility and other research infrastructure for testing of various oceanographic equipment; and coastal engineering related activities. The emphasis of NIOT would on societal applications of various ocean sciences related technologies, and development of necessary infrastructure and skill base to support and maintain the deep ocean systems. Indian National Centre for Ocean Information Services, Hyderabad, would be strengthened for providing reliable coastal ocean services and to meet the requirement of a wide range of user communities in India. User-oriented data/data products such as species specific Potential Fishing Zone advisories and Coastal Ocean State forecast would be generated and disseminated using existing and upcoming satellites and in-situ data, on an operational basis. Electronic display boards and information kiosks would be established in every coastal village covering the entire coast of India for providing various ocean information services including storms, cyclones, weather, sea state, and so on. Special focus would be on the development of an effective early warnings system for oceanogenic disasters such as storm surges and tsunami. Under the Integrated Coastal Marine Area Management and Coastal Ocean Monitoring Area and Prediction Systems programmes, focus would be on the demonstration of ideal coastal protection measures, coastal circulation, ecosystem modelling, marine ecotoxicology, carbon cycling in coastal waters and preparation of a coastal risk atlas; and modelling of movement of oil spills along the western and eastern Exclusive Economic Zone of India.

8.85. Under atmospheric science and technology, emphasis would be on modernization of the observation networks in a phased manner. This will facilitate rendering of various services relating to weather and climate to the public (by setting up a dedicated weather channel) and to other specific sectors like agriculture, aviation and hydrology. Focus would on the development of expertise both for numerical models and assimilated models. This is essential for making an accurate forecast of local-scale weather which is highly diverse in India due to its climatic and topographic condition. In addition, strengthening of infrastructure facilities for numerical weather modelling; undertaking state-of-the-art climate and atmospheric research by setting up a Centre of Climate Studies to act as a dynamic feedback to improve weather forecast and services; and climate research and monitoring with focus on the computing and data requirements to build a credible climate service facility in India, have also been envisaged. Focus will also be on Numerical Weather Prediction based on a global Atmospheric General Circulation Model of horizontal resolution of 25 km in order to generate a district/taluk level Agromet Advisory Service. Seismic monitoring for earthquake detection and support to a tsunami warning system and other related hazards would be initiated, and a state-of-the-art network to augment real time connectivity with major analysis and decision support centres will be established at Delhi. Micro-zonation activity would be strengthened to study hazard potential in a few cities and hot spots with respect to seismigenic areas would be identified. Micro-zonation of specific geo-hazards like land slides, inundation and damage potential by cyclones and floods, would be taken up in a project mode. IMD will cover all the 127 agro climatic zones and provide forecast to these units on a bi-weekly basis.

8.86. The Eleventh Five Year Plan outlay of the MoES has been tentatively fixed at Rs 6193 crore at 2006–07 constant price and Rs 7004 crore at current price.

8.87. The Progress of Plan Outlays/Expenditure during the Tenth Five Year Plan and Eleventh Plan Outlays of the central scientific departments is given in Annexure 8.1. In absolute terms, the Eleventh Five Year Plan proposed allocation for scientific departments is almost 3–4 times that of the Tenth Plan. The major deliverables of the scientific departments are given in Annexure 8.2.

ANNEXURE 8.1
Progress of Plan Expenditure of Central Scientific Departments

(Rs in crore)

S. No.	S&T Department/ Agencies	Tenth Plan (2002–07) Outlay	Annual Plan 2002–03		Annual Plan 2003–04		Annual Plan 2004–05		Annual Plan 2005–06		Annual Plan 2006–7		Tenth Plan (2002–07)		Eleventh Plan (2007–12) Projected Outlay (at current price)
			BE	Actuals	BE	Actual	BE	Actual	BE	Actual	BE	RE	Total BE	Anti Expdr.	
1	2	3	4	5	6	7	8	9	10	11	12	13	15	16	17
1	Dept. of Atomic Energy (R&D Sector)	3501.35	535.00	405.56	464.00	409.94	703.58	609.52	872.74	770.80	1003.00	1032.72	3578.32	3228.54	11000.00
2	Ministry of Earth Sciences	1125.00	175.00	138.69	175.00	147.38	200.00	198.88	340.00	225.04	438.00	417.49*	1328.00	1127.48	7004.00
3	Dept. of Science & Tech.	3400.00	625.00	537.10	800.00	602.37	900.00	896.26	1250.00	1024.24	1367.00	964.16 #	4942.00	4024.13	11028.00
4	Dept. of Biotechnology	1450.00	225.00	203.25	260.00	248.76	310.00	319.27	445.00	386.36	521.00	496.00	1761.00	1653.64	6389.00
5	Dept. of Scientific & Industrial Research, incl. CSIR	2575.00	440.00	366.96	520.00	380.15	650.00	596.25	846.00	730.33	975.00	775.00	3431.00	2848.69	9000.00
6	Dept. of Space	13250.00	1950.00	1846.71	2050.00	1941.00	2400.00	2194.70	2800.00	2294.30	3220.00	2600.00	12420.00	10876.71	30883.00
	Grand Total	25301.35	3950.00	3498.27	4269.00	3729.60	5163.58	4814.88	6553.74	5431.07	7524.00	6285.37	27460.32	23759.19	75304.00

Note: * including outlays for IMD, NCMRWF & IITM; # excluding outlays for IMD, MCMRWF & IITM.

ANNEXURE 8.2

Major Deliverables of Scientific Departments during the Eleventh Five Year Plan

- Department of Space (DoS)
  - Development of satellite launch capabilities to GSLV Mk-III
  - Indigenous development and initiation of cryogenic engine and stages
  - Enhancing INSAT systems capacity for communications and broadcasting to 500 transponders
  - Development of critical technologies for manned missions in space
  - Exploration of the lunar environment through Chandrayaan
  - Establishing Diurnal All Weather Microwave Imaging Capability, crucial for Natural Resource Management (NRM) applications in agriculture and disaster management
  - Establishing Regional Satellite Navigational System and providing Global Positioning Services
  - Setting up a constellation of state-of-the-art high-resolution remote sensing satellites for NRM, weather forecasting and disaster management
  - Enlarging societal applications of space technology in areas of education, health care, rural development, agriculture and disaster management
  - Capacity building for advanced space missions and infrastructure, creation of ground facilities and technology upgradation

- Department of Atomic Energy (DAE)
  - Development of a new campus for Bhaba Atomic Research Centre (BARC) at Vishakhapatnam
  - Infrastructure upgradation at—
    - (i) Tata Institute of Fundamental Research (TIFR), Mumbai
    - (ii) Institute of Plasma Research (IPR), Gandhinagar
    - (iii) Variable Energy Cyclotron Centre (VECC), Kolkata
    - (iv) Saha Institute of Nuclear Physics (SINP), Kolkata
  - Participation in the International Thermo-nuclear Experimental Reactor
  - Setting up of a National Institute of Science Education and Research (NISER)
  - Intensification of Uranium exploration and development of aerial electromagnetic survey capability
  - Thorium fuel cycle development
  - Life extension of existing nuclear/heavy water power plants
  - Fuel cycle and safety related R&D
  - Development of new energy systems such as Advance Heavy Water Reactor (AHWR), Indian High Temperature Reactor (IHTR) and a multi-purpose research reactor with facility to accommodate a Proton beam-driven neutron source
  - Setting up Scientific Frontier Research Facilities such as or Radioactive Ion Beam (RIB) or Indian Neutrino Observatory (INO)
  - Participation in international mega-science projects like:
    - (i) Facility for Anti Proton and Ion Research (FAIR)
    - (ii) International Linear Collider (ILC)
    - (iii) X-Ray Free Electronic Laser (XFEL)

- Department of Earth Sciences
  - Comprehensive modernization of India Meteorological Department (IMD) with a network of state-of-the-art weather observation systems—Automatic Weather Stations, Rain Gauges and Data Buoys connected with Doppler Weather Radars. This network will be serviced by an IT-based decision support system using 10 Teraflop Supercomputing facilities at IMD, NCMRWF and IITM
  - Provision of comprehensive atmospheric, hydrological, land surface and oceanic data services to client communities
  - Dissemination of weather forecasts/warnings, flood and cyclone warnings, tsunami early warnings for coastal communities, and so on, and providing agro-met services to all farmers
  - R&D on climate change and cloud seeding
  - Seismic research on earthquake precursors and micro-zonation of major earthquake prone cities
  - Polar science R&D; a third Indian station in Antarctica and a dedicated Arctic Expedition; acquisition of an ice–class vessel

- Development and exploitation of Exclusive Economic Zone or EEZ and the continental shelf; acquisition of state-of-the-art technologies for deep-sea mining and manned missions, particularly for gas hydrates and polymetallic nodules
- Upscale sea water desalination technology up to 25 million litres/day to meet the potable water supply requirements of coastal cities and areas affected by coastal salinity

- **Department of Science and Technology (DST)**
  - National Mission on development of nanotechnology
  - Creation of new R&D institutes on Molecular Materials, and Glaciology
  - Modernize existing R&D institutions
  - Modernization of SoI and Creation of a seamless GIS in digital format
  - Promote innovation and creation of Intellectual Property and National Innovation clusters
  - Attracting bright young students to take up science as career by launching a new scheme INSPIRE to cover 100000 scholarships of Rs 1 lakh per year each for students joining Universities and dedicating themselves for scientific research. INSPIRE will also fund innovation in schools (one million young innovators) and provide assured opportunity schemes for proven talent and for retention of talent in public funded research through PPP.
  - Building research capabilities in the academic sector

- **Department of Scientific and Industrial Research**
  - Creation of Centres of Excellence in CSIR laboratories
  - Expanding the New Millennium Technology Leadership Initiative (NMTLI)
  - Providing fellowships for research in basic sciences and interdisciplinary areas
  - Setting up Translational Research Centres
  - R&D on Photovoltaics and solar energy
  - Technology development in the strategic aerospace sector
  - Development of alternative energy source for a cleaner and green environment
  - Expanding scientific frontiers in areas such as Plasma Proteomics, bioactive molecules, bio-energy technology, cancer biotechnology and gene environment

- **Department of Biotechnology (DBT)**
  - Creation of new institutes for
    - (i) Stem Cell Research
    - (ii) Marine Biotechnology
    - (iii) Centre for Translational Research in Public Health
    - (iv) Seri Biotechnology
    - (v) Animal Biotechnology
    - (vi) National Institute for Agri-food Biotechnology at Punjab Knowledge City
  - Human Resource Development—Biotechnologists with expertise in Genomics, Proteomics and Metabolomics, Development of 'Info-bio' and 'Info-bio-nano' manpower
  - Creation of a SPV for Small Business Innovation Research Initiative (SIBRI) to pursue technological innovation
  - Creation of: Large animal house facilities for testing candidate vaccines; DNA and stem cell banks and depositories of biological materials.

9

Environment and Climate Change

9.1 ENVIRONMENT

9.1.1. Protection of the environment has to be a central part of any sustainable inclusive growth strategy. This aspect of development is especially important in the Eleventh Plan when consciousness of the dangers of environmental degradation has increased greatly. Population growth, urbanization, and anthropogenic development employing energy-intensive technologies have resulted in injecting a heavy load of pollutants into the environment. More recently, the issue assumed special importance because of the accumulation of evidence of global warming and the associated climate change that it is likely to bring.

9.1.2. An important feature of any environmental strategy is that environmental objectives require action in several areas, which typically lie in the purview of different ministries. The Ministry of Environment and Forests (MoEF) has the important role of monitoring the development process and its environmental impact in a perspective of sustainable development and to devise suitable regulatory structures to achieve the desired results. While this role is crucial, environmental objectives can only be achieved if environmental concerns are internalized in policymaking in a large number of sectors. This would require sharing of responsibility at all levels of government and across sectors with respect to monitoring of pollution, enforcement of regulations, and development of programmes for mitigation and abatement. Regulatory enforcement must also be combined with incentives, including market and fiscal mechanisms to encourage both industry and people in their day-to-day working lives to act in a manner responsive to environmental concerns. Sustainable use of natural resources also requires community participation with a responsible role assigned to the communities for conservation.

9.1.3. In this chapter, we outline the main issues in the traditional area of environment and also consider the new challenges posed by climate change.

OVERVIEW

9.1.4. The Tenth Plan was a period of extensive review of environmental processes and law. The first National Environment Policy was put into place in May 2006. Also, the re-engineering of the environmental clearance process and Environmental Impact Assessment (EIA) Notification and review of the Coastal Regulation Zone Notification were undertaken to improve the quality of environmental governance. The Eleventh Plan must build on this experience by integrating environment considerations into policymaking in all sectors of the economy—infrastructure, transport, water supply, sanitation, industry, agriculture, and anti-poverty programmes. It also calls for strengthening the oversight and regulatory framework for environment management so that development decisions do not impinge adversely on sustainability.

9.1.5. Some initiatives needed to integrate environmental concerns into planning and developmental activities across all the sectors are given below:

- Environment is a residual Central subject. Since regulation and enforcement in this area cannot be handled by the Central Government alone and the responsibility of maintaining the environment rests at all levels of government, we need to consider whether environment can be made a concurrent subject in the constitution. This will help the State Governments and the local authorities to enact and notify their own enforcement laws and rules to ensure compliance of relevant environmental norms.

- There is a case for setting up an independent, statutory body on sustainable development with the specific responsibility of guiding government policies and programmes for making them more socially and environmentally sustainable, and to monitor and evaluate their outcomes. This body should comprise eminent environmental experts and citizens with a long and publicly known record in environmental research or action. It should have adequate powers to address environment concerns and not be a purely advisory body.
- The State Pollution Control Boards should be restructured into statutory Environment Protection Authorities with the mandate of developing regulations, standards and upgraded facilities for enforcing compliance.
- At the district level, the scheme of Paryavaran Vahinis, or committees of concerned citizens, should be revived to serve as environmental watchdogs and undertake selective first hand monitoring of the environmental situation in the districts.
- For improving the quality and transparency of the environmental clearance process, prior informed consent of the local self governments of the respective area, as specifically provided in PESA, may be introduced for proposals requiring environmental clearance. Public hearing should also be made mandatory for the activities specified in the EIA notification.

ENVIRONMENTAL IMPACT ASSESSMENT (EIA)

9.1.6. EIA is an important management tool for integrating environmental concerns in the development process and for improved decision making. The MoEF in 1994 issued the first EIA Notification prescribing mandatory environmental clearance for 32 categories of developmental activities. The process involved consideration of environmental consequences before starting projects and included procedures like EIA study, public hearing in certain cases, and consideration of the outcome by expert groups before issuing of final clearance by MoEF. This process takes time, often causing long delays in commencement of projects. MoEF organized a re-engineering of the process and a fresh notification was issued in September 2006. The specific modifications made in the EIA notification are summarized in Table 9.1.1.

TABLE 9.1.1
Changes in Environment Clearance Notification, 2006

Step	Pre 2006 Notification position	As per 2006 Notification
Activities requiring clearance	32 activities including infrastructure in respect of petroleum and chemicals, exploration, hazardous industries, large tourism projects, thermal power plants, construction and industrial estates.	39 activities in eight categories including mining/ exploration/power generation, primary processing, material processing, material production, manufacturing/ fabrication, service sector, infrastructure, and construction.
Process	Clearance based on recommendation of Expert Committees set up by the Ministry.	Clearance by designated EIA authorities at the Central or State level based on prescribed dimensions of the projects in the Notification. At the Central and State level, Expert Appraisal Committees provide recommendations for decision-making.
Categories of projects	No categories defined as MoEF was the sole authority for granting clearance.	Two categories prescribed namely, (i) to be dealt at the Central level and (ii) delegated to the State EIA Authority for clearance.
Processing time excl. EIA/EMP	180 days.	Cat. A: 120 days. Cat. B: 30 days.
Public Consultation	Requirement of public hearing at the discretion of government.	Public hearing prescribed for all Category A and some of the Category B projects (defined as B1).

Source: Environment Clearance Notifications, 1994 and 2006.

9.1.7. The new process came into effect on 14 September 2006. As State level authorities and committees are in the process of being set up, the impact of the new process is yet to be seen.

AFFORESTATION

9.1.8. Forests play a critical role in environment protection in two ways. They help to absorb carbon dioxide in the atmosphere thus mitigating the build up of GHGs. They also help to cope with water stress by trapping water that would otherwise run off and this is especially so when forests exist in upper ends of catchments. Unfortunately, both benefits are eroded by deforestation largely as a result of human pressure to exploit forest resources. While some exploitation of forests may be appropriate, the sustainability of forest resources is determined by the quantum of withdrawals.

9.1.9. The existing information on forest/tree cover based on the satellite data of 2002 indicates a green cover of 23.68%. There has been a net improvement of 0.65% between 2000 and 2002. Presuming that the same growth rate continues till 2007, the Tenth Plan target of 25% may have been achieved by 2007. This will be variable in the data of 2008, to be used for the *State of Forest Report* (*SFR*) 2009.

9.1.10. The present extent of forest lands in the country is 77.47 million ha. However, not all the forest lands are under the tree canopy and trees grow outside forests also. *SFR* 2003 of Forest Survey of India indicates a tree cover of over 67.83 million ha, that is, 20.64% of the land area. This extent aggregates the blocks of more than 1 ha area under tree cover. Outside this, nearly 10 m ha area has been assessed as under tree cover in smaller than 1 ha patches outside forests. This brings the total green cover up to 77.83 million ha or 23.68% of the total area. Out of this, dense forests have declined from 416809 sq km in 2001 to 390564 sq km, that is, a fall of 6%. Though over the last few years the extent of forest cover has stabilized, the low extent of good forests is a matter of concern.

9.1.11. Severe pressure for meeting growing livelihood, industrial, and development needs have been some of the critical contributing factors. A demand–supply gap of almost 64 million cubic meters has been projected for timber in 2006. The shortage is being met through import since 1985 amounting to nearly Rs 9000 crore (2003–04). Against a sustainable availability of fuel wood of only 17 million tonnes from the forests, the annual fuel wood requirement has been estimated to be above 200 million tonnes. With development of technologies for use of even smaller sizes of wood for structural uses, small wood is also not available for fuel. India may have sufficient food to eat but it does not have sufficient fuel wood to cook it. Forests also meet about one-third of fodder requirement. The total production of Non Timber Forest Produce (NTFP) has been assessed as worth about Rs 4188 crore annually (Institute of Economic Growth, 2002). Ever increasing herbal markets are only to put further pressures.

9.1.12. While the gaps are huge, potential for improvement of productivity exists. The status of green cover is an indicator of status of productivity of forests. The following strategies have been evolving in the sector for improving the status of green cover.

Participatory Forest Management or Joint Forest Management (JFM)

9.1.13. Initiated with the circular of the MoEF on 1 June 1990 on people's involvement in forest conservation and management, the JFM regime has evolved gradually and at present 106479 such committees (22 million participants) are functioning in 28 States covering 22.02 million ha of forests. This participatory regime is seen as a potential strength of forest management for the forest fringes. The challenge now is to effectively empower the local communities with appropriate rights and responsibilities, and ensure that substantial benefits from forest conservation accrue to them.

9.1.14. A similar approach has been attempted in wildlife management also. In Project Tiger, India, Eco-development Project was implemented during 1995–2005 under Global Environment Facility (GEF) with focus on village eco-development through optimum use of local resources and involvement of local people in conservation of protected areas. Integration of this approach to protected area management through shared decision-making and full integration of conservation and livelihoods across the landscape are yet to be realized. Also, the recognition of a large range and diversity of community traditions or new initiatives towards conservation is very weak.

Social Forestry

9.1.15. The First Five Year Plan, as far back as 1951, indicated the scope for establishment of village plantations. Subsequently, a series of externally aided social forestry projects during the 1980s and allocation of 25% of District Rural Development Agency funds under National Rural Employment Programme, Rural Landless Employment Guarantee Programme, and so on, for social afforestation provided impetus to social forestry. This provision was not pursued since the Eighth Plan. Regeneration of forests and growing of trees being a long-term activity, did not receive due focus in the rural development programmes. Even the Watershed Management Programme aims more at equitable sharing and caring of watershed benefits, and afforestation remains a latent component. The cost norms of these programmes are not able to support substantial afforestation activities requiring strong wage contribution.

Agro and Farm Forestry

9.1.16. The social forestry programmes also include extension and promotion of agro and farm forestry in the farm sector. The farmers of the States like Punjab, Haryana, Himachal Pradesh, Uttar Pradesh, Karnataka, and Tamil Nadu have adopted agro forestry. However, the forward linkages with the user industry and facilitation by the State agencies have not existed. Thus, the sector suffers from problems of unorganized markets driven by middlemen, depriving the farmers of optimum prices for their produce. Conservative exim regulations, cutting and transit controls act as disincentives for diversification into the species which face controls but are economically important.

Strategy for the Eleventh Plan

9.1.17. The monitorable target of the Eleventh Five Year Plan is to increase the forest cover by 5% of the total geographical area. This would require an additional cover of about 16 million ha. Out of this, 5 million ha could be brought under the tree cover within the recorded forest area while the rest would be added through agro forestry and social forestry. However, the policy target is to have 33% forest and tree cover ultimately which will require additional coverage of about 10–11 million ha. This will have to be done mainly outside the recorded forest area.

9.1.18. The target of 33% forest and tree cover reflects the tree component without accounting for other vibrant non-tree natural biomes like grasslands. The amendment of the target of the 1952 policy, of one-third area under *forests*, to *forest/tree cover* resulted in a shift of focus from ecological habitats to tree cover. Further recognition of biodiversity characteristics and ecological services rendered by habitats like grasslands, natural desert ecosystems, alpine, and riparian habitats suggests that several biomes, even if devoid of tree component, can be recognized as 'green cover' and accounted so. Recognizing these facts, the following strategic principles will be adopted for dealing with the green cover.

9.1.19. The policy objective of 33% tree/forest cover should be revisited for its definition on ecological considerations. The green cover should include the existing natural ecosystems within which the tree cover constitutes a sub-set.

9.1.20. Enabling environment for social and participatory regimes should be the aim of Central efforts, as is being done through the JFM mode under the National Afforestation Programme.

9.1.21. Implementation of the Central programmes has met with difficulties on fund flow management at the State level. It is advisable to undertake activities in project mode with earmarked funding, as is done in the externally aided projects.

Improving Air Quality

9.1.22. The Air (Prevention and Control of Pollution) Act, 1981 is the main legislation for regulating air quality, through the Pollution Control Boards (PCBs) in the States. The Central Pollution Control Board (CPCB) has identified 2301 medium and large scale polluting industrial units under 17 highly polluting categories. The requisite pollution control devices are reported to have been provided in 1927 units, while 235 have been closed and the 139 are still defaulting. CPCB also monitors ambient air quality at 308 stations covering 115 cities/towns in 28 States and four UTs in the country to: (i) determine the status and trend in ambient air quality on significant parameters like benzene and polyaromatic hydrocarbons (PAH); (ii) assess health hazard and the damage to materials; (iii) develop preventive and corrective measures; and (iv) understand the natural cleansing process. Presently, the criteria pollutants monitored by Central/State PCBs and associate agencies include sulphur dioxide (SO_2), NOx, and Respirable Suspended Particulate Matter (RSPM). Other parameters for toxic trace matters PAH are also monitored for select cities.

9.1.23. A programme for real time air quality monitoring for cities with population of more than 1 million was started during the Tenth Plan. The automatic air quality monitoring systems are operational in Jodhpur, Patna, Pune, and Sholapur while those in Kanpur, Varanasi, Jharia, and Kolkata will be functional soon. As many as 76 cities/towns are found to exceed acceptable limits of these parameters mainly due to vehicular and industrial pollution measured in terms of ambient air quality in residential, industrial and sensitive areas for SO_2, oxides of nitrogen, Suspended Particulate Matter, RSPM, ammonia, and carbon monoxide.

9.1.24. Figure 9.1.1 displays the average air quality levels of select Asian cities between 2000 and 2004. The chart shows that New Delhi, Mumbai, and Kolkata have failed to meet the WHO standards as far as Total Suspended Particulate Matter and RSPM are concerned. Beijing and Shanghai, though better than Indian cities, also could not meet the WHO standards in this respect. The other Asian cities which failed to meet the required standards were Jakarta, Katmandu, Seoul, Dhaka, and Colombo. As far as SO_2, and NO_2 are concerned, New Delhi and Mumbai were much better than the prescribed WHO standards whereas several Asian cities exceeded the safe limits.

9.1.25. Action Plans for improvement of air quality have been drawn for 16 identified cities on the advice of the Supreme Court. Based on the basic format prepared by CPCB for this purpose, the State PCBs have been asked to evolve such plans for their respective areas.

9.1.26. During the Eleventh Plan period, all Central programmes on outdoor pollution should be reorganized under a National Air Quality Plan, which will cover (i) City based Clean Air Action Plans (CAAPs) and (ii) Pollution Control and Prevention in Industrial Areas programmes. The ongoing national programme for monitoring air quality will be taken forward for achieving real time data. This would help in creating early warning systems and thus enforcing the Plan target of conforming air and water quality to WHO standards.

9.1.27. The entire Air Quality Monitoring network should be expanded from the current 308 stations to 1000 stations. Real time monitoring of PM2.5 (Particulate Matter 2.5 micron), ozone, VOCs (Volatile Organic Compounds), PAH, secondary pollutants—sulphates and nitrates—will be organized in about 15 cities per year, to cover the 76 cities which currently exceed the four specified levels of air pollution. Source monitoring of VOC, BTX (benzene, toluene, and xylene), and toxic heavy metals will be initiated to develop control measures.

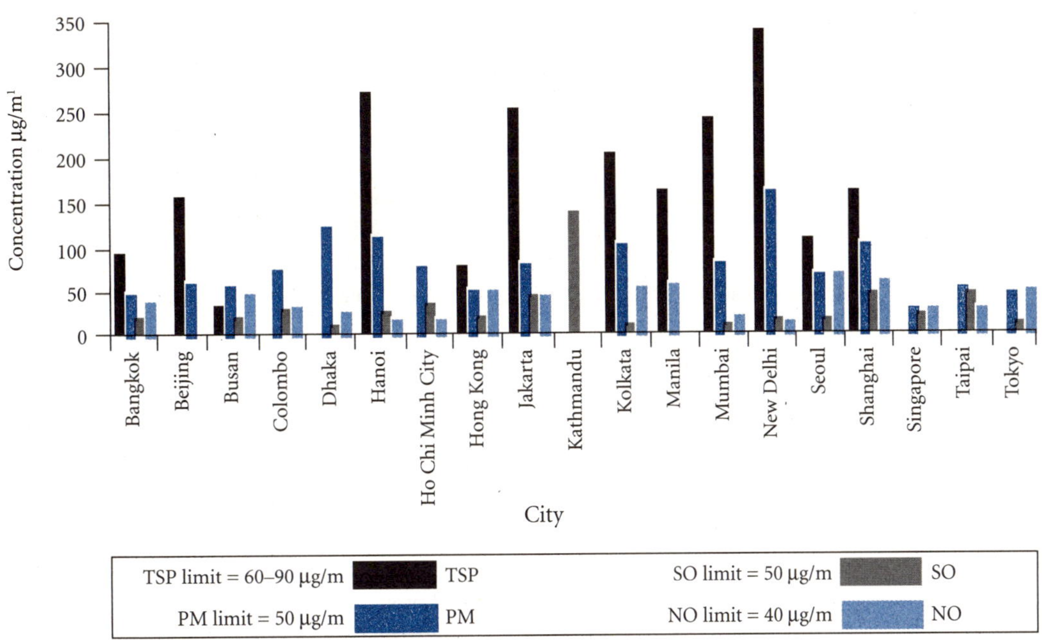

Source: CAI-Asia (2006c).

FIGURE 9.1.1: Urban Air Quality in Select Asian Cities, 2000–04

9.1.28. Vehicular pollution is a major source of air pollution in our cities and control of vehicular pollution should have high priority in planning for a clean urban environment. Some of the initiatives needed to control vehicular emissions are listed in Box 9.1.1.

9.1.29. More generally, effective urban transport planning, with appropriate initiatives for the development of public transport is particularly important. CAAP should therefore be integrated with the National Urban Transport Policy and the JNNURM to ensure optimal development of public transport including both bus and rail based mass rapid transit systems. CAAP should also be the basis of all Central and State funding with appropriate provision of penalties for non-compliance.

9.1.30. The monitorable target in air quality should be to achieve WHO standards of air quality in all major cities by 2011–12.

Box 9.1.1
Strategy to Control Vehicular Emissions

- There should be uniform fuel quality and emission standards across India. The road map proposed in the government's Auto Fuel Policy must be accelerated and tightened to cover all cities and to implement Euro IV standards.
- The use of diesel in private vehicles must be discouraged. The present distortions in pricing under which diesel is much cheaper than petrol, encourages the growth of diesel vehicles leading to cheap and toxic motorization.
- All Central funding for the transport sector must be linked to the implementation of car restraint measures including parking charges designed to recover the full cost of using parking space (linked to the real estate and construction costs) and rationalization of road and other transportation related taxes (such as passenger tax, sales tax, and so on) to reduce the tax burden on public transport and increase it for the personal motorized transport.
- The government should impose higher annual taxes on personal transport, which should be used to create a dedicated fund for public transport.

TABLE 9.1.2
Notified Standards for Water Quality

Designated-Best-Use	Class of water	Criteria
Drinking water source without conventional treatment but after disinfection	A	1. Total Coliform—Most Probable No. (MPN)/100ml < 50 2. pH – 6.5–8.5 3. DO > 6mg/litre 4. BOD (5 days 20°C) – < 2mg/litre
Outdoor bathing (Organized)	B	1. Total Coliform (MPN)/100ml – < 500 2. pH – 6.5–8.5 3. DO – > 5mg/l 4. BOD – (5 days 20°C) – < 3mg/l
Drinking water source after conventional treatment and disinfection	C	1. Total Coliform (MPN)/100ml – < 5000 2. pH – 6.5 – 9.0 3. DO > 4mg/litre 4. BOD – (5 days 20°C) – < 3mg/l
Propagation of wildlife and fisheries	D	1. pH – 6.5–8.5 2. DO – > 4mg/litre 3. Free Ammonia (as N) – < 1.2 mg/l
Irrigation, industrial cooling, controlled waste disposal	E	1. pH – 6.5–8.5 2. Electrical Conductivity—(25°C) micro mhos/cm < 2250 3. Sodium Absorption Ratio Max. 26 4. Boron Max. 2mg/l
	Below-E	Not Meeting A, B, C, D & E Criteria

Source: CPCB.

WATER QUALITY

Monitoring Water Pollution

9.1.31. The Water (Prevention and Control of Pollution) Act, 1974 regulates water quality through the State PCBs. The CPCB, under MoEF, has established a nationwide network for water quality monitoring comprising 1019 stations in 27 States and six UTs. The monitoring is done on a monthly or quarterly basis for surface water and on a half-yearly basis for groundwater. The monitoring network covers 200 rivers, 60 lakes, five tanks, three ponds, three creeks, 13 canals, 17 drains, and 321 wells. Water samples are analysed for 28 parameters including physical parameters, nutrients, major ions, and organic and bacteriological parameters.

National River Conservation Plan (NRCP)

9.1.32. The different standards of water quality required for drinking, bathing, and irrigation are given in Table 9.1.2.

9.1.33. Out of the various parameters monitored, Biochemical Oxygen Demand (BOD) and Coliforms are critical. Maintenance of certain level of flow that could ensure a minimum assimilative capacity in water bodies remains a matter of concern, especially in the light of increasing consumptive demands of various sectors such as household, industry, and agriculture. Based on monitoring done during the last 10 years, 14% of riverine length is highly polluted (BOD more than 6 mg/litre) and 19% moderately polluted (BOD—3 to 6 mg/litre). A total of 86 polluted stretches have been identified and action plans for improving the water quality in them are being prepared.

9.1.34. As small-scale industries do not have adequate resources, space or skilled manpower to treat their wastewater, a scheme of Common Effluent Treatment Plants (CETPs) was initiated in June 1990. The CETPs are partially funded by the GoI. Eighty-eight CETPs covering more than 10000 polluting industries have been set up during the Tenth Plan. However, the performance of these units has been generally unsatisfactory largely due to improper operation and maintenance. This calls for strengthening of enforcement. Charters on Corporate Responsibility on Environmental Protection in respect of 17 categories of highly polluting industries have also been formulated in collaboration with the concerned industries.

9.1.35. It is necessary to consider rivers holistically to evolve plans to restore their ecological health and improve the water quality to bathing standards. Cities and towns located on the banks have been found to be gross polluters and these have been taken up for planning and implementing schemes to ensure that only treated wastewater is discharged into the rivers.

9.1.36. Untreated sewage dumped into our rivers is a major cause of river pollution. The total sewage generation in the country is about 33000 MLD (million litres per day). Against this, the total average treatment capacity is only 6190 MLD and 40% of that capacity is in Delhi. This underlines the urgent need to expand the sewage treatment capacity in the country.

9.1.37. The NRCP has covered 160 towns along 34 polluted river stretches in 20 States and has created 2055 MLD of sewage treatment plant (STP) capacity till now, which is approximately 38% of the approved capacity of 5435 MLD to be set up under the Plan. The average capacity utilization of existing STP capacity is reported to be about 72% against the desirable capacity utilization of 100%. Under-utilization of capacity is due to factors like irregular power supply, absence of connections between domestic sewage drains and STPs, failure of States to provide for maintenance costs of STPs, and so on.

9.1.38. Under the Ganga Action Plan (GAP) Phase-I, sewage treatment capacity of 869 MLD was set up covering 25 Class-I towns in Uttar Pradesh, Bihar, and West Bengal. This amounted to 35% of the total sewage treatment capacity needed. As a result of the implementation of GAP I, the length of the polluted stretch of the river was reduced from 740 km to 437 km (Kannauj to Varanasi). Phase-II (1993) covered Ganga's tributaries (Yamuna, Damodar, and Gomti) in 96 towns in seven States. It is estimated that another 20% of the pollution load of Ganga would be covered on completion of the on-going works under NRCP. However, there will still be a gap of nearly 45% of the pollution load to be addressed in the future.

9.1.39. Other major river cleaning projects cover Gomti river in Uttar Pradesh; Yamuna River in Delhi; Musi River in Hyderabad and Pamba River in Kerala. The 22 km stretch of the Yamuna in Delhi between Wazirabad and Okhla, is critically polluted. A sewage treatment capacity of 2960 MLD was required to handle the entire discharge load in Delhi. However, the STP capacity created is about 2500 MLD only, leaving a gap of about 460 MLD. More importantly, the existing STPs are able to treat only about 1600 MLD (about 64% capacity utilization) due to dilapidated condition of trunk sewers.

9.1.40. The impact reported by MoEF reveals that BOD is within the prescribed standards (BOD less than 3 mg/l and Dissolved Oxygen [DO] more than 6 mg/l for Bathing Quality) at most major cities along the Ganges. However, as shown in Table 9.1.3 below, the stretch from Kannauj to Allahabad has not yet achieved bathing quality standard. As shown in Table 9.1.4, the stretch of Yamuna river between Delhi and Etawah in Uttar Pradesh is not even of bathing standard.

9.1.41. The rivers Narmada, Mahanadi, Brahmini, Baitarni, Subarnrekha, Beas, and Chambal maintain DO levels of 4.0 mg/l or above throughout the year. In the Ganga, Yamuna, Krishna, Sabarmati, Tapi, Sutlej however, the DO level goes as low as 0.3 mg/l.

TABLE 9.1.3
Water Quality Data for River Ganga
(Summer Average, March–June)

Station/Location	1986		2006	
	DO (mg/l)	BOD (mg/l)	DO (mg/l)	BOD (mg/l)
Rishikesh	8.10	1.70	8.30	1.00
Haridwar D/S	8.10	1.80	8.10	1.30
Garhmukteshwar	7.80	2.20	7.70	2.10
Kannauj U/S	7.20	5.50	7.35	1.11
Kannauj D/S	na	na	6.45	4.20
Kanpur U/S	7.20	7.20	6.20	6.80
Kanpur D/S	6.70	8.60	3.90	6.80
Allahabad U/S	6.40	11.40	7.10	4.90
Allahabad D/S	6.60	15.50	8.50	3.20
Varanasi U/S	5.60	10.10	8.70	2.10
Varanasi D/S	5.90	10.60	8.65	2.25
Patna U/S	8.40	2.00	7.40	2.05
Patna D/S	8.10	2.20	8.10	2.30
Rajmahal	7.80	1.80	7.20	1.95
Palta			6.96	2.58
Uluberia			6.46	2.64

Source: CPCB.

TABLE 9.1.4
Water Quality Data for River Yamuna
(Summer Average, March–June)

Station/Location	1986		2006	
	DO (mg/l)	BOD (mg/l)	DO (mg/l)	BOD (mg/l)
Tajewala	11.70	1.20	11.20	1.50
Kalanaur	10.40	1.05	7.30	2.50
Sonepat	9.75	3.00	8.40	2.50
Palla	13.95	6.00	8.00	4.80
Nizamuddin Bridge	0.30	25.00	0.00	31.30
Agra Canal	0.35	26.50	0.00	28.30
Majhawali	0.50	22.00	3.05	26.00
Mathura	8.10	4.00	5.40	15.30
Mathura D/S	8.50	2.50	5.77	15.00
Agra U/S	10.65	4.50	8.40	15.00
Agra D/S	1.65	9.00	8.17	14.80
Batteshwar	13.90	11.00	9.68	14.00
Etawah	11.16	7.00	16.90	15.50
Udi	9.71	2.00	13.30	3.00
Auraiya Juhika	8.14	5.00	8.40	1.80

Source: CPCB.

Strategy for the Eleventh Plan

9.1.42. The country's first river action programme—GAP—completes over 20 years and the NRCP completes 10 years in 2007. The experience of the first 20 years needs to be used to design an effective and affordable river cleaning programme for the future.

- A basic objective must be to maintain minimum flows, which are threatened by withdrawal of water to meet the needs of agriculture and industry, and to ensure treatment of sewage and effluents.
- As urban sewage load is the dominant factor causing river pollution, integration of the NRCP and National Lake Conservation Plan (NLCP) with the urban development programmes and agencies is essential. It should be ensured that by 2011–12 no untreated sewage is drained into the rivers.
- For receiving assistance under the NRCP/NLCP, ULBs should be fully involved in developing the programme along with specific statutory responsibility for operating and maintaining the treatment facilities created.
- The City Development Plans should incorporate environmental management services as the number one priority in JNNURM and Urban Infrastructure

Development Scheme for Small and Medium Towns (UIDSSMT). Mechanisms are needed to ensure that the urban areas covered under these programmes provide for full treatment of the sewage generated.

- For the plan period, the River Conservation Programme should aim at completing the projects in hand and new projects should be considered only in towns which are not covered under JNNURM and UIDSSMT.
- The NRCP should encourage installations on command area basis to facilitate investment in the treatment of maximum quantity of sewage and reuse in the vicinity. In other words, decentralized systems of wastewater treatment need to be encouraged as against centralized, large, end-of-pipe treatment units.
- The wastewater management strategy needs to emphasize the use of state-of-the-art Geographical Information System (GIS)-based decision support systems.
- Water efficiency in flushes and gadgets should be planned in order to reduce wastewater generation. Recycling/reuse of treated sewage in cities should be promoted. Resident groups should be sensitized towards water conservation, recycling, and reuse.

National Lake Conservation Plan (NLCP)

9.1.43. The NLCP was approved as a 100% Centrally funded scheme during the Ninth Plan with the objective of restoring the polluted and degraded lakes of the country. To begin with, NLCP proposed to cover urban lakes of tourist importance. The scope of work has been expanded during the Tenth Plan to include rural water bodies also. Under the programme, conservation of 46 lakes in 13 States has been taken up through 31 projects. So far, projects for 10 lakes have been completed and 10 more are likely to be completed. Improvement in the quality of water in the lakes in the completed projects is more marked than in the river conservation projects. The scheme now provides assistance to States on a 70:30 sharing basis and till date the estimated approved cost is about Rs 565 crore.

9.1.44. The activities covered under NLCP include interception and treatment of pollution loads entering the lake, lake cleaning interventions such as desilting, de-weeding, bioremediation, catchment area treatment, lake front eco-development like bunding, fencing, shore line development, and creation of facilities for public recreation and entertainment.

Dal Lake Conservation Project (DLCP)

9.1.45. The DLCP was approved by the government at a cost of Rs 298.76 crore in September 2005. As an exception, this project is being implemented entirely by the Central Government. The expected date of completion of the project is March 2010. The works envisaged include interception and diversion of pollutants entering the lake, setting up of six STPs, desilting, de-weeding, removal of encroachments in the project area, and so on. The GoI has released Rs 70 crore for the project till 2006–07. Utilizing this, three out of six STPs have been made operational. The remaining three STPs are expected to be commissioned by December 2007. The progress of implementation is, however, slow due to delay in relocation of families who need to be shifted from the project area of the lake.

9.1.46. While the lakes conservation plan focuses on pollution abatement in lakes, the larger objective of conservation of lakes is the maintenance of the aquatic ecosystems. Keeping this in view, wetlands will be integrated with NLCP and the programme's objectives will cover conservation of life forms apart from mitigating pollution and augmenting catchments.

Water Pollution

9.1.47. Effluent standards, environmental laboratories, and government analysts have been notified under the Environment (Protection) Act. There is a need for much stronger monitoring and enforcement for expanded coverage by both the Central and State Pollution Control Boards. Greater awareness and involvement of local (affected) communities and local governments in compliance and monitoring is critically important. While compliance will cover treatment and recycling of used water, monitoring should include the extent and quality of the treated water, and water quality of the water bodies providing or receiving the water in treated or untreated form.

9.1.48. The Joint Parliamentary Committee on pesticide residues in and safety standards for soft drinks, fruit juice, and other beverages has suggested notifying quality standards for drinking water. These quality standards should be made mandatory.

WASTE MANAGEMENT

9.1.49. Municipal Solid Waste (Management and Handling) Rules, 2000 stipulated that these were to be complied by December 2003. Under these rules, all local bodies were expected to undertake segregation of waste and its collection, storage, transportation, processing, and disposal. While the Ministry of Urban Development reported that Jodhpur in Rajasthan, Sirsa in Haryana, and Namakkal in Tamil Nadu have been making good efforts towards compliance, no other city/town in the country has taken the required steps. Some local bodies are reported to have taken initiatives to set up waste processing and disposal facilities. These local bodies are generating about 1.2 lakh tonnes of municipal solid waste every day and treatment is not a priority in their plans.

Urban Solid Waste Management

9.1.50. Management of industrial and municipal waste is a serious challenge because of its magnitude and the resources required. The JNNURM covers programmes for urban waste disposal. The scheme of Balanced Use of Fertilizer under the Ministry of Agriculture strengthens the soil-testing programme in the country and encourages efficient fertilizer use and composting of urban biodegradable waste. The Ministry of New and Renewable Energy (MNRE, previously MNES) has formulated a National Programme on Energy Recovery from urban and industrial waste. These programmes need convergence and exploitation of synergies.

Strategy for the Eleventh Plan

9.1.51. Collection, treatment and disposal of solid waste are the responsibility of the ULBs. These bodies must be made specifically accountable in this respect. The Supreme Court directions for municipal solid waste collection and management which require segregation, sanitary landfills, and other safe options of treatment should be part of a Master Plan. The following measures also need to be taken.

- Processes for waste minimization and segregation should be promoted and pursued. The existing regulations have to be revisited to see the changes needed and the investments required.
- The role of CPCB and MoEF must be clarified. They should be charged with enforcing the rules through the ULBs and not rest satisfied solely from being the key standard setting and pollution monitoring agency.
- Assistance for projects for treatment and disposal of hazardous and biomedical waste should be provided as incentive for compliance.
- Avoidance of waste going to the landfill should be the priority for all ULBs.
- For smaller and medium towns and cities, regional/shared landfills/waste processing infrastructure should be considered. For larger cities, the problem of availability of land should be addressed.
- Programmes like JNNURM and UIDSSMT need to link assistance to the progress in solid waste management. During the Plan period, all Class I cities should have sanitary landfills in place.

9.1.52. The PCBs are responsible for enforcing Management of Hazardous Waste and Biomedical Wastes (Management and Handling) Rules. It is assessed that about 4.4 million tonnes of hazardous waste are generated annually by over 13000 units. At the instance of the Supreme Court, an inventory of dumpsites is being carried out. MoEF provides assistance for installing Transport, Storage, and Disposal Facilities (TSDF) for management of hazardous waste generating industrial clusters. So far, six such systems have been supported in PPP mode. The average capacity of these units is 1–1.2 lakh tonnes per annum. Biomedical waste is generally disposed of by incinerators or conventional methods. At least 17 units, mostly incinerators, were set up by industry associations. Some health care facilities have installed their own biomedical waste treatment facilities and others are availing the services of Common Bio-medical Waste Treatment Facilities (CBWTF). There were 157 CBWTFs, including eight under installation, in the country as on March 2007.

9.1.53. During Eleventh Plan period, an institutional mechanism would be required to be put in place to ensure that issues related to handling of industrial, hazardous and bio-medical wastes are also dealt under JNNURM and UIDSSMT. Funding through these two umbrella schemes should be made conditional upon appropriate measures being taken in respect of these issues. In places not covered under JNNURM and UIDSSMT, an effective mechanism should be put into place to ensure strict monitoring and compliance by the concerned local authorities. A framework for management of e-waste also needs to be put into place.

BIODIVERSITY

9.1.54. Habitat conversion or land use changes, land degradation, and pollution result in the decline of ecological goods and services needed for human welfare. The Biological Diversity Act, 2002 and Rules, 2004 provide for constitution of State Boards (SBBs) and Management Committees (BMCs) for conservation, documentation and sustainable utilization of biodiversity and for building up capacities of these bodies. Chronicling in the form of

People's Biodiversity Registers will be the only way we can identify changes happening due to climate change. There is a need to develop appropriate methodology and models for conducting such an exercise. Documentation of traditional knowledge should also include adaptation of such knowledge in line with the present needs of conservation.

Biosphere Reserves

9.1.55. This programme was started in 1986 with UNESCO (Management and Biosphere) support for integrating social, cultural, and ecological values of ecologically rich landscapes. The primary focus was on monitoring and designing conservation strategies. With a Tenth Plan outlay of Rs 35 crore, the programme has not been able to deliver an effective outcome for the existing biosphere reserves. There is a need to reinforce the information and strategic back up for the management of protected areas in the core of biosphere reserves.

9.1.56. Keeping in view the facts that village eco-development and participatory management of habitats are part of protected areas management schemes, the primary objectives of this programme will be research, documentation, and monitoring of the dynamics of human ecosystem interface. The programme should focus on cross-sectoral linkages between biochemical resources and human livelihood.

Mountain Ecosystems

9.1.57. The MoEF has established an autonomous institute, the G.B. Pant Institute of Himalayan Environment and Development (GBPIHED), with the overall mandate of dealing with issues relating to the environment of the Indian Himalayan Region. The results of project studies of the Institute also have implications on issues such as climate change and land degradation. However, the output falls far too short of what is needed to be done for the Himalayan ecosystems.

9.1.58. During the Eleventh Plan period, GBPIHED should reorient its activities to evolve as a resource centre for the Himalayan States and GoI for advice on sustainable development of the Indian Himalayan Region. The focus of research should include socio-economic development of the mountain habitations. An Indian Alpine Initiative should also be started for tracking the dynamics of alpine biomes in the context of climate change.

Coastal Zone Management

9.1.59. The earlier Coastal Regulation Zone notification prescribed regulation of activities based on uniform principles of vulnerability of coastal areas against human activity. Coastal areas are currently classified in four categories (CZ 1 to 4) with different principles for development activities. Category 1 includes ecologically sensitive areas, category 4 includes islands, and categories 2 and 3 permit construction activities based on vulnerability. The Swaminathan Committee prescribed that the local circumstances and vulnerabilities should be the basis of coastal zone management and regulations. For this purpose, use of scientific, social, and local information should be made in environmental management plans for coastal areas. Conservation of life forms (and their habitats such as nesting/spawning sites) and integration of their environments with human well-being should be essential components of such plans. Participation of civil society and fishing/coastal communities in the State level coastal zone management committees should be ensured for conservation and sustainable harvests.

Botanical Survey of India (BSI) and Zoological Survey of India (ZSI)

9.1.60. The Botanical and Zoological Survey of India are today facing major challenges in view of the new regime on genetic resources, provisions of the Biochemical Diversity Act, and fast evolving knowledge and information environment. Use of recent trends in organizing information and modern skills in exploration and documentation will be given priority. These institutions will develop into prime repositories of information on plants and animals, and as referral institutes. Collaboration and linkages with other institutions as part of a network will be encouraged.

ENVIRONMENTAL AWARENESS AND EDUCATION

9.1.61. The Environment Education in School System project initiated in 1999 strengthens environment education in the formal school curriculum through infusion of appropriate education material. Introduction of environmental concepts in Business/Management Education is another focus area. A committee comprising representatives from management institutions, AICTE, UGC, industry, and MoEF is working on this.

9.1.62. During the Eleventh Plan, the programme of Environmental Education, Training, and Extension may be continued with further linkages with the publicity and awareness mechanisms of State forest departments.

This may include a manual on public participation in all activities of MoEF. Public transport like railways, buses, and even airways can be extensively used for environmental awareness through well designed awareness material. Information generated by student activities on local environmental issues may be integrated with the database under the National Environmental Monitoring Programme (NEMP). Capacity building, such as training of trainers, should also be focused on.

9.1.63. The National Museum of Natural History (NMNH), New Delhi, and three regional museums at Mysore, Bhubaneshwar, and Bhopal will be made more effective in natural history education and awareness with the introduction of the state-of-the-art education and interpretation methods. The MoEF has contemplated setting up of a new regional museum at Sawai Madhopur with focus on the life forms of the region, the details of which are being worked out.

National Environmental Monitoring Programme (NEMP)

9.1.64. The Steering Committee on Environment and Forests for the Eleventh Plan has suggested a unified NEMP for ecology, environmental chemistry, public health, and socio-environmental studies. This programme would track the status and change in the socially relevant biophysical parameters and their social impacts, wherever possible. NEMP may have sub-programmes on forest cover and ecosystem services, apart from air and water pollution. The programme may have linkages with educational, scientific, and social organizations working in the relevant fields. Accordingly, the existing programme for Environment Information System (ENVIS) will be reshaped to provide information in interactive formats for effective use. Real time sharing of data on environmental parameters collected under NEMP will be implemented. A special portal could also be organized for environmental data from school and college student projects.

Environmental Research And Development

9.1.65. The MoEF supports nine Centres of Excellence in research which need to be strengthened.

9.1.66. During the Eleventh Plan period, environmental policies and programmes will need strong research backup. The identified research priorities will be met by a combination of open, competitive research grant programmes, and dedicated support to special organizations and centres of excellence.

- An 'Environmental Research Grants' programme should focus on the relevant areas such as clean technologies, preventive strategies, hazardous substances management, and so on. There should be special programmes on Ecosystem Health, Pollution and Health, Ecological Footprint, NTFP regeneration ecology, Invasive species, Fire Ecology, and Forest-Watershed Services.
- Documentation of traditional and community knowledge should be a special area of research.
- Special mechanisms may be set up for co-ordination and management of research amongst agencies like Indian Council of Forestry Research and Education (ICFRE), ICAR, CSIR, DBT, DST, and UGC, as well as multilateral and bilateral donors and private foundations.
- The All India Coordinated Project on Taxonomy (AICOPTAX) needs strengthening in order to bring more taxa of lower organisms and issues like molecular taxonomy.

Taxonomy Capacity Building

9.1.67. The implementation of the Biological Diversity Act, 2002 and Rules, 2004 and National Environmental Policy, 2006 calls for an adequate number of trained taxonomists. Existing programmes on botanical gardens and taxonomic capacity building assume immense significance in this respect. MoEF provided assistance to 72 botanical gardens during the Tenth Plan and under an AICOPTAX, 11 coordinating centres and two centres for training have been supported at various institutions.

9.1.68. AICOPTAX should be augmented for capacity building (including human resources) in Taxonomy. The ZSI and BSI will be the key institutions to organize taxonomic capacity building programmes and train young Indian taxonomists for forest, wildlife and management.

Conservation of Natural Resources and Ecosystems

9.1.69. Inland aquatic systems (excluding paddy fields) cover 5.3% of the country's land area but harbour 15% and 20% of India's floral and faunal diversities, respectively. There are wide gaps in knowledge relating to hydrological parameters, ecosystem processes, and aquatic life forms in these systems. Information on the physico-chemical aspects of water quality in rivers and lakes has become available largely because of the support from the National River Conservation Directorate (NRCD) and the CPCB, but that on aspects such as area, depth, hydrology, and ecosystem processes (functions) is practically non-existent. The existing programmes on conservation accordingly need a revamp.

9.1.70. The Scheme on Conservation and Management of Mangroves, Coral Reefs, and Wetlands has been too small to make an impact on the conservation of these ecosystems. Mangroves and coral reefs are mainly found on government lands. Development of appropriate institutions to motivate people to cooperate in the conservation efforts of these systems will be a priority area. More protected areas are needed for the conservation of coral reefs. Restoration and plantation programmes for mangroves are necessary to make these eco-systems function as effective barriers against invasion of land by sea. The existing programmes on wetlands, mangroves, and coral reefs will be extended to mountains, grasslands, and alpine ecosystems.

9.1.71. Initiatives on conservation need to be more effectively integrated with development and poverty reduction. The principles of Community Reserves under the Wild Life (Protection) Act may be useful in such efforts. Long-term plans for conservation of such habitats will be important. Wetlands will be part of NLCP and the objectives will cover conservation of life forms apart from mitigating pollution and augmenting catchments.

- An information system will be set up for islands, coral reefs, mangroves, and wetlands by developing a consolidated and easily accessible database of all recorded species.
- Support activities will include participatory research for inventory and valuation of freshwater ecosystems, measures to tackle serious threats to them and ensure conservation, as also the livelihood security of dependent communities.
- With regard to linkage between biodiversity and climate change, it should be recognized that biodiversity is an important tool to find solutions for tackling the impact of climate change on rural populations that depend on biomass for their livelihood.
- There is a need to recognize the potential of biodiversity to provide solutions for adaptation in the form of traditional crop varieties and donors for creating GMOs.
- National agro biodiversity hotspot mapping and identification of important agro biodiversity landscapes will be undertaken for conservation with the participation of farmers and pastoralist groups. Regions with high concentration of genetic diversity on major and important crops may be declared as 'gene sanctuaries' for conservation and enrichment of diversity, involving communities through diversity based income generation and incentives.
- The regulatory mechanism for trials and adoption of GMOs will be required to be based on scientific, socio-economic, and EIA in the long as well as short term. The process of a regulatory regime, therefore, should be consultative and transparent, based on the prescribed scientific, logical, and progressive norms, taking into account factors of human health and environmental health.
- Awareness generation will be important for ensuring effective outreach of the prescribed process for promotion of appropriately and adequately tested GMOs, mechanisms for enforcement of procedures, and processes for safeguarding ecological and health safety will be established.

Other Programmes

9.1.72. Several ongoing programmes of NoEF on specific subjects will continue to be pursued during the Eleventh Plan period. This includes the Environment Planning and Coordination project for Madhya Pradesh and Nagaland, Environmental authorities and tribunals, the Taj Protection Mission, National Natural Resource Management systems, IT, Adaptation and Capacity Building on Climate Change, and so on. Such programmes, with specific mandate derived from the Supreme Court or externally aided projects, will continue till their logical conclusion.

9.2 CLIMATE CHANGE

9.2.1. Global Climate Change due to rising levels of GHGs in the atmosphere is one of the most serious environmental concerns of our time. The Intergovernmental Panel on Climate Change (IPCC), established in 1988 by the World Meteorological Organization and the United Nations Environment Programme, has worked extensively on evaluating past trends and the future prospects of climate change. The synthesis report of the Fourth Assessment Report (AR4) of the Panel was released in November 2007.

9.2.2. The IPCC reports present a grim picture. It is estimated that the Earth's surface temperature has risen by 0.6 ± 0.2°C over the twentieth century. In the last 50 years, the rise has been 0.13 ± 0.07°C per decade and the recent years have been the warmest since 1860, the year from which regular instrumental records are available. The Panel has concluded that the fact of global warming is unequivocal and there is enough evidence to indicate that this is due to anthropogenic reasons. Although some of these conclusions have been disputed, the assessment of the IPCC represents a broad and growing consensus in the scientific community worldwide. The current level of atmospheric CO_2 is estimated as 379 parts per million (ppm) compared with the pre-industrial level of only 280 ppm. The annual growth rate of CO_2 concentration has been greater in the last 10 years (1.9 ppm/yr) compared to the last 40 years (1.4 ppm/yr). Halocarbons (chloro-flouro-carbons etc.) in the atmosphere, however, are observed to be decreasing due to their phase out under the Montreal Protocol.

9.2.3. Since warming depends upon the total stock of GHG in the atmosphere, continued emissions beyond the earth's absorptive capacity necessarily imply a rise in temperature. If emissions continue to increase as at present, a warming of about 0.2°C per decade is projected by IPCC. If emissions are stabilized at the 2000 level, the warming could be about 0.1°C per decade. The Special Report on Emission Scenarios projects that surface air temperatures could rise by between 1.1 and 6.4°C over the twenty-first century. In most cases, the temperature rise may be 2–4°C. The sea level rise is projected to be 18 to 59 cm.

Impact and Implications of Climate Change

9.2.4. Climate changes noted in the IPCC Assessment reports include recession of glaciers, thawing of permafrost, lengthening of mid- to high-latitude growing seasons, pole-ward and altitudinal shifts of plant and animal ranges, decline in some plant and animal populations, early flowering of trees, and changes in insect populations and egg-laying in birds. Associations between changes in regional temperatures and the observed changes in physical and biological systems have been documented in many aquatic, terrestrial, and marine environments.

- The water cycle is totally dependent on the temperature regime. Increasing global temperature and resultant faster retreat of most glaciers is expected to affect the snow fed perennial water regimes. Accordingly, the vegetation status of catchments, magnitude and frequency of floods, precipitation, runoff and groundwater recharge may all be affected. These changes may substantially affect hydropower generation, and may also require an increase in irrigation due to higher crop evaporative demand.
- Through the twentieth century, the average rate of global sea level rise has been 1.7 $\pm$ 0.5 mm/yr. The maximum rise since 1992 has been observed in the Western Pacific and the Eastern Indian Ocean. This trend could result in loss of land due to inundation, erosion, floods, and salt-water intrusion, adversely affecting coastal agriculture, tourism, fisheries and aquaculture, human settlements, and health.
- Changing environmental attributes are sure to affect the species spectrum and the profile and composition of forests is also likely to change. The degree to which terrestrial ecosystems will continue to be net sinks for carbon is uncertain. In arid or semi-arid areas, productivity is expected to decrease. Trends of drying up of wetlands and degradation of ecosystems have been observed.
- Estimated crop yield responses to climate change vary widely, depending upon species, cultivation practices and soil properties; pests, and pathogens; the direct effects of carbon dioxide (CO_2) on plants; and interactions between CO_2, air temperature, water stress, mineral nutrition, air quality, and adaptive responses. Even though increased CO_2 concentration can stimulate crop growth and yield, this benefit may not always overcome the adverse effects of excessive heat and drought. The AR4 projects a decline in global rice production by 3.8% by the end of the twenty first century.
- Changes in the severity and frequency of extreme heat and cold, and of floods and droughts, coupled with local air pollution and aero allergens may result in changes in infectious disease occurrence, in local food production and also cause under nutrition, leading to impaired child development. There will also be health consequences of population displacement and economic disruption. For India, the risks of malaria and heat stress related mortality have been projected by IPCC. Increase in flooding and droughts are associated with increased risk of drowning, diarrhoeal and respiratory diseases, and hunger and malnutrition. Adaptive options like health-oriented management of the environment (including air and water quality, food safety, urban and housing design, and surface water management), and appropriate medical interventions are normally related to income levels. Therefore, the poor are more vulnerable. Human settlements are also expected to be affected by changes in resource productivity or market demand for goods and services causing structural and functional adaptations leading to migration, which in turn would result in changes in living conditions.

9.2.5. Global warming will affect us seriously. For South Asia, warming has been projected to be above the global mean and in South East Asia, equal to the global mean. The impact projections for India indicate a rise of 0.68°C in the twentieth century with an increasing trend in the annual mean temperature. Precipitation is likely to increase and extreme rainfall and other climatic events may occur more frequently. Extreme rains in the South West monsoon and fewer rainy days along the East Coast have been projected. An increase in temperatures of 0.5°C to 1.5°C could produce a decline of between 2.5% in wheat and maize production in India.

9.2.6. Existing research based on formal modeling suggests that a scenario of warming between 2–3°C would lead to a permanent loss of up to 3% in the global output. In countries with predominantly agrarian economies, the projected increase in temperature and reduction in precipitation could, in the absence of adaptive responses such as increased irrigation, related agricultural research and related infrastructural interventions, dampen economic growth by reducing agricultural productivity. These impacts can be moderated by efforts at adaptation but these are expected to be costly and will impose a burden on both producers and consumers. Climate change would therefore result in lower incomes of the vulnerable populations and increase in the absolute number of people at risk of hunger unless these outcomes can be countered through the development of cost effective technologies.

Responses to Climate Change

9.2.7. The serious consequences of climate change, including especially the consequences for India, lead naturally to the question of what should be our response. Two types of responses need to be considered. The first relates to adaptation, i.e., measures that have to be taken given the very high likelihood that climate change will occur and will have adverse effects. The second relates to mitigation, i.e., steps to be taken that might reduce the extent of climate change.

9.2.8. Recognizing the importance of climate change issues, the Prime Minister established a Council on Climate Change under his chairmanship in June 2007 to co-ordinate national action for assessment, adaptation, and mitigation of climate change. Earlier, the government had set up an expert committee to study the impact of climate change. One of the important decisions taken by the Prime Minister's Council is that a National Action Plan will be prepared compiling action taken by India for addressing the challenge of climate change and the action that needs to be taken in the future.

Adaptation

9.2.9. Since a substantial adverse change in climate appears unavoidable even with the optimal mitigation response, the process of adaptation to climate change must have priority. The most important adaptation measure is development itself. A stronger economy is more able to adapt both in terms of the cost of adaptation and technological capability. Achieving rapid economic growth as targeted in the Eleventh Plan is therefore a key element in adaptation. As mentioned earlier, the Prime Minister's Council on Climate Change has decided that a National Action Plan on Climate Change compiling action taken by India for addressing the challenge of climate change and the action that it proposes to take, should be prepared as India's National Report on Climate Change. The Action Plan will deal with key vulnerabilities of India to Climate Change and, in particular, the impact on water resources, forests, coastal areas, agriculture, and health. An action plan for adaptation to climate change would require (i) action in the area of agricultural research to evolve varieties that can cope with likely climate changes, (ii) action to cope with likely increases in water stress, (iii) action to be able to cope with a greater frequency in natural disasters. The institutional network created at the time of preparation of India's initial National Communication to United Nations Framework Convention on Climate Change (UNFCCC) exists and is currently engaged in the preparation of information on India's second National Communication.

9.2.10. In the changing temperature and water regimes, improvement of productivity potential and water use efficiency of agricultural crops, specifically in regimes of water shortage and extreme variations of temperature, will be priority areas of research.

9.2.11. The adaptation response needs to be incorporated in the relevant programmes, including those relating to watershed management, coastal zone planning and regulation, forestry management, agricultural technologies and practices, and health.

9.2.12. Work on the potential impact, forecasting systems and adaptations in response to Climate Change will be the key concerns for future development. For projections and early warning systems, understanding of the processes which could show discernible changes well before the actual impact starts is essential.

Mitigation

9.2.13. Recognizing the need for international co-operation in devising an effective mitigation strategy, in 1992, the international community established the UNFCCC which established the principle of 'common but differentiated responsibility' between the industrialized countries (Annex 1 countries) and the developing countries (non-Annex 1 countries), taking account of the respective capacities. The Annex 1 countries were required to bring down their GHG emissions to 1990 levels by 2000. In 1997, the Kyoto Protocol under the UNFCCC was adopted, which set legally binding targets for GHG reduction by individual industrialized countries totaling 5.2% below their aggregate 1990 emissions during the 'first commitment period', 2008–12. Under the provisions of the Kyoto Protocol, non Annex I Parties (India is in this category) are not obliged to reduce emissions of GHG. So far, 176 countries, including India (and the regional economic organization EEC), have ratified the Protocol. The US and some other countries have not ratified the Protocol till now. Most of the industrialized countries thus far have not achieved significant progress in reducing their GHG emissions in the manner required in the first commitment period.

9.2.14. An optimum approach to mitigation from a global perspective is only possible if all countries cooperate to facilitate collective action. This is because mitigation actions are characterized by the classic problem of externality—the benefits of the action of any one country do not accrue only to the country itself but to the entire global community, while the costs of mitigation are fully internalized. Without co-operative action, all countries taken together will do less mitigation than is collectively optimum. The challenge lies in determining a basis for collective action which is fair, provides equitable entitlement to the global environment space with burden sharing in a manner which recognizes the very different levels of development and also the very different degrees of historical responsibility for causing the problem in the first place. Such differenciation among the countries of the world has been accepted by the UNFCCC and the Kyoto Protocol. This must be effectively operationalized to create an environment of trust and co-operation.

9.2.15. The first commitment period of the Kyoto Protocol is 2008–2012 and as per the provisions of the Kyoto Protocol and discussion at the 13th Conference of Parties at Bali in December 2007, Bali Action Plan was commenced which intends to enable the full, effective, and sustained implementation of the Convention through long-term co-operative action, now, upto and beyond 2012. As part of the Bali Action Plan, a process has also been initiated to determine the GHG reduction commitments of industrialized countries (Annex 1 countries) under the Kyoto Protocol, beyond 2012. The precise nature of the outcomes of this process would be determined in a two year negotiating time table ending in 2009.

9.2.16. There is no doubt that the accumulation of GHG, which is the cause of global warming, has occurred overwhelmingly due to the emissions of industrial countries and it is therefore entirely appropriate that the burden of mitigation must fall on them. It is for this reason that the first commitment period in the Kyoto Protocol entailed commitment for reduction only by the industrialized countries.

9.2.17. With a share of just 4% of global emissions, any amount of mitigation by India will not affect climate change. A substantial commitment to reduce emissions by the major industrialized countries will be required. Nevertheless, as contribution to the global emissions reduction effort, the Eleventh Plan would focus on efforts to ensure that the emissions intensity of India's GHG continues to decline. The correct approach in mitigation is to define the obligations of different parties on the basis of common but differentiated responsibility and differences in respective capabilities. India's view on burden sharing is based on this approach. Our National Environmental Policy of 2006 requires 'equal per capita entitlements of global environmental resources to all countries'. At the meeting of the G 8 +5 in Heiligendamm in July 2007, Prime Minister Manmohan Singh indicated that we are determined to see that India's per capita emissions never exceed the per capita emissions of the industrialized countries. This formulation focuses on per capita emissions rather than total emissions as the relevant variable, and also provides industrial countries with an incentive to reduce their level of emissions as quickly as possible.

9.2.18. While optimal mitigation strategies will no doubt evolve in time from the ongoing international negotiations, India is already taking a number of initiatives in clean energy including renewable energy and action to increase energy efficiency and conservation.

One of the objectives of the Eleventh Plan is to reduce the energy intensity per unit of GHG by 20% from the period 2007–08 to 2016–17. We will also initiate action to increase our access to cleaner and renewable energy by fully exploiting existing resources (e.g., hydropower and wind power) developing nuclear power, and also supporting research in newer areas such as biofuels from agro-waste, solar energy, etc.

9.2.19. The CDM is a flexible arrangement under the Kyoto Protocol which enables industrialized countries to meet their emission reduction obligations by encouraging adoption of sustainable and environmentally friendly technologies in developing countries. India's CDM potential is a significant component of the global CDM market. Till 14 February 2008, out of a total of 871 projects accorded Host Country Approval, 314 projects in India have been registered by the CDM Executive Board, so far the highest in any country. However, in terms of the corresponding Certified Emission Reduction (CERs), India is second to China.

ALLOCATIONS IN THE ELEVENTH PLAN

9.2.20. The total projected GBS in the Eleventh Plan for the MoEF is Rs 8842 crore (at 2006–07 price) and Rs 10000 crore (at current price).

9.3 DISASTER MANAGEMENT

OVERVIEW

9.3.1. Many regions in India are highly vulnerable to natural and other disasters on account of geological conditions. About 60% of the landmass is susceptible to earthquakes and over 8% is prone to floods. Of the nearly 7500 kilometers long coastline, approximately 5700 kilometers is prone to cyclones. 68% area is susceptible to drought. All this entails huge economic losses and causes developmental setbacks. Disasters are no longer limited to natural catastrophes. Man-made emergencies often cause bigger disasters in terms of fatalities and economic losses. With urbanization and concentration of population in metropolitan cities, more and more people are becoming vulnerable to locational disasters. So, the development process needs to be sensitive towards disaster prevention, preparedness and mitigation. Disaster management has therefore emerged as a high priority for the country. Going beyond the historical focus on relief and rehabilitation after the event, there is a need to look ahead and plan for disaster preparedness and mitigation in order to ensure that periodic shocks to our development efforts are minimized.

9.3.2. Disaster risk reduction has not been highlighted in the policies and programmes of various plan schemes. The country's commitment to mainstreaming disaster risk reduction into the process of development planning at all levels so as to achieve sustainable development is yet to be carried forward across sectors through actionable programmes for achieving the desired result.

TENTH FIVE YEAR PLAN STRATEGY AND APPROACH

9.3.3. The Tenth Five Year Plan (2002–07), prepared in the backdrop of the Orissa super cyclone, Gujarat earthquake, and end of the International Decade of Natural Disaster Reduction, recognized disaster management as a development issue for the first time. The Plan devoted a separate chapter to disaster management and made a number of important prescriptions to mainstream disaster risk reduction into the process of development.

9.3.4. The Tenth Plan prescriptions on disaster management can broadly be divided into three categories:

(i) Policy guidelines at the macro level that would inform and guide the preparation and implementation of development plans across sectors;
(ii) Operational guidelines for integrating disaster management practices into development plans and programmes, and
(iii) Specific developmental schemes for prevention and mitigation of disasters.

9.3.5. At the macro level, the Plan emphasized that 'while hazards, both natural or otherwise, are inevitable, the disasters that follow need not be so and the society can be prepared to cope with them effectively whenever they occur' and called for a 'multi-pronged strategy for total risk management, comprising prevention, preparedness, response and recovery, on the one hand, and for initiating development efforts aimed towards risk reduction and mitigation, on the other'. It stated that only then could we look forward to 'sustainable development'.

9.3.6. At the operational level, the Plan made a number of very important suggestions, as given below:

- Streamlining institutional arrangements for disaster response by an integrated approach involving civilian and military resources; setting up a modern, permanent national command centre or operations room with redundant communications and data links to all State capitals; establishing a quick response team particularly for search and rescue operations; developing standard operating system for dealing with humanitarian and relief assistance from non-government sources; and formulating a unified legislation for dealing with all types of disasters.

- Building disaster prevention and preparedness in development planning by introducing a rigorous process of vulnerability analysis and risk assessment, maintaining comprehensive database and resource inventories at all levels, developing state-of-the-art infrastructure for mitigation planning, and establishing a Disaster Knowledge Network for the use of disaster managers, decision makers, community, and so on.
- Developing a nation-wide culture of prevention by introducing disaster management in the school curriculum, including relevant aspects of disaster management in professional courses, enhancing the capacity of disaster managers by better training facilities and creating a massive awareness at all levels.
- Encouraging community level initiatives for disaster preparedness by involving people at the grass roots, particularly those who are more vulnerable, for better preparedness and response.
- Developing appropriate zonal regulations, design standards, building codes, and performance specifications for safe construction.
- Inclusion of disaster mitigation analysis in all development schemes in vulnerable areas through which the feasibility of a project is assessed with respect to vulnerability of the area.
- Building disaster mitigation components into all development projects financed under the Plan.

9.3.7. The Tenth Plan felt that planned expenditure on disaster mitigation and prevention measures was required in addition to a Calamity Relief Fund. The Plan, however, stopped short of recommending any specific plan scheme for prevention, mitigation or preparedness for disasters nor did it allocate any amount for such scheme, except making a general recommendation that '*Creation of faculties in disaster management in all 28 states is proposed to be taken up in the Tenth Plan in addition to community mobilization, human resource development, establishment of Control Rooms and forging international cooperation in disaster management. There is also an urgent need for strengthening the disaster management pedagogy by creating disaster management faculties in universities, rural development institutes and other organizations of premier research.*'

IMPLEMENTATION OF SCHEMES IN THE TENTH PLAN

9.3.8. A Central Sector Plan Scheme, the National Disaster Mitigation Programme (NDMP), has been implemented since 1993–94. The scheme mainly provided for training and capacity building of government functionaries and other stakeholders to manage disasters in an effective manner. This scheme was transferred from the Ministry of Agriculture to the Ministry of Home Affairs in June 2002. The allocation for this scheme was raised from Rs 6.30 crore in the Eighth Plan to Rs 16.32 crore in the Ninth Plan and to Rs 30.77 crore in Tenth Plan. The annual allocations under various components of the scheme during the Tenth Five Year Plan are in Table 9.3.1.

9.3.9. Out of the eight components of the above scheme, only two components namely 'Grants-in-Aid' and 'Professional Services' were developmental in nature, while the remaining components were on revenue expenses. The major activities under the grants-in-aid include the setting up of the National Centre for Disaster Management at the Indian Institute of Public Administration, now upgraded as a statutory organization

TABLE 9.3.1

National Disaster Mitigation Programme—Year-wise Allocation of Funds in the Tenth Five Year Plan

(Rs in lakh)

S. No.	Head	2002–03	2003–04	2004–05	2005–06	2006–07	Total
1.	Grants-in-aid	262.00	349.00	474.00	505.00	600.00	2190.00
2.	Professional Services	20.00	29.00	54.00	110.00	150.00	363.00
3.	Machinery & Equipments	2.00	20.00	30.00	15.00	10.00	77.00
4.	Foreign Travel	80.00	30.00	25.00	40.00	50.00	225.00
5.	Contribution	20.00	20.00	20.00	17.00	20.00	97.00
6.	Office Expenses	2.50	3.00	2.00	2.00	2.00	11.50
7.	Advertisement & Publicity	20.00	10.00	25.00	1.00	1.00	57.00
8.	Other Charges	0.50	26.00	10.00	10.00	10.00	56.50
	Total	407.00	487.00	640.00	700.00	843.00	3077.00

Source: Disaster Management Division (MHA).

known as National Institute of Disaster Management (NIDM), creation of 29 disaster management faculties/ Centres in 28 States, research and consultancy services, and documentation of major disaster events. The faculties did not have sufficient back-up from the States with the result that only limited activities are undertaken by the Centres. Even meagre allocations provided by the Central Government as grants-in-aid were not fully utilized in many of the States. The allocation of Rs 21.90 crore to the training institutes during the Tenth Five Year Plan was mainly used on NIDM which incurred an expenditure of Rs 11.56 crore. Nearly 71000 persons have been imparted training under the programme (Table 9.3.1).

9.3.10. The National Cyclone Risk Mitigation Project is another Plan Scheme proposed to be implemented with World Bank assistance. The project is presently at the stage of preparation of Detailed Project Report. It covers all 13 cyclone prone coastal States and UTs. Investments are to be made in upgradation of cyclone forecasting, tracking and warning systems, construction work of cyclone shelters, road linkages, plantation, retro-fittings of vital lifeline installations, strengthening of national and regional training institutions, setting up a techno-legal regime for cyclone mitigation and for strong management and monitoring system. As regards upgradation of cyclone forecasting, tracking and warning systems, this activity is proposed to be taken up either as part of the project or independently by the IMD.

9.3.11. The Ministry of Home Affairs is also implementing Phase II of a Community based Disaster Risk Mitigation (DRM) Programme in 169 multi hazard districts in 17 States/UTs with the support of UNDP under a multi-donor programme at a total estimated cost of Rs 153 crore (US$ 34 million). Under this programme, disaster management plans are being prepared from village to district; village volunteers are being trained in first-aid, search and rescue, evacuation and relief and shelter management; disaster management teams are being constituted at the district and sub-district levels and mock drills are being conducted at all levels. This 100% externally funded programme is, however, outside the framework of the Plan and is being implemented on the non-Plan side. It is the largest community based DRM programme in the world. Phase I of the programme was implemented in the three States of Gujarat, Orissa, and Bihar during 2002–06 and has been rated well in a recent evaluation conducted by a team of consultants. While the general feedback on Phase II of the programme is good, there is a definite need to increase the scope to cover other deficient areas too, in order to draw the full benefit from this.

Institutional and Other Initiatives in the Tenth Plan

9.3.12. The following significant initiatives on disaster management were taken during the Tenth Five Year Plan period:

- The Disaster Management Act, 2005 has been enacted for establishing requisite institutional mechanisms for drawing up and monitoring the implementation of disaster management plans, ensuring measures by various wings of the government for prevention and mitigating the effects of disasters, and for undertaking a holistic, co-ordinated, and prompt response to any disaster situation.
- The National Disaster Management Authority (NDMA), under the Chairmanship of the Prime Minister, has been set up in terms of the Act. NDMA is an apex body responsible for laying down of policies, plans and guidelines on disaster management so as to ensure timely and effective response to disasters. The Authority has prepared a Draft National Policy on Disaster Management and has taken up preparation of guidelines on prevention, mitigation, response, and recovery in regard to various types of disasters such as earthquake, flood, landslides, industrial disaster, and so on. The guidelines on management of earthquake, chemical disasters, and chemical (industrial) disasters have been finalized and circulated.
- The State Governments are in the process of setting up State and district Disaster Management Authorities. The provisions of the Act relevant to the States/UTs have been brought into force w.e.f. 1 August 2007. While Arunachal Pradesh, Goa, Gujarat, Himachal Pradesh, Kerala, Mizoram, Puducherry, Punjab, and Uttar Pradesh are reported to have constituted SDMAs as per the Act, the other States/UTs are in the process of constituting the same.
- An eight battalion-strong National Disaster Response Force has been set up comprising of 144 specialized response teams on various types of disasters of which 72 teams are for nuclear, biological, and chemical (NBC) disasters.
- The Civil Defence set-up in the country is proposed to be revamped to strengthen local efforts for disaster preparedness and effective response. Similarly, the Fire Services are also proposed to be strengthened/

modernized to convert them into a multi-hazard response force.

- The National Institute of Disaster Management has been set up for training, capacity building, research, and documentation on various natural and manmade disasters. A comprehensive Human Resource Plan for Disaster Management has also been developed.
- Disaster Management has been included in the curriculum of middle and secondary school education. The subject has also been included in the post-induction and in-service training of civil and police officers. Modules have also been identified to include disaster management aspects in the course curriculum for engineering, architecture, and medical degrees.
- A committee of experts has finalized the Model building by-laws for town and country planning legislations, land use zonation, and development control legislations. The municipalities and city development authorities all over the country have been advised to make necessary changes in their respective by-laws and regulations in accordance with the model laws.
- The Bureau of Indian Standards has issued building codes for construction of different types of buildings in different seismic zones in the country. The National Building Code has also been revised, taking into consideration the natural hazards and risks of various regions of the country.
- The National Programme for Capacity Building of Engineers in Earthquake Risk Management to train 10000 engineers and 10000 architects on safe construction techniques and architectural practices is under implementation.
- A Web-enabled centralized inventory of resources has been developed to minimize response time in emergencies. Over 110000 records from 600 districts have been uploaded.
- Safe construction practices and dos and don'ts for various hazards are being disseminated for creating public awareness.

ELEVENTH PLAN

Vision and Strategy

9.3.13. The Tenth Plan has set into motion the process of shift in focus from response-centric disaster management covering rescue, relief, rehabilitation, and reconstruction to laying greater emphasis on the other elements of disaster management cycle—prevention, mitigation, and preparedness—as a means to avert or soften the impact of future emergencies. The Eleventh Plan aims at consolidating the process by giving impetus to projects and programmes that develop and nurture the culture of safety and the integration of disaster prevention and mitigation into the development process. The guidance and direction to achieve this paradigm shift will need to flow from NDMA, and in the true spirit of the Disaster Management Act, to all stakeholders including State Governments and UTs, right up to the PRIs. Communities at large will need to be mobilized to achieve this common objective as they are the first responders. Even the best of isolated efforts will not bear fruit unless they are part of an overall, well- considered approach, and responsibilities of all stakeholders are clearly spelt out and accountability and sustainability factored in.

9.3.14. Projects and programmes undertaken may be such that they address the felt national needs and with well acknowledged prioritization. With scarce resources, it will be imperative to put in place suitable mechanisms which will facilitate systematic project and programme appraisal. Support will have to be lent to programmes and projects that will lead to sustainable development, with assurance of disaster risk reduction built in. The question of vulnerability will also have to be considered, not only in the physical sense but in a comprehensive sense; vulnerability could also be social, ecological, organizational, educational, attitudinal, political, cultural, and economical.

9.3.15. For an objective screening and scrutiny of development projects in a speedy manner, it is essential that professionalism in project formulation is insisted upon. Well-considered and well-drafted, need-based project proposals with in-built disaster prevention and mitigation features, as brought out above, should usually sail through the decision making process. These projects would need to be based on sufficient studies, reliable assumptions, and have regard for the latest advances in science and technology.

9.3.16. To ensure thoroughness in project formulation, all the expected requirements need to be clearly articulated and the project appraisal procedure kept simple and straightforward. One set of standard guidelines may not be adequate in addressing all the complex set of issues and there is clearly a need to evolve a multi-pronged approach to address a host of interlinked issues.

9.3.17. For the assessment of impact of any major development scheme in a given zone of hazard, it is imperative that the proposal takes in its stride what all could go wrong (damage scenarios) and shows how the project design is fashioned to counter that likely damage scenario. Conceptualization of damage scenarios will require quality scientific studies in a multi-disciplinary environment, and generation of new data, besides filling data gaps.

9.3.18. The SoI needs to be entrusted with the responsibility of generating large-scale maps which will form the basis for disaster management studies. They will also need to generate a Digital Elevation Map (DEM) of high resolution (1/2m interval along vertical) for the purpose of 3D terrain modelling. There will be a need to carry out prioritization of the areas on which the SoI will carry out the 1:10000 mapping for the whole country and map all towns and cities on 1:2000 scales. Coastal zones and flood prone areas of the country will need to get priority in the preparation of DEM. NDMA, in consultation with National Informatics Centre (NIC), National Spatial Data Infrastructure, National Remote Sensing Agency, and DoS is actively promoting the use of GIS in all institutions concerned with disaster management. Priority will have to be given to highly vulnerable areas for generating the database for mapping as well as hazard vulnerability and risk assessment related to disasters like cyclone, flood earthquake, chemical and industrial, etc.

9.3.19. Data-sharing among the various data generators is an even more important aspect and needs to be addressed. All such schemes getting Plan funds will be treated as national asset and data would be made available without any pre-condition for use for disaster management authorities and others.

9.3.20. The national emergency communication network, involving the contemporary space and terrestrial-based technologies, in a highly synergistic configuration and with considerable redundancy, needs to be developed and deployed countrywide. With almost a 100% reliability, this network must ensure real-time dissemination of warnings and information direct to the affected community and local authorities.

9.3.21. Research on all aspects of disaster mitigation which has the potential to save lives and property needs to be encouraged. NDMA could provide the necessary policy direction to Science related ministries and departments both at the Central and State levels to foster, promote, and sustain research and development work through need-based disaster mitigation and management projects.

9.3.22. A well sensitized and prepared community forms one of the most important links in the process of better management of disasters. For that reason, 'Extended Disaster Risk Mitigation Project' has been identified for being taken up for preparation of a Project Report during the Plan. This will be supplemented by activities under various other national/State level mitigation projects. As far as Community Based Disaster Management is concerned, a degree of convergence is required to be brought into community mobilization, participation, awareness, and capacity building aspects of all concerned social sector schemes like women and child development, rural development, drinking water, sanitation, and so on. The concerned ministries may consider inclusion of disaster management content into their plans and make provision of funds in their respective schemes.

9.3.23. It is essential that while clearing plans for State Governments, there is an integrated approach, particularly for creation of adequate capacity for relief and rescue operations.

9.3.24. There is need for evolution of a broad classification of anticipated projects that would come up for clearance by the Planning Commission. One possible classification could be:

- Projects specifically designed in response to the NDMA Strategy, Guidelines and Action Plan, and
- Development projects with built-in environmental preservation and disaster mitigation features in tune with the philosophy of mainstreaming mitigation measures into development projects.

9.3.25. Assistance is needed for State level mitigation projects, especially drafting of State, district, and panchayat level disaster management plans and in continuous sustenance, modernization, and upgradation of disaster management capacity.

9.3.26. In view of the focus on disaster mitigation of projects, institution building, aimed at training a new breed of disaster managers, and establishment of centres/ institutes fully equipped to carry out specialized investigations and post-disaster studies, would need to be encouraged. The training and skills of the 72 teams for NBC disasters in the eight battalions of the National Disaster Response Force have to be improved and sharpened.

9.3.27. Out of the eight battalions of the National Disaster Response Force already sanctioned by the government, two Battalions already have the basic infrastructure. While the existing infrastructure has to be upgraded for these two Battalions, completely new infrastructure has to be created for the remaining six Battalions.

Mainstreaming Disaster Management into Development Planning

9.3.28. Mainstreaming disaster management into the development planning process essentially means looking critically at each activity that is being planned, not only from the perspective of reducing the disaster vulnerability of that activity, but also from the perspective of minimizing that activity's potential contribution to the hazard. Every development plan of a ministry/department should incorporate elements of impact assessment, risk reduction, and the 'do no harm' approach. Examples of this approach are urban planning and zoning, upgradation of building codes and their effective enforcement, adoption of disaster resilient housing designs and construction of school and hospitals, flood proofing, response preparedness planning, insurance, establishment of early warning systems for various types of disasters, generating community awareness, creating technical competence and promoting research among engineers, architects, health experts, and scientists.

9.3.29. State governments need to give priority in their plans for schemes regarding hazard identification and risk assessment once they have prepared the project paper, completed preliminary work, and drawn up the details of the scheme. Hazard identification and risk assessment across the country must be bound by uniformly followed procedures, fine-tuned to local conditions. In the absence of such procedures, any sporadic activity based on some ad hoc procedure carries the potential of doing more harm than good. It will be essential that while clearing plans of State Governments, there is an integrated approach particularly for creation of adequate capacity for relief and rescue operations, for example, for funding projects for construction of school buildings. Some school buildings need to be identified which will be used as relief centres and buildings designed so that they withstand the impact of disasters and also have adequate capacity to provide space as relief centres. Such schools should be equipped with essential services which become important at the time of a disaster.

9.3.30. State governments will need to make comprehensive Management Action Plans for achieving long-term results in a phased manner. To make these plans more meaningful, workshops and training programmes are to be organized at local/regional/national levels for capacity building and awareness generation/community participation.

9.3.31. Outside the framework of Plan schemes, many innovative measures can be adopted to encourage disaster risk reduction measures by the corporate sector, non-government organizations, and individuals. Fiscal measures like rebates on income and property tax for retrofitting unsafe buildings, compulsory risk insurance for bank loan on all types of properties, and so on, shall definitely help to mobilize resources for safe construction and retrofitting of existing constructions in all disaster prone areas. Similarly, many innovative measures may be taken for promoting public–private–community partnership for disaster risk reduction.

Principles for Project Appraisal from the Disaster Management Perspective

9.3.32. To assist the Planning Commission in appraisal of projects, broad and generic guidelines which are not disaster or theme specific have to be adopted. Conceptualization of hazard scenarios and associated vulnerability and risk assessments in a given situation will necessarily have to depend on available maps, Master Plans and building and land use regulations, National Building Code of India, and the various safety Standards and Codes of the Bureau of Indian Standards. The guidelines will have to cover the following aspects:

- The location of the project is to be carefully considered, especially if this is in a multi-hazard prone area/district recognized by the NDMA. Multi-hazard prone districts are reported in the latest National Building Code of India of the Bureau of Indian Standards. The listing has been revised by the Building Materials Technology Promotion Council of India, currently under the consideration of NDMA.
- The project/scheme should be based on a detailed hazard and risk assessment; wherever required, environmental clearance will also be taken. The risk assessment will usually involve the following factors:

- Assessment of degree of hazard, based on high resolution single/multiple hazard maps interpreted in the light of all available historic records, publications, site-specific information, and studies. For all major projects/schemes, where such maps are presently unavailable, the project/scheme should be supported by adequate site-specific seismo-tectonic, geological, geo-physical, and geotechnical studies and analyses. Data gaps, assumptions made, and their implications should be brought out. Where high resolution multi-hazard maps are not available, multi-hazard assessment is to be made by coalescing the information on single hazards.
- All such site specific risk assessment studies should be referenced to a national high resolution geospatial database so as to facilitate temporal analysis of future assessment impact studies in the area and also enable integration of all other assessment studies carried out in the vicinity. Through such a process it will be possible to evolve a national database of assessment studies which, in turn, will facilitate refinement of National Hazard and Vulnerability Mapping.
- Assessment of vulnerability against a hazard of a given magnitude should be carried out. The vulnerability of an individual or a group of individuals or of any element or an infrastructure like a flyover or a bridge, for a hazard of a given magnitude, will vary from 0 to 1 depending on the degree of mitigation built into the design. For example, an earthquake of magnitude 7 on the Richter scale may render very unsafe school children in a poorly built school (vulnerability = 1) whereas the residents of an earthquake-resistant neighbouring house for the same magnitude of earthquake, may be safe (vulnerability = 0). This distinction is essential because existence of hazard does not automatically mean vulnerability, and vulnerability does not necessarily have to be 1. The question of vulnerability has to be considered not only in a physical sense but in a comprehensive sense. Vulnerability could be physical, social, ecological, organizational, educational, attitudinal, political, cultural, or economical. Vulnerability assessment may also take note of medical care and casualty management that would be possible in the vicinity in case of natural or man-made disaster.
- Assessment of risk against a given hazard will be a function of hazard and vulnerability.
- Identification of elements at risk like population, properties, economic activities, public services, is to be brought out. By overlaying the infrastructure map of an area on the corresponding hazard map of the same scale, elements at risk can be identified.
- Particularly while carrying out hazard identification and risk assessment for industrial estates, issues like release scenario, consequences in terms of heat generation over pressure and toxicities, identification of hazardous chemicals, processes and operations, identification of important receptors, both environmental and physical, classification of units which have potential for creating an off site emergency, and so on, need to be addressed.

• The reliability of hazard, vulnerability, and risk assessments will depend upon the quality of maps and other investigational data and various uncertainties involved due to inadequacy of data and other factors. It is therefore important that all major stages of project/scheme development, namely, planning, site investigations and designs, are subject to a process of rigorous peer review and accordingly certified.

9.3.33. Where projects specifically identified and designed for disaster management are to be appraised, the following factors would need to be considered:

• The proposed project or scheme (i) is to be need based and demand driven; (ii) must fall within the high priority bracket, linked with the development plan of the area; (iii) should have well stipulated goals, clearly identified stakeholders and beneficiaries; (iv) should be fully backed with analyses of risks and quantified benefits in terms of disaster safety; and (v) should clearly reflect implications of not taking up the project in terms of disaster related risks, environmental protection, and economic development.
• Projects/schemes which yield multiplier effect for the greatest good of the largest number will deserve priority. For example, a well drafted practical disaster emergency plan for a school or disaster management plan for a district can inspire other schools and districts to yield the snow-balling (multiplier) effect. Similarly, development of a knowledge based, multi-media disaster mitigation product when translated in different vernacular languages may at once multiply benefits.
• Project merit rating should also depend on the following factors:
  - Breaking new ground in terms of scientific, technological or management innovation, including peoples' participation. For instance, development

of an innovative early warning system against a particular type of disaster using simple, readily monitored indicators.
  - Delivering 'Best Practices' for others to emulate and getting inspired by them. For example, best practices of engineered constructions in a given earthquake-affected hilly area.
  - Choice of appropriate technology. For example, partially prefabricated construction technology will be more appropriate than the cast-in-place construction technology in a post-disaster reconstruction programme in a given situation.
  - Employment generation. For example, a judicious man-machine mix in the construction of flood prevention works may help generate employment in an area without unduly compromising on efficiency of work.
  - Sustainable capacity building. It is the key to empowering a village, district, State, or a region so that each one of them can, as far as possible, manage their own affairs in the event of a disaster. For example, water sampling and testing capacity at local level when post-disaster situations threaten epidemics.
  - Pro-active engagement of communities and spreading the culture of safety in communities and other levels. Disaster education and community leadership development, public awareness development, gender mainstreaming, special focus on the needs of women and children, vocational training of unemployed youth, and concern for physically challenged persons will add weight to the project/scheme.
- Since disasters know no district or State boundaries, projects of interest to two or more districts or States may score over those yielding localized benefits. By the same logic, national level mission-mode projects/schemes should get preference over others.

Financial Provisions for Disaster Management

9.3.34. It is important that a portion of the Plan funds is earmarked for efforts that directly or indirectly help in disaster management. Ideally, each project should provide adequately for the disaster mitigation and management expenditure that is identified by the appraisal process described in the previous section as being necessary. In addition, Central and State Governments may, depending upon their own hazard assessments, earmark a suitable and adequate amount for disaster mitigation schemes that are implemented over a definite time period.

9.3.35. The projects to be taken up should include:

- All schemes for generating basic input data for hazard and vulnerability impact analysis.
- Stand-alone disaster management projects such as mitigation projects, awareness programmes, capacity building projects, community based disaster management projects, upgrading early warning systems, failsafe disaster management communication network, micro-zoning, and so on.
- Mainstreaming disaster reduction into already approved projects in sectors of education, housing, infrastructure, urban development, and the like. For example, projects already under implementation such as the SSA, which caters to the construction of school buildings, could be reviewed. The design of the school building under the programme could include hazard resistant features, at least in multi-hazard prone (earthquake, cyclone, flood), high-risk areas so that these are safe. Similarly, existing infrastructure like bridges and roads will need to be strengthened and upgraded to mitigate disaster at a subsequent stage.

Schemes/Programmes Identified/Proposed to be taken up in the Eleventh Five Year Plan

9.3.36. National level initiatives/projects for disaster management, identified and recommended by the Working Group on Disaster Management and the NDMA for being taken up during the Eleventh Five Year Plan are indicated at Annexure 9.3. However, details of these projects/schemes will have to be worked out through preparation of project reports. Thereafter, such schemes as are approved for implementation during the Eleventh Five Year Plan will have to be accommodated within the sectoral allocations of the ministries concerned.

9.3.37. Apart from the projects/schemes mentioned above, a number of ongoing and proposed schemes of various ministries and departments of the GoI have a direct or indirect bearing on disaster management as these add to preparedness for responding to disasters or constitute the efforts towards recovery from the impact of disasters. Similarly, many developmental projects/schemes take care of the vulnerability to different kinds of disasters and provide for mitigation of their effects.

ANNEXURE 9.1
Financial Performance in the Tenth Plan

S. No.	Schemes/Programmes	Financial Performance Tenth Plan (Rs in crore)			
		Outlay	BE	RE	Actual Exp.
	Environment				
1	Central Pollution Control Board (CPCB)	100.00	147.90	138.90	140.06
2	Industrial Pollution Abatement through Preventive Strategies	5.00	4.60	4.48	1.48
3	Common Effluent Treatment Plants (CETP)	25.00	20.27	20.25	20.10
4	Environmental Management in Heritage Pilgrimage and Tourism Centres, including Taj Protection	170.00	59.02	25.03	25.00
5	Establishment of Environment Protection Authorities and Environment Commission and Tribunal	15.00	18.80	18.22	13.83
6	Assistance for Abatement of Pollution and Environment Policy and Law	19.67	21.00	24.69	25.00
7	Environmental Health	10.00	2.00	0.05	1.03
8	Clean Technologies	25.00	12.50	9.19	5.18
9	Environmental Impact Assessment (EIA)	13.00	11.80	11.07	12.35
10	Industrial Pollution Prevention Project (EAP)	10.00	10.00	13.54	13.55
11	Hazardous Substances Management	70.00	37.00	32.91	30.71
12	Botanical Survey of India (BSI)	85.00	61.50	49.54	47.89
13	Zoological Survey of India (ZSI)	45.00	49.37	50.87	45.51
14	G.B. Pant Institute of Himalayan Environment and Development	35.00	34.00	36.96	37.00
15	Biosphere Reserves	35.00	37.20	37.87	36.62
16	Conservation and Management of Mangroves, Coral Reefs, and Wetlands	54.00	55.00	57.55	57.11
17	Assistance of Botanical Gardens	15.00	9.50	7.25	6.96
18	Biodiversity Conservation	12.00	15.00	17.00	15.51
19	Taxonomy Capacity Building Project	10.00	8.50	8.34	8.96
20	Institute of Biodiversity	16.00	1.00	0.00	0.00
21	Research and Development	24.00	20.07	20.83	20.78
22	Environment Education, Training, and Awareness	125.00	143.00	125.25	118.16
23	National Museum of Natural History (NMNH)	40.00	31.50	28.56	26.71
24	Centres of Excellence	45.00	38.00	36.56	33.28
25	Environmental Information System (ENVIS)	14.00	17.50	20.03	19.55
26	National Natural Resource Management System (NNRMS)	7.00	23.50	22.50	22.74
27	Environment Management Capacity Building Project (EMCB) (EAP)	48.98	80.00	48.29	46.14
28	Indo-Canada Environment Facility (ICEF) (EAP)	35.00	0.05	0.04	0.00
29	GoI-UNDP-CCF Programme (EAP)	3.00	13.00	9.50	9.06
30	Global Environment Facility (EAP)	0.05	0.01	0.01	0.00
31	International Co-operation Activities	8.00	9.20	9.92	10.13
32	Canada Assisted Centre for Excellence in Environmental Science, Technology, and Policy (EAP)	1.00	0.11	0.02	0.00
33	Indo-German Technical Co-operation Project (EAP)	6.00	0.50	0.01	0.00
34	State of Environment Project	6.00	6.15	7.26	6.26

(Annexure 9.1 contd.)

(Annexure 9.1 contd.)

S. No.	Schemes/Programmes	Financial Performance Tenth Plan (Rs in crore)			
		Outlay	BE	RE	Actual Exp.
35	Information Technology (IT)	25.00	46.73	29.96	29.69
36	Adaptation and Capacity Building Project on Climate Change (ACPCC)	30.00	21.83	28.05	26.99
37	Strengthening of Plan Coordination	0.30	0.06	0.01	0.00
38	Civil Construction Unit (CCU)	12.00	8.98	9.71	8.75
NEW SCHEMES					
39	EPCO-Madhya Pradesh and Strengthening Natural Resource Management and Farmers Livelihood in Nagaland (EAP)		1.59	0.94	0.90
40	Strengthening of Environment Information Centre		0.10	0.00	0.00
41	National Coastal Management Programme		0.10	0.00	0.00
42	Capacity building EIA and Revised Environmental Clearance Process		0.10	0.00	0.00
43	Promotion of Bilateral Cooperation		0.00	0.00	0.00
Total Environment		1200.00	1078.04	961.16	919.99
NRCD					
44	NRCD	33.00	27.00	27.00	24.35
45	NRCP	1342.00	1199.96	1207.27	1134.89
46	NRCP (EAP)	75.00	337.00	185.76	218.91
47	NLCP	220.00	250.00	202.37	164.62
Total NRCD		1670.00	1813.96	1622.40	1542.77
FORESTRY & WILDLIFE					
48	Indian Council for Forestry Research and Education (ICFRE)	210.00	226.86	228.57	227.95
49	Grant-In-Aid to Indian Plywood Industries Research and Institute (IPIRTI)	10.00	12.10	14.20	14.15
50	Indian Institute of Forest Management (IIFM)	20.00	21.00	22.77	23.46
51	Training to IFS Officers	6.00	6.75	6.25	5.94
52	Indira Gandhi National Forest Academy (IGNFA)	30.00	27.25	26.68	23.61
53	Directorate of Forestry Education (DFE)	10.00	11.73	12.69	15.06
54	Gregarious flowering of Muli (*Melocanna baccifera*) Bamboos		60.00	43.00	42.82
55	Forest Survey of India (FSI)	35.00	29.50	26.97	27.15
56	Integrated Forest Protection Scheme	445.00	279.84	224.47	208.01
57	Strengthening of Forestry Divisions	34.00	31.50	32.94	33.79
58	Afforestation through PRIs (NCMP—related scheme)	0.00	0.10	0.10	0.00
59	Strengthening of Wildlife Divisions and outside Protected Areas	10.00	15.00	14.51	11.23
60	Development of National Parks and Sanctuaries	350.00	230.50	240.11	234.65
61	Wildlife Institute of India (WII)	50.00	45.00	49.47	46.07
62	National Zoological Parks (NZP)		2.50	4.80	4.37
63	Project Tiger	150.00	149.00	160.96	160.44

(Annexure 9.1 contd.)

(Annexure 9.1 contd.)

S. No.	Schemes/Programmes	Financial Performance Tenth Plan (Rs in crore)			
		Outlay	BE	RE	Actual Exp.
64	Biodiversity Conservation and Rural Livelihood Improvement Project (EAP)		4.00	3.33	2.03
65	Eco-development around Protected Areas (EAP)	45.00	80.25	58.05	56.59
66	Project Elephant	60.00	67.25	66.00	63.83
67	Central Zoo Authority (CZA)	75.00	76.00	83.85	86.38
68	Protection of Wildlife outside Protected Areas	60.00	10.11	0.01	0.00
Total Forests & Wildlife		1600.00	1386.24	1319.73	1287.53
69	Animal Welfare	175.00	70.50	81.02	75.22
	NAEB				
70	National Afforestation and Eco-development Board (NAEB)	80.00	106.00	86.19	71.60
71	National Afforestation Project (NAP)	1115.00	1224.10	1164.42	1179.07
72	National Action Programme to Combat Desertification	30.00	3.00	0.02	0.00
73	Eco-development Forces	75.00	42.00	41.04	42.96
Total NAEB		1300.00	1375.10	1291.67	1293.63
Grand Total		5945.00	5723.84	5275.98	5119.14

Source: Ministry of Environment and Forest (MOEF).

ANNEXURE 9.2
Physical Performance of Important Plan Schemes of the Tenth Plan

S. No.	Schemes/Programmes	Physical Performance	
		Targets	Achievements
1	Central Pollution Control Board (CPCB)	National Ambient Air Quality Monitoring Program (NAMP)	Ambient air quality monitoring at 321 locations; water quality monitoring at 1019 locations.
2	Environmental Management in Heritage Pilgrimage and Tourism Centres Including Taj Protection		Moratorium due to court case.
3	Clean Technologies	Life Cycle Assessment (LCA) studies and demonstration projects	Ten projects on Clean Technologies for food preservation, arsenic removal, bio-remediation of lakes, recycling of marble slurry, development of natural dyes; adhesives from forest waste; development of bamboo composites; utilization of anode muds and chips; air pollution control package for medium-scale lime kilns and development of eco-friendly welding machines.
4	Hazardous Substances Management	Management of chemical emergencies and hazardous substances	6 TSDFs set up.
5	Environment Education, Training and Awareness	Assistance to 100000 eco-clubs and 10000 organizations	33778 eco-clubs created (total 91378); 9784 organizations.
6	National River Conservation Plan (NRCP)	Projects for 34 polluted river stretches in 160 towns for treating 5435 MLD sewage.	308 projects completed; creating treatment capacity for 2055 MLD sewage.
7	National Lake Conservation Plan	Conservation of 35 lakes, 28 projects	Approved works in 42 new lakes; projects for 10 lakes completed.
8	Indian Council for Forestry Research and Education (ICFRE)	Co-ordinating research, education in institutes/universities	414 research projects initiated; 23 universities supported.
9	Integrated Forest Protection Scheme	Assistance to States and UTs for identified activities	Assistance for fire protection (196819 km) and forest boundary (219418 nos) consolidation.
10	Development of National Parks and Sanctuaries	Assistance to States and UTs for national parks and sanctuaries (total 606)	Assistance to 342 national parks and sanctuaries being provided.
11	Project Tiger	Funding support to 28 Tiger Reserves	Funding support to 28 Tiger Reserves covered in the area of 37761 sq km.
12	Project Elephant	Assistance to 15 States for elephant conservation.	Funds released for 25 Elephant Reserves in 15 States.
13	Central Zoo Authority (CZA)	Assistance for management of zoos	293 zoos evaluated; 42 supported.
14	Animal Welfare	Animal Welfare Board and construction of National Institute of Animal Welfare.	Animal Welfare Board and National Institute of Animal Welfare functioning.
15	National Afforestation and Eco-development Board (NAEB)	Evaluation of projects and assistance to NGOs for afforestation.	650 projects evaluated.
16	National Afforestation Project (NAP)	Afforestation project-based assistance to JFMCs.	729 projects involving 6.45 lakh ha in 29 States taken up.
17	Eco-development Forces	Support to 4 Eco Task Force battalions	4 Eco Task Force battalions supported.

Source: MOEF.

ANNEXURE 9.3

Projects/Schemes Identified by the Working Group/ NDMA for being taken up by NDMA/MHA for Implementation during the Eleventh Plan

S. No.	Name of the Project/Programme/Scheme	Objective
1	National Cyclone Risk Mitigation Project (with World Bank Assistance)	For mitigating hazard risks in the country & enhancing capabilities at various levels.
2	National Earthquake Risk Mitigation Project	Strengthening structural & non-structural earthquake mitigation efforting and reducing risk and vulnerability in high risk districts.
3	National Flood Mitigation Project	Multi-objectives including effective preparedness and improved promptness and capability, strengthening community capacity, and reduction in consequences of floods.
4	National Landslide Mitigation Project	Strengthen the structural and non-structural landslide mitigation efforts and reduce the landslide risk and vulnerability in the hilly districts prone to landslides and mudflows.
5	Expanded Disaster Risk Mitigation Project	Strengthen the structural and non-structural disaster preparedness and mitigation efforts to reduce the risk and vulnerability in the disaster-prone districts with community participation.
6	National Disaster Communication Network (NDCN)	Dedicated communication & IT support for pro-active disaster support functions including for early warning & forecasting.
7	Information, Education, and Communication (IEC) Programme	Disaster risk and vulnerability reduction, disaster preparedness, structural and non-structural mitigation efforts and disaster response by developing ICT materials, print and electronic media products, campaigns, exhibitions, etc.
8	Micro-zonation of Major Cities	To carry out micro-zonation of High Risk Cities in Seismic Zones IV and V to prepare strategies to reduce earthquake risk and vulnerability in the high risk districts.
9	Project Preparation Facility/Research Programme Studies	Take up mitigation projects for disaster risk reduction and also undertake special studies and research programmes.
10	Vulnerability Assessment Schemes	Gujarat has undertaken vulnerability analysis of different parts of the State to different forms of disasters. Such an analysis is urgently required to be carried out by other States too.
11	International Co-operation	India needs to adopt a proactive approach for providing necessary support to the neighbouring countries through multilateral co-operation and involvement of regional organizations.
12	Infrastructure of 8 NDRF Battalions	Completely new infrastructure has to be built for 6 battalions @ Rs 80 crore per bn and existing infrastructure has to be upgraded for the 2 battalions @ Rs 25 crore per bn.
13	Upgradation of NIDM and other Institutes	The institute requires space and equipments for state-of-the-art emergency operations centre, disaster mitigation workshop, mock drill exercise, library, GIS laboratory, etc.

ANNEXURE 9.4
Tenth Plan Outlay and Actual Expenditure in Environment and Forest Sectors (States and UTs)

(Rs lakh)

S. No.	State/ UT	State Plan Outlay	Forestry & Wildlife			Ecology & Environment		
			Projected Outlay	Agreed Outlay	Actual Expenditure	Projected Outlay	Agreed Outlay	Actual Expenditure
1	Andhra Pradesh	4661400	123779	113262.86	80076.85	620	203.72	316.29
2	Arunachal Pradesh	388832	7700	9529.87	8403.42	42	208.91	38.46
3	Assam	831522	7736	11235	9076.1	65	79	29.45
4	Bihar	2100000	4514	7953.92	6267.25	0	0	0
5	Chhattisgarh	1100000	32718	39180	46844.04	783	679.5	370.13
6	Goa	320000	2500	2908.95	2880.93	300	795.45	799.33
7	Gujarat	4000700	93634	75445.7	66076.37	2766	2196	1010.44
8	Haryana	1028500	12733	32125	30612.03	283	407	277.46
9	Himachal Pradesh	1030000	42377	36748.49	36344.2	50	27	82.59
10	Jammu & Kashmir	1450000	36358	23794.13	23096.74	3619	465.42	288.4987
11	Jharkhand	1463274	46277	49802	46875.73	0	0	0
12	Karnataka	4355822	73396	51408.83	46677.84	1285	5535	2417.584
13	Kerala	2400000	17500	22789	21348.75		0	0
14	Madhya Pradesh	2618993	35275	64458.82	81330.29	5112	9663.63	8388.896
15	Maharastra	6663200	68279	10997.81	10729	1200	627.71	500
16	Manipur	280400	1744	3704.66	3560.81	495	1714	556.75
17	Meghalaya	300900	5250	6596	6093.89	275	300	174.34
18	Mizoram	230001	2846	4285	4515.88	19	20	11.04
19	Nagaland	222765	2250	2535	2828.24	100	178	272
20	Orissa	1900000	69446	22899.95	6083.94	2030	2482.29	2561.305
21	Punjab	1865700	28075	40800.6	30500.46	572	203.1	26.08
22	Rajasthan	2731800	115320	52592.87	31584.73	464	100.95	35.8972
23	Sikkim	165574	3500	3564.2	3510.45	500	160	125.97
24	Tamilnadu	4000000	134810	63561.93	64601.18	11305	1578.16	486.2261
25	Tripura	450000	4835	4273.65	4113.03	446	209	243.3531
26	Uttar Pradesh	5970800	120800	49784	48642.5	235525	24979	2628.58
27	Uttaranchal	763000	20693	56223.18	62063.17	5902	2900	1505
28	West Bengal	2864100	16443	12908.12	6823.73	1688	1259.99	2487.03
Total (States)		56157283	1130788	875369.54	791561.55	275446	56972.83	25643.7
UTs								
29	Andaman & Nicobar	248300	7243	6369	6097.71	0	40	32.88
30	Chandigarh	100000	1733	2455	1916	270	323	188.13
31	Dadra & Nagar Haveli	30400	1200	1657	1733.87	0	0	0
32	Daman & Diu	24500	278	200	173.38	0	5	13.1
33	Delhi	2300000	2600	2300	14791.16	4800	2705	998.6
34	Lakshadweep	43700	92.3	91.7	46	400.3	163.3	102.52
35	Pondicherry	190649	500	859	819.54	176	244	257.13
Total (UTs)		2937549	13646.3	13931.7	25577.66	5646.3	3480.3	1592.38
Total (States/UTs)		59094832	1144434.3	889301.24	817139.21	281092.3	60453.13	27236.08
Percentage to Total		100	1.94	1.50	1.38	0.48	0.10	0.05

Source: Planning Commission.

ANNEXURE 9.5

State-wise and Scheme-wise Releases of Central Funds to Ongoing CSS under MoEF during the Tenth Plan

(Rs crore)

Name of the State/Scheme	CETPs	Indus. Polln. Prevention	Taj Protection	Biosphere Reserve	Mangroves, Coral Reefs & Wetlands	NRCP	NLCP	Tiger Project	India Eco-development Project	Project Elephant	IFPS	Dev. of National Parks & Sanctuaries	NAP	Gregarious Flowering	Total 2002–07
1	2	3	4	5	6	7	8	9	10	11	12	13	14	15	16
Andhra Pradesh	0.30	3.24			1.20	115.85	0.80	1.74		2.78	6.94	4.91	53.18		190.94
Arunachal Pradesh				1.13	0.00			5.49		3.05	10.34	5.91	14.18	0.75	40.84
Assam				0.89	2.88			3.15		4.95	11.67	8.24	33.07	3.25	68.10
Bihar						0.66		2.36		3.93	3.80	0.35	12.98		24.09
Chhattisgarh		1.58						2.65		0.64	12.08	13.53	44.55		75.03
Goa					1.20	8.56					0.99	0.93	0.64		12.33
Gujarat	4.28	1.01			8.40	42.54			13.67		9.46	9.71	48.80		137.87
Haryana						16.78				0.50	5.11	1.73	40.99		65.12
Himachal Pradesh					1.41						3.70	11.52	38.89		55.53
Jammu & Kashmir					2.26		70.00				3.78	5.89	31.01		112.94
Jharkhand								5.77	4.48		8.08	3.86	46.15		68.33
Karnataka		4.38		2.73	3.07	31.48	22.93	16.07	10.42	7.65	4.55	28.05	101.62		232.95
Kerala				3.64	2.18	0.75	4.30	5.61	2.35	8.07	7.51	12.73	25.09		72.23
Madhya Pradesh		1.21		3.78	0.30	39.90	4.58	41.47	8.56		11.93	21.82	71.08		204.63
Maharashtra	15.24				57.93	66.73	5.50	17.46		0.25	3.03	9.07	61.93		237.14
Manipur					0.86						6.78	4.31	26.99	5.44	44.39
Meghalaya				1.34						2.67	2.30	3.16	13.45	1.71	24.62
Mizoram					0.25			4.66		0.05	17.94	11.40	62.47	13.33	110.10
Nagaland										2.20	12.81	2.01	35.64	6.32	58.98
Orissa				2.53	6.53	28.99	1.21	5.92		5.85	4.27	13.07	67.54		135.91
Punjab					1.88	88.40					1.01	0.03	10.17		101.49
Rajasthan		0.37			2.04	0.44	15.00	9.86	8.64		2.70	12.28	27.69		79.02
Sikkim				2.64		1.79					6.82	5.75	27.80		44.80
Tamil Nadu	0.11			1.81	6.86	480.30	0.73	4.85		5.38	8.14	8.37	76.53		593.08
Tripura							0.50	0.50		0.36	10.40	4.28	21.26	11.32	48.61

(Annexure 9.5 contd.)

(Annexure 9.5 contd.)

(Rs crore)

Name of the State/Scheme	CETPs	Indus. Polln. Prevention	Taj Protection	Biosphere Reserve	Mangroves, Coral Reefs & Wetlands	NRCP	NLCP	Tiger Project	India Eco-development Project	Project Elephant	IFPS	Dev. of National Parks & Sanctuaries	NAP	Gregarious Flowering	Total 2002–07
1	2	3	4	5	6	7	8	9	10	11	12	13	14	15	16
Uttar Pradesh			0.24		1.00	121.07	1.49	7.37		0.18	5.61	12.25	89.01		238.22
Uttaranchal				3.50	0.42	20.02	31.94	9.12		6.10	13.37	4.28	44.41		133.
West Bengal				3.52	7.53	135.56	5.11	9.10	4.14	6.97	8.45	14.26	27.79		222.42
Total States	19.93	11.79	0.24	27.50	108.21	1199.82	164.09	153.16	52.26	61.58	203.58	233.70	1154.91	42.12	3432.88
Union Terrotories															
Andaman & Nicobar				2.50	0.83							2.11			5.45
Chandigarh				0.95								0.14			1.09
Dadra & Nagar											0.52	0.70			1.22
Delhi						121.25						0.20			121.45
Lakshadweep					0.30										0.30
Total UTs				3.45	1.13	121.25					0.52	3.15			129.50
Total States/UTs	19.93	11.79	0.24	30.95	109.34	1321.07	164.09	153.16	52.26	61.58	204.10	236.84	1154.91	42.12	3562.38

Source: MOEF.

10

Governance

INTRODUCTION

10.1. The Eleventh Plan vision of inclusive growth, reducing poverty and bridging the various divides that continue to fragment our society can only be achieved if there is a significant improvement in the quality of governance. There are many different definitions of good governance but it is generally agreed that good governance must be broadly defined to cover all aspects of the interface between individuals and businesses on the one hand and government on the other.

10.2. In our situation, good governance should cover the following distinct dimensions.

- As a democratic country, a central feature of good governance is the constitutionally protected right to elect government at various levels in a fair manner, with effective participation by all sections of the population. This is a basic requirement for the legitimacy of the government and its responsibility to the electorate.
- The government at all levels must be accountable and transparent. Closely related to accountability is the need to eliminate corruption, which is widely seen as a major deficiency in governance. Transparency is also critical, both to ensure accountability, and also to enable genuine participation.
- The government must be effective and efficient in delivering social and economic public services, which are its primary responsibilities. This requires constant monitoring and attention to the design of our programmes. In our situation, where the responsibility for delivery of key services such as primary education and health is at the local level, this calls for special attention to ensuring the effectiveness and efficiency of local governments.
- Governments at lower levels can only function efficiently if they are empowered to do so. This is particularly relevant for the PRIs, which currently suffer from inadequate devolution of funds as well as functionaries to carry out the functions constitutionally assigned to them.
- An overarching requirement is that the rule of law must be firmly established. This is relevant not only for relations between the government and individuals enabling individuals to demand their rights but also for relations between individuals or businesses. A modern economic society depends upon increasingly complex interactions among private entities and these interactions can be efficiently performed only if legal rights are clear and legal remedies for enforcing these rights are swift.
- Finally, the entire system must function in a manner which is seen to be fair and inclusive. This is a perceptional issue but it is real nonetheless. Disadvantaged groups, especially the SCs, STs, minorities and others, must feel they have an equal stake and should perceive an adequate flow of benefits to ensure the legitimacy of the State.

10.3. Achieving a successful outcome in all these dimensions is not easy, and the effects of initiatives taken today will take time to manifest themselves. Nor is it easy to measure the extent of progress achieved. It is also important to recognize that perceptions are important and perceptions of the state of governance depend upon the expectations of the people. These expectations are rising as indeed they should, and from this perspective, we need to recognize that while increased concern about inadequacies of governance may not reflect an absolute deterioration in the quality of governance, they do point to rising demands that need to be met.

TENTH PLAN EXPERIENCE

10.4. The Tenth Plan drew attention to the implementation of good governance in the following terms:

'Governance relates to the management of all such processes that, in any society, define the environment which permits and enables individuals to raise their capability levels on the one hand, and provide opportunities to realize their potential and enlarge the set of available choices, on the other. These processes, covering the political, social and economic aspects of life impact every level of human enterprise, be it the individual, the household, the village, the region or the nation. It covers the State, civil society and the market, each of which is critical for sustaining human development. The State is responsible for creating a conducive political, legal and economic environment for building individual capabilities and encouraging private initiative. The market is expected to create opportunities for people. Civil society facilitates the mobilization of public opinion and people's participation in economic, social and political activities.'

10.5. A number of steps were taken in the Tenth Plan period aimed at improving the quality of governance.

- The RTI, 2005 was brought into force. This applies to Union and local agencies, local governments and societies which receive public funds, and empowers citizens.
- The All India Service Rules were amended, providing a certain fixed tenure for specified posts to be notified by the State and Central Government. It will help promote accountability.
- A new Value Added Tax regime was introduced which simplifies the tax systems and has enormous positive implications for major reforms in the tax structure.
- Electoral funding reforms were introduced, promoting transparency and fairness and creating tax incentives to donors and disclosure of antecedents of candidates contesting for public office.
- An e-Governance Plan for 27 major areas was adopted designed to assist, improve delivery of services and digitization of information.
- Initiatives on participatory governance were introduced under the NREGA, NRHM and other measures.
- A policy for VOs was announced by the Central Government, reflecting the importance of the voluntary sector in promoting participatory systems.
- A NDMA was established to bring more focused attention to this important area and to initiate preparatory work to make responses to disasters more effective.

10.6. In 2005, the Second Administrative Reforms Commission (ARC) was constituted to prepare a detailed blue print for revamping the public administration system. The First ARC, was constituted in 1966 and subsequently several committees and commissions have examined and given recommendations on various aspects of reforming governance. The Second ARC has been given very comprehensive Terms of Reference and it has been asked to suggest measures to achieve a proactive, responsive, accountable, sustainable and efficient administration for the country at all levels of government. The Commission has already submitted six reports on different aspects of administration. It is also working on several other areas including civil service reforms, citizen centric administration, and reorganizing the structure of the government.

10.7. The Department of Administrative Reforms and Public Grievances has proposed a framework for good governance in the form of a Code of Governance. The main components of this Code are: (i) improving service delivery; (ii) development of programmes for weaker sections and backward areas; (iii) technology and system improvement; (iv) financial management and budget sanctity; (v) accountability and transparency; (vi) public service morale and anti-corruption; and (vii) incentivizing reforms.

10.8. The federal structure of the country provides an opportunity for measuring different States on an index of good governance. It is important to measure the performance of the States on developmental schemes apart from the indicators mentioned above, give them appropriate weightage and index them on this basis. The process could be finalized by a high-level independent expert group and it is important that it be part of the discussions with the States so as to bring to the centre stage issues relating to governance which, otherwise, in the absence of any specific financial outlays, go unrecognized. The index can also be used for giving incentives to the States.

CHALLENGES FOR THE ELEVENTH PLAN

10.9. The Eleventh Plan must build on the initiatives already taken and seek to achieve a decisive improvement in governance in the Plan period. Some of the major challenges are:

- The Plan accords priority to providing access to quality health care and education, particularly in the rural areas and for girls, minorities, SCs and STs, backward classes and BPL families. It also emphasizes programmes of employment under the Rural Employment Guarantee Programme. Access to clean and good quality water, sanitation, housing and electricity are also critical. These services are delivered at the local level and this calls for both empowerment and accountability of the relevant authorities and effective monitoring of service delivery, particularly for low income groups.
- Effective administration of the rule of law resulting in efficient criminal and civil justice system delivering swift decisions and, particularly, ensuring access to the poor is of extreme importance. An effective security and policing system is required for Naxalite affected and communally sensitive areas.
- The Plan relies heavily on a dynamic private sector to expand investment and create new employment opportunities. This requires developing a business-friendly environment, enabling setting up and exiting of business and promoting efficiency, matching world standards.
- Space must be provided to VOs for developing citizen initiatives, acting as a watchdog on government systems and strengthening group initiatives. This can only be done if full transparency is assured.
- Finally, it is necessary to tackle the problem of corruption which is widely perceived as being all pervasive and is a major source of complaint about the quality of governance.

10.10. To meet these challenges it is necessary to take initiatives on a broad range as discussed in the rest of this chapter.

DECENTRALIZATION AND STRENGTHENING PANCHAYATI RAJ INSTITUTIONS (PRIs)

10.11. As pointed out earlier, a large part of Plan expenditure is now accounted for by development programmes and schemes for rapid eradication of poverty and delivery of various services that are mostly in the realm of local government functions. Some of these are State sector schemes and others are CSS which are part of the Central budget, but deal with areas which are in the realm of the States. In spite of the massive flow of funds, there is widely shared concern that the results have not been commensurate with the investments. A comprehensive reform of how these schemes are implemented is necessary.

CENTRALLY SPONSORED SCHEMES (CSS)

10.12. A critical assessment of the performance of CSS reveals the following deficiencies:

- Most of them exist as silos planned and implemented as stand-alone schemes with little horizontal convergence or vertical integration, resulting in multiple sub-sectoral district plans, unrelated to each other. At times they are even mutually conflicting, prepared without any integrated vision or perspective of what is needed at the district level.
- The schemes are often too rigid and do not provide the flexibility needed for adaptation according to the different development needs at the local level. There is also too much micro management without any mechanism to understand the local situation and respond to it properly.
- There is no consistent approach in the design of delivery mechanisms. At times, independent structures are created for each scheme resulting in multiplicity of such structures at the local level with no interaction or coordination among them.
- The extent of professional support to the design, implementation and monitoring of these schemes is quite weak at the national, State and local levels. Often, line departments with generalist approaches control the implementation process without having the necessary competence.
- In spite of stated objectives aiming at the quality of outputs and outcomes, there is not enough outcome-based evaluation and the programmes are mostly monitored on an expenditure basis.

10.13. The architecture of the continuing and new CSS will need to be radically altered and the instrumentality of implementation fundamentally changed. In this context, there are a number of arguments in favour of giving local governments a pivotal place in CSS in keeping with their constitutional mandate of economic development and social justice.

- By their very nature, local governments are democratic systems, especially at the level of Gram Sabhas and Ward Committees. They are laboratories of multi-level pluralist democracy, facilitating the achievements of consensus on development issues at the lowest level of government. At the local level, groups learn to co-exist, cooperate, negotiate and arrive at acceptable decisions and even marginalized groups can gain confidence and move on from token participation to higher forms of direct social action for the collective good.

- Local governments are in a better position to appreciate problems holistically and come out with cross-sectoral solutions. They are better suited to exploit local production possibilities and adopt technologies which can be handled locally. They also have quicker outreach and can provide faster feedback.
- As local governments are closer to the people, they are capable of identifying local priorities and entering into partnership with communities for the management of assets and facilities.

10.14. These arguments show that there is a strong case for strengthening PRIs so that they could bring about the desired results through effective planning and implementation of CSS. This, however, does not mean that things would happen naturally. Assiduous preparation is called for and a conscious strategy of capacity building is needed, accompanied by intense monitoring.

District Planning

10.15. In order to achieve the best outcome in terms of balanced development with convergence of resources and enforcement of inter-sectoral priorities, it is necessary to shift to integrated planning at the grass roots level leading to the preparation of District Plans. The CSS which lend themselves to effective grass roots level planning are:

- Poverty reduction programmes like the SGSY, SGRY, National Rural Employment Guarantee Scheme (NREGS).
- Human Development schemes like SSA, Mid-day Meals, Literacy, Rural Health Mission and ICDS.
- Social Assistance Schemes like the NSAP and National Old Age Pension (NOAP).
- Schemes for provision of minimum needs like Accelerated Rural Water Supply Programme and Swajaladhara, TSC, IAY, PMGSY and RGGVY.
- Area development schemes like BRGF, Hariyali, National Watershed Development Project for Rainfed Areas, WGDP, DDP and Drought Prone Areas Programme.
- Schemes in the productive sectors like agriculture, horticulture, and animal husbandry.

10.16. These and other sector schemes need across the board restructuring to facilitate the following:

- Assignment of responsibilities to different levels of PRIs for planning, implementation and monitoring.
- Harmonization of existing planning and implementation arrangements and institutions with the Panchayati Raj setup.
- Evolution of criteria for allocation of funds to different levels of PRIs as may be appropriate.
- Introducing enabling provisions to make available technical support for planning and implementation.
- Introduction of a common planning process facilitating an integrated approach to the identification of problems and preparation of plans for tackling them by pooling resources from the relevant schemes. This has to be attempted in the Eleventh Five Year Plan.

10.17. Typically, the process of decentralized planning would involve the following steps:

- Needs assessment and priority setting through participatory fora like Gram Sabhas and SHG networks.
- Situation analysis using locally available data through simple methods supplemented by Participatory Rapid Appraisal techniques.
- Resource assessments from the various sources of funds available to them, including from various CSS.
- Formulation of a vision of development as well as strategies for attaining the vision by PRIs through a process of interaction with stakeholders and local experts.
- Development of project ideas based on need assessment and situation analysis by expert Working Groups at different levels of PRIs.
- Consolidation of development proposals of the Working Groups.
- Prioritization of proposals and allocation of resources to the prioritized proposals.
- Preparation of project reports in detailed formats.
- Vetting of project reports on technical and financial aspects by Technical Advisory Groups of DPC.
- Integration of projects into plans by PRIs.
- Consolidation of PRI Plans into District Plans
- Clearance of the Plan by the DPC.

10.18. In order to ensure that the proposals of different PRIs merge into a District Plan, it will be necessary to develop a framework, both sectoral and cross-sectoral, at the district level through a multi-level and iterative planning process with assessment and prioritization being made at the lowest level and then consolidated at higher levels. There will be areas where differences may arise on relative priorities but it is possible to evolve a reasonable consensus through dialogues and discussions which are then reflected in actual plan preparation. For decentralized planning to happen the following are essential:

- DPCs, which are a constitutional requirement, need to be fully strengthened. They need to function not just as Committees but as full-fledged institutions.
- DPCs should be assisted by Technical Advisory Groups for different sectors consisting of professionals from Government, academic institutions and non-government organizations as well as civil society.
- DPCs should be encouraged to network with academic and research institutions within the district.
- The Planning Commission, with the approval of line Ministries, should issue common guidelines for preparation of plans in a converged manner, utilizing the resources of CSS in the functional area of local governments.
- State governments should issue detailed guidelines for decentralized planning leading to District Plans within the framework stipulated in the report of the Expert Group.

10.19. To support decentralized planning, the Planning Commission would consider the following:

- Provide assistance to States to set up offices of the DPC as well as to provide technical support.
- Over a period of time, generate a local statistical system by increasing the sample size of National Sample Surveys so that interpretation is possible at least at the level of the Block, if not the village.
- Identify one expert institution in each State as was done for the preparation of the State Development Report, and assign it the task of preparation of pilot District Plans through action research, in partnership with the States and local governments.

Empowering Panchayati Raj Institutions (PRIs)

10.20. For the PRIs to meet their obligations, they need to be adequately empowered through the devolution of functions, finances and functionaries. They also need to be answerable to the Gram Sabhas. Empowerment along these lines is the single most significant reform of governance that could change for the better, the relationship between government and its interaction with the ordinary citizen. Several steps to ensure the centrality of Panchayats in planning and implementation of key CSS have been taken in the period leading up to the Eleventh Plan.

- The NREGA provides guaranteed employment in rural areas, with PRIs as the principal authorities for planning and implementation.
- The ambitious plans for universal elementary education and primary health care are to be delivered with full involvement of the local community through PRIs.
- BRGF is planned for and implemented by the Panchayats and Nagar Palikas in 250 backward districts.
- In the Eleventh Plan, in the agriculture and allied sectors, preparation of district and local level agriculture plans have been mandated for utilization and resources available under all new programmes and schemes. To fulfil this ambitious mandate, Panchayati Raj will require substantial, enhanced backing by the Central Government, in association with State Governments, for training and capacity building of PRIs, as also the provision of attractive incentives to States for the empowerment of PRIs

10.21. States can no longer delay or sidestep the devolution of functions, funds and functionaries to the Panchayats. Activity mapping, resulting in the assignment of activities relating to a function to each level of the Panchayats, is a critical trigger for effective devolution. There are two central principles that underlie a good activity mapping exercise. First, is the principle of subsidiarity, in terms of which tasks are placed at that level alone where it is best performed and no other. Second, is that activity mapping should touch all levels of the government and not merely the three levels of Panchayats. Constitution of the DPCs is mandatory under the Constitution. States must therefore quickly meet the obligations of completing activity mapping and constituting DPCs.

10.22. Unfortunately, a major weakness thus far is that the devolution through legislative or executive order of functions to Panchayats is not matched by a concomitant transfer of funds to them. Panchayats have also not utilized effectively whatever limited powers of taxation they possess. The key to ensuring effective devolution of States and Central Plan Funds to Panchayats at all levels lies in the creation of a Panchayat sector in the plans and budgets of both the State and Union Governments. This will provide a repository within the accounting structure which makes clear the financial resources that are placed with the Panchayats for them to efficiently perform the functions devolved upon them. The demarcation of a Panchayat sector in State and Central budgets will make it easier to ensure that there is no mismatch between functional and fiscal devolution.

PARTICIPATION AND HARMONIZING COMMUNITY-BASED ORGANIZATIONS WITH PRIS

10.23. Decentralization allows direct citizen participation in different aspects of development and governance. The Gram Sabha is, in a sense, the fourth tier of governance facilitating direct democracy and face-to-face accountability. This critical institution of Panchayati Raj has to be further strengthened through action, research and semi-structured processes of developmental dialogue, needs assessment, priority setting, oversight monitoring and social audit.

10.24. In addition to Gram Sabhas, several other fora such as SHGs, management committees, anganwadis and similar stakeholders' institutions enhance participation and accountability. In addition, the mechanism for securing transparency and accountability at all levels needs to be strengthened and made a critical component in implementation

10.25. For PRIs to be effective, they have to reach out to communities, especially the poor, and involve them in the development process. So their relationship with various people's groups becomes important. Over the last two decades, several CBOs have sprung up, sometimes as spontaneous people's groups for developmental action or as consciously organized ones as part of a development project or programme. The objectives behind setting up such groups include:

- Participatory planning
- Local resource mobilization
- Efficiency in implementation
- Inculcating a culture of self help
- Facilitating NGO involvement
- Ensuring sustainability through takeover of operation and maintenance functions
- Potential to develop as interest groups
- Empowerment of communities

10.26. It is important to be clear about the relationship between community-based organizations, which includes SHGs and user groups, and PRIs as people's institutions. Community-based organizations cannot be equated with PRIs, nor should they be viewed legally as people's institutions. These are as 'efficient' substitutes of 'weak' or 'partisan' PRIs. Project-based CBOs are largely uni-dimensional, socio-economic groups focused on benefits from a particular project. They can certainly be efficient delivery vehicles for development programmes. But PRIs have a broader reach as local governments performing a range of governance and developmental functions. They are political entities and their function entails reconciling and satisfying the development aspirations of different groups of people. As such they are accountable to the entire population within their jurisdiction and not to a small circle of beneficiaries of a project or a programme.

10.27. It is often not understood that CBOs can perform their stated objectives even more efficiently without devaluing their social capital or reducing their capacity for public action, if they are seen as thematic and functional sub-systems of PRIs and conceptualized as community wings of PRIs. The creation and strengthening of CBOs could become the next step in democratic decentralization, after the strengthening of PRIs.

10.28. Conceptually, structurally and procedurally, CBOs should draw their powers and resources from PRIs, not in a relationship of subordination or agency functioning but in a spirit of social contract. This would ensure accountability to PRIs even while protecting the autonomy of CBOs; in such a scenario, CBOs could complement and strengthen PRIs even while carrying on their social action to retard negative tendencies like partisanship and corruption.

10.29. For achieving the linkages between PRIs and CBOs, massive capacity building efforts are required. The PRIs should be trained on the role and mode of functioning of CBOs, especially entry norms, procedures of functioning, MIS norms and accountability systems. The CBOs should be sensitized on the legal and functional role of PRIs and on the need to work closely with them.

REHABILITATION AND RESETTLEMENT

10.30. Problems related to land acquisition for development projects and rehabilitation and resettlement of those displaced have been a source of considerable dissatisfaction, and perceived unfairness of past policies and practices has been an important example of perceived weakness in governance. There is an obvious need for striking a fair balance between those whose land is being acquired and are thereby affected vitally, and the need for land for development. The issues relating to the Sardar Sarovar Project in Gujarat and more recently, on Nandigram in West Bengal and in the Posco Plant in Orissa, have reinforced the need for a policy based on a comprehensive consideration of various issues.

10.31. The National Policy on Resettlement and Rehabilitation was effective from February 2004 after it was notified by the government. This laid down immediate provisions for resettlement and rehabilitation of project-affected families and the States, public sector undertakings or public bodies were free to offer better packages. The entire issue has subsequently been considered in pursuance of the Common Minimum Programme (CMP), which called for a 'more effective' system of resettlement and rehabilitation for tribal and other groups displaced by development projects. A new rehabilitation policy has, therefore, been formulated. In order to further strengthen this process, proper amendments in the Land Acquisition Act are to be undertaken.

10.32. Some of the salient features of the new Policy are:

- The Policy, which was notified in October 2007, aims to promote, as far as possible, non-displacement or least displacement alternatives;
- Adequate rehabilitation package, and acceptance and implementation of the rehabilitation process with the active participation of affected persons.
- Special care for protecting the rights of and ensuring affirmative State action for the weaker sections of society, especially the members of SCs/STs along with an obligation on the State for their treatment with concern and sensitivity.
- Providing a better standard of living than before and sustaining their income above poverty-line, to the affected families. It also aims to integrate the rehabilitation concerns into the developmental planning and implementation process.

10.33. Other salient features of the Policy are:

- A social impact assessment of projects involving physical displacement of 400 or more families or 200 or more families in tribal or hilly areas, desert development programme blocks or other Schedule I and II areas. Public hearing in the affected areas will be mandatory and the report will be examined by experts in the field, including social sciences and rehabilitation.
- Special concern for vulnerable populations by having lifetime monthly pension to affected persons above 50 years or age, disabled, orphans, unmarried girls, and so on.
- Special provisions for SCs and STs.
- People's participation right from the mandatory public hearing stage to consultation with Gram Sabhas and public hearing at the social life assessment stage.
- The benefit of allotment of land for all those who propose to become marginal farmers. However, this benefit has been made subject to the availability of government land.
- House sites and at least one job for each affected families.

10.34. Implementation of the new policy will protect the interests of those whose property is being acquired and provide more generous compensation and rehabilitation. The policy will be monitored effectively during the Plan, and based on the experience of its functioning and inputs from various stakeholders, such changes would be considered as may be appropriate.

SHIFT IN FOCUS FROM INPUTS TO OUTCOMES

10.35. Traditionally, government schemes are evaluated in terms of expenditure incurred and adherence to process requirement. It is necessary to shift the focus from vertical input controls to horizontal coordination and monitoring of outcomes. The need for horizontal coordination is evident from the fact that interventions in one area, say, rural drinking water and sanitation, affect outcomes in health, which affect outcomes in education. These examples can be multiplied. Given the manner in which government structures are organized at the Centre and States, horizontal coordination is very necessary to achieve the desired outcomes. Mechanisms for this coordination, convergence and synergy at all levels have atrophied or are non-existent. Reinstating dynamic coordination, to break through excessive hierarchy and securing teamwork and mechanisms for vertical coherence and horizontal coordination to achieve outcomes is a major challenge at all levels of government. Emphasis will be laid on effective monitoring on outcome at all levels. The district level and other functionaries will need to be strengthened with authority and powers so that they are made fully accountable for the outcomes.

MONITORING AND EVALUATION

10.36. Since the Eleventh Plan substantially increases public investment in many critical sectors, a major concern would be that of monitoring the quality of expenditure. A

Committee with representations of both the Centre and States would be set up to formulate a plan of action to improve the quality of public expenditure in key result areas and enable its public monitoring. This Committee would have a time frame of three months to give its report and would be part of the Eleventh Plan monitoring.

10.37. Ever since the concept of planning was introduced in India, the task of evaluating development schemes and programmes for improved and effective implementation has been recognized. Accordingly, the Programme Evaluation Organization (PEO) was established in 1952 and functioned relatively independently for about four decades. However, since then, the capacity of PEO has suffered even though the need for proper evaluation of plan programmes has grown and is likely to grow further for the Eleventh Plan. Keeping this in mind, the Eleventh Plan will need to substantially strengthen monitoring and evaluation capacity. While monitoring is an internal activity of programme management carried out by the implementing department, evaluation is the assessment of the appropriateness of design and implementation of ongoing projects and programmes which can be done concurrently during implementation of a programme by the agency involved, but also requires independent agencies like PEO to conduct studies from time to time. Given the current weakness of PEO and the even worse State of State Evaluation Organizations, it is necessary during the Eleventh Plan to rejuvenate the existing organizations and also network with evaluation capacity that exists outside the government. For this, the following need to be addressed:

- **Lack of Baseline Data**
  The baseline data for many schemes/programmes are not available, which becomes a serious bottleneck in measuring the performance indicators of the programme's outcome and impact. New schemes should, as far as possible, be approved only after the baseline has been determined.

- **Identification of Inappropriate Indicators**
  In almost all the cases, the process and outcome indicators of the programmes are not appropriately identified for collection of relevant information, which makes it difficult to attempt the meaningful analysis of the monitored data. New schemes should indicate clearly the indicators that could be monitored.

- **No follow-up Action on M&E of Results**
  There is an in-built mechanism introduced in each of the flagship programmes for earmarking a certain percentage of total allocation of funds annually for monitoring and evaluation. Yet, there is a complete lack of follow-up action on the results of monitoring and evaluation of these programmes. There should be a transparent data depository of results of in-house monitoring which could also be utilized by independent evaluators.

- **No Mechanism for Data Analysis**
  There is no in-built mechanism introduced in the programmes for making an analysis of the monitored information. This aspect, including proper impact analysis of programme components utilizing results of pilots for the purpose, needs to be emphasized during the Eleventh Plan. For this, the outside government would need to be harnessed.

10.38. With the renewed importance attached to evaluation, a new Central plan scheme, namely, Strengthening Evaluation Capacity in government, was introduced in 2006–07. The allocation for the scheme in 2007–08 was Rs 26 crore. To enable PEO to undertake evaluation of prioritized programmes and schemes at the behest of the Planning Commission as well as various ministries of the GoI, this outlay will be stepped up substantially in Eleventh Plan. Quality evaluation of various programmes and projects would not only bring improvement in public sector performance, but would also address a broad range of issues relating to economy, efficiency, sustainability and relevance of public sector funding and development intervention.

E-GOVERNANCE FOR BETTER SERVICE DELIVERY AND PROGRAMME DESIGN, IMPLEMENTATION AND MONITORING

10.39. Since good governance is about all aspects of governments' interface with (i) Citizens (G2C) and (ii) Businesses (G2B), e-Governance aims at the use of technology and process re-engineering for more efficient service delivery to both citizens and business, and also for more effective delivery of various programmes, projects and schemes.

10.40. In an increasingly connected virtual world of knowledge in cyberspace and with increasing spread of

Internet and web-based information systems, time and distances have shrunk, and service delivery is now possible on 'anytime, anywhere' basis. Sequential steps in service delivery can in some cases be processed in parallel, making simultaneous delivery possible. Government interface with people can be re-engineered in a manner that human discretion is minimized. In programmes like e-seva, government functionaries do not interface with the public and private providers man the front-end service-delivery kiosks. The service provider does not have authorization to alter government records and those who manage the records do not interface with the people. In the process, corruption gets minimized and the entire service delivery process becomes more transparent.

10.41. If attributers of good governance are transparency, efficiency, responsiveness cost effectiveness and accountability, e-Governance is the means to attain these attributers through application of technology.

10.42. The National Knowledge Commission had, in the context of e-Governance, suggested that to make an immediate impact on citizens, it is critical to identify and simplify important processes and services, say 15 to 20 to begin with, which are currently cumbersome, bureaucratic and prone to unnecessary delays and corruption. Initially these services could include providing online record of land rights, computerized land registration, computerized transfers, computerization of social security schemes, birth and death certificates, proof of residence, issue of ration and ID cards, and so on.

PROCESS RE-ENGINEERING

10.43. The first and most crucial element of this agenda has to be a change in the procedures of various government departments. Over a period of years, very few of these procedures has been reviewed. Recently, when the review of procedures applicable for passports was undertaken, it was observed that for ordinary citizens, availing passport facilities is well night impossible unless they take the help of intermediaries. The form for getting a passport was quite complicated. Further, the procedures which were prescribed envisaged verification by police at various places where the persons were staying in the past few years. This led to enormous delays and harassment. Similar, complicated procedures for issue of ration cards, caste certificates, driving licences or depositing taxes are also in vogue. There is a strong need to revise them and make these more citizen-centric.

10.44. While the above processes could be prioritized, it will be necessary to have a comprehensive review of all those deliverables which impact on the availability of services to the common citizen.

E-GOVERNANCE INFRASTRUCTURE

(i) Unique Identifiers

10.45. In a citizen-centric system of governance, the citizen's satisfaction becomes the measure of success of both service delivery as well as programme delivery. A citizen's identity, therefore, becomes important both in developmental as well as regulatory administration. The absence of a reliable system for such purposes has been an impediment to improving targeting of developmental schemes and reducing leakages in the delivery system. Many major individual-oriented government programmes incorporate a provision for collection of information at the individual/family level. In most cases, this is undertaken as a de novo exercise without reference to similar exercises undertaken in the past by other government departments and sometimes even by the same department. The absence of a system of updation of such purpose-specific databases and the lack of a system for corroboration among such departments are also factors leading inevitably to expensive, time consuming and error-prone de novo surveys for data collection for each scheme. To create a common platform for service/programme delivery, it is proposed to create a unique ID (UID) in the G2C domain and Corporate Identity Number (CIN) in G2B domains as unique identifiers of citizens and businesses, respectively.

• UID FOR INDIAN RESIDENTS

It is important for both service delivery and programme delivery in the G2C domain.

10.46. The long-term objective of the UID Project is to create a Core Database (CDB) for all residents, each having a unique identification number, which is regularly updated and is easily accessible to, and is used by, all departments for identification of residents in the country. This CDB would be used as the basis for identifying a person and enabling cross-linkage of major databases in the country. It is envisaged that the UID could significantly reduce identity related fraud, reduce leakages and allow for better targeting of government schemes. The implementation strategy involves creation of Central and State UID authorities who would be responsible for implementation and maintaining the UID.

- UID FOR INDIAN CORPORATES/BUSINESS ENTITIES—MCA 21:

In the G2B domain.

10.47. The Ministry of Company Affairs (MCA) is implementing an e-Governance initiative called 'MCA 21 e-Governance Project'. The objective of the MCA 21 programme is to improve speed and certainty in the delivery of MCA services. All available services from MCA—including filing of documents, registration of companies and public access to corporate information—are provided through a secure portal with the help of secured electronic filing through e-Form. The use of digital signatures has been mandated to carry out e-filing in conformity with the Information Technology Act, 2000.

10.48. At the time of registration of a company, they are given a CIN, which works as a unique identifier of a company, in the case of an Indian Company. To facilitate better outreach, the Ministry has introduced a scheme of Certified Filing Centres (CFC) wherein the practicing professionals (Chartered Accountants, Company Secretaries and Cost Accountants) have been authorized to set up the CFCs and provide services to the stakeholders on a user charge basis.

10.49. The concept of a Director Identification Number (DIN) has also been introduced for the first time with the insertion of Sections 266A to 266G of the Companies (Amendment) Act, 2006. As such, all the existing and intending Directors of Corporate entities have to obtain a DIN.

- SMART CARDS

10.50. The UID Project will eventually become the underpinning of the Citizens Smart Card Project of the Ministry of Home Affairs—both are aimed at identifying citizens, providing them a unique identity and in case of the MHA project, also will provide a Smart Card which has all this information.

10.51. The smart card would have a memory partitioned into distinct modules representing different entitlement groups for which free services or implicit/explicit subsidies are given. These include food and nutrition, energy (kerosene, LPG, electricity), education services, health services, civic amenities and services (drinking water, latrines/sanitation), employment (National Rural Employment Guarantee) and economic/farming (fertilizer, irrigation water, MSP). These separate modules could, in principle, be managed by the ministry/department under which the group falls. They would be responsible for setting up and maintaining the back-end financial and database system that is vital to eliminating errors of omission and commission and improving delivery efficiency. These departments/ministries would control the entry of data into their own module of the smart card.

10.52. Any subsidy received by any individual would be entered on his/her smart card when the goods or service is delivered/charged for by the authorized supplier (for example, the fair price shop, kerosene/LPG dealer, fertilizer outlet). The rules and regulations for delivery of subsidy and its reimbursement to the goods/service supplier would be defined by the concerned department. The data entered on the smart card should, however, be accessible by all monitoring/evaluating agencies so that they can put together a picture of what subsidies are being received by whom, as well as those who are not receiving a subsidy for which they are eligible.

10.53. The smart card initiative for service delivery may encounter many initial teething problems. It will be necessary to conduct pilot studies before extending it to all parts of the country.

(ii) Service Delivery Infrastructure

10.54. While the Mission Mode Projects (MMPs) would enable the back-end computerization of various departments, thereby e-enabling them for 'any time, any where' service delivery, to achieve the vision of providing government services at the doorstep of the citizen, a common service delivery platform is being created. The three important elements that form the basis of this effective service delivery framework are, State-Wide Area Networks (SWANs), the front-end outlets for the service delivery, that is, the CSCs and the SDCs, as discussed in the following sections.

- STATE-WIDE AREA NETWORKS (SWANS)

The government has approved the scheme for establishing SWANs in 29 States and six UTs across the country at a total cost of Rs 3334 crore. This scheme envisages the establishment of an intra-government network with a minimum of 2 Mbps connectivity from the State headquarters to block headquarters through the District headquarters. The SWAN project provides the connectivity to facilitate the rolling out of citizen-centric services under various MMPs under the National e-Governance Plan (NeGP). The SWAN Scheme is at an advanced stage of implementation and it is expected that the SWAN would be ready in most States by end 2008.

• COMMON SERVICE CENTRES (CSCS)

The government has approved the scheme of establishing CSCs across the country. The CSC scheme envisages the establishment of 100000 broadband Internet enabled kiosks in rural areas which would deliver government and private services at the doorstep of the citizens. An additional 10000 CSCs would be set up in semi-urban/urban areas. Visualizing a honeycomb pattern with one village surrounded by six villages, this implies that each village would have a CSC either within its own area or in an adjoining village. The CSC Scheme would be a bottom-up model for delivery of content and services like e-Governance, education, entertainment, tele-medicine, agriculture, and so on, and is being implemented in an entrepreneur driven, PPP mode. CSCs are also expected to be operational in most States by end 2008.

• CONNECTIVITY FOR THE LAST MILE

The CSC Scheme is the first step towards ubiquitous broadband reaching up to the village level. The connectivity infrastructure is being created through three distinct initiatives. The first two seek to use the infrastructure already created by BSNL for last mile connectivity, and the third seeks to use the resources available under Universal Service Obligation Fund (USOF).

Leveraging BSNL rural exchanges

Existing BSNL rural OFC exchanges (approx. 20000) are being upgraded to allow them to provide broadband (512 Kbps) connectivity to about 25000 CSCs, with partial funding support from the Department of Information Technology (DIT). These exchanges, once upgraded, would also be able to provide connections within a radius of 4–5 km to other users as well.

Wireless Connectivity from BSNL

In those areas where there are no other existing telecom service providers, BSNL towers are being used to provide wireless broadband connectivity, with partial funding support from DIT. It is expected that a further 25000 CSCs would be able to be connected in this manner.

Last mile connectivity through USOF

The USOF will be inviting existing TSPs to provide last mile connectivity with funding provided by the USOF. This initiative would provide connectivity to the remaining 50000 CSCs.

• STATE DATA CENTRES (SDCS)

State Data Centres are proposed to be established across 29 States and six UTs in the country, along with Disaster Recovery (DR), in order to provide shared, secured and managed infrastructure for consolidating and securely hosting State-level data and applications. SDC would provide better operations and management control and minimize the overall cost of data management, IT management and deployment. SDCs would ordinarily be located at the State headquarters and help the State Government, State line ministries and departments in providing central repository (database consolidation), application consolidation, State Intranet/Internet portal, State messaging infrastructure, remote management and business continuity site needed for their G2G, G2C and G2B services. The various MMPs, both at the Central level, State level and also the integrated services of the NeGP are expected to use SDCs to deliver their services. This infrastructure would be created during the Eleventh Five Year Plan.

NATIONAL E-GOVERNANCE PLAN FOR BETTER SERVICE DELIVERY AND MISSION MODE PROGRAMMES

10.55. The Government approved the National e-Governance Plan (NeGP) in May 2006 with the following vision: 'Make all Government services accessible to the common man in his locality, throughout common service delivery outlets and ensure efficiency, transparency and reliability of such services at affordable costs to realize the basic needs of the common man.' As can be seen, the one major difference from the 'computerization' initiatives of the past is the focus on delivery of services to citizens.

10.56. The architecture for e-Governance envisaged in NeGP aims to leverage e-Governance optimally to radically change the way government delivers services to citizens; addresses developmental challenges in key areas like education, health and agriculture; implements major programmes; and even the way it conducts its own business. In fact, key governance objectives like citizen-

TABLE 10.1
List of Mission Mode Projects

S. No.	Central Government Category	State Government Category	Integrated Services Category
01.	Income Tax	Land Records	EDI (e-Commerce)
02.	Passport Visa and Immigration	Road Transport	e-Biz
03.	MCA21	Property Registration	CCSs
04.	Insurance	Agriculture	India Portal
05.	National Citizen Database and UID Project	Treasuries	EG Gateway
06.	Central Excise	Municipalities	e-Courts
07.	Pensions	Gram Panchayats	e-Procurement
08.	Banking	Commercial Taxes	
09.	e-office	Police (UTs initially)	
10.		Employment Exchanges	
11.		e-district	

Source: DIT/GoI.

centricity, transparency and efficiency cannot be achieved without extensive and pervasive use of technology.

10.57. The NeGP currently consists of 27 MMPs and eight support components to be implemented at the Central, State and local government levels. The full list of MMPs and components may be seen in Table 10.1.

10.58. The NeGP seeks to lay the foundation and provide impetus for the long-term growth of e-Governance in the country. It also seeks to create the right governance and institutional mechanisms, lay down appropriate policies and set up the core infrastructure, all of which would facilitate implementation of various programmes and projects of the government. A body under the Chairpersonship of the Prime Minister has been constituted to prescribe deliverables and milestones, and monitor periodically the implementation of NeGP.

ICT Applications for Better Programme Implementation and Monitoring

10.59. ICT interventions are a pre-requisite for effective implementation and delivery of flagship programmes. The proposed NREGS stipulates the provision of employment for a minimum of 100 days a year for at least one adult per rural household. For this scheme to be properly implemented, it will be necessary for every village Panchayat to maintain a register enumerating eligible adult individuals in every family. This would need to be converted into a workers' register. All government departments with works programmes in rural areas would have to create village-wise works registers, which would then have to be centrally aggregated and catalogued village-wise at the district/block headquarters.

10.60. Each potential worker would have to be given a UID and would have to be assigned to the aggregated village-wise works register so that an account can be kept for 100 days of employment for one member from each family. In a nutshell, this would require works and workers inventories to be created and stored in a central data depository at the district headquarters. ICT solutions are all the more needed to plug the following loopholes:

- Inflated Schemes
  - Inflated quantity of work, depressed productivity, inflated person day estimates
  - Bogus registrations
  - Registration of dead persons, minors and medically unfit persons, duplicate and/or proxy registration, fictitious registrations
- Fraudulent Requisition of Funds
  - False measurement, inflated progress of works, omitting an operation or work item
- Inflated Muster
  - Ghost workmen, bogus attendance
- Fraudulent Wage Payment
  - Under payments, dependant fraudulent payments

10.61. The following schematic diagram depicts a possible technology enabled delivery system for implementation of the NREGP.

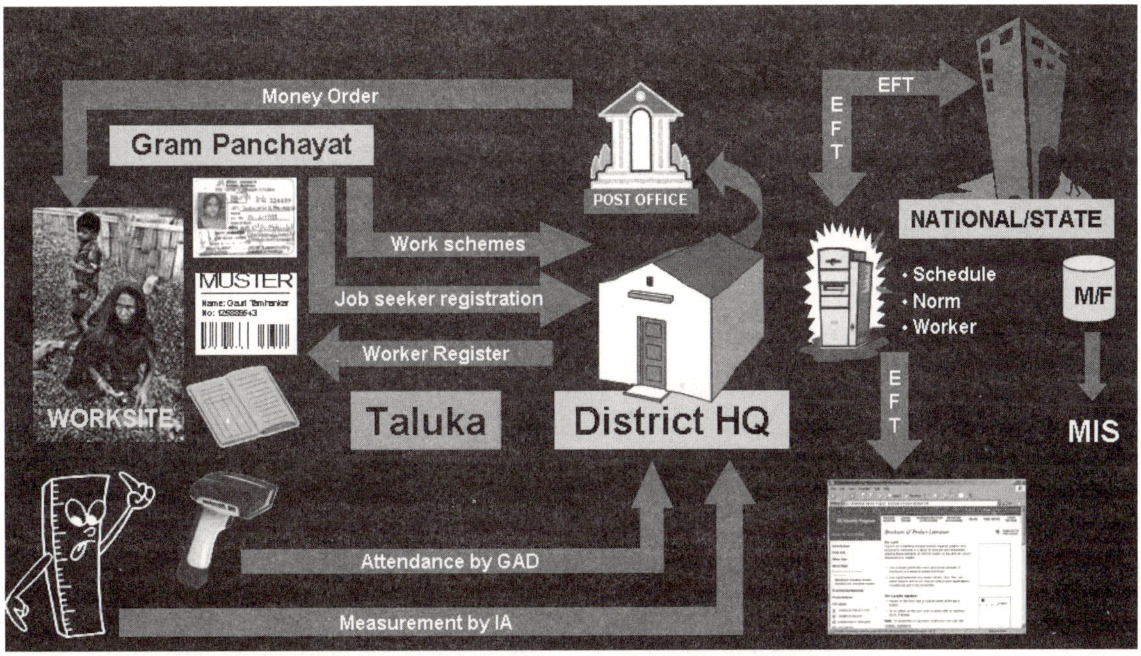

FIGURE 10.1: Delivery System for Implementation of NREGP

• Use of ICT in Major Flagship Programmes

While approving the NeGP, the government directed that for major projects like Bharat Nirman and Rural Employment Guarantee Schemes, the concerned line Ministry concerned should make use of e-Governance and automation techniques in implementation from the inception stage. Significant steps have been taken by the Ministry of Rural Development to use ICT in the implementation and monitoring of the NREGA and PMGSY, through its NREGASoft and Online Management Monitoring and Accounting System (OMMAS) applications developed by the NIC.

• NREGASoft and OMMAS

The MoRD, with the assistance of NIC, is capturing information related to NREGA right from the stage of registration of the worker. This information is also linked to the Rural Household Survey database of the concerned State. Information relating to worker registration, demand for work, payment of wages, and so on, can be captured through this application. Similarly, information relating to fund transfer and payments made, as well as information relating to the status of various works can also be captured. Currently, at the national level, information on the status of works under NREGA is being captured and is available on the Web. Similarly, information relating to road data, district rural road plan, proposal formulation and submission to the Ministry and clearance/sanction/release of funds is being captured through OMMAS. All districts are carrying out data entry using the online package from district HQs.

• Smart Technologies and Flagship Programmes

The use of Global Positioning Systems in the construction industry, Radio-frequency Identification for logistics and biometrics and smart cards for identification and security purposes is now well established. Handheld devices as a means of delivering real time information from the field has also come of age on account of the telecom revolution in the country in the private domain and the explosive growth and innovation in the handheld devices sector, making them affordable on a mega scale.

Location-Specific Planning using Geographical Information System

10.62. Planning for sustainable development has been a challenge, as it requires substantial amount of data on all aspects of development. In emerging technology paradigm, GIS has emerged as a powerful tool which has the potential to organize complex spatial data into layered information with tabular relationships.

10.63. The Planning Commission has put in place a Web-enabled 23-layered GIS database to facilitate location specific planning by creating hierarchical spatial database and application services. The multi-layered GIS database provides comprehensive data village wise—geographical data, river basin/watersheds/micro watersheds data, physical infrastructure (roads/electricity/rail roads), social infrastructure (education and health facilities), urban and rural settlements, demographic data, amenities data, soil/forest cover data, and so on.

10.64. The Planning Commission has also taken up a project, being implemented by the NIC, for creating computer aided digital utility mapping for six mega cities—Ahmedabad, Bangalore, Chennai, Hyderabad, Kolkata, and Mumbai. The project envisions collating information from all concerned organizations and analysing the same for each utility, for example, water, sewerage, electricity, roads, communication, gas pipeline, and so on, by creating large-scale digital maps for the concerned cities, with an aim to help in urban planning, disaster preparedness and infrastructure management. The database is expected to be a major aid to planning, development and management of urban utilities. It will also provide the GIS information base for a vehicle navigation/tracking system based on GPS. The Ministry of Urban Development has a project for carrying GIS to other cities of India. Both these projects will help decision makers in effective planning by making a paradigm shift in resource allocation from the broadcast mode to a location specific, need based mode.

VOLUNTARY ORGANIZATIONS (VOs)

10.65. A National Policy on VOs has been notified by the Central Government in July 2007, which aims to further strengthen, promote and develop such institutions. The Policy has the following objectives:

- To create an enabling environment for VOs that stimulate their enterprise and effectiveness and safeguard their autonomy.
- To enable VOs to legitimately mobilize necessary financial resources from India and abroad.
- To identify systems by which the government may work together with VOs on the basis of the principles of mutual trust and respect, and with shared responsibility.
- To encourage VOs to adopt transparent and accountable systems of governance and management.

10.66. In a democracy, VOs act as public 'watch dog' and a major check on arbitrary exercise of power by the Executive and other organs. Many such organizations are also doing remarkable work in implementing certain projects, some of which are funded by the government. During the course of the Plan, efforts will be made to strengthen such institutions and integrate their vigilance supervision over many of the programmes which affect the common citizen. Effective measures must be taken to implement the policy for improving governance.

CORRUPTION

10.67. One of the biggest challenges in improving governance is to act against corruption, which is widely seen as having seeped into the administrative fabric. This is a stupendous task but if a nation wishes to move forward rapidly, provide efficient services to all its citizens and especially aim at inclusive growth, it must address this question quickly and seriously. Some international agencies have rated India among nations with a high degree corruption. For example, the Transparency International Index for 2006 ranks India at 70th position (Index 3.3) along with Brazil, China, Egypt, and Mexico. This is an improvement over 2005 when it was rated at the 88th rank (Index 2.9), but the scale of the problem is too large to allow any complacency. Corruption in public services has today assumed serious dimensions. In the last few decades, its scale, growth and spread have significantly increased. Different levels of governments have become implicated in corrupt practices in mutually reinforcing ways. At each of these levels, corruption has tarnished the image of government functionaries. Serious introspection and decisions are required to meet the challenge.

10.68. It is necessary to act on two fronts. First, the punitive approach of identifying those guilty and punishing them must be strengthened. Second, and as important, is the need to make concerted efforts to develop systems which are less vulnerable to corruption. Reduced administrative discretion of greater transparency at all levels, combined with a vigilant civil society and Press can make a substantial difference.

10.69. Corruption not only undermines the moral fibre of the society but can have serious and irreversible practical consequences for politics, economic development and governance. In an overwhelmingly corrupt society, value-based politics loses its meaning. The legitimacy of government based on impartial application of the rule of law no longer holds. Resources which ought to be available to the exchequer for welfare and development are diverted into the private coffers of certain individuals. Honest public servants are demoralized while the corrupt are rewarded. Corruption is a major factor in the wastefulness, inefficiency and inequities we find in public administration today. It particularly affects the poor who cannot afford to pay. The burden of corruption saddles the private sector, and ultimately the consumer, with high costs and an inefficient infrastructure. Many more ramifications of corruption can be identified, but what is important to appreciate is that as corruption intensifies and accelerates, it tends to perpetuate itself in even widening and deeper forms. No time can, therefore, be lost in efforts to arrest and roll back this pernicious process.

10.70. There is widespread concern in India about the scale, spread and consequences of corruption. However, the daunting nature of the problem has generated a feeling of helplessness and apathy in the public mind, resulting in cynicism, fatalism or in arguments that rationalize corruption. Alternatively, escape is sought in sweeping solutions such as, for example, radical constitutional changes, wholesale deregulation and privatization of the economy and decentralization of most governmental activities. An agenda for removing corruption will thus far have to be worked upon in the Plan.

10.71. Some suggestions which need to be seriously worked upon are:

- The Prevention of Corruption Act, 1988 and other related laws need to be reviewed with an effective role assured for the Central and State Vigilance Commissions. They should have wide powers with independent budgets and staff so as to be able to initiate and pursue investigations on their own.
- Strengthening the 'watch dog' role of the Comptroller and Auditor-General of India and his establishment in order to ensure probity, transparency and accountability in all public financial transactions. This will involve, inter-alia: (i) wider powers for audit, (ii) prompt publication and discussion of audit reports, (iii) follow-up by the vigilance machinery of financial irregularities brought to light by audit, and (iv) provision for audit based on references from citizens and investigative reports in the media.
- Tackling corruption in public utilities and in municipal and other services provided by the State and its agencies. This will involve (i) the adoption of clear and verifiable standards for performance, (ii) institution of transparent practices and systems and (iii) adequate mechanisms—such as Ombudsman—for the redressal of public complaints and grievances.
- A thorough and systematic review of all legislations, rules and executive orders which involve discretionary decisions, thereby creating financial stakes and inducements for the giving and taking of bribes. The objectives will be to eliminate, or considerably reduce the role for discretion in governmental actions, discipline the exercise of discretion, where inescapable, through objective and transparent guidelines, and provide public access to information relating to discretionary decisions having direct or indirect financial implications.
- Formulation and enforcement of a code of conduct to regulate relations between government and private enterprises, domestic and multi-national. Enterprises which violate the code of conduct should be blacklisted with due publicity.
- Appropriate self-policing arrangements should be developed by independent authorities and professions such as the judiciary, lawyers, doctors, media persons, chartered accountants, architects and contractors.

10.72. In addition to the above suggestions, it is also necessary to consider initiatives, which would address aspects of the political system, which often encourage corruption. These include the following:

- To provide State funding for candidates to an appropriate extent and subject to appropriate criteria, drawing upon practices followed in a number of other democracies.
- To tighten the anti-defection law to ensure that legislators are not bought and sold. No split in the legislature parties should be recognized unless it is followed by a split in the parent political organization on the basis of issues. There should also be a bar on defectors being rewarded with political office.

CIVIL SERVICE REFORMS

10.73. A serious effort will have to be made to protect honest civil servants. Protecting the public services from political interference and abuse of power on the part of politicians will involve: (i) enforcement of objective and transparent criteria and procedures for appointments and promotions; (ii) definite tenure for civil servants holding senior positions. The abridgement of tenure through transfers should be for objective reasons to be recorded in writing; (iii) Public Service Commissions/Administrative Tribunals should have a role in monitoring tenure, transfers and promotions; (iv) no civil servant should be suspended without the prior concurrence of the Public Service Commission; (v) rules of business in government should be strictly enforced, particularly the recording of reasoned orders in writing; and (vi) protection for civil servants who expose corrupt practices.

10.74. An important question today is developing a climate of probity in public life. Codes of ethics, therefore, need to be developed for civil servants and other public functionaries. A number of countries, like the UK and Spain, have developed their code of ethics. The ARC has made extensive recommendations on these issues.

10.75. Some of the values which a civil servant could be mandated, to follow are objectivity, integrity, neutrality, dedication to public service, transparency, exemplary conduct, accessibility and efficiency.

10.76. These values have also been studied in the context of developing an Act for the Civil Services. Some principles which they should observe in their functioning are:

- Allegiance to the various ideals enshrined in the preamble to the Constitution;
- Apolitical functioning;
- Good governance for the betterment of the people to be the primary goal of civil service;
- Duty to act objectively and impartially;
- Accountability and transparency in decision making;
- Maintenance of the highest ethical standards; and
- Ensuring economy and avoidance of wastage in expenditure.

RULE OF LAW: POLICE AND JUDICIARY

10.77. Rule of Law requires equality before law and equal protection of the law. The sine qua non of fairness of Criminal Justice Administration is that law should be enforced by Police without fear or favour. Furthermore, the judicial system must protect innocents and punish the guilty. Even though the police and judiciary are conventionally considered as non-developmental and regulatory arms of the State, the Eleventh Plan takes these to be upholders of the rule of law, which is the bedrock of democracy and development. Respect for human rights and equality for all social groups are the preconditions for political participation and a peaceful society. Viable institutions based on the rule of law improve the chances of settling conflicts peacefully. The legal system provides certainty and the necessary framework for sustainable economic and social development. For instance, establishing and enforcing property rights clears the way for capital formation and a market economy. In addition, a reliable legal and judicial system reduces uncertainties and related investment risks. Thus, transparent predictable legal provisions lay the foundation for vigorous economic activity, investment and growth. Accordingly, capacity building in the police and judicial system has been accepted as a legitimate activity for Plan funding in the Eleventh Plan.

10.78. The police is the instrument of coercive power of the State and this power has to be exercised transparently, with maximum restraint but with telling effect. The effectiveness of the beat constable, as well as the station house officer, has only declined progressively since Independence. Over the years, increasing politicization and corruption, overstretched duty hours and low policing intensity (that is, ratio of police personnel to population) have only contributed to the decline in their credibility. In the 1950s, a single beat constable used to effect the arrest of several offenders, but today a posse is needed for the same task. If this trend is to be reversed, the majesty of law must be re-established and public perception will have to be changed so that a policeman is seen as the person responsible for the public safety, an ace investigator and a professional crime-buster. His achievements will have to be rewarded and misconducts punished relentlessly. Once this is done, it will be necessary to change the legal system so that it gives greater credence to the policeman deposing in a court of law. In special circumstances, his solitary evidence should be relied upon for securing convictions. Conversely, it will be necessary to hold the police officer fully accountable for the depositions made by him. Any falsification of evidence should make him liable to the severest punishment. This change is fundamental to realigning the criminal justice administration system.

10.79. Once this is achieved, the conviction rate will increase, perpetrators of crime will get punished and judicial processes will start buttressing the deterrent effect of law. The current vicious circle of poor policing, poor investigation, half-hearted prosecution, hostile witnesses and high acquittal rate will get converted into a virtuous cycle of greater professionalism in investigation, more responsible prosecution, higher conviction rate and lesser crime. A more orderly society is the bedrock of planned development.

10.80. The police need to stay ahead of crime and criminals and counter the threats posed by destabilizing forces. Police also need to be equipped to effectively handle emergent challenges of newer criminal and economic offences. Increased reliance on science and technology will also be central to contemporary developments in policing. Today, technology enables us to view crime perpetration, detection, registration, investigation, prosecution, adjudication and incarceration as a seven-stage continuum. It is possible to follow and monitor the crime and the criminal from the time of the perpetration of crime to the time of its adjudication and resultant conviction.

10.81. This requires a unified database on a shared network to monitor the progress of each case till the delivery of the punishment. It will also enable evaluation of the performance of investigators and prosecutors more systematically and enable High Courts to supervise the subordinate courts more effectively. State governments should be encouraged to establish an integrated portal for crime and punishment. The portal will have two tracks:

- The Crime and Punishment Tracking System will monitor crime from the time of its detection, through registration, investigation, prosecution and adjudication.
- The Criminal Tracking System will create a nation-wide system of biometric data capture relating to criminals at the time of arrest, with digital equipment for lifting, recording and storage of fingerprints at the police station level and a powerful search engine for matching fingerprints with those in the database across the country. This will help in creating comprehensive criminal history sheets of individual criminals, habitual offenders and perpetrators of repeat-crimes. Subsequently, more sophisticated databases could be built based on DNA fingerprinting and other biometric identifiers, such as retinal image identification system and Lambdoid Sutures. These could be handled by suitable equipment at district HQs. Fingerprint data capture should be provided for in each police station, as well as in jails.

10.82. It is proposed to provide Rs 2000 crore towards a scheme for Technology Upgradation of the Investigation and Prosecution function, Crime and Criminal Tracking Network, which will establish a secured database on a Web-based, secured network containing information on crimes and criminals and will provide extensive infrastructure for biometric data capture. In all, Rs 7000 crore has been provided in the Plan for various schemes of the Ministry of Home Affairs.

10.83. Wide-ranging reforms in the field of police administration at senior levels are already on the anvil after the Supreme Court had intervened in matters of transparency relating to the appointment of Director Generals of Police and other police functionaries and their tenures. The recommendations of the Soli Sorabjee Committee on some of the issues would form an important input in further strengthening reforms in this area.

10.84. There is today a serious problem posed by Naxalism. A number of districts in the States of Bihar, Jharkhand, Chhattisgarh, Orissa, Maharashtra, and Andhra Pradesh are afflicted by it. The delivery of public services in many of these areas is a serious issue. Resources will be provided to the States to supplement their efforts and ensure access to the people who are suffering from the effect of Naxalism. It is not merely a law and order problem but also a developmental challenge, and the affected States require a combination of political, developmental and perception management responses as part of a holistic strategy. Some of these could be in the field of education and health. Employment of more resources for them for development for the region would be a key issue during the Plan to gradually change the environment in such regions. A new initiative on the Plan side is proposed with an outlay of Rs 500 crore for improving village connectivity and meeting critical gaps in physical and social infrastructure and addressing unmet livelihood concerns in the Naxalite-affected areas.

10.85. Though India has a robust judicial system based on the Anglo-Saxon legal tradition, the process of delivery of justice to the common man is long and tortuous. The long list of pending cases in courts, frequent adjournments, dilatory tactics by some counsels and the practice of charging the client per court hearing/per diem and not on the outcome, are resulting in interminable litigation and unacceptable delays in adjudication.

10.86. As per the Supreme Court newsletter of July–September 2007, 44819 cases are pending in the Supreme Court and 3712715 cases are pending in the High Courts. Special attention will be paid to reforms that would speed up the judicial process. The Mid Term Appraisal had suggested certain initiatives, which need to be pursued. Briefly, these were:

- Empowering the presiding officers of the courts to exercise better control over their case-lists or Lists of Business in a transparent manner. The List of Business Information System developed by the NIC can help courts monitor whether hearings are getting fixed with predictable periodicity and are beyond manipulation of court staff.
- More courts should be opened to tackle the large backlog of cases.
- Laws need to be reviewed for facilitating out-of-court settlements in civil cases and plea-bargain in criminal cases.
- The counsel–client relationship and counsel fee payment system need to be brought under some principled regulation to make the judicial process more client-friendly, creating an incentive for counsels to ensure early delivery of decisions.
- There is also a need to provide greater finality to adjudicatory processes. Currently, judicial processes meander through an interminable process of interlocutory injunctions and appeals against interlocutory orders. This can be simplified by enhancing the power of the court to review its own orders, to enable it to bring about a self-correction at the interlocutory stage.
- There is a strong case for moving from a two-appeal system to a single appeal system to give finality to judicial pronouncements. Furthermore, frivolous recourse to filing appeals can be discouraged by imposing a heavy fee.

10.87. The application of information technology can bring about a sea change in the quality of management of casework and can substantially reduce the time taken in the disposal of cases. Under the directions of the Supreme Court and the Conference of Chief Justices, NIC has initiated COURTSIS (Courts Information System) covering all 18 High Courts. The Supreme Court has also started the use of e-signature. This has already enabled them to improve the court–litigant interface, with prompt delivery of copies of judgments, daily orders, case status information, and so on.

10.88. In the Tenth Plan, an ambitious target had been set to computerize all 14948 subordinate courts in the Districts (including 1734 fast track courts). The actual expenditure during the Tenth Plan was Rs 519 crore and the entire amount spent was on computerization of the courts. In the Eleventh Plan, it is proposed to provide Rs 1470 crore to the Department of Justice. Of this, Rs 740 crore is being assigned for computerizing and networking of district and subordinate courts and for establishing e-courts and video-conferencing facilities in courts and jails, and Rs 700 crore for capacity building and infrastructure for Judiciary. An e-Committee has been set up for this purpose, which has prepared an ambitious computerization project to be implemented in three phases over the Five Year Plan period. The Department has also prepared a new scheme on the 'Study of Judicial Reforms and Assessment of Status' that will address the needs of capacity building and training of judicial officers, at all levels.

10.89. While computerization and networking of all courts will enable better administrative supervision and control by High Courts over the disposal of cases in subordinate courts on a daily basis, the full benefits of IT will be realized when the judicial processes start getting re-engineered in the following manner:

- Allowing e-filing of plaints, written statements, affidavits, counter-affidavits and rejoinder affidavits.
- E-filing of examination-in-chief is made admissible in evidence.
- Permitting cross-examination of witnesses in remote locations (that is, outside courts) through video-conferencing and making it admissible in evidence.
- Providing touch screens in witness boxes to enable witnesses to draw site-plans of scenes of occurrence in complicated sessions cases.
- Allowing audio-recorded/audio-video-recorded versions of evidence in order to reduce the time of the court in recording evidence. Once the technology is perfected, speech to text transcripts can also be made admissible in evidence.
- Video-conferencing can be deployed by courts more effectively as an aid to judicial processes in following situations:
  - Securing evidence of witnesses in remote locations or those not able to attend the court.
  - Securing evidence of vulnerable witnesses like rape victims, who may want to avoid the public gaze.

- Conducting identification proceedings.
- Physically distancing the witnesses from the criminals in the identification parade. This will enable the witness to identify the offender fearlessly.
- Dispensing with the transportation of undertrials to and from jail for periodic appearances before magistrates. This will reduce instances of custodial escapes.

10.90. In order to implement these proposals, the judicial processes will need to be re-engineered and amendments made in the Evidence Act, 1872; Criminal Procedure Code (CrPC) and Civil Procedure Code (CPC). This should not be difficult, considering that Singapore, which had similar legislation/regulations in place because of the shared British colonial past, has successfully re-engineered its judicial processes to enable e-courts in order to bring about expeditious disposal.

NEW REGULATORY STRUCTURES

10.91. A new area, which is relevant to determine the quality of governance, is the growth of independent regulators who now perform some of the functions earlier performed by governments. Their role is particularly evident in the infrastructure sectors where the economic policy changes of the past ten years or so have led to a shift from the earlier system, where infrastructure was provided almost exclusively by the public sector to a system where private suppliers of infrastructure services are actively encouraged. The reasons for the shift and its potential benefits have been extensively discussed elsewhere in the Plan document. In this chapter we focus on the fact that the shift has involved the development of new regulatory structures which perform some of the functions earlier performed by governments and which, therefore, have governance implications. The emergence of the regulatory State in the area of infrastructure is the natural consequence of the fact that infrastructure sectors have an element of natural monopoly. Consumers do not always have the choice of choosing alternative service suppliers (there is usually only one airport or road servicing an area) and when they do, as in the case of telecommunications, each service provider must be part of a network where access and connectivity become important. For these reasons, it is necessary for sectors which have opened up to private suppliers, to have regulators who can ensure that the interests of the consumers are adequately protected and also that the producers are fairly treated. Competing suppliers have to be assured a level playing field, and where government entities are also suppliers only regulators independent of government can carry credibility.

10.92. Economic regulation in such situations should be designed to achieve the effective functioning of competitive markets and, where such markets are absent, to mimic competitive market outcomes to the extent possible. Regulation can also be used to achieve a range of non-market objectives, which include ensuring universal and equitable access, consumer protection and maintaining safety and health standards.

10.93. The regulatory framework that has emerged in the infrastructure sectors is characterized by the establishment of independent regulatory commissions. However, the system has developed autonomously within each sector, with relatively little coordination or cross fertilization of ideas. Box 10.1 captures the broad legislative and institutional framework currently prevailing in different sectors. It is evident that there are significant differences across sectors. An issue that needs to be addressed is whether a fresh look is needed at the regulatory structures that have evolved, taking account of the experience gained thus far.

CONSTITUTIONAL AND LEGAL FRAMEWORK

10.94. The three general principles which are critical to regulatory institutional design are discussed below.

Separation of Power

10.95. The separation of powers principle is complied with when rule-making and administration of rules are vested in the regulatory institution without combining judicial functions, which are reserved for a differently constituted body. Such a regulatory institution would essentially perform the erstwhile role of the government in making rules and enforcing them through licensing and other mechanisms. The administration of these rules would require the regulator to function in a quasi-judicial manner in conformity with the principles of administrative law. However, the adjudicating tribunal must be headed by a judicial member whose appointment and conditions of service are comparable to those holding similar positions in the Judiciary. This adjudication tribunal must be insulated from the rest of the regulatory system and must adopt a process of the highest judicial standards to resolve the disputes before it. The institutional framework that has emerged in the telecom and electricity sectors broadly conforms to the doctrine of separation of powers with the regulators functioning as quasi-judicial bodies while appeals against their orders are heard by Appellate Tribunals that resemble judicial bodies in form and character. This principle has also been applied to the competition and securities regulatory regimes.

Box 10.1
Legislative and Institutional Framework

Sector	Relevant Statutes	Regulatory Authority
Transport • Roads • Rail • Airports • Ports	– National Highways Act of India, 1998 – Central Road Fund Act, 2000 – The Control of National Highways (Land and Traffic) Act, 2002 – Indian Railway Board Act, 1905 – Railways Act, 1989 – Aircraft Act, 1934 – Airports Authority of India Act, 1994 – Air Corporations (Transfer of Undertakings and Repeal) Act 1994 – Indian Ports Act, 1908 – Major Port Trusts Act, 1963	No transport sector regulatory authority. • National Highways Authority of India acts as the regulator as well as the operator. • States have floated their own corporations or agencies. • Investors have no recourse to an independent roads regulator. • Indian Railways act as the operator as well as the regulator. • Investors have no recourse to an independent railways regulator. • Airports Authority of India is the operator as well as the regulator. Director General of Civil Aviation and the Bureau of Civil Aviation Security (BCAS) regulate safety and technical aspects only. • Investors have no recourse to an independent airports regulator. • Proposal to set up the Airports Economic Regulatory Authority (AERA). • Tariff Authority for Major Ports (TAMP) has the sole function of tariff setting. • Investors and users have no recourse to an independent ports regulator on other matters such as dispute resolution, performance standards, consumer protection and competition.
Energy • Power	– Electricity Act, 2003	No energy sector regulator • Regulatory commissions at the Centre and States with very extensive functions and powers. • Track record not as yet convincing.
• Oil and Gas • Coal and Lignite	– Petroleum and Natural Gas Regulatory Board Act, 2006. – Petroleum Act, 1934 – Oilfields (Regulation and Development) Act 1948 – Petroleum and Minerals Pipelines (Acquisition of Right of User in Land) Act, 1962 – Coal Bearing Areas (Acquisition and Development) Act 1957 – Mines and Minerals (Regulation and Development) Act 1957 – Coal Mines Nationalization Act, 1973 – Coal Mines Conservation and Development Act, 1974	• The Petroleum and Natural Gas Regulatory Board regulates the refining, processing, storage, transportation, distribution and marketing of petroleum, petroleum products and natural gas. • Director General of Hydrocarbons licenses and regulates the exploration and optimal exploitation of hydrocarbons. • No regulatory authority for coal. Control by Ministry (Coal Controller) and through nationalized corporations.

(Box 10.1 contd.)

(Box 10.1 contd.)

Sector	Relevant Statutes	Regulatory Authority
Communication • Posts • Broadcasting • Cable TV • Telecom and Internet	– Communication Convergence Bill, 2001 – Indian Post Office Act, 1898 – Prasar Bharati (Broadcasting Corporation of India) Act, 1990 – Sports Broadcasting Signals (Mandatory Sharing with Prasar Bharati) Act 2007 – Cable Television Networks Regulation Act, 1995 – Telecom Regulatory Authority of India Act, 1997 – Indian Telegraph Act 1885 – Indian Wireless Telegraphy Act 1933 – Information Technology Act 2000	No communication regulatory authority. • The draft Bill proposes a sectoral regulator to promote, facilitate and develop the carriage and content of communications (including broadcasting, telecommunications and multimedia). It is currently being reviewed in consultation with stakeholders. • No posts regulatory authority. Proposal to create a new regulatory body. A draft amendment bill is open for consultation. • Private participation allowed in the FM radio sector through licensing. No regulatory authority exists for radio and TV broadcasts. A draft bill is currently being subjected to consultations with stakeholders. • Draft Broadcasting Services Regulation Bill, 2007, is open for consultation. It proposes setting up a Broadcast Regulatory Authority of India. • TRAI has the responsibility of tariff setting and interconnection for cable operators. • TRAI has been given the responsibility to regulate telecom and Internet service providers. • Provides for the regulation of carriage and content of cable TV broadcasts.

Democratic Accountability

10.96. In the earlier model of public sector provision of infrastructure services, the Ministry was responsible for setting policy and for various aspects of the delivery of services by the suppliers and was accountable to Parliament for all these functions. With the emergence of private suppliers, the various functions have been unbundled. The Ministry is responsible for policy but the regulator is responsible for many of the functions earlier performed by the Ministry, especially on issues such as price caps, quality of service, etc. The Ministry is responsible for service delivery by the public sector suppliers but not by private sector suppliers. It is also not responsible for balancing the competition between suppliers, which is left to the regulator. This raises the question of the regulator's accountability. To be truly independent the regulator must not be accountable to the Ministry. However, if it is not accountable to the Ministry then perhaps it should be made responsible to the Legislature. This raises the issue of how precisely such accountability can be established. Legislative oversight cannot be absolute. In particular, it must be limited in one significant respect: those decisions of a regulator which are open to appeal before an appellate tribunal or court should be exempt from legislative scrutiny to avoid a clash of jurisdictions. However, it would remain open to the Legislature to review the regulations or policies underlying such decisions.

10.97. Second, the regulator needs to be made responsible to the people at large. This is possible by adopting processes and systems whereby interested citizens or groups of citizens may seek and acquire information, make representations and be accorded full process and participation rights. This capacity of citizens must be extended to both the rule making and quasi-judicial aspects of regulatory functions. The role of CSOs should also be recognized and enhanced. Requiring the regulator to rest decision making on publicly articulated rationale and persistently making them engage with the people at large, is the most effective way for regulatory institutions to earn democratic legitimacy. Further, this is an effective safeguard against regulatory capture by special interest groups. However, it should be recognized that the requirement of engaging with CSOs would by itself fail to achieve the desired results unless the regulators are themselves made accountable to the Legislature.

Federal Principle

10.98. The Constitution distributes legislative and executive power vertically between the Union, State and local government. As the subjects of economic regulation are often divided between Union and State competencies, the regulatory structure should reflect this distribution. An elementary glance at the different regulatory structures for telecom and power may suggest that, so far, the federal principle has been grasped and accommodated. However, problems remain in other areas. Wherever a multi-level regulatory framework is created, as in the electricity sector, a common policy approach backed by uniform enforcement and dispute resolution processes must be ensured. As domain knowledge and regulatory expertise is scarce, a centralized knowledge bank can be maintained in every sector so that all regulators are able to access sufficient information. These initiatives will help promote consistent and coordinated regulation of crucial sectors of the economy.

UNIFORM REGULATORY FRAMEWORK

10.99. As indicated in Box 10.1, the creation of independent regulatory agencies in the last 15 years has proceeded on a sectoral basis, where each line ministry or State Government has constituted a regulator for a particular sector of the economy. This sectoral approach has resulted in an uneven regulatory environment. There is no regulator in some sectors (for example, roads and railways), partial regulators in others (ports and airports) and relatively comprehensive regulators in some (telecommunications and electricity). It is appropriate to review the experience in these sectors and benchmarking them against international best practices to see what changes, if any, are needed. Several issues arise.

Objectives

10.100. There is need for clear articulation of the objectives of regulating the infrastructure sectors so that divergent mandates for sectoral regulators are eliminated. In particular it is important to emphasize that competition is the best safeguard for consumer interests and, therefore, regulation should aim at removing barriers to competition and eliminating the abuse of market power. In those segments of infrastructure services that are amenable to competition, regulation should be light handed and tariff-setting could be left to competitive markets whereas segments that have elements of monopoly should be subjected to close regulation. In all cases, performance standards should be regulated for ensuring quality of service. Regulation should also extend to determination of tariffs for the supply of goods and services, like railways and coal, so long as the market structure remains monopolistic.

10.101. Competition can be promoted by operating on the assumption that each of the infrastructure sectors can be broadly divided into carriage and content segments, and while the carriage element may involve a natural monopoly, content lends itself to competition. Content normally refers to electricity, gas, data or voice. On the other hand, carriage refers to transmission lines, networks, exchanges, airports, ports, highways and other fixed assets. While carriage is typically regarded as a natural monopoly, content is eminently amenable to competition. In order to enable competition in the content segment, the carriage should be subjected to non-discriminatory open access under close regulatory oversight, including determination of tariffs. Where technology or market structure enables adequate competition in carriage, its regulation could remain light handed. These aspects must be clearly addressed in the overarching approach to regulation.

Institutional Framework

10.102. To be effective, all regulatory institutionsshould normally be empowered to make regulations, issue licenses, set performance standards and determine tariffs. They should also have the powers to enforce their regulations, licence conditions and orders by imposing punitive measures, including suspension or cancellation of licences. They may adjudicate on disputes among licensees and between the licensees and government, subject to review in appeal before an Appellate Tribunal that is headed by a judicial person. In the discharge of their functions, the regulatory commissions should be governed by the principles of administrative law and should be expected to act as quasi-judicial entities.

Independence and Autonomy

10.103. Efficient and credible regulation requires that the regulatory authority should be independent and that the regulators should be persons of competence and integrity. To achieve this, it is necessary to review the existing system from this point of view. This includes a review of the qualifications laid down for regulators and the procedures for selection, the remuneration of regulators and their terms of service to see whether they are capable of attracting the most suitable persons instead of naturally leading to the appointment of retiring civil servants, the degree of autonomy which the regulator has from the administrative Ministry concerned, which is linked to the extent of financial autonomy they enjoy. The Planning Commission has consulted extensively on these issues and will come up with comprehensive proposals for change for the consideration of the government.

Participatory Regulatory Process

10.104. An important aspect of the system of independent regulation is that it provides a structured method of participation. This requires the regulator to adopt a consultative process that ensures avenues for participation by stakeholders. Its proposed annual plan of action and its consultation papers should be freely available on the Internet. The two central functions of the regulator, rule making and the enforcement of rules, should be standardized across regulators to ensure that opportunities for intervention are made available at every stage of the regulatory process.

Regulation and Competition

10.105. Defining a workable division of labour between the regulator and the competition authority is a key to predictability as also for eliminating the possibilities of forum shopping. Presently, competition and regulation laws ignore the potential jurisdictional overlaps between the two areas of law. Sections 3, 4, 5, and 6 of the Competition Act, 2002 which are the key substantive provisions of law, are not market specific and apply generically to regulated and unregulated markets. So it is inevitable that sectoral regulators and the competition authority will issue directives to the same market players, which are likely to conflict given the diverse perceptions of the respective authorities.

10.106. There is a minimal institutional interface between the regulator and competition authorities. Though Section 21 allows any statutory body, which includes a regulator, to refer matters that may potentially violate the competition law, this is optional and regulators may choose not to do so. Further, by creating an interface which is limited to dispute resolution, the statute leaves open a wide scope for disagreements, which may best be resolved before they have matured into legal disputes.

10.107. The Competition Commission of India (CCI) has conducted its own analysis of the interface between regulation and competition in India and explored three possible modes of interaction. First, mandatory consultation between regulators and competition authorities before any action is taken in regulated industries may be a formal and effective technique. This may be institutionalized by allowing some members of each institution to participate in the decision-making processes of the other. Second, each authority must have the right to intervene in any dispute adjudication before the other. If such a participation right is prescribed by allowing each institution an intervention right in any dispute, this will allow for a reasonable degree of inter-institutional communication. Finally, the competition authority and regulator may be given precise roles in any regulated industry.

Multi-Sectoral Regulators

10.108. Another important issue is whether we should consider establishing multi-sectoral regulators for (i) communications; (ii) electricity, fuels and gas; and (iii) transport. This would eliminate proliferation of regulatory commissions, help build capacity and expertise, promote consistency of approach and save on costs. In the case of States, a single regulatory commission for all infrastructure sectors may be more productive and cost-effective as compared to sectoral regulators for each sector. States should be encouraged to consider this approach and the scope of their existing electricity regulators could be extended to other sectors.

Appellate Tribunals

10.109. The effectiveness of regulators can be severely compromised if their decisions get locked up in appellate courts. Constitution of appellate tribunals on the lines of the telecom and electricity appellate tribunals would help address this concern. These tribunals should be headed by eminent persons of judicial background and may consist of subject matter specialists. Separate appellate tribunals could be constituted for the three major segments, that is, energy, communication and transport. Another approach could be to constitute a single appellate tribunal for all regulatory commissions with regional benches. The respective merits of these two options could be evaluated before arriving at a conclusion.

11

Consumer Protection and Competition Policy

CONSUMER PROTECTION

11.1. Promotion of consumer welfare is the common goal of consumer protection and competition policy. At the root of both consumer protection and competition policy is the recognition of an unequal relationship between consumers and producers. Protection of consumers is accomplished by setting minimum quality specifications and safety standards for both goods and services and establishing mechanisms to redress their grievances. The objective of competition is met by ensuring that there are sufficient numbers of producers so that no producer can attain a position of dominance. If the nature of the industry is such that dominance in terms of market share cannot be avoided, it seeks to ensure that there is no abuse on account of this dominance. Competition policy also seeks to forestall other forms of market failure, such as formation of cartels, leading to collusive pricing, division of markets and joint decisions to reduce supply. Mergers and acquisitions also need to be regulated as they reduce competition.

CONSUMER PROTECTION POLICY

11.2. The consumer movement in India is as old as trade and commerce. In Kautilya's *Arthashastra*, there are references to the concept of consumer protection against exploitation by the trade and retailer with respect to quality, short weight, measurement and adulteration of goods. Yet until the late 1970s, there was no systematic movement in the country for safeguarding the interest of consumers. But now it is widely acknowledged that the level of consumer awareness and protection is a true indicator of development of the country and progressiveness of civil society. The main reason for this is the rapidly increasing variety of goods and services which modern technology has made available. In addition, the growing size and complexity of production and distribution systems, the high level of sophistication in marketing and selling practices and in advertising and other forms of promotion, mass marketing methods and consumers' increased mobility resulting in reduction of personal interaction between buyers and sellers, have contributed to the increased need for consumer protection.

11.3. Protection of consumer rights in modern times dates back to 1962. On 15 March 1962, the Consumer Bill of Rights was proclaimed by the United States President in a message to the Congress. The message proclaimed: (i) the right to choice, (ii) the right to information, (iii) the right to safety, and (iv) the right to be heard. Subsequently, the right to consumer education, the right to a healthy environment and the right to basic needs (food, clothing, and shelter) were added by Consumer International. In India, 24 December is celebrated as National Consumer Rights Day as the Consumer Protection Act, 1986 was enacted on that day. 15 March is observed as World Consumer Rights Day since 1983, when International Organization of Consumer Unions declared it so. In India, 15 March was also adopted as the National Consumers Day and has been observed since then. Another significant day in the history of world consumer movement is 9 April 1985, when the General Assembly of the United Nations adopted a set of guidelines for consumer protection and the Secretary General of the United Nations was authorized to persuade member countries to adopt these guidelines through policy changes or law. These guidelines constituted a comprehensive policy framework outlining what governments need to do to promote consumer protection in the following areas: (i) physical safety, (ii) protection and promotion of consumer economic interests, (iii) standards for safety and quality of consumer goods and services, (iv) measures enabling consumers to obtain redressal, (v) measures relating to specific areas (food, water, and pharmaceuticals); and (vi) consumer education and information programme.

11.4. These guidelines provided an internationally recognized set of basic objectives, particularly for governments of developing countries, enabling them to identify the priorities and structure of their consumer protection policy and legislation. Subsequently, the guidelines were expanded to include 'sustainable consumption' which was an important subject in the changed social, political and economic scenario. The importance of 'sustainable consumption' is aptly highlighted in Mahatma Gandhi's words, 'the rich must live more simply so that the poor may simply live'. Sustainable development is crucially dependent on sustainable consumption. Article 21 of the Constitution requires the State, inter alia, to protect life, which must be construed as including the right to a healthy and safe environment. A healthy and safe environment is inalienably linked with sustainability and promotion of sustainable consumption.

11.5. The concern in the Indian Constitution for protection and promotion of an individual's rights, and for the dignity and welfare of the citizen makes it imperative to provide for the welfare of the individual as a consumer, a client and a customer. The rights under the Consumer Protection Act, 1986 flow from the rights enshrined in Articles 14 to 19 of the Constitution of India. The RTI, 2005 which has opened up governance processes of our country to the common public also has far-reaching implications for consumer protection.

11.6. The consumer protection policy creates an environment whereby the clients, customers, and consumers receive satisfaction from the delivery of goods and services needed by them. Good governance requires efficiency, effectiveness, ethics, equality, economy, transparency, accountability, empowerment, rationality, impartiality and participation of citizens. The concern of consumer protection is to ensure fair trade practices; quality of goods and efficient services with information to the consumer with regard to quality, quantity, potency, composition and price for their choice of purchase. Thus, proper and effective implementation of consumer protection law promotes good governance.

11.7. Education is the most powerful tool for the progress of the country and is a social and political necessity. Education helps an individual—as a consumer—in making rational choices and protects him from trade and business-related exploitation. But more is needed for the effective functioning of the national market to create an increased level of awareness of consumer rights, and for this consumers have to be educated about rights and responsibilities through concerted publicity and awareness campaigns. In the awareness campaigns, special emphasis needs to be given to vulnerable groups such as women and children, students, farmers and rural families and the working class. The report of the study on the Consumer Protection Act commissioned by the Comptroller and Auditor General (C & AG) of India and conducted in July–August 2005, brought out that 66% of consumers were not aware of consumer rights and 82% were not even aware of the Consumer Protection Act. In rural areas, only 13% of the population had heard of the Consumer Protection Act.

11.8. Standards, which are the essential building block for quality, play a key role in consumer protection. Standards could be on technical requirements (specifications), standard terminology (glossary of terms), good practices (codes of practice) or test methods or management system standards. Developed countries generally rely on management system standards like ISO 9001 (Quality Management System), ISO 14001 (Environmental Management Systems) and hazard analysis and critical control points (HACCP) as an indicator of the ability of an organization to meet quality needs and address environmental concerns. These standards are set generally by governmental or inter-governmental bodies but there are some private initiatives as well, which are widely used such as OHSAS 18000 (Occupational Health and Safety), SA 8000 (Social Accountability) and WRAP (Worldwide Responsible Apparel Production).

11.9. Setting standards is not enough for assuring the consumer of quality. For this, governments need to establish the full quality infrastructure, embracing standardization, conformity assessment and enforcement. The constituents of quality infrastructure are :

- Standardization
- Standard development
- Standard information
- Metrology
- Quality assurance/conformity assessment
- Testing
- Inspection
- Product certification
- Management Systems Certification (ISO 9000/14000/ 22000/27001/ OHSMS, etc.)
- Regulation and enforcement
- Accreditation

Consumer Protection in India

11.10. The Consumer Protection Act was enacted in 1986 based on United Nations guidelines with the objective of providing better protection of consumers' interests. The Act provides for effective safeguards to consumers against various types of exploitations and unfair dealings, relying on mainly compensatory rather than a punitive or preventive approach. The Act applies to all goods and services unless specifically exempted, and covers the private, public, and cooperative sectors and provides for speedy and inexpensive adjudication. The rights provided under the Act are:

- The right to be protected against marketing of goods and services which are hazardous to life and property
- The right to be informed about the quality, quantity, potency, purity, standard and price of goods and services, as the case may be, to protect the consumer against unfair trade practices
- The right to be assured of access to a variety of goods and services at competitive prices
- The right to be heard and assured that consumer interest will receive due consideration at appropriate fora
- The right to seek redressal against unfair or restrictive trade practices or unscrupulous exploitation of consumers
- The right to consumer education

11.11. Under the Consumer Protection Act, 1986 a three-tier, simple, quasi-judicial machinery has been established at the national, State, and district levels for hearing cases raised by consumers. The Act had been amended in 1991 and again in 1993. A comprehensive amendment was last made in 2002 for making the Act effective, functional and purposeful. The amended Act, inter alia, provides for the attachment and subsequent sale of the property of a person not complying with an order.

11.12. Although implementation of the Consumer Protection Act can be viewed as a success, there are still serious shortfalls in achieving consumer welfare because of the deficiencies in quality infrastructure in the country. First, there is a regulatory deficit in many products and services which impact on the health, safety and environment of the consumers and mandatory standards have not been prescribed for such products as electrical and electronic goods, IT and telecom equipment, industrial and fire safety equipment and toys. There is a multiplicity of regulatory/standardization/conformity assessment bodies and proliferation of certification and inspection bodies. At present, the Quality Council of India (QCI) is the main accreditation body for conformity assessment bodies taking up product or system certification or for inspection bodies, and the National Accreditation Board for Laboratories performs the same function for laboratories. However, there is no compulsion on the conformity assessment bodies, inspection bodies or laboratories to obtain accreditation, thus creating a lack of certainty about the existence of quality products, systems, inspections and laboratories. Laboratory infrastructure is weak in terms of international norms. Quality professionals lack the skills to guide quality improvement efforts in industry. There is apathy among businesses towards standardization in general, and lack of awareness among them about the impact of standards on quality, competitiveness, and profitability. There is absence of consumer demand for quality goods and services primarily because of lack of awareness among them regarding quality issues. In short, there is absence of a quality culture in the country. At a time when tariff barriers are falling worldwide as a result of multilateral trade negotiations and in the context of Foreign Trade Agreements (FTAs), and technical barriers to trade have become more significant as determinants of trade flows, urgent action has become necessary to correct the situation in the country as described above. If the quality of Indian products and their conformity with international standards is to be accomplished by Indian producers, the impulse must be generated from within the country. Nothing can have a more powerful impact on the producers than the demand for quality products by quality-conscious domestic consumers.

STRATEGY FOR THE ELEVENTH FIVE YEAR PLAN

Establishment of National Quality and Standardization Authority

11.13. As of today, the Bureau of Indian Standards (BIS), set up under the BIS Act, 1986 functions as the National Standards Body. Apart from the BIS, there are other organizations which are formulating specifications for their own internal use. In some areas, regulators are also prescribing the standards to be observed by the industry concerned. There is need to have a mechanism for the declaration of a harmonized Indian standard in different areas. For this purpose, the establishment of a National Quality and Standardization Authority through appropriate legal framework to ensure uniformity of approach for setting of standards and ensuring regulation of conformity assessment, is necessary. The framework should provide for setting voluntary standards in all areas of economic and social activities, and mandatory regulations in areas that impact on health, safety, and the environment. A national system of conformity assessment and compliance should be established to bring in complete synergy in standardization, conformity assessment and enforcement. In sectors critical to health and safety like food or drugs, infrastructure upgradation should be supported for MSE sectors to attain national/international standards/regulations like GMP/Good Hygienic Practice (GHP)/HACCP. A National Regulatory System Database should be developed. More specifically, the following are the measures that need to be undertaken:

(I) STRENGTHENING REGULATION

11.14. Some of the priority elements that should be considered by the concerned ministries or their agencies (Regulatory Bodies) for strengthening the regulation are:

- Mandatory standards for products which impact on health and safety of the consumer and on the environment such as electrical appliances, electronic, IT and telecom products, medical devices, industrial safety and fire safety equipment, helmets, plastic and other material used for food packaging.
- GHP/GMP/HACCP being made mandatory as a rule under the PFA Rules/ Integrated Food Law for the food industry and for hotels and restaurants.
- Mandatory national standards for compliance by all water agencies—rural or urban.
- Introduction of law for product liability provisions including punitive damages as a deterrent for sub-standard goods.
- Laying down residue limits for contaminants for raw materials as well as food products.
- Mandatory compliance with Good Agricultural Practices or Good Animal Husbandry Practices (GAHP) by commercial farms.

(II) EXTENDING VOLUNTARY STANDARDS INTO THE SERVICES SECTOR

11.15. For consumer protection, voluntary standards should be extended to the area of services, in particular, medical and hospital services, financing and investor services provided by non-banking financial companies, real estate services, e-commerce, and so on.

(III) NATIONAL STANDARDS SYSTEM

11.16. The Bureau of Indian Standards (BIS) may be made the national standards body and repository of all voluntary national standards. Wherever voluntary standards are being formulated by other standards development organizations which are recognized as national (like Indian Roads Congress or Agmark), these may be published as national standards by BIS while these bodies continue to make these standards.

(IV) POLICY ON CONFORMITY ASSESSMENT

11.17. The policy should be laid down for the government recognizing only one National Accreditation Body for conformity assessment for each area of activity. All conformity assessment bodies should be required to obtain accreditation either from national or international accreditation bodies within a reasonable period. As a general rule, functions of regulation, standardization and conformity assessment should be performed separately. Similarly, there is need to enlarge consumer choice in the matter of certification. Appropriate mechanism would need to be evolved for this purpose.

Setting up of National Consumer Protection Authority

11.18. There is need to deal effectively with deceptive practices, including misleading advertisements. Besides, there would be a gap in legislation to be caused by the proposed winding up of the Monopolies and Restrictive

Trade Practice Commission (MRTPC) with respect to unfair trade practices. The gap can be filled in by establishing a National Consumer Protection Authority through enactment of a National Consumer Protection Authority Act.

Enhancing Consumer Awareness

11.19. There is necessity for continuing consumer awareness campaigns on a large scale to sensitize the population on basic aspects such as Maximum Retail Price (MRP), Gold Hall Marking, Indian Standard Institute (ISI) mark on products, and expiry dates. As and when voluntary standards are extended into the services sector or regulations are imposed for mandatory compliance with standards for reasons of health, safety or environment, the content of awareness campaigns would need to be expanded.

COMPETITION POLICY

11.20. The Approach Paper to the Eleventh Five Year Plan recognized the need for creating a competitive environment to stimulate private investment. It emphasized the need for increased reliance on competitive markets subject to appropriate, transparent and effective regulations. A major objective of the Eleventh Plan is to recommend policies that spur private sector investment while ensuring fair competition by guarding against restrictive business practices.

11.21. A review of cross-country literature suggests that there is a positive association between GDP growth and competition. Empirical studies have suggested that competition enhances productivity at industry level, generates more employment and lowers consumer prices. A pro-competitive policy environment has been found to be positively associated with long-term growth. Competition-enhancing policies have pervasive and long-lasting effects on economic performance by affecting economic actors' incentive structure, by encouraging their innovative activities and by selecting more efficient ones from less efficient ones over time. The positive effects of competition are well illustrated by the recent experiences in India in several sectors such as telecommunications, automobiles, newspapers and consumer electronics, where there has been a fall in real prices/tariffs and marked improvement in the quality of goods/services. This experience demonstrates the benefits of ensuring competition in other sectors of the economy.

11.22. The reforms initiated since 1991 recognized the need for removing fetters on trade and industry with the view to unleash the competitive energies. The Industrial Policy Statement of 1991 emphasized the attainment of technological dynamism and international competitiveness. It noted that Indian industry could scarcely be competitive with the rest of the world if it had to operate within an over-regulated environment. To enhance competition in the domestic markets and to generate/promote a culture of competition in the country is part of this broader agenda on reforms. The economic reforms undertaken by the government have been generally on a sector by sector basis and the progress across sectors has not been uniform. While some sectors have successfully imbibed a strong competition culture, relatively weak competitive pressure exists in a number of sectors, such as electricity, in India. There are several policies and laws that can have significant bearing on competition. These should be made competition-friendly as far as possible.

11.23. To strengthen the forces of competition in the market, both competition law and competition policy are required. The two complement each other. The competition law prohibits and penalizes anti-competitive practices by enterprises functioning in the market; that is, it addresses market failures. Sector regulatory laws mimic competition in the areas of natural monopolies. Other regulatory laws, such as those for intellectual property or anti-dumping or even capital markets, too have an important interface with competition. The aim of the competition policy is to create a framework of policies and regulations that will inform other policies to facilitate competitive outcomes in the market. Competition policy is a critical component of any overall economic policy framework. Competition policy is intended to promote efficiency and to maximize consumer/social welfare. It also promotes creation of a business environment, which improves static and dynamic efficiencies, leads to efficient resource allocation and consumer welfare, and in which abuse of market power is prevented/curbed. It also promotes good governance by restricting rent seeking practices of economic actors.

11.24. During the Tenth Plan period, the Competition Act, 2002 was enacted. The Act established the CCI to eliminate practices having adverse effect on competition, promote and sustain competition in markets, protect the interest of consumers and ensure freedom of trade carried on by other participants, in markets in India. The Competition (Amendment) Act, 2007 passed by the Parliament in September 2007 has incorporated some changes in the Competition Act, 2002 including the establishment of a Competition Appellate Tribunal to hear appeals from the orders of the CCI. Until recently, as the substantive provisions were not notified, CCI was engaged, inter alia, in promotion of competition advocacy and creating awareness about competition issues. This activity will continue, even after the operationalization of the Competition Commission, which should happen soon.

11.25. During the mid-term appraisal of the Tenth Plan, it was recognized that there is an urgent need for articulating a National Competition Policy (NCP) in India, which should fully reflect the national resolve to accelerate economic growth, improve both the quality of life of the people of the country, national image and self-esteem. It further noted that NCP would bring about a competition culture amongst economic entities to maximize economic efficiency, protect consumer interests and improve international competitiveness.

11.26. The Planning Commission, in the context of the formulation of the Eleventh Plan, constituted a Working Group on Competition Policy with wide representation of professionals from government and non-government organizations. As suggested by the Working Group, there is a need for the government to adopt a broad-based, overarching and comprehensive NCP to promote coherence in the reforms process, to establish uniform competition principles across different sectors and to harmonize all other policies keeping in view the competition dimensions.

11.27. The broad objectives of the NCP should be: (i) to preserve the competitive process and to encourage competition in the domestic market so as to optimize efficiency, (ii) promote innovation and maximize consumer welfare, (iii) to promote, build and sustain strong competition culture within the country; (iv) to achieve harmonization in policies, laws and procedures regarding competition dimensions at all levels of governance, (v) to ensure competition in regulated sectors and to establish an institutional mechanism for synergized relationship between the Competition Commission and sectoral Regulators, and (vi) to strive for a single national market.

11.28. The NCP should be based on the following principles: (i) there should be effective control on anti-competitive conduct which undermines competition in markets in India; (ii) there should be competitive neutrality or a level playing field among all players, whether these be private enterprises, PSEs or government departments engaged in non-sovereign commercial activity; (iii) the procedures should be rule bound, transparent, fair and non-discriminatory; (iv) there should be institutional separation between policy making, operations and regulation; (v) where a separate regulatory arrangement is set up, it should be consistent with the principles of competition; (vi) third party access to essential facilities on fair terms should be available; (vii) any deviation from the principles of competition should be only to meet desirable social, environmental, developmental or other national objectives which are clearly defined, transparent, non-discriminatory, rule based and having the least competition restricting effect. The above principles of competition should be applicable across all sectors of the economy and be incorporated in policies, which govern them.

11.29. Several existing policies, statutes and regulations of the Central Government restrict or undermine competition. A review of such policies, statutes and regulations from the competition perspective (this is referred to as 'regulatory impact assessment' in several countries) may be undertaken with a view to remove or minimize their competition restricting effects. Proposed policies, statutes, regulations that impact competition should also include a competition impact assessment through an internal mechanism which should form one of the inputs in any decision-making process in this regard. Regulatory impact analysis should be a pre-condition for introducing regulatory changes in any sector. Any disinvestment or privatization attempt should take into account the competition dimension. In a globalizing economy, incorporation of competition clauses in trade agreements will go a long way to check anti-competitive behaviour and potential anti-competitive cross-border transactions/mergers having an adverse effect in India.

11.30. The initiatives at the State Government level would require undertaking pro-competition reforms, keeping in mind the principles of NCP. There are many economic areas of State policies and regulations that impact or inhibit competition in the market. These restrictions also tend to fragment the national market and undermine the freedom of economic actors. The State Governments should be encouraged to undertake a review of existing policies, laws or regulations from the competition perspective and also undertake a competition impact assessment of proposed policy, law and regulations before these are finalized; while seeking expert assistance of CCI and other expert agencies. Similarly, the statutes, laws and procedures which govern the sub-State authorities need to be reviewed so as to align them with the principles of NCP. All State Governments have, at the instance of CCI, established Nodal Points within their administrations to deal with the subject of competition; the State Governments are encouraged to give these Nodal Points an effective role in this regard.

11.31. Given the wide canvas of NCP, a suggestion has been made by the Working Group on Competition Policy for setting up an institutional arrangement for monitoring the progress of the implementation of the policy. A small and compact Competition Policy Council of about 25 members could be set up which would be advisory, non-statutory and autonomous in its functioning and be headed by an eminent non-official person and comprising key officials from economic Ministries/Departments, and non-officials from media, academia and civil society. The task of the Competition Policy Council would be to review the progress in the implementation of NCP such as reviews of policies, regulations and practices, and the competition impact assessment of new laws, regulations and policies.

11.32. An incentive scheme could be instituted by the government under which financial grants may be given to State Governments linked to the progress in aligning their policies and laws with the principles of NCP. The grants could be released based on the progress made by the various State Governments on the recommendations received from the Competition Policy Council.

11.33. The interface between the Competition Commission vis-à-vis sectoral regulators is critical. The basic premise to be recognized is that sectoral regulators have domain expertise in their relevant sectors. The Competition Commission, established under the Competition Act, 2002 on the other hand, has been constituted with a broad mandate to deal with competition for which certain very specific parameters are laid down under the Act. A formal mechanism for coordination between the Competition Commission and the sectoral regulators is, therefore, of key importance. Coordination between sectoral regulators and Competition Commission should be made mandatory through suitable provisions in the Competition Act, 2002 and sectoral laws.

11.34. Regulation may be justified or warranted in sectors which have natural monopolies or network industries; more so where a universal service obligation exists. However, regulation may not be required where these features do not prevail. Such sectors should ideally be left to the forces of competition. Even in sectors where regulation is required, it should be competition based or competition driven. One of the objectives of the regulation should be to create a competitive market in so far as this is feasible. As competition in the regulated sectors expands, the regulation should ideally become lighter and ultimately economic regulation may not be necessary. Therefore, a sunset clause based on considered timelines appropriate to the regulated sector may be considered in all economic regulatory laws so as to leave the industry to market forces once effective competition is achieved. Any anticompetitive conduct can always be addressed by the Competition Act, 2002.

11.35. Successful implementation of competition policy and law largely depends upon its acceptance by the people. Competition advocacy buttressed by good enforcement plays a vital role in securing the willingness and acceptability of a competition policy and law. Competition advocacy can also be looked at as law enforcement without intervention. An important tool of advocacy is the ability of many competition authorities to give an opinion on proposed legislation and public policy on their own, so that the law makers and policy makers consider the competition dimension and give reasons for deviating from them for the benefit of the public. The assistance of CCI and other expert bodies could be utilized for conducting studies in this regard.

11.36. The concept and the role of competition are relatively new to the Indian business community. There is, therefore, a pressing need to increase the level of awareness about the benefits of competition and the contribution of the competition law in this respect among the public, more particularly among the business community. The Commission has been given, under the Act, the mandate to generate public awareness; its efforts in this area may be further strengthened. The Commission should formulate, publish and post in the public domain, guidelines covering various dimensions related to competition law for enhancing public awareness. Such guidelines will help enterprises by bringing greater clarity about the provisions of the competition law and the manner of its enforcement. The Commission should also engage in Compliance Education for business.

11.37. There is strong commonality between competition policy and law on the one hand and consumer protection policy and law on the other. An effective competition policy lowers entry and exit barriers and makes the environment conducive to promoting entrepreneurship, which also provides space for the growth of small and medium enterprises and consequent employment expansion. Competition law concentrates in maintaining the process of competition between enterprises and tries to remedy behavioural or structural problems in order to re-establish effective competition in the market. The consequence of this is higher economic efficiency, greater innovation and enhancement of consumer welfare. Thereby the consumer experiences wider choices and greater availability of goods at affordable prices. On the other hand, the consumer protection policy and law are primarily concerned with the nature of consumer transactions, trying to improve market conditions for effective exercises of consumer choice. Thus, the two disciplines focus on different market failures and offer different remedies, but are both aimed at maintaining well functioning, competitive markets that promote consumer welfare. The two disciplines are mutually re-enforcing.

12

Development of Infrastructure

INTRODUCTION

12.1. The fast growth of the economy in recent years has placed increasing stress on physical infrastructure such as electricity, railways, roads, ports, airports, irrigation, and urban and rural water supply and sanitation, all of which already suffer from a substantial deficit from the past in terms of capacities as well as efficiencies in the delivery of critical infrastructure services. The pattern of inclusive growth of the economy projected for the Eleventh Plan, with GDP growth averaging 9% per year can be achieved only if this infrastructure deficit can be overcome and adequate investment takes place to support higher growth and an improved quality of life for both urban and rural communities.

12.2. This chapter provides a broad picture of investment requirements in each subsector, as well as the split between the Centre and the States and the role of the private sector in meeting the investment targets in these sectors. For the purpose of this chapter, infrastructure has been defined to include electricity (including non-conventional energy), telecommunications, roads and bridges, railways (including MRTS), ports, airports, irrigation (including watershed development), water supply and sanitation, storage and gas distribution sectors.

INVESTMENT IN INFRASTRUCTURE

12.3. The total investment in infrastructure, defined as above, in 2006–07 was estimated to be around 5% of GDP. From a macroeconomic perspective and taking account of investment in infrastructure in other relatively fast growing countries, it can be argued that the gross capital formation (GCF) in infrastructure should rise as a share of GDP from 5% in 2006–07 to 9% by the end of the Plan period (see Table 12.1). The experience of many other emerging developing countries would suggest that GCF in infrastructure may need to be accelerated to an even higher level—around 11%—by the terminal year of the Eleventh Plan. However, an increase of this order cannot be achieved starting from a level of less than 5% of GDP observed in 2005–06. Moreover, it may not be a necessary condition for achieving a 9% growth in the Eleventh Plan period since many East Asian countries have invested more than is essential. The target of 9% by the end of the Eleventh Plan seems reasonable.

12.4. On the above basis, the aggregate capital formation in infrastructure required to achieve India's targeted annual average growth in GDP of 9% over the Eleventh Plan period, would have to rise from Rs 259839 crore in 2007–08 to Rs 574096 crore in 2011–12 at constant 2006–07 price. Over the Eleventh Plan period, as a whole, this estimate aggregates to Rs 2011521 crore or US$ 502.88 billion (at an exchange rate of Rs 40/$).

12.5. The aggregate investment target derived above is broadly consistent with estimates of investment requirements based on sector specific requirements emerging from reports of the Working Groups constituted by the Planning Commission and by Inter-Ministerial Committees under the aegis of the Committee on Infrastructure. The relevant quantitative targets for these sectors in the Eleventh Plan are presented in Box 12.1 and the resulting investment totals and sector-wise details are presented in Tables 12.3 and 12.4. Total investment in infrastructure on this basis during the Eleventh Plan

TABLE 12.1
GCF in Infrastructure Based on Growth Targets (Top-down Estimates)

(at 2006–07 price)

	Year	2006–07	2007–08	2008–09	2009–10	2010–11	2011–12
				Eleventh Plan Period			
1.	GDP at market prices (Rs crore)	4145810	4518933	4925637	5368944	5852149	6378843
2.	Rate of growth of GDP (%)	9.00	9.00	9.00	9.00	9.00	9.00
3.	GCF in infrastructure as % of GDP	5.00	5.75	6.50	7.25	8.00	9.00
4.	GCF in infrastructure (Rs crore)	207291	259839	320166	389248	468172	574096
5	GCF in infrastructure (US$ billion)	51.82	64.96	80.04	97.31	117.04	143.52
6	Total GCF in Eleventh Plan			Rs 2011521 crore or US$ 502.88 billion			

Source: CSO for estimates for 2006–07, and computations of the Planning Commission.

Box 12.1
Infrastructure—Deficit and Eleventh Plan Physical Targets

Sector	Deficit	Eleventh Plan Targets
Roads/Highways	65590 km of NH comprise only 2% of network; carry 40% of traffic; 12% 4-laned; 50% 2-laned; and 38% single-laned	6-lane 6500 km in GQ; 4-lane 6736 km NS-EW; 4-lane 20000 km; 2-lane 20000 km; 1000 km Expressway
Ports	Inadequate berths and rail/road connectivity	New capacity: 485 m MT in major ports; 345 m MT in minor ports
Airports	Inadequate runways, aircraft handling capacity, parking space and terminal buildings	Modernize 4 metro and 35 non-metro airports; 3 greenfield in NER; 7 other greenfield airports
Railways	Old technology; saturated routes; slow speeds (freight: 22 kmph; passengers: 50 kmph); low payload to tare ratio (2.5)	8132 km new rail; 7148 km gauge conversion; modernize 22 stations; dedicated freight corridors
Power	13.8% peaking deficit; 9.6% energy shortage; 40% transmission and distribution losses; absence of competition	Add 78577 MW; access to all rural households
Irrigation	1123 BCM utilizable water resources; yet near crisis in per capita availability and storage; only 43% of net sown area irrigated	Develop 16 mha major and minor works; 10.25 mha CAD; 2.18 mha flood control
Telecom/IT	Only 18% of market accessed; obsolete hardware; acute human resources' shortages	Reach 600 m subscribers—200 m in rural areas; 20 m broadband; 40 m Internet

is projected at Rs 2056150 crore (or US$ 514.04 billion at Rs 40/$).

12.6. The strategy for infrastructure development in the Eleventh Plan reflects the dominant role of the public sector in building infrastructure. However, it also recognizes that the total resources required to meet the deficit in infrastructure exceed the capacity of the public sector. It is, therefore, necessary to attract private investment through appropriate forms of public private partnerships to meet the overall investment requirements.

12.7. The relative role of the public and private sectors will vary. In some sectors such as irrigation and water resources management, construction of rural roads, capital dredging at major ports, as well as in certain economically or situationally disadvantaged regions, the bulk of the investment in infrastructure would have to come from the public sector. Available public sector resources must therefore be directed to these sectors as a matter of priority. Precisely for this reason, PPPs must be seriously explored in other areas.

12.8. In building infrastructure for the future, it is also necessary to develop capacity that comes up to world-class performance standards. Both the Centre and the States must keep their policies under close review to ensure that new infrastructure, whether built by the public sector or the private sector, comes up to these standards.

12.9. A beginning has been made in the public sector, by setting targets for various infrastructure sectors to address the gaps in quantity and quality. Going in to the Eleventh Plan, the strategy would entail strengthening and consolidating these infrastructure-related initiatives, such as Bharat Nirman for building rural infrastructure, and sectoral initiatives, such as the RGGVY, APDRP, Accelerated Irrigation Benefit Programme (AIBP), NHDP, National Maritime Development Programme (NMDP) and the JNNURM.

12.10. The strategy for the Eleventh Plan also encourages private sector participation directly as well as through various forms of PPPs where desirable and feasible. As shown in Table 12.4, the share of the private sector in infrastructure investment will have to rise substantially from about 20% anticipated in the Tenth Plan to around 30% in the Eleventh Plan. It is expected that as in the case of the telecommunications sector, competition and private investment will not only expand capacity but also improve the quality of service in Indian infrastructure.

12.11. Achieving high volumes of private investment in infrastructure is not easy. It is necessary to develop an environment which is both attractive to investors and also seen to be fair to consumers, especially since many (but not all) infrastructure projects have an element of monopoly. This calls for an environment in which either the market itself is competitive giving consumers a choice among different suppliers, as in the case with telecommunications or freight container carriers; or concessions are given to the most competitive bidders in an environment where regulatory system limits user charges to reasonable levels and regulations set appropriate standards of service as in the case of airports, ports and roads.

12.12. The approach to PPPs must remain firmly grounded in principles which ensure that PPPs are formulated and executed in public interest with a view to achieving additional capacity and delivery of public services at reasonable cost. These partnerships must ensure the supplementing of scarce public resources for investment in infrastructure sectors, while improving efficiencies and reducing costs. As noted in the Approach to the Eleventh Plan, PPPs must aim at bringing private resources into public projects, not public resources into private projects.

12.13. The government's current initiatives in the area of PPPs are designed to achieve these objectives. Private investment in infrastructure is being encouraged in an environment which ensures competition and transparent regulation. Protection of public interest is being ensured by institutionalizing the necessary frameworks and processes for due diligence, checks and balances. Unless governance issues, such as those related to competition in service provision, collection of user charges, institutional capacity, regulation and dispute resolution are adequately addressed, financing or mobilization of sufficient resources for the requisite infrastructure investment may not be possible.

PROJECTIONS OF INVESTMENT IN INFRASTRUCTURE

12.14. The investment required by the Central and State Governments and the private sector in each of the ten major physical infrastructure sectors for sustaining a growth rate of 9% in GDP over the Eleventh Plan (2007–08 to 2011–12) and corresponding to the quantitative targets for the Eleventh Plan as presented in Box 12.1 is given in Table 12.4. The total investment amounts to Rs 2056150 crore. This level of investment amounts to an average of 7.6% of GDP (Table 12.2) during the Eleventh Plan as a whole.

12.15. A comparative picture of the sector-specific allocations in these two Plan periods is given in Table 12.3. Compared with investment levels achieved in the Tenth Plan period, the expected infrastructure investment in the Eleventh Plan is 2.36 times the amount of Rs 871445 crore or US$ 217.86 billion at constant 2006–07 price.

12.16. The telecom, transportation (comprising ports and airports), and storage improve their share in the total investment in the Eleventh Plan as compared to their share in the Tenth Plan. Irrigation, electricity and the transportation sectors comprising roads and railways are expected to invest more than double the actual absolute

TABLE 12.2
Projected Investment as Percentage of GDP (Bottom-up Estimates)

(Rs crore at 2006–07 price)

Years	Base year (2006–07 of Tenth Plan) (BE/RE)	2007–08	2008–09	2009–10	2010–11	2011–12	Total Eleventh Plan
GDP	4145810	4518933	4925637	5368944	5852149	6378843	27044506
Public Investment	175388	192107	227327	273543	332355	411226	1436559
Private Investment	49858	78166	94252	115724	146762	184687	619591
Total investment	225246	270273	321579	389266	479117	595913	2056150
				Investment as Percentage of GDP			
Public	4.23	4.25	4.62	5.09	5.68	6.45	5.31
Private	1.20	1.73	1.91	2.16	2.51	2.89	2.29
Total	5.43	5.98	6.53	7.25	8.19	9.34	7.60

Source: CSO for 2006–07, and computations of the Planning Commission.

TABLE 12.3
Sector-wise Investment Anticipated in the Tenth Plan and Projected for the Eleventh Plan

(Rs crore at 2006–07 price)

Sectors	Tenth Plan (Anticipated investment)			Eleventh Plan (Projected investment)		
	Rs crore	US$ billion @ Rs 40/$	Shares (%)	Rs crore	US$ billion @ Rs 40/$	Shares (%)
Electricity (incl. NCE)	291850	72.96	33.49	666525	166.63	32.42
Roads and Bridges	144892	36.22	16.63	314152	78.54	15.28
Telecommunication	103365	25.84	11.86	258439	64.61	12.57
Railways (incl. MRTS)	119658	29.91	13.73	261808	65.45	12.73
Irrigation (incl. Watershed)	111503	27.88	12.80	253301	63.32	12.32
Water Supply and Sanitation	64803	16.20	7.44	143730	35.93	6.99
Ports	14071	3.52	1.61	87995	22.00	4.28
Airports	6771	1.69	0.78	30968	7.74	1.51
Storage	4819	1.20	0.55	22378	5.59	1.09
Gas	9713	2.43	1.11	16855	4.21	0.82
Total (Rs crore)	871445	217.86	100.00	2056150	514.04	100.00

Source: Annual Plans and other Planning Commission documents and CSO.

investment in the Eleventh Plan, but would register some decline as a proportion in the overall pie. The need for investment in the electricity sector is greater than what has been projected in this chapter. However, a realistic assessment suggests that even the projections made in this chapter would pose serious policy and implementation challenges. If these challenges can be overcome in time, actual investments could exceed these projections.

PUBLIC PRIVATE BALANCE

12.17. Table 12.4 presents a breakup of investment in the public sector component showing the Centre and States separately and the private sector component for each sector for the Tenth Plan and for the Eleventh Plan. The anticipated public sector share of investment in the Tenth Plan across the ten major sectors was 80% and the balance 20% was contributed by the private sector. In the Eleventh Plan, the private sector's contribution would have to grow to around 30% or Rs 619591 crore (US$ 154.90 billion). Roads and bridges, telecommunications, ports, airports, storage and gas distribution are projected at higher than average private sector contribution ranging upwards of 30%, with over 60% in ports, airports and telecommunications. In the Eleventh Plan, private sector participation in asset

TABLE 12.4
Projected Investment in Infrastructure during Eleventh Five Year Plan

(Rs crore at 2006–07 price)

Sector	Tenth Plan (Anticipated Expendr.)	2007–08	2008–09	2009–10	2010–11	2011–12	Total Eleventh Plan	Share (%)
Electricity (incl. NCE)	291850	81954	101553	126380	158027	198611	666525	
Centre	102463	37808	43469	49989	57631	66420	255316	38.31
States	97553	20978	29729	41357	56670	76963	225697	33.86
Private	91834	23168	28355	35034	43726	55228	185512	27.83
Roads and Bridges	144892	51822	54789	59200	68370	79971	314152	
Centre	71534	18318	19446	20673	22618	26304	107359	34.17
States	66354	17534	18150	18889	20613	24815	100000	31.83
Private	7004	15970	17193	19638	25140	28852	106792	33.99
Telecommunications	103365	31375	38134	48593	61646	78690	258439	
Centre	49013	13525	14037	16061	17728	19401	80753	31.25
Private	54352	17850	24098	32532	43918	59289	177686	68.75
Railways (incl. MRTS)	119658	34225	40964	49525	60393	76701	261808	
Centre	108950	25925	31176	37974	46685	59693	201453	76.95
States (MRTS)	10402	1575	1788	1979	2170	2489	10000	3.82
Private	307	6725	8000	9572	11537	14519	50354	19.23
Irrigation (incl. Watershed)	111503	27497	35916	47189	62266	80433	253301	
Centre	13617	3367	4006	4782	5726	6879	24759	9.77
States	97886	24130	31911	42407	56540	73554	228543	90.23
Water Supply & Sanitation	64803	19298	22781	27323	33266	41063	143730	
Centre	42316	5152	6411	7991	9976	12474	42003	29.22
States	21465	13500	15558	18308	21995	26945	96306	67.00
Private	1022	646	812	1024	1295	1645	5421	3.77
Ports	14071	12409	14822	17374	19980	23410	87995	
Centre	2185	4898	5698	6243	6350	6700	29889	33.97
States	1530	598	658	724	796	850	3627	4.12
Private	10356	6913	8466	10407	12833	15860	54479	61.91
Airports	6771	5208	5520	5904	6646	7690	30968	
Centre	3823	1146	1369	1894	2205	2674	9288	29.99
States	12	50	–	–	–	–	50	0.16
Private	2936	4012	4151	4010	4441	5016	21630	69.85
Storage	4819	3777	4098	4446	4824	5234	22378	
Centre	577	755	820	889	965	1047	4476	20.00
States	866	1133	1229	1334	1447	1570	6713	30.00
Private	3377	1888	2049	2223	2412	2617	11189	50.00
Gas	9713	2708	3003	3332	3700	4111	16855	
Centre	8713	1714	1874	2049	2240	2450	10327	61.27
Private	1000	995	1129	1283	1460	1661	6528	38.73
Total (Rs crore)	871445	270273	321579	389266	479117	595913	2056150	
Centre	403189	112608	128305	148545	172123	204041	765622	37.24
States	296068	79499	99022	124998	160232	207186	670937	32.63
Private	172188	78166	94252	115724	146762	184687	619591	30.13

(Table 12.4 contd.)

(Table 12.4 contd.)

(Rs crore at 2006–07 price)

Sector	Tenth Plan (Anticipated Expendr.)	2007–08	2008–09	2009–10	2010–11	2011–12	Total Eleventh Plan	Share (%)
Total (US$ bn) @Rs 40/$	217.86	67.57	80.39	97.32	119.78	148.98	514.04	
Centre	100.80	28.15	32.08	37.14	43.03	51.01	191.41	37.24
States	74.02	19.87	24.76	31.25	40.06	51.80	167.73	32.63
Private	43.05	19.54	23.56	28.93	36.69	46.17	154.90	30.13
Total (Rs crore)	871445	270273	321579	389266	479117	595913	2056150	
Public	699257	192107	227327	273543	332355	411226	1436559	69.87
Private	172188	78166	94252	115724	146762	184687	619591	30.13
Total (US$ bn)@Rs 40/$	217.86	67.57	80.39	97.32	119.78	148.98	514.04	
Public	174.81	48.03	56.83	68.39	83.09	102.81	359.14	69.87
Private	43.05	19.54	23.56	28.93	36.69	46.17	154.90	30.13

Source: Annual Plans and other documents of the Planning Commission and CSO for the Tenth Plan period and computations of the Planning Commission for the Eleventh Plan period.

creation in roads and bridges, storage and gas distribution ranges between 34 and 50%, with electricity somewhat lower at 28% even as compared to the overall private sector average of 30%.

12.18. Central share in the overall infrastructure investment would decline from 46% in the Tenth Plan to 37.24% in the Eleventh Plan and the States' share will slightly decline to 32.63% compared to 34% anticipated in the Tenth Plan. Sector-wise, public and private shares as well as the shares of the Centre and States anticipated to be realized for the Tenth Plan are presented in Annexure 12.1. Comparable details for the projections of infrastructure investment for each year of the Eleventh Plan are shown in Table 12.4.

Rural Infrastructure

12.19. Improvement in rural infrastructure is crucial for broad-based inclusive growth of the economy and for bridging the ruralurban divide. The government has launched in 2005, a special programme, Bharat Nirman, for upgradation of rural infrastructure which aims to provide electricity to the remaining 125000 villages and to 23 million households; to connect the remaining 66802 habitations with all weather roads and construct 146185 km of new rural roads network; to provide drinking water to 55067 uncovered habitations; to provide irrigation to an additional 10 million hectares; and connect the remaining 66822 villages with telephones. It is estimated that out of the total projected investment of Rs 1436559 crore to be incurred by the Centre and the states in the Eleventh Plan, Rs 435349 crore (or 30.3%) would be spent exclusively towards improvement of rural infrastructure. The distribution across sectors is indicated in Table 12.5.

TABLE 12.5
Projected Investment in Rural Infrastructure

(Rs crore at 2006–07 price)

Sector	Projected Investment
Electricity	34000
Rural Roads	41347
Telecommunications	16000
Irrigation (incl. Watershed)	253301
Water Supply and Sanitation	90701
Total	435349

Source: Computations of the Planning Commission.

Role of the Public Sector

12.20. The public sector, including the public corporate sector, would continue to play a dominant role in investment for infrastructure. The total public sector investment envisaged in the Eleventh Plan is Rs 765622 crore by the Centre and Rs 670937 crore by the States. Investment by the private sector, which includes PPP projects, makes up the balance of Rs 619591 crore, which is 30% of the required investment during the Eleventh Plan a much higher share than the anticipated 20% during the Tenth Plan.

12.21. Of the projected investment of Rs 765622 crore by the Central Government, Rs 565622 crore is likely to be funded out of IEBR. In the case of States, Rs 444671 crore is expected from budgetary resources while about Rs 226266 crore is expected from their IEBR, as per details in Table 12.6. This would require a much higher scale of effort by the public sector undertakings, especially for raising debt on commercial terms.

THE NEED FOR DEBT FINANCING

12.22. The total requirement of debt by the public and private sectors is likely to be Rs 988035 crore (US$ 247.01 billion). However, the availability of debt financing for infrastructure during the Eleventh Plan is estimated at Rs 825539 crore or US$ 206.38 billion. There is a funding gap of Rs 162496 crore or US$ 40.62 billion for the debt component, the details of which are given in Table 12.7. Measures would have to be taken for addressing this gap.

12.23. The required investment in infrastructure would be possible only if there is a substantial expansion in internal generation and extra-budgetary resources of the public sector, in addition to a significant rise in private investment. The share of the private sector in total

TABLE 12.6
Source-wise Projected Investment

(Rs crore at 2006–07 price)

	2007–08	2008–09	2009–10	2010–11	2011–12	Total Eleventh Plan
1. Centre	112608	128305	148545	172123	204041	765622
Central Budget	29416	33517	38804	44963	53301	200000
Internal Generation (IEBR)	24958	28437	32922	38148	45222	169687
Borrowings (IEBR)	58234	66352	76819	89012	105518	395936
2. States	79499	99022	124998	160232	207186	670937
States Budgets	52689	65628	82844	106195	137315	444671
Internal Generation (IEBR)	8043	10018	12646	16211	20961	67880
Borrowings (IEBR)	18767	23376	29508	37826	48910	158386
3. Private	78166	94252	115724	146762	184687	619591
Internal Accruals/Equity	23450	28726	34717	44029	55406	185877
Borrowings	54716	65976	81006	102733	129281	433713
4. Total Projected Investment	270273	321579	389266	479117	595913	2056150
Non-Debt	138555	165875	201933	249546	312205	1068114
Debt	131718	155704	188333	229571	283709	988035

Source: Computations of the Planning Commission.

TABLE 12.7
Likely Sources of Debt

(Rs crore at 2006–07 price)

	2007–08	2008–09	2009–10	2010–11	2011–12	Total Eleventh Plan
1 Domestic Bank Credit	49848	63207	80147	101626	128862	423691
2 Non-Bank Finance Companies	23852	31485	41560	54859	72415	224171
3 Pension/Insurance Companies	9077	9984	10983	12081	13289	55414
4 External Commercial Borrowing (ECB)	19593	21768	24184	26868	29851	122263
5 Likely Total Debt Resources	102370	126444	156874	195435	244416	825539
6 Estimated Requirement of Debt (from Table 12.6)	131718	155704	187333	229571	283709	988035
US$ Billion	32.93	38.93	46.83	57.39	70.93	247.01
7 Gap between Estimated Requirement and Likely Debt Resources (6–5)	29348	29260	30460	34136	39292	162496
US$ Billion	7.34	7.31	7.61	8.53	9.82	40.62

Source: Computations of the Planning Commission.

infrastructure investment of around 30% overall, is far higher in some sectors, for instance in telecommunications, ports and airports where over 60% of the investments would have to come from the private sector. As a pre-requisite, this would require large infrastructure projects to be structured on sound commercial principles in an enabling policy and regulatory environment. If these initiatives succeed, India would deliver a large programme of PPPs, even by international standards, details of which are given in the next section.

Committee on Infrastructure

12.24. In order to provide direction to the effort to prioritize infrastructure development including, especially, the PPP effort, Government constituted a Committee on Infrastructure (CoI) in August 2004 under the chairmanship of the Prime Minister, with the objectives of initiating policies that would ensure time-bound creation of world class infrastructure, delivering services matching international standards, developing structures that maximize the role of PPPs and monitoring progress of key infrastructure projects to ensure that established targets are realized. The CoI is serviced by the Planning Commission through the Secretariat for the Committee.

12.25. CoI has identified several areas of reforms. The following Model Concession Agreements, Reports and Guidelines finalized under the aegis of CoI have been published by the Planning Commission:

- Guidelines for Financial Support to PPPs in Infrastructure.
- Guidelines on Formulation, Appraisal and Approval of PPP Projects.
- Scheme for Financing Infrastructure Projects through the India Infrastructure Finance Company Ltd. (IIFCL).
- MCA for PPPs in Highways.
- Report of the Task Force on the Delhi-Mumbai and Delhi-Howrah Freight Corridors.
- Report of the COS on Road Rail Connectivity of Major Ports.
- Report of the Core Group on Financing of the NHDP.
- Report of the Task Force on Financing Plan for Airports.
- Report of the Inter-Ministerial Groups on Customs Procedures and Functioning of Container Freight Station and Ports.
- Report of the Inter-Ministerial Group on Restructuring of National Highways Authority of India (NHAI).
- Report of the Task Force on Tariff Setting and Bidding Parameters for PPPs in Major Ports.
- Report of the Expert Committee on Road Safety and Traffic Management.
- MCA for Container Train Operation.
- Report of the Task Force on Financing Plan for Ports.
- Manual of Specifications and Standards for Two-Laning of Highways through PPPs
- MCA for PPPs in Ports.
- MCA for PPPs in the Operation and Maintenance of Highways.
- MCA for PPPs in State Highways.
- Guidelines for Pre-Qualification, including Model Request for Qualification (RFQ) of Bidders, for PPP projects.
- Guidelines for Invitation of Financial Bids, including Model Request for Proposal Document (RFP) for PPP projects.

Public–Private Partnership Appraisal Committee (PPPAC)

12.26. PPP projects typically involve transfer or lease of public assets, delegation of government authority for recovery of user charges, operation and/or control of public utilities/services in a monopolistic environment and sharing of risk and contingent liabilities by the government. With a view to conducting a thorough scrutiny and due diligence in the formulation, appraisal and approval of PPP projects, the Ministry of Finance in consultation with the Planning Commission has constituted a PPPAC consisting of the Secretary, Department of Economic Affairs, as chairman and Secretaries of the Planning Commission, Department of Expenditure, Department of Legal Affairs and the Administrative Department concerned, as members of the Committee.

12.27. PPP project proposals costing Rs 100 crore and above received from ministries/departments of the GoI are considered for approval by PPPAC. The PPP project proposals costing less than Rs 100 crore are considered for approval by the existing EFC mechanism.

12.28. A PPP Appraisal Unit (PPPAU) has also been set up within the Secretariat for CoI in the Planning Commission to appraise PPP projects received from Central and State/UT governments for VGF under the Scheme for Financial Support to PPPs in infrastructure.

India Infrastructure Finance Company Limited (IIFCL)

12.29. IIFCL was incorporated by the Ministry of Finance in consultation with the Planning Commission for providing long-term loans for financing infrastructure projects that typically involve long gestation periods. IIFCL provides financial assistance up to 20% of the project cost both through direct lending to project companies and by refinancing banks and financial institutions. IIFCL raises funds from both domestic and overseas markets on the strength of government guarantees, which are extended, if considered necessary.

Model Concession Documents

12.30. Because of the nature of the risks and the involvement of many participants in PPPs including project sponsors, lenders, government agencies and regulatory authorities, the terms of the project agreements as well as the tendering arrangements are usually complex. Given the complexity of PPP contracts and the exposure of government in such contracts, standardized documents and arrangements that provide predictability and mitigate risk to private capital are regarded as the best option for implementing a PPP programme of the magnitude envisioned under the Eleventh Plan. The use of standard documents also simplifies and expedites decision-making by the authorities. The CoI has, therefore, mandated the adoption of model documents. Projects that are based on duly approved MCAs do not require in-principle clearance from PPPAC prior to inviting expressions of interest.

12.31. The MCA for PPP projects in national highways was approved by the CoI and published in 2006. The Planning Commission has also published MCAs for ports, state highways, and operation and maintenance of highways that will serve as best practice guidance for the ministries and State Governments undertaking PPPs. Similarly, MCA for Operation of Container Trains has also been approved and adopted. MCAs for PPPs in other sectors, such as urban rail systems, airports, re-development of railway stations and public accommodation are under preparation. Standardized guidelines that incorporate key principles relating to the bid process for PPP projects have also been developed. Guidelines for the pre-qualification of bidders along with a Model Request for Qualification Document have been approved by CoI for application to all PPP projects. Guidelines for inviting financial bids on the basis of a Model RFP have also been approved and notified.

Financing

12.32. Recognizing that externalities engendered by infrastructure projects cannot always be captured by project sponsors, the VGF Scheme was notified in 2006 to enhance the commercial viability of competitively bid infrastructure projects which are justified by economic returns, but do not pass standard thresholds of financial returns. Under the scheme, grant assistance of up to 20% of project capital costs can be provided by the Central government to PPP projects, thus leveraging budgetary resources to access a larger pool of private capital. An additional grant of up to 20% of project costs can be provided by the sponsoring ministry or State Government.

Co-operation of State Governments

12.33. In a federal country like India, cooperation and support of State Governments is essential for development of world class infrastructure. The State Governments' support in maintenance of law and order, land acquisition, rehabilitation and settlement of displaced persons, shifting of utilities and obtaining environmental clearances is necessary. Many State Governments have also initiated several PPP projects to improve infrastructure.

ANNEXURE 12.1
Anticipated Plan Investment in Infrastructure in the Tenth Plan

(Rs crore at 2006–07 price)

	2002–03 (Actual)	2003–04 (Actual)	2004–05 (Actual)	2005–06 (Actual/RE)	2006–07 (BE/RE)	Tenth Plan Anticipated	Share (%)
Electricity (incl. NCE)	47612	53485	56956	62268	71529	291850	
Centre	14219	17336	19708	22867	28332	102463	35.11
States	20467	20566	18819	18329	19372	97553	33.43
Private	12926	15583	18428	21071	23825	91834	31.47
Roads	26605	20564	21379	34278	42065	144892	
Centre	15869	8761	8442	17509	20953	71534	49.37
States	9724	9693	11321	16083	19534	66354	45.80
Private	1013	2111	1616	686	1578	7004	4.83
Telecommunication	21644	12924	18108	24599	26090	103365	
Centre	15690	8649	9508	7957	7208	49013	47.42
Private	5954	4274	8600	16642	18882	54352	52.58
Railways (incl. MRTS)	18260	20366	22327	26117	32589	119658	
Centre	16644	18671	20362	23626	29647	108950	91.05
States	1616	1695	1964	2327	2800	10402	8.69
Private	–	–	–	165	142	307	0.26
Irrigation (incl. Watershed)	17467	18651	24770	25548	25068	111503	
Centre	2303	2318	2911	2884	3200	13617	12.21
States	15163	16333	21859	22663	21868	97886	87.79
Water Supply and Sanitation	9616	11040	12681	13749	17716	64803	
Centre	6936	7292	8470	8370	11248	42316	65.30
States	2520	3391	3925	5217	6411	21465	33.12
Private	159	357	286	162	57	1022	1.58
Ports	823	1379	4013	4516	3339	14071	
Centre	573	350	377	434	451	2185	15.53
States	250	280	300	340	360	1530	10.87
Private	-	749	3336	3742	2529	10356	73.60
Airports	535	659	691	1858	3029	6771	
Centre	533	653	670	927	1040	3823	56.46
States	–	–	–	–	12	12	0.18
Private	2	6	21	931	1977	2936	43.36
Storage	1851	1906	64	149	850	4819	
Centre	511	240	(-) 143	(-) 128	96	577	11.97
States	767	360	(-) 214	(-) 192	144	866	17.96
Private	574	1305	421	469	609	3377	70.07
Gas	1051	3399	464	1826	2972	9713	
Centre	921	3239	254	1586	2712	8713	89.70
Private	130	160	210	240	260	1000	10.30
Total (Rs crore)	145465	144372	161453	194909	225246	871445	
Centre	74201	67508	70560	86033	104887	403189	46.27
States	50507	52318	57974	64767	70501	296068	33.97
Private	20757	24546	32918	44108	49858	172188	19.76

(Annex 12.1 contd.)

(Annex 12.1 contd.)

(Rs crore at 2006–07 price)

	2002–03 (Actual)	2003–04 (Actual)	2004–05 (Actual)	2005–06 (Actual/RE)	2006–07 (BE/RE)	Tenth Plan Anticipated	Share (%)
Total (US$ bn)	36.37	36.09	40.36	48.73	56.31	217.86	
Centre	18.55	16.88	17.64	21.51	26.22	100.80	46.27
States	12.63	13.08	14.49	16.19	17.63	74.02	33.97
Private	5.19	6.14	8.23	11.03	12.46	43.05	19.76
Total (Rs crore)	145465	144372	161453	194909	225246	871445	
Public	124708	119827	128535	150800	175388	699257	80.24
Private	20757	24546	32918	44108	49858	172188	19.76
Total (US$ bn)	36.37	36.09	40.36	48.73	56.31	217.86	
Public	31.18	29.96	32.13	37.70	43.85	174.81	80.24
Private	5.19	6.14	8.23	11.03	12.46	43.05	19.76

Source: Annual Plans and other documents of the Planning Commission and CSO.

13

External Environment
Opportunities, Challenges and Risks

13.1. The strategy for Eleventh Plan must take into account the fact that our economy is now much more open to foreign trade and capital flows than it was fifteen years ago and is therefore more linked to the global economy. A globalized world is clearly one in which individual countries are more influenced by what happens elsewhere in terms of world prices, changes in world trade patterns and prices, changes in global capital market conditions and associated investor perceptions, changes in technology etc. The impact of globalization on developing countries has been much discussed and it is generally accepted that it presents both opportunities and also poses challenges and risks. These challenges are not identical for each country, because individual country circumstances differ. In this chapter we review the experience with managing trade and capital flows in the Tenth Plan and discuss some of the critical challenges arising from the external environment which we are likely to face.

MANAGING TRADE AND CAPITAL FLOWS

13.2. Managing the balance of payments is obviously one important challenge and an assessment of prospects in this dimension has been one of the basic functions of macroeconomic planning. This challenge is particularly large because of the changes that have taken place in our system of economic management since the liberalization of the economy in the Eighth Plan. It is important to note that transition to the new liberalized system has not posed problems on the external front. We have not had a balance of payments crisis since 1991, despite the global slow down after the East Asian crisis of 1997 and the sharp rise in oil prices in 2005. Contrary to the traditional fears that liberalization would exacerbate the scarcity of foreign exchange and make it difficult to manage the external of payments position, our actual experience has been a surfeit of riches.

13.3. Imports of goods and services have indeed increased as a percentage of GDP from about 10% in 1990–91 to 26% in 2006–07. However this increase has been paralleled by a corresponding increase in the exports of goods and services, particularly the latter, with the ratio as a percentage of GDP moving from 7.3% in 1990–91 to 22.8% in 2006–07. The current account deficit in recent years has varied from a small surplus, for example, 1.25% in 2002–03 and 2.31% in 2003–04 to a small deficit thereafter. The deficit is expected to be only –1.05 % of GDP in 2006–07. This compares with a deficit of –3.05% in 1990–91. Fortunately, managing deficit of this order will not present problems given the growing recognition of India's potential attractiveness as an investment destination. However, openness to capital flows can present problems for policy which need to be carefully calibrated. As far as trade is concerned, we need to exploit export opportunities opened by access to global markets by expanding our export of goods and services thus generating high quality employment. Countries such as China have exploited these opportunities very well and we need to learn from their experience. On the import front we need to be aware of the potentially disruptive effect of exposing domestic producers especially small producers to competitive pressure without giving them time for adjustment and assisting them where possible to improve their competitive capacity. Fortunately, the graduated pace of change followed thus far has avoided serious negative effect but much more needs to be done in this area to ensure that the benefits of trade expansion and access to global opportunities are more broadly shared and that special attention is paid to its gender aspects.

REVIEW OF EXPORTS IN THE TENTH PLAN

13.4. The broad composition of exports during the Tenth Plan is shown in Table 13.1. Total exports grew at about 24% per year but this was largely because petroleum products grew at 54.32%. Manufactured goods recorded an impressive compound annual growth rate of 19.92% and exports of agricultural and allied products also rose at a healthy rate of 16.22%. The share of petroleum products in the export basket rose substantially at the expense of manufactured and agricultural goods. Supported by strong commodity prices, the share of ores and minerals was stable around 6% during the last three years as compared to about 3.7% during first two years.

TABLE 13.1
Composition of Exports during the Tenth Plan

Commodity Group	2002–03		2003–04		2004–05		2005–06		2006–07*		CAGR
	% share	% growth	% share	% growth	% share	% growth	% share	% growth	% share	% growth	
Agri. and Allied Products	12.73	13.71	11.8	12.27	10.14	12.5	9.91	20.52	9.91	22.53	16.22
Ores and Minerals	3.78	58.12	3.71	18.67	6.08	114.4	5.98	21.36	5.57	14.11	40.99
Manufactured Goods	76.33	20.62	75.95	20.5	72.7	25.24	70.38	19.48	65.51	14.05	19.92
Petroleum Products	4.89	21.58	5.59	38.5	8.37	95.87	11.29	66.53	14.69	59.39	54.32
Others	2.27	1.15	2.95	57.37	2.71	20.28	2.44	11.15	4.29	115.43	35.60
Total	100	20.29	100	21.1	100	30.85	100	23.41	100	22.54	23.58

Note: *Figures are provisional.
Source: DGCI&S.

13.5. The growth rate of exports of agriculture and allied products picked up during the last two years of the Tenth Plan supported by a sudden and substantial spurt in the exports of raw cotton and continued good performance by the 'agriculture and allied products' group. The share of manufactured products in the export basket was affected by the slowing down of exports in two major sectors, that is, textiles and clothing and gems and jewellery. The textiles and clothing sector grew at a healthy pace of 12.14 % during the four years of the Tenth Plan but the growth slowed down to 3.65% during the final year when the industry was adversely affected by the exchange rate movement. The gems and jewellery sector recorded only a negligible growth during the terminal year of the Tenth Plan. Gems and jewellery, which has been a leading item in India's export basket sustained a reverse because of the decision of the US Government to withdraw the GSP benefit, whereby Indian exports have lost the preferential tariff advantage over some of the competing supplying countries that were not receiving the benefits earlier. The deceleration of manufacturing sector exports during the last two years is also a reflection of the fact that petroleum products are not classified as a manufactured product. If these products are added to manufactured goods, as they should be, the share of manufactured goods has been retained at over 80% throughout the Tenth Plan period.

13.6. The direction of India's exports may be seen in the Table 13.2. America and Europe continued to be important destinations of Indian exports although their combined share declined from 48.62 to 42.12%. There was a marginal decline also in the already low share of Commonwealth of Independent States (CIS) countries. On the other hand, the share of Asia and ASEAN steadily increased during the Tenth Plan and the region accounted for nearly half of India's exports during the last three years of the Plan period. Exports to Africa also registered a steady increase.

REVIEW OF IMPORTS IN THE TENTH PLAN

13.7. Imports recorded a compound annual growth rate of 29.96% in dollar terms during the Tenth Plan period. The high growth of imports was mainly on account of increase in oil prices. The quantity of crude oil imported rose from about 90 MMT in 2002–03 to 130 MMT during the year 2006–07. However the dollar value of crude oil

TABLE 13.2
Direction of India's Exports

	Percentage Share				
Region	2002–03	2003–04	2004–05	2005–06	2006–07*
Europe	24.17	24.54	23.55	24.16	22.89
EU Countries (27)	22.55	22.74	21.85	22.53	21.26
Other WE Countries	1.58	1.73	1.65	1.58	1.57
East Europe	0.04	0.07	0.05	0.05	0.06
Africa	4.65	4.82	5.05	5.27	6.63
Southern Africa	1.21	1.24	1.51	1.88	2.23
West Africa	2.02	1.99	1.98	1.84	1.91
Central Africa	0.22	0.24	0.19	0.16	0.16
East Africa	1.20	1.35	1.37	1.39	2.33
America	24.45	20.97	20.10	20.72	19.23
North America	21.99	19.19	17.52	17.82	15.85
Latin America	2.46	1.78	2.58	2.90	3.38
Asia	44.39	47.60	49.50	48.38	49.78
East Asia	1.15	1.10	1.03	0.97	1.18
ASEAN	8.76	9.12	10.09	10.10	9.95
WANA	14.28	15.95	17.04	16.19	18.22
NE Asia	14.92	14.70	15.83	15.74	15.31
South Asia	5.28	6.73	5.51	5.38	5.12
CIS & Baltics	1.75	1.63	1.31	1.21	1.17
CARs Countries	0.16	0.24	0.21	0.16	0.15
Other CIS Countries	1.59	1.39	1.10	1.05	1.02
Unspecified Region	0.59	0.44	0.49	0.24	0.27
Total	100.00	100.00	100.00	100.00	100.00

Note: Figures are provisional.
Source: DGCI&S.

imports in 2006–07 was more than US$ 57 billion, against about US$ 17.6 billion in 2002–03, that is, a more than three-fold increase over the period. The price of the Indian Basket of crude oil has increased from around US$ 26.6/bbl in 2002–03 to US$ 62.40 /bbl in 2006–07.

13.8. The broad composition of imports during the Tenth Plan may be seen in Table 13.3 given below. Bulk imports continued to account for a significant share of the total imports during the Tenth Plan mainly on account of crude oil. The crude oil and petroleum products taken together were the single most important category of imports during the Plan period. This group registered a compound annual growth rate of 32.45% during the Plan period accounting for about 26% to 30% of the total value of imports by India during the Tenth Plan. The share of 'other bulk items', which include important commodities like fertilizers, edible oils, non-ferrous metals, metal ores and products and iron and steel, witnessed a perceptible increase over the Plan period with a compound growth rate of 34.85%. The share of this group increased from 10.3% in 2002–03 to 13.6% in 2006–07. Iron and steel and metalliferrous ores and products are the two most important commodities of imports under the category of 'other bulk items'.

13.9. The share of machinery and project goods registered a significant increase during the Tenth Plan, increasing from 11.3% of total imports in 2002–03 to 18.1% in 2006–07. Imports of pearls, precious and semi-precious stones contracted sharply in the last two years of the Plan period after three years of very rapid growth reflecting the stagnation of exports of gems and jewellery.

13.10. The direction of the major imports may be seen in Table 13.4 The major change is that Asia and the ASEAN region recorded a significant increase during this

TABLE 13.3
Broad Composition of Imports

Commodity Group	2002–03		2003–04		2004–05		2005–06		2006–07*		CAGR
	% share	% growth	% share	% growth	% share	% growth	% share	% growth	% share	% growth	
A. Bulk Imports	38.98	20.74	37.44	22.21	38	44.82	40.9	43.96	43.59	36.16	33.17
(i) Petroleum Crude & Products	28.72	25.99	26.32	16.61	26.76	45.09	29.48	47.31	29.95	29.82	32.45
(ii) Other Bulk Items	10.26	8.13	11.12	37.9	11.24	44.19	11.42	35.98	13.64	52.51	34.85
B. Non-Bulk Imports	61.01	18.64	62.56	30.48	62.01	41.43	59.1	27.51	56.42	21.94	27.76
(i) Pearls, Precious & Semi-Precious Stones	9.87	31.16	9.12	17.58	8.45	32.18	6.12	–3.06	3.93	–18.03	10.13
(ii) Machinery & Project Goods	11.26	26.3	12.41	40.24	12.16	39.76	14.96	64.58	18.08	54.42	44.46
(iii) Others	39.88	13.99	41.03	30.91	41.4	43.98	38.02	22.86	34.41	15.6	25.00
Of which											
– Electronic Goods	9.12	48.05	9.60	34.05	8.96	33.13	8.88	32.51	8.37	20.42	33.35
– Gold & Silver	6.98	–6.42	8.77	59.89	10.00	62.62	7.59	1.50	7.69	29.40	26.16
Total	100.00	19.45	100.00	27.25	100.00	42.70	100.00	33.76	100.00	27.75	29.96

Note: Figures are provisional.
Source: DGCI&S.

TABLE 13.4
Direction of India's Imports

Percentage Share

Region	2002–03	2003–04	2004–05	2005–06	2006–07*
Europe	24.98	24.04	22.98	21.18	23.64
EU Countries (27)	20.90	19.29	17.31	17.44	18.25
Other WE Countries	4.07	4.73	5.66	4.72	5.36
East Europe	0.01	0.02	0.01	0.02	0.03
Africa	4.71	3.50	3.02	2.71	5.97
Southern Africa	3.52	2.51	2.06	1.77	1.53
West Africa	0.88	0.74	0.74	0.78	4.30
Central Africa	0.01	0.01	0.02	0.01	0.02
East Africa	0.30	0.24	0.20	0.15	0.12
America	9.86	8.90	8.81	8.75	10.59
North America	8.16	7.37	6.97	6.96	7.41
Latin America	1.70	1.53	1.84	1.79	3.18
Asia	30.12	35.36	36.18	34.58	57.51
East Asia	2.32	3.52	3.63	3.54	3.89
ASEAN	8.39	9.51	8.17	7.30	9.49
WANA	5.84	6.30	8.54	7.28	26.85
NE Asia	12.71	15.12	14.95	15.51	16.49
South Asia	0.86	0.91	0.89	0.95	0.79
CIS & Baltics	1.37	1.61	1.76	1.98	1.86
CARs Countries	0.06	0.06	0.06	0.05	0.08
Other CIS Countries	1.31	1.55	1.70	1.93	1.78
Unspecified Region	28.96	25.59	27.25	29.82	0.43
Total	100.00	100.00	100.00	100.00	100.00

Note: *Figures are provisional.
Source: DGCI&S.

period mainly on account of increase of import share of West Asia due to increase in all prices. The combined share of imports from America and Europe was steady during the Plan period.

TRADE BALANCE

13.11. The merchandise trade deficit widened sharply during the Tenth Plan as can be seen from Table 13.5, mainly on account of the growing oil import bill.

13.12. The extent to which the rising oil import values influenced the merchandise trade balance can be seen from Table 13.6 below. The substantial exports of petroleum products made a large contribution toward ameliorating the trade deficit.

TABLE 13.5
India's Trade Balance

(Value: US$ billion)

Year	Total Exports	Total Imports	Trade Balance
2002–03	52.7	61.4	–8.7
2003–04	63.8	78.1	–14.3
2004–05	83.5	111.5	–28.0
2005–06	103.1	149.2	–46.1
2006–07*	126.3	185.6	–59.3

Note: *Provisional.
Source: DGCI&S.

TABLE 13.6
Balance of Trade and Petroleum Products

(Value: US$ billion)

	2002–03	2003–04	2004–05	2005–06	2006–07*
BoT (Billion)	–8.7	–14.3	–28.0	–46.1	–59.3
BoT (without petroleum imports)	8.9	6.3	1.9	–2.1	–7.2
BoT (excluding petroleum from import and export)	6.4	2.7	–5.1	–13.8	–25.7

Note: P= Provisional.
Source: DGCI&S.

THE BALANCE OF PAYMENTS IN THE ELEVENTH PLAN

13.13. Projections of the balance of payments (BoP) for the Eleventh Plan have been discussed in Chapter 2. Exports are projected to grow at about 20% per year in US$ terms which is marginally lower than the rate at which they have been growing over the Tenth Plan. The current account deficit projected for the Eleventh Plan period could range between 1.2% and 2% of GDP. Financing a current account deficit of this order should not present a problem given the foreign capital inflows that are taking place and which can be expected to continue barring unexpectedly severe downside shock to the world economy. In fact, the capital flows we have been experiencing in recent years have proved difficult to manage leading to a sharp build up in foreign exchange reserves and upward pressure on the exchange rate which has adverse consequence.

STRATEGY FOR EXPORTS

13.14. A vigorous strategy for promoting exports must be an important part of our strategy for managing the balance of payment in the years ahead. An enhanced target of US$ 160 billion has been fixed for 2007–08 (the first year of the XI Plan) indicating a growth rate of 26.6%. On an average, the exports are projected to grow at the rate of about 20% or more during the Eleventh Five Year Plan period in current US$ terms.

13.15. To achieve this target, it is necessary to achieve the general conditions that would promote rapid growth of the economy, including especially the development of efficient infrastructure services. Of these, reliable power supply is perhaps the most important especially if we wish to strengthen the competitive capacity of our middle and small enterprises. In addition it is necessary to ensure the following:

- Promoting production and exports of commercial crops and agri-based processed products.
- Facilitating the provision of critical specialized infrastructure necessary for promoting exports of various commodities including agricultural and marine products in collaboration with State Governments where necessary.
- Expansion and modernization of infrastructure and quality control mechanisms through upgradation of technology and greater use of IT.
- Strengthening of various institutions involved in consultancy, design, human resource development and information services needed for export promotion. This is especially important for exploiting the export potential of medium and small exporters.
- Strengthening the institutions providing general support services to the exporters.

13.16. In line with government's policy of according a high priority to agriculture, the Eleventh Plan must place special emphasis on promoting production and exports of commercial crops and agro-based processed products. Ageing bushes/ plants are acting as a major constraint to the growth of the plantation sector leading to decline in productivity, high cost of production and deterioration in the quality of products. With a view to ensuring healthy growth and improved productivity in the plantation sector, a Special Purpose Tea Fund (SPTF) has been set up under the Tea Board for funding assistance for re-plantation and rejuvenation of old tea . The Scheme will be implemented during the Eleventh Plan period. Similar initiatives are envisaged to be put in place for other plantation crops viz. coffee, rubber, spices, cashew and coconut.

13.17. The following areas should receive special attention during the Eleventh Plan: (i) Simplification of procedures, (ii) streamlining of documentary requirements, (iii) accelerated implementation of EDI initiatives, (iv) fuller neutralization of taxes, (v) improving infrastructure facilities to international standards, and (vi) initiating necessary institutional and structural changes. Streamlining trade data infrastructure to remove anomalies and to enable providing a sound and timely basis for policy formulation along with improved trade infrastructure would be the focus of Eleventh Five Year Plan.

13.18. In order to reduce transaction costs, time limits must be fixed for various clearances/approvals/filing of documents.

OPPORTUNITIES IN EXPORTS OF GOODS AND SERVICES

13.19. Globalization provides us with a number of opportunities which we can exploit to our advantage provided we can take appropriate steps domestically.

PROSPECTS FOR MANUFACTURING EXPORTS

13.20. Manufacturing was the most heavily protected sector of the Indian economy with the most extensive Quantitative Restrictions (QRs) and the highest tariff rates till the end of the 1980s. Since the early 90s , one of the objectives of Trade Policy reforms has been to enable the manufacturers of exported products to functioned in an effectively free trade regime so that that they have access to inputs at international prices and customs duties and internal taxes borne by the exported product are fully rebated. As mentioned earlier competitive restrictions on imports were progressively abolished (except for reasons of safety and security) and import duties were broght down steeply. This trend of tariff reduction continued during the Tenth Plan period and the peak basic customs duties applying to a majority of non-agricultural products were reduced every year, from 30% at the beginning of 2002–03 to 10% at the end of 2006–07. As a result the simple average applied tariff rates on non agricultural products declined sharply during the Tenth Plan as shown in Table 13.7.

TABLE 13.7
Simple Average Applied Rate (Total)

	2001–02	2002–03	2003–04	2004–05	2005–06	2006–07
Agricultural Products	44.2	41.3	41.3	36.8	36.9	36.9
Non-agricultural products	35.9	32.6	29.5	20.8	15.5	13.3
All commodities	37.1	33.7	31.3	22.9	18.3	16.5

Source: Calculations based on Data from Budget Document.

13.21. The Eleventh Plan will address the various issues involved so as to facilitate quicker and hassle-free movement of goods by road in order to reduce the time taken for transportation of goods from the production centres to the port of export, which is an important factor in determining the cost of transaction. To facilitate trade further, One Stop Documentation Centres (OSDCs) will be established in all major airports/ seaports/ ICDs. Full neutralization of indirect taxes including those imposed at the State level will be ensured in the Eleventh Five Year Plan so that Indian exports do not become uncompetitive by carrying the burden of internal and border taxes.

13.22. With the complete elimination of QRs and reduction of 'peak tariff' rates to 10% in non-agricultural products (with some exceptions), it is the manufacturing sector that has seen the most noteworthy trade liberalisation . After removal of most domestic controls on this sector, it has also been a significant beneficiary of the opening up of the capital account and the consequent flows of FDI, FII, and ECB. Though the initial surge in manufacturing GDP, following the domestic and import liberalization from 1991–92 to 1993–94, petered out around 1997–98, the manufacturing sector has again performed well after 2003–04. As competitive pressures on this sector were balanced by greater access to higher quality imported inputs, capital goods, finance and technology, the global competitiveness of this sector has increased significantly. This is reflected in the restoration of high growth in manufacturing GDP and in the surge in outward FDI in the form of acquisition of foreign companies by Indian ones.

13.23. To ensure that this trend is strengthened and expanded it is necessary to reduce peak tariffs to 5%, for non-agricultural products eventually, make progress towards fuller capital account convertibility, accelerate the liberalization and development of the financial sector (e.g., long-term debt market) and complete the elimination of restrictions and controls (e.g., SSI reservation). Consideration of possible reduction of tariffs on agricultural products will have to await an international compact for reform of world trade in agriculture at the WTO negotiations.

13.24. The fact that manufacturing growth is high does not automatically mean that the sector does not suffer from some distortions. Inappropriate labour laws and cumbersome and pointless rules and procedures impose a cost that is separate from and over and above the wages that are paid to the worker. There are often high transactions cost of implementing the laws and the losses imposed by labour inflexibilities when demand falls. This may be one of the reasons why the historically natural shift of labour from agriculture to manufacturing has not taken place at the rate expected and the share of labour force in agriculture is so much higher than the share of GDP from agriculture.

13.25. The modern organized manufacturing sector has responded to the higher direct and indirect cost of labour (life time employment guarantee) by adopting more capital- and skill-intensive technology than it would have otherwise. It has also organized production processes so that labour-intensive stages of production and services are carried out in the unregistered sector. The more innovative entrepreneurs have focused on niche export markets by adopting technology to replace large numbers of unskilled labour with fewer semi-skilled workers. This has happened in conventional labour-intensive sectors like textiles as well as in labour intensive segments of sectors such as automobiles (components) and chemicals. Manufacturing has therefore developed some comparative advantage in what may be termed relatively skilled labour-intensive manufacturing. This is what will drive the growth of manufacturing GDP, outward FDI and manufactured exports. Though the private sector has geared up to exploit these opportunities, regulatory systems must be modernized (e.g. testing of drugs) and infrastructure support provided wherever necessary (e.g. specialized ports/berths for auto export) so as to support private efforts.

13.26. However the rate of growth of unskilled employment in the organized sector could continue to suffer as long as labour rigidities are not appropriately addressed.

PROSPECTS FOR SERVICES EXPORTS

13.27. In the first 30 years of independence the emphasis on higher education coupled with slow GDP growth created an excess supply of highly educated manpower that could not be absorbed productively within the country. A small part of this stock of educated manpower migrated to the West and participated in the high tech wave linked to IT and internet. At a later stage, domestic entrepreneurship was able to couple the stock of highly educated manpower available domestically with network linkages with highly skilled NRI manpower abroad to generate the IT export boom in the 1990s.

13.28. India witnessed a steady growth in proportion of trade in services to total trade and this can be largely attributed to trade in IT and ITES. Services trade share has grown at the same rate as goods trade over the 1990s, that is, about 6.5% and the share of services in total trade is about 24%. Services exports grew by 71% in 2004–05 and reached US$46 billion. While India's share in world merchandise exports in 2004 was 0.8%, the corresponding share in world commercial services exports was 1.9%. India's share in world markets for IT software and services (including BPO) increased from 1.7% in 2003–04 to 2.3% in 2004–05 and an estimated 2.8% in 2005–06.[1]

13.29. An important reason for growth of the services sector, is the impact of trade liberalization and reforms on growth of services. According to one study[2] sectors that were open for FDI, external trade, or private ownership, etc. were the ones which experienced faster growth. Lower tariff (adjusted for changes in real effective exchange rate) and lower non-tariff barriers (in terms of import coverage ratio) were also found to have led to an increase in the usage of services in manufacturing sector. The process appears to have been aided by other reforms undertaken in this decade.

[1]See *Economic Survey 2005–06*.

[2]Gordon, J. and P. Gupta (September 2004), Understanding India's Services Revolution, IMF working Paper WP/04/171.

13.30. At the disaggregated level, exports of communications, computer & information services have more than doubled since the turn of the century (Table 13.7).

13.31. Studies confirm that India exhibits a strong revealed comparative advantage (RCA) in services as compared to goods. Between 1996 and 2000, the RCA index for services increased by 74% while that for goods declined by 15% [World Bank (2004)]. This increase in RCA of services was mainly on account of 'other business services' which include software exports, finance, communication, management, consultancy and telecommunication sectors.

13.32. At the disaggregated level, we find that India has a revealed comparative advantage vis-à-vis rest of the world in commercial services and other services (Table 13.8). In contrast India's RCA in transport and travel services has declined overtime.

TABLE 13.8
India's Exports and Imports of Disaggregated Services, 1990–2003

	Exports (US$ million)					
	1990	1995	2000	2001	2002	2003
Communications	....	....	598.8	1103.9	779.4	1065.9
Construction	....	....	501.9	65.1	231.4	284.1
Insurance	123.3	170.2	257.0	282.0	331.9	408.9
Financial	....	....	276.0	306.1	598.2	392.1
Computer & Information	....	....	4727.4	7407.4	8889.3	11365.7
Royalities & Licence Fees	1.3	1.4	82.6	37.2	20.2	25.2
Other Business Services	1967.1	2119.7	4147.8	2349.0	2699.1	2601.0
Personal, Cultural & Recreational	....	....	....	....	....	....
Government, N.I.E	15.4	11.5	653.7	537.9	352.9	305.1
	Imports (US$ million)					
	1990	1995	2000	2001	2002	2003
Communications	....	....	104.8	266.8	1002.6	610.5
Construction	....	....	127.1	470.3	601.0	1208.9
Insurance	343.9	558.8	813.2	810.9	892.6	1168.9
Financial	....	....	1277.2	1780.1	1434.3	488.0
Computer & Information	....	....	576.8	910.9	905.3	659.3
Royalities & Licence Fees	72.5	90.3	282.5	317.0	345.2	420.8
Other Business Services	1715.0	2713.8	4320.7	3732.5	4084.0	8088.1
Personal, Cultural & Recreational	....	....	....	....	....	....
Government, N.I.E	147.0	205.7	290.4	306.9	262.9	199.2

Source: Reserve Bank of India.

TABLE 13.9
Revealed Comparative Advantage (RCA)* of India in Services

	1980	1990	1998	1999	2000	Average (1998–2000)
Commercial Services	1.6	1.1	1.3	1.5	1.6	1.4
Transport Services	0.4	0.7	0.6	0.6	0.5	0.6
Travel Services	2.0	1.0	0.9	0.7	0.6	0.7
Other Services	0.9	1.2	1.3	1.5	1.6	1.4

Note: * RCA = (India's Export of ith Services to world /total export of Indian services)/(world export of ith services /total world export of services).
Sources: RBI 2005; World Bank, 2004.

13.33. Software services constitute around 50% of total exports while travel and transportation services constitute around 30%. Together these three services constitute around 80% of India's exports of services (Table 13.9). The high share of travel services in export earnings but a declining RCA and a falling share of travel in total exports of services highlight the urgency of formulating trade-boosting policies with respect to travel and tourism.

TABLE 13.10
Composition of India's Services Exports

	Service export (million US$)		Share in service exports (%)	
	2000–01	2003–04	2000–01	2003–04
Travel	3497	4122	22	17
Transportation	2046	3260	13	13
Insurance	270	420	2	2
Communication Services	1138	1047	7	4
Construction services	536	465	3	2
Financial services	347	315	2	1
Softwware services	6341	12200	41	49
News agency services	114	59	1	0

Source: RBI 2005.

IT AND ITES

13.34. Trade in IT and ITES has emerged as the main driver of India's growth of trade in services. Both domestic and international market for Indian IT-ITES has been increasing steadily. Exports have increased rapidly in the last six years (i.e., from US$4 billion in 2000 to around US$ 24 billion in 2006). Total market for Indian IT-ITES is around US$30 billion in 2006.

13.35. The competitiveness of India in IT and ITES trade has been examined by many analysts. For 2005, the Global Services Location Index[3] showed that India remained the best offshore location by a wide margin, although wage inflation and the emergence of lower-cost countries have decreased its overall lead.[4] Close competitors in this field were China and Thailand. Improved infrastructure and relevant people skills have increased the attractiveness of China as a low-cost option for servicing Asian markets. Thailand jumped from 13th to 6th in the 2005 Index and Southeast Asian countries had four of the top six locations on the Index.

[3]previously known as the Offshore Location Attractiveness Index
[4]A.T Kerney Global Services Location Index,2005

13.36. The rise and expansion of the Indian IT and ITES services industry is a much talked about subject the world over. Total export revenues earned by this sector have grown from US$ 7.7 billion 2001–02 to US$ 31.3 billon in 2006–07, thus showing a near 32 % compounded growth. India now accounts for 65% of the global market in offshore IT and 46% of the ITES market . A majority of the Fortune 500 and Global 2000 corporations are sourcing IT and ITES from India. Export forecast for the Eleventh Plan period is estimated at US$ 37.6 billion for 2007–08 which is expected to increase to US$ 86.6 billion in 2011–12 according to NASSCOM McKinsey Report 2005. The domestic software services market however is growing at a lower rate compared to software exports. From US$ 3 billion in 2002–03 the domestic market grew to nearly US$ 5 billion in 2004–05. Clearly Indian software services are a globalized and outward looking sector.

13.37. In the past three years, the reputation of the Indian IT and ITES industry has grown worldwide fuelled by greater commercial presence of the Indian IT companies in the US, UK, and other EU countries, more numbers of cross-border acquisitions by Indian companies, more business processing outsourcing by global companies from India and a movement by Indian companies towards a higher value added products and services.

13.38. The growth of IT/ITES industry has helped to create both direct and indirect employment. Indirectly the industry employs about three million people. Indirect employment arises out of expenditure on vendors including telecom, power, construction, facility management, IT, transportation, catering and other services. The industry has also created induced employment arising out of consumption expenditure of employees on food, clothing, utilities, recreation, health and other services.

13.39. Technological changes at a global level have led to the tremendous growth in the IT sector with the emergence of a number of new services (e.g. software development or internet access) and increasing tradability of existing services (e.g. cross-border medical diagnosis using online or video conferencing medium). The Indian software sector has been able to keep pace with changes at the global level, which is demonstrated by the double digit growth in the software and related services sector since the later half of 1990s and emergence of new services sector activities (e.g. BPO centres). Government policies including deregulation (such as tax exemption, reduction of tariffs on software from 114% to zero, amendment of the copyright law etc) and incentives at the right time in right measures facilitated the growth of the Indian software industry since the 1990s. India's main advantage in its software sector story is that the sector has been able to tap into the pool of human resources that includes, engineering graduates, software professionals and English-speaking young graduates prepared to work in BPO centers.

13.40. India has a comparative advantage in Mode 1 as captured by outsourcing activities, Mode 3 as seen in increasing outward investment by Indian companies in US, UK and other developed and developing country markets and Mode 4 as captured by movement of Indian software professionals in the US, EU, etc. While a part of the movement by the software professionals is permanent and thus falls under migration, a significant part is temporary as demonstrated by a growing number of Indian software professionals returning to India from Silicon Valley of the US and other places.

13.41. Along with the rising opportunities in this sector, there are also many challenges faced by this sector in the recent years. These include:

- The prospect of protectionist legislations in developed countries and backlash against the BPO industry for the fear of loss of jobs in developed countries are some of the impediments to increasing exports of these services.
- A rise in the concerns over the security of data on customers which BPO professionals have access to and emerging shortages of skilled professionals.
- The Indian IT/ITES industry has been engaged more in developing low value and low technology products and services and less in innovation and back office processing work.
- An inadequate regime for preventing piracy in the IT/ITES industry is also viewed as a possible hindrance to foreign multinationals from moving their R&D outsourcing units to India.

13.42. Several initiatives have been taken to further enhance the availability of and access to suitable talent for IT-ITES in India. An image-enhancement programme is also in place to build greater awareness about the career opportunities in this segment. A comprehensive skill assessment and certification programs for entry-level talent and executives (low-middle level management) has been launched.

13.43. For India to fully capitalize on the opportunity and sustain its present lead in the global IT/ITES space, there is a need to focus on skill development to enhance the talent pool advantage, strengthening infrastructure to lower the transaction costs of business; and improve the domestic regulatory provisions.

HEALTH SERVICES

13.44. Rising income levels and the emergence of health insurance has facilitated the growth of high quality health care sector in India although the capacity to pay for health services remains limited to middle and high income brackets. With the opening of the insurance market in 2000 to private players, health and medical insurance has shown significant growth. Though at present, only 2.5 million people are covered under voluntary medical insurance. Cashless claim facilities offered by many players have led to a significant rise in health insurers.

13.45. The public health care system is not able to meet the growing demands for health care facilities. The gap between demand and supply has to be bridged by the private players, and this has facilitated the growth of the corporate health care industry in India. Emergence of strong corporate players in health care is not a substitute for expansion of public sector health facilities especially for the bulk of our population but it has led to professionalization of the industry, better hospital management and higher investments in infrastructure facilities.

13.46. An international dimension of the growth of the health care industry is the phenomenon of what is called medical tourism. Thailand has been able to attract more than one million medical tourists due to world-class infrastructure facilities in Thailand. India should be able to replicate the Thailand example by focusing on development of good-quality medical as well as tourism infrastructure. India certainly has the potential and the capacity to attract more than one million tourists per annum.

13.47. There are two clear advantages for India in the field of medical tourism. The first and the foremost is the cost advantage. The second unique advantage of India is that it offers holistic medicinal services. With yoga, meditation, ayurveda, allopathy and natural herbal treatments, India offers a unique basket of services to foreign patient-tourists that is difficult to match by other countries. Kerala has been the pioneering State in this area as evidenced by the fact that Kerala and ayurveda have virtually become synonymous with each other. The preference for health tourism in Kerala is so strong that Kerala Ayurveda Centre (KAC) has been established at multiple locations in various major cities. Karnataka has also taken some very pioneering steps in promoting medical tourism. The Government of Karnataka has planned to setup Bangalore International Health City Corporation in order to cater to international patients for a wide variety of health care products and treatments. The recent operations of children from Pakistan in Bangalore have not only helped boost the medical economy in the State, but also helped in fostering goodwill, peace and harmony between India and Pakistan.

13.48. In Maharashtra, there is a wide array of speciality and super-speciality hospitals that can help promote medical tourism. Some of the major hospitals already in the business of medical tourism are Lilavati Hospital, Jaslok Hospital, Breach Candy, Hinduja Hospital, Wockhardt Hospital, and Apollo NUSI Wellness Retreat. The Asian Heart Institute at Mumbai's Bandra-Kurla Complex offers state-of-the-art facilities for all types of heart ailments. Hotels such as Hyatt, JW Marriott, Renaissance and Resort offer extensive spa facilities for both domestic and international tourists.

13.49. The Indian Health care Federation has prepared a roadmap for making India a world-class destination for medical tourism. Accreditation of Indian hospitals is paramount for medical tourism. This will help in ensuring quality standards across a spectrum of specialty and super-specialty hospitals. In order to encourage medical tourism, air connectivity needs to be strengthened for all the major cities in the country especially Delhi, Chennai, Bangalore, Pune, Hyderabad and Kolkata. Health-support infrastructure also needs to be created at the airports and other travel junctions. It is also essential to establish Indian health care brand synonymous with safety, trust and excellence. One-stop centres need to be established in key international markets to facilitate inflow of foreign patients, and immigration process needs to be streamlined for medical visitors.

13.50. A related area which can be exploited is provision of back end health care related services. Health care majors in the developed world, especially the US, are already outsourcing back-end health care services to Indian BPO firms. The major health care BPO operations in the country are Hinduja TMT (claims adjudication), Apollo Health Street (claims adjudication, billing and coding), Comat Technologies (transcription), Datamatics (transcription and forms processing) and Lapiz (medical billing).

MULTILATERAL TRADE NEGOTIATIONS

13.51. Since India is today much more integrated in the world economy than it was in the past, it needs a well-functioning rule based trading system more than in the past. Working constructively towards a fair and balanced agreements in the Doha Round is therefore an essential part of managing globalization. Since India had taken major strides toward liberalization of its trade and investment regime after the conclusion of the Uruguay Round on an autonomous basis, it entered into the Round with a strong bargaining position of being able to offer tariff bindings (which is what trade negotiations are about) without much threat of disruption. Although our bound tariffs on agricultural products are high, since domestic support is incomparably lower in India than in the industrialized countries, we have considerable leverage in agricultural negotiations as well.

13.52. Unfortunately the Doha Round currently appears to be in serious difficulty because of continued differences among the principal participants. India's priority in agriculture must remain seeking steep reduction in the levels of agricultural subsidies prevailing in the industrialized countries. The agreement to eliminate all forms of export subsidies was no doubt a very positive development. However, the fact remains that export subsidies have been and will be effectively substituted by domestic support. Obtaining cuts in this pillar therefore constitutes the key to success. It is important for access not only in the subsidizing country but in third country markets as well. Participants have so far focused on the level of cuts in Overall Trade Distorting Support and the Total Aggregate Measurement of Support.

13.53. The negotiations have not given adequate attention to one important point that has been made by G20 for putting some limitation on decoupled income payments. The architecture of the Agreement on Agriculture was based on the belief that fully decoupled income support caused no or minimal distortion to trade and production. Since then, two aspects have come to light. First, that in the real world there is no such thing as fully decoupled income support. Second, economists now agree that it was not quite right to characterize even fully decoupled income payments as minimally distorting. As observed in a OECD study 'any policy that transfers income to producers could conceivably have some effect on production decisions by increasing farm incomes and farmers' wealth, by reducing income risks and by altering farmers' expectations. Unless deep reform is accomplished in domestic support by the developed countries developing countries cannot be expected to reduce tariffs on important agricultural products, which provide the means of livelihood to a large section of the population. In India the dependence on agriculture for employment and livelihood is very high and this is the central reason why India will need flexibility through special safeguards and in special products, both in coverage and treatment, unless radical reform in domestic support is adopted by the major industrialized countries encompassing not only steep reduction in what has been hitherto regarded as trade distorting but also strict disciplines on the Green Box payments which put money in the hands of the farmer from publicly funded government programmes.

13.54. In services, India's major interest is the liberalization of cross-border trade (Modes 1&2) and also in Mode 4 which relates to movement of person. In cross-border trade India has requested for broad-based commitments across a wide range of service sectors. In Mode 4 the main request by India is in respect of admission of independent professionals and contractual service suppliers for provision of services. It has been pressing for reduction of impediments such as visa and immigration procedures, economic needs test, work permit norms, etc. Its main trading partners have not been forthcoming in offering openings for professionals under Mode 4. Most members have not offered any commitment in the categories of contract service providers and independent professionals. Where a response has been forthcoming it is lacking in sectoral spread. Efforts to take up visa and immigration matters in the discussions on Domestic Regulations have also not gone very far.

13.55. India has autonomously liberalized Mode 3 in many sectors. Today FDI is allowed in all but a few service sectors such as retail trade, and establishment restrictions exist in accountancy and legal services. Among important service sectors, foreign equity caps of less than 50% apply only to insurance, print and electronic media covering news and current affairs, air transport and higher caps apply to telecommunications and private sector banking at 74%. India should be in a position to bind most of these, and perhaps go even further in exchange for comparable concessions in the areas of India's interest.

13.56. Since the Doha Round began, India has brought down its import tariffs on non-agricultural products successively every year and the peak tariffs for non-agricultural products at the beginning of the Eleventh Plan period are 10% (except for a handful of products). While the Swiss formula has been accepted for effecting cuts in tariffs, the negotiations are stalled by disagreement on the coefficients that should be applicable and particularly on the difference between the coefficients to be adopted by the developing and developed countries. The objection about accepting a lower co-efficient in the Swiss formula arises from the need to provide assurance that India is dealt with fairly. The World Trade Organizaton (WTO) rules and the Doha Ministerial Declaration speak of less than full reciprocity in reduction commitments being expected from the developing countries. Past practice suggests that reciprocity is a function of two factors viz., trade coverage and depth of reduction. When all the trade is being covered the extent of reduction becomes the sole measure of reciprocity. If the coefficients suggested by the developed countries (10 for the developed and 15 for the developing) were to be adopted India would be reducing its bound tariffs by 73%, the EC by 33% and the USA by 35%. This is clearly not consistent with the principle of reciprocity in trade negotiations and far removed from the agreed standard of less than full reciprocity from the developing countries.

13.57. Developed countries argue that the developing countries must lower their tariffs by a larger proportion because their bound tariffs were higher at the outset. However this ignores the fact that trade negotiation must start from the balance that was struck during the last Round. India has been autonomously reducing tariffs since the launching of the Round but it has a right to receive negotiating concessions for converting the applied levels into contractual commitments under the WTO Agreement. If the proportionate reduction by the developed countries is less, a reciprocal balance can be established in one of two ways. Either the developed countries deliver additional concessions in other areas (Mode 4 in services for instance) or India should be allowed to restore parity in reciprocity by adopting an appropriately high coefficient.

13.58. India has a strong interest in a successful conclusion of the Doha Round and should aim at the negotiations ending at a high level of ambition even if the impasse may need to be prolonged to accomplish such an outcome. We should not be deterred by the fear that the trend toward regional arrangements would strengthen and trade conflicts would intensify. The geopolitical dynamic which drives regional arrangements will remain unaltered as it did despite the successful conclusion of the Uruguay Round and such arrangement were broadened and strengthened and new ones were created with redoubled vigour at that time. There is no doubt a distinct possibility of increased trade disputes especially in agriculture after the demise of the Peace Clause, but India should not be daunted by the possibility of increased trade disputes as the major subsidizing countries are likely to face disputes and trade friction could eventually prove to be a tonic for the trading system if it helps to create a sense of urgency among the major players and a political will to effect deep reform in agriculture by the time they return to the negotiating table.

REGIONAL TRADE AGREEMENTS

13.59. Paradoxically, the successful conclusion of the Uruguay Round and the establishment of the WTO, was followed by a wave of regional trade agreements in the world. India too took similar steps. The India-Sri Lanka FTA was formed in 1998, and South Asian Preferential Trade Agreement was replaced by South Asian Free Trade Agreement (SAFTA) in January 2004. Several initiatives were taken for PTA or FTA with trading partners not only in the region but also outside the region. The new direction of trade policy toward regional trade agreements was given during the Ninth Plan period but the move intensified during the Tenth Plan. The position at the beginning of the Eleventh Plan is the following:

- Three FTAs are in existence viz., India-Sri Lanka FTA, SAFTA, and Indo-Singapore Comprehensive Economic Cooperation Agreement. Within SAFTA unilateral preferences have been extended to Bangladesh and Nepal.
- Apart from Asia-Pacific Trade Agreement (APTA) and Global System of Trade Preferences (GSTP) India has entered into four PTAs viz., Indo-Afghanistan PTA, India-Thailand Framework Agreement, Indo-Mercosur PTA and India-Chile PTA, the latter two not having been implemented until the beginning of the Eleventh Plan. Negotiations are ongoing for FTAs with the ASEAN, Thailand, Gulf Cooperation Council, Mauritius, South Korea, Japan, Israel, and the European Union. In the case of Mauritius it is envisaged that there would be PTA in goods and FTA in Services and investment. Another initiative is the Bay of Bengal Initiative Multi-Sector Technical and Economic Cooperation Framework Agreement, which envisages an FTA among Bangladesh, India, Sri Lanka, Myanmar, and Thailand. Negotiations are underway also for broadening the FTA in goods with Sri Lanka into a comprehensive economic cooperation agreement, embracing services and investment as well.
- Joint Study Groups have been set up for closer economic cooperation with China, Malaysia and Russia and a similar initiative has been taken in the context of India-Brazil-South Africa (IBSA)

13.60. India's engagement in a large number of regional trade initiatives raises some issues. There are strong geopolitical reasons for promoting close economic cooperation in South Asia and also with the countries of South East Asia and East Asia. India must aim to be a partof a future East Asian Free Trade Area, which could eventually evolve out of the ASEAN plus Six. But in order to avoid disruptions in domestic agriculture and industry a great deal of preparatory work needs to be done before we start implementing the FTAs. First, our infrastructure, both social and physical must be brought on par with the trading partner with whom we are entering into an agreement. It is particularly necessary to raise the level of education and skills and to improve power and transport infrastructure in the country, as otherwise an FTA would result in the flight of capital from the country. Efficiency in manufacturing in particular is a function of the quality of physical infrastructure and of skill development. Second, a level playing field must be created on the fiscal side. A great deal of progress has no doubt been made by the changeover from the cascade system of taxation and the introduction of Central Value Added Tax and State VAT. But in order to ensure that our industries do not suffer a disadvantage in an FTA the introduction of GST must be put firmly on course. There must be an understanding on the exchange rate policy as well, before we can have a soundly functioning FTA as a market driven exchange rate policy in one partner country cannot co-exist with a substantially controlled exchange rate policy in another. When the time is ripe for negotiating FTAs both goods and services must be considered together so that balanced results are obtained. These fundamental aspects need to be attended to in parallel with operationalizing FTAs.

13.61. The easy way of going ahead with FTAs on the basis of exemptions of a long list of products needs to be avoided except in agriculture where there is a particular problem because of the dependence of majority of the population on the sector for their livelihood and the lack of alternatives for them for redeployment. Furthermore, in FTAs sufficient time should be given to manufacturing industries to adjust to new conditions of competition and the temptation to show quick results through 'early harvest' resisted. It has to be borne in mind also that in a rapidly globalizing world, manufacturers are keenly searching for cheaper inputs and it is very difficult to ensure that imports from a particular trading partner qualify as an 'originating' product. Strict rules of origin have been put in place, but the certificates of compliance with these rules are issued by authorities in the exporting country and the customs authorities in India do not have the wherewithal to verify the accuracy of the information on which the certificates are based.

13.62. If FTAs need preparation and time for adjustment, PTAs need to be shunned altogether. As demonstrated in the now defunct Tripartite Agreement and the Trade Negotiating Protocol among developing countries PTAs can have adverse effects through trade diversion. In addition PTAs can result in an inverted duty structure to the detriment of domestic industry, as has been the experience in the Indo-Thailand Agreement, which was in reality a PTA because of the operationalization of preference on selected products subject to 'early harvest'. The selective and partial preference in PTAs such as the GSTP and APTA and those envisaged in the Indo-Mercosur Agreement, while not resulting in any trade flows clutter up the tariff schedule of the country.

FOREIGN DIRECT INVESTMENT (FDI)

13.63. The liberalization of the FDI policy and the steady growth of the Indian economy contributed to a large increase in FDI inflows during the Tenth Plan period as can be seen from Table 13.11.

APPROVAL MECHANISM UNDER FDI POLICY

13.64. **Automatic route**—In most sectors FDI is permitted on the automatic route. FDI in such sectors/activities does not require any prior approval and only requires notification to the Reserve Bank of India within thirty days of such receipt of inward remittance; and filing of required documents within thirty days of issue of shares to foreign investors. FEMA Regulations prescribe specific formats for notifying foreign investments, transfer of shares to non-residents and payment for foreign technology/use of trademark/brand name made under the automatic route.

13.65. **Government approval route**—Limited activities require prior Government approval. Proposals for FDI are considered by the Foreign Investment Promotion Board (FIPB), now functioning under the Department of Economic Affairs, and decisions are conveyed in most cases within 6–8 weeks of receipt of complete application. Approval for foreign technology collaboration, where required, is considered by the Project Approval Board (PAB) under the Department of Industrial Policy and Promotion.

TABLE 13.11
Foreign Investment Flows during Tenth Plan Period

(Value: US$ million)

S. No.	Financial Year (April–March)	Equity		Reinvested earnings +	Other capital +	Total FDI Inflows	% age growth over previous
		FIPB route/ RBI's Automatic	Equity capital of unincorporated bodies#				
1.	2002–03	2574	190	1833	438	5035	() 18
2.	2003–04	2197	32	1460	633	4322	() 14
3.	2004–05	3250	528	1904	369	6051	(+) 40
4.	2005–06 (P)	5540	280	1676	226	7722	(+) 28
5.	2006–07 (P)*	15585	480	2936	530	19531*	(+) 153

Note: '#' Figures for equity capital of unincorporated bodies for 2005–06 and 2006–07 are estimates. '+' Data in respect of re-invested earnings and Other capital for the years 2005–06 and 2006–07 are estimated as average of previous two years; 'P' All figures are provisional; * Include swap of shares US$ 3.1 billion.

13.66. A comprehensive review of the FDI policy was undertaken in 2006 with a view to consolidate the liberalization already effected and further rationalize the FDI policy governing various activities. New sectors/activities viz. Single Brand Product retailing, Power Trading, Coffee and Rubber processing and warehousing were opened for FDI.

13.67. As a result of the various rationalization measures, the FDI Policy has become progressively more liberal, transparent and investor-friendly. A liberal and transparent FDI policy has been put in place for the industry, services and infrastructure sectors under which FDI up to 100% is permitted in most sectors on the automatic route. Caps on foreign equity apply only in a few service sectors viz. 20% on FM radio broadcasting, 26% on insurance, defence production, print and electronic media covering news and current affairs, 49% on air transport services, asset reconstruction companies, cable network, DTH, hardware for up-linking, HUB etc., 51% for single brand retailing of products and 74% for atomic minerals, private sector banking, telecom services and the establishment and operation of satellites. A proposal for foreign investment/technical collaboration requires prior government approval only if the foreign investor has an existing Joint Venture or technology transfer/trademark agreement in the 'same' field (determined on the basis of 4 digit NIC 1987 code) unless the investments are made by SEBI registered venture capital funds or where the existing investment by either of the parties is less than 3% or where the existing venture/collaboration is defunct or sick. This requirement does not apply for IT Sector, investments by multinational financial institutions and in the mining sector.

FDI Outlook

13.68. A.T.Kearney FDI Confidence Index 2006 based on a seven-year survey of top 1000 firms, covering 68 countries receiving 90% of the FDI has rated India ahead of the US in terms of business confidence index. The top honours go to China. US is the fourth in the list. 45% of global investors are upbeat about India compared to last year. The report predicts India to be on the cusp of FDI take off, in view of the government focus on reforms, overcoming narrow business interests, de-bottlenecking infrastructure, logistics and regulatory barriers.

13.69. India has improved its position by two places in the World Economic Forum's Global Competitive Index (GCI) rankings for 2006–07, coming in 43rd, well ahead of Brazil (66), China (54), and Russia (62).

Strategy for FDI during the Eleventh Five Year Plan

13.70. Given the current scenario, FDI could increase significantly during the Eleventh Plan. During the Eleventh Plan steps would need to be taken to consolidate the gains from FDI by reducing the delays in State-level clearances required by investors to establish enterprises. Progress towards elimination of FDI limits in key sectors also needs to continue in order to increase FDI flows and stimulate transfer of technology, which is critical for improving competitiveness.

Foreign Technology Transfer Policy

13.71. FDI brings along with capital, modern technologies and best practices. The GoI has announced a liberal foreign technology transfer policy as well. The policy on foreign technology transfer is regulated on the basis of the quantum of payments allowed for technology transfers. Payments for technology transfer from a foreign collaborator are allowed to a joint venture with an Indian partner as also to wholly owned Indian subsidiaries of a foreign company. There is no time limit prescribed for the duration of payments to be made. The technology payments are governed by the Foreign Exchange Management (Current Account Transaction) Regulations, 2000. These do not cover the FDI Scheme which is governed by Foreign Exchange Management (Transfer or Issue of security by a Person Resident outside India) Regulations, 2000 except where specifically notified. In other words, there is no restriction on technology collaboration in areas, which are prohibited for foreign equity or which attract foreign equity caps under the FDI policy except where such a restriction has been notified.

13.72. At present, foreign technology collaboration involving payment of lump-sum amount of up to US $2 million and/or royalty at the rate of 5% on domestic sales and 8% on exports are allowed under the automatic route. In addition, the current policy also allows payment of royalty up to 2% on exports and 1% on domestic sales under the automatic route for use of trademark and brand names of the foreign collaborator without technology transfer. Cases involving payment of lump-sum amount or royalty beyond the limits prescribed under the automatic route are considered by the government on the recommendations of the PAB.

MANAGING CAPITAL FLOWS

13.73. A major issue that most emerging market countries need to address is how to cope with a world of greater capital mobility. There is general agreement that the emergence of large pools of international capital, highly mobile across borders, provides an important opportunity for developing countries to access additional capital to finance their development in both the private and the public sectors. However, it is also true that free capital mobility brings with it the risk of volatility. This risk is particularly great for developing countries because investor perceptions of the prospects of individual developing countries are more vulnerable to contagion effects which could lead to volatility that is not justified by underlying fundamentals. Developing countries also face problems because they typically lack financial system strong enough to deal with inward and outward capital mobility.

13.74. The difficult choices facing developing countries are usually described in terms of a 'trilemma' or the 'impossible trinity' which asserts that in a world of internationally integrated capital market flows, a country cannot simultaneously achieve all three objectives of free capital mobility, a stable exchange rate, and an independent monetary policy. It is possible to have an independent monetary policy (i.e., a target interest rate or money supply growth) and exchange rate stability, but in that case capital flows have to be controlled. Alternatively, if capital flows are completely free it is necessary to give up either exchange rate stability or the ability to set monetary policy independently. In practice, few governments make firm choices for all times, and a mixed strategy is often adopted. The exchange rate is flexible but not fully flexible, capital flows are moderated in various ways or monetary policy is forced to adjust in various ways. All these choices involve costs. However, there is general agreement that it is undesirable to allow too large an appreciation in the exchange rate in response to capital inflows that may be temporary. Efforts to avoid appreciation by unsterilized intervention run the risk of increasing liquidity and money supply with a possible increase in inflationary pressure. On the other hand, resort to sterilised intervention imposes interest cost on the Budget.

13.75. These problems illustrate the merit of the cautious approach adopted by the government in the matter of liberating capital inflows. The advantages of accessing pool of capital to finance development are recognized in the commitment to move gradually to fuller capital account convertibility. But the move is to be made gradually at a pace which enables the authorities to deal with unexpected volatility. In controlling capital flows it is important to recognize the relative attractiveness of different types of flows. In this regard direct foreign investment is the most preferred form of flow. Investments in Indian firms through the stock market and by venture capital funds in unlisted companies are also potentially beneficial. ECB and other short term flows are areas where one can introduce an element of control to moderate sudden surges. However, even with capital calibration it is not easy to manage a surge in capital inflows, if it occurs. In such situations, it is necessary to explore ways of limiting the fiscal cost of sterilizing large growth of reserves; either by making these flows less attractive or by means that do not require costly sterilization.

Eleventh Five Year Plan (2007–2012)

Social Sector

Volume II

सत्यमेव जयते

Planning Commission
Government of India

OXFORD
UNIVERSITY PRESS

YMCA Library Building, Jai Singh Road, New Delhi 110 001

Oxford University Press is a department of the University of Oxford. It furthers the University's objective of excellence in research, scholarship, and education by publishing worldwide in

Oxford New York

Auckland Cape Town Dar es Salaam Hong Kong Karachi Kuala Lumpur Madrid Melbourne Mexico City Nairobi New Delhi Shanghai Taipei Toronto

With offices in

Argentina Austria Brazil Chile Czech Republic France Greece Guatemala Hungary Italy Japan Poland Portugal Singapore South Korea Switzerland Thailand Turkey Ukraine Vietnam

Oxford is a registered trademark of Oxford University Press in the UK and in certain other countries

Published in India
By Oxford University Press, New Delhi

© Planning Commission (Government of India) 2008

The moral rights of the author have been asserted

First published 2008

All rights reserved. No part of this publication may be reproduced or transmitted, in any form or by any means, electronic or mechanical, including photocopying, recording or by any information storage and retrieval system, without permission in writing from Planning Commission, Government of India

ISBN-13: 978-0-19-569650-9
ISBN-10: 0-19-569650-6

Typeset in Minion in 11/13
by Excellent Laser Typesetters, Pitampura, Delhi 110 034
Printed by Tara Art Printers Pvt. Ltd., Noida
Published by Oxford University Press
YMCA Library Building, Jai Singh Road, New Delhi 110 001
On behalf of Planning Commission, Government of India, Yojna Bhawan,
Sansad Marg, New Delhi 110 001

Contents

Tables

Figures

Boxes

Annexures

Acronyms

A&N Islands	Andaman and Nicobar Islands
AABY	Aam Admi Bima Yojana
AAY	Antyodaya Anna Yojana
AICTE	All India Council for Technical Education
AIDS	Acquired Immune Defficiency Syndrome
AIE	Alternative and Innovative Education
ANC	Antenatal Care
ANM	Auxiliary Nurse Midwife
APL	Above Poverty Line
ARI	Acute Respiratory Infections
ARV	Antiretroviral
ARWSP	Accelerated Rural Water Supply Programme
ASCs	Academic Staff Colleges
ASHA	Accredited Social Health Activist
ASI	Archaeological Survey of India
ASU&H	Ayurveda, Siddha, Unani, and Homeopathy
AUWSP	Accelerated Urban Water Supply Programme
AVIs	Accredited Vocational Institutes
AWW	Anganwadi Worker
AYUSH	Ayurveda, Yoga and Naturopathy, Unani, Siddha, and Homeopathy
BFC	Budget for Children
BITS	Birla Institute of Technology & Science
BMI	Body Mass Index
BPL	Below Poverty Line
BRCs	Block Resource Centres
CACP	Commission for Agricultural Costs and Prices
CBHI	Community Based Health Insurance
CBSE	Central Board of Secondary Education
CCIM	Central Council of Indian Medicine
CCRAS	Central Council for Research in Ayurveda & Siddha
CCRT	Centre for Cultural Resources and Training
CEC	Consortium for Educational Communication Centre
CEP	Continuing Education Programmes
CG	Commonwealth Games
CGHS	Central Government Health Scheme
CHCs	Community Health Centres
CICT	Central Institute of Classical Tamil
CIIL	Central Institute of Indian Languages
CIP	Central Issue Prices
CME	Continuing Medical Education
CP	Community Polytechnics
CRCs	Cluster Resource Centres
CS	Central sector scheme
CSIR	Council of Scientific and Industrial Research
CSO	Civil Society Organization
CSO	Central Statistical Organization
CSS	Centrally sponsored scheme
CSWB	Central Social Welfare Board
CTE	College of Teacher Education

CTSs	Central Tibetan Schools
CU	Central University
CVDs	Cardiovascular Diseases
CWSN	Children with Special Needs
CYG	Commonwealth Youth Games
CYP	Commonwealth Youth Programme
D&N Haveli	Dadra and Nagar Haveli
DAE	Department of Atomic Energy
DBT	Department of Biotechnology
DCPU	District Child Protection Unit
DDWS	Department of Drinking Water Supply
DIETs	District Institutes of Education and Training
DISE	District Information System for Education
DIT	Department of Information Technology
DLHS	District Level Health Surveys
DMHP	District Mental Health Programme
DOC	Department of Culture
DoT	Department of Telecommunications
DOTS	Directly Observed Treatment, Short Course
DPA	Dowry Prohibition Act
DPEP	District Primary Education Programme
DRC	District Resource Centre
DST	Department of Science and Technology
EBB	Educationally Backward Blocks
ECCE	Early Childhood Care and Education
ECG	Electrocardiogram
EDUSAT	Education Satellite
EFA	Education For All
EGS	Education Guarantee Scheme
EmOC	Emergency Obstetric Care
EPFO	Employees' Provident Fund Organization
ESIC	Employees State Insurance Corporation
FCI	Food Corporation of India
FPS	Fair Price Shop
FRUs	First Referral Units
GBS	Gross Budgetary Support
GDP	Gross Domestic Product
GER	Gross Enrolment Ratio
GLV	Green Leafy Vegetables
GMP	Good Manufacturing Practices
GO	Government Organization
GoI	Government of India
HAMA	Hindu Adoption and Maintenance Act
HBNC	Home Based Newborn Care
HIV	Human Immunodeficiency Virus
HLC	High-level Committee
HMIS	Health Management Information System
IASE	Institute of Advanced Study in Education
ICAR	Indian Council of Agricultural Research
ICDS	Integrated Child Development Services
ICMR	Indian Council of Medical Research
ICPS	Integrated Child Protection Scheme
ICTs	Information and Communication Technologies
IDA	Iron Deficiency Anaemia
IDD	Iodine Deficiency Disorders
IDSP	Integrated Disease Surveillance Project
IEC	Information, Education, and Communication
IEDC	Integrated Education for the Disabled Children
IEDSS	Inclusive Education for the Disabled at Secondary Stage
IFA	Iron Folic Acid
IGNCA	Indira Gandhi National Centre for Arts
IGNOU	Indira Gandhi National Open University
IIIT	International Institute of Information Technology
IIM	Indian Institute of Management
IIPS	International Institute for Population Sciences
IISc	Indian Institute of Science
IISER	Indian Institute of Science Education and Research
IISFM	Integrated Information System for Foodgrains Management

IIT	Indian Institute of Technology
ILO	International Labour Organization
IMNCI	Integrated Management of Neonatal and Childhood Illness
IMR	Infant Mortality Rate
INDEST	Indian National Digital Library for Engineering Sciences and Technology
INFLIBNET	Information for Library Network
IOL	Intra Ocular Lens
IPERPO	Intellectual Property Education, Research, and Public Outreach
IPHS	Indian Public Health Service Standards
IPR	Intellectual Property Right
ISM	Indian Systems of Medicine
ISRO	Indian Space Research Organization
IT	Information Technology
ITPA	Immoral Traffic (Prevention) Act
J&K	Jammu and Kashmir
JNNURM	Jawaharlal Nehru National Urban Renewal Mission
JRF	Junior Research Fellowship
JSK	Jansankhya Sthirata Kosh
JSS	Jan Shikshan Sansthan
JSS	Jan Swasthya Sahyog
JSY	Janani Suraksha Yojana
KGBVS	Kasturba Gandhi Balika Vidyalaya Scheme
KVs	Kendriya Vidyalayas
LBW	Low Birth Weight
LEAP	Lifelong Education and Awareness Programme
LF	Lymphatic Filariasis
LHVs	Lady Health Visitors
LKA	Lalit Kala Akademi
LNIPE	Laxmibai National Institute of Physical Education
LPCD	Litres Per Capita per Day
M/o WCD	Ministry of Women and Child Development
MASCs	Multi-Application Smart Cards
MBA	Master of Business Administration
MCA	Master of Computer Applications
MCH	Maternal and Child Health
MCI	Medical Council of India
MDA	Mass Drug Administration
MDGs	Millennium Development Goals
MDM	Mid-Day Meal
MDMS	Mid-Day Meal Scheme
ME	Monitoring and Evaluation
MHRD	Ministry of Human Resources Development
MIS	Management Information System
MLD	Million Litres per Day
MMR	Maternal Mortality Ratio
MOEF	Ministry of Environment and Forests
MoHFW	Ministry of Health and Family Welfare
MO	Medical Officers
MoRD	Ministry of Rural Development
MoU	Memorandum of Understanding
MP	Madhya Pradesh
MP	Member of Parliament
MPCC	Multipurpose Cultural Complexes
MPWs	Multipurpose Workers
MS	Mahila Samakhya
MSP	Minimum Support Price
MTP	Medical Termination of Pregnancy
NAAC	National Accreditation Assessment Council
NABH	National Accreditation Board for Hospitals and Health Care Providers
NACO	National AIDS Control Organization
NACP	National AIDS Control Programme
NAI	National Archives of India
NBA	National Board of Accreditation
NBE	National Board of Examinations
NBT	National Book Trust
NCCP	National Cancer Control Programme
NCDs	Non-communicable Diseases
NCDC	National Centre for Disease Control
NCERT	National Council of Educational Research and Training
NCEUS	National Commission for Enterprises in the Unorganized Sector
NCF	National Curriculum Framework
NCF	National Culture Fund
NCMH	National Commission on Macroeconomics and Health
NCMP	National Common Minimum Programme
NCSM	National Council of Science Museums
NCTE	National Council for Teacher Education

NCW	National Commission for Women
NDA	National Drug Authority
NE	North East, North Eastern
NER	North Eastern Region
NERIST	North Eastern Regional Institute of Science and Technology
NET	National Education Testing
NFHS	National Family Health Survey
NGCP	National Goitre Control Programme
NGO	Non-Governmental Organization
NHA	National Health Account
NIC	National Informatics Centre
NICD	National Institute of Communicable Diseases
NIDDCP	National Iodine Deficiency Disorders Control Programme
NIOS	National Institute of Open Schooling
NITs	National Institutes of Technology
NITTTRs	National Institutes of Technical Teachers Training and Research
NLM	National Literacy Mission
NLSI	New Linguistic Survey of India
NMBS	National Maternity Benefit Scheme
NMHP	National Mental Health Programme
NMPB	National Medicinal Plants Board
NNAP	National Nutritional Anaemia Prophylaxis
NNMB	National Nutrition Monitoring Bureau
NMR	Neonatal Mortality Rate
NOAPS	National Old Age Pension Scheme
NPE	National Policy of Education
NPEGEL	National Programme for Education of Girls at Elementary Level
NPTEL	National Programme on Technology Enhanced Learning
NREGA	National Rural Employment Guarantee Act
NREGP	National Rural Employment Guarantee Programme
NRHM	National Rural Health Mission
NSAP	National Social Assistance Programme
NSERB	National Science and Engineering Research Board
NSFs	National Sports Federations
NSS	National Service Scheme
NSS	National Sample Surveys
NSSO	National Sample Survey Organization
NSVS	National Service Volunteers Scheme
NUEPA	National University of Educational Planning Administration
NUHM	National Urban Health Mission
NVs	Navodaya Vidyalayas
NVQ	National Vocational Qualification
NYKS	Nehru Yuva Kendra Sangathan
O&M	Operation and Maintenance
OBC	Other Backward Classes
OPD	Out Patient Department
OP/IP	Out Patient/In Patient
ORS	Oral Rehydration Solution
OSC	Oversight Committee
PC&PNDT Act	Pre-Conception and Pre-Natal Diagnostic Techniques Act
PDS	Public Distribution System
PEM	Protein-Energy Malnutrition
PEO	Programme Evaluation Organization
Pf	*Plasmodium falciparum*
PFA	Prevention of Food Adulteration
PGDM	Post Graduate Diploma in Management
PHC	Primary Health Centre
PHFI	Public Health Foundation of India
PIP	Project Implementation Plan
PLP	Post Literacy Projects
PLWHA	People Living With HIV/AIDS
PMR	Physical Medicine and Rehabilitation
PMSSY	Pradhan Mantri Swasthya Suraksha Yojana
PPP	Public–Private Partnership
PRIs	Panchayati Raj Institutions
PSE	Pre-school Education
PTR	Pupil Teacher Ratio
PUB	Public Utilities Board
PWDVA	Protection of Women from Domestic Violence Act
PYKKA	Panchayat Yuva Krida Aur Khel Abhiyan
R&D	Research and Development
RCH	Reproductive and Child Health

RGNDWM	Rajiv Gandhi National Drinking Water Mission
RGNIYD	Rajiv Gandhi National Institute of Youth Development
RHP	Rural Health Practitioners
RMP	Registered Medical Practitioner
RNTCP	Revised National Tuberculosis Control Programme
RSY	Rashtriya Sadbhavana Yojana
RTI	Reproductive Tract Infections
RTE	Ready To Eat
S&T	Science and Technology
SA	Sahitya Akademi
SAI	Sports Authority of India
SBAs	Skilled Birth Attendants
SC	Sub-centre
SC	Scheduled Caste
SCERT	State Council for Educational Research and Training
SCSP	Scheduled Caste Sub-Plan
SDM	Skill Development Mission
SET	State Eligibility Test
SEWA	Self Employed Women's Association
SFDs	Special Focus Districts
SHGs	Self-help Groups
SIEs	State Institutes of Education
SLIET	Sant Longowal Institute of Engineering Technology
SNA	Sangeet Natak Akademi
SNP	Supplementary Nutrition Programme
SOS	State Open Schools
SOUs	State Open Universities
SRB	Sex Ratio at Birth
SRCs	State Resource Centres
SRS	Sample Registration System
SSA	Sarva Shiksha Abhiyan
ST	Scheduled Tribe
STD	Sexually Trasmitted Disease
STEP	Support to Training and Employment Programme
STI	Sexually Transmitted Infections
SUCCESS	Scheme for Universalization of Access and Improvement of Quality of Secondary Education
SWM	Solid Waste Management
TA	Technical Assistance
TBAs	Traditional Birth Attendants
TEQIP	Technical Education Quality Improvement Programme
TFC	Twelfth Finance Commission
TFR	Total Fertility Rate
THRs	Take Home Ration
TISS	Tata Institute of Social Sciences
TLC	Total Literacy Campaigns
TLE	Teaching Learning Equipment
TMSSML	Thanjavur Maharaja Serofji Saraswati Mahal Library
TPA	Third Party Administrator
TPDS	Targeted Public Distribution System
TSC	Total Sanitation Campaign
TSP	Tribal Sub Plan
TTIs	Teacher Training Institutions
UEE	Universalization of Elementary Education
UFW	Unaccounted For Water
UGC	University Grants Commission
UIDSSMT	Urban Infrastructure Development Scheme for Small and Medium Towns
UIT	Urban Improvement Trust
ULB	Urban Local Body
UNESCO	United Nations Educational, Scientific and Cultural Organization
UNICEF	United Nations International Children's Emergency Fund
UP	Uttar Pradesh
UPS	Upper Primary Schools
UPS	Uninterrupted Power Supply
UT	Union Territory
VAD	Vitamin A Deficiency
VAW	Violence Against Women
VE	Vocational Education
VECs	Village Education Committees
VHSCs	Village Health and Sanitation Committees
VO	Voluntary Organization
WB	West Bengal
WCD	Women and Child Development
WCU	World Class Universities
WHO	World Health Organization
ZBB	Zero Based Budgeting
ZCCs	Zonal Cultural Centres

1

Education

1.1 ELEMENTARY EDUCATION AND LITERACY

1.1.1 The role of education in facilitating social and economic progress is well recognized. It opens up opportunities leading to both individual and group entitlements. Education, in its broadest sense of development of youth, is the most crucial input for empowering people with skills and knowledge and giving them access to productive employment in future. Improvements in education are not only expected to enhance efficiency but also augment the overall quality of life. The Eleventh Plan places the highest priority on education as a central instrument for achieving rapid and inclusive growth. It presents a comprehensive strategy for strengthening the education sector covering all segments of the education pyramid.

1.1.2 Elementary education, that is, classes I–VIII consisting of primary (I–V) and upper primary (VI–VIII) is the foundation of the pyramid in the education system and has received a major push in the Tenth Plan through the Sarva Shiksha Abhiyan (SSA).

1.1.3 In view of the demands of rapidly changing technology and the growth of knowledge economy, a mere eight years of elementary education would be grossly inadequate for our young children to acquire necessary skills to compete in the job market. Therefore, a Mission for Secondary Education is essential to consolidate the gains of SSA and to move forward in establishing a knowledge society.

1.1.4 The Eleventh Plan must also pay attention to the problems in the higher education sector, where there is a need to expand the system and also to improve quality.

1.1.5 The Eleventh Plan will also have to address major challenges including bridging regional, social, and gender gaps at all levels of education.

ELEMENTARY EDUCATION IN THE TENTH PLAN

Major Schemes in the Tenth Plan

1.1.6 The Tenth Plan laid emphasis on Universalization of Elementary Education (UEE) guided by five parameters: (i) Universal Access, (ii) Universal Enrolment, (iii) Universal Retention, (iv) Universal Achievement, and (v) Equity. The major schemes of elementary education sector during the Tenth Plan included SSA, District Primary Education Programme (DPEP), National Programme of Nutritional Support to Primary Education, commonly known as Mid-Day Meal Scheme (MDMS), Teacher Education Scheme, and Kasturba Gandhi Balika Vidyalaya Scheme (KGBVS). The schemes of Lok Jumbish and Shiksha Karmi were completed but DPEP will extend up to November 2008. KGBV has now been subsumed within SSA.

Sarva Shiksha Abhiyan (SSA)

1.1.7 SSA, the principal programme for UEE, is the culmination of all previous endeavours and experiences in implementing various education programmes.

While each of these programmes and projects had a specific focus—Operation Blackboard on improving physical infrastructure; DPEP on primary education; Shiksha Karmi Project on teacher absenteeism, and Lok Jumbish Project on girls' education—SSA has been the single largest holistic programme addressing all aspects of elementary education covering over one million elementary schools and Education Guarantee Centre (EGS)/Alternate and Innovative Education (AIE) Centres and about 20 crore children.

Performance of SSA and Related Schemes in Tenth Plan

1.1.8 The specific goals of SSA during the Tenth Plan period were as follows:

- All children to be in regular school, EGS, AIE, or 'Back-to-School' camp by 2005;
- Bridging all gender and social category gaps at primary stage by 2007 and at elementary education level by 2010;
- Universal retention by 2010;
- Focus on elementary education of satisfactory quality with emphasis on education for life.

UNIVERSAL ACCESS

1.1.9 SSA has brought primary education to the doorstep of millions of children and enrolled them, including first generation learners, through successive fast track initiatives in hitherto unserved and underserved habitations. According to the VII Educational Survey (2002), the number of habitations that had a primary school within a distance of 1 km was 10.71 lakh (87%), the uncovered habitations numbered 1.61 lakh (13%), whereas, the number of habitations that had an upper primary school within a distance of 3 km was 9.61 lakh (78%). With the opening up of 1.32 lakh primary schools and 56000 EGS/AIE centres access to primary education is nearly achieved. About 0.89 lakh upper primary schools (UPS) have been provided up to 2006–07. At primary and at upper primary level the number of habitations remaining to be covered is estimated at almost 1 lakh.

1.1.10 The number of primary schools (PS) in the country increased from 6.64 lakh in 2001–02 to 7.68 lakh in 2004–05. In the same period, the number of UPS increased at a faster rate from 2.20 lakh to 2.75 lakh. The sanction of 2.23 lakh new PS/UPS, 1.88 lakh new school buildings, and 6.70 lakh additional classrooms has made a big dent in reducing the school infrastructure gap.

UNIVERSAL ENROLMENT

1.1.11 SSA had a sluggish start as States took considerable time to prepare district perspective plans. By the time the States realized the full potential of SSA, two and a half years had already rolled on. The urgency called for fast track initiatives. Household surveys, school mapping, constitution of Village Education Committees (VECs), setting up of Mother Teacher Associations and Parent Teacher Associations, and a series of campaigns for enrolment and context-specific strategies, all learnt from the experience of implementing DPEP, were used for good results in the next two and a half years. As a result, the second phase of enrolment drive by the States/union territories (UTs) was more systematic with household survey data reflecting substantially improved Gross Enrolment Ratio (GER) and a significant reduction in the number of out-of-school children. The strategy of providing AIE grants to Maktabs/Madarsas for introducing teaching of general subjects to minority children was also very fruitful.

1.1.12 Consequently, the total enrolment at elementary education level increased from 159 million in 2001–02 to 182 million in 2004–05, an increase of over 23 million (Figure 1.1.1).

1.1.13 The following Table 1.1.1 shows GER for primary, upper primary, and elementary level from 2001–02 to 2004–05.

1.1.14 Social and gender disparity, existing at both primary and upper primary education levels, continues to be an issue to be tackled with more concerted and sustained efforts, especially in Bihar, Rajasthan, Jharkhand, Madhya Pradesh (MP), Gujarat, and Uttar Pradesh (UP).

1.1.15 SSA interventions have brought down the number of out-of-school children from 32 million in 2001–02 to 7.0 million in 2006–07 (Figure 1.1.2). 48 districts in 10 States accounted for over 50000 out-of-school

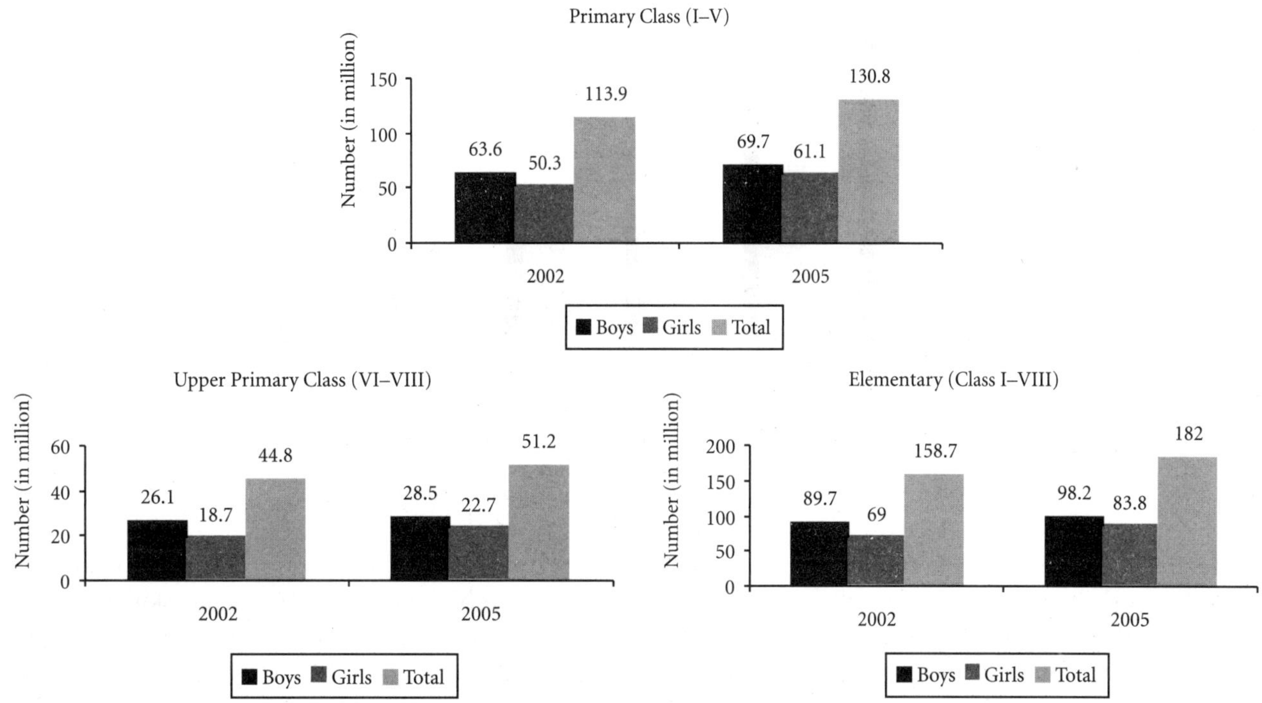

Source: Selected Educational Statistics, 2004–05.

FIGURE 1.1.1: Enrolment in Elementary Education

TABLE 1.1.1
GER in Primary and Upper Primary Schools

Stages	Gross Enrolment Ratio				%age point increase
	2001–02	2002–03	2003–04	2004–05	
Primary (I–V)					
Boys	105.3	97.5	100.6	110.7	5.4
Girls	86.9	93.1	95.6	104.7	17.8
All	96.3	95.3	98.2	107.8	11.3
Upper Primary (VI–VIII)					
Boys	67.8	65.3	66.8	74.3	6.5
Girls	52.1	56.2	57.6	65.1	13.0
All	60.2	61.0	62.4	69.9	9.7
Elementary (I–VIII)					
Boys	90.7	85.4	87.9	96.9	6.2
Girls	73.6	79.3	81.4	89.9	16.3
All	82.4	82.5	84.8	93.5	11.1

Source: Selected Educational Statistics, 2004–05.

children, each. The number of such districts declined to 29 in 2005–06. An independent study[1] estimated that about 6.9% of the total children in the 6–13 age groups were out of school and of them 2.1% accounted for dropouts and 4.8% for never-enrolled children, a bulk of whom apparently belonged to the poorer segments of rural households.

1.1.16 The social composition of out-of-school children indicates that 9.97% of Muslim children, 9.54% of Scheduled Tribes (STs), 8.17% of Scheduled Castes (SCs), and 6.97% of Other Backward Class (OBC) children were out of school and an overwhelming majority (68.7%) was concentrated in five States, viz., Bihar (23.6%), UP (22.2%), West Bengal (WB) (9%), MP (8%), and Rajasthan (5.9%).

UNIVERSAL RETENTION

1.1.17 It is increasingly realized that retaining the disadvantaged children enrolled in schools is a far more challenging task than enrolling them into educational system. Around 22% children dropped out in classes I and II. Several factors, apart from their adverse socio-economic conditions are responsible for this. The opportunity cost of girl-child education is quite high in the rural set up and she is often a 'nowhere child',

[1] Social and Rural Research Institute (2005), New Delhi.

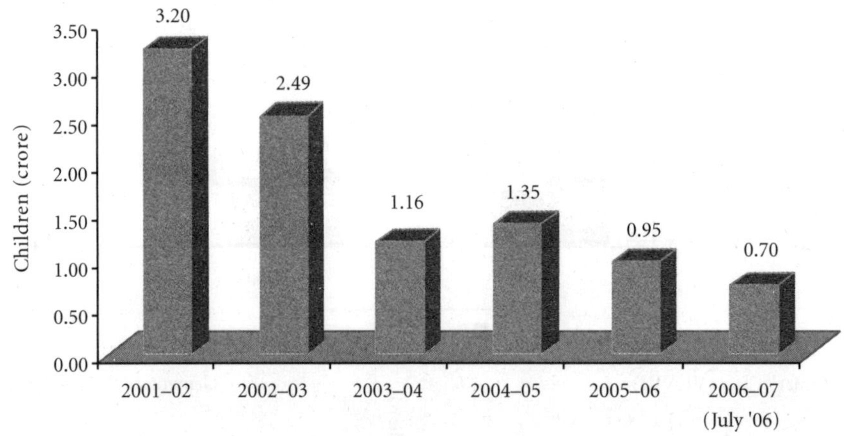

Source: Ministry of Human Resources Development (MHRD).

FIGURE 1.1.2: Reduction in Out-of-School Children

neither in the school nor in the labour force but doing domestic work, mostly sibling care. It is well documented that the presence of female teachers often serves as a role model for girls and positively influences their enrolment and attendance. But, then, in the educationally backward States, there are few women teachers to particularly attract girls to school and retain them.[2]

1.1.18 SSA stipulates that 50% of additionally recruited teachers should be women. Given the emphasis on improving girls' enrolment, which is critically dependent upon the presence of female teachers, there is a need to increase the proportion to 75% in the recruitment of female teachers in educationally fragile States.

1.1.19 The fact that children drop out of school early or fail to acquire basic literacy and numeracy skills partially reflects poor quality of education.[3] The average school attendance was around 70% of the enrolment in 2004–05. In States like UP and Bihar, the average attendance was as low as 57% and 42%, respectively. One-third of the teachers in MP, 25% in Bihar, and 20% in UP do not attend schools.[4] Besides, the repetition rates in such States are also very high, resulting in wastage of human and material resources. Teacher attendance, ability, and motivation appear to be the weakest links of elementary education programmes. Lack of universal pre-schooling (Early Childhood Care and Education, ECCE) and consequent poor vocabulary and poor conceptual development of mind makes even enrolled children less participative in the class, even for learning by rote.[5]

TABLE 1.1.2
Number of Female Teachers per 100 Male Teachers

States	High	States	Low
Goa	454	Bihar	24
Kerala	273	Jharkhand	26
Pondicherry	279	MP	36
Tamil Nadu	221	Rajasthan	38
Delhi	221	UP	40

Source: Selected Educational Statistics, 2004–05.

TABLE 1.1.3
Dropout Rates by Social Composition, 2004–05

Categories	Primary (I–V)			Elementary (I–VIII)		
	Boys	Girls	Total	Boys	Girls	Total
SCs	32.7	36.1	34.2	55.2	60.0	57.3
STs	42.6	42.0	42.3	65.0	67.1	65.9
All	31.8	25.4	29.0	50.5	51.3	50.8

Source: Selected Educational Statistics, 2004–05.

[2] UNESCO (2007), EFA-Global Monitoring Report.
[3] ibid.
[4] MHRD (2007), PPT Presentation in the Steering Committee meeting held in Planning Commission.
[5] Lynn Erickson (2007), *Concept Based Curriculum and Instruction for the Thinking Classroom*, Crowing Press, A Sage Publication Company, Thousand Oaks, California, chapter 5, p. 98.

1.1.20 The dropout rate in primary classes which has been decreasing at a very low average rate of 0.5% per annum since 1960s showed a steeper decline by 10.03% over the first three years of the Tenth Plan (29% in 2004–05 as compared to 39.03% in 2001–02). The dropout rate reduction has been faster for girls as compared to that for boys. However, the dropout rate at the elementary level (classes I–VIII) has remained very high at 50.8%.

1.1.21 The dropout rates at primary levels for SCs (34.2%) and STs (42.3%) are substantially higher than the national average (29%) (Table 1.1.3). The gap in respect of SCs is very wide in Goa, UP, Tamil Nadu, WB, Haryana, and Himachal Pradesh. The gap in respect of STs is very large in Maharashtra, Andhra Pradesh, Orissa, and Gujarat. The social gap in dropout rate is acute in respect of girls. Two-thirds of the tribal students just do not go beyond class VIII.

UNIVERSAL ACHIEVEMENT AND EQUITY

1.1.22 Two major issues yet to be addressed satisfactorily under UEE are quality and equity. The results of learning achievement surveys conducted by National Council for Education Research and Training (NCERT) (Table 1.1.4) and also by independent agencies (Annual Status of Education Report, 2005) highlight poor quality of learning.

TABLE 1.1.4
Learning Achievements at Elementary Level

(Percentage)

Stages of education	Math.	Language	EVS/ Science	Social Science
At the end of Class III	58.25	63.12	–	–
Class V	46.51	58.57	50.3	–
Class VII	29.87	53	35.98	32.96
Class VIII	38.47	52.45	40.54	45

Source: NCERT (2004–05).

1.1.23 SSA did attempt to strengthen a range of inputs that impact on quality, viz. recruitment of 7.95 lakh additional teachers to improve the pupil teacher ratio (PTR) from 44 to 40:1 at primary level, regular annual in-service training of teachers for a period of 20 days, curriculum renewal and textbook development, free distribution of textbooks for primary and upper primary classes to about 6.69 crore SCs, STs, and girl students, computer-aided learning in over 20000 schools, regular academic support to primary and UPS through 6746 Block Resource Centres (BRCs) and 70388 Cluster Resource Centres (CRCs), monitoring of performance of schools including the pass percentage at exit levels; at least 10% better achievement in pass percentage as in 2006–07 over the benchmarking level in 2005–06, and running of learning enhancement programmes especially for the early primary grades in 19 States. However, the impact has not been very encouraging.

1.1.24 314 Special Focus Districts (SFDs) have been identified for need-based interventions in resource allocation, micro-planning, and development. There is a focus on girls' education by targeting additional resources to Educationally Backward Blocks (EBBs) under National Programme for Education of Girls at Elementary Level (NPEGEL). Under KGBV scheme 2180 residential schools for girls belonging to SCs, STs, OBCs, minorities, and below poverty line (BPL) families were sanctioned in the EBBs.

Parameters for EBBs as per Census 2001

- Rural Female Literacy below the national average (46.13%);
- Gender gap in literacy more than the national average (21.59%).

1.1.25 Such EBBs total up to 3073. Another 212 Blocks with SC concentration, 142 Blocks with ST concentration, and 52 Blocks with minority concentration have been identified, making the total number of EBBs to 3479. NPEGEL has its own EBBs. There seem to be different criteria and definitions of EBBs. Relevant criteria would be framed in the Eleventh Plan and EBBs re-identified.

1.1.26 During the Tenth Plan, 11542 primary and UPS and 32250 EGS centres were sanctioned in the minority concentration districts. EGS and AIE centres enrolled 120.90 lakh and 11.3 lakh children, respectively. The Madarsas (8309) affiliated to the State Boards were assisted and 4867 Maktabs/Madarsas were taken up under EGS/AIE. Free textbooks are provided to all minority girls from classes I–VIII and Urdu textbooks are provided for Urdu medium schools. The number of KGBVs sanctioned in minority Blocks is 270.

1.1.27 The 86th Constitutional Amendment Act has given a new thrust to Children with Special Needs (CWSN). A multi-option model for educating CWSN is being adopted. The programme has been successful in enrolling 1.99 million out of the identified 2.4 million CWSN (81%) in schools.

1.1.28 Although SSA was launched in November 2000, only three States in the North East (NE) (Assam, Mizoram, and Nagaland) could start it in 2001–02; by 2004–05, Meghalaya, Sikkim, Tripura, Arunachal Pradesh, and Manipur had also started the programme. Lack of capacities to handle various components of SSA and default on States' share and its subsequent effect on the flow of funds from the Government of India (GoI) affected full utilization. A one-time special dispensation was provided for the years 2005–06 and 2006–07 to the NE States whereby Non Lapsable Central Pool of Resources provided three-fifth of the State share and the NE States contributed only two-fifth under SSA. Learning achievements of children in schools in North East Region (NER) are very low.

Outlay and Expenditure in SSA in the Tenth Plan

1.1.29 The Tenth Plan outlay for Elementary Education and Literacy was Rs 30000 crore. The actual expenditure has been Rs 48201 crore, out of which SSA (Rs 28077 crore) and MDMS (Rs 13827 crore) account for 88%. Prarambhik Shiksha Kosh, a non-lapsable fund for crediting the education cess proceeds, has been set up.

1.1.30 The States of UP (19%), MP (10%), Rajasthan and Bihar (7% each), Maharashtra and WB (6% each), Andhra Pradesh, Tamil Nadu, and Karnataka (5% each) accounted for 70% of the total expenditure incurred by the Central and State Governments under SSA during the Tenth Plan.

SECTORAL EXPENDITURE UNDER SSA

1.1.31 A pragmatic decision was taken to relax the civil works ceiling (33%) under SSA to accelerate bridging school infrastructure gaps in selected States. Consequently, the share of expenditure on civil works increased from 35.5% in 2003–04 to 46.2% in 2006–07 and that on teacher's salary from 15.7% to 20.8%. With EGS centres being converted into regular primary schools, their share has declined from 10.3% in 2003–04 to 6.8% in 2006–07 (see Table 1.1.5).

Table 1.1.5
Distribution of SSA

S. No.	Expenditure	Percentages		
		2003–04	2006–07	Tenth Plan
1	Civil Works	36	46	43.84
2	Teacher's Salary	16	21	19.37
3	EGS/AIE	10	7	5.00
4	Teacher's Training	5	3	2.92
5	Text Books	6	3	4.89
6	BRC/CRC	3	3	3.64
7	TLE	4	1	2.07
8	Management Cost	3	4	2.67
9	Innovative Activities	3	2	0.91
10	Others	14	10	14.69

Source: MHRD.

1.1.32 Low expenditures on components relating to quality dimensions of the programme, such as Teacher's Training, Teaching Learning Equipment (TLE) (including Information and Communication Technology, ICT) Innovative Activities, School/Teacher Grants etc., need to be sharply stepped up during the Eleventh Plan. Moreover, SSA should not fund teachers appointed in the Tenth Plan but pay only for the new teachers, with a view to addressing the serious problem of single-teacher and multi-grade teaching.

Kasturba Gandhi Balika Vidyalaya Scheme (KGBVS)

1.1.33 The KGBVS was launched in July 2004 for setting up of residential schools at upper primary level for girls, predominantly belonging to the SCs, STs, OBCs, and minorities in EBBs. A minimum of 75% of the enrolment in KGBVS is reserved for girls from the target groups and the remaining 25% is open for girls belonging to the BPL category. The Tenth Plan allocation for the scheme was Rs 427 crore.

1.1.34 As soon as the schools were sanctioned under KGBV, the States rented premises and sought funds without waiting for the buildings to come up. The targeted 750 schools (Model I—364 schools, Model II—117 schools, and Model III—269 schools) were sanctioned between December 2004 and May 2005. By December 2006, 1039 schools were operational with a total enrolment of 63921 girls. In February 2006, 430 schools and in March 2007 additional 1000 schools were sanctioned, raising the total to 2180 schools. The allotments of KGBVs to States were not in proportion to the number of EBBs. The skewed distribution of KGBVs would be set right in the Eleventh Plan.

District Primary Education Programme (DPEP)

1.1.35 DPEP, an externally aided project, aimed at the holistic development of primary education, covering classes I to V. It has specific objectives of reducing the dropout rate to less than 10%, reducing disparities among gender and social groups in the enrolment to less than 5%, and improving the level of learning achievement compared to the baseline surveys. However, these ambitious targets could not be achieved.

1.1.36 Nevertheless, DPEP has brought a sea change in the implementation of school education programme with its decentralized approach and focus on community participation and provided complete wherewithal for handling ECCE, Non-formal Education Centres, BRCs, CRCs, out-of-school children, and education of girls. The success of SSA owes much to DPEP. Since its inception, external assistance of Rs 6938 crore—comprising Rs 5137 crore as credit from IDA and Rs 1801 crore from development partners, European Commission, Department for International Development, UNICEF, and Netherlands—has been tied up for DPEP. At its peak, DPEP covered 273 districts in 17 States. Now it continues in only 17 districts of Orissa and Rajasthan where it would be completed in 2008.

Mahila Samakhya (MS)

1.1.37 MS, an externally aided project for women's empowerment, was started with Dutch assistance in 1989. Since 2005–06 it is being funded by GoI. The programme endeavours to create an environment for women to learn at their own pace, set their own priorities, and seek knowledge and information to make informed choices. It has strengthened women's abilities to effectively participate in village level education programmes. The programme is implemented in 9 States covering 83 districts, 339 blocks, including 233 EBBs, and 20380 villages. The States of MP and Chhattisgarh have registered MS societies through which the programme is initiated. It provides for vocational and skill development as well as educational development of adolescent girls and women in rural areas. MS runs residential schools, bridge courses, viz., Jagjagi and Mahila Shikshan Kendras.

Mid-Day Meal Scheme (MDMS)

1.1.38 MDMS was launched in 1995 to enhance enrolment, retention, and participation of children in primary schools, simultaneously improving their nutritional status.

1.1.39 The MDMS was revised and universalized in September 2004 and central assistance was provided at the rate of Re. 1.00 per child per school day for converting food grains into hot cooked meals for children in classes I–V in government, local body, and government-aided schools, and EGS and AIE centres. MDMS provided nutritional support to students in drought-affected areas during summer vacation. The maximum permissible transport subsidy was revised for Special Category States from Rs 50 to Rs 100 per quintal and for other States to Rs 75 per quintal.

1.1.40 The scheme was further revised in June 2006 to enhance the minimum cooking cost to Rs 2.00 per child per school day to provide 450 calories and 12 grams of protein. The revised scheme also provided assistance for construction of kitchen-cum-stores at the rate of Rs 60000 per unit in a phased manner in primary schools and procurement of kitchen devices (utensils, etc.) at the rate of Rs 5000 per school. Besides providing free foodgrains, cooking cost, transport subsidy, and Management Monitoring and Evaluation, 94500 schools were also sanctioned kitchen sheds and 2.6 lakh schools were sanctioned kitchen equipment.

1.1.41 The number of children covered under the programme has risen from 3.34 crore in 3.22 lakh schools in 1995 to 12 crore in 9.5 lakh primary schools/ EGS centres in 2006–07.

1.1.42 A review of MDMS indicates absence of proper management structure in many States. Even the reported average number of school days on which meals are provided varied widely. National University of Educational Planning Administration (NUEPA) reports 209 days per annum, while Ministry of Human Resource Development (MHRD) reports 230 days at the national level. Steering Committees at State/

Box 1.1.1
Best Practices under MDMS

In Tamil Nadu, Health Cards are issued to all children and School Health Day is observed every Thursday. Curry leaves and drum-stick trees are grown in the school premises. In Karnataka, all schools have gas-based cooking. In Pondicherry, in addition to the mid-day meal (MDM), Rajiv Gandhi Breakfast Scheme provides for a glass of hot milk and biscuits. In Bihar, Bal Sansad (Child Cabinet) is actively involved in the orderly distribution of MDM. In Uttaranchal, mothers are appointed as Bhojan Mata and Sahayika in primary schools. In Gujarat, Chhattisgarh, and MP children are provided micronutrients and deworming medicines under MDMS.

district levels for effective monitoring are yet to be set up in some States. There are no details on coverage and facilities in EGS/AIE centres in urban areas. The Planning Commission has undertaken a detailed evaluation study in 2006–07 to assess the impact of the MDMS. On the whole, despite the prevalence of good practices, a systematic supervision and monitoring of the programme and transparency in implementation are lacking in most of the States.

1.1.43 Notwithstanding these shortcomings, MDMS appears to have had a positive impact on school attendance and nutritional status of children through removal of classroom hunger.[6] The latest National Sample Survey (NSS) (61st Round) covered MDMS along with Annapurna Integrated Child Development Services (ICDS) Scheme, and Food for Work Programme. It is reported that MDMS has benefited 8.1% of rural population and 3.2% of urban population. The total coverage of all the four programmes was 11% in rural and 4.1% in urban areas. MDMS has catered to the nutritional needs of low-income groups in both rural and urban areas.

Eleventh Plan: Goals, Targets, and Strategies in Elementary Education

1.1.44 The Constitution of India was amended in 2002 to make elementary education a justiciable Fundamental Right. However, 7.1 million children being out of school and over 50% dropping out at elementary level are matters of serious concern. SSA would, therefore, be reoriented to meet the challenges of equity, retention, and high-quality education. This would require a strong rights orientation within the programme. It is necessary to consider passing appropriate legislation for this purpose. SSA would be restructured into a National Mission for Quality Elementary Education to ensure minimum norms and standards for schools (both government and private). It would address access, quality, and equity holistically though a systems approach.

1.1.45 The backlog for additional classrooms is about 6.87 lakh. Opening of about 20000 new primary schools and upgradation of about 70000 primary schools are required.

TABLE 1.1.6
Schools without Basic Facilities, 2005–06

(Percentages)

Facilities	Primary		Upper Primary	
	2004–05	2005–06	2004–05	2005–06
Building	3.5	3.0	2.8	2.4
Toilets	51.4	44.6	16.8	15.3
Drinking water	16.3	15.1	4.7	4.8

Source: DISE data, 2005–06, NUEPA.

1.1.46 Unless there is a strong effort to address the systemic issues of regular functioning of schools, teacher attendance and competence, accountability of educational administrators, pragmatic teacher transfer and promotion policies, effective decentralization of school management, and transfer of powers to Panchayati Raj Institutions (PRIs), it would be difficult to build upon the gains of SSA. It is important to focus on good quality education of common standards, pedagogy, and syllabi to ensure minimum learning levels.

TABLE 1.1.7
Elementary Schools by Management

(in lakh)

Stages of Education	Govt.	Local Bodies	Private Aided	Private Unaided	Total
I–V	3.32	3.60	0.20	0.55	7.67
VI–VIII	1.18	0.80	0.18	0.59	2.75
I–VIII	4.50	4.40	0.38	1.14	10.42

Source: Selected Educational Statistics, 2004–05.

[6] J. Dreze and A. Goyal (2003), The Future of Mid-day Meals, *EPW*, 38(44), Nov. 1–7, pp. 4673–84.

1.1.47 In the liberalized global economy where there is a pursuit for achieving excellence, the legitimate role of private providers of quality education not only needs to be recognized, but also encouraged. Public–Private Partnership (PPP) need not necessarily mean only seeking private investments to supplement governmental efforts, but also encouraging innovation in education that the government schools may lack. Schools under private management (unaided) have been expanding at a faster rate (Table 1.1.7). However, a vast majority of the poor, particularly in rural areas, is solely dependent on government schools.

Box 1.1.2
National Commission on Education

The Kothari Commission (1964–66) was the last commission set up on education. As regards school education, the salient features of the report, submitted in 1966, advocated, inter alia (i) improving the system in existence, (ii) setting up State Boards of Education, (iii) levelling of institutions for equality, (iv) setting up area-specific neighbourhood schools, and (v) a statutory School Education Commission. While there has been progress in the last three decades on (i) and (ii) mentioned above, the same cannot be said of (iii), (iv), and (v).
There is a need for setting up a new Education Commission for deliberating on the emerging perspectives on education in the changing global context.

1.1.48 The substantial step up in the Eleventh Plan outlay in the Central sector would increasingly be invested in improving quality of elementary education, recruiting additional teachers (particularly science and mathematics), seeking technology upgradation including ICT in schools, and Technical Assistance (TA) including the educationally fragile States. The issue of poor performing schools would be addressed by grading schools through a composite index and by providing TA.

1.1.49 It has been found that students who often do not perform well in conventional subject examinations demonstrate high success levels in the use of Information Technology (IT) and IT-enabled learning. IT could provide new directions in pedagogical practices and students' achievement. The idea is not merely making children computer literate but also initiating web-based learning through modern software facilities.

1.1.50 Keeping the above in view, the following targets have been set for elementary education in the Eleventh Plan.

Eleventh Plan Targets for Elementary Education

- Universal enrolment of 6–14 age group children including the hard to reach segment.
- Substantial improvement in quality and standards with the ultimate objective to achieve standards of Kendriya Vidyalayas (KVs) under the Central Board of Secondary Education (CBSE) pattern.
- All gender, social, and regional gaps in enrolments to be eliminated by 2011–12.
- One year pre-school education (PSE) for children entering primary school.
- Dropout at primary level to be eliminated and the dropout rate at the elementary level to be reduced from over 50% to 20% by 2011–12.
- Universalized MDMS at elementary level by 2008–09.
- Universal coverage of ICT at UPS by 2011–12.
- Significant improvement in learning conditions with emphasis on learning basic skills, verbal and quantitative.
- All EGS centres to be converted into regular primary schools.
- All States/UTs to adopt NCERT Quality Monitoring Tools.
- Strengthened BRCs/CRCs: 1 CRC for every 10 schools and 5 resource teachers per block.

Quality Improvement in SSA

1.1.51 In the Eleventh Plan, the quality of education imparted in the primary and UPS would be improved through a range of coherent, integrated, and comprehensive strategies with clearly defined goals that help in measuring progress. These include the following:

- Restructure SSA with a clear goal of providing a quality of education equivalent to that of KVs under the CBSE pattern.
- Ensure basic learning conditions in all schools and acquisition of basic skills of literacy and numeracy in early primary grades to lay a strong foundation for higher classes.

- Give special focus on Maths, Science, and English (core) where students tend to be weak and universally introduce English in Class III onwards.
- Implement a Common Syllabi, Curriculum, and Pedagogy and carry out the consequent textbook revisions.
- Support more quality-related activities and improve interactive classroom transaction.
- Address fully all teacher-related issues—vacancies, absenteeism, non-teaching assignments, and fix accountability for learning outcomes of pupils.
- Achieve 100% training for teachers including para-teachers. Revise PTR to 30:1 from 40:1.
- Recruit additional teachers to deal with single teacher schools and multi-grade teaching with mandatory two-third new teachers to be female for primary classes.
- National Eligibility Test (NET)/State Eligibility Test (SET) for teacher recruitment by NCERT/State Council for Educational Research and Training (SCERT)/CBSE/State Boards to enable decentralized recruitment of high-quality teaching faculty at district/block levels.
- Make District Institutes of Education and Training (DIETs)/SCERTs fully functional and organically linked with BRC/CRC and NCERT.
- Enhance learning levels by at least 50% over baseline estimates (2005–06 District Information System for Education [DISE]).
- 'Improved Quality' to be defined in operational terms through clearly identified outcome indicators, viz. learning levels of students, teacher competence, classroom processes, teaching learning materials, etc.
- The National Curriculum Framework (NCF) 2005 and the syllabi prepared by NCERT to be the guiding documents for States for revising their curricula/syllabi with SCERTs playing a more active role in ensuring common standard.
- Introduce monetary and non-monetary incentives for recognizing good teachers with block/district and State awards.

Sharing of SSA Expenditure and Reprioritization of SSA Components

1.1.52 The approved SSA programme provided for an 85:15 sharing between Centre and the States till the end of the Ninth Plan period, 75:25 sharing during the Tenth Plan period, and 50:50 thereafter. In view of persistent demand from the States and the urgency in filling up the infrastructure gap in the educationally fragile States, the funding pattern between Centre and States/UTs for SSA Phase II has been modified to 65:35 for the first two years of the Eleventh Plan, 60:40 for the third year, 55:45 for the fourth year, and 50:50 thereafter. The special dispensation for NE States during 2005–06 and 2006–07 will continue for the Eleventh Plan whereby each of the NE States contributes only 10% of the approved outlay as State share.

1.1.53 The restructuring of SSA will include ensuring that all teachers, including para teachers, are trained, the norms for civil works are the same throughout a State, there is 1 CRC for every 10 schools, 10 CRCs per BRC, and 5 resource teachers per block, there is no single teacher school and no multi-grade teaching. The curricula/syllabi will be revised as per the NCF and the NCERT guidelines.

Special Interventions for the Disadvantaged Groups

1.1.54 Young learners from socially marginalized sections experience education in a distinctly different form than those who occupy mainstream positions of power and privilege.[7] They face overt and covert forms of rejection in schooling.[8] The Eleventh Plan will lay special focus on disadvantaged groups and educationally backward areas. This focus will include not only higher resource allocation but also capacity building for preparation and implementation of strategies based on identified needs, more intensive monitoring and supervision, and tracking of progress. Specific measures will include:

- Top priority in pre-primary schooling to habitations of marginalized sections.

[7] Sunil Batra (2006), Equity in Education in India: A distant Dream or an Elusive Reality? National Seminar on Universalising Elementary Education in India, IHD, New Delhi.

[8] K Kumar (1983), Educational Experience of Scheduled Castes and Tribes, *EPW*, 18, pp. 328–47.

- Setting up additional 500 KGBVs in blocks with higher concentration of SC, ST, OBC, and minority population.
- Special attention to districts with high SCs, STs, and minority population. Innovative funds for SFDs to be doubled.
- Focus on improving the learning levels of SC, ST, minority children through remedial coaching in schools and also in habitations through educated youth of Nehru Yuva Kendra Sangathan (NYKS), NSS, Self-help Groups (SHGs), and local non-governmental organizations (NGOs).
- Special schools for slum children in 35 cities with million plus population.
- Special intervention for migrating children, deprived children in urban slum areas, single parent's children, physically challenged children, and working children.
- Creation of capacity within the school for dealing with students lagging in studies.
- Setting up 1000 hostels in EBBs with the resident PG teacher as the warden to provide supplementary academic support.
- Sensitizing teachers for special care of weaker sections and CWSN.
- Intensive social mobilization in SCs, STs, OBCs, and predominantly tribal and minority habitations through community support.
- Housing for teachers in tribal and remote habitations.

Pre-school Education (PSE)

1.1.55 The PSE component of ICDS-Anganwadi is very weak with repetition high and learning levels low. This in turn discourages many children from continuing their education. SSA will have a component of one-year pre-primary, which can be universalized to cover 2.4 crore children in a phased manner.[9] This is critical for school readiness/entry with increased basic vocabulary and conceptual abilities that help school retention. Besides, it will free the girl child of sibling care. The existing coverage of pre-primary classes in schools is over 11 million. A large number of primary schools in States like UP and Rajasthan already have ECCE. Primary schools within the habitations are ideal for such ECCE. In other habitations, ICDS-Anganwadi will be supported.

Madarsas/Maktabs

1.1.56 In the Eleventh Plan additional madarsas maktabs will be supported for modernization under AIE component and it should be possible to cover all the 12000 odd Madarsas during the Plan period.

1.1.57 Education in human moral values, civic duties, environmental protection, and physical education will be built into the system whereby every child is prepared to face the future with a healthy frame of mind and body and become a responsible citizen. Education will foster the spirit of liberty, freedom, patriotism, non-violence, tolerance, national unity and integration, cultural harmony, inquisitive reasoning, rationality, and scientific temper in young minds. Every school and EGS/AIE centre will receive a special grant to celebrate national festivals of Independence Day and Republic Day. Hoisting of national flag on these days should be made mandatory in all educational institutions including private schools with discipline.

KGBV and DPEP

1.1.58 These schemes will be subsumed within SSA in the Eleventh Plan. Expansion of 500 KGBVs in district/ blocks with high concentration of SCs, STs, OBCs, and minorities will be taken up. Also, an in-depth evaluation of the functioning of the existing KGBVs will be undertaken. The programme of civil works under KGBV appears to be slow in many States. DPEP will end in November 2008 and will be subsumed under SSA as per the existing procedure. The external commitments will however be met.

Mid-Day Meal Scheme (MDMS)

1.1.59 The scheme has been extended to UPS (government, local body, and government-aided schools, and EGS/AIE centres) in 3479 EBBs from 1 October 2007 to cover 17 million additional children and will be extended to all UPS from April 2008 to cover 54 million children. Thus, MDMS will cover about 18 crore children by 2008–09. The nutritional value of meals for upper primary children will be fixed at

[9]Mid-Term Appraisal of the Tenth Five Year Plan, 2005, Planning Commission, New Delhi.

700 calories derived from 150 gm of cereals and 20 gm of protein.

MDMS: ACTION POINTS

- MDM to be managed by the local community and PRIs/NGOs, and not contractor-driven: civic quality and safety to be prime considerations.
- Sensitize teachers and others involved in nutrition, hygiene, cleanliness, and safety norms to rectify observed deficiencies.
- Involve nutrition experts in planning low cost nutrition menu and for periodic testing of samples of prepared food.
- Promote locally grown nutritionally rich food items through kitchen gardens in school, etc.
- Revive the School Health Programme; disseminate and replicate best practices adopted by States.
- Provide drinking facilities in all schools on an urgent basis.
- Display status regarding supplies, funds, norms, weekly menu, and coverage in schools to ensure transparency.
- Central assistance to cooking cost should be based on the actual number of beneficiary children and not on enrolment.
- Promote social audit.
- Online monitoring.

Mahila Samakhya (MS)

1.1.60 The MS programme will be continued as per the existing pattern and expanded in a phased manner to cover all the EBBs and also in urban/suburban slums, as it contributes to educational empowerment of poor women. There is a need to operationalize the National Resource Centre of MS to support training, research, and proper documentation. The documentation and dissemination of MS needs its strengthening. It is desirable to conclude negotiations with the development partners as EAP comes with excellent project design and measurement system, capacity building, and TA.

LITERACY AND ADULT EDUCATION: PERFORMANCE IN TENTH PLAN

1.1.61 Literacy is the most essential prerequisite for individual empowerment. A new thrust was given to adult literacy in the National Policy on Education 1986 and the Plan of Action 1992, which advocated a three-pronged strategy of adult education, elementary education, and non-formal education to eradicate illiteracy. The National Literacy Mission (NLM) was set up in 1988 with an initial target to make 80 million persons literate by 1995, which was later enhanced to 100 million by 1997 and the revised target is to achieve a threshold level of 75% literacy by 2007.

1.1.62 Dominant strategies of the NLM and the Total Literacy Campaigns (TLC) were 'area specific, time bound, volunteer based, cost effective and result oriented.' The efforts made by the TLCs and Post Literacy Projects (PLP) to eradicate illiteracy yielded commendable results: rise in literacy from 52.2% in 1991 to 64.8% in 2001. The urban–rural literacy differential also decreased during the period. The literacy rates for females increased at a faster rate than that for males. However, gender and regional disparities in literacy still continue to persist.

1.1.63 The national overall literacy rate for Muslims is 59.1% (males 67.6% and females 50.1%). The literacy rate among Muslims is higher than the national literacy rate of 64.8% in 17 States/UTs.

1.1.64 Female literacy rates among Muslims are particularly low in Haryana (21.5%), Bihar (31.5%), Nagaland (33.3%), and Jammu and Kashmir (34.9%).

1.1.65 The Tenth Plan had set a target of achieving a sustainable threshold level of 75% literacy by 2007, to cover all left-over districts by 2003–04, to remove residual illiteracy in the existing districts by 2004–05, to complete PLP in all districts and to launch Continuing Education Programmes (CEP) in 100 districts by the end of the Plan period

TLC and PLP

1.1.66 The TLC has been the principal strategy of NLM for eradication of illiteracy. The TLCs are implemented through Zilla Saksharata Samitis (District Literacy Societies), independent and autonomous bodies having due representation of all sections of society. A total of 597 districts are presently covered under various literacy programmes The Central:State share for TLCs and PLPs is in the ratio of 2:1 for general districts and

4:1 for tribal districts. During the Tenth Plan period, the total number of districts under TLC and PLP were 95 and 174, respectively. Special project undertaken through these agencies are:

Accelerated Female Literacy Programme

1.1.67 As per 2001 census, 47 districts had a female literacy rate below 30%. These districts are concentrated in UP, Bihar, Orissa, and Jharkhand. Special innovative programmes were taken up in identified districts for improvement of female literacy.

Projects for Residual Illiteracy

1.1.68 In many cases despite the completion of the TLC campaigns, a large number of illiterates remained unreached. Projects for Residual Illiteracy were launched after the conclusion of TLCs for covering the remaining illiterates in districts of Rajasthan (10), Andhra Pradesh (8), Bihar (4), Jharkhand (3), MP (9), Karnataka (2), UP (13), and WB (4).

Special Literacy Drive in 150 Districts

1.1.69 A special literacy drive was launched in 150 districts in April 2005, which had the lowest literacy rates in the country. These districts are mainly in UP, Bihar, Jharkhand, Rajasthan, MP, Chhattisgarh, and Orissa. The special drive aimed to cover nearly 36 million illiterates during 2005–07. So far, 134 districts have been completed.

Continuing Education Programme (CEP)

1.1.70 The Continuing Education Scheme provides a learning continuum to the efforts made by TLC/PLP. The main thrust is on providing further learning opportunities to neo-literates by setting up Continuing Education Centres that provide area-specific and need-based opportunities for basic literacy, upgradation of literacy skills, pursuit of alternative educational programmes, vocational skills, and promotion of social and occupational development. The total number of districts covered under CEP is 328.

Jan Shikshan Sansthan (JSS)

1.1.71 The objective of JSS Scheme is educational, vocational, and occupational development of socio-economically backward and educationally disadvantaged groups of urban/rural population, particularly neo-literates, semi-literates, SCs, STs, women and girls, slum dwellers, migrant workers, etc. By linking literacy with vocational training, JSSs seek to improve the quality of life of the beneficiaries. JSSs offered around 284 different types of vocational courses—from candle and agarbatti making to computer training and hospital/health care. The total number of JSSs is 198.

Major Weaknesses in Adult Education Programmes

1.1.72 The constraints in the implementation of adult education programmes include inadequate participation of the State Governments, low motivation and training of voluntary teachers, lack of convergence of programmes under CEP, and weak management and supervision structure for implementation for NLM. Besides, the funding for various components of NLM schemes was also inadequate and the level of community participation was low.

ADULT EDUCATION AND LITERACY: GOALS, TARGETS, AND STRATEGIES FOR THE ELEVENTH PLAN

Adult Education

1.1.73 The NLM programmes will be revamped in the Eleventh Plan. The targets and special focus areas are given in Box 1.1.3 below.

Box 1.1.3
Eleventh Plan Targets and Special Focus Areas

Eleventh Plan Targets	Special Focus Areas
• Achieve 80% literacy rate, • Reduce gender gap in literacy to 10%, • Reduce regional, social, and gender disparities, • Extend coverage of NLM programmes to 35+ age group	• A special focus on SCs, STs, minorities, and rural women. • Focus also on low literacy States, tribal areas, other disadvantaged groups and adolescents.

Revamped Strategy of NLM in Eleventh Plan

1.1.74 The main features of the revamped NLM will be:

- Integrating Zilla Saksharata Samitis with the PRIs.

- Bringing literacy programmes at various levels under PRI structures at Block/Gram Panchayat levels, through Panchayat Saksharata Samitis.
- Revamping of NLM integrating TLC, PLP, and CEP and introducing a broad-based Lifelong Education and Awareness Programme (LEAP). The LEAP will offer diverse learning programmes, functional skills, Quality of Life Improvement Programmes, Vocational Skills, and Equivalency Programmes.
- Centres for Lifelong Education and Awareness will be multifunctional and multidimensional seeking to provide a variety of learning programmes to beneficiaries.
- ICTs will be more widely used to spread literacy in the country.
- About 250 new JSS will be set up in the Eleventh Plan. The sanction of new JSS will be contingent upon independent evaluation of the existing JSS with regard to their utility.
- To ensure transparency in the functioning of JSS, an accreditation process will be evolved in partnership with States and only accredited NGOs with good track record will implement JSS. The management of dysfunctional JSS will be changed. The quality of JSS training programme will be improved with the help of professional technical institutions of the district and the programmes tuned to meet local demand. Placement record of the trainees in the self employment will be maintained.
- A stronger synergy would be ensured between the State Resource Centres (SRCs) and the Adult Education Departments in universities for sound academic and research inputs.
- Existing SRC/District Resource Centre (DRC) will be strengthened as per the assessed needs and new SRCs will be set up only in the States where they do not exist. There will be no more than one SRC per State irrespective of the size of the State's population so that uniform standards are maintained including production of Teaching Learning Materials (TLM).
- All NGO-operated schemes will be sanctioned to accredited institutions only. The accreditation process will invariably involve State Governments and the accredited institutions will be listed on the MHRD website.

1.2 SECONDARY EDUCATION AND VOCATIONAL EDUCATION (VE)

1.2.1 The success of SSA in achieving large scale enrolment of children in regular and alternate schools has thrown open the challenge of expanding access to secondary education. Rapid changes in technology and the demand for skills also make it necessary that young people acquire more than eight years of elementary education to acquire the necessary skills to compete successfully in the labour market. Moreover, secondary education serves as a bridge between elementary and higher education.

1.2.2 The stage is thus set for universalization of secondary education. The population of children in the age group (14–18 years) is estimated at 107 million in 2001, 119.7 million in 2006, and 121.1 million in 2011, where as, the current enrolment in secondary and senior secondary education together is around 37 million only (2004–05).

SECONDARY EDUCATION: REVIEW OF PERFORMANCE IN THE TENTH PLAN

1.2.3 The thrust of secondary education during the Tenth Plan period was on improving access and reducing disparities by emphasizing the Common School System in which it is mandatory for schools in a particular area to take students from low-income families in the neighbourhood. The Tenth Plan also focused on revision of curricula with emphasis on vocationalization and employment-oriented courses, expansion and diversification of the open learning system, reorganization of teacher training, and greater use of ICTs. These objectives have been achieved only partly.

Access

1.2.4 The enrolment in 1.02 lakh secondary and 0.50 lakh higher secondary schools is 24.3 million and 12.7 million, respectively (2004–05). The GER for secondary education (IX and X) is 51.65% and that for higher secondary 27.82%. The combined GER for both the levels is only 39.91%. The dropout rate at secondary level is as high as 62% (Table 1.2.1).

1.2.5 There are glaring inter-State and intra-State variations in enrolment, dropouts, and access to secondary and higher secondary schools (Annexure 1.2.1). At the national level, the average number of secondary/higher secondary schools per 1 lakh population is as low as 14 and it is lower than the national average in Bihar (4), UP (7), WB (10), and also Jharkhand (4) and Chhattisgarh (12). The national average number of secondary and higher secondary schools per 100 sq. km is only four, and Bihar, UP, Rajasthan, MP, Chhattisgarh, and Jharkhand fall below this national average. Consequently, the GER in these States is lower than the national average of 39.91%.

TABLE 1.2.1
Secondary Education—Enrolment and Dropout, 2004–05

S. No.	Indicators Enrolment (in crore)	Boys	Girls	Total
1	Secondary (IX–X)	1.42 (57.39)	1.01 (45.28)	2.43 (51.65)
2	Hr Secondary (XI–XII)	0.74 (30.82)	0.53 (24.46)	1.27 (27.82)
3	Secondary & Hr Sec. (IX–XII)	2.16 (44.26)	1.54 (35.05)	3.70 (39.91)
4	Dropout (%) Rates (I–X)	60.41	63.88	61.92

Note: Figures in the parentheses are GER.
Source: Selected Educational Statistics (2004–05), MHRD.

1.2.6 During the decade ending 2004–05, enrolment at the secondary and higher secondary levels increased at an average annual rate of 5.32%. During the three years of the Tenth Plan upto 2004–05, it increased at a faster rate of 6.75% per annum and an additional 7.5 million children were enrolled. There will be further acceleration in secondary enrolments during the Eleventh Plan period as the primary dropout rates are declining and the transition rate from primary to upper primary is getting closer to 90%.

1.2.7 Nearly 60% of secondary schools are with private management both aided and unaided, almost in equal proportions. The share of government and local body schools and private aided schools has shown a declining trend with private unaided schools showing an increase from 15% in 1993–94 to 24% in 2001–02 and further to 30% in 2004–05 (see Figure 1.2.1). The doubling of the share of private unaided schools indicates that parents are willing to pay for education that

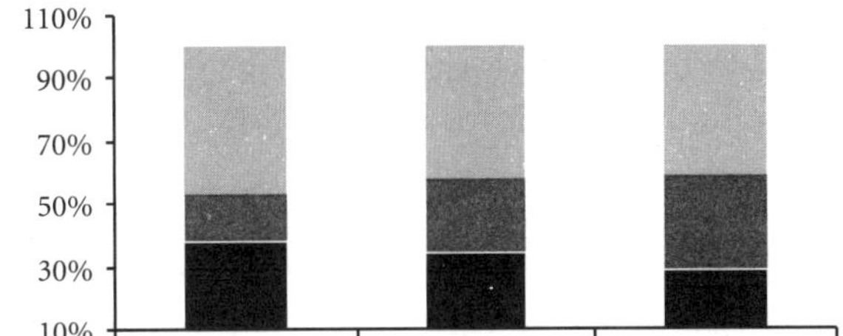

	1993–94	2001–02	2004–05
Govt	47	42	41
Unaided	15	24	30
Aided	38	34	29

Source: Selected Educational Statistics (2004–05), MHRD.

FIGURE 1.2.1: Secondary Schools by Management

is perceived to be of good quality. The factors underlying this perception include better English teaching, better monitoring and supervision of students' performance, better attention, attendance and accountability of teachers. There is, however, no evidence to show that the enrolments in these schools are additional. Only those who can afford to pay apparently opt for these schools and their average enrolment is much lower than that in the aided and government schools. Public sector investment in secondary schools has therefore to be increased even for incentivizing PPP.

SC and ST Enrolments

1.2.8 The secondary education GER for SCs and STs 45.4% and 37.2%,are respectively, as compared to the overall GER of 51.6% indicating a substantial social gap in enrolments for these groups. The GER for girls belonging to SCs and STs is 37.6% and 30.5%, respectively, indicating a substantial gender gap in enrolment for these groups.

Girls' Education

1.2.9 The Central Advisory Board of Education Committee Report on Girls Education noted a gross shortage of secondary schools for girls (both co-educational and girls' schools). The dropout of girls is extremely high mainly in the northern States, not only because the parental priority for girls' education is low, but also due to the poor access to schools in the rural areas. Opening of schools exclusively for girls appears to be necessary to overcome the gender disparity. States have to undertake, on priority, school mapping for girl's education, especially for Muslim girls.

1.2.10 The Union Government has been implementing the scheme 'Strengthening of Boarding and Hostel Facilities for Girl Students of Secondary and Higher Secondary Schools (Access & Equity)'. Under the scheme, financial assistance is given to societies and NGOs to provide boarding and hostel facilities to girls, predominantly belonging to the rural, desert, and hilly areas, and particularly for those belonging to SCs, STs, and educationally backward minorities. The performance of the scheme is not up to the mark. The scheme will be restructured and merged with the new umbrella scheme of 'Universalization of Access and Improvement of Quality of Secondary Education'.

Quality Improvement in Schools

1.2.11 During the Tenth Plan, a composite Centrally sponsored scheme (CSS) of 'Quality Improvement in Schools' was introduced by converging the following five existing schemes: (i) Improvement of Science Education in Schools, (ii) Promotion of Yoga in Schools, (iii)Environmental Orientation to School Education, (iv) National Population Education Project, and (v) International Science Olympiads. Improvement of Science Education in Schools has since been transferred to the States as a State sector scheme and the remaining four components are being implemented by NCERT. It appears that very few States implement this scheme at present.

National Curriculum Framework (NCF)

1.2.12 Mathematics, Science, and English are the three core subjects in which a large number of students do not fare well in examinations. In fact, nearly 50% fail in these subjects. This is perhaps the biggest shortcoming of both the elementary and secondary education system. The NCF—2005 NCERT addresses this issue. The National Focus Group on 'Teaching of Science' suggested prevention of marginalization of experiment-based learning in school science curriculum. Investment is required for improving school libraries, laboratories, and workshops to promote culture of experiment-based learning while reducing the importance of external examinations. There is also a need to have computer-interfaced experiments and projects utilizing database from public domain.

Education for Disabled

1.2.13 The scheme 'Integrated Education for the Disabled Children (IEDC)' is being implemented with a view to integrating children and youths with mild and moderate disabilities in the formal school system. It provides 100% financial assistance to States/UTs and NGOs. About 2.84 lakh children from 1.0 lakh schools were benefited under the scheme.

Central Sector Schemes (CS)

1.2.14 The Central Government is managing and fully funding four types of schools viz., KVs, Navodaya Vidyalayas (NVs), Central Tibetan Schools (CTSs), and National Institute of Open Schooling (NIOS). There are 972 KVs with an enrolment of 9.54 lakh and staff strength of about 46000. KVs are to cater to the educational needs of the wards of transferable Central Government and public sector employees. There are 548 NVs with a total enrolment of 1.91 lakh students, selected through entrance tests. These are pace setting residential co-educational schools providing quality education to talented children predominantly from rural areas. The enrolment of SC and ST children in these schools is 23.9% and 16.2%, respectively. There are 79 CTSs with a total enrolment of 9755 children. NIOS provides opportunities for continuing education to those who missed completing school education. 14 lakh students are enrolled at the secondary and senior secondary stages through 11 Regional Centres, 1943 accredited institutions for academic courses, and 1002 accredited vocational institutions (AVIs) for programme delivery through open learning and distance learning. NIOS centres have also been set up in UAE, Kuwait, Nepal, and China.

Allocation and Expenditure of the Tenth Plan

1.2.15 As against the total Tenth Plan allocation of Rs 4325.00 crore, the anticipated expenditure was Rs 3766.90 crore.

SECONDARY EDUCATION: GOALS, TARGETS, AND STRATEGIES FOR THE ELEVENTH PLAN

1.2.16 The Eleventh Plan aims to: (i) raise the minimum level of education to class X and accordingly universalize access to secondary education; (ii) ensure good quality secondary education with focus on Science, Mathematics, and English; and (iii) aim towards major reduction in gender, social, and regional gaps in enrolments, dropouts, and school retention. The norm will be to provide a secondary school within 5 km and a higher secondary school within 7–8 km of every habitation. The GER in secondary education is targeted to increase from 52% in 2004–05 to 75% by 2011–12 and the combined secondary and senior secondary GER from 40% to 65% in the same period.

Scheme for Universal Access and Quality at the Secondary Stage (SUCCESS)

1.2.17 The erstwhile schemes of ICT in schools, girls child incentive, IEDC, VE, etc. will be subsumed under a new umbrella CSS named SUCCESS. The principal objectives of SUCCESS will be (i) universalizing access with major reduction in gender, social, and regional gaps in enrolment, dropout, and retention and (ii) improving quality with focus on Science and Maths. Specific interventions will include:

- Setting up 6000 high quality Model Schools at block level to serve as benchmark for excellence in secondary schooling.
- Upgrading 15000 existing primary schools to secondary schools.
- Increasing the intake capacity of about 44000 existing secondary schools.
- Strengthening infrastructure in existing schools with 3.43 lakh additional classrooms and additional 5.14 lakh teachers.
- Encouraging establishment of good quality schools in deficient areas in both public and more in PPP mode.
- Expansion of KVs and NVs in underserved areas.
- 100% trained teachers in all schools and reaching PTR of 25:1 by 2011–12.
- Revamped ICT in secondary and higher secondary schools.

1.2.18 The 6000 Model Schools will be set up in two distinct streams. Under both the streams, land will be provided by the State/UTs free of cost. The first stream will consist of 3500 public funded schools (3000 in KVs and 500 in NVs template) to be launched in the EBBs which have a significant SC, ST, OBC, and Minority population. The second stream of about 2500 schools would be set up through PPP in other blocks with emphasis on geographical, demographic, gender, and social equity. These schools will be managed and run by involving corporates, philanthropic foundations, endowments, educational trusts, and reputed private providers.

Substantial Improvement in Quality of Secondary Education

1.2.19 The other measures for improving quality in secondary education will include adoption of NCF 2005, adoption of NET/SET of NCERT/CBSE/SCERT/State Boards to enable recruitment of quality teaching faculty; long pending institutional reforms in school management, and ensuring accountability at all levels.

Revamped ICT in Schools

1.2.20 There has been a significant impact of ICT in the delivery of educational services across the world. ICT infrastructure will be established at government and government-aided secondary and senior secondary schools during the Eleventh Plan period. There are about 1.4 lakh such schools out of which 1.08 lakh are government and government-aided schools. About 28000 schools are in far flung areas. About 80000 schools are proposed to be connected on Internet through terrestrial/wireless broadband mode and the remaining 28000 schools will be provided Internet connectivity through broadband Very Small Aperture Terminals. The latter mode of connectivity (satellite) has been proposed as the terrestrial infrastructure in the far flung and Schedule V regions is quite weak and service providers have no immediate plans to extend the broadband infrastructure in these regions. UPS with battery backups and solar power panels for uninterrupted power supply will also be provided as per requirements.

1.2.21 An amount of Rs 5000 crore is being provided during the Eleventh Plan for providing ICT infrastructure in schools. Under this programme, each school will be provided with ICT infrastructure consisting of a networked computer lab with at least ten computers, a server, a printer connected on Local Area Network and broadband Internet connectivity of 2 Mbps. Every school will also have a technology classroom, with audio visual equipment for enhancing the learning. A dedicated programme for content creation as per the curricula will be undertaken as an integral part of this initiative. In addition, educational content on CDs for embellishing classroom teaching will also be made available. Training of teachers in the use of computers and teaching through computers will be another important component of this initiative.

1.2.22 This revamped scheme of ICT in schools will be implemented in partnership with the States and private providers. This will be a sub-Mission of the National Mission of ICT of MHRD.

Education for Girls

1.2.23 Most of the States implement incentive schemes for education of girls, but generally with very limited coverage. Measures will be undertaken to overcome obstacles to girls' education posed by factors such as poverty, domestic/sibling responsibilities, girl child labour, low preference to girls' education, preference to marriage over the education of girls, etc. A Girl Child Incentive Scheme will be launched on a pilot basis in the selected EBBs. On the basis of quick evaluation, its expansion will be considered in the Eleventh Plan period. The merger of all girl child incentives schemes will be ensured.

Bridging Social Disparities

1.2.24 In order to bridge social gaps in secondary education in respect of SCs, STs, minorities, and OBCs, the Eleventh Plan will address specific areas including (i) upgradation of elementary schools to secondary schools in geographic concentration areas of relevant social groups, (ii) supply of free uniforms, text books, footwear, (iii) supply of bicycle/wheelchairs, (iv) hostels for boys and girls, (v) stipends to the deserving children, (vi) support to all Madrasas for adoption of general curriculum of States, (vii) pre-matric and post-matric scholarships, (viii) special remedial coaching within/outside school for weaker students, and (ix) an area-intensive approach with community participation.

Education of Children with Disabilities

1.2.25 The scheme of Inclusive Education for the Disabled at Secondary Stage (IEDSS) will enable all students with disabilities completing eight years of elementary schooling an opportunity to complete four years of secondary schooling (classes IX–XII) in an inclusive and enabling environment. The IEDSS will also support the training programmes for general school teachers to meet the needs of children with disabilities.

Levy of Fees

1.2.26 Even in public schools, there is a need to encourage some fees for students for enabling school management to raise resources for quality improvement. This should be accompanied by a generous provision of scholarships to those who cannot afford such fees, particularly girl students who are at the risk of dropping out and marrying early.

National Institute of Open Schooling (NIOS)

1.2.27 During the Eleventh Plan, the thrust of the Open Schooling system will be on (i) developing NIOS as a potential Resource Organization in Open Schooling at the national and international level, besides offering courses of study, (ii) up-scaling programmes of the existing 10 State Open Schools (SOSs), and (iii) setting up SOSs in the remaining 19 States. In order to ensure quality in Open Schooling, there will be a full-time coordinator with ancillary staff on contract basis in each Study Centre under the Open Schooling system. During the Eleventh Plan, 1000 AVIs will be set up as a part of the Skill Development Mission (SDM). All AVIs will be rated for their performance before continuation.

Teacher Education

1.2.28 During the Tenth Plan, the thrust areas for Teacher Education are development and strengthening of teacher education institutes, improvement in quality of pre-service and in-service teacher education, professional development of teacher education, and assessment of students. All these were to ensure that teacher education leads to qualitative improvement of schools. The performance of teacher education programmes has not, however, been satisfactory. The objective of setting up DIETs was to influence the quality of teacher education through innovative pre-service and in-service education programmes. However, there seems to be no evidence of DIETs taking off, constrained as they are by several factors that are proposed to be addressed in the Eleventh Plan. The scheme of Restructuring and Reorganizing of Teacher Education, a CSS, has built up a large infrastructure base with 571 DIETs/DRCs, 104 Colleges of Teacher Education (CTEs), and 31 Institutes of Advanced Study in Education (IASEs) up to 2006–07. However, in view of the acute shortage of teachers, States have appointed a large number of para-teachers through VECs.

1.2.29 DIETs have not justified their existence in terms of outcomes despite their existence for about two decades. DIETs were in acute shortage of quality faculty and several DIETs were headless during the Tenth Plan. Structural problems and the absence of linkages with higher education seem to have isolated DIETs from current trends in research as well as from the academic community. The quality of teacher training leaves much to be desired. SCERTs have also not yet measured up to their expectations. It appears that quality faculty for DIETs needs to be outsourced or else DIETs should adopt the PPP mode, in partnership with reputed institutions to take up intensive and useful training activities. The Eleventh Plan should ensure that the DIETs fulfil their mandate.

1.2.30 A holistic framework cross-connecting various teacher education institutions ranging from those run by universities and research organizations to SCERTs, DIETs, BRCs, and CRCs is needed. A core team drawn from apex agencies and universities should be set up to evolve linkages and to draw up standards for teacher education, along with a plan for academic support at each level. This team will also formulate detailed guidelines for recruitment of teacher educators, academic responsibility, affiliation, and accountability.

1.2.31 A grading system of DIETs/SCERTs will be evolved through NCERT/State Institute of Educational Management and Training (SIEMAT). All teacher training for elementary education will be brought under a single major head. All in-service training, pre-service training, special courses, training for remedial coaching, training of master trainers, etc., will be brought under the aegis of DIETs. BRCs and CRCs will be organically linked with DIETs. All training institutions (NCERT to CRCs) will be properly strengthened and funded to enable them to conduct programmes of high standards.

1.2.32 The vacant faculty positions in DIETs will be filled on a drive basis. A broad-based faculty development programme for continuous teacher training and master trainers will be in place. DIETs will develop their own model institutions or set benchmarks in collaboration with renowned teacher training institutions (TTIs). There will be full-fledged teacher training capacity building from CRCs to NCERT with adequate funding. A special package for improving teacher education in NE States needs to be initiated. The Regional Centre of Indira Gandhi National Open University (IGNOU) and the newly created North East Regional Institute of Education of NCERT may be entrusted with this task. Special support to NE States should also be extended to establish additional teacher education institutions. MHRD will create a teacher education portal giving details of all teacher education institutions, their calendar of training programmes, curriculum, best teaching/learning practices, self-learning material, theoretical and practical teaching material, etc.

1.2.33 The Teacher Education Scheme should be implemented in partnership with States. Recurring expenditure on the scheme, including salaries and contingencies during the Eleventh Plan period will be met by GoI to the extent of 100% in 2007–08 and thereafter progressively reduced by 10% each year to be 90% in 2008–09; 80% in 2009–10; 70% in 2010–11, and 60% in 2011–12 so that gradually the States can take up their committed liabilities and hold establishment expenditure. The GoI will bear 100% of the new establishment and programme components expenditure.

1.2.34 The Eleventh Plan would be a Quality Plan in respect of the education sector. The following specific programmes are proposed to be taken up in teacher education during the Eleventh Plan.

- Strengthening Teacher Education by (i) developing Teacher Education Information Base in Public

Domain, (ii) creating additional support systems in the field, and (iii) strengthening academic capacity.

- Continuation of existing scheme relating to SCERTs.
- Continuation of support to IASEs and CTEs.
- Conducting training of Educational Administrators including Head Teachers.
- Introducing substitute/stipend scheme for enabling teachers and educational administrators to enhance their academic qualifications.
- Continuation of support to DIETs.
- Augmenting Teacher Education capacity in SC/ST and minority areas.
- Professional Development of teacher through training programmes.
- Professional Development of Teacher Educators through Refresher Courses and Fellowship programmes.
- Support to NGOs.
- Technology in Teacher Education.
- Integrating Elementary Teacher Education with Higher Education.

NCTE, SCERTs, CTEs, and IASEs

1.2.35 National Council for Teacher Education (NCTE) is a statutory body vested with the responsibility of maintaining quality standards in teacher education institutions. Performing this task is obviously linked to regulating the establishment of TTIs in accordance with specified norms and matching the need for qualified teachers. Uncontrolled growth in the number of private TTIs in recent years has led to unevenness in the quality of teacher training institutions. There has been a mushroom growth of low-quality private institutions. While NCTE has been very active in southern States and Maharashtra, it is virtually dormant in the eastern States. The existing mechanism for regular monitoring has proved inadequate.

1.2.36 SCERTs have been in existence in practically all States of the country. Though SCERTs were envisaged as apex institutes for educational research and training, the older State-created institutions such as the State Institutes of Education (SIEs) also continue to function in some States. SIEs and SCERTs will be merged. New SCERTs could be set up in States that are yet to establish them. Expansion of CTEs and IASEs will be undertaken only on the basis of evaluation by independent bodies.

1.2.37 Pre-service and in-service training programmes, the annual conference of Directors of SCERTs/SIEs, NCERT Awards for innovative practices in teacher education/school education, etc., have continued to be organized by the NCERT. Besides NCERT organizes orientation programme for librarians of SCERTs/DIETs. However, NCERT has contributed very little to the capacity building of the SCERTs. The schemes implemented by NCERT, particularly those relating to grants needs to be evaluated by an independent professional agency.

There is a need to address the teacher training requirements in polytechnics. Teachers in polytechnics have to be trained to upgrade their teaching skills due to the changes in technology. Further, in order to keep pace with industry, the curriculum of diploma courses will be revised and its periodic updation made compulsory.

Vocational Education: Review of Performance in Tenth Plan

1.2.38 The Kothari Commission on Educational Reforms, 1964–66, had visualized that 25% of the students at the secondary stage would go for the vocational stream. The Kulandaiswamy Committee Report had targeted this figure at 15% to be achieved by 2000. According to the recent National Sample Survey Organization (NSSO) data, only 5% of the population of 19–24 age group in India have acquired some sort of skills through VE. The corresponding figure for Korea is 96%.

1.2.39 The CSS of Vocationalization of Secondary Education at +2 level is being implemented since 1988. The revised scheme is in operation since 1992–93. The scheme provides financial assistance to States for setting up administrative structures, carrying out area-vocational surveys, preparing curriculum guides training manuals, organizing teacher training programmes, strengthening technical support system for research and development (R&D), etc. It also provides financial assistance to NGOs and voluntary organizations (VO) for implementation of specific innovative projects for conducting short-term courses. Under the scheme, an enrolment capacity of over 10 lakh students in 9583 schools with about 21000 sections have been created so far.

VOCATIONAL EDUCATION: STRATEGY AND TARGETS IN THE ELEVENTH PLAN

Strategy

1.2.40 The National SDM is on the anvil. It is envisaged to evolve a comprehensive scheme for creating a diverse and wide range of skills for our youth that would enable the country to reap the scientific and demographic dividend. The emphasis will be on demand-driven VE programmes in partnership with employers. The current programmes will be restructured with emphasis on hands-on training/exposure, vertical mobility, and flexibility.

1.2.41 Greater emphasis will be placed on the services sector and, therefore, on soft skills, computer literacy, and flexi-time. There will also be emphasis on development of generic and multiple skills so that persons may respond to changes in technology and market demands. Generic skills that cut across a number of occupations would enable an individual to transfer from one field to another during his/her working life. Other features will include compulsory partnership with employers who could provide trainers and arrange for internships, give advice on curricula, and participate in assessment and certification.

1.2.42 Only 5% of the population can receive skill training through the formal system. The remaining about 4.0 crore unskilled and semi-skilled persons, who are already working, will be given continuous or further training for upgradation of their skills through a variety of delivery systems, including part-time, sandwich system, day release system, block release system, open and distance learning system, etc.

1.2.43 VE programmes preparing for occupations in Farming, Artisan Trades, Crafts, Small and Medium Enterprises, particularly for self-employment, will include entrepreneurship development and elementary training in ICT to enable persons to take responsibility for production, marketing, management, and rational organization of enterprise.

1.2.44 VE could be offered in flexible mode through modular courses of varying durations, with credit transfer facility. Clear strategies for encouraging access to Vocational Education and Training (VET) for marginalized groups, including SCs, STs, OBCs, minorities, girls, street children, working children and differently abled children will be adopted.

1.2.45 A National Vocational Qualification (NVQ) system, in which public and private systems of VE collaboratively meet the needs of industry and individuals, will be developed. Under this, modular competency based vocational courses will be offered along with a mechanism of testing skills. Bridge courses to facilitate people without any formal education to get enrolled in the regular system of courses will also be developed through NVQ system.

1.2.46 The functioning of the Central Institute of Vocational Education, Bhopal, will be reviewed and the institute restructured to serve as a national resource institution for policy, planning, and monitoring of VE programmes and for developing a NVQ system in the country.

1.2.47 An integrated institutional mechanism for effective implementation of vocational programmes, with quality checks at the State, district, and block levels could be established as a distinct wing of the existing institutional arrangements of SCERT, DIETs, and BRCs. These institutions will be strengthened in a convergent mode.

Physical Targets

1.2.48 During the Eleventh Plan, VE will be expanded to cover 20000 schools with intake capacity of 25 lakh by 2011–12. The programme will ensure mobility between vocational, general, and technical education and multiple entry and exit options.

1.3 HIGHER AND TECHNICAL EDUCATION

1.3.1 The investment made in higher education in the 1950s and 1960s has given us a strong knowledge base in many fields and contributed significantly to economic development, social progress, and political democracy in independent India. At the time of independence, the number of universities was no more than

20, of colleges around 500 and the total enrolment was less than 1.0 lakh. By the end of the Tenth Plan, the Indian higher education system has grown into one of the largest in the world with 378 universities, 18064 colleges, a faculty strength of 4.92 lakh, and an estimated enrolment of 140 lakh students. The higher education institutions include 23 Central universities (CU), 216 State universities, 110 deemed universities, 11 private universities, and 33 institutions of national importance established through central legislation and another 5 institutions established through State legislations.

1.3.2 Despite the expansion that has occurred, it is evident that the system is under stress to provide a sufficient volume of skilled human power, which is equipped with the required knowledge and technical skills to cater to the demands of the economy. The accelerated growth of our economy has already created shortages of high-quality technical manpower. Unlike the developed countries, where the young working age population is fast shrinking with higher dependency ratios, India has a demographic advantage with about 70% of the population below the age of 35 years. But this advantage can only be realised if we expand opportunities for our youth on a massive scale and in diverse fields of basic science, engineering and technology, health care, architecture, management, etc. This is possible only if we initiate rapid expansion along with long overdue reforms in the higher, technical, and professional education sectors.

1.3.3 Expansion, inclusion, and rapid improvement in quality throughout the higher and technical education system by enhancing public spending, encouraging private initiatives, and initiating the long overdue major institutional and policy reforms will form the core of the Eleventh Plan effort. *Our long-term goal is to set India as a nation in which all those who aspire good quality higher education can access it, irrespective of their paying capacity.*

Higher Education: Review of the Tenth Plan

Expansion

1.3.4 The focus of the Tenth Plan was on primary education with an expenditure of over Rs 50000 crore, whereas, the expenditure on university and higher education was below Rs 8000 crore. The growth of higher education system during the Tenth Plan is given in Table 1.3.1.

TABLE 1.3.1
Growth of Higher Education System

No. of Institutions	2002	2007
Universities	201	378
Colleges	12342	18064
NAAC Accredited:		
(i) Universities	61	140
(ii) Colleges	198	3492
Enrolment(lakh)	75	140

Source: UGC-NAAC.

1.3.5 Our GER of around 11% is very low compared to the world average of 23.2%, 36.5% for countries in transition, 54.6% for the developed countries, and 22% for Asian countries. Further, with high disparities (Table 1.3.2), inclusive education has been an elusive target. 370 districts with GER less than the national average need enrolment drives and rapid expansion of higher education institutions.

TABLE 1.3.2
Disparities in GER, 2004–05

Disparities	GER
Area:	
(i) Rural	6.70
(ii) Urban	19.90
Gender:	
(i) Male	12.40
(ii) Female	9.10
Social:	
(i) SCs	6.57
(ii) STs	6.52
(iii) OBCs	8.77
(iv) Others	17.22
ALL	11.00

Source: UGC.

1.3.6 We should aim to increase the GER to 21% by the end of the Twelfth Plan with an interim target of 15% by 2011–12. To achieve this, the enrolments in universities/colleges need to be substantially raised at an annual rate of 8.9% to reach 21 million by 2011–12.

This requires an additional enrolment of 8.7 lakh students in universities and 61.3 lakh in colleges.

Private Institutions

1.3.7 A welcome development during the Tenth Plan is that the share of private unaided higher education institutions increased from 42.6% in 2001 to 63.21% in 2006. Their share of enrolments also increased from 32.89% to 51.53% in the same period. This trend is likely to continue in the Eleventh Plan and therefore, it is reasonable to expect that about half of incremental enrolment targeted for higher education will come from private providers.

1.3.8 Though the emergence of the private sector has helped expand capacity, it is characterized by some imbalances. Private institutions have improved access in a few selected disciplines such as engineering, management, medicine, IT, etc. where students are willing to pay substantial fees. However, the distribution across country is uneven, with some States receiving most of the growth in private institutions.

Grant to Colleges/Universities

1.3.9 Out of the 18064 colleges that exist today, only 14000 come under the purview of the University Grants Commission (UGC) system, with permanent and temporary affiliations. UGC assists only 40% (5625) of these 14000 colleges recognized under Section 12(b) of UGC (permanent affiliation) Act, which meet the minimum eligibility norms, mostly in terms of physical facilities and infrastructure.

Central Universities (CU)

1.3.10 The existing State universities of Allahabad, Manipur, Tripura, and Arunachal Pradesh and the Central Institute of English and Foreign Languages (CIEFL) have been converted into CU, while a new CU has been established in Sikkim. The National Institute of Education Planning and Administration has been converted into a deemed university and is now called the NUEPA.

UGC

1.3.11 The UGC, a statutory body, established in 1956, operates over 100 schemes, providing a wide range of development grants to institutions, running day care centres for children, promotion of sports, travel grants for Vice-Chancellors and researchers, area studies, cultural exchange, adult education, women studies, academic staff colleges (ASCs), hostels for women, innovative programmes in frontier research and career oriented education, etc. The schemes implemented by UGC have not yet been evaluated by any external professional agencies. There is an urgent need for such in-depth evaluation and streamlining the range of schemes, and rationalizing the procedures and delivery mechanism including the disbursal of grants.

The National Accreditation Assessment Council (NAAC)

1.3.12 NAAC was set up in 1994 to make quality an essential element through a combination of internal and external quality assessment and accreditation. During the Tenth Plan, NAAC was strengthened with the opening of four regional centres so as to speed up the accreditation process. NAAC has so far completed accreditation of only 140 out of the 378 universities and 3492 out of the 14000 colleges. The results of the accreditation process thus far indicate serious quality problems. Only 9% of the colleges and 31% of the universities are rated as A grade and the rest fall in 'B' and 'C' categories.

ASCs

1.3.13 At present there are 55 ASCs which conduct orientation programmes of four weeks for newly appointed teachers and refresher courses of three weeks for in-service teachers. The refresher courses provide opportunities for serving teachers to learn from each other and serve as a forum for keeping abreast with the latest advances in various subjects. The functioning of ASCs has not yet been evaluated.

ICT

1.3.14 A number of steps have been taken for leveraging the use of ICT in higher education. UGC INFONET allows teachers and students to have access to e-formatted journals, besides links to other research. The network is run and managed by ERNET India. Information for Library Network (INFLIBNET), an autonomous Inter-University Centre for UGC, is the nodal agency for coordination and facilitation of the linkage between ERNET and universities. States have

Box 1.3.1
Private Sector Participation in Higher Education

Past experience shows that private mechanism has been responsible for setting up of some first rate institutions:

- Indian Institute of Science (IISc), Bangalore and Tata Institute of Fundamental Research (TIFR), Mumbai were established by J.N. Tata with the vision and aim of advancing the scientific capabilities of the country.
- The renowned Santiniketan, presently Viswa-Bharati University, was founded by Nobel Laureate Rabindranath Tagore in early 1900s.
- Xavier Labour Relations Institute (XLRI), one of the finest management schools in India, was founded in 1949 by Fr Quinn Enright in the Steel City of Jamshedpur with a vision of 'renewing the face of the earth'.
- The Birla Institute of Technology & Science (BITS), Pilani, whose founder is the noted industrialist G.D. Birla, was started in early 1900s as a small school that grew to become a premier engineering institution. Today, BITS has campuses in Goa, Hyderabad, and Dubai. The Birla Education Trust is one of the biggest educational trusts in the private sector in our country.
- The Tata Institute of Social Sciences (TISS) was established in 1936, as the Sir Dorabji Tata Graduate School of Social Work. It was the first school of social work in India and in 1944 was renamed as TISS. In 1964 it was recognized as a deemed university by UGC.
- The International Institute of Information Technology (IIIT), Hyderabad is an autonomous, self-supporting institution with major national and international IT companies being actively involved in its academic programmes through their corporate schools on the campus.
- Vidyanagari in Baramati offers courses from Primary Education to Masters Degree. The Trust runs a Law College, Engineering College, Biotechnology College, and an Institute of Information Technology.

agreed to encourage their universities, colleges, and technical institutes to become members of INFLIBNET and Indian National Digital Library for Engineering Sciences and Technology (INDEST).

Autonomous Status

1.3.15 During the Tenth Plan, the target was to accord autonomous status to 10% of eligible colleges. At present 132 colleges under 29 universities are autonomous. However, the number of institutions that have utilized their autonomous status in launching new courses and innovative methods either in teaching or management appears to be extremely limited.

Science Education

1.3.16 The proportion of students opting for Science courses is far too low. Consequently, a large segment of our graduates are inadequately equipped to meet the changing needs of the emerging labour market.

All India Council for Technical Education (AICTE)

1.3.17 The AICTE was set up in 1945, and was given statutory status in 1987 for coordinated development of Technical Education, promotion of qualitative improvement, and maintenance of norms and standards.

National Board of Accreditation (NBA)

1.3.18 NBA has also become a provisional member of the Washington Accord. This will ensure acceptance of its accreditation procedure amongst the member countries of the Accord. So far about 1924 programmes have been considered for accreditation.

HIGHER EDUCATION: TARGETS AND STRATEGIES IN ELEVENTH PLAN

Setting a Reforms Agenda

1.3.19 An Inter-Ministerial Working Group should be set up to work out a detail reforms agenda on outlines given below.

(i) ADMISSION, CURRICULUM, AND ASSESSMENT

- Common calibration and admission based on Common Entrance Test and/or other relevant criteria for at least professional and PG courses in CU in the first phase.
- Universalizing the semester system.
- Continuous internal evaluation and assessment to eventually replace annual examinations.
- Introducing Credit System to provide students with the possibility of spatial and temporal flexibility/mobility.

- Curriculum revision at least once in every three years or earlier to keep syllabi in tune with job market dynamics and advancement in research.

(ii) ACCREDITATION AND RATINGS

- Introduction of a mandatory accreditation system for all educational institutions;
- Creation of multiple rating agencies with a body to rate these rating agencies.
- Department-wise ratings in addition to institutional rating.

(iii) TEACHERS' COMPETENCE AND MOTIVATION

- Restructuring of NET/SET with greater emphasis on recruitment of adequate and good quality teachers.
- Revamping ASCs and upgrading teachers capabilities through short and long term courses.
- Expansion of research programmes/projects and incentivizing research faculty through funded projects/research.

(iv) MISCELLANEOUS

- UGC in consultation with stakeholders to arrive at optimum size of universities and the number of college affiliations.
- Setting up of a new Inter-university Centre on higher education to undertake specialized research for policy formulation.

Autonomy and Accountability in Higher Educational Institutions

1.3.20 The issues of autonomy and accountability are very critical. While many initiatives have already been taken on various aspects, a lot has to be done in the near future with full determination.

1.3.21 Autonomy is the sine qua non of excellence. Erosion of autonomy adversely impacts quality. Autonomy must, however, be linked to accountability. Furthermore, the government must ensure that fee structures do not lead to profiteering. Beyond this, the State/government must not interfere in institutional governance.

1.3.22 Higher education institutions must subject themselves to internal accountability to their stakeholders with respect to their performance and outcomes. They need to set their own goals and targets to assess their achievements and subject themselves to peer review. They should be subject to an apex regulatory institutional mechanism that must be at an arm's-length from the government and independent of all stakeholders. The main function of the regulatory mechanism would be of setting and maintenance of standards as also to evaluate performance and outcomes. The regulatory framework must be conducive to innovation, creativity, and excellence in higher education.

1.3.23 Autonomy has three inter-related dimensions:

(i) Institutional autonomy in Academic Matters envisages that there will be a Governing Board in the each institution that will be free to decide future strategies and directions, the processes governing admissions, curriculum updating, examinations, classroom processes, and the interface with the external environment as well as to determine the standards and degree of excellence. The Board should consist of people of eminence and should not have more than one third of its members from the government, with the others coming from industry, the professions, and alumni to enable it to draw upon the services of persons of eminence and provide representation to all stake-holders.

(ii) Governance related autonomy enables the Governing Board and its Academic Councils to decide on personnel policies of the institutes, faculty recruitment and development plans, core areas of academics, research and consultancy related strengths, delegation of administrative authority, and its performance review processes for faculty and non-faculty personnel.

(iii) Financial Autonomy will enable institutions to mobilize resources from user fees, review fee-structures, consultancy services, and donations. They can rationalize their fee structures according to the degree of excellence achieved both in terms of academic achievement and market value. It will also unshackle the institutions, enabling them to take bold initiatives regarding campus accretions/additions, starting new faculties and new disciplines, creating competencies in new knowledge domains, expanding infrastructure, and enlarging student outreach. The Governing Board should be left free to evolve policies relating to donations, endowments, scholarships, instituting Chairs, accumulation and deployment of reserves and surpluses, keeping in mind the overarching principle of equity while fixing fees and determining the amount of scholarships.

Quantitative Expansion

1.3.24 Quantitative expansion in enrolment will be achieved through: expansion of existing institutions, both government and private; creation of new government (Central and States) funded universities and colleges; facilitating/removing barriers in creation of new universities and colleges; special programmes for targeted expansion in CU; support to State universities and colleges, and additional assistance to under-funded institutions; the implementation of recommendations of the Oversight Committee (OSC), would be subject to final order of the Supreme Court. Focus on access and affordability in SCs, STs, OBCs, and minority concentration districts and implementation of the recommendations of the Sachar Committee with respect to educational development of the Muslim community.

Inclusive Education

1.3.25 The objective of inclusiveness will be achieved through the following:

- Reduction of regional imbalances;
- Support to institutions located in border, hilly, remote, small towns, and educationally backward areas;
- Support to institutions with larger student population of SCs, STs, OBCs, minorities, and physically challenged;
- Support to the SCs, STs, OBCs, minorities, physically challenged, and girl students with special scholarships/fellowships, hostel facilities, remedial coaching, and other measures;
- Setting up of an 'Equal Opportunity Office' in all universities to bring all schemes relating to this group under one umbrella for effective implementation.

Quality Improvement

1.3.26 Quality improvement in higher education will be brought about through restructuring academic programmes to ensure their relevance to modern market demands; domestic and global linkages with employers and external advisory resource support groups and tracer studies; greater emphasis on recruitment of adequate and good quality teachers; complete revamping of teaching/learning methods by shifting from traditional repetitive experiments to open-ended design-oriented work for encouraging invention and innovation; compulsory interactive seminar-tutorials, broadening the content of Science and engineering programmes to strengthen fundamental concepts, improving learning opportunities and conditions by updating text books and learning material; and improving self-directed learning with modern aids and development of IT network.

New CU

1.3.27 30 CU will be set up including 16 on the basis of one CU in each of the 16 uncovered States such as Bihar, Chhattisgarh, Goa, Gujarat, Haryana, Himachal Pradesh, J&K, Jharkhand, Karnataka, Kerala, MP, Orissa, Punjab, Rajasthan, Tamil Nadu, and Uttarakhand. The Indira Gandhi National Tribal University will be set up as a CU. In addition, it is proposed to establish 14 new CU aiming at world class standards. These universities will be set up through a single umbrella Central legislation and will be subject to the State providing land free of cost and signing a Memorandum of Understanding (MoU) for a minimum set of educational reforms in its university system whereby the new institutions serve as benchmarks of excellence for other universities and colleges.

1.3.28 The proposed 14 World Class Universities (WCU) need to be carefully planned to have various schools including medical and engineering. Their establishment should be implemented in a creative mode, by setting up an autonomous project team comprising eminent people for each of the proposed WCU, who would design and implement the project creatively. The location of these institutions should be determined by competitively evaluating alternative offers of land by State. The location decision should balance the desire for achieving a greater geographical spread and the potential synergies arising from co-location with the existing reputed institutions and laboratories (e.g., Council of Scientific and Industrial

Research [CSIR] laboratories). The setting up of WCU will take time, especially for them to come up to full strength. But locations and initiation of work should get top priority during the Eleventh Plan so as to enable India to become the global knowledge hub and set benchmark for Central and other universities.

Supporting State Universities and Colleges

1.3.29 About 8800 affiliated colleges of State universities, mainly undergraduate colleges, are technically under the purview of UGC but do not get assistance as they do not meet the minimum eligibility norms in terms of physical facilities and human resources. During the Eleventh Plan, about 6000 colleges and 150 universities with focus on under served areas will be strengthened to enable these institutions to fulfil the criteria for UGC assistance. Each college and university will be provided Rs 2.0 crore and Rs 10 crore, respectively, based on DPR. But there must be corresponding funds from States plus willingness to raise funds internally.

1.3.30 Although assistance is provided through UGC to about 160 State universities and 5625 colleges through development grants, due to the budgetary constraints the funding is low and insufficient affecting the quality of interventions. During the Eleventh Plan, these colleges and universities will be provided one-time assistance at the rate of Rs 1.0 crore and Rs 5.0 crore, again based on DPR. This support will be subject to the matching commitments on funding and reforms from the Centre, States, and institutions.

Correcting Regional Imbalances: Establishing 370 New Degree Colleges

1.3.31 States like Bihar, MP, and Orissa have low GER. To ensure better access with equity, a new CSS will be launched with a Central–State funding pattern of 1:2 (1:1 for Special Category States) for increasing intake capacity in the existing institutions or starting new institutions. Further, 370 new degree colleges will be established in districts with low GER based on careful selection.

Initiatives for Inclusive Education in States

1.3.32 Focus on the disadvantaged sections (SCs, STs, OBCs, and minorities) holds the key to achieving the GER of 15% for the Plan. Financial assistance will be provided to the States on the basis of specific projects submitted for these social groups. Girl's hostels will be constructed in districts with low female GER and high concentration of SCs STs, OBCs, and minorities. About 2000 hostels with a unit cost of Rs 1.0 crore will be provided during the Eleventh Plan subject to the recurrent expenditure being borne by the States/beneficiaries and hostels being managed by the respective institutions.

TECHNICAL EDUCATION

Status

1.3.33 India's technical education institutions comprise:

- 7 Indian Institutes of Technology (IITs) and 6 Indian Institutes of Management (IIMs), which are Institutions of National Importance;
- 20 National Institutes of Technology (NITs);

Box 1.3.2
Basic Features of a Model CU

- CU should provide education and research opportunities in a variety of disciplines.
- These universities should admit students on an all-India basis and through a nationwide test by an independent testing body.
- Degrees should be granted on basis of completion of a requisite number of credits.
- Syllabi should be revised every two year to keep up with changes.
- Appropriate system of appointments and incentives should be put in place to maximize the productivity of faculty.
- Mechanisms should be set up to monitor and evaluate performance and progress of teachers.
- Strong linkages should be built between teaching and research, the university and industry and research laboratories.
- The CU should be department-based and should have no affiliated colleges.
- Non-teaching functions should be outsourced wherever possible.
- Administrative processes should be streamlined and made transparent and accountable by use of ICTs.

- 1617 engineering and technology colleges, 1292 polytechnics,
- 525 institutions for diploma in pharmacy,
- 91 Schools for Hotel Management and 4 Institutions for Architecture in 2006.
- For postgraduate courses, these are 1147 educational institutions, for Master of Business Administration (MBA)/Post Graduate Diploma in Management (PGDM) and 953 for Master of Computer Applications (MCA).
- 7 Deemed-to-be-Universities, namely, Indian Institute of Science (IISc), Bangalore, Indian School of Mines, Dhanbad, School of Planning and Architecture, New Delhi, Indian Institute of Information Technology and Management, Gwalior and Indian Institute of Information Technology (IIIT), Allahabad, Indian Institute of Information Technology, Design and Manufacturing, Jabalpur and Kanchipuram.
- 4 Boards of Apprenticeship Training, etc.
- National Institute of Foundry and Forge Technology, Ranchi.
- National Institute of Industrial Engineering, Mumbai.
- Sant Longowal Institute of Engineering and Technology (SLIET).
- North Eastern Regional Institute of Science and Technology (NERIST), Itanagar.
- 4 National Institute of Technical Teachers Training and Research (NITTTRs).

1.3.34 Many central programmes/schemes contribute significantly to technical education. These include:

- Programme for Apprenticeship Training (Scholarships and Stipends),
- Community Polytechnics (CP),
- Technician Education Project-III assisted by the World Bank for Improvement of Polytechnic Education,
- Technical Education Quality Improvement Programme (TEQIP),
- Polytechnics for Disabled Persons,
- National Programme on Technology Enhanced Learning (NPTEL).
- National Programme for Earthquake Engineering Education,
- INDEST,
- Consortium and Technology Development Missions.

1.3.35 The dispersal of degree level technical institutions in the country is however highly skewed. Andhra Pradesh, Tamil Nadu, Karnataka, and Maharashtra account for nearly 55% of the engineering colleges and 58% of enrolments in the country. The State-wise distribution of national institutions is even worse (Annexure 1.2).

Tenth Plan Performance

1.3.36 The Tenth Plan period saw a big increase in the number of technical and management institutions, mainly due to private initiatives. During the Tenth Plan, the number of AICTE approved Degree Engineering/Technology institutions has risen from 1057 to 1522 and the annual intake from 2.96 lakh to 5.83 lakh. The aggregate number of technical institutions and the intake capacity by the end of Tenth Plan were 4512 and 7.83 lakh, respectively.

1.3.37 During the Tenth Plan the University of Roorkee was upgraded to an IIT and the number of IITs increased to seven. Seventeen RECs, two Indian Institutes of Science Education and Research (IISERs) at Pune and Kolkata were also set up and three other institutions were upgraded to NIT level. A new Indian Institute of Information Technology, Manufacturing and Design was established at Jabalpur making it the third institute in the series. All the four Technical Teacher Training Institutes were upgraded as NITTTR. Several engineering colleges were conferred with Deemed to-be-University status. Many private universities became operational imparting technical education through legislation of various State Governments. Bengal Engineering College, a deemed university, was conferred with the status of unitary university and redesignated as Bengal University of Science and Technology. In several States, technical institutions were brought under the purview of new Technical Universities and this improved quality and standards.

1.3.38 The AICTE and INDEST have joined hands to form a combined AICTE-INDEST Consortium.

The AICTE has set up 106 virtual classrooms in identified technical institutions under Education Satellite (EDUSAT) scheme to share the knowledge of premier and well-established institutions with other institutions.

1.3.39 To enhance learning effectiveness and to expand access to high-quality digital video-based courses, an NPTEL has been launched. The TEQIP aims at up-scaling and supporting ongoing efforts of the GoI to improve quality of technical education. Under the scheme, 40 lead institutions (including 18 Centrally funded NITs) and 88 State engineering/network institutions (including 20 polytechnics) in 13 States have participated. The programme targets 10000 graduating students each year. It also imparts superior skills and training to enhance the professional development of 1000 teachers. TEQIP Phase II is still under negotiation and it is expected to be substantially enlarged, diversified, made more flexible and allow for greater involvement of States in design and implementation.

1.3.40 The Tenth Plan outlay for the technical education sub-sector was Rs 4700 crore, against which an expenditure of only Rs 3416 crore was incurred (73%).

TECHNICAL EDUCATION: GOALS AND TARGETS IN ELEVENTH PLAN

1.3.41 During the Eleventh Plan, intake of technical education institutions needs to grow at an estimated 15% annually, to meet the skilled manpower needs of our growing economy.

Schemes for Expansion and Upgradation

1.3.42 The Eleventh Plan envisages setting up of 8 new IITs, 7 new IIMs, 10 new NITs, 3 IISERs, 20 IIITs, and 2 new SPAs. In establishing these institutions the scope for PPPs will be explored. Seven selected technical institutions will be upgraded subject to their signing MoU on commitments to making reforms in governance structure, admission procedure, etc. and aligning with character of the national institutions. In the location and selection of sites for the new institutions, clustering will be a key consideration and the States will be incentivized for co-locating institutions in strategic locations.

Expansion of Intake Capacity in the Existing Central Institutions

1.3.43 The recent recommendations of the OSC to increase the intake capacities of the Cen-trally funded technical institutions in the categories of IITs, NITs, IIITs, NITTTRs, and IIMs provide for an opportunity for major capacity expansion of high level technical and management institutions while providing for social equity.

1.3.44 Considering the urgency in expanding the intake capacity due to the acceleration in demand for technical education, a quick feasibility study will be undertaken to decide upon the optimum intake capacity of the Central institutions and support them for additional infrastructure, etc. In view of the increasing demand particularly for MBAs, Departments/Institutes of Management and Business Administration in the university system will also be strengthened.

Strengthening State Technical Institutions

1.3.45 The State Engineering Colleges suffer from severe deficiencies in academic infrastructure, equipment, faculty, library facilities, and other physical facilities. Top ranking students in entrance examination of the States opt for these institutions in view of relatively low fee structure and government recognition. These are supposed to be model institutions for the private sector institutions to benchmark their standards. If standards and norms are insisted upon for private institutions, the government cannot keep its institutions in unsatisfactory condition.

1.3.46 TEQIP Phase II is expected to be substantially enlarged to cover additional 200 State engineering institutions, diversified, made more flexible and allow for greater involvement of States in design and implementation. There will be one-time assistance for project-based support and funds will be released on performance and the State Government accepting a minimum set of reforms including curriculum revision, internal assessments, faculty upgradation, adoption of seminar-tutorials, and the semester system, etc. Proper appraisal system of the projects and effective Monitoring and Evaluation (ME) system will be established . TEQIP-II projects will be on log frame.

Box 1.3.3
Mohali Knowledge City—Advantages of Clustering

- It is planned to build a knowledge city in Mohali, Punjab with a vision to promote innovation and startup companies. The cluster includes, on a single campus, the Indian Institute of Science Education and Research (IISER), National Agri-food Biotechnology Institute, Nanotechnology Institute, Management School, Technology and IP Management Centre, Business Centre, an Informatics Centre, Centralized Platform, Technology facility, a Good Manufacturing Practices (GMP) compliant Bio process Facility for Food and Nutriceuticals, a Technology Park for start-ups, and a host of other shared facilities. Governance, as a cluster is so designed as to allow dynamic contact and collaboration within the cluster and with all existing local institutes and enterprises.
- Building cluster in strategic location enables innovation. Characteristically, in a cluster, research, technology management, investment and business skills, technology incubators and parks for startups are co-located, functionally linked, based on a common vision. The vision of such a cluster is to create necessary synergies and sharing of resources, ideas, and facilities.

1.3.47 Efforts will be made to establish 50 centres for training and research in frontier areas like Biotechnology, Bio-informatics, Nano-materials and Nano–technologies, Mechatronics, MEMS, High Performance Computing, Engineering, etc. However, these will be funded on the basis of specific proposals and on a competitive basis.

SCIENCE AND TECHNOLOGY (S&T): THE CUTTING EDGE

1.3.48 In the current knowledge era, our development depends crucially on the ability to harness S&T to find innovative solutions. Capabilities in S&T, therefore, are reckoned as a benchmark for establishing the status of the development of a nation. India must occupy a frontline position in this listing. The Eleventh Five Year Plan approach to S&T will be guided by this ambition and emphasis will be on:

- Evolving an integrated S&T Plan involving UGC, Department of Science and Technology (DST), CSIR, Indian Council of Agricultural Research (ICAR), Departments of Atomic Energy and Space to provide the resources needed for substantially stepping up support to basic research, setting up a national level mechanism for evolving policies, and providing direction to basic research.
- Enlarging the pool of scientific manpower and stren-gthening the S&T infrastructure. Focused efforts will be made to identify and nurture bright young students who can take up scientific research as a career.
- Promoting strong linkages with other countries in the area of S&T, including participation in mega international science initiatives.
- Evolving an empowered National Science and Technology Commission responsible for all matters relating to S&T (Administrative, Financial, and Scientific) including scientific audit and performance assessment of scientists and scientific institutions through peer review.
- Supporting the schemes suggested by the Empowered Committee on the Science Education.

Faculty Development and Research

1.3.49 The world over, it is recognized that R&D efforts are imperative for sustained economic growth and social development. However, in India there has been a low level of R&D efforts, mainly due to the inadequate number of highly trained and knowledgeable R&D personnel—particularly at the level of PhDs—relatively low investment in R&D by the corporate sector, and the lack of synergy among R&D institutions and universities. The present output of about 450 doctorates per annum in Engineering and Technology, should increase several folds with the expanded technical education capacity, offering substantial scope for postgraduate and doctoral level programmes.

National Science and Engineering Research Board (NSERB)

1.3.50 Upgradation of science education and research infrastructure in the universities is a major challenge. The DST would adopt a two-pronged strategy to achieve this objective: (i) expansion and strengthening of S&T base in the universities through appropriate HRD measures and building up of research capabilities of the academic sector and (ii) funding for undertaking internationally competitive and front-ranking major research programmes. For this purpose, the existing Science and Engineering Research Council mechanism of the DST would be restructured into NSERB and a special program for rejuvenation of research in universities would be initiated. The proposed Board will address these issues and follow global best practices.

Reducing Wide Regional Disparities

1.3.51 Southern States have successfully attracted capital and students from all over the country. Government schemes and AICTE will proactively encourage establishment of higher (technical) institutions in deficient States (Annexures 1.2.1 and 1.3.1).

OVERSIGHT COMMITTEE (OSC)

1.3.52 In pursuance of the 93rd amendment to the Constitution of India aiming to provide statutory reservations to SCs, STs, and OBCs in Central Educational Institutions, the Central Educational Institutions (Reservation in Admission) Act has been enacted and has been notified in January 2007. The OSC (Moily Committee), constituted in May 2006 recommended an investment of Rs 17270 crore over a period of five years for the Central Educational Institutions to increase their intake capacity by 54% so as to provide 27% reservation to OBCs without affecting the number of general seats. Of this, Rs 7035 crore will be non-recurring expenditure, the bulk of which will be spread over year 1, 2, and 3, whereas, the recurring expenditure will be Rs 10235 crore spread over five years, increasing progressively subject to the final order of the Supreme Court. An Inter-Ministerial Monitoring Committee will be constituted in the Planning Commission to oversee and review the progress. (See Annexure 1.3.2.)

FEES IN HIGHER EDUCATION, SCHOLARSHIPS, FELLOWSHIPS, AND LOAN SCHEMES

1.3.53 The national commitment 'to ensure that nobody would be deprived of higher education opportunities due to lack of financial resources' necessitates a serious look at the issues of fees, scholarships, and loan schemes.

1.3.54 At present, fees vary across universities, but generally these have been kept very low, in many cases not even covering 5% of the operating cost. The Centre and State Governments must either be able to subsidize university education massively or try to mobilize a reasonable amount from those who can afford it by way of fees that cover a reasonable part of the running cost. Since most university students come from the top 10% of the population by income levels, they would be able to pay fees amounting up to 20% of the operating cost of general university education. The fees for professional courses could be much higher. The fee levels

Box 1.3.4
Faculty Augmentation and Development in Science and Technology

- Substantial increase in the intake in Junior Research Fellowship (JRF);
- Enhance research fellowship for PhD students if they are given additional responsibility to also take up teaching as lecturer and make eligible non-NET PhD scholars also for fellowship;
- Increase the number of fellowships and the quantum of assistance for MTech students;
- Make the teaching system attract and retain the best talent with better pay/perks and funded research. Performance-based rapid career progression;
- Increase industry–institution interface including provision for tenure jobs in industry for faculty;
- Set aside a share of project funds as incentive payments for the researchers/fellows;
- Selected top class institutions to undertake special programmes for best faculty development;
- Infusion of knowledge capital in the Centres of Excellence through MoU;
- Institutions to open up for international faculty, visiting programmes, and faculty exchange;
- Recruitment policy of faculty reviewed for providing more flexibility in appointments, short-term contracts, assignments, and possibility of outsourcing select faculty that is in short supply;
- A major expansion of faculty development programme.

should, therefore, be increased gradually in existing institutions but the new norms could be implemented in new institutions from the start. It may be noted that the new institutions will take time to start.

1.3.55 It must be recognized that there will be some students who cannot afford to pay the increased fees and they should receive scholarships. From a fiscal perspective, the government has to bear the cost either by undercharging fees or providing scholarships. The latter method is most preferable because not all students need scholarships and those that do should be able to avail of the scholarship at any recognized university, thus providing an incentive for universities to compete and attract students rather than have all their costs covered. With a portable scholarship system, the demand for admission in the better universities will signal their preferred standing.

1.3.56 The operating cost of providing technical and medical education is much higher then general education and fees in these institutions will have to be higher. However, these courses also provide opportunities for much higher earnings for most graduates. The additional cost to the student of taking these courses, beyond the basic level of fees referred to above, can be met through student loan programmes. Banks are currently providing student loans but there are operational problems. Students at premier institutions such as the IITs or IIMs find no difficulty in getting bank loans, but in other institutions, loans are often linked to providing collateral.

Increasing Affordability through Scholarships, Fellowships, and Loans

- Scholarships to colleges/universities students.
- Effective fellowship programme and substantial increase in coverage of PhD research students under Junior Research Fellowship (JRF).
- Encourage NET qualified and PhD students to take to research as a career and for creation of intellectual property.
- Establish interlink of research faculty with research students in universities by offering research fellowships.
- A framework for facilitating student loans for professional programmes including a Higher Education Loan Guarantee Authority for covering bank loans to students of accredited universities.

1.3.57 It is necessary to move to a position where banks will lend freely to students who have achieved admission to certified institutions against a loan guarantee given by a National Student Loan Guarantee Corporation.

Reforms in Apex Regulatory Institutions of Higher Education

1.3.58 The government has created an elaborate institutional arrangement by establishing the UGC as an umbrella organization for coordination and maintenance of standards of higher education, as also other professional statutory councils for regulating professional and technical education and determining their quality and standards. These include AICTE, Medical Council of India (MCI), Bar Council of India, NCTE, etc. These institutions have played an important role in laying down a strong foundation of higher, professional, and technical education and expanding its base throughout the country. However, consequent upon the major structural changes that have taken place during the last 25 years or so in the domestic education system and its growing linkages and involvement with the international education providers, the context of higher, professional, and technical education has undergone a paradigm shift.

1.3.59 It is, therefore, imperative to review the changing role that these organizations are expected to perform in the context of global changes, with a view to enabling them to reach out, regulate and maintain standards, and meet the challenges of diversification to enhance access and maintain the quality and standards of higher, professional, and technical education. This would help create and expand the relevant knowledge base from the point of view of the expanding individual entitlements and increasing the capacity of the economy to take full advantage of the domestic and global opportunities.

1.3.60 A high-level committee will be set up to suggest a specific reforms agenda in this context. Similar exercises will have to be carried out with respect to State level institutional arrangements.

National Mission in Education through ICT

1.3.61 A National Mission in Education through ICT will be launched to increase ICT coverage in all the 378 universities and 18064 colleges. The Mission will focus on digitization and networking of all educational institutions, developing low cost and low power consuming access devices, and making available bandwidth for educational purposes. MHRD-Department of Information Technology (DIT)-Department of Tele Communications (DoT) collaborative efforts are needed to ensure fully electronic universities and digital campuses. Advanced computational facilities will be provided in select institutions.

1.3.62 The outputs envisaged from these efforts include:

- Availability of e-books in English language for most of the subjects.
- EDUSAT teaching hub at each of the CU.
- 2000 broadband Internet nodes at each of the 200 Central Institutions.
- One Satellite Interactive terminal for providing network connectivity in 18000 colleges.
- Each department of 378 universities and each of the 18064 colleges to be networked through broadband Internet modes of adequate bandwidth.
- Digitization of large volume of video contents of Teaching Learning Materials generated overtime.
- Spreading Digital Literacy.

1.3.63 National Knowledge Network and Connected Digital Campuses for plunging into knowledge cyberspace:

- The move from the old economy to a knowledge economy is characterized by collaborations and sharing of knowledge. Today, the R&D activities are becoming multi-disciplinary and moving onto collaborative mode amongst researchers spread across countries. The Eleventh Plan must, therefore, aim at creating a world-class ambience by establishing a dynamically configurable national multi-gigabit network connecting all educational institutions, R&D institutions, hospitals, libraries, or agricultural institutions.
- A provision of Rs 5000 crore has been made in the Eleventh Five Year Plan for 'Education Mission through ICT'. This would adequately take care of the recommendations of the 'Oversight Committee on Reservations in Higher Educational Institutions' for harnessing ICT and creating digital campuses to cope with the challenges of the age of networked intelligence, as well as the recommendation of the National Knowledge Commission for networking 1000 institutions in the first phase.
- The Integrated National Knowledge Network shall be designed to support Overlay Networks, Dedicated Networks, create country wide classrooms, and empower campuses through campus wide network. The entire network will seamlessly integrate with global science at multiple gigabits per second speed. In the first phase 1000 institutions would be brought under this network.
- A suitably structured Empowered Committee consisting of stakeholders will also be required to coordinate activities of creation and implementation of the content, applications, and establishment of network. The Empowered Committee shall be assisted by a Technical Advisory Committee.
- The National Knowledge Network will enable our institutions of higher learning to have digital campuses, video-conference classrooms, and wireless hot-spots campus wide. Students of all professional/science programmes should be encouraged to have their own laptops/desktop computers, with hostels providing wi-fi connectivity.

Polytechnics

Present Status

1.3.64 Polytechnics in the country offer three year generalized diploma courses in conventional subjects such as civil, electrical, and mechanical engineering. The courses are now diversified to include electronics, computer science, medical lab technology, hospital engineering, etc. Women's polytechnics offer courses in garment technology, beauty culture, textile design, etc.

1.3.65 The number of polytechnics has increased slowly from 1203 in 2001–02 to 1292 in 2005–06 with corresponding rise in intake from 2.36 lakh to 2.65 lakh. The proportion of polytechnics is high in the southern States (46%). Further, the proportion of public sector institutions at degree level in the country is very low around 20% and on the other hand around 80% of diploma level institutions are in public sector. 125 districts do not have even a single polytechnic.

1.3.66 Even the existing polytechnics seem to struggle for survival. Over the years, the diploma courses have lost the skill components and are perceived as diluted version of degree education. The Eleventh Plan will have to address several issues including static curricula, poor industry interface, lack of flexibility to respond to needs obsolescence of equipment, lack of trainers, and inadequate funding.

1.3.67 CP are wings of the existing polytechnics intended to provide a platform for transfer of appropriate technologies to rural masses and to provide technical support and services to the local community. At present, there are 669 CP in the country. During the Tenth Plan period, about 13 lakh persons had been trained in various job-oriented non-formal skills/trades.

Eleventh Plan Proposals

1.3.68 New polytechnics will be set up in every district not having one already on priority basis. These polytechnics will be established primarily with Central funding and over 700 will be set up through PPP and private funding. All these new polytechnic institutes will have a CP wing. Women's hostels will also be set up in all the government polytechnics. The existing government polytechnics will be incentivized to modernize in PPP mode. Efforts will also be made to increase intake capacity by using space, faculty, and other facilities in the existing polytechnics in shifts.

1.3.69 There is a shortage of qualified diploma holder in several new areas. Therefore, engineering institutions will be incentivized and encouraged to introduce diploma courses to augment intake capacity. Diploma programmes could be run in evening shifts when the laboratory, workshop, equipment, and library are free. The faculty could be incentivized for institutions running diploma programmes in an optimal manner. This will also restore the credibility of diploma programmes and also support vertical mobility for higher education. In fact, Sant Longowal Institute and NERIST, Itanagar, already have vertically integrated certificate, diploma, and degree programmes.

1.3.70 Teachers in the polytechnics will be trained continuously to upgrade their teaching knowledge and skill to keep pace with the industry. The curriculum of diploma courses will be revised. Polytechnics will be encouraged to involve industrial and professional bodies in developing linkages with industries in their vicinity.

1.3.71 Setting up of additional 210 community colleges, mainly in northern, western, and eastern parts of the country will be supported on placement based funding. Existing 190 community colleges (largely in southern States, some of which offer diploma courses) will also be supported for capacity building, training cost (equipment, faculty development, TLM, stipend, etc., but not for civil works and other capital costs). Funding will based on MoU between community colleges, States, and MHRD.

Distance Learning

IGNOU

1.3.72 Access to education through the open and distance learning system is expanding rapidly. IGNOU now has a cumulative enrolment of about 15 lakh. It has a network of 53 regional centres and 1400 study centres with 25000 counsellors. Besides, there are 28 FM radio stations and 6 television channels. The university introduced 16 new programmes during 2006–07. The Distance Education Council, an authority of IGNOU is coordinating the activities of 13 State Open Universities (SOUs) and 119 Institutes of Correspondence Courses in the conventional universities.

1.3.73 The pilot project of 'SAKSHAT'—one-stop education portal—has been launched in October 2006 to facilitate lifelong learning of students, teachers, and those of employment or in pursuit of knowledge, free of cost to them. The vision is to scale up the pilot project to cater to the learning needs of more than 50 crore people. The portal contains the virtual class that has four quadrant approaches to learning, which include written course materials, animations, simulations, video lectures, related web links, question answers, confidence building measures, etc.

1.3.74 The Eleventh Plan will support IGNOU, existing SOUs and the States setting up new SOUs. Considering the dismal performance of some of the statutory bodies, in-depth and independent evaluation of these statutory bodies will be undertaken urgently.

1.3.75 Consortium for Educational Communication Centre (CEC) will set up a technology enabled system of mass higher education by taking advantage of Vyas 24-hours Education Channel for one way communication, EDUSAT network for two-way communication and Internet for 'any time anywhere' education. The thrust areas will include strengthening of the existing media centres, setting up of new media centres in those States where no centres exist, strengthening of the concepts of packaging knowledge in video and e-content form in need-based subject areas, transforming the CEC and media centre into a virtual university system.

Language and Book Promotion

Language Promotion

1.3.76 The development of languages occupies an important place in the National Policy on Education 1986 and the Programme of Action 1992. There are 122 other languages having at least 10000 speakers and nearly 234 identifiable mother tongues (as per the figures given in the 2001 Census Report). Promotion and development of 22 languages listed in the Schedule VIII of the constitution, including classical languages on the one hand and English and foreign languages on the other, have received due attention and will continue to do so. Some of the important programmes that continued during the Tenth Plan are promotion and development of Sanskrit and Hindi through different institutions, training of Hindi teachers for non-Hindi speaking States, and the use of ICT in the sector.

1.3.77 New Linguistic Survey (NLSI) of India will be undertaken during the Eleventh Plan as a CS. The original Linguistic Survey of India is more than 100 years old, supervised by Sir George Abraham Grierson who produced a monumental document consisting of 19 volumes between 1894 and 1927. It had identified 179 languages and 544 dialects.

1.3.78 The proposed NLSI will focus on 22 languages in the Eighth Schedule and their geo-space but would also pay special attention to the top 15 Non-Scheduled languages and also to the sign languages that are as complex as spoken languages. The Survey will be conducted by the Central Institute of Indian Languages (CIIL), Mysore, and the Departments in select universities that have a strong base in sociology, anthropology, etc.

1.3.79 At present there is no scheme or organization devoted exclusively for the development of Non-Schedule VIII languages. A new scheme for the preservation and development of languages not covered by the Eighth Schedule, namely the Bharat Bhasha Vikas Yojana would be taken up.

1.3.80 The National Translation Mission would cover Translators' Education: running short-term training programmes; creating a course for translators as a part of language teaching programme; developing specialized courses in translation technology and related areas; information dissemination; etc.

1.3.81 A Central Institute of Classical Tamil (CICT) at Chennai will be set up during the Eleventh Plan to develop Tamil as a classical language. The Tenth Plan scheme for development of Tamil language will be subsumed in CICT.

1.3.82 The following Central sector institutional schemes will continue to be supported by the MHRD but all the schemes will be evaluated in-depth for further funding: (i) Central Hindi Directorate, (ii) Commission for Scientific and Technical Terminology, (iii) Kendriya Hindi Sansthan, (iv) CIIL, Mysore, (v) National Council for Promotion of Urdu Language, (vi) National Council for Promotion Sindhi Language, and (vii) Mahrishi Sandipani Rashtria Ved Vidya Pratishthan (viii) Rashtriya Sanskrit Sansthan.

Book Promotion

1.3.83 An outlay of Rs 434 crore for the Languages and Rs 67 crore for Book Promotion Sectors have been allocated for the Tenth Plan and expenditures during the Plan period were Rs. 578.16 crore and Rs. 45.92 crore, respectively.

1.3.84 The main schemes under the sector are two: (i) National Book Trust (NBT) that undertakes the activities such as promotion of Indian books abroad, assistance to authors and publishers, and promotion of children's literature (National Centre for Children Literature) and (ii) Intellectual Property Education, Research, and Public Outreach (IPERPO) run by the Book Promotion and Copyright Division, MHRD.

1.3.85 The existing schemes of IPERPO were operationalized in the Tenth Plan for effective implementation of the cause of promoting awareness/research on copyright/Intellectual Property Rights (IPRs) and WTO matters. The Scheme will review the present IPR in the area of Education, Research, Literacy and strengthen it to suit the objectives of a knowledge-based economy. New initiatives need to be taken to strengthen the Copyright Office, establish new IPR Chairs in all universities, other IPR Centre/Cells in Government Departments, PSUs, develop appropriate Internal Monitoring Systems, hold National Seminars and celebrate World Intellectual Property Day, and Public awareness programmes.

1.3.86 During the Eleventh Plan the NBT will strengthen its three regional offices at Bangalore, Mumbai, and Calcutta and also strengthen its activities in the North Eastern Region. The subsidy project for assistance to authors and publishers for producing books of an acceptable standard at reasonable prices for students and teachers will continue.

FINANCING EDUCATION IN THE ELEVENTH PLAN

1.3.87 The government has pledged to raise public spending on education to 6% of Gross Domestic Product (GDP). For accelerating public expenditure, the Central Budget 2004 introduced a cess of 2% on major central taxes/duties for elementary education and Budget 2007 a cess of 1% for secondary and higher education. In the Eleventh Plan, Central Government envisages an outlay of about Rs 2.70 lakh crore at current price (Rs 2.37 lakh crore at 2006–07 price) for education. This is a four-fold increase over the Tenth Plan allocation of Rs 0.54 lakh crore at 2006–07 price. The share of education in the total plan outlay will correspondingly increase from 7.7% to 19.4%. Around 50% of Eleventh Plan outlay is for elementary education and literacy, 20% for secondary education, and 30% for higher education (including technical education). The scheme wise details are given in Appendix to Volume III.

1.3.88 This reflects the high priority being given to the education sector by the Central Government and represents a credible progress towards raising the public spending of the Centre and the States combined to 6% of GDP. However, it is a shared responsibility between the Centre and States to raise education expenditure to the targeted level. The State Governments should also accord a high priority to education in the sectoral plan priorities/allocation.

ANNEXURE 1.2.1
Major Education Statistics, 2004–05

S. No.	State/UT	Population (Cr)			GER	Drop-out	PTR		Schools per lakh population		Tenth Plan SSA Exp.			Lakh of Population per Institution		
		Total Census 2001	6–14 age 2004	Literacy 2001	Classes (I–VIII)	Classes (I–X)	Primary	UP	Elem.	Sec./ Hr Sec	(Rs cr)	% of Total	Per capita 6–14 age	Univ-ersity	College	Tech-nical
1	2	3	4	5	6	7	8	9	10	11	12	13	14	15	16	17
1.	Andhra Pradesh	7.62	1.30	60.5	86.99	63.69	33	31	99	22	1806.75	5.09	1387	31.6	0.59	1.97
2.	Arunachal Pradesh	0.11	0.02	54.3	106.70	70.79	34	30	163	19	187.30	0.53	8179	11.4	1.14	5.70
3.	Assam	2.67	0.53	63.3	91.92	74.96	42	16	137	19	1165.14	3.28	2186	46.5	0.88	25.34
4.	Bihar	8.30	1.88	47.0	65.16	83.06	104	75	57	4	2479.49	6.99	1319	46.2	1.18	43.87
5.	Chhattisgarh	2.08	0.41	64.7	112.63	0.00	48	46	203	12	1439.83	4.06	3513	43.8	1.03	18.25
6.	Goa	0.13	0.02	82.0	106.04	40.65	21	17	76	31	19.03	0.05	1119	14.1	0.61	1.57
7.	Gujarat	5.06	0.89	69.1	101.70	59.29	35	39	73	14	972.75	2.74	1096	26.6	1.05	5.55
8.	Haryana	2.11	0.41	67.9	80.01	32.48	44	30	63	23	732.96	2.07	1800	24.9	1.35	2.20
9.	Himachal Pradesh	0.61	0.10	76.5	108.74	-6.98	24	30	212	37	366.50	1.03	3658	9	0.71	7.00
10.	Jammu & Kashmir	1.01	0.19	55.5	74.45	53.75	34	16	153	13	482.54	1.36	2518	11.8	2.12	6.64
11.	Jharkhand	2.69	0.58	53.6	75.82	0.00	81	61	76	4	1429.56	4.03	2480	35.5	2.43	18.93
12.	Karnataka	5.28	0.89	66.6	98.76	59.38	26	37	97	21	1707.17	4.81	1909	20.3	0.59	1.84
13.	Kerala	3.18	0.44	90.9	95.35	7.15	28	27	30	16	390.72	1.10	893	40.9	1.76	2.68
14.	Madhya Pradesh	6.03	1.24	63.7	114.09	64.70	43	30	205	13	3534.59	9.96	2844	30.5	0.84	6.15
15.	Maharashtra	9.69	1.66	76.9	105.70	54.16	37	37	67	18	2205.65	6.22	1327	24.8	0.84	2.99
16.	Manipur	0.22	0.04	70.5	129.65	43.02	30	20	150	31	52.07	0.15	1389	11.25	0.39	11.25
17.	Meghalaya	0.23	0.05	62.6	121.93	79.15	44	16	317	29	94.10	0.27	1897	24.1	0.45	24.1
18.	Mizoram	0.09	0.02	88.8	109.51	66.95	17	8	263	56	141.21	0.40	8826	9.2	0.35	4.60
19.	Nagaland	0.20	0.04	66.6	75.76	97.29	19	16	97	18	69.86	0.20	1708	20.7	0.56	6.90
20.	Orissa	3.68	0.65	63.1	108.47	64.42	53	44	162	23	1506.65	4.25	2315	25.4	0.54	7.05
21.	Punjab	2.43	0.41	69.7	72.57	44.06	43	19	62	16	602.66	1.70	1486	28.2	1.20	5.52
22.	Rajasthan	5.65	1.22	60.4	102.67	73.87	49	34	137	17	2540.85	7.16	2089	24	0.98	10.71
23.	Sikkim	0.05	0.01	68.8	111.49	82.30	22	25	155	29	29.33	0.08	2848	2.8	2.8	1.87
24.	Tamil Nadu	6.24	0.89	73.5	113.96	55.19	33	41	63	14	1742.08	4.91	1965	16.4	1.44	1.51
25.	Tripura	0.32	0.06	73.2	109.59	73.36	54	15	84	20	214.40	0.60	3622	33.2	2.37	16.6

(*Annexure 1.2.1 contd.*)

(*Annexure 1.2.1 contd.*)

1	2	3	4	5	6	7	8	9	10	11	12	13	14	15	16	17
26.	Uttar Pradesh	16.62	3.64	56.3	87.04	43.77	58	35	95	7	6836.31	19.27	1878	45.2	1.75	11.76
27.	Uttaranchal	0.85	0.16	71.6	106.39	0.00	25	18	207	21	533.95	1.51	3258	9.9	1.04	4.46
28.	West Bengal	8.02	1.43	68.6	94.67	78.03	54	44	63	10	2051.18	5.78	1438	34.7	2.23	8.86
29.	Andaman & Nicobar Islands	0.03	0.01	81.3	107.97	36.97	20	18	69	24	15.29	0.04	2592		1.3	1.95
30.	Chandigarh	0.09	0.01	81.9	71.87	16.73	41	29	3	12	16.04	0.05	1146	3.33	0.83	3.33
31.	Dadra & Nagar Haveli	0.02	0.00	57.6	113.70	67.06	62	43	91	9	3.90	0.01	975			2.39
32.	Daman & Diu	0.06	0.00	78.2	128.85	43.43	43	29	40	15	0.91	0.00	479		1.9	1.90
33.	Delhi	1.38	0.25	81.7	91.84	46.92	40	26	20	11	88.91	0.25	358	1	2.4	3.69
34.	Lakshadweep	0.01	0.00	86.7	58.75	18.88	21	16	38	16	0.10	0.00	53			
35.	Pondicherry	0.1	0.01	81.2	121.34	16.89	24	21	45	22	13.83	0.04	981	10.1	0.92	1.01
	India	102.86	19.46	64.8	93.54	61.92	46	35	97	14	35473.61	100.0	1823	27.4	1.04	4.36

Note: GER: Gross Enrolment Ratio; PTR: Pupil Teacher Ratio; UP: Upper Primary.
Source: Selected Educational Statistics, 2004–05.

ANNEXURE 1.3.1
National Institutions

S. No.	State/UT	Population (Cr)	IITs	IIMs	CU	CSIR	ICAR	DST	ICMR	Others*	Total
1	2	3	4	5	6	7	8	9	10	11	12
1	Andhra Pradesh	7.62			3	3	9	1	3	2	20
2	Arunachal Pradesh	0.11			1		1				2
3	Assam	2.67	1		2	1	1		1		6
4	Bihar	8.30					2		1		3
5	Chhattisgarh	2.08									0
6	Goa	0.13				1	1			1	3
7	Gujarat	5.06		1		1	2		1	1	6
8	Haryana	2.11					6			1	7
9	Himachal Pradesh	0.61				1	2				3
10	Jammu & Kashmir	1.01				1	1				2
11	Jharkhand	2.69				3	1				4
12	Karnataka	5.28		1		3	5	4	1		14
13	Kerala	3.18		1		1	5	1		2	10
14	Madhya Pradesh	6.03		1		1	4		1	1	8
15	Maharashtra	9.69	1		1	2	8	2	7	5	26
16	Manipur	0.22			1					1	3
17	Meghalaya	0.23			1		1				2
18	Mizoram	0.09			1						1
19	Nagaland	0.20			1		1				2
20	Orissa	3.68				1	4		1	3	9
21	Punjab	2.43					1				1
22	Rajasthan	5.65				1	6		1		8
23	Sikkim	0.05			1		1				1
24	Tamil Nadu	6.24	1			4	3		3	3	14
25	Tripura	0.32			1						0
26	Uttar Pradesh	16.62	1	1	4	4	14	1	2	1	28
27	Uttarakhand	0.85	1			2	4	2			9
28	West Bengal	8.02	1	1	1	3	3	3	1	2	15
29	A&N Islands	0.03					1		1		2
30	Chandigarh	0.09				2					2
31	Dadar & Nagar Haveli	0.02									0
32	Daman & Diu	0.06									0
33	Delhi	1.38	1		4	5	8		4	2	24
34	Lakshadweep	0.01									0
35	Pondicherry	0.1			1				1		2
	India	102.86	7	6	23	40	95	14	29	25	237

Note: * Others include DBT, DOC, DAE, MOEF.
Source: Selected Educational Statistics, 2004–05.

ANNEXURE 1.3.2
Oversight Committee—Sector-wise Expenditure

(Rs crore)

S. No.	Sector	No. of Institutions	Total Expenditure
1.	Agriculture	5	133
2.	Central Universities	17	3298
3.	Management	7	285
4.	Medical	11	1877
5.	Engineering	39	6746
	Total	79	12338
6.	Merit Scholarship scheme	–	1680
7.	Research Fellowship	–	1500
8.	IT Infrastructure	–	1752
	Grand Total	79	17270

Note: Items 1–5: For infrastructural and physical facilities.
Item 6: To cover at least 100000 students a year @ Rs 12000 per student per year from class IX to a post-graduate programme.
Item 7: For a National Science Talent for Research and Innovation Scholarships of Rs 100000 a year for 10000 students.
Item 8: For ICT enabled networked digital campuses with each student having access to a personal computer.
Source: OSC Recommendations.

2

Youth Affairs and Sports and Art and Culture

2.1 YOUTH AFFAIRS AND SPORTS

YOUTH AND ADOLESCENT DEVELOPMENT

2.1.1 The adolescents and youths are the most vibrant and dynamic segment as well as potentially most valuable human resource of every country. While the youth population is fast shrinking with higher dependency ratios in the developed world, India is blessed with 70% of her population below the age of 35 years. In the next few decades India will probably have the world's largest number of young people. The population between the age of 10–19 years is approximately 242 million, the largest ever cohort of young people to make a transition to adulthood. The time has never been better to invest in our young people. Efforts, therefore, need to be made to harness the energy of the youth towards nation-building through their active and responsive participation.

Existing Schemes and Programmes

2.1.2 At present, 12 schemes and programmes are being implemented for the development of youth and adolescents. These schemes can be broadly categorized into two groups, viz., youth based organizations and youth development activities. The NYKS and National Service Scheme (NSS) are the two flagship programmes encompassing a major part of its activities in institutional, functional, and financial terms (60%). The Rajiv Gandhi National Institute of Youth Development (RGNIYD), established in 1993, has been engaged in education, training, and research on youth development. The scheme of Youth Hostel aims at promoting youth travel and provides boarding and lodging facilities at very subsidized rates. The National Service Volunteers Scheme (NSVS) and Rashtriya Sadbhavana Yojana (RSY) aim at providing opportunities to educated youths other than students to involve themselves voluntarily in youth and community developmental activities. The schemes are for performing activities related to vocational training, development of adolescents, national integration and adventure, for which financial assistance is provided to NYKS and other NGOs/institutions. Grant-in-aid is provided to Bharat Scouts and Guides for conducting training camps and holding of jamborees, etc., throughout the country. The scheme of 'Cultural Youth Programmes with Commonwealth Countries' is an effective institution for promoting exchange of ideas, values, and culture among youth and strengthens better relations.

Performance during the Plan Period

2.1.3 In the temporal context, to harness the *Yuva Shakti* in nation-building several programmes for national discipline, leadership training, expansion and strengthening of the NSS and NYKS, launching NSVS, effective coordination amongst different programmes were introduced in successive Plan periods. However, the sector received a boost in the Seventh Plan, when a National Youth Policy was enacted and a Plan of Action formulated in 1992. The thrust in the Eighth and Ninth Plans was on harnessing youth power by involving them in various community-based nation building activities.

2.1.4 The major thrust of the Tenth Five Year Plan was on involving the youth in the process of planning and development and making them a focal point of the development strategy, by providing proper educational and training opportunities, access to information on employment opportunities including entrepreneurial guidance and financial credit and the programmes for developing among the youth qualities of leadership, tolerance, open mindedness, patriotism, etc. The NYKS was to be expanded to cover all the districts in the country together with expanding the network of Youth Clubs to cover at least 50% of the more than six lakh villages. At least one Youth Development Centre was to be set up in each of the country's 6200 blocks. Besides, 500 rural Information Technology Youth Development Centres were envisaged to be set up. The NSS was to be expanded to cover all degree colleges and +2 schools, while the RSY was to extend its reach to 500 districts. RGNIYD was to be developed into an apex national centre for information, documentation, research and training in respect of youth related issues. However, desired expansion and envisaged activities for various institutes could not materialize fully. Hence, the review of Planning Commission suggested restructuring and overhauling the institutional arrangement to meet the stated goals. A major drawback was the lack of involvement of State Government in various programmes of Ministry of Youth Affairs and Sports. Other dysfunctionalities include over centralized system and procedures, acute problems of utilization certificate, and sub-optimal performance of scheme activities.

2.1.5 The NSS has been included as one of the priority areas under the National Common Minimum Programme (NCMP), which emphasizes the need to provide opportunities for the youth to involve themselves in national and social development through educational institutions. Under the revised 20-Point Programme, RSY and NSS have been made a part of the specific monitorable targets. The NSS motto 'you, not me' seeks to invite a spirit of volunteerism and community service in youth minds.

Review of Performance during the Tenth Plan

2.1.6 As against the Tenth Plan outlay of Rs 677.64 crore, an amount of Rs 642.06 crore was provided in the annual plans and the aggregate expenditure was Rs 522.64 crore accounting for 77% of outlay and 81% of allocations (Annexure 2.1.1). The physical achievements under the various schemes were short of the target. The NYKS could not extend its activities beyond 500 districts that were covered by end of the Ninth Plan. A logical linkage between grassroots youth organizations such as youth clubs, sports clubs, *mahila mandals*, etc., and NYKS could not fully materialize. Although the progress of NSS has been relatively better, it had not kept pace with desired expansion to universities, colleges, and +2 school networks. RGNYID continued to suffer teething problems and could start functioning only during the latter part of Tenth Plan. Presently, there are 72 youth hostels, 18 are under construction, and 32 have been approved in-principle. Only a few government-owned youth hostels could get affiliation to the International Youth Hostels Association as they failed to meet the prescribed standards on accommodation, reception, hygiene, security, etc. The mega youth exchange programme with China, as a part of the activities during the India–China Friendship Year, 2006, has however, been a major success.

2.1.7 Considering huge and ever-increasing youth population in India, and to achieve the goals set for the Tenth Plan, the National Youth Policy 1998 was replaced by a New National Youth Policy-2003 with four thrust areas, viz. (i) Youth Empowerment; (ii) Gender Justice; (iii) Inter-sectoral Approach; and (iv) Information and Research Network.

2.1.8 The policy accords priority to the following groups of young people including (i) Rural and Tribal Youth; (ii) Out-of-School Youth; (iii) Adolescents, particularly female adolescents; (iv) Youth with disabilities; and (v) Youth under especially difficult circumstances like victims of trafficking, orphans, and street children.

Approach and Strategy for the Eleventh Plan

2.1.9 The Eleventh Plan envisages a holistic approach and comprehensive strategy to enable the development and realization of the full potential of the youth in the country and channelize their energy towards socio-economic development and growth of the nation. To achieve the goals of empowering and enabling the youth to become effective and productive participants in the socio-economic changes, a de novo look at the existing policies, instruments and institutions, initiation of innovative policies, efficient and effective instruments, and creative ways to rejuvenate institutions would be taken up. Synergy and convergence of efforts will be ensured. Evaluation of existing schemes/programmes, through an independent agency, would be mandatory and restructuring of schemes under Zero Based Budgeting (ZBB) will be a regular annual budgetary exercise.

Programmes for the Eleventh Plan

(i) NEHRU YUVA KENDRA SANGATHAN (NYKS)

2.1.10 The thrust of the NYKS would be on a consolidating, expanding, and energizing the youth club movement. There would be a paradigm shift in the manner of its functioning and implementation. The services of NYKS would be utilized for fostering secular values, national unity, and against extremism in the country through a number of existing and new programmes. A flexible approach would be adopted to register active clubs. The youth clubs would be regrouped into three categories 'A', 'B', and 'C' as per their performance and activeness. Focus would be on encouraging the clubs to move up the ladder and become active and self-sustaining/self-reliant. The reach of NYKS would be extended to all 609 districts in the country. Female membership would be increased through special campaigns. Computerized Management Information System (MIS) would be introduced for monitoring purposes. The selection procedure for filling up the posts would be reviewed. NYKS would involve State Governments in implementation of various programme activities.

Box 2.1.1
Objectives of the Eleventh Plan—Youth Affairs

- Holistic adolescent development through convergence of schemes;
- Overall personality development of youth and provision of life skills;
- Youth empowerment through restructuring and expansion of youth programmes;
- Greater female participation in youth development programmes;
- Special focus on engaging rural youths in nation-building activities transcending beyond social, economic, religious, and linguistic boundaries.

(ii) NATIONAL SERVICE SCHEME (NSS)

2.1.11 NSS would be strengthened and expanded from 2.60 million to 5.10 million volunteers and made more effective through qualitative improvements in the programme activities. NSS would be extended to uncovered universities, colleges, technical institutes, and senior secondary schools. The feasibility of extending NSS to class IX will be examined separately. The funding pattern would be revised from the existing 70:50 to 75:25, at par with National Cadet Corps, for normal States and 90:10 in the case of NE States.

(iii) RAJIV GANDHI NATIONAL INSTITUTE OF YOUTH DEVELOPMENT (RGNIYD)

2.1.12 RGNIYD would be developed as the apex institution with the status of Deemed National Youth University in the country. The Institute would provide special focus on youth leaders from PRIs and will be developed as an International Centre of Excellence on youth development. The collaboration of RGNIYD with the Commonwealth Youth Programme (CYP) Asia Centre, Chandigarh, would be strengthened to enable a higher level of international participation.

(iv) YOUTH HOSTELS

2.1.13 To encourage youth travel, youth hostels are envisaged at historical, cultural, and tourist places in the country as a joint venture between the Central and the State Governments. The construction and maintenance and operations could be taken up in a self-sustaining manner in the PPP/franchising mode. Some portion of the hostels could also be earmarked with differential tariff and facilities so as to generate additional resource to meet maintenance and up keep of the campus.

(v) NATIONAL PROGRAMME FOR YOUTH AND ADOLESCENT DEVELOPMENT

2.1.14 The programmes/schemes being funded through grant-in-aid/financial assistance under 'Yuva

Shakti Abhiyan' for youth and adolescent development will be restructured and placed under a single scheme namely, 'National Programme for Youth and Adolescent Development'. Considering increasing population of adolescents in future, Eleventh Plan recognizes adolescents as individuals with their own rights, aspirations and concerns, thus emphasizing a shift away from the welfare approach to a rights and empowerment oriented approach. The thrust areas of Eleventh Plan will consist of highlighting the need to extend coverage to adolescents in the various schemes of the Ministry of Youth Affairs and Sports and strengthening of the existing scheme of Financial Assistance for Development and Empowerment of Adolescents on holistic approach.

(vi) OTHER SCHEMES

2.1.15 The volunteers under NSVS and RSY are the backbone of NYKS. These schemes should be merged with NYKS and should be renamed as 'National Volunteer Scheme'. The existing scheme, namely, CYP would be strengthened. The mega youth exchange programme with China will be continued as a regular feature. Scouting and Guiding would be continued with renewed focus to develop the character of young boys and girls and inculcate in them a spirit of patriotism, social service, and communal harmony. There is a wider scope for PPP especially in respect of adventure sports, tourism, and eco-tourism. A road map will be drawn through a stakeholders' consultative process to broad-base the movement and mainstream it as a part of a larger India Youth Network.

SPORTS AND PHYSICAL EDUCATION

2.1.16 Every civilization has evolved and developed its own indigenous modes of physical endeavour and healthy social interaction through a variety of games and sports forms and events. There has been an intrinsic component of education and development of the human personality in philosophical texts of ancient Greece, the progenitor of the Olympic movement. In India, sports and games as a vital component of social and cultural life are embedded in the heritage right from Vedic as well as in Buddhist and Jain literature. Swami Vivekanand has been the principal exponent of sports culture in the country. He advised 'Be strong my young friends, that is my advice to you. You will be nearer to heaven through football than through the study of the Gita'.

2.1.17 The Eleventh and Twelfth Plan periods would be full of international sports events in the country. The World Military Games are proposed to be held at Hyderabad in 2007, the Commonwealth Youth Games (CYG) would be held in Pune in 2008, followed by the main Commonwealth Games (CG), 2010 in Delhi. The main aim behind the organization of such games has to relate to development of a sports culture and world-class sports facilities across the country, and a significant improvement in the levels of excellence, in terms of performance and medal-winning abilities of our sportspersons at the national and international levels. The existing policy and programmes need to be reviewed and the strategy and activities chalked out accordingly.

Box 2.1.2

Commonwealth Games (CG) 2010 and Commonwealth Youth Games (CYG) 2008

- The CG will be held in Delhi during 3–14 October 2010.
- CG 2010 will host 17 disciplines that will be held in the newly constructed and existing indoor/outdoor stadiums, developed by various agencies like Delhi Development Authority, Delhi University, Sports Authority of India (SAI), All India Tennis Association, and National Capital Territory of Delhi. The New Delhi Games Village will be set up on a 63.5 acre site with the accessible capacity of 8500 athletes and officials. The residential Zones of the Games are being developed on PPP basis. The tentative estimated outlay is Rs 6304 crore.
- The existing stadiums will be used for sports, viz., Archery, Aquatics, Athletics, Badminton, Boxing, Cycling, Elite Athletes with Disability events, Gymnastics, Hockey, Lawn Bowls, Netball, Rugby 7s, Shootings, Squash, Table Tennis, Tennis, Weightlifting, and Wrestling.
- Prior to CG 2010, third CYG will be held from 12–18 October 2008 at Pune. The CYG covers Athletics, Badminton, Boxing, Shooting, Swimming, Table Tennis, Tennis, Weightlifting, and Wrestling. Planning Commission provided Rs 210 crore and Government of Maharashtra Rs 100 crore for sports infrastructure development of CYG, Pune.

Performance during Plan Period

2.1.18 The National Sports Policy, 1984, was the first move towards developing an organized and systematic framework for the development and promotion of sports in the country, and the precursor of the present National Sports Policy, 2001. The policy, inter alia, emphasized the need for making sports and physical education an integral part of the curriculum. This resolve has also been stated in the National Policy of Education 1986, which calls for making sports and physical education an integral part of the learning process, and provides for its inclusion in the evaluation of performance. However, a review of Eighth Plan investments in Youth Affairs and Sports both at the national and State levels showed gross inadequacy considering the magnitude of youth population as indicated in Table 2.1.1.

TABLE 2.1.1
Plan Expenditure on Youth Affairs and Sports

(Rs crore)

Government	Eighth Plan	Ninth Plan	Tenth Plan
Centre	434 (38)	895 (44)	1832 (41)
States/UTs	712 (62)	1143 (56)	2649 (59)
Total	1146 (100)	2038 (100)	4481 (100)

Note: The figures in parenthesis indicate percentage.
Source: Planning Commission, State Plans Division.

2.1.19 The per capita plan expenditure at the central and State level works out to only Rs 8.94 and Rs 12.92 per youth per annum, respectively, and the national per capita expenditure at Rs 21.86 per youth per year during Tenth Plan. The per capita State Plan expenditure was much lower than the national average in several major States like Kerala, Haryana, UP, Orissa, Gujarat, MP, and Bihar. It has also been observed from the structure of Plan expenditure, the State share of Plan expenditure has declined from 62% in the Eighth Plan to 59% in the Tenth Plan (Figure 2.1.1). Among the major States, while Andhra Pradesh, Karnataka, West Bengal, Maharashtra, and Tamil Nadu topped the Plan expenditure, Gujarat, Rajasthan, Himachal Pradesh were in the lower order of expenditure.

2.1.20 There is a need for reforms in sports management and governance to make it dynamic, responsive, and result-oriented. Some of the problems and issues identified by Parliamentary Standing Committee include: (i) Lack of a sports culture and consciousness in the country; (ii) Non-integration of sports with education; (iii) Lack of proper co-ordination amongst the Centre, States, federations/associations, and various private and public sector undertakings; (iv) Lack of infrastructure in the rural areas and its concentration in urban/metropolitan centres; (v) Under-utilization of available infrastructure and its poor maintenance and upkeep; (vi) Lack of good quality and affordable sports equipments; (vii) Absence of adequate incentives for the youth to take up sports as a career; (viii) Unfair selection procedure and last minute finalization of teams; and (ix) Lack of adequate exposure and specialized training/coaching of international standards. It is noted that most of the State Governments do not have their State Sports Policy. These would be addressed in the Eleventh Plan.

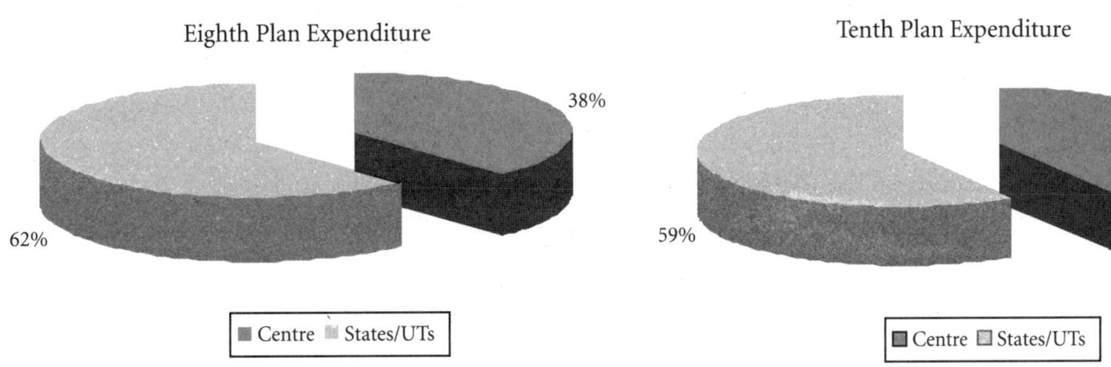

Source: Planning Commission, State Plans Division.

FIGURE 2.1.1: Centre vs State Share of Plan Expenditure

Performance Review of Tenth Plan

2.1.21 The thrust areas identified for the Tenth Plan were creation of infrastructure, training facilities, upgradation of coaching skills, promotion of research and scientific support systems, creation of a drug-free environment, welfare and incentives for sportspersons, and tapping of resources from the private/public sector and individuals for the development of sports. Sports Authority of India (SAI) is an apex body for promotion of sports excellence in the country. The qualitative performance of SAI has to be seen in the light of three distinct aspects, i.e. (i) academics, which include the schemes for the training of coaches and other scientific staff, and programmes related to physical education; (ii) the collaboration with the National Sports Federations (NSFs) pertaining to the training of identified elite athletes and teams in different disciplines; and (iii) operations, which include schemes pertaining to the spotting and nurturing of talent. There is an acute shortage of coaches in the country. Efforts made by SAI under its Training centres and Special Area Games scheme have not yet yielded results.

2.1.22 The CSS related to sports infrastructure was transferred to States w.e.f. 1.4.2005 with provision for meeting the committed liability of continuing projects till the end of the Tenth Plan. The performance of district and State level competitions under Rural Sports Programme and Promotion of Sports and Games in Schools had not been satisfactory. Adequate participation from corporate/private sector could not forth come under National Sports Development Fund and for setting up of State Sports Academies. The scheme relating to Talent Search and Training was a bit slow to take off, but in the last two to three years, the scheme helped a number of players in achieving excellence at the international level. The progress of pre-project activities for the development of infrastructure for CG 2010, Delhi, and CYG 2008, Pune, is satisfactory.

2.1.23 Against the outlay of Rs 1145.36 crore and allocation of Rs 1463.69 crore for Sports and Physical Education, the anticipated expenditure was Rs 1306.41 crore (89.25%) during Tenth Plan (Annexure 2.1.1). SAI incurred 47% of expenditure followed by assistance to NSFs (16%), CG-2010 (15%), and infrastructure schemes (9%).

Approach and Programmes for Eleventh Plan

2.1.24 The approach and strategy for the Eleventh Plan would encompass the twin objectives of 'Broad-basing of Sports' and 'Promotion of Sports Excellence'. Despite initiating of a variety of steps taken by the Central Government, in terms of establishing structures and schemes for the development and promotion of sports, the desired results seem exclusive and therefore, there is an urgent need to review and reorient the system and procedures pertaining to coaching and organizing camps, provision of scientific back-up, and support during training/coaching camps and at the competition stage.

2.1.25 There is also a need for clear delineation of the roles and responsibilities of the related organizations/institutions, viz., SAI, Indian Olympic Association, and NSFs, together with action to co-opt the private sector in the form of adoption of disciplines/teams, sponsorship, etc., to supplement the efforts of the government. To achieve this, a close coordination and convergence would be required of all stakeholders.

Box 2.1.3
Objectives for Eleventh Plan—Sports and Physical Education

- Creation of sports infrastructure at grass-root level in rural and urban areas;
- Creating sports culture through organizing competitive events and involvement of educational institutions;
- Creating a pool of talented sports persons and providing them world class training facilities;
- Improving coaching facilities;
- Reformulating sport policy and action plan;
- Involvement of corporate sector;
- Creating career opportunities and social security for sports persons.

There is a need for transparency and accountability in the functions of sports bodies. The facilities under SAI would need systematic and scientific expansion and upgradation. The management aspects pertaining to development of various individual sports disciplines will also need to be reviewed and made more effective.

BROAD-BASING: INTRODUCTION OF PANCHAYAT YUVA KRIDA AUR KHEL ABHIYAN (PYKKA)

2.1.26 Broad-basing of Sports is the key to the promotion and development of a sports culture. The emphasis on sports should be on fitness of body of every individual and particularly youth and not relegated to entertainment and related activities as listed in the concurrent list. In order to make sports as mass movement, a new CSS under the title of 'Panchayat Yuva Krida Aur Khel Abhiyan (PYKKA)' would be launched for filling up the gaps at the sub-district level. The objective of the scheme is to create basic infrastructure and facilities for sports and games at the village and town levels, generating a sports culture among the rural youth, organizing competition and non-competition sporting activities at the village level, and developing a competition structure up to the district level. PYKKA would be implemented during Eleventh and Twelfth Plan in a Mission Mode with the involvement of the PRIs and the 2.50 lakh Rural Youth and Sports Clubs under NYKS and other schemes of the State Governments in a phased manner. The existing scheme of Rural Sports Programme will be subsumed in PYKKA. As the sports and games is State subject, the State Governments should also share costs and be accountable.

2.1.27 For purposes of funding under the scheme, it is proposed to bring in the greatest possible synergy and convergence between various schemes of the Central Government, such as the National Rural Employment Guarantee Scheme, Backward Regions Grant Fund, relevant schemes of the Ministry of Tribal Affairs and Department for the Development of the North Eastern Region, MP Local Area Development Scheme (and similar schemes of State Governments), funds available to the PRIs through devolution and the schemes of the State Governments for development of sports infrastructure.

PROMOTION OF SPORTS EXCELLENCE

2.1.28 The broad-basing of sports could gradually yield a pool of one lakh talented youth at the Sub-Junior, Junior, and Senior levels, who would require systematic and scientific nurturing and focused training to achieve excellence at the national/international levels. This would require multiple measures, including spotting/identification of national probables based on proficiency, performance, and potential; establishment of training infrastructure arrangements; coaching facilities; strengthening scientific and technical supports system; supply of quality sports goods and equipment; and use of media to bring sports consciousness. There is a need to maintain a computerized inventory of assets relating to sports at State, district, and block levels. NGOs, outstanding sportspersons, and corporate entities would be encouraged to get involved in the creation of facilities to promote sports excellence, in the form of academies, etc.

2.1.29 Recognizing the role of media in creating sports consciousness in the country, all efforts would be made to ensure their support in promoting and broad-basing of sports, particularly rural sports. The government will have to build in some regulations to ensure covering of sporting events apart from cricket and tennis to make good lack of adequate sponsorship. Special programmes and capsules also need to be prepared and aired, from time to time, about excellence promotion programmes such as coaching camps, talent-spotting exercise, selection trials, etc., to generate awareness about the development of sports in the country.

2.1.30 As regards the development of physical education, steps would need to be taken to develop and bring about an integral relationship between related institutions, including the possible reorganization of Laxmibai National College of Physical Education, Thiruvananthapuram as a Regional Centre (South) of the Laxmibai National Institute of Physical Education (LNIPE), Gwalior, which itself is a Deemed University. This would be in addition to other measures pertaining to synergy and complimentary between LNIPE and SAI. LNIPE would set up regional centres in the north east, east, west, and north. Besides, the infrastructure facilities at LNIPE itself would be strengthened, upgraded, and modernized. The recommendation of NCERT that Health and Physical Education should be a core subject up to class X and an elective subject up to plus two levels should be implemented.

2.1.31 Considering the growing menace of doping, two separate autonomous entities, namely, National Anti-Doping Agency and National Dope Test Laboratory will be set up for ensuring quality testing of samples, etc. In view of 2.13% of Indian population is physically or mentally challenged and the impressive performance of Indian Elite Athletes with Disability at the international level, a comprehensive scheme would be formulated to ensure planned and systematic promotion of excellence in this field.

NE States

2.1.32 The approved outlay Tenth Plan was Rs 192.50 crore for NE States including Sikkim against which the expenditure is Rs 167.22 crore indicating a utilization of about 87%. NE region has a tremendous potential to excel in sports has been proved by the National Games at Guwahati in Assam. There is need for greater investment in improving games facilities in this region.

The Path Ahead

2.1.33 Despite Youth Affairs and Sports being a State subject, it has not got adequate support from the State Governments. Only few State Governments have their own Youth and Sports Policies. It is necessary that all States/UTs formulate State-specific Youth and Sports Policies and Action Plan for development of youth. State Sports Academies should be set up to select the best talent in sports. Perhaps, Sports could be brought in the concurrent list to supplement the State efforts. However, Plan expenditure of States will have to step up to arrest the declining trends.

2.1.34 The total projected Gross Budgetary Support (GBS) for the Eleventh Plan for the Ministry of Youth Affairs and Sports is given in Appendix of Volume III.

2.2. ART AND CULTURE

Introduction

2.2.1 The Constitution of India stipulates that it shall be the duty of every citizen to value and preserve the rich heritage of our composite culture. The art and culture of India are a vast continuum, evolving incessantly since time immemorial. Therefore, preservation and conservation of India's rich cultural heritage and promotion of all forms of art and culture, both tangible and intangible, including monuments and archaeological sites, anthropology and ethnology, folk and tribal arts, literature and handicrafts, performing arts of music-dance-drama, and visual arts of paintings-sculpture-graphics assume considerable importance. On a larger scale, cultural activities also address issues relating to national identity in conjunction with several other sectors such as education, tourism, textiles, external relations, etc.

Thrust During Plan Periods

2.2.2 Since Independence the crux of all culture development plans has been the preservation of cultural heritage with emphasis on the thread of continuity binding the dissimilarities into a synergistic whole. The main focus in the early Five Year Plans, up to the Sixth Plan, was on the establishment of cultural institutions in the field of archaeology, anthropology and ethnography, archives, libraries, museums, and performing arts including academies. Since the Seventh Plan there was also special emphasis on the pursuit of contemporary the creativity.

Achievements in the Plan Periods

Performing Arts

2.2.3 The ongoing schemes under the performing arts spanning disparate fields of classical/traditional and folk music/theatre and dance—showcased by organizations like Sangeet Natak Akademi (SNA), National School of Drama, and Zonal Cultural Centres (ZCCs)—have played a crucial role in supporting and facilitating the performing arts traditions in the country. Several schemes continue to be implemented under the performing and visual arts with a view to supporting creative individuals and institutions in their new ventures/productions.

Museums and Visual Arts

2.2.4 Modernization of museums involved laying emphasis on digitization and documentation of artworks as part of Plan activities and on strengthening of networking among Central museums. The scheme of financial assistance for strengthening of regional and local museums has been revised with a view to widening its scope for assisting smaller museums. The National Council of Science Museums (NCSM) has been engaged in popularizing Science and Technology amongst students through a wide range of activities and interactive programmes implemented by 26 Science Museums/Centres.

Archaeology, Anthropology, and Ethnology

2.2.5 Successive Five Year Plans focused on preservation and development of heritage sites and monument complexes. Major strategies included (i) involvement of university departments of History and Archaeology in survey of heritage sites; (ii) modernization of galleries, digital documentation of antiquities, publication of catalogues, museum guides, and picture postcards by the Archaeological Survey of India (ASI); (iii) publication of excavation reports; (iv) setting up a new Underwater Archaeology Branch; and (v) demarcation of protected limits of archaeological monuments and provisions to safeguard against encroachments.

Archives, Libraries, and Literature

2.2.6 The National Archives of India (NAI) has been the custodian of Central Government records of enduring value for permanent preservation and use by administrators and scholars. Preservation and conservation of rare books and other documents is one of the chief activities of the National Library and Central Reference Library (Kolkata), Central Secretariat Library and Delhi Public Library (New Delhi), State Central Library (Mumbai), Thanjavur Maharaja Serofji Saraswati Mahal Library (TMSSML) (Thanjavur) and Raja Ram Mohun Roy Library Foundation (Kolkata), which are engaged in digitization of old books and manuscripts and retro-conservation of catalogues. Developing a National Bibliographic Database in electronic format to encourage resource sharing, networking and to improve reader services is the hallmark of modernization activities in the library sector.

Education, Research and Others

2.2.7 Achievement of Plan schemes have been substantial under the education and research fields, viz. Buddhist and Tibetan Institutions, National Museum Institute, Centenary and Memorials, Centre for Cultural Resources and Training (CCRT), etc. Other initiatives included building projects and construction activities at National Museum (New Delhi) and at National Gallery of Modern Art (Bangalore and New Delhi). Under National Culture Fund (NCF), projects were undertaken in collaboration with private houses, viz. Shaniwarwara (Pune), Jnana Pravaha (Varanasi), Humayun's Tomb (Delhi), Durgapur Children's Society (WB), five heritage sites in five States in collaboration with Indian Oil Corporation, Taj Mahal (Agra) in collaboration with Taj Group of Hotels, and Jantar Mantar (New Delhi) in collaboration with APJ Group.

Progress During the Tenth Plan

2.2.8 The thrust areas during the Tenth Plan included implementation of a comprehensive plan for the preservation of archaeological heritage and development of monument complexes; modernization of museums and preservation of archival heritage; promotion of classical, folk and tribal art crafts, and oral traditions. Computerization of museums with the assistance of National Informatics Centre (NIC), digitization of collections, micro filming of manuscripts and the introduction of equipment for audio tours received special focus. Networking amongst Central museums, undertaking in-service staff training and organizing exhibitions were other priority areas.

2.2.9 The Tenth Plan (2002–07) allocation for Art and Culture was Rs 1720 crore. The total expenditure during the Tenth Plan at Rs 1526.30 crore accounted for 88.74% of Plan outlay (see Annexure 2.2.1). Lack of proper phasing of expenditure and activities under various cultural organizations hindered full utilization of Plan allocation. There were cost and time over-runs in some of the major civil work projects.

Scheme-wise/Sector-wise Analysis

Promotion and Dissemination of Art and Culture

2.2.10 Promotion and dissemination of art and culture have been mainly done through seven ZCCs.

During the Tenth Plan, the CCRT trained about 22000 in-service teachers and 700 teacher-educators. The SNA, Sahitya Akademi (SA), and Lalit Kala Akademi (LKA) organized Golden Jubilee Celebrations to commemorate their fiftieth anniversaries. About 21000 books were added to the SA libraries in Delhi, Mumbai, Kolkata, and Bangalore during the Tenth Plan. SNA organized Music, Dance and Theatre Festivals, Seminars and Workshops, Yuva Utsavs and Puppetry Shows. LKA organized exhibitions in India and abroad. The National School of Drama conducted more than 300 production-oriented theatre workshops and organized a Satellite Theatre Festival in Bangalore. The expenditure under Promotion and Dissemination of Art and Culture at Rs 454.99 crore exceeded the Tenth Plan outlay of Rs 362.43 crore by 25.5%.

Archaeology

2.2.11 Several excavation projects undertaken during the period include those at Dholavira (Kachchh, Gujarat), Dhalewa (Punjab), Sravasti (UP), Kanaganahalli Sannati (Karnataka), Hathab (Saurashtra, Gujarat), Udaigiri (Orissa), Boxanager (Tripura), Karenghar (Sibsgar, Assam), Arikamedu (Pondicherry), Dum Dum (Kolkata), and Bellie Guard (Lucknow). Major works for conservation and integrated development in respect of 15 monuments were taken up by the ASI. Collaboration with the corporate sector such as Taj Group of Hotels and the World Monument Fund was also initiated. Initiatives undertaken by the ASI included protection of 3667 monuments and signing an MoU with Government of Kampuchea for the conservation of Ta-Prohm Temple in Siem Reap. Under Archaeology, the plan expenditure of Rs 304.11 crore exceeded the Tenth Plan outlay of Rs 284.83 crore by 7%.

Archives and Records

2.2.12 The NAI has revitalized its programmes of expansion of records management and repair and reprography. Other scheme components under Archives and Records, viz., Khuda Baksh Oriental Public Library, Rampur Raza Library, Asiatic Societies at Kolkata and Mumbai, and the TMSSML have performed well during the Tenth Plan. However, the Plan expenditure of Rs 60.32 crore showed a shortfall of 18.61% as compared to the Tenth Plan outlay of Rs 74.11 crore.

2.2.13 It was during the Tenth Plan that attention was drawn towards the manuscript wealth of the country and on the need for special attention on their conservation and upkeep. The National Mission for Manuscripts was launched for inventorization and protection of Indian manuscripts. The mission has taken up the task of compiling a national database of manuscripts (being made available online) by initiating a national survey of about 2 million manuscripts. More importantly, 45 most unique manuscripts recording India's achievements in science, philosophy, scripture, history, and the arts have been selected by a committee of selectors as national treasure. Software has been prepared by NIC in Visual Basic Net for cataloguing of manuscripts. About 2 lakh illustrated manuscripts have been digitized.

Museums

2.2.14 Out of the Tenth Plan outlay of Rs 304.13 crore for Museums, Plan expenditure at Rs 314.21 crore exceeded the outlay by 3.3%. The thrust was on the strengthening of networking among Central museums, enabling these institutions to share their experiences and resources in undertaking in-service training, and organizing exhibitions. The National Museum paid increased attention on modernizing its permanent galleries. Three new galleries, viz., Nizam Jewellery Gallery, Folk and Art Gallery, and Central Asian Antiquities were set up in the National Museum.

Public Libraries

2.2.15 Out of the Tenth Plan outlay of Rs 131.05 crore, an expenditure of Rs 121.76 crore was incurred, which indicates a shortfall of 7.1%. This scheme includes National Library of India, Central Research Library, Raja Rammohun Rai Library Foundation, Kolkata; Delhi Public Library and Central Secretariat Library, New Delhi; State Central Library, Mumbai; Connemara Library, Chennai, and National Policy on Library and Information Centre.

Indira Gandhi National Centre for Arts (IGNCA)

2.2.16 The mandate of IGNCA is to explore, study and revive the dialogue between India and her neighbours in areas pertaining to the arts, especially in South and South East Asia. IGNCA has six functional units, viz., Kalanidhi (multi-form library); Kalakosh (Indian language texts); Janapada Sampada (lifestyle studies); Kaladarshan (visible forms of IGNCA researches); Culture Informatics Lab (technology tools for cultural preservation); and Sutradhara (coordinating IGNCA activities). IGNCA had a plan outlay of Rs 90.00 crore. IGNCA's performance suffered a setback due to administrative and other reasons including lack of credible Plan schemes. By the time the factors responsible for dismal performance and other issues were sorted out and IGNCA re-railed, the Tenth Plan closed with an expenditure only Rs 4.12 crore.

Institutions of Tibetan and Buddhist Studies

2.2.17 Out of the Tenth Plan outlay of Rs 45.70 crore, an expenditure of Rs 45.11 crore was incurred indicating 98.7% utilization. The scheme consists of Central Institute of Buddhist Studies (Leh), Central Institute of Higher Tibetan Studies (Sarnath), Centre for Buddhist Cultural Studies (Tawang), Tibet House (New Delhi), and Scheme of Financial Assistance for the Preservation and Development of Buddhist/ Tibetan Culture and Art.

Memorials

2.2.18 The scheme comprises Gandhi Smriti, Darshan Samiti, and Nehru Memorial Museum and Library (New Delhi), Maulana Abul Kalam Azad Institute of Asian Studies (Kolkata), and Nava Nalanda Mahavihar (Bihar). Actual expenditure at Rs 61.73 crore exceeded the plan outlay of Rs 49.35 crore by 25.1%.

Activities for North East Region (NER)

2.2.19 As against the targeted expenditure of Rs 154.00 crore in the NER, the actual expenditure was only Rs 134.19 crore (87.1%). With the aim of creating cultural awareness in the NER and identifying/ promoting vanishing folk art traditions in rural/ semi-urban areas the North Eastern ZCC has been set up at Dimapur. The progress under the scheme of Multipurpose Cultural Complexes (MPCC) has been slow and the scheme not yet been evaluated in any of the States. The MPCC did not meet any criteria for a CSS and only about 25% of the projects sanctioned have been completed. As per the ZBB exercise, the scheme was discontinued in Budget 2007–08. Initiatives were taken to set up the Central Institute of Himalayan Cultural Studies at Dahung (AP) for promoting traditional Buddhist Studies. The approach towards utilization of earmarked funds, save for few activities listed above, was far from satisfactory. It is essential that the 10% earmarked resources are not only invested for the NE States but also in the NER.

Perspective of the Eleventh Plan

2.2.20 Given the challenges inherent in the enormity a country of India's size, the monumental diversity of its people and their languages, and the plurality of faiths and belief systems, it is imperative to embark on a planned development of cultural conservation and promotion activities in the Eleventh Five Year Plan. There is a need for a long-term perspective plan for each major sector within which the medium term and annual plans are built up to fulfil the vision.

2.2.21 Diversity is the hallmark of India's rich cultural heritage. Therefore, all forms of art and culture should have an equal footing and deserve financial and other support. Conventional support should yield to relative merits in terms of the need to preserve, protect, and promote the cultures of different parts of the country. In this context, it is essential to view culture as 'ways of living together', as means to the end of promoting and sustaining human progress, with intrinsic value. Accordingly, the imbalances in flow of funds for various activities under promotion and dissemination of performing arts will have to be set right, particularly in favour of vanishing folk arts and crafts that cannot be pitted against classical arts to compete for resources and media attention. Popular forms of art and culture, particularly in terms of patronage, could find resources of their own via PPP.

2.2.22 Many art forms are in the peril of withering away due to the lack of State patronage. Market forces can also extend support to creative arts, but these are necessarily selective and limited. There is a need for greater support for performing arts and for correcting the distortions induced by selective support of market forces. It is with this perspective that the existing schemes in the area of art and culture including Performing Arts, in addition to being reviewed and strengthened, have been appraised and recommended for continuation in the Eleventh Plan with modifications.

PRIORITIES IN THE ELEVENTH PLAN

2.2.23 The two UNESCO Conventions, one 'to safeguard and protect Intangible Heritage' and the other on 'Cultural Diversity', have urged governments to initiate proactive measures to safeguard and protect cultural diversity and the various expressions of intangible heritage facing the risk of disappearance. The spirit of these two conventions would permeate the schemes of Ministry of Culture and its bodies during the Eleventh Plan period.

2.2.24 The upkeep and maintenance of museums and archaeological sites will be considerably improved with introduction of modern technology and redeployment of existing staff. Security services are already outsourced. The possibility for outsourcing in areas like consultancy and maintenance needs to be examined. PPP models may be explored for development of monuments not protected by ASI with the involvement of States. Delhi should be developed as a heritage city by making some of its monuments world-class, preferably before 2010 CG. Publication through private sector should be encouraged as they have modern technology and know-how to produce the best. Repository work is done well by the private sector. As Ministry of Culture has been facing recurrent cuts in outlay due to poor spending during the first two quarters, proper expenditure planning including phasing of expenditure in sub-sectors other than Akademies and ASI. In the field of art and culture, several schemes are being implemented without assessing the process and impact. Therefore, all the schemes will be evaluated.

RESTRUCTURING OF SCHEMES AND SECTORAL THRUSTS

Performing Arts

2.2.25 The existing scheme of 'Financial Assistance to Professional Groups and Individuals for Specified Performing Art Projects' will be bifurcated into two schemes, viz., Salary and Production Grants with revisions in the cost structure. The scheme of 'Financial Assistance for Research Support to Voluntary Organizations engaged in cultural activities' will be modified as the scheme of 'Financial Assistance for Research, Seminar and Performance to voluntary organizations engaged in cultural activities'. The existing scheme of 'Award of Senior/Junior Fellowship to Outstanding Artists in the field of Performing, Literary and Classical Arts' would be added with a new component, namely 'Fellowship of National Eminence', with fellowships to outstanding scholars selected through a search process and peer review.

Box 2.2.1
Strategies for the Eleventh Plan

- Tapping of PPP models for sustenance of Arts and Crafts.
- Greater involvement of universities in schemes of Lalit Kala, Sangeet Natak, and Sahitya Akademies; Fine Arts to be included as a subject in universities.
- SA to work out operational modalities of promoting Hindi and getting it recognized as a UN language.
- SNA to promote and correct the imbalance in extending patronage to varied forms of art with focus on group and dances like Bihu, Bhangra, Nautanki, Dandiya, Bamboo and folk dances besides classical forms.
- Protection of monuments not notified for protection by ASI and involvement of States/PRIs in protecting unprotected monuments.
- Preserving and promoting India's rich intangible cultural heritage by inventorizing and documenting oral traditions, indigenous knowledge systems, guru-shisya parampara, Vedic chanting, Kuddiattam, Ramlila, folklores and tribal, oral traditions.
- Publication of reports of archaeological excavations undertaken in last 20 years.
- Greater momentum and funding to the library movement in the country and the National Mission on Libraries launched.
- Set up one museum in each district with separate chambers for visual and other forms of art, architecture, science, history and geography with regional flavour.
- Enhancing assimilative capabilities to adapt to emergent challenges of globalization and technological innovations.

Box 2.2.2
Specific Plan of Action for Art and Culture

- Promoting regional languages with focus on translation of regional/vernacular literature and integration with National Translation Mission.
- Dovetailing of cultural and creative industries—media, films, music, handicraft, visual and performing arts, literature, heritage, etc., for growth and employment.
- Generating demand for cultural goods and services as a matter of sustenance rather than patronage, thus bringing art and culture sector in the larger public domain.
- Restructuring some existing schemes to encourage PPP.
- Development of Sanskriti Grams for giving basic amenities to indigent urban artists.
- Promoting export of core cultural goods and services for taking the country in the list of first 20 countries ranked by UNESCO for export of culture.
- Recognizing 'cultural heritage tourism' as an upcoming industry with mutually supportive activities.
- Building cultural resources with adaptation of scientific and technological knowledge to local circumstances, and forming partnerships between local and global.
- Infusion of knowledge capital in cultural institutions through flexible engagements.
- Housing segments on cultural resources in the national museums and Science Cities/Centres set up by the NCSM.
- Documentation of unprotected monuments, other than the 3667 protected ASI monuments.

2.2.26 A new component under performing arts is the creation of a 'National Artists Welfare Fund'—with a corpus of Rs 5.00 crore for meeting medical emergencies of artists—as an independent administered fund with facilities to receive contributions from any lawful sources.

2.2.27 The Akademies and the ZCCs will have a new scheme called 'Protecting the Intellectual Property Rights of the artists and of cultural industries'—especially of folk and tribal artists—along with the creation of a national apparatus to work as a watchdog and facilitator in this area. A Cultural Centre at Kolkata will be set up in PPP with Calcutta Museum of Modern Art in collaboration with the State Government with provision for funding by the three Akademies.

Museums and Visual Arts

2.2.28 The ongoing schemes/institutions in the field of museums will continue in the Eleventh Plan along with the modernization/strengthening/upgradation of various museums. The museums in four metros, viz., Delhi, Kolkata, Mumbai, and Chennai will be modernized. Gandhi Darshan Memorial at Rajghat will be developed as a Centre of Excellence for promoting research in Gandhian studies. Also, during the Eleventh Plan, a comprehensive development of Jallianwala Bagh National Memorial, befitting its status and importance in the history of Indian freedom struggle, will be undertaken.

Archaeology, Anthropology, and Ethnology

2.2.29 Specific tasks for the ASI include undertaking a time-bound programme to complete all pending excavation reports and drawing up a phased programme for qualitative upgradation of all 41 site museums besides completing and operationalizing new museums that are built at Chanderi, Khajuraho, and Shivpuri. ASI will undertake an intensified conservation programme for 2000 Centrally protected monuments and excavated archaeological remains and a program-me of integrated development of all World Heritage Cultural Sites. The Regional Centres of ASI will be strengthened.

2.2.30 A research/conservation laboratory at Aurangabad for further improving the condition of Ajanta-Ellora monuments and a centralized Cell for Archaeological Investigation using modern scientific methods will be set up. A new scheme providing fellowships for two years' duration to young archaeologists in the age group of 25–35 years will be launched. A new scheme for providing Financial Assistance to

State Protected Monuments and for Unprotected Monuments will be launched leveraging State and private sector funds for protection and preservation of monuments.

2.2.31 The Anthropological Survey of India will take up four new Plan schemes, viz., Indigenous Knowledge and Traditional Technology, Oral Traditions/Folk Taxonomies, Social Structure and Bio-Cultural Adaptations with Gender Perspectives, and Man in the Biosphere and National Repository of Human Genetic Resources. Indira Gandhi Rashtriya Manav Sangrahalaya will take up new programmes for upgradation of existing exhibition galleries and development of new exhibitions on the theme 'India and the World', National Documentation Centre and Archive for Intangible Cultural Heritage and establishment of four Regional Outreach Centres.

Literature, Libraries, and Archives

2.2.32 The development of Public Libraries in the Eleventh Plan includes Rural Public Libraries and provision for handicapped and under-privileged in District Libraries. A National Library Mission will be set up. National, State/district libraries will develop special collections and technological support for visually challenged and hearing-impaired.

Education, Research, and Others

2.2.33 A Cultural Heritage Volunteers Forum will be set up in schools/colleges/universities in convergence with NSS for integrating the basic tenets of India's cultural heritage. A Pilot Scheme for Cultural Industries will be launched by selected ZCCs for providing market information, design, packaging, training, and e-commerce facilities. The schemes of CCRT, Assistance for Preservation and Development of Cultural Heritage of Himalayas, and Assistance for Preservation and Development of Buddhist/Tibetan Organization will be restructured.

National Translation Mission

2.2.34 A new scheme will be launched in partnership with States for cultural exchange to strengthen the composite culture through translation of a minimum five good literary works in every language into all other major languages.

The Path Ahead

2.2.35 The strengthening of inter-organizational networks and introduction of management-oriented approaches in the administration of cultural institutions are the two cardinal prerequisites for improving efficiency in the working of the cultural institutions. The Ministry of Culture's Modernization and Computerization Scheme should develop a module for exclusively dealing with increasing inter-organizational cooperation, networking, and sharing of information amidst disparate cultural organizations. There is a need to emulate networking systems in scientific institutions with a view to repositioning India's rightful place in the comity of Knowledge Superpowers.

2.2.36 Resuscitating India's dwindling higher institutions of art and culture poses a real challenge and an action plan to strengthen these institutions needs to be worked out during the Eleventh Plan. Outstanding scholars from India and abroad could be encouraged to get associated with these organizations. However, it is important that institutions must be autonomous and develop a conducive working environment. In this context, it is desirable to formulate norms and procedures for flexible engagement of scholars in higher institutions of art and culture. There is an urgent need for adopting the idea of concept makers. In other words, creating an Ideas Bank, which could explore and scrutinize the ideas that originated in India first and then spread across the globe. The Ideas Bank could generate new research designs and modules with inter-disciplinary linkages to develop the growth of innovative research.

2.2.37 The dynamics of the infusion of knowledge capital into the designated Knowledge Institutions through flexible engagements needs to be worked out during the Eleventh Plan. The key elements of this infusion will include (i) evolving a broad framework for infusion of knowledge capital, both domestic and global, (ii) setting out guiding principles that are conducive to flexible engagements and are free from crippling rules and regulations, (iii) redefining the role of knowledge institutions as facilitators of production of knowledge, (iv) extending enhanced autonomy to the institutions for flexible engagements, (v) attracting global creative talents in specialized disciplines and exploring the possibilities of institutionalizing linkages, (vi) ownership of knowledge outputs including inalienable rights of creative talents over output and dissemination and (vii) freeing institutions from budgetary constraints by creating a Knowledge Fund with a reasonable corpus to begin with. Hence, there is a need for (i) assessment of requisite competencies and criteria such as eligibility/suitability and scholarship, (ii) level playing field and (iii) development and nurturing of domestic creative talents with attachments, assignments and partnerships in projects.

2.2.38 Major scheme-wise break up of the GBS for the Eleventh Plan for the Ministry of Culture is given in Appendix of Volume III.

ANNEXURE 2.1.1

Youth Affairs and Sports—Outlay and Expenditure of the Tenth Plan

(Rs Crore)

S. No.	Sub-Sector	Tenth Plan (2002–07)	
		Outlay	Expenditure
A.	Youth Affairs	677.64	522.62
B.	Sports and Physical Education	1145.36	1306.41
C.	Others	2.00	3.05
	Total	1825.00	1832.08

Source: Ministry of Youth Affairs and Sports.

ANNEXURE 2.2.1

Culture—Outlay and Expenditure of the Tenth Plan

(Rs Crore)

S. No.	Scheme/Major Head	Tenth Plan (2002-07)	
		Outlay	Expenditure
1	Modernization & Computerization	4.39	2.73
2	Promotion & Dissemination	362.43	454.99
3	Archaeology	284.83	304.11
4	Archives & Records	74.11	60.32
5	Museums	304.13	314.21
6	Anthropology & Ethnology	40.02	42.06
7	Public Libraries	131.05	121.76
8	IGNCA	90.00	4.12
9	Inst. of Buddhist & Tibetan Studies	45.70	45.11
10	Other Exp. (Memorials)	49.35	61.73
11	Activities for NER	154.00	134.19[@]
12	Building Projects/Capital outlay	180.00	115.16
	Total	1720.00	1526.30

Note: [@]An expenditure of Rs 134.19 crore included under respective sectors.

Source: Ministry of Culture.

3

Health and Family Welfare and AYUSH

3.1 HEALTH AND FAMILY WELFARE

INTRODUCTION

3.1.1 The health of a nation is an essential component of development, vital to the nation's economic growth and internal stability. Assuring a minimal level of health care to the population is a critical constituent of the development process.

3.1.2 Since Independence, India has built up a vast health infrastructure and health personnel at primary, secondary, and tertiary care in public, voluntary, and private sectors. For producing skilled human resources, a number of medical and paramedical institutions including Ayurveda, Yoga and Naturopathy, Unani, Siddha, and Homeopathy (AYUSH) institutions have been set up.

3.1.3 Considerable achievements have been made over the last six decades in our efforts to improve health standards, such as life expectancy, child mortality, infant mortality, and maternal mortality. Small pox and guinea worm have been eradicated and there is hope that poliomyelitis will be contained in the near future. Nevertheless, problems abound. Malnutrition affects a large proportion of children. An unacceptably high proportion of the population continues to suffer and die from new diseases that are emerging; apart from continuing and new threats posed by the existing ones. Pregnancy and childbirth related complications also contribute to the suffering and mortality.

3.1.4 The strong link between poverty and ill health needs to be recognized. The onset of a long and expensive illness can drive the non-poor into poverty. Ill health creates immense stress even among those who are financially secure. High health care costs can lead to entry into or exacerbation of poverty. The importance of public provisioning of quality health care to enable access to affordable and reliable heath services cannot be underestimated. This is specially so, in the context of preventing the non-poor from entering into poverty or in terms of reducing the suffering of those who are already below poverty line.

3.1.5 The country has to deal with rising costs of health care and growing expectations of the people. The challenge of quality health services in remote rural regions has to be urgently met. Given the magnitude of the problem, we need to transform public health care into an accountable, accessible, and affordable system of quality services during the Eleventh Five Year Plan.

VISION FOR HEALTH

3.1.6 The Eleventh Five Year Plan will provide an opportunity to restructure policies to achieve a New Vision based on faster, broad-based, and inclusive growth. One objective of the Eleventh Five Year Plan is to achieve good health for people, especially the poor and the underprivileged. In order to do this, a comprehensive approach is needed that encompasses individual health care, public health, sanitation, clean drinking water, access to food, and knowledge of hygiene, and feeding practices. The Plan will facilitate convergence and development of public health systems and services that are responsive to health needs and aspirations of people. Importance will be given to reducing disparities in health across regions and communities by ensuring access to affordable health care.

3.1.7 Although it has been said in plan after plan, it needs to be reiterated here that the Eleventh Five Year Plan will give special attention to the health of marginalized groups like adolescent girls, women of all ages, children below the age of three, older persons, disabled, and primitive tribal groups. It will view gender as the cross-cutting theme across all schemes.

3.1.8 To achieve these objectives, aggregate spending on health by the Centre and the States will be increased significantly to strengthen the capacity of the public health system to do a better job. The Plan will also ensure a large share of allocation for health programmes in critical areas such as HIV/AIDS. The contribution of the private sector in providing primary, secondary, and tertiary services will be enhanced through various measures including partnership with the government. Good governance, transparency, and accountability in the delivery of health services will be ensured through involvement of PRIs, community, and civil society groups. Health as a right for all citizens is the goal that the Plan will strive towards.

Time-Bound Goals for the Eleventh Five Year Plan

- Reducing Maternal Mortality Ratio (MMR) to 1 per 1000 live births.
- Reducing Infant Mortality Rate (IMR) to 28 per 1000 live births.
- Reducing Total Fertility Rate (TFR) to 2.1.
- Providing clean drinking water for all by 2009 and ensuring no slip-backs.
- Reducing malnutrition among children of age group 0–3 to half its present level.
- Reducing anaemia among women and girls by 50%.
- Raising the sex ratio for age group 0–6 to 935 by 2011–12 and 950 by 2016–17.

(Actions to be taken to achieve the goals related to clean drinking water, malnutrition, and anaemia have been indicated in detail in other chapters.)

CURRENT SCENARIO, CONCERNS, AND CHALLENGES

India in the International Scenario

3.1.9 The comparative picture with regard to health indicators such as life expectancy, TFR, IMR, and MMR points that countries placed in almost similar situations such as Indonesia, Sri Lanka, and China have performed much better than India (Table 3.1.1).

TABLE 3.1.1
Health Indicators among Selected Countries

Country	IMR (per 1000 live births)	Life Expectancy M/F (in years)	MMR (per 100000 live births)	TFR
India	58	63.9/66.9*	301	2.9
China	32	70.6/74.2	56	1.72
Japan	3	78.9/86.1	10	1.35
Republic of Korea	3	74.2/81.5	20	1.19
Indonesia	36	66.2/69.9	230	2.25
Malaysia	9	71.6/76.2	41	2.71
Vietnam	27	69.5/73.5	130	2.19
Bangladesh	52	63.3/65.1	380	3.04
Nepal	58	62.4/63.4	740	3.40
Pakistan	73	64.0/64.3	500	3.87
Sri Lanka	15	72.2/77.5	92	1.89

Note: * Projected (2001–06).
Source: India—RGI, Government of India (GoI) (Latest Figures); Others—State of World Population (2006).

Scenario in Relation to Tenth Plan Goals

3.1.10 Of the 11 monitorable targets for the Tenth Plan, three were related to the health sector. Their goals and achievements are summarized in Table 3.1.2.

DECADAL RATE OF POPULATION GROWTH/ TOTAL FERTILITY RATE (TFR)

3.1.11 The decadal growth of population during 1991–2001 had been 21.5%, on account of the momentum built from high levels of fertility in the past. The good news is that we are right on course with respect to the first of the three Tenth Plan monitorable targets related to the health sector. The projected decadal population growth rate is 15.9% for 2001–11. The two important demographic goals of the National Population Policy (2000) are: achieving the population replacement level (TFR 2.1) by 2010 and a stable population by 2045. TFR, which in the early 1950s was 6.0, has declined to 2.9 in 2005. Thus, India is moving towards its goal of replacement-level fertility of 2.1. The percentage of married women using contraception has increased from a level of just over 10% in the early 1970s to 41% in 1992–93, 48% in 1998–99, and to 56% by 2005–06 (Figure 3.1.1). However, there are huge differentials amongst various States.

MATERNAL MORTALITY RATIO (MMR)

3.1.12 The MMR during 2001–03 has been 301 per 100000 live births (RGI, 2006). Levels of maternal mortality vary greatly across the regions due to variation in access to emergency obstetric care (EmOC), prenatal care, anaemia rates among women, education level of women, and other factors. There has been a substantial decline during the seven year period of 1997–2003. However, the pace of decline is insufficient. At the present rate of decline, it will be difficult to achieve the goal of 100 by 2012 (Figure 3.1.2). This reinforces that rapid expansion of skilled birth attendance and EmOC is needed to further reduce maternal mortality in India.

INFANT MORTALITY RATE (IMR)

3.1.13 IMR is 58 per 1000 live births (Sample Registration System [SRS], 2005). It is higher in rural areas (64) and lower in the urban areas (40) of the country. It also varies across States. Neo-natal mortality (at 37 per 1000 live births) constitutes nearly 60%–75% of the IMR in various States. The coverage of immunization has increased marginally from 42% in 1998–99 to 44% in 2005–06 (Figure 3.1.3). Polio continues to be a problem and usage of Oral Rehydration Solution (ORS) among children with diarrhoea continues to be low (according to NFHS-3, 26.2% of children with diarrhoea in the last two weeks received ORS). The trend of reduction in IMR has been shown in Figure 3.1.4. Concerted efforts will be required under Home Based Newborn Care (HBNC) to reduce the IMR and Neonatal Mortality Rate (NMR) further.

TABLE 3.1.2
Goals and Achievements during the Tenth Plan

Indicator	Goal for Tenth Plan	Achievements
Decadal Rate of Population Growth	16.2%	15.9% for 2001–11 (Projected)[1]
IMR	45 per 1000 live births	58 per 1000 live births[2]
MMR	2 per 1000 live births	3.01 per 1000 live births[3]

Notes: 1. Technical Group on Population Projections set up by National Commission on Population (December 2006), RGI, GoI; 2. SRS 2005; 3. 2001–03 Special Survey of Deaths using RHIME (routine, re-sampled, household interview of mortality with medical evaluation), RGI (2006), GoI.

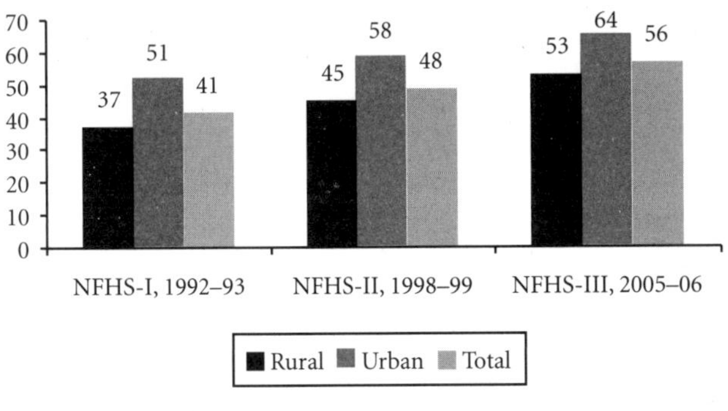

Source: NFHS-3, IIPS (2005–06).

FIGURE 3.1.1: Trends in Contraceptive Use (%) (currently married women in 15–49 age group)

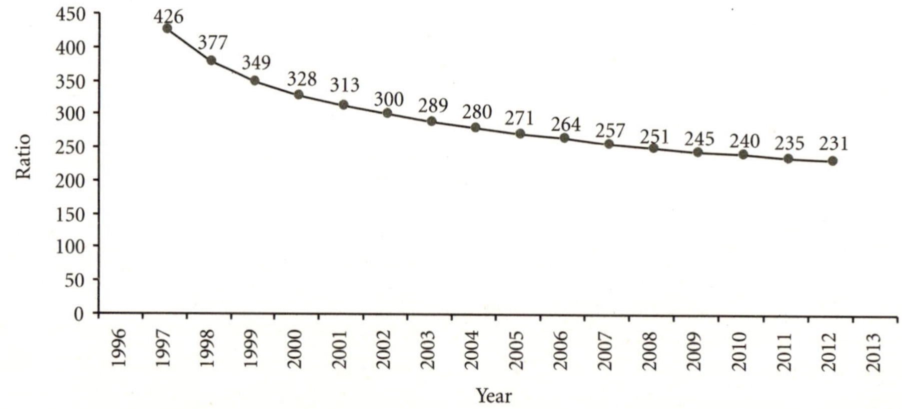

Source: RGI (2006).

FIGURE 3.1.2: MMR in India: Trends Based on Log-linear Model, 1997–2012

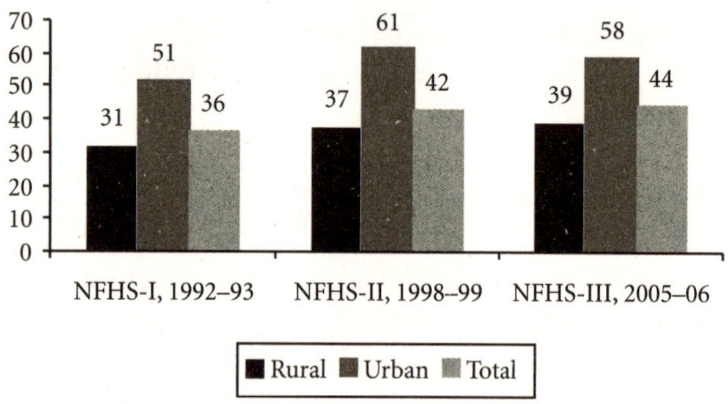

Source: NFHS-3, IIPS (2005–06).

FIGURE 3.1.3: Trends in Full Immunization Coverage

access to care as well as health outcomes. Kerala's life-expectancy at birth is about 10 years more than that of MP and Assam. IMRs in MP and Orissa are about five times that of Kerala. MMR in UP is more than four times that of Kerala and more than three times that of Haryana. Crude death rates among States also reveal wide variations. Crude death rates in Orissa and MP are about twice the crude death rates in Delhi and Nagaland. This high degree of variation of health indices is itself a reflection of the high variance in the availability of health services in different parts of the country.

Disparities and Divides

3.1.14 Within the country, there is persistence of extreme inequality and disparity both in terms of

3.1.15 Approximately a quarter of the districts account for 40% of the poor, over half of the malnourished, nearly two-thirds of malaria and kala-azar, leprosy,

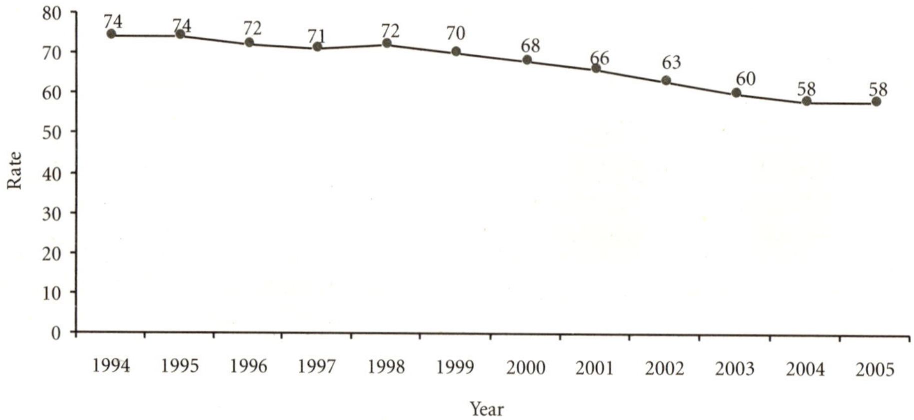

Source: SRS Bulletin, RGI (October 2006).

FIGURE 3.1.4: IMR in India

infant and maternal mortality, and diseases (National Commission on Macroeconomics and Health, NCMH, 2005). The challenge is to provide these areas with access to low-cost public health interventions such as universal immunization services and timely treatment. These States are also the ones that have acute crises of human and financial resources.

3.1.16 Public health care system in rural areas in many States and regions is in shambles. Extreme inequalities and disparities persist both in terms of access to health care as well as health outcomes (Table 3.1.3). This large disparity across India places the burden on the poor, especially women, scheduled castes, and tribes. Inequity is also reflected in the availability of public resources between the advanced and less developed States.

3.1.17 Urban growth has led to increase in number of urban poor. Population projections postulate that slum growth is expected to surpass the capacity of civic authorities to respond to their health and infrastructure needs. As per 2001 census, 4.26 crore lived in urban slums spread over 640 towns and cities. The number is growing. Though the coverage of health and family welfare services in urban areas is much better than the rural, lack of water and sanitation and the high population density in slums leads to rapid spread of infections. These settlements have high incidence of vector-borne diseases, asthma, tuberculosis, malaria, coronary heart diseases, diabetes, etc. Poor housing conditions, exposure to heat and cold, air and water pollution, and occupational hazards add to the environmental risks for the poor. They are vulnerable as they have no backup savings, food stocks, or social support systems to tide over the crisis of illness. Despite the presence of many private and government hospitals in urban areas, a large chunk of the homeless and those living in slums or temporary settlements are left out of the proper health care system. Thus, even though there is a concentration of health care facilities in urban areas, the urban poor lack access; initiatives in the country to date have been limited and fragmented.

Disease Burden

3.1.18 India is in the midst of an epidemiological and demographic transition with increasing burden of chronic diseases, decline in mortality and fertility rates, and ageing of the population. An estimated 2–3.1 million people in the country are living with HIV/AIDS, a communicable disease, with a potential to undermine the health and developmental gains India has made since Independence. Non-communicable diseases (NCDs) such as cardiovascular diseases (CVDs), cancer, blindness, mental illness, etc., have imposed the chronic disease burden on the already over-stretched health care system of the country. The NCMH 2005 figures of disease burden are given in Table 3.1.4.

COMMUNICABLE DISEASES

3.1.19 AIDS is acquiring a female face, that is, gradually the gap between females and males is narrowing as far as number of cases and infections are concerned. The youth are becoming increasingly vulnerable. The prevalence rate of more than 1% amongst pregnant women was reported from five States, that is, Andhra Pradesh, Maharashtra, Karnataka, Manipur, and Nagaland. GoI responded to HIV/AIDS threat by preventive awareness, targeted interventions, and care and support programmes. As on 31 December 2006, a total of 162257 cases of AIDS were reported. The risk of tuberculosis infection in HIV positive

TABLE 3.1.3
Urban/Rural Health Indicators

	Crude Birth Rate (per 1000)	Crude Death Rate (per 1000)	IMR (per 1000 live births)	Prevalence of Anaemia among Children (6–35 months) (%)	Prevalence of Anaemia among Pregnant Women (%)
Urban	19.1	6.0	40	72.7	54.6
Rural	25.6	8.1	64	81.2	59.0
Total	23.8	7.6	58	79.2	57.9

Source: Ministry of Health and Family Welfare (MoHFW), GoI (2006) and NHFS-3, IIPS (2005–06).

TABLE 3.1.4
Disease Burden Estimation, 2005

Disease/Health Condition	Estimate of Cases/lakh	Projected number (2015) of Cases/lakh
Communicable Diseases		
Tuberculosis	85 (2000)	NA
HIV/AIDS	51 (2004)	190
Diarrhoeal Diseases Episodes per Year	760	880
Malaria and other Vector Borne Diseases	20.37 (2004)	NA
Leprosy	3.67 (2004)	Expect to be Eliminated
Otitis Media	3.57	4.18
Non-Communicable Conditions		
Cancers	8.07 (2004)	9.99
Diabetes	310	460
Mental Health	650	800
Blindness	141.07	129.96
CVDs	290 (2000)	640
COPD and Asthma	405.20 (2001)	596.36
Other Non-Communicable		
Injuries—deaths	9.8	10.96
Number of Hospitalizations	170	220

Source: NCMH (2005).

persons increased manifold. National AIDS Control Organization (NACO) is working closely with Revised National Tuberculosis Control Programme (RNTCP) for promoting cross referrals for early diagnosis and prompt treatment. The strategies of National AIDS Control Programme Phase II (NACP-II) have yielded positive results. The HIV prevalence is stabilizing and States like Tamil Nadu, Andhra Pradesh, Karnataka, Maharashtra, and Nagaland have started showing declining trends. The State-wise distribution of number of AIDS cases in India during 2006 is shown in Figure 3.1.5. The lessons learnt have been utilized in formulating NACP-III, which will be implemented in the country during the Eleventh Five Year Plan.

3.1.20 Tuberculosis remains a public health problem, with India accounting for one-fifth of the world incidence. Every year 1.8 million people in India develop tuberculosis, of which 0.8 million are infectious smear positive cases. The emergence of HIV-TB co-infection and multi drug resistant tuberculosis has increased the severity and magnitude of the problem. RNTCP has achieved nation wide coverage in March 2006. Since the inception of the programme, over 6.3 million patients have been initiated on treatment, and the programme has achieved all the proposed goals in terms of expansion of Directly Observed Treatment, Short Course (DOTS) services, case finding, and treatment success during the Tenth Plan.

3.1.21 A National Vector Borne Disease Control Programme was initiated during the Tenth Plan with the convergence of ongoing programmes on malaria, kala-azar, filariasis, Japanese encephalitis, and dengue.

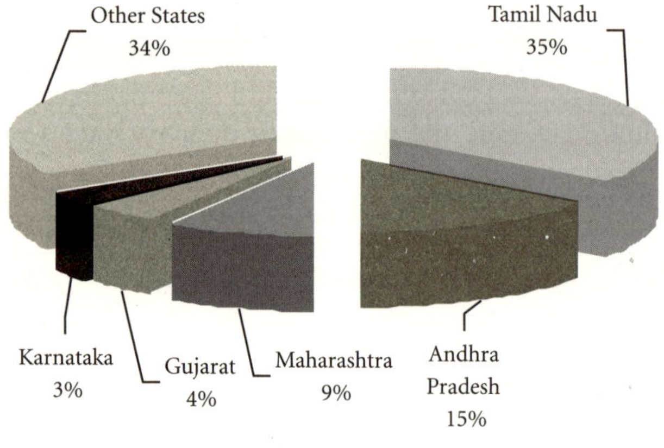

Source: National Health Profile (2006).

FIGURE 3.1.5: Number of AIDS Cases in States, 2006

Malaria cases in India declined from 3.04 in 1996 to 1.82 million cases in the year 2005. The number of *Plasmodium falciparum* (*Pf*) cases has also been decreasing (Figure 3.1.6). More than 80% of malaria cases and deaths are reported from NE States, Chhattisgarh, Jharkhand, MP, Orissa, Andhra Pradesh, Maharashtra, Gujarat, Rajasthan, WB, and Karnataka. Under the Enhanced Malaria Control Project, 100% support was provided in 100 districts of 8 States, predominantly inhabited by tribal population. These areas reported a 45% decline in malaria cases.

3.1.22 An estimated population of 130 million is exposed to the risk of kala-azar in the endemic areas. The annual incidence of disease has come down from 77099 cases in 1992 to 31217 cases in 2005 and deaths from 1419 to 157, respectively. Lymphatic Filariasis (LF) remains endemic in about 250 districts in 20 States and UTs. The population at risk is over 500 million. To achieve elimination of LF, the GoI has launched nationwide Annual Mass Drug Administration (MDA) with annual single recommended dose of diethylcarbamazine citrate tablets in addition to scaling up home based foot care and hydrocele operations. In 2005, 243 endemic districts implemented MDA targeting a population of about 554 million with a coverage rate of 80%. Dengue fever and Chikungunya are emerging as major threats in urban, peri-urban, and rural areas in many States/UTs.

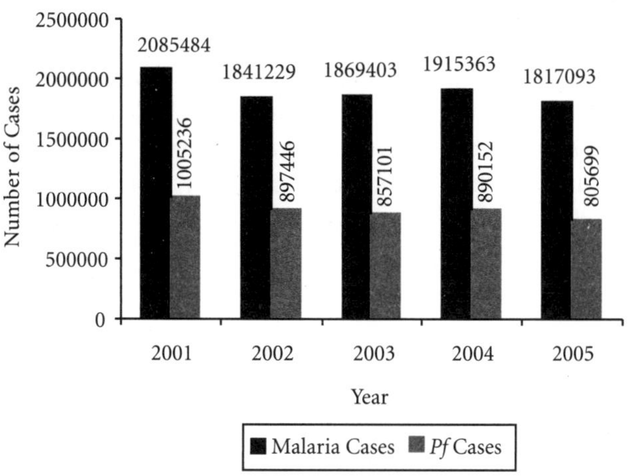

Source: MoHFW, GoI (2006).

FIGURE 3.1.6: Malaria Cases and *Pf* Cases, India

3.1.23 The goal of leprosy elimination at national level (<1 case/10000 population) as set by National Health Policy (2002) was achieved in the month of December 2005. Even though the disease came down to a level of elimination, still it is prevalent with moderate endemicity in about 20% of the districts. During 2005–06, a total of 1.61 lakh new leprosy cases were detected.

NON-COMMUNICABLE DISEASES (NCDs)

3.1.24 India is experiencing a rapid epidemiological transition, with a large and rising burden of chronic diseases, which were estimated to account for 53% of all deaths and 44% of Disability Adjusted Life Years lost in 2005. NCDs, especially diabetes mellitus, CVDs, cancer, stroke, and chronic lung diseases have emerged as major public health problems due to an ageing population and environmentally-driven changes in behaviour.

3.1.25 Cancer has become an important public health problem in India with an estimated 7 to 9 lakh cases occurring every year. At any point of time, it is estimated that there are nearly 25 lakh cases in the country. The strategy under the National Cancer Control Programme (NCCP) was revised in 1984–85 and further in 2004 with stress on primary prevention and early detection of cancer cases. In India, tobacco related cancers account for about half the total cancers among men and 20% among women. About one million tobacco related deaths occur each year, making tobacco related health issues a major public health concern.

3.1.26 In India, more than 12 million people are blind. Cataract (62.6%) is the main cause of blindness followed by Refractive Error (19.70%). There has been a significant increase in proportion of cataract surgeries with Intra Ocular Lens (IOL) implantation from <5 % in 1994 to 90% in 2005–06 (Figure 3.1.7).

3.1.27 Oral Health Care has not been given sufficient importance in our country. Most of the district hospitals have a post of dental surgeon but they lack equipment, machinery, and material. Even where the equipment exists, the maintenance is poor, hence service delivery is affected.

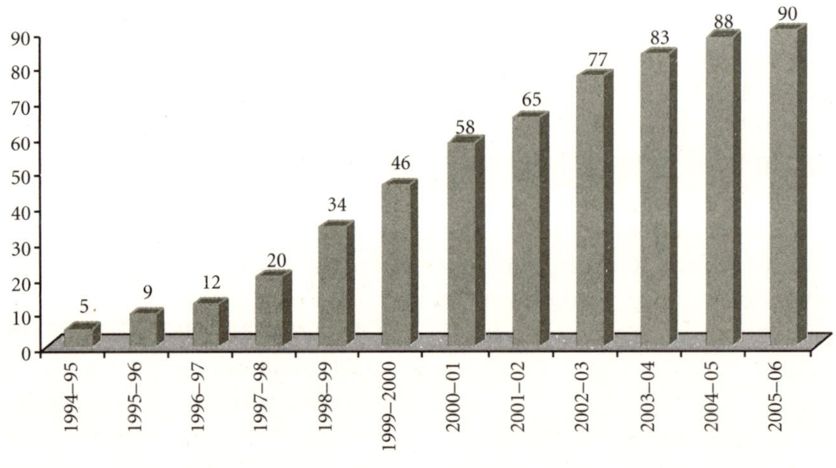

Source: Annual Report, MoHFW (2006–07).

FIGURE 3.1.7: Percentage of Cataract Surgeries with IOL

Health Care Infrastructure and Human Resources: The Gaps

3.1.28 To address the gaps in health infrastructure and human resources, the National Rural Health Mission (NRHM) was launched on 12 April 2005. A generic public health delivery system envisioned under NRHM from the village to block level is illustrated in Figure 3.1.8.

3.1.29 The details of existing and required physical infrastructure have been provided in Table 3.1.5. Maximum shortage at the Community Health Centres (CHCs) level is adversely affecting the secondary health care and linkages.

3.1.30 Availability of appropriate and adequately trained human resources is an essential concomitant of Rural Health Infrastructure. The present position, requirement, and shortfall regarding public health care human resources have been shown in Table 3.1.6. Across rural areas, there are considerable shortfalls plus a large number of vacant positions of doctors, nurses, and paramedical personnel. There is also wide variation in number of persons served by a specialist in rural areas (Figure 3.1.9). Despite the existing shortages, whatever few formally trained and qualified doctors are available, are mainly through the public health care system. A large proportion of population visits private providers for their health care needs. The challenge is to resolve these problems and provide the poor access to subsidized or free public health services.

3.1.31 During the last few years there has been a great change in the availability of secondary and tertiary health care facilities in the country. Number of government hospitals increased from 4571 in 2000 to 7663 in 2006, that is, an increase of 67.6%. Number of beds in these hospitals increased from 430539 to 492698, that is, an increase of 14.4%. Current figures are not available on number of private and NGO hospitals as well as on human resources in the

TABLE 3.1.5
Shortfall in Health Infrastructure—All India

As per 2001 Population	Required	Existing	Shortfall	% Shortfall
Sub-Centres	158792	144998	20903	13.16
PHCs	26022	22669	4803	18.46
CHCs	6491	3910	2653	40.87

Notes: All India shortfall is derived by adding State-wise figures of shortfall ignoring the existing surplus in some of the States.

Source: Bulletin of Rural Health Statistics in India, Special Revised Edition, MOHFW, GoI (2006).

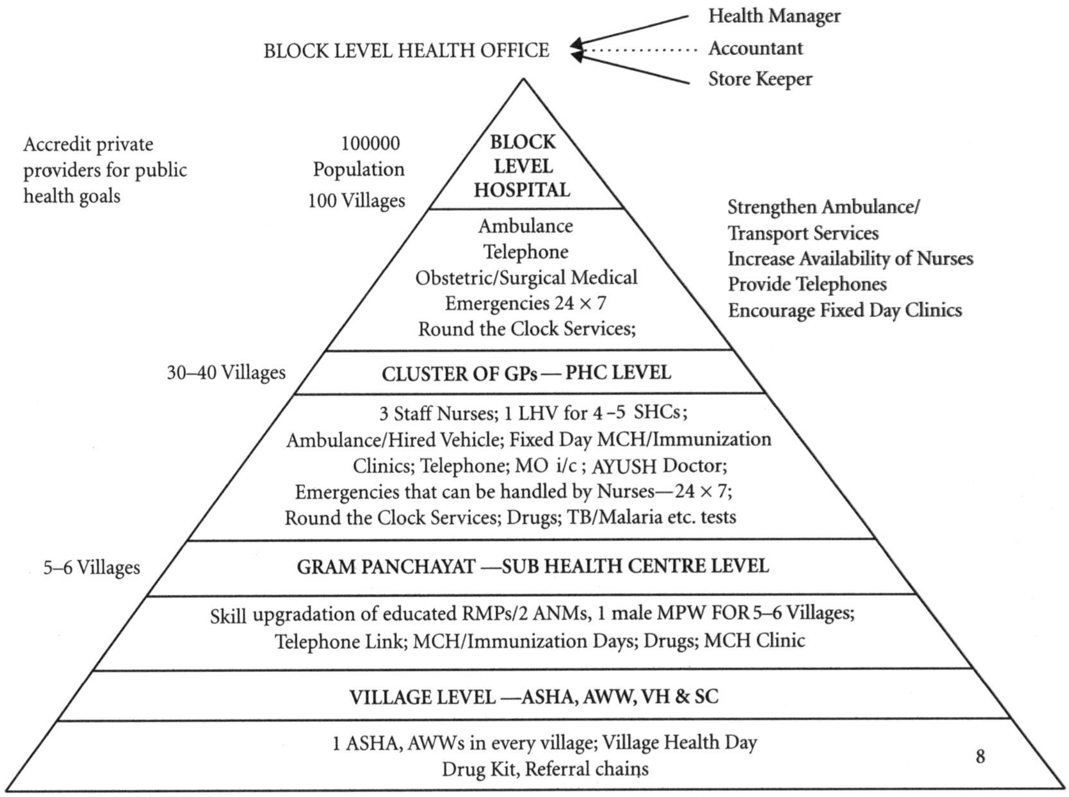

Notes: TB = Tuberculosis, MO = Medical Officer, MCH = Maternal and Child Health.

FIGURE 3.1.8: NRHM–Illustrative Structure

private sector but in 2002, the country had 11345 private/NGO hospitals (allopathic) with a capacity of 262256 beds. These are mostly in the private sector located in cities and towns.

Drawbacks of the Public Health System

3.1.32 The public health system in our country has various drawbacks (see Box 3.1.1). The conceptualization and planning of all programmes is centralized instead of decentralized using locally relevant strategies. The approach towards disease control and prevention is fragmented and disease-specific rather than comprehensive. This leads to vertical programmes for each and every disease. These vertical programmes are technology-centric and work in isolation of each other (Box 3.1.2). The provision of infrastructure is based on population norms rather than habitations leading to issues of accessibility, acceptability, and utilization. Inadequate resources also lead to lack of client conveniences and non-availability of essential consumables and non-consumables. The gap between requirement and availability of human resources at various levels of health care is wide and where they are available, the patient–provider interactions are beset with many problems, in addition to waiting time (opportunity cost) for consultation/treatment. The system lacks a real and working process of monitoring, evaluation, and feedback. There is no incentive for those who work well and check on those who do not. Quality assurance at all levels is not adhered to due to lacunae in implementation. This results in semi-used or dysfunctional health infrastructure. There is lack of convergence with other key areas affecting health as the system has been unable to mobilize action in areas of safe water, sanitation, hygiene, and nutrition. Despite constraints of human resources, practitioners of Indian Systems of Medicine (ISM), Registered Medical Practitioners (RMPs), and other locally available human resources have not been adequately mobilized and integrated in the system.

TABLE 3.1.6
Shortfall in Health Personnel—All India

For the Existing Infrastructure	Required (R)	Sanctioned (S)	In Position (P)	Vacant (S-P)	Shortfal (R-P)
Multipurpose Workers (Female)/ANM at Sub-Centres and PHCs	167657	162772	149695	13126 (8.06%)	18318 (10.93%)
Health Workers (Male)/MPWs (M) at Sub-Centres	144998	94924	65511	29437 (31.01%)	74721 (51.53%)
Health Assistants (Female)/LHV at PHCs	22669	19874	17107	2781 (13.99%)	5941 (26.21%)
Health Assistants (Male) at PHCs	22669	24207	18223	5984 (24.72%)	7169 (31.62%)
Doctors at PHCs	22669	27927	22273	5801 (20.77%)	1793 (7.91%)
Total Specialists at CHCs	15640	9071	3979	4681 (51.60%)	9413 (60.19%)
Radiographers at CHCs	3910	2400	1782	620 (25.83%)	1330 (34.02%)
Pharmacists at PHCs and CHCs	26579	22816	18419	4445 (19.48%)	4389 (16.51%)
Lab Technician at PHCs and CHCs	26579	15143	12351	2792 (18.44%)	9509 (35.78%)

Note: For calculating the overall percentages of vacancy and shortfall, the States/UTs for which the human resources position is not available, have been excluded. Also, all India shortfall is derived by adding State-wise figures of shortfall ignoring the existing surplus in some of the States.

Source: Bulletin of Rural Health Statistics in India, Special Revised Edition, MOHFW, GoI (2006).

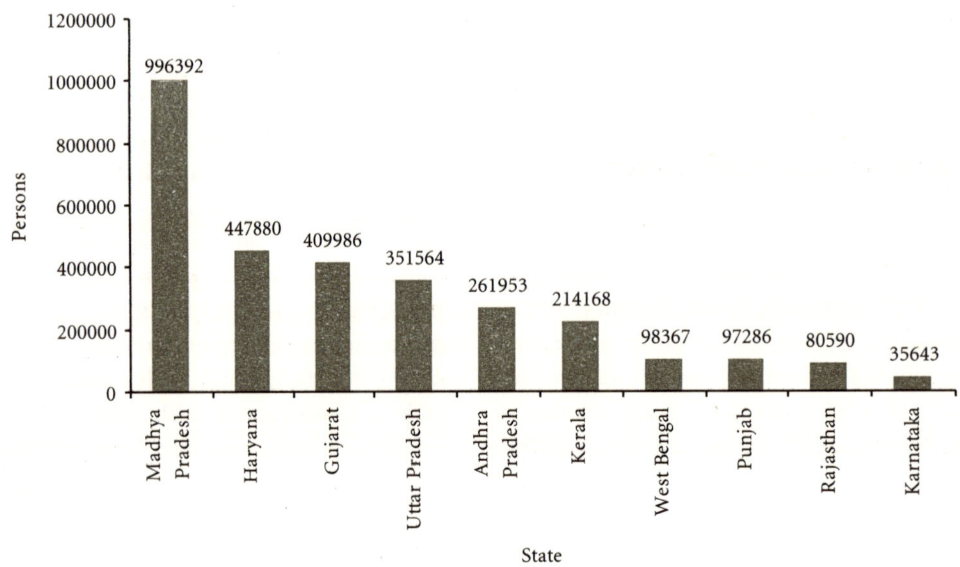

Source: Bulletin of Rural Health Statistics in India, Special Revised Edition, MOHFW, GoI (2006).

FIGURE 3.1.9: Number of Persons per Specialist at CHCs, 2006

Box 3.1.1
Drawbacks of the Public Health System

- Centralized planning instead of decentralized planning and using locally relevant strategies
- Institutions based on population norms rather than habitations
- Fragmented disease specific approach rather than comprehensive health care
- Inflexible financing and limited scope for innovations
- Semi-used or dysfunctional health infrastructure
- Inadequate provision of human resources
- No prescribed standards of quality
- Inability of system to mobilize action in areas of safe water, sanitation, hygiene, and nutrition (key determinants of health in the context of our country)—lack of convergence
- Inability to mobilize AYUSH and RMPs and other locally available human resources

Box 3.1.2
Vertical Programmes

Technology-centric
- See the disease as being caused by an agent (parasite/virus/bacteria) and fail to see its social and ecological setting.
- Response is heavily dependant on technology.

Fragmented
- Only one or two of all the factors that go into the disease setting (and that too in isolation) are addressed.

Administration
- The entire planning and packaging is done centrally.
- Only local aspect is the application (under a chain of command).
- Limited role for community participation.

The Result
- An inappropriate package for local needs.
- Local people are indifferent—sometimes even resistant.
- Even the administration cannot in perpetuity keep its attention on the programme alone.

Growth of Private Sector, Health Care Utilization, and Cost

3.1.33 The growth of private health sector in India has been considerable in both provision and financing. There is diversity in the composition of the private sector, which ranges from voluntary, not-for-profit, for-profit, corporate, trusts, stand-alone specialist services, diagnostic services to pharmacy shops and a range of highly qualified to unqualified providers, each addressing different market segments.

3.1.34 We have a flourishing private sector, primarily because of a failing in the public sector. The growth of private hospitals and diagnostic centres was also encouraged by the Central and State Governments by offering tax exemptions and land at concessional rates, in return for provision of free treatment for the poor as a certain proportion of outpatients and inpatients. Apart from subsidies, private corporate hospitals receive huge amounts of public funds in the form of reimbursements from the public sector undertakings, the Central and the State Governments for treating their employees.

3.1.35 The cost of health care in the private sector is much higher than the public sector. Many small providers have poor knowledge base and tend to follow irrational, ineffective, and sometimes even harmful practices for treating minor ailments. Bulk of the qualified medical practitioners and nurses are subject to self-regulation by their respective State Medical Councils under central legislation. In practice, however, regulation of these professionals is weak and close to non-existent.

3.1.36 Public spending on health in India is amongst the lowest in the world (about 1% of GDP), whereas its proportion of private spending on health is one of the highest. Households in India spend about 5–6% of their consumption expenditure on health (NSSO). The cost of services in the private sector makes it unaffordable for the poor and the underprivileged.

HEALTH CARE UTILIZATION

3.1.37 Despite a steady increase in public health care infrastructure, utilization of public health facilities by population for outpatient and inpatient care has not improved. The NSSO (1986–2004) data clearly show a major decline in utilization of the public health facilities for inpatient care and a corresponding increase in utilization of the same from private health care providers in both rural and urban areas (Figures 3.1.10 and 3.1.11). With the exception of a few States, there has been very low utilization for outpatient care as well (Figure 3.1.12). Despite higher costs in the private sector, this shift shows the people's growing lack of trust in the public system. Critical shortage of health personnel, inadequate incentives, poor working conditions, lack of transparency in posting of doctors in rural areas, absenteeism, long wait, inconvenient clinic hours, poor outreach, time of service, insensitivity to local needs, inadequate planning, management, and monitoring of service/facilities appear to be the main reasons for low utilization.

COST OF TREATMENT BY HOUSEHOLDS

3.1.38 According to NSSO (60th Round), the average expenditure for hospitalized treatment from a public hospital was less than half that of private hospital in rural areas and about one-third in urban areas (Figure 3.1.12). There are also inter-State variations. The cost per hospitalization in government hospital was lowest in Tamil Nadu (Rs 637 in rural areas and Rs 1666 in the urban areas) and highest in rural Haryana (Rs 11665) and urban Bihar (Rs 30822). The cost of hospitalization in private hospitals was highest in Himachal Pradesh (Rs 14652 in rural areas and Rs 23447 in urban areas) and lowest in rural Kerala (Rs 4565) and urban Chhattisgarh (Rs 4359), respectively.

3.1.39 As per NSSO 60th Round, during 2004, 24% of the episodes of ailments among the poor were untreated in rural areas and 22% in urban areas. Lack of finances was cited as a reason by 28% of persons with untreated episodes in rural areas and 20% in urban areas. It is also notable that 12% cited lack of medical facility as the cause of not receiving treatment in rural areas.

Review of Tenth Plan Schemes

3.1.40 The Tenth Five Year Plan (2002–2007) indicated the dismal picture of the health services infrastructure and emphasized the need to invest more on building good primary-level care and referral services. The plan emphasized on restructuring and developing the health infrastructure, especially at the primary level. The plan highlighted the importance of the role of decentralization but did not state how this would be achieved. Programme-driven health care was in focus. Verticality and technical solutions were

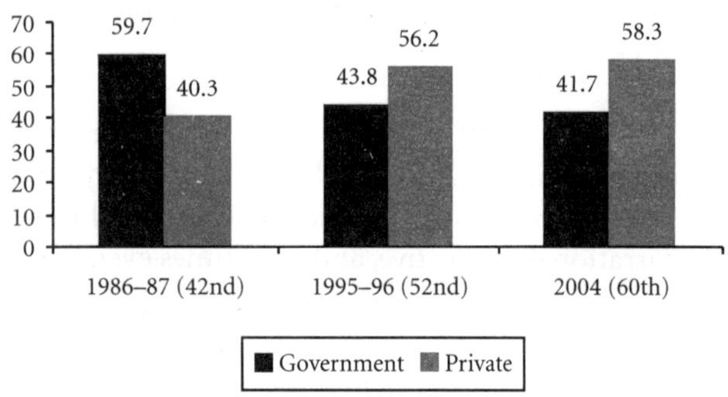

Source: NSSO 60th Round (2004).

FIGURE 3.1.10: Percentage of Cases of Hospitalized Treatment by Type of Hospital in Rural Areas

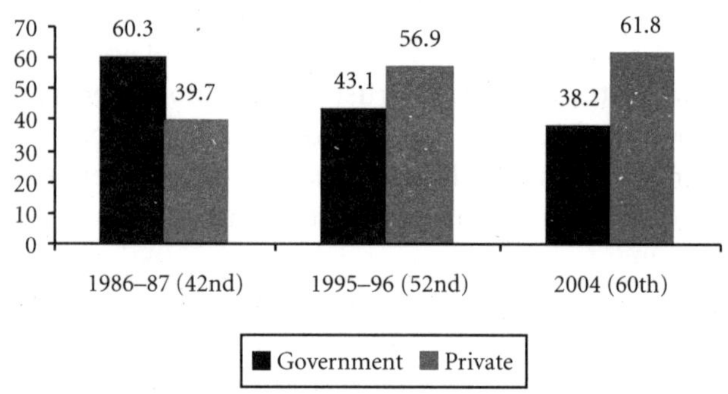

Source: NSSO 60th Round (2004).

FIGURE 3.1.11: Percentage of Cases of Hospitalized Treatment by Type of Hospital in Urban Areas

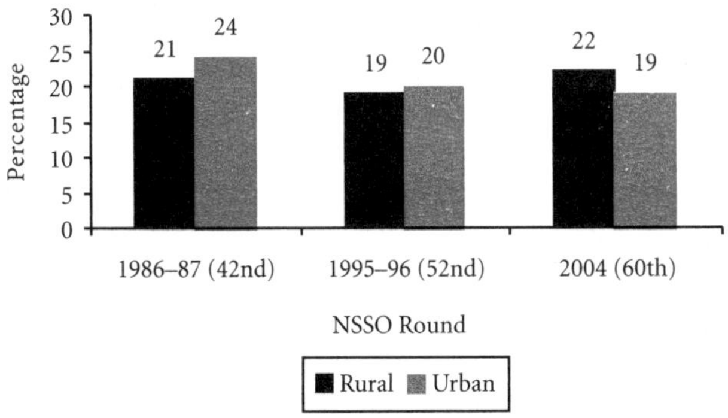

Source: NSSO 60th Round (2004).

FIGURE 3.1.12: Percentage of Treated Ailments Receiving Non-hospitalized Treatment from Government Sources

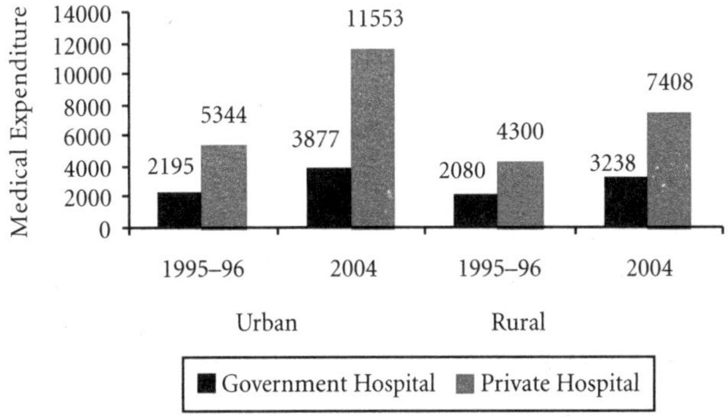

Source: NSSO 60th Round (2004).

FIGURE 3.1.13: Average Medical Expenditure (Rs) per Hospitalization Case

given more importance than comprehensive primary health care. The review of the plan not only throws light on the gap between the rhetoric and reality but also the framework within which the policies were formulated.

3.1.41 It was important to question whether it is only the low investment in health that is the main reason for the present status of the health system or is it also to do with the framework, design, and approach within which the policies were formulated. Keeping this in view the NRHM was launched.

3.1.42 The original approved health and family welfare outlay for the Tenth Plan CSS and CS was Rs 36378 crore. However, the sum of annual outlay increased to Rs 41585 crore. Against this, the actual expenditure has been Rs 34950.45 crore, that is, 84.05% of the sum of annual outlay. In 2005–06, all family welfare schemes and major disease control programmes were put under the umbrella of the NRHM. Scheme-wise details of Tenth Plan outlay and expenditure are provided in Annexures 3.1.1 and 3.1.2. State Plan outlay and expenditure during Tenth Plan have been provided in Annexure 3.1.3.

3.1.43 Review of the NRHM at the end of the Tenth Plan reveals that in order to improve the public health delivery, the situation needs to change on a fast track mode at the grassroots. The status as on 1 April 2007 is as under:

- 17318 Village Health and Sanitation Committees (VHSCs) have been constituted against the target of 1.80 lakh by 2007.
- No untied grants have been released to VHSCs pending opening of bank accounts by the Committees.
- Against the target of 3 lakh fully trained Accredited Social Health Activists (ASHAs) by 2007, the initial phase of training (first module) has been imparted to 2.55 lakh. ASHAs in position with drug kits are 5030 in number.
- Out of the 52500 Sub-centres (SCs) expected to be functional with 2 Auxiliary Nurse Midwives (ANMs) by 2007, only 7877 had the same.
- 9000 Primary Health Centres (PHCs) are expected to be functional with three staff nurses by 2007. This has been achieved at 2297 PHCs.
- There has been a shortfall of 9413 (60.19%) specialists at the CHCs. As against the 1950 CHCs expected to be functional with 7 specialists and 9 staff nurses by 2007, none have reached that level.
- CHCs have not been released untied or annual maintenance grant envisaged under the NRHM as they have not reached upto the expected level.
- Number of districts where annual integrated action plan under NRHM have been prepared for 2006–07 are 211.

Towards Finding Solutions

3.1.44 The Eleventh Five Year Plan will aim for inclusive growth by introducing National Urban Health

Mission (NUHM), which along with NRHM, will form *Sarva Swasthya Abhiyan.*

National Rural Health Mission (NRHM)

3.1.45 NRHM was launched to address infirmities and problems across primary health care and bring about improvement in the health system and the health status of those who live in the rural areas. The Mission aims to provide universal access to equitable, affordable, and quality health care that is accountable and at the same time responsive to the needs of the people. The Mission is expected to achieve the goals set under the National Health Policy and the Millennium Development Goals (MDGs).

3.1.46 To achieve these goals, NRHM facilitates increased access and utilization of quality health services by all, forges a partnership between the Central, State, and the local governments, sets up a platform for involving the PRIs and the community in the management of primary health programmes and infrastructure, and provides an opportunity for promoting equity and social justice. The NRHM establishes a mechanism to provide flexibility to the States and the community to promote local initiatives and develop a framework for promoting intersectoral convergence for promotive and preventive health care. The Mission has also defined core and supplementary strategies.

3.1.47 STRATEGIES OF NRHM

Core Strategies

- Train and enhance capacity of PRIs to supervise and manage public health services.
- Promote access to improved health care at household level through the female health activist (ASHA).
- Health Plan for each village through Village Health Committee of the Panchayat.
- Strengthen SC through an untied fund to enable local planning and action and more Multipurpose Workers (MPWs).
- Strengthen existing PHCs and CHCs and provide 30–50 bedded CHC per lakh population for improved curative care to a normative standard (Indian Public Health Service Standards [IPHS] defining personnel, equipment, and management standards).
- Prepare and implement an intersectoral District Health Plan prepared by the District Health Mission, including drinking water, sanitation, hygiene, and nutrition.
- Integrate vertical health and family welfare programmes at national, State, and district levels.
- Technical Support to National, State, and District Health Missions for Public Health Management.
- Strengthen capacities for data collection, assessment, and review for evidence-based planning, monitoring, and supervision.
- Formulate transparent policies for deployment and career development of Human Resources for health.
- Develop capacities for preventive health care at all levels for promoting healthy life styles, reduction in consumption of tobacco and alcohol, etc.
- Promote non-profit sector particularly in underserved areas.

Supplementary Strategies

- Regulation of private sector including the informal rural practitioners to ensure availability of quality service to citizens at reasonable cost.

Box 3.1.3
Sarva Swasthya Abhiyan

- NRHM has been launched for meeting health needs of all age groups and to reduce disease burden across rural India.
- NUHM will be launched to mmet the unmet needs of the urban population (28.6 crore in 2001 and 35.7 crore in 2011). As per the 2001 Census, 4.26 crore lived in urban slums spread over 640 towns and cities. The number is growing.
- NUHM based on health insurance and PPP will provide integrated health service delivery to the urban poor. Initially, the focus will be on urban slums. NUHM will be aligned with NRHM and existing urban schemes.
- Besides, Sarva Swasthya Abhiyan aims for inclusive growth by finding solutions for strengthening health services and focusing on neglected areas and groups.

Box 3.1.4
Five Planks of the NRHM

The Mission is expected to address the gaps in the provision of effective health care to rural population with a special focus on 18 States, which have weak public health indicators and/or weak infrastructure.

The Mission is a shift away from the vertical health and family welfare programmes to a new architecture of all inclusive health development in which societies under different programmes will be merged and resources pooled at the district level.

The Mission aims at the effective integration of health concerns with determinants of health like safe drinking water, sanitation, and nutrition through integrated District Plans for Health. There is a provision for flexible funds so that the States can utilize them in the areas they feel are important.

The Mission provides for appointment of ASHA in each village and strengthening of the public health infrastructure, including outreach through mobile clinics. It emphasizes involvement of the non-profit sector, especially in the under-served areas. It also aims at flexibility at the local level by providing for untied funds.

The Mission, in its supplementary strategies, aims at fostering PPPs; improving equity and reducing out of pocket expenses; introducing effective risk-pooling mechanisms and social health insurance; and taking advantage of local health traditions.

- Promotion of PPPs for achieving public health goals.
- Reorienting medical education to support health issues including regulation of Medical Care and Medical Ethics.
- Effective and viable risk-pooling and social health insurance to provide health security to the poor by ensuring accessible, affordable, accountable, and good quality health care.

3.1.48 The expected outcomes of NRHM are listed below:

- IMR—reduced to 30/1000 live births by 2012.
- Maternal Mortality—reduced to 100/100000 live births by 2012.
- TFR—reduced to 2.1 by 2012.
- Malaria Mortality Reduction—50% up to 2010, additional 10% by 2012.
- Kala-azar Mortality Reduction—100% by 2010 and sustaining elimination until 2012.
- Filaria/Microfilaria Reduction—70% by 2010, 80% by 2012, and elimination by 2015.
- Dengue Mortality Reduction—50% by 2010 and sustaining at that level until 2012.
- Cataract operations—increasing to 46 lakh until 2012.
- Leprosy Prevalence Rate—reduce from 1.8 per 10000 in 2005 to less that 1 per 10000 thereafter.
- Tuberculosis DOTS—maintain 85% cure rate through entire Mission Period and also sustain planned case detection rate.
- Upgrading all health establishments in the district to IPHS.
- Increase utilization of First Referral Units (FRUs) from bed occupancy by referred cases of less than 20% to over 75%.

3.1.49 Under the NRHM, it is planned to have:

- Over 5 lakh ASHAs, one for every 1000 population/large habitation, in 18 Special Focus States and in tribal pockets of all States by 2008
- All SCs (nearly 1.75 lakh) functional with two ANMs by 2010
- All PHCs (nearly 30000) with three staff nurses to provide 24 × 7 services by 2010
- 6500 CHCs strengthened/established with seven specialists and nine staff nurses by 2012
- 1800 Taluka/Sub Divisional Hospitals and 600 District Hospitals strengthened to provide quality health services by 2012
- Mobile Medical Units for each District by 2009
- Functional Hospital Development Committees in all CHCs, Sub Divisional Hospitals, and District Hospitals by 2009
- Untied grants and annual maintenance grants to every SC, PHC, and CHC released regularly and utilized for local health action by 2008

- All District Health Action Plans completed by 2008

3.1.50 In the Eleventh Five Year Plan, the emphasis under NRHM will not be on numerical achievements only but also on IPHS and enforcement of guidelines for improving the functioning of infrastructure being strengthened and created. It has been felt that the Mission Directors, both at the Centre and the States, should be officials with public health background, supported by the Civil Service cadres.

JANANI SURAKSHA YOJANA (JSY)

3.1.51 To change the behaviour of the community towards institutional delivery, the GoI, under NRHM in 2005, modified the National Maternity Benefit Scheme (NMBS) from that of a nutrition-improving initiative to the JSY. The scheme has the dual objectives of reducing maternal and infant mortality by promoting institutional deliveries. Though the JSY is implemented in all States and UTs, its focus is on States having low institutional delivery rate. The scheme is 100% centrally sponsored and integrates cash assistance with maternal care. It is funded through the flexi-pool mechanism. Under the NRHM, out of 184.25 lakh institutional deliveries in the country (as on 1 April 2007), JSY beneficiaries were 28.74 lakh.

3.1.52 While the JSY scheme is meant to promote institutional delivery, it has to take two critical factors into account, one being that India does not have the institutional capacity (International Institute of Population Sciences [IIPS], 2003) to receive the 26 million women giving birth each year, and the other being that around half of all maternal deaths occur outside of delivery, during pregnancy, abortions, and postpartum complications. If institutions are preoccupied with handling the huge numbers of normal childbirths, there will be inevitable neglect of life-threatening complications faced by women. They will be compelled to vacate beds in the shortest time. Consequently, complications during pregnancy and after childbirth will not be given attention. Second, JSY money sometimes does not reach hospitals on time, and as a result, poor women and their families do not receive the promised money.

National Urban Health Mission (NUHM)

3.1.53 The NUHM will meet health needs of the urban poor, particularly the slum dwellers by making available to them essential primary health care services. This will be done by investing in high-caliber health professionals, appropriate technology through PPP, and health insurance for urban poor.

3.1.54 Recognizing the seriousness of the problem, urban health will be taken up as a thrust area for the Eleventh Five Year Plan. NUHM will be launched with focus on slums and other urban poor. At the State level, besides the State Health Mission and State Health Society and Directorate, there would be a State Urban Health Programme Committee. At the district level, similarly there would be a District Urban Health Committee and at the city level, a Health and Sanitation Planning Committee. At the ward slum level, there will be a Slum Cluster Health and Water and Sanitation Committee. For promoting public health and cleanliness in urban slums, the Eleventh Five Year Plan will also encompass experiences of civil society organizations (CSO) working in urban slum clusters. It will seek to build a bridge of NGO–GO partnership and develop community level monitoring of resources and their rightful use. NUHM would ensure the following:

- Resources for addressing the health problems in urban areas, especially among urban poor.
- Need based city specific urban health care system to meet the diverse health needs of the urban poor and other vulnerable sections.
- Partnership with community for a more proactive involvement in planning, implementation, and monitoring of health activities.
- Institutional mechanism and management systems to meet the health-related challenges of a rapidly growing urban population.
- Framework for partnerships with NGOs, charitable hospitals, and other stakeholders.
- Two-tier system of risk pooling: (i) women's *Mahila Arogya Samiti* to fulfil urgent hard-cash needs for treatments; (ii) a Health Insurance Scheme for enabling urban poor to meet medical treatment needs.

3.1.55 NUHM would cover all cities with a population of more than 100000. It would cover slum dwellers; other marginalized urban dwellers like rickshaw pullers, street vendors, railway and bus station coolies, homeless people, street children, construction site workers, who may be in slums or on sites.

3.1.56 The existing Urban Health Posts and Urban Family Welfare Centres would continue under NUHM. They will be marked on a map and classified as the Urban Health Centres on the basis of their current population coverage. All the existing human resources will then be suitably reorganized and rationalized. These centres will also be considered for upgradation.

3.1.57 Intersectoral coordination mechanism and convergence will be planned between the Jawaharlal Nehru National Urban Renewal Mission (JNNURM) and the NUHM.

Strengthening Existing Health System

3.1.58 There is need to shift to decentralization of functions to hospital units/health centres and local bodies. The States need to move away from the narrow focus on the implementation of budgeted programmes and vertical schemes. They need to develop systems that comprehensively address the health needs of all citizens. Thus, in order to improve the health care services in the country, the Eleventh Five Year Plan will insist on Integrated District Health Plans and Block Specific Health Plans. It will mandate involvement of all health related sectors and emphasize partnership with PRIs, local bodies, communities, NGOs, Voluntary and Civil Society Organizations.

PRIMARY HEALTH CARE

3.1.59 During the Eleventh Five Year Plan, major focus will be on NRHM initiatives. Efforts will be made for restructuring and reorganizing all health facilities below district level into the Three Tier Rural Primary Health Care System. These will serve the populations in a well-defined area and have referral linkages with each other. Population-centric norms, which continue to drive the provisioning of health infrastructure, will be modified. These will be replaced with flexible norms comprising habitation-based needs, community-based needs, and disease pattern-based needs. Steps will also be taken to reorganize Urban Primary Health Care Institutions and make them responsible for the health care of people living in a defined geographic area, particularly slum dwellers.

3.1.60 The Approach Paper on Eleventh Five Year Plan stated accessibility as a major issue, especially in rural areas, where habitations are scattered and women and children continue to die en route to hospital. Policy interventions, therefore, have to be evidence based and responsive to area specific differences as shown in Assam (Box 3.1.5). Concerted action will be taken such as enabling pregnant women to have skilled attendance at birth and receive nutritional supplements. PHCs and CHCs will be connected by all weather roads so that they can be reached quickly in emergencies (accessibility to hospital would be measured in travel time, not just distance from nearest PHC). Home-based neonatal care will be provided, including emergency life saving measures. Achievement of health objectives will, therefore, involve much more than curative or even preventive health care, an integrated approach will be adopted.

3.1.61 The Eleventh Five Year Plan will ensure availability of essential drugs and supplies, vaccines, medical equipment, along with the basic infrastructure like electricity, water supply, toilets, telecommunications, and computers for maintaining records. All States will be encouraged to implement the Tamil Nadu model in which close to 58% of the health centres are functioning round the clock. Success models of various States such as higher salary to health workers posted in tribal regions of Himachal Pradesh and KBK districts of Orissa can be considered and replicated.

3.1.62 Tribal population in India is considered to be the most socio-economically disadvantaged group. The National Population Policy (2000) has made special mention of tribal areas in terms of improving basic health and Reproductive and Child Health (RCH) services. In order to ensure adequate access to health care services for the tribal population, apart from dispensaries and mobile health clinics, 20284 SCs, 3230 PHCs, and 750 CHCs have been established.

Box 3.1.5
***Akha*—Ship of Hope**

On the *saporis* or river islands of Assam that are inundated with floods every time the mighty Brahmaputra unleashes its fury, life is a constant struggle against disease and deprivation. Some 30 lakh people live in 2300 remote, floating villages on the Brahmaputra in Upper Assam. Here, there are no functional *anganwadis*, no health centres, no schools, no power, not even drinking water. Till recently, immunization, Antenatal Care (ANC), disease management, and treatment were all unheard of. Then in 2005 the Centre for North East Studies and Policy Research intervened. They partnered with NRHM, UNICEF, and the government of Assam, to start Akha (meaning hope in Assamese)—a 22-metre long, four-metre wide ship that carries hope and health care to 10000 forgotten people in Tinsukhia, Dhemaji, and Dibrugarh districts of Upper Assam. The 120 hp powered Akha has an Out Patient Department (OPD) room, cabins for medical staff and ship crew, medicine storage space, a kitchen, two toilet cum bathrooms, and a general store. A generator set and 200 litre water reservoir are also installed to ensure that the medical team that travels to the saporis has adequate power and water supply.

The idea behind Akha is simple—use the river to tackle the problems and challenges created by it. Doctors and ANMs who are unwilling and unable to survive on these remote islands, live on this ship stocked with medicine and other supplies and hold health camps on the saporis. They immunize, treat, provide medicines, and advise people on preventive measures. They even take critically ill patients to the nearest health centre in Dibrugarh.

In less than two years, Akha has provided succour to many. If we can upscale this innovative intervention under NRHM, health care will no longer be a distant reality for the people living on this highly volatile river. It can be upscaled to include a hospital ship with diagnostic facilities, in patient ward and operation theatre. Then health care would become truly inclusive.

Most of the centrally sponsored disease control programmes have a focus on the tribal areas. In spite of all this, tribal communities have poor access to health services and there is also underutilization of health services owing to social, cultural, and economic factors. Some of the problems include difficult terrain, locational disadvantage of health facilities, unsuitable timings of health facilities, lack of Information, Education, and Communication (IEC) activities, lack of transport, etc.

3.1.63 Challenges such as demand side constraints, human resource development issues, and the providers' attitude are particularly acute in tribal areas. During the Eleventh Five Year Plan, therefore, renewed efforts will be made to provide need-based quality integrated health and family welfare services, improvement of service coverage, promotion of community participation, encouragement of tribal system of medicine under AYUSH and replication of successful efforts (See Box 3.1.6).

3.1.64 The challenge of increasing urbanization with growth of slums and low-income families in cities has made access to health care for the urban poor a priority of the Eleventh Five Year Plan. Therefore, the thrust during the Eleventh Five Year Plan will be to locate the services in or around urban slums, Minorities, and SC *bastis* and SC concentration areas having 20% or more SC/ST population. With a view to improving health status of people in urban slums, the Eleventh Five Year Plan will provide support to the Comprehensive Project Implementation Plan (PIP) for vulnerable groups, which covers population in urban slums and other vulnerable groups in cities and towns with a population up to one lakh. The Plan will develop mechanism to address this particular issue. This will be in addition to the NUHM described above.

3.1.65 In order to meet the objectives of reducing various types of inequities and imbalances, interregional and rural–urban, the Eleventh Five Year Plan will increase the sectoral outlay in the primary health sector. While recognizing the role of primary heath sector, the National Health Policy (2002) sets out an increased allocation of 55% of the total public health outlay for primary care; the secondary and tertiary health sectors being targeted for 35% and 10% respectively. The Policy also states that the increased aggregate outlays for primary health care should be utilized for strengthening existing facilities and opening additional public health service outlets, consistent with the norms.

Box 3.1.6
Cultural Alignment

Often cultural alienation coupled with the apathy of doctors drives the tribals away from big hospitals and government health care facilities. The best way of delivering health care to the tribals is to do so in an environment that is familiar to them. This is what has been done in Gadchiroli. The SEARCH hospital is a habitat of huts built between trees. The reception area resembles a *Ghotul*—the traditional place for social and cultural events in a Gond village. The patients don't stay in wards but in individual huts with their families. Everything from bedsheets to towels is of khadi. The tribals often feel isolated and scared in big buildings. Here, surrounded by their natural environment and loved ones, patients feel at home. The result: thousands of tribal patients from 10 blocks of Chandrapur and Gadchiroli flock to this hospital for treatment.

SEARCH has also demonstrated how tribal beliefs can be used to disseminate health education. Every year, a *jatra* is organized in Shodhgram (SEARCH campus at Gadchiroli) in honour of Goddess Danteshwari, the deity revered by tribals. Representatives from as many as 40 tribal villages participate in this jatra. At the end of it, an *Aarogya Sansad* is held where the tribals are asked to enumerate their health concerns. After voting, one health problem is identified as the year's priority. Representatives then go back to the villages and start working on the identified problem. This is regarded as a command from the Goddess herself which no one can oppose. For instance, one year, the tribals voted for eradication of malaria. They were shocked to learn that malaria was caused by a mosquito bite and immediately wanted to know how to check the breeding of mosquitoes. By communicating with the tribals in a language that they understand, SEARCH has been able to tackle many superstitions and unhealthy practices.

3.1.66 Under the NRHM, emphasis has been given to allocate 70% of the total financial resources to below district level (block level and below), 20% at district level, and 10% at State level. Efforts will be made to allocate funds under various schemes and programmes as per NRHM guidelines. Further, the requirements of funds for a fully functional primary health care system (defined as all services at block level and below, including field-based implementation of disease control and preventive activities, but not administration) will also be worked out.

SECONDARY AND TERTIARY HEALTH CARE

3.1.67 Secondary and Tertiary health care will receive attention. There is an urgent need to take a fresh look at how public and private sector can be better utilized during the Eleventh Five Year Plan. The NRHM addresses these issues through a few strategies. Priorities will be given to strategies involving PPPs, risk-pooling mechanisms, and cross subsidization.

3.1.68 Administration of the secondary and tertiary care hospitals will be professionalized and trained professionals posted as Medical Superintendents. Hospitals will be allowed to recruit various staff including junior doctors on ad hoc and contract basis. Drugs purchase should be made through centralized rate contract and decentralized distribution with zero stock at headquarter level. Emergency and disaster stock should be located at each hospital. Drugs at all levels with minimum of one year shelf life should be supplied.

3.1.69 District hospitals, which play a key role in providing health services to the poor, need substantial improvement in infrastructure and other facilities to perform their role more effectively. This would also be a key intermediate step in the health strategy, till the vision of health care through PHCs and community health centres is fully realized. The Plan will also complete setting up of 6 AIIMS-like institutions, upgrading 13 existing medical institutes under the *Pradhan Mantri Swasthya Suraksha Yojana* (PMSSY) and strengthening the Central Government hospitals. Adoption of PPP mode will be explored for these activities.

3.1.70 It is often observed that Government Medical Colleges and Hospitals are on the verge of de-recognition mainly because they fail to adhere to the infrastructure, equipment, and staff norms, as laid down by MCI. This is thought to be due to lack of funding. The Centre and States will have to make provisions for strengthening these institutions.

3.1.71 During the Eleventh Five Year Plan period, the following will receive priority:

- Establishment of Hospital Development Committees in all government hospitals.
- Improvement of infrastructure and facilities in district hospitals.
- Provision of high-quality secondary health care services for every block in the country.
- Creation of state-of-the-art medical education, research, and care institutions in all disciplines of medicine.
- Creation of new institutions and upgradation of existing tertiary care hospitals.
- Mainstreaming of AYUSH systems to actively supplement the efforts of the allopathic systems.

ACCESS TO ESSENTIAL DRUGS AND MEDICINES

3.1.72 Drugs and medicines form a substantial portion of the out-of-pocket spending on health by households (Table 3.1.7). The poor are the worst affected because they are frequently affected by diseases and are least able to purchase and utilize the health services, such as drugs. On the other hand, the component of drugs and medicines accounts for a mere 10% of the overall health budget of both the Central and State Governments. Timely supply of drugs of good quality that involves procurement as well as logistics management is of critical importance in any health system.

3.1.73 An essential component of strengthening primary health facilities will be a system of guaranteeing essential drugs. Standard treatment guidelines will be available for doctors at PHCs and CHCs. Under the NRHM, experiences of efficient procurement and distribution could be rapidly adapted and generalized to all States. Although the World Health Organization (WHO) has its essential list of drugs yet all of these are not required at all levels. Each State will decide for each level the essential list based on epidemiological situation. Availability of essential drugs in every PHC and CHC will increase people's confidence in the public health system.

3.1.74 Analysis of drug prices indicates that publicly procured drugs are cheaper. Assuring regular supply of drugs in public facilities would improve utilization of public sector services and reduce out-of-pocket expenditures. The NCMP also committed to ensure availability of life saving drugs at reasonable prices. During the Eleventh Five Year Plan, all efforts will be made to encourage States to model the public procurement systems on the lines of the Tamil Nadu Medical Services Corporation (Box 3.1.7). Efforts will be made to experiment available models in Rajasthan and Delhi for making drugs available to hospital at cheaper rates. In order to take up drug pricing, quality, clinical trials, etc. as recommended by the Mashelkar Committee (2003) and NCMH (2005), a National Drug Authority (NDA) with an autonomous status was to be set up during the Plan. Accordingly, Central Drugs Authority of India has been set up. The present National Pharmaceutical Pricing Authority, created under the aegis of the Ministry of Chemicals and Fertilizers, is proposed to be merged with the NDA. The Central Government will provide assistance to States for strengthening the drug regulatory system. During the Plan, the following will be emphasized:

- Developing essential drug lists for all levels of institutions
- Making available essential drugs of good quality in adequate quantities in all government health facilities
- Increasing efficiency, economy, and transparency in drug procurement, warehousing, and distribution
- Initiating strategies in coordination with professional and consumer bodies to ensure safe drugs and rational use of drugs
- Disseminating information on essential drugs to medical professionals, pharmacists, and to the people
- Including all essential drugs under a system of price monitoring
- Implementing and reinforcing the concept of Standard Treatment Guidelines in the in-service and pre-service training programmes of the doctors and health workers.

FOOD SAFETY AND QUALITY CONTROL

3.1.75 To tackle the issues of pesticide residues in food/beverages, additives and contaminants, and nutritional

TABLE 3.1.7
Percentage Share of Household Expenditure on Health and Drugs in Various States

State	Share of Health to Total Household Expenditure		Share of Drug Expenditure to Total Household Health Expenditure	
	Rural	Urban	Rural	Urban
Andhra Pradesh	6.56	4.13	72.42	71.36
Assam	2.47	4.04	70.65	68.49
Bihar	4.40	2.96	89.14	82.16
Delhi	3.34	3.34	61.83	72.69
Goa	4.28	5.16	79.19	73.87
Gujarat	5.03	4.22	63.90	69.56
Haryana	6.99	6.56	76.80	76.28
Himachal Pradesh	5.25	3.91	88.96	74.39
J&K	2.90	3.61	90.39	81.33
Karnataka	4.58	4.17	68.75	55.96
Kerala	7.79	7.15	71.83	64.05
MP	6.05	5.25	81.28	78.21
Maharashtra	7.50	5.98	68.75	59.08
Orissa	5.46	4.51	90.64	90.26
Punjab	7.66	5.60	79.47	73.90
Rajasthan	4.79	4.70	89.43	83.88
Tamil Nadu	5.80	4.45	61.41	61.44
UP	8.20	5.64	86.76	81.47
WB	4.64	4.84	72.89	67.80
All India	6.05	4.91	77.33	69.18

Source: NCMH (2005).

Box 3.1.7
Essential Drug Supply—Tamil Nadu Experience

Activities

Finalizing list of Essential Drugs selected from the model list by the WHO
Ensuring adequate funds and human resources for supply of drugs from its warehouses to various points of health care delivery
Testing drugs for quality
Supplying drugs only in strips and blister packing
Selecting drugs on the basis of disease pattern, safety, effectiveness, and cost
Including only generic drugs
Making proper arrangements for storage of drugs in modern warehouses
Training the pharmacists regarding storage and distribution of drugs
Revising store keeping procedures and storing drugs according to the first come-first out basis and according to their generic name

Achievements

Preparation of the Essential Drugs list, catering to varying needs of different levels of health care
Provision of good quality, generic drugs
Provision of drugs specific to the need and level of health care
Rational use of drugs
Availability of accurate up to date stock information on the computer
Linkage of all warehouses telephonically with the TNMSC headquarters in Chennai

labelling, following actions will be undertaken during the Eleventh Five Year Plan:

- Creating Food Safety Authority for speedy enforcement of safety standards.
- Ensuring implementation of Capacity Building Project with the objective to enhance capacities in laboratories, awareness of food safety, and hygiene.
- Strengthening State labs, capacity building, food portal, comprehensive and informative/analytical database.
- Rationalizing protocol for establishment of labs for food safety.
- Implementing the Food Safety and Standards Act, 2006.

Decentralized Governance

ROLE OF PRIs

3.1.76 PRIs have the mandate to manage the primary health system. Communiza-tion through ownership by PRIs is necessary for an efficient and effective health system. Implementation of the NRHM will have to be closely watched to ensure that the involvement of Panchayats is total and complete. The various tiers of PRIs will decide the local priorities and also supervise functioning of health facilities, functionaries, and functions through their participation in various committees.

3.1.77 Since one-third of elected members at the local bodies are women, this is an opportunity to promote a gender-sensitive, multi-sectoral agenda for population stabilization with the help of village level health committees. All this will remain rhetoric until the elected women are trained and empowered. Under the NRHM, ASHAs are envisaged to be selected by and be accountable to the village Panchayats. Involvement of PRIs will also be necessary to improve the coverage and quality of registration of births, deaths, marriages, and pregnancies in all States.

3.1.78 During the Eleventh Five Year Plan, decentralization of resources to Panchayats or local representative bodies will be implemented in a phased manner to make decentralized planning a living reality.

ROLE OF CIVIL SOCIETY

3.1.79 Community Based Health Partnership is the key to sustaining health action even with limited resources. This can take many forms, through the PRIs, community-based and NGOs, and of people participating at all levels of health interventions. This cannot be achieved only by giving financial and administrative powers to the Panchayats, it needs active participation of the people for local action. Partnership with community groups (through youth, *mahila mandals*, SHGs, and Gram Sabhas) is necessary for local solutions to local problems. In this regard, successful communitization of health services in Nagaland should be studied and replicated (Box 3.1.9).

3.1.80 The NRHM envisages community participation such as described above. Under the framework for implementation, the Mission tries to ensure that more than 70% of the resources are spent through bodies that are managed by peoples' organizations and at least 10% of the resources are spent through grants-in-aids to NGOs. The mechanism of untied funds at the local level is meant to give them a little flexibility. During the Eleventh Five Year Plan, efforts will be made to promote various community-based initiatives.

Affecting Convergence

3.1.81 Clean drinking water is vital as unsafe water increases the risk of diseases and malnutrition. Waterborne infections hamper absorption of food even when intake is sufficient. Rural water supply is beset with the problem of sustainability, maintenance, and water quality. Though more than 95% coverage was achieved prior to Bharat Nirman, out of the 14.22 lakh habitations in the country about 1.66 lakh have slipped back to a position where people do not have adequate water to drink and have to walk more than 2 km to fetch potable water. Similarly, about 1.86 lakh habitations are dependent on contaminated water supply, which leads to various health problems.

3.1.82 Lack of sanitation is directly responsible for several waterborne diseases. Rural sanitation coverage was 1% in the 1980s. With the launch of the Central Rural Sanitation Programme in 1986, the coverage improved

Box 3.1.8
Role of PRIs

Nearly three-fourths of the population of the country lives in villages. This rural population is spread over more than 10 lakh habitations of which 60% have a population of less than 1000. For the success of Sarva Swasthya Abhiyan, the reform process would have to touch every village and every health facility. This would be possible only when the community is sufficiently empowered to take leadership in health matters.

PRIs, right from the village to district level, would have to be given ownership of the public health delivery system in their respective jurisdictions. Some States like Kerala, WB, Maharashtra, and Gujarat have already taken initiatives in this regard and their experiments have shown the positive gains of institutionalizing involvement of PRIs in the management of the health system.

The NRHM empowers the PRIs at each level that is, Gram Panchayat, Panchayat Samiti (Block), and Zilla Parishad (District) to take leadership to control and manage the public health infrastructure at district and sub district levels in the following ways:

- A VHSC in each village within the over all framework of Gram Sabha in which proportionate representation from all the hamlets would be ensured. Adequate representation is given to the disadvantaged categories like women, SCs, STs, OBCs, and Minorities.
- Sub Health Centre is accountable to the Gram Panchayat and shall have a local committee for its management, with adequate representation of VHSCs.
- PHC, which is not at the block level, will be responsible to the elected representative of the Gram Panchayat where it is located. All other Gram Panchayats covered by the PHCs would be suitably represented on its management.
- The Block level PHC and CHC will have involvement of Panchayati Raj elected leaders in its management. The *Rogi Kalyan Samiti* would manage day-to-day affairs of the hospital.
- The Zilla Parishad at the district level will be directly responsible for the budgets of the health societies and for planning for people's health needs.
- With the development of capacities and systems, the entire public health management at the district level would devolve to the District Health Society which would be under the effective leadership and control of the district Panchayat, with participation of the block Panchayats.

To empower and facilitate local action, the NRHM provides untied grants at all levels, namely, Village, SC, PHC, and CHC. Monitoring committees will be formed at various levels, with participation of PRI representatives, user groups, and CBO/NGO/VO representatives to facilitate their inputs in the monitoring planning process. They will enable the community to be involved in broad-based review and suggestions for planning. A system of periodic *Jan Sunwai* or *Jan Samvad* at various levels has been built in to empower community members to engage in giving direct feedback and suggestions for improvement in public health.

Box 3.1.9
Communitization in Nagaland

The health SC in Mopungchuket village in Mokokchung district of Nagaland is a beautifully and aesthetically constructed building made from local materials. This village of almost 6000 people felt an acute need for health care. So, in 2002 when communitization started, the community collected Rs 2.83 lakh through contributions to run the SC. They donated a building. Two ANMs, one ASHA, and a pharmacist run the SC. They are always present. The building is spic and span. A room has been created and a few beds put in for patients. Deliveries also take place here. The records of all patients, along with their health problems, line of treatment, and medications prescribed are meticulously maintained in neat registers. The centre never falls short of medicines and essential drugs. If the government supply is delayed, the community pools in money to purchase drugs.

to 4% in 1988 and then to 22% in 2001. It is now acknowledged that unless 100% coverage is achieved and proper solid waste management (SWM) carried out, health indicators will not show significant improvement. Toilets are essential also for ensuring the safety and dignity of girls and women. Lack of adequate number of toilets with privacy affects the school dropout rate of girl child. The solution, therefore, is to provide clean drinking water and adequate sanitation coverage throughout the country by adoption of a convergent approach by VHSCs under the NRHM.

3.1.83 During the Eleventh Five Year Plan, the Ministry of Health and Family Welfare (MoHFW) will take up a Programme for Prevention and Control of Water Borne Diseases as a part of Sarva Swasthya Abhiyan, which will establish a mechanism of collaboration with other departments (for supplying safe water to community and carry out water quality monitoring), with specific responsibilities. The targets are: (i) by 2010, to reduce the burden of waterborne diseases to 75% of the present level; and (ii) by 2015, to reduce the burden of waterborne diseases to 50% of the present level. In order to achieve 100% coverage of clean water and sanitation, Eleventh Five Year Plan strategies include:

- Convergence of health care, hygiene, sanitation, and drinking water at the village level through VHSCs under NRHM.
- Renewed efforts under NUHM to cover primary health care, safe drinking water, and sanitation in urban areas.
- Participation of stake holders at all levels, from planning, design, and location to implementation and management of the projects.
- Institutionalization of water quality monitoring and surveillance systems by involving PRIs, community, NGOs, and other CSO.
- Increased attention to Behavioural Change Communication.
- Linking treatment of sewage and industrial effluents to development planning.

Enhancing PPP

3.1.84 During the last few years, the Centre as well as the State Governments have initiated a wide variety of PPP arrangements to meet peoples' growing health care needs (few examples provided in Box 3.1.10). Besides these examples, services like cleaning and maintenance of buildings, security, waste management, scavenging, laundry, diet have been contracted out to the private sector by many States.

3.1.85 The existing evidence for PPP does not allow easy generalization. Contracting is the predominant model for PPP in India. Some partnerships are simple contracts (like laundry, diet, cleaning, etc.), others are more complex involving many stakeholders with their respective responsibilities. For example, the Yeshaswini Health Insurance scheme for farmers in Karnataka includes the State Department of Cooperatives, the Yeshaswini Trust with its almost 200 private hospitals, a corporate Third Party Administrator (TPA), and beneficiaries with the eligibility conditions. It is seen that in most partnerships, the State Health Department is the principal partner with limited stakeholder consultation. However, true partnerships that mean equality among partners, mutual commitment to goals, shared decision making, and risk taking are rarely seen.

3.1.86 Findings of existing case studies also bring forth concerns such as absence of the beneficiary in the entire process, lack of effective governance mechanisms for ensuring accountability, non transparent mechanisms, lack of appropriate monitoring and governance systems, and institutionalized management structures to handle the task. For example, while contracting out PHCs, the State Governments sometimes hand over the worst performing PHCs to NGOs. Not paying the initial instalment to NGOs at the start of the project is another problem. The NGOs are never sure whether the money will eventually be released and if so, how much to expect. Management of health facilities should be handed over to NGOs only if the process is completely transparent and there is a strong local monitoring mechanism. This is the objective of Government–NGO partnership envisaged in the Eleventh Five Year Plan.

3.1.87 During the Eleventh Five Year Plan, the experience of PPP initiatives in selected States will be studied thoroughly. Based on evidence, efforts will be made

Box 3.1.10
Public–Private Partnership (PPP)

- Rajasthan:
  Partners: Medicare Relief Society, SMS Hospital, Jaipur, and Vardhman Scanning and Imaging Private Ltd.
  Services: Contracting in Radiological diagnostic services in the public hospitals.
  Provision of quality drugs and supplies cheaper than market rate. All this free for BPL patients above 70 years of age and freedom fighters; pre-negotiated rates for others.
- West Bengal:
  Partners: Government of West Bengal, Mediclue, District Health & FW Societies, Private partners, M/S Doctors Laboratory and Non Profit NGOs.
  Services: CT Scan in seven medical colleges, MRI in one medical college hospital, diagnostic facilities in 30 rural hospitals, and running of 133 ambulances for emergency transport under management of NGOs/CBOs at the level of Block PHCs.
- Uttarakhand:
  Partners: Government of Uttarakhand, DST, GoI and Uttaranchal Institute of Scientific Research, Bhimtal (NGO).
  Services: Mobile Health Services—Diagnostic, Laboratory, and Clinical Services through mobile vans. Dedicated health camps in 6 districts of western part of Uttarakhand.
- Karnataka:
  Partners: Government of Karnataka and Apollo Hospitals Enterprises Ltd, Hyderabad Rajiv Gandhi Super Specialty Hospital, Raichur handed to Apollo Hospital under management contract.
  Services: 350 bedded hospital. Free services to BPL patients, 40% beds for BPL (government reimburses the charges) and remaining patients treated under special rates.
  Partners: Government of Karnataka & Karuna Trust.
  Services: Contracting out adoption and management of PHCs and affiliated SCs in remote, rural, and tribal areas in the State.
  24 hrs health services—OPD, emergency services, electrocardiogram (ECG), X-ray, laboratory, immunization, national health programmes, RCH programme, 20 bed patient ward, and ambulance.
- Gujarat:
  Partners: Government of Gujarat and Private Doctors (Obstetricians and Gynecologists).
  Services: Chiranjeevi Yojana: Private Doctors (Obstetricians) are contracted for deliveries both normal and caesarian of BPL women at their facilities.
- Arunachal Pradesh:
  Partners: Government of Arunachal Pradesh & VHAI, Karuna Trust, Future Generations, and Prayas.
  Services: Management of selected PHCs.
- Andhra Pradesh:
  Partners: Government of Andhra Pradesh and Social Action for Integrated Development Services, Adilabad (NGO)
  Services : Urban Slum health care project. Contracting in (performance contract but without any public premises being handed over to the private partner).
  Partners: Government of Andhra Pradesh & New India Assurance Company.
  Services : Arogya Raksha Scheme based on vouchers.
  Funded by the government, operational management by the public sector company, and service delivery by private health service providers.
- Tamil Nadu:
  Partners: Government of Tamil Nadu & the Seva Nilayam Society in association with Ryder-Cheshire Foundation (NGOs).
  Services: Performance contract for the provision of emergency ambulance services in the region. Ambulances are owned by the government.

Note: FW = Family Welfare.

to develop a generic framework for different categories of PPPs at primary, secondary, and tertiary levels of health care to improve cost-effectiveness, enhance quality, and expand access through extensive stakeholder consultations. Contracting out well-specified and delimited projects such as immunization can help enhance accountability. Setting up of diagnostic and therapeutic centres (facilities that are not available in hospital) by private players in hospital premises will be encouraged. Government may consider giving them an infrastructure status in those geographical areas by providing incentives like land at concessional rates, increasing floor area ratio and ground coverage, tax holiday, and loan at concessional rates. However, emphasis would be on model contractual agreements with specific performance requirements to be measured by the civil society. Costs will be built in.

Health Insurance: Protecting the Poor

3.1.88 In India, due to huge geographical area, very large population, and inequity of resources, ensuring good health for all, particularly the poor, is a complex issue. Our health system is a mix of the public and private sectors, with the NGOs and civil society still playing a very small (though important) role.

3.1.89 The 60th Round of the NSSO (2004–05), has clearly brought out the fact that in rural government hospitals, an out-of-pocket expenditure of more than Rs 3000 is made during every hospitalization. In rural private hospitals, it is more than Rs 7000. The expenditure in the urban areas in private hospitals is more than Rs 11000 and about three times higher than the public hospitals. Today, this expenditure would have increased substantially. Private out-of-pocket expenditure can be reduced through Comprehensive Health Insurance, on a risk pooling basis for all, particularly the poor.

3.1.90 Coverage of health insurance in India is pathetically limited. Current health insurance in government and private sector covers around 11% of the population. The existing Employees State Insurance Scheme, Central Government Health Scheme (CGHS), and Ex-Servicemen Contributory Health Scheme provide services to industrial workers, government employees, and ex-Armed Forces Personnel along with their families. Mediclaim covers mainly the upper-middle income groups. Private health insurance schemes are mainly urban oriented and they have problems like unaffordable premiums, delay in settling claims, non-transparent procedures in deciding reimbursements, etc. Even though the system of TPAs has facilitated cash payments and expanded access to providers it is yet to show evidence of having been able to control cost or provide appropriate care.

ENCOURAGE COMMUNITY RISK-POOLING

3.1.91 Providing financial protection to the poor during hospitalization will have an immediate impact on alleviating indebtedness. Local governments will identify population at risk and provide a revolving fund to be managed by a consortium of SHGs. This consortium would also encourage small savings by households and whenever required, give needy households, a cash support of Rs 5000 to Rs 10000 for hospitalization, catastrophic illness, and death. This will save households from immediate financial debt at the point of crisis. They would repay this money at a modest interest rate within an appropriate time frame so that the village health risk pool does not fall below Rs 1 lakh. During the Plan, pilots will be undertaken in selected States under NRHM and NUHM. The scheme will empower SHGs, enable households to access micro-credit, and also recover from financial stress during treatment of illness.

COMMUNITY BASED HEALTH INSURANCE (CBHI)

3.1.92 Evidence suggests that well-designed and managed CBHI schemes coupled with behavioural change campaigns and other interventions increase the quality of health care. Easy and low cost accessibility to health care can protect the households from indebtedness arising from high medical expenditure. These schemes can be implemented in areas where institutional capacity is too weak to organize mandatory nation-wide risk pooling.

3.1.93 CBHI is 'any not-for-profit insurance scheme that is aimed primarily at the informal sector and formed on the basis of a collective pooling of health risks and the members participating in its management'. What distinguishes these schemes from public or private-for-profit insurance schemes is that the targeted community is involved in defining the contribution amount and collecting mechanism, content of benefit package, and allocating the scheme's financial resources.

3.1.94 CBHI schemes in India are very diverse in nature in terms of design, management, and size of the targeted population. ACCORD, BAIF, Karuna Trust, Self Employed Women's Association (SEWA), DHAN Foundation, and VHS are some examples. Experience of current CBHI schemes in India reveals that area specific schemes should be developed according to the local requirements. These schemes should be tailored to the reality of the poor, and organized according to their convenience. During the Plan, CBHI schemes through the public system and by accredited private providers will be encouraged.

HEALTH INSURANCE FOR THE UNORGANIZED SECTOR

3.1.95 We have a huge working population of about 400 million. Almost 93% of this work force is in the unorganized sector. There are numerous occupational groups in economic activities, passed on from generation to generation, scattered all over the country with differing employer–employee relationship. Those in the organized sector of the economy, whether in the public or private sector, have access to some form of health service coverage. The unorganized sector workers have no access. The National Commission for Enterprises in the Unorganized Sector (NCEUS) has recommended a specific scheme for health in incidences of illness and hospitalization for workers and their families.

3.1.96 The Eleventh Five Year Plan will introduce a new scheme based on cashless transaction with the objective of improving access to health care and protecting the individual and her family from exorbitant out-of-pocket expenses. Under the scheme, coverage will be given to the beneficiary and her family of five members. Providers will be both public and private.

MATERNITY HEALTH INSURANCE

3.1.97 During the Eleventh Five Year Plan, the Maternity Health Insurance Scheme as an initiative across a few States is expected to be implemented. This scheme is premised on capitation-based financing, where the provider is assured a fixed per capita payment in respect of all those who enrol for maternity care. All pregnant women belonging to BPL families will be covered under this scheme. They would register with the ANM and simultaneously identify from a list of diverse accredited providers, any institutional facility in the public or private sector, which will look after her during her pregnancy. The ANM will complete the antenatal check in consultation with the facility identified. The capitation fee for the pregnant women in the BPL category will be borne by government. This intervention will improve outcomes for maternal and infant mortality by ensuring that the complete cycle of maternity care in particular for the poor, is handled by a qualified institutional provider. More specifically, this intervention will increase institutional deliveries and lower maternal mortality, empower women with improved access to reproductive health care, enable and facilitate women to adopt postpartum terminal methods of family planning if they need to. It will stimulate development of accredited health infrastructure accessible in rural and remote areas, facilitate partnerships, and finally, improve the responsiveness and accountability of public sector facilities.

Central Government Health Scheme (CGHS)

3.1.98 CGHS was started in 1954 and at present 24 cities are covered with total of 9.12 lakh card holders and 33.01 lakh beneficiaries (as on 31 March 2006). 72.5% card holders are serving employees, 25.4% are pensioners, and rest belong to the categories such as freedom fighters, Members of Parliament (MPs), ex-MPs, journalists, and others. Services covered under CGHS include hospitalization, outpatient consultation and treatment, diagnostics, drugs, etc. For these services there are 247 allopathic dispensaries, 82 AYUSH dispensaries, 19 polyclinics, and 65 laboratories in the cities covered. For hospitalization, the services are largely outsourced to selected private hospitals, all government hospitals are included. Out Patient Department (OPD) and diagnostic services are also partly outsourced to selected private hospitals and diagnostic centres.

3.1.99 Mid Term Appraisal for the Tenth Plan has made the following recommendations regarding CGHS:

- Restructure, reform, and rejuvenate.
- Existing subscribers be given the option to either continue or switch over to a system of health insurance.
- Greater autonomy to the CGHS to enable it to develop various options for reducing costs in providing services and trying different models of service delivery.

3.1.100 To reform CGHS, a number of new initiatives have been taken. A pilot project on computerization has been completed. This would help weeding out large number of duplicate cards, online indenting, and billing of medicines, reducing supply time from three days to one day, and reduction in waiting time for the beneficiaries. All dispensaries are being networked to allow beneficiary treatment from any dispensary. Database on disease profile of beneficiary, reimbursement claims, prescribing and referring, pattern of medical officers (MO), billing pattern of panel hospitals, diagnostic centres are also computerized. Other new initiatives proposed to be taken are delegation of enhanced financial powers to ministries. Within CGHS, local advisory committees at dispensary level, empanelment process of hospitals, and diagnostic centres as a continuous process, outsourcing of sanitation of CGHS dispensaries, PPP for setting diagnostic/radiological services in GGHS buildings, procurement of drugs on rate contract system with stringent penalties for delay, TPAs for processing of claims, and medical audit will also be taken up.

3.1.101 Fixed subscription is contributed by the beneficiary irrespective of the size of the family and the magnitude of services being availed. Present subscription rates are based upon the basic pay or pension of the government servant or pensioner. Since there is no linkage between subscription rates (fixed) and cost of services (dynamic), the already huge gap between beneficiary contributions and actual expenditure is progressively widening. To arrest the increasing trend, following options will be considered during Eleventh Five Year Plan:

- Linking the rate of subscription to total cost of CGHS system so that beneficiaries contribute a fixed percentage of CGHS cost and remaining cost is borne by the government.
- Contribution should be per person/beneficiary and not per CGHS card issued to the family.
- In addition to the monthly subscription, each beneficiary should bear the first 20% of the total admissible bill/amount and the balance 80% would be paid by CGHS.
- Phasing out the direct budgetary support for the CGHS through the introduction of health insurance system. Health insurance scheme(s) would cover both serving employees as well as pensioners particularly in non-CGHS areas, on optional basis. Employees joining after a cut off date (to be decided) would compulsorily be covered under health insurance scheme. Health insurance scheme would cover both OPD and hospitalization services. Premium on coverage in the insurance scheme would be on sharing basis.
- Gradually shifting Central Government employees from CGHS to system of health insurance, through which they may access the CGHS or any other clinical health care provider of their choice.

Regulation and Accreditation

3.1.102 There is a need to empower PRIs to monitor the minimum standards for clinical establishments. Participation of NGOs in such efforts will be ensured.

3.1.103 All State Councils will be encouraged to shift to a system of periodical renewal of registration, possibly every three to five years. A specialist's or a super specialist's qualifications should also be required to be registered. These details should get transferred to a National Register to be maintained and updated by each apex council. There is need for a system of accreditation of various courses offered by Medical, Dental, and Nursing educational institutions. The Human Resource Development Ministry has already established a system for accreditation and rating of universities. Such a system is also needed in the medical education sector. The proposed Health Sciences Grants Commission should be given this responsibility.

3.1.104 In the field of paramedical education, priority will be given for establishment of National Para

Medical Council as an apex body to determine standards and to ensure uniform enforcement throughout the country. On similar lines, councils for physiotherapy and occupational therapy should also be established.

3.1.105 National Accreditation Board for Hospitals and Health care Providers (NABH), a constituent Board of Quality Council of India, has adopted standards and accreditation process in line with worldwide accreditation practices. Academy of Hospital Administration had formulated a standard for NABH. Other organizations like Indian Confederation for Health Care Accreditation and financial rating organizations like ICRA have started the process of accreditation and rating the health institutions.

3.1.106 Of late, the government has given approval for introducing the Clinical Establishments (Registration and Regulation) Bill in the Parliament. The proposed legislation will cover all clinical organizations in different streams of medicine including AYUSH systems. Under this legislation, all the clinical establishments including diagnostic centres will be registered and regulated by the National Council of Standards. The council will prescribe minimum standards for health services and maintain national register of clinical establishments.

3.1.107 Efforts will be made to enforce standards for government hospitals at all levels. Priority will be given for development of Standard Operating Procedures and Standard Treatment Guidelines for all specialties and all systems of medicines. A National Advisory Board for Standards will be set up and financial assistance will be provided to States for setting up infrastructure for registration of clinical establishments.

3.1.108 The following activities will be accorded priority during the Eleventh Five Year Plan:

- Legislation for registration of clinical establishments in the country.
- Development of uniform standards for infrastructure and service delivery.
- Re-registration in case of additional and higher qualifications.
- Creation of National Registers of all medical and paramedical personnel.
- Setting up a National Paramedical and other Councils for regulating education and service delivery.
- Recognition of RMPs as *sahabhaagis* in NRHM.

Emerging Technologies

LOW COST AND INDIGENOUS TECHNOLOGIES

3.1.109 For quality health service, development and utilization of appropriate technologies for diagnosis and treatment of diseases is essential. Over the last few years, health-related technology has developed at a rapid pace. But its impact on indices of public health has been minimal. There is a need to develop cheaper technologies that are as effective as the existing ones. Many technologies are expensive, so alternatives are badly needed. It should be of prime concern to find technological solutions for making crucial equipment affordable, for example, anaesthesia machine, surgical equipment and lighting, sterilization equipment, defibrillator, ventilator, electrocardiogram (ECG), blood pressure monitoring equipment, pulse oxymeter. Benefits of reduced cost of such technologies should reach village health care providers.

3.1.110 Apart from the secondary and tertiary care, there is need and scope to introduce the use of public health related technologies and public health related practices at all levels of health care. Use of the technologies like those indicated in Box 3.1.11 would help to prevent outbreaks of waterborne diseases, maternal mortality related to unsafe deliveries and postpartum infections, anaemia, prevent acquisition of malaria, and deaths due to childhood pneumonias, etc. Efforts will be made in the Eleventh Five Year Plan to promote public health related technologies.

ROLE OF e-HEALTH

3.1.111 Appropriate use of IT for an enhanced role in health care and governance will be aimed at during the Eleventh Five Year Plan. It is feasible to set up a National Grid to be shared by health care providers, trainers, beneficiaries, and civil society. The country already has the advantage of a strong fibre backbone and indigenous satellite communication technology with trained human resources in this regard. A number of pilot projects on e-Health over the past years by private concerns, corporate, NGOs, medical colleges, and research institutions have been set up. The successful outcome of many of these initiatives needs to be evaluated and scaled up.

3.1.112 Health Management Information System (HMIS) would be an important new initiative utilizing developments in the field of IT. A computerized web enabled data capturing and analytical system will be established to provide valid and reliable data and reports for use at all levels. This would not only facilitate proper ME of different programmes under implementation but will also help in various aspects of service delivery. The HMIS will also integrate the various vertical systems having their own reporting machinery into an integrated umbrella of holistic ME to cater to the needs of Sarva Swasthya Abhiyan. The data will flow directly from the periphery. The Integrated Disease Surveillance Project (IDSP) will eventually be a by-product of the HMIS. As the system stabilizes and the penetration of computerization at the block level increases, the system will be modular enough to expand the scope to the remotest areas. Wastage of drugs due to date expiry also needs to be curtailed by demand-driven management and redistribution of medicines nearing date of expiry. HMIS when fully developed and implemented will track demand and supply and continuously monitor the drug situation.

3.1.113 Telemedicine could help to bring specialized health care to the remotest corners of the country. Telemedicine is likely to provide the advantages of tele-diagnosis, especially in the areas of cardiology, pathology, dermatology, and radiology besides continuing medical education (CME). It will be of immense use for diagnostic and consultative purposes for patients getting treatment from the secondary level health care facilities. The efficacy of telemedicine has already been shown through the network established by the Indian Space Research Organization (ISRO) that has connected 42 super-specialty hospitals with 8 mobile telemedicine vans and 200 rural and remote hospitals

Box 3.1.11
Making Health Care Affordable—
The Experience of *Jan Swasthya Sahyog* (JSS)

For the last seven years, a group of dedicated young doctors from institutes like CMC, Vellore and AIIMS have been working to make health in the hinterlands, available, accessible, and affordable. The JSS team has given up lucrative jobs, sparkling city lights, and hefty pay packets to develop cheap, accurate and easy-to-use technology that can be used for prevention, diagnosis, and treatment of diseases in remote, tribal areas of Bilaspur and Chhattisgarh. So, the JSS method for early detection of UTIs costs less than Rs 2 per test, anaemia Re 1, diabetes Rs 2, pregnancy Rs 3. They have also developed low cost mosquito repellent creams, breath counters for detection of pneumonia among children, easy-to-read BP instruments to prevent preeclampsia, and a simple water purification method whereby one can cycle for 15 minutes and get a bucket of potable water treated by UV light. Low cost delivery kits with everything needed for the mother and child in the first 24 hours—gloves, large plastic sheets, soap, disinfectant, blade, gauze, sterilized threads, cotton cloth to wrap the baby, thick sanitary pads for women—are available for just Rs 40. These simple techniques are so designed that they can be used by illiterate and semi-literate village women and school students. Then there are the more complicated tests like sputum concentration system for increasing the sensitivity of microscopic diagnosis of tuberculosis and electrophoresis for detection of sickle cell anaemia, a common malady in the area. While electrophoresis costs Rs 300 in the market, using JSS technology it costs just Rs 20.

The most innovative strategy put in place by JSS, however, is the malaria detection system. They have trained village health workers in taking blood smears. These are labelled and neatly packed in small soap cases which are handed over through school children to bus drivers. On their way to school, the drivers drop the smears at the Ganiyari hospital run by JSS. Here they are immediately tested and the reports are sent back through the same buses on their return trip. This courier system has been operational in 21 villages in the area for the last 5 years and has saved many lives. It is now being extended for tuberculosis detection. These simple, innovative technologies developed by JSS can be used by all health workers to make diagnosis in peripheral, remote areas more rational and decrease misuse of drugs.

across the country through its geostationary satellites. So far about 3 lakh people have benefited from this programme. Facility of telemedicine will be provided in district hospitals and government medical colleges.

3.1.114 The e-Health initiatives to be taken up during the Eleventh Five Year Plan are:

- Training, Education, and Capacity Building for e-Health
- Monitoring by e-enabled HMIS to ensure timely flow of data and collation to be used at various levels
- Geographical Information System (GIS) Resource Mapping of various health facilities (Allopathic and AYUSH), Laboratories, Training Centres, Health Manpower, and other inputs to optimize utilization
- Providing service delivery and other e-enabled activities like, disease surveillance, tele-consultations, health helpline, district hospital referral net, and e-enabled mobile medical units

Gender Responsive Health Care

3.1.115 The GoI has taken several policy measures to reduce gender bias. The practice of gender budgeting in Health will be made mandatory in all programmes of the Centre and the States. The performance of different health programmes will be judged on the basis of gender disaggregated data.

Box 3.1.12
Telemedicine

Telemedicine programmes are being actively supported by:

ISRO
DIT
NEC Telemedicine programme for NE States
State Governments
NGOs

Various projects have been commissioned. Few examples are:

NE Project
Jammu & Kashmir (J&K) Project
Southern India Project
Armed Forces Medical Services Project
Asia Heart Foundation South India Project
Sankara Netharalaya Telemedicine Project
Wockhardt Hospital and Heart Institute Project
Apollo Hospitals Project

3.1.116 To reduce maternal mortality, several initiatives have been taken to make the maternal health programme broad based and client friendly. The major interventions include providing additional ANMs and Staff Nurses in certain health care facilities; referral transport; 24-hours delivery service at PHCs and CHCs; essential and emergency obstetric care; and optimal operationalization of FRUs. All these interventions will have to actually be done on a large scale during the Eleventh Five Year Plan. The goal is to reduce MMR to 100 per 100000 live births by 2012. State specific goals have also been suggested (Annexure 3.1.4).

SEX RATIO

3.1.117 The Eleventh Five Year Plan target is to raise the sex ratio for age group 0–6 to 935 by 2011–12 and subsequently to 950 by 2016–17. State-specific goals have also been suggested (Annexure 3.1.5). Apart from ensuring effective implementation of the Pre-Conception and Pre-Natal Diagnostic Techniques (PC & PNDT) Act, relentless public awareness measures will be undertaken. Other steps for integrating the issue of prenatal sex selection in the initiatives and programmes include the following:

- Increasing community awareness through ASHAs
- Including these issues in training modules and programmes and in IEC
- Adding sex selection information in medical curriculum
- Including indicators on improvement in sex ratios and birth registration as monitoring targets
- Ensuring inclusion of these issues in district level programme planning and implementation
- Ensuring convergence with other ministries such as Women and Child Development (WCD), Panchayati Raj, and Youth Affairs
- Evoking a community response to the issue

3.1.118 During the Eleventh Five Year Plan, the following additional strategies will be adopted:

- Develop clear targets of natural sex ratio at birth (SRB) which is 105 males per 100 females and give financial benefits to States that have improved SRB. From 2007 onwards, the Annual Health Survey will include estimates of SRB at the district level. Planning Commission will obtain independent estimates of the SRB at the district level each year. The States will be asked to monitor the SRB of the institutional deliveries, by parity, for each facility as well as for the districts. Improvement in SRB will be considered one of the indicators for arriving at decisions on plan assistance to States.

- Improve availability of data plus its access and quality on SRB. The option of PHC level enumeration will be considered to monitor the SRB on a routine basis.
- Provide financial support for capacity building, awareness generation and strict enforcement of PC & PNDT Act
- Amend the PC & PNDT Act to provide for the independence of the Appropriate Authorities at the district level.
- A National Research and Resource Centre in health for women will be developed under NRHM.

ANTENATAL CARE (ANC)

3.1.119 Universal screening of pregnant women using appropriate ANC is essential for the detection of problems and risk during pregnancy for referral to appropriate hospital for treatment. Under the NRHM, efforts are being made to improve the coverage, content, and quality of ANC in order to substantially reduce maternal and perinatal morbidity and mortality. Every effort will be made to operationalize the strategy for prevention and management of anaemia during the Eleventh Five Year Plan so that the target of reducing anaemia among women and girls by 50% is achieved by the end of 2012.

3.1.120 Emphasis will be given to screening all women during pregnancy to detect those with problems and referring them at the appropriate time to pre-designated institutions for management and safe delivery. This will reduce maternal and perinatal morbidity and mortality.

SAFE DELIVERY

3.1.121 Since child birth at home costs less than that at a private hospital or a public health facility, it is reasonable that families opt for home deliveries. Emphasis will therefore be given on training Traditional Birth Attendants (TBAs) and turn them into Skilled Birth Attendants (SBAs). They would ensure proper deliveries, whether at home or in an institution. Home delivery by trained persons will be encouraged if the families so desire. TBAs will be taught to recognize complications and refer them to hospitals. This strategy will help in reduction of maternal and neonatal deaths and perhaps pave the way for good ANC.

3.1.122 Attention will be paid by ASHAs, Anganwadi Workers (AWWs), and TBAs to make arrangements for transport to hospital for EmOC, early detection, and management of infections. All pregnant women from poor households will be covered by social insurance schemes to facilitate access to reliable maternal care. In this context, all States will be encouraged to experiment with schemes for maternity care (like *Chiranjeevi* scheme in Gujarat). Positive outcomes will be upscaled and replicated. Every district will have fully equipped Mother and Child Hospital. The existing maternal and child hospitals in the districts will also be upgraded.

3.1.123 It is now recognized globally that the countries successful in bringing down maternal mortality are the ones where the provision of skilled attendance at every birth and its linkage with appropriate referral services for complicated cases has been ensured. This has also been ratified by WHO. Guidelines for normal delivery and management of obstetric complications at PHCs and CHCs for MO and guidelines for ANC and skilled birth attendance at birth for ANMs and Lady Health Visitors (LHVs) have been formulated and disseminated to the States. During the Eleventh Five Year Plan, emphasis will be given to ensure the services of skilled birth attendant at child birth, both for home deliveries and in institutional settings. Since home deliveries will remain the norm across many States, effort will be made to provide skilled birth attendant training to *dais* who are ubiquitous in every nook and corner of the country.

ESSENTIAL AND EMERGENCY OBSTETRIC CARE

3.1.124 Operationalization of FRUs and skilled attendance at birth go hand in hand. Therefore simultaneous steps have been taken to ensure tackling obstetric emergencies. Under the NRHM, efforts are being made to make FRUs operational for providing Emergency and Essential Obstetric Care. Other steps include training of MBBS doctors in life saving anaesthetic skills for EmOC, establishment of blood storage at FRUs, and guidelines for operationalization of the FRUs. There is also a plan for training MBBS doctors in management of obstetric cases including caesarean section with the help of professional organizations of obstetricians and gynaecologists. Over the next five years, efforts will be made to improve the Emergency Obstetric Care in all CHCs in a phased manner. CHCs will have well equipped operation theatre, access to safe banked blood, qualified obstetricians, paediatricians, and anaesthetists. Roads linking habitations to CHCs will get special attention. The objective is to ensure availability of EmOC facilities within two hours of travel time.

ESSENTIAL POSTPARTUM CARE

3.1.125 Early postpartum care is essential to diagnose and treat complications such as puerperal infections, secondary postpartum haemorrhage, and ecclampsia, which are major causes of postpartum mortality. Postpartum care provides an opportunity to check the general well-being of mother and infant and to ensure that the infant is nursing well and there is enough supply of breast milk. Exclusive breastfeeding should be started within the first hour of birth. It can save many infant lives by preventing malnutrition and infections. Birth spacing and methods of contraception need to be discussed at this time. During the Eleventh Five Year Plan, Community Health Workers (ASHAs) will be appropriately oriented to this and their remuneration would also be linked to health checks of both the mother and newborns.

SAFE ABORTION SERVICES

3.1.126 The Medical Termination of Pregnancy (MTP) Act was passed by the Indian Parliament in 1971 and came into force from 1 April 1972. The aim of this Act was to reduce maternal mortality and morbidity due to unsafe abortions. The MTP Act, 1971 laid down conditions under which a pregnancy can be terminated and the place where such terminations can be performed. A recent amendment to the Act (2003) includes decentralization of power for approval of places and enlarging the network of safe MTP service providers. The amendment also provides for specific punitive measures for performing MTPs by unqualified persons and in places not approved by the government.

3.1.127 States are being provided flexibility to adopt strategies for the delivery of services to suit their local situations. Interventions for safe abortion services that were being provided in RCH Programme will however continue to be available and implemented more effectively during the Eleventh Five Year Plan.

REPRODUCTIVE TRACT INFECTIONS/SEXUALLY TRANSMITTED INFECTIONS (RTI/STI)

3.1.128 The spread of HIV infection and the role that RTI/STI play in the transmission of HIV has focused urgent attention on the problem. Identification and management of RTI is an important objective of the RCH Programme. The RCH strategies, under NRHM, for prevention, early detection, and effective management of common lower RTI through the existing primary health care infrastructure; and provision of the RTI/STI services at sub-district level will be implemented during the Eleventh Five Year Plan.

3.1.129 During the Eleventh Five Year Plan, for improving maternal health, special attention will be focused on the following areas:

- Ensuring universal provision of comprehensive ANC
- Providing widespread screening for anaemia and high-risk conditions
- Ensuring comprehensive training programme for skilled birth attendants
- Ensuring the services of skilled birth attendant at child birth, both for home deliveries and in institutional settings
- Providing SBA training to dais who are ubiquitous in every nook and corner of the country
- Enhancing availability of facilities for institutional deliveries and effective EmOC
- Providing 24-Hours Delivery Service at PHCs and CHCs
- Training of health personnel at PHCs and CHCs to

perform emergency obstetrical procedures, especially c-sections
- Providing additional ANMs and Public Health and Staff Nurses in certain SCs, PHCs, and CHCs
- Providing skilled human resources on contractual basis
- Improving EmOC in all CHCs in a phased manner (CHCs will have well equipped operation theatre, access to safe banked blood, qualified obstetricians, paediatricians, and anaesthetists)
- Operationalizing FRUs through supply of drugs in the form of Emergency Obstetric drugs kits
- Providing special attention to roads linking habitations to CHCs
- Providing Referral Transport
- Orienting ASHAs to postpartum care and linking her remuneration to health checks of both the mother and newborns
- Providing Safe Abortion Services
- Preventing, detecting, and effectively managing common lower RTI through the existing primary health care infrastructure

Child Health

3.1.130 Under the RCH Programme, newborn and child health services are implemented in the country with the aim of reducing neonatal, infant, and child mortality. In order to reduce these, a continuum of care is needed at the community as well as facility level. The Eleventh Five Year Plan goal is to reduce IMR to 28 per 1000 live births by 2012. State-specific goals have also been suggested (Annexure 3.1.6).

HOME BASED NEWBORN CARE (HBNC)

3.1.131 Efforts to improve home based care have proven successful at improving child survival. Home Based Newborn and Child Care is to be provided by a trained Community Health Worker (such as the ASHA) who guides and supports the mother, family, and TBA in the care of newborn, and attends the newborn at home if she is sick. The worker is supervised by a field person (ANM/LHV or a doctor) who visits the community once in 15 days. Community acceptance and coverage of such care has been quite good.

3.1.132 The GoI has recently approved the implementation of HBNC based on the Gadchiroli model (Box 3.1.13), where appreciable decline in IMR has been documented on the basis of work done by a VO called SEARCH. Gadchiroli has shown how ordinary women can do extraordinary things: a well-trained local woman can not only lower neonatal mortality but can also bring about attitudinal change. The women *Shishu Rakshaks* of Gadchiroli have managed to dispel many myths surrounding pregnancy and have been able to ensure better nutrition, care, immunization, and hygiene.

3.1.133 During the Eleventh Five Year Plan, ASHAs will be trained on identified aspects of newborn care during their training. This initiative will be initially implemented in the five high focus States (MP, UP, Orissa, Rajasthan, and Bihar). To supervise and provide onsite training and support to ASHAs, mentor-facilitators will be introduced for effective implementation. The national strategy during the Plan will be to introduce and make available high-quality HBNC services in all districts/areas with an IMR more than 45 per 1000 live births. Apart from performance incentive to ASHAs, an award will be given to ASHAs and village community if no mother–newborn or child death is reported in a year. For effective linkages, model Intensive Care Units will also be set up at the district level, particularly in States with poor health indicators, in order to make facility based curative newborn care available.

INTEGRATED MANAGEMENT OF NEONATAL AND CHILDHOOD ILLNESS (IMNCI)

3.1.134 IMNCI strategy encompasses a range of interventions to prevent and manage five major childhood illnesses, that is, Acute Respiratory Infections (ARI), Diarrhoea, Measles, Malaria, and Malnutrition and the major causes of neonatal mortality, which are prematurity and sepsis. It focuses on preventive, promotive, and curative aspects. The major components of this strategy are:

- Strengthening the skills of the health care workers
- Strengthening the health care infrastructure
- Involvement of the community

3.1.135 The first two components of the strategy are the facility based IMNCI and the third is the

Box 3.1.13
Home Based Newborn Care—Gadchiroli Model

Requirements

- Transparent selection of best motivated
- Rigorous training
- Intensive supervision
- Curative role for CHWs
- Performance-based remuneration

Interventions

- Health education of mothers and the community
- Attending home delivery with TBA
- Care of baby at birth
- Home visits and support to mother and baby up to 28 days
- Management of newborn sicknesses

Interventions Aimed at Prevention and Management of

- Birth asphyxia
- Sepsis/Pneumonia
- Low Birth Weight (LBW)/Preterm
- Breast feeding problems
- Hypothermia

Achievements

- NMR reduced by 51%
- IMR reduced by 47%
- High community acceptance and beneficiary preference to CHW as the source of newborn care at home (85%)

Lessons Derived

- CHWs could be trained to provide HBNC in villages and urban slums
- 85% mothers and newborns can be covered
- The various components of HBNC including the management of birth asphyxia in home deliveries and the diagnosis and treatment of newborn sepsis by using injectable gentamicin could be safely and effectively delivered by trained CHWs working under supervision

community based IMNCI. 104 districts all over the country have initiated implementation of IMNCI. During the Eleventh Five Year Plan, efforts will be made to implement the IMNCI programme coupled with home-based neonatal care throughout the country in a phased manner.

HBNC AND IMNCI: DIFFERENT BUT COMPLEMENTARY ROLES

3.1.136 In order to reduce infant and child mortality a continuum of care is needed at the community as well as facility level. Of the two main packages available for reducing child mortality, the HBNC operates at the community level and has a strong evidence of feasibility and reducing child mortality. It should be used to deliver care at home through ASHAs and ANMs. IMNCI training is primarily facility-based and has been shown to improve neonatal care. Hence the IMNCI should focus on improving newborn and child care in the district hospitals and CHCs. This will avoid duplication of efforts and, at the same time, provide continuum of care.

SKILLED CARE AT BIRTH

3.1.137 The underlying principle of effective care at birth is that wherever she is born whether at home or facility, she is provided clean care, warmth, resuscitation, and exclusive breastfeeding. She is weighed and examined, and if clinical needs are not manageable at the place of delivery, she is referred and managed at an appropriate facility. Programme for newborn care is relatively easy to implement in facilities because of the presence of doctors, nurses, ANM/LHV, and supporting environment.

3.1.138 It is also true that a large proportion of deliveries would continue to take place at home by the TBAs. Under NRHM, newborn care skills should also be imparted to TBAs in areas with high rate of home deliveries. For this they should be provided with delivery kits. There are many good practices all over the country related to low cost hygienic kits which can be taken on board and replicated, e.g. the one developed by Jan Swasthya Sahyog (JSS). The overall effort during the Eleventh Five Year Plan will be to promote childbirth by skilled attendants at home and in institutions, both in the public and private sector.

BREAST FEEDING PRACTICES

3.1.139 Exclusive breastfeeding for the first six months of life is the single most important child survival intervention. Successful breastfeeding also requires the initiation of breastfeeding within an hour after birth, and avoidance of prelacteals, supplementary water, or top milk. Continued breastfeeding for two years or more, with introduction of appropriate and adequate complementary feeding from the seventh month onwards, further improves child survival rates by a considerable percentage. According to NFHS-3, the proportion of exclusively breast fed infants at 6 months of age was only 46.3%. Only 23.4% of mothers initiated breastfeeding within the desired one hour after birth, as against the Tenth Plan goal of 50%. Therefore, the Eleventh Five Year Plan will concentrate on promoting optimal breastfeeding practices among women at home and in health facilities. Baby Friendly Hospital Initiative and Breastfeeding Partnership, two programmes involving all the key partners will be encouraged.

ARI, DIARRHOEA, AND VACCINE PREVENTABLE DISEASES

3.1.140 Research has shown that most of the cases of ARI are not severe; community health workers can effectively manage them and bring down IMR. Severe ARI cases require urgent referral to a facility for injectable antibiotic therapy and supportive care. Co-trimoxazole tablets are being provided at SCs and ANMs are being trained to treat children with the infection. During the Eleventh Five Year Plan, attempt will be made to eradicate polio from the country along with strengthening the routine immunization. Studies have shown that the entire context, strategy, and implementation of polio eradication activities need to be reanalysed. The option of injectable polio vaccine should also be kept open. Reduction will be done in the mortality associated with diarrhoea and ARI through HBNC and IMNCI.

3.1.141 During the Eleventh Five Year Plan, thus, IMNCI and HBNC will be rigorously implemented across the country. The major strategies will be:

- Essential new born care (home and facility based)
- Standard case management of diarrhoea and pneumonia
- Timely initiation of breastfeeding, exclusive breastfeeding for six months and continued breastfeeding with appropriate complementary feeding from the seventh month onwards
- Increased usage of ORS and strengthened immunization.

School Health

3.1.142 School Health Programme should aim at helping children in attaining optimal potential for growth in physical, mental, educational, and emotional development. The programme should provide health knowledge and improve the health of children. Its components will include school health services, health promoting school environment, and health education curriculum. In this area as well there are good practices all over the country that can be taken on board and replicated. Eleventh Five Year Plan will work on school going children's health. One innovative School Health Programme is under implementation, in PPP mode, in Udaipur district of Rajasthan. In view of the low cost versus achievements, it is a good case for replicating in other parts of the country. However, to make it comprehensive, preventive, and promotive components of school health care will have to be added to this programme. Some of the key features of the programme are given in Box 3.1.15.

Box 3.1.14
Strengthening Immunization

- Strengthening routine immunization programme
- Improving awareness through various channels of communication
- Involving community and CSO in routine immunization
- Achieving 100% coverage for the six vaccine preventable diseases
- Eradicating polio
- Eliminating neonatal tetanus
- Expanding the coverage of Hepatitis B vaccine

Adolescent Health

3.1.143 Adolescents in India represent nearly one-third of the population. The last two decades witnessed a rapid increase in their population. Some of the public health challenges for adolescents include pregnancy, excess risk of maternal and infant mortality, STI, RTI, and the rapidly rising incidence of HIV. The use of health services by adolescents is limited due to poor knowledge and lack of awareness. Pregnancy is associated with significantly higher obstetric risk in adolescent girls. Many of them suffer from malnutrition and anaemia. This combined with poor ANC leads not only to increased morbidity in the mother but also to high incidence of Low Birth Weight (LBW) and perinatal mortality. Poor child-rearing practices add to the morbidity and undernutrition in infants, thus perpetuating the inter-generational cycle of undernutrition and ill health. Thus, ill health during adolescence has profound implications for maternal and infant morbidity and mortality.

3.1.144 The urgent need for appropriate nutrition and health education for adolescents will be met by advocacy for delay in age at marriage and optimum health and nutrition interventions during pregnancy. Knowledge and skills will be given to health service delivery personnel catering to the adolescents' reproductive and sexual health needs.

3.1.145 During the Eleventh Five Year Plan, adolescent issues will be incorporated in all the RCH training programmes. Materials will be developed for communication and behavioural change. The existing services at PHCs and CHCs will be made adolescent friendly by providing special window for their needs.

Health Care for Older Persons

3.1.146 An area of growing importance and demanding attention is the health of older persons. It requires comprehensive care providing preventive, curative, and rehabilitative services. Unlike developed countries, India does not have a Geriatric Health Service as a component of health services. According to the 2001

Box 3.1.15
Innovative School Health Programme—Udaipur Model

- Target Group: 40000 students from 222 government/aided schools in Udaipur.
- Care: Screening, outpatient as well as inpatient, and also specialty care.
- Screening: Camps held in school, free dental kits, and ID card issued.
- Outpatient care: one room in selected 28 schools and mobile team.
- Inpatient: a ward (7 ICU and 12 general beds), redesigned/furnished with NGO in government hospital).
- Specialty care: Tie up with good private hospitals.
- 24×7 service: toll free number and ambulances.
- Human resources: 9 doctors, 12 paramedical, and 38 support staff.
- Cost: Check up Rs 4 lakh (borne by GoR and NGO @ 50:50), Cost of OP/IP facility Rs 25 lakh (by NGO), and recurring cost Rs 72 lakh (NGO, Nagar Parishad, and UIT @ 50:25:25). It amounts to 50 paise per child per day.
- Achievements: 17500 treated in OP, 150 treated in IP for different disease including serious/chronic and 4 cardiac cases operated.

Note: GoR = Government of Rajasthan, OP/IP = Outpatient/Inpatient, UIT = Urban Improvement Trust.

Census, there are 76.6 million people over the age of sixty, constituting about 7.4 % of the total population. Life expectancy has been increasing and the proportion of older persons in India will rise in the next few decades.

3.1.147 The health services need to be responsive to the special needs of older persons. Provision of specialty based clinics in secondary and tertiary care facilities would help. A counselling and medical care facility to look after health needs of older persons and an emergency facility to reach those in acute need and transport them to a hospital is needed. This will include acute care, long-term care, and community-based rehabilitation.

3.1.148 To improve the access to promotive, preventive, curative, and emergency health care among older persons, a range of services will be provided under the programme for health care of older persons. First, a home health service, which means home visits intended to detect health problems, and as a psychological support by health personnel sensitized on such issues. Second, a community-based health centre for them for educational and preventive activity. This will be integrated with the NRHM and an allocation made specifically for geriatric care. The ASHAs under the NRHM will be trained in geriatric care. Third, the outpatient medical service that serves as the base for home health service will be enhanced. Finally, an improved hospital-based support service focused on their health care needs will be established. Specific provisions will also be made for widows and a few centres on geriatric health especially focused on elderly women.

Box 3.1.16
Older Persons' Health

- Prevalence and incidence of diseases as well as hospitalization rates are much higher in older people than the total population.
- 8% of older Indians are confined to their home or bed (immobile)
- Women are more frequently afflicted with immobility
- Many older people take ill health in their stride as a part of 'usual/normal ageing'.
- Self perceived health status is an important indicator of health service utilization and compliance to treatment interventions.

3.1.149 During the Eleventh Five Year Plan, thus, following actions will be taken:

- Providing comprehensive health care to the older persons
- Training health professionals in Geriatrics, including supportive care and rehabilitation
- Developing scientific solutions to specific health problems by research in Geriatrics and Gerontology
- Developing two National Institutes for Research in Ageing and Health, one in the North and the other in South

Voluntary Fertility Regulation

3.1.150 The percentage of married women using contraception has increased. Yet the gender imbalance in the family planning programme is evident by the fact that despite being the most invasive and tedious contraceptive intervention, female sterilization remains the most common method of family planning. Men are not being addressed as responsible partners and the use of condoms or male sterilization remains very low. There are also inter-State differences in the magnitude of unmet need for contraception (Figure 3.1.14).

3.1.151 Even meeting half of the unmet need could lead to an appreciable decline in the birth rate. ANMs and ASHAs will identify the couples with unmet need in their area, and address their concerns. During the Eleventh Five Year Plan, all strategies adopted under RCH programme will be continued with a greater focus in areas of high unmet need.

3.1.152 The Eleventh Five Year Plan goal is to achieve a reduction of TFR to 2.1 by 2012. State specific goals have also been suggested (Annexure 3.1.7). The Plan will ensure that all issues of demographic change, the population policies, and programmes to achieve population stabilization are addressed without violating the peoples' rights of decision making and choices. Most importantly this should be done without adversely affecting the sex ratio.

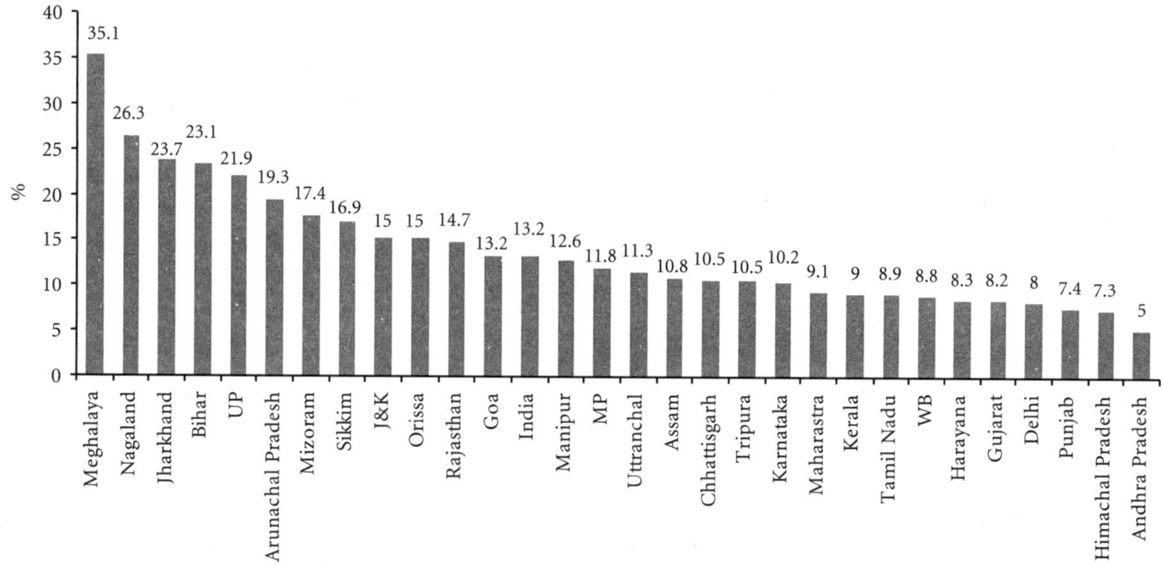

Source: NFHS-3, IIPS (2005–06).

FIGURE 3.1.14: Unmet Need for Family Planning (currently married women, age 15–49)

INVOLVEMENT OF CIVIL SOCIETY AND NGOS

3.1.153 As per the NFHS data, less than 10% of rural women report that they are visited by the ANMs during a year. On the other hand, there is a large pool of formally or informally qualified Rural Health Practitioners (RHPs) who meet the day-to-day health care needs of people in 6 lakh villages, 24×7. In the Eleventh Five Year Plan, it is proposed to enlist their services for many tasks including the delivery of non-clinical methods of contraception and referring the clinical cases to the PHCs or FRUs. The successful experiment by a VO, *Janani*, in Bihar may be studied and replicated.

3.1.154 There is an urgent need to increase the involvement of CSO, VOs, and NGOs including private sector in the delivery of family planning services, especially in areas where the public sector is weak. *Jansankhya Sthirata Kosh* (JSK) (National Population Stabilization Fund) is a registered society of the MoHFW to accelerate population stabilization efforts. JSK is expected to work in close cooperation with the government, private, and voluntary sectors to promote small and healthy families. State governments, district officials, and other organizations will be encouraged to suggest innovations in enhancing family planning services which can be supported by JSK on a pilot scale. Expertise of the Population Foundation of India will be sought to scale up good pilots in the country. Centres of excellence (such as one in Tamil Nadu—Box 3.1.18) can also play a vital role.

3.1.155 During the Eleventh Five Year Plan greater focus will be on the following for voluntary fertility reduction:

Box 3.1.17
Janani—Using RHPs

An NGO, Janani, set up a network of more than 21000 Titli (Butterfly) centres and more than 500 Surya (Sun) clinics in the States of Bihar, Jharkhand, and MP. Surya clinics are referral clinics run in towns by formally qualified, State-registered doctors. Titli centres are situated in villages and run by RHPs who have been trained to provide family planning counselling and sell non-clinical contraceptives. Since RHPs are males, they work with a Woman Health Partner who is generally a member of their family (in most cases, wife). RHPs and their female counterparts hold a two-day training programme on family planning counselling. Female partners help reach out to the village women who are hesitant to approach male health providers on reproductive health matters.

Box 3.1.18
Facilitating Action by Private Sector

Tamil Nadu Government established a Centre of Excellence, 'Sterilization and Recanalization Training-cum-Service Centre' at Kilpauk Medical College, Chennai, in 1987 with core officers—a female gynaecologist and a male urologist. It conducts workshops and trains doctors in standard procedures of male and female sterilizations. The centre also provides services by conducting sterilization and recanalization operations for males and females.

In Tamil Nadu, private sector participation is strengthened to improve family welfare programmes in the State. Private nursing homes have been approved to provide family welfare services in the State. Nearly 25% of the sterilizations are performed by voluntary and approved private institutions. Contraceptive stocks are freely supplied to these institutions to provide better services to needy couples to improve spacing between births.

- Expanding the basket of contraceptive choices
- Improving social marketing
- Increasing male involvement
- Enhancing role of mass media for behavioural change
- Disseminating through satisfied users

Human Resources for Health

3.1.156 Given the present scarcity of human resources, the next decade will posit newer opportunities and challenges for medical and health education. The country has to train an adequate number of health professionals with appropriate knowledge, skill, and attitude to meet the future health care needs of the people and the increasing disease burden. Additionally, there is the opportunity for India to become an important destination for health care services. Given the rising demand and growing need for expanding health services, systematic studies need to be launched for estimating requirements. In the Eleventh Five Year Plan, efforts will be made to develop an effective human resource MIS by involving concerned Ministries, Professional Councils, Technical Councils, UGC, Central and State Universities, Public Health Institutions, and knowledgeable individuals from Civil Society.

3.1.157 NCMH (2005) has recommended additional funding for establishment of new medical, nursing, and other institutions, training of village level functionaries, and in-service training of health personnel. The resource requirements for development of human resources for health during the Eleventh Five Year Plan will be shared by the Centre and the States. The NRHM will also contribute. Efforts will be made to mobilize additional resources through suitable partnership arrangements with the private sector and also through other available options.

3.1.158 Measures will be taken during the Eleventh Five Year Plan period to solve the problem of shortage of basic education infrastructure and human resources. The role and functions of apex bodies like MCI need to be reviewed. The following strategies will be accorded priority during the Plan:

- Ensure availability of medical professionals in rural areas on a permanent basis, posting of doctors with adequate monetary as well as non-monetary incentives, such as suitable accommodation, class I status, preferential school admissions for children of doctors living in remote areas, transfer or posting of choice after a stipulated length of stay and training opportunities.
- States to expand the pool of medical practitioners including a cadre of Licentiate Medical Practitioners and practitioners of Indian Systems of Medicine and Homeopathy (AYUSH).
- Increase age of retirement of doctors (all Central and State Government including Defence, Railways, etc.) to 62 years. States will be encouraged to retain public health doctors on contract basis for further period of three years till the age of 65 years, especially in the notified hardship areas.
- A series of one-year duration Certificate Courses for MBBS graduates will be launched in deficit disciplines like public health, anaesthesia, psychiatry, geriatric care, and oncology. The private sector will also be encouraged to participate in this venture.

Box 3.1.19
Human Resources for Health

Issues

- Growing shortage of all key cadre in rural areas—Doctor, Paramedicals, ANMs, Nurses, Lab Technicians, and OT Assistants.
- Problems of absenteeism and irregular staff attendance.
- Non-availability of drugs and diagnostic tests at health facility leading to demotivation of doctors.
- No motivation or will to serve in rural areas.
- Weak or non-existent accountability framework leading to powerlessness of local communities and Panchayat vis-à-vis the health system functionaries.
- Non-transparent transfer and posting policy leading to demoralization.
- Inadequate systems of incentive for all cadres especially in difficult area postings.
- Lack of career progress leading to demotivation and corruption.
- Lack of standard protocols to promote quality affordable care and full utilization of human resources.

Possible Solutions

- State-specific human resource management policy and transparency in management of health cadres.
- Training and utilization of locally available paramedics, RMPs, and VHWs to meet the gaps in rural areas. Allow them to prescribe basic medication.
- Reintroducing Licentiate course in Medicine
- Incentives for difficult areas and system for career progression.
- Accountability to local communities and Panchayats.
- Devolution of power and functions to local health care institutions—provide resources and flexibility to ensure service guarantee.
- Resources, flexibility, and powers to ensure that IPHS are achieved.
- Adequate staff nurses and a minimum OPD attendance and service provision
- Improved and assured tele-linkages.

- Efforts of the National Board of Examinations (NBE) will be enhanced for overcoming the shortage of specialists and also to improve the quality of training.
- Councils to create a scientific data bank of health professionals.
- Re-registration of all medical and dental practitioners including specialists after every five years till they are practising or serving.
- New medical, nursing, and dental colleges will be established in the underserved areas.
- As recommended by the NCMH (2005), priority will be given to reducing the existing inequality by establishing 60 medical colleges in deficit States (UP, Rajasthan, MP, Orissa, Chhattisgarh, etc.) and 225 new nursing colleges in underserved areas. PPP will be used to bridge this gap.
- Experiences of University of Health Sciences set up in various States during the Tenth Plan, against medical colleges that are part of the general universities to be evaluated before more such universities are set up during the Eleventh Five Year Plan.
- Implementation of recommendations of OSC for development of Human Resources for health.
- Equip medical graduates with the skills essential for providing broad-based community health care.
- Stem the high rate of attrition of academics; teaching in professional colleges to be made attractive. Need to enhance the salary structure and provide an innovative programme of incentives. Private OPDs in the medical colleges to be considered as one such incentive.
- RMPs, after training, can contribute towards activities under NRHM. Few suggested roles have been listed in Box 3.1.20.

Public Health Education

3.1.159 Currently several institutions are engaged in imparting public health and related education in the country. Various medical organizations are in the process of starting new Public Health Courses at the Masters level, namely Indian Council of Medical Research (ICMR), AIIMS, PGIMER, etc. The supply position is bound to improve after institutions of Public Health under Public Health Foundation of India (PHFI) and new Public Health Schools are set up within the existing Medical Institutions.

3.1.160 During the Eleventh Five Year Plan, benefits of knowledge and skills of modern Public Health will be made available at all levels. For the development of public health, multiple independent centres with a common regulatory body will be a suitable approach. Some of these centres could be located in universities of health sciences and some with the multidisciplinary universities. This would enable greater input from different disciplines to enrich the subject. During the Plan, therefore, efforts will be made to set up new public health schools within the existing medical colleges. MBA Programmes specially tailored for the health care and MD (Hospital Administration)/Diplomate National Board (Hospital and Health Administration)/ MD (Community Health Administration)/Masters (Hospital Administration) Programmes will be encouraged.

Health Systems and Bio-Medical Research

3.1.161 With the development and use of sophisticated tools of modern biology, a better understanding of complex interplay between the host, agent, and environment is emerging. This is resulting in the generation of new knowledge. This scientific knowledge is to be used to develop drugs, diagnostics, devices, and vaccines that should find a place in the health systems of the country. A vibrant inter-phase between the research community, the industry, and the health systems is the only way to facilitate this. It is not only the technological advances in public health and medicine that influence health of the population. The epidemiology of disease extends beyond biology. A sociological perspective is important to understand the occurrence, persistence, and cure of a disease. The diseases are not rooted in biological causes alone, but are multifactorial. This calls for an inter-disciplinary approach to health research.

3.1.162 The Eleventh Five Year Plan, therefore, will mark a departure in orientation to research in health. No amount of pure bio-medical research will be able to find solutions to health issues unless it addresses upfront the social determinants of health. While health research has made appreciable progress, there remains an unacceptable lag time in translating the research outcomes into tangible health products or in application of the knowledge generated through research. Thus, the task is how best to mobilize research to bridge the gap between what is known and what is done—the 'know-do' gap. Equally important is to ensure that the products of health research reach and are used for and by the people who need it most. Health research during the Eleventh Five Year Plan will be directed to provide ways and means of bringing about equity and improving access to health technologies.

3.1.163 With a view to re-organize the medical research establishments in the country in order to keep

Box 3.1.20
Role of RMPs as Sahabhaagis in NRHM

- Running social awareness programmes in schools to cover topics like: ill effects of tobacco and alcohol, advantages of good sanitation, hygiene, nutrition, and safe drinking water
- Running free camps for: vision tests, health check-ups, immunization
- Training rural people in association with SHGs about: Hygiene, Sanitation, Nutrition, Safe drinking water, Needs of pregnant women, Protection against unsafe sex, awareness about locally prevalent communicable and non communicable diseases
- Providing non clinical contraceptives and referring for clinical cases
- Acting as drug distribution depots and fever treatment centres
- Supervising spray activities, water treatment, sanitary landfill, and sanitary latrines
- Providing emergency primary health services and referrals

abreast with the dynamic international health research environment and to address the current and future health challenges, the Central Government is creating a new Department of Health Research under the MoHFW. The newly created Department will deal with promotion and co-ordination of basic, applied, and clinical research including clinical trials and operations research in areas related to medical, health, biomedical and medical profession, and education through development of infrastructure, human resources, and skills in the cutting edge areas and management of related information thereto; promote and provide guidance on research governance issues including ethical issues in medical and health research; inter-sectoral coordination and promotion of PPP in medical, biomedical, and health research areas; advanced training in research areas concerning medicine and health including grant of fellowship for such training in India and abroad; international co-operation in medical and health research including work related to international conferences in related areas in India and abroad; technical support for dealing with epidemics and natural calamities; investigation of outbreaks due to new and exotic agents and development of tools for prevention; matters relating to scientific societies and associations, charitable and religious endowments in medicine and health research areas; coordination between organizations and institutions under the Central and State Governments in areas related to the subjects entrusted to the Department and for promotion of special studies in medicine and health, and ICMR.

3.1.164 The following priority areas for the health system research have been identified for the Eleventh Five Year Plan:

- Impact of PPPs in health on the public health services, State finances, and whether PPPs really bring about equity in health access.
- Studies on modalities and impact of health insurance.
- Issues of health care access in urban areas, health problems of urban poor, the migrants, homeless, street, and working children.
- Health care in situations of violence and conflict.
- Gender issues in disease prevalence, access to health care, and education.
- Studies on the innovation, diffusion, use, and misuse of medical technologies, research on their relevance or appropriateness, misuse and irrational use, the additional financial burden on the users due to misuse. Such studies should cover prescription practices to the new medical technologies such as genetics, assisted reproduction, life prolonging technologies, stem cell research, and organ donation and transplantation.
- Medical audit to establish various ways of improving health care service delivery at different levels.
- Nursing research to be undertaken by the nursing as well as social science and bioethics institutions in India.
- Audit of research, that is, whether research is justified and relevant.

3.1.165 During the Plan, clinical and operational research in both the modern and AYUSH systems will continue. The major thrust in Allopathy as well as AYUSH will be given to the following areas:

- Improving diagnosis, treatment delivery, and development of new tools for the diagnosis and treatment
- Integrating disease control programmes within primary health care system
- Cost effectiveness analysis of different regimen for prevention and treatment of diseases
- Quality of lab-diagnosis, lab related factors, periodic training, adequacy of reagents, kits and good microscopy
- Delayed diagnosis: community factors, surveillance factors, lab factors, and health system factors
- Upgradation of drug delivery system: surveillance mechanisms
- Research on poor drug compliance rate: community, social, educational, ethnic, cultural, and health system factors
- Research on social determinants of health, health care seeking, and the epidemiological web

3.1.166 The institutions and organizations like ICMR involved in research, should be committed to an agenda that recognizes that future improvements in health and well-being will depend on research that does the following:

- Increases understanding of both the molecular and biological mechanisms underlying diseases as well as the psychosocial, economic, and environmental determinants of health
- Develops new vaccines, diagnostic tools, and cost effective therapies
- Deepens understanding of underlying social and behavioural causes of injuries and lifestyle diseases
- Links health with S&T, engineering, and related disciplines
- Promotes healthy living and reduces risk behaviours

From Vertical to Horizontal: Affecting Integration

3.1.167 The Eleventh Five Year Plan will not allow any vertical structures to be created below district level under different programmes. The existing programmes will be integrated horizontally at the district level, as the emphasis during the Plan would be system-centric rather than disease centric. Already under NRHM, some programmes like the ones dealing with vector-borne diseases, tuberculosis, leprosy, blindness, and iodine deficiency disorders (IDD) have been integrated under a single District Health Society. Other programmes and activities described below will also be brought under one umbrella.

NATIONAL AIDS CONTROL PROGRAMME (NACP)

3.1.168 During the Eleventh Five Year Plan, the NACP has set the goal to halt and reverse the epidemic in India over the next five years by integrating programmes for prevention, care, support, and treatment and also addressing the human rights issues specific to people living with HIV/AIDS (PLWHA). The specific objectives are to reduce new infections by 60% in high prevalence States so as to obtain reversal of the epidemic and by 40% in the vulnerable States so as to stabilize the epidemic.

3.1.169 In order to achieve the objectives, the following strategies will be adopted:

- Preventing new infections in high risk groups and general population through:
  - Saturation of coverage of high risk groups with targeted interventions.
  - Scaled up interventions in the general population.
- Increasing the proportion of PLWHA who receive care, support, and treatment.
- Strengthening the infrastructure, system, and human resource in prevention, care, support, and treatment programmes at the district and national levels.
- Enacting and enforcing national legislation prohibiting discrimination against PLWHA and their families in health facilities, schools, places of employment, and other institutions.
- Including mechanisms for victims and their guardians to lodge complaints and receive quick redressal.
- Ensuring that women and children living with HIV/AIDS receive medical care, including antiretroviral (ARV) treatment and use all possible means to remove barriers to their receiving care.
- Strengthening a nation-wide strategic information management system.
- Advancing R&D of vaccines suitable for the strains of HIV prevalent in India.

NATIONAL CANCER CONTROL PROGRAMME (NCCP)

3.1.170 During the Tenth Five Year Plan, a taskforce comprising experts from across the country was constituted. Based on recommendations from the national taskforce a comprehensive NCCP will be implemented during the Plan. The main activities during the Plan will be:

- Establishing new Regional Cancer Centres
- Upgradation of the existing Regional Cancer Centres based on their performance and linkages with other cancer organizations in the region.
- Creating skilled human resources for quality cancer care services
- Training health care providers for early detection of cancers at primary and secondary level
- Increasing accessibility and availability of cancer care services
- Providing behavioural change communication along with provision of cost effective screening techniques and early detection services at the door step of community

- Propagating self-screening of common cancers (oral, breast)
- Upgrading Oncology Wings in government medical colleges
- Creating and upgrading Cancer detection and Surgical and Medical Treatment facilities in District Hospitals/Charitable/NGO/Private Hospitals
- Promoting research on effective strategies of prevention, community-based screening, early diagnosis, environmental, and behavioural factors associated with cancers and development of cost effective vaccines
- Creating Palliative Care and Rehabilitation Centres
- Monitoring, Evaluation, and Surveillance

NATIONAL PROGRAMME FOR PREVENTION AND CONTROL OF DIABETES, CVDs, AND STROKE

3.1.171 Common risk factors for both CVD and diabetes are unhealthy diet, physical inactivity, and obesity. There is evidence-based information that NCDs are preventable through integrated and comprehensive interventions. Cost-effective interventions exist and have worked in many countries. The most successful ones have employed a range of population wide approaches combined with interventions for the individuals. Thus, the programme will aim to prevent and control common NCDs risk factors through an integrated approach and to reduce premature morbidity and mortality from diabetes, CVD, and stroke. Up scaling based on pilot results will be done during the Eleventh Five Year Plan.

3.1.172 During the Plan, the objectives of the programme will be:

- Primary prevention of major NCDs through health promotion
- Surveillance of NCDs and their risk factors in the population
- Capacity enhancement of health professionals and health systems for diagnosis and appropriate management of NCDs and their risk factors
- Reduction of risk factors in the population
- Establishment of National guidelines for management of NCDs
- Development of strategies and policies for prevention by intersectoral coordination
- Community empowerment for prevention of NCDs

NATIONAL MENTAL HEALTH PROGRAMME (NMHP)

3.1.173 A multipronged strategy to raise awareness about issues of mental health and persons with mental illness with the objective of providing accessible and affordable treatment, removing ignorance, stigma, and shame attached to it and to facilitate inclusion and acceptance for the mentally ill in our society will be the basis of the NMHP. Its main objective will be to provide basic mental health services to the community and to integrate these with the NRHM. The programme envisages a community and more specifically family-based approach to the problem.

3.1.174 The Plan will strengthen District Mental Health Programme (DMHP) and enhance its visibility at grass root level by promoting greater family and community participation and creating para professionals equipped to address the mental health needs of the community from within. It will fill up human resource gap in the field of psychiatry, psychology, psychiatric social work, and DMHP. The plan will strive to incorporate mental health modules into the existing training of health personnel. It will also harness NGOs' and CSOs' help in this endeavour, especially family care of persons with mental illness, and focus on preventive and restorative components of Mental Health. The Eleventh Five Year Plan, recognizing the importance of mental health care, will provide counselling, medical services, and establish help lines for people affected by calamities, riots, violence (including domestic), and other traumas. To achieve these, a greater outlay will be allocated to mental health.

3.1.175 During the Eleventh Five Year Plan, the Re-strategized NMHP will be implemented all over the country with the following objectives:

- To recognize mental illnesses at par with other illnesses and extending the scope of medical insurance and other benefits to individuals suffering with them
- To have a user friendly drug policy such that the psychotropic drugs are declared as Essential drugs

- To give greater emphasis to psychotherapeutic and a rights based model of dealing with mental health related issues
- To include psychiatry and psychology, and psychiatric social work modules in the training of all health care giving professionals
- To empower the primary care doctor and support staff to be able to offer psychiatric and psychological care to patients at PHCs besides educating family carers on core aspects of the illness.
- To improve public awareness and facilitate family-carer participation by empowering members of the family and community in psychological interventions.
- To provide greater emphasis on public private participation in the delivery of mental health services.
- To upgrade psychiatry departments of all medical colleges to enhance better training opportunities
- To improve and integrate mental hospitals with the whole of health delivery infrastructure that offer mental health services thus lifting the stigma attached
- To provide after care and lifelong support to chronic cases.

INJURIES AND TRAUMA

3.1.176 Data from Survey of Causes of Death and Medical Certification of Causes of Deaths reveals that 10–11% of total deaths in India were due to injuries. It is estimated that nearly 850000 persons die due to direct injury related causes including road traffic injuries every year in India, with 17 million hospitalizations and 50 million requiring hospital care for minor injuries. Most of the hospitals do not have integrated facilities for treatment of trauma victims and the casualty services are generally ill equipped, poorly managed, and over worked. A scheme to upgrade and strengthen emergency care in State hospitals located on national highways has been under implementation with a view to provide treatment to road accident victims in hospitals as near the site of accident as possible.

3.1.177 During the Eleventh Five Year Plan, the emphasis will also be given for development of a comprehensive trauma care system covering the entire nation with State wide emergency medical service and trauma care The components will include provision of equipment, communication system, training and provision of human resources, registry and surveillance. Eventually the plan is to start a National Programme for Medical Emergencies Response. The strategy during the Eleventh Five Year Plan will be:

- To identify health care facilities along highways and upgrade them to specific levels of trauma care
- To establish a life support ambulance system
- To plug gaps in human resource training and availability for trauma care
- To establish communication linkages between various levels of health care
- To assist the States in developing and managing an appropriate trauma referral system
- To develop, implement, and maintain State-wise and nation wide trauma registry as an integral part of e-Health.

DISABILITY AND MEDICAL REHABILITATION

3.1.178 With the ongoing health, demographic, and socio-economic transitions, the Disability Profile is changing, with an alarming rise in the number of people suffering from chronic disorders and associated morbidity and disability. According to census (2001), there were 2.19 crore persons with visual, hearing, speech, locomotor, and mental disabilities in India. Of the disabled population, locomotor disabled constitute 28%, speech and hearing 13%, visual 49%, and mental 10%. Population over 60 years of age has disabilities affecting multiple organs.

3.1.179 The Eleventh Five Year Plan aims at building capacity in Medical Colleges and District Hospitals to train adequate human resources required for medical rehabilitation programme at all three levels of Health Care Delivery System. Towards this end the following steps are planned:

- To upgrade and develop two Physical Medicine and Rehabilitation (PMR) departments in the country to act as Model Centres
- To set up PMR Departments in 30 Medical Colleges/Teaching Institutions (at least one in each State) and each such department to adopt districts, CHCs,

and PHCs for developing medical rehabilitation services
- To train medical and rehabilitation professionals in adequate number for providing secondary and tertiary level rehabilitation services
- To introduce training programme on Disability Prevention, Detection, and Early Intervention at diploma, undergraduate, and postgraduate level
- To provide Rehabilitation Services in Medical Hospitals and evolve strategy of care in the domiciliary and community set up.

PREVENTION AND CONTROL OF DEAFNESS

3.1.180 As per WHO estimates, in India, there are 63 million hearing impaired, with an estimated prevalence as 6.3%. A larger percentage of our population suffers from milder degrees of hearing impairment, adversely affecting productivity, both physical and economic. The objectives in the Eleventh Five Year Plan will be to prevent avoidable hearing loss; identify, diagnose, and treat conditions responsible for hearing impairment; and medically rehabilitate all hearing impaired.

3.1.181 The strategies during the Eleventh Five Year Plan will be:

- Strengthening service delivery including rehabilitation
- Developing human resources for ear care
- Promoting outreach activities and public awareness using innovative IEC strategies
- Developing institutional capacity of District Hospitals/CHCs/PHCs for ear care services

OCCUPATIONAL HEALTH

3.1.182 Exposure to chemicals, biological agents, physical factors and adverse ergonomic conditions, allergens, safety risks, and psychological factors often afflict working population of all ages. People also suffer from injuries, hearing loss, respiratory, musculoskeletal, cardiovascular, reproductive, neurotoxic, dermatological, and psychological effects. Such risks are often preventable. The illness resulting from such exposures is not identified properly due to lack of adequate expertise. The work up of the cases by physicians lacking skills to identify such illness leads to unnecessary use and waste of scarce medical resources as well as their own time. Freedom from occupational illness is essential in today's competitive world where workers' productivity is an important determinant of growth and development.

3.1.183 The objectives of occupational health initiative during the Eleventh Five Year Plan will be to promote and maintain highest degree of physical, mental, and social well-being of workers in all occupations; identify and prevent occupational risks of old as well as newer technologies such as Information and Nano technology; build capacity for prevention, that is, early identification of occupational illness; create an occupational health cell under NRHM in each district headquarter, well-equipped to be able to promote primary, secondary, as well as tertiary prevention; and establish occupational health services in agriculture, health and other key sectors for placement of workers in suitable work and propagating adaptation of work to humans.

3.1.184 During the Eleventh Five Year Plan, following strategies will be implemented to reduce occupational health problems:

- Creating awareness among policymakers on the cost of occupational ill health including injuries
- Ensuring use of technologies that are safe and free from risks to health of the workers
- Sensitizing employers as well as workers' organizations for their right to safety and the implication of injuries in their lives
- Instituting legislation and ensuring proper enforcement for prevention and control of occupational ill health and compensating those who suffer intractable illness due to work
- Building a national data base of occupational illness and injuries
- Monitoring and evaluating programmes and policies related to pollution prevention and control
- Establishing surveillance and research on occupational injuries and building capacity in health sector to be able to participate in preventing work related illness and injuries
- Enforcing safety regulations and standards
- Introducing no-fault insurance schemes for all workers in the formal and informal sectors

BLOOD AND BLOOD PRODUCTS

3.1.185 A well-organized Blood Transfusion Service is a vital component of any health care delivery system. An integrated strategy for Blood Safety is required for elimination of transfusion transmitted infections and for provision of safe and adequate blood transfusion services to the people.

3.1.186 During the Eleventh Five Year Plan, the programme for Blood and Blood Products to be initiated, will have following objectives:

- To reiterate firmly the government commitment to provide safe and adequate quantity of blood, blood components, and blood products.
- To make available adequate resources to develop and reorganize the blood transfusion services in the entire country.
- To make latest technology available for operating the blood transfusion services and ensure its functioning in an updated manner.
- To launch extensive awareness programmes for donor information, education, motivation, recruitment, and retention in order to ensure adequate availability of safe blood.
- To encourage appropriate clinical use of blood and blood products.
- To encourage R&D in the field of Transfusion Medicine and related technology.
- To take adequate regulatory and legislative steps for ME of blood transfusion services and to take steps to eliminate profiteering in blood banks.

Pilot Projects

3.1.187 During the Eleventh Five Year Plan, a few pilot projects would be taken up that will be eventually, depending on the success and experience gained, upscaled and most put under NRHM/NUHM. These relate to:

- Sports Medicine
- Deafness
- Leptospirosis Control
- Control of Human Rabies
- Organ Transplant
- Oral Health
- Fluorosis
- Disability and Medical Rehabilitation

National Centre for Disease Control (NCDC)

3.1.188 It has been planned to strengthen the National Institute of Communicable Diseases (NICD) as the NCDC to fulfil its role as an apex institute in the country. The NCDC will have two main divisions under its head. One division will look after communicable diseases while the other will look after coordination of non-communicable disease activities. Budgetary provisions have been made for this.

Health Financing

FINANCING HEALTH SERVICES

3.1.189 The existing level of government expenditure on health in India is about 1%, which is unacceptably low. Effort will be made to increase the total expenditure at the Centre and the States to at least 2% of GDP by the end of the Eleventh Five Year Plan. This will be accompanied by innovative health financing mechanisms (Box 3.1.21). The providers in public health system are not given any incentive, which affect the quality, efficiency, and drives them to greener pastures in the private sector. Therefore, incentives that link payment to performance will be introduced in the public health system.

3.1.190 The Eleventh Five Year Plan will experiment with different systems of PPPs, of which examples already exist. The State Governments may have an entitlement system for pregnant women to have professionally supervised deliveries. If properly implemented, it will empower them to exercise choice, as well as create competition in the health service sector. Contracting out well-specified and delimited projects such as immunization may also help increase accountability.

3.1.191 The problems of indebtedness due to sickness will be handled by sensitively devised and carefully administered health insurance. CBHI is a promising idea. Existing experiences in different States show that well-managed prepayment systems with risk pooling could be effective in protecting people from impoverishment. CBHI initiatives based on some individual contribution to the premium, along with a government subsidy, will be supported as they would improve the health care quality and expand interventions as per need of the people. In the Eleventh Five Year Plan we will consider approaches such as comprehensive risk pooling packages through the public system and through accredited private providers. This is an area where many experiments need to be encouraged to discover what can work best for people.

HEALTH SPENDING

3.1.192 Health spending in India is estimated to be in the range of 4.5–6% of GDP. The results from the National Health Account (NHA) for the year 2001–02 (Figure 3.1.15) showed that total health expenditure in the country was Rs 105734 crore, accounting for 4.6% of its GDP. Out of this, public health expenditure constituted Rs 21439 crore (0.94%), private health expenditure constituted Rs 81810 crore (3.58%) and external support 2485 crore (0.11%).

3.1.193 Of the private health expenditure during 2001–02, households' out-of-pocket health expenditure was Rs 76094 crore, which accounts for 72% of the total health expenditure incurred in India. This includes out-of-pocket payments borne by the households for treating illness among any member in the household and also insurance premium contributed by individuals for enrolling themselves or family members in health insurance schemes. The data shows that a majority of expenditure (87.7%) goes towards curative care.

3.1.194 Studies have shown that the poor and other disadvantaged groups in both rural and urban areas spent a higher proportion of their income on health care than those who are better-off. The burden of treatment is high on them when seeking inpatient care (NSSO 60th Round). Very often they have to borrow at very high interest to meet both medical and other household consumption needs. The Eleventh Five Year Plan will explore mechanisms for providing universal coverage of population for meeting the cost of hospitalization, particularly for those who cannot afford it. It will provide public-sector financed universal health insurance, for which private and public-sector provider organizations can compete.

TREND IN HEALTH FINANCING BY THE CENTRE AND STATES

3.1.195 The financial allocation for the health sector over the past decade indicates that the public expen-

Box 3.1.21
Some Innovative Financing Mechanisms

Kerala:	In Kozhikode, risk pools constituted around professionals or occupational groups, SHGs or micro credit groups, weavers, fishermen, farmers, agricultural labourers, and other informal groups. Almost 90% of the population is covered under some form of network or the other.
Uttar Pradesh:	Voucher scheme for RCH services piloted in seven blocks of Agra for BPL population. The scheme was launched in March 2007 and funded by State Innovations in Family Planning Services Agency.
Jharkhand:	In order to promote institutional delivery and routine immunization, a voucher scheme was introduced in December 2005 in all 22 districts. Vouchers are issued to BPL pregnant women at the time registration of pregnancy. She is entitled to have the delivery at any government facility or at accredited private health providers.
Haryana:	Vikalp—an innovative approach to financing urban primary health care for the poor through a combination of PPPs and risk pooling using capitation fees for a package of primary health care services with the State Health Department and private providers.
Karnataka:	Yeshasvini Co-operative Health Care Scheme is a health insurance scheme targeted to benefit the poor. The scheme was initiated by Narayana Hrudayalaya, a super-specialty heart-hospital in Bangalore and by the Department of Co-operatives of the Government of Karnataka. All farmers who have been members of a cooperative society for at least a year are eligible to participate, regardless of their medical histories. The scheme provides coverage for all major surgeries.

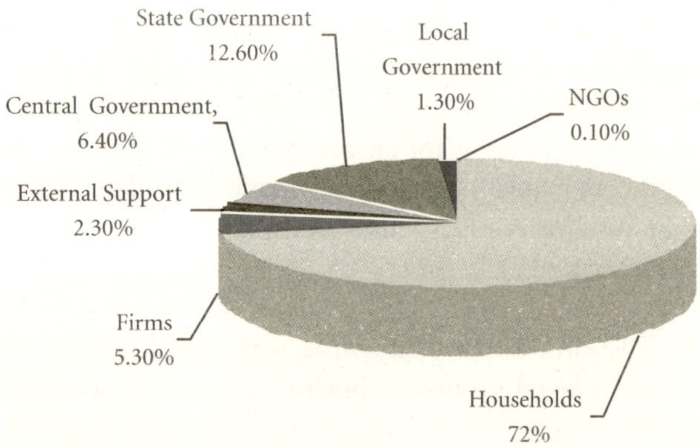

Source: NHA Cell, MoHFW, GoI (2005).

FIGURE: 3.1.15: Source of Health Care Financing in India, 2001–02

ditures on health (through the Central and State Governments), as a percentage of total government expenditure, have declined from 3.12% in 1992–93 to 2.99% in 2003–04. Similarly, the combined expenditure on health as a percentage of GDP has also marginally declined from 1.01% of GDP in 1992–93 to 0.99% in 2003–04. In nominal terms, the per capita public health expenditure increased from Rs 89 in 1993–94 to Rs 214 in 2003–04, which in real terms is Rs 122 (Figure 3.1.16).

3.1.196 Health care is financed primarily by State Governments, and State allocations on health are usually affected by any fiscal stress they encounter. Besides chronic under funding, the sector has been plagued with instances of inefficiencies at several levels resulting in waste, duplication, and sub optimal use of scarce resources. All these factors combined have had an adverse impact on the public health sector's ability to provide health care services to the people.

3.1.197 There was also a gradual decline in the proportion of funds released to States by Central Government when the States were themselves under fiscal stress. This resulted in sharp reduction in capital investment in public hospitals, low priority to preventive and promotive care, and inefficiencies in allocations under national health programmes. The financing system is equally dysfunctional as funds are released in five-year cycles, divided under different and complex budget heads—revenue, capital, etc., providing for little flexibility to respond to any health emergency. To address these issues, government has initiated several interventions under the NRHM such as District Health Action Plan, National Health Accounting systems, management capacity at all levels, improved financial management, and close monitoring.

3.1.198 It is estimated that in order to meet the target expenditure level, total Plan expenditure will need to grow at 29.7 % annually during the first three years of the Eleventh Five Year Plan, which breaks down to 30.2 % for the Centre and 29.2 % for the States. As a result, total health expenditure of the Centre and States, respectively, will rise to 0.55% of GDP and 0.85% of GDP in 2009–10. In the last two years of the Plan, total Plan expenditure will need to rise at about 48% annually. This will result in a total health expenditure of 0.87% of GDP by the Centre and 1.13% by States in 2011–12. Therefore, during the Eleventh Five Year Plan, while the Central Government makes every effort to augment resources for health, State Governments will be persuaded to assign at least 7–8% of State expenditures towards health care.

3.1.199 During the Plan, the objective of every State will be to increase competition among providers, create options for consumers, and ensure oversight through elected local bodies and Panchayats. State governments will also focus on integrating public health programmes with other public health interventions like drinking water, sanitation, nutrition, primary education, roads, and connectivity. State governments will be persuaded to allocate more resources for these sectors through better fiscal management and reprioritization.

MONITORING OUTCOMES VERSUS OUTLAYS

3.1.200 The allocation of funds among different levels (namely primary, secondary, and tertiary) and disease control programmes has been changing. The manner in which resources are allocated shows a wide disparity in spending and outcomes. It is therefore necessary to focus on health outcomes rather than health outlays, including a disaggregated examination by gender, class, caste, etc. to assess their impact on different groups. During the Eleventh Five Year Plan,

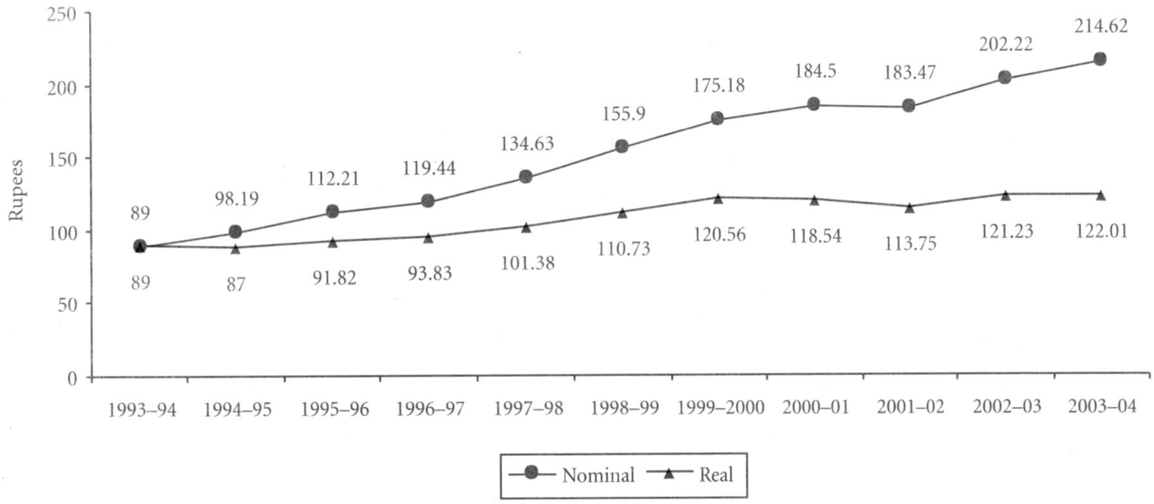

Source: NCMH (2005).

FIGURE 3.1.16: Growth of per capita Health Expenditure by Centre and States—Nominal and Real Terms

norms and indicators for outputs and outcomes will be developed to enable government and other agencies to measure the efficiency of health spending by the Centre and the States and allocations adjusted accordingly. The practice of gender budgeting by the States will be necessary.

BLOCK BUDGETING

3.1.201 Data from available surveys and studies reveal that there are major inequities in access to health care between the rich and the poor, between urban and rural areas, and between various regions of the country. Presently allocation of public funds is also quite iniquitous, with urban areas often receiving much larger per capita public health resources than rural areas, and certain States (Bihar, UP, MP, Orissa, Chhattisgarh, Jharkhand) having per capita public health expenditure less than half of other States (Himachal Pradesh, Punjab, Goa, Delhi, Mizoram).

3.1.202 One approach to address this situation is to follow the equity principles of 'equal resources for equal need' and 'greater resources for greater need'. With this approach, it is possible to work out a system of block budgeting wherein people in either urban or rural areas, whether in developed or less developed States anywhere in the country would receive the same baseline level of public health resources eliminating existing inequities in public health resource allocation. Added to this, there would need to be recognition of special needs (for women, children, *adivasis*, and other disadvantaged groups) that would merit additional resources being allocated for services for these groups. During the Plan, block budgeting will be piloted in selected districts.

SCHEMES AND OUTLAYS FOR ELEVENTH FIVE YEAR PLAN

3.1.203 To achieve the desired outcomes in the health sector, a substantially enhanced outlay for the Department of Health and Family Welfare has been earmarked during the Eleventh Five Year Plan (2007–2012). The total projected GBS for the Eleventh Plan is Rs 120374.00 crore (at 2006–07 prices) and Rs 136147.00 crore (at current prices). This enhanced outlay is about four times the initial outlay for the Tenth Plan (Rs 36378.00 crore). A large proportion of this amount, i.e., Rs 89478.00 crore (65.72 %) is for NRHM, the flagship of the GoI. Another Rs 625 crore is to be contributed by the Department of AYUSH to make a total of Rs 90103 crore for NRHM during the Eleventh Five Year Plan. For the other ongoing schemes, a total of Rs 23995.05 crore has been earmarked. For the new initiatives it is Rs 20846.95 crore. Rs 1827.00 crore has also been earmarked for OSC.

3.1.204 Annexure 3.1.8 indicates the number of schemes that were in operation during 2006–07 and the schemes that will be operational during the Eleventh Five Year Plan. The scheme-wise outlays of Department of Health and Family Welfare during the Eleventh Five Year Plan are given in Appendix of Volume III.

Eleventh Five Year Plan Agenda

3.1.205 Thrust areas to be pursued during the Eleventh Five Year Plan are summarized below:

- Improving Health Equity
  - NRHM
  - NUHM
- Adopting a system-centric approach rather than a disease-centric approach
  - Strengthening Health System through upgradation of infrastructure and PPP
  - Converging all programmes and not allowing vertical structures below district level under different programmes
- Increasing Survival
  - Reducing Maternal mortality and improving Child Sex ratio through Gender Responsive Health care
  - Reducing Infant and Child mortality through HBNC and IMNCI
- Taking full advantage of local enterprise for solving local health problems
  - Integrating AYUSH in Health System
  - Increasing the role of RMPs
  - Training the TBAs to make them SBAs
  - Propagating low cost and indigenous technology
- Preventing indebtedness due to expenditure on health/protecting the poor from health expenditures
  - Creating mechanisms for Health Insurance
  - Health Insurance for the unorganized sector
- Decentralizing Governance
  - Increasing the role of PRIs, NGOs, and civil society
  - Creating and empowering health committees at various levels
- Establishing e-Health
  - Adapting IT for governance
  - Establishing e-enabled HMIS
  - Increasing role of telemedicine
- Improving access to and utilization of essential and quality health care
  - Implementing flexible norms for health care facilities (based on population, distance, and terrain)
  - Reducing travel time to two hours for EmOC
  - Implementing IPHS for health care institutions at all levels
  - Accrediting private health care facilities and providers
  - Redeveloping hospitals/institutions
  - Mirroring of centres of excellence like AIIMS
- Increasing focus on Health Human Resources
  - Improving Medical, Paramedical, Nursing, and Dental education, and availability
  - Reorienting AYUSH education and utilization
  - Reintroducing licentiate course in medicine
  - Making India a hub for health care and related tourism
- Focusing on excluded/neglected areas
  - Taking care of the Older persons
  - Reducing Disability and integrating disabled
  - Providing humane Mental Health services
  - Providing Oral health services
- Enhancing efforts at disease reduction
  - Reversing trend of major diseases
  - Launching new initiatives (Rabies, Fluorosis, Leptospirosis)
- Providing focus to Health System and Bio-Medical research
  - Focusing on conditions specific to our country
  - Making research accountable
  - Translating research into application for improving health
  - Understanding social determinants of health behaviour, risk taking behaviour, and health care seeking behaviour.

3.2 AYURVEDA, YOGA AND NATUROPATHY, UNANI, SIDDHA, AND HOMEOPATHY (AYUSH)

INTRODUCTION

3.2.1 There is a resurgence of interest in holistic systems of health care, especially, in the prevention and management of chronic lifestyle related non-communicable diseases and systemic diseases. Health sector trends suggest that no single system of health care has the capacity to solve all of society's health needs. India can be a world leader in the era of integrative medicine because it has strong foundations in Western biomedical sciences and an immensely rich and mature indigenous medical heritage of its own.

VISION FOR AYUSH

3.2.2 To mainstream AYUSH by designing strategic interventions for wider utilization of AYUSH both domestically and globally, the thrust areas in the Eleventh Five YearPlan are: strengthening professional education, strategic research programmes, promotion of best clinical practices, technology upgradation in industry, setting internationally acceptable pharmacopoeial standards, conserving medicinal flora, fauna, metals, and minerals, utilizing human resources of AYUSH in the national health programmes, with the ultimate aim of enhancing the outreach of AYUSH health care in an accessible, acceptable, affordable, and qualitative manner.

CURRENT SCENARIO AND CHALLENGES

3.2.3 During the Tenth Plan, the Department continued to lay emphasis on upgradation of AYUSH educational standards, quality control, and standardization of drugs, improving the availability of medicinal plant material, R&D, and awareness generation about the efficacy of the systems domestically and internationally. Steps were taken in 2006–07 for mainstreaming AYUSH under NRHM with the objective of optimum utilization of AYUSH for meeting the unmet needs of the population.

Health Care Services under AYUSH

3.2.4 The AYUSH sector across the country supported a network of 3203 hospitals and 21351 dispensaries. The health services provided by this network largely focused on primary health care. The sector has a marginal presence in secondary and tertiary health care. In the private and not-for-profit sector, there are several thousand AYUSH clinics and around 250 hospitals and nursing homes for in patient care and specialized therapies like *Panchkarma*.

3.2.5 In clinics and nursing homes there are anecdotal reports of the role of AYUSH in the successful management of several communicable and non-communicable diseases. However, there is no macro-data available about the contribution of AYUSH to major national programmes for the management of communicable and NCDs. System and State-wise details of hospitals and dispensaries under AYUSH have been provided in Annexures 3.2.1 and 3.2.2. A major challenge in Eleventh Five Year Plan is to identify reputed clinical centres and support upgradation of their facilities via PPP schemes so that the country can boast of a national network of high-quality clinical facilities developed for rendering specialized health care in strength areas of AYUSH.

AYUSH under NRHM

3.2.6 Despite having a different scheme of diagnosis, drug requirements, and treatments as compared to the mainstream health care system, preliminary efforts to integrate AYUSH in NRHM were initiated during the Tenth Plan. The AYUSH interventions under NRHM have been depicted in Box 3.2.1. It is too early to assess if the AYUSH interventions in NRHM have had significant health impact by way of complementing the conventional national health programmes. Integrating AYUSH into NRHM has the potential of enhancing both the quality and outreach of NRHM, especially with the availability of a large number of practitioners in this field (Table 3.2.1). Supporting strategic pilot action research projects in the Eleventh Five Year Plan to evolve viable models of integration seems necessary.

Box 3.2.1
AYUSH Interventions under NRHM

- Co-location of AYUSH dispensaries in 3528 PHCs in different States.
- Appointment of 452 AYUSH doctors and paramedics (pharmacists) on contractual basis in the primary health care system.
- Inclusion of AYUSH modules in training of ASHA.
- Inclusion of *Punarnavdi Mandoor* in the ASHA Kit for management of anaemia during pregnancy.
- Inclusion of seven Ayurvedic and five Unani medicines in the RCH programme.
- Establishment of specialty clinics, specialized therapy centres, and AYUSH wings in district hospitals supported through CSS.

TABLE 3.2.1
Registered Medical Practitioners under AYUSH

System	Number of Practitioners
Ayurveda	453661
Unani	46558
Siddha	6381
Naturopathy	888
Homeopathy	217850
Total	725383

Source: Department of AYUSH, status as on 1 January 2007.

Human Resources Development in AYUSH

3.2.7 There are a total of 485 government and non-government AYUSH educational institutions in India (Table 3.2.2). There are Undergraduate and Postgraduate Regulations of Central Council of Indian Medicine (CCIM) for Minimum Standards of Ayurveda, Siddha, and Unani education. The teaching institutions are required to provide the infrastructure specified in the regulations, which include building for the college, hostel, library, hospital with requisite bed strength, teaching and non-teaching staff, etc. Despite a very large educational infrastructure, the quality of education in most of the institutions does not meet prescribed standards set by CCIM. The major challenge in the Eleventh Five Year Plan will be to initiate reforms in undergraduate and postgraduate education that can make AYUSH education more contemporary and to provide generous support to centres of excellence in governmental and non-governmental sector. The functioning of regulatory bodies requires vast improvement for proper regulation and development of professional education in these systems. Initiatives like institution of National Education Testing type testing for AYUSH teachers and NAAC type assessment and accreditation for AYUSH colleges are required.

3.2.8 There are, as of today, practically no formal accredited programmes for training of AYUSH para-medics viz., nurses, pharmacists, and panchakarma therapists.

3.2.9 Continuing Medical Education/Reorientation and Training Programme were initiated with two sub-components (i) reorientation programme for AYUSH personnel and (ii) short-term CME programme for AYUSH physicians/practitioners. Government/Private/NGO institutions of AYUSH are eligible to take up this training programme. The programme has been restructured for Eleventh Five Year Plan with more components including use of IT tools to modernize CME.

AYUSH Industry

3.2.10 System-wise details of manufacturing units have been provided in Table 3.2.3. The turnover of AYUSH industry is estimated to be more than Rs 8000 crore. 70% of the Indian exports from the AYUSH sector consist largely of raw materials and are estimated to be of the order of Rs 1000 crore per annum. The balance (around 30%) consists of finished products including herbal extracts. Indian exports are at present led by a trader's vision rather than a vision inspired by value added knowledge products. The major challenge for industry is to transform its global image from that of a raw material supplier to a knowledge products industry. This transformation will call for major

TABLE 3.2.2
Details of Educational Institutions and their Capacity

	Ayurveda	Yoga	Unani	Siddha	Homeopathy	Naturopathy	Total
Undergraduate Colleges	240	–	39	7	183	10	479
Admission Capacity	11225	–	1750	350	13425	385	27135
Colleges with Postgraduate Courses	62	–	7	3	33	–	105
Admission Capacity	991	–	67	110	1084	–	2252
Exclusive Postgraduate Institutes	2	–	1	1	2	–	6
Admission Capacity	40		28	30	99	–	197
Total Institutions	242	–	40	8	185	10	485

Source: Department of AYUSH, status as on 1 April 2007.

TABLE 3.2.3
System-wise Details of Manufacturing Units

System	Manufacturing Units	
	Numbers	Proportion
Ayurveda	7621	85.68
Unani	321	3.61
Siddha	325	3.65
Homeopathy	628	7.06
Total	8895	100.00

Source: Department of AYUSH, status as on 1 April 2007.

investments in upgrading processing technology, R&D including collaborative research with reputed international institutions and quality control. It will also call for intersectoral cooperation among AYUSH, CSIR, ICMR, private sector R&D, NGOs, and Ministry of Commerce for meeting global requirements of quality and safe natural medicinal products. Technical and financial support to the industry in this direction could go a long way in improving our exports.

Standardization and Quality Control of Ayurveda, Siddha, Unani, and Homeopathy (ASU&H) Drugs

3.2.11 Four different Pharmacopoeia Committees are working for preparing official formularies/ pharmacopoeias to evolve uniform standards in preparation of drugs of ASU&H and to prescribe working standards for single drugs as well as compound formulations. Standards for around 40% of the raw materials and around 15% of formulations have been published by these committees. Drug Control Cell (AYUSH) is working in the Department of AYUSH to deal with the matters pertaining to licensing and regulation of Ayurvedic, Unani, and Siddha Drugs. Setting up of the Central Drug Authority for centralized licensing and enforcement of the provisions of Drugs and Cosmetics Act and Rules would go a long way in ensuring quality and safety of ASU&H drugs. Department of AYUSH intends to convert Pharmacopoeial Committees of various systems into a modern pharmacopoeial commission with adequate representation of stakeholders and to develop standards that are in line with internationally acceptable pharmacopoeial standards and quality parameters of Ayurveda, Siddha, and Unani drugs.

Research Activities

3.2.12 The Central Government has established research councils for Ayurveda and Siddha (Central Council for Research in Ayurveda and Siddha, CCRAS), Unani (Central Council for Research in Unani Medicine), Homeopathy Central Council for Research in Homeopathy, and Yoga and Naturopathy (Central Council of Yoga and Naturopathy). These Councils have carried out a wide range of research activities. Other government departments like ICMR, CSIR, DST, Department of Biotechnology (DBT), and ICAR also have research centres and focused programmes related to specific aspects of AYUSH. Department of AYUSH also administers an Extramural Research Scheme supporting project based research studies from accredited scientific and medical institutions.

3.2.13 One of the socially important outputs of research in the AYUSH sector has been the pharmacopeias and formularies of the various systems of medicine. Whereas numerous important research projects have been undertaken in the last three decades across the various research councils on important public health problems like malaria, filariasis, hepatitis, anaemia, there is no critical report on the quality or impact of these projects on the health sector in India. The current research investments are extremely low. One challenge is to step up research investments and support reputed research organizations in the government, non-government, and private sector and promote collaborative research with reputed international institutions. The challenge of addressing strategic research needs in disease areas of national and global importance is attempted to be met through Golden Triangle Research Programme from development of ASU&H drugs.

Natural Resource Base of AYUSH

3.2.14 The resource base of AYUSH is largely plants. Around 6000 species of medicinal plants are documented in published medical and ethno-botanical literature. Wild populations of several hundreds of these species are under threat in their natural habitats. In the Tenth Plan, a National Medicinal Plants Board (NMPB) was established for supporting conservation of gene pools and large scale cultivation of medicinal plants. The NMPB has also promoted the creation of

Box 3.2.2
Research Initiatives

Literary Research

Medico-historical studies, Transcription/translation of rare works

Fundamental Research

Pharmacopoeial work and standardization of formulations/therapies.

Drug Research

Medico-Botanical survey, Pharmacognostical/Phytochemical studies

Clinical Research

Therapeutic trials of drugs for specified diseases
Drug proving or Homeopathic Pathogenetic Trials

Tribal Health Care Research Programme, Family Welfare and RCH Related Research

Oral Contraceptive (*Pippalyadi Yoga*)
Spermicidal Agent (*Neem oil*)
Bal Rasayan and *Ayush Ghutti* for children's health
Scientific validation of Ayurvedic and Siddha Medicines for RCH Programme
Development of cosmaceutical/neutraceutical products based on traditional medicine knowledge

State Medicinal Plants Boards in most of the States. In addition to plants, there are also around 300 species of medicinal fauna and around 70 different metals and minerals used by AYUSH. However, there have been no official efforts so far to conserve these resources. The key challenges in the Eleventh Five Year Plan will be to conserve gene pools of red listed species, support large-scale cultivation of species that are in high trade, involve forestry sector in plantation of medicinal tree species, and establish modern processing zones for post-harvest management of medicinal plants.

Centrally Funded Institutions

3.2.15 Institutions for all the core functions (Regulatory, Research, Education, Laboratory, and Manufacture) have been established and/or strengthened by Central funding for establishing benchmarks for others to follow.

Review of Tenth Plan Schemes

3.2.16 Original approved outlay for the Department for the Tenth Plan was Rs 775.00 crore, which was increased to Rs 1214.00 crore. Year-wise allocation and corresponding expenditure substantially increased during Tenth Plan, particularly from the year 2004–05 onwards. Scheme wise details for Tenth Plan have been provided in Annexure 3.2.3.

TOWARDS FINDING SOLUTIONS

3.2.17 Apart from core areas for the AYUSH sector like education, research, industry, and medicinal plants, four important dimensions have been added to AYUSH in the Eleventh Five Year Plan viz., (i) mainstreaming of AYUSH in public health, (ii) technology upgradation of AYUSH industry, (iii) assistance to Centres of Excellence, and (iv) revitalization and validation of community-based local health traditions of AYUSH. All these dimensions will serve to enhance the social and community outreach of AYUSH in the Eleventh Five Year Plan at domestic and global level.

Systems Strengthening

3.2.18 The ongoing schemes namely, strengthening the Department of AYUSH, Statutory Institutions, hospitals and dispensaries, strengthening of pharmacopoeial laboratories, IEC, and other programmes and schemes have been merged as 'Systems Strengthening'. Adequate budgetary provisions will be made for this in the Eleventh Five Year Plan.

Educational Institutions

3.2.19 National Institutes of various AYUSH systems have been set up by the Central Government to set benchmarks for teaching, research, and clinical practices. Keeping in view the need for upgrading these national institutes into Centres of Excellence, a substantial increase in outlay will be made in the Eleventh Five Year Plan. This increase is also on account of setting up a state-of-the-art tertiary Ayurveda centre in the national capital with R&D focus and tertiary health care facilities.

3.2.20 Most of the AYUSH undergraduate and postgraduate colleges in the government sector suffer from a variety of infrastructure constraints. As low quality of AYUSH education is one of the crucial factors for lack of public confidence in AYUSH system, selected institutions in governmental and non-governmental sector having better track records will be upgraded into Centres of Excellence. An increased outlay will be provided to ensure that AYUSH institutions are brought up to the minimum standards prescribed by the Statutory Body within the Eleventh Five Year Plan period.

Research and Development (R&D)

3.2.21 The infrastructure and capacities of AYUSH research councils will be upgraded to enable them to carry out state-of-the-art scientific work related to drug standardization and quality control, botanical standardization, laying down of pharmacopoeial standards, and clinical trials.

3.2.22 Golden Triangle Research partnership initiated by Department of AYUSH with collaboration of CCRAS, ICMR, and CSIR is aimed at scientific validation and development of R&D based drugs as well as development of herbal drugs based on traditional medicinal knowledge for prioritized disease conditions. Ayurveda, Siddha, Unani, and Homoeopathy drug industry is being associated with this initiative. For expediting the work of laying down pharmacopoeial standards of single drugs and poly-herbal formulations, the research councils have been declared as the Secretariats of the Pharma-copoeias Committees. Various peripheral units/laboratories of research councils will be upgraded for undertaking sophisticated scientific work relating to development of marker compounds and biologically active ingredients for drug standardization and development.

Medicinal Flora and Fauna

3.2.23 The NMPB is functioning with a very small component of staff as an extension of the Department. Manifold increase in outlay for the Eleventh Five Year Plan is to restructure the NMPB as an autonomous body and provide sufficient manpower to undertake its wide mandate. A Centrally Sponsored component for cultivation, processing, and marketing of medicinal plants is being started from the outlay of NMPB. This will have sub components for financial allocation: cultivation of prioritized medicinal plants species over 75000 hectares; raising of 50 lakh seedlings; setting up of Centralized Seed Centre and Nursery for cultivating planting materials for 15 States; setting up of six medicinal plants zones in agro-climatic zones of the country; and market development assistance fund for plan building and marketing support. Another existing Central Sector component is regarding programme for in-situ conservation, creation of Gene Bank for medicinal plants, ex-situ conservation of prioritized medicinal plants, R&D for quality standards, and certification and programme for IEC.

Hospitals and Dispensaries

3.2.24 This Scheme has now been subsumed under the NRHM, as it aims at creating AYUSH facilities in PHCs, CHCs, and district hospitals for the purpose of mainstreaming of AYUSH under NRHM. The ambit of the scheme is widened to provide support for strengthening of AYUSH dispensaries, hospitals and for supply of AYUSH medicinal kits in rural areas and for development of specialized AYUSH treatment centres under PPP mode.

Industry

3.2.25 AYUSH industry at present suffers from small scale of operation and low technology that needs to be upgraded. Majority of the 5000 GMP compliance manufacturing units are of small and medium size. Even though back ended subsidy to these units under the Centrally sponsored component 'Drug Quality

Control' for establishing in-house quality control will be provided, these units also require other infrastructure like sophisticated packing machine, medicinal plants storage, testing facilities, other common quality control R&D facilities, and marketing assistance. Therefore 20 AYUSH industry clusters have been identified and an initiative for development of common facilities for these clusters will be made during the Eleventh Five Year Plan. They will be able to set benchmarks for quality control, packaging, testing of medicinal plants, brand development, and marketing development network, which are very necessary for globalizing AYUSH industry to capture a fair share of the global herbal market.

Drugs Quality Control

3.2.26 An increased outlay will be made during Eleventh Five Year Plan for strengthening the regulatory mechanism with a view to ensure safety, control, and efficacy of AYUSH medicines as a priority area. It is also proposed to reimburse to the States expenditure incurred on testing of AYUSH drugs through the network of National Accreditation Board for Testing and Calibration Laboratories accredited laboratories in the country. This is again a high priority to strengthen the enforcement of Drugs and Cosmetics Act in the country with regard to Ayurveda, Siddha, Unani, and Homoeopathy manufacturing units to create public confidence in India and abroad.

Financing AYUSH

3.2.27 The total Central Government investments in the AYUSH sector at the national level since the First Five Year Plan have ranged from 1% to 3% of the national health budget. In the States too, a small proportion of the health budget is assigned to AYUSH. The private sector investment in AYUSH industry (Rs 8800 crore turnover) is relatively large, while the private investments on research and education, public health services, and community health are relatively small. Gradually public investments for the AYUSH sector will be increased. The additional investments in AYUSH sector will not be exclusively put into government institutions. The government sector needs to be supplemented by appropriate investments through PPP and supported by non-government initiatives in strategic fields.

3.2.28 The new initiatives will be: International Co-operation including global market development; support for revitalization of local health traditions; assistance to accredited AYUSH Centres of Excellence in governmental and non-governmental sector engaged in AYUSH education, drug development and scientific validation and clinical research; AYUSH and Public Health; Cataloguing, digitization, and AYUSH IT network.

3.2.29 Some of the important new initiatives for Eleventh Five Year Plan are shown in Box 3.2.3.

3.2.30 ZBB exercise has been done for the Eleventh Five Year Plan (Annexure 3.2.4). The exercise was done to arrive at greater convergence among schemes with similar objectives for improving the efficacy and efficiency of Plan spending. The total projected GBS for the Eleventh Plan for the Department of AYUSH is Rs 3526 crore (at 2006–07 prices) and Rs 3988 crore (at current prices). Scheme-wise financial details for the Eleventh Five Year Plan have been provided in Appendix of Volume III.

Box 3.2.3
Important New Initiatives during the Eleventh Plan

- Development of common drug testing and other infrastructure facilities for AYUSH industry clusters
- Financial assistance to ASU&H Units for capacity building to improve quality control and R&D
- Support to centres of excellence in AYUSH education/drug development/clinical research/tertiary care
- Support for validation and revitalization of local health traditions
- Development of backward and forward linkages for in-situ conservation and ex-situ cultivation of medicinal plants for a sustainable ASU&H Industry
- Provision of marketing and value-added services to medicinal plant farmers
- Expansion of international cooperation and exchange programme with focus on global positioning of AYUSH systems and facilitation of cooperation with other countries in the areas of AYUSH education, research, and exports

Eleventh Five Year Plan Agenda

3.2.31 Successful implementation of the abovementioned initiatives will enable AYUSH systems to contribute significantly to the health care of population while being an integral component of the health care system of our country.

3.2.32 The key interventions and strategies in the Eleventh Five Year Plan are enumerated below:

- Documenting measurable outputs for annual plan as well as for the five year plans that will facilitate designing and implementing systematic ME systems.
- Training in Public Health for AYUSH personnel is envisaged as an essential part of education and CME.
- Mainstreaming the system of AYUSH in National Health Care Delivery System by co-locating AYUSH facilities in primary health network.
- Restructuring Public Health Management to integrate AYUSH practitioners into the national health care system.
- Formulating a two-tiered research framework for AYUSH to interface with modern science while giving due cognizance and importance to development and application of theoretical foundations of the traditional knowledge systems and practices.
- Promoting scientific validation of AYUSH principles, remedies, and therapies.
- Revitalizing, documenting, and validating local health traditions of AYUSH.
- Improving the status of pharmacopoeial standards by setting up Pharmacopoeia Commission.
- Improving the status of quality of clinical services by creating specialty AYUSH Secondary and Tertiary Care Centres.
- Upgrading AYUSH undergraduate and postgraduate educational institutions by better regulation and establishing a system for NET type testing of AYUSH teachers and NAAC type assessment and accreditation of AYUSH undergraduate/postgraduate colleges.
- Ensuring conservation of medicinal plants gene pools as well as promoting cultivation of species in high trade and establishment of medicinal plants processing zones.
- Strengthening regulatory mechanism for ensuring quality control, R&D, and processing technology involving accredited laboratories in the government and non-government sector.
- Establishing Centres of Excellence.
- Promoting international co-operation in research, education, health services, and trade, and market development.
- Digitizing India's vast corpus of medical manuscripts in collaboration with the National Manuscripts Mission.
- Promoting public awareness about the strengths and contemporary relevance of AYUSH through IEC.

ANNEXURE 3.1.1

Department of Health and Family Welfare (Other than NRHM)—
Scheme-wise Outlay and Actual Expenditure during the Tenth Plan

(Rs in Crores)

S. No.	Name of the Schemes/Institutions	Outlay Tenth Plan (2002–07)	Tenth Plan (2002–07) Sum of Annual Outlay	Tenth Plan (2002–07) Actual Exp.
1	2	3	4	5
I.	CENTRALLY SPONSORED PROGRAMMES	2045.80	3097.82	2718.36
	Control of Communicable Diseases	1392.80	2165.17	2055.55
	1 NACP and National STD Control Programme	1392.80	2165.17	2055.55
	Control of NCDs	405.00	516.00	359.13
	2 Cancer	266.00	333.00	252.63
	(i) NCCP	266.00	333.00	252.63
	(ii) Tobacco Control Programme	0.00	0.00	0.00
	3 NMHP	139.00	183.00	106.50
	Other Programmes	248.00	355.65	299.45
	4 Assistance to State for Capacity Building for Trauma Care	110.00	140.00	142.03
	5 Assistance to States for Drug & PFA Control	138.00	215.65	157.42
	(i) Drugs Control	60.00		
	(ii) PFA Control	78.00		
	New Initiatives under CSS	0.00	61.00	4.23
	6 Initiatives during 2006–07	0.00	61.00	4.23
	(i) Telemedicine	0.00	15.00	0.00
	(ii) National Programme for Prevention and Control of Diabetes, (iii) CVD, and Stroke	0.00	5.00	0.00
	(iv) National Programme for Deafness	0.00	15.00	4.23
	(v) Other Initiatives	0.00	26.00	0.00
II	CENTRAL SECTOR SCHEMES (CS)	5176.20	4926.58	3858.60
	Control of Communicable Diseases	199.80	203.63	161.48
	7 NICD	65.00	62.17	49.93
	(i) Ongoing Activities (including Guineaworm & Yaws Eradication)	50.00		
	(ii) Strengthening of the Institute	15.00	4.00	0.00
	8 National Tuberculosis Institute, Bangalore	10.30	9.73	3.49
	9 BCG Vaccine Laboratory, Guindy, Chennai	19.50	17.27	9.48
	10 Pasteur Institute of India, Coonoor	35.00	44.00	31.18
	11 Lala Ram Sarup Institute of Tuberculosis and Allied Diseases, Mehrauli, Delhi	54.50	52.55	55.54
	12 Central Leprosy Training & Research Institute, Chengalpattu (Tamil Nadu)	5.50	7.00	4.73
	13 Regional Institute of Training, Research & Treatment under Leprosy Control Programme:	10.00	10.91	7.13
	(i) RLTRI, Aska (Orissa)	2.00	2.35	0.37
	(ii) RLTRI, Raipur (MP)	1.00	0.96	0.71
	(iii) RLTRI, Gauripur (WB)	7.00	7.60	6.05

(Annexure 3.1.1 contd.)

(Annexure 3.1.1 contd.)

1	2	3	4	5
	Hospitals & Dispensaries	567.00	796.03	609.22
	14 Central Government Health Scheme	80.00	132.50	122.43
	15 Central Institute of Psychiatry, Ranchi	50.00	62.20	30.17
	16 All India Institute of Physical Medicine & Rehabilitation, Mumbai	20.00	17.60	13.60
	17 Safdarjung Hospital and College, New Delhi	230.00	367.09	270.46
	18 Dr RML Hospital, New Delhi	150.00	175.64	138.35
	19 Institute for Human Behaviour & Allied Sciences, Shahdara, Delhi	7.00	4.00	0.00
	20 All India Institute of Speech & Hearing, Mysore	30.00	37.00	34.21
	Medical Education, Training, & Research	2981.10	3077.17	2774.62
	(a) Medical Education:	1951.00	1992.19	1649.56
	21 All India Institute of Medical Sciences and its Allied Departments, New Delhi	675.00	787.12	636.50
	22 PGIMER, Chandigarh	200.00	153.00	234.00
	23 JIPMER, Pondicherry	150.00	182.00	118.61
	24 Lady Hardinge Medical College & Smt. SK Hospital, New Delhi	200.00	95.00	68.33
	25 Kalawati Saran Children's Hospital, New Delhi	140.00	39.56	34.39
	26 Indira Gandhi Institute of Health & Medical Sciences for North East Region at Shillong	380.00	447.78	274.99
	27 NIMHANS, Bangalore	120.00	173.96	180.98
	28 Kasturba Health Society, Wardha	50.00	56.80	59.57
	29 National Medical Library, New Delhi	35.00	45.00	34.82
	30 NBE, New Delhi	1.00	11.97	7.37
	(b) Training	95.00	110.39	73.82
	31 Development of Nursing Services	82.00	102.00	70.14
	32 Nursing Colleges	13.00	8.39	3.68
	(i) RAK College of Nursing, New Delhi	11.00	6.46	2.69
	(ii) Lady Reading Health School	2.00	1.93	0.99
	(c) Research	870.00	841.00	962.00
	33 ICMR, New Delhi	870.00	841.00	962.00
	(d) Public Health	27.50	83.35	48.83
	34 PHFI	5.00	73.00	43.00
	35 All India Institute of Hygiene & Public Health, Kolkata (AIIH&PH) and Serologist and Chemical Examiner, Kolkata	22.50	10.35	5.83
	(i) AIIH&PH, Kolkota	20.00	8.90	5.22
	(ii) Serologist & Chemical Examiner, Kolkata	2.50	1.45	0.61
	(e) Others	37.60	50.24	40.41
	36 Indian Nursing Council	2.10	3.20	2.50
	37 VP Chest Institute, Delhi	23.00	30.30	31.80
	38 National Academy of Medical Sciences, New Delhi	2.50	2.74	1.75
	39 MCI, New Delhi	5.00	5.00	4.36
	40 Medical Grants Commission	5.00	9.00	0.00
	Other Programmes	429.30	441.75	283.02
	(a) Health Education, Research, & Accounts	19.40	16.64	3.37
	41 Health Education	12.60	8.20	0.79
	42 Health Intelligence and Health Accounts	6.80	8.44	2.58

(Annexure 3.1.1 contd.)

(Annexure 3.1.1 contd.)

1	2	3	4	5
	(i) Intelligence	3.80	4.44	2.58
	(ii) Accounts	3.00	4.00	0.00
	(b) Strengthening of DGHS/Ministry:	20.00	23.40	16.55
43	I. Strengthening of Departments under the Ministry	12.00	15.00	11.68
	II. Strengthening of DGHS	8.00	8.40	4.87
	(c) Emergency Medical Relief	30.00	87.00	35.96
44	Health Sector Disaster Preparedness and Management	30.00	47.00	23.25
45	Emergency Medical Relief (including Avian Flu)	0.00	40.00	12.71
	(d) Miscellaneous	359.90	314.71	227.14
46	Central Research Institute, Kasauli	50.00	30.88	23.37
47	National Institute of Biologicals, Noida (UP)	170.90	166.50	152.13
48	PFA	78.00	47.20	14.95
49	Central Drug Standard & Control Organization (CDSCO)	52.00	62.90	35.37
50	Port Health Authority	9.00	7.23	1.32
	(i) Jawaharlal Nehru Port Sheva	1.50	2.03	1.30
	(ii) Setting up of offices at 8 newly created international airports	7.50	5.20	0.02
51	PMSSY	999.00	385.00	20.94
	Dropped/Transferred Schemes	43.00	62.40	44.62
1	Hospital Waste Management	10.00	10.00	10.82
2	UNDP Pilot Initiatives for Community Health	0.00	8.90	0.00
3	Training of MO of CHS	0.00	0.00	0.01
4	RHTC, Najafgarh	0.00	0.00	1.48
5	Drug De-addition Control Programme	33.00	20.50	22.99
6	Bhuj Hospital	0.00	23.00	9.32
	Grand Total	7265.00	8063.80	6612.26

Note: Exp. stands for Expenditure; MO stands for Medical Officers.
Source: MoHFW.

ANNEXURE 3.1.2
Department of Health (H) and Family Welfare (FW)—NRHM#

(Rs in Crores)

S. No.	Name of the Schemes	Outlay Tenth Plan (2002–07)	Tenth Plan (2002–07) Sum of Annual Outlay	Tenth Plan (2002–07) Actual Exp.
1	2	3	4	5
	CENTRALLY SPONSORED SCHEMES (CSS) OF FAMILY WELFARE	24169.20	28011.97	23854.74
1	Direction & Administration	1100.00	1176.66	999.93
2	Rural FW Services (SCs)	9663.00	8881.29	7561.01
3	Urban FW Services	580.00	638.17	539.48
4	Grants to State Training Institutions	480.00	500.37	411.08
5	Free Distribution of Contraceptives	940.00	760.22	627.97
6	Sterilization (Beds)—(Weeded)	12.00	10.25	8.78
7	Family Welfare Linked Health Insurance	150.00	105.10	10.63
8	Training	250.00	143.81	71.60
9	Procurement of Supplies and Materials	994.98	1141.30	335.14
10	Routine Immunization	1557.88	1625.50	783.44
11	Pulse Polio Immunization	3110.00	3887.70	3999.56
12	IEC	539.50	569.87	542.42
13	Area Projects	1750.00	1838.14	1250.60
14	Flexible Pool for State PIPs	3041.84	6733.59	6713.10
	CENTRAL SECTOR SCHEMES (CS) OF FAMILY WELFARE	1367.80	1611.53	1180.69
1	Social Marketing Area Projects	20.00	35.00	0.00
2	Social Marketing of Contraceptives	660.00	790.04	599.70
3	FW Training and Res. Centre, Bombay	10.00	10.53	2.31
4	NIHFW, New Delhi	20.00	25.45	19.91
5	IIPS, Mumbai	10.00	9.57	8.09
6	Rural Health Training Centre, Najafgarh	45.00	12.42	1.56
7	Population Research Centres	45.00	39.13	30.01
8	CDRI, Lucknow	12.00	12.65	12.85
9	ICMR and IRR	100.00	150.00	162.44
10	Travel of Experts/Conference/Meetings etc. (Melas)	57.00	17.00	47.84
11	International Co-operation	9.00	8.44	6.73
12	NPSF/National Commission on Population	100.00	116.00	104.08
13	NGOs (PPP)	130.00	241.61	88.95
14	Other Schemes	149.80	143.69	96.22
	TRANSFERRED TO STATES/WEEDED DURING TENTH PLAN	589.00	417.50	291.12
1	District Projects	51.00	105.00	40.95
2	Community Incentive Scheme	200.00	62.00	0.00
3	Transport	313.00	223.00	248.02
4	New Initiatives	25.00	27.50	2.15
	TO NACO	0.00	200.00	265.99
	FAMILY WELFARE (TOTAL)	26126.00	30241.00	25592.54
	DISEASE CONTROL PROGRAMMES OF HEALTH	2987.00	3280.20	2745.65
1	Vector-borne (CSS)	1349.00	1496.03	1186.11
2	Tuberculosis (CSS)	662.00	758.17	756.88
3	Leprosy (CSS)	236.00	288.00	224.54
4	IDD (CSS)	35.00	49.00	42.71
5	Blindness (CSS)	445.00	439.00	458.15
6	Integrated Disease Surveillance (CS)	260.00	250.00	77.26
	GRAND TOTAL	29113.00	33521.20	28338.19

Note: # Includes corresponding H&FW schemes of NRHM up to 2004–05. To accommodate PMSSY, the approved Tenth Plan Outlay of the Department of Family Welfare was reduced from 27125 crore to Rs 26126 crore (Rs 999 crore was transferred to the Department of Health).

Source: MoHFW.

ANNEXURE 3.1.3
Health—State Plan Outlays and Expenditure

(Rs lakhs)

State/UT	Tenth Plan	2002–03		2003–04		2004–05		2005–06		2006–07	
	Outlay	Outlay	Exp.	Outlay	Exp.	Outlay	Exp.	Outlay	Exp.	Outlay	RE
1	2	3	4	5	6	7	8	9	10	11	12
Andhra Pradesh	133024.00	24309.00	22008.16	40995.00	35362.36	40995.44	31427.72	43269.24	33964.48	53574.24	53574.24
Arunachal Pradesh	23129.00	2181.00	2181.01	2201.00	2099.23	2781.35	3185.00	1828.82	1478.36	1970.00	3850.00
Assam	57069.00	8648.00	8194.35	7682.00	7882.00	6529.00	6529.00	5687.00	4203.54	21399.00	21399.00
Bihar	107920.00	13703.00	10731.11	13699.00	12343.11	14182.02	14389.78	12721.80	15426.00	13700.00	13822.00
Chhattisgarh	43418.00	6935.00	5550.00	8083.00	8083.00	15076.00	12462.52	14287.44	10035.86	33249.90	25165.69
Goa	13135.00	1895.00	1888.48	3175.00	2568.54	3521.33	3149.21	4132.99	4579.65	4495.00	4495.00
Gujarat	116616.00	21387.00	15192.32	25221.00	21472.13	25294.00	25294.00	43494.00	43494.00	45994.00	45994.00
Haryana	96062.00	6280.00	2233.22	7800.00	5757.51	7124.00	5843.76	10200.00	10000.50	11450.00	11450.00
Himachal Pradesh	78772.00	13414.00	12905.15	19517.00	18066.07	18295.79	19734.27	18476.60	19629.56	19948.92	19948.92
J&K	79666.00	13000.00	12861.04	14864.00	13752.90	16330.87	17748.78	21061.70	21954.04	21864.25	21864.25
Jharkhand	65000.00	11575.00	6498.00	9700.00	6339.98	14040.00	13371.59	15000.00	14020.07	26800.00	16225.00
Karnataka	153052.00	19247.00	17715.31	13974.00	19189.66	18011.51	15731.51	33239.29	26602.68	34098.61	48151.64
Kerala	40840.00	7135.00	7916.65	9748.00	5170.31	10130.00	6813.87	10035.00	10196.62	9650.00	9650.00
MP	71533.00	14016.00	14520.93	18105.00	15444.43	20298.09	17763.95	20587.00	20747.97	16961.91	23193.47
Maharashtra	110666.00	40740.00	21632.92	76435.00	33244.78	18663.93	31192.05	77874.10	35138.73	88228.54	88228.54
Manipur	8173.00	1415.00	304.23	2280.00	940.96	1915.91	789.52	499.00	558.20	2837.00	3215.00
Meghalaya	18000.00	3020.00	3219.79	3550.00	3773.09	4042.00	4071.31	4484.00	4676.31	4750.00	4750.00
Mizoram	12370.00	2860.00	2725.99	2975.00	4185.67	3000.00	2950.10	3480.00	3378.10	4000.00	4102.06
Nagaland	7965.00	1548.00	1562.14	2383.00	2514.00	2207.15	2114.87	2263.00	1991.93	2363.00	2578.00
Orissa	52139.00	12777.00	7283.09	21694.00	9256.11	11739.19	10281.41	14348.19	7659.27	4052.20	3002.20
Punjab	53081.00	9298.00	6483.49	10450.00	5971.99	7508.93	2133.32	2743.13	1247.13	5019.10	5019.10
Rajasthan	56892.00	12778.00	4034.19	8236.00	5434.80	10811.56	9736.64	18605.59	15384.70	20615.60	21822.16
Sikkim	8000.00	1600.00	1408.04	1606.00	1454.87	2210.00	2200.56	1840.00	1984.87	1690.00	1790.00
Tamil Nadu	70000.00	10440.00	14285.27	16314.00	15963.39	19400.66	17402.60	26874.17	39745.00	46564.75	38074.55
Tripura	25072.00	1480.00	1407.34	2013.00	2243.86	2535.36	3040.42	2662.21	4831.84	6459.60	8376.42
UP	240543.00	27826.00	25950.00	33927.00	19745.93	33009.00	38352.82	85421.00	91526.63	188763.00	189570.00
Uttaranchal	38767.00	4286.00	5768.50	7359.00	6302.53	8759.31	9978.76	8790.92	17710.21	18600.00	18600.00
WB	103618.00	27898.00	14137.89	21193.00	18590.41	23739.80	15392.06	40207.80	25440.14	44289.68	38482.68
A&N Islands	11400.00	2050.00	2119.64	2150.00	2312.26	2390.00	2382.96	3321.00	2832.22	3657.00	3657.00
Chandigarh	22426.00	3803.65	3944.93	3111.00	3546.75	3477.00	3355.33	3392.00	2983.27	3587.00	3587.00
D&N Haveli	1225.00	238.00	269.57	266.00	301.67	343.00	403.20	400.00	561.27	470.00	470.00
Daman & Diu	1750.00	194.15	217.68	228.00	282.85	290.00	301.03	350.00	462.84	414.00	424.50
Delhi	238150.00	38970.00	33043.43	42692.00	38942.11	53775.00	46989.16	60600.00	54336.37	69120.00	76160.30
Lakshadweep	901.30	275.20	232.33	227.00	264.90	225.00	166.73	242.00	236.70	178.00	178.00
Pondicherry	16360.00	3272.09	3000.21	3205.00	3259.04	4160.00	4196.59	5635.00	5665.74	9485.00	12681.40
Total	2176734.30	370494.09	293426.40	457058.00	352063.20	426812.20	400876.40	618053.99	554684.80	840299.30	843552.12

Note: RE stands for Revised Estimate.
Source: Planning Commissioin.

ANNEXURE 3.1.4
Maternal Mortality Ratio—India and Major States

(per 100000 live births)

India & Major States	MMR 1998	MMR 2001–03	Eleventh Five Year Plan Goal
India	407	301	100
Assam	409	490	163
Bihar/Jharkhand	452	371	123
MP/Chhattisgarh	498	379	126
Orissa	367	358	119
Rajasthan	670	445	148
UP/Uttarakhand	707	517	172
Andhra Pradesh	159	195	65
Karnataka	195	228	76
Kerala	198	110	37
Tamil Nadu	79	134	45
Gujarat	28	172	57
Haryana	103	162	54
Maharashtra	135	149	50
Punjab	199	178	59
WB	266	194	64

Source: 2001–03 Special Survey of Deaths, RGI (2006).

ANNEXURE 3.1.5
Sex Ratio (0–6 Years) (India and States/UTs)

S. No.	State/UT	Current Level	Goal by 2011–12	Goal by 2016–17
1	2	3	4	5
	India	927	935	950
1	A&N Islands	957	965	981
2	Andhra Pradesh	961	969	985
3	Arunachal Pradesh	964	972	988
4	Assam	965	973	989
5	Bihar	942	950	965
6	Chandigarh	845	875	900
7	Chhattisgarh	975	983	999
8	Dadra & Nagar Haveli	979	987	999
9	Daman & Diu	926	934	949
10	Delhi	868	875	900
11	Goa	938	946	961
12	Gujarat	883	891	905
13	Haryana	819	850	875
14	Himachal Pradesh	896	904	918
15	J&K	941	949	964
16	Jharkhand	965	973	989
17	Karnataka	946	954	969
18	Kerala	960	968	984
19	Lakshadweep	959	967	983
20	MP	932	940	955
21	Maharashtra	913	921	936
22	Manipur	957	965	981
23	Meghalaya	973	981	997
24	Mizoram	964	972	988
25	Nagaland	964	972	988
26	Orissa	953	961	977
27	Pondicherry	967	975	991
28	Punjab	798	850	875
29	Rajasthan	909	917	932
30	Sikkim	963	971	987
31	Tamil Nadu	942	950	965
32	Tripura	966	974	990
33	UP	916	924	939
34	Uttarakhand	908	916	931
35	WB	960	968	984

Source: Curent Level, Census 2001.

ANNEXURE 3.1.6
Infant Mortality Rate—India and States/UTs

(per 1000 live births)

S. No.	State/UT	Current Level	Eleventh Five Year Plan Goal
	India	58	28
1	Andhra Pradesh	57	28
2	Assam	68	33
3	Bihar	61	29
4	Chhattisgarh	63	30
5	Delhi	35	17
6	Gujarat	54	26
7	Haryana	60	29
8	J&K	50	24
9	Jharkhand	50	24
10	Karnataka	50	24
11	Kerala	14	7
12	MP	76	37
13	Maharashtra	36	17
14	Orissa	75	36
15	Punjab	44	21
16	Rajasthan	68	33
17	Tamil Nadu	37	18
18	UP	73	35
19	WB	38	18
20	Arunachal Pradesh	37	18
21	Goa	16	8
22	Himachal Pradesh	49	24
23	Manipur	13	6
24	Meghalaya	49	24
25	Mizoram	20	10
26	Nagaland	18	9
27	Sikkim	30	14
28	Tripura	31	15
29	Uttarakhand	42	20
30	A&N Islands	27	13
31	Chandigarh	19	9
32	Dadra & Nagar Haveli	42	20
33	Daman & Diu	28	14
34	Lakshadweep	22	11
35	Pondicherry	28	14

Source: Current level—SRS Bulletin, Vol. 41, No. 1, October 2006.

ANNEXURE 3.1.7
Total Fertility Rate—India and Major States

S. No.	State	Current Level	Eleventh Five Year Plan Goal
	India	2.9	2.1
1	Andhra Pradesh	2.1	1.8
2	Assam	2.9	2.3
3	Bihar	4.3	3.0
4	Chhattisgarh	3.3	2.4
5	Delhi	2.1	1.8
6	Gujarat	2.8	2.2
7	Haryana	3.0	1.9
8	Himachal Pradesh	2.1	1.8
9	J&K	2.4	2.0
10	Jharkhand	3.5	2.5
11	Karnataka	2.3	1.8
12	Kerala	1.7	1.7
13	MP	3.7	2.6
14	Maharashtra	2.2	1.9
15	Orissa	2.7	2.1
16	Punjab	2.2	1.8
17	Rajasthan	3.7	2.6
18	Tamil Nadu	1.8	1.7
19	UP	4.4	3.0
20	WB	2.2	1.8

Note: Figures for other States are not available.
Source: Current level—Statistical Report, RGI (2004).

ANNEXURE 3.1.8
Schemes under Health and Family Welfare

S. no.	Ministry/ Department	No. of Schemes Towards the End of Tenth Plan	Weeded/Transferred Towards the End of Tenth Plan	To be Continued During Eleventh Five Year Plan	New Schemes During Eleventh Five Year Plan	Total Schemes During Eleventh Five Year Plan
Central Sector Schemes (CS)						
1	Health	49	3	6 (Ongoing Schemes clubbed as 6 Schemes)	6	12
2	Family Welfare	14	Nil	– (Ongoing Schemes clubbed with above)		
Centrally Sponsored Schemes (CSS)						
1	Health	14	3	6 (Ongoing Schemes merged into 6 Schemes)	7	13
2	Family Welfare	14	1	– (Ongoing Schemes merged with above)		

ANNEXURE 3.2.1

State-wise/System-wise Number of AYUSH Hospitals with their Bed Strength in India as on 1.4.2007

S. No.	States/UTs & others	Ayurveda		Unani		Siddha		Yoga		Naturo-pathy		Homoeo-pathy		Total	
		Hosp.	Beds	Hosp.	Beds	Hosp.	Beds	Hosp.	Beds	Hosp.	Beds	Hosp.	Beds	Hosp.	Beds
(1)	(2)	(3)	(4)	(5)	(6)	(7)	(8)	(9)	(10)	(11)	(12)	(13)	(14)	(15)	(16)
1	Andhra Pradesh	9	584	6	310	0	0	0	0	1	120	6	300	22	1314
2	Arunachal Pradesh	1	10	0	0	0	0	1	10	0	0	1	50	3	70
3	Assam	1	100	0	0	0	0	1	25	0	0	3	105	5	230
4	Bihar	11	1356	4	459	0	0	0	0	0	0	11	510	26	2325
5	Chhattisgarh	8	365	1	90	0	0	0	0	1	50	3	100	13	605
6	Delhi	10	643	2	111	0	0	2	65	4	125	2	150	20	1094
7	Goa	1	40	0	0	0	0	0	0	0	0	1	25	2	65
8	Gujarat	48	1855	0	0	0	0	0	0	0	0	14	873	62	2728
9	Haryana	8	835	1	10	0	0	0	0	0	0	1	50	10	895
10	Himachal Pradesh	24	420	0	0	0	0	0	0	1	10	1	25	26	455
11	J&K	2	155	3	200	0	0	0	0	0	0	0	0	5	355
12	Jharkhand	1	160	0	0	0	0	0	0	0	0	2	82	3	242
13	Karnataka	122	8147	13	402	1	10	3	15	5	276	20	896	164	9746
14	Kerala	124	3987	0	0	2	170	0	0	1	40	33	1130	160	5327
15	MP	34	1626	3	250	0	0	0	0	0	0	20	1105	57	2981
16	Maharashtra	51	7673	6	635	0	0	0	0	0	0	44	3080	101	11388
17	Manipur	0	0	0	0	0	0	0	0	2	65	1	10	3	75
18	Meghalaya	1	10	0	0	0	0	0	0	0	0	7	70	8	80
19	Mizoram	0	0	0	0	0	0	0	0	1	14	0	0	1	14
20	Nagaland	0	0	0	0	0	0	0	0	0	0	1	10	1	10
21	Orissa	8	488	0	0	0	0	0	0	0	0	6	185	14	673
22	Punjab	15	1214	0	0	0	0	0	0	0	0	6	270	21	1484
23	Rajasthan	100	914	3	30	0	0	1	20	2	22	8	205	114	1191
24	Sikkim	1	10	0	0	0	0	0	0	0	0	0	0	1	10
25	Tamil Nadu	7	580	1	54	275	2131	0	0	0	0	9	460	292	3225
26	Tripura	1	10	0	0	0	0	0	0	0	0	1	10	2	20
27	UP	1771	10288	209	1585	0	0	0	0	0	0	8	350	1988	12223
28	Uttrakhand	7	319	2	8	0	0	0	0	0	0	1	50	10	377
29	WB	4	409	1	60	0	0	0	0	0	0	12	630	17	1099
30	A&N Islands	1	10	1	5	1	5	0	0	0	0	1	10	4	30
31	Chandigarh	1	120	0	0	0	0	0	0	0	0	1	25	2	145
32	Dadra & Nagar Haveli	0	0	0	0	0	0	0	0	0	0	0	0	0	0
33	Daman & Diu	0	0	0	0	0	0	0	0	0	0	0	0	0	0
34	Lakshadweep	0	0	0	0	0	0	0	0	0	0	0	0	0	0
35	Puducherry	1	10	0	0	0	0	0	0	0	0	0	0	1	10
36	CGHS	1	25	0	0	0	0	0	0	0	0	0	0	1	25
37	Research Council	24	600	12	280	2	85	0	0	0	0	6	85	44	1050
38	Ministry of Railways	0	0	0	0	0	0	0	0	0	0	0	0	0	0
39	Ministry of Labour	0	0	0	0	0	0	0	0	0	0	0	0	0	0
40	Ministry of Coal	0	0	0	0	0	0	0	0	0	0	0	0	0	0
	Total	2398	42963	268	4489	281	2401	8	135	18	722	230	10851	3203	61561

Note: Figures are provisional; Hosp. = Hospitals.

Source: State governments and certain Central Government organizations.

ANNEXURE 3.2.2
State-Wise/System-wise Number of AYUSH Dispensaries in India as on 1.4.2007

S.No.	States/UTs and Others	Ayurveda	Unani	Siddha	Yoga	Naturopathy	Homoeopathy	Total
(1)	(2)	(3)	(4)	(5)	(6)	(7)	(8)	(9)
1	Andhra Pradesh	620	193	–	–	–	283	1096
2	Arunachal Pradesh	2	–	–	1	–	44	47
3	Assam	380	1	–	25	2	75	483
4	Bihar	311	144	–	–	–	179	634
5	Chhattisgarh	634	6	–	–	–	52	692
6	Delhi	148	25	–	4	2	98	277
7	Goa	11	–	–		–	3	14
8	Gujarat	501	–	–	1	8	216	726
9	Haryana	472	19	–	–	–	20	511
10	Himachal Pradesh	1105	3	–	–	–	14	1122
11	J&K	273	235	–	–	–	0	508
12	Jharkhand	122	30	–	–	–	54	206
13	Karnataka	589	51	–	–	5	42	687
14	Kerala	740	1	6	–	–	580	1327
15	MP	1427	50	–	–	–	146	1623
16	Maharashtra	490	25	–	–	1	0	516
17	Manipur	0	–	–	–	–	9	9
18	Meghalaya	12	–	–	–	–	10	22
19	Mizoram	0	–	–	–	–	1	1
20	Nagaland	–	–	–	–	–	–	0
21	Orissa	624	9	–	35	30	603	1301
22	Punjab	507	35	–	1	–	107	650
23	Rajasthan	3496	92	–		4	147	3739
24	Sikkim	1	–	–	–	–	1	2
25	Tamil Nadu	32	21	435	1	1	43	533
26	Tripura	55	–	–	–	–	93	148
27	UP	340	49	–	–	–	1482	1871
28	Uttrakhand	467	3	–	–	–	60	530
29	WB	295	3	–	–	–	1220	1518
30	A&N Islands	1	–	–	–	–	8	9
31	Chandigarh	6	–	–	–	–	5	11
32	Dadra & Nagar Haveli	3	–	–	–	–	1	4
33	Daman & Diu	1	–	–	–	–	–	1
34	Lakshadweep	2	–	–	–	–	1	3
35	Puducherry	16	–	16	–	–	7	39
36	CGHS	31	9	2	3	3	34	82
37	Research Council	6	5	2	–	–	40	53
38	Ministry of Railways	39	–	–	–	–	129	168
39	Ministry of Labour	127	1	3	–	–	29	160
40	Ministry of Coal	28	–	–	–	–	–	28
	Total	13914	1010	464	71	56	5836	21351

Note: Figures are provisional; – = Nil.
Source: State governments and certain Central Government organizations.

ANNEXURE 3.2.3
Department of AYUSH—Scheme-wise Tenth Plan Outlay and Expenditure

(Rs in crore)

S. No.	Name of Scheme	2002–07 Tenth Plan Approved Outlay	2002–07 Sum of Annual Outlay	2002–07 Sum of Actual Expenditure
1	2	3	4	5
1	Development of Institutions	120.00	155.72	120.81
2	Hospitals and Dispensaries	59.00	243.85	310.15
3	Drugs Quality Control	45.40	43.56	56.67
	Total CSS	224.40	443.13	487.63
1	Strengthening of Department of AYUSH	22.50	28.56	27.02
2	Statutory Institutions	2.65	2.75	0.69
3	Hospitals and Dispensaries	28.94	61.69	15.72
4	Strengthening of Pharmacopoeial Laboratories	26.50	36.17	9.97
5	IEC	19.00	18.71	19.27
6	Educational Institutions	116.50	147.75	125.18
7	Research Councils	140.50	206.78	195.64
8	Medicinal Plants	93.50	134.21	141.47
9	Other Programmes and Schemes	100.46	134.20	6.95
10	New Initiatives	0.05	0.05	0.01
	Total CS	550.60	770.87	541.92
	Total: (CSS + CS)	775.00	1214.00	1029.55

ANNEXURE 3.2.4
Schemes under Department of AYUSH

S. No.	Ministry/ Department	Number of Schemes towards the end of Tenth Plan	Weeded/ Transferred towards the end of Tenth Plan	To be continued during Eleventh Plan	New Schemes during Eleventh Plan	Total Schemes during Eleventh Plan
Central Sector Schemes (CS)						
1	AYUSH	10	0	5 (Ongoing Schemes clubbed as 5 Schemes)	3	8
Centrally Sponsored Schemes (CSS)						
1	AYUSH	3	0	1 (Ongoing Schemes merged into 1 Scheme)	2	3

4

Nutrition and Social Safety Net

4.1 FOOD AND NUTRITION

INTRODUCTION

4.1.1 At the beginning of the Eleventh Plan period there are serious concerns around food and nutritional security. Agriculture has performed well below expectations during the two recent Plans. Cereal production has declined in per capita terms. The number of the poor has barely declined by 20 million people over three decades, 1973–2005, from 320 million to 300 million; and most of this decline has occurred during the most recent decade (1993/94–2004/05). Low and stagnating incomes among the poor has meant that low purchasing power remains a serious constraint to household food and nutritional security, even if food production picks up as a result of interventions in agriculture and creation of rural infrastructure (discussed in Volume III).

4.1.2 Outcomes in terms of protein-energy malnutrition (PEM) speak for themselves: in 1998–99, according to National Family Health Survey-2 (NFHS-2), as much as 36% of the adult population of India had a body mass index (BMI) below 18.5 (the cut-off for adult malnutrition); eight years later (2005–06) that share had barely fallen to 33% of the population, despite a decade of robust economic growth. Similarly, share of the under-weight children under-3 in the total child population under-3 had not fallen at all (47% in 1998–99 and 46% in 2004–05/06). There is a need to look at food security issues not in isolation as being confined to cereal production and consumption, but to examine how nutritional outcomes can be improved for the vast majority of the poor.

4.1.3 Ensuring food and nutritional security, however, cannot be enough. There are far too many vulnerabilities in the lives of the poor and those just above the poverty line. Around 93% of our labour force works in the informal sector, without any form of social protection, especially against old age. With growing migration of younger rural residents to urban and fast-growing rural areas, elderly parents are often left behind in the village to cope on their own, or are dependent upon women who also have to tend to the family farm, as agriculture feminizes with growing male migration. Old-age pension is thus becoming a crying need for those dependent on insecure employment in the informal economy as well as for parents left behind. Moreover, vulnerability in respect of health arises from the under-funding of the public health system and its inability to provide comprehensive care, which is a major concern for the majority of the population.

MALNUTRITION: A CONCEPTUAL AND EMPIRICAL ANALYSIS

Some Conceptual Issues

4.1.4 Malnutrition reflects an imbalance of both macro and micro-nutrients that may be due to inappropriate intake and/or inefficient biological utilization due to the internal/external environment. Poor feeding practices in infancy and early childhood, resulting in malnutrition, contribute to impaired cognitive and social development, poor school performance, and reduced productivity in later life. Malnutrition therefore is a major threat to social and economic development as it is among the most serious obstacles to attaining and maintaining health of this important age group.

4.1.5 When poor nutrition starts in utero, it extends throughout the life cycle, particularly in girls and women. This not only amplifies the risks to the individual's health but also increases the likelihood of damage to future generations, through further foetal retardation. Low birth weight increases the risk of infant and child mortality and those who survive are usually undernourished, fall ill frequently, and fail to develop optimally, both physically and mentally. Further, undernourished adults are functionally impaired and unable to sustain productive physical activity throughout the day. Nutrition-related disabilities, such as memory disturbances, osteoporosis, etc., are found among elderly.

4.1.6 When nutritional needs are not met, recovery from an illness also takes longer. Malnutrition is also linked to the growing HIV/AIDS pandemic. Malnutrition makes adults more susceptible to the virus. Inadequate infant feeding aggravates its transmission from mother to child; and evidence suggests that malnutrition makes ARV drugs less effective. In addition, good nutrition can help to extend the period when the person with HIV/AIDS is well and working. There are also new dimensions to the malnutrition problem. The epidemic of obesity and diet-related NCDs is spreading in India slowly but steadily. India is beginning to suffer from a double burden of undernutrition and obesity. This phenomenon, called 'nutrition transition', means that the national health systems now have to cope with the high cost of treating diet-related NCDs and at the same time, fight under nutrition and the traditional communicable diseases.

4.1.7 Therefore the challenges that still remains include:

- High levels of adult malnutrition affecting a third of the country's adults,
- Inappropriate infant feeding and caring practices,
- High levels of undernutrition, particularly in women and children,
- Micronutrient undernutrition,
- Emerging diet-related diseases,
- Inadequate access to health care.

Empirical Evidence

4.1.8 The absolute weights and heights of Indians on average have not shown significant improvement over the last 25 years. A staggering percentage of babies in India are born with LBW, a problem that began in utero. A mean deficit of 1.4 to 1.6 kg in weight at one year worsens to a deficit of about 9 kg at 10 years and 13–18 kg when adults. A similar trend is seen in the case of heights (where a deficit of 1cm at 1 year reaches 12–13 cm when adult). It is therefore, not surprising that about half of children are under weight (moderate to severe under nutrition) or are stunted. There are no differences in the nutritional status between girls and boys; however, the mean heights and weights of children from SC/ST and other marginalized sections are below the national mean values. In addition, about 30% of all adults have BMI<18.5 (33% of women and 28% of men), which defines adult malnutrition.

4.1.9 Some of the reasons for this grim picture in India are as follows: With a 500–600 kcal deficit in energy intake (almost 40% of their requirement) and multiple nutrient deficiencies such as fat, calcium, iron, riboflavin, vitamin C (all 50% deficit), and vitamin A (70% deficit), it is not surprising that there is massive inadequacy/hunger leading to malnutrition in children and adolescents. Studies from 10 States show that less than 30% of children have protein-calorie adequacy (Table 4.1.1).

4.1.10 On further scrutiny of the diet surveys, it is obvious that over 70 to 80% of the calories consumed by the children (even though inadequate) are derived from cereals and pulses. This results in two things:

(i) Children cannot consume more cereals to make up for the calorie deficiency because of its sheer monotony and lack of energy density.
(ii) In the absence of fats, milk, eggs, and sources of iron, children starve themselves. The resultant

TABLE 4.1.1
Distribution of Children by Protein-calorie Adequacy Status

(%)

Age (yrs)	%	
1–3	31.8	
4–6	28.2	
7–9	28.1	
	Boys	Girls
10–12	26.0	32.9
13–15	34.7	43.1
16–17	50.2	64.0
Adult Sedentary	Men—68.8	Women—81.8
Pregnant Women	64.3	
Lactation Women	62.2	

Source: National Nutrition Monitoring Bureau (NNMB) Reports 2002.

iron deficiency anaemia (IDA), further worsens their appetite.

4.1.11 Therefore in the absence of foods other than cereals and pulses in the diets of children and the inability of children in the age groups of (1–18 years) to derive and satisfy their protein-calorie and other nutrient needs from cereals, the malnutrition scenario can only get worse. Even fats that provide energy density in the diets are not available in adequate quantities (normally fats should provide 30–40% of calorie needs). It is therefore not surprising that there is massive hunger leading to multiple nutrient deficiencies. This is not hidden hunger; it is hunger for nutrient-rich foods.

Trends in All-India Pattern of Consumption Food Expenditure since 1972–73

4.1.12 Per capita cereal consumption of the Indian population has been declining in both rural and urban areas over the past two or three decades. Table 4.1.2 gives per capita quantity of cereal consumption per month in 15 major States as estimated from the 50th (1993–94), 55th (1999–2000), and 61st (2004–05) rounds of NSS, (Ministry of Statistics and Programme Implementation, GoI). It shows that the decline is spread over all the major States

TABLE 4.1.2
Changes in Average per capita Cereal Consumption in 15 States in Physical Terms over the Last Decade in Major States

RURAL — Monthly per capita cereal consumption (kg.) in

Year	AP	ASM	BHR*	GUJ	HAR	KTK	KRL	MP#
1993–94	13.3	13.2	14.3	10.7	12.9	13.2	10.1	14.2
1999–2000	12.65	12.63	13.75	10.19	11.37	11.53	9.89	12.94
2004–05	12.07	13.04	13.08	10.07	10.66	10.73	9.53	12.16
	MAH	ORS	PUN	RAJ	TN	UP^	WB	IND
1993–94	11.4	15.9	10.8	14.9	11.7	13.9	15.0	13.4
1999–2000	11.32	15.09	10.58	14.19	10.66	13.62	13.59	12.72
2004–05	10.50	13.98	9.92	12.68	10.89	12.87	13.18	12.12

URBAN — Monthly per capita cereal consumption (kg.) in

Year	AP	ASM	BHR*	GUJ	HAR	KTK	KRL	MP#
1993–94	11.3	12.1	12.8	9.0	10.5	10.9	9.5	11.3
1999–2000	10.94	12.26	12.70	8.49	9.36	10.21	9.25	11.09
2004–05	10.51	11.92	12.21	8.29	9.15	9.71	8.83	10.63
	MAH	ORS	PUN	RAJ	TN	UP^	WB	IND
1993–94	9.4	13.4	9.0	11.5	10.1	11.1	11.6	10.6
1999–2000	9.35	14.51	9.21	11.56	9.65	10.79	11.17	10.42
2004–05	8.39	13.11	9.01	10.84	9.48	10.94	10.39	9.94

Note: *includes Jharkhand; # includes Chhattisgarh; ^ includes Uttaranchal

Source: NSS 50th, 55th, and 61st Rounds.

and affects both rural and urban sectors to a similar extent.

4.1.13 In both rural and urban India, the share of food in total expenditure continued to fall throughout the three decades prior to 2004–05. The overall fall was from 73% to 55% in rural areas and from 64.5% to 42% in urban areas (Table 4.1.3). In urban India, not only the shares of cereals and pulses have fallen, but there has been a fall in the shares of other food groups as well, such as milk and milk products, edible oil, and sugar. In rural India, however, the shares of milk and milk products, egg, fish and meat, and fruits and nuts have increased by about 1 percentage point each, the share of vegetables has increased by 2.5 percentage points, and that of beverages, refreshments, and processed food has increased by 2 percentage points since 1972–73; only the shares of sugar and pulses (the latter, largely during the last decade) have declined noticeably, apart from cereals. In any case, the increase in the share of non-cereals is not enough to compensate for the decline in cereal consumption.

TABLE 4.1.3
Composition of Food Consumption, All-India, Rural, and Urban, 1972–73 to 2004–05

Sector	Year	% share of major food groups in total expenditure									
		All food	Cereals	Pulses	Milk and milk products	Edible oil	Egg, fish and meat	Vege-tables	Fruits and nuts	Sugar	Beve-rages, etc.
Rural	72–73	72.9	40.6	4.3	7.3	3.5	2.5	3.6	1.1	3.8	2.4
	87–88	64.0	26.3	4.0	8.6	5.0	3.3	5.2	1.6	2.9	3.9
	93–94	63.2	24.2	3.8	9.5	4.4	3.3	6.0	1.7	3.1	4.2
	99–00	59.4	22.2	3.8	8.8	3.7	3.3	6.2	1.7	2.4	4.2
	04–05	55.0	18.0	3.1	8.5	4.6	3.3	6.1	1.9	2.4	4.5
Urban	72–73	64.5	23.3	3.4	9.3	4.9	3.3	4.4	2.0	3.6	7.6
	87–88	56.4	15.0	3.4	9.5	5.3	3.6	5.3	2.5	2.4	6.8
	93–94	54.7	14.0	3.0	9.8	4.4	3.4	5.5	2.7	2.4	7.2
	99–00	48.1	12.4	2.8	8.7	3.1	3.1	5.1	2.4	1.6	6.4
	04–05	42.5	10.1	2.1	7.9	3.5	2.7	4.5	2.2	1.5	6.2

THE PROBLEM WITH CHILD MALNUTRITION

4.1.14 Sixty years after independence, nearly half of India's children under three are malnourished (see Table 4.1.4). India has the largest number of children in the world who are malnourished. Even more significantly, India's rate of malnutrition is worse than that in Africa on average. In fact, South Asian countries have the world's worst rate of malnutrition, and India's rate of malnutrition is among the worst in South Asia (together with Nepal and Bangladesh). Even the best State in India, Kerala, has a rate of child malnutrition comparable to that for Africa's average rate.

4.1.15 Even more worrying is the fact that the rate of malnutrition, defined as underweight children relative to an internationally accepted reference population, has not declined significantly over the last decade and a half. In 1992–93 (NFHS-1) it was 54%; in 1998–99 (NFHS-2), it was 46%, and in 2005–06 (NFHS-3) it was 46%—hardly any change over a period in which the economy has been growing at over 6% p.a. on average. Naturally, given the increase in population,

TABLE 4.1.4
Trends in Childhood (0–3 Years of Age)—Malnutrition in India

Nutritional Parameter	1992–93 NFHS-1	1998–99 NFHS-2	2005–06 NFHS-3
Stunted	52.0	45.5	38.4
Wasted	17.5	15.5	19.1
Underweight	53.4	47.0	45.9

Note: Figures of NFHS-1 above are for 0–4 years. However, NFHS-1 later generated data for below 3 years children with 51.5% children being underweight.

Source: NFHS surveys, IIPS, MoHFW, GoI.

the number of malnourished is likely to have actually increased.

4.1.16 Bihar, Jharkhand, MP, Chhatisgarh, and UP are the States with malnutrition rates well above the national average of 46% (Annexure 4.1.1). Some of these States have actually seen an increase in the share of malnourished children in the 0–3 year-old child population between 1998–99 (NFHS-2) and 2005–06 (NFHS-3). A concerted effort is planned, therefore, in the Eleventh Plan to reduce the child malnutrition rate in each State to the extent identified in Annexure 4.1.2.

4.1.17 NFHS-3 shows that anaemia among children and women is on the rise. As much as 74.2% of the children of 6–35 months were anaemic (NFHS-2) that has increased to 79.2% (NFHS-3). Similarly, the percentage of married women in the age group 15–49 who were anaemic has increased from 51.8% in 1998–99 to 56.2% in 2005–06 and that of pregnant women of 15–49 years has increased from 49.7% in 1998–99 to 57.9% in 2005–06 (see later section on Micronutrient deficiencies).

A Summary of the Situation Analysis

4.1.18 In other words, what emerges is that first, per capita availability of cereals has declined, and second, the share of non-cereals in food consumption has not grown to compensate for the decline in cereal availability. Even if the latter has grown there may well be a problem for significant sections of the population who may be feeling the distress caused by falling per capita cereal availability, and who also do not have the purchasing power to diversify their food consumption away from cereals.

4.1.19 In any case, the significant point is that overall per capita intake of calories and protein has declined consistently over a 20-year period from 1983 to 2004–05, according to NSS data (see Table 4.1.5). Rural calorie consumption per day has fallen from 2221 to 2047, an 8% decline. Similarly, the urban calorie consumption fell by 3.3%, from 2080 to 2020. The rural protein consumption fell by 8% over the same period and urban consumption remained the same over the 20-year period. Since this data is for households, it does not capture the impact of intra-household food distribution. It is well known that women and girls in poor households receive poorer quality food and less food in a normal, patriarchal household.

TABLE 4.1.5
Per Capita Intake of Calorie and Protein

	Calorie (K cal/day)		Protein (gm/day)	
	Rural	Urban	Rural	Urban
1983 (NSS 38th Round)	2221	2089	62.0	57.0
1993–94 (NSS 50th Round)	2153	2071	60.2	57.2
1999–2000 (NSS 55th Round)	2149	2156	59.1	58.5
2004–05 (NSS 61st Round)	2047	2020	57.0	57.0

Source: NSS Report No. 513, Nutritional Intake in India, 2004–05.

4.1.20 So taken together we have a set of overlapping problems in the country. First, the calorie consumption *on average* in rural areas has fallen way below the calorie-norm for the rural poverty line (2400 calories). It was lower than that norm 20 years ago and it has actually fallen since then on average. Similarly, the poverty line threshold for urban areas for calorie consumption is 2100 and urban consumption too was lower on average than the norm two decades ago and has also fallen. It is obvious that the non-poor consume more calories on average than the poor. Hence, to allow for distributional inequity that prevails in any society, calorie availability on average in the country as a whole should be at least 20% higher than the per capita requirement (i.e. 2100 calories for urban and 2400 calories for rural areas). Even 20 years ago, Indian consumption of calories on average was way below the requirements. So inevitably the poor, let alone the extremely poor, were and still are consuming calories that are way below the norm. And the intra-household allocation, not just among the poor but also among those who are marginally above the poverty line, is likely to be highly skewed against women and girls. When one combines this fact with the well-known fact (established in repeated NFHS since the early 1990s) that women and girls are less likely to access health services when they fall sick, it is hardly surprising that the sex ratio in the population is as low as it is, and falling.

4.1.21 The state of PEM has shown little no or signs of improvement over several decades. It is in this context that the Minimum Support Price (MSP) and the Public Distribution System (PDS) become significant.

Minimum Support Price, Food Procurement Policy, and the Public Distribution System

4.1.22 Food security is the outcome of both production and distribution decisions. Agricultural production issues are discussed in the 'Agriculture' chapter of the Eleventh Plan (Volume III). In fact, the GoI has in 2007 taken the decision to introduce a Food Security Mission, which will focus on increasing production of cereals and pulses. This chapter focuses on the distribution, affordability, and availability issues in respect of calories. This section discusses what changes need to happen in the PDS in order to both improve food security as well as reduce fiscal subsidies.

Minimum Support Price (MSP)

4.1.23 Foodgrains are procured at the MSP fixed by the government mostly in a small number of grain-surplus States in the north of India, which are then transported across the country to deficit States (the latter mostly in the south and west of the country). MSPs are fixed on rates recommended by Commission for Agricultural Costs and Prices (CACP), which are set using mainly cost of cultivation. These grain stocks essentially supply the PDS of the country. Through the PDS, cereals are made available to BPL households, as well as to Above Poverty Line (APL) households—at differential prices. There is a third category of beneficiaries—*Antyodaya* card holders. Under the *Antyodaya Anna Yojana* (AAY), 35 kg of foodgrains are being provided to the poorest of the poor families at the highly subsidized rate of Rs 2 per kg for wheat and Rs 3 per kg for rice.

4.1.24 During the years of accumulation of stocks in the Central Pool until 2001–02, it was believed that excess procurement was on account of the government's decision to fix the MSP for paddy and wheat in excess of the levels prescribed by the CACP. Grain stocks have declined since then.

Stabilization

4.1.25 Given the limited purchasing power of the poor, there is a need to contain cereal price rises. For this purpose government maintains foodgrains buffer stocks through the Food Corporation of India (FCI). Stocks had reached to 256.17 lakh tonnes (rice) and 324.15 lakh tonnes (wheat) for the year 2001–02. But in 2007, the stocks of these two foodgrains fell to 131.71 lakh tonnes (rice) and 45.63 lakh tonnes (wheat), respectively.

4.1.26 To achieve the cereal price stabilization objective of PDS, food stocks with FCI should be at a reasonable level. In recent years, both procurement and stocks with FCI have tended to fall. If the needs of procurement to maintain adequate stocks requires procurement prices to be higher than MSP, a transparent mechanism is needed that enables government to undertake commercial purchases at prices comparable to those paid by private traders. This could be done if the procurement price (i.e. MSP plus bonus) was announced at the beginning of the purchase season, along with a procurement target in terms of quantity. After the procurement target was met, the bonus would be suspended. However, if procurement quantities, even with bonus are not met, FCI should be able to tender from both domestic as well as international markets, after standard procurement operations, to make up the deficit to maintain stocks with the FCI.

Decentralized Procurement

4.1.27 Unlike the mid-1990s, cereal procurement was earlier concentrated in a few northern States. However, under the decentralized procurement scheme introduced in 1997–98, the State Governments themselves undertake direct purchase of paddy and wheat and procurement of levy rice on behalf of the GoI. Purchase centres are opened by the State Governments and their agencies as per their requirements. The State Governments procure, store, and distribute foodgrains under Targeted Public Distribution System (TDPS) and other welfare schemes. In the event of the total quantity of wheat and rice thus procured falling short of the total allocation made by the Central Government, FCI meets the deficit out of the Central Pool stocks. Under this scheme, State-specific economic cost is determined by the GoI and the difference between the economic cost so fixed and the central issue prices (CIP) is passed on to the State as food subsidy.

4.1.28 The Decentralized Procurement Scheme, which is presently in operation in 11 States, has been very successful in increasing procurement of rice in many non-traditional States, as can be seen below in Table 4.1.6.

4.1.29 There is a need for States to increase procurement to reduce their requirement of foodgrains from the Central Pool. There is also a need for more States with large production, such as Bihar for wheat and rice and Assam for rice, to adopt the Decentralized Procurement scheme. If this were to happen, there could be a considerable saving in terms of transportation costs.

with higher MSPs declared more recently, there is a danger that the subsidy is likely to rise (see Table 4.1.7) due to increase in MSP, announcement of bonus, and carrying cost of FCI. The Table 4.1.7 gives the figures of food subsidy of the GoI.

Public Distribution System

4.1.32 The PDS is a major State intervention in the country aimed at ensuring food security to all the people, especially the poor. The PDS operates through a large distribution network of around 4.89 lakh fair price shops (FPS), and is supplemental in nature. Under the PDS, the Central Government is responsible for the procurement and transportation of foodgrains up to the principal distribution centres of the FCI while the State Governments are responsible for the identification of families living below the

TABLE 4.1.6
Procurement of Rice in DCP States during Kharif Marketing Season

(Figures in lakh tonnes)

S. No.	State	2002–03	2003–04	2004–05	2005–06	2006–07*
1	WB	1.26	9.25	9.44	12.75	5.19
2	UP	13.60	25.54	29.71	31.51	21.01
3	Chhattisgarh	12.91	23.74	28.37	32.65	25.20
4	Uttaranchal	2.32	3.23	3.61	3.36	1.74
5	A&N Islands	-	Neg.	0.01	-	-
6	Orissa	8.90	13.73	15.90	17.85	14.18
7	Tamil Nadu	1.07	2.07	6.52	9.26	10.38
7	Kerala	-	-	0.33	0.94	1.05
8	Karnataka	-	-	0.21	0.48	0.12
	Total (a)	40.06	77.56	94.10	108.80	78.86

Note: *Position as on 19.04.07.

Food Subsidy

4.1.30 Food subsidy is provided in the Budget of the Department of Food and Public Distribution to meet the difference between the economic cost of foodgrains procured by FCI and their sales realization at CIP for TPDS and other welfare schemes. In addition, the Central Government also procures foodgrains for meeting the requirements of buffer stock. Hence, part of the food subsidy also goes towards meeting the carrying cost of buffer stock.

4.1.31 The food subsidy bill of the GoI peaked in 2004–05 and declined as stocks declined. However,

TABLE 4.1.7
Food Subsidy

Year	Food Subsidy (Rs in crore)
1996–97	5166
1997–98	7500
1998–99	8700
1999–2000	9200
2000–01	12010
2001–02	17494
2002–03	24176
2003–04	25160
2004–05	25746
2005–06	23071
2006–07	23827

poverty line, the issue of ration cards, and the distribution of foodgrains to the vulnerable sections through FPSs. *PDS seems to have failed in serving the second objective of making foodgrains available to the poor. If it had, the consumption levels of cereals should not have fallen* on average—as it has consistently over the last two decades.

4.1.33 With a view to improving its efficiency, the PDS was redesigned as TDPS with effect from June 1997. The TPDS envisages identifying the poor households and giving them a fixed entitlement of foodgrains at subsidized prices. Under the TPDS, higher rates of subsidies are being given to the poor and the poorest among the poor. The APL families are also being given foodgrains under TPDS but with lower subsidy. The scale of issue under TDPS for Antyodaya cardholders began with 10 kg per family per month, which has been progressively increased to 35 kg per family per month with effect from April 2002.

4.1.34 Under the TPDS, the identification of BPL families was to be carried out by the State Governments based on criteria adopted by the Ministry of Rural Development (MoRD). However, the total number of beneficiaries was to be limited to the State-wise poverty estimates (1993–94) of the Planning Commission projected to the population as on 1.03.2000. Against a total ceiling of 6.52 crore BPL households (as per the poverty estimates of the Planning Commission for 1993–94 and population projection of the Registrar General as on 01.03.2000), more than 8 crore BPL ration cards have been issued. Similarly against the figure of 18.03 crore households in the country (as per the population projections as on 1.03.2000 of the Registrar General of India), the total number of ration cards issued is around 22.32 crore. This does raise problems at the field level.

Major Deficiencies of TPDS

4.1.35 As identified by various studies, the major deficiencies of the TPDS include: (i) high exclusion and inclusion errors, (ii) non-viability of FPSs, (iii) failure in fulfilling the price stabilization objective, and (iv) leakages.

(I) HIGH EXCLUSION AND INCLUSION ERRORS

4.1.36 The Programme Evaluation Organization's (PEO's) Study (2005) establishes large-scale exclusion and inclusion errors in most States (see Box 4.1.1). It also questions the BPL methodology used for

Box 4.1.1
Performance Evaluation of TPDS

- Only 22.7% FPSs are viable in terms of earning a return of 12% on capital.
- The offtake by APL cardholders was negligible except in Himachal Pradesh, Tamil Nadu, and West Bengal.
- The offtake per BPL card was high in WB, Kerala, Himachal Pradesh, and Tamil Nadu.
- The offtake by the poor under TPDS was substantially higher than under universal PDS.
- There are large errors of exclusion and inclusion and ghost cards are common.
- High exclusion errors mean a low coverage of BPL households. The survey estimated that TPDS covers only 57% BPL families.
- Errors of inclusion are high in Andhra Pradesh, Karnataka, and Tamil Nadu. This implies that the APL households receive an unacceptably large proportion of subsidized grains.
- Leakages vary enormously between States. In Bihar and Punjab, the total leakage exceeds 75% while in Haryana and UP, it is between 50 and 75%.
- Leakage and diversion imply a low share of the genuine BPL households of the distribution of the subsidized grains. During 2003–04, it is estimated that out of 14.1 million tonnes of BPL quota from the Central Pool, only 6.1 million tonnes reached the BPL families and 8 million tonnes did not reach the target families.
- Leakage and diversion raised the cost of delivery. For every 1 kg that was delivered to the poor, GoI had to issue 2.32 kg from the Central Pool.
- During 2003–04, out of an estimated subsidy of Rs 7258 crore under TPDS, Rs 4123 crore did not reach BPL families. Moreover, Rs 2579 crore did not reach any consumer but was shared by agencies involved in the supply chain.

identification of households at State level. There are two problems here. One is the criterion used for allocation of foodgrains by the Central Government to States. The Central Government allocates foodgrains to States based on a narrow official poverty line. There is a need to look at this allocation criterion to States. If we go by the official poverty ratio criterion, only 28% of the population is eligible under PDS at all-India level in 2004–05. However, food-insecure households may be much higher than the official poverty ratios. For example, undernutrition among children and households is much higher than this figure. The use of BPL estimates to determine Central allocations should be revisited because there is a significant mass of households just above the poverty line.

4.1.37 A second problem is the use of BPL method for identifying households by the States. This identification differs from State to State. For example, some of the south Indian States do not follow the official poverty ratio for limiting the ration cards. In Andhra Pradesh, more than 70% of the households have ration cards. This is one of the reasons for high inclusion errors in Andhra Pradesh.

(II) VIABILITY OF FPSs

4.1.38 An important institutional concern is that of the economic viability of FPSs, which appears to have been badly affected by the exclusion of APL population from the PDS (which happened after PDS became TPDS in 1997). The virtual exclusion of the APL population has led to a big decline in offtake. With fewer ration cards to serve, lower turnover, and upper bounds on the margins that can be charged to BPL consumers, the net profits of FPS owners and dealers are lower under the TPDS than before. Since there are economies of scale here, for instance, with respect to transport, the distribution of smaller quantities is likely to make many shops unviable. When FPSs are economically viable, there are fewer incentives to cheat.

4.1.39 Some of the steps suggested by the High-level Committee (HLC) on Long Term Grain Policy to revive the retail network were the following:

'Relax restriction on eligibility to be a licensed FPS; make NGOs and village-level retailers eligible to undertake licensed PDS distribution, and in particular, encourage women; remove restrictions on the range of commodities that can be sold in a FPS; and allow registered associations of FPS dealers to purchase the grain allocated directly from the FCI'.

(III) REGIONAL ALLOCATION AND PRICE STABILIZATION OBJECTIVE

4.1.40 One of the objectives of the PDS has always been to ensure price stabilization in the country by transferring grain from cereals-surplus to cereals-deficit regions. Targeted PDS has reduced the effectiveness of this objective. This is because under TPDS, the demand for cereals is no longer determined by State Governments (based on their requirements and in practical terms on past utilization) but on allocations decided by the Central Government (based on poverty estimates prepared by the Planning Commission). The new system of allocation, as pointed out by the HLC, has led to imbalances between actual allocations and 'allocations necessary to meet the difference between cereals production and requirement'.

(IV) LEAKAGES AND DIVERSION

4.1.41 Undoubtedly, in many parts of India, the current system of delivery has weaknesses resulting in leakages at different stages. As the Programme Evaluation Organization, PEO Study (2005) points out, 'the share of leakages in offtake from the Central Pool is abnormally high, except in the States of West Bengal and Tamil Nadu'. Further, 'in terms of leakages through ghost BPL cards, there are fewer problems in Andhra Pradesh, Haryana, Kerala, Punjab, Rajasthan and Tamil Nadu than in other States'. At the FPS level, leakages were found to be high in Bihar, Punjab, and Haryana.

4.1.42 The study goes on to identify the factors associated with relatively low leakages at the FPS level and concludes that 'general awareness of the beneficiaries, high literacy and strong grass root-level organizations (particularly PRIs) have helped States like West Bengal and Himachal Pradesh in minimising FPS level leakage, while in the case of Tamil Nadu, it is the elimination of private retail outlets'. It has been documented that strong political commitment and careful monitoring by the bureaucracy are the key elements of the success of PDS in Tamil Nadu.

4.1.43 Leakages cannot be lowered by finer targeting using official poverty criterion. They require political commitment and participation of the people in the delivery process. The nexus between officials, the mafia, and ration shop dealers must be broken in order to reduce leakages. Monitoring and accountability of TPDS (food security watch) should be improved in a significant way. The TPDS needs to be strengthened by means of the effective use of IT including introduction of a unique ID-based smart card system.

Coverage of Commodities Supplied through TPDS

4.1.44 If nutrition security is one of the considerations of TPDS, the government may explore the possibility of including more commodities under TPDS. For example, cereals such as jowar, bajra, and also pulses could be introduced in TPDS because of nutritional considerations. The consumption of pulses is low for the poor. Operational details of supplying these commodities, particularly, pulses have to be worked out. It is true that presently the country has a shortage of these commodities. However, the introduction of these commodities may encourage production of these crops especially in dry land areas. The National Food Security Mission has identified pulses as an area of focus.

Steps Taken to Strengthen the TPDS and Plan Schemes

4.1.45 The GoI has taken following measures to strengthen TPDS and check diversion of foodgrains meant for TPDS:

CITIZEN'S CHARTER

- A Citizens' Charter has been issued in November 1997 for adoption by the State Governments to provide services in a transparent and accountable manner under PDS. Instructions have been issued for involvement of PRIs in identifications of BPL families and in Vigilance Committee.

PDS (CONTROL) ORDER, 2001

- The Order, inter alia, covers a range of areas relating to correct identification of BPL families, issue of ration cards, proper distribution, and monitoring of PDS-related operations. Contraventions of the provisions of the Order are punishable under the Essential Commodities Act, 1955. Clearly, these do not seem to have had much impact, since the NSSO estimates of 2006 suggest that the extent of leakage and diversion of grain has only increased.

4.1.46 In addition, a number of Plan Schemes have been introduced.

(I) CONSTRUCTION OF GODOWNS

4.1.47 The Scheme was conceived during the Fifth Five Year Plan to build and increase the storage capacity available with FCI for storage of foodgrains.

(II) INTEGRATED INFORMATION SYSTEM FOR FOODGRAINS MANAGEMENT (IISFM)

4.1.48 The main objective of the IISFM project in the FCI, initiated in 2003–04, is to put in place an online MIS that would give the stock position in any depot at any given point of time.

(III) STRENGTHENING OF PDS

Food Credit Cards/Computerization of PDS Operations

4.1.49 A new scheme 'Computerization of PDS Operations' with a token provision of Rs 5 crore was introduced in 2006–07. The computerization of PDS operations would be an improvement on the existing system of ration cards, that is, the present manual system of making entries, etc. The new system will have personal details of all members of the family including their entitlement and the entire network of PDS from taluk to State level will be linked. With this kind of system in place, the objectives of Food Credit Card Scheme of checking diversion of foodgrains and eliminating the problem of bogus ration cards are expected to be met.

Curbing Leakages/Diversion of Foodgrains Meant for TPDS

4.1.50 This is a new scheme introduced during the Eleventh Five Year Plan to strengthen the PDS. The scheme aims at taking effective measures to curb diversion and leakages through Global Positioning System, Radio Frequency Identification Device, etc.

Generating Awareness amongst TPDS Beneficiaries about their Entitlement and Redressal Mechanism and Monitoring

4.1.51 A mass awareness campaign on the rights and entitlements of TPDS beneficiaries is proposed through newspaper advertisements, bill boards, posters, printing of annual calendar on the themes of TPDS, and audio-visual publicity measures such as short spots/quickies, audio jingles/radio spots, TV serials/documentaries.

Training and Awareness of Negotiable Warehouse Receipt System

4.1.52 This is a new scheme for the Eleventh Five Year Plan. The warehousing receipts at present do not enjoy the fiduciary trust of depositors and banks, as there is fear of not being able to recover the loans in events such as fraud or mismanagement on behalf of the warehouse or insolvency of depositor. The legal remedies are also time consuming and inadequate. In this context, it is proposed to develop a negotiable warehouse receipt system for commodities including agricultural commodities. The negotiable warehouse receipt system will result in increase in the liquidity in the rural areas, encouragement of scientific warehousing of goods, lower cost of financing, etc.

(IV) VILLAGE GRAIN BANK SCHEME

4.1.53 The Village Grain Bank Scheme, which was hitherto with the Ministry of Tribal Affairs, has been transferred to the Department of Food and Public Distribution w.e.f. The objective of the scheme is to establish Grain Banks in chronically food-scarce area and to provide safeguard against starvation during the lean period. The scheme is also to mitigate drought-induced migration and food shortages by making foodgrains available within the village during such calamities. During 2006–07, there was a budget provision of Rs 50 crore for setting up 8591 Village Grain Banks in food-scarce areas.

Further Innovations Needed to Strengthen TPDS and the Way Forward

4.1.54 One of the long-standing criticisms of the TPDS has been that offtake of PDS cereals (rice and wheat) by States from FCI does not match with NSS estimates of PDS consumption of those same grains (as we noted earlier). For instance, Table 4.1.8 shows that, according to NSS, over 1993–94, 1999–2000, and 2004–05, consumption of PDS grains rose. It also shows that offtake of PDS grain from FCI by States increased much more than consumption over the same decade. The difference between the two shows the extent of leakage of PDS wheat and rice. This leakage [defined as 1—{ratio of (a) to (b)}] was 28% for wheat and rice together in 1993–94, but it had risen to 54% by 2004–05—a very significant increase in leakage. These facts clearly show that TPDS is in urgent need of reform.

TABLE 4.1.8
PDS Implied Leakage—Offtake vs Consumption

	1993–94	1999–2000	2004–05
(a) NSS PDS consumption (m. tons)			
Rice	7.20	9.30	9.98
Wheat	3.44	2.99	3.55
Total	10.64	12.29	13.53
(b) PDS offtake (m. tons)			
Rice	8.84	11.35	16.62
Wheat	5.86	5.76	13.02
Total	14.70	17.11	29.65
Ratio of (a) to (b)			
Rice	0.81	0.82	0.60
Wheat	0.59	0.52	0.27
Total	0.72	0.72	0.46

Source: NSS.

4.1.55 These facts are further underlined by Annexure 4.1.4, which demonstrates the massive leakage of the fiscal subsidy to the non-poor on the one hand and the ineffective targeting of the poor by the cardholder-based TPDS system.

4.1.56 Annexure 4.1.5 drives home the point about the poor targeting by TPDS benefits. It estimates the benefits in rupees per household of PDS grain beneficiaries [calculated as PDS quantity consumed* (PDS Price—Average Market Price)]. It shows that the benefits to the household are dependent upon whether you have a card or not (and which card you have—APL, BPL, or Antyodaya), and not on whether you are poor or non-poor. In fact, it demonstrates that there is very little difference between the benefits (in Rs/household) of poor and non-poor households when one compares poor BPL cardholders with non-poor BPL cardholders, or when comparing poor AAY cardholders with non-poor AAY cardholders.

4.1.57 The TPDS in its current form as a anti-poverty programme clearly is not doing very well. Given these facts, a restructuring of the TPDS has been suggested.

4.1.58 In this context, a recommendation of the HLC on Long Term Grain Policy (2000) was that instead of the current distinction between APL, BPL, and Antyodaya in terms of issue pricing for rice and wheat, there should be a single issue price for grain issued by the FCI from its warehouses. This recommendation, sometimes identified with the return to universal PDS from TPDS adopted in 1997, has been criticized on a number of grounds. First, that if the same price for BPL and APL households was charged, this would not be financially viable for the BPL. If existing AAY and BPL cardholders were charged a higher price, there would be a diversion of benefits from the relatively poor to the relatively rich. Second, there might be pressure to keep the uniform CIP low as high common price for BPL and APL would have adverse consequences for the poor. On the other hand, a low CIP would increase even further the fiscal subsidy. Third, any widening in the effective reach of PDS due to its universalization would put unbearable pressures for the supply of grain into the PDS.

4.1.59 It needs, however, to be noted that the HLC had not altogether ruled out the continuation TPDS in States where this might be the best option. Its recommendation was that there should be a single CIP as far as FCI is concerned for each grain fixed at FCI's acquisition cost and that the existing subsidy beyond this should be passed on to the States on the condition that this be used for food based schemes.

4.1.60 The key issue here is whether or not the existing subsidies that the HLC recommended should be given to the States as cash or best targeted to the intended beneficiaries by means of the existing differential pricing system with lowest prices for Antyodaya, slightly higher price for BPL, and higher still for APL cardholders. The view of the HLC was that although this differential pricing system may work well for some States, it was not necessarily the case in most others and that removing the price differentials in PDS would enable FCI to concentrate on its proper role of price stabilization rather than get involved, as it has, with the complexities of an anti-poverty programme. Also, the HLC had pointed out that differential pricing of the same grain is an invitation to corruption and, therefore, to leakages and other deadweight losses—as already shown by the PEO study cited above as well as more recent evidence emerging from the NSSO. The HLC had suggested that large savings were possible if the subsidy on FCI account could be used to expand other food-based schemes like ICDS, Mid Day Meals, and food entitlement in employment programmes. However, as already mentioned, the HLC left this choice to the States allowing them to continue with the existing TPDS if they so wish to do, by having their own differential prices rather than differential price at the FCI stage.

4.1.61 As we have noted in the tables above, data available from the 61st Round of NSS supports some of the concerns expressed by the HLC. NSS 61st Round also enables an assessment of how effectively PDS and other food based schemes such as MDM, ICDS, and Food for Work are able to reach the poor. This shows that: (i) only about 36% of the poor have either BPL or Antyodaya cards, and also that about 40% of such cards are with the non-poor (Annexure 4.1.4); (ii) possession of appropriate cards (e.g. BPL or Antyodaya) rather than actual poverty status is the determinant of the benefits derived from targeted TPDS (Annexure 4.1.5); (iii) in more self-selecting schemes such as MDM, ICDS, and Food for Work, the total number of beneficiaries is similar to the number currently benefiting from a BPL or AAY status and indeed these self-targeted schemes are somewhat better reaching the poor than the assignment of BPL cards (Annexure 4.1.6). Although not conclusive, this observation taken together suggests that the *leakages of physical grain could be reduced without greater fiscal cost and with somewhat better targeting towards the poor by redirecting subsidies currently in the PDS to better funding of the other schemes (i.e. the MDM, the ICDS).* However, it was noted by the HLC that the incident of leakages and the effectiveness of PDS targeting varies considerably from State to State, suggesting that a one-size-fits-all approach to food and nutrition management is highly mistaken.

Other Measures Needed to Reform TPDS

INTRODUCTION OF FOOD STAMPS

4.1.62 If markets are integrated, food stamps system may be introduced, which is supposed to be more effective than the present system. On food stamps/coupons, the HLC has observed as follows: 'In the long run, as markets get better in tegrated, the PDS function need not remain restricted to designated FPS and a food coupon system valid even outside PDS outlets may become possible. Food coupons may allow wider choice of consumers in terms of commodities and outlets. In the Committee's view, this is a course which should be followed with considerable caution in view of the experience of other countries, and the possibility of counterfeiting. However, the more important reason food stamps have not been successful elsewhere has been the erosion in the value of the coupons where it was fixed in nominal terms. If the coupon system is to succeed the PDS suggested above, the value of the coupon should be indexed to food inflation. The coupon system should not lead to a dilution of the Central Government commitment to food security'. Cash for food subsidies (sometimes known as food stamps) eliminate the need for dual retail marketing mechanisms. This can resolve the endemic problem of uneconomic viability of FPS. As a way of restoring economic viability, the HLC on Grain Policy recommended that FPS should be allowed to sell other commodities. This recommendation of the HLC needs to be considered by the States.

MULTI-APPLICATION SMART CARDS (MASCS)

4.1.63 MASCs is one of the technological breakthroughs of recent times. MASCs facilitate simplification of procedures and enhancing the efficiency in administering various schemes. The National e-Governance Policy fully recognizes the significance of this technological revolution. On-the-spot availability of proof of identity, authentic transaction history, and entitlement details are required at the point of service delivery. It will also allow other innovations/experiments such as the division of the PDS food entitlement between the Head of household and his/her (non-earning) spouse or transfer of entire household entitlement to the housewife/mother. Similarly, different models can be used for kerosene supply and fertilizer supply to farmers. In other words, the precise model for delivery of the subsidy or income transfer to individuals/households can be decided separately and/or modified overtime.

WEB-ENABLED SYSTEMS

4.1.64 Many departments of the Central Government, notably the MoRD, are in the process of developing web-enabled systems that provide information about government programmes to beneficiaries and also details of the benefits received by the targeted beneficiaries. Easy access to such information is the most effective means to empower the beneficiaries and their well-wishers/representatives. Such web-enabled systems can be created for the PDS.

Way Forward

- NSS 61st Round enables an assessment of how effectively PDS and other food based schemes such as MDM, ICDS, and Food for Work are able to reach the poor. This shows that in more self-selecting schemes such as MDM, ICDS, and Food for Work, the total number of beneficiaries is similar to the number currently benefiting BPL or AAY status and indeed these self-targeted schemes are somewhat better reaching the poor than the assignment of BPL cards. Thus the leakages of physical grain could be reduced without greater fiscal cost and with somewhat better targeting towards the poor by redirecting subsidies currently in the PDS to better funding of the other schemes (i.e. the MDM, the ICDS).
- However, a one-size-fits-all approach to food and nutrition management is mistaken. As there are large differences in the efficiency of implementation of the PDS among the States, it may be desirable to introduce State-specific designs and implementation strategies rather than continuing with a uniform design. Separate designs and implementation strategies may be thought of for areas with high concentration of the poor.
- Since some distinction needs to remain between the 'poor' and 'non-poor', the nature of exclusion/inclusion errors suggests that it is much better to

define 'poor' for PDS purposes as much larger than current Planning Commission estimates of the number of poor, and exclude altogether the residual 'non-poor'. If the current allocation of 35 kg per household per month continues, the present PDS offtake (rice + wheat) of about 40 million tonnes would meet PDS requirements of nearly 10 crore households, that is, roughly 60% more households than those defined to be poor by current official poverty estimates.

- The effectiveness of the system can also be improved by better management with the help of IT. Computerization of PDS operations and introduction of a unique ID-based Smart Card System would help in addressing the issues related to bogus ration cards, diversion of foodgrains, etc. The Eleventh Plan will therefore focus on improving the delivery mechanisms and the monitoring arrangements based on IT.
- There is also a need to make concerted efforts for minimizing the operational costs of the FCI from the present high levels through better management practices so that major part of the food subsidy actually accrues to the beneficiaries.
- Attention should also be given to streamlining and standardizing the State level taxes on procurement of foodgrains. Decentralized procurement will be further encouraged and extended to other States with potential for procurement. It is also necessary to strengthen both domestic and international trade in foodgrains by means of appropriate changes in trade policies.

4.1.65 The centralized system involving FCI's stabilization operations would need to be strengthened. This would be helped if FCI is relieved of having to operate the system involving differential prices (i.e. between BPL and APL prices). The total projected GBS for the Eleventh Plan for the Department of Food and Public Distribution is Rs 614 crore (at 2006–07 prices) and Rs 694 crore (at current prices).

Malnutrition: Addressing It through a Revamped ICDS

4.1.66 The ICDS, which has been in existence for over three decades, was intended to address the problem of child and maternal malnutrition, but has clearly had limited impact. Child malnutrition has barely declined at all in a decade and a half, anaemia among women and children has actually risen (see Annexure 4.1.3) and a third of all adult women were undernourished at the end of 1990s and also in 2005–06. It has also had limited coverage. Therefore, the answers are increasing coverage to ensure rapid universalization; changing the design; and planning the implementation in sufficient detail that the objectives are not vitiated by the design of implementation. Besides, all its original six services have to be delivered fully for the programme to be effective: (i) supplementary nutrition programme (SNP), (ii) immunization, (iii) health check-up, (iv) health and nutrition education, (v) referral services, and (vi) PSE.

4.1.67 First, the ICDS has to be universalized. Second, the current scheme does not focus on 0–3 year children. But malnutrition sets in in utero and is likely to intensify during the 0–3 year period, if not addressed. In fact, this window of opportunity never returns in the lifetime of the child. A child malnourished during 0–3 years will be marred physically and mentally for life. The design of the scheme has to address this problem frontally. This has several implications:

- *Mother's malnutrition and its knock-on effects on child malnutrition:* Malnutrition begins in utero, as Indian mothers on average put on barely 5 kg of weight during pregnancy. This is a fundamental reason underlying the LBW problem. They should put on at least 10 kg of weight, which is the average for a typical African woman. Middle class Indian women tend to put on well over 10 kg weight during pregnancy. But this is not the only problem; LBW is also partly explained by low BMI of women in general, prior to their becoming pregnant. Small women (who are small before they become pregnant) give birth to small babies. In 1998–99 as much as 36% of all Indian women (48% in Orissa and Chhattisgarh) had a below normal BMI; the share had barely dropped to 33% in 2005–06 (according to NFHS-3).
- *Breastfeeding in the first hour:* Within the first hour of birth, the infant must be breastfed. Only 23% of Indian babies were breastfed within the first hour

(in 2005–06). If Indian mothers enhance early initiation of breastfeeding within one hour, we can save 250000 babies from death annually by just this action; this would reduce the overwhelming share of neonatal mortality in our IMR.

- *Exclusive breastfeeding for six months* is necessary to avoid unnecessary infections to the baby, develop the baby's immunity, and ensure growth. Only 46% of Indian babies are exclusively breastfed; the remaining half is exposed to unhygienic methods of feeding (see Annexure 4.1.2).
- *Solid food six months on.* The baby must begin to receive solid, mushy food at 6 months (i.e. together with breastfeeds) for the baby to continue to grow in the way nature intended her to grow. Only 56% of mothers introduce appropriate solid, mushy food in a timely manner after 6 months. Not surprising that NFHS-2 data shows that the proportion of underweight children rises from 16% to more than 60% between the ages of 6 months and 2 years. This malnutrition also affects the mental development of the child for life. About 90% of the development of the brain takes place before a child reaches the age of two years (see Annexure 4.1.2).

4.1.68 The ICDS scheme accordingly needs to be restructured in a manner that addresses some of the weaknesses that have emerged and is suitable for universalization. The programme must effectively integrate the different elements that affect nutrition and reflect the different needs of children in different age groups. For the purpose the programme needs to be restructured in a Mission Mode with a Mission Structure at the central level and a similar structure at the State level. The Ministry of Women and Child Development (MoWCD) will prepare proposals for restructuring along the following lines so that the restructured programme can become effective on 1 April 2008.

- 0–3 year old children. Without prejudicing the interest of the 3–6 year olds, the focus of the entire ICDS has to shift to a much greater extent than before to the 0–3-year-olds. The AWWs in all anganwadi centres could focus on children under three years of age, pregnant, and lactating mothers. The tasks of this AWW would include breastfeeding counselling, nutrition and health education and counselling to ensure solid, mushy food is introduced by six months to all infants, growth monitoring, provision of SNP to children in the six months to three years age group and pregnant and lactating mothers, and motivation for ANC, immunization, and related matters.
- 3–6 years. At present SNP is provided to children in the age group of 3–6 years. A major factor adversely affecting the success of ICDS is leakages which at least in part is due to centralized procurement of ready to eat (RTE) foods. Centralized procurement of food has the additional problem of irregular supply of food in the anganwadis, and thrusting food items on beneficiaries irrespective of their taste and preferences. Very often this leads to non-acceptance or rejection of the food distributed. The food distributed has to be hygienically prepared and culturally acceptable. Some States, for example Tamil Nadu and Maharashtra, are successfully serving hot cooked meals.
- Accordingly, it is necessary that the existing mechanism of fund flow to States for implementation of the scheme of ICDS be reviwed and restructured in the Eleventh Plan. In the vision for the Eleventh Plan outlined in Volume I, funds should ideally be released directly by the Centre through States to districts, with DPC and PRI institutions involved. The District Planning process will be strengthened if Gram Panchayats were involved for local level procurement of food items and supervision of AWWs. The Women and Child Development (WCD) prefers a fund release mechanism involving State, district, and block level societies working in Mission mode. The actual restructuring in the Eleventh Plan would need to keep in view both the urgency implicit in the Mission-mode approach and the convergence aspects that are implied in the overall Eleventh Plan vision for effective delivery.
- The feeding components present some choices. One approach is to rely on hot cooked meals according to local taste and provided at the anganwadi centres. Preparation of meals will be entrusted to Self-help Groups (SHGs) or Mothers' Groups, as per decision of the Village Committee. An alternative approach is to rely upon RTE micronutrient

fortified hygienically prepared food. The decision between these two options need to be based on a careful evaluation of pros and cons and will be an important part of the proposed restructuring. The choice between the two could also be left to decentralized decision making.

- Poor sanitation leads to high incidence of diarrhoeal disease in the early years, undermining whatever little poor nutrition the infant taking in; hence, the Total Sanitation Campaign (TSC) must force its pace, particularly in urban areas where the density of population is high and the risk of fecal contamination even higher than in rural areas.
- Convergence between nutrition and health interventions needs to be ensured. An institutional mechanism should be put in place to ensure better delivery of the services through regular periodic meetings of the functionaries of the two programmes at village, block, district, State, and Central level. Even more importantly, joint training of ICDS and Health Department staff, including the Accredidated Social Health Activists (ASHAs), is necessary.
- Micronutrients do not work unless the child and mother are consuming sufficient calories through proper quantity of fat, protein, etc. For children between 3–6 years food diversification is necessary, that is, addition of egg, milk, fruits, leafy vegetables to their meal. There is also need for fortification in the diet of adolescent children especially girls. This is especially needed to address iron deficiency. It would be desirable to have an area-specific approach to the issue of micronutrients, rather than a thin spread across the country. There has been very little research on the efficacy of different forms of fortified foods/micronutrient supplementation for resolving micronutrient deficiencies. There needs to be much greater research into the strategy of providing fortified foods to address micronutrient deficiencies. The Eleventh Plan will support food fortification based on scientific evidence.
- LBW. It is necessary to improve the nutritional status of adolescent girls to make a significant dent on LBW babies and infant/child maternal mortality. The fact that the Mid Day Meal programme is being extended to UPS from 2007–08 will provide SNP to all girls between the ages of 12–14, which will go someway towards meeting the additional calorie requirements of adolescent girls. However, on its own, this intervention will not suffice, and more serious thought needs to be given on how to address the LBW problem.
- Maternity benefit. Poor women continue to work to earn a living for the family right upto the last days of their pregnancy, thus not being able to put on as much weight as they otherwise might. They also resume working soon after childbirth, even though their bodies might not permit it—preventing their bodies from fully recovering, and their ability to exclusively breastfeed their new born in the first six months. Therefore, there is urgent need for introducing a modest maternity benefit to partly compensate for their wage loss. This could be an extension of the scheme of JSY of the MoHFW or part of a restructured ICDS.
- PSE is the weakest link of the ICDS. There is incontrovertible research that preschool education is critical to improve primary school readiness of the child of functionally illiterate parents, and thus improving dropout rates. Keeping in view the potential of PSE in enhancing enrolment and reducing school dropout rates, the component of PSE has to be necessarily strengthened (either under ICDS or in the primary school).

If this is to be done under ICDS, AWWs will need to be provided adequate training to upgrade their skills for imparting Pre-school Education (PSE) at anganwadis and the issues of their work-load and incentives would need to be considered. It may also be advisable to train and involve adolescent girls to impart PSE to supplement efforts of existing AWWs, for which too incentives will be required.

4.1.69 The aim should be to halve the incidence of malnutrition by the end of the Eleventh Plan to the level noted in Annexure 4.1.3 and to reduce anaemia among pregnant women and children to under 10%. There has to be provision made for annual or biennial surveys throughout the country to measure the incidence of underweight (mild, moderate, and severe), stunting, and wasting. There should also be a regular measurement of the status of anaemia among women and children. This task could be assigned to the National Institute of Nutrition, Hyderabad.

MICRONUTRIENT MALNUTRITION CONTROL: CURRENT SCENARIO

4.1.70 The National Nutrition Monitoring Bureau (NNMB) Report of December 2006 reveals that the consumption of protective foods such as pulses, green leafy vegetables (GLV), milk, and fruits was grossly inadequate. Consequently, the intakes of micronutrients such as iron, vitamin A, riboflavin, and folic acid were far below the recommended levels in all the age groups. The data from nutritional survey of children under five years shows that the prevalence of signs of moderate vitamin A deficiency (VAD) (Bitot spots on conjunctiva in eyes) and that of B-complex deficiency (angular stomatitis) was about 0.6% and 0.8% respectively among the preschool children. Among the school age children, Bitot Spots were found in 1.9%, and the prevalence of B-complex deficiency and of mottling of teeth (dental fluorosis) was 2% each.

4.1.71 We look at some of the specific micronutrient deficiencies in the country that are of a magnitude that causes public health concerns.

Anaemia

4.1.72 IDA is the most widespread micronutrient deficiency in the world affecting more than a billion people. It affects all age groups irrespective of gender, race, caste, creed, and religion, with higher incidence among vulnerable groups in developing world. Anaemia is associated with increased susceptibility to infections, reduction in work capacity, and poor concentration. In India, this silent emergency is rampant among women belonging to reproductive age group, children, and low socio-economic strata of the population. IDA reduces the capacity to learn and work, resulting in lower productivity and loss of wages, limiting economic and social development. Anaemia in pregnant women leads to adverse pregnancy outcomes such as high maternal and neonatal mortality, LBW, increased risk of obstetrical complications, increased morbidity, and serious impairment of the physical and mental development of the child. Anaemia remains one of the major indirect causes of maternal mortality in India. In children, anaemia causes low scholastic skills leading many of them to be below average in classes or premature dropping out from schools. It also triggers increased morbidity from infectious diseases.

4.1.73 It is also seen that children born to mothers who were illiterate or who belonged to scheduled castes/tribes were more likely to be anaemic than their counterparts. Further, children born to moderately and severely anaemic mothers were also anaemic, reflecting the consequences of poor maternal health status on the health of the children. Research studies have suggested that severe IDA during the first two years of life, when the brain is still developing, may cause permanent neurologic damage adding further sense of urgency to the current efforts to prevent IDA in children.

4.1.74 As per District Level Health Survey (DLHS) (2002–04), the prevalence of anaemia in adolescent girls is very high (72.6%) in India with prevalence of severe anaemia among them much higher (21.1%) than that in preschool children (2.1%). In adolescent girls, educational or economic status does not seem to make much of a difference in terms of prevalence of anaemia. Prevention, detection, or management of anaemia in adolescent girls has till now not received much attention. In view of the high prevalence of moderate and severe anaemia in this group and the fact that many of them get married early, conceive, and face the problems associated with anaemia in pregnancy, it is imperative to screen them for anaemia and treat them.

4.1.75 Low dietary intake and poor iron and folic acid intake are major factors responsible for high prevalence of anaemia in India. Poor bioavailability of iron in Indian diet aggravates the situation. High levels of infection such as water—and food-borne infections, malaria, and hook worm infestations further aggravate the situation.

4.1.76 Prevalence of anaemia is very high among young children (6–35 months), ever married women (15–49 years), and pregnant women (Annexure 4.1.3). Overall, 72.7% of children up to the age of three in urban areas and 81.2% in rural areas are anaemic.

Also, the overall prevalence has increased from 74.2% (1998–99) to 79.2% (2005–06). Nagaland had the lowest prevalence (44.3%), Goa was next (49.3%), followed by Mizoram (51.7%). Bihar had the highest prevalence (87.6%) followed closely by Rajasthan (85.1%), and Karnataka (82.7%). Moderate and severe anaemia is seen even among the educated families both in urban and rural areas. There are inter-State differences in prevalence of anaemia that are perhaps attributable partly to differences in dietary intake and partly to access to health care.

4.1.77 While analysing the data for States with anaemia level of 70% among children it was found that, except for Punjab, all other States had more than 50% prevalence of anaemia among pregnant women. This again reiterates the strong relationship between anaemia levels of mothers and children.

4.1.78 India was the first developing country to take up a National Nutritional Anaemia Prophylaxis Programme (NNAP) in 1972 to prevent anaemia among pregnant women and children. However, coverage under the programme needs improvement as only 22.3% of pregnant women consumed iron and folic acid for 90 days and only 50.7% had at least three antenatal visits for their last child birth (NFHS-3, 2005–06).

4.1.79 The current strategy, included as part of RCH Programme under NRHM, recommends that pregnant and lactating women, 6–12 months infants, school children, 6–10 year olds, and adolescents (11–18 year old) should be targeted in the NAPP as per the recommended dosage.

Iodine Deficiency Disorders (IDD)

4.1.80 IDD is a major public health problem for populations throughout the world, particularly for pregnant women and young children. They are a threat to the social and economic development of countries. The most devastating outcomes of iodine deficiency are increased perinatal mortality and mental retardation. Iodine deficiency is the greatest cause of preventable brain damage in childhood, which is the primary motivation behind the current worldwide drive to eliminate it. The main factor responsible for iodine deficiency is a low dietary supply of iodine. It occurs in populations living in areas where the soil has low iodine content as a result of past glaciation or the repeated leaching effects of snow, water, and heavy rainfall. Crops grown in this soil, therefore, do not provide adequate amounts of iodine when consumed.

4.1.81 Goitre is the most visible manifestation of IDD. In severely endemic areas, cretinism may affect up to 5–15% of the population. While cretinism is the most extreme manifestation, of considerably greater significance are the more subtle degrees of mental impairment leading to poor school performance, reduced intellectual ability, and impaired work capacity.

4.1.82 IDDs have been recognized as a public health problem in India since the 1920s. No State in India is completely free from IDDs. A third of all children in the world that are born with IDD-related mental damage live in India.

4.1.83 The Indian National Goitre Control Programme (NGCP) was started in 1962 with a focus on the goitre belt in the country. However, the programme of universal iodization was introduced only in 1984, when all edible salt in the market was required to offer 30 ppm (parts per million) iodine at the production level. This was legalized through the PFA (Prevention of Food Adulteration) Act of 1988 that also banned the availability of crystalline salt (non-iodized) as an edible product. It was accepted variably by the different States, some putting only a partial ban and others none at all. Based on the recommendations of the Central Council of Health, the government took a policy decision to iodise the entire edible salt in the country by 1992. Since 1992, the National Iodine Deficiency Disorders Control Programme (NIDDCP) is the new name given to the erstwhile NGCP. This change has been effected with a view to cover the wide spectrum of iodine deficiency such as mental and physical retardation, deaf-mutism, and cretinism under the programme. Due to various research reports, the Central Government lifted the ban on the sale of non-iodized salt in 2000. The States chose to retain or revoke the ban depending upon their own assessment.

In 2005, a country-wide universal ban on sale of non-iodized salt for human consumption has again been promulgated by the Central Government.

4.1.84 Studies indicate that after a certain level, the prevalence of goitre does not decrease by iodination alone due to role of various other factors like goitrogens in food, pollutants in water, etc. Definite identification of the active agents and knowledge of their biological and physicochemical properties may permit public health officials to develop procedures for eliminating these compounds at the community level and eradicating goitre from endemic areas.

4.1.85 Evidence also provides basis to have a fresh look about: iodine as the sole factor in causality; magnitude of the problem as a major public health problem universally; effectiveness of universalization of iodized salt as a measure that leads to decreasing goitre and other IDD by itself; and possible negative impacts on health like increase in hyperthyroidism and hypothyroidism, and interaction with other minerals like iron.

Vitamin A Deficiency

4.1.86 VAD has been recognized as a major controllable public health and nutritional problem. An estimated 5.7% children in India suffer from eye signs of VAD. Recent evidence suggests that even mild VAD probably increases morbidity and mortality in children, emphasizing the public health importance of this disorder.

4.1.87 Vitamin A is an important micronutrient for maintaining normal growth, regulating cellular proliferation and differentiation, controlling development, and maintaining visual and reproductive functions. VAD is one of the major deficiencies among lower income strata population in India. Human beings cannot produce this micronutrient in the body itself. Hence it has to be externally provided. This deficiency is seen greater in preschool children and pregnant and lactating women due to higher need for this micronutrient. In severe cases it can even lead to total blindness.

4.1.88 Though the prevalence of severe forms of VAD such as corneal ulcers/softening of cornea (keratomalacia) has in general become rare, Bitot spots were present in varying magnitudes in different parts of the country (NNMB 2003). The prevalence was higher than the WHO cut-off level of 0.5%, indicating the public health significance of the problem of VAD. There is huge inter-State variation in the prevalence of VAD among children. It is also a matter of concern that only 21% children of age 12–35 months received a vitamin A dose in last six months. Less than 10% coverage is reported in Nagaland (8.7%) and UP (7.3%). Only States such as Tamil Nadu (37.2%), Goa (37.3%), Tripura (38.0%), Kerala (38.2%), WB (41.2%), and Mizoram (42.2%) have better coverage, though substantially low.

4.1.89 In India way back in 1970 a National Programme for Prevention of Nutritional Blindness was initiated to fight this deficiency. The beneficiaries of this programme were preschool children (1–5 years). Further, the programme was modified in 1992 to cover children in the age group of nine months to three years only. Since Tenth Five Year Plan Vitamin A Supplementation exists as an integral component of RCH programme that is a part of NRHM.

4.1.90 During the past few years, series of expert consultations were held among various stakeholders. In view of disaggregated age-wise prevalence of VAD in children (NNMB reports), all these stakeholders recommended extending the programme to cover children up to five years. Consequently, MoHFW, GoI, issued guidelines to the States in November 2006 extending the programme to cover up to five years.

4.1.91 The programme focuses on:

- Promoting consumption of vitamin A rich foods by pregnant and lactating women and by children under five years of age and appropriate breast-feeding.
- Administering massive doses of vitamin A up to five years.
  - First dose of 100000 IU with measles vaccination at nine months.
  - Subsequent doses of 200000 IU each every six months.

4.1.92 Vitamin A supplementation and nutrition education is being implemented through the PHCs, Sub Centres, and the Anganwadis. The services of ICDS Programme, under the MoWCD, are utilized for the distribution of vitamin A to children in the ICDS blocks and for educa-tion of mothers in prevention of VAD.

Other Micronutrient Deficiencies

4.1.93 Recently, GoI examined the issue of use of zinc in the management of diarrhoea for the children and recommended to administer zinc as part of ORS in the management of diarrhoea for children older than three months. It is expected that introduction of zinc for diarrhoea will go a long way in reducing IMR in the country.

4.1.94 Apart from major macro and micronutrients there exist more than 300 nutrients, which are vital for the body. In recent years micronutrients and phyto nutrients (nutrients in edible plants having anti-oxidant and anti-inflammatory) have acquired centre stage in the field of nutrition. Phyto nutrients in the foods have biological property for disease prevention and health promotion. Truly nutritious diet is one that promotes health and prevents diseases. There is considerable interaction between different micronutrients with respect to metabolic function. Diets of the poor and even of some rich people may be deficient in a number of nutrients. Evidences based on research suggest that consumption of balanced food including protective foods like milk; varied kind of fruits, vegetables, etc. will meet the nutritional needs of the body. However, limited data is available regarding causes of deficiencies, interactions among various micronutrients when given as supplements, modalities of prevention and management of deficiencies, stability of micronutrients in fortified foods, etc.

4.1.95 ISSUES OF CONCERN

- Micronutrient malnutrition continues unabated in the country leading to heavy economic loss.
- Exact mapping of micronutrient deficiencies has not been done for the country.
- Existing programmes do not address the problem in a holistic manner. Only nutrient supplementation programmes are in existence and that too not covering the entire high risk group.
- There is inadequate monitoring of micronutrient deficiencies in the country. NFHS undertaken every six years covers only anaemia levels in women and children under three years and projects only State-level picture. NNMB exists only in few States giving State-level projections for the eight States only.
- Dietary diversification and nutrition education have not been given the required thrust.
- Food fortification has not been studied adequately.
- Nutrition-oriented horticultural interventions to promote production of fruits and vegetables at household and community level are yet to be taken up.
- Awareness generation on consequences of micronutrient malnutrition, its prevention, and management is not being addressed adequately.

TOWARDS FINDING SOLUTIONS

4.1.96 A five-pronged strategy will be adopted during the Eleventh Plan to accelerate the programmes to overcome micronutrient deficiency in the country. These relate to:

(i) Dietary Diversification: It means increasing the range of micronutrient-rich foods consumed. In practice, this requires the implementation of programmes that improve the availability and consumption of, and access to, different types of micronutrient-rich foods (such as animal products, fruits, and vegetables) in adequate quantities, especially among those who are at risk for, or vulnerable to, micronutrient malnutrition. Attention also needs to be paid to ensure that dietary intakes of oils and fats are adequate for enhancing the absorption of the limited supplies of micronutrients. It includes activities that improve production, availability, and access to micronutrient-rich and locally produced foods as a major focus of this type of intervention. Equally important is the use of communication and education activities to motivate changes in behaviour that increase consumption of beneficial foods, increase food production, and improve feeding practice in infants and children. Many dietary diversification activities operate at the community level where they are more likely to be sustainable and cause enduring behaviour change in micronutrient consumption. Such efforts are primarily to be taken up by the Ministries of Health and Family Welfare, WCD, and Information and Broadcasting.

(ii) Nutrient Supplementation: It concerns the Ministries of Health and Family Welfare, WCD, and Department of School Education and Literacy and could be achieved through biannual campaigns for administration of vitamin A to children between nine months to five years, providing iron and folic acid supplements to children from six months to two years and to adolescent girls of 10–19 years, administering iron tablets to all pregnant and lactating women and by emphasizing breastfeeding of infants up to six months under the NRHM implementation plans. While single supplements for various deficiencies are being used world over, evidence for a shift to multiple micronutrient supplementation is conflicting.

(iii) Horticulture Intervention: Although India is one of the leading producers of vegetables; GLV constitute only 16% of the total vegetable production. Horticulture intervention will include increasing the nutrient-rich crops to meet the requirements. Promotion of home gardening is important to increase availability at the household level. Emphasis should be put on perennial varieties of GLVs that are relatively easy to grow. It includes training farmers in agriculture technologies to improve production and also providing them incentives to move away from cash crops. There is a need to develop a mechanism of coordination between the various departments involved in horticultural and educational activities for optimum benefit of the community. The activities also include increasing both production and productivity through adoption of improved technologies for ensuring quality, post-harvest activities, and food processing. Horticulture Intervention will also involve the Ministry of Agriculture for the supply of seeds, extension, and storage support.

(iv) Public Health Measures: These will involve the Ministries of Health and Family Welfare, WCD, Commerce, Rural Development, and Urban Development. This would require streamlining procedures of procurement and supply, building institutional capacity in organizations for monitoring and mapping micronutrient deficiencies, deworming children at regular intervals, and providing safe drinking water and sanitation.

(v) Food Fortification: The activities involve the addition of one or more essential nutrients to a food, whether or not it is normally contained in it, for the purpose of preventing or correcting a demonstrated deficiency of one or more nutrients in the population or specific population groups. Examples of food fortification include adding specific micronutrients to commercially processed staple foods, such as vitamin A in sugar and margarine, iron and B vitamins in wheat and corn flour, and iodine in salt. The activities would involve the Ministries and Department of Health, Food Processing Industries, Food and Public Distribution, Consumer Affairs, Finance, Panchayati Raj, and State Governments. While fortification of foods supplied by the PDS has been suggested by some, the implications of this are not yet clear. The effects of fortification when there is a calorie gap are suspect. There are definitely some issues regarding the proposed forms of food fortification such as providing fortified atta instead of grain under the PDS; as grain can be stored for a longer period. Clearly, there needs to be much greater research into the strategy of providing fortified foods to address micronutrient deficiencies. The Eleventh Plan will support food fortification based on scientific evidence.

4.1.97 During the Eleventh Plan importance would be given to the following strategies and measures:

- High priority to micronutrient malnutrition control, specifically so to tackle anaemia, will be accorded at Centre and State levels. The goal is to reduce anaemia among women and girls by 50% by the end of the Eleventh Plan. State-specific goals have also been suggested (Annexure 4.1.1).
- DLHS of RCH Programme will recognize malnutrition including micronutrient as a serious public health problem and monitor prevalence of micronutrient deficiencies on priority.

- NNMB of ICMR will be expanded to all States/UTs to assist in monitoring micronutrient deficiencies through existing programmes.
- Existing Iron and Folic Acid Supplementation Programmes under RCH (NRHM) to cover infant and young children, by providing IFA in syrup form, and adolescent girls (10–19 years) by providing weekly iron supplements with immediate effect.
- Vitamin A Supplementation Programme to cover all children between nine months to five years of age and existing low coverage to be brought to 90% by 2009.
- Promotion of breastfeeding will be taken up for prevention of VAD.
- The NIDDCP will balance between preventing the ill-effects due to iodine deficiency and aggravation of other forms of hypothyroidism or hyperthyroidism that have been ignored until now. Multi-causality and regional diversity requires a range of approaches rather than a universal mono-solution. Based on this epidemiological understanding, the rational approach will be used to evolve a differential strategy for regions above and below the threshold levels.
- Research will be encouraged regarding causes of micronutrient deficiencies, understanding the complex web of causality, preventive strategies, and health behaviour regarding diet need to be carried out for a holistic view.
- Studies will be undertaken for collection of evidence regarding interaction amongst micronutrients, taste, smell, and shelf life of fortified foods, regional variations in deficiency, differing requirements of individuals, etc. before implementation of any multiple micronutrient supplementation and food fortification strategies.
- Community and household level production of fruits and vegetables will be promoted.
- Public health measures like deworming of all children every six months will be undertaken through schools and ICDS.
- Environmental sanitation and hygiene will be promoted vigorously and safe drinking water to be made universally accessible.
- A vigorous awareness campaign in the form of *Poshan Jagriti Abhiyan* will be launched utilizing all available channels of communication.
- A high level inter-agency coordination mechanism will be set up to enable policy directions to the concerned sectors.

4.2 SOCIAL SECURITY

Issues in Social Security for Workers

4.2.1 In India, traditionally, the aspects of social security were taken care of by the set up of family/community. Rapid industrialization/urbanization that began in the early twentieth century has largely led to the collapse of the joint family set up, thus necessitating institutionalized intervention in the form of State-cum-society regulated social security arrangements. The need has been felt for social security arrangements for workers and their families to enable them to deal with transient poverty/vulnerability caused by shock/adversity. Social protection could be instrumental in motivating the workers to work better and to increase productivity insofar as it would enable them to work free from domestic worries to a great extent. Indisputably, the best strategy to improve the condition of unorganized labour is to improve the demand for labour. Employment is the best form of social protection.

4.2.2 Institutionalized social security was available in India before 1947 to only a handful of government employees who had the benefit of retirement pension or contributory provident fund together with other complementary support for them and their family members. Few of the industrial/commercial sector establishments had extended certain measures in this regard on voluntary basis for their employees. The majority of workers remained uncovered and were left to fend for themselves. The situation worsened with the weakening of family support system due to various social and economic factors. The need assumes greater relevance with longer life span and the changing economic environment.

4.2.3 The concept of social security is to provide a safety mechanism through series of public intervening against the economic and social distress that is caused by the stoppage or substantial reduction of earnings resulting from sickness, maternity, employment injury, occupational distress, unemployment, invalidity, and old age. In the Eleventh Plan social security will be treated as an inclusive concept that also covers housing, safe drinking water, sanitation, health, educational, and cultural facilities for the society at large. It is necessary to ensure living wages, distinct from the concept of minimum wages, which can guarantee the workers a decent life. A number of schemes implemented by the government, both in the rural and urban areas seek to provide many services that supplement incomes of the people, which otherwise are fairly low.

CONSTITUTIONAL PROVISION

4.2.4 Articles 39(a) and 41 of the constitution require that the State should within the limits of its economic capacity, make effective provision for securing the right to work, to education, and to public assistance in case of unemployment, old age, sickness, and disablement. Though social security is not viewed as a fundamental right, Article 42 requires that the State should make provision for securing just and humane conditions of work and for maternity relief. Article 43 states that States shall endeavour to secure to all workers—agricultural, industrial, or otherwise, a living wage, such conditions of work that ensure a decent standard of life. Article 47 requires that the State should, as its primary duty, raise the level of nutrition and the standard of living of its people and improve public health.

LEGISLATIVE SUPPORT

4.2.5 Currently, there are contributory and non-contributory social security laws in our country. The contributory laws are those that provide for financing of the social security programmes by contributions paid by workers and employers and in some cases supplemented by contribution/grants from the government. The important contributory schemes include the Employees State Insurance Act, 1948 and the Provident Fund, Pension and Deposit linked insurance schemes framed under Employees Provident Funds and Miscellaneous Provisions Act, 1952. The major non-contributory social security measures are provided for under the Workmen's Compensation Act, 1923, the Maternity Benefit Act, 1961, and the Payment of Gratuity Act, 1972.

EXISTING SOCIAL SECURITY SCENARIO

4.2.6 The existing social security system in India exhibits diverse characteristics. There are a large number of schemes, administered by different agencies, each scheme designed for a specific purpose and target group of beneficiaries, floated as they are by the Central and State Governments as well as by VO in response to their own perceptions of needs, of the particular time. The result is often ambiguous. Many a time some scheme(s) might be responsible for creating 'exclusion' of the large number of those 'in most critical need for support from the planning process', on grounds of practicability or to protect the interests of those who are already 'in'. There are wide gaps in coverage (a large population is still uncovered under any scheme) and overlapping of benefits (a section of the population is covered under two or more schemes). In the existing system, coverage varies from scheme to scheme, with different groups of people receiving different types of benefits. In other words, no one is insured against all risks of life.

4.2.7 Over the years, both Central and State Governments have been taking initiatives for the welfare and social security of the workers in the unorganized sector. The Ministry of Labour and Employment is implementing welfare schemes for certain categories of unorganized sector workers like beedi workers, cine workers, and certain non-coal mine workers. Similarly, several insurance/poverty alleviation schemes are being implemented by various ministries/departments, as well as by States like Kerala and Tamil Nadu, which have constituted Welfare Funds for some occupational groups. Some States have launched group insurance schemes for their workers. Yet, some States like West Bengal initiated State-Assisted Provident Fund Schemes for the unorganized workers.

WORKERS WITH INSTITUTIONALIZED SOCIAL SECURITY COVER

4.2.8 The organized sector includes primarily those establishments that are covered by the Factories Act, 1948, the Shops and Establishments Acts of the States, Industrial Employment Standing Orders Act, 1946, etc. This sector already has a structure through which social security benefits are extended to its workers. While some of them such as Provident Fund, pension, insurance, medical and sickness benefits are contributory (workers alone, or workers and employers, sometimes supported by the State), others like employment injury benefits, gratuity, maternity benefit are purely non-contributory and are met by the employers alone. Most workers under the organized sector are covered under the Institutionalized social security provided through Employees Provident Fund Organization (EPFO), and the Employees State Insurance Corporation (ESIC).

4.2.9 The EPFO is one of the largest provident fund institutions in the world in terms of members and volume of financial transactions that it has been carrying on. The EPFO caters to: (i) every establishment that is engaged in any one or more of the industries specified in the Act or any activity notified by Central Government, employing 20 or more persons, (ii) all cinema theatres employing five or more persons, other than those under the control of Central/State/local government that provide equivalent/better benefits of social security, and co-operative societies employing less than 50 persons and working without the aid of power, and (iii) any other establishment seeking coverage under the scheme voluntarily. As on 31.03.2006, 429.53 lakh persons were members of the Employees' Provident Fund, while 323.89 lakh persons were members of the Pension Fund.

4.2.10 The ESI Act was originally applicable to non-seasonal factories using power and employing 20 or more persons; but it is now applicable to non-seasonal power using factories employing 10 or more persons and non-power using factories employing 20 or more persons. The ESI Scheme has now been extended to shops, hotels, restaurants, cinemas including preview theatre, road motor transport undertakings, and newspaper establishments employing 20 or more persons. The existing wage limit for coverage is Rs 10000 per month (with effect from 1.10.2006). The ESI Scheme is being implemented area-wise by stages and it now covers all the States except Nagaland, Manipur, Tripura, Sikkim, Arunachal Pradesh, and Mizoram; and in Union Territories of Delhi, Chandigarh, and Pondicherry.

4.2.11 A scheme for providing employment to persons with disabilities in the organized sector has been proposed to be launched. The main objective of the scheme is to provide incentives to the employers in the organized sector for promotion of regular employment to persons with disabilities. Under this scheme, the government would reimburse the employers' contribution of EPF and ESI for the first three years, aiming at creation of one lakh jobs for the physically challenged persons.

Workers without Institutionalized Social Security Cover

4.2.12 Workers in the informal economy include: (i) the vast majority of the workers in the unorganized/informal as well as; (ii) the workers employed in an informal capacity in the organized sector—the two together account for 93% of workforce. This category of the workforce is excluded from the institutionalized social security cover referred to above.

4.2.13 A number of schemes and systems are in operation in the nature of social security to workers in the informal economy, following four different major models. However, the major deficiency in this approach is the limited coverage (geographical areas and industrial activity). The benefits are confined to only about 5–6% of the informal sector workers. The National Farming benefit scheme that provides an assistance of Rs 10000 in the event of death of family breadwinner and the National Old Age Pension to destitutes above 65 years of age are other elements of existing social security structure.

4.2.14 The Social Insurance Schemes available to the unorganized sector are operated through the LIC such as Social Security Group Insurance Scheme. All persons in the age group of 18 to 60 years belonging to the 24 approved occupation groups, that is, beedi workers, brick-kiln workers, carpenters, cobblers, fishermen, hamals, handicraft artisans, handloom weavers, handloom and khadi weavers, lady tailors, leather and tannery workers, papad workers attached to Self-Employed Women's Association (SEWA), physically handicapped self-employed persons, primary milk producers, rickshaw pullers/auto drivers, safai karmcharies, salt growers, tendu leaf collectors, urban poor, forest workers, sericulture, toddy tappers, powerloom workers, women in remote rural hilly areas are covered. The most important and comprehensive scheme that has been launched is the Janashree Bima Yojana providing insurance cover of Rs 20000 in case of natural death, Rs 50000 in case of death or total permanent disability due to an accident, and Rs 25000 in case of partial disability. The premium for these benefits is Rs 200 per beneficiary, of which 50% of the premium, that is, Rs 100 is contributed from the 'Social Security Fund' and 50% contributed by the beneficiary/State Government/nodal agency. Janashree Bima Yojana is available to persons in the age group of 18 to 60 years and living below or marginally above the poverty line. The scheme is extended to a group of 25 members or more. The limited reach of the schemes' benefits to the unorganized workers and the absence of direct link between a beneficiary and LIC have been the major drawbacks of these schemes.

NEED FOR AN INCLUSIVE SOCIAL SECURITY SYSTEM

4.2.15 More than 91% of India's workforce consists of informal workers working either in the unorganized informal sector (85%) or in the organized formal sector (6%). A large majority of them face the problem of 'deficiency' or capability deprivation (of basic needs) as well as the problem of 'adversity' (arising out of such contingencies as sickness and accidents). As stated earlier, the social security schemes that are currently in place hardly cover even 5 to 6% of the estimated number of total informal workers of 362 million (as of 1999–2000). With the exception of a small number of States with some social security cover for workers in the unorganized sector, a majority of the States do not offer any cover, especially for addressing such core concerns as health care and maternity. Among the Central and State Government initiatives that address the social security needs of the population, there are very few schemes addressed specifically for the unorganized workers. Kerala and Tamil Nadu are the only States that offer some reasonable coverage of both old age pension for the aged poor and other protective social security schemes for the workers in the unorganized sector. Some States like Maharashtra, Gujarat, West Bengal, Punjab, Haryana, Tripura, Karnataka, and Goa have a number of schemes for the aged poor and vulnerable population, but except in MP, no State has social security schemes specifically meant for the unorganized sector workers.

ISSUES ON SOCIAL SECURITY IN THE CONTEXT OF INCLUSIVE GROWTH

4.2.16 The majority of workers in the unorganized/informal sector come from the socially backward communities. Viewed in this light, the provision of social security to these workers should be seen as a form of social uplift. Further, the absence of a viable and comprehensive social security arrangement is not merely the problem of individual workers and their families. It also has wider ramifications for the economy and society. Economically speaking a worker with no social security cover is likely to have more domestic worries than the one with a reasonable cover. This, as noted above, debilitates the worker's efficiency and productivity. Lack of purchasing power, as a result of low earning power, along with vulnerabilities will have the effect of reducing the aggregate demand in the economy. Socially, the demonstration effect of the prospering section is likely to lead the uncovered section to disillusionment, dissatisfaction, and disaffection. The overall well-being of the country as measured by health, education, longevity of life, and access to resources will be affected adversely, at times manifesting itself in crimes and other illegal activities.

PROVISION OF SOCIAL SECURITY IN THE PERSPECTIVE PERIOD—RECENT INITIATIVES

4.2.17 The Recent Initiatives on Social Security consist of the Unorganized Sector Workers Social Security Bill, 2007, the *Aam Admi Bima Yojana* (*AABY*), 2007, and Health Insurance Scheme for Unorganized Sector BPL workers, 2007. The major features are listed below:

Unorganized Sector Workers Social Security Bill, 2007

4.2.18 The Unorganized Sector Workers Social Security Bill, 2007, which has been introduced in the Rajya Sabha, seeks to provide statutory backing to the various social security schemes of the Central government included in the Schedule to the Act. These relate to: (i) life and disability cover, (ii) health and maternity benefits, (iii) old age protection, and (iv) any other benefits to be determined by the Central government. The State Governments may formulate schemes for: (i) provident fund, (ii) employment injury benefits, (iii) housing, (iv) educational schemes for children,

(v) skill upgradation of workers, (vi) funeral assistance, and (vii) old age homes. There will be a National Social Security Advisory Board and State Social Security Advisory Boards to make recommendations to the governments on suitable schemes for different sections of unorganized workers. The Boards will also monitor the administration of the schemes, review the processes of registration, issue of identity cards, recordkeeping, and the expenditure under the schemes, and also advise the governments on administration of the schemes. The benefits shall be admissible to all persons above 14 years of age based on a self-declaration that he/she is an unorganized sector worker. Upon an application to the District Administration in the prescribed form, such persons will be given an identity card in the form of a smart card. The law also requires the governments to make their contributions under the schemes regularly. The Schedule to the Act will have 11 schemes including the AABY and the Health Insurance Scheme for Unorganized Sector BPL workers.

Aam Admi Bima Yojana (AABY), 2007

4.2.19 Group Insurance Schemes do not attract unorganized sector workers or the organizations working for their welfare and development because the schemes do not provide the annuity in the cases of survivor members. All categories of unorganized workers are not covered under the existing schemes of social security. Further, lack of awareness about schemes amongst rural population and the poor delivery mechanism at the village level contribute to the ineffectiveness of the programmes.

4.2.20 Taking the above factors into account, the government has announced the AABY. The members of All Rural Landless Households, in the age group of 18–59 years will be eligible. The premium of Rs 200 per member will be borne by the Centre and States equally. The State Government will be the Nodal Agency. A sum of Rs 30000 in case of natural death and Rs 75000 in case of accidental death will be payable. A compensation of Rs 75000 will be payable in case of total permanent disability and of Rs 37500 in case of partial permanent disability. The scheme also has a provision for the payment of a scholarship of Rs 300 per quarter per child for two children of the beneficiaries studying in 9th to 12th standard for its beneficiaries.

4.2.21 The AABY scheme also proposes the creation of a fund of Rs 1000 crore to be operated by LIC for meeting the liability of Central government towards its share of premium payment. As per the NSS, the number of rural landless households in the country is 1.5 crore. It is expected that in the first year approx. 70 to 80 lakh of rural landless households would be covered under the scheme requiring an expenditure of Rs 70–80 crore by the Central government towards its share of 50% premium. With an 8% per annum return expected on the Rs 1000 crore fund, the amount would be sufficient to meet the liability of premium payment.

4.2.22 A separate Rs 500 crore fund will be created for the purpose of providing scholarships to children of beneficiaries. This will make available Rs 40 crore for the full year at 8% per annum return. This amount would suffice for the coverage of 333000 children of the beneficiaries.

4.2.23 This scheme would extend the benefit of life insurance coverage as well as coverage of partial and permanent disability to the head of the family or an earning member of the family of rural landless households in the States and also educational assistance to their children studying from 9th to 12th standard as an extended benefit.

Health Insurance Scheme for Unorganized Sector BPL Workers, 2007 (Rashtriya Swasthaya Bima Yojana)

4.2.24 In order to provide accessible, affordable, and accountable quality health services to households in rural areas, the government has launched the NRHM. The principle thrust of NRHM is to make public system fully functional at all levels and to place a framework that would reduce the distress of households in seeking health care system through Health Insurance Scheme. Many efforts in the past for providing health insurance for the rural poor have not been successful because of inadequacies in design and implementation. The cost of insurance coupled with lack of perception of the benefits in the target group, and the procedure for claiming reimbursements have posed serious challenges in the administration. A transparent scheme that lists the entitlements, administered through a smart card obviating the need for out-of-pocket expenses is expected to streamline the administration, ensuring the benefits. With these objectives in view, the government has introduced the *Rashtriya Swasthya Bima Yojana* to cover all BPL unorganized sector workers and their families (of five members), whose identity will be verified by the implementing agency and be issued a smart card. The cost of smart card will be borne by Central government, and the beneficiary will be required to pay Rs 30 per annum as registration/renewal fee. The prescribed premium of Rs 750 per member-family will be borne by the Central and State Governments in the ratio of 75:25. The package of benefits will include: (i) cashless attendance to all covered ailments; (ii) hospitalization expenses, taking care of most common illnesses, (iii) all pre-existing diseases to be covered, (iv) transportation costs subject to prescribed limits payable to the beneficiary. Flexibility is provided to the States to add to the benefits by meeting the additional premium requirements from their own resources. State governments would decide the Implementing Agency and also bear the administrative costs.

4.2.25 There are 6 crore BPL families. They will be covered in five years (1.2 crore per annum). The total cost of the scheme over the Eleventh Five Year Plan is estimated at Rs 7078.25 crore.

Extension of National Old Age Pension Scheme (NOAPS)

4.2.26 The National Social Assistance Programme (NSAP) came into effect from 15 August 1995 as a 100% Centrally Sponsored Programme, with three components namely, NOAPS, National Family Benefit Scheme, and NMBS. The NMBS has since been transferred to the MoHFW with effect from 1.4.2001. The NSAP aims at providing social security in case of old age, death of primary breadwinner, and maternity. The main objective of the NOAPS is ensure a minimum national standard of social assistance in addition to the benefit that States are already providing, without displacing the expenditure by States on social protection schemes. The scheme is aimed at senior citizens, that is, over 65 years or above, who are destitute in the sense of having little or no regular means of subsistence from his/her own sources of income or through support from family members or other sources. Major modifications in NSAP are being proposed in the Eleventh Plan to provide more comprehensive coverage to the old (details in Chapter 3, Vol. III).

Unorganized Sector Workers—Conditions of Service Law

4.2.27 The unorganized section of agricultural sector (consisting of crop cultivation and other agricultural activities such as forestry, livestock, and fishing), not protected under the Plantations Workers Act, has neither formal system of social security nor regulation of conditions of work. The government has taken note of the concerns expressed by the NCEUS and is examining the desirability of enacting laws regulating the minimum conditions of work of agricultural wage workers and provide a measure of social security to agricultural wage workers and marginal and small farmers in the unorganized sector. Similar provisions would be made for other workers in the non-agricultural unorganized sector as well as informal/unorganized workers in the organized sector consisting of wage workers, independent self-employed, and workers who are self-employed at home, whose minimum conditions of work are not regulated by any other legislation. The provision of a statutory package of National Minimum Social Security to which all unorganized (agricultural and non-agricultural) workers are entitled need to be considered. There may be Social Security Advisory Boards and dispute resolution mechanisms to oversee and monitor the implementation and ensure that each such worker has the sense of being provided with what is due to him/her.

SOCIAL SECURITY: APPROACH AND STRATEGY FOR THE ELEVENTH FIVE YEAR PLAN

4.2.28 A protective social security mechanism, taking care of the adversity aspects of ill-health, accidents/death, and old age would be established at the core. The other vulnerability aspects due to in-built deficiencies as they exist now, such as lack of access for the poor to credit/finance (especially for the self-employed), loans for upgrading skills, loans for housing, children's education, etc. shall be tailored to meet the social security concerns of workers qua workers in the unorganized/ informal sector, subject to the availability of resources. The National Old Age Pension presently covers persons who are destitute and old aged. Some States cover the old aged BPL persons. NSAP would be made more comprehensive.

4.2.29 Considering the achievements made by the ESIC and the EPFO in providing institutionalized social security cover to a majority of the workers in the organized sector, attempt would be made to widen their coverage and strengthen them. To cover more number of beneficiaries, measures should be taken to enhance the capability of these institutions to cope with the workload. To reduce harassment and corruption in these institutions, the government will strive to streamline the delivery system in these institutions.

4.2.30 A national policy for fixing minimum wages would be crystallized and made effective. Discrimination in wages based on gender and age would be abolished/penalized. The recovery of minimum wages would be simplified and be equated with recovery due of land revenue. An information network will also be built to promote awareness, to educate employers (some of whom do alternate as wage labour too), and to prevent malpractices (perpetrated by design or by ignorance) with the help of the media, NGOs, and PRIs.

4.2.31 Assigning an identity to the beneficiary is an essential condition to create empowerment to lay a claim to what one is expected to receive. The National Social Security Numbers schemes shall be extended to all citizens in the country, so that the most vulnerable people who need it the most, including migrant labour and nomads could use it. In fact, considering that such persons do not even get the rations under the PDS, which is an important social security measure, this exercise will be taken up urgently.

ANNEXURE 4.1.1
Malnutrition of Children (0–3 Years), by State

S.No.	State	Current level of Wt-for-age below–2 SD	Eleventh Plan Goal-redn. by 50%
1	Andhra Pradesh	36.5	18.3
2	Arunachal Pradesh	36.9	18.5
3	Assam	40.4	20.2
4	Bihar	58.4	29.2
5	Jharkhand	59.2	29.6
6	Goa	29.3	14.7
7	Gujarat	47.4	23.7
8	Haryana	41.9	21.0
9	Himachal Pradesh	36.2	18.1
10	J&K	29.4	14.7
11	Karnataka	41.1	20.6
12	Kerala	28.8	14.4
13	MP	60.3	30.2
14	Chattisgarh	52.1	26.1
15	Maharashtra	39.7	19.9
16	Manipur	23.8	11.9
17	Meghalaya	46.3	23.2
18	Mizoram	21.6	10.8
19	Nagaland	29.7	14.9
20	Orissa	44.0	22.0
21	Punjab	27.0	13.5
22	Rajasthan	44.0	22.0
23	Sikkim	22.6	11.3
24	Tamil Nadu	33.2	16.6
25	Tripura	39.0	19.5
26	UP	47.3	23.7
27	Uttarakhand	38.0	19.0
28	WB	43.5	21.8
29	Delhi	33.1	16.6
	INDIA	45.9	23.0

Note: 1. Figures for current level are that of NFHS 2005–06.
2. For State level figures, pro-rata reduction has been applied on the basis of targeted reduction at All India level. Figures for other States are not available.
Source: NFHS 2005–06.

ANNEXURE 4.1.2
State-wise Malnutrition Rate of Children in Various Age Groups

State	Children age 0–5 months exclusively breastfed (%)	Children age 6–9 months receiving solid or semi-solid food and breast milk (%)	Children under 3 years who are underweight (%)
India	46.3	55.8	45.9
Andhra Pradesh	62.7	63.7	36.5
Arunachal Pradesh	60.0	77.6	36.9
Assam	63.1	59.6	40.4
Bihar	27.9	57.3	58.4
Chhattisgarh	82.0	54.5	52.1
Delhi	34.5	59.8	33.1
Goa	17.7	69.8	29.3
Gujarat	47.8	57.1	47.4
Haryana	16.9	44.8	41.9
Himachal Pradesh	27.1	66.0	36.2
J&K	42.3	58.3	29.4
Jharkhand	57.8	65.3	59.2
Karnataka	58.0	72.5	41.1
Kerala	56.2	93.6	28.8
Maharashtra	53.0	47.8	39.7
MP	21.6	51.9	60.3
Manipur	61.7	78.1	23.8
Meghalaya	26.3	76.3	46.3
Mizoram	46.1	84.6	21.6
Nagaland	29.2	71.0	29.7
Orissa	50.2	67.5	44.0
Punjab	36.0	50.0	27.0
Rajasthan	33.2	38.7	44.0
Sikkim	37.2	89.6	22.6
Tamil Nadu	33.3	77.9	33.2
Tripura	36.1	59.8	39.0
UP	51.3	45.5	47.3
Uttaranchal	31.2	51.6	38.0
WB	58.6	55.9	43.5

Source: NFHS-3 (2005–06), IIPS, MoHFW, GoI.

ANNEXURE 4.1.3
Anaemia among Women (15–49 Years)

S. No.	State	Current Level	Eleventh Plan Goal: reduction by 50%
	India	56.1	28.1
1	Delhi	43.4	21.7
2	Haryana	56.5	28.3
3	Himachal Pradesh	40.9	20.5
4	J&K	53.1	26.6
5	Punjab	38.4	19.2
6	Rajasthan	53.1	26.6
7	MP	57.6	28.8
8	Chattisgarh	57.6	28.8
9	UP	50.8	25.4
10	Uttarakhand	47.6	23.8
11	Bihar	68.3	34.2
12	Jharkhand	70.4	35.2
13	Orissa	62.8	31.4
14	WB	63.8	31.9
15	Arunachal Pradesh	48.9	24.5
16	Assam	69.0	34.5
17	Manipur	39.3	19.7
18	Meghalaya	45.4	22.7
19	Mizoram	38.2	19.1
20	Nagaland	30.8	15.4
21	Sikkim	46.8	23.4
22	Goa	38.9	19.5
23	Gujarat	55.5	27.8
24	Maharashtra	49.0	24.5
25	Andhra Pradesh	62.0	31.0
26	Karnataka	50.3	25.2
27	Kerala	32.3	16.2
28	Tamil Nadu	53.3	26.7
29	Tripura	67.4	33.7

Notes: 1. Figures for current level are that of NFHS 2005–06.

2. For State-level figures, pro-rata reduction has been applied on the basis of targeted reduction at All India level.

3. Figures for other States are not available.

Source: NFHS 2005–06.

ANNEXURE 4.1.4
Distribution of Cardholders among Poor and Non-poor

	% poor having no ration card	% of poor having BPL/AAY cards	% BPL/AAY cards with non-poor	% non-poor having BPL/AAY cards
J&K	7.9	55.1	85.4	17.2
Himachal Pradesh	3.3	45.1	73.6	13.7
Punjab	15.8	19.5	83.0	8.5
Uttranchal	6.1	35.2	34.2	12.0
Haryana	4.4	32.6	74.8	15.2
Rajasthan	5.0	23.6	65.2	12.1
UP	16.4	22.9	48.7	10.6
Bihar	25.5	21.2	45.1	12.6
Assam	25.7	23.3	56.0	7.6
WB	11.2	40.5	60.7	20.6
Jharkhand	22.1	31.9	42.4	17.0
Orissa	29.3	54.8	38.1	29.4
Chhatisgarh	24.1	47.9	47.0	29.4
MP	30.0	41.9	46.2	22.2
Gujarat	10.9	48.1	71.2	24.2
Maharashtra	19.2	39.9	51.1	18.4
Andhra Pradesh	24.1	66.8	81.3	50.3
Karnataka	20.7	59.6	65.6	36.5
Kerala	10.0	48.4	74.8	25.0
Tamil Nadu	9.0	29.7	63.1	15.0
All India	19.1	36.0	59.8	20.7

Source: NSS, 61st Round, 2004–05.

ANNEXURE 4.1.5
PDS Benefits—Rice and Wheat

(Rs per Household)

	Poor				Non poor			
	No card	APL card	BPL card	Antyodaya card	No card	APL card	BPL card	Antyodaya card
J&K	33.73	78.19	278.72	333.96	22.77	53.89	206.43	286.26
Himachal Pradesh	0.00	43.83	124.94	262.10	2.72	21.84	122.38	204.55
Punjab	0.00	0.00	1.96	111.54	-0.58	-0.07	1.38	0.00
Uttranchal	0.00	8.32	88.22	202.61	0.06	10.52	54.73	115.10
Haryana	0.00	0.04	12.09	114.36	0.00	0.00	11.61	75.15
Rajasthan	6.23	6.42	70.93	169.27	-6.18	3.77	54.35	93.80
UP	2.48	0.92	39.96	132.88	0.17	0.68	23.79	107.40
Bihar	-0.29	0.32	3.86	47.27	-0.05	0.01	6.10	44.26
Assam	8.27	4.71	81.33	184.81	2.45	1.43	47.98	21.30
WB	50.69	-0.03	30.78	86.65	14.82	0.31	24.15	46.06
Jharkhand	0.00	0.48	30.43	112.80	0.15	0.94	10.84	65.06
Orissa	2.17	3.09	31.93	129.92	0.25	0.81	12.04	120.67
Chhatisgarh	5.72	13.69	70.05	213.53	2.97	6.36	43.01	104.49
MP	4.27	8.02	60.37	146.03	0.80	1.42	40.20	100.32
Gujarat	4.38	1.99	86.17	182.58	0.57	1.86	79.17	29.02
Maharashtra	3.02	8.75	97.16	192.23	1.87	4.25	80.77	158.83
Andhra Pradesh	1.71	56.75	113.67	260.27	4.17	31.23	95.72	249.61
Karnataka	8.79	63.08	199.43	230.81	1.29	46.29	180.99	231.85
Kerala	22.04	68.16	166.06	242.23	4.82	18.33	94.03	209.85
Tamil Nadu	43.83	182.85	198.06	349.04	13.56	126.08	177.58	314.68
All India	6.69	15.64	81.45	176.18	2.28	12.56	74.59	146.92

Source: NSS 61st Round, 2004–05.

ANNEXURE 4.1.6
Beneficiaries of any Programme (Annapurna, FFW, ICDS, MDM)

(%)

	Poor			Non-poor		
	No card	APL	BPL/AAY	No card	APL	BPL/AAY
J&K		4.5	12.7	1.0	2.1	7.8
Himachal Pradesh	23.3	70.0	72.2	23.8	34.7	37.8
Punjab		6.2	13.9	1.8	3.3	8.3
Uttranchal	33.9	41.9	57.5	6.2	20.4	37.0
Haryana	13.8	37.1	31.3	9.6	19.5	34.3
Rajasthan	19.2	29.8	54.5	9.2	24.6	45.2
UP	21.8	24.1	31.5	10.5	13.7	27.5
Bihar	7.1	18.4	23.6	6.9	13.1	31.6
Assam	24.5	49.2	42.5	8.5	24.7	28.9
WB	47.3	52.6	52.1	21.8	27.0	43.3
Jharkhand	16.7	13.3	20.2	8.4	9.7	18.4
Orissa	41.9	50.1	56.4	25.3	32.3	46.8
Chhatisgarh	59.8	59.3	73.3	36.9	39.4	50.3
MP	40.5	42.6	52.1	18.9	26.1	42.7
Gujarat	42.0	67.0	65.7	20.8	25.7	37.5
Maharashtra	49.8	38.8	52.6	25.9	22.5	39.2
Andhra Pradesh	23.5	40.1	50.1	18.1	15.9	33.3
Karnataka	35.5	35.6	62.6	19.4	23.2	44.2
Kerala	56.2	45.2	58.4	30.9	23.4	33.9
Tamil Nadu	54.2	56.7	57.1	26.9	27.1	39.2
All India	31.6	34.2	49.0	17.4	20.6	36.9

Source: NSS, 61st Round, 2004–05.

5

Drinking Water, Sanitation, and Clean Living Conditions

INTRODUCTION

5.1 Provision of clean drinking water, sanitation, and a clean environment are vital to improve the health of our people and to reduce incidence of diseases and deaths. Women and girls spend hours fetching water and that drudgery should be unnecessary. Drudgery is undesirable in itself and it also takes away other opportunities for self-development. Drinking water is less than 1% of the total water demand and should have the first priority among all uses of water.

5.2 Lack of covered toilets nearby imposes a severe hardship on women and girls. Also provision of clean drinking water without at the same time of provision for sanitation and clean environment would be less effective in improving health. The two should be treated together as complementary needs.

5.3 The status of provision of water and sanitation has improved slowly. According to Census 1991, 55.54% of the rural population had access to an improved water source. As on 1 April 2007, the Department of Drinking Water Supply's figures show that out of a total of 1507349 rural habitations in the country, 74.39% (1121366 habitations) are fully covered and 14.64% (220165 habitations) are partially covered. Further, present estimates shows that out of the 2.17 lakh water quality affected habitation as on 1.4.05, about 70000 habitations have since been addressed for providing safe drinking water. Also, from the reported coverage, there are slippages in the prescribed supply level, reducing the per capita availability due to a variety of reasons.

5.4 Water supply in urban areas is also far from satisfactory. As on 31 March 2004, about 91% of the urban population has got access to water supply facilities. However, this access does not ensure adequacy and equitable distribution, and the per capita availability is not as per norms in many areas. Average access to drinking water is highest in class I towns (73%), followed by class II towns (63%), class III towns (61%), and other towns (58%). Poor people in slums and squatter settlements are generally deprived of these basic amenities. The population coverage in the past decades and as of March 2004 is as shown in Table 5.1 below:

5.5 The quantity of urban water supply is also poor. Water is supplied only for few hours of the day that

TABLE 5.1
Percentage of Population Covered with Water Supply Facilities

Year	Urban Population (million)	Percentage of Population Covered with Water Supply
1981	152	78
1991	217	84
2001	285	89
2004	308 (projected)	91

leads to a lot of waste as taps are kept open and water is stored not all of which is used. This is so, despite the fact that per capita availability of water in cities like New Delhi exceeds that in Paris, where water is supplied round the clock.

5.6 The access to toilets is even poorer. As per the latest Census data (2001), only 36.4% of the total population has latrines within or attached to their houses. However in rural areas, only 21.9% of population has latrines within or attached to their houses. An estimate based on the number of individual household toilets constructed under the TSC programme (a demand-driven programme implemented since 1999) puts the sanitation coverage in the country at about 49% (as on November 2007). An evaluation study on the programme conducted in 2002 shows 80% of toilets constructed were put to use. This use is expected to be much higher as awareness has improved much since 2002.

5.7 63% of the urban population has got access to sewerage and sanitation facilities (47% from sewer and 53% from low cost sanitation) as on 31.3.2004. As a consequence, open defecation is prevalent widely in rural areas but also significantly in urban areas too.

5.8 We look at the Eleventh Plan approach to deal with the problems of rural water supply, urban supply, rural sanitation, and urban sanitation.

RURAL WATER SUPPLY

PAST PROGRAMMES AND OUTLAYS

5.9 The GoI's major intervention in water sector started in 1972–73 through Accelerated Rural Water Supply Programme (ARWSP) for assisting States/UTs to accelerate the coverage of drinking water supply. In 1986, the entire programme was given a mission approach with the launch of the Technology Mission on Drinking Water and Related Water Management. This Technology Mission was later renamed as Rajiv Gandhi National Drinking Water Mission (RGNDWM) in 1991–92. In 1999, Department of Drinking Water Supply (DDWS) was formed under the MoRD to give emphasis to rural water supply as well as on sanitation. In the same year, new initiatives in water sector had been initiated through Sector Reform Project, later it was scaled up as *Swajaldhara* in 2002. With sustained interventions, DDWS remains an important institution to support the States/UTs in serving the rural population with water and sanitation related services all across India.

5.10 An investment of about Rs 72600 crore has been made (under both State and Central Plans) from the beginning of the planned era of development in rural water supply sector. As per available information, this investment has helped to create assets of over 41.55 lakh hand pumps, around 15.77 lakh public stand posts, around 1.60 lakh mini-piped water supply schemes, and 45000 multi village schemes in the country under the Rural Water Supply Programme. Of these systems, 88.21% hand pumps, 93.49% stand posts, 91.95% mini schemes, and 96.26% multi village schemes are reported functional by the States. During the Tenth Plan, the approved outlay for the programme was Rs 13245 crore. The programme was well funded during the Tenth Plan (being a part of Bharat Nirman Programme) and by the end of March 2007, an amount of Rs 16,103 crore was released to the States under the scheme. On the physical achievement side, 352992 habitations have been reported covered by the States during Tenth Plan.

5.11 The Swajaldhara programme was launched in 2002–03. The programme involves a community contribution of 10% of the project cost to instil a sense of owner ship among the people and also to take over the Operation and Maintenance (O&M) of the schemes constructed under the programme. The Centre provides 90% of the project cost as grant. Under the Swajaldhara programme, out of the 19385 schemes included under the programme with an estimated cost of Rs 1069 crore, only 11046 schemes could be completed in the Tenth Plan with an expenditure of Rs 610 crore. The monitorable target of covering all habitations in the Tenth Plan, which was aimed to be achieved in 2004, could not be achieved. During the Eleventh Plan, the Swajaldhara principles are to be adopted by the State Governments as per local conditions and adequate flexibility has been provided to incorporate such principles under the ongoing ARWSP itself.

MAJOR ISSUES IN RURAL WATER SUPPLY

5.12 The main problems are of sustainability of water availability and supply, poor water quality, centralized versus decentralized approaches, and financing of O&M costs.

Sustainability

5.13 Habitations that are covered in the earlier years slip back to not covered or partially covered status due to reasons such as sources going dry or lowering of groundwater, sources which are quality affected, systems working below their capacity due to poor O&M, and normal depreciation. Increasing population leading to emergence of new habitations also increase the number of unserved habitation.

5.14 Sustainability of the Rural Water Supply Programme has emerged as a major issue and the Eleventh Plan aims at arresting the slip backs. The rate of habitation slippages from fully covered to partially covered and partially covered to not covered is increasing. In addition to this the increase in the number of quality-affected habitations that are dependent on ground water source is adding to these slippages. This can be gauged from the fact that there are about 6.83 lakh partially covered and not covered habitations as per the 2003 survey. The Mid-Term Appraisal of the Tenth Plan observed that over-reliance on groundwater for rural water supply programme has resulted in the twin problem of sustainability and water quality and suggested a shift to surface water sources for tackling this issue. Restoration of tanks can provide a local solution (see Box 5.1). It is important to apply the principle of subsidiarity to collect water, store water, use water, and manage waste water as close to the source as possible.

Water Quality

5.15 There are about 2.17 lakh quality-affected habitations in the country with more than half of the habitations affected with excess iron (118088). This is followed by fluoride (31306), salinity (23495), nitrate (13958), arsenic (5029) in that order. There are about 25000 habitations affected with multiple problems. About 66 million population is at risk due to excess fluoride in 200 districts of 17 States. Arsenic contamination is widespread in West Bengal and it is now seen in Bihar, eastern UP, and Assam. The hand pump attached de-fluoridation and iron removal plants have failed due to in appropriate technology unsuited to community perceptions and their involvement. Desalination plants have also met a similar fate due to lapses at various levels starting with planning to post implementation maintenance.

5.16 The Bharat Nirman Programme aims at addressing water quality problems in all the quality-affected habitations by 2009. It has given a sign of hope for addressing the issue. While higher allocation (20% of ARWSP funds committed for water quality) of funds is addressed, the next important step is to achieve convergence, ensure community participation, and an

Box 5.1
Success Stories in Sustainability—*Ooranis*—The Lifelines of Rural Tamil Nadu

For the people of Tamil Nadu the traditional ooranis or ponds have truly proved to be a blessing. The ooranis were developed as the main supply systems in Tamil Nadu centuries back. These earthen bunded ponds were constructed by the collective efforts of the people over the ages and have been designed hydrologically to have adequate and assured inflow of surface runoffs. Almost all ooranis are well connected with irrigation tanks called Kanmoi.

In recent years however the ooranis were neglected and dilapidated due to implementation of new water supply facilities such as handpumps, deep borewell, and Combined Water Supply Schemes. Initiatives were taken therefore to improve and strengthen them under the Ministry of Rural Development's RGNDWM, *Pradhan Mantri Grameen Yojana*, ARWSP programmes. These included measures like desilting the pond, treatment of catchment areas, clearing of the supply channel, provision of filter media, and providing draw well arrangements and fencing of the oorani. 360 ooranis have been rejuvenated in several districts with the combined efforts of the government, the community, technical expertise from the Anna University, and NGO participation. Water shortages have now become a thing of the past in these areas, and with the harvested rainwater flowing into the ooranis, a sustainable water supply system has thus become a reality.

IEC campaign. Convergence would offer twin benefits, that is, sustain the source (also provide alternative surface source) and dilute the groundwater chemical contamination.

Decentralization

5.17 Whenever the community has been involved from planning stage, the programme has always become sustainable. While our programmes have elaborate guidelines for community involvement, it is obvious that field-level adoption is far from satisfactory. The 73rd and 74th constitutional amendments have devolved the water supply responsibility to PRIs/local bodies. Due to their inherent weaknesses like funding constraints, low technical ability, etc. the devolution of power is yet to make a desirable impact on the ground. While sporadic success stories are trickling in, this concept has yet to go a long way. States have to play an important role in placing the Twelfth Finance Commission (TFC) grants devolved to Panchayats and placing the implementation agency at the command of local bodies. The second is simply absent in many States.

Financing of the Capital Cost and O&M (Rural Water Supply Programme)

5.18 States have been expressing constraints in providing adequate matching share for availing ARWSP funds. The DDWS has suggested that funding pattern of the programme should change from the current 50:50 (Centre:State) to 75:25 for Non Special Category States and 90:10 for Special Category States.

5.19 The Bharat Nirman Programme has nearly doubled the funds available for the sector through the ARWSP. The Centre is also encouraging external assistance for this sector. The average cost of coverage of not covered, slipped back, and quality-affected habitations have gone up considerably.

5.20 The TFC has provided enough funds for the O&M of the water supply systems in rural areas. Also the rural community is not averse to paying charges for a reliable supply. Convergence of various programmes would also bring additional funds. While the funding for the programme would be provided for through various sources, what is more important for the success of the programme is the change in the approach (community-based local solutions) and mindset (moving away from the pure asset creation towards service delivery approach).

Eleventh Five Year Plan Targets for Rural Water Supply

The Targets

5.21 To 'provide clean drinking water for all by 2009 and ensure that there are no slip-backs by the end of the Eleventh Plan' is one of the monitorable targets of the Eleventh Five Year Plan. The first part of the goal coincides with the terminal year of Bharat Nirman Programme under which it is proposed to provide safe drinking water to all habitations. Under the Bharat Nirman Programme 55067 not covered habitations, 2.8 lakh slipped back habitations, and 2.17 lakh quality-affected habitations are proposed to be covered. The first two years of the Eleventh Plan forms the second-half period of the Bharat Nirman Programme. While the coverage reported by the States under not covered and slipped back habitations are encouraging, the coverage under water quality-affected habitations is far from satisfactory. This would be one of the major challenges during the Eleventh Plan. The States have done well in covering the slipped back habitations (1.63 lakh habitations covered) and not covered habitations (23000 habitations covered). However, achievement in the quality-affected habitations is way below the target. Against 2.17 lakh habitations, as on 1.4.05, about 70000 habitations have since been addressed. The States find it difficult to establish alternate sources of water supply to the quality-affected habitations, as either the source is very far off or simply not available, nearby.

5.22 The government is also committed to provide 100% coverage of water supply to rural schools. The ARWSP includes school water supply also. The DDWS has estimated that by April 2005, there are 2.31 lakh uncovered rural schools in the country, which needs to be covered with water supply. While the ARWSP has provision of water supply to existing schools, the new schools are covered under other programmes like *Sarva SSA* of the MHRD. The funds required to cover the schools at the rate of Rs 40000 per school works out to Rs 924 crore. The coverage of schools could be best achieved by convergence of various programmes of the Department of the Elementary Education and Literacy and the Department of Women and Child Development.

The Way Forward

5.23 The problems of sustainability of water availability, maintenance of supply system, and dealing with the issue of water quality are the major challenges in the Eleventh Five Year Plan. The conjunctive use of groundwater, surface water, and rooftop rainwater harvesting systems will be required to be encouraged as the means of improving sustainability and drinking water security. While convergence of various programmes for funds and physical sustenance is most important, States should put in place an effective coordinating mechanism for attaining success. Otherwise the vicious cycle of coverage and slip back would continue in the next plan also. The Eleventh Five Year Plan proposes to deal with the various issues as follows:

5.24 The TFC awards for maintaining the water supply systems by local bodies must be implemented and schemes transferred to Panchayats. State can share a part of the O&M cost of such Panchayat as a hand-holding support for first few years before the local bodies become self-sustainable. To enable local bodies, an effective MIS for knowing the status of water supply in every habitation in the State should be put in place and every State should earmark funds for this purpose. All the States' information systems should be connected to the all-India server at Delhi and this MIS should be web-enabled for moving to the larger objective of public monitoring. Also adequate training at local bodies' level should be undertaken for enhancing their technical capacities for maintaining the water supply systems. The implementing agencies must be made accountable to the local bodies for providing water supply services. However major engineering schemes can continue to be with the State-level agencies.

Local Participation and Convergence

5.25 In order to universalize access to safe drinking water, it needs to be isolated from agriculture and other uses wherever possible. To prevent lowering of water tables due to excessive extraction, cooperation with agricultural users becomes necessary. A cooperative mechanism of water users and Panchayat representatives has to regulate use within average annual recharge level. All groundwater-based resources should be provided with a recharge structure that would help keep the source alive. Also rainwater harvesting in schools and community buildings should be made compulsory and individual household rooftop rainwater harvesting system like individual household toilets should be promoted, if necessary, special funds should be earmarked for this purpose.

5.26 Where groundwater quality and availability is unsatisfactory, surface water sources need to be developed. Restoration and building of tanks and other water bodies along with rainwater harvesting structures for recharge and for direct collection at community and household levels constitute an attractive option. The Central Government should support the States for tapping the maximum external assistance for this purpose, a part of the assistance could be shared by the Centre as decided in the case of the external assisted Water Bodies Restoration programme (WBRP) wherein 25% grant of the project cost is passed on to the States. The assistance here could be restricted to covering the quality-affected habitations in various States.

5.27 Another alternative is to bunch the habitations into large numbers and involve the technically sound private service providers to cover the quality-affected habitations on an annuity basis for a certain period. Meanwhile parallel efforts to restore the source through water augmentation programme should continue in these habitations as an alternative arrangement, provided such systems are proposed by and have the consent of the PRIs and local bodies.

5.28 Involvement of the community in the monitoring of the water supply works should be made a primary condition for release of funds for completed work. The DDWS has initiated monitoring of the water quality under the National Rural Drinking Water Quality Monitoring and Surveillance Programme (NRDWQMSP) under which the Gram Panchayat/Village Water and Sanitation Committee provided with user-friendly field test kits for testing both bacteriological and chemical contaminants followed by testing of the samples at district- and State-level laboratories. Such initiatives need to be extended to the other regular programmes under the ARWSP also. Involving the community in bringing quality and sustainability to the village-level drinking water supply systems should be encouraged, rewarded, and recognized in an appropriate manner along the lines of the *Nirmal Gram Puraskar* that has galvanized communities and local bodies for an enthusiastic and effective response to the TSC of the GoI.

5.29 While our programme guidelines do recognize the role of women in planning and post implementation maintenance with some success stories of women maintaining the hand pumps and tube wells, the success has to spread far and wide. Of late, the country is realizing the potential of women in the form of SHGs. Women SHGs are functioning well in States such as Tamil Nadu and Gujarat. Women SHGs also should be given the responsibility for collection of maintenance funds after the source is handed over to them for maintenance. Women SHGs should be encouraged for taking up the O&M of the existing functional systems. If the source is dysfunctional, the State should incur one-time expenditure to set it right and encourage SHG to take them over.

5.30 The resources required could be easily mobilized if the various programmes can be converged to work in complementary ways.

5.31 The National Rural Employment Guarantee Programme has seven identified work component related to water. The Rural Development Ministry is implementing major watershed schemes through the Department of Land Resources. There are other programmes such as Backward Region Grant Fund, artificial recharge of groundwater schemes and rain water harvesting, restoration of water bodies scheme (both pilot and external assisted) by the Ministry of Water Resources, the National Project for Renovation of Water Bodies and schemes such as the National Afforestation Programme, River Valley Project, Flood Prone River Programme, Integrated Wasteland Development Programme, Grants under TFC, *Hariyali*, and the States' own schemes. Convergence of these programmes should help to augment funds and bring institutions together for sustainable water supply.

URBAN WATER SUPPLY

PAST PROGRAMMES AND OUTLAYS

5.32 The coverage of urban population with water supply facilities in the past had not been very impressive, due to various reasons, including the fact that the investment made in the urban water supply sector had been inadequate. The Tenth Plan projected a requirement of Rs 28240 crore for achieving population coverage of 100% with drinking water supply facilities in the 300 Class I cities by 31.3.2007. The estimated outlay for the Tenth Plan period, however, was only Rs 18749 crore in the State sector, and Rs 900 crore in Central sector making a total outlay of Rs 19649 crore only.

5.33 The Tenth Five Year Plan envisaged augmentation of water supply in urban areas to reach the prescribed norms, higher degree of reliability, assurance of water quality, a high standard of operation and management, accountability to customers, and, in particular, special arrangements to meet the needs of the urban poor, and levy and recovery of user charges to finance the maintenance functions as well as facilitate further investment in the sector. The achievement of these tasks depends to a large extent on the willingness of the State Governments and urban local bodies to restructure water supply organizations, levy reasonable water rates, take up reforms in billing, accounting, and collection, and become creditworthy in order to have access to market funding. Measures were suggested for water conservation, reuse, and recycling of waste water.

5.34 While there were progress in some of the suggestions of Tenth Five Year Plan like adoption of the rainwater harvesting, tariff revision for sustaining O&M, augmenting the water supply, reducing the leakages, etc. This progress is, however, confined to some pockets of the country. Thus, for example, the southern metropolitan water supply and sanitation service providing institutions of Chennai and Bangalore are meeting their O&M expenditure from the revenue generated from water tariff. The capital city of Delhi's service provider Delhi Jal Board is performing far below the desirable levels both in terms of service provision, persistence of large amount of unpaid and unaccounted for water (UFW) as well as in tariff realization.

5.35 However the Tenth Five Year Plan has triggered the realization that institutions have to be self-sustaining and efficient service is the key to realize that. The lesson to be learnt is in today's scenario, in urban areas, people are willing to pay for the services, provided they are reliable both in quantity as well as in quality. The experience of Bangalore is reflected in Box 5.2 below.

Box 5.2
Urban Slum Water Supply

The Social Development Unit of Bangalore Water Supply and Sewerage Board (BMWSSB) under the AusAID Master Plan project has helped to cover 10000 households with water supply in 43 Bangalore slums. This was made possible by reducing the connection fee, tariff, and effecting changes in the proof of residency. This way the illegal water connections were connected to revenue earning ones. All these connections were metered and with individual connections, dependence on public stand posts reduced. BMWSSB then cut down the wastages also. The most significant part was the assessing the willingness and capacity to pay by slum dwellers and the tariff made acceptable to the community by ensuring reliable service.

5.36 To extend financial support to the State Government/local bodies and to provide water supply facilities in towns having population less than 20000 (as per 1991 census), the centrally sponsored Accelerated Urban Water Supply Programme (AUWSP) was launched in March 1994. These towns are often neglected during normal times and are worst hit during the period of drought.

5.37 So far, water supply schemes for 1244 towns have been sanctioned at a cost of Rs 1822.38 crore under AUWSP since its inception from 1993–94 and 639 schemes have been completed/commissioned. Since 2005–06, no schemes are being sanctioned under the programme since scheme has been merged with the Urban Infrastructure Development Scheme for Small and Medium Towns (UIDSSMT). An amount of Rs 828.60 crore (till September 2006) was released to the States and they have reported incurring an expenditure of Rs 805.83 crore and the total expenditure reported is Rs 1412.88 crore.

5.38 An evaluation study carried out in 62 towns in 24 States has shown that the programme has resulted in water supply augmentation and improved health outcomes but indicated the need for some design flexibility and institutional strengthening of local bodies for managing the completed schemes.

MAJOR ISSUES IN URBAN WATER SUPPLY

Sustainability and Equity

5.39 Sustainability in the urban water supply is addressed mainly through supply side augmentation. Distant perennial sources are identified and long distance piped water transfer to the cities and towns are common. Augmentation plans are generally gigantic and engineering-oriented and has greater acceptability at all levels. The demand management is the least preferred option. However when it comes to payment of water charges, the decision is invariably with the elected government and not with the executing agency, which has to depend on the grants for O&M, for sustaining the quantity and quality.

5.40 It is not uncommon that pockets of urban areas would get higher service levels both in terms of number of hours of water availability as well as per capita availability. The UFW due to leaking water supply systems and illegal tapping reduces water availability. The average water loss in the leaking water supply systems varies from place to place and it is generally between 20–50%. Dedicated efforts to plug the leakages are required in addition to demand management measures for achieving the sustainability and equity.

5.41 Long distance water transfer has brought in the attendant issues of dependence on other States for urban water supply. For example, Delhi depends on Haryana and UP for its water supply. Chennai gets 15 TMC of Krishna River Water from Andhra Pradesh. Bangalore water supply is fully dependent on Cauvery waters. There are a few instances when even within the State people object to transfer of water from one district to another. Some times, these issues have a serious implication on the sustainability of supplies to the cities.

Demand and Supply Management

5.42 There is a huge gap between the demand and supply of water in urban areas, which is also growing due to population and urbanization. Norms for various places depending upon the level of development have been established and it is maximum for metropolitan cities. The regular Plan programmes by the States are heavily tilted in favour of supply side management. Recycling and reuse of water, reducing the water demand through rainwater harvesting, using water-efficient household equipment, including flushing cisterns would go a long way in conserving water and reducing demand. Proper metering of water and rational tariff would reduce water demand and encourage conservation. We need to have a concept of water-efficient homes in urban areas and for this there is a need to have a well-orchestrated information campaign. Long distance piped water transfer and desalination of water in coastal areas as augmentation measures are very capital-intensive. Demand management is necessary to achieve sustainability. An integrated water supply and use strategy such as used in Singapore (see Box 5.3) should be encouraged.

Financing and Institutional Issues

5.43 Provision of water supply in urban areas is basically a responsibility of urban local bodies. The PPP efforts to attract financing of water supply projects are finding its place, though so far only in few cases (see Box 5.4). PPP is important to leverage government investments and to access private sector management efficiencies. Reforms are a necessary precondition for gaining success through PPP. It is paradoxical that urban utilities receive funds from institutions such as HUDCO, LIC, government, etc. without any reform conditionalities but on the other hand, States are given additional financial support towards implementing reforms through schemes like JNNURM.

Box 5.3
Public Utilities Board (PUB) Singapore

PUB is the National Water Agency in Singapore charged with water, wastewater, and storm water management in the city state. The public agency services about 4.5 million people and a number of major industries with intensive water use. The development and implementation of the complete management system is ongoing but has taken over a period of about 40 years.PUB's holistic approach has resulted in a lower dependence on external water sources by diversification of water sources including water reuse, desalination, storm water storage in new water storages, and supply of very high-quality recycled water to industry with some internal reuse of this supply. Singapore presents a challenging environment for water resources management, as it is a small but densely populated island city state.In its own operations PUB has significantly reduced water losses due to leakage in pipes and inaccurate meters. It has 100% servicing of its population with water and waste water services and strong political and public acceptance of its policies and services.It has been accompanied by a major change in water pricing and access policy, which aims to use the rate structure to encourage the more efficient use of water. PUB has been able to provide lowered costs of delivered water of improved higher quality to industry and the community. Reclaimed water branded *NEWater* in Singapore is recognized for its high quality. Singapore has also been able to maintain low water costs for households on the lowest tariff water supply despite the major capital investments in new equipment and systems. Its household directed campaign of 'Water-efficient homes' helps residents to save water at home and reduce their water bills.Through an extensive partnering programme with the water industry in all aspects of implementation it has been a model of outsourcing skills. From this it has developed an industry capable of transferring this knowledge and skills to the region as well as attracting a broad rage of industry skills and capabilities as well as research in Singapore.The PUB story would fit well as a study example in the education of water managers. PUB has won the prestigious 2007 Stockholm Industry Water Award.

PUB website: *www.pub.gov.sg*

Box 5.4
PPP in Urban Water Supply

Tamil Nadu has emerged as forerunner in attracting PPP in urban water supply sector. At 42%, it is a highly urbanized State in the country. The State has already commissioned the 'Tirupur Water Supply and Sewerage project' at a cost of Rs 1023 crore. The cost per kilo litre of water at estimate stage is Rs 30, which is high due to recovery of the sewerage capital cost, operating expenses, and capital cost. The next project on PPP is 100 million litres per day (MLD) desalination project for Chennai Water Supply.

5.44 The large number of institutional issues in water supply sector discussed during the formulation of the Tenth Plan are still valid. The rationale of financing water supply schemes fully or partly as grant, inability of the urban local bodies (ULBs) to raise funds due to low tariff recovery, their weak financial position preventing any augmentation efforts, tossing around the responsibility of water supply from the State level utility to local bodies/Panchayats with large liabilities, etc. are continuing.

5.45 Despite the large grants by TFC for local bodies to maintain the water supply systems, things have yet to improve a lot on the ground. Overlapping of responsibilities between various institutions like ULBs, State-level agencies, and departments dilutes the accountability and responsibility to the customers.

Tariff and O&M

5.46 Evolving realistic water tariff so as to discourage excessive use of treated/potable water is one of the important management tools for demand management. Not much has been done on this important aspect in many urban local bodies in the country except a few larger cities that have undertaken some measures by way of installing water meters for consumers. The major reason for slow progress in this regard is that good quality meters are not available on a large scale since the meter manufacturing facility is vested with small-scale industries at present, which do not have the capacity to produce meters on a large scale.

5.47 Poor O&M due to inadequate financial resources is one of the primary reasons for low sustainability and equity in water supply. The responsibility of operation, maintenance, and revenue collection is generally vested with the elected ULB, while the specialized bodies are not able to raise the water tariff without the approval of the provincial governments. The local bodies generally receive grant assistance ranging from 10% to 60% for capital works on water supply and sanitation from the State Government. Usually, they do not receive any grant assistance for O&M of water supply and sewerage. Municipal bodies in many parts of the country suffer from inadequate resources. Assessment of demand and 'willingness to pay' by the communities would help to arrive at a basis for pricing water management services and to clarify the scope for adopting 'full cost recovery' policies to achieve financial sustainability.

Eleventh Five Year Plan Programmes for Urban Water Supply

5.48 With a view to provide 100% water supply accessibility to the entire urban population by the end of the Eleventh Plan in 2012, it has been estimated that Rs 53666 crore is required. With a view to provide reform-linked infrastructure facilities in the urban areas, the GoI has launched the two new programmes namely—

(i) JNNURM covering 63 cities with population above one million as per 2001 census, including 35 metro cities and other State capitals and culturally important towns.
(ii) UIDSSMT for the remaining 5098 towns having population less than one million to cover all the towns as per 2001 census, irrespective of the population criteria.

5.49 JNNURM is envisaged for implementation over a seven-year period starting from 2005 to 2012 with a tentative outlay of Rs 100000 crore, which includes contribution of Rs 50000 crore to be made by the States and ULBs. Water supply and sanitation is accorded priority under the programme and is likely to receive 40% of plan funds. It is important to tap the other sources like higher Central and State sector outlays, institutional financing, PPP, and external assistance.

5.50 Sea water desalination has emerged as an alternative option for water supply augmentation in coastal areas. Many research institutes have embarked upon this programme for producing cheap water from the abundant source. While the Chennai Desalination Plan of 100 million litres per day (MLD) is large version being tried with PPP mode by the Government of Tamil Nadu, Central institutes such as Bhabha Atomic Research Centre (BARC) and National Institute of Ocean Technology (NIOT) have already established desalination plants at various places (see Box 5.5). The research needs to be advanced to bring down the cost of water produced from such systems.

THE WAY FORWARD

5.51 The Eleventh Five Year Plan will address the issues faced by the sector and strive to achieve the goal of universal water supply coverage and sustainability as follows:

Priority for Drinking Water

- While designing and constructing multipurpose dams/reservoirs, adequate care would be taken to reserve/apportion sufficient quantity of water for domestic use in the urban areas. Keeping in view the National Water Policy, topmost priority would be given by the State Governments to the drinking water supply needs of cities and towns from the available water sources. This needs to be operationalized by all States in the form of State Water Policy as desired in National Water Policy, 2002.
- Under JNNURM and UIDSSMT programmes, special attention will be given to towns and cities affected by surface and groundwater contamination due to the presence of chemicals such as iron, manganese, fluoride, salinity, arsenic, pesticides, etc. in excess of the prescribed limits. Such drought-prone and water shortage areas as well as the cities and towns having water quality problems would be given top priority in the selection process by State Governments/ULBs.

Maintenance of Assets

- Adequate thrust may be given to the O&M of the assets created for their optimal and efficient use by evolving suitable strategy and creating adequate infrastructure facilities within State departments/ concerned ULBs.
- Computerized MIS is a must for developing a strong data base at local, State, and Central levels on Urban Water Supply and Sanitation sector for decision making, planning, and mid-course corrections from time to time. In most States, elaborate computerized MIS is not in place. It is recommended that MIS cells may be created with central funding at State and Central levels for exchanging information and to develop good data base for the sector.

Metering of Water for Volumetric Change

- Telescopic water tariff/user charges should be formulated and levied to discourage excessive use of water while providing a basic quantity of water at a low tariff. Metering of water supplies should be made mandatory in a phased manner with a view to conserve water as well as to generate revenue on a realistic basis.

Box 5.5

Sea Water Desalination Initiative by National Institute of Ocean Technology (NIOT), Chennai, Pure Water at Six Paise per Litre

The NIOT, Chennai, has succeeded in putting together and operating a desalination system with a capacity of 1 million litres a day. The quality of water is tested and found above international standards. For instance, the total dissolved solids was found to be less than 10 parts per million (PPM) as against international standard of 500 ppm. The system that works on the principle of flash evaporation works on mounted barge off shore, drawing water from sea at different levels to accomplish the task. The technology involved was turning surface sea water into vapour in a vacuum chamber and then condensing the vapour using the cold water drawn from the sea itself from a depth of 600 m. For transporting the one million litre water from offshore barge to the shore, specially designed water bags of special material were made that could hold and carry 2 lakh litres and could be towed to shore using small fishing boats. The NIOT would now focus on desalination plant with 10 MLD with the help of private sector. The water costs 6 paise per litre. The NIOT has already installed one lakh litre desalination plant at Lakshadweep Island during 2006.

- The ULBs need to be given greater autonomy in respect of fixing tax rates, user charges, etc. and also ensure regular revision of such rates. The 74th constitutional amendment needs to be implemented in its entirety. There is a need for regulatory regime in water supply and sanitation sector to enthuse confidence among the private players.

Reducing Waste and Promoting Conservation

- Intensive leak detection and rectification programme should receive priority. Severe penalties should be levied on those found responsible for leakage and wastage of water. ULBs may be asked to enact necessary changes in the municipal Acts.
- To reduce wastage of water, adoption of low volume flushing cisterns, waste not taps, etc. should be adopted so as to minimize the need for fresh water. Ministry of Urban Development/Town and Country Planning Organization (TCPO) may take up the matter with the States and ULBs to promote usage of such cisterns so as to conserve fresh water. Central Public Works Department may also widely use such cisterns in the buildings constructed by them.

Augmenting Availability

- It must be made mandatory to install rainwater harvesting systems in both public and private buildings including industrial and commercial establishments so as to conserve water. The ULBs should make it a point not to approve building plans having no provision for such systems. It is also equally important to ensure proper implementation of the approved system by the builders.
- The State Governments and ULBs may implement schemes for artificial recharge of ground water as per techniques developed by the Central Ground Water Board.

Water Quality

- Water quality surveillance and monitoring should be given top most priority by the State Governments/ULBs so as to ensure prevention and control of water-borne diseases. For this purpose, water quality testing laboratories have to be set up in every city and town backed by qualified personnel to handle such laboratories and where such labs already exist, they should be strengthened with equipment, chemicals, manpower, etc., if necessary.

Finance

- Efforts should be made to step up the quantum of funds through institutional financing, foreign direct investment, assistance from bilateral, multilateral agencies, newly launched Pooled Finance Development Scheme, tax-free municipal bonds, Member of Parliament Local Area Development (MPLAD) funds, etc. apart from involving private entrepreneurs.

Human Resources

- Trained technical human resources are a must for successful implementation and maintenance of various water supply and sanitation schemes. However, in some States as well on in many ULBs the water utilities do not have adequate trained technical personnel, due to which the sector is affected badly. Under the circumstances, the Public Health Engineering (PHE) training programme of the Ministry of Urban Development has to be toned up further with adequate funds to enable Central Public Health and Environmental Engineering Organization (CPHEEO) to impart training to the various technical personnel of the State Governments/ULBs on a variety of technical subjects and management aspects.

RURAL SANITATION

5.52 Sanitation is to be seen as a basic need, as basic as drinking water or food. A sanitary toilet, within or near home, provides privacy and dignity to women. Mahatma Gandhi emphasized the link between sanitation and health as a key goal for our society.

5.53 Sanitation coverage, which ought to be a way of life to safeguard health, is inadequate in our country. In fact, problems like open defecation continue to remain the only form of sanitation for the majority of the population in rural areas. The practice of open defecation in India is due to a combination of factors—the most prominent of them being the traditional behavioural pattern and lack of awareness of the people about the associated health hazards.

5.54 Recognizing the link between healthy environment and sanitation, the MDGs stipulate, inter alia, halving, by 2015, the proportion of people without sustainable access to safe drinking water and basic sanitation. The TSC programme, the flagship programme of the government, has set an ambitious target beyond the MDGs and aims to achieve universal sanitation coverage in the country by the end of the Eleventh Plan.

Performance Review of Rural Sanitation Sector—TSC in Tenth Plan

5.55 The TSC is being implemented in 578 districts of 30 States/UTs with support from the Central Government and the respective State/UT governments. Against a target of 10.85 crore individual household toilets, the toilets reported completed is about 2.89 crore up to January 2007. In addition, about 3.12 lakh school toilets, 8900 sanitary complex for women, and 99150 *balwadi* toilets have been constructed. The approved outlay for the programme in the Tenth Plan was Rs 955 crore and the anticipated financial utilization is about Rs 2000 crore. The Eleventh Five Year Plan targets to complete 7.29 crore individual toilets for achieving universal sanitation coverage in rural areas.

Major Issues in Rural Sanitation Coverage

5.56 Though the current programme emphasis on construction of household toilets is laudable, it needs to reorient itself to a vigorous Information and Education Campaign mode to bring about a change in mindset. The evaluation study of the programme has shown that 20% of the toilets are not used or used for other purposes like storage. The superstructure for the toilet, the one that guarantees privacy and dignity, was provided funds under the programme starting only in March 2006.

5.57 The issue of convergence of the programme with health awareness received a boost only after the launch of the NRHM. While it was introduced earlier at school level, at the community level it was expanded later. However, the school programme had a cascading effect on the individual household and children helped to change attitudes. The awareness is now picking up and the programme needs to capitalize on this for increasing the sanitation coverage. Lack of priority for the programme by many States leading to inadequate provision of funds for the State share for the TSC, lack of emphasis on personal communication on sanitation at the village level, and inadequate capacity building at the grassroot level are some of the common issues seen across the States that hinder expansion of sanitation coverage.

Eleventh Plan Priorities

5.58 While the hardware part of the programme for assisting the States in providing the various types of sanitation would continue, the focus now should be more on changing behaviour patterns. The Nirmal Gram Puraskar (described later) has brought a sea change in the attitudes of the community and it is promoting a healthy competition among the Panchayats for achieving total sanitation. Low-cost technology options for constructing the toilets should be tried and community should be given freedom to choose the various options. The focus on school sanitation needs to continue. In addition, SWM in villages should be the next focus area. Ten per cent of the TSC funds are earmarked for this purpose already. Adequate funding for the programme would have to be provided so that the momentum generated is not lost.

IEC and Nirmal Gram Puraskar (NGP)—Success Stories

5.59 To add vigour to the TSC, in June 2003, the GoI initiated an incentive scheme for fully sanitized and open defecation free Gram Panchayats, blocks, and districts called the NGP. The incentive pattern is based on population criteria. The NGP is given to the following:

- Gram Panchayats, blocks, and districts that achieve 100% sanitation coverage in terms of 100% sanitation coverage of individual households, 100% school sanitation coverage, making the village, block, district free from open defecation and with clean environment.
- Organizations that have been the driving force for effecting full sanitation coverage in the respective geographical area.

5.60 The incentive scheme has caught on like wild fire and the number of Panchayats who have received this Puraskar is steadily going up. From a mere 40 village/block panchayats from six States that received the award in 2005, in the year 2007, the number of awardees have gone up to 4959 from 22 States. Maharashtra, which got 13 awards in 2005, received 1974 awards in 2007—a significant achievement—followed by Gujarat with 576 awards. Box 5.6 highlights the efforts of Suravadi Panchayat in this area.

Beyond Nirmal Gram—Monitoring for Sustainability

5.61 Once the village, block, or district Panchayat has received the Puraskar, there is a responsibility thrust on them, to maintain the Nirmal Gram status. The sustainability features mentioned in the Maharashtra success story on sanitation are worth emulating. Specially, community involvement with women and children would sustain the Nirmal Gram status. Such grams have to move now to the next stage of sustained SWM and proper street drainages.

5.62 The Way Forward

- Open defecation-free status is the basic objective of the programme. The sanitation campaign should focus on creating awareness about the importance of sanitation among people with special emphasis on children. Awareness can spread rapidly from children to parents to community, which will create demand for sanitation. The software component of the programme like IEC, NGP will receive more priority.
- Once individual or community toilets are provided demand for water would increase.
- Rural sanitation has to be promoted on low water, low-cost, and eco-sanitation models without causing further stress on water resources. Such systems will be actively promoted, encouraged, incentivized, and rewarded.

Box 5.6

How Suravadi Panchayat in Phaltan Block in Satara District of Maharashtra won the Nirmal Gram Puraskar (NGP)

This Panchayat that has a population of 2891 people has 412 households out of which 112 are BPL households. The Panchayat has a village primary school, an anganwadi centre, and a Primary Health Centre five km away. There was no community toilet facility in the village. Men, women, and children used to defecate in the open. Out of 47 individual toilets 34 were not in use (used only for other purposes). Village was always highly stinking, no drainage, many ill with diseases like jaundice, flu, cholera, etc. Several village meetings were held for stoppage of open defecation. It looked like a Herculean task in the beginning, as people were not coming forward for construction of toilets.

Things began to change when Sant Gadge Baba Gram Swachhata Abhiyan started in year 2000 and motivational campaign and meetings were organized by Panchayat. The school teachers and students were involved in this campaign. Sanitation campaign started with making a 28-seater complex and few individual units. Persons still going for open defecation were penalized with no distribution of wheat and kerosene from FPS. It was also decided to give Rs 500 to every family to construct its own latrine. Construction of toilets geared up slowly but taken up in later stages by community participation. The Gram Panchayat and youth group of the same village monitored the sanitation programme.

Everybody is using toilets in the village today. Recognition of community is shown by painting all houses using toilets in pink colour. With the campaign, people also gained knowledge on bio-gas plants and about conservation of sources. The scheme was also linked with and benefited through other rural developmental schemes like Yaswant Gram Samruddhi Yojana.

To sustain the programme women and children get regular knowledge on cleanliness through school. Extra classes have been organized for students on promotion of sanitation and hygiene activities in the schools. The village now has a better school facility and the Panchayat is fully involved, as it had initiated this campaign. There is a feeling of pride with their becoming the first village in the entire State to get the NGP award.

Present sanitation status in the village is as follows:

Number of Households:	412
Status of Toilets:	100% using toilets
	Community Complexes (28 users)
	10 Gobar gas plants linked to toilets

- As an incentive mechanism, the Nirmal Grams should be provided funds under the ARWSP for higher service levels from 40 litre per capita per day (LPCD) to 55–60 lpcd per capita. This should be with commitment for meeting the O&M cost from the society.
- Specific policy directives for sanitation campaigns to include special needs of women, adolescent girls, infants, disabled, and the aged will be given.
- Sufficient focus of rural sanitation should be laid on the needs of disaster-prone areas such as hills, mountains, coastal areas, etc.
- The investments required in training, skill development for production of low-water, low-cost sanitation appurtenances suitable for rural areas, and training of self-groups of women, youth, etc. as masons and mistries for embarking on large-scale simple toilet construction activities throughout the country will be made available. The community should be encouraged to avail soft micro credits from the SHGs and for which a separate revolving fund should be provided.
- There is a need to have a monitoring system for the villages, which received the Nirmal Gram Puraskar award so that the success obtained is sustained. Community monitoring with women and children would be the primary choice. A close monitoring mechanism to oversee the coverage of BPL household and in SC/ST household also should be put in place at every State level.
- Schools provided with sanitation facilities should have a separate rain water harvesting system to meet the water requirement for the sanitation purposes.
- The Nirmal Gram Puraskar model of recognizing and rewarding entire village panchayats and PRIs that have been able to bring about total sanitation in many villages through awareness, peer pressure, and local competitive spirit amongst the PRIs will continue to be promoted.
- Segregation of degradable and non-degradable solid waste, black and grey liquid wastewater, and holistic environmental protection and cleanliness through rural sanitation, solid and liquid waste programmes will be promoted as the next area of focus.
- Decentralized sanitation solid and liquid waste management as business models under various employment and self-employment programmes with appropriate incentives will be encouraged.

URBAN SANITATION INCLUDING SWM

5.63 The major issues in urban sanitation are how to expand sewerage and sanitation facility to cover all the people in all cities and towns; how to find resources to do that; how to create awareness about the importance of sanitation and SWM; how to prepare and execute plans that keep up with growing population; and how to finance the O&M costs of the facilities created?

STATUS OF URBAN SANITATION AND SOLID WASTE DISPOSAL

5.64 On the basis of information furnished by the State agencies in charge of Urban Water Supply and Sanitation Sector, about 91% of the urban population has got access to water supply and 63% to sewerage and sanitation facilities (47% from sewer and 53% from low cost sanitation) as on 31.3.2004. However, adequacy, equitable distribution, and per capita provision of these basic services may not be as per prescribed norms in most of the cities. For instance, the poor, particularly those living in slums and squatter settlements, are generally deprived of these basic facilities.

5.65 As per assessment made by the Central Pollution Control Board on the status of wastewater generation and treatment in Class I cities and Class II towns during 2003–04 (Table 5.2), about 26254 MLD of wastewater is generated in 921 Class I cities and Class II towns in India (housing more than 70% of urban population). The wastewater treatment capacity developed so far is about 7044 MLD—accounting for 27% of wastewater generated in these two classes of urban centres.

5.66 The pollution effect of sanitation is enormous. Three-fourths of the surface water resources are polluted and 80% of the pollution is due to sewage alone. Poor sanitation conditions, particularly in slums, are often linked to outbreaks of cholera and gastroenteritis. Water-borne diseases are one of the major causes of mortality throughout India and impose a huge burden in terms of loss of life and productivity.

TABLE 5.2
Status of Water Supply, Wastewater Generation, and Treatment in Class I Cities/Class II Towns in 2003–04

Parameters	Class I Cities	Class II Towns	Total
Number (as per 2001 census)	423	498	921
Population (millions)	187	37.5	224.5
Water Supply (MLD)	29782	3035	32817
Water Supply (LPCD)	160	81	146
Wastewater generated (MLD)	23826	2428	26054
Wastewater generation (LPCD)	127	65	116
Wastewater treated (MLD)	6955 (29%)	89 (3.67%)	7044 (27%)
Wastewater untreated (MLD)	16871 (71%)	2339 (96.33%)	19210 (73%)

Water and sanitation diseases are responsible for 60% of the environmental health burden. The single major cause of this burden of disease is diarrhoea, which disproportionately affects the children under the age of five.

5.67 It is estimated that about 115000 MT of municipal solid waste is generated daily in the country. Per capita waste generation in cities varies from 0.2 kg to 0.6 kg per day depending upon the size of population. An assessment has been made that per capita waste generation is increasing by about 1.3% per year. With growth of urban population ranging between 3 to 3.5% per annum, the annual increase in overall quantity of solid waste generated in the cities is assessed at about 5%. The collection efficiency ranges between 70 to 90% in major metro cities, whereas in several smaller cities it is below 50%. It has been estimated that the ULBs spend about Rs 500 to Rs 1500 per tonne on solid waste collection, transportation, treatment, and disposal. About 60–70% of this amount is spent on street sweeping, 20–30% on transportation, and less than 5% on final disposal of waste, which shows that hardly any attention is given to scientific and safe disposal of waste. Landfill sites have not yet been identified by many municipalities and in several municipalities, the landfill sites have been exhausted and the respective local bodies do not have resources to acquire new land. Due to lack of disposal sites, even the collection efficiency gets affected.

5.68 SWM is a part of public health and sanitation, and according to the Indian constitution, it falls under State list. Since this activity is non-exclusive, non-rivalled, and essential, the responsibility for providing the service lies within the public domain. As this activity is of local nature, it is entrusted to the ULBs. The ULB undertakes the task of solid waste service delivery, with its own staff, equipment, and funds. In a few cases, part of the said work is contracted out to private enterprises. The management of municipal solid waste is one of the most important obligatory functions of the urban local bodies, which is closely associated with urban environmental conditions. The 74th constitutional amendment gives constitutional recognition for local self government institutions specifying the powers and responsibilities.

5.69 Very few ULBs in the country have prepared long-term action plans for effective SWM in their respective cities. For obtaining a long-term economic solution, planning of the system on long-term sustainable basis is very essential. The Ministry of Environment and Forests (MoEF), GoI, has notified Municipal Solid Waste (Management and Handling) Rules, 2000 to tackle this problem. The increase in quantity of municipal solid waste generation with increase in the urban population is quite obvious. Efforts towards waste recycle, reuse, and resource recovery for reduction in waste and adoption of more advanced technological measures for effective and economical disposal of municipal solid waste is the need of the hour.

5.70 There has been no major effort in the past to create community awareness, either about the likely perils due to poor waste management or the simple steps that every citizen can take, which will help in reducing waste generation and promote effective management of solid waste generated. The degree of community sensitization and public awareness is low.

5.71 Since in most of our cities there are many unauthorized housing colonies that are not provided sewerage facilities, their waste go untreated polluting the water bodies in which it is drained. Cities need to treat the sewage from the entire city.

5.72 Growing urbanization has made storm water draining systems inadequate increasing the frequency of flooding of cities like Mumbai.

PERFORMANCE REVIEW OF THE SECTOR IN TENTH PLAN

5.73 The Tenth Plan targeted a coverage of providing sewerage and sanitation facilities to 75% of the population from 57% at the beginning of the Plan. An investment requirement of Rs 23157 crore was worked out for sanitation and Rs 2322 crore for SWM. There was no scheme at the beginning of the Tenth Plan to assist the States in the sanitation sector and the Plan recommended an enhanced scope for the AUWSP to include sanitation. With the launch of JNNURM and UIDSSMT, the AUWSP programme is subsumed in UIDSSMT and the scheme now includes funding for sanitation also.

5.74 The Central Scheme of Solid Waste Management and Drainage in airfield towns was also launched in the Tenth Plan. Bird hits are among the major causes of air crashes in our country leading to the loss of costly defence aircrafts and loss of invaluable lives of pilots. An Inter-Ministerial Joint Sub-Group constituted by the Ministry of Defence recommended to provide proper sanitation facilities, including SWM and drainage to over-come the bird menace in the following 10 towns having airfields of the Indian Air Force at Gwalior (MP), Ambala (Haryana), Hindon (UP), Jodhpur (Rajasthan), Tezpur (Assam), Dundigal (AP), Sirsa (Haryana), Adampur (Punjab), Pune (Maharashtra), and Bareilly (UP).

5.75 All the schemes are under execution and are at different stages of execution and were expected to be completed in the Tenth Plan itself, but have not been completed.

ELEVENTH FIVE YEAR PLAN TARGETS FOR URBAN SANITATION

5.76 The target fixed for urban sanitation is 100% population coverage with 70% by sewerage facility and 30% by low-cost sanitation. For SWM 100% population is proposed to be covered with appropriate SWM. It has been estimated that the fund requirement for these programmes is Rs 53168 crore for sanitation and Rs 2212 crore for SWM.

5.77 While funds to the tune of Rs 40000 crore would be available from the JNNURM for water supply and sanitation, at this stage it would be difficult to predict the availability for sanitation and SWM separately. External assistance could be tapped and States/UTs should increase their outlays in their regular budget for these programmes. Some amount of contribution by beneficiaries is desirable as it reflects their need. Leverage of funds through PPP should also be used.

5.78 The importance of effective administration and citizen cooperation in SWM cannot be overestimated. The case of Surat shows what these can be accomplished (see Box 5.7).

5.79 Initiatives Required in Eleventh Five Year Plan

- Recycling and reuse of sewage after the desired degree of treatment (depending upon the end use) for various non-potable purposes should be encouraged. Industries and commercial establishments must be persuaded to adopt reuse of treated sewage and recycle treated trade effluents to the extent possible in order to cut down the fresh water demand.

Box 5.7
Success in SWM—The Case of Surat

The outbreak of a plague-like disease in Surat in 1994 brought solid waste to the attention of the public. The contrast between the scrupulously clean Indian homes and the heaps of rubbish and filth commonly found in the urban public spaces was much discussed in the newspapers of the day. Urban filth was deemed to be bad for both public health and the urban economy.

Accordingly, the situation created an intense political will to clean up the city. Money and professional management was mobilized on a PSP/PPP basis and there was a major cleaning of the urban areas. Today, Surat is one of the cleanest cities in India, indicating how rapidly and effectively this can be achieved if political will and the organization are present.

Moreover, incentives in the form of rebate on water cess, concessions in customs and excise duty on equipment and machinery, tax holiday, etc., should be considered by the GoI for agencies dealing with planning, developing, and operating such reuse treatment plants as well as users of treated sewage and trade effluents. Similarly, for dense urban neighbourhoods, decentralized waste treatment systems that are cheaper and reduce the distance that the sewage is transported form a viable alternative to large treatment plants.

- Targeted subsidy may be made available to the SCs and STs, and other disadvantaged groups living in urban slums on taking house service connections for water supply/sewerage, metering, construction of latrine, subsidized water rates, etc. and accordingly adequate funds may be earmarked for the purpose so as to avoid any possible diversion of funds by the State Governments/ULBs. At the same time internal earmarking of funds for the urban slums under JNNURM/UIDSSMT schemes should be made mandatory. It is also very much necessary to monitor the physical and financial progress of the implementation of such programmes on a regular basis by the funding agencies so as to ensure fulfilment of the envisaged objectives.
- Comprehensive storm water drainage system has to be provided in all the cities and towns based on need, in order to avoid water logging in residential areas/flooding of streets during the monsoon period.
- There is a need to have a national centre for water excellence, which looks at especially the drinking water and sanitation sector in rural and urban water areas.
- We need to find a way to provide sewerage facilities to unauthorized housing colonies without giving them a right to the land by implication.

SOLID WASTE MANAGEMENT (SWM)

- Urban waste management by ULBs is already under stress because of paucity of resources and inadequacies of the system. Unless concerted efforts are made to improve the flow of resources to SWM and build up systems that incorporate the basic requirements of a proper waste management practice, the problem of urban waste will be further aggravated and cause environmental health problems.
- It is recommended that all the cities and towns have to be provided with appropriate SWM facilities giving due emphasis to the magnitude of the problem.
- Soil fertility is being badly affected by excessive use of chemical fertilizers and inadequate use of organic fertilizers. Large quantities of urban waste can be a useful solution to this problem. Compulsory production of compost from urban solid waste in cities and towns and promotion of application of this organic manure in agriculture and horticulture should be implemented, as this may have a significant positive impact on soil fertility.
- The Report of the Inter Ministerial Task Force on the 'Integrated Plant Nutrient Management using city compost' constituted by the Ministry of Urban Development in March 2005 as per the directive of the Hon'ble Supreme Court of India has recommended technical, financial, qualitative, marketing, and sustainability aspects of utilization of Municipal Solid Waste for compost purpose. Recommendations of the Task Force need to be implemented through provision of various fiscal incentives/concessions.
- Quality standards for compost will have to be prescribed by Bureau of Indian Standards at the earliest. At the same time, it should be made mandatory that compost sold in the market should clearly indicate the exact chemical composition (Nitrogen, Phosphorus, and Potassium, NPK, etc.) on the bags for the benefit of users.
- To the extent possible materials such as metal, glass, plastic, rubber, tin, and paper available in the municipal waste must be recycled back as they have adequate salvage value. Inorganic and inert material such as sand, grit, stones, bricks, concrete, rubble, etc. may also be used for making low-cost bricks, road material, aggregates, etc. As such, efforts should be made to reuse the same and enough incentives in the form of tax concessions, subsidies, etc. may be given to the entrepreneurs dealing with such materials/processes.
- Our cities are littered with uncollected solid waste and no public place or street is free of litter. Though much recycling takes place by rag pickers and waste

collectors, a lot is left to be disposed off. To keep cities clean, citizen involvement is essential to sort waste at source and minimize waste that needs to be collected and disposed. A programme should be implemented to obtain citizens' cooperation. NGOs should be encouraged to provide organizational support and identity to the rag pickers so that better recycling occurs. Adequate land should be earmarked/allotted at the planning stage itself by the respective ULBs for setting up of sanitary landfills, compost plants, and other processing units including provision for future expansion.

- Awareness campaigns on various aspects of water quality, importance of safe drinking water, its handling and storage, water conservation in homes, use of sanitary toilets, separate storage of dry and wet garbage and its hygienic disposal, vector control, personal hygiene, etc. should be mounted.

PPP in Urban Sanitation and SWM

5.80 Though privatization of water supply and sanitation sector could not make significant progress as of now, there is substantial potential and urgent need for the same in near future. By and large, the tariff rates being charged from the consumers are very low and there is a general reluctance for enhancing the same. Under the circumstances, without aiming at full cost recovery, privatization cannot be a successful proposition. It is felt that it would be easier and convenient to introduce privatization in new areas where the private companies will have a free hand to take up the task of planning, designing, execution, O&M, billing, and collection including tapping of raw water from the selected source either on Build Own Operate (BOO) or Build Own Operate Transfer (BOOT) basis. Few examples to infuse confidence in private entrepreneurs are—the successful award of Chennai service contract for O&M of 61 sewage pumping stations in the city, and of Rajkot and Surat contracting out a number of municipal services to private firms as well as community groups.

5.81 There were some public concerns on PPP projects in the water supply sector in the country because of which the projects were either stalled or dropped. If the community could be involved in PPP projects there would be more acceptability to such projects. PPP can be redesigned as Public–Private Community Partnership to overcome the hurdle.

CLEAN LIVING CONDITIONS

Introduction

5.82 Achievement of health objectives involves much more than curative or preventive medical care. Many of the communicable diseases in India can be prevented through a combination of health and non-health interventions. We need a comprehensive approach that encompasses individual health care, public health, sanitation, clean drinking water, access to food and knowledge about hygiene and feeding practice, etc. A direct relationship exists between water, sanitation, and health. Safe drinking water and sanitation are critical determinants, which directly contribute nearly 70–80% in reducing the burden of communicable diseases. Inadequate provision of safe drinking water, improper disposal of human waste, and lack of adequate systems for disposal of sewage and solid wastes leads to unhealthy and unhygienic conditions. This coupled with overall ignorance of personal and environmental hygiene are the main causes of a large number of water-borne diseases in the country.

Clean Water Supply

5.83 The water supply and sanitation sector will face enormous challenges over the coming decades. In India, the groundwater is consumed directly without any sort of treatment and disinfection. Its quality is therefore a cause of concern. The national objectives of reducing morbidity and mortality largely depend on the reduction of diarrhoea, jaundice, etc. In fact, no water supply and sanitation programme can be successful if water-related illnesses are not reduced. It is a matter of concern that despite the progress made with water supply, the level of water-related illnesses continues to be high. Approximately 10 million cases of diarrhoea, more than 7.2 lakh typhoid cases, and 1.5 lakh viral hepatitis cases occur every year (Annexure 5.1). A majority of them are contributed by unclean water supply and poor sanitation. Micro-level studies revealed that availability of clean water; sanitation, and hygiene interventions reduce diarrhoeal diseases on average by between one-quarter and one-third.

5.84 Causes of contamination of water are indiscriminate use of chemical fertilizers and chemicals, poor hygienic environment of the water sources, improper disposal of sewage and solid waste, pollution from untreated industrial effluents, and over-exploitation leading to quality degradation. Thus, the supply of additional quantity of water by itself does not ensure good health, proper handling of water and prevention of contamination are also equally important.

SANITATION

5.85 Sanitation covers the whole range of activities including human waste disposal, liquid and solid wastes from household, and industrial waste. Lack of drains and the presence of ditches create unsanitary conditions, which contaminate water, breed mosquitoes, and cause water-borne diseases. Malaria, typhoid, jaundice, cholera, dengue, and diarrhoea are all connected to unsanitary conditions (Annexure 5.2). Chikungunya fever has emerged as an epidemic outbreak after more than three decades. These diseases can be prevented by appropriate sanitation system. Unfortunately, access to sanitation facilities continues to be grossly inadequate.

5.86 Census 2001 indicates that of the 200 million dwelling units across the country, only some 40 million dwelling units have a toilet inside the house. Only 61% households in urban areas and 17% households in rural areas have access to improved sanitation.[1] While households having bathroom facility within the house is abysmally low in rural areas and urban areas in the poor performing States, the position in respect of connectivity for wastewater outlet is even more alarming. While closed drainage is available in the urban areas at least in the developed States, a large percentage of bathrooms across all States in the country have no drainage system particularly in the rural areas. This percentage is as high as 73.88 in Orissa, 72.69 in Assam and 71.81 in Chhattisgarh. The non-availability of toilets within the house is as high in Bihar (71.94%), Chhattisgarh (76.78%), and in Jharkhand (73.03%). In urban areas, the percentage of households not having toilet is marked in the case of Goa (15.26%), Maharashtra (17.75%), Chandigarh (17.83%), Delhi (19.58%), and Tamil Nadu (14.84%).[2] Top priority needs to be accorded to improving sanitary conditions and ensuring a clean microenvironment at home and at the workplace, which must now include factories, coalmines, quarries, and roads. The TSC aims to eliminate the practice of open defecation completely by 2012.

ENVIRONMENTAL POLLUTION

5.87 Serious environmental health problems affect millions of people who suffer from respiratory and other diseases caused or exacerbated by biological and chemical agents, both indoors and outdoors. Millions are exposed to unnecessary chemical and physical hazards in their home, workplace, or wider environment. Concern about the health effects of the high levels of air pollution observed in many mega cities is growing; moreover, it is likely that this problem will continue to grow because countries are trapped in the trade-offs of economic growth and environmental protection. Population in urban areas are at risk of suffering adverse health effects due to rising problems of severe air and water pollution.

5.88 Cooking and heating with solid fuels on open fires or traditional stoves results in high levels of indoor air pollution. Indoor smoke contains a range of health-damaging pollutants, such as small particles and carbon monoxide.

5.89 Indian women spend nearly 60% of their reproductive life in either pregnancy or breast-feeding.[3] Most of the women keep their children in the kitchen when they are cooking, thereby exposing the children to the pollutants too. This, combined with malnutrition may retard growth and lead to smaller lungs and a greater prevalence of chronic bronchitis. There is an urgent need for the implementation of control programs to reduce levels of particulate and other

[1] Census of India 2001, Registrar General of India.

[2] Census of India 2001, Registrar General of India.

[3] A. Kotwal (2007), Environment and Health, in O.P. Gupta and O.P. Ghai (eds), Text Book of Preventive & Social Medicine, 2nd edn, New Delhi: C.B.S Publishers.

pollutant emissions. To be effective, these programs should include the participation of the different stakeholders and initiate activities to identify and characterize air pollution problems, as well to estimate potential health impacts. A full understanding of the problem and its potential consequences for the local setting is essential for effectively targeting interventions to reduce the harmful impacts of air pollution.

5.90 Monitoring of air and water quality is crucial for devising programmes and policies related to pollution management. Establishing a reasonably adequate monitoring network with contemporary technology will be given priority. Ways of linking treatment of sewage and industrial effluents to the urban and industrial development planning need to be worked out. The goal should be to ensure that by the end of the Eleventh Plan no untreated sewage or effluent flows into rivers from cities and towns.

Strategies during the Eleventh Five Year Plan

5.91 In order to achieve 100% coverage of clean water and sanitation in rural areas, rural sanitation programme will be linked with the NRHM. The strategies include:

- Convergence of health care, hygiene, sanitation, and drinking water at the village level
- Participation of stakeholders at all levels, from planning, design and location to implementation and management of the projects
- Instituting water quality monitoring and surveillance systems by involving PRIs, community, NGOs, and other CSOs
- Increased attention to IEC campaign

5.92 Efforts will be made to launch a *Sarva Swasthya Abhiayan* in the county that will cover the primary health care, safe drinking water, and sanitation in urban areas.

Eleventh Five Year Plan Recommended Outlays

5.93 The full coverage of rural drinking water supply is to be achieved by March 2009 and 100% sanitation coverage by the end of the Eleventh Plan (2012) with mass awareness and NGP. The Eleventh Plan Central sector GBS for rural water supply and sanitation is Rs 41826 crore (at 2006–07 prices) and Rs 47306 crore (at current prices) (including Rs 6000 crore for Nirmal Gram Puraskar) and this provision will draw matching provision in the State Plan to the tune of Rs 48875 crore. Thus the total outlays in the Eleventh Five Year Plan for Rural Water Supply and Sanitation sector would be close to Rs 100000 crore. The total outlay for Urban Water Supply and Sanitation sector would be Rs 75000 crore.

ANNEXURE 5.1
Cases and Deaths due to Water-borne Diseases in Various States

States	Diarrhoeal Disease (2006)		Viral Hepatitis (2006)		Typhoid (2006)	
	Cases	Deaths	Cases	Deaths	Cases	Deaths
Andhra Pradesh	1215659	124	17846	28	135550	12
Arunachal Pradesh	32032	30	553	6	9098	23
Assam	..	..	..	..	..	..
Bihar	..	..	..	..	..	..
Chhattisgarh	95202	13	1491	2	21474	6
Goa	7631	0	15	0	68	0
Gujarat	382056	4	9396	16	7290	0
Haryana	285342	42	3983	11	5688	4
Himachal Pradesh	347055	28	835	11	26327	5
J&K	519317	32	5882	0	42369	0
Jharkhand	14752	1	51	0	4707	284
Karnataka	939221	1279	14980	24	96147	5
Kerala	475510	4	7018	6	6219	2
MP	318935	88	2499	9	28654	29
Maharashtra	695723	93	43215	131	39663	8
Manipur	13614	17	346	0	2421	2
Meghalaya	178260	33	294	2	6709	1
Mizoram	18063	20	546	11	1392	2
Nagaland	9176	0	112	0	2328	0
Orissa	373748	40	2687	38	15387	9
Punjab	182451	64	3829	17	17008	3
Rajasthan	318169	21	3869	78	14084	131
Sikkim	51433	8	290	2	428	2
Tamil Nadu	116062	12	4523	0	36973	0
Tripura	150750	47	2520	14	18547	19
Uttarakhand	94746	6	3381	0	15020	2
UP	284709	55	3716	6	42648	13
WB	2622968	964	7433	205	110835	70
A&N Islands	22752	2	213	4	3055	0
Chandigarh	..	..	..	..	..	..
D&N Haveli	74661	4	126	3	646	0
Daman & Diu	109	0	3	0	33	0
Delhi	94398	85	4080	42	13774	18
Lakshadweep	7316	0	86	0	6	0
Pondicherry	137443	8	615	7	1936	1
Total	10079263	3124	146433	673	726484	651

Note: '..' means not reported.

Source: MoHFW, GoI, 2006.

ANNEXURE 5.2
Burden of Major Communicable Diseases in Various States

States	Malaria (2005)		TB (2006)		ARI	
	Cases	Deaths	Cases	Deaths	Cases	Deaths
Andhra Pradesh	39099	0	142057	1184	2465743	434
Arunachal Pradesh	31215	0	1593	38	43426	1
Assam	67885	113	..	..	..	..
Bihar	2733	1	..	..	..	..
Chhattisgarh	187950	3	8689	12	132276	25
Goa	3747	1	2228	0	25559	0
Gujarat	179023	54	41730	238	833339	17
Haryana	33262	0	29900	227	1269205	178
Himachal Pradesh	129	0	14705	140	1545057	161
J&K	268	0	2346	28	383069	0
Jharkhand	193144	21	15516	5	23470	1
Karnataka	83181	26	76687	745	2544300	196
Kerala	2554	6	13840	181	7897043	165
MP	104317	44	18866	132	478278	180
Maharashtra	47608	104	52998	795	657432	192
Manipur	1844	3	482	20	12602	1
Meghalaya	16816	41	1900	29	304097	25
Mizoram	10741	74	936	28	41018	26
Nagaland	2987	0	838	0	11792	0
Orissa	396573	255	11443	178	768445	69
Punjab	1883	0	20612	106	601038	66
Rajasthan	52286	22	71180	695	1299772	126
Sikkim	69	0	2155	36	65304	7
Tamil Nadu	39678	0	28979	73	380708	220
Tripura	18008	20	971	27	279702	98
Uttarakhand	1242	0	3522	8	130683	11
UP	105303	0	109898	161	502869	81
WB	185964	175	89276	820	2020983	894
A&N Islands	3954	0	2898	10	32405	13
Chandigarh	432	0	..	..	..	..
D&N Haveli	1166	0	1544	36	118461	0
Daman and Diu	104	0	25	3	0	0
Delhi	1133	0	13544	993	323392	276
Lakshadweep	0	0	39	0	32093	0
Puducherry	44	0	7738	125	584161	1
Total	1816342	963	789135	7073	25807722	3467

Note: '..' means not reported.

Source: National Health Profile 2006, CBHI, DGHS—MoHFW.

6

Towards Women's Agency and Child Rights

INTRODUCTION

6.1 Women are significant contributors to the growing economy and children are assets of the future. Almost 50% of our population today comprises women while 42% is under the age of 18. For growth to be truly inclusive, we have to ensure their protection, well-being, development, empowerment and participation.

6.2 India has committed to meeting the MDGs and is a signatory to many international conventions, including Convention for Elimination of all forms of Discrimination against Women and the Convention on the Rights of the Child. Yet, at the start of the Eleventh Five Year Plan, women and children continue to be victims of violence, neglect, and injustice. The Eleventh Plan will address these problems by looking at gender as a cross-cutting theme. It will recognize women's agency and the need for women's empowerment. At the same time it will ensure the survival, protection, and all-round development of children of all ages, communities and economic groups.

APPROACH TO THE ELEVENTH FIVE YEAR PLAN

6.3 The vision of the Eleventh Five Year Plan is to end the multifaceted exclusions and discriminations faced by women and children; to ensure that every woman and child in the country is able to develop her full potential and share the benefits of economic growth and prosperity. Success will depend on our ability to adopt a participatory approach that empowers women and children and makes them partners in their own development. The roadmap for this has already been laid in the National Policy on Women 2001 and the National Plan of Action for Children 2005.

6.4 The Eleventh Plan recognizes that women and children are not homogenous categories; they belong to diverse castes, classes, communities, economic groups, and are located within a range of geographic and development zones. Consequently, some groups are more vulnerable than others. Mapping and addressing the specific deprivations that arise from these multiple locations is essential for the success of planned interventions. Thus apart from the general programme interventions, special targeted interventions catering to the differential needs of these groups will be undertaken during the Eleventh Plan.

6.5 The gender perspectives incorporated in the plan are the outcome of extensive consultations with different stakeholders, including a Group of Feminist Economists. In the Eleventh Plan, for the first time, women are recognized not just as equal citizens but as agents of economic and social growth. The approach to gender equity is based on the recognition that interventions in favour of women must be multi-pronged and they must: (i) provide women with basic entitlements, (ii) address the reality of globalization and its impact on women by prioritizing economic empowerment, (iii) ensure an environment free from all forms of violence against women (VAW)—physical, economic, social, psychological etc., (iv) ensure the participation and adequate representation of women at the highest policy levels, particularly in Parliament and State assemblies, and (v) strengthen existing institutional mechanisms and create new ones for gender main-streaming and effective policy implementation.

6.6 The child development approach in the Eleventh Plan is to ensure that children do not lose their childhood because of work, disease, and despair. It is based on the understanding that the rights of all children, including those who do not face adverse circumstances, must be protected everywhere and at all times so that they do not fall out of the social security net. Successful integration of survival, development, protection, and participation policies are important for the overall well being of the child. The essence of the Eleventh Plan strategy for Women Agency and Child Rights is summarized in Box 6.1.

MONITORABLE TARGETS FOR THE ELEVENTH PLAN

6.7 The Eleventh Plan lays down six monitorable targets

- Raise the sex ratio for age group 0–6 from 927 in 2001 to 935 by 2011–12 and to 950 by 2016–17.
- Ensure that at least 33% of the direct and indirect beneficiaries of all government schemes are women and girl children.
- Reduce IMR from 57 to 28 and MMR from 3.01 to one per 1000 live births.
- Reduce malnutrition among children of age group 0–3 to half its present level.
- Reduce anaemia among women and girls by 50% by the end of the Eleventh Plan.
- Reduce dropout rate for primary and secondary schooling by 10% for both girls as well as boys.

Box 6.1
Essence of the Approach

- Recognition of the right of every woman and child to develop to her/his full potential
- Recognition of the differential needs of different groups of women and children.
- Need for intersectoral convergence as well as focused women and child specific measures through MoWCD
- Partnership with civil society to create permanent institutional mechanisms that incorporate the experiences, capacities and knowledge of VOs and women's groups in the process of development planning.

STATUS OF WOMEN: A BRIEF OVERVIEW

6.8 Due to the untiring efforts of the women's movement, the country amended and enacted women-related legislations during the Tenth Plan. The Married Women's Property Act (1874), the Hindu Succession Act (1956) were amended and the Protection of Women from Domestic Violence Act (PWDVA) (2005) was passed. The Union Budget 2005–06, for the first time, included a separate statement highlighting the gender sensitivities of the budgetary allocation under 10 demands for grants. Gender Budgeting Cells were set up in 52 Central ministries/departments to review public expenditure, collect gender disaggregated data, and conduct gender-based impact analysis. Under Women Component Plan (WCP), efforts were made to ensure that not less than 30% of funds/benefits under various schemes of all ministries/departments were earmarked for women. The performance however has been far from satisfactory. The Mid Term Appraisal of Tenth Plan revealed that while 42.37% of the GBS to the Department of Education flowed to women under WCP, only 5% of the GBS of Ministry of Labour (against 33.5% in the Ninth Plan) went to women in the first three years of the Tenth Plan. Several ministries and/or departments that had

Box 6.2
Schemes (major) for Women during Tenth Plan

- *Swayamsidha*—Implemented in 650 selected blocks. Target: 16000 SHGs. Achievement: 1767.
- Support to Training and Employment Programme for Women (STEP)—Target: provide training to 2.5 lakh. Achievement: 2.31 lakh.
- *Swawlamban Scheme*—Target: 5 lakh. Achievement: 2.32 lakh.
- Hostels for Working Women—Target: construct 125 hostels benefiting 12500 women. Achievement: 111 hostels were constructed during the Plan benefiting 6976 women.
- *Swadhar*—To provide shelter, food, clothing, and care to the women living in difficult circumstances. No specific target. Achievement: 21464 women benefited.

earlier reported on the WCP in their sectoral budgets stopped doing so. Within the Ministry of WCD, the financial allocation for women specific schemes during the Tenth Plan was Rs 1246 crore. As a result of this modest allocation of resources and ineffective implementation of existing schemes, we have fallen far short of our Tenth Plan targets. Selected development indicators relating to women may be seen at Annexure 6.1.

DEMOGRAPHY

6.9 Female population of the country rose marginally from 48.1% of the total population in 1991 to 48.3% of the total population in 2001, an increase of 89.4 million. At 23.08%, the growth rate of female population for the 1991–2001 decade was slightly higher than the male population decennial growth rate of 22.26%. This is because life expectancy at birth for women has been rising steadily from 58.6 years in 1987–91 to 66.91 years in 2001–06; it is higher than the male life expectancy of 63.87 years. Demographic imbalances between men and women, however, continue to exist, even worsen, in certain regions.

6.10 While the overall sex ratio improved slightly from 927 in 1991 to 933 in 2001, the Child Sex Ratio (0–6 years) plummeted from 945 to 927. At 880, the SRB for 2003–05 was even lower.[1]

6.11 During the decade 1991–2001, 70 districts in 16 States and union territories recorded more than a 50 points decline in sex ratio. Fatehgarh Sahib district in Punjab[2] registered the lowest sex ratio at 754. What is truly worrying is the dip in child sex ratio in economically prosperous States like Punjab (793),[3] Delhi (865), Haryana (820), and Gujarat (878).[4] This negates the popular belief that female foeticide stems from illiteracy and poverty and will cease with economic growth (see Box 6.3). The Census of 2001 and Sachar Committee report (2006) also reveal that the sex ratio varies across communities and social groups. At 950, child sex ratio for Muslims is much higher than Hindus (925).

HEALTH AND FAMILY WELFARE

6.12 Discrimination against women and girls impinges upon their right to health and manifests itself in the form of worsening health and nutrition indices. Thus, India continues to grapple with unacceptably high MMR, IMR, and increasing rates of anaemia, malnutrition, HIV/AIDS among women. According to NFHS-3, incidence of anaemia has risen from 49.7% to 57.9% in pregnant women and from 51.8% to 56.2% in ever-married women within a period of seven years (1998–99 to 2005–06). This has raised anaemia among children by 5 percentage points (to 79.2%) and is also partially responsible for the high MMR. Maternal mortality has a direct correlation with lack of accessibility to health care facilities. Paucity of resources and age old discriminatory practices deny large number of women access to good nutrition and care before, during, and after child birth, thus increasing their mortality. Only 22% of mothers consume Iron Folic Acid (IFA) tablets for 90 days or more, and less than half of them receive three ANC visits. As many as 51.7% births take place without assistance from any health personnel. Practices such as female foeticide also affect women's health, as they are forced to go through multiple pregnancies and abortions. As a result, although MMR has fallen from 398 in 1998 to 301 in 2001–03 (SRS), we are far from meeting the Tenth Plan target of reducing MMR to 200 per 100000 live births. States like UP(707), Uttaranchal (517), Assam (409), and MP (498) have very high MMRs.[5]

6.13 While the mean age of marriage of women has increased from 15.5 years in 1961 to 19.5 in 1997, 44.5% of women are still married off by the age of 18.

[1] Registrar General of India 2003.

[2] *Missing: Mapping the Adverse Child Sex Ratio in India*, 2003, Booklet compiled by Registrar General of India and Census Commissioner, the M/o Health and Family Welfare and UNFPA.

[3] Sansarwal village of Patiala District, Punjab. A health survey showed an alarming figure of 438 girls for 1000 boys (*Hindustan Times*, 11 November 2007).

[4] *Missing: Mapping the Adverse Child Sex Ratio in India*, 2003.

[5] India, Registrar General and Census Commissioner (2004). Primary Census Abstract Total Population: Census of India 2001, New Delhi, p. iii.

Box 6.3
Learn More, Earn More, Discriminate More

A report by Infochange India (CCDS) uses data from Census 2001 to question the popular belief that literacy rates have a direct bearing on population and that literate people are less prone to gender bias. Although this may be true in some cases like high population growth rates, the same logic does not hold true for child sex ratio.

HAVE MONEY, WILL RAISE ONLY BOYS

	Overall Sex ratio*	Child sex ratio*	Proportion in India's total population**	Overall literacy rate**	Female literacy rate**	Female work participation rate**
Hindus	931	925	81.4	65.1	53.2	27.5
Muslims	936	950	12.4	59.1	50.1	14.1
Jains	940	870	0.4	94.1	90.6	9.2
Sikhs	893	786	1.9	69.4	63.1	20.2
Christians	1009	964	2.3	80.3	76.2	28.7
Buddhists	953	942	0.8	72.7	61.7	31.7
Others	992	976	0.7	47	33.2	44.2

Notes: *as number of females per 1000 males; **as %

THE NORTH–SOUTH DIVIDE

Punjab	798	Kerala	960
Haryana	819	Tamil Nadu	942
Delhi	868	Karnataka	946
Chandigarh	845	Andhra Pradesh	961

Child sex ratio (0–6) as number of girls per 1000 boys

Source: The disappearing girl child—Info Change India News and Features Development News India, October 2004.

Certain States such as Jharkhand (61.2%), Bihar (60.3%), and Rajasthan (57.1%) have a much higher percentage of underage marriage among girls. Among other things, this results in early pregnancies and takes its toll on the health of the woman as well as the child.

6.14 Women also disproportionately lack access to health services. Inaccessibility of health centres and poverty prevent them from getting timely medical aid. Absence of toilets and drinking water adversely impacts their health. NFHS-3 data reveals that only 27.9% households in rural areas and 70% in urban areas have access to piped water. Further, only 25.9% households in rural areas have access to toilets.

6.15 Inadequacies of clean cooking fuels adversely impacts women and children's work burden, health, and nutrition. Till date, 92% of rural domestic energy comes from unprocessed biofuels (firewood, crop waste, cattle dung), and 85% of rural cooking fuel is gathered from forests, village commons, and fields. Women and girls spend a great deal of time gathering fuel, adversely affecting their productivity and education. Use of firewood and inferior fuels such as weeds or crop wastes leads to smoke-related ailments including respiratory diseases, cancer, and cataracts resulting in blindness.

6.16 Then there are sexually transmitted diseases (STDs). NACO estimates that one in three persons living with HIV in India is a woman. The National Council for Applied Economic Research survey shows that women account for more than 70% of the caregivers, 21% of who are themselves HIV positive. Disowned by family and disinherited from property, they are unable to access drugs to prevent mother-to-child-transmission. Nearly 60% of HIV-positive widows are less than 30 years of age and live with their natal families; 91% of them receive no financial support from their marital homes. Thus not only are women more vulnerable to getting infected, but when they are found positive they face much greater discrimination than their male counterparts.

EDUCATION

6.17 The growth rate for female literacy in the last decade has been 3% higher than the growth rate for male literacy resulting in a decline in the absolute numbers of illiterate women—from 200.7 million in 1991 to 190 million in 2001. Gender differential in education, however, continues to be high at 21.7%. This can be attributed to a number of factors—lack of access to schools, lack of toilets and drinking water, parents feeling insecure about sending girl children, poor quality of education in government schools, and high fees charged by the private ones. Also with increasing feminization of agriculture, the pressure of looking after younger siblings, collecting cooking fuel, water and maintaining the household, all fall upon the girl child, putting a stop to her education and development.

WORK AND EMPLOYMENT

6.18 Entrenched patriarchal norms and customs mean that women's work goes unnoticed and is unpaid for. The double burden of work placed on her (unrecognized household work and low pay in recognized work) coupled with social norms that prevent her from getting the requisite educational and technical skills result in a low female work participation rate, either real or statistical. Female workforce participation rate in India was 28% (2004) as compared to other developing nations like Sri Lanka (30%), Bangladesh (37%), and South Africa (38%).[6] As per NSSO, however, (Table 6.1) work participation rate for female in rural areas has increased from 28.7% in 2000–01 to 32.7% in 2004–05, whereas in urban areas it has increased from 14% in 2000–01 to 16.6% in 2004–05. The work participation rate remains lower for women than for men both in rural and urban areas.

6.19 A sectoral breakdown of women workers reveals that 32.9% are cultivators, 38.9% agricultural labourers (as against 20.9% men) and 6.5% workers in the household industry.[7] Much of the increase in employment among women has been in the form of self-employment; 48% of urban and 64% of rural women workers describe themselves as 'self-employed'.[8] The Tenth Plan has, however, seen a welcome increase in the share of regular employment among female workers in urban India.

TABLE 6.1
Work Participation Rates by Sex (1972 to 2005)

(in %)

Year	Rural		Urban	
	Female	Male	Female	Male
1972–73	31.8	54.5	13.4	50.1
1987–88	32.3	53.9	15.2	50.6
1996–97	29.1	55.0	13.1	52.1
2000–01	28.7	54.4	14.0	53.1
2004–05	32.7	54.6	16.6	54.9

Source: NSSO.

6.20 As in the case of education, women's employment characterization differs across communities. The Sachar Committee Report shows that work participation rate among Muslim women is 25%, and as low as 18% in urban areas. A larger proportion (73%) of Muslim women is self-employed compared to 55% Hindu women. A much smaller proportion of SC/ST women are self-employed; 45% of SC/ST women are casual workers compared to around 20% Muslim and 15% of upper caste Hindu women.

6.21 Another worrying fact is that despite a slight increase in employment, the average earning for rural women has declined between 1999–2000 and 2004–05. This decline is more pronounced among poorer women, that is, illiterate women and women who have dropped out of primary, secondary, or higher secondary (see Table 6.2). The average wage for men has, on the other hand, shown an increase across all categories, leading to a widening of the wage disparity ratio (ratio of female wage/male wage) from 0.89 in 1999–2000 to 0.59 in 2004–05 for rural and 0.83 in 1999–2000 and 0.75 in 2004–05 in urban areas, for all categories.

[6] Gender Statistics, World Bank 2004.
[7] Census of India 2001.
[8] NSSO 2004–05.

TABLE 6.2
Average Wage/Salary Earnings (Rs Per Day) Received by Regular Wage/Salaried Employees of Age 15–59 Years for Different Education Levels

Category	Rural males		Rural females		Urban males		Urban females	
	1999–2000	2004–05	1999–2000	2004–05	1999–2000	2004–05	1999–2000	2004–05
Not literate	71.2	72.5	40.3	35.7	87.6	98.8	51.8	48.7
Literate upto primary	91.6	98.6	161.5	97.8	105.1	111.4	64.4	64.8
Sec/H.Sec	148.2	158.0	126.1	100.2	168.2	182.6	145.7	150.4
Dip/Cert	–	214.4	–	200.4	–	274.9	–	237.0
Graduate and others	220.9	270.0	159.9	172.7	281.6	366.8	234.7	269.2
All	127.3	144.9	113.3	85.5	169.7	203.3	140.3	153.2

Source: NSSO 55th and 61st Round.

Unorganized Sector

6.22 On an average, unorganized sector workers earn one-fourth the wage of organized sector workers, often doing similar jobs. It is estimated that 118 million workers or 97% of the female workforce are involved in the unorganized sector. Agriculture is the main employer of women informal workers. 75% of the total female workforce and 85% of rural women are employed in agriculture as wage workers or workers on own/contracted household farms.[9] As men migrate to non-farm jobs, there has been an increasing feminization of agriculture. But even as the face of the farmer becomes increasingly female, few women have direct access to agricultural land affecting their ability to optimize agricultural productivity.

6.23 The non-agriculture segment of the informal sector engages 27 million workers or 23% of the female workforce.[10] It is estimated that more than half of the 31 million construction workers in India (90% of them informal) are women. The seasonality of work and the lack of alternate avenues lead to exploitation and ensure that these women remain the poorest and most vulnerable.

Home-Based Workers

6.24 Due to lack of qualifications and training, absence of childcare support, loss of formal employment, social and cultural constraints and absence of alternatives, around 57% of working women are home-based workers. As home-based work is sometimes the only alternative for the poorest communities, it inevitably involves children, especially girls.

Services Sector

6.25 The number of women in the services sector has increased. According to NSSO data, in 2000, 12% of the female workforce was employed in the tertiary sector. Women, however, remain underrepresented in higher level and higher paid jobs. The biggest single increase after apparels has been among those employed in private households. More than 3 million women or over 12% of all women workers in urban India work as domestic servants.[11] These women are poorly paid and often are forced to work under harsh conditions. It is also important to note that nearly 60% of the women from the organized sector are employed in community, social, and personnel services.

Government Sector

6.26 Women's representation in government sector has improved from 11% in 1981 to 18.5% in 2004 (Table 6.3). At the grass roots level, women are playing a more active role in Panchayati Raj bodies and their representation in Panchayats has gone up from 33.5% in 1995 to 37.8% in 2005. Women's presence in Parliament has, however, only increased slightly; from 6.1% in 1989 to 9.1% in 2004. The issue of reservation of seats for women in Parliament remains unresolved. In 2004, only six Ministers of State and one Cabinet Minister were women.

[9] Planning Commission: Report of the Sub Group on Gender and Agriculture, 2007.
[10] Jeemol Unni (2003), 'Gender Informality and Poverty', *Seminar*, 531, November 2003.
[11] Women Workers in Urban India, *Macroscan*, C.P. Chandrashekhar and Jayati Ghosh (2007).

TABLE 6.3
Women in the Government Sector

Year	Central government			State government			Local bodies			Total (In million)		
	Female	Total	Female %	Female	Total	Female %	Female	Total	Female %	Female	Total	Female%
1981	0.14	3.19	4.3	0.65	5.67	11.4	0.41	2.04	20.4	1.2	10.91	11
2004	0.25	3.03	8.25	1.46	7.22	20.22	0.58	2.13	27.23	2.29	12.38	18.5

Source: Directorate General of Employment and Training, Ministry of Labour, New Delhi.

Violence against Women (VAW)

6.27 Despite improving education levels and consistent economic growth, every form of violence against women including female foeticide, rape, abduction, trafficking, dowry death, domestic violence, and witch-hunting, has been increasing. We have 10 million missing girls in India and this number is rising. Dowry deaths rose from 6822 in 2002 to 7026 in 2004. In 2005, highest number of dowry deaths were registered in UP, followed by Bihar, and MP. NFHS-3 shows that more than half of all Indian women believe that husbands can beat wives if they have an appropriate reason and 37% admit to being victims of spousal violence. Data from NCRB reveals little or no change in crime trends in rape and molestation. In 84–89% of the rape cases in the years 2002–04, the victim knew the offenders. In 9% cases, the offender was the father, family member, or close relative, highlighting the prevalence of incestuous and child sexual abuse. Abduction and trafficking for sexual and other exploitations accounted for 19.4% and 7.2% cases registered in 2005. Campaigns and stricter laws notwithstanding, 8.3% of registered cases in 2005 were dowry deaths, a fall of 0.3% from 2004.

Despite the high incidence of VAW, reporting is rare and conviction rates for reported cases, abysmally low; conviction rate for cruelty by husband was 19.2% and 25.5% each for dowry and rape.[12]

CHALLENGES IN THE ELEVENTH PLAN

6.28 The challenges for gender equity and the roadmap for the Eleventh Five Year Plan can be clubbed under a five-fold agenda.

(i) Ensuring economic empowerment.
(ii) Engineering social empowerment.
(iii) Enabling political empowerment.
(iv) Effective implementation of women-related legislations.
(v) Creating institutional mechanisms for gender mainstreaming and strengthening delivery mechanisms.

ENSURING ECONOMIC EMPOWERMENT

Employment

WOMEN IN THE UNORGANIZED SECTOR

6.29 The Eleventh Plan recognizes that women in the unorganized sector need social security covering issues of leave, wages, work conditions, pension, housing, childcare, health benefits, maternity benefits, safety and occupational health, and complaints committee for sexual harassment. While it is difficult to tackle some of these issues immediately due to the nature of unorganized enterprises, steps will be taken to ensure safety, childcare facilities, toilets, etc. for women. The Plan will ensure increased availability of micro-credit to women in the unorganized sector.

WOMEN IN AGRICULTURE

6.30 The challenge in the Eleventh Plan is to improve the availability of agricultural inputs, credit, marketing facilities, technology, and skill training for the increasing number of women farmers. Resource pooling and group investment, financial and infrastructural support will be provided. Women in agriculture will be on the top of the Eleventh Plan agenda and a two-pronged strategy will be adopted: (i) ensuring effective and independent land rights for women, and (ii) strengthening women's agricultural capacities.

6.31 A specific scheme will be devised by MoWCD for identifying and helping women in States where

[12] National Crime Record Bureau, 2005.

TABLE 6.4
Women's Political Participation: Global Picture

Country	Women in Government/ Ministerial Level(2005)	Gender Empowerment measure	Seats in parliament held by women	Female legislator	Female Professional workers	Ratio estimated Female/male earned income
India	3.4	–	9.2	–	–	0.31
Nepal	7.4	–	6.7	–	–	0.50
Pakistan	5.6	0.377	2.04	2	26	0.29
Bangladesh	8.3	0.374	14.8	23	12	0.46
Sri Lanka	10.3	0.372	4.9	21	46	0.42
Malaysia	9.1	0.500	13.1	23	40	0.36
UnitedStates	14.3	0.808	15.0	42	55	0.62
Mexico	9.4	0.597	25	25	42	0.39

Source: Human Development Report 2006, UNDP.

agrarian crisis has ravaged families. Women's vulnerabilities resulting from farmer suicides due to crop failure and inability to pay loans will be addressed.

LAND

6.32 Land rights not only empower women economically but strengthen their ability to challenge social and political inequities. The Eleventh Plan will carry out a range of initiatives to enhance women's land access. It will ensure direct transfers to them through land reforms, anti-poverty programmes, and resettlement schemes. It will include individual or group titles to women in all government land transfers, credit support to poor women to purchase or lease land, records and legal support for women's inheritance rights, incentives and subsidies on women owned land. The group approach to women's ownership of land and productive assets will be explored and appropriate linkages will be made with the SHG movement. In case of displacement, a gender sensitive rehabilitation policy that includes equitable allocation of land to women will be devised. The Eleventh Plan will also ensure the rights of poor, landless, and tribal women over forest land, commons, and other resources.

IMPACT OF GLOBALIZATION AND ELEVENTH PLAN STRATEGY

6.33 Liberalization has led to a paradigm shift in the country's economy. While this has provided many increase in opportunities, it has also posed challenges. We have moved towards technology dominated sectors. Many traditional livelihoods that have high employment potential like handlooms and other home based non-agro enterprises that are women-dominated have become unviable. Wage differentials, job vulnerability, and unpaid work burden for women has increased, while their social safety nets have been eroded. Unequal access for women to schooling, land, credit facilities, alternate employment, skill training, and technology has led to the crowding of women in the lowly paid jobs of most sectors. The Eleventh Plan will examine the impact of globalization on women, especially poor women including gender differentials in wage rates, exploitation of women in the unorganized sector, lack of skill training, technology, and marketing support, etc. While seeking to provide relief to deprived and women-dominated sectors, such as agriculture and small enterprises, the Plan will also work towards mainstreaming women in new and emerging areas of the economy through necessary skill training, vocational training, and technology education. It will work towards a social security policy that mitigates the negative impact of globalization on women.

WOMEN IN THE SERVICES SECTOR

6.34 The challenge in the Eleventh Plan is to promote women's participation, especially in areas where there is a poor gender ratio. This will entail special tax incentives for women headed enterprises, women employees, firms employing more women, and women entrepreneurial ventures. The Plan will encourage public–private partnerships and corporate social responsibility programmes for women's training, capacity building and empowerment.

6.35 In view of the large number of women employed as domestic workers, the plan will make attempts to organize them and frame regulations with respect to hours of work, holidays, etc. for them. Cases of brutality and abuse will be registered immediately and legal support will be provided to the domestic workers to prevent their exploitation.

SKILL DEVELOPMENT

6.36 Globalization has put a premium on skills and higher levels of education, which are often out of reach of women in the unorganized sector. A key issue in the Eleventh Plan is to enable these women to secure higher level and better paid jobs through vocational training and skill development. Women need technology support, credit facilities, and marketing support to take up entrepreneurial activities in new and emerging trades. At the same time, women's traditional skills such as knowledge of herbal plants, weaving, food processing, or providing 'care' will be recognized and marketed.

MAKING EMPLOYMENT AND NATIONAL RURAL EMPLOYMENT GUARANTEE ACT (NREGA) GENDER RESPONSIVE

6.37 Currently, most of the works included under NREGA require strenuous physical labour and women are sometimes effectively 'disqualified'. The Eleventh Plan will ensure that wage works conducive to women and their skills are also included under NREGA.

6.38 It will guarantee that if they demand, women will be provided employment opportunities under NREGA. It will also ensure that the Minimum Wages Act, 1948 and Equal Remuneration Act, 1976 are implemented by all States and that their implementation is monitored by the Ministry of Labour and Employment. It will encourage higher representation of women among Labour Officers. Besides ensuring equal pay for work, it will also ensure that no work is defined as 'man's' work and hence denied to women.

ACCESS TO RESOURCES AND ECONOMIC ASSETS

6.39 International evidence shows that women's access to land or homestead is positively linked to the family's food security, child survival, health, education, and children's exposure to domestic violence. Women with land and house are also at lower risk from spousal violence, have greater bargaining power in the labour market, and are better able to protect themselves and their children from destitution if the father dies from ill health, natural disaster, or HIV/AIDS. Indirectly, it also reduces maternal mortality both by enhancing women's nutrition and medical support and reducing the risk of domestic violence during pregnancy. These synergies and interlinkages are what make asset creation in women's hands a critical part of the Eleventh Plan agenda for women's economic empowerment.

Amenities for Urban Poor Women

6.40 The Eleventh Plan recognizes slum dwellers, most of whom are employed in the informal sector, as important contributors to cities' economy. Even though relocation of slums may sometimes be inevitable, appropriate measures need to be taken to ensure that the slum dwellers, especially women, do not lose access to livelihood opportunities and basic amenities. Today, almost 30–40% of India's urban population lives in slums. Over 62% of this population does not have access to sanitation services and 25% does not have access to water.[13] Since it is generally women who fetch water, they spend much of their time and energy at water pumps, in water queues, or walking to other colonies. The Asian Development Bank (2007) estimates that India's housing shortage is as high as 40 million units, suggesting that more than 200 million people are living in chronically poor housing conditions or on the pavements. In the absence of toilets, poor women are forced to defecate in public places such as railway tracks, parks, open spaces, or even public pavements. Not only do they feel ashamed by this, but it is a serious health and security hazard as they can only use these public spaces in the dark. Thus provision of clean drinking water, toilets, and sanitation in urban slums will be an important challenge for ensuring gender justice in the Eleventh Plan.

Homes and Homesteads for Poor Women

6.41 Home ownership not only provides shelter but also serves as collateral in credit markets and increases social status and security in the event of natural or manmade disasters. As more than half the women workers in the unorganized, non-agricultural sector

[13] World Bank, 2007.

work from their own homes, a home is a productive and wealth-generating asset for millions of low-income women. There is well-documented evidence to show that in both the urban and rural context, women's ownership of housing offers a vital form of security against poverty and enhances associated economic and social status. There are three main sources of access to land: family, State, and market. The challenge in the Eleventh Plan is to tap all these three sources. With the amendment of the Hindu Succession Act we have already taken the first step towards enhancing women's claims through inheritance. This should be strengthened by enacting gender-equal laws, adopting vigilance in recording women's claims, increasing legal awareness, and providing legal aid. All housing provided by the government during the Eleventh Plan should either be half in the name of the woman in the household or in the single name of the woman. Single women, widows, and women in difficult circumstances will be given priority. Finally, the Eleventh Plan agenda will strive to support women's access via banks by developing a system of reaching housing finance at reasonable rates to poor women. This will require provision of subsidized credit, changes in land tenure policies, and in norms for mortgages and housing loans.

ENSURING FOOD SECURITY

6.42 During the Eleventh Plan attempts will be made to strengthen the PDS system and revise BPL census norms to ensure that women in vulnerable situations, particularly widows, single women, internally displaced women, and women in conflict situations are covered.

6.43 The agrarian crisis is taking a heavy toll on women, with farmer suicides leaving women behind to take care of family and indebtedness. The Eleventh Plan will have a comprehensive package of inputs from various sectors like agriculture, rural development, Khadi and Village Industries Commission (KVIC), MoWCD, along with micro-credit facilities, and capacity building inputs for women from affected families.

Self-help Groups (SHGs)

6.44 While strengthening SHG initiatives, policies and schemes the Eleventh Plan will simultaneously increase women's awareness, bargaining power, literacy, health, vocational, and entrepreneurial skills. It will prioritize training, capacity-building inputs, and the creation of backward-forward linkages, which are essential to generate sustainable livelihood opportunities. Given the scale of the phenomenon, there is a need to review the SHG interventions and ground realities to determine how SHGs may better serve the interests of poor women, and suggest changes required in overall SHG policy frameworks. The Eleventh Plan recognizes the importance of this issue and proposes a HLC to conduct a review of SHG-related policies and programmes.

ENGINEERING SOCIAL EMPOWERMENT

Health

6.45 Health care access remains low for many women, especially the poor and marginalized who suffer from multiple exclusions and stigmatized groups such as sex workers and women with alternative sexualities. The

Box 6.4
Ordinary Women Who Did the Extraordinary

Making women partners in their own health care has proved to be an effective strategy for ensuring good health and well-being of the society in general. This is what the experience from places like Gadchiroli (Nagpur, Maharashtra), Ongna (Udaipur, Rajasthan), Khajrana (Indore, MP), and Ganiyari (Bilaspur, Chattisgarh) demonstrates. In Gadchiroli, ordinary women, most of them class 5 or 6 pass, have managed to reduce the NMR by half. They have also managed to bring about an attitudinal change. Women now get better nutrition during pregnancy. Many unhealthy and unsafe practices traditionally carried out during childbirth have been curtailed. In Ongna, a cadre of *Swasthyakarmis* have spread the message of good health and sanitation. They have led to increased coverage of the Directly Observed Treatment Short (DOTS) course programme. In small forest fringe villages in the Achanakmaar National Park in Chhattisgarh, illiterate and semi-literate Baiga, Gond, and other tribal women proudly flaunt their satchels replete with medicines like chloroquine, amoxicin, pictorial charts explaining their use, breath counters for pneumonia detection, dressing for wounds, and pregnancy kits. These women have managed to provide much needed medical relief to the local population. In Khajrana, in Indore, slum women have got together under the Rehbar Society to ensure that slum dwellers get access to medical aid and medicines.

Plan recognizes the gender dimension of health problems and seeks to address issues of women's survival and health through a life cycle approach. Making ordinary women partners in their own health care is an underpinning of Women's Health in the Eleventh Plan.

6.46 The Eleventh Plan agenda is to move beyond the traditional focus on family planning and reproductive health, to adopt a holistic perspective on women's health. For this, allocation towards health is being stepped up. Details of the Eleventh Plan roadmap for women are available in Chapter 3.

6.47 The high rates of MMR and IMR, poor prenatal and postnatal care, combined with the low proportion of institutional deliveries is a grave cause of concern. Empowering adolescent girls through information about health, sexuality, and increased awareness to negotiate rights with families, future partners, and in the workplace is equally important. The challenge is to create an enabling environment with information, services, and health programmes for women to exercise their rights and choices. The Eleventh Plan commitment to reduce MMR and IMR is detailed in Chapter 3.

6.48 The effect on women of HIV/AIDS is a critical area. There is an increase of mother to child transmission of HIV and paediatric HIV cases. The Eleventh Plan will commit resources to move towards a multi-sectoral, decentralized, gender-sensitive, community-based health service of which HIV/AIDS prevention and treatment is an integral part. It will prioritize information dissemination on a mass scale for prevention and treatment of HIV/AIDS. Resources will have to be made available to address the socio-economic problems faced by HIV positive women, including access to ARV treatment, medical services, child care, and livelihood security. Enacting legislation that protects HIV-positive women against discrimination in education, livelihood opportunities, workplace, medical treatment, and community will be the gender equity agenda for the Eleventh Plan.

6.49 Many other factors affect the health of women. For instance women's risk of mortality from indoor air pollution resulting from use of unprocessed fuels is estimated to be 50% higher than of men. While over time, community investment in low cost clean fuel such as biogas will be encouraged, in the interim, firewood needs to be made available. Provision of clean drinking water and sanitation facilities are also important for good health. Intersectoral convergence to ensure the health and well being of women in this regard is a major challenge before the Eleventh Plan.

Curbing Increasing Violence against Women (VAW)

6.50 During the Eleventh plan period, the justice delivery mechanism as well as the legislative environment under the PWDVA 2005 will be strengthened. VAW will be articulated as a Public Health issue and training will be provided to medical personnel at all levels from public health facilities (PHCs) to premier health facilities. It will be included in medical education because the medical and health establishments are often the first point of contact for women in a crisis situation. Training and sensitization of health personnel will include recognizing and dealing with injuries resulting from VAW and providing psychological support. Multiple forms of sexual VAW in conflict zones and in communal or sectarian violence, where they are specifically targeted as embodiments of community honour are cause for great concern. In the Eleventh Plan period, a National Task Force on VAW in Zones of Conflict will be set up under the National Commission for Women (NCW) with adequate budgetary allocations to make it effective in monitoring VAW in conflict zones and facilitating relief and access to justice for affected women.

MENTAL HEALTH

6.51 Mental health has long been a neglected and invisible area. NFHS-3 shows disturbing evidence that women have internalized domestic violence leading to intense mental illness. The chapter on Health details the Eleventh Plan direction in this regard.

Education

6.52 The challenge in the Eleventh Plan is to retain girls in school and to bridge gender disparities in educational access, specifically for SC, ST, and Muslim communities through allocation of greater resources

Box 6.5
Ensuring Equality for Muslim Women: A Big Challenge

Even today, 59% Muslim women have not attended school and 60% are married by the age of 17. Overall, Muslims have a literacy rate of 59.1%, 5.7 percentage points lower than the national average. While in Haryana, one-fifth of Muslim women are literate, the figure is about one-third in Bihar and UP. In 15 States, the literacy level among Muslim women is less than 50%. Muslims register the lowest work participation rate of 31.3%, and just about 14% of Muslim women are registered as workers. Even in Kerala and Tamil Nadu, which have high literacy rates among all communities, including Muslims, the work participation rate of Muslims is 14 percentage points lower than that of Hindus.

Ensuring that Muslim women get access to education, health, and livelihoods, not just at par with Muslim men but with female and male counterparts from other religions will be a critical challenge for the Eleventh Plan.

and more context-specific programming. This calls for strategies to increase the number of women and girls from these socially disadvantaged communities in professional, technical, and higher education and in posts of teachers.

6.53 The Eleventh Plan will make concerted efforts to examine why young girls, especially those belonging to particular socio-economic and cultural groups, are unable to access education despite the SSA. Through provision of crèches, scholarships, and adequate infrastructure, especially toilets in schools, it will facilitate enrolment and retention of girls in the education system. Details of Education for girl children and women are available in the Education Chapter.

Women and Media

6.54 Much of television programming propagates patriarchal values and portrays women roles in detrimental ways. As the nodal agency for the empowerment of women, one of the important tasks for the MoWCD during the Eleventh Plan will be to curtail the harmful effects of television on women's lives through a gender-informed media policy. It will harness this powerful medium to promote the message of gender equity through positive programming and information dissemination on laws and schemes. For this, the Ministry might engage in a professional PPP with media experts with gender specialization. In order to operationalize an aggressive and professional multi-media strategy, there may be a need to set up a separate media unit within the MoWCD, with the participation of professional media consultants and women's media groups.

Reaching Marginalized and Vulnerable Women

6.55 Intersections between gender and other social and economic variables reinforce vulnerability of more than one type and result in double and triple discrimination amongst women belonging to particular groups. Sectoral planning often fails to capture this. Our ability to recognize these intersections and address the specific deprivations will be the real test of the Eleventh Plan agenda of inclusive growth. For example, women in the NER continue to be excluded from traditional decision-making bodies like Durbars and Village Councils. To attain inclusive growth for them, support services like counselling centres, shelter homes, drug rehabilitation centres, particularly for victims of HIV/AIDs, working women's hostels etc., have to be provided.

Zero Tolerance for Discrimination against SC/ST Women

6.56 It is critical that the Ministries of WCD, Social Justice and Empowerment, and HRD join hands to enforce penalties for blatant violations of the constitution and the Scheduled Caste and Scheduled Tribes (Prevention of Atrocities) Act, 1989. Crimes of caste-based discrimination, untouchability, *devadasi/jogini*, and manual scavenging will be strictly punished according to law. Institutions like NCW, National Human Rights Commission, SC/ST Commission, Safai Karmacharis Commission will be urged to take up SC/ST women's issues as priority. Implementation of the Scheduled Caste Sub-Plan (SCSP) and Tribal Sub-Plan (TSP) will be maximized by earmarking of the funds in proportion to the SC/ST population under all schemes of the various line Departments. Distinct provisions for SC women will be made in the planning of programmes, allocation of finances, and in distribution of reservation facilities in education and employment.

6.57 An important agenda for the Eleventh Plan is to ensure that the rights of tribal women over community land and forest produce are recognized and established. The economic base of tribal and other villages will be strengthened to prevent migration. The plan also purports to encourage, document, and popularize tribal women's knowledge of indigenous, traditional healing practices. It will try to include voices of tribal women in both national and State-level planning forums that deal with women's issues. Details of Eleventh Plan commitment to SC/ST women are available in the Social Justice chapter.

MINORITY WOMEN

6.58 Minority women are typically engaged in home-based, subcontracted work with lowest levels of earnings. The Sachar Committee Report has pointed out the absence of adequate social and physical infrastructure and civic amenities in Muslim-dominated habitations and the multiple discriminations faced by Muslim women. To fulfil its agenda for inclusive growth, the Eleventh Plan will ensure that Muslim localities are provided with universal benefits of primary and elementary schools, water, sanitation, electricity, public health facilities (PHCs), anganwadis, ration shops, roads, transport facilities, access to government development schemes and facilities, such as BPL cards and widow pensions. Education will be made accessible for Muslim girls by locating educational institutions near Muslim areas, establishing some girls' schools, and increasing scholarships for Muslim girls. The challenge is to make technical and higher education opportunities available to minority women and to link them to employment. Access to low interest credit, markets, technical training, leadership training, and skill development for Muslim female home-based workers and entrepreneurs will be ensured. Representation of religious minorities in public employment will be increased and minority women will be provided access to institutional and policy level decision-making.

6.59 In view of the double discrimination faced by Muslim women, the Prime Minister's 15-point programme for the minorities is a critical statement of intent. To further this agenda of inclusive growth, MoWCD will work on a pilot scheme for 'Minority Women' to empower them and place them in the forefront of making the government system at the grassroots responsive to the needs of the minority community. Such a scheme will provide critical learning and benchmarks to launch more ambitious programmes for minority women in subsequent plans. In addition to this, targeted development of SC, ST, and minority women will be made a stated part of implementation strategies of all WCD programmes/ schemes and of the SSA. It will be made a mandatory part of their parameters of review and monitoring guidelines.

Box 6.6
Leadership Development of Minority Women: A Proposed Pilot Scheme

To tackle the double discrimination faced by Muslim women, the MWCD will formulate and implement a pilot scheme for 'Leadership Development for Life, Livelihood, and Civic Empowerment of Minority Women'. This scheme will reach out to minority women and provide them with support, leadership training, and skill development so that they can move out of the confines of home and community and assume leadership roles in accessing services, skills, and opportunities that will improve their lives and livelihoods. The scheme will give them training, inputs, information, and the confidence to interact with the government system, banks, and intermediaries at all levels. Implementation of the scheme through NGOs in the initial phase will also encourage the NGO sector to take up work with this neglected community. Initially the pilot scheme can be launched in five States with large minority populations. It is expected that this scheme will reach 35000 to 50000 women directly and hundreds of thousands indirectly.

INTERNALLY DISPLACED WOMEN

6.60 Internal displacement due to social strife and upheaval affects men and women differently. Adult and adolescent males are separated from families and the number of female-headed households increases. Even when families remain together, trauma and stress of displacement may destroy the unit leading to increased incidence of domestic violence and abuse. Internally displaced women are at greater risk of gender-based violence including physical and sexual attacks. They

Box 6.7
Hope for Single Women

Tagore's poem 'Ekla Chalo Re', which exuded confidence in self, truth, and dignity, finds echo in the ideals of the *Ekal Nari Shakti Sangathan*—Association of Strong Single Women established in January 2000 in Rajasthan. This grass roots mass membership organization has widows, separated, abandoned, and abused women as its members. In the last seven years, the Sangathan has sought to address every day issues of these women. It has altered the destiny of many, fighting injustice, red-tapism, and parochial mindsets. By mid-2007, Ekal Nari had 21325 members in 26 of the 32 districts of Rajasthan.

This organization is a mass movement. These Ekal women have achieved the impossible—from closing down liquor shops and revolting against age-old practices to increasing pensions and assistance for widows. The group has also introduced pension for low income, separated women. Using both satyagraha and open defiance as strategy, the Sangathan has ensured employment to women who were facing manipulation and threats. Today the movement has spread to Himachal Pradesh, Jharkhand, and Gujarat.

suffer psychological and physical trauma. The Eleventh Plan is committed to mitigating the negative impact on women of displacement due to natural or manmade calamities, incidents of communal violence, or social upheaval and development projects. It will formulate gender-sensitive relief and rehabilitation policies; women will have joint rights to any land or assets that are part of rehabilitation packages.

WOMEN WITH DISABILITY

6.61 Women with disabilities are considered a financial burden and social liability by their families; denied opportunities of mobility and access to education; viewed as asexual, helpless, and dependant; taken advantage of and abused; denied aspirations for marriage and motherhood; and are isolated and neglected with no hope of a normal life. Although a rights-based approach today defines the disability rights movement, the specific concerns of women with disabilities have to be adequately reflected in the planning process. RCH programmes will pay attention to reproductive health needs of women with disabilities. Violation of their reproductive rights through forced sterilization, contraception and abortion especially in institutions will be dealt with severely. In the Eleventh Plan, women with disabilities will be specifically included in gender equity programmes, both as beneficiaries and as project workers. The Eleventh Plan sensitization prog-rammes of government departments, police, and health care personnel will include sensitization to the needs of women with disabilities. Laws will be strictly enforced in cases of discrimination.

WOMEN AFFECTED BY DISASTERS

6.62 Disasters, both natural and manmade, have the worst impact on women. Their lower social status often results in various kinds of exclusions from rehabilitation and relief benefits. This posits a serious challenge to the Eleventh Plan goal of gender equity and gender justice. To overcome this, disaster management policies in the Eleventh Plan will ensure representation of women in relief committees. Resource allocations will be made for sensitization of government, aid workers, armed forces and all personnel involved in relief work. Social equity audits will be conducted. The Plan will promote the collection and use of gender-disaggregated data to inform relief and rehabilitation policies. It will also examine and review the Relief Code and Disaster Management Bill to ensure gender mainstreaming.

6.63 In addition to the categories of vulnerable and marginalized women discussed above, the Eleventh Plan will also have to pay special attention to other categories including migrant women, urban poor women, and single women to fulfil its commitment of equality and gender justice.

6.64 To tackle the problem of child marriage, the Eleventh Plan will call for compulsory registration of marriages and verification of age at the time of marriage.

ENABLING POLITICAL EMPOWERMENT

A. Panchayati Raj Institutions (PRIs)

6.65 Notable constitutional, legislative, and policy reforms, and continued administrative decentralization have demonstrated the government's commitment to increase women's grass roots political participation. Although only one-third of seats were reserved for women by the 73rd and 74th constitutional amendments, the actual representation is higher at all levels. Women's increased political participation has yielded a range of positive results, not only for women, but also for their families and communities. Central issues in development such as health, nutrition, family income, and education are finding their way to the top of the agenda for action. Women's participation brings about more inclusive governance and effective community-centred development. Yet in many places, especially in States like UP, Bihar, and Rajasthan, women continue to serve as proxies. The challenge for the Eleventh Plan is to ensure that women panchayat members are empowered to take their own decisions.

6.66 The Eleventh Plan will undertake the following measures to accelerate the process of women's political empowerment and participation in PRIs:

- The no-confidence clause is often used to remove women *sarpanches*. State governments will be advised to ensure that women sarpanches cannot be removed for at least a year and a half by a no-confidence motion. If a no-confidence vote is passed, the replacing incumbent should also be a woman from the same social group as the earlier incumbent;
- States should revisit the two-child norm laws that prevent those who have more than two children from holding office. This law has been repealed across some States because it was found to be used against women in that it disproportionately impacted poor, SC, ST, Muslim, and tribals. More tragically, the norm led to increasing female foeticide;
- Increase resource allocation for capacity building of all PRI members (male and female) in diverse areas pertaining to gender sensitization and women's rights, as well as in the political skill-building of women members of PRIs;
- Greater effort to include poor and other excluded women on State Planning Boards and Commissions;
- Funds for time-series evaluations of the impact of women on PRIs, and on enabling policy conditions and contextual factors for women's political participation;
- Accelerate the State Governments' process of devolution and decentralization of powers, so that PRIs are not handicapped in carrying out their mandated duties.

EFFECTIVE IMPLEMENTATION OF WOMEN-RELATED LEGISLATIONS

6.67 During the Tenth Plan period, some important legislations have been passed and amended. For example, besides the Hindu Succession (Amendment) Act 2005 and PWDVA 2005 mentioned earlier, the Dowry Prohibition Act was reviewed. A very active civil society has been relentlessly campaigning on these

Box 6.8
Panchayat Women: Ground Realities

Till some time back, Kanjiguzhy village panchayat in Allepey district of Kerala was a backward area of the district. Today it has an annual turnover of over Rs 10 crore, thanks to an active Panchayat Samiti headed by a dynamic woman *pradhan* Jalaja Chandra. Ask her about the number of families in her area, number of SHGs, employment statistics, net profit, amount spent on different development works and she answers confidently. It is not difficult to see why this village has prospered. Kotli village in Fatehgarh Sahib district of Punjab is headed by Paramjeet Kaur who has managed to convince her villagers to let their girl children live. So in a district that made headlines for having the worst child sex ratio in the country, Kotli now boasts of a positive sex ratio. While these and many such women have clearly demonstrated what political empowerment of women can achieve, in many parts of the country woman panchayat members are yet to get their due.

In Bhimra village of Barmer district of Rajasthan, the sarpanch is a woman. She never opens her mouth; it is always the husband who speaks. The fate of her *ghoonghat*-clad counterpart in a Kol village in eastern UP is no different. Here the *Pradhanpati* makes all decisions. In Bihar, power rests with the MPs and SPs—*Mukhiyapati*s and Sarpanchpatis i.e. husbands of women Mukhyas and Sarpanches. In Ongna village of Udaipur district (Rajasthan), the women panchayat members rue the day they were elected. 'We have no powers; we are never allowed to attend meetings. When villagers come and ask us why we haven't done anything, what do we say?' they question.

issues. Their experiences and recommendations will be taken on board to ascertain that the rights of every woman are enshrined in laws.

6.68 Under the Eleventh Plan budgetary allocations will be made for publicity and for creating the required infrastructure for effective implementation of these legislations. MoWCD will appoint Protection Officers and set up district-level cells to be responsible for monitoring and implementation of Protection of Women from Domestic Violence Act (PWDVA) and other Acts under its charge.

6.69 Ministry of WCD will also try and ensure the enactment of other legislations that benefit women. The government is already contemplating the unorganized sector bill to provide social security to unorganized sector workers; besides this the schemes for life and health insurance have already been introduced. These should be implemented with a special emphasis on safeguarding the interests of women. The DPA will be reviewed to clarify existing provisions relating to the definition of the dowry and penalties for guilty parties. Implementation of PWDVA with DPA will be linked to enable PWDVA protection officers to take action under the DPA. The Eleventh Plan will also have provisions for sensitization of medical professionals on recording of evidence in cases of dowry deaths, training and capacity building of law enforcement functionaries and awareness generation about problems of dowry. Efforts will be made to ensure effective monitoring and enforcement of Pre-Conception and Pre-natal Diagnostic Techniques (Prohibition of Sex Selection) (PC and PNDT) Act, 2002 through Central and State Supervisory Boards and adequate allocation of funds. Public awareness and community mobilization will be generated along with training the authorities to deal with the issue of sex determination and sex selective abortions.

6.70 The MoWCD will ensure the enactment of the bill to prevent sexual harassment at the workplace. The Immoral Traffic (Prevention) Act (ITPA) is already being reviewed to ensure that women in prostitution are not victimized further. In addition to this, the Eleventh Plan will strengthen inter-regional networks to check forced migration and trafficking. Special police officers will be appointed to promote community level vigilance to reduce trafficking. There will be special training modules on trafficking for police, judiciary, and other government personnel. More rehabilitation homes will be established.

6.71 To tackle the conflict-related VAW, the Eleventh Plan will ensure the inclusion of provisions of sexual violence in the draft law on the prevention of communal violence. It will look into setting up Special Courts to deal with cases of VAW in conflict situations, including those involving security personnel. It will encourage women's involvement in peace keeping, community dialogues, and conflict resolution. There will be special measures for compensation, financial assistance, and support to widows and female headed households in conflict areas.

6.72 The Eleventh Plan will foster women's access to legal services through a range of measures. Women will be exempted from paying fees to fight cases of human rights violations. Funds for legal assistance will be provided to poor women seeking legal redress. Legal awareness programmes will be carried out in all States in collaboration with NGOs working at the grassroots level. Legal Aid Cells consisting of committed and gender-sensitive lawyers will be set up at the Panchayat level to provide information and support to rural women, especially poor women. *Lok Adalats* will be organized to encourage alternate dispute settlement mechanisms for efficacious settlement of cases. The Plan will also work towards increasing the percentage of women in police and judicial services. Training on use of gender specific laws will be provided to all Members and Authorities involved in providing legal services. Concept of *Jan Sunwaiye* will be adopted to listen to people's voices.[14]

Creating Institutional Mechanisms for Gender Mainstreaming and Strengthening Delivery Mechanisms

6.73 In the Eleventh Plan, institutional mechanisms will carry forward the process of gender mainstreaming

[14] Jan Sunwaiye is a forum of CSO, Government Functionaries and People for hearing and redressal of grievances.

and will be strengthened. National Commission for Women (NCW) and State Commissions for Women will be strengthened to enable them to effectively play their role as the nodal agencies for the protection of rights of women. Towards this end, efforts will be made in the Eleventh Plan to suitably amend the NCW Act to give the Commission more powers. The States likewise, will be urged to review the powers of their Women's Commissions. In addition to this, more functional and financial autonomy and a statutory base will have to be ensured for these organizations to strengthen their legal status. This will not only ensure that these bodies remain non-partisan, it will also increase their credibility. A mechanism will be created to periodically report to the National Development Council the progress on Women's Plans with respect to the National Policy for Empowerment of Women. Action Plans for Women's Empowerment at national and State levels will be drawn up in consultation with all sectoral agencies and civil society including women's groups, lawyers, activists, women's study centres, etc. Cross-cutting issues such as unpaid work, land and asset entitlements, skill development and vocational training, child care, occupational health, wages, VAW will be mainstreamed. *Parivarik Mahila Lok Adalat*[15] will be organized, which will supplement the efforts of District Legal Service Authority. Resource Centres for women will be set up at national and State levels and linked with Women's Study Centres.

6.74 Gender Budgeting and Gender Outcome assessment will be encouraged in all ministries/departments at Central and State levels. Gender Budgeting helps assess the gender differential impact of the budget and takes forward the translation of gender commitments to budgetary allocations. During the Eleventh Plan efforts will continue to create Gender Budgeting cells in all ministries and departments. Data from these cells will be collated on a regular basis and made available in the public domain.

6.75 Gender outcome assessment of fund flows has been made a mandatory part of the outcome budget prepared by every ministry/department as part of their budget documents. In 2005–06, this exercise covered 10 departments and the total magnitude of the Gender Budget (that is, women specific allocations) was recorded at 4.8% of total Union Government expenditure. In 2006–07, 24 departments of the Union Government were included and the magnitude of the Gender Budget was 3.8% of total budget estimates. It was found that schemes, which do not have a 100% women's component, also found a mention as women specific schemes. The Eleventh Plan will therefore ensure that each ministry/department of both Centre and State should put in place a systematic and comprehensive monitoring and auditing mechanism for outcome assessment. In addition, the Ministry of WCD, Ministry of Finance, and Planning Commission will facilitate national level gender outcome assessments through spatial mapping of gender gaps and resource gaps. They will undertake gender audits of public expenditure, programmes, and policies, and ensure the collection of standardized, gender disaggregated data (including data disaggregated for SC/ST and minority women) at national, State, and district levels.

6.76 In the Eleventh Plan period, the existing system of gender-based planning will be extended to other ministries and departments and not confined only to those that have historically been perceived as 'women-related'. Ministries and departments, such as Education, Health and Family Welfare, Agriculture, Rural Development, Labour, Tribal Affairs, Social Justice, and Empowerment, which have the potential to exceed the 30% WCP requirement, will be encouraged to administer more women related programmes. During the Eleventh Plan, efforts will be made to extend the concept of gender based plan component to PRIs and to the 29 subjects transferred to them under the 73rd constitutional amendment. Recognizing that some women suffer greater deprivation and discrimination than others, the Eleventh Plan will refine the norms of WCP to prioritize the most vulnerable as beneficiaries, particularly SC, ST women, Muslim women, single women, differently abled, and HIV-positive women, among others.

6.77 The Eleventh Plan period will seek to make all national policies and programmes gender sensitive

[15] It is a special court, which is mainly concerned with resolving family disputes separately from general criminal cases.

right from their inception and formulation stages. The MoWCD is the nodal Ministry for Gender Budgeting and the coordination mechanism for gender budgeting will ensure that all policies including fiscal and monetary policies, agricultural policies, non-farm sector, information and technology policies, public policy on migration, health insurance schemes, disaster management policies, media policy, and the legal regime among others are relevant from a gender perspective and are thoroughly examined. It will ensure that all legislations before they are presented to Parliament for enactment are cleared by the Parliamentary Committee on Women's Empowerment.

6.78 The Eleventh Plan is committed to ensuring the participation of women in governance through the smooth passage of the much-delayed Women's Reservation Bill. There will be simultaneous training and inputs for women in the PRIs to enable them to influence gender sensitive local planning and implementation. Gender disaggregated data on the participation of women, especially SC/ST and minority women, in Parliament, State legislative assemblies, Council of Ministers, premier services, and in the overall government sector will be collected and made available in the public domain. The Plan will also make proactive efforts to provide competitive exam training and prioritize recruitment of women to All India Services especially IAS, IFS, and IPS.

6.79 The MoWCD will take the lead in creating and maintaining a comprehensive gender-disaggregated data base, for quantitative and qualitative data. The purpose would be: (i) to base new initiatives on facts and figures, (ii) assess the gender impact of programmes, and (iii) assess the level of women's participation in planning and implementing programmes.

ELEVENTH PLAN SCHEMES

6.80 *Swayamsiddha*, an integrated scheme for women's empowerment through SHGs will be the major scheme to be implemented by the Ministry of WCD in the Eleventh Plan. Swayamsidha Phase-II will be launched as a countrywide programme with larger coverage in States lagging behind in women development indices. The lessons learnt from Swayamsiddha Part 1 and *Swashakti*, especially regarding capacity building of poor women through SHGs, promoting thrift and credit activities amongst the women themselves, emphasizing on participatory approach towards poverty alleviation, and addressing common problems and issues through the SHGs, will be incorporated in the universalized Swayamsidha.

6.81 Support to Training and Employment Programme (STEP), a scheme for skill training of women, will be revamped during the Eleventh Plan based on evaluation results (under way) and will be integrated with Swayamsidha to ensure adequate outlay for countrywide implementation as a CSS. The *Rashtriya Mahila Kosh* will also be integrated with STEP and Swayamsidha for credit linkages, but will be reviewed in the Eleventh Plan period before considering any further expansion.

6.82 A separate Women Empowerment and Livelihood Project assisted by United Nations' International Fund for Agricultural Development will be implemented during the Eleventh Plan in four districts of UP and two districts of Bihar.

6.83 Various social empowerment schemes for women will be implemented during the Eleventh Plan. Condensed courses of education will be run to facilitate skill-development and vocational training of adult girls and women who could not join mainstream education system or were forced to dropout from formal schools. This will improve their social and economic status by making them employable. The Ministry will use mass media to run an Awareness Generation Project on issues relating to the status, rights, and problems of women. Through this project it will also try to ensure a balanced portrayal of women in newspapers, media channels, serials, films, etc.

6.84 The most important programme for women to be run by the Ministry of WCD during the Eleventh Plan will be the provision of Maternity Benefits. The ICDS scheme will have a component of conditional maternity benefits under which pregnant and lactating mothers will be entitled to cash incentives for three months before birth and three months after the birth of the child. This will encourage and enable mothers to avoid physically stressful activities, meet medical and nutrition supplementation expenses during the last trimester, and spend time with the child after birth. The benefits under the scheme will be conditional to the mother being registered with the Anganwadi, undergoing regular health check up and immunization.

6.85 Ministry of WCD will continue to run its earlier schemes offering support services. Under a revised Working Women's Hostel scheme, financial assistance will be provided to NGOs, co-operative bodies, and other agencies for construction/renting of buildings for hostels to provide safe and affordable accommodations to working women. The scheme of *Swadhar* homes for destitute women and women in difficult circumstance will continue, albeit with modifications. A women's helpline foundation will also be set up. Under the Short-Stay Home Scheme, suitable accommodation with basic amenities and services like counselling, legal aid, medical facilities, vocational training, and rehabilitation will be provided for women and girls who are victims of marital conflict, crime, or homelessness.

6.86 The Central Social Welfare Board (CSWB) will continue financing NGOs for implementation of various women and child-related schemes. But during the Plan, all the existing schemes of the CSWB will be reviewed and restructured in the light of current requirements. If necessary, some of them will also be merged with schemes of WCD.

National and State Machineries

Relief and Rehabilitation of Rape Victims

6.87 The Hon'ble Supreme Court in Delhi Domestic Working *Women's Forum* vs *Union of India* and others writ petition (CRL) No. 362/93 had directed the NCW to evolve a 'scheme so as to wipe out the tears of unfortunate victims of rape'. It observed that given the Directive principles contained in the Article 38(1) of the constitution, it was necessary to set up a Criminal Injuries Compensation Board. Besides the mental anguish, rape victims frequently incur substantial financial loss and in some cases are too traumatized to continue in employment. The Court further directed that compensation for victims shall be awarded by the Court on conviction of the offender and by the Criminal Injuries Compensation Board irrespective of whether or not a conviction has taken place. The Board shall take into account pain, suffering, and shock as well as loss of earnings due to pregnancy and the expenses of child birth if this occurs as a result of rape. Accordingly, NCW has drafted a scheme titled 'Relief and Rehabilitation of Rape Victims'. This scheme will be initiated in the Eleventh Plan as 'Scheme for Relief and Rehabilitation of Victims of Sexual Assault'. For this, the Eleventh Plan will allocate sufficient resources to sensitize law enforcement agencies, medical establishments, etc. It will ensure immediate online filing of FIR and recording of the victim's statement by female police officers. It will set up more forensic labs and DNA testing centres in various districts and provide special care for minor rape victims. It will also ensure the safety of rape victims to testify in courts and appoint a specially designated Judge in the District Court to deal with rape cases.

6.88 These schemes along with the measures suggested above will ensure that when we enter the Twelfth Plan, women are no longer seen as 'Victims', but as agents of socio-economic growth and development for the country.

CHILD RIGHTS

6.89 Development of children is at the centre of the Eleventh Five Year Plan. The Plan strives to create a protective environment, which will ensure every child's right to survival, participation, and development.

STATUS OF CHILDREN: A BRIEF OVERVIEW

Progress During the Tenth Plan

6.90 Some landmark inter-ministerial and intersectoral steps towards child development were taken during the Tenth Plan period. The Sarva Siksha Abhiyan was launched to increase enrolment of children in schools and to ensure that every child has access to quality education. Coverage under the ICDS scheme increased and National Programme for Adolescent Girls was initiated. Schemes like NREGA, TSC, and NRHM were introduced to ensure food security and access to health services for poor households and the children therein.

Box 6.9
Tenth Plan Schemes for Children

Rajiv Gandhi National Crèche Scheme is for children of working mothers. Eight lakh crèches are required to meet the child care needs of an estimated 22 crore women in the informal sector. Till September 2006, 23834 crèches were sanctioned under this scheme.

Integrated Programme for Street Children aims to prevent destitution of children and engineer their withdrawal from streets by providing basic facilities like shelter, nutrition, health care, education, recreation, and protection against abuse and exploitation. During the Tenth Plan, over 2 lakh children benefited from this.

Scheme for Welfare of Working Children in Need of Care and Protection provides non-formal education, vocational training to working children to facilitate their entry/re-entry into mainstream education and prevent their exploitation. The scheme is implemented through NGOs. Between 2005 and 2007, 6996 children benefited from this programme

Scheme of 'Assistance to Homes (Shishu Greh) for Children' provides grant-in-aid through Central Adoption Resource Agency to government institutions and NGOs for increasing and promoting adoptions within the country. During the Tenth Plan period there were 2650 beneficiaries under this scheme.

Nutrition Programme for Adolescent Girls was launched by the Planning Commission, in 51 districts, on a pilot project basis, in 2002–03. The scheme was transferred to MoWCD. It envisages that all adolescent girls (10–19 years) will be weighed four times a year and families of girls weighing less than 35 kg will be given 6 kg of foodgrains/month for three months.

Kishori Shakti Yojana provides self-development, nutrition, health care, literacy, numerical skills, and vocational skills to adolescent girls between 11 and 18 years of age.

Programme for Juvenile Justice provides 50% assistance to State Governments and UT administrations for establishment and maintenance of various levels of institutions for juveniles in conflict with law and children in need of care and protection. Almost 2 lakh children were covered during the Tenth Plan.

ICDS

6.91 In accordance with the NCMP commitment and SC directive for universalization, the coverage under ICDS was expanded from 5652 sanctioned projects at the beginning of the Tenth Plan to 6291 projects and 10.53 lakh anganwadi centres sanctioned up to March 2007. Of this, 5670 projects were operational through 7.81 lakh Anganwadi Centres by the end of Tenth Plan. Until December 2006, 6.62 crore beneficiaries comprising 5.46 crore children and 1.16 crore pregnant and lactating mothers were covered.

6.92 In addition to the above schemes, the Tenth Plan adopted new policies like the National Charter for Children, 2003. In 2005, the National Commission for the Protection of Child Rights Act was passed to provide for the constitution of a National Commission and State Commissions for protection of child rights and for children's courts for speedy trial of offences against children or violation of child rights. The National Plan of Action for Children 2005 was also formulated to address the specific commitments set out in the MDGs. Further important amendments were carried out in the Juvenile Justice (Care and Protection of Children) Act, 2000 in 2006.

6.93 Despite these measures we have fallen short of the Tenth Plan targets, partly because they were unrealistic and partly because of poor implementation of schemes. For instance it took two decades to reduce the gender gap in literacy from 26.62 % in 1981 to 21.69% in 2001, but the Tenth Plan envisaged a reduction by 50% in five years.

6.94 Lack of adequate budgetary allocations (as seen from Table 6.5 below on Sectoral allocation and expenditure in Budget for Children, BFC as percentage of the Union Budget), has also impacted on the country's ability to meet the MDGs with respect to children.

6.95 Table 6.5 on BFC clearly demonstrates that despite the alarming increase in various forms of crimes against children, child protection remains a largely neglected sector.

Box 6.10
State of ICDS

In Tarana village of MP, the AWC is a *kutchcha* house with slush outside. Foodgrains are stored in the house of the AWW who States that, 'There are rats at the centre. So I can't leave food there.' Meanwhile villagers complain that their children fall ill if they eat at the AWC.

In Gohilaon in Bhadohi District of UP, the AWC runs from an empty room with broken furniture in the primary school premises. The registers are missing, AWW is seldom present and grain is stored in the helper's house next door.

Gokarnapur ICDS centre in Ganjam district of Orissa has been running from the AWWs' house for over five years now. A handful of rice and dal provides meal to 30 children. Immunization, weighing scales, growth charts, PSE, etc. are all unheard of here.

In Barmer district of Rajasthan, ICDS workers are illiterate. Some, like the AWW at village Rawatsar can't even fill growth registers. In Chizami village of Phek district in Nagaland, the centre runs from a dank and cold building. Children receive two glucose biscuits as SNP. And six AWCs with 150 children run from a single verandah in Maalab village of Mewat in Haryana.

In Jehangirpuri, in Delhi, ICDS centres do not have weighing scales and they have not received deworming capsules and IFA tablets for 10 years.

In States like Himachal, Kerala, and Tamil Nadu, the ICDS programme is doing better. In Chamba in Himachal, toilets are being built at AWCs. In Tamil Nadu, there is a proper preschool curriculum followed by the AWW. Children are well fed and stay at the AWC for almost six hours. They have sleeping mats, toys, even mirrors to comb their hair and stay clean. In Chamarkundi village of Ganjam district of Orissa, women's SHG supplement the Anganwadi food with eggs and vegetables.

TABLE 6.5
Sectoral Allocation and Expenditure in Budget for Children (BFC) as percentage of the Union Budget

Year	Health		Development		Education		Protection		*BfC*	
	BE	AE	BE	AE	BE	AE	BE	AE	BE	AE
2000–01	0.542	0.38	0.358	0.39	1.466	1.34	0.023	0.02	2.389	2.14
2001–02	0.469	0.37	0.407	0.43	1.414	1.39	0.029	0.03	2.319	2.2
2002–03	0.505	0.35	0.448	0.48	1.452	1.40	0.036	0.03	2.441	2.25
2003–04	0.497	0.40	0.501	0.41	1.468	1.51	0.031	0.02	2.497	2.35
2004–05	0.646	0.52	0.421	0.46	1.644	1.96	0.033	0.03	2.745	2.96
2005–06	0.762	NA	0.659	NA	2.629	NA	0.034	NA	4.084	NA
2006–07	0.837	NA	0.829	NA	3.534	NA	0.035	NA	5.236	NA
Average	0.61	0.41	0.52	0.44	1.94	1.55	0.03	0.03	3.10	2.42

Note: Actual Expenditure is available till 2004–05, so the average for the actual expenditure has been calculated for that period only.
Source: Demand for Grants—All Ministries, HAQ: Centre for Child Rights, New Delhi.

SOCIO-ECONOMIC INDICATORS

Health

6.96 Almost 2.5 million children die in India every year accounting for one in five child deaths in the world. In almost all cases girl children are 50% more likely to die than boys. India also accounts for 35% of the developing world's LBW babies and 40% of child malnutrition. According to the report on the *State of India's Newborns*,[16] India has the highest number of births as well as neonatal deaths in the world. Inherent in the health system is a strong gender bias against the female at all levels. The report also reveals that for every two sick male newborns admitted to a facility; only one female infant was admitted.

[16] *State of India's New Born*, Report of National Neonatology Forum of India and Save the Children, 2004.

TABLE 6.6
Monitorable Targets for the Tenth Plan and Achievements

S. No.	Indicators	Target Set	Current Status
1.	IMR	45 by 2007 and 28 by 2012	57 (NFHS-3) 58 (SRS 2005)
2.	MMR	2 by 2007 and 1 by 2012	3.01 (SRS 1997–2003)
3.	Gender gaps in literacy	Reduce by at least 50% by 2007	21.70% (Census of India 2001)
4.	Gender differential in wage rates	Reduce by 50% by 2007	Ratio of female wage/male wage reduced to 0.59 for rural and 0.75 for urban areas (NSSO, 2004–05). Therefore indicating increase in gender differential in wage rates
5	Literacy	All children in school by 2003	0.95 crore out of school children
6.	Five years of schooling	For all children by 2007	Drop out rate for Primary level—29%; Middle Level—50.8% (2004–05)

Source: Selected Educational Statistics, MoHRD, 2004–05.

TABLE 6.7
Health Status of Children in India vis-à-vis in Other E-9 Countries

Country Name	Under-5 mortality rate (per thousand)		Progress towards MDG for reducing under-5 and Infant Mortality Rates by two-thirds	%ageof under-5s with stunting (1995–2001)	GDP per capita (PPP US$, 2001)
	1960	2001			
Bangladesh	248	77	On track	45	1610
Brazil	177	36	On Track	11	7360
China	225	39	Far Behind	17	4020
Egypt	282	41	On Track	19	3520
India	242	93	Lagging	46	2840
Indonesia	216	45	On Track	–	2940
Mexico	134	29	On Track	18	8430
Nigeria	207	183	Far behind	46	850
Pakistan	227	109	Far behind	–	–
E9 Average	218	72		29	3717

Source: The State of the World's Children (2003), UNICEF; Human Development Report (2003), UNDP in ECCE in E-9 Countries: Status and Outlook. Prepared for the Fifth E-9 Ministerial Meeting.

6.97 A study by International Labour Organization (ILO) in 2002,[17] found that children of HIV-infected parents are forced to face significant decline in income and heavy discrimination. Children orphaned by AIDS, especially girls, tend to become vulnerable to prostitution due to their disadvantaged socio-cultural status. In India, of the 70000 children in urgent need of ARV treatment, only 1048 (1.5%) are currently receiving this lifesaving therapy.[18] NACO with support from UNICEF, Indian Academy of Paediatrics, Clinton Foundation, WHO, and the GoI has recently launched a new initiative that had, till May 2007, reached out to 4100 children needing ARV.

6.98 India also has the largest percentage as well as the largest absolute number of vitamin A deficient children. Water-borne diseases afflict a large number of children leading to numerous child deaths. Only 42% of Indian households have access to piped water (NFHS-3) and in the absence of potable water, children continue to suffer from stomach ailments. Diarrhoea, often caused by unsafe drinking water or

[17] Assessing the Socio-economic Impact of HIV/AIDS on People Living with HIV/AIDS, ILO, 2002.
[18] Stop HIV/AIDS in India Initiative, 2005.

Box 6.11
Socio-Economic Status of Children

- IMR is as high as 57 per 1000 live births (NFHS-3)
- Birth registration in India is just 62% (Registral General of India, 2004)
- MMR is equally high at 301 per 100000 live births (SRS, 2001–03)
- Only 43.5% children in the age group of 12–23 months are fully immunized
- The number of children orphaned in India is approaching 2 million (World Bank 2005)
- Only 21% children in the age group of 12–35 months receive a dose of vitamin A
- Nearly 60000 newborns are infected every year from 189000 HIV-positive women
- Only 26% children who had diarrhoea got ORS (NFHS-3) as compared to 27% in NFHS-2.

Box 6.12
Child Immunization: South Asia Performance

India has the lowest child immunization rate in South Asia. The proportion of children who have not had a BCG vaccine in India is twice as high as in Nepal, more than five times as high as in Bangladesh, and almost 30 times as high as in Sri Lanka.

Child immunization is virtually universal in Sri Lanka. This success is largely based on public intervention. Sri Lanka has an IMR of only 12 per 1000. The contrast in immunization rates between Bangladesh and India reflecting the proportion of children who have not been vaccinated is two to five times as high in India as in Bangladesh.

National averages often hide major disparities between regions and socio-economic groups. For a child born in Tamil Nadu, the chance of being fully immunized by age one is around 90%. Chances of being fully immunized are only 42% for the average Indian child, dropping further to 26% for the average 'ST' child, and a shocking 11% for the average Bihari child. When different sources of disadvantage (relating, for instance, to class, caste, and gender) are combined, immunization rates dip to abysmally low levels. For instance, among 'ST' children in Bihar only 4% are fully immunized and 38% have not been immunized at all.[19]

poor sanitation, is the second leading cause of death among children. Yet only 58% of children with diarrhoea were taken to a health facility, down from 65% seven years earlier (NFHS-3).

Child Diabetes

6.99 A cause for alarm is that diabetes is now being detected in very small children. According to hospital statistics, in 2002, Delhi alone had about 4000 to 5000 diabetic children and it is estimated that there might be an equal number of undiagnosed cases.

Nutrition

6.100 One of every three malnourished children in the world lives in India; every second child is underweight. NFHS-3 data shows that despite various interventions, incidence of under-nutrition, stunting, and wasting among children continues to be very high with an increase in the number of under-weight children in States of Bihar, Haryana, and Gujarat. As children grow up, poor nutrition and ill health affects their learning abilities and preparedness for schooling. An assessment of diet and nutritional status carried out by the NNMB in 2006 revealed that the proportion of adolescent girls who could be considered 'at risk' due to stunting was 35.5% and those under weight was 38.5%.

6.101 Childhood anaemia below 3 years has gone up from 74.2% in NFHS-2 to 79.2% in NFHS-3 while Bihar has seen an increase of 7% in rates of anaemia in this age group. This is partly because of food insecurity at the household level. Poor breastfeeding practices together with lack of complementary feeding also aggravates child malnutrition.

[19] Infochangeagenda-June 2007.

Education

6.102 The education strategy in primary and secondary schooling is the most important intervention for giving children their due rights. The Eleventh Plan strategy in this respect is discussed in the chapter on Education. The Plan envisions to reach out to all categories of children, including children with disabilities, who are discriminated against in the education system. According to the 2001 Census Report, 1.67% of the total population in the 0–19 age group is differently abled. The SRI-IMRB report (2005) estimates that 38% of CWSN are out of school. The percentage of children with disability, both in primary and upper primary classes, is below 1% of the total enrolment in classes. Yet only 4.50% primary schools and 8.15% integrated higher secondary schools have the provision for ramps.

Exploitation, Violence, and Abuse

6.103 India has the highest number of child labourers.The Census report clearly point to the increase in the number of child labourers in the country from 11.28 million in 1991 to 12.59 million in 2001.[20] Although the number of children employed in the agricultural sector, in domestic work, roadside restaurants and sweet meat shop, automobile mechanic units, rice mills, Indian-made foreign liquor outlets and most such sectors considered as 'non-hazardous', there is ample evidence to suggest that more and more children are entering the labour force and are also exploited by their employers. In many cases such children are forced to work for long durations, without food and for very low wages. Many of the live-in domestic workers are in a situation of near slavery with constant violation of their human rights. There is a need to address the rehabiliatation of these children including shelter, education, food, health and other needs and return to families based on review of their situations.

Box 6.13
Nutrition Status of Children

- Three out of four children in India are anaemic
- Every second new born has reduced learning capacity due to iodine deficiency
- Children (0–3 years) underweight are 46% in NFHS-3, a marginal decrease from 47% in NFHS-2
- Children under 3 with anaemia are 79% (NFHS-3), an increase from 74.2% in NFHS-2
- Only 23.4% children are breastfed within the first hour of birth and 46.3% are exclusively breastfed for 6 months (NFHS-3)

6.104 Crimes against children continue to spiral with rising figures for kidnapping and abduction (3518 in 2005), infanticide (187 in 2005), and foeticide (86 in 2005). Children's vulnerability to physical abuse is exposed in the grim statistics of child rapes that have increased from 2532 cases in 2002 to 4026 cases in 2005.[21] Porous borders and increasing poverty has increased procuring, buying, and selling of girls for prostitution. Falling sex ratios and annihilation of the girl child has led to an increase in child marriages.

6.105 Over 44000 children go missing every year, of which more than 11000 children remain untraced. Traditional forms of violence and abuse against children such as child marriage, economic exploitation, *Devadasi* tradition continues in many parts of the country. Further physical and psychological punishment in the name of discipline is rampant and even culturally acceptable in schools and homes across the country.

6.106 Violent situations, circumstances like forced evictions, displacement due to development projects, war and conflict, communal riots and natural disasters, all take their toll on children and affect their physiological and social development.

Voicelessness

6.107 In spite of legislations in the past, children have no right to be heard in either administrative or judicial processes. This limits their access to information and to choice, and often to the possibility of seeking help outside their immediate circle.

[20] RGI, Census of India 1991, 2001.
[21] NCRB, 2005.

CHALLENGES, STRATEGIES, AND THE ROAD AHEAD

6.108 All strategies for Child Rights and Development in the Eleventh Plan must be cognizant of the slowing decline in poverty, and an unsettling of traditional, 'pre-modern' livelihoods and local economies. This has constrained the caring capacity of millions of families and impacted children. Cosmetic measures targeting only children and not their milieu are therefore not enough to correct this situation.

6.109 Successful integration of survival, development, protection, and participation is closely linked to all aspects of a child's well being. Often, the same child is prone to malnutrition and illness, deprived of early stimulation, is out-of-school, and more likely to be abused and exploited. An immunized child who is constantly beaten will not be healthy; a school-going child taunted and abused for his or her ethnicity won't enjoy a good learning environment; and an adolescent sold into prostitution will not be empowered to participate in and contribute to society. Sexual abuse and violence in schools can be a hidden factor behind low retention rates. Violence can be behind many of the unexplained injuries that are treated at health centres, or even the cause of long-term disability. These links have to be recognized to ensure a holistic approach to child rights, particularly children's right to protection.

6.110 At the same time it is important to remember that while children have equal rights, their situations are not uniform. Their needs and entitlements are area-specific, group-specific, culture-specific, setting-specific, and age-specific and demand different sets of interventions. They live and struggle for growth and well-being in the contextual frame of who they are and where they are located, and how that identity includes or excludes them from social and State provisions and benefits. While some children are in difficult circumstances and have suffered violence, abuse, and exploitation, there are others who are not in any of these adverse situations and yet need to be protected in order to ensure that they remain within the social security net. It is critical that interventions destined for children do not 'exclude' anyone.

6.111 In the light of the above, the following strategies will be adopted during the Eleventh Plan to ensure that every child enjoys her childhood and all her rights without any fear and without the need to work:

- Developing specific interventions to address malnutrition, neonatal, and infant mortality.
- Creating child-friendly protective services.
- Identifying the most vulnerable and marginalized children and ensuring age and situation-specific interventions.
- Reviewing all legal provisions for children and undertaking necessary amendments based on international commitments.
- Ensuring effective implementation of laws and polices by personnel trained to work with children.
- Establishing child impact as a core indicator of Eleventh Plan interventions, with special emphasis on the status of the girl child.
- Creating a protective environment for children through implementation of schemes and programmes based on *the best interest of the child.* Some of the current initiatives only address the needs of children once they have fallen through the protective net. While these initiatives to identify such children and rehabilitate them are critical, there is an equal need for legislative changes and programmatic interventions, so that prevention is foregrounded and children grow up in a protective environment.
- Undertaking a child rights review of all existing developmental policies and plans to assess their impact on children and to ensure that children are not further marginalized.
- Recognizing that crèches and day care are important for child development, empowerment of women, and retention of girls in schools.
- Ensuring survival of the girl child and her right to be born. Shift to 'lifecycle and capability approach' where the girl child's contribution in economic and social terms is recognized.
- Ensuring multi-pronged programme, focusing on preventing children from falling out of the protective net, ameliorative initiatives for children who are already out of the protective net, and ensuring long-term and sustainable rehabilitation by upgrading quality of services and addressing regional imbalances.

- Recognizing that children are best cared for in their own families, strengthening family capabilities to care and protect the child.
- Ensuring institutional care to those children who need the same.
- Involving PRIs, VOs, and urban local bodies in implementation, monitoring, and evaluation by devolving powers and resources to the Panchayat level, and providing them with technical and administrative support.
- Recognizing 'Child Budgeting' as an important policy analysis tool to take stock of development investments for children and identify gaps in resource investment and utilization.
- Strengthening capacity of families and communities, police, judiciary, teachers, PRI representatives, bureaucrats, and other implementation personnel who deal directly with children.

ELEVENTH PLAN INITIATIVES

DEFINING AGE OF THE CHILD

6.112 Recognizing everyone below the age of 18 as children and respecting their rights will be an important Eleventh Plan initiative. The challenge will be to amend all legislations and laws to ensure a uniform definition of children, as stipulated under UNCRC and JJ Act. The Child Labour Act and related legislations like The Factories Act, 1948, The Mines Act, 1952, The Plantation Labour Act, 1951, The Merchant Shipping Act, 1958, The Motor Transport Workers Act, 1961, The Beedi and Cigar Workers (Conditions of Employment) Act, 1966, The Bonded Labour System (Abolition) Act, 1976 continue to *prohibit employment of children under 14 years only.* The ITPA, 1956 draws heavily from the Indian Penal Code 1860, which define a child as someone who is less than 16 years of age under ITPA as well.

ENSURING EARLY CHILDHOOD DEVELOPMENT AND CARE

6.113 As per Census 2001, the country has approximately 60 million children in the age group of 3–6 years. The 86th amendment to the constitution, making education for children in the 6–14 age group a fundamental right, leaves out under six years of age. It is for this age group that early childhood care in the form of childcare programmes, crèche programmes, and preschool interventions are critical. Current figures suggest that preschooling under ICDS and other private initiatives covers about 34 million children; approximately 26 million children are left out of preschool activities. Thus, the gap between the number of preschool children and available preschool services is large. Moreover, there are disparities in provision of ECCE in rural and urban areas. As per findings of a study conducted by the National Institute of Urban Affairs (year), though the share of urban population in the country is approximately 27.78% (expected to go up by 33%), corresponding provision of ECCE facilities in these areas is insufficient. Urban slums are under-represented in ICDS.

6.114 Early childhood care and rights of working mothers are interconnected. Exclusive breastfeeding, recommended for the first six months of life, before complementary feeding is introduced, requires constant proximity of mother and child. The Eleventh Plan will, hence ensure Maternity Entitlements to support exclusive breastfeeding.

ICDS

6.115 Currently ICDS is the only programme that reaches out to millions of women and children living in remote villages, *dhanis* (small settlements), and *saporis* (river islands) in our country. It is and will continue to be the flagship programme of the MoWCD. However, during the Eleventh Plan, ICDS needs to be restructured in a manner that addresses some of the weaknesses that have emerged and is suitable for universalization. The programme must effectively integrate the different elements that affect nutrition and reflect the different needs of children in different age groups. For the purpose the programme needs to be restructured in a Mission Mode with a Mission Structure at the central level and a similar structure at the State level. The MoWCD will prepare proposal for restructuring along these lines so that the restructured programme can become effective on 1 April 2008.

6.116 Universalization with quality entails that the existing ICDS scheme is thoroughly examined and evaluated to identify gaps. Various surveys show that high expectations from the ICDS scheme along with lack of proper training, implementation, monitoring, and financial resources are the reasons why our anganwadis have been unable to deliver. At present, the AWW is expected to perform 21 tasks. In addition to this, given her proximity to the people in the villages, she is often used for non-ICDS duties. So, in the Eleventh Plan targets for child nutrition, health care, immunization, early childhood education, etc. will be set for AWWs. Since the condition of children and their problems vary from region to region and even within districts in the country, these targets and objectives will be district or block specific. At the district-level a committee comprising the District Collector, District Health Officer, women Panchayat members, and mothers groups will be set up to decide the targets for ICDS. Performance of the ICDS centres will be evaluated against these targets and well-performing centres will be rewarded. Besides, streamlining the work and expectations from the AWW, the new ICDS will also tackle issues of programme design, implementation, and financial allocations.

6.117 In the Eleventh Plan, community involvement will be the strategy for ensuring better functioning of ICDS centres. Communitization of education has proved to be a success in Nagaland. Involving the local community not only creates a sense of ownership and facilitates monitoring, it also ensures that the program-me is tailored according to local needs. A Village Committee comprising mothers or representatives 'of mothers' groups, AWW, ANM, ASHA, women Panchayat members will be constituted to look at issues like appointment of AWWs and helpers (which should take place through an open *Gram Sabha* with at least 60% attendance), content of SNP, procurement and preparation, meeting the targets set for the ICDS, and organization of monthly Mother and Child Health Days. The AWW will be answerable to this committee and the committee should have the power to recommend to the district-level committee (which will have the power to remove non-performing workers) removal of the AWW, ANM, ASHA, or helper by a simple majority. It is this committee that would be entrusted with the proper use of flexi-funds being suggested for AWCs. Since many of the issues are interlinked, the Eleventh Plan proposes the merging of this committee with the VHSC.

6.118 The modalities for the feeding component present some choices. One approach is to rely on hot cooked meals according to local taste and provided at the anganwadi centres. Preparation of meals will be entrusted to SHGs or mothers' groups, as per decision of the Village Committee. An alternative approach is to rely upon RTE micronutrient fortified hygienically prepared food. The decision between these two options needs to be based on a careful evaluation of pros and cons and will be an important part of the proposed restructuring. The choice between the two could also be left to decentralized decision making.

6.119 Since malnutrition sets in before the age of two, it is very difficult to reverse the process. It is this age group (the under threes') that is often left out of the ambit of ICDS. Most centres only provide some form of nutrition to children in the 3–6 years age group. It is therefore, important to recognize the different target groups under ICDS and to understand their varying needs. Malnutrition and the cycle of ill-health often start with the mother. The first task of the ICDS will be to ensure the health nutritional status, ANC, and immunization of pregnant women. It will also address the need of proper counselling, iron, folic acid supplements, vital for the health of both the mother and the child. The AWW and ASHA will promote exclusive breastfeeding for children up to six months of age. For this purpose some form of Conditional Maternity Benefits could be introduced in the Eleventh Plan. Lactating women will also be counselled and provided with adequate nutrition.

6.120 The second important target group for checking malnutrition is children in the six months to three years age group. They need proper care and growth monitoring. Currently, the ICDS programme only provides Take Home Rations (THRs) and in some cases, weaning foods for these children. To tackle malnutrition the Eleventh Plan will introduce an intensive malnutrition control programme within the ICDS scheme. Under this, 6–8 hour crèches for children under three will be provided in the most nutritionally backward

Box 6.14
Balwadis and Phoolwaris:
Focussing on Under Threes

Sewa Mandir in Udaipur has been running *Balwadis* for young children under three. For a meagre monthly fee, often Rs 5, poor tribal women leave their children at the Balwadis. The centres run from 6–8 hours; timings are decided by the community. Often other women from the community chip in to help the worker take care of the children.

In the tribal hinterlands of Bilaspur in Chattisgarh, the *JSS* has started *Phoolwaris*. Two to three women from the community volunteer to take care of children below age three. The community provides them with premises. Sarees are made into slings, where the little ones are lulled to sleep by the workers. They have neat little kerchiefs pinned to their front and are fed by the volunteers with love and affection. The doctors who run the programme are confident that this is the way to fight malnutrition. The programme also enables the poor tribal women to carry on with their work so that the family does not lose income.

districts of the country. The Village Health Sanitation and Nutrition Committee will be funded for providing at least three meals per child per day at these crèches. It will also be provided money for crèche workers. From appointment of crèche workers, to crèche timings and constitution of meals, everything will be left to the Village Committee. They will even be allowed to collect a small user fee, if the village Panchayat agrees. The Committee will be responsible for ensuring that the health workers visit the crèche on a monthly basis for immunization and health check-ups of children. Continuation of the scheme in the village will depend on the performance of the village crèches. In areas where the new programme is not introduced, children under three will continue to get THRs and will be provided home-based care through the ASHA.

6.121 PSE for children in the 3–6 years age group is another important issue. The approach paper to the Eleventh Plan had suggested that this component be taken up under SSA to streamline the functioning of ICDS centres. There are varying opinions on this but the basic proposal that children will get preschool education must be implemented.

6.122 The final target group under the ICDS is adolescent girls. It is extremely important to reach out to this segment of the population to break the cycle of ill-health. As of now, however, this group is most neglected. In addition to SNP, and IFA tablets, these girls require proper counselling. The ANM and AWW will conduct a monthly meeting to educate and counsel this group.

Training, Monitoring, and Surveillance

6.123 Recruiting a second AWW or converging the ASHA and ANM alone will not make the AWCs effective. During the Eleventh Plan, the AWW and helper, along with the ASHA, will receive on-going training in child care, health, nutrition, and hygiene.

6.124 The ICDS centres will collect a host of data that can provide valuable insights into the State of health and nutrition in the villages. If collected properly and checked regularly (through random sampling) this data can also indicate the performance of the AWCs. DLHS will be used to gauge the impact of ICDS and other interventions. Based on this information, a performance appraisal system for AWCs will be worked out. Well-performing AWCs will be incentivized. Efficient AWWs and helpers will be encouraged by providing monetary incentives and by getting promotions to senior posts of supervisors, etc. Social audits by NGOs and by Village Level Committees will be encouraged. At the same time, a system of concurrent third party evaluation through professional bodies will be established.

Financial Allocation

6.125 In the Eleventh Plan, allocation of resources under ICDS has been increased substantially to not just expand coverage but to ensure availability of adequate infrastructure. For the proper functioning of an ICDS centre, it should be housed in a building with a kitchen, have baby-friendly toilet, drinking water facilities, and with adequate space for children to play. Availability of toys, utensils, weighing machine, mats, and IFA tablets might be ensured in the Eleventh Plan. Every AWC will be provided with a flexi-fund administered by the Village Committee.

6.126 Finally, NGOs and even corporate houses will be encouraged to adopt local anganwadi centres and to augment their resources. For instance, they could provide buildings, toys, additional SNP (like a glass of milk or eggs), impart training, sponsor severely malnourished children, offer the services of a teacher to strengthen the preschool component, etc. They could also help with the management of AWCs.

6.127 No amount of restructuring will however be able to bring about a change in the health status of children unless it is supported by parallel measures outside the ICDS system. Diarrhoea caused due to unavailability of clean drinking water is the leading cause of childhood morbidity and consequently malnutrition and death. Providing clean drinking water at Anganwadis is essential but we must remember that the child primarily drinks water at home. Unless clean drinking water is available all day, diarrhoea diseases will continue. Similarly, toilets at ICDS centres are important to inculcate the habit among children, but unless the homes have toilets, children will continue to defecate in the open and be susceptible to worms and diseases. Detection of diseases and referral services at ICDS centre will be effective if and only if there is a functioning PHC where the child can get treatment. Thus ICDS will provide results only in a conducive environment. Currently, there are many schemes to tackle the multifarious problems which assail our villages, towns and cities. Convergence is the key.

RAJIV GANDHI CRÈCHE SCHEME

6.128 The scheme in its present form is neither widespread nor able to provide meaningful day care services to children below 6. The Eleventh Plan will therefore review and restructure the scheme. Some changes proposed are:

- Eligibility criteria will be widened to allow diverse agencies/organizations to participate, for example, SHGs, *Mahila Mandals*, women's organizations, labour unions, cooperatives, schools, panchayats, and tribal associations.
- Programme standards that are measurable through input and process indicators will be laid down.
- Results will be monitored through output and outcome indicators.
- Pattern of funding will be revised.
- Upgrading infrastructure and materials, regular training of crèche workers, lateral linkages with the local PHC or sub-PHC in the area and tie up with the Anganwadi centres for inputs like immunization, polio-drops, and basic health monitoring will be carried out.

PROVIDING CHILD PROTECTION

6.129 Provision of Child Protection will be a key intervention in the Eleventh Plan. 'Child Protection' refers to protection from violence, exploitation, abuse, and neglect. India has recognized the right to protection for its children through its constitutional commitments and the laws, policies, and programmes it has put in place over the years. It has also recognized that some children are in 'especially difficult circumstances', such as child labour, street children and children under the juvenile justice system, and has made specific programme interventions for them. This

Box 6.15
Child Protection

- Initiation of a new Centrally Sponsored Integrated Child Protection Scheme (ICPS) with adequate allocation
- Review of existing legal provisions and necessary amendments
- Strengthening and implementation of law
- Intersectoral and inter-ministerial convergence for protection of children (such as integration of protection with Creche and Day Care Programme)
- Review and reorganization of Adoption System in India
- Human resource development for strengthening counselling services
- Data systems, research, advocacy, and communication
- Child impact audit to ensure that government interventions do not decrease protection for children making them more vulnerable to abuse and exploitation
- Strengthening the National and State Commissions for the Protection of Child Rights.

recognition is underpinned by the fact that every child has a right to protection, even if he/she is not in difficult circumstances. Thus the Eleventh Plan intervention for Child Protection takes both a preventive and a protective approach.

The Integrated Child Protection Scheme

6.130 During the Eleventh Plan, the Ministry of WCD will launch an Integrated Child Protection Scheme. The existing schemes of: (i) An Integrated Programme for Street Children, (ii) A programme for Juvenile Justice, (iii) Shishu Greha scheme, etc. will be merged with Integrated Child Protection Scheme (ICPS). The proposed scheme is planned to be implemented in the States/UTs. ICPS will be principled on child protection, which is a shared responsibility of government, family, community, professionals, and civil society.

6.131 Its several facets will be the following:

- Reducing child vulnerability by focusing on systematic preventive measures to address protection failures at various levels. Provisions and services of various sectors will be converged—like health, child day care, education to strengthen families and reduce the likelihood of child neglect, abuse, and vulnerability.
- Promoting non-institutional care: Institutionalization will be used as a measure of last resort. Constant review of cases to encourage release from institutions will be carried out.
- Creating a network of services at community level
- Establishing standards for care and protection: All protection services will have prescribed standards, protocols for key actions, and will be monitored regularly.
- Building capacities: Capacities of all those in contact with children will be strengthened on a continuing basis. Thrust will be on strengthening the family's capabilities to care for and protect the child by capacity building, family counselling, and support services and linking it to development and community support services.
- Providing professional child protection services at all levels: Special services for the many situations of child neglect, exploitation, and abuse, including shelter, care, psychological recovery, social reintegration, legal services, etc. will be provided.
- Strengthening crisis management system at all levels: First response and coordinated intersectoral actions for responding to crisis will be established and institutionalized.
- Addressing protection of children in urban poverty: Developing a strong social support and service system.
- Child impact monitoring and social audit: Programmes and services will be undertaken in order to promote transparency.
- Protecting children in conflict situations: Children in conflict-prone areas like Jammu and Kashmir (J&K), NER, and Naxal-affected regions, where they are often victims, must be provided care and protection under the Juvenile Justice Act.

Components of ICPS

6.132 Towards integrating child protection

- 24-hour emergency helpline Childline to be extended to all districts/cities and setting up of drop-in shelters in urban areas.
- Steps to streamline adoption process by addressing identified bottlenecks; reaching out to children whose parents are unable to care for them.
- Setting up of Cradle Baby Reception Centres in each district linked to PHCs, hospitals, *Swadhar* units, short stay homes, and in the office of District Child Protection Unit (DCPU) to receive abandoned babies, those in crisis and vulnerable to trafficking.
- ICPS will support the creation of new institutional facilities and maintenance of existing facilities for children. It will also provide additional components to institutions that cater to CWSN. Further it will support need-based innovative programmes in districts/cities by grant-in-fund to State Child Protection Units, for example, for children of sex workers or for post-disaster rescue and relief.
- Providing financial and human resource support to the States/UTs for setting up statutory bodies under the Juvenile Justice (Care & Protection of Children) Amendment Act, 2006, i.e., Juvenile Justice Boards (JJBs), Child Welfare Committees (CWCs), Special Juvenile Police Units (SJPUs) in

each district and strengthen their service delivery. It will also take up training and capacity building of all personnel involved in child protection sectors throughout the country.

- Facilitating comprehensive research to assess the cause, nature, and extent of specific child protection issues and documentation of best practices.
- Initiating web-enabled child protection data management system and a national website for missing children
- Developing comprehensive advocacy and communication strategy for child rights and protection.

CHILD LINE

6.133 In the Eleventh Plan Childline-1098, will be extended to rural areas and to all districts of the country. Expansion of Childline will require stronger partnership with VO and higher investment of resources and capacity building of the allied systems to reach out to every child in distress.

NATIONAL AND STATE COMMISSIONS FOR THE PROTECTION OF CHILD RIGHTS

6.134 The National Commission for Protection of Child Rights has been notified. The process for setting up the full Commission is underway. One of the major responsibilities of the Commission is to monitor and report on implementation of child rights in India. The Eleventh Plan will ensure that similar Commissions for protection of child rights are constituted in all States and UTs at the earliest.

ENDING DISCRIMINATION AGAINST GIRL CHILD

6.135 The Eleventh Plan will set out proactive, affirmative approaches and actions necessary for realizing the rights of the girl child and providing equality of opportunity. The situation of the girl child in this country is a result of deep-rooted biases that can only improve with a change in attitudes. This will be the overarching philosophy cutting across many schemes of the Eleventh Plan that will entail coordination with other sectors plus monitoring and documentation of the impact of measures undertaken by the State. The status of the girl child and recommendations for the Eleventh Plan have been discussed in the Women's Agency's part of this chapter. Her status will be used to gauge the effectiveness of development measures in reaching out to all children and in removing inequalities. Panchayats, Gram Sabhas, community-based organizations and local self-government bodies will be brought into this surveillance. At district level, the District Magistrate, District Collector will take responsibility for monitoring the overall progress of the girl children. The Eleventh Plan will also examine sectoral communication strategies and how they reflect the rights of the girl child. Ministry of WCD will pilot special measures for this as well as initiate actions for assessing the impact of such measures on the actual condition and status of girls. The following measures will be taken:

Ensuring a Balanced Sex Ratio

6.136 Sex selection/female foeticide will be treated as a crime and not just a social evil. Preventive, corrective/regulatory, and punitive actions to address foeticide and sex selection will be strengthened by ensuring coordination with the MoHFW. It will seek the review of the PC & PNDT Act with law enforcement authorities to ensure its implementation. It will also review the current Appropriate Authorities under the PC & PNDT Act for granting, suspending or cancelling registration of Genetic Counselling Centres and investigating complaints. It will ensure stringent penalties and punitive action against erring persons. Capacity building for State and WCD officials and their participation in Appropriate Authorities for monitoring implementation of the Act will be ensured. The nationwide sensitization and advocacy campaign with specific focus on the girl child will continue.

Education

6.137 Community Vigilance Committees formed at village level under the SSA will ensure that every girl child in the village is enrolled and attends school regularly. The Ministry of WCD will work in close collaboration with Department of Elementary Education and Literacy and ancillary bodies to ensure that curricula and syllabi are gender sensitive. The department will start bridge schools with quality education packages for girl children and street children, child labourers, seasonal migrants and all those who are out of the formal education system.

Pilot Scheme on Conditional Cash Transfer for Girl Child with Insurance Cover

6.138 The Eleventh Plan will introduce a pilot scheme in selected backward districts of the country wherein conditional cash will be provided to the family of the girl child (preferably the mother) on fulfilling certain conditionalities for the girl child, such as birth registration; immunization; enrolment retention in school; and delaying the marriage age beyond 18 years. The scheme will also include a sub-component for providing insurance cover to the girl child. This will be in addition to the various existing incentives provided by the Centre and State. This scheme will be monitored closely to support desirable behaviour and practices and study its impact on community attitudes and practices.

Prevention of Girl Child Abuse, Exploitation and Violence

6.139 The ICPS of the MoWCD along with enabling legislations like Offences Against Children Bill is expected to prevent girl child abuse and violence by strict enforcement of laws for rape, sexual harassment, trafficking, domestic violence, dowry, and other related crimes. Community Vigilance Groups along with Self-Help and Youth Groups will be created to ensure that girl children are protected. These groups will work closely with Panchayats and DCPUs being proposed under ICPS. Public discourse on abuse, exploitation, and violence against the girl child will be promoted to break the silence around these issues. At the same time, well thought out 'rehabilitation packages' for specific types of abuse/violence perpetuated will be prepared with the assistance of VOs.

Trafficking for Commercial Sexual Exploitation

6.140 In the Eleventh Plan, MoWCD will focus on a multi-pronged approach to combat trafficking. This will include reform in the laws, preventive measures, rescue and rehabilitation measures, awareness generation, and sensitization. The Eleventh Plan will address trafficking in women and children through a 'Comprehensive Scheme for Prevention of Trafficking, Rescue, Rehabilitation and Re-integration of Victims of Trafficking for Commercial Sexual Exploitation' that will be based on the results of small pilot projects initiated during the Tenth Plan. Three pilot projects have already been initiated; two in source areas (rural area, where it is a traditional practice) and one in destination area. All projects under the scheme are one-year pilots. The lessons learnt will be replicated and up-scaled for wider outreach during the Eleventh Plan period.

Prohibition of Child Marriage

6.141 Enforcement mechanisms for implementation of the Prohibition of Child Marriage Act, 2006 will be strengthened. MoWCD will partner with Civil Society groups, PRIs, community-based organizations, SHGs, *maulvis*/*pandits*/priests/ other religious leaders to mobilize, develop, and promote community initiatives to support delayed marriage. Compulsory Registration of Marriages will be ensured.

CONSUMERISM AND THE GIRL CHILD

6.142 The Eleventh Plan will fund initiatives that raise awareness to ensure that the market economy, increasing consumerism, and resultant family planning practices do not enhance gender inequality and lead to 'male child planning'.

REACHING OUT TO THE MARGINALIZED AND MOST VULNERABLE

Child Workers

6.143 Statistics show that the number of child workers has gone up from 11.28 million in 1991 to 12.66 million in 2001. This increase is primarily attributed to States like Uttar Pradesh, Bihar, Rajasthan, and West Bengal (Figure 6.1).

Eliminating Child Labour

6.144 Child labour as such is not illegal in India except in specific hazardous occupations. With effect from October 2006, the Ministry of Labour has included domestic work and employment in *dhabas*, tea stalls, and restaurants in the schedule of prohibited occupations under the Act. As a result a large number of children may be laid off, especially in metropolitan cities and big towns. It will be necessary to take adequate measures for the protection, rehabilitation, and education of these children.

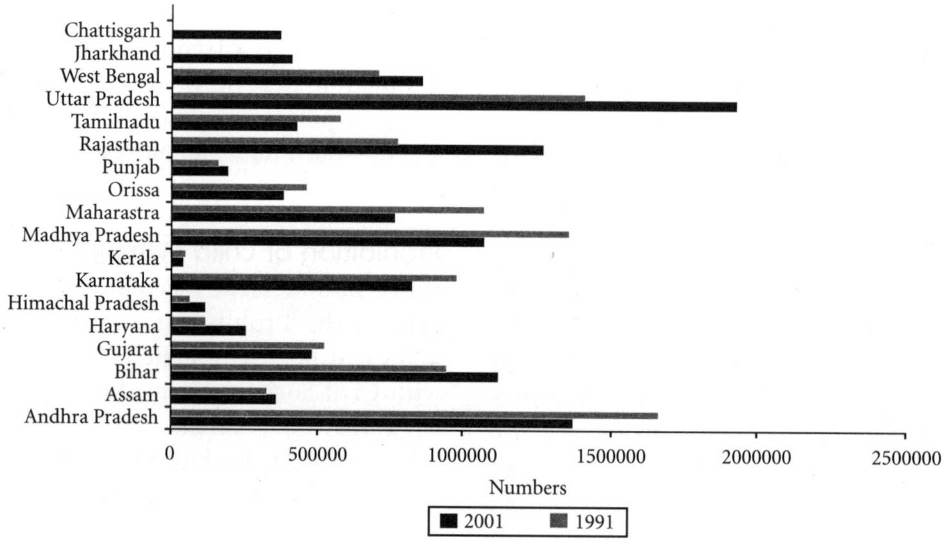

Source: Census of India

FIGURE 6.1: Child Workers

Eliminating Child Trafficking, Commercial Sexual Exploitation of Children, Child Pornography, Child Sex Tourism

6.145 NHRC reports[22] that about 44000 children in India go missing every year. They are being trafficked for prostitution, marriage or illegal adoption, child labour, begging, recruitment to armed groups, and for entertainment (circus or sports). With the opening up of the markets and increase in tourism, children have fallen prey to operating paedophiles and sex abusers. With more women being forced into prostitution, the condition of children of sex workers is also a matter of concern. It is necessary to take affirmative action to ensure that these children have access to basic services and rights that will protect them from becoming victims of sexual exploitation. Efforts must also be made towards rehabilitation and reintegration of trafficked children.

HIV/AIDS-Infected/Affected Children

6.146 Among the estimated 5.7 million people in India living with HIV/AIDS, 220000 (15%) are children under 15 years of age.[23] There are many affected children whose parents are infected and alive. Stigma and discrimination, often associated with HIV infection, can lead to exclusion and isolation along with emotional and psychological distress. It ruins a child's chances to receive an education or a normal childhood. Economic hardship resulting from their parents' inability to work may cause children to drop out of school or become child labourers. Children orphaned by HIV/AIDS are exposed to exploitation, abuse, and violence. The challenge in the Eleventh Plan is to end the discrimination and reach out to children affected/infected by HIV/AIDS to ensure that they are protected, treated, and get an opportunity to develop according to their full potential. The chapter on Health details Eleventh Plan commitment in this regard.

Children in Conflict with Law—Social Integration

6.147 The Eleventh Plan will review the conditions of State-run homes and fund their development through the new ICPS scheme. The basic mandate of rehabilitating and reintegrating children in conflict with law will be upheld, by urging training for law enforcement and child welfare officers. The Plan will stress on the protection of children from violence, abuse, and exploitation inside institutions, and will adopt a paradigm that recognizes that children in conflict with law also need care and protection. The challenge for the Eleventh Plan is to condense the long judicial process

[22] NHRC Action Research on Trafficking, Orient Longman, 2005, New Delhi.

[23] UNAIDS 2004.

for children, appoint more child-friendly officers, and ensure the proper implementation of the JJ Act.

Special Provisions for Children in Distress/ Difficult Circumstances

6.148 Migration to cities by families forces children to drop out of schools who then find themselves on the streets. Most are unable to continue their education and end up becoming child labourers or beggars. Away from the secure environment of the villages, many are exposed to substance, drug, and sexual abuse.

6.149 Street children or children living and working on the streets are a common phenomenon in urban India. Yet despite their relatively high visibility, very little information is available on their exact numbers. Given the limited number of shelters in the cities, these children are often exploited and harassed by the police. They are vulnerable to hunger, malnutrition, lack of health care and education, physical and sexual abuse, substance abuse, and STD/HIV/AIDS. There is neither ICDS nor school for them. Many are forced into begging. The Eleventh Plan proposes setting up of walk-in ICDS centres at railway stations and bus stands (where most migrant children arrive and where many street children and beggars are found). These centres will offer food to any child who walks in after a proper health check-up and distribution of appropriate medicines and identity cards.

6.150 Another set of children who are often neglected are the children of prisoners. The fact that a large number of women prisoners are with children (or have children in prisons), means that this category of deprived children suffer from social isolation and absence of healthy interaction. Those separated from their imprisoned mothers and fathers have different problems. Their problems are largely the hidden and uncalculated costs of imprisonment. The National Plan of Action 2005 as well as the Juvenile Justice (Care and Protection) Act has now finally recognized their need for care and protection.

Providing for Special Needs of Differently Abled Children

6.151 Ministries of Social Justice and Empowerment and Health and Family Welfare deal with the subject of disability. Yet it is critical to see disability as a child protection issue as well. Even today, data related to disability among children varies with source. It is estimated that hardly 50% disabled children reach adulthood, and no more than 20% survive till the fourth decade of life.[24] Although there is very little information regarding the nutritional status of children with disabilities, it is recognized that disabled children living in poverty are among the most deprived in the world. Discrimination and often abandonment is a reality for them. Data of disabled children in school reveals that integration of the disabled into the education system is a distant reality. Ensuring access to education, health, and nutrition for children with disabilities is a formidable challenge for the Eleventh Plan. The Plan will ensure among other things, provision of ramps in schools, development of disabled friendly curricula, and training and sensitization of teachers.

Rehabilitating Children Affected by Substance Abuse

6.152 A survey reveals that out of all the children who came for treatment to various NGOs, 63.6% were introduced to drugs before the age of 15 years. According to recent data, among those involved in drugs and substance abuse in India, 13.1% are below 20 years of age.[25] This problem is especially widespread in the NER and Punjab. In the Eleventh Plan, children of this group will get special attention. Measures for rehabilitation backed by proper counselling and sensitive de-addiction camps will be undertaken.

Ensuring Child Mental Health

6.153 At any given time, 7–15% or 65 million Indian children suffer from significant mental disorder.[26] This is in addition to the stress-related suicides and deaths that are a leading cause of mortality among young adults. There is currently no budgetary allocation for

[24] M.L. Kataria, 'War against disability-fighting for the right of the child', 29.5.2002, *www.tribuneindia.com*

[25] UNDOC, Rapid Assessment Survey: The Extent, Pattern and Trend of Drug Abuse in India.

[26] ICMR, 2001; Malhotra, 2005.

child and adolescent mental health. Mental health of children is an issue that the Eleventh Plan will fund and take up on priority basis. Counsellors will be appointed in all schools and helplines will be set up especially during exams.

Simplifying Adoption Procedures and Preventing Unscrupulous Practices

6.154 Despite recognition of adoption as the most important mechanism for provision of alternative care and family to a child, procedures and laws were, till recently, cumbersome and inadequate. Adoptions took place under the Hindu Adoption and Maintenance Act (HAMA) 1956 and Guardians and Wards Act 1890. HAMA's applicability is restricted to Hindus (including Buddhists, Jains, and Sikhs). Since the enactment of the Juvenile Justice (Care and Protection of Children) Act 2000 adoption, both domestic as well as inter-country, is now also possible under it and this amendment allows everyone without any bias of caste, creed, religion, or gender to adopt. The Eleventh Plan will promote adoption under the JJ Act 2000 that ensures adopted child the same status as that of a biological child.

Promoting Inter-Sectoral and Inter-Ministerial Action

6.155 In the Eleventh Plan every ministry/department will review its own policies, programmes, services, laws, budgets, and procedures to examine how it can incorporate and integrate better development and protection of children. Some of the general principles of such a review will include monitoring exclusion/disparity in access by groups and communities, availability of gender disaggregated child data, enforcement of law and guidelines for protection and development of children, integration of children' participation in policies and programmes, and specific provision for the girl child. Further, each sector will be advised to take up child budget analysis and publish reports on the progress of child indicators.

6.156 In order to ensure adequate coordination and convergence for achieving the goals for children, M/oWCD will ensure wider representation and invigorated participation in the National Coordinating Group at the central level; establishment of similar groups at State level will be encouraged. The effective functioning of this mechanism is most important for ensuring better outcomes for children and safeguarding their rights.

CHILD BUDGETING

6.157 The MoWCD has been analysing allocations and expenditures on children since 2002–03. In the Eleventh Plan this exercise in child budgeting will be carried out regularly to monitor the 'outlays to outcome' and examine the adequacy of investments in relation to the situation of children in India.

CONCLUSION

6.158 The Eleventh Plan marks a big step forward in the area of women agency and child rights. It is entrenched in a rights framework that views women and children as agents, not recipients. It recognizes heterogeneity within groups, acknowledges multiple discriminations, and suggests pilots to tackle them. Some of these pilots, it is hoped will develop into full-fledged schemes after the mid-term appraisal of the Plan. The aim of these schemes, pilots and the Plan in general is not just to meet the monitorable targets set out; rather to develop a new paradigm wherein women and children find place within all sectors, ministries, departments, and schemes. This alone can ensure that the status of women and children grows exponentially at the beginning of the Twelfth Plan. This alone can carry forward the momentum for justice and equality set by the government through several Eleventh Plan initiatives.

6.159 The total projected GBS for the Eleventh Five Year Plan for the MoWCD is Rs 48420 crore (at 2006–07 prices) and Rs 54765 crore (at current prices). Details are given in Appendix to Volume III.

ANNEXURE 6.1
Selected Development Indicators Relating to Women

Sl. No.	Indicators	Women	Men	Total	Women	Men	Total
Demography							
1.	Population (in million in 1991 & 2001)	407.07	439.23	846.30	496.4	532.1	1028.6
2.	Decennial Growth (1971 & 2001)	24.03	25.52	24.80	23.08	22.26	22.67
Vital Statistics							
3.	Sex Ratio (1991 & 2001)	927	–	–	933	–	–
4.	Expectation of Life at Birth (1991–96 to 2001–05)	61.7	60.6	–	66.1	63.8	–
5.	Mean Age at Marriage (1991 & 1997)	19.5	23.9	–	19.5	NA	–
Health							
6.	Birth Rate (1991 & 2005)	–	–	29.5	–	–	23.8
7.	Death Rate (1991 & 2005)	–	–	9.8	7.1	8.0	7.6
8.	IMR (1991 & 2005)	–	–	80	61	56	58
9.	Child Mortality rate (1991 & 2005)	–	–	26.5	18.2	16.4	17.3
10.	MMR (1997–98 & 2001–03)	398	–	–	301	–	–
Literacy and Education							
11.	Literacy Rates (1991 & 2004–05)	39.3	64.1	52.2	57.00	77.00	67.30
	Literacy Rates, SCs	23.8	49.9	37.4	41.9	66.6	54.7
	Literacy Rates, STs	18.1	40.7	29.6	34.8	59.2	47.1
12.	Gross Enrolment Ratio (1990–91 & 2004–05)						
	Classes I–V	85.5	114.0	100.1	104.67	110.70	107.80
	Classes I–VIII	70.8	100.0	86.0	89.87	96.91	93.54
	Classes VI–VIII	47.0	76.6	62.1	65.13	74.30	69.93
13.	Dropout Rate (1990–91 & 2004–05 [Provisional])						
	Classes I–V	46.0	40.1	42.6	25.42	31.81	29.00
	Classes I–VIII	65.1	59.1	60.9	51.28	50.49	50.84
	Classes I–X	76.9	67.5	71.3	63.88	60.41	61.92
	SC Classes I–X	83.4	74.3	77.7	74.17	69.11	71.25
	ST Classes I–X	87.7	83.3	85.0	80.66	77.75	78.97
Work and Employment							
14.	Work Participation Rate (1991 & 2001)	22.3	51.6	–	25.7	51.9	–
15.	Organized Sector (No. in lakh in 1991 & 1999)	3.8	23.0	26.7	4.8	23.3	28.1
16.	Government (No. in lakh in 1997)	1.6	9.1	10.7	–	–	–
Decision Making (Administrative & Political)							
17.	Administrative (IAS in 1997 & 2000)	512 (10.2%)	4479	4991	535 (10.4%)	4624	5159
18.	PRIs (Figures in thousand for 2006)				916.61 (42.8% of total)	1225	2141.61
19.	Parliament (No. in 2001 & 2005)	70 (8.5%)	750	820	73 (9.24%)	717	790
20.	Central Council of Ministers (1985 & 2001)	4 (10.0%)	36	40	8 (10.8%)	66	74
Crime against women							
21.	2001 & 2005	143795	–	–	155553	–	–

Source: 1 to 4—Census of India; 5—SRS, Registrar General of India; 6 to 10—Family Welfare Statistics in India, 2006; 11 to 13—Selected Educational Statistics, 2004–05; 14 to 16—Census of India, Registrar General of India; 17, 19, 20—NRCW Website; 18—Statistics on Women, National Institute of Public Cooperation and Child Development 2007; 21—NCRB Website.

Eleventh Five Year Plan
(2007–2012)

Agriculture, Rural Development, Industry, Services and Physical Infrastructure

Volume III

सत्यमेव जयते

Planning Commission
Government of India

OXFORD
UNIVERSITY PRESS

YMCA Library Building, Jai Singh Road, New Delhi 110 001

Oxford University Press is a department of the University of Oxford. It furthers the University's objective of excellence in research, scholarship, and education by publishing worldwide in

Oxford New York

Auckland Cape Town Dar es Salaam Hong Kong Karachi Kuala Lumpur Madrid Melbourne Mexico City Nairobi New Delhi Shanghai Taipei Toronto

With offices in

Argentina Austria Brazil Chile Czech Republic France Greece Guatemala Hungary Italy Japan Poland Portugal Singapore South Korea Switzerland Thailand Turkey Ukraine Vietnam

Oxford is a registered trademark of Oxford University Press in the UK and in certain other countries

Published in India
By Oxford University Press, New Delhi

© Planning Commission (Government of India) 2008

The moral rights of the author have been asserted

First published 2008

All rights reserved. No part of this publication may be reproduced or transmitted, in any form or by any means, electronic or mechanical, including photocopying, recording or by any information storage and retrieval system, without permission in writing from Planning Commission, Government of India

ISBN-13: 978-0-19-569650-9
ISBN-10: 0-19-569650-6

Typeset in Minion in 11/13
by Excellent Laser Typesetters, Pitampura, Delhi 110 034
Printed by Tara Art Printers Pvt. Ltd., Noida
Published by Oxford University Press
YMCA Library Building, Jai Singh Road, New Delhi 110 001
On behalf of Planning Commission, Government of India, Yojna Bhawan,
Sansad Marg, New Delhi 110 001

V. Physical Infrastructure

Appendix

Contents

Tables

Figures

Boxes

Annexures

Acronyms

3G	Third Generation
A&N Islands	Andaman and Nicobar Islands
AAI	Airports Authority of India
AAUI	Automobile Association of Upper India
ABB	Asea Brown Boveri Ltd
ACA	Additional Central Assistance
ACI	Aero Club of India
ACZs	Agro-Climatic Zones
ADB	Asian Development Bank
AGR	Adjusted Gross Revenue
AI	Air India
AIBP	Accelerated Irrigation Benefit Programme
AICL	Air India Charters Limited
AICRP	All-India Co-ordinated Research Project
AIDS	Acquired Immuno Deficiency Syndrome
AIR	All-India Radio
ALHW	Andaman Lakshadweep Harbour Works
ALIMCO	Artificial Limbs Manufacturing Corporation
AMR	Addition, Modification and Replacement
ANDA	Abbreviated New Drug Application
AP	Annual Plan
AP	Andhra Pardesh
APDRP	Accelerated Power Development and Reforms Programme
APEDA	Agricultural and Processed Food Products Export Development Authority
APES	Apparel Parks for Exports Scheme
API	Active Pharmaceutical Ingredient
APM	Administered Price Mechanism
APMC	Agricultural Product Marketing Committee
ARAI	Automotive Research Association of India
ASI	Annual Survey of Industries
AT&C	Aggregate Technical and Commercial
ATF	Aviation Turbine Fuel
ATI	Automotive Training Institutes
ATM	Air Traffic Management
ATMAs	Agriculture Technology Management Agencies
AUWSP	Accelerated Urban Water Supply Programme
AVT	Artisan, Village, and Tiny
AWBI	Animal Welfare Board of India
BALCO	Bharat Aluminium Co. Ltd
BARC	Bhabha Atomic Research Centre
BC	Business Correspondents
BCAS	Bureau of Civil Aviation Security
BCCL	Bharat Coking Coal Limited
bcm	billion cubic metre
BCPL	Brahmaputra Cracker and Polymer Ltd

BCPL	Bengal Chemicals and Pharmaceuticals Limited
BDDS	Bomb Detection and Disposal Squad
BE	Budget Estimate
BEE	Bureau of Energy Efficiency
BG	Broad Gauge
BHEL	Bharat Heavy Electricals Ltd
BIFR	Bureau of Industrial and Financial Reconstruction
Bih	Bihar
BIFR	Bureau of Industrial and Financial Reconstruction
BIS	Bureau of Indian Standards
BkWh	billion kilowatt hours
BLA	BLA Industries
BMI	Body Mass Index
BMTC	Bangalore Metropolitan Transport Corporation
BMTPC	Building Materials and Technology Promotion Council
BMS	Basic Minimum Services
BOO	Build–Own–Operate
BOT	Build, Operate, and Transfer
BPCL	Bharat Petroleum Corporation Ltd
BPL	Below Poverty Line
BPO	Business Process Outsourcing
BRDB	Border Roads Development Board
BRGF	Backward Regions Grant Fund
BRK	Brick Kiln
BRO	Border Roads Organization
BRPL	Bongaigaon Refineries and Petrochemicals Ltd
BRPSE	Board for Reconstruction of Public Sector Enterprises
BS	Budgetary Support
BSNL	Bharat Sanchar Nigam Ltd
BSUP	Basic Services to the Urban Poor
Bt	Billion tonne
BTKM	Billion Tonne Kilometre
btu	British Thermal Unit
BU	Billion Unit
C-DOT	Centre for Development of Telematics
CAA	Constitution Amendment Act
CACP	Commission for Agricultural Costs and Prices
CAD	Command Area Development
CAD	Computer Aided Design
CADWM	Command Area Development and Water Management
CAGR	Compound Annual Growth Rate
CAMPA	Compensatory Afforestation Fund Management and Planning Authority
CARA	Central Adoption Resource Agency
CART	Credit Appraisal and Rating Tool
CAS	Conditional Access System
CBM	Coal Bed Methane
CBOs	Community Based Organizations
CBSP	Capacity Building for Service Provider
CBVS	Chanderi Bunkar Vikas Samiti
CBWE	Central Board for Workers' Education
CCA	Culturable Command Area
CCBs	Central Co-operative Banks
CCDA	Coal Conservation and Development Act
CCEA	Cabinet Committee on Economic Affairs
CCL	Central Coalfields Limited
CCO	Coal Controller Organization
CDI	Coal Dust Injection
CDMA	Code Division Multiple Access
CDP	City Development Plan
CDSCO	Central Drugs Standard Control Organization
CEA	Central Electricity Authority
CERC	Central Electricity Regulatory Commission
CENVAT	Central Value-Added Tax
CERT-In	Indian Computer Emergency Response Team
CFC	Common Facility Centre
CFS	Container Freight Station
CFt	Cubic Feet
CGWB	Central Ground Water Board
Cha	Chhattisgarh
CHMS	Complaints Handling Management System
CIC	Community Information Centre
CIDC	Construction Industry Development Council

CII	Confederation of Indian Industries
CIL	Coal India Limited
CIPET	Central Institute of Plastics Engineering and Technology
CIRT	Central Institute of Road Transport
CITES	Convention on International Trade in Endangered Species of Wild Fauna and Flora
CLA	Central Loan Assistance
CLCS	Credit-Linked Capital Subsidy
CLCSS	Credit Linked Capital Subsidy Scheme
CLIFF	Community-linked Finance Facility
CMTI	Central Manufacturing Technology Institute
CNS	Communication, Navigations and Surveillance
CoI	Committee on Infrastructure
COIN	Co-operative Bank Information Network
COSCAP	Co-operative Development of Operational Safety and Continuing Airworthiness Programme
CPCL	Chennai Petroleum Corporation Ltd
CPCSEA	Committee for the Purpose of Control and Supervision of Experiments on Animals
CPDS	Chemical Promotion and Development Scheme
CPL	Commercial Pilot Licence
CPP	Calling Party Pays
CPP	Captive Power Plant
CPPRI	Central Pulp and Paper Research Institute
CPSE	Central Public Sector Enterprise
CPSU	Central Public Sector Undertaking
CRC	Chawki Rearing Centre
CRF	Central Road Fund
CRRI	Central Road Research Institute
CSB	Central Silk Board
CSC	Common Service Centre
CSD	Cutter Suction Dredger
CSIR	Council of Scientific and Industrial Research
CSL	Cochin Shipyard Ltd
CSO	Central Statistical Organization
CSS	Centrally Sponsored Schemes
CST	Central Sales Tax
CTL	Coal To Liquid
CTSA	Central Tibetan School Administration
CUM	Cubic Metre
CUSP	Cryogenic Upper Stage Project
CVs	Commercial Vehicles
CWC	Central Water Commission
CWDB	Central Wool Development Board
CZA	Central Zoo Authority
DAC	Department of Agriculture and Co-operation
DAE	Department of Atomic Energy
DAHDF	Department of Animal Husbandry, Dairying, and Fisheries
DAP	Di-Ammonium Phosphate
DARE	Department of Agricultural Research and Education
DBT	Department of Biotechnology
DC	Development Commissioner
DCI	Dredging Corporation of India
DD	Doordarshan
DDHPY	Deen Dayal Hathkargha Protsahan Yojana
DDP	Desert Development Plan
Del	Delhi
DFC	Dedicated Freight Corridor
DFID	Department for International Development
DFP	Directorate of Field Publicity
DFPD	Department of Food and Public Distribution
DGCA	Directorate General of Civil Aviation
DGH	Directorate General of Hydrocarbon
DGLL	Directorate General of Lighthouses and Lightships
DGMS	Directorate General of Mines Safety
DGPS	Differential Global Positioning Systems
DG (S)	Directorate General of Shipping
DHI	Department of Heavy Industry
DIL	Direct Industrial License

DIPP	Department of Industrial Policy and Promotion
DIT	Department of Information Technology
DMF	Drug Master File
DMIC	Delhi–Mumbai Industry Corridor
DPAP	Drought Prone Area Programme
DPC	District Programme Co-coordinator
DPE	Department of Public Enterprises
DPR	Detailed Project Report
DoDWS	Department of Drinking Water Supply
DOE	Directorate of Extension
DoNER	Development of North East Region
DoP	Department of Posts
DoRTH	Department of Road Transport and Highways
DoT	Department of Telecommunications
DRDA	District Rural Development Agency
DRM	Digital Radio Mondiale
DSIR	Department of Scientific and Industrial Research
DSL	Digital Subscriber Lines
DSM	Demand Side Management
DTH	Direct To Home
DTO	District Transport Office
DVC	Damodar Valley Corporation
DWCUA	Development of Women and Children in Urban Areas
DWT	Dead Weight Tonnage
E&I	Roads of Economic and Interstate Importance
E&P	Exploration and Production
EAPs	Externally Aided Projects
EBR	Extra Budgetary Resources
EC	Expert Committee
ECBC	Energy Conservation Building Codes
ECE	Economic Commission for Europe
ECL	Eastern Coalfields Limited
EDI	Electronic Data Interchange
EDP	Entrepreneurship Development Programme
EFC	Expenditure Finance Committee
EFR	Environment Flow Releases
EGS	Education Guarantee Scheme
EIA	Environmental Impact Assessment
EIC	Export Inspection Council
EMSC	Environmental Measures and Subsidence Control
EOR	Enhanced Oil Recovery
ERC	Expenditure Reform Committee
ERM	Extension, Renovation, and Modernization
ERP	Enterprise Resource Planning
ESA	External Support Agencies
EU	European Union
EV	Electric vehicle
EWS	Economically Weaker Sections
FAB	Fabrication Units
FAO	Food and Agricultural Organization
FAR	Floor Area Ratio
FASAL	Forecasting Agriculture Output using Space, Agro-Meteorology, and Land-based Observation
FBRs	Fast Breeder Reactors
FCI	Food Craft Institute
FCRI	Fluid Control Research Institute
FDA	Forest Development Agency
FDDI	Footwear Design and Development Institute
FDI	Foreign Direct Investment
FICCI	Federation of Indian Chambers of Commerce and Industry
FM	Frequency Modulation
FO	Furnace Oil
FOB	Free On Board
FOIS	Freight Operation Information System
FPI	Food Processing Industry
FPR	Flood Prone River
FR	Feasibility Report
FRM	Fertilizer Raw Material
FSI	Floor Space Index
FSI	Forest Survey of India
FTA	Free Trade Agreement
FTII	Film and Television Institute of India
FTL	Fluorescent Tube Light
FWW	Four Wheeler Wagon
G&P	Ginning and Pressing
GAIL	Gas Authority of India Ltd
Gbps	Gigabits per second
GBS	Gross Budgetary Support
GCF	Gross Capital Formation
GCV	Gross Calorific Value

GDCF	Gross Domestic Capital Formation
GDP	Gross Domestic Product
GER	Gross Enrolment Ratio
GHz	Gigahertz
GI	Geographical Indication
GIS	Geographic Information Systems
GLP	Good Laboratory Practices
GMP	Good Manufacturing Practice
GoI	Government of India
GoM	Group of Ministers
GP	Gram Panchayat
GPS	Global Positioning System
GQ	Golden Quadrilateral
GRE	Graduate Record Examination
GSI	Geological Survey of India
GSM	Global System for Mobile Communications
GSPC	Gujarat State Petroleum Corporation Limited
GSRDC	Gujarat State Road Development Corporation
GST	Goods and Service Tax
GT	Gross Tonnages
Guj	Gujarat
GVA	Gross Value Added
GW_e	Gigawatt Electrical
GW-Yr	Gigawatt Year
ha	Hectare
HACCP	Hazard Analysis and Critical Control Point
Har	Haryana
HCI	Hotel Corporation of India
HCL	Hindustan Copper Ltd
HCR	Headcount Ratio
HDTV	High Definition Television
HEMM	Heavy Earth Moving Machinery
HEP	Hydro Electric Project
HFC	Housing Finance Company
HH	Household
HMCPs	Hardware Manufacturing Cluster Parks
HP	Himachal Pradesh
HOCL	Hindustan Organics Chemicals Limited
HPC	High Powered Inter-Ministerial Committee
HPCL	Hindustan Petroleum Corporation Ltd
HPL	Hindustan Prefab Limited
HR	Human Resource
HRD	Human Resource Development
HSL	Hindustan Shipyard Ltd
HUDCO	Housing Urban Development Corporation
HZL	Hindustan Zinc Ltd
I&B	Information and Broadcasting
I&M	Industry and Minerals
IAY	Indira Awaas Yojana
IBM	Indian Bureau of Mines
IBP	Indo Burma Petroleum Company Ltd
IC	Integrated Circuits
ICAR	Indian Council of Agricultural Research
ICDS	Integrated Child Development Services
ICE	Information, Communication and Entertainment
ICFRE	Indian Council of Forestry Research and Education
ICML	Integrated Coal Mining Ltd
ICPS	Integrated Child Protection Scheme
ICRIER	Indian Council for Research on International Economic Relations
ICT	Information and Communication Technology
ID	Industrial Dispute
IDA	International Development Association
IDLS	Integrated Development of Leather Sector
IDSMT	Integrated Development of Small and Medium Towns
IDTR	Institute of Driving Training and Research
IEBR	Internal and Extra Budgetary Resource
IEC	Information, Education, and Communication
IEM	Industrial Entrepreneur Memoranda
IEPR	Integrated Energy Policy Report

IFFCO	Indian Farmers Fertilizer Co-operative Ltd
IGCAR	Indira Gandhi Centre for Atomic Research
IGCC	Integrated Gasification Combined Cycle
IGRUA	Indira Gandhi Rashtriya Uran Akademi
IHM	Institutes of Hotel Management
IHSDP	Integrated Housing and Slum Development Programme
IID	Integrated Infrastructure Development
IIFM	Indian Institute of Forest Management
IIM	Indian Institute of Management
IIMC	Indian Institute of Mass Communication
IIP	Index for Industrial Production
IISCO	Indian Iron and Steel Company
IIT	Indian Institute of Technology
IITM	Indian Institute of Tropical Metereology
IITTMs	Indian Institute of Tourism and Travel Management
IIUS	Industrial Infrastructure Upgradation Scheme
IL&FS	Infrastructure Leasing and Financial Services Ltd
ILCS	Integrated Low Cost Sanitation Scheme
ILD	International long distance
ILDP	Indian Leather Development Programme
IMD	Indian Meteorological Department
IMF	Irrigation Maintenance Fund
IMO	Instant money-order
IMR	Infant Mortality Rate
IMU	Indian Maritime University
INCOIS	Indian National Centre for Ocean Information Services
Indal	Indian Aluminium Company Limited
INSA	Indian National Shipowners' Association
IOC	Indian Oil Corporation
IODP	Integrated Ocean Drilling Programme and Geotechnoic
IOR	Improved Oil Recovery
IP	Internet Protocol
IPE	Institute of Public Enterprise
IPEA	International Preliminary Examining Authority
IPFT	Institute of Pesticides Formulation Technology
IPIRTI	Indian Plywood Industries Research and Training Institute
IPM	Integrated Pest Management
IPO	Indian Intellectual Property Office
IPRs	Intellectual Property Rights
IPTV	Internet Protocol Television
IR	Internal Resources
IRDA	Insurance Regulatory and Development Authority
IREDA	Indian Renewable Energy Development Agency
IREP	Integrated Rural Energy Programme
IRMRA	Indian Rubber Manufacturers Research Association
IRQP	Improvement of Riding Quality Programme
ISA	International Searching Authority
ISO	International Organization for Standardization
ISP	Internet Service Provider
IT	Information Technology
ITC	Industrial Training Centres
ITES	IT-enabled Services
ITI	Industrial Training Institute
ITS	Intelligent Transportation System
IWAI	Inland Waterways Authority of India
IWDP	Integrated Wasteland Development Project
IWT	Inland Water Transport
J&K	Jammu and Kashmir
JBIC	Japan Bank for International Cooperation
JFM	Joint Forest Management
Jha	Jharkhand
JKML	Jammu and Kashmir Mineral Ltd
JNNURM	Jawaharlal Nehru National Urban Renewal Mission
JNPT	Jawaharlal Nehru Port Trust
JSMDCL	Jharkhand State Mineral Development Corporation

JSPL	Jindal Steel and Power Ltd
JV	Joint Venture
JVC	Joint Venture Company
K–G	Krishna–Godavari
Kar	Karnataka
KBK	Koraput, Bolangir, and Kalahandi
Kcal	Kilocalorie
KCCs	Kisan Credit Cards
Ker	Kerala
Kg	Kilogram
Kgoe	Kilogram of oil equivalent
Km	Kilometre
KPO	Knowledge Process Outsourcing
KRIBHCO	Krishak Bharati Co-operative Limited
KRL	Kochi Refineries Ltd
KV	Kilo Volt
KVI	Khadi and Village Industries
KVIC	Khadi and Village Industries Commission
KVK	Krishi Vigyan Kendra
KW	Kilowatt
KWh	Kilowatt hour
KWp	Kilowatt peak
LEAP	Lifelong Education and Awareness Programme
LED	Light-emitting diode
LIC	Life Insurance Corporation
LIG	Low-Income Groups
LMT	Lakh Metric Tonnes
LNG	Liquefied Natural Gas
LOI	Letter of Intent
LSIs	Large-Scale Industries
m	metre
m^2	square metre
m^3	cubic metres
Mah	Maharashtra
MAMID	Mine Accident Analysis and Modernization of information Database
MAP	Medicinal and Aromatic Plant
MAT	Management Aptitude Test
MBC	Mail Business Centre
MCA	Model Concession Agreement
MCA	Ministry of Corporate Affairs
MCDR	Mineral Conservation and Development Rules
MCuM	Million Cubic Metres
MDM	Mid-day Meal
MDF	Mineral Development Fund
MDR	Major District Road
MECL	Mineral Exploration Corporation Ltd
MEMU	Mainline Electric Multiple Unit
MFI	Micro Finance Institution
MFPI	Ministry of Food Processing Industries
MGIRI	Mahatma Gandhi Institute for Rural Industrialization
MH	Million Hectare
MHRD	Ministry of Human Resources Development
MI	Minor irrigation
MICE	Meetings Incentives Conventions and Exhibitions
MIS	Management Information Systems
MITI	Model Industrial Training Institute
ML	Mining Lease
MLAs	Members of Legislative Assembly
MMA	Macro Management Scheme
MMBtu	Million British Thermal Unit
MMI	Major and Medium Irrigation
MMP	Mission Mode Project
MMDR Act	Mines and Minerals (Development and Regulation) Act
MMSCMD	Million Standard Cubic Metres per Day
MNC	Multi-National Company
MNRE	Ministry of New and Renewable Energy
MoA	Union Ministry of Agriculture
MoC	Ministry of Coal
MoCA	Ministry of Civil Aviation
MoEF	Ministry of Environment and Forest
MoHUPA	Ministry of Housing and Urban Poverty Alleviation
MoI&B	Ministry of Information and Broadcasting
MoP	Ministry of Power
MOP	Muriate of Potash
MORD	Ministry of Rural Development
MoSRTH	Ministry of Shipping, Road Transport, and Highways
MoT	Ministry of Tourism

MoU	Memorandum of Understanding
MoWR	Ministry of Water Resources
MP	Madhya Pradesh
MPC	Metropolitan Planning Committee
MPLAD	Member of Parliament Local Area Development Programme
MPP	Marketing Promotion Programme
MPP	Multipurpose Project
MRIN	Marketing Research Surveys and Information Network
MRO	Maintenance, Repair, and Overhaul
MRPL	Mangalore Refineries and Petrochemicals Ltd
MRP	maximum retail price
MRTD	Marine Research and Technology Development
MRTS	Mass Rapid Transit System
MSE	Micro and Small Enterprise
MSME	Micro, Small, and Medium Enterprise
MSMED Act	Micro, Small, and Medium Enterprises Development Act
MSP	Minimum Support Prices
mt	metric tonnes
MTA	Mid-Term Appraisal
MTNL	Mahanagar Telephone Nigam Ltd
Mtoe	Million Tonne of Oil Equivalent
MU	Million Unit
MUTP	Mumbai Urban Transport Project
MUV	Multi-Utility Vehicle
MVA	Million Volt Amperes
MW	Megawatt
MW_e	Megawatt Electrical
NABARD	National Bank for Agriculture and Rural Development
NAEB	National Afforestation and Eco-development Board
NAEEB	National Afforestation, Ecorestoration, and Eco-development Board
NAEP	National Afforestation and Eco-Development Project
NAFUS	National Fund for the Unorganized Sector
NAIS	National Agricultural Insurance Scheme
NAL	National Aerospace Laboratories
NALCO	National Aluminium Company Ltd.
NAP	National Afforestation Programme
NARDCO	National Real Estate Development Council
NARS	National Agricultural Research System
NASSCOM	National Association of Software and ServiceCompanies
NATRIP	National Automotive Testing and R&D Infrastructure Project
NBC	Net Bank Credit
NBCC	National Building Construction Corporation
NBFC	Non-banking Financial Company
NBO	National Building Organization
NBS	Net Budgetary Support
NCA	Normal Central Assistance
NCAER	National Council for Applied Economic Research
NCAOR	National Centre for Antarctic and Ocean Research
NCCBM	National Council for Cement and Building Materials
NCDC	National Climatic Data Centre
NCERT	National Council of Educational Research and Training
NCEUS	National Commission for Enterprises in the Unorganized Sector
NCIWRD	National Commission on Integrated Water Resources Development
NCL	Northern Coalfields Ltd
NCLT	National Company Law Tribunal
NCMP	National Common Minimum Programme
NCMRWF	National Centre for Medium Range Weather Forecast
NCPCR	National Commission for Protection of Child Rights
NCR	National Capital Region
NCRPB	National Capital Region Planning Board
NDC	National Development Council
NDE	Non-Departmental Enterprise
NDDB	National Dairy Development Board
NDMA	National Disaster Management Authority
NE	North East/Eastern

NEC	North Eastern Coalfields
NEDFI	North Eastern Development Finance Corporation Ltd
NEF	National Electricity Fund
NEF	National Equity Fund
NEF (R&D)	National Energy Fund
NeGP	National e-Governance Plan
NEIP	North East Industrial Policy
NEKRTC	North East Karnataka Road Transport Corporation
NELP	New Exploration Licensing Policy
NER	North Eastern Region
NFBS	National Family Benefit Scheme
NFDB	National Fisheries Development Board
NFHS	National Family Health Survey
NGN	Next Generation Networks
NGOs	Non-Governmental Organizations
NH	National Highway
NHAI	National Highways Authority of India
NHB	National Housing Bank
NHDP	National Highway Development Programme
NHFDC	National Handicapped Finance and Development Corporation
NHM	National Horticulture Mission
NH (O)	National Highways (Original)
NHPC	National Hydroelectric Power Corporation Ltd
NIAM	National Institute of Agricultural Marketing
NIC	National Informatics Centre
NIC	National Industrial Classification
NICFS	National Institute of Criminology and Forensic Sciences
NICNET	National Informatics Centre Network
NID	National Institute of Design
NIFM	National Institute of Finance Management
NIFT	National Institute of Fashion Technology
NIOT	National Institute of Ocean Technology
NIPER	National Institute of Pharmaceutical Education and Research
NITs	National Institutes of Technology
NITA	National Institute of Tribal Affairs
NLC	Neyveli Lignite Corporation
NLCPR	Non-Lapsable Central Pool of Resources
NLD	National Long Distance
NLDCP	National Livestock Disease Control Programme
NLI	National Labour Institute
NLW	Non Linked Washery
NMBS	National Maternity Benefit Scheme
NMCC	National Manufacturing Competitiveness Council
NMDFC	National Minorities Development and Finance Corporation
NMT	Non-motorized Transport
NNM	National Nutrition Mission
NOAPS	National Old Age Pension Scheme
NOCs	National Oil Companies
NOVOD	National Oilseeds and Vegetable Oils Development Board
NPC	National Productivity Council
NPCIL	Nuclear Power Corporation of India Limited
NPK	Nitrogen–Phosphorus–Potassium
NPPA	National Pharmaceutical Pricing Authority
NPS	New Pricing Scheme
NRAA	National Rainfed Area Authority
NRC	National Referral Centre
NRC	National Research Centre
NRCP	National River Conservation Plan
NREG	National Rural Employment Guarantee
NREGA	National Rural Employment Guarantee Act
NREGP	National Rural Employment Guarantee Programme
NREGS	National Rural Employment Guarantee Scheme
NRHM	National Rural Health Mission
NRI	Non-Resident Indian
NRM	Natural Resource Management
NRSA	National Remote Sensing Agency
NS–EW	North–South and East–West
NSAP	National Social Assistance Programme

NSC	National Seed Corporation
NSDP	National Slum Development Programme
NSDP	National State Domestic Product
NSIC	National Small Industries Corporation
NSS	National Sample Survey
NSSO	National Sample Survey Organization
NSVS	National Service Volunteer Scheme
NTFP	Non-Timber Forest Produce
NTH	National Test House
NTKM	Net Tonne Kilometre
NTP	New Telecom Policy
NTPC	National Thermal Power Corporation
NUIF	National Urban Infrastructure Fund
NUIS	National Urban Information System
NW	National Waterway
NWDA	National Water Development Agency
NWDPRA	National Watershed Development Project for Rainfed Area
NWKRTC	North West Karnataka Road Transport Corporation
NWP	National Water Policy
NYKS	Nehru Yuva Kendra Sangathan
O&M	Operation and Maintenance
O&OEG	Oil and Oil Equivalent of Gas
OBCs	Other Backward Classes
OECD	Organization for Economic Co-Operation and Development
OEM	Original Equipment Manufacturer
OFC	Optical Fibre Cable
OIL	Oil India Ltd
OMIFCO	Oman India Fertilizer Company
OMS	Output per Man-Shift
OMT	Operation, Maintenance, and Tolling
ONGC	Oil and Natural Gas Corporation
OOH	Out-of-Home
OOIS	Ocean Observation and Information System
OSVs	Offshore Supply Vessels
OTC	Open Technology Centre
OVL	ONGC Videsh Ltd
PAP	Project-Affected Person/People
PBITEP	Profit before interest, tax, and EP
PCC	Pulverized Coal Combustion
PCO	Public Call Office
PCPDS	Pharma and Chemical Promotion and Development Scheme
PCPIRs	Petroleum, Chemicals, and Petrochemical Investment Regions
PCS	Port Community System
PCUs	Passenger Car Units
PDS	public distribution system
PEPSURTC	Punjab and East Punjab States Union Road Transport Corporation
PESA	Panchayat (Extension to Scheduled Areas) Act
PFDF	Pooled Finance Development Fund
PFMs	Postal Finance Marts
PGE	Platinum Group of Elements
PHE	Public Health Engineering
PHED	Public Health Engineering Department
PHHL	Pawan Hans Helicopters Ltd
PHM	Post-harvest Management
PHWR	Pressurized Heavy Water Reactor
PIA	Programme Implementation Agency
PIB	Public Investment Board
PIM	Participatory Irrigation Management
PIU	Programme Implementation Unit
PL	Prospecting License
PLF	Plant Load Factor
PLR	Prime Lending Rate
PMEGP	Prime Minister's Employment Generation Programme
PMGSY	Pradhan Mantri Gram Sadak Yojana
PMN	Polymettalic Nodules
PMRY	Prime Minister's Rozgar Yojana
PMS	Pavement Management Systems
POL	Petroleum, Oil, and Lubricants
PPP	Public–Private Partnership
PRIs	Panchayati Raj Institutions
PRODIP	Product Development, Design Intervention, and Packaging
PSCs	Powerloom Service Centres
PSCI	Postal Staff College India
PSE	Public Sector Enterprise
PSP	Pump Storage Project

PSU	Public Sector Undertaking
Pun	Punjab
PURA	Provision of Urban Amenities in Rural Areas
PVC	Polyvinyl Chloride
PWC	Pricewaterhouse Coopers
PWD	Persons With Disabilities
PWD	Public Works Department
QCI	Quality Council of India
Qts	Quintals
R&D	Research and Development
R&M	Renovation and Modernization
Raj	Rajasthan
RAS	Reclamation of Alkali Soil
RBI	Reserve Bank of India
RCF	Rashtriya Chemicals and Fertilizers Ltd
RCPs	Rural Community Phones
RCSRC	Regional Cyber Security Research Centre
RDG	Route Dispersal Guidelines
RE	Revised Estimate
REACH	Registration, Evaluation, and Authorization of Chemicals
REC	Rural Electrification Corporation Ltd
REGP	Rural Employment Generation Programme
RF	Radio Frequency
RFI	Radio Frequency Identification
RGGVY	Rajiv Gandhi Grameen Vidyutikarn Yojana
RGSY	Rashtriya Gram Swaraj Yojana
RIDF	Rural Infrastructure Development Fund
RINL	Rashtriya Ispat Nigam Ltd
RISC	Rural Industries Service Centes
RKM	Route Kilometres
RKVY	Rashtriya Krishi Vikas Yojana
RMC	Ready-Mix Concrete
RMK	Rashtriya Mahila Kosh
RMS	Risk Management System
RNI	Registrar of Newspaper for India
ROB	Road Over Bridge
RP	Reconnaissance Permit
RPO	Regional Project Office
RPS	Retention Price Scheme
RR	Rural Roads
RRBs	Regional Rural Banks
RSVY	Rashtriya Sam Vikas Yojana
RSY	Rashtriya Sadbhavana Yojana
RTA	Regional Trading Arrangement
RTKM	Revenue Tonne Kilometres
RTOs	Regional Transport Authorities
RUB	Road Under Bridge
RVP	River Valley Project
RW	Road Wing
S&T	Science and Technology
SAIL	Steel Authority of India Ltd.
SARDP-NE	Special Accelerated Road Development Programme for the North Eastern Region
SARS	Severe Acute Respiratory Syndrome
SAT	Scholastic Aptitude Test
SAUs	State Agricultural Universities
SBIRI	Small Business Innovation Research Initiative
SBLP	SHGs–bank linkage programme
SC	Scheduled Caste
SCA	Special Central Assistance
SCB	Scheduled Commercial Banks
SCCL	Singareni Collieries Company Ltd
SCDC	Scheduled Caste Development Corporation
SCI	Shipping Corporation of India
SCP	Special Component Paln
SDA	State Designated Agency
SDC	Strategic Distribution Centre
SDD	Song and Drama Division
SDF	Sustainable Development Framework
SDF	Sugar Development Fund
SEB	State Electricity Board
SECL	South Eastern Coalfields Ltd
SEI–CMM	Software Engineering Institute–Capacity Maturity Model
SERCs	State Electricity Regulatory Commissions
SES	Selected Educational Statistics
SEWA	Self Employed Women's Association
SEZ	Special Economic Zone
SFCI	State Farm Corporation of India

SFURTI	Scheme of Fund for Regeneration of Traditional Industries
SGRY	Sampoorna Grameen Rozgar Yojana
SGSY	Swaranjayanti Gram Swarozgar Yojana
SH	State Highway
SHG	Self-help Group
SHPI	SHG Promoting Institution
SHTP	Special Handicrafts Training Project
SIAs	State Implementing Agencies
SIDBI	Small Industries Development Bank of India
SISI	Small Industries Service Institutes
SITP	Scheme for Integrated Textile Parks
SJSRY	Swarna Jayanti Shahri Rozgar Yojana
SLDB	State Land Development Bank
SLNA	State-level Nodal Agency
SLPEs	State-level Public Enterprises
SME	Small and Medium Enterprise
SMP	Statutory Minimum Price
SOCFOD	Strengthening of Core Functions of DGMS
SPA	School of Planning and Architecture
SPS	Sanitary and Phytosanitary
SPUs	State Power Utilities
SPV	Special Purpose Vehicle
Sq M	Square Metre
Sq Km	Square Kilometre
SRs	State Roads
SREP	Strategic Research Extension Plans
SRFTI	Satyajit Ray Film and Television Institute
SRR	Seed Replacement Rate
SRSF	Special Railway Safety Fund
SRTUs	State Road Transport Undertakings
SRU	Ship Repair Unit
SS	Secondary School
SSA	Sarva Shiksha Abhiyan
SSCP	Sethusamudram Channel Project
SSIs	Small-Scale Industries
ST	Scheduled Tribe
STD	Sexually Transmitted Disease
STPI	Software Technology Parks of India
SWAN	State-Wide Area Network
T&CS	Thrift and Credit Societies
T&D	Transmission and Distribution
T&T	Travel and Tourism
TAT	Technical Assistance in Telecom Sector
TB	Tuberculosis
TCD	Metric Tonnes crushed per day
TCF	Trillion Cubic Feet
TCIDS	Textile Centres Infrastructure Development Scheme
TDSAT	Telecom Disputes Settlement and Appellate Tribunal
TEC	Telecom Engineering Centre
TETC	Telecom Testing and Security Certification Centre
TFC	Twelfth Finance Commission
TISCO	Tata Iron and Steel Company
TMC	Technology Mission on Cotton
TMT	Thousand Metric Tonne
TN	Tamil Nadu
TPD	Tonnes Per Day
TPY	Tonne per Year
TRAI	Telecom Regulatory Authority of India
TSC	Total Sanitation Campaign
TSD	Trailer Suction Dredger
TSP	Tribal Sub-Plan
TUFS	Technology Upgradation Fund Scheme
TVEs	Town and Village Enterprises
TWh	Trillion Watt hour
UAE	United Arab Emirates
UCG	Underground Coal Gasification
UGC	University Grants Commission
UHV	Useful Heat Value
UIDSSMT	Urban Infrastructure Development Scheme for Small and Medium Towns
UIP	Ultimate Irrigation Potential
UK	United Kingdom
ULBs	Urban Local Bodies
UMA&N	Undersea Cabling between Mainland and Andaman & Nicobar (A&N) Islands
UMBVS	Urmul Marusthali Bunkar Vikas Samiti
UMPP	Ultra-mega Power Project
UNCCD	United Nations Convention to Combat Desertification

UNCTAD	United Nations Conference on Trade and Development
UNDP	United Nations Development Programme
UNFC	United Nations Framework Classification
UNIDO	United Nations Industrial Development Organization
UP	Uttar Pradesh
UPA	United Progressive Alliance
URIF	Urban Reform Incentive Fund
US/USA	United States of America
USAID	United States Agency for International Development
USFDA	United Sates Food and Drug Administration
USO	Universal Service Obligation
USOF	Universal Service Obligation Fund
USP	Unique Selling Point
UT	Union Territory
Utt	Uttarakhand
VAMBAY	Valmiki Ambedkar Awas Yojana
VAT	Value-Added Tax
VGF	Viability Gap Funding
VLCC	Very Large Crude Carrier
VLF	Village Level Federation
VoIP	Voice over Internet Protocol
VPN	Virtual Private Network
VPT	Village Public Telephone
VRS	Voluntary Retirement Scheme
VSAT	Very Small Aperture Terminal
VSE	Village and Small Enterprises
VSNL	Videsh Sanchar Nigam Limited
WB	West Bengal
WCCU	World Class Central University
WCD	Women and Child Development
WCL	Western Coalfields Ltd
WDF	Watershed Development Fund
WDPSCA	Watershed Development Project for Shifting Cultivation Area
WHO	World Health Organization
WiFi	Wireless Fidelity
WII	Wildlife Institute of India
WiMAX	Worldwide Interoperability for Microwave Access
WLL	Wireless in Local Loop
WMO	Wireless Monitoring Organization
WPC	Wireless Planning & Co-ordination
WTO	World Trade Organization
WUA	Water Users Association
ZBB	Zero Based Budgeting

I
Agriculture

1

Agriculture

INTRODUCTION

1.1 Although its share in Gross Domestic Product (GDP) has declined from over half at Independence to less than one-fifth currently, agriculture remains the predominant sector in terms of employment and livelihood with more than half of India's workforce engaged in it as the principal occupation. Agriculture still contributes significantly to export earnings and is an important source of raw materials as well as of demand for many industries.

1.2 India's agriculture sector has an impressive long-term record of taking the country out of serious food shortages despite rapid population increase. This was achieved through a favourable interplay of infrastructure, technology, extension, and policy support backed by strong political will. The main source of long-run growth was technological augmentation of yields per unit of cropped area. This resulted in tripling of foodgrain yields, and foodgrain production increased from 51 million tonnes in 1950–51 to 217 million tonnes in 2006–07. Production of oilseeds, sugarcane, and cotton have also increased more than four-fold over the period, reaching 24 million tonnes and 355 million tonnes and 23 million bales, respectively, in 2006–07.

1.3 But, although GDP from agriculture has more than quadrupled, from Rs 108374 crore in 1950–51 to Rs 485937 crore in 2006–07 (both at 1999–2000 price), the increase per worker has been rather modest. GDP per agricultural worker is currently around Rs 2000 per month, which is only about 75% higher in real terms than in 1950 compared to a four-fold increase in overall real per capita GDP. While slower growth of GDP in agriculture than non-agriculture is expected, the main failure has been the inability to reduce the dependence of the workforce on agriculture significantly by creating enough non-farm opportunities to absorb the labour surplus in rural areas and equipping those in agriculture to access such opportunities. Half of those engaged in agriculture are still illiterate and just 5% have completed Higher Secondary education. Incomes and education are of course least among agricultural labourers. Even families operating farms now suffer from much smaller holdings (70% below 1 hectare in 2003 compared to 56% in 1982), and farming members in such families are twice as likely to be illiterate as non-farming members. Ensuring food security and farmer welfare thus require support systems to extend technology and scale benefits in a sustainable manner to a huge existing workforce in agriculture that lacks non-farm skills and is also ageing and getting feminized.

RECENT TRENDS AND CONCERNS

1.4 The Mid-Term Appraisal (MTA) for the Tenth Five Year Plan had drawn attention to the loss of dynamism in agriculture and allied sectors after the mid-1990s. In fact, during the last decade or so Indian agriculture has faced a number of severe challenges, superimposed on the long-term demographics. Recent trends that have raised concern regarding food security, farmers' income, and poverty are:

- Slowdown in growth.
- Widening economic disparities between irrigated and rain-fed areas.
- Increased vulnerability to world commodity price volatility following trade liberalization. This had an adverse effect on agricultural economies of regions growing crops such as cotton and oilseeds.
- Uneven and slow development of technology.
- Inefficient use of available technology and inputs.
- Lack of adequate incentives and appropriate institutions.
- Degradation of natural resource base.
- Rapid and widespread decline in groundwater table, with particularly adverse impact on small and marginal farmers.
- Increased non-agricultural demand for land and water as a result of the higher overall GDP growth and urbanization.
- Aggravation in social distress as a cumulative impact of the above, reflected in an upsurge in farmers' suicides.

1.5 Growth of agricultural GDP decelerated from over 3.5% per year during 1981–82 and 1996–97 to only around 2% during 1997–98 and 2004–05 (see Table 1.1). This deceleration, although most marked in rain-fed areas, occurred in almost all States and covered almost all major sub-sectors, including those such as horticulture, livestock, and fisheries where growth was expected to be high (see Table 1.3). Consequently, growth of agricultural GDP has been well below the target of 4% set in both Ninth and Tenth Plans. In fact, Tenth Plan growth averaged even less than that during

TABLE 1.1
Average GDP Growth Rates—Overall and in Agriculture
(% per Year at 1999–2000 Price)

Period	Total Economy	Agriculture and Allied Sectors	Crops and Livestock
1. Pre-green revolution 1951–52 to 1967–68	3.69	2.54	2.65
2. Green revolution period 1968–69 to 1980–81	3.52	2.44	2.72
3. Wider technology dissemination period 1981–82 to 1990–91	5.40	3.52	3.65
4. Early reforms period 1991–92 to 1996–97	5.69	3.66	3.68
5. Ninth Plan 1997–98 to 2001–02	5.52	2.50	2.49
6. Tenth Plan period 2002–03 to 2006–07	7.77	2.47	2.51
of which 2002–03 to 2004–05	6.60	0.89	0.89
2005–06 to 2006–07	9.51	4.84	4.96

Source: National Accounts Statistics 2008 (New Series), Central Statistical Organization, Ministry of Statistics and Programme Implementation, New Delhi.

TABLE 1.2
Growth Rates of National State Domestic Product (NSDP) from Agriculture
(States Ranked by % of Rainfed Area)

State	Growth Rate in NSDP Agriculture		Rainfed (%)	State	Growth Rate in NSDP Agriculture		Rainfed (%)
	1984–85 to 1995–96	1995–96 to 2004–05			1984–85 to 1995–96	1995–96 to 2004–05	
1	2	3	4	5	6	7	8
Punjab	4.00	2.16	3	Gujarat	5.09	0.48	64
Haryana	4.60	1.98	17	Rajasthan	5.52	0.30	70
Uttar Pradesh	2.82	1.87	32	Orissa	–1.18	0.11	73
Tamil Nadu	4.95	–1.36	49	Madhya Pradesh	3.63	–0.23	74
West Bengal	4.63	2.67	49	Karnataka	3.92	0.03	75
Bihar	–1.71	3.51	52	Maharashtra	6.66	0.10	83
Andhra Pradesh	3.18	2.69	59	Kerala	3.60	–3.54	85
All-India	3.62	1.85	60	Assam	1.65	0.95	86

Source: National Accounts Statistics, (State Series) Central Statistical Organization, Ministry of Statistics and Programme Implementation, New Delhi.

TABLE 1.3
Growth Rate in Output of Various Sub-sectors of Agriculture
(Gross Value of Output at 1999–2000 Price)

Period	Cereals	Pulses and Oilseeds	Fruits and Vegetables	Other Crops	All Crops	Livestock	Fishery
1951–52 to 1967–68	4.19	2.98	2.67	2.42	3.00	1.02	4.68
1968–69 to 1980–81	3.43	0.97	4.82	2.98	3.00	3.26	3.08
1981–82 to 1990–91	3.52	5.41	2.84	1.71	2.97	4.78	5.74
1991–92 to 1996–97	2.36	2.92	6.07	2.18	3.09	4.00	7.05
Ninth Plan 1997–98 to 2001–02	1.49	–1.43	4.11	3.82	2.25	3.53	2.63
Tenth Plan 2002–03 to 2006–07	1.28	4.29	2.97	3.58	2.46	3.69	3.23
of which 2002–03 to 2004–05	–1.27	5.95	0.30	1.57	0.42	3.32	1.77
2005–06 to 2006–07	3.52	1.61	6.97	6.59	5.53	4.23	5.49

Source: New Series of National Accounts Statistics, Central Statistical Organization, Ministry of Statistics and Programme Implementation, New Delhi.

Ninth Plan because, as was noted in the MTA, growth plummeted to below 1% during its first three years, that is from 2002–03 to 2004–05. There has been some upturn since then and growth has averaged more than 4% in the subsequent two years, with early indications that this is likely to be maintained in 2007–08 also. This revival gives hope that at least some of the causes of recent poor agricultural performance are being reversed and that the Eleventh Plan target, set at 4%, may actually be attainable.

1.6 The improved performance in the second half of Tenth Plan is a welcome development, but there is no reason for complacency. Not only is the period too short to reach firm judgment on trends, the prolonged deceleration over several years has meant that despite the improvements, per capita output of cereals, pulses, oilseeds, and also of some major vegetables and fruits (e.g., potatoes and bananas) in 2006–07 remained below 1996–97 levels. Moreover, despite significant imports, food prices flared up in 2006. This was unlike during 2000–05 when, although production was even lower, prices remained subdued because of low domestic demand and depressed world prices. Part of the recent production upturn is clearly price-led, following a marked hardening of world commodity prices and possibly also responding to the fact that domestic food demand has responded positively to higher overall GDP growth and the introduction of Rural Employment Guarantee. However, although important in the short-run, such price response alone cannot be the basis of sustained agricultural growth at 4%. The recent trend towards diversion of food crops for biofuels in surplus countries means that food security needs a stronger production response based on tackling supply side problems in the foodgrains sector.

1.7 The supply side performance of agriculture is affected by a large number of factors, several of which interact among each other. These factors are the natural resource base (including rainfall), technology, infrastructure (including irrigation), and the economic environment comprising price signals and institutions (Table 1.4). Analysis by the Steering Group for the Eleventh Plan has identified technological change (using yield potential of varieties of major crops released by the National Agricultural Research System [NARS] as a proxy), public investment (including investment on irrigation), and diversification (represented by area under fruits and vegetables) as the most important proximate determinants of growth. The Steering Group analysis shows (Table 1.4) that progress on first two of these factors slowed down from early 1990s. However, the negative effect in growth was offset by private investment, which was the fourth most important factor in the analysis, because the terms of trade, which affect profitability and thus private investment, improved during 1990–97. As a result, growth continued to be relatively high in this period. However, terms of trade turned against agriculture from 1999–2000 to 2004–05 and reduced profitability of farming quite sharply. This occurred partly because of low domestic food demand and partly because removal of quota

TABLE 1.4
Trend Growth Rate in Area, Input Use, Credit and Capital Stock in Agriculture—1980–81 to 2005–06

(% per Year)

Period	1980–81 to 1990–91	1990–91 to 1996–97	1996–97 to 2005–06
Technology#	3.3	2.81	0.00
Public sector net fixed capital stock	3.86	1.92	1.42*
Gross irrigated area	2.28	2.62	0.51*
Electricity consumed in agriculture	14.07	9.44	–0.53@
Area under fruits and vegetables	5.60	5.60	2.71@
Private sector net fixed capital stock	0.56	2.17	1.17*
Terms of trade	0.190	0.95	–1.69*
Total net fixed capital stock	2.00	2.06	1.28*
NPK use	8.17	2.45	2.30
Credit supply	3.72	7.51	14.37*
Total cropped area	0.43	0.43	–0.10
Net sown area	–0.08	0.04	–0.22
Cropping intensity	0.51	0.39	0.12

Note: # Yield potential of new varieties released of paddy, rapeseed/mustard, groundnut, wheat, maize, and cotton; * Upto 2003–04; @ Upto 2004–05.

restrictions under World Trade Organization (WTO) made Indian farm prices to become more aligned with corresponding international prices at a time when these were in decline. Private investment in agriculture stagnated as a result, the area cultivated fell, and diversification slowed down—all leading to deceleration. Moreover, public investment remained low and technology generation became negligible. Cutbacks following the Fifth Pay Commission in 1997 may have contributed to the problem as these cutbacks severely weakened the reach of critical support institutions—notably co-operatives, seed farms, and the extension system.

1.8 An important reason for recent farm distress was that after improving steadily from 1980 to 1997, terms of trade turned against agriculture from 1999 and, almost for the first time in post-independent India, farm prices actually fell at the same time that farm production decelerated. This not only depressed incomes, but also increased farm debt considerably. More generally, farmers are now subject to greater risk because variability of world prices is much higher than what Indian farmers have been used to in the past. There is need to evolve a clear policy on how to deal with this situation and some suggestions are made later in this chapter.

1.9 In the meantime, commodity futures markets that can potentially reduce price variability have grown massively in crop coverage and trading volume. At Rs 36.76 lakh crore in 2006–07, futures volumes now far exceed the volume of actual physical trade in agricultural commodities. But direct participation of farmers is negligible and price volatility does not appear to have reduced. A reason why futures markets are not being able to perform efficiently could be that these markets are very new and still in a learning phase. Quality specifications, delivery norms, margin, and lot size of most commodities traded at the bourses make it difficult for the average farmers to directly participate in exchange trading as hedgers. There is also a need to look at legal and regulatory regime and modify these to enable direct farmers' participation. For example, the passage of the Warehousing (Development and Regulation) Act 2006 makes possible the introduction of a regulated system of warehouse receipts which, along with investment in rural marketing infrastructure, can improve the effective reach of futures trading. Besides the poor direct participation of farmers, which is not unusual, available evidence is also that indirect benefit through reduced spot price volatility has been insignificant so far and the cash–future linkage is not very strong. However, futures markets do appear to have better integrated different spot market prices with each other and with world prices. This can benefit farmers by reducing local monopsony power, but it can also be problematic if the policy objective is to insulate domestic prices from full variability of world prices. Unless trade policy is broadly predictable in advance, futures can too quickly transmit international price shocks leading to controversy and knee-jerk reactions.

1.10 Another important development of market institutions is the rise of modern food retailing which offers the prospect of lower marketing costs and reduced spoilage leading to lower prices for consumers and higher realization for farmers. Modern retailing has become controversial partly because those involved in existing trading mechanisms feel their vested interests threatened. However, although there is room for mutually beneficial modernization in this area and this will undoubtedly evolve, a legitimate area of concern is that if front-end investment outpaces the backward linkage with farmers, the immediate outcome may simply be higher imports and lower farm prices. Clearly, efforts must be made to ensure more efficient spot and futures markets and more rapid development of the backward farm linkages of retailing.

1.11 An unfortunate trend over the past two decades has been that expenditure control efforts following fiscal shocks such as the Pay Commissions awards have led to cutbacks in agricultural investment and extension, but not in subsidies. Budgetary subsidies to agriculture have increased from around 3% of agriculture GDP in 1976–80 to about 7% in 2001–03. During the same period, public investment in agriculture declined from over 4% of agriculture GDP to 2%. Most of the subsidies are on fertilizer, power, and irrigation water and these have actually contributed to the degradation of natural resources. Further, a considerable amount of Plan expenditure on agriculture is not on investment but on subsidies not accounted for in the above list. Simplistic fiscal rules such as protecting Plan expenditures more than non-Plan expenditures add to the problem. For example, although the Plan share in States' total expenditure on agricultural and allied sectors has improved considerably from a low just after Fifth Pay Commission, much of this represents increase in Plan subsidies at the cost of essential staff, particularly in the extension system and the co-operative sector. With hindsight, it appears that the policy of restraining new hiring may have been excessive, as is evident from the age composition and high vacancies among extension staff and reduced reach of co-operatives. Even a relatively small percentage reduction in subsidies can finance relatively large increase in public investment in crucial areas such as soil amelioration, watershed development, groundwater recharge, surface irrigation, and other infrastructure and can also allow substantial expansion in the reach of critical farm support systems.

1.12 Nonetheless, an important policy gain of recent years is the turnaround in public investment in later years of the Tenth Plan, reversing years of decline. Overall capital formation in the sector is now 12% of agricultural GDP, which is the highest in 25 years. This must have contributed to the recent upturn in growth. But figures in Table 1.5 also imply that Incremental Capital Output Ratio has risen from about 2.5 to around 4. Unless efficiency of investment is restored, investment would need to increase much further, to about 16% of agricultural GDP, to achieve the 4% agricultural growth target.

1.13 In light of the above, the Eleventh Plan certainly needs to increase public investment further, from 3% of agricultural GDP to about 4%. But it also needs to do much more to ensure that future growth is more efficient, sustainable, and inclusive. This can be achieved by focusing on the following:

- With availability of land and water fixed, growth in agriculture can be achieved only by increasing productivity per unit of these scarce natural resources through effective use of improved technology. The research system has so far focused mainly on breeding varieties that increase the yield potential of individual crops by enabling more intensive use of inputs. Although such research did increase potential yields substantially in the past, it put less emphasis on efficient and sustainable use of soil nutrients and water, or on identifying location-specific farming systems with proper mix of crops and livestock, especially for rain-fed areas. Besides, the potential yields of new varieties being released

TABLE 1.5
Investment in Agriculture
(Rs in Crore at 1999–2000 Price)

Year	GDP from Agriculture	Gross Capital Formation (GCF) in Agriculture			GCF in Agriculture as % of GDP from Agriculture		
		Public Sector	Private Sector	Total	Public Sector	Private Sector	Total
1980–81 to 1984–85	239678	12007	13132	25139	5.0	5.5	10.5
1985–86 to 1989–90	274034	9601	14370	23971	3.5	5.2	8.7
1990–91 to 1994–95	325957	7915	19348	27263	2.4	5.9	8.4
1995–96 to 1999–2000	383330	7724	22631	30354	2.0	5.9	7.9
2000–01	407176	7155	31872	39027	1.8	7.8	9.6
2001–02	433475	8746	39468	48215	2.0	9.1	11.1
2002–03	398206	7962	38861	46823	2.0	9.8	11.8
2003–04	441360	9376	35457	44833	2.1	8.0	10.2
2004–05	441183	12273	36835	49108	2.8	8.3	11.1
2005–06	468013	15006	39899	54905	3.2	8.5	11.7
2006–07	485939	17749	43013	60762	3.7	8.9	12.5

Source: National Accounts Statistics 2008 (New Series), Central Statistical Organization, Ministry of Statistics and Programme Implementation, New Delhi.

seem to have plateaued suggesting that the current system is no longer leading to adequate outcomes. This 'technology fatigue' has to be countered by changing research priorities suitably.

- At the same time, frontline trials of various research departments provide clear evidence of large gaps between what can be attained at the farmer's field with adoption of available technology as compared to what is obtained with existing practices. Exploiting this potential must be the main source of yield growth in the Eleventh Plan because overcoming technology fatigue will take time. Moreover, since yield gaps vary considerably from crop-to-crop and from region-to-region, the strategy must enable specific plans for each agro-climatic region. As Table 1.6 shows, constraints vary considerably even by very aggregate zones. This will also require much stronger links between research, extension, and farmers.
- The pressing need to accelerate agriculture growth should not be at the cost of sustainability of our natural resource base, which is starkly limited. Deforestation has affected both soils and water and this is compounded by soil degradation and overexploitation of groundwater. Besides watershed development in watersheds where agriculture is important, a concerted effort is needed to afforest upper catchments at higher elevations of river basins. In addition to erosion, salinity, and alkalinity, soils are losing soil carbon and micronutrients due to irrational and unbalanced fertilizer use (Table 1.6). This must be addressed urgently since this directly affects input use efficiency. The seriousness of the problem can be seen from the fact that nearly two-thirds of our farmlands are in some way either degraded or sick and only about one-third are in good health. Rapid expansion of groundwater use for irrigation was a key factor in the relatively rapid growth of agriculture between the mid-1960s and late 1980s. But further expansion should be strictly monitored, especially in regions where aquifer levels have dropped causing concern about future sustainability. Action on the environmental front cannot wait in face of a possibly looming adverse climate change due to global warming.

1.14 For growth to be at all inclusive, the agricultural strategy must focus on the 85% of farmers who are small and marginal, increasingly female, and who find it difficult to access inputs, credit, and extension or to market their output. While some of these farmers may ultimately exit from farming, the overwhelming majority will continue to remain in the sector and the objective of inclusiveness requires that their needs are attended to. For example, credit has grown at unprecedented rates (30% per annum) to other sectors but not to small and marginal land holders and women who lack collateral security. Besides issues such as rights to land (especially for women), it is now well recognized that the poor are best empowered if they function as a group rather than as individuals. Hence there

TABLE 1.6
Region-specific Factors Causing Low Productivity

Agro-climatic Region	States/Parts of States	Region-specific Constraints
Western Himalayan region-I	J&K, HP, Uttaranchal	Severe soil erosion, degradation due to heavy rainfall/floods and deforestation, low SRRs, poor road, poor input delivery, inadequate communication infrastructure and marketing
Eastern Himalayan region-II	Assam, NE States, Sikkim	Aluminium toxicity and soil acidity, soil erosion and floods, shifting cultivation, low SRRs, non-availability of electricity, poor road, poor input delivery system and communication infrastructure
Lower and middle gangetic plains regions-III and IV	West Bengal, Bihar, Eastern UP	Flood/water logging, improper drainage, salinity/alkalinity, arsenic contamination, low SRRs, non-availability of electricity, high population growth, poor road and communication infrastructure
Upper and trans-gangetic plains region-V and VI	Western UP, Punjab, Haryana	Groundwater depletion, decreasing total factor productivity, micronutrient deficiency, non-availability of electricity, and high population density
Eastern plateau and hills region-VII	Orissa, Jharkhand, Chhattisgarh	Moisture stress, drought, and soil acidity, iron toxicity, low SRRs, non-availability of electricity, high population growth, poor road, poor input delivery and communication infrastructure

Source: Cited in Report of the Working Group of Sub-Committee of National Development Council on Agriculture and Related Issues on Region/Crop Specific Productivity Analysis and Agro-Climatic Zones, Planning Commission, Government of India (February 2007).

is a need to encourage a 'group approach' for the poor and for women to reap economies of scale and be effective farmers. A group approach could also improve the bargaining power of small cultivators in contract farming. The few examples where small and marginal farmers have benefited from contract farming are those where they have entered into contracts collectively rather than individually. In Punjab, Mahindra Shubhlabh Services Ltd followed this approach for maize farming with a number of safeguards for risk protection, etc., built in. Again in South India, the United Planter's Association of South India signed contracts with women's self-help groups (SHGs) for tea cultivation. One way forward to encourage marginal farmers and women to form groups for purposes of farming would be to shift at least some of the current subsidies to be available only to groups of such farmers rather than to individuals.

TENTH PLAN OUTLAYS AND EXPENDITURE

1.15 Against the projected Tenth Plan outlay of Rs 58933 crore on agriculture and allied sectors, the utilization is about the same as outlay in current price but likely to be only around 84% at the 2001–02 price. The utilization in the case of irrigation and flood control sector is also of the same order, that is 85%. In both the cases, much larger shortfalls in the first two years of the Plan were made up in subsequent years. Plan outlays in agriculture and allied sectors and in irrigation and flood control for the Centre, States, and union territories (UTs) are presented in Annexure 1.1.

1.16 The progress of outlay and expenditure during the Plan period for the three departments of the Union Ministry of Agriculture (MoA), namely, the Department of Agriculture and Co-operation (DAC), the Department of Animal Husbandry, Dairying, and Fisheries (DAHDF), and the Department of Agricultural Research and Education (DARE) is given in Table 1.7.

1.17 As may be seen, a substantial increase in outlay was provided to the Ministry of Agriculture since 2004–05 taking the Central Government's share of total plan expenditure on agriculture and allied sectors (Centre and States) from 33% in 2002–03 to 44% in 2006–07. The Ministry has introduced several new programmes during Tenth Plan aimed at diversification of agriculture, strengthening technology validation, demonstration and dissemination, water saving, and development of infrastructure. These include:

- The National Horticulture Mission (NHM) approved by the Cabinet Committee on Economic

TABLE 1.7
Outlay and Expenditure of Ministry of Agriculture during the Tenth Five Year Plan

(Rs Crore)

S. No.		Current Price				2001–02 Price			
		DAC	DAHDF	DARE	TOTAL	DAC	DAHDF	DARE	TOTAL
1.	Tenth Plan outlay (2002–07)*	13200.00	2500.00	5368.00	21068.00	13200.00	2500.00	5368.00	21068.00
2.	2002–03 (Expenditure)#	1655.94	238.90	650.75	2536.95	1593.9	221.6	626.4	2441.9
3.	2003–04 (Expenditure)#	2050.34	271.76	748.98	3068.67	1901.4	249.8	694.6	2845.8
4.	2004–05 (Expenditure)#	2656.26	566.22	816.01	4035.72	2360.2	500.6	725.1	3585.9
5.	2005–06 (Expenditure)#	3817.46	589.37	1046.75	5453.37	3247.5	501.2	890.4	4639.2
6.	2006–07 (RE)#	4860.00	679.32	1430.00	7040	3909.1	603.2	1150.2	5662.5
7.	Total expenditure	15040.00	2345.57	4692.49	22134.71	13012.1	2076.5	4086.7	19175.4
8.	Total expenditure as % of Tenth Plan outlay	114%	94%	87%	105%	99%	83%	76%	91%
9.	2007–08 BE	5520.00	910.00	1600	8030	–	–	–	–

Note: RE = Revised Estimate, BE = Budget Estimate.
Sources: * Tenth Five Year Plan (2002–07), Planning Commission, Government of India; # Union Expenditure Budgets, Vol. I, Ministry of Finance, Government of India, from 2002–03 to 2007–08.

Affairs (CCEA) on 19 May 2005 became operational during 2005–06.

- The government approved a Centrally sponsored ‘Micro Irrigation’ programme to help spread the network of water-saving implements such as sprinkler and drip irrigation throughout the country.
- A National Gender Resource Centre in Agriculture was set up in the directorate of extension as a focal point for convergence and co-ordination of gender-related issues within the DAC.
- Jute Technology Mission was approved in June 2006.
- The National Agricultural Innovation Project was launched by the Indian Council for Agricultural Research in July 2006. A National Fund for Basic and Strategic Research in Agricultural Sciences has also been set up in 2005–06. Both these will support agricultural research in project mode.
- The National Fisheries Development Board (NFDB) was formally set up at Hyderabad in September 2006 with the main objectives of bringing major activities relating to fisheries and aquaculture for focused attention and professional management.
- A new Centrally sponsored scheme (CSS) ‘National Mission on Bamboo Technology and Trade Development’ was approved in October 2006.
- The government decided to set up a Krishi Vigyan Kendra (KVK) in each rural district (578) in the country. So far over 537 KVKs have been established. These Kendras disseminate farm technologies to farmers and provide training to enhance the productivity and hence the income earning capacity of the farmers.
- Technology dissemination efforts are being strengthened further by establishing Agriculture Technology Management Agencies (ATMAs), which are autonomous bodies for extension planning and reform, in 252 districts. These will be extended to all rural districts.
- The National Rainfed Area Authority (NRAA) was constituted as an expert body to bring technical focus to problems of rainfed agriculture and to advise on design and convergence of various watershed development schemes.
- The Constitution (106th) Amendment Bill 2006 in respect of co-operatives was introduced in Lok Sabha on 22 May 2006.
- The government approved a rehabilitation package amounting to Rs 16978.69 crore for the farmers in distress in 31 selected districts in the four States, namely, Andhra Pradesh, Karnataka, Kerala, and Maharashtra. The package comprises relief from the Prime Minister’s Relief Fund, strengthening institutional credit support, irrigation development, promotion of micro irrigation, watershed development, extension services, enhancing seed replacement rate (SRR) and income augmentation through horticulture, livestock, and fishery in these districts.

AREAS OF CONCERN IN IMPORTANT EXISTING PLAN SCHEMES

1.18 Among major ongoing schemes of DAC, the largest is the Macro Management Scheme (MMA) which was initiated in 2000–01 by integrating 27 CSS so as to provide flexibility to the States to develop and pursue a mix of activities on the basis of their regional priorities. The approved pattern of assistance is in the ratio of 90:10 for the Centre and the States, respectively, except in the case of North Eastern States that get 100% Central assistance. With the launching of NHM in the year 2005–06, 10 schemes pertaining to horticulture development were taken out of the purview of this scheme. An evaluation of the scheme (in August 2004) by three institutions, namely, the Indian Institute of Management, Kolkata, the National Bank for Agriculture and Rural Development (NABARD) Consultancy Services Limited, and the Agricultural Finance Corp. Ltd brings out that the objective of flexibility was achieved but the work plans prepared by the States did not necessarily originate from the grass root level. These were generally prepared in a top-down process, and often did not reflect State priorities, thrust areas, and the initiatives for agricultural development. Further, there appeared to be lack of co-ordination among different departments. The funds were mainly retained by the nodal department, that is the Agriculture Department, resulting in neglect in some of the States of the schemes that were in the areas of Natural Resources Management and Co-operative Departments.

1.19 The Technology Mission on Oilseeds, Maize, Oil palm, and Pulses is being implemented for two decades for oilseeds. Pulses, oil palm, and maize were brought under the ambit of the mission in 1990–91, 1992, 1995–96. Although there has been a fairly substantial increase in production of oilseeds since its inception in 1986, domestic production of oilseed is short of the demand of edible oils in the country. The pulses production in the country has continued to be stagnant for decades suggesting that the pulses mission has not been effective.

1.20 Crop insurance was introduced in the country two decades ago. The present version, the National Agricultural Insurance Scheme (NAIS) has been available since 1999–2000. The Scheme's coverage is limited to a few States and a few crops only. If NAIS is to be retained, it is important to impart a measure of permanency to the Scheme by shifting it to non-Plan, with banks that are its principal beneficiaries contributing to the subsidy. If so, new additional actuarial schemes with subsidy on premia, involving larger number of service providers and wider menu of insurance products, can be considered for Plan financing. Some further details of agricultural insurance have been discussed later in the chapter.

1.21 The National Project on Cattle and Buffalo Breeding is the flagship scheme of DAHDF. Initiated in October 2000 for a period of 10 years, this envisages genetic upgradation of indigenous cattle and buffaloes, development and conservation of important indigenous breeds, and to evolve sustainable breeding policy. The project is being implemented by State Implementing Agencies (SIAs) in 26 States and 1 UT. This scheme suffers from many shortcomings, particularly quality of progeny bulls and inadequate attention to tagging and registry. Further, feed and fodder are a perennial problem for exotic breeds and efforts made during the Tenth Plan to improve feed and fodder resources for livestock were not very successful. The performance of the Central Fodder Development Organization was evaluated by The Centre for Management Development, Thiruvanthapuram and found to be unsatisfactory. Moreover, with the completion of 'Operation Flood' Project by National Dairy Development Board (NDDB), the pace of investment in dairy sector has slowed down. The allocation for dairy development by the Central and State Governments has also diminished over the last two plans. Assistance from Government of India under CSS, Intensive Dairy Development Programme, has gone to non-viable areas without conducting proper feasibility studies and has been implemented without proper technical supervision. Delicensing and the subsequent decision to do away with the concept of milk sheds were expected to boost private sector investment in dairying, but this has not happened. Furthermore, there appears to have been no concentrated efforts to invest in technology for development of value-added and innovative milk products. Consequently, in the first four years of the Tenth Five Year Plan, the growth rate of milk has been less than 3% per annum.

CHALLENGES FOR THE ELEVENTH PLAN

AGRICULTURAL RESEARCH

1.22 The major challenges facing us in formulating policy for the Eleventh Plan are discussed below.

1.23 The DARE has an extensive network comprising 48 Central Institutes, 5 National Bureaux, 12 Project Directorates, 32 National Research Centres (NRC), and 62 All-India Co-ordinated Research Projects (AICRP). It also supports research and education in 41 State Agriculture Universities, 5 Deemed Universities, and 1 Central Agriculture University. During Tenth Plan period 2 Indian Council of Agricultural Research (ICAR) institutes, 1 National Bureau, 3 Project Directorates, and 10 State Agricultural Universities (SAUs) have been established. Over the years, its co-ordinated trials have helped the nation improve varieties of sugarcane, rice, wheat, maize, sorghum, groundnut, mustard, etc., considering the ecological variations with respect to each crop. However, two glaring features are now obvious. First, the productivity achieved on farms has fallen short of those in the field trials. Clearly, the KVKs that have the mandate of technology validation and transfer have not delivered their full potential. Second, as observed earlier, there is some evidence of technological fatigue in terms of yields obtainable with the newest varieties being delivered by the NARS. Since access to international research is now much more circumscribed by intellectual property rights (IPRs), this will have to be addressed largely by toning up NARS capacity.

1.24 The following are critical research gaps:

- Integrating methods of traditional and modern biology giving attention to both yield and quality aspects.
- An orientation of public sector research in 'hybrid development with commercial viability' has to be reintroduced on a mission mode at least in crops like pigeon pea, soybean, and mustard.
- Indigenous plant types that inherently possess genes responsible for higher nutritive value (more protein, micronutrients, etc.) need to be identified and used for enriching nutrients in rainfed crops.
- The implications of climate change on agriculture and vice versa need to be studied and a dedicated research programme should be initiated to combat global warming.
- A major research thrust is warranted in areas of balanced and site-specific nutrient supply and efficient water management strategies.
- Integrated Pest Management (IPM) needs greater emphasis. The existing package of practices is not fully integrated between various plant protection sciences. This results in duplication, overlapping as well as unrealistic recommendations in the name of IPM. There is a need for interdisciplinary research in plant protection to elucidate basic issues of herbivory as well as to develop suitable mitigations.
- In horticulture, the research agenda needs to emphasize survey of indigenous biodiversity for resistance to various biotic and abiotic stresses for improvement in production, productivity, and quality of produce.
- In livestock, there is an urgent need to reorient research and assess the genetic potential of indigenous breeds. Intensive research work needs to be undertaken for genetic identification of traits of excellence in Indian breeds, such as Jaffarabadi buffalo, Black Bengal goat, Garole sheep, etc., and identify the functional genomics associated with their traits of excellence.
- With endemic shortage of animal feeds, research should explore technologies to augment feed resources, including genetic modification of microorganism to utilize high lignin forage grasses.
- With large quantities of animal products now being produced, research on process technologies, value addition, packaging, storage, transportation, and marketing should receive high priority. In the absence of a proper slaughter regime, there is considerable wastage and an effective package of practices for management of slaughterage needs to be evolved. Prevention of animal losses due to disease should be the major area of focus with emphasis on development of diagnostic kits and vaccine. The health of the human population is intimately connected to the health of the animal with several fatal and debilitating diseases being common to both man and animal. Serious attention to animal health care, disease diagnosis, and

prophylactics will go a long way in ensuring human health also.

- Overall, there is a need to identify integrated farming systems in different agro-ecological regions, internalizing synergies of different components to enhance resource utilization, income, and livelihood generation and minimize environmental loading.

1.25 It is necessary to take a comprehensive view of the functioning of the agricultural research system and make systemic changes in the course of the Eleventh Plan. Thus far, research has tended to focus mostly on increasing the yield potential by more intensive use of water and bio-chemical inputs. Far too little attention has been given to the long-term environmental impact or on methods and practices for the efficient use of these inputs for sustainable agriculture. These features are widely known but efforts to correct them have not been adequate; at any rate they have not made much of a difference.

1.26 Agricultural research is underfunded but lack of resources is not the only problem. Available resources also have not been optimally utilized because of lack of a clearly stated strategy that assigns definite responsibilities, prioritizes the research agenda rationally, and recognizes that the research mode is not always best suited for product development and delivery:

- Dominance of commodity-based research and development (R&D), that is lack of a holistic approach involving a matrix of farm enterprises.
- Strict compartmentalization of R&D agencies, i.e., lack of effective bilateral flow of information among research, extension, and implementation departments.
- Lack of large-scale on-farm validation of techniques and feedback thereon, leading to practically no scope for their refinement.

1.27 As far as possible, ICAR institutes should mainly undertake basic, strategic, and anticipatory research in line with national priorities, while SAUs do applied and adaptive research addressing location-specific problems, with complementarities also found between the public and private sectors in product development. A distinction also needs to be made between basic research which has knowledge advancement and scientific curiosity as its major focus and strategic research which is aimed at well-defined researchable problems which are of high development priority and worthy of multi-discipline and multi-institution effect on a mission mode.

1.28 A major paradigm shift is needed to transform the present commodity-based research to a systems approach. Since farm-level problems are specific to agro-climatic zones (ACZs), what is needed is a convergence between R&D agencies within individual ACZs so as to bring region-specificity in technologies and their time-bound assessment. This requires a seven-step mechanism:

- Problem identification and prioritization;
- Convergence of existing technologies to match the need;
- Generation of need-based viable technologies using the holistic farming system approach;
- On-farm assessment and evaluation;
- Feedback on the technologies;
- Refinement of technologies, if necessary;
- Ensuring timely availability of inputs.

1.29 This kind of approach will help in establishing a research-development-technology transfer continuum involving all stakeholders.

1.30 SAUs are the key to regionally relevant research and for generating quality human resources. Unfortunately, SAUs are so poorly funded by their own State Governments that some are in chronic overdraft, only a quarter are accredited, and almost all rely mainly on ICAR funding for research. This situation, where States still provide salary and establishment costs but SAUs look to ICAR for other funds, not only affects their education function adversely but it also distances SAUs from State Agricultural Departments and reduces relevance of their research for local problems. Thus, although Central support for revamping SAUs is justified, this is likely to be effective only where States recognize the value of agricultural education and research. An important criterion for identifying SAUs for support from the Centre should be the investment that the State itself is making. Moreover, the biggest problem with NARS remains that it is strictly governed by the same rules and regulations relating to expenditure and filling up of positions as operative in government departments of States and the Centre. This robs the system of flexibility and discretion which are essential for healthy functioning of scientific institutions.

EXTENSION

1.31 Frontline demonstrations of various departments provide clinching evidence of large gaps between what can be attained at farmers' fields with the adoption of improved technology and what is obtained with the existing practices followed by the farmers. This is a clear pointer to the large potential for raising output through the effective dissemination of technology, especially in the eastern Gangetic plains. But this is not happening because of the absence or weak research–extension–farmer linkages. While technologies more adaptable to wider regional variations are required, effective extension remains vital for realization of demonstration trials yields at farmers' field on a large scale.

1.32 The challenge before extension agencies is how to deliver knowledge to all farmers, and especially how to involve and motivate the resource-poor farmers with a holding size below 1 hectare to take command of their situation and reduce the innovation adoption period. Given the meagre marketable surplus at individual farmer level for small farmers, there is need to organize the farmers around the commodity for getting them the benefits both mutually within the community and in interaction with external agencies supporting the development process. Developing farmer's organizations and federating them at block/district/State level and linking their economic activities with the market assumes special significance as it helps to attain the power of scale economies and collective bargaining to the advantage of farmers.

1.33 Public extension system has a key role in educating farmers and helping them to take right decisions. In this context, it is to be noted that extension should be treated as a service delivery mechanism and not be viewed as a revenue-generating programme. Hence, the principles governing business models of revenue-generating programmes should not be made applicable for extension services. Adequate fund allocation to reach large number of small and marginal farmers by extension agency is essential. Infrastructure below district level is needed to support capacity building of farmers. In view of the above, it is essential to upscale the ATMA to all 588 development districts by incorporating the modifications and taking consideration of all the pre-requisites to meet the emerging and imminent changes in the context of 'Wake up Call' given by the National Commission on Farmers and 'Regaining Agricultural Dynamism'. These provisions are expected to enhance the acceptability of the scheme by States and effective operationalization of the scheme in original spirits.

1.34 There are many extension service providers in the field, providing different kinds of useful services such as information and service support to farmers. They are State Government and Central Government agencies, agri-business companies, agripreneurs, input dealers, manufacturing firms, non-governmental organizations (NGOs), farmers' organizations, and progressive farmers. There is duplication of efforts with multiplicity of agents attending extension work without convergence. There should be co-ordinated attempt to synergize and converge these efforts at the district level and below to improve the performance of various stakeholders. It is essential to route all the State and Central Government extension funds through single agency like ATMA for effective utilization of crucial resources.

1.35 At zonal level, institutions like Zonal Research Stations and line departments need to prepare a zonal agricultural development strategy through consultative approach. At district/block/village level, the key institutions such as KVK, ATMA, and farmers' organizations need to have a close link with each other for technology assessment, refinement, and for creating a platform between farmers' organization and market opportunities. The research and extension agenda of the district needs to be set by multi-disciplinary team involving scientists, extension workers, farmers, and other stakeholders who would ensure research–farmer–extension–market linkage.

1.36 Public–private partnership (PPP) in extension has to be promoted for convergence and sharing of resources. Horizontal expansion of private sector increases through partnership with the public extension system, while vertical expansion of public extension increases through partnership with the private sector. The potential private extension service providers could be identified and made partners in PPP mode for effective management of services and for nurturing a plurality of institutions. Under extension reform, minimum 10% of the fund allocation is made to undertake extension activities through private extension agencies. This needs to be continued and, where appropriate, even expanded by framing suitable guidelines.

PRICE POLICY

1.37 Pricing policy concerns arising from the volatility of international prices need to be addressed. In periods of falling international prices, as for example in the case of edible oils after the East Asian crisis, farmers experience income losses although consumers benefit. In a period of rising international prices, as for example in the case of wheat at present, farmers stand to benefit but consumers lose. It is logical for government to want to balance producer and consumer interests and this can be done through careful calibration of import duties and minimum support prices (MSP) . Our policy has not been entirely consistent in this respect. For example, import duties on edible oils were lowered in the mid-1990s when international edible oil prices were high, but they were not adjusted when edible oil prices declined sharply after 1997. Domestic producers of oil seeds experienced a substantial price shock. The reaction to the recent increase in wheat prices has been different in the sense that farmers did not experience the full benefit of higher prices because efforts were made to protect consumer interests by wheat imports for the public distribution system (PDS) that were undertaken at what are implicitly subsidized rates.

1.38 A symmetric approach would be to moderate price fluctuation both for upswings and downswings. This requires a clear understanding of how to calibrate import tariffs and the MSP depending upon how international prices move. For downward movements in international prices beyond a certain level, import tariffs should be adjusted automatically to stabilize Cost, Insurance, and Freight prices. No change needs to be made in the MSP once announced, but persistence of high or low prices internationally should be taken into account by the Commission for Agricultural Costs and Prices (CACP) to adjust the MSP for the next year. As a general rule, we should not impose bans on exports but rely only on export taxes to ease domestic price pressure by moderating export if this is felt to be needed. In case international prices rise sharply, there is a case for lowering tariffs. In such situations, for food products supplied through the PDS, there is a case for offering a bonus on the MSP before the marketing season begins to ensure adequate supplies for the PDS. This could be supplemented by imports on the government account for meeting PDS requirements and/or rebuilding depleted stocks. This amounts to a targeted subsidy for PDS consumers. If high international prices continue, the CACP should take this into account in fixing the MSP for next year. An important feature of the system must be that increases in import tariffs in periods of low international prices must be accompanied by a simultaneous upward revision of duty drawback rates to ensure that exporters are not hurt. This is essential in cases such as cotton where the absence of such adjustment would hurt the competitiveness of our textile or garment export. A coherent policy along these lines would provide an internally consistent and predictable way for dealing with international price volatility in a manner which balances producer, consumer, and exporter interests.

SOIL HEALTH MANAGEMENT AND FERTILIZER SUBSIDY

1.39 Soil degradation through use of agro-chemicals is a serious issue that needs to be addressed on a priority basis during Eleventh Plan. Imbalanced use of chemical fertilizer has led to declining fertilizer response in the fertile irrigated regions. Excess use of some nutrients, driven in part by imbalanced subsidies, has led to depletion of other nutrients from the soil leading to deterioration of the soil health. The nature and extent of problem differ in different of parts of the country.

1.40 Lack of knowledge on the part of the farmers about the importance of soil health and information about the status of the soil on his particular farm is an important constraint. Soil health cards, giving regularly updated information on major and micro nutrient, should be issued to all the farmers. This would require strengthening of soil testing labs in all parts of the country and expanding their testing capacity to cover micro-nutrients as well. Initial capital investment will have to be made by the government and subsequent maintenance may be funded out of the fee to be charged for the services rendered by these labs. The PPP mode can be explored wherever possible to expand reach and ensure accountability.

1.41 The present system of fertilizer subsidy is irrational and has become counter-productive. Fertilizer is sold at almost the same controlled price throughout the country. However, because nitrogenous fertilizers are subsidized more than potassic and phosphatic fertilizers, the subsidy tends to benefit more the crops and regions which require higher use of nitrogenous fertilizer as compared to the crops and regions which require higher application of potassic and phosphatic fertilizers. The imbalance in the use of nitrogen–phosphorus–potassium (NPK) brought about by distortions in prices ratio in favour of nitrogenous fertilizer is creating serious problem of soil degradation and adversely affecting productivity. Balanced use of fertilizer can be achieved either by redistributing the present amount of fertilizer subsidy over NPK in a manner which is nutrient neutral or by increasing subsidy on P and K in such a way that farmers are induced to use NPK in the right proportion. The price control system also discourages producers from adding micro-nutrients to standard fertilizer eligible for subsidy because the controlled price parameter for that fertilizer cannot be adjusted to cover the cost of micro-nutrient added. Immediate steps should be taken to allow the major producers to charge costs for adding micro-nutrients. Many of the micro-nutrients are also reserved for small-scale production. This segment should be dereserved in the interest of the agricultural community.

SEEDS

1.42 Seed management is a very crucial element for growth in productivity and the present situation is highly unsatisfactory. There is practically no change in the SRR in the States of Orissa, Bihar, Uttar Pradesh, Jharkhand, Assam, Madhya Pradesh, and Chhattisgarh. At present the SRRs in respect of various crops in different States are still relatively low and need to be raised. The desirable SRRs, without which it is not possible to achieve higher productivity, are 25% for self-pollinated crops, 35% for cross-pollinated crops, and 100% for hybrids.

1.43 Production of breeder seeds, foundation seeds, distribution of certified seeds for the year 2004–05 to 2006–07 as compared to those in the triennium ending 1996–97 and 2001–02 are given in Table 1.8. Although the production of breeder seeds has increased significantly, the production of foundation seeds has not. There is a large increase in the distribution of certified seeds but the quality of these seeds is often questioned by farmers.

1.44 There are missing links in the seed production system. There is very little focus on hybrid seed production in public sector. However the private sector has expanded to fill the gap. The private sector seed industry in India is growing appreciably and has made significant contributions to BT cotton, hybrids of maize, rice, sunflower, etc. As shown in Table 1.9, the share of private sector in seed production is increasing whereas that of public sector is decreasing.

TABLE 1.8
Production and Distribution of Seeds

Programme		Use/Production in Triennium Ending				
	Unit	1996–97	2000–01	2004–05	2005–06	2006–07
Production of breeder seeds	Thousand Qts	43.72	44.27	66.46	64.88	73.83
Production of foundation seeds	Lakh Qts	6.45	5.77	6.90	7.40	8.00
Distribution of certified/quality seeds	Lakh Qts	79.01	86.41	120.26	126.74	191.98

Source: Report of the Working Group on Crop Husbandry, Agricultural Inputs, Demand and Supply Projections and Agricultural Statistics for the Eleventh Five Year Plan (2007–12), Planning Commission, Government of India (December 2006).

TABLE 1.9
Changing Share of Private and Public Sector in Seeds Production

Year	Share in Seed Production	
	Private (%)	Public (%)
2004	49.11	50.89
2005	58.00	42.00
2006	57.75	42.25

Source: Report of the Working Group on Crop Husbandry, Agricultural Inputs, Demand and Supply Projections and Agricultural Statistics for the Eleventh Five Year Plan (2007–12), Planning Commission, Government of India (December 2006).

During the Tenth Plan the private seed supply had overtaken the seed sourcing from public sources. However, not surprisingly, the private sector remains absent in the production of seeds of self-pollinating varieties.

HORTICULTURE

1.45 While the first few Five Year Plans assigned priority to achieving self-sufficiency in foodgrain production, over the years, horticulture has emerged as an indispensable part of agriculture, offering a wide range of choices to the farmers for crop diversification. It also provides ample opportunities for sustaining large number of agro-industries which generate substantial employment opportunities. The horticulture sector contributes around 28% of the GDP in agriculture from about 13.08% of the area. It also provides 37% of the total exports of agricultural commodities. The sector encompasses a wide range of crops namely fruit crops, vegetables crops, potato and tuber crops, ornamental crops, medicinal and aromatic crops, spices, and plantation crops. New introductions such as mushroom, bamboo, and bee keeping (for improving the crop productivity) has further expanded the scope of horticulture.

1.46 India accounts for an area of 4.96 million hectares (MH) under fruit crops with a production of 49.29 million metric tonnes (mt). During the period 1991–92 to 2001–02 growth in area, production, and productivity of fruits was observed at the rate of 3.4%, 4.2%, and 0.7%. Area growth accelerated between 2001–02 and 2004–05 to 7.37% but with negligible acceleration in production growth. Among various States, Maharashtra ranks first and contributes 27% in area and 21.5% in production. Andhra Pradesh ranks second in area and production contributing 13% and 16% of fruits. The maximum productivity was observed in Madhya Pradesh (22.6 mt/hectare), followed by Tamil Nadu (19.9 mt/hectare), Gujarat (15.9 mt/ hectare), Karnataka (15.9 mt/hectare), and West Bengal (12.8 mt/hectare). The growth in productivity was maximum (5%) in Kerala from 1991–92 to 2001–02 while it was 10.2% in Uttar Pradesh from 2001–02 to 2004–05.

1.47 Total vegetable production in India before independence was 15 million mt and since Independence for decades the growth rate was stabilized around 0.5%. The impetus on vegetable research and policy intervention to promote vegetable crops witnessed a sudden spurt in growth rate of 2.5%, a hike of five times during the last decade. The potential technological interventions with improved gene pool and precise management can take growth rate to nearly 6% per annum. The area under vegetables increased from 5.59 MH in 1991–92 to 6.76 MH during 2004–05. The production in this period increased from 58.53 million mt to 101.43 million mt. During the period, productivity of vegetables increased from 10.5 mt/ hectare to 15.0 mt/hectare. While West Bengal continues to be the leading State in area and production, the productivity is higher in Tamil Nadu followed by Uttar Pradesh and Bihar.

1.48 India is the second largest producer of flowers after China. The traditional flower sector registered an impressive growth during the Eighth, Ninth, and Tenth Plan periods and grew from 71000 hectares at the end of the Eighth Plan period to 106000 hectares by the end of the Ninth Plan. During the Tenth Plan an additional 10000 hectares has been brought under the traditional flowers sector by the end of 2004–05 to register an overall area of 115921 hectares. The productivity per hectare is the highest in Bihar (17.05 mt) followed by Haryana (11.55 mt). On the other hand, the productivity of flowers is the least in Rajasthan (0.59 mt). The overall productivity of the country during 2004–05 was recorded at 5.64 mt. Nearly 77% of area under floricultural crops is concentrated in seven States comprising Tamil Nadu, Karnataka, Andhra Pradesh, West Bengal, Maharashtra, Haryana, Uttar Pradesh, and Delhi. The production of cut flowers increased over Plan periods to attain a production of 1952 million flowers during the Tenth Plan period from 615 million cut flowers during the end of Eighth Plan period.

1.49 The medicinal plants-based industry is growing at the rate of 7%–15% annually. According to a conservative estimate, the value of medicinal plants-related trade in India is to the tune of about Rs 5000 crore per annum while the world trade is about 62 billion US dollars and is expected to grow to the tune of 5 trillion US dollars by the year 2050. The Indian Systems of Medicine have identified 1500 medicinal plants, of which 500 species are mostly used in the preparation of drugs. At present different Medicinal and Aromatic Plant (MAP) species are under cultivation in the country out of which about 32 are listed in the priority list of the National Medicinal Plant Board, Ministry of Health and Family Welfare for commercial cultivation and processing in the country. However, unorganized collection from forest area has been banned in many states; the trade in this important sector is far from being organized and is also under private hands leading to distress sale by the growers and causing loss making ventures for new growers. Hence, in this sector it is important that only need-based cultivation of any medicinal and aromatic crops is taken up with assured buy back arrangements. Furthermore, in some Council of Scientific and Industrial Research (CSIR) institutes the plants are available but the costs are higher and not affordable for the growers. There is dearth of planting material in many key species and limited improved varieties are available. Hence, different institutions under public domain are required to multiply plants for supply to the growers. The centres to be entrusted with this task are NRC on MAP, Anand, Central Institute for Medicinal and Aromatic Plants, Lucknow, AICRP Centres of the network projects; Madhya Pradesh, West Bengal, Orissa, Jharkhand, Chhattisgarh, etc.

1.50 In the area of horticulture, a major beginning has been made with the NHM. Already the government is implementing Technology Mission for Integrated Development of Horticulture in North Eastern States, Sikkim, Jammu and Kashmir, Himachal Pradesh, and Uttaranchal. The most important constraints to establish the required linkages are in the area of agricultural marketing and processing. Since high-value agriculture is based on perishable commodities, large investments are required in modern methods of grading, post-harvest management (PHM), and development of cold chains. Such investment in turn requires that new players, including large corporate players, be able to enter existing markets and set up new marketing channels. The NHM therefore incentivizes the ongoing marketing reforms based on amending existing Agricultural Product Marketing Committee (APMC) Acts to allow this. This process has started in earnest, with many business houses investing in the area and with most States having already made APMC amendments. However, this must be taken to its logical conclusion. Many States have made APMC amendments but are yet to frame the necessary rules. This uncertainty needs to be removed as soon as possible.

1.51 Most States have also endorsed, and many have encouraged, contract farming. This can be a useful instrument for linking farmers to corporate buyers who can provide information and also inputs and extension tailored to the specific crops. It needs to be backed by ensuring effective mechanisms for contract registration and dispute resolution, along with adequate information and support so that small farmers are able to enter into collective contracts.

1.52 Planting material is the single most important factor around which the entire gamut of horticultural activities revolves. It is of special significance especially in perennial horticultural crops which have a long juvenile/gestation phase and any mistake committed by the grower in the initial stage will result in enormous loss in the later stages. Hence, genuineness, quality, and health of plant material are the major requirements of multiplication, sale, and adoption of any plant material. At present, farmers have to depend on private sources of which the majority of the units are not regulated or monitored in most of the States. Hence, farmers do not have access to genuine and disease-free elite to certified planting material in different crops and as a result suffer with respect to production, productivity, and quality of the produce. Most of the old existing nurseries lack modern infrastructure such as greenhouses, mist propagation units, cold storage, mist irrigation systems, efficient nursery tools, implements, and machineries and even facilities for soil sterilization, etc. Ignorance of the farmers, acute shortage of mother plants of improved varieties, and absence of quality testing and monitoring mechanisms make the situation complex.

1.53 The situation is comparatively better in the case of vegetables with the private sector taking a major share of the production and supply of seeds of hybrids/ improved varieties, and enforcement of the provision of Seed Act by the government agencies. However, the gap between the demand and supply of genuine quality material is too large to be met out of the present efforts. Therefore, in the Eleventh Plan it is envisaged that a massive programme on planting material be initiated so that a sound basis for further growth and development of this sector can be taken up. The government would also consider setting up a Central Certification Agency and a Planting Material Authority to take care of good quality planting material.

1.54 There are at present 10 Central institutes with 27 regional stations, 12 NRC, 9 multi-disciplinary institutes, 15 AICRPs with 223 centres, 1 full-fledged SAU on horticulture and forestry, 25 SAUs with horticulture discipline, 5 network projects, 330 ad hoc research projects, and 29 revolving fund schemes which are dealing with research on different horticultural crops. Besides the above, a large number of CSIR laboratories and centres aided by Department of Biotechnology (DBT), Bhabha Atomic Research Centre (BARC), and Indian Space Research Organization are also undertaking basic and strategic research on horticultural crops. In addition, the Ministry of Commerce has established one research institute each for coffee, rubber, and spices and two research institutes for tea which work on different aspects of these commodity crops. In spite of several research leads, there are still gaps that require focused attention. Development of improved varieties/hybrids of fruits, vegetables, plantation crops, medicinal and aromatic crops, flowers and ornamental crops, spices, cashew, oil palm with high production potential, biotic and abiotic stress resistance is the need of the hour. There is also need to evolve appropriate horticultural-based cropping systems for different agro-climatic areas. Although the private sector has emerged as a major supplier of new varieties, there is a need to evolve appropriate horticulture-based cropping systems for different agro-climatic areas.

1.55 Protected cultivation/greenhouse/low poly tunnels production techniques are now available for growing cut-flowers and vegetables. Crops, such as tomato, cucurbits, cabbage, cauliflower, cucumber, lettuce, onion, spinach, brinjal, pepper, turnip, radish, can be successfully grown achieving high quality under protected cultivation. It has enabled farmers to produce vegetables in places such as Leh and also off-season production of vegetables in north India. Technology for protected cultivation of flowers such as rose, chrysanthemum, gerbera, and carnation in polyhouse, shade net, etc., has been perfected. Low-cost greenhouse technology has also been developed for high quality flower production in hilly States of Jammu and Kashmir, Himachal Pradesh, Uttaranchal, and North Eastern States. These structures are now used commercially for export of quality flower production in plains of Maharashtra and Karnataka.

Plant Protection

1.56 IPM, inter alia, aims at employment of alternate methods of pest control like cultural, mechanical, and biological control in a compatible manner. Chemical control which has several ill-effects should be resorted to only when other control methods fail to provide desired results. IPM is economical and ecologically safe, an important consideration since food safety issues are an area of growing concern all over the world. To ensure ecologically safer food products, it is necessary to control pesticide residue contents by fixing maximum residue limits so as to bring them down to internationally accepted minimum tolerance levels. At present implementation of IPM itself is disintegrated as IPM component in different Plan schemes. These fragmented elements need to be co-ordinated.

1.57 The Plant Quarantine (Regulations of Import into India) Order 2003, made operational from 1 January 2004, contains adequate provisions to prevent the introduction of exotic pests, diseases, and weeds into India. Other allied responsibilities are the issuance of a Phytosanitary Certificate as per the International Plant Protection Convention 1951, of the Food and Agricultural Organization (FAO), and to undertake the Post Entry Quarantine inspections in cases of imports of agricultural products. These functions should be enlarged with a view to facilitating international trade in agricultural products.

AGRICULTURAL CREDIT

1.58 Credit is an essential requirement for revitalizing agriculture and there have been some important positive developments in this area. The total credit to agriculture increased from Rs 62045 crore during 2001–02, the terminal year of the Ninth Five Year Plan, to Rs 200000 crore during 2006–07, the final year of the Tenth Five Year Plan. This was a more than threefold increase over five years. The share of commercial banks in total agricultural credit increased from 54% in 2001–02 to around 69% in 2005–06. The share of investment credit increased from 35% in 2001–02 to around 41% in 2004–05, despite the negative growth achieved by the long-term co-operative credit structure. As against a target of Rs 736570 crore, the total institutional credit flow to agriculture during the Tenth Five Year Plan is expected to be above Rs 650000 crore, that is, a likely compound annual growth rate (CAGR) of 26%. This is much better than the CAGR of 18% achieved during the Ninth Five Year Plan.

1.59 The growth of credit was especially impressive during the last two years of the Tenth Plan on account of the 'Farm Credit Package' announced by the Government of India (GoI). A Special 'Farm Credit Package' as enunciated by the GoI on 18 June 2005 for doubling the credit flow to agriculture, contained various innovative propositions for credit growth. As per provisional figures available for 2005–06, the ground-level credit flow to agriculture during 2005–06 was Rs 180446 crore; 128% of the target of Rs 141000 crore, and registering an annual growth of 44%. While commercial banks registered a growth of 54% during the year, co-operative banks recorded 25% growth, followed by regional rural banks (RRBs) at 22%.

1.60 However, although the total agricultural credit has increased during the Tenth Plan period, there are serious quantitative as well as qualitative concerns. The outreach of the formal institutional credit structure is very limited. The findings of the National Sample Survey Organization (NSSO) 59th Round (2003) revealed that only 27% of the total number of cultivator households received credit from formal sources while 22% received credit from informal sources. The remaining households, comprising mainly small and marginal farmers, had no credit outstanding. It is unlikely that the situation has changed much since 2003.

1.61 Comprehensive measures aimed at financial inclusion in terms of innovative products and services to increase access to institutional credit are urgently required. Issues such as credit flow to tenant farmers, oral lessees and women cultivators, complex documentation processes, high transaction costs, inadequate and ineffective risk mitigation arrangements, poor extension services, weak marketing links, and sectoral and regional issues in credit are also required to be addressed expeditiously. The agrarian crisis also led to default by many farmers, and a consequent freeze on their ability to access institutional credit. The overhang of such non-performing debt also needs to be reduced.

1.62 The share of direct accounts with a credit limit of less than Rs 25000 in total direct accounts declined from 97% in 1990 to 67% in 2005, while their share in direct credit has declined precipitously. The coverage of operational holdings needs to be increased significantly, with sub-targets for the less developed States and small and marginal farmers. Considering that for small and marginal farmers the only alternate sources of finance are expensive loans from moneylenders, the share of direct accounts with a credit limit of Rs 25000 in total direct finance may be targeted at a substantially higher level.

1.63 At present direct finance to agriculture under priority sector lending includes credit for the purchase of trucks, mini-trucks, jeeps, pick-up vans, bullock carts, and other transport equipment to assist the transport of agricultural inputs and farm produce. Direct finance also includes credit for the construction and running of cold storage facilities, warehouses, and godowns. As alternate formal sources of finance are available for these activities, their inclusion under direct finance for agriculture needs to be reconsidered.

1.64 Special credit packages with varying and flexible repayment periods may be thought of for the agriculture sector to take care of mismatches of income and expenditure flows of farmers and the seasonal nature of agricultural income. Doorstep banking implemented through designated agent of commercial banks has now been facilitated by recent decision of the Reserve Bank of India (RBI) and provides an opportunity for farmers to interact with banks with timings suitable to the farming community. The banks are currently allowed to extend financial outreach by utilizing the services of civil society organizations, Farmers' clubs, NGOs, post offices, etc., as 'Business Facilitators' or as 'Business Correspondents'. NABARD could look into the reasons which are coming in the way of the banks using intermediaries as facilitators/correspondents and approach RBI for necessary changes/amendments in the instructions on the subject.

Co-operatives

1.65 The credit disbursal by commercial banks covers only 11.7% of operational holdings in the country. As may be seen from Table 1.10, credit growth by the co-operatives to the agriculture sector has gradually picked up during the course of the Tenth Five Year Plan. The number of loan accounts have, however, declined from 224.6 lakh in 2004–05 to 192.8 lakh in 2005–06. The most potent means *for widening and deepening access to institutional* credit to the innumerable small and marginal farmers are the co-operative credit societies that are autonomous and democratic. The revitalization of the co-operative credit structure in order to transform them into vibrant and viable democratic financial institutions is therefore vital. It is, therefore, extremely important, that the restructuring of co-operative credit now in progress, on the lines of the recommendations of the A. Vaidyanathan Committee are implemented speedily and rigorously. Memorandum of Understanding (MoU) has been signed by 13 State Governments and the process of auditing of accounts is under way. It is necessary to move quickly to take the next steps in depoliticizing the system.

TABLE 1.10
Credit Flow to Agriculture Sector by Co-operatives

Year	Credit (Rs in Crore)	Growth (%)	Number of Loan Accounts (Lakh)
2001–02	23604	–	–
2002–03	23716	–	–
2003–04	26959	14	–
2004–05	31424	17	224.6
2005–06	39404	25	192.8
2006–07	42480	8	188.7

Source: Various Issues of *Economic Survey*, Department of Economic Affairs, Ministry of Finance, and information provided by Department of Agriculture and Co-operation, Krishi Bhawan, New Delhi.

Risk Management

1.66 The frequency and severity of risks in agriculture particularly in last few decades have increased on account of climate variability. The principal evidence of climatic change has been rising temperatures, erratic rainfall pattern, and increase in the severity of droughts, floods, and cyclones which have caused huge losses in agricultural production and the livestock population. India has developed response mechanisms for primary (crop failures) and to some extent secondary (livestock deaths) consequences of climate variability. However, a tertiary mechanism which goes beyond resource transfer to resource assessment and management, through climate forecasting, climate information generation and dissemination, early warning system, mapping of agricultural losses through remote sensing technology, and a pre- and post-climate change response need to be put in place on a decentral-ized basis. Such a response mechanism must include putting in place a catastrophe protection insurance mechanism as also provision of bankruptcy legislation for the farmers.

1.67 Crop insurance was introduced in the country two decades ago. The present version, the NAIS is available since 1999–2000. Despite States' support for coverage of the NAIS being tardy, NAIS is a useful device, especially for farmers growing relatively risky crops. The main problem is that NAIS is not really actuarial insurance. Premiums for most important crops are fixed at all-India level irrespective of risk and the government pays for entire excess of claims over premium received. Moreover, being compulsory for all borrowers from banks in States where it is in force, and with relatively few non-loanee farmers involved, it mainly insures banks against default following poor harvest. Further, its popularity with farmers is limited since it is based on crop-cutting experiments, which delays claims payments until well after harvest and the risk covered is only of yield shortfalls at the block level. There is a scope for improving the coverage of NAIS in terms of regions and crops, substitution of long-term yield rate as a benchmark, and ensuring prompt payment of the indemnities. Decision to devolve the area of damage assessment from blocks to smaller units may be done with care, as the costs of such decentralization and the moral hazards will be very high compared to the likely benefits. Other indicators, such as rainfall, could be used for assessing the damage due to natural factors. Some States are devising their own crop insurance policies including weather insurance, which can be supported in suitable ways. However, for the next few years they should not be treated as a substitute to NAIS.

1.68 An important lacuna, which many researchers have pointed out, is the rather indifferent attitude of the banks towards crop insurance. All commercial banks, RRBs, and the co-operative banks should make crop insurance mandatory for all agricultural loanees, especially because such insurance can indirectly contribute to the viability of rural banking. An equally important aspect is the need for much larger involvement of the States in the functioning of the scheme. The government needs to take up agricultural reinsurance more extensively with appropriate insurance products. Recently some of the successful insurance products like Weather based Insurance have been developed by Agriculture Insurance Company of India Ltd (AIC), ICICI-Lombard General Insurance Company, and by IFFCO-Tokyo General Insurance Company. Under the scheme, coverage for deviation in rainfall index is extended and compensations for economic losses due to the less or more than normal rainfall are paid. There is a lot of interest in private sector for insurance business. Necessary incentives should be devised for insurance companies to design suitable products for the agriculture sector.

MARKETING

1.69 The agriculture sector needs well-functioning markets to drive growth, employment, and economic prosperity in rural areas. Currently agricultural markets are regulated under respective State Agricultural Produce Marketing (Regulation) Acts, generally known as APMC Act. Besides, there are other regulations, viz. Essential Commodities Act and various Control Orders issued thereunder. All these have created restrictive and monopolistic marketing structures, which have resulted in inefficient operation and high degree of marketing costs. They have also had an adverse impact upon agricultural production and system, inefficient flow of commodities, and lack of competitiveness.

1.70 The markets lack even basic infrastructure at many places. When the APMCs were first initiated there was significant gain in market infrastructure development. However, this infrastructure is now out of date, especially given the needs of a diversified agriculture. At present only one-fourth of the markets have common drying yards, trader modules, viz., shop, godown, and platform in front of shop exist in only 63% of the markets. Cold storage units are needed in the markets where perishable commodities are brought for sale. However they exist only in 9% of the markets at present and grading facilities exist in less than one-third of the markets. The basic facilities, viz., internal roads, boundary walls, electric lights, loading and unloading facilities, and weighing equipment are available in more than 80% of the markets. Farmers' rest houses exist in more than half of the regulated markets. Covered or open auction platforms exist in only two-thirds of regulated markets. It is evident from the above that there is considerable gap in the facilities available in the market yards. Also the farmers have to deal with non-transparent methods of price discovery and there is often lack of auction of graded items. Some modern markets with electronic auctioning have been introduced, but they are the exception. A major modernization of this aspect of the infrastructure is urgently needed.

1.71 On the basis of the recommendation of the Inter-Ministerial Task Force, Ministry of Agriculture drafted a model law on marketing which would allow new markets to be established by private entities or co-operatives. Several State Governments have already amended their APMC Acts allowing varying degrees of flexibility. The present status of the amendment in the APMC Acts by the States is given at Table 1.11. However several States are yet to notify the relevant rules that would make the amendment fully operational. These steps should be speedily completed to provide a boost to promotion of direct marketing, contract farming, and setting up of markets in private and co-operative sectors. Some of the important issues relating to agricultural marketing which would be addressed during the Eleventh Plan include marketing system improvement and conducive policy environment; strengthening of marketing infrastructure and investment needs; improving market information system with the use of Information and Communication Technology (ICT); human resource development for agricultural marketing; and promotion of exports/external trade. We should move to a regime of professionally managed wholesale markets.

1.72 In the context of market regulation and development, all States and UT governments should:

- Hold regular elections of agricultural produce market committees and bring professionalism in the functioning of existing regulated markets.
- Plough back the market fee for development of marketing facilities and investments for creation and/or upgradation of infrastructure in market yards/sub-yards.
- Extend greater flexibility to stakeholders, sellers, as well as buyers to interact in the markets.
- Promote grading, standardization, packaging, and certification in the market area.
- Ensure transparency in auction system, penalization on arbitrary deductions from the farmers' realization, prompt payments to farmers, dissemination of market intelligence, and speedier and hassle free transactions in the market.
- Improve weighing systems by installing bulk weighment system and handling in a time-bound manner.

1.73 There are issues concerning legal framework and fiscal matters which will have to be attended to during the Eleventh Plan. Some of these include a need for bringing uniformity in the State-level tax structure in agricultural commodities for improving the market efficiencies; rationalizing taxes and fees on raw agricultural commodities, and removing de facto restrictions on movement of goods across State borders by harmonizing State-level taxes and providing for their hassle free collection at convenient points. Further, the country should be conceptualized as a unified

TABLE 1.11
Progress of Reforms in Agricultural Markets (APMC Act) as on March 2008

Stage of Reforms	Name of States/Union Territories (UTs)
1. States/UTs where reforms to APMC Act has been done for direct marketing, contract farming, and markets in private/co-operative sectors	Andhra Pradesh, Arunachal Pradesh, Assam, Chhattisgarh, Goa, Gujarat, Himachal Pradesh, Karnataka, Madhya Pradesh, Maharashtra, Nagaland, Orissa, Rajasthan, Sikkim and Tripura
2. States/UTs where reforms to APMC Act have been done partially	(i) *Direct Marketing:* National Capital Territory of Delhi (ii) *Contract Farming:* Haryana, Punjab, and Chandigarh (iii) *Markets in Private/Co-operative Sectors:* Punjab and Chandigarh
3. States/UTs where there is no APMC Act and hence not requiring reforms	Kerala, Manipur, Andaman and Nicobar Islands, Dadra and Nagar Haveli, Daman and Diu, and Lakshadweep. Bihar has recently repealed the APMC Act w.e.f. 1.9.2006
4. States/UTs where APMC Act already provides for the reforms	Tamil Nadu
5. States/UTs where administrative action is initiated for the reforms	Mizoram, Meghalaya, J&K, Uttarakhand, West Bengal, Pondicherry, Jharkhand, and Uttar Pradesh

Source: Information provided by Department of Agriculture and Co-operation, Krishi Bhawan, New Delhi.

integrated national market. Essential Commodities (Amendment) Act should be modified to provide for imposition of trade and marketing restrictions only during the exceptional situations of demand–supply dislocation, market aberration, and price volatility.

1.74 The rules and regulations under the Food Safety and Standards Act 2006, which has been passed by the Parliament, should be expeditiously formulated and notified. The Warehousing (Development and Regulation) Bill 2005 has been passed by the Parliament. This will facilitate early introduction of negotiable warehousing receipt system. There is need to set up an accreditation agency for certified warehouses and warehouse receipts; encourage private sector, co-operatives, and Panchayats to set up rural godowns and specify standards and permit warehousing receipt system.

POST-HARVEST MANAGEMENT (PHM)

1.75 At present, the post-harvest losses are about 20%–30% in different horticultural crops. This happens because of inadequate infrastructure development for PHM including pre-cooling. Packing materials like corrugated fibreboard boxes, perforated punnettes, cling films, sachets, wraps, etc., have been standardized for fresh horticultural produce. Tetra packs of different products are now household items.

AGRO-PROCESSING

1.76 Demand for horticultural products will be sustained by developments in agro-processing. In fact there is a rising demand for new products such as dried powder fruit based milk mix, juice punches, banana chips and fingers, mango nectar, and fruit kernel derived cocoa substitute, essential oils from citrus, fruit wines, dehydrated products from grape, pomegranate, mango, apricot and coconut, grape wines, value-added coconut products like snowball tender coconut, milk powder, and pouched tender coconut water (Cocojal). Improved blending and packaging of tea and coffee have opened new markets. Consumer-friendly products such as frozen green peas, ready-to-use salad mixes, vegetable sprouts, ready-to-cook fresh cut vegetables are major retail items. The private corporate sector has a major role to play in developing this aspect in the agriculture–consumer linkage. Technology development has been in vogue but its adoption is far below the requirements.

MECHANIZATION

1.77 To keep pace with improved production and productivity, different machines have been developed for effective cultivation, intercultural operations, harvesting, grading, packaging, and value-addition. Machines such as mango harvesters, kinnow clippers, potato diggers, coconut peelers, etc., are being adopted by the growers. Machines have also been developed/installed for different specialized uses such as cool sterilization (irradiation) for sprouting in potato and onion, dehydration of different produce, vapour heat treatment in major mango growing belts, packaging of coconut water, banana fig, and chip-making machine, etc.

ANIMAL HUSBANDRY, DAIRYING, AND FISHERIES

1.78 Livestock plays an important role in Indian economy and is an important sub-sector of Indian agriculture. The contribution of livestock to the GDP is about 4.5% and the sector employs about 5.5% of the workforce. Livestock provides stability to family income especially in the arid and semi-arid regions of the country and is an insurance against the vagaries of nature due to drought, famine, and other natural calamities. Major part of the livestock population is concentrated in the marginal and small size of holdings. Growth during the Tenth Plan has been at the rate of 3.6%.

1.79 The goals for the Eleventh Five Year Plan for the livestock sector would be (i) to achieve an overall growth between 6% and 7% per annum for the sector as a whole with milk group achieving a growth of 5.0% per annum and meat and poultry group achieving a growth of 10% per annum; (ii) the benefit of growth should be equitable, benefiting mainly the small and marginal farmers and landless labourers and should benefit poorly endowed areas like draught prone, arid, and semi-arid areas; (iii) to provide adequate animal health services for effective disease control; (iv) the sector should generate additional employment opportunity to people in the rural areas especially to the female population; (v) livestock should provide major source of income in the selected areas having potential for mixed crop-livestock farming system; and (vi) the growth in the sector should result in the improvement of environment, specially in the rural areas. Market opportunities have opened up for the livestock sector following the economic liberalization. But the sector's ability to capitalize on new market opportunity is constrained by the availability and quality of support services which, at present, are mainly provided by the government. Moreover, these services are not available at the doorsteps of the producers. There is a need to restructure service delivery mechanism to become conducive to the requirement of the rural livestock producers. Lack of credit for livestock production has been a major problem. Public sector lending is very low. The strategy should be to correct these distortions and ensure timely availability of inputs and services including credit to livestock farmers.

1.80 Presently, fisheries and aquaculture contribute 1.04% to the national GDP of the country and 5.34% to agriculture and allied activities. The fisheries sector has been providing employment to over 9 lakh full time and 11 lakh part time fishermen whose occupation is highly prone to natural calamities. The projected exports from the fisheries sector by end of the Eleventh Plan is 1.06 million tonnes in quantity and Rs 15000 crore in value. The future of fisheries export would be influenced by the consistent compliance with food safety measures (Hazard analysis and Critical Control Point [HACCP] and Sanitary and Phytosanitary [SPS] standards).

1.81 Seed, being the critical input for successful culture practices, needs focused attention with regard to strengthening of the existing infrastructure for production and rearing, transport, and quality aspects. The projected requirement of seed of carps, in pond culture, wetland, and reservoir fisheries that are mostly carp-based, is to the tune of 34400 million annually. Sustainable fisheries can only be achieved through improvement of the quality, technical skills, and management of human resource managing fisheries in the country, in consonance with the rapidly changing needs. Raising a cadre of officers at various levels to plan and execute fishery development programmes is critically important. Fishes in waters, whether seas or inland waters, are impacted by a number of processes, both natural and anthropogenic. While fisheries is a State subject like agriculture, it is necessary to develop a broad framework for harmonizing the various acts under which fisheries is administered. This would enable addressing international issues.

Rainfed Agriculture

1.82 Rainfed areas in the country, which account for 60% of the cultivated area and are home to majority of our rural poor and marginal farmers, have suffered neglect in the past in not having received differentiated technological, institutional, infrastructural, and investment support. These areas are characterized by high incidence of poverty, low education and health status, high distress in the farming sector, distress migration, low employment opportunities, and vulnerability to a variety of high risks. Apart from these conditions, the population in these areas also suffers from various exploitative social structures and practices, poor attention by government departments, poor quality of service delivery, and so on. Repeated water scarcities leading to large-scale droughts have severely affected livelihoods of these rural poor. The challenge, therefore, is to improve rural livelihoods through participatory watershed development projects, reinforced by an integrated farming system approach that would increase productivity in a sustainable manner and contribute to livelihood security.

1.83 After a high growth in rainfed agriculture during 1985–96, the deceleration in its growth since 1996 was more than that of the irrigated sector partly due to liberated trade policies in vegetable oils and ineffective domestic support prices of rainfed crops. Therefore, stabilization of domestic support price is called upon for internalizing improved technology. Efforts will have to be made to fill up productivity gaps of the existing technologies and their scaling up through proper extension mechanisms, supply of inputs, institutions, and proper governance. The coarse cereals in these areas are being diversified into a better option of pulses crops which need to be promoted by providing improved seeds of pulses, availability of specific nutrients of sulphur and phosphorous, and better market linkages. Improving productivity of rainfed rice in eastern India would also help in ensuring food security in the country. Similarly, sweet sorghum for ethanol production could be more competitive in the relatively dry regions of southern and western States. Crop residues could be used as fodder or feed stock to add more value to the cultivation of sweet sorghum. Risk moderation through in situ rain water conservation, rejuvenation of traditional water bodies, and improving efficiency of harvested water may be given high priority to reduce vulnerability to climatic variability. Livestock, agro-forestry, and dryland horticulture and value addition through processing, storage etc., of these commodities are significant coping mechanisms of managing risk and uncertainties. Diversification and expansion of predominantly rainfed crop of soybean by market linkage is an excellent example to be pursued in other commodities. There are some niche attribute crops like seed spices, guar, and medicinal crops which are very relevant at micro level in which contract farming needs to be promoted to avoid periodic crash in prices. Credit requirement of rainfed regions are also more specific. The repayment strategies should be planned to cover the risks; for example, total livelihood portfolio with extended repayment period would be more appropriate. Convergence with employment guarantee schemes, Backward Regions Grant Fund, Artificial Groundwater Recharge, as well as renovation of existing water bodies may be promoted to have complementarities of different programes. Upgradation of skills of the landless, assetless, artisans, and small and marginal farmers should be promoted keeping in view the new marketing demands. Intensification of biofuels in farming system in these areas can add significantly to livelihood security. Comprehensive District Agricultural Plans have been initiated on pilot basis to capture such variations and develop appropriate strategies.

1.84 Systematic reviews and appraisals conducted on watershed development projects by various organizations and departments have established the merits of the watershed-based approach. These are:

- Soil loss and surface runoff reduced by 52% to 58% respectively in completed watersheds.
- Area under irrigation increased from 34% to 100% in different watersheds.
- The area under sowing increased. The cropping intensity increased.
- Productivity/yields of crops increased and the net returns also increased (up to 63%).
- The Benefit Cost Ratio of watershed ranged from 1.10 to 15.72, depending on the above factors.
- The availability of drinking water and groundwater situation improved in all project villages.
- Other benefits such as fodder availability, employment opportunities (and also equal wages in limited number of cases), and income generation opportunities improved significantly in all villages where watershed projects were implemented.
- Human and cattle migration reduced significantly.

1.85 These findings suggest that there is a strong case for a massive expansion of the rainfed areas programme in the country.

1.86 The integrated watershed development projects implemented since 1994 have unique strengths in project management, project content, and processes which need to be reinforced (see Box 1.1).

1.87 The analysis of benefits/strengths and weaknesses of the watershed development projects implemented so far establish the following essential principles for guiding policy and its execution in the future. These are:

- Equity: Watershed Development Projects should be considered as instruments for increased land productivity and inclusiveness.
- Decentralization: Establishing suitable institutional arrangements within the overall framework of the Panchayati Raj Institutions (PRIs), professional and dedicated human resources, and operational flexibility in norms to suit varying local conditions will enhance decentralized decision making.
- Facilitating Agencies: Social mobilization, community organization, building capacities of communities in planning and implementation, ensuring equity arrangements, etc., need intensive facilitation by professional teams. They need to be provided financial support to perform the above specific functions.
- Centrality of Community Participation: The community organizations should be closely associated and accountable to the Gram Sabha in project

Box 1.1
Strengths and Weaknesses of Watershed Development Projects in India after 1994

Strengths

- Project Management Related:
  - All ministries issued guidelines.
  - Community-based Project Management including financial aspects.
  - Support for capacity building agenda (Community Organization and Training).
  - Provisions for maintenance of assets.
  - Formal role for NGO and partnerships between government and NGOs.
  - Several models emerged at operational level for project management at State/district level.
- Project Content Related:
  - Integrated NRM approach with a focus on area of micro watershed.
  - Bilateral projects joined the ongoing projects and diversified the scope of the projects.
- Process Related
  - Community-level decision making, planning, and execution of watershed projects.
  - Fund management at community level.
  - Specific roles of PRIs and other Community Based Organizations (CBOs).
  - Building block approach (user groups, SHGs form the building blocks of institutional arrangements).
  - Clear support and institutional arrangement for project facilitation (Project Implementation Agency [PIA] and Watershed Development Teams).

Weaknesses

- Project Management Related:
  - No dedicated project management teams at State/district levels.
  - Poor delivery of capacity building services.
  - Fluctuating partnerships between government organizations (GOs) and NGOs.
  - State/district level offices gave low priority to watershed projects.
  - Good experiences could not be up scaled effectively.
- Project Content Related:
  - Strong focus on engineering treatment at the cost of integrated approaches.
  - Little formal support to productivity and livelihoods related agenda.
  - Post-project sustainability is grossly neglected.
- Process Related:
  - Low level of internalization of participatory approaches by project teams.
  - Lip service to equity and gender concerns at operational level.
  - Weak institutional arrangements at community level and reducing role of CBOs.

implementation and get the support of the Gram Panchayat (GP) for convergence of all programmes in the area.

- Monitoring, Evaluation, and Learning: Laying specific milestones, institutionalizing the process of participatory evaluation and learning are important instruments. A participatory, outcome/impact-oriented and user-focused approach has to be instituted.
- Capacity Building and Software Support: Ensuring effective capacity building inputs to all key stakeholders at multiple levels (national to local) through long-term institutional arrangements with competent capacity building organizations and allocation of financial resource for the purpose are key instruments.
- Organizational Restructuring: Establishing appropriate technical and professional support structures

at national, State, district, and project levels and developing effective functional partnerships among project authorities, implementing agencies and support organizations is essential for ensuring effective project management.

1.88 Estimates of the extent of degraded land vary from 55 MH to 175 MH depending upon the definition of wasteland and also the source of information. As per the 25 year perspective plan of the Planning Commission (1997), 88.5 MH was to be developed under watershed programme by the end of Thirteenth Five Year Plan. Out of the above, 22.2 MH has already been developed during Ninth and Tenth Plan through a watershed approach. The latest attempt to harmonize the above data (ICAR–National Remote Sensing Agency [NRSA]–NRAA Expert Group 2007) has brought out that the degraded land which has the potential for development under watershed development projects amounts to a total of 64 MH consisting of 50 MH of water eroded, 5 MH of wind eroded, and 9 MH in notified forest. It is proposed to develop 36.6 MH during the Eleventh Plan through integrated watershed approach. The rest of the area, that is 29.7 MH, would be considered for development in the subsequent Five Year Plans.

1.89 The major thrust in the Eleventh Plan must be laid on developing the untreated area in Desert Development Plan (DDP) and Drought Prone Areas Programme (DPAP) blocks and watershed development projects of the Ministry of Agriculture. In addition, special attention is to be devoted to developing villages where groundwater is over exploited. For this purpose, priority would be laid to work in 425 blocks in 100 districts, where groundwater depletion is very high and the number of dug wells is also high. The priority for Integrated Watershed Development projects during the Eleventh Plan would be arid, semi-arid, and dry sub-humid areas.

1.90 In order to develop an integrated approach for rainfed areas a farming system approach would be emphasized. Common guidelines for watershed management programmes in different ministries are being prepared to be put before the newly created NRAA. The Authority will also work towards developing a watershed plus approach for improving agricultural productivity. This would involve an emphasis on integrating crop husbandry, livestock, horticultural, and other sub-systems appropriate to the agro-climatic conditions. A new programme on Rainfed Farming would be launched for the purpose of augmenting the existing programmes of Ministry of Rural Development (MoRD) and Ministry of Agriculture.

1.91 The investment requirement for treatment of 36.6 MH in Eleventh Plan is estimated at approximately Rs 36600 crore. Although only about Rs 23000 crore is likely to be available from concerned Central ministries (Rs 17000 crore from MoRD and Rs 6000 crore from Ministry of Agriculture), it is envisaged that substantial additional resources can became available through convergence with National Rural Employment Guarantee (NREGA) and Backward Regions Grant Fund (BRGF) programmes. The possibility of some additional funding by the State Governments would also be explored.

The Social Context: Need to Modernize Agrarian Relations for Equity and Efficiency

1.92 Land is the prime resource of the vast majority of the poor in India deriving livelihood from agriculture. The Land Administration is plagued by many infirmities. Unclear titles, informal tenancy arrangements, and other related problems have not only affected productivity of agriculture, they have also forced migration of people, both landless and marginal farmers, in search of employment to urban areas as well as of the landed gentry, giving rise to absentee landlordism, who do not lease out land for fear of losing the land titles. Therefore, an efficient and corruption free land administration, coupled with a dynamically adaptive land policy, has a vital role in increasing agriculture growth and poverty reduction. The key elements of an effective land policy are the following:

- Modernization of management of land records.
- Reforms relating to land ceiling.
- Security of homestead rights.
- Reforms relating to tenancy laws.
- Protection of the rights in land of tribals.
- Access to agricultural services.

Modernization of Management of Land Records and Titles

1.93 Correct and updated land records are crucial for the security of land rights and to encourage investment. These result in fewer disputes and conflicts, allow land to be used as collateral, lower transaction costs and corruption, ensure efficient land markets, and help in implementation of land reforms and planning for various development programmes.

1.94 Efforts thus far have remained focused on the system of computerization of textual land records. However, by itself it has limited benefits, unless the land records are accurate and updated in real time. The steps to be taken to put in place effective and modern land administration system are:

- The process of registration and mutation should be integrated into one function of registration of deeds. Before registering the deed, the concerned officer should check the legality of the transaction and competence of parties to take part in the transaction. Computerization should also be taken up of records of the previous 50 years, or such length of time as may be prescribed in this regard in the relevant State laws, so that the title being registered is clear and uncontested.
- The computerization of spatial records should be taken up in all the States and all the cadastral maps should be digitized.

1.95 Setting up a system on the above lines in all States and UTs would facilitate citizen services based on land data, such as providing records of rights with maps-to-scale; other land-based certificates such as caste certificates, income certificates (particularly in rural areas), domicile certificates, etc.; information for eligibility for development programmes; land passbooks with the relevant land information for access to agricultural credit; and access to the data to the co-operative banks and other credit institutions.

1.96 In addition to the above steps, it would also be desirable to integrate three layers of data: (i) forest summary maps, (ii) cadastral maps, and (iii) revenue records, and harmonize them on a Geographic Information System (GIS) pattern, so as to provide a comprehensive tool for planning developmental, regulatory, and disaster management activities and for any other purpose where location-specific information is needed.

1.97 The modernization of the land administration system through computerization of textual and spatial records and integration of the registration office should open the doors to exploring, by setting up a few pilot projects, the possibility of shifting to the 'Torrens' system which is 'title' based rather than the present 'deed' based system. This will ensure that the deed document is a proof of title and reflects reality; search costs for ascertaining title will thus reduce to negligible and title guarantee by the State would be feasible.

1.98 Two CSS currently under implementation are the computerization of land records and strengthening of Revenue Administration. These would be subsumed in the proposed National Land Records Management Programme, which would be launched shortly as a pilot project in one district in each State. After the validation of the proof of concept within the next two years, the scheme would be extended to the entire country. It is expected that digitization of land records after undertaking comprehensive land survey would be completed by the end Twelfth Plan period. It is expected that after availability of this basic record, the country could move towards the Torrens system in the Thirteenth Five Year Plan.

Reforms Related to Land Ceilings

1.99 One of the basic objectives of land reforms was to bring about a more equitable distribution of land. The main instrument for realizing this objective was the imposition of ceiling on land. In line with the prescription of the five year plans, laws on imposition of ceiling on agricultural holdings were enacted by several States during the 1950s and 1960s. These were implemented with varying degrees of effectiveness in different States. The quantum of land declared surplus is far short of land which was estimated to be surplus on the basis of various national surveys. Thus, it is clear that reform measures have not been able to achieve the desired impact. The total area declared surplus so far has been 73.5 lakh acres only, of which 53.9 lakh acres have been distributed. The distribution of the remaining area of land declared surplus is held up mainly due to litigation.

1.100 There are also widespread complaints that lands allotted to the rural poor under the ceiling laws are not in their possession. In some cases, it has also been alleged that *patta*s were issued to the beneficiaries but possession was not delivered in respect of the lands shown in the pattas or corresponding changes in the records of rights were not made. It has also been the experience that rural poor allottees of ceiling surplus land are dragged into litigation by the erstwhile land-owners and against which the allottees are unable to defend themselves. Besides, a number of *benami* and clandestine transactions have resulted in illegal possession of significant amounts of lands above ceiling limits. For all these reasons the results of implementation of the ceiling laws are far from satisfactory. The following measures can be taken up:

- Since large areas of good quality ceiling surplus land are unlikely to be available for distribution to the landless poor, efforts must be made to take steps to release and distribute the land locked in litigation through speedy disposal of court cases.
- In such cases where the land has been distributed but the beneficiary is not in a position to enjoy the land due to being dispossessed or not having a well-defined title to the land, these cases should be surveyed and reopened and such land be restored.
- A special squad of revenue functionaries and Gram Sabha members should be set up for identification of benami and fictitious transactions in a time-bound manner.
- There should be a survey of the government land encroached by ineligible persons and such land should be identified and distributed to the landless. An inventory of the government lands should be made and wherever surplus land is available, it should be distributed to the landless persons.
- Asset in the form of land can lead to poverty reduction. However, to the extent that distributing government lands is not an option, acquisition of land through purchase by the State and distribution to the poor as individuals or in a group may be considered.

Protection of Rights in Land of Tribal People

1.101 Land is the major tangible productive asset that members of scheduled tribes (STs) possess. Tribals also have very strong emotional attachment to their land. Some of the social practices and religious rituals of tribals are also connected with land, which occupies a pivotal place in their psyche. An important fact is that community ownership of tribal land continues to be the dominant mode in tribal societies and takes precedence over individual ownership.

1.102 The increase in extremist activities in many tribal districts can be linked to issues related to land including alienation of tribal land. These are:

- Sale and transfer of land by tribals to other tribals and non-tribals.
- Indebtedness and consequent sale of land.
- Forcible eviction of tribals from land or unauthorized occupation of tribal land by non-tribals or by public authorities.
- Conversion of land from communal ownership to individual ownership.
- Treating tribals traditionally occupying forest lands as encroachers.
- Government land allotted to tribals under various schemes but substantive possession not given.
- Large-scale displacement on account of development projects, such as multi-purpose irrigation and power projects, mining, industry, highways, and urbanization.
- Environment-disturbing developments taking place close to tribal habitats, forcing the tribals to move out, though there is no formal transfer and acquisition of land.

1.103 The following measures are necessary for preventing alienation of tribal land and restoration of alienated tribal land:

- Highest priority should be accorded to the preparation and updating of land records in tribal areas, and with active participation of tribal communities.
- The legal provisions prohibiting the alienation of tribal land in Schedule V areas and its restoration should be extended to the non-Scheduled areas also. A cut-off date should be prescribed while

extending these provisions to the non-Scheduled areas.

- A complete ban on all forms of transfers of tribal lands should be enforced.
- The district authorities should be empowered to take suo moto action for the detection and restoration of land belonging to the STs. It should be ensured that once order of restoration is passed by the competent authority, land is speedily restored to the tribal.
- At present Panchayat (Extension to the Scheduled Areas) Act 1996 (PESA) is applicable only to the Scheduled areas, but a large part of the tribal population lives outside the Scheduled areas. Therefore, provisions of PESA should be applicable mutatis mutandis to villages/areas where majority of the population consists of STs.
- Major alienation of tribal land in the scheduled areas has taken place through the means of compulsory acquisition using the government process of land acquisition. As provided under PESA, no acquisition should take place without the prior concurrence of the Gram Sabha.

1.104 The present arrangements of resettlement and rehabilitation are detrimental and prejudicial to the interests of the tribals. The process of erosion of corpus of tribal land continues at an accelerated pace under the new economic dispensation while the policy options are being debated. The proposed revisions to the Land Acquisition Act and to the current policy and practices relating to resettlement and rehabilitation would provide the much desired policies and packages for more humane and relevant approach in dealing with displacements. There is a strong need for enactment by Parliament of an enabling legislation (like PESA) regarding alienation of land belonging to STs. Incorporating the provisions of the enabling legislation should be mandatory in all laws/regulations made by the respective State Governments.

1.105 Implementation of the Scheduled Tribes and other Traditional Dwellers (Recognition of Forest Rights) Act 2006, passed by the Parliament, and rules framed under it, will provide the much needed protection and respite from exploitation for large numbers of those whose rights could not be recorded or recognized for generations.

Security of Homestead Rights

1.106 An estimated 13 to 18 million families in rural India today are reported to be landless, of which about 8 million lack homes of their own. They either live in a house constructed on the land of others or provided by landowners in return for some forced labour. Some of these persons do not have land to construct a house, while others may have small patches of land but no resources to build a hutment.

1.107 The right to a roof over one's head needs to be seen as a basic human right, along with the right to freedom from hunger and right to education. The Supreme Court, in *UP Avas Evam Vikash Parishad* vs *Friends Co-operative Housing Society* (List All India Reporter [AIR], 1997, Supreme Court [SC] 152), held that right to shelter is a fundamental right. The Eleventh Five Year Plan provides the opportunity to realize this vision.

1.108 Several State Governments have already taken steps to provide each family with a minimum size of land (10–15 cents), so that they have enough space to live and, also a little space extra for supplementary livelihood activities, such as growing fodder and keeping livestock, planting fruit trees or vegetables, or undertaking other land-based economic activities (farm or non-farm) to improve their food, nutrition, and livelihood security. Kerala has a scheme of providing 10 cents of land to each landless family and this has had a notable impact on poverty reduction in the State. Similarly, in 2005, the governments of Karnataka and West Bengal initiated schemes to give homestead-cum-garden plots to landless families. These experiments should be generalized across all States.

1.109 The following steps are needed to ensure this objective:

- All landless families with no homestead land as well as those without regularized homestead should be allotted 10–15 cents of land each. Female-headed families should have priority.
- Some of the required resources could be arranged

through reallocation of the resources from existing schemes, such as the Indira Awas Yojana, NREGA, etc. This must be completed during the Eleventh Five Year Plan.

- When regularizing the homesteads of families occupying irregular and insecure homesteads, the homesteads so regularized should be in the name of the wife.
- The beneficiaries should be given homestead land in a contiguous block, within 1 km or less of their existing village habitation, with proper roads and infrastructural connectivity. In such a consolidated block, essential facilities should also be provided, such as primary school, primary health centre, drinking water, etc.
- The beneficiaries of homestead-cum-garden plot should be assisted by Panchayats and line departments of government to develop plans and receive financial assistance for undertaking suitable economic activities, such as livestock rearing, fodder development, and planting of high-value trees if water is available.

TENANCY REFORMS

1.110 Tenancy legislations were introduced after independence to confer ownership on the tenant and some measure of security of tenure, coupled with rent regulation to prevent exploitation of tenants and increase agricultural productivity in such farms. There is a need for giving a fresh look at the tenancy legislations to reflect changes that have occurred in a manner which balances the interest of the landowner and the tenant and improves access to land, its utilization and releases the forces of production leading to improved agricultural productivity.

1.111 Legislative provisions have been made in many States, providing for conferment of ownership rights on tenants or for allowing cultivating tenants to acquire ownership rights on payment of a reasonable compensation to the landowners. Some States have acquired ownership of land from the landowners and have transferred them to the tenants who have to pay a certain amount or premium to the State. The national policy, however, permits landowners who are members of the Defence Services, widows, unmarried women, minors, and persons suffering from physical and mental disability to lease out lands to tenants without loss of ownership. Provisions for security of tenure have been made even in States which do not provide for conferment of ownership rights on tenants, sub-tenants, and sharecroppers.

1.112 Although agricultural tenancies are banned in most States, the incidence of some type of tenancy, particularly in various forms of crop sharing, is still substantial in some regions. As tenancy is contracted orally, and in most cases in violation of law, the tiller's position is precarious and she/he has no incentive to cultivate land efficiently. In several regions, the existing provisions lead landowners to keep the land fallow for fear of losing their rights. It also restricts poor peoples' access to land through leasing in. Experience has shown that measures to ban tenancy are not usually effective and large amount of oral/concealed tenancy continues to exist among all categories of rural households. Thus decrease in lease market participation with economic growth indicates that tenancy restrictions are constraining the supply of land in the rental market. Tenancy legislation has also led to the demise of longer term contractual arrangements and led to even seasonal tenancy in some areas. This discourages the use of farm yard manure and investments which have a long-lasting effect.

1.113 In a majority of States landless and marginal farmers are net leasers in of land. On the other hand, in some of the States, large and medium farmers lease in land from smaller farmers, giving rise to 'reverse tenancy'. This indicates that the transactions for leasing in and leasing out pervade all along the farm size continuum and it appears that it is economic factors rather than power relationships which are defining these leasing arrangements.

1.114 Security of tenure is necessary for producers to have the incentive for investment for productivity and security of tenure should not be confused with ownership rights. Land tenure security should signify that legitimately held rights-to-use in land will not be disturbed without legitimate cause and without due process, and any such contested rights will be resolved by an appropriate dispute settlement mechanism. For protecting the interests of tenants and landowners and also to increase agricultural productivity, the following reforms in tenancy legislation should be undertaken:

- Tenancy should be legalized in a 'limited' manner. It should provide security to the tenant for the contractual period, which could be long enough to encourage long-term investment by the tenant. It should also protect the rights to the land of the landowner so that he has an incentive to lease his land instead of keeping it fallow or underutilizing it. Long-term tenure arrangements should thus maximize agricultural production and increase the returns to both the farmer, the landlord, and the tenant.
- Instead of prescribed rentals, which are violated in informal tenancies, an upper and lower bound of rents may be prescribed at the State level. If these bands are wide enough, this will do away with the need for illegal arrangements, ensure that the rents are determined by market forces within the prescribed band, and thus increase efficiency and cooperation of both the willing parties.
- Legalizing of tenancy within the above framework will result in increasing the supply of land and will encourage all categories of rural households to participate in the lease market based upon resource endowment, education, employment prospects, prevailing wage levels, and the institutional backup available.
- As agrarian conditions vary across the States, a one-size fit-all prescription cannot be advocated. In cases where the landlords are dominant and there is strong likelihood that interests of tenants may not be safeguarded, special clauses could be necessary.
- Small land-owners who would otherwise have to operate small uneconomic holdings should have the opportunity to legally lease out land to other farmers with the assurance of being able to resume possession at the end of the stated period of tenancy.
- The marginal and small landowners should be assisted with adequate institutional support and rural development schemes, so that they are not compelled to lease out land to big farmers or corporate houses, thereby creating conditions for involuntary reverse tenancy. In the case of sharecroppers, they should have access to credit, once they enter into long-term contracts.

ACCESS TO AGRICULTURAL SERVICES

1.115 Small and marginal farmers often lack access to major agricultural services, such as credit, extension, insurance, and markets. This is especially true of women farmers since there is pervasive male bias in provision of such services. With almost all sharecroppers and most marginal farmers unable to access credit from the formal system, a key issue relating to agricultural credit is the utter lack of financial inclusiveness. Recent suicides by farmers in many parts of India are linked with increase in indebtedness to non-institutional sources.

1.116 Small and marginal farmers, particularly women, have lower literacy levels compared to the bigger farmers. This limits their access to information sources like media, TV, etc. The government extension machinery also tends to focus on progressive or bigger farmers. Small and marginal farmers are also deprived of MSP because of low surpluses, and at times pledge of produce to moneylenders at less than market price.

1.117 Agricultural technology for enhancing efficiency should normally be scale neutral if markets exist for water and for rental use of lumpy machinery. In fact, small-sized farms actually have an advantage in using surplus family labour and saving monitoring costs, and this is the main argument for land reforms. But lack of access often results in significant yield gaps between bigger and smaller farmers. One solution is strong public intervention in favour of small producers, enabling them to access and benefit from the relevant markets and extension services. But while instructions from above can help, this is not a substitute for empowerment of the beneficiaries themselves.

1.118 The most potent vehicle that can empower the poor is group action. Among success stories, the Deccan Development Society has provided subsidized credit to landless scheduled caste (SC) women's groups for land purchase using an AP government scheme. Many groups have purchased land through this scheme and are farming it collectively. This has enhanced agricultural output, food security, and employment for poor women and their families. Many have brought uncultivated land into productive use. Another example is a Government of India–United Nations Development Programme (GoI-UNDP) programme which covered 1357 villages and 50000 women in Andhra Pradesh, UP, and Orissa promoting group access to land and collective cultivation by women. This involved collective cultivation on land acquired in many ways: leasing in, releasing mortgaged land, etc. Undertaken in partnership with State Governments, women's groups, and NGOs, support for this programme has ended. It needs revising and extending.

THE WAY AHEAD

1.119 The strategy to accelerate agricultural growth to 4% per annum in the Eleventh Plan requires action in the following broad areas.

- Bringing technology to the farmers.
- Improving efficiency of investments, increasing systems support, and rationalizing subsidies.
- Diversifying, while also protecting food security concerns.
- Fostering inclusiveness through a group approach by which the poor will get better access to land, credit, and skills.

TECHNOLOGY

1.120 It is necessary to prepare a long-term vision envisaging synergy between SAU/ICAR institutions with other relevant research funded by CSIR, DBT, the Ministry of Earth Sciences, etc., especially to cope with longer climate change from global warming. It is also necessary to impart a strategic focus to adaptive research making it location-specific and aimed at identifying regionally relevant best practice.

1.121 Immediate action points are the following:

- Priority in agriculture research should be given to strategic research.
- Research priorities have to shift towards evolving cropping systems suited to various agro-climatic conditions and towards enhancing the yield potential in rainfed areas through development of drought- and pest-resistant varieties.
- The ICAR needs to restructure accordingly and to increase its accountability.
- SAUs also need to be made more accountable, and strengthened to develop, refine, and promote location-specific technologies. Their teaching capacity also requires to be strengthened.

1.122 Public expenditure (both Plan and non-Plan, Centre and States) on agriculture research will need to increase from around 0.7% of agriculture GDP at present to 1% by end of Eleventh Plan. Increased allocation by the Centre would take this to 0.9%. Additional investment by States would lead to public expenditure on agricultural research to 1% of agricultural GDP. To avoid business as usual, the additional resources should be conditional on:

- Improving the governance of the National Strategic Research Fund within the Ministry of Agriculture. An expert body independent of the NARS can assess potential and constraints, including climate change, and set the priorities for the much enhanced strategic research required.
- High-level expert committees at the Centre and in States should also be formed to oversee extended but incentivized SAUs to revitalize their teaching and location-specific research to enable stronger links with farmers. This, in turn, should have a demand-led component whereby States and districts could finance [from schemes such as Rashtriya Krishi Vikas Yojana (RKVY)] specific problem-oriented research arising from the district plans.

IRRIGATION

1.123 The scope for new large surface irrigation projects is getting smaller and the focus should be therefore on completing ongoing irrigation projects and on modernizing existing ones. In particular, much greater emphasis is required on investments in physical rehabilitation and on modernization of systems essential for improving the efficiency of water use. With these considerations in view, it is suggested:

- The allocation to Accelerated Irrigation Benefit Programme (AIBP) during Eleventh Plan should be increased but with much more effective monitoring using remote sensing data to incentivize the Central funds flow to the States.
- States should shift to 'fixed-time fixed-cost' contracts.

- One model modernization project should be in each State.
- More emphasis must be placed on Participatory Irrigation Management (PIM), including collection and retention of water rates by water user associations, to reduce the gap between potential created and the actual utilized.
- Comprehensive water balance accounts must be prepared of current use, both at the system level and at the level of water user associations, to highlight the extent of avoidable waste and identify possibilities of reducing this through better regulation of water deliveries and conjunctive use.
- The subsidy structure on micro-irrigation equipment must be restructured to enable promotion of community sprinkler systems by water user associations.
- National Rural Employment Guarantee (NREG)/ BRGF funds must be used to supplement Command Area Development.

1.124 As far as groundwater is concerned, the priority should be to exploit the abundant availability in Assam, Bihar, Chhattisgarh, Orissa and parts of Jharkhand, Uttar Pradesh, and West Bengal. The ongoing programme of rural electrification in this region under Bharat Nirman will help. The scope of Rajiv Gandhi Grameen Vidyutikaran Yojana (RGGVY) must be expanded to include energization of pump-sets by converging resources from BRGF and the newly formed RKVY.

1.125 However, it is vital to ensure both that adequate credit is available for pump-sets and that electricity rates are not reduced to the unsustainable levels reached elsewhere.

1.126 In other parts of the country where withdrawal currently exceeds recharge, the following are essential:

- There must be regular and accurate assessment of actual groundwater use in both rural and urban areas to correlate this with recharge and extraction.
- Separation of feeders for domestic and agricultural power and its timely but controlled supply for irrigation can help regulate water use.
- Ways must be explored to empower and entrust village communities with the right and responsibility to collect electricity charges and in dark blocks to regulate access through, for example, obligation on groundwater users to undertake rainwater harvesting and groundwater recharge.

Natural Resources Management and Watershed Development

1.127 Much of the country's agricultural area will remain rainfed even if we utilize irrigation potential fully. It is this area that has witnessed the largest deceleration although the untapped potential from existing yield gaps is high. Government has now constituted the NRAA to bring focus to the problems and potentials of these huge but hitherto neglected areas. The NRAA is expected to harmonize across the different Central Government efforts and offer expert advice to States on how to integrate these in their own agricultural plans.

1.128 The pace of watershed development must be accelerated to cover about 37 MH in the Eleventh Plan. To sustain people's participation, it is necessary to have longer treatment and inclusion of a farming systems component. With the higher unit costs envisaged, and including soil conservation measures, this would require a minimum investment of Rs 36000 crore on Natural Resource Management (NRM) during the Eleventh Plan. This magnitude of investment is feasible if the combined investment on irrigation and NRM increases at 12% per annum from their 2006–07 base, but only if the States progressively shift some of the resources currently expended on irrigation to NRM. States could utilize resources available from the RKVY for this purpose. At the same time, existing Central Sector NRM programmes under Macro Management and Sustainability of dry land farming will be linked to a new and larger programme for rainfed farming systems with a much wider focus so as to bring the watershed-plus element into programmes of the Ministry of Agriculture and of Rural Development. The National Rainfed Authority will provide guidelines and technical inputs.

Strengthening Input and Support Services and Rationalizing Subsidies

1.129 The present unbalanced and irrational system of fertilizer subsidy is an important cause of deteriorating soil quality. There is an urgent need to rationalize subsidy across nutrients and also examine methods by which the delivery of some part of the presently huge subsidies can be transferred from fertilizer producers to farmers or a group of farmers directly.

1.130 Soil health awareness must be promoted through a credible system of soil testing and of advice on nutrient needs based on soil tests.

1.131 Agricultural extension is critical for narrowing the more general knowledge gaps that exists in our agriculture. States must begin by filling up field-level vacancies in extension and provide much better training, including at SAUs. At the same time, the Centre's plan to support the KVKs and ATMAs should be synergized and made part of a comprehensive and participatory district planning process. Alternate delivery channels spanning Rural Knowledge Centres, ICT-based extension, farmer-to-farmer extension, NGOs, and the private sector should also be promoted simultaneously. ATMAs capacity in relatively neglected areas, such as animal husbandry must be increased and the scope of Strategic Research Extension Plans (SREP) enlarged. The SREP and ATMAs will form a core part of agricultural district planning to be incentivized by the RKVY.

1.132 There is also a need to ensure adequate and timely supply of the quality inputs of which the supply of seed needs the most urgent attention. The seed production and distribution system must be revamped by strengthening public sector seed agencies and by involving private trade in seed multiplication and distribution system. States must simultaneously strengthen their systems to check quality of inputs since there is evidence that sale of spurious seed, fertilizer, and farm chemicals is on the rise.

1.133 An associated issue is that of credit outreach. In order to revamp the co-operative credit structure, all the States must act urgently to implement the Vaidyanathan Committee recommendations. Early reports are promising, but monitorable deadlines must be set to meet the required commitments.

1.134 Promoting financial inclusion should receive higher priority than the demand for lower interest rates. We need to move towards universal banking, including group lending and a rural credit information system aimed at smart Kisan Credit Cards (KCCs) for all. Although arbitrary debt waivers should be avoided, the present situation on farm debt requires that banks and State Governments act together to set up some appropriate formal mechanism to expedite one-time settlements.

1.135 The existing NAIS is a Plan Scheme with very limited coverage and there is strong demand to expand this massively and to reduce the basis of assessment from block to the village. This involves high cost if it is done in an actuarial basis and also raises issues of moral hazard. However, new insurance providers and products are emerging and could offer more choice than currently. Expansion of insurance should be a State initiative, which the Centre should support through an Additional Central Assistance (ACA)/CSS, while retaining the existing NAIS on the non-Plan side.

1.136 Another aspect of risk mitigation is to reduce price uncertainty. MSP exist, and farmers in every region need to be supported in at least one food and one non-food crop in each marketing season. The flexibility provided by our WTO bound tariffs should be used symmetrically to protect farmers from excessive international price volatility.

Food Security

1.137 Food security considerations remain an immediate priority. In view of this, and the large existing potential from yield gaps in eastern and central India, the Central Government has launched the National Food Security Mission as a Central sector scheme in mission-mode aimed at increasing foodgrains production by at least 20 million tonnes by the end of Eleventh Plan. This programme concentrates particularly on increasing seed replacement and the replacement of older varieties by newer ones. Adequate emphasis will also be given to better ground water utilization and linkage with RGGVY. A feature of this scheme is that it provides much more than earlier programmes on capacity building, monitoring, and planning and that the execution of the programme would be within the district planning framework.

Diversification

1.138 Available demand projections suggest that the demand for foodgrains, including for uses other than for direct human consumption, will grow at 2–2.5% per annum during Eleventh Plan, traditional cash crops such as oilseeds, fibres, and sugarcane at 3–4% per annum and livestock and horticulture at 4–6% per annum. Diversification towards horticulture and livestock therefore will have to be a very major element in the strategy for achieving 4% agricultural growth. Such diversification not only offers opportunity for raising farm incomes significantly, employment elasticity for these activities is quite high and these are also likely to put less pressure on natural resources.

1.139 The NHM is already the largest single scheme of the Union Ministry of Agriculture (MoA), with more allocation than for all other crops put together. However, this still largely excludes vegetable production and there is still a shortage of quality planting material. Moreover, horticulture statistics continue to be very weak so that there is inadequate benchmark to assess either the selections made regarding crop clusters or the Mission's overall impact. Although States have welcomed the NHM, their own efforts are still inadequate, for example, on possibilities of converging with other schemes such as integrating with watershed development, using the NREG to develop orchards or using the Mid-day Meals (MDM) scheme to provide a stable local source of demand. There is danger that full opportunities of horticulture may be missed if horticulture has less than full co-operation from other relevant departments. For this reason the district plans incentives by RKVY will put broad emphasis on such convergence.

1.140 Agricultural marketing is a critical element of the diversification strategy. Since high-value agriculture is based on perishable commodities, large investments are required in modern methods of grading, PHM, and development of cold chains. Such investment in turn requires that new players, including large corporate players, be able to enter existing markets and set up new marketing channels. The NHM therefore incentivizes the on-going marketing reforms based on amending existing APMC Acts to allow this. This process has started in earnest, with many business houses investing in the area and with most States having already made APMC amendments. However, this must be taken to its logical conclusion. Many States that have made APMC amendments are yet to frame the necessary rules. This uncertainty needs to be removed as soon as possible.

1.141 Contract farming is another mechanism whereby the private corporate sector can establish linkages between farmers and markets. This needs to be backed by ensuring effective mechanisms for contract registration and dispute resolution, along with adequate information and support so that small farmers are able to enter into collective contracts.

1.142 Food processing also needs to be strengthened to create demand for agricultural produce, cut down or eliminate post-production losses and provide value added products. Investment in food processing, especially in rural areas would lead to a higher realization to farmers as this would generate additional demand farm products as well as create employment opportunities in the non-farm sector crating a virtuous cycle in the process.

1.143 Livestock and fishery development need a major step-up in infrastructure and policy support. There is need to massively expand the breeding infrastructure for cattle and buffalo, utilizing scope for improvement through selective breeding using better quality indigenous stock. India needs a comprehensive disease control programme, including for small ruminants and poultry, and a definite policy to cope with the growing problem of surplus male cattle. New initiatives contemplated during Eleventh Plan include salvaging and rearing of male buffalo calves, entrepreneurial development for commercial rearing of small ruminants and pigs, a separate poultry capital venture fund to promote establishment of poultry estates, retail poultry outlets, and other poultry activities. During Eleventh Plan new initiatives are envisaged to provide infrastructure for deriving economic gains from the fallen animals and also for training of the primary producers to create awareness regarding acceptable level of food safety at various levels of animal husbandry. In fishery, there is need to establish more hatcheries and ensure stockable sizes of seed for ponds, tanks, and reservoir sites. All this would require much more commitment from States than is indicated by their current annual plan (AP) allocation of only around Rs 2100 crore for all these activities, including dairy. The Centre, too, will require stepping up its efforts, especially in areas of feed/fodder supply, disease control, and in ensuring progeny testing and traceability.

1.144 The recently set up NFDB has huge potential and requires being up-scaled rapidly. It is also necessary to reduce the present duplication of efforts between the Department of Animal Husbandry and the NDDB and resolve the associated disagreements on a long-term strategy for dairy development. The NDDB has proposed a National Dairy Plan. This needs to be considered seriously by the States and their views incorporated in the Eleventh Plan.

EQUITY ISSUES

SMALL FARMERS' NEEDS

1.145 Given that 80% of farmers are small and marginal, and, increasingly female, special steps will be needed to improve their effective access to inputs, credit, extension services, and output markets. It is now well recognized that the poor are best empowered if they function as a group rather than as individuals and that this is also the best way to secure economies of scale. Hence for the poor and for women to gain and be effective farmers we should encourage a 'group approach'. This could range from low levels of collective functioning such as joint investments in lumpy inputs such as tube wells or co-operatives for input purchase and marketing, to high levels of collective functioning such as land pooling or even joint purchase of leasing of land and joint farming. A group-oriented approach could benefit small farmers on many different fronts:

- Investment in irrigation and irrigation delivery systems.
- Information and input delivery.
- Product marketing.
- Promoting land access.
- Land pooling of owned land, or joint purchase or joint leasing in and group farming.
- Contract farming.

1.146 An important task in this context will be to examine the nature of subsidies in current schemes. There is a strong case to redesign these subsidies, giving greater benefits to PRIS/farmers groups than individuals, so as to incentivize group formation particularly amongst small, marginal, and female farmers.

1.147 Managing vulnerabilities and demographic change: All precaution must be taken to ensure that the poor do not get further excluded as a result of contingencies, whether natural or a part of the economic growth strategy. In particular, there should be no fear that they will lose their lands involuntarily to larger entities:

- Survey/settlement should be completed and land titles and their mutations issued and recorded properly. If this is done, modern IT/GIS technologies could be used to build an online registry of farmers and their land status. This would not only bring confidence but also enable better credit linkage and eventually allow subsidies to be passed on to farmers directly.
- There is no justification, at this stage, for encouraging corporate farming by relaxing the existing ceiling on land ownership. In fact, if the registry above is done properly, some ceiling-surplus land will be available for distribution. In any case, since many richer farmers are exiting agriculture voluntarily, small farmers should be assisted to buy land through the provision of institutional credit on long-term basis at a low rate of interest.
- At the same time, the land-lease market should be liberalized. The two major elements of such reform are: security of tenure for the tenants during the period of contract and the right of the land-owner to resume land after the period of contract is over. The right should be especially firmly available to small farmers.
- Special programmes need to be designed and implemented to enable small farmers to improve their capacity to go for high value commercial activities in crop production, dairy, poultry, fisheries, etc.

1.148 Gender equity: With the share of female workforce in agriculture increasing, and increased incidence of female-headed households, there is an urgent need to ensure women's rights to land and infrastructure support:

- Women's names should be recorded as cultivators in revenue records on family farms where women operate the land having ownership in the name of male members.
- The gender bias in functioning of institutions for information, extension, credit, inputs, and marketing should be corrected by gender-sensitizing the existing infrastructure providers.
- Women's co-operatives and other forms of group effort should be promoted for the dissemination of agricultural technology and other inputs, as well as for marketing of produce.
- Wherever possible a group approach for investment and production among small scale women farmers, be it on purchased or leased land, should be promoted. Women farmers are typically unable to access inputs, information, and market produce on an individual basis. A group approach would empower them.

1.149 Regional balance: A problem, not peculiar to agriculture, is that poorer States that have poor infrastructure not only miss out on private investment but also cannot avail many Central government programmes. The Bharat Nirman initiative is attempting to rectify some of this so far as rural areas are concerned but two sources of bias in agriculture against poorer States need to be corrected:

- The Rural Infrastructure Development Fund (RIDF) recycles to States for infrastructure creation banks' shortfall in agricultural lending from priority lending norms. This should ideally go to those States and benefit those who have least access to credit. In fact, most RIDF funds go to States where rural credit–deposit ratios are relatively high. This should be corrected, along with RIDF allocations changed from being year-to-year to a longer allocation so that this can be built properly into State and district plans.
- Regions with poor market infrastructure are usually excluded from MSP operations by Central agencies. Since this leads to a double disadvantage for farmers in such regions, some arrangement needs to be made, for example a revolving price stabilization fund, so that short-term credit from this can be easily availed by PRIs to do their own MSP purchase which can then be delivered to the Central agencies involved.
- The new Eleventh Plan schemes will put special emphasis on regional balance. For example the RKVY gives special weightage to rainfed areas and the selection of districts under National Food Security Mission especially targets districts with currently low yields but high potential.

Restructuring Agriculture Planning

1.150 An important innovation during the Eleventh Plan is the new RKVY with an outlay of Rs 25000 crore, which is designed to give more flexibility to States, and incentivize them to spend more on agriculture on the basis of properly designed district and State plans. The RKVY provides a framework to achieve this objective since it requires that every district should draw up a district plan that fully utilizes an initial resource envelope available from all existing schemes, State or Central, including resources at district level from Central schemes such as those of Rural Development, Ministry of Panchayati Raj, Ministry of Water Resources (MoWR), and other ministries. The District Agricultural Plan should include livestock and fishing and be integrated with minor irrigation (MI) projects, rural development works, and with other schemes for water harvesting and conservation. The State agricultural plan should be based on these initial district plans, subject to reasonable resources from its own plan and adding those available from the Centre, aimed at achieving the State's agricultural growth objective, keeping in view the sustainable management of natural resources and technological possibilities in each agro-climatic region. This plan should then determine each district's final resource envelope, their production plan, and the associated input plan. Annual targets at the start of the fiscal year should be fixed and funds for relevant schemes ensured, with implementation reviewed every quarter both at district and State level.

1.151 Most agricultural activities figure in Schedule XI of the Constitution and form part of the domain of PRIs. The 74th Constitutional Amendment Act stipulates District Planning Committees at the district level to integrate sectoral plans of a district which then get further integrated into the State plans. The Planning Commission has already issued detailed guidelines of Plan process which needs to be followed by the States while preparing District Agriculture Plan as well.

1.152 Unfortunately, State Agricultural Plans today are far from this ideal. In many cases these are only little more than an aggregation of the States' share of CSS whose guidelines are Centrally determined and whose release is often a problem. Moreover, since Central funds flow through different channels and to different levels, district plans are no more than a collection of proposals to different Central departments and since each Central department clears proposals on its own priorities, the resulting State and district plans lose the application of minds which can come up with better region-specific solutions. Things are, of course, somewhat better where the State plan component of total Plan expenditure on agriculture is high, but this is getting rare.

1.153 There is, therefore, a need to ensure that adequate resources are available for agriculture from both Centre and State and that this be known adequately in advance for meaningful planning at district and State levels. The RKVY is an attempt to address these issues. It is conditional on States adopting appropriate district planning and also on States maintaining a baseline share for agriculture in total Plan expenditure. The guidelines already issued strongly incentivize higher State expenditure on the sector and also stresses almost all the priorities outlined earlier in the chapter.

1.154 In this format, not only RKVY but also the work plans of existing schemes of macro-management and extension (including district-level SREPs) will be integrated into the district plans. On the basis of these, the State plan can be the basis for early discussion between the State, the Ministry of Agriculture, and the Planning Commission so that resource envelopes can accordingly be communicated to the districts. It would allow much more integration especially with NRM, on which the NRAA could advise and also provide incentives for States to maintain the share of agriculture in their own plans. The Planning Commission, along with Ministry of Agriculture and Panchayati Raj, has already started intensive consultation with States to put into effect adequate and comprehensive district agricultural planning. If this works, the Centre could consider, in consultation with States, decentralizing the administration of its CSS through empowered Regional Production Commissioners acting alongside ICAR regional co-ordinators so that the Central role in both R&D becomes more consistent, with the agro-economic requirements. However, the workability of this needs to be further discussed in detail with the State Government.

Financing of the Eleventh Plan

1.155 The Eleventh Plan strategy of inclusive growth rests upon substantial increase in public sector outlay. The Eleventh Plan allocation at 2006–07 price is projected at Rs 54801 crore as against a Tenth Plan outlay of Rs 20513 crore at 2001–02 price. The total projected Gross Budgetary Support (GBS) for the Eleventh Plan for Department of Agriculture and Cooperation is Rs 36549 crore (2006–07 price) and Rs 41337 crore (current price), for DAHDF is Rs 7121 crore (2006–07 price) and Rs 8054 crore (current price) and for Department of Agriculture Research and Education is Rs 11131 crore (2006–07 price) and Rs 12588 crore (current price). (Details at Annexure 1.3.)

As has been highlighted in the chapter, in addition to this, the government has already initiated measures to incentivize State Governments to increase investment in agriculture sector by provision of Rs 25000 crore ACA to States over the plan period through the RKVY. In addition to these budgetary supports provided to Ministry of Agriculture, Rs 17205 crore would be made available to MoRD for Natural Resource Management and support to the States for setting up an efficient Land Administration System. Investments in NREGA, BRGF, and Rural Infrastructure under Bharat Nirman would also strengthen the growth impulse in the agriculture sector. These measures are expected to create conditions for drawing in private investment as well which has been seen to be complementary to public investment in agricultural sector.

ANNEXURE 1.1
Plan Outlays for the Centre, States and UTs

(Rs Crore)

	Total Plan Outlay	Agriculture and Allied Sectors	Irrigation and Flood Control	Total (3) + (4)	Total Plan Outlay	Agriculture and Allied Sectors	Irrigation and Flood Control	Total (7) + (8)
		At Current Price				At 2001–02 Price		
(1)	(2)	(3)	(4)	(5)	(6)	(7)	(8)	(9)
Eighth Plan (1992–97) outlay	434100.0	22467.2 (5.2%)	32525.3 (7.5%)	54992.5 (12.7%)	853898.25	44194.2 (5.2%)	639793.0 (7.5%)	108173.2 (12.7%)
Ninth Plan (1997–2002) outlay	859200.0	42462.0 (4.9%)	55420.0 (6.5%)	97882.0 (11.4%)	1094541.7	54092.7 (4.9%)	70599.9 (6.5%)	124692.7 (11.4%)
Tenth Plan (2002–07) outlay	1525639.0	58933.0 (3.9%)	103315.0 (6.8%)	162248.0 (10.6%)	1525639.0	58933.0 (3.9%)	103315.0 (6.8%)	162248.0 (10.6%)
Annual Plan 2002–03 (Actual)	210202.9	7655.1 (3.6%)	11964.8 (5.7%)	19620.3 (9.3%)	202333.92	7368.5 (3.6%)	11516.9 (5.7%)	18885.8 (9.3%)
Annual Plan 2003–04 (Actual)	224827.0	8776.0 (3.9%)	12900.3 (5.7%)	21676.3 (9.6%)	208497.1	8138.6 (3.9%)	11963.3 (5.7%)	20101.9 (9.6%)
Annual Plan 2004–05 (Actual))	263665.2	10962.6 (4.2%)	19024.5 (7.2%)	29987.1 (11.4%)	234279.1	9740.8 (4.2%)	16904.2 (7.2%)	26644.9 (11.4%)
Annual Plan 2005–06 (RE)	351629.5	13439.8 (3.8%)	25007.0 (7.1%)	38446.8 (11.2%)	299132.7	11433.3 (3.8%)	21273.6 (7.1%)	32706.8 (11.2%)
Annual Plan 2006–07	441285.2	16162.8 (3.7%)	33189.4 (7.5%)	49352.2 (11.2%)	354941.2	13000.3 (3.7%)	26695.4 (7.5%)	39695.7 (11.2%)
Total Tenth Plan expenditure	1491616.2	56996.3 (3.82%)	102086.00 (6.84%)	159082.7 (10.67%)	1299183.98	49681.5 (3.82%)	88353.3 (6.84%)	138035.2 (10.67%)
Tenth Plan expenditure as % of outlay	97.8%	96.7%	98.8%	98.1%	85.1%	84.3%	85.5%	85.1%

Note: Figures in brackets indicate % of total Plan outlay.

Source: *Economic Survey 2006–07.*

ANNEXURE 1.2
Degraded Lands Developed under Various Watershed Development Programmes—since Inception upto the Tenth Five Year Plan

(Area in Lakh Hectares and Expenditure in Rs Crore)

S. No.	Ministry/Scheme and Year of Start	Progress since Inception up to Ninth Plan		Progress in Tenth Plan* (2002–07)		Total since Inception up to Tenth Plan*	
		Area	Expr.	Area	Expr.	Area	Expr.
(A) Ministry of Agriculture (Department of Agriculture and Co-operation)							
	NWDPRA (1990–91)	69.79	1877.74	23.30	1147.82	93.09	3025.56
	RVP and FPR (1962 and 1981)	54.88	1516.26	9.98	727.98	64.86	2244.24
	WDPSCA (1974–75)	2.58	166.27	1.35	129.31	3.93	295.58
	RAS (1985–86)	5.81	76.39	1.30	45.35	7.11	121.74
	WDF (1999–2000)	0.00	0.00	0.59	26.02	0.59	26.02
	EAPs	13.35	2039.81	4.80	1927.54	18.15	3967.35
Subtotal		146.41	5676.47	41.32	4004.02	187.73	9680.49
(B) Ministry of Rural Development (Department of Land Resources)							
	DPAP(1973–74)	68.95	3284.74	68.32	1557.76	137.27	4842.50
	DDP(1977–78)	33.56	797.38	45.17	1152.50	78.73	1949.88
	IWDP(1988–89)	37.34	616.51	62.22	1821.64	99.56	2438.15
	EAPs	1.40	18.39	3.60	274.28	5.00	292.67
Subtotal		141.25	4717.02	179.31	4806.18	320.56	9523.20
(C) Ministry of Environment and Forests							
	NAEP(1989–90)	0.70	47.53	0.00	0.00	0.70	47.53
Total (A+B+C)		288.36	10441.02	220.63	8810.20	508.99	19251.22

Note: * Includes tentative achievement of 2006–07.

Source: Report of the Working Group on Natural Resources Management for the Eleventh Five Year Plan (2007–12), Planning Commission, Government of India (February 2007).

ANNEXURE 1.3
Projection for Central Sector GBS—Ministry-wise for the Eleventh Plan

(Rs Crore)

S. No.	Ministry/Department	Tenth Plan BE (2001–02) Price	Eleventh Plan Base Year 2006–07 BE	Eleventh Plan	
				Constant (2006–07)	Current Price
1.	Department of Agriculture and Co-operation	13883	4800	36549	41337
2.	Department of Agricultural Research and Education	4422	1350	11131	12588
3.	Department of Animal Husbandry, Dairying, and Fisheries	2208	777	7121	8054

Note: In addition, Rs 25000 crore will be provided as Central Assistance to States through RKVY, to be administered by DAC.

2

Water Management and Irrigation

INTRODUCTION

2.1 Sustainable development and efficient management of water is an increasingly complex challenge in India. Increasing population, growing urbanization, and rapid industrialization combined with the need for raising agricultural production generates competing claims for water. There is a growing perception of a sense of an impending water crisis in the country. Some manifestations of this crisis are:

- There is hardly any city which receives a 24-hour supply of drinking water.
- Many rural habitations which had been covered under the drinking water programme are now being reported as having slipped back with target dates for completion continuously pushed back. There are pockets where arsenic, nitrate, and fluoride in drinking water are posing a serious health hazard.
- In many parts, the groundwater table declines due to over-exploitation imposing an increasing financial burden on farmers who need to deepen their wells and replace their pump sets and on State Governments whose subsidy burden for electricity supplies rises.
- Many major and medium irrigation (MMI) projects seem to remain under execution forever as they slip from one plan to the other with enormous cost and time overruns.
- Owing to lack of maintenance, the capacity of the older systems seems to be going down.
- The gross irrigated area does not seem to be rising in a manner that it should be, given the investment in irrigation. The difference between potential created and area actually irrigated remains large. Unless we bridge the gap, significant increase in agricultural production will be difficult to realize.
- Floods are a recurring problem in many parts of the country. Degradation of catchment areas and loss of flood plains to urban development and agriculture have accentuated the intensity of floods.
- Water quality in our rivers and lakes is far from satisfactory. Water in most parts of rivers is not fit for bathing, let alone drinking. Untreated or partially treated sewage from towns and cities is being dumped into the rivers.
- Untreated or inadequately treated industrial effluents pollute water bodies and also contaminate groundwater.
- At the same time water conflicts are increasing. Apart from the traditional conflicts about water rights between upper and lower riparians in a river, conflicts about quality of water, people's right for rainwater harvesting in a watershed against downstream users, industrial use of groundwater and its impact on water tables and between urban and rural users have emerged.

2.2 India with 2.4% of the world's total area has 16% of the world's population; but has only 4% of the total available fresh water. This clearly indicates the need for water resource development, conservation, and optimum use. Fortunately, at a macro level India is not short of water. The problems that seem to loom large over the sector are manageable and the challenges facing it are not insurmountable.

AVAILABILITY OF WATER

WATER RESOURCES

2.3 The water resource potential of the country has been assessed from time to time by different agencies. The different estimates are shown in Table 2.1. It may be seen that since 1954, the estimates have stabilized and are within the proximity of the currently accepted estimate of 1869 billion cubic metre (bcm) which includes replenishable groundwater which gets charged on annual basis.

TABLE 2.1
Estimates of Water Resources in India

Agency	Estimate in bcm	Deviation from 1869 bcm
First Irrigation Commission (1902–03)	1443	–23%
Dr A.N. Khosla (1949)	1673	–10%
Central Water and Power Commission (1954–66)	1881	+0.6%
National Commission on Agriculture	1850	–1%
Central Water Commission (1988)	1880	+0.6%
Central Water Commission (1993)	1869	–

UTILIZABLE WATER RESOURCES POTENTIAL

2.4 Within the limitations of physiographic conditions, socio-political environment, legal and constitutional constraints, and the technology available at hand, the utilizable water resources of the country have been assessed at 1123 bcm, of which 690 bcm is from surface water and 433 bcm from groundwater sources (CWC, 1993). Harnessing of 690 bcm of utilizable surface water is possible only if matching storages are built. Trans-basin transfer of water, if taken up to the full extent as proposed under the National Perspective Plan, would further increase the utilizable quantity by approximately 220 bcm. The irrigation potential of the country has been estimated to be 139.9 MH without inter-basin sharing of water and 175 MH with inter-basin sharing.

2.5 While the total water resource availability in the country remains constant, the per capita availability of water has been steadily declining since 1951 due to population growth. The twin indicators of water scarcity are per capita availability and storage. A per capita availability of less than 1700 cubic metres (m^3) is termed as a water-stressed condition while if per capita availability falls below 1000 m^3, it is termed as a water-scarcity condition. While on an average we may be nearing the water-stressed condition, on an individual river basin-wise situation, nine out of our 20 river basins with 200 million populations are already facing a water-scarcity condition. Even after constructing 4525 large and small dams, the per capita storage in the country is 213 m^3 as against 6103 m^3 in Russia, 4733 m^3 in Australia, 1964 m^3 in the United States (US), and 1111 m^3 of China. It may touch 400 m^3 in India only after the completion of all the ongoing and proposed dams.

ULTIMATE IRRIGATION POTENTIAL (UIP)

2.6 The demand for irrigation water in India is very large. However, the limits to storage and transfer of water restrict the potential for irrigation. UIP reassessed by the Committee constituted by the MoWR in May 1997, the potential created, and the potential utilized up to end of the Tenth Plan are given in Table 2.2.

2.7 The assessment of UIP needs to be periodically reviewed to account for revision in scope, technological advancement, inter-basin transfer of water, induced recharging of groundwater, etc. The creation of irrigation potential depends upon the efficiency of the system for delivering the water and its optimal use at the application level. With the modern techniques of integrating micro irrigation with canal irrigation as has been done in the case of Narmada Canal Project, Rajasthan, the UIP can further be increased. Similarly in the case of groundwater, innovative methods of recharging the groundwater and also storing water in flood plains along the river banks may enhance the UIP from groundwater to more than 64 MH.

WATER FOR NATURE

2.8 The question of a trade-off between competing claims on water becomes most important in the context of ecological requirement. The National Water Policy (NWP) places ecology in the fourth place in the order of priorities for water use. Yet, there is a general agreement amongst all that any water diversion

TABLE 2.2
Ultimate Irrigation Potential, Potential Created and Potential Utilized

(in MH)

Sector	Ultimate	Potential Created		Potential Utilized	
	Irrigation Potential	Till End of Ninth Plan	Anticipated in Tenth Plan	Till end of Ninth Plan	Anticipated in Tenth Plan
MMI	58.47	37.05	5.3	31.01	3.41
MI					
Surface water	17.38	13.6	0.71	11.44	0.56
Groundwater	64.05	43.3	2.81	38.55	2.26
Subtotal	81.43	56.9	3.52	49.99	2.82
Total	139.9	93.95	8.82	81.00	6.23

needs to take care of river ecosystem downstream. The problem is of quantifying the Environment Flow Releases (EFR), that is the flow required for maintaining ecosystems. Usable water will be reduced to that extent. During 2004–05, the Ministry of Environment and Forests (MoEF) appointed a committee headed by Member, Central Water Commission (CWC), to develop guidelines for determining the EFR. The committee submitted its report in 2005. Depending on what the final accepted recommendation is, the minimum flow required for maintaining the river regime and environment will be decided and considered in water resources development and management.

Climate Change and Uncertainty in Water Availability

2.9 The threat of climate change is now considered an established fact. General Circulation Models simulate the behaviour of the atmosphere and paint 'what if' scenarios for various levels of greenhouse gas emissions. Using these models the weather experts have predicted that global warming will intensify the hydrologic cycle; more intense rainfall will occur in fewer spells; floods and droughts both will become more intense; the floods will be more frequent; the rainfall will shift towards winter; and there may be a significant reduction in the mass of glaciers, resulting in increased flows in the initial few decades but substantially reduced flows thereafter.

2.10 The MoWR has already initiated some studies in co-operation with research institutions and reputed academic institutions to assess the impact of climate change on water resources.

2.11 The hydrologists are yet to translate what climate change means for the water availability, its distribution in time and space, and changes in demand. An increase in mean temperatures would increase the energy flux for evapo-transpiration. The increased potential evapo-transpiration in the forests could trigger major changes in the environment, and it would result in an increased crop water requirement in the farms. The changes in seasonal temperatures could change the crop seasons. Enough data is now available to paint 'what if' scenarios for different possibilities, and to formulate some tentative plans to respond to these possibilities.

2.12 In the post-climate change scenario, systems that are more resilient will fare better than systems that are less resilient. Engineering infrastructure that enables the water managers to store and transfer water with greater certainty can reduce the impact of uncertainty. Climate change considerations need to be factored in as we plan water resource infrastructure.

Water Requirement

2.13 The requirement of water for various sectors has been assessed by the National Commission on Integrated Water Resources Development (NCIWRD) in the year 2000. This requirement is based on the assumption that the irrigation efficiency will increase to 60% from the present level of 35–40%. The Standing Committee of MoWR also assesses it periodically. These are shown in Table 2.3.

TABLE 2.3
Water Requirement for Various Sectors

Sector	Water Demand in km³ (or bcm)					
	Standing Sub-Committee of MoWR			NCIWRD		
	2010	2025	2050	2010	2025	2050
Irrigation	688	910	1072	557	611	807
Drinking water	56	73	102	43	62	111
Industry	12	23	63	37	67	81
Energy	5	15	130	19	33	70
Others	52	72	80	54	70	111
Total	813	1093	1447	710	843	1180

WATER RESOURCES DEVELOPMENT AND USE: IRRIGATION

HISTORICAL DEVELOPMENT

2.14 The planned development of irrigation sector started in a big way since the First Five Year Plan (1951–56). New projects were taken up in the Second Five Year Plan, the Third Five Year Plan, and the Annual Plans 1966–69. During the Fourth Five Year Plan emphasis was shifted to the completion of ongoing schemes. The widening gap between potential creation and utilization was felt in the Fifth Plan (1974–78) and accordingly Command Area Development (CAD) programme was launched. The Annual Plans 1978–80 and the Sixth Plan witnessed new starts and then the focus was shifted towards completion of irrigation projects. By the end of the Eighth Plan (1996–97), central assistance was provided under AIBP to help the State Governments in early completion of the projects.

2.15 Although plan expenditure on irrigation has increased from Rs 441.8 crore in the First Plan to Rs 95743.42 crore (outlay) in the Tenth Plan, the share in total plan expenditure has decreased from 23% in the First Plan to 6.3% in the Tenth Plan. The trends in change of per cent of total plan expenditure on irrigation sector are shown in Figure 2.1.

2.16 The anticipated irrigation potential created up to March 2007 is 102.77 MH, which is 73.46% of the UIP of 140 MH. MMI projects have an UIP of 58.47 MH against which irrigation potential created is 42.35 MH. MI potential created is 60.42 MH against the UIP of 81.43 MH. The irrigation potential creation and its corresponding utilization during the plan periods is given in Annexure 2.1.

2.17 The gross irrigated area in the country is only 87.23 MH. With an average irrigation intensity of 140%, the actual net irrigated area is likely to be around 62.31 MH, which is only 43% of the net sown area of the country (142 MH). Even after achieving the UIP of 139.89 MH. and considering the average irrigation intensity of 140%, the ultimate irrigated area in the country would be only 70% of the net sown area.

2.18 The increasing difference between irrigation potential created and utilized is ascribed to a number of reasons. Irrigation systems are designed for extensive irrigation for a 75% confidence level. Thus water availability in some basins would be less the designed amount. Excess withdrawal by farmers near the head

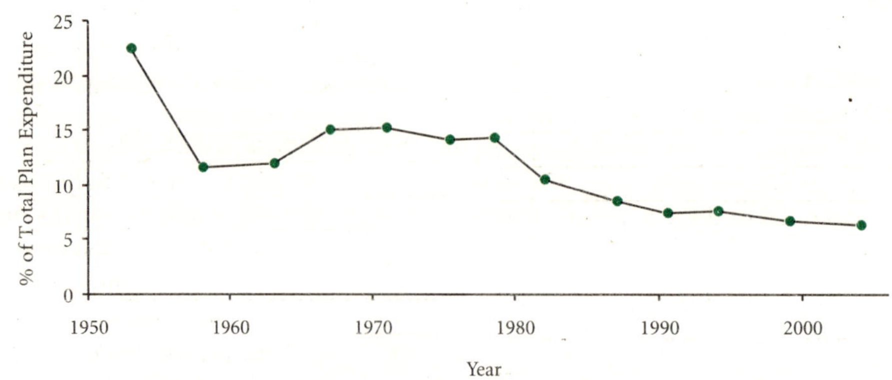

FIGURE 2.1: Expenditure on Irrigation

of canals deprives farmers at the tail end of water. Inadequate development of field channels, required to be developed by farmers, contribute to the gap. The missing links or breaks in the canal network may also reduce utilization. A part of this gap can be reduced by command area development programmes. Under the CAD Programme, 311 projects [with total culturable command area (CCA) of 28.58 MH] have been included so far. Till the end of March 2006, the construction of field channels has been completed in an area of 17.43 MH. The programme is presently being implemented in 136 projects with total CCA of 17.06 MH.

2.19 Details of the physical progress achieved in respect of core components under the Command Area Development and Water Management (CADWM) Programme during the Tenth Plan till the end of March 2006 and progress likely to be achieved till end of Tenth Plan are given in Table 2.4.

2.20 The total anticipated State share expenditure for the Tenth Plan under the CADWM Programme works out to Rs 1591.57 crore.

MAJOR AND MEDIUM PROJECTS

Physical and Financial Performance

2.21 The potential creation target fixed for the Tenth Plan by the Planning Commission was 9.93 MH. It was revised to 6.5 MH during the MTA of the Plan. The performance during the first three years of the Tenth Plan and anticipated performance for remaining two years is given in Table 2.5.

Completion of Projects

2.22 A total number of 490 projects spilled into the Tenth Plan from previous plans, and another 231 projects were to be taken up during the Tenth Plan. Besides, based on the current financial and physical status of the projects, it was also anticipated that 103 major, 210 medium, and 62 extension, renovation, and modernization (ERM) projects could be completed with adequate provision of funds. Since irrigation is a State subject, the projects are largely executed by State Governments. The Working Group for Water Resources for the Eleventh Five Year Plan has now assessed that 179 new projects have been taken up in the Tenth Plan, while 178 projects including 48 major, 91 medium, and

TABLE 2.4
Physical Progress under CAD and Water Management (CADWM) Programme in the Tenth Plan

(in MH)

S. No.	Item	Progress till the End of March 2006	Anticipated Progress during 2006–07	Total Anticipated Progress for Tenth Plan
1	Field channels	1.671	0.373	2.044
2	Field drains	0.476	0.108	0.584
3	*Wara Bandi*	0.929	0.124	1.053
4	Land levelling*	0.050	–	0.050

Note: * This component was discontinued w.e.f. 1 April 2004.

TABLE 2.5
Physical and Financial Performance of MMI Sector during the Tenth Plan

Year	Physical (in MH)		Financial (in Rs Crore)	
	Potential Created	Potential Utilized	Revised Outlay	Expenditure
2002–03	0.812	0.532	13131.51	9655.68
2003–04	0.922	0.639	12334.79	11046.40
2004–05#	1.064	0.685	15483.05	15483.05
2005–06#	1.069	0.625	30263.83	30263.83
2006–07*	1.428	0.928		
Total	5.295	3.409	71213.18	66448.96

Note: # anticipated; * targeted.

39 ERM projects would be completed during the Tenth Plan. The reasons for non-completion of the projects from the projected level include inadequate funds due to thin spread of funds over many projects, revision in the estimated costs, change in scope of the works, unforeseen bottlenecks involving other agencies, opposition by the project-affected persons (PAPs), etc.

Spillover Projects into Eleventh Five Year Plan

2.23 In the course of analysing the status of ongoing projects likely to spill over, it is observed that a number of previously unreported projects have now been reported; some of the ongoing projects deferred while some of the projects have been interchanged among the classified heads of major, medium, and ERM projects. After accounting for the number of new projects taken up in the Tenth Plan, projects likely to be completed in the Tenth Plan, and other factors inducing changes in the number of projects, the number of spillover projects into the Eleventh Five Year Plan works out to be 477 including 166 major, 222 medium, and 89 ERM projects. The status is given in Table 2.6.

2.24 Projects of all three types have been under execution for many years, some from as far back as the Second Five Year Plan. Around 63% of the above 477 projects are unapproved by the Centre and are ineligible for central assistance.

TABLE 2.6
Spillover Major, Medium and ERM Projects into the Eleventh Plan

Plan of Start of Project	Major	Medium	ERM	Total
I	0	0	0	0
II	2	0	0	2
III	5	1	0	6
1966–69	2	0	0	2
IV	8	5	4	17
V	33	19	1	53
1978–80	2	9	3	14
VI	25	19	6	50
VII	10	13	11	34
1990–92	2	2	0	4
VIII	19	48	11	78
IX	20	40	17	77
X	38	66	36	140
Total	166	222	89	477

Major and Medium Projects in Drought-prone Areas and Tribal Areas

2.25 Projects in drought-prone areas and tribal areas are approved with a lower cut-off ratio of benefits to costs to reflect the higher weight given to benefits accruing to these areas. About one-third of the total geographical area of the country is recognized as drought-prone area. A total of 99 districts in 14 States are identified as drought prone. These districts have cultivable area of about 77 MH which is 42% of the country's total cultivable area of 184 MH. Among the States, Gujarat and Rajasthan are the most drought-prone States followed by Karnataka and Maharashtra. At the beginning of Eleventh Five Year Plan, of the 477 projects under implementation, 148 major and 195 medium projects envisaged benefits to drought-prone districts. Among these, 76 major and 102 medium projects benefit tribal areas as well.

Unapproved Projects

2.26 The schemes under the Plan sector require formal investment clearance from the Planning Commission before execution. Accordingly, major schemes are scrutinized for techno-economic feasibility, inter-state and international aspects, ecology and environmental aspects, and rehabilitation aspects by the concerned Central ministries. Recommendations of various expert agencies are then considered by the Advisory Committee of the MoWR. Thereafter the proposal is considered by the Planning Commission for investment clearance. In case of MMI projects the State Planning Boards are empowered to clear the proposals if inter-state issues are not involved. In spite of well-defined policy and guidelines in place, a large number of major and medium projects have been under execution without investment clearance from Planning Commission. The unapproved projects in the Tenth Plan comprising 90 major, 136 medium, and 74 ERM projects are likely to spill over into the Eleventh Five Year Plan. Expenditure likely to be incurred on these projects up to the Tenth Plan will be about Rs 41128 crore with the break-up as shown in Table 2.7.

ACCELERATED IRRIGATION BENEFIT PROGRAMME (AIBP)

2.27 The additional irrigation potential created in the country from the beginning of the Sixth Plan (i.e. 1980)

TABLE 2.7
Unapproved Major, Medium and ERM Projects

	Number of Unapproved Projects	Latest estimated cost (Rs in Crore)	Expenditure up to Tenth Plan (Rs in Crore)	Ultimate Potential (thousand hectare)	Potential created up to Tenth Plan (thousand hectare)
Major projects	90	100017.85	31004.66	5960.58	930.85
Medium projects	136	12947.09	5943.78	809.82	153.16
ERM	74	9095.30	4234.31	1177.07	135.10
Total	300	122060.24	41127.75	7947.47	1219.11

to the end of the annual rolling plan of 1992 for the period of 12 years was 24.48 MH, which is at the rate of 2.04 MH per annum. This rate of creation sharply came down to 1.03 MH per annum during the Eighth Plan. Responding to this sudden decline in the rate of creation of irrigation potential as well as allocation to the irrigation sector in the States Annual Plan, the Central Government initiated AIBP from the year 1996–97 under which Central assistance is being extended to large irrigation schemes for the early completion and accelerating creation of additional irrigation potential.

2.28 Under this programme all the projects which have the investment approval of the Planning Commission are eligible for assistance. The programme which was entirely a loan from the Centre in the beginning had been modified as per programmes of the Normal Central Assistance (NCA) with a grant and loan component (mixed) from 2004–05. Also reform measures such as revision of water rates to cover Operation and Maintenance (O&M) charges have been introduced but the results were not satisfactory because of the sluggish efforts of State Governments to comply with the reform measures. Moreover, the incentive to the State Government, that is 70% loan, was not attractive enough to carry out the reforms. In the year 2005–06, the GoI launched Bharat Nirman Programme where 10 MH of additional irrigational potential creation was targeted in a period of four years and to achieve this target, the AIBP guidelines were further modified in December 2006 wherein Central assistance has been kept in the form of 25% grant of project cost under AIBP for non-special category States and 90% grant of project cost for special category States and projects benefiting drought-prone and tribal areas. It was also decided to treat projects in the undivided Koraput, Bolangir, and Kalahandi (KBK) districts of Orissa at par with special category States.

Performance of AIBP

2.29 A total of 229 MMI projects have been included under AIBP, out of which, 91 have been reported completed by July 2007. The UIP of the AIBP-assisted major and medium projects/components is 82.76 lakh hectare. Out of this, the irrigation potential created up to March 2007 is 43.56 lakh hectare which is about 53% of the UIP of all AIBP projects. Up to March 2007, 6205 MI schemes were provided assistance under AIBP of which 4418 schemes have been completed. The UIP of MI schemes included in AIBP was 3.85 lakh hectare and potential of 1.87 lakh hectare has been created up to March 2007. The completion rate has been quite satisfactory in respect of AIBP-assisted MI schemes as these have low gestation periods.

2.30 However, the performance of MMI projects in terms of completion of the projects as well as the potential creation is not very satisfactory. The outlays under the AIBP have been continuously stepped up since 1996–97. Creation of irrigation potential in the country under major and medium sector received a fillip after commencement of AIBP. During the Eighth Plan period, irrigation potential of 22.10 lakh hectare was created in the country under major and medium sector at an annual rate of 4.4 lakh hectare per annum. During the Ninth Plan, when AIBP was in operation, irrigation potential created in the major and medium sector was 41.0 lakh hectare out of which 16.5 lakh hectare (nearly 40%) was through AIBP schemes. The highest creation of irrigation potential from the First Plan to the Eighth Plan is in the Fifth Plan and

TABLE 2.8
Performance of AIBP Projects

(Rs Crore/Thousand Hectare)

Year	Central Loan Assistance (CLA)/ Grant Released	Potential Created (Normal)	Potential Created (Fast Track#)	Total Potential Created under AIBP	Total Potential Created
1996–97	500.00	72.08		72.08	559.97
1997–98	952.19	200.02		200.02	645.18
1998–99	1119.18	257.41		257.41	592.15
1999–2000	1450.48	220.21		220.21	666.04
2000–01	1856.20	531.43		531.43	983.53
2001–02	2601.98	443.37	0.00	443.37	1214.59
2002–03	3061.70	272.43	182.93	455.36	812.00
2003–04	3128.50	357.20	89.83	447.03	1004.00
2004–05	2867.34	408.67	82.58	491.25	1000.00*
2005–06	1900.31	735.85	144.09	879.94	1500.00*
2006–07	2301.97				
Total	21739.85	3498.67	499.43	3998.10	

Note: # Projects which are to be completed in two agricultural season (one year) with higher Central assistance; * Tentative.

this is 40.28 lakh hectare. With the introduction of AIBP the same pace of additional irrigational potential could be restored in the Ninth Plan and subsequently in the Tenth Plan. The year-wise funds released and potential created are shown in Table 2.8.

MINOR IRRIGATION (MI)

2.31 Over the period 1951–2007, irrigated area from major projects has increased to 3.47 times, from tanks 1.9 times, and from groundwater 6.3 times. Groundwater use has expanded as it provides control over irrigation to the farmer and its growth stimulated by spread of electrification and subsidized power. Even in the command area of major irrigation projects, farmers often use groundwater as a matter of routine to supplement canal water to maximize agricultural production.

2.32 The outlay provided for the Tenth Plan by the Planning Commission was Rs 13873 crore for a target of 6.8 MH. The outlay has been subsequently revised to Rs 14764 crore and during MTA the target was revised to 4.0 MH. However, it is now anticipated that the achievement may be around 3.5 MH, out of which 2.81 MH is anticipated through groundwater development. The performance during the first three years of the Tenth Plan and anticipatory performance for remaining two years is given in Table 2.9.

TABLE 2.9
Physical and Financial Performance of MI Sector during the Tenth Plan

Year	Physical (in MH)		Financial (in Rs Crore)	
	Potential Created	Potential Utilized	Revised Outlay	Expenditure
2002–03	0.687	0.548	1950.45	1639
2003–04	0.628	0.502	2634.63	1957
2004–05	0.740	0.592	2780.35	2780.35
2005–06#	0.545	0.440	7398.75	7398.75
2006–07*	0.918	0.734		
Total	3.518	2.816	14764.18	13775.1

Note: # anticipated; * targeted.

2.33 The broad reasons for low performance are mentioned below:

- Poor economic status of small and marginal farmers.
- Non-availability of assured power supply.
- Highly subsidized water rates in canal command, whereas, no provision of subsidy for development of groundwater.
- In hard rock areas, probability of obtaining groundwater resource is low.
- Over-extraction in critical areas which has caused depletion of water tables resulting in failure of wells.

2.34 The rapid development of groundwater has led to over-exploitation of groundwater in the country. In 15% of the blocks the annual extraction of groundwater exceeds annual recharge and in 4% of the blocks it is more than 90% of recharge. As the groundwater recedes wells have to be deepened and more energy has to be used to pump water. Figure 2.2 shows the status of groundwater use in the country. The map shows two challenges: first, how to restrain groundwater use to sustainable level in over-exploited regions and second, how to develop the large untapped ground water potential in eastern India.

2.35 Rural electrification through the RGGVY is being completed in Eastern Uttar Pradesh, Bihar, and West Bengal. In the Eleventh Plan the objective should be to bring large part of the cultivable area in these States under irrigation through electrified agricultural pump sets. This would be the key to the breakthrough in the agricultural production and food security. As this is a viable action plan would need to be drawn up by the States involving provision of (i) adequate power for irrigation, (ii) soft credit for farmers to install tubewells, and (iii) subsidized rates for grant of electricity connections. With the implementation of the tariff policy of differential pricing for peak and off-peak supply of electricity, it should be possible to have modest rates for supply of off-peak electricity to agriculture.

MINOR IRRIGATION SURFACE WATER SCHEMES

2.36 Surface water schemes based on tanks and ponds have developed slowly. Due to the success of the Government in providing canal irrigation and heavily subsidized electricity for use of ground water there has been neglect of local storage through village ponds, tanks, etc. Many of these have begun to disappear. This is partly due to village communities losing a sense of their own responsibility for managing water optimally. Restoration of water bodies has been taken up in 24 districts of 14 States, namely, Andhra Pradesh, Chhattisgarh, Gujarat, Himachal Pradesh, Jammu and Kashmir, Jharkhand, Karnataka, Kerala, Madhya Pradesh, Maharashtra, Orissa, Rajasthan, Tamil Nadu, and West Bengal. In the Eleventh Five Year Plan 20000 water bodies are likely to be renovated and restored.

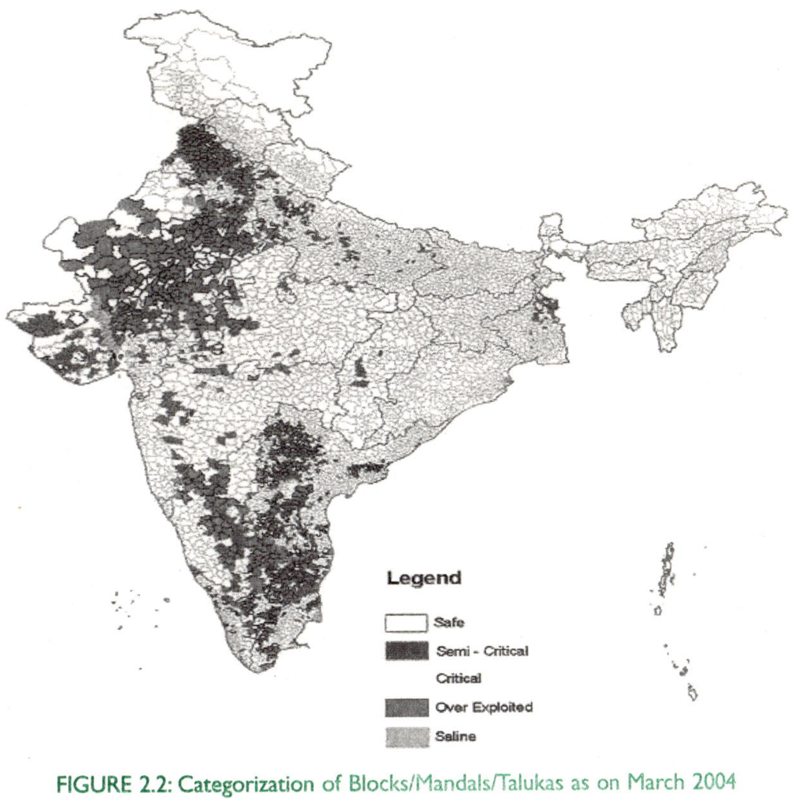

FIGURE 2.2: Categorization of Blocks/Mandals/Talukas as on March 2004

FLOOD MANAGEMENT

Physical Achievements

2.37 At the beginning of the Tenth Plan (2002), the area benefited or the area provided with a reasonable degree of protection was about 16.44 MH. The Planning Commission approved an outlay of Rs 4619 crore for State sector to protect 1.93 MH. The area likely to be protected as reported by the States in their respective annual plan documents is 1.78 MH. Thus, total area reasonably protected against flood by end of the Tenth Plan is likely to be 18.22 MH. The physical achievements per unit investment follow a reducing trend because of cost escalation and increased allocation for stabilization of existing works.

2.38 The year-wise outlays of the State and Central sectors for the Tenth Plan and the actual/anticipated expenditures are given in Table 2.10.

Flood Damages and Relief

2.39 During the first three years of the Tenth Plan, the flood damages as reported by the States and the relief fund released are given in Table 2.11.

2.40 The aforementioned relief funds also include assistance for cyclones and other such natural calamities. It would be seen from the above table that during the first three years of the Tenth Plan, the expenditure on relief was significantly high and the corresponding Plan outlays were inadequate. It is necessary that a more rational approach and optimum programme of works is adopted for flood management.

2.41 The preceding paragraphs describe the situation analyses of the irrigation sector in the country. As has been indicated at the beginning of the chapter, water scarcity and uncertainty in availability of water are important constraints that would need to be addressed in the Eleventh Five Year Plan. The strategy to be followed in the Eleventh Five Year Plan for this sector is described in the following section.

ELEVENTH FIVE YEAR PLAN STRATEGY FOR MAJOR, MEDIUM, AND MINOR IRRIGATION

2.42 The GoI launched Bharat Nirman Programme in 2005–06. The irrigation component of the programme envisages creation of an additional 6.2 MH of irrigation potential. This target will be achieved through major, medium, and minor projects for surface water and ERM schemes. Owing to comparatively low allocation by the States for irrigation projects, intervention of the Centre for creation of irrigation potential will be required. AIBP is the only programme under MoWR to assist State Governments to achieve the targets set under the surface water component of irrigation programme of Bharat Nirman.

TABLE 2.10
Financial Performance in Flood Management during the Tenth Plan

(Rs Crore)

Year	Approved/Revised Outlay			Expenditure (Actual/Anticipated)		
	States	Centre	Total	States	Centre	Total
2002–03	624	151	775	698	86	785
2003–04	496	156	652	523	96	619
2004–05	669	184	853	644	100	744
2005–06	933	232	1165	830	181	1011
2006–07	1034	680	2520	1116	194	1310
Total	4562	1403	5965	3811	657	4468

TABLE 2.11
Flood Damage and Relief in the Tenth Plan

(Rs Crore)

Year	Flood Damage Reported	Recommended Calamity Relief Fund
2002–03	2575	1600
2003–04	4434	1587
2004–05	3337	1286

2.43 The Prime Minister has announced a rehabilitation package for agrarian distress districts of Andhra Pradesh, Karnataka, Kerala, and Maharashtra which includes early creation of irrigation facilities in these districts. The package includes 65 MMI projects to be completed through assistance to be provided under AIBP out of which 28 projects are already included under AIBP assistance. It has also been decided to provide assistance under AIBP to the projects providing irrigation facilities to drought-prone tribal areas as well as to States which are having irrigation development of their potential below national average.

Linkage of AIBP with Command Area Development

2.44 It has been observed that utilization of the created irrigation potential through AIBP is not up to the expected level. One of the reasons for non-utilization or low utilization of created irrigation potential is non-completion of CAD work in the area where irrigation facilities have been created. The CAD Programme should be integrated with the project implementation and upon completion of the project the water should reach to the farm gate instead of creating the irrigation potential which is not immediately utilized. It is also pertinent to mention that the cost of land development works should also be integrated with the project cost which may be funded under AIBP. The inclusion of CAD component with the cost of the project may affect the benefit–cost ratio of the project.

National Projects

2.45 For quite sometime many State Governments have been raising the issue of declaring some irrigation projects as 'National Projects'. The criteria for the selection of these projects, their mode of implementation and pattern of funding, etc. are yet to be finalized. However, it is obvious that the projects which are on international borders and the projects benefiting two or more States should figure as National Projects.

Monitoring of the Projects with Remote Sensing

2.46 During the end of the Tenth Plan, the Planning Commission insisted on monitoring of the project funded under AIBP through remote sensing. Accordingly a pilot scheme for monitoring Teesta and Upper Krishna projects through remote sensing has been taken up. The results of remote sensing have been matched with the ground realities and were found to the extent of 90% close to actuals. Accordingly the MoWR has assigned the job of monitoring of 53 projects covering the area of 5 MH for remote sensing monitoring.

STRATEGY

2.47 The following steps could be taken for major, medium, and minor irrigation sector for the Eleventh Five Year Plan.

Major and Medium Irrigation Projects

- Funds would be earmarked by the Planning Commission in the State plans so that the ongoing schemes under AIBP can be completed in time and cost over-run is avoided.
- Since the fund requirement for medium or minor irrigation projects are less, adequate funds may be made available for completion of these projects, without jeopardizing the programme for major projects. ERM projects should be given due priority where the eroded potential can be restored with moderate expenditure.
- Foremost priority should be given for completion of the ongoing projects.
- Ongoing projects which have already achieved 90% or more of the ultimate potential should be considered as completed. It is also neceesary to critically review all such projects which are having only marginal benefit left or are near impossible to complete because of various problems, and declare them completed or curtailed or deleted. The balance cost of the remaining projects should be updated realistically for consideration during the Eleventh Plan.
- Inter se priority should be decided considering various aspects such as externally aided projects, inter-state projects, projects benefiting drought-prone or tribal areas, etc. as per the guidelines prepared by National Commission for Integrated Water Resources Development Plan.
- High priority should be accorded to the Pre-Seventh and Seventh Plan Projects for funding under AIBP to complete these projects during the Eleventh Plan.
- Schemes should be given out on fixed cost time certain contract basis with incentive and penalty clause.
- Remote sensing satellite monitoring should be the

basis for the performance of the implementation and accordingly the next release of funds should be made.

- The CAD works and project execution should be in one package to ensure the availability of water upon completion of the project.
- The ERM projects are being funded under AIBP assistance and their funding should be linked with improvement in efficiency of the irrigation system and for this purpose minimum threshold target efficiency should be considered.
- To improve efficiency, irrigation projects should be benchmarked for performance evaluation by an independent expert group so that optimum use of water is realized. The AIBP assistance in the form of grant should be made according to the performance parameters.
- A separate budget head up to 15% of Plan fund may be provided as Irrigation Maintenance Fund (IMF) and full amount of irrigation revenue as collected should be credited to the IMF.
- In addition to the liabilities of completed projects and provision for ongoing and new projects, the State plan proposals should incorporate provisions for special repairs of existing irrigation systems, dam safety measures, improved water management, and water development aspect encompassing survey and investigation, R&D, training, and National Hydrology Project.
- System maintenance and revenue realization should be handed over to beneficiaries groups or Water Users Associations (WUAs).
- The existing regional and State-level institutions such as Water and Land Management Institutes should be strengthened and brought into mainstream activities for irrigation management improvement.
- Dam safety measures should be taken up systematically for Disaster Prevention and Management. 5% of plan fund may be allocated for undertaking dam safety activities to ensure that dams in distress get special and timely attention.
- The performance evaluation of completed projects needs to be continued for benchmarking and improvement in irrigation efficiency.
- New projects should be undertaken only after confirming that adequate funds for ongoing programmes are available, in the State plan as well as the availability of Central assistance by the Planning Commission.
- Introduce the concept of National Projects.
- Review the requirements and process of environmental clearance.

Minor Irrigation Sector

- Renovation and restoration of old tanks as well as old diversion channels in hilly regions may be given high priority.
- Micro irrigation system in water deficit areas should be promoted.
- Groundwater development in areas having untapped and unutilized potential, particularly in the Eastern Region should be promoted through a time-bound programme.
- A comprehensive strategy as recommended by the expert group for regulation of groundwater development and use on sustainable basis should be implemented.

GROUNDWATER EXPLOITATION AND GOVERNANCE FOR PREVENTING OVER-EXPLOITATION OF GROUNDWATER

2.48 The two concerns about groundwater are over-exploitation in parts of the country and under-utilization in large parts of the country. The region-wise potential is as follows.

- Alluvial areas of the east and north east regions (NER) (particularly Assam, Bihar, West Bengal, and Uttar Pradesh) with low stage of groundwater development have an additional potential of around 2.7 MH from the unconfined aquifers.
- Hard rock areas of peninsular India have an additional potential of around 0.8 MH by judicious and scientific development of groundwater in Andhra Pradesh, Chhattisgarh, Jharkhand, Kerala, Maharashtra, Orissa, Tamil Nadu, and parts of Madhya Pradesh.
- Hilly areas of the north and the NER have a marginal additional potential of around 0.04 MH in Arunachal Pradesh, Himachal Pradesh, Jammu and Kashmir, Manipur, Tripura, and Uttaranchal.
- Deeper confined aquifers in the alluvial plains of Uttar Pradesh, Haryana, and Punjab have an

additional potential of 1.0 MH by tapping deeper confined aquifers. However, there is need to undertake detailed studies to establish the 'Safe Yield' from such aquifers to avoid any adverse environmental impacts.

2.49 Sustainable groundwater development and management need to be taken up by incorporating studies on artificial recharge to groundwater and rainwater harvesting, management of salinity ingress in coastal regions, sustainable management in areas with high levels of groundwater development, conjunctive use of surface water and groundwater, and regulation of groundwater development. There are number of groundwater extraction structures in the country which are very old, have outlived their working life, and are not functional. These structures, in reality, do not contribute to irrigation potential. Such structures need replacement for restoration of old/already created potential. As suggested by NABARD, replacement may be planned at 0.5 MH during the Eleventh Five Year Plan in only safe and semi-critical blocks/units.

2.50 MI and groundwater development provide plenty of scope for employment of unskilled labour forces. It is, therefore, very important to link National Rural Employment Guarantee Programme (NREGP) with MI and groundwater development.

2.51 The UIP through ground- water resources has been assessed to be about 64 MH in the country, out of which 46.03 MH has been created upto the end of the Tenth Plan. Since groundwater is an open access resource and everyone is entitled to pump water below his own land, it is over-exploited in a number of blocks in the country and the water table is going down. This increases the cost of irrigation and farmers are required to periodically deepen their wells.

2.52 In order to address the issues of sustainable use of groundwater and the question of ownership of the groundwater, the Planning Commission has set up an expert group on 'GroundWater Management and Ownership' chaired by Member (Water and Energy) Kirit S. Parikh. The group recommended that the ownership of the groundwater below the land will continue to remain with the owner of the land as per the Easement Act 1882 as long as the exploitation of groundwater is not causing depletion in the ground water levels so the similar rights of the adjoining landowners and public at large are not encroached upon. Centre's intervention would be required when the groundwater level falls below the replenishable level. In such events, the affected area will be declared as an area under threat and any exploitation will be regulated. The Central Ground Water Authority, under the provisions of Environment Act 1986, is empowered to make such declarations and it would be the responsibility of the State Government to ensure that the exploitation in the area is regulated.

2.53 The group has noted that the experiences at national and international levels have shown that a command and control mechanism has not yielded good results in protecting the groundwater resources from over-exploitation. The regulation/reduction/restriction on the groundwater usage can be made effective by the State Government only with the co-operation of user groups and community participation involving PRIs. The user groups will be responsible for regulating the ground water usage among various sectors, that is irrigation, drinking, and industrial. Such regulations by the user group can be made effective only if the State/Central Ground Water Board (CGWB) monitors and provides information on safely extractable water on the basis of water table levels recorded scientifically.

AUGMENTING UTILIZABLE WATER

2.54 Usable water availability can be increased by tapping water that otherwise would have run-off to the sea. Water storage above ground through dams and diversion through weirs are the conventional means. However, water can also be stored underground by enhancing percolation through artificial recharge. Rain water harvesting in many small ponds through construction of bunds can also add to water availability. Inter-basin transfer of water through inter-linking of rivers can substantially expand availability.

ARTIFICIAL RECHARGE AND RAIN WATER HARVESTING

2.55 The groundwater levels are declining in many parts of the country. Artificial recharge of groundwater with rainwater is an important strategy to arrest this trend. The CGWB has already prepared a master plan to recharge 36 bcm of rainwater into groundwater at a cost of Rs 24500 crore. Except for pilot projects in the Eighth and Ninth Plans, no serious effort has been made to implement this on a mission mode. In urban areas, many cities have by-laws making rainwater harvesting compulsory for new buildings. However in rural areas there is no such programme.

2.56 Local storage is cost effective. There is significant potential for increasing the overall utilizable water through rainwater harvesting, construction of check dams, watershed management, and restoration of traditional water bodies as well as creation of new ones. In areas where groundwater is under severe stress, artificial recharging would need to be undertaken with proper technical support. Resources under the NREGP, BRGF, etc. are available for this purpose. The multilateral agencies such as World Bank and Asian Development Bank (ADB) have also been requested to provide financing for this purpose. Alternatively, a cess on the bottled water (since many negative externalities are associated with it like generation of plastic waste, their improper disposal, etc.) can be levied and funds from such levy could be used for revival of traditional water bodies or for recharging ground water with community participation. The challenge is to motivate the local communities to undertake this work on priority basis and to build their capacity for this purpose. Technical support systems for developing an optimal water management master plan for a micro watershed/ hydrological unit need to be created. Groundwater mapping, GIS mapping, satellite imagery, etc. need to be utilized for assisting the village community in preparing water resource development and management of master plans. With broadband connectivity expected to reach all over rural India in the Eleventh Plan this is feasible. It does however pose a difficult challenge in creating the institutional systems and delivery mechanisms for providing technical back-up support to the village community for preparing water management master plans.

2.57 The flood plains in the vicinity of rivers can be good repositories of groundwater. A planned management of groundwater in the flood plain aquifers offers an excellent scope of its development to meet the additional requirements of water. The development of groundwater in the Yamuna flood plain area in Delhi is an example of scientific management of water resources. During rainy season, the flood water spreads over the plains but due to very shallow water table the recharge is small and the rejected recharge result in river out flows. CGWB constructed 95 tubewells in Palla Sector in the depth range of 38–50 m for Delhi Jal Board. The total pumpage during the pre-monsoon period of 2002 was 40 million gallons per day which created a regional drawdown of about 5 m in the flood plain area. It was observed that immediately after rainy season, the depleted aquifer fully recouped. Thus over-development of shallow aquifers in flood plains creates the necessary subsurface space for augmentation of groundwater from the river flows during the monsoon. Induced recharge is an effective management tool to meet the gap of demand and supply in areas adjacent to rivers with active flood plains.

Inter-Basin Transfers through Inter-linking of Rivers

2.58 The inter-linking of rivers and the transfer of surplus water, especially in the monsoon period from the surplus basins to the deficient basins has been championed by many experts over time. The task force on the inter-linking of rivers has drawn up a set of project proposals. The total amount of water that can be usefully transferred is estimated to be about 220 bcm. However, there are apprehensions that the assessed surplus is somewhat illusory for many basins and future generations would actually need all the water. Sceptics have reservations about the economic viability of such large projects. Environmental concerns would need to be addressed through the environmental appraisal process of each project. For these reasons the pace of progress in the Tenth Plan period has been quite modest and is summarized in Table 2.12.

2.59 The availability of water in the country has vast variation both in time and space. The bulk of the rainfall is concentrated in the monsoon months June to September. While 51.12 MH is affected by droughts, mainly in peninsular India, 40 MH is affected by floods mainly in Bihar and Assam. The per capita availability of water is 1820 m^3 which is above the water

TABLE 2.12
Progress of Inter-linking of Rivers

S. No.	Item of Work	Progress Made So Far
1	Preparation of feasibility reports (FRs) by National Water Development Agency (NWDA)	NWDA has already prepared 16 FRs (14 under Peninsular Component, 2 under Himalayan Component). Draft FR of 4 links under Himalayan Component in advance stage of completion and remaining are in progress.
2	Inter-linking of rivers is to be pursued continuously with a focus on peninsular component	The MoWR is laying special emphasis on undertaking the works of the peninsular components on priority and accordingly NWDA is working on this component.
3	Priority links Ken–Betwa	(i) After signing of MOU by concerned states of UP and MP for preparation of DPR for Ken–Betwa link on 25 August 2005, work started by NWDA.
	Parbati–Kalisindh–Chambal	(ii) Concerned States of MP and Rajasthan are discussing bilaterally to sort out differences for MOU of Parbati–Kalisindh–Chambal link.
4	Identification of another priority link	NWDA has identified three more links in Peninsular Component namely Damanganga–Pinjal and Par–Tapi–Narmada and Polavaram–Vijayawada link as priority links.

stress condition threshold value of 1700 m^3. However the per capita availability varies from 18417 m^3 in the Brahmaputra river to 380 m^3 in some east-flowing rivers in Tamil Nadu showing that many basins in the country are already critically starved of water. Out of the annual precipitation and snowfall of 4000 bcm, 747 bcm runs waste to the sea, mainly from the Ganga and Brahmaputra rivers systems, which have 60% of the water potential. Only 19% of the water potential is available in Mahanadi, Godavari, Krishna and Cauvery.

2.60 In the above backdrop, inter-linking of rivers assumes importance as a part of the 747 bcm running waste to sea (about 160–220 bcm) is proposed to be transferred through a series of 30 inter-linking proposals from surplus basins to deficit basins. Long-distance, trans-basin transfer of water is not a new concept. Many examples of existing projects can be given in this regard—Western Yamuna canal, Periyar project, Kurnool Cuddapah canal, Indira Gandhi canal, and Sardar Sarovar canal. International examples can be given of California water transfer project from north to central and southern parts of the US, China, the erstwhile USSR, Sri Lanka, and Mexico. Pioneering work was earlier done on a National Water Grid by K.L. Rao and Capt. Dastur. These were refined by the MoWR and 30 links identified—16 as peninsular component and 14 as Himalayan component. Pre-feasibility studies of 16 links (14 in peninsular component) have also been completed.

2.61 Before detailed project reports (DPR) are taken up, consensus among States is required so that implementation can smoothly begin after the DPRs are appraised. Five links have already been identified for DPR preparation and dialogue with concerned States initiated by MoWR. Co-operation of States is thus a sine qua non for success of the inter-link projects. The National Common Minimum Programme (NCMP) also stresses for a consultative approach to the project. One could even think of monetary compensation to the donor States in the form of a royalty as is being done for other natural resources such as coal and oil.

2.62 Since water will be transferred at a great cost, the economics of the proposal will need a careful evaluation taking into consideration not only primary benefits but also secondary and tertiary benefits. The environmental impacts of such a large-scale transfer will also need a very careful study and integration into the economic evaluation. Stress needs to be laid on promotion of drip and sprinkler irrigation and horticulture crops from the point of view of water saving and optimum returns. The funding will have to come from a mix of budgetary support, market borrowings, and external assistance. For the implementation of such a mega project, an authority may have to be set up akin to the National Highways Authority of India (NHAI) with full autonomy for raising loan, approvals, etc. The maintenance of the created assets will have to be properly done with required revenues generated from the project.

2.63 Inter-linking of rivers is a challenging project and is essential for meeting the looming water crisis in future. The syndrome of drought and floods is hampering the required growth in agriculture and inter-linking of rivers offers an effective solution to the problem. In the Eleventh Plan the inter-basin transfer of water needs to be pursued more vigorously. Where a consensus emerges regarding the prima facie feasibility of specific projects their DPR preparation, environmental appraisal and decision on investment as well as execution modalities need to be completed in a time-bound manner. The execution of some projects should commence in the Eleventh Plan period.

IMPROVING WATER USE EFFICIENCY

2.64 For a gross irrigated area of about 87 MH, the water use is 541 bcm which gives a delta of 0.68 m per ha of gross irrigated area. The average annual rainfall is 1170 mm (1.17 m). Taking 70% of the rainfall as effective for crop consumptive use, the gross water use is about 1.45 m (4.8 feet) per ha of the gross irrigated area. This is very high as compared to water use in irrigation systems in say the US where water allocation is about 3 feet. This overuse in the country reflects a low irrigation efficiency of about 25% to 35% in most irrigation systems, with efficiency of 40% to 45% in a few exceptional cases. A basin-wise study conducted by A. Vaidyanathan and K. Sivasubramaniam of the Madras Institute of Development Studies (MIDS) using potential evapotranspiration data and gross water withdrawals reports the overall irrigation efficiency in the country as 38%. The study reveals that the Krishna, Godavari, Cauvery, and Mahanadi systems have a very low efficiency of around 27% while the Indus and Ganga systems are doing better with efficiencies in the range of 43%–47%. This is understandable as the peninsular rivers have large areas under irrigation in delta areas, where the water management practices are poor, while the rotational water supply (wara bandi) is practised in the Indus and Ganga systems. However, this is only a macro-level study. Project-level data available on irrigation efficiency unfortunately is minimal. It needs to be appreciated that 55% of the area irrigated is by groundwater sources where the efficiencies are quite high (70%–80%) in view of absence of long conveyance systems. Consequently the efficiencies in surface irrigation systems must be much lower than the average figure of 38%.

REASONS FOR LOW IRRIGATION EFFICIENCY

2.65 The reasons that contribute to low irrigation efficiency can be identified as follows:

- Completion of dam/head works ahead of canals.
- Dilapidated irrigation systems.
- Unlined canal systems with excessive seepage.
- Lack of field channels.
- Lack of canal communication network.
- Lack of field drainage.
- Improper field levelling.
- Absence of volumetric supply.
- Inadequate extension services.
- Low rate for water.

2.66 The equitable and optimal use of water from canal irrigation has been a matter of continuing concern. The traditional approach of pursuing these objectives through the field-level functionaries of irrigation department had its limitations. The participation of actual beneficiaries through PIM and the maintenance of village-level distribution channels through WUAs have been found useful. There is broad consensus that this has been a step in the right direction. This needs to be pursued more vigorously with genuine empowerment of WUAs. The objective should be to cover the entire command of all major and medium projects with WUAs by the end of the Eleventh Plan. The experience across States has been uneven. It is reported that 55501 users associations has been created and their State-wise position is indicated in Table 2.13.

ON-FARM WATER MANAGEMENT

2.67 On-farm water management covers a gamut of areas such as field channels, field drains, land levelling,

TABLE 2.13
State-wise Number of WUAs Formed and Irrigated Area Covered

S. No.	Name of State	Number of WUAs Formed	Area Covered (Thousand Hectare)
1	Andhra Pradesh	10790	4800.00
2	Arunachal Pradesh	2	1.47
3	Assam	37	24.09
4	Bihar	37	105.80
5	Chhattisgarh	945	NA
6	Goa	42	5.00
7	Gujarat	576	96.68
8	Haryana	2800	200.00
9	Himachal Pradesh	875	35.00
10	Jammu and Kashmir	1	1.00
11	Karnataka	2279	1052.41
12	Kerala	3930	148.48
13	Madhya Pradesh	1470	1501.45
14	Maharashtra	1299	444.00
15	Manipur	62	49.27
16	Meghalaya	99	NA
17	Nagaland	25	NA
18	Orissa	11020	907.00
19	Punjab	957	116.95
20	Rajasthan	506	219.65
21	Tamil Nadu	7725	474.28
22	Uttar Pradesh	24	10.55
23	West Bengal	10000	37.00
	Total	55501	10230.08 (say, 10.23 MH)

and irrigation scheduling with the objective of reducing field application losses. The works below the outlet are traditionally taken as CAD works and are not included as a part of the scope of the irrigation project which stops at the outlet. Out of an investment of Rs148000 crore in major, medium, and minor irrigation till the Ninth Plan, the investment in CAD works has been only Rs 6800 crore or 4.6%. This low outlay is an important contributory factor to poor on-farm water management, viz. low application efficiency and shortage in supplies to tail-enders. Since stepping up of CAD allocations by the States will be difficult, one measure that could be taken is to include all CAD works as a part of the project itself so that infrastructure required for irrigation water to reach every field is implemented alongwith the dam. This, together with conjunctive use, will no doubt hike project cost but since compartmentalized approach has not succeeded, an integrated approach will have to be seriously considered. There is an option to dovetail these works with the rural development programmes such as NREGP, BRGF, district plan, etc.

MICRO IRRIGATION

2.68 Micro irrigation, comprising drip and sprinkler, has emerged as a tool for effective management of resources which save water, fertilizer as well as electricity and distribute water evenly unlike other irrigation systems. Drip irrigation is ideally suited for horticulture crops such as pomegranate, grapes, mango, banana, guava, coconut, *amla*, and cash crops such as sugarcane. Drip irrigation saves 25%–60% water and upto 60% increase in yield can be obtained. Sprinklers are useful in undulating land with cereals crops and save 25%–33% of water. Out of the 69 MH net irrigated area in the country, only 0.5 MH under drip and 0.7 MH under sprinkler has been achieved. Maharashtra has 46% of the area under drip in the country. Karnataka, Tamil Nadu, and Andhra Pradesh follow with percentage area of 21%, 14%, and 12%, respectively. Drip irrigation methods range from simple bucket kit systems for small farms to automated systems linking release of water to soil moisture conditions measured continuously by tensiometers.

2.69 It is suggested that while sanctioning new irrigation projects, it would be made obligatory for project authorities to implement micro irrigation in at least 10% of the command area. The various suggestions of the Task Force on Micro Irrigation also need to be taken note of as micro irrigation has the potential to transform Indian agriculture.

RURAL AND URBAN DRINKING WATER AND SANITATION

2.70 These issues and programmes are discussed in Volume II, Chapter 5, 'Drinking Water, Sanitation, and Clean Living Conditions'.

MEETING INDUSTRIAL WATER DEMAND

2.71 Industrial demand for water is growing. Also disposal of waste water from industries without appropriate treatment pollutes water bodies, underground aquifers, and soils. In addition long-term land use planning for urbanization and industrialization is now a necessity and provision of water on a sustainable long-term basis should be a key factor in such planning exercises. In the absence of such planning demand for water emerges in areas where the provision of water requires enormous investments in carriage systems over long distances or even treatment of sea water. With proper long-term planning in terms of location of special economic zones (SEZs), industrial parks, and townships it should be possible to optimize costs of industrial development. For meeting the water needs of industry the approach discussed next appears appropriate.

2.72 New industries should ideally be located only in planned industrial areas, industrial parks, townships on industrial/zones identified in township Master Plans. They should be provided water by the local authorities who should charge prescribed rates on a volumetric basis. These rates should fully cover:

- the cost of supply.
- a premium to reflect the scarcity value of water in areas where there is water shortage.
- the cost of treatment to enable the discharge to go back into the water system through drainage into irrigation canals, rivers, lakes, etc.

2.73 Where groundwater is the source of supply and is under stress, the cost of supply should include the cost of recharge wherever such recharge is required and the recharge component should be credited to a dedicated Recharge Fund (RF) so that its utilization is suitably monitored. For new and existing industries which would use groundwater on their own there should be a system of IT-based volumetric metering of actual extraction by water-intensive industries in those areas where ground water levels have become critical. For these areas, there should be prescribed rates for ground water use by industry in a particular hydrological unit. The option of recycling the water and using it for secondary needs, that is other than drinking, should be a strategy for the Eleventh Plan.

FLOOD MANAGEMENT

2.74 Every year some part or other of the country gets flooded. A multi-pronged approach consisting of measures of prevention, protection, management, forecasting, and early warning are needed.

PREVENTION AND PROTECTION

2.75 Floods can be prevented or significantly moderated by watershed management of the catchment area of rivers. Agriculture, which is the nodal ministry for the watershed management works, should work out a detailed programme in consultation with the MoWR. For international rivers originating in Nepal and Bhutan, a joint mechanism for watershed management needs to be evolved. Another way is to preserve and augment flood cushions like natural swamps and lakes which can be developed into detention basins. Also, capacity of existing depressions can be improved for absorbing flood waters. Special drives for development of Tal and Diara areas are needed. Construction of dams and reservoir schemes with adequate flood cushion provide long-term solution of flood problems. Efforts should also be made for utilizing the existing reservoirs in the country for flood moderation to the extent possible. Even in reservoirs constructed for power or other purposes, the rule curves may be framed in such way that effective flood moderation is achieved. Rule curves guide the operation of a reservoir and ensure that a desired level of storage cushion is maintained to absorb floods of specified probability. Raising and strengthening of the existing embankments, if required after detailed studies of hydrological, morphological, topographical, and developmental aspects, provide some protection.

2.76 Watershed management in the hilly catchments of the rivers originating in Nepal, Bhutan, and hilly areas of India should be selectively chosen and fully funded. Implementation should be done through a joint mechanism.

2.77 The ideal solution for flood control is the creation of adequate storages in flood prone river systems. The Damodar Valley Corporation (DVC) is the best example of a series of storage projects which have made floods in the Damodar river basin a matter of history. The Ganga–Brahmaputra–Barak basins are our most flood-prone basins. There is clearly a need to build storage reservoirs in the northern tributaries of the Ganga and in the Brahmputra and its tributaries in the NER. These storage projects need to be investigated designed and executed expeditiously.

For the northern tributaries of the Ganga, cooperation with Nepal would be required. Negotiations would need to be pursued with vision and constructive pragmatism.

2.78 The strategy of flood control through embankments has been pursued by the States over the years. A holistic view of an entire tributary or a large stretch of a tributary needs to be taken. Wherever feasible a one time decisive investment for a flood protection project should be made. The recommendations of expert groups and contemporary international experience in other rivers in Asia with monsoon climate need to be looked into.

MANAGING FLOODS

2.79 Construction at appropriate location of spilling sections/sluices in the flood embankment for the controlled flooding of the protected areas for restoring fertility, recharge of soil moisture and groundwater can be useful. Drainage sluices should be integral part of embankments to prevent water-logging in the protected areas. Flood management schemes should be integrated with other infrastructural development programmes in the sectors of roads, railways, inland waterways, and canal/command area development works. Drainage improvement in critical areas in the country should be given priority. Also dredging at selective locations, that is outfalls, etc. in the rivers and the tributaries, helps reduce flood levels in low-lying areas and also helps in quick drainage. Erosion of land by rivers should be minimized through suitable cost effective measures. The Centre should continue to assist the States in the Ganga and Brahmaputra Valleys through Plan Funds to counter land erosion by river action. In order to give adequate emphasis on the O&M of the flood protection measures already created, a percentage of outlay of the flood sector should be earmarked for this purpose. R&D activities for improved flood management need to be encouraged.

2.80 To the extent groundwater is intensively utilized for irrigation for multiple cropping in north Bihar and Bengal and local water bodies are restored, the capacity for recharge of groundwater in the monsoon period would increase and flooding would get mitigated partially. In other parts of India flash floods would get minimized if local drainage and restoration/creation of local water bodies was done with watershed planning under NREGP, BRGF, etc.

FORECASTING AND EARLY WARNING

2.81 Development of digital elevation model of flood-prone areas for taking up schemes for inundation forecast, preparation of flood risk maps, planning of flood management schemes, etc. should be taken up. Steps should be taken to ensure implementation of Action Plan prepared by National Disaster Management Authority (NDMA) for flood management.

SUSTAINABILITY

2.82 Two major challenges are being faced in ensuring sustainability of water, that is quality and quantity, to meet the needs. Groundwater use has to be restricted to average recharge and quality of water has to be improved and should be protected from biological and chemical contamination. Sustainable use of groundwater has been already discussed.

PRESERVING WATER QUALITY

2.83 The threats to water quality are from untreated industrial effluents and municipal wastes from habitations, pollution from open defecation, and run-off from farms containing fertilizers and pesticides. Upscaling total sanitation campaign (TSC) programme for rural sanitation (see Volume II, Chapter 5), strict enforcement of industrial effluent standards, and treatment of all municipal wastes are needed. At the same time farming practices have to be adjusted to use as little chemical fertilizers and pesticides and apply them in ways that minimize residues in run-off water, which is a waste for the farmer, are called for.

CONVERGENCE

2.84 The subject of water is presently being dealt at the Centre by a number of Ministries/Departments. The linkages of water with other sectors are many. Water availability and quality impact on social, human development and economic activities. Effective coordination among different ministries and convergence of programmes is essential. Suitable institutional arrangements would be made in the Eleventh Plan in this regard.

FINANCING THE ELEVENTH PLAN

2.85 The total projected GBS for the Eleventh Plan for MoWR is Rs 2870 crore (2006–07 price) and Rs 3246 crore (current price). As per the constitution, irrigation is a State subject; hence, the substantial investment will be contributed by the State Governments in this sector. The details of the recommended outlays for the Eleventh Five Year Plan and physical targets are indicated in Tables 2.14 and 2.15.

TABLE 2.14
The Overall Outlay for the Eleventh Five Year Plan

(Rs Crore)

State plan	182050
State sector schemes, i.e. AIBP and others	47015
Central plan	3246
Total	232311

2.87 In recognition of the fact that the actual requirements of the water resources sector, in general, and above schemes, in particular, could exceed the provisions made in the plan document, the size of the actual yearly allocations may exceed the pro rata allocation during AP discussion and the issue of an overall increase could be revisited at the time of MTA.

EMPLOYMENT GENERATION

2.88 When irrigated area increases it generates additional employment year after year. Water resources projects, particularly irrigation development and flood control works, generate significant employment opportunities during construction period as well as in the post-project phase. The overall employment potential likely to be generated in the Eleventh Five Year Plan in irrigation sector is as per Table 2.16 below.

TABLE 2.15
Physical Target

No. of Projects included in Eleventh Plan	Major	Medium	ERM
(i) Completion of Projects			
Tenth Plan projects spilling into Eleventh Plan	166	222	89
New projects of Eleventh Plan	78	145	86
Total	244	367	75
Projects likely to be completed in Eleventh Plan	72	133	132
(ii) Creation of Potential (in MH)			
MMI sector	9.00		
MI sector	7.00		
Surface water	1.50		
Ground water	4.50		
Restoration of water bodies and ERM	1.00		
(iii) Physical Targets for CADWM (in MH)			
Development of CCA	3.5		
Correction of conveyance deficiency	6.25		
Reclamation of water logged, saline, and alkaline lands	0.5		
(iv) Physical Target under Flood Control Works (MH)			
Area to be benefited against flood: 2.18 MH			

2.86 The following five core programmes of MoWR have been identified as important:

- River management activities and works related to border rivers.
- CAD and water management.
- AIBP.
- Repair renovation and restoration of water bodies.
- Flood management programmes other than border rivers.

TABLE 2.16
Overall Employment Potential

(Million Person Years)

	Direct Employment	Indirect Employment
MMI	2.1	10.1
MI	5	1.05
Flood Control	2.5	–
Total	9.6	11.15

THE WAY FORWARD

2.89 The measures suggested for the Eleventh Plan address the whole range of issues concerning water management and irrigation. The long gestation period in building irrigation infrastructure and thin spread of resources are the main reasons for delay in completion of a number of ongoing projects. During the Eleventh Plan a total of 477 projects including 166 major, 222 minimum, and 89 ERM projects are likely to spill-over. The spill-over cost of these projects during the Eleventh Plan is estimated to be about Rs 133746 crore. There is a need for reducing the gestation period and making available the benefits of irrigation to the users by way of integrating CAD programme with the projects. The projects should be implemented on a construction schedule not more than four to five years. The land acquisition and R&R works should be taken simultaneously with the project formulation. Irrigation efficiency in the systems needs to be upgraded from the present level of 35% to about 60% in case of surface water system and from about 65% to 75% in groundwater system. The efforts of the other departments such as Rural Development and Agriculture, etc. should be converged and an integrated approach for water resources development and conservation should be adopted. The various schemes of MoRD for rain water harvesting, watershed development, and NREG Act should be implemented in consultation with MoWR and Department of Drinking Water Supply (DoDWS). There is a need for (PPP) in development of water resource projects as this issue has already been addressed by NWP, 2002. The modern scientific development of water resources conservation, transfer, and application to the field is needed to be applied in the irrigation command. In flood management, the recurrence interval of the floods should be the guiding factor for taking up flood control measures. The flood control measures should not be taken in isolation but it should be based on master plan approach in an integrated manner. The sustainability of ground water is one of the core areas which require attention for meeting irrigation and drinking water requirements. Use of ground water should be limited and linked with the quantum of water being recharged. The issue of monitoring ground water levels through scientific methods such as Piezo meters, etc. should be left to the group of beneficiaries with proper technical support from the Central Government and the State Governments.

ANNEXURE 2.1
Plan-wise Cumulative Potential Created and Utilized

(In MH)

Plan	Potential Created					Potential Utilized				
	Major and Medium	SW	Minor GW	Total	Total	Major & Medium	SW	Minor GW	Total	Total
Upto 1951 (Pre-Plan)	9.7	6.4	6.5	12.9	22.6	9.7	6.4	6.5	12.9	22.6
First Plan 1951–56	12.2	6.43	7.63	14.06	26.26	10.98	6.43	7.63	14.06	25.04
Second Plan 1956–61	14.33	6.45	8.3	14.75	29.08	13.05	6.45	8.3	14.75	27.8
Third Plan 1961–66	16.57	6.48	10.52	17	33.57	15.17	6.48	10.52	17	32.17
Annual Plan 1966–69	18.1	6.5	12.5	19	37.1	16.75	6.5	12.5	19	35.75
Fourth Plan 1969–74	20.7	7	16.5	23.5	44.2	18.39	7	16.5	23.5	41.89
Fifth Plan 1974–78	24.72	7.5	19.8	27.3	52.02	21.16	7.5	19.8	27.3	48.46
Annual Plan 1978–80	26.61	8	22	30	56.61	22.64	8	22	30	52.64
Sixth Plan 1980–85	27.7	9.7	27.82	37.52	65.22	23.57	9.01	26.24	35.25	58.82
Seventh Plan 1985–90	29.92	10.9	35.62	46.52	76.44	25.47	9.97	33.15	43.12	68.59
Annual Plan 1990–92	30.74	11.46	38.89	50.35	81.09	26.31	10.29	36.25	46.54	72.85
Eighth Plan 1992–97	32.95	12.51	40.8	53.31	86.26	28.44	11.07	37.7	48.77	77.21
Ninth Plan 1997–2002	37.05	13.6	43.3	56.9	93.95	31.01	11.44	38.55	49.99	81
Tenth Plan 2002–2007	42.35	14.31	46.11	60.42	102.8	34.42	12	40.81	52.81	87.23

3

Forest

INTRODUCTION

3.1 National Forest Policy 1988 acknowledged the importance and primacy of local communities and provided for a sustainable management approach with maintenance of environmental stability as the prime objective. Commitment to conservation of nature is highlighted by the targets of maintaining one-third of land under the forest/tree cover. The social concerns are targeted through increasing productivity to meet local and national needs and creating a people's movement for afforestation. Industries have been advised to network with farmers for industrial raw material.

3.2 Forest cover is critical for a living environment as it influences the quality and quantity of air and water. The role of forests as carbon sinks endows them added recognition as an important environmental factor. Therefore, forest cover and afforestation have been dealt with in Volume I, Chapter 9, 'Environment and Climate Change'.

3.3 In India, per capita forest area is only 0.064 ha against the world average of 0.64 ha. (FAO). The productivity of our forests is only 1.34 m^3/ha/year against the world average of 2.1 m^3/ha/year. While 78% of the forest area is subjected to heavy grazing and other unregulated uses, adversely affecting productivity and regeneration, nearly 10 MH of forest area is subjected to shifting cultivation. Land use changes such as diversion of community areas for non-biomass purposes have directed nearly all biomass needs towards forests.

3.4 Plan investment in forestry and wildlife sector so far, including State and Central plan, has been about 1% of the total plan outlay. The National Forestry Commission (2006) has recommended an investment of 2.5% of the plan outlay in the forestry and wildlife sector.

3.5 As the State forest administration is responsible for management of forests, the focus of Central interventions should be on reinforcing the capacity of States to undertake the national policy mandates towards conservation and sustainable use. The strategy for the Eleventh Plan will, therefore, be to create an environment for achieving sustainable forestry and wildlife management with specific focus on the socio-economic targets. Accordingly, the following scenario will be the core of the forestry sector development strategy:

- The objective of enhancing the green cover will be integrated with livelihood opportunities. Suitable policy and legal measures for this purpose will back-up the programmatic interventions. The Tenth Plan strived to universalize Joint Forest Management (JFM). The resolve of the Eleventh Plan is to strengthen the regime by incorporating the concepts of harvesting, value addition, and facilitated marketing of forest produce.

- The ultimate aim of the State forest management will be to achieve optimally productive forests capable of providing timber and non-timber products, apart from the ecological services without unnatural change in the composition of the forests.
- The forests in the vicinity of habitations will be managed for livelihood needs of the neighbouring populations. For this, adequate support and empowerment will be ensured.
- The harvest of forest products will be governed by the availability. However, strategy for widening the production base beyond forests will be pursued to ensure sustainable use of the land resources of the country.
- Protected areas will be integrated with the sensitivities of local populations and protected area management planning will be based on the optimization of local community resources and the use of non-invasive benefits from the PAs directed towards the neighbouring population, on village eco-development principles.
- Support systems for attaining these results will be evolved in terms of R&D, capacity building, and strong information system for long as well as short term objective monitoring.

LINKING FORESTS TO LIVELIHOOD AND STRENGTHENING PARTICIPATORY PROCESSES

NATIONAL AFFORESTATION PROGRAMME

3.6 The CSS National Afforestation Programme (NAP) of National Afforestation and Eco-development Board (NAEB) assists rehabilitation of degraded forests through JFM Committees. Forest Development Agencies (FDAs) have been created at the district level to function as a link between the Ministry of Environment and Forest (MoEF) and JFM Committees for the scrutiny of projects, release of funds, and implementation of the sanctioned programmes.

3.7 NAP, as a CSS, has been the epicenter of the JFM movement. Out of about 22 MH forest area looked after by 1.07 lakh JFM Committees, NAP covers about 9 lakh ha through 23750 committees, which represents only 24% of the total committees and 4.20% of the total area under JFM. NAP as a stand-alone scheme may not have any impact unless it is able to influence the States to orient their programmes towards strengthening JFM.

3.8 There have also been certain shortcomings in the way JFM has been functioning. The modalities of JFM do not recognize the existing informal traditional institutions engaged in conservation. At the national level, centralized control on activities for NAP components has resulted in a slow pace of awareness and development of interface between the forest managers and community institutions.

3.9 In a national-level study conducted by the Indian Institute of Bio-Social Research and Development in 2004–05, JFM was evaluated in about 500 JFM Committee areas in 13 States across the country. The criteria were clarity and purpose of roles, institutional mechanisms, capacity of JFM Committees, and resource management. Impact on forest profile, socio-economic aspects such as household income, village development, women empowerment, and social unity were studied. The average score for institutionalization is 51% with high scores for West Bengal (68%), Rajasthan (62%), and Maharashtra (56%). However, no State has reached the state of incorporating and routinization of JFM. The effectiveness of the institutions has been rated as 50.28% with strong correlation with resource management. To achieve success the need for more motivation than mechanisms has been felt. Highest effectiveness was observed in Uttaranchal, West Bengal, Orissa, and the least in Karnataka, Andhra Pradesh, and Chhattisgarh.

3.10 Close analysis has revealed that conflicts and failures have been more where the benefits from managed resources are scarce or not clearly visible. This situation demands investment for improving productivity of the resources and rationalizing the modalities of sharing. Products from the forests could form a share of communities while ecological benefits including aperpetual green cover could be the national share. Products can then be accounted as the value paid by the State to the communities for the environmental services rendered by them for conserving forests.

3.11 National Afforestation/Eco-restoration Programme, as the flagship programme of the Central Government, will be designed for augmenting ecological resources and resultant benefits will accrue to the participating community. The main objective will be to empower all participatory institutions to ensure forest conservation.

- For improving the outreach of the Programme, States will also need to implement their forest improvement programmes through the Forest Development Agency (FDA) mechanism.
- It will be ensured that the micro plans evolve from the JFM Committees and the decisions on species for afforestation are based on a naturally compatible combination of species with local ownership.
- The JFM framework will duly recognize the existing Van Panchayat and other community forestry institutions and honour their democratic decisions related to management of forests. The gram sabhas under the PESA in Schedule V areas and the traditional institutions in the North East can act as community forestry institutions. The green cover of the community forests and the environmental services will be treated as the share of the State and the harvested products as the share of the community.
- The programme may also include a component for encouraging forest-based small enterprises with appropriate mechanisms for accessing forest produce. Self-employment programmes will be supported with training and capacity building of educated unemployed youth.
- The social component in the Programme can also include specific projects on decentralized energy solutions such as biomass gasification-based electricity, solar systems, etc., for improvement of community services, linking these to planting projects.
- The programme for afforestation/eco-restoration should leverage part of allocation under NREGP for augmenting the ecological resource base.

National Afforestation, Eco-restoration, and Eco-development Board

3.12 The NAEB may be renamed as the National Afforestation, Eco-restoration, and Eco-development Board (NAEEB) to broaden its vision to include non-tree ecosystems. The NAEEB programme will have the following components:

- Grants-in-Aid for Greening India Scheme will include assistance for setting up well-equipped nurseries for quality planting material, supported by well-networked genetic improvement plans and well-monitored seed/clone testing and certification programme, apart from afforestation efforts by NGOs.
- Monitoring and evaluation of the state of desertification and afforestation/eco-restoration programmes and co-ordination of programmes for combating desertification based on the defined criteria and indicators, as mandated within United Nations Convention to Combat Desertification (UNCCD).
- Support to regional centres of the NAEB to assist in dissemination of technologies and NAEEB programmes through mass awareness and studies.
- **Eco task forces** for afforestation/eco-restoration of the areas where afforestation/eco-restoration is not possible with participation of people due to harsh conditions.

Augmenting Common Biomass Resources

3.13 More than four lakh villages in the country do not have a forest in the vicinity. For augmenting the biomass resource base, community controlled and other accessible lands need to be made optimally productive.

3.14 Panchayat Raj Institutions should identify such available lands and empower the community groups for their regeneration and management on locally relevant terms. States will provide technology and wages through the social forestry wing, with the support of the Central Government through a new CSS. Thus the funds and technical support under this programme will be available where Panchayats are willing to put the underproductive lands under productive regimes.

3.15 The NREGP can be linked for building these common resources. However, this would presuppose proactive action by fund users and sustained supply of manpower till the establishment of the plantations.

Promotion of Agro-Forestry

3.16 Agro-forestry offers ancillary opportunities of sustained income per unit investment in agricultural lands as subsidiary to the main crops. While in commercial agriculture, bund planting has been popular, net returns are better than conventional practices in many situations in rainfed areas. Subsistence or commercial agro-forestry has thus scope to grow from the existing indicative contribution of about 3% to about 10% of the forest/tree cover.

3.17 India today imports large quantities of timber as well as pulp. For ensuring impetus in greening in farm sector, organizing markets and facilitating fair trade will be the priority. Concessions for cheap and duty-free import of pulp need to be reviewed. Market options and incentives including overseas markets should be available to the farmers. R&D for enhancing productivity and testing indigenous alternatives to conventional agro-forestry species such as Eucalyptus and Acacias, suitable for the farm sector, should be taken up.

MITIGATION OF DEGRADATION OF FORESTS

3.18 The management of government forests is handled by the State Governments whereas capacity building and research have been with the Central Government.

3.19 Apart from a network of regional centres of MoEF for monitoring the compliance of central regulations, a CSS Integrated Forest Protection was launched in the Tenth Plan. The programme could be made fully operational only in 2005–06 and is yet to show an impact. Assistance provided under this programme needs to be thoughtfully used for building modern sustainable forest management capacity of the states. This will include management information, inventory and assessment, and adoption of modern methods for planning and monitoring. Accordingly the following two programmes of MoEF, viz., Integrated Forest Protection, and Strengthening Forestry Divisions, are proposed to be reoriented in the Eleventh Plan.

INTENSIFICATION OF FOREST MANAGEMENT SCHEME

3.20 The Integrated Forest Protection Scheme will be redesigned to provide assistance to the states for building capacity and basic infrastructure for modern forest management. Improving Management Planning and Survey (land records) set-up will be the first priority for Central assistance. The following components will be provided for modernization of the State forest management:

- Modernization of the management planning (Working Plan) units with equipment, infrastructure, and manpower. This may include forest inventories, training and satellite imagery processing, and GIS facilities. This will also include professional services such as ecologists and sociologists for relevant inputs.
- Forest Land Information System for land records, with modern and empowered survey, and land record maintaining mechanisms for documenting the legally recognized individual rights, concessions, ownerships including those under the Scheduled Tribes and other Forest Dwellers (Recognition of Forest Rights) Act.
- Forest boundary demarcation by providing assistance for the state-of-the-art infrastructure, training/outsourcing survey work, fixing permanent boundary pillars, updating the forest block indices and compartment histories.
- Installation of forest fire surveillance and warning systems, along with fire management planning in participatory mode. This fire management system will also be integrated with a national network for forest fire surveillance and monitoring.
- Assistance for general infrastructure for accommodation in remote areas, communication, improvement of road network, etc., will also be a part of this programme.

STRENGTHENING FOREST MANAGEMENT

3.21 The programme will cover consultations and studies on relevant matters for efficient management of the sector including monitoring of compliance through the network of regional offices of the Ministry. Following specifically earmarked components should be part of this programme:

- A National Forestry Information system may be set up, along with networking with the States, for tracking the changes in forest development, harvesting, trade, and utilization scenarios. This will include information on non-timber forest produce

(NTFP) resources including medicinal and aromatic plants.
- The National Working Plan Code may be revisited for incorporating aspects dealing with ecological and biodiversity concerns of the forest areas. This will also include NTFP, medicinal, and aromatic plant resources.
- A mechanism for internationally recognized independent sustainable forest management certification regime for forest resources and products may be set-up.

Management of Gregarious Flowering in the North East

3.22 Muli bamboo, *Melocanna baccifera*, grows over an area of approximately 18000 square kilometre (sq km) in the States of Mizoram, Tripura, Manipur, and parts of Assam, Nagaland, and Meghalaya. The largest population of the species exists in Mizoram covering about 6700 sq km. Gregarious flowering has commenced after a flowering cycle of about 48 years and the whole flowered bamboo population will dry off after seed setting. This may result in ecological, economic, and social problems in the area due to destruction of large tracts, rendering them vulnerable to forests fires, depletion of important bamboo resources for the artisans and industry, and increase in rodent population causing further destruction and health hazards. For working out a strategy for management of gregarious flowering in the North East, consultations began in April 2002 which resulted in the launching of a CSS for which a sum of Rs 85 crore was approved by the Central Government as part of an action plan of Rs 366 crore. The programme actually took off in 2005–06 and will continue till 2008–09. The action plan has the following priorities:

- Resource survey and mapping be taken up for assessment of the growing stock affected.
- Harvesting of the standing crop of bamboo to the extent possible before flowering, including arrangements to facilitate transport by road, railway, waterways, etc. Effective ways of disposal of the harvested bamboo by linkages with paper mills like Hindustan Paper Corporation Ltd, promoting bamboo-based cottage industries and establishing mini mechanical chipping and pulping units in small-scale industrial sector.
- Regeneration of flowered areas including introduction of economically important bamboo species for subsequent use.

CAPACITY BUILDING AND RESEARCH

Capacity Building

3.23 The ongoing paradigm change in the forestry sector necessitates fundamental orientation and attitudinal changes of the personnel in line with multifarious roles of forests, corresponding variety of externalities, and for coping with traditional forestry management practices. This includes social sensitivities along with the scientific basis of the processes of nature.

3.24 An integrated capacity building programme will be designed for forestry personnel including training of trainers for State frontline staff training institutions and will also enable stakeholders to understand the perspective of conservation in human well being by providing them state-of-the-art information and knowledge base.

Indian Institute of Forest Management (IIFM)

3.25 IIFM has emerged as a premier forestry institution and has contributed to the development of criteria and indicators for sustainable forest management and participatory forest management processes. Based on an evaluation, IIFM intends to enlarge its educational and management development programmes as well as policy-relevant research focused on forestry and its linkages with rural institutions and natural resource-based rural livelihoods. The Institute will take up policy and development research including the valuation of ecosystem services, evaluation of the economy of participation in natural resource, especially forest management, and modelling of impact of climate change on livelihood and forest resources.

Wildlife Institute of India (WII)

3.26 Apart from the training, research, and advisory role of WII, the new approaches would include developing workable framework for mainstreaming conservation in development projects and policies, empirical studies on processes for ecological impacts of developmental projects and human activities, strengthening common property resource management, and developing expertise in managing wildlife in isolated and fragmented landscapes. The use of modern tools and technology and development of analytical capabilities will be undertaken.

INDIAN COUNCIL OF FORESTRY RESEARCH AND EDUCATION (ICFRE)

3.27 The Council was created in 1986 to evolve a scientific environment in forestry, in view of the new scope of genetic, ecological, climatic, and economic roles, compared to pre-1988 mandates, of largely silviculture-based management systems, and ancillary aspects on regeneration, harvest, and utilization. Accordingly, the management of research and education needs to be supported by enabling decision-making through consultation and in a professional capacity.

- The Council should have specific separate mandates regarding the administration of its institutes and co-ordination of research. For this purpose, a task group may be set up, involving top-level research managers, forest managers, and policy makers, to propose a working mechanism including resource mobilization for its research and education components. This group may also deliberate on integrating wildlife, biodiversity, and habitat/landscape/ ecological research concerns within the Council.
- For the plan period, 50% of the total grants-in-aid to ICFRE will be earmarked exclusively for research and education. The Council will encourage its institutes to collaborate with other institutions of repute in relevant fields including State Forest Research Institutes.
- Research programmes will be oriented towards meeting the priority areas of productivity, genetic improvements, ecosystem research, and updating growth and yield parameters required for analysis in management planning. Management of natural forests for improvement of their profile will be the main focus. The research and education programme in the field of utilization of wood and wood products should also include Indian Plywood Industries Research and Training Institute (IPIRTI).
- Nation-wide long-term genetic improvement programmes for indigenous species, screening of Indian species for fast growing, short rotation alternatives for traditional species for industry and protocols for survey, inventory, and management planning for NTFP, medicinal, and aromatic plants in forests will be launched.
- Specific thrust will be given for developing technologies and processes for agro-forestry and social forestry. Quality seed and planting material programmes in public or private sector will be supported by credible testing and certification regimes.
- A forest biodiversity network will be established for integrating the available information on one platform and for studies in the left out areas. It will be compatible with the management planning systems of forest administration and the other existing/ evolving information resources.
- Inter-sectoral impacts, trade, and market aspects of forest economics, ecosystem research, policy research, and concerns of climate change including carbon trade methodologies, will be taken up.

INDIAN PLYWOOD INDUSTRIES RESEARCH AND TECHNOLOGY INSTITUTE (IPIRTI)

3.28 Besides the specific mandate of developing technologies for efficient utilization of wood in structural material, development and promotion of technologies for alternative and efficient use of residual waste like bamboo, husk, wood waste, small wood, etc., will be the thrust areas. Better utilization of the agro-forestry species including treatments for longevity of the products will be the focus of research for utilization. Apart from its own grants in aid, IPIRTI will be integrated with ICFRE for wood utilization research and technology. Technology transfer being the mandate of IPIRTI, professional courses on wood technology should be planned.

FOREST SURVEY OF INDIA (FSI)

3.29 Present scope of the FSI is limited to the assessment of tree canopy cover. The information is not sufficient for objective assessment and planning for the sector.

3.30 Scope of interpretation of satellite data for tree cover will include separate canopy status in forest lands, patterns of degradation, and state of commercial plantations. With redefined green cover, appropriate indicators compatible with the technologies used by FSI need to be developed. Monitoring of ecological status of landscapes/habitats in terms of the dynamics of vegetation and early warning systems, productivity, consumption, and supply from forest and non-forest resources will be taken up. On the basis of these priorities, rationalization of the present network of regional units and manpower will be taken up. The scope, definition, and components of FSI inventories will be decided at an expert group level, in order to render them compatible with various national and international formats, definitions, and organizations for collaboration.

SOCIO-ECONOMIC AND POLICY IMPERATIVES

TRIBALS, NTFP, AND PESA

3.31 State governments will need to provide support for implementation of the Scheduled Tribes and other Forest Dwellers (Recognition of Forest Rights) Act for preparing the forest land records for the recognized rights, mapping of common forests for community management, and developing management plans.

3.32 To maximize economic benefits to the communities with sustainable forest use, the available mechanisms for dealing with NTFP will be reviewed. As the large volume NTFPs require dealing and trading at higher scale, professional services can be organized through the marketing federations of NTFP gatherers/processors. Nationalized system of collection through corporations and contracts will be dealt with in the light of the settled policy and legal position. Improving livelihood through gainful employment opportunities will be encouraged by organizing value addition of NTFP at community level under the NAP. For capacity building and technology assistance, linkages with voluntary organizations and programmes such as National Bamboo Mission, National Mission on Bamboo Applications, Village and Small Scale Industries, and institutes of rural development and technologies will be established.

GENDER PERSPECTIVE

3.33 Women are the principal stakeholders in natural resource use and management. It is crucial to ensure equal representation of women in the decision making and implementation processes in participatory planning and development programmes. JFM principles indicate 50% participation of women in JFM institutions. However, the models vary among States. The participation of women should be ensured in all community activities and the decisions should be based on their considered opinions. This should hold good for not only JFM but also processes such as afforestation through Panchayats, protected area management, planning, and use of common property resources including NTFP under the Tribal Rights Act or PESA. Thus gender perspective should be a visible component of any community-based programme.

MOBILIZATION OF RESOURCES FOR AFFORESTATION

3.34 Apart from enrichment activity for forests, afforestation/eco-restoration helps in sustaining the livelihood of the rural poor. Developing multipurpose resources in underproductive forest or non-forest areas must be a component of any employment generation programme. A shelf of afforestation/eco-restoration programmes will be generated for village communities for implementation under the NREGP. Necessary institutional initiatives will include notification of afforestation as one of the activities, and dovetailing afforestation programmes with the NREG programme.

COMPENSATORY AFFORESTATION FUND MANAGEMENT AND PLANNING AUTHORITY (CAMPA)

3.35 While considering the proposals for diversion of forest lands for non-forestry purposes under Forest (Conservation) Act, 1980, MoEF generally levies cost of compensatory afforestation in equivalent non-forest lands offered by the user agencies or in degraded forest land. Net present value of the land allowed to be diverted is also realized from the user agency. The funds thus accrued were to be made available by the respective States for identified compensatory afforestation and other forest development activities. The Apex Court had, however, observed that the funds were not appropriated to the implementing authorities. It, therefore, directed the Central Government in 2002 to constitute an authority for management of the funds received from the user agencies and their exclusive and prompt utilization for the intended purpose. MoEF notified the constitution of CAMPA on 23 April 2004 for management and use of this fund for forest development. However, the mechanism is yet to take effect. It is understood that presently an amount of about Rs 5000 crore is available with CAMPA for utilization in forest conservation activities. The amount should be made available in the current plan period on the basis of specific project proposals from the States.

FOREST PLANTATIONS

3.36 For sustaining forest cover, existing commercial plantations should be intensively managed for optimum productivity and provided with scientifically designed inputs including quality planting material, cultural/silvicultural treatments, etc. Harvesting and replanting should be the interlinked operations. In the context of the required thrust on agro-forestry, it should be ensured that plantation projects in forest lands avoid agro-forestry species.

3.37 On the other hand, afforestation works should be taken up with a specific context and habitat profile in mind and only in participatory mode with local communities. The species selection should be a part of the micro plans. The Central Government is responsible for the approval and monitoring of Working Plans. Therefore, MoEF should ensure that no new commercial plantations are created in the name of afforestation/eco-restoration.

PRIVATE FORESTRY INITIATIVES

3.38 The Central Government has been deliberating on modalities of PPP. The concept of multi-stakeholder partnership in forestry is primarily based on granting tenure on degraded lands (including forest lands) to investors with benefit-sharing arrangements. Considering the multiple stakes of local communities over the forest lands, and the accepted position of first charge of communities on natural resources, such partnership with industry for forest lands is not desirable. However, with the explicit consent of the communities in public-hearing mode, possibilities of such ventures in non-forest wastelands can be explored.

3.39 Encouraging industry as a dedicated destination for agro-forestry products will be desirable and focus should be on establishing appropriate linkages with the farmers for cultivation of tree crops as suggested in the National Forest Policy 1988. The examples of ITC-Bhadrachalam and other similar initiatives within the private sector are worth emulating in this context.

AREAS UNDER SHIFTING CULTIVATION

3.40 The North Eastern hill areas need to be viewed as cultivated and uncultivated domains—both with extensive tree cover owned by people, individually or collectively. The length of the *jhum* cycle is the main determinant of degradation of jhum lands. The reduced amount of land available for jhum shortens the fallow period and results in increased economic pressure on low-income families. Most of the shifting cultivation is practiced on lands with customary community rights. In such areas, any afforestation activity beyond fallow management is expected to face resistance. Replacement of these practices by settled agriculture or horticulture has resulted in alienation of the lands from common categories, putting further pressure on the remaining commons.

3.41 For the areas with jhum cycles above 10 years, the tree farming model of Nagaland Environmental Protection and Economic Development Project may be studied. It provides for planting of fast-growing indigenous trees along with main crop to ensure that the trees attain harvestable girths by the subsequent slash and burn stage, and find demand in the timber market. While tree planting can be supported under NAP, appropriate market linkages for ensuring economic benefits to the farmers from the tree products will be quite useful. For this, opening up markets beyond NER with appropriate safeguards is important.

ECO-TOURISM

3.42 Eco-tourism, including homestead tourism, offers excellent possibilities of taking the benefits of nature conservation to local communities in many ways. The protected areas and the adjoining terrestrial and wetland ecosystems have the potential to contribute to the rural economy and community development. A long-term policy is needed on eco-tourism, complementary with the conservation objectives and participation of the local stakeholders from the serving communities.

3.43 The eco-tourism plans should include modalities of managing the ecological and socio-economic integrity of the area, designs to strengthen the capacities of locally formed institutions, such as land management committee, waste management committee, alternative fuel technology institutions, tour operators committee, etc. The programmes should be taken up with the tourism sector and build on community ownership to promote equitable distribution of the net benefits.

PRESERVATION OF WILDLIFE AND FOREST BIODIVERSITY

3.44 The 1952 National Forest Policy provided for setting up of sanctuaries and national parks for preservation of wildlife. Enactment of the Wildlife (Protection) Act, 1972, launch of Project Tiger in 1973, Project Elephant in 1992, and the Biological Diversity Act 2002 are other milestones. Indian Ivory is banned and India is a member of the Convention on International Trade in Endangered Species of Wild Fauna and Flora. On the R&D front, WII, Central Zoo Authority (CZA), the new Tiger Conservation Authority, and National Wildlife Crime Control Bureau show the increasing Central resolve to support the responsibility of States for conservation.

3.45 The public forests dedicated to the protection of wildlife habitats include 96 national parks and 509 wildlife sanctuaries. The total area of 15.7 MH, which is about 4.78% of the geographical area of the country covering about 20% of the total forests, is maintained under this protected area network. Scientific assessments of biodiversity of fauna, flora, and micro-organisms and well-organized retrievable databases for these are yet to be achieved.

3.46 During the Eleventh Plan, initiatives will be taken for mitigation of wildlife–human conflicts, involving and compensating local communities, management of habitats outside PAs, rehabilitation of displaced communities, and strengthening and protection of indigenous knowledge while improving research and monitoring systems.

INTEGRATED DEVELOPMENT OF WILDLIFE HABITATS

3.47 The CSS 'Development of National Parks and Wildlife Sanctuaries' provides assistance to the States for conservation activities in the wildlife areas. During the Tenth Plan, out of the outlay of Rs 350 crore, Rs 240 crore was allocated and 342 PAs have been covered. MoEF has prioritized the PAs on conservation value basis. However, all PAs do not have scientifically drafted management plans. At present, about 204 PAs

Box 3.1
Avoided Deforestation Incentive Mechanism for States

- There is no incentive to the States to protect forests. In the era of climate change, India has to depend on avoided deforestation as a mitigation step. In this context, there should be a mechanism that supports and encourages avoided deforestation. This money must be shared between the States and the forest dwelling communities.
- Satellite imagery can be used for determining the extent of avoided deforestation. The aim would be to pay for existing dense forest cover, at rates which reflect the opportunity costs of the forests. This will create local stakes and economic interest in dense forest protection.
- It is important to develop a compensation structure for the State Government and the local community. The Central Government should create a system for cess on all tax payers—a forest services tax (replace the road cess) to fund this mechanism.
- If such a strategy is developed internally in India, it can provide the framework to source carbon funds for avoided deforestation that can enhance economic benefits of protection and livelihood security.

are reported to have approved management plans. The principal objective of Central assistance being developing efficient management, the assistance needs to have linkages with the management plans.

3.48 The scheme may be renamed as 'Integrated Development of Wildlife Habitats' with wider scope for conservation. The support for management, protection, and development of PAs can be augmented by the following initiatives by MoEF:

- Evaluation of the non-recurring investment in the PAs should form the basis of further non-recurring assistance. The Central assistance can also be linked to the deployment of sanctioned frontline staff strength in the first place. The concept of project-based assistance with a provision of mid-course third-party appraisal may be considered.
- States should constitute specialized units for undertaking surveys, inventories, and the socio-economic analysis required for management planning and baseline landmarks for the PAs including the community and conservation reserves.
- Assistance for development of PAs should be based on the management plan and assessment of outcomes of the past interventions. Participatory management with village eco-development will be an earmarked component of the programme. Ministry will issue an eco-development resolution to the States with guiding principles, as was done in case of JFM in 1990.
- Assistance should also be provided for management of the identified special vulnerable habitats of high conservation value outside PAs on similar terms. This may include assisted regeneration for the vegetation components of such habitats.
- Species recovery and conservation programmes should also be supported for endangered species/ecosystems such as the Snow Leopard, the Great Indian Bustard, the Dolphin, and their habitats. Wide consultation will be undertaken for threat assessment and project formulation, considering the larger landscapes and socio-economic issues involved.
- Management of human–wildlife conflict may include compensation for damage from wildlife, measures to mitigate and avoid ingress of wildlife movement into habitations, tracking, capture, and translocation of wildlife from high conflict areas in excess of carrying capacity, to other suitable habitats on case to case basis.

STRENGTHENING WILDLIFE MANAGEMENT

3.49 The Directorate of Wildlife Preservation with a network in major ports of import/export has been reinforced with National Wildlife Crime Control Bureau. The following components may be added to the programme.

- Studies and consultations needed for important areas of concern such as conservation values, biodiversity impact assessments, cost–benefit analysis of relocation proposals of habitations from wildlife areas, etc.
- Pilot projects for species focused initiatives and relocation of viable populations of wildlife species to new habitats, monitoring of the impact of rescue/conservation/outreach efforts, etc.
- A programme for rehabilitation of traditional hunting communities with the participation of NGOs, activists, forest department, and the revenue department.

CENTRAL ZOO AUTHORITY (CZA)

3.50 The CZA provides financial assistance to recognized public sector zoos having adequate land, potential, and willingness to develop as modern zoos. A laboratory for conservation of endangered species at the Centre for Cellular and Molecular Biology Hyderabad and five veterinary centres for zoo animal health care have been supported. The assistance to zoos includes modern housing and upkeep of animals including relocation of the existing zoos. During the Eleventh Plan, this may also include the following components.

- Support for rehabilitation and upkeep of animals of seven rescue centres created by CZA for rehabilitation of captive animals from the circuses.
- Development of a National Referral Centre at the Indian Veterinary Research Institute, Izatnagar (Bareilly) for specialized services and diagnostic facilities for health care of wild animals in Indian zoos.

PROJECT TIGER

3.51 The Tenth Plan period saw the depletion of tiger population from the Sariska Tiger reserve, resulting in the introspection through the Tiger Task Force. The methods of monitoring the status of wildlife have been found primitive. The recommendations of the Tiger Task Force are relevant for not only protected area management but also general forest management. The follow-up of the recommendations has resulted in the constitution of the Tiger Conservation Authority and Wildlife Crime Control Bureau at the Centre. Critical activities such as identification of areas feasible for relocation and inclusive protection strategies remain to be worked on. Out of about 1500 villages in tiger reserves, only 80 have been relocated so far including nine during the Tenth Plan period.

3.52 India eco-development project was taken up in seven tiger reserves during the Ninth Plan and the Tenth Plan at a cost of Rs 142 crore. The investments made for evolving a protected area management strategy with village eco-development as an important component are yet to be evaluated for sustainability. The evaluation of the project remains to be analysed for utility and cost efficiency in the context of extension to other protected areas.

3.53 The National Tiger Conservation Authority provides an institutional mechanism for Project Tiger. The prerequisites for efficient management, namely, filling up vacancies of frontline staff, capacity building for working in conservation areas, management planning on the acceptable principles of participatory processes, and scientifically sound systems for documentation and monitoring of the key constituents of the habitats should be ensured:

- Relocation of villages from the existing tiger reserves is a priority. The resources for this purpose will be earmarked in the annual plans on the basis of the project reports and feasibility.
- Specific arrangement for documentation of landmarks and progress on the basis of the socio-economic, population, habitat, and ecological indicators should be laid down for effective monitoring of the impact of management inputs in the tiger reserves.
- Village eco-development should be the core activity in the project. The assistance for the tiger reserves can be linked to the eco-development activities based on micro plans developed with full participation of local communities.
- Notification of any new tiger reserves should be considered based on the scientific data analysis as well as assessment of impact on local communities.

PROJECT ELEPHANT

3.54 The aim of Project Elephant is long-term conservation of viable elephant populations in the larger landscapes through strengthening or creation of corridors. Not enough attention has been paid to reduce human–wildlife conflicts. Much of the activities have been short-term responses to conflict situations. With increasing population, wild elephants are observed to be increasing their range by dispersing into new areas.

3.55 The project should focus on strategies for strengthening and developing elephant movement corridors. Possibility of relocation from the areas with the potential of restoration of habitats should be explored. For the captive elephant population, a complete database for monitoring the status of health and productivity should be aimed at. For State Governments maintaining domestic elephants, component for improving the *kraals* and training of *mahouts* may also be provided.

ANIMAL WELFARE

3.56 The Animal Welfare Board of India (AWBI) has been working on ensuring a humane dealing of animals in experimentation, during stress, of stray animals, and general protection from cruelty. The Animal Welfare movement has been largely based on NGO participation. The following components of animal welfare are dealt with by the Ministry under the plan:

- Provision of shelter houses.
- Provision of ambulance services for animals in distress.
- Animal birth control and immunization of stray dogs.
- Scheme for relief to animals during natural calamities and unforeseen circumstances.
- Assistance to AWBI.

- Assistance to Committee for the Purpose of Control and Supervision of Experiments on Animals.
- National Institute of Animal Welfare.

3.57 Proposed programmes for rabies control, *gaushalas*, and capacity building should be structured within the existing components. An information base along with fact sheets on the voluntary groups working in the field of animal welfare should be prepared. For National Institute of Animal Welfare, curricula need to be designed based on the larger scope of career opportunities and subject related courses. A good programme of monitoring the status of stray dog population in the country can be taken up through collaborative, free, public domain knowledge resources based on student projects.

3.58 The total projected GBS for the Eleventh plan for the MoEF is Rs 8842 crore (at 2006–07 price) and Rs 10000 crore (at current price).

II
Rural Development

4

Rapid Poverty Reduction

THE POOR IN INDIA: A PROFILE

4.1 India is a nation with over 300 million poor people, a number that has barely declined over the last three decades of development. It is therefore essential that the Eleventh Five Year Plan address the task of reducing the numbers of the poor frontally. It is clear that rapid growth will be essential to reduce the number of the poor and for sustainable poverty reduction, but for growth to benefit the poor disproportionately, it will have to be accompanied by more rapid employment expansion than hitherto, greater investment in health, education, water/sanitation, and child nutrition than so far, and directly targeted poverty-reduction programmes.

MEASURING AND PROFILING THE POOR IN INDIA

THE HEADCOUNT RATIO (HCR)

4.2 India has successfully reduced the share of the poor in the population by 27.4 percentage points from 54.9 in 1973 to 27.5 in 2004. Between 1973 and 1983, the HCR of the poor had declined from 54.9% to 44.5%, and it fell further to 36% in 1993–94 and to 27.5% by 2004–05 (Table 4.1). Thus, 60 years after independence, over a quarter of our population still remains poor. There is growing consensus that the poverty line (Rs 356 monthly per capita consumption expenditure for rural areas and Rs 539 for urban areas in 2004–05) in India is much too low, and continues to be based on a consumption basket that is too lean. If the poverty line was higher, the share of the population below the poverty line would be accordingly higher.

TABLE 4.1
Percentage of People Below Poverty Line in India (1973–2004)

Years	Rural	Urban	Combined
1973	56.4	49.0	54.9
1983	45.7	40.8	44.5
1993	37.3	32.3	36.0
2004	28.3	25.7	27.5

Source: Planning Commission.

4.3 Some States have been particularly successful in reducing the share of the poor in the total population. In 2004–05, the States with the lowest HCR were J&K (5.4%), Punjab (8.4%), Himachal Pradesh (10%), Haryana (14%), Kerala (15%), Andhra Pradesh (15.8%), and Gujarat (16.8%); at the other end of the spectrum are Orissa (46.4%), Bihar (41.4%), Madhya Pradesh (38.3%), and Uttar Pradesh (32.8%)—which also happen to be among the most populous States of India. The States that were formed recently (Chhattisgarh 40.9%, Jharkhand 40.3%, Uttarakhand 39.6%) also have among them the highest poverty ratio (Annexures 4.1 to 4.3).

THE ABSOLUTE NUMBER OF POOR

4.4 Over time, while the HCR of the poor fell, the number of the poor barely changed over the last three decades, remaining constant over two decades before falling (3213 lakhs in 1973, 3229 lakhs in 1983, 3204 lakhs in 1993–94) to 3017 lakhs in 2004–05 (Table 4.2). Therefore, number of poor in the country has declined over the last decade (1993–94 to 2004–05) by 1.86.

TABLE 4.2
Number of Persons Below Poverty Line in India (1973–2004)

(in Lakh)

Years	Rural	Urban	Combined
1973	2612.90	600.46	3213.36
1983	2519.57	709.40	3228.97
1993	2440.31	763.37	3203.68
2004	2209.24	807.96	3017.20

Source: Planning Commission.

4.5 In some States, the absolute numbers of the poor in the population has actually increased over the last three decades: in Uttar Pradesh (including Uttaranchal) from 535.7 lakhs in 1973 to 626 lakhs in 2004–05; in Rajasthan from 128.5 lakhs to 134.9 lakhs; in Maharashtra from 287.4 lakhs to 317.4 lakhs, and in Nagaland from 2.9 lakhs to 4.0 lakhs. The total number of poor has also increased in Madhya Pradesh (including Chhattisgarh) taken together from 276 lakhs to 341 lakhs and in Bihar (including Jharkhand) from 370 lakhs to 485.5 lakhs over the same period. There are many States where the number of poor overall has remained roughly constant over the last two decades: Haryana, Himachal Pradesh, Orissa, and Mizoram. However, there are also States that have succeeded in reducing the absolute number of the poor in rural areas over the three decades from 1973 to 2004–05: Andhra Pradesh from 178.2 lakhs to 64.7 lakhs; Karnataka from 128.4 lakhs to 75 lakhs; Kerala from 111.4 lakhs to 32.4 lakhs; Tamil Nadu from 172.6 lakhs to 76.5 lakhs; and West Bengal from 257.9 lakhs to 173.2 lakhs (Annexures 4.1 to 4.3), and Assam and Gujarat to a much smaller extent. These are the relative success stories in reducing the numbers of the poor in India.

4.6 Overall, the number of poor in *rural* areas in the country as a whole has declined from 2613 lakhs in 1973 to 2209 lakhs in 2004–05, i.e., by just 404 lakh people over a 31 year period. That means the rate of decline in the numbers of the poor has been 13 lakhs per year. But in *urban* areas the numbers of the poor has gone on increasing from 600.5 lakhs in 1973 to 808.0 lakhs in 2004–05 (Annexures 4.1 to 4.3); this is hardly surprising since the share of the urban population in India's total population has also gone on increasing, driven partly by rural urban migration.

4.7 The fact that the numbers of the poor have declined in rural areas, and increased in urban areas over the last three decades suggests that to escape rural poverty, the poor migrate to urban areas. In fact, the total number of *migrant workers* in India in 1999–2000 was 10.27 crore—a staggering number. The number of seasonal or cyclical migrants in India may be 2 crore or so. But migration, both rural–rural (from relatively poor to relatively richer States and districts) and rural–urban, has the effect of disenfranchising the poor, leaving them without a safety net. Nevertheless, rural–urban migration will, and should continue; the policy imperative is that migrants are provided the basic social services that all citizens are entitled to according to the Constitution of India.

4.7(a) While the earlier two subsections examined the headcount ratio and the absolute numbers of the poor, it is also useful to examine which States contribute most of India's Poor. Four States account for nearly 58% of India's poor population in 2004–05: Uttar Pradesh (19.6%), Bihar (12.23%), Madhya Pradesh (8.3%) and Maharashtra (10.5%). In 1983, these States (including undivided Bihar and Madhya Pradesh) accounted for 49% of India's total poor population (Annexure 4.1).

COMPOSITION OF THE POOR

4.8 The composition of the poor has been changing and rural poverty is getting concentrated in agricultural labour and artisanal households and urban poverty in casual labour households. Agricultural labour households accounted for 41% of rural poor in 1993–94 as well as in 2004–05. The share of self-employed in agriculture among the rural poor had fallen from 32% to 21.6%. Casual labour households accounted for 62.6% in 1993–94 in urban areas and 56.5% in 2004–05.

4.9 The occupational composition of rural poor varied across the States. In general, in developed States poverty was highly concentrated among agricultural labour households, and in contrast in backward States poverty extended to other occupational groups including self employed in agriculture.

4.10 Among social groups, SCs, STs, and backward castes accounted for 80% of the rural poor in 2004–05, considerably more than their share in the rural population (Working Group on Poverty, Planning Commission, 2006). In 2004–05, while the HCR of the poor in the total rural population was 28.3%, among the SCs it was 36.8%. In urban areas, the HCR overall was 25.7%, but among SCs it was even higher than in rural areas at nearly 40%.

4.11 The proportion of STs population among the rural population living in poverty is high. It is about 15% in 2004–05—double that of their share in the total population of India. For rural population, the incidence of poverty among STs had fallen from 51.94% in 1993–94 to 47.3 % in 2004–05 whereas it had fallen from 37.3% to 27.5% in the total population. In 2004–05, the incidence of poverty among the STs had barely fallen compared to a decade earlier and it was a good 20 percentage points higher for the STs than for the rest of the population.

4.12 The share of poor in the total urban population in 2004–05 was 25.7% but 33.3% of the STs in urban areas were poor. The HCR of the STs (47.3%) is higher than that of SCs (36.8%) in rural areas, but the situation is the other way around in urban areas, i.e., of all STs living in rural areas a higher proportion is poorer than all SCs living in rural areas. On the other hand, of all SCs living in urban areas, more SCs are poor than all STs. In rural areas SCs don't have access to land and therefore are forced to migrate to urban areas more often. On the other hand, STs (unlike SCs) in rural areas have much better access to land, especially in the forested areas, but the quality of that land, and its productivity is low, and yields low incomes. In terms of assets, unlike SCs, the STs have less of a problem in respect to land. Thus, in the total rural population, 63.2% of households held land, and that share was 61.3% for STs.

4.13 In terms of both income poverty and other indicators of human development (such as education and health) the STs are at the bottom. The increasing concentration of the tribals among those who suffer from multiple deprivations is a matter of concern.

Multiple Deprivations of the Poor

4.14 Deprivation of SCs and STs shows itself also in the form of inequalities of wealth. SCs own fewer assets than the rest of the population. Most SCs live in rural areas, where land is the main asset. In the overall population, 60% of the rural households were cultivator households. But SC households are more disadvantaged among rural households; only 47% were cultivators and a quarter of the SC households were agricultural labour households (Table 4.3). About 6% to 7% of the SC households were artisan households. If we examine the value of assets held by social groups in rural areas, we find that in the total population about 12% of the households in the 'Other category' (i.e., non-SC, non-ST, and non-OBC) have assets worth less than Rs 30000; but 22% of rural SCs have assets worth less than Rs 30000. Conversely, only 9% of SC households have assets worth Rs 3 lakh and above, while 37% of households in the 'Other category' (who are not either SC or ST or OBC) hold such assets. This difference in asset holdings becomes sharper in urban areas, with as much as 29% of SC households with assets less than Rs 30000. Only 16.7% of SC households hold assets worth Rs 3 lakh, while 43.5% of 'other households' hold such assets in urban areas.

TABLE 4.3
Percentage of Households by Asset-holding Categories, by Social Group

Social Group	Household Asset-holding (Rs in '000s)			
	Rural		Urban	
	less than 30	300 and above	less than 30	300 and above
ST	23.5	9.1	32.5	20.1
SC	22.1	9.0	29.1	16.7
OBC	13.3	24.4	23.7	28.5
Others	11.9	37.1	20.0	43.5
All	15.9	24.8	23.0	33.7

Source: All-India debt and investment survey, Ministry of Statistics and Programme Implementation, GoI, NSS 59th Round, 2003.

4.15 Land is the most important asset for rural people. Although SCs were 21.6% of the rural households, they held only 9% of the land (Table 4.4). On average SC households barely owned 0.3 ha of land in rural areas. Land distribution was even further skewed against the SCs in urban areas. Other Backward Classes (OBCs) on average held 0.758 ha (or approx. 1.5 acres) per household, although the share of total rural land held by them was comparable to their share in the population.

4.16 With fewer assets, it was also not possible for SCs and STs to borrow (Table 4.5), and thus emerge out of poverty. This is true for both sets of communities in both rural and urban areas.

4.17 SCs and STs have much worse health, education, and nutrition indicators than the rest of the population, followed by OBCs, and others (Table 4.6). While infant mortality rates (IMR) were 49 for Others, for SCs it was 66, for STs 62 and for OBCs 57. Their nutritional status is also worse; the mean body mass index (BMI) for SCs, STs, and OBCs is 5–10% below that for Others, and very close to the cut-off for malnutrition (>18.5). (BMI is a measure of a person's nutritional status [weight for height, measured in kg per square metre, sq m, of height.])

4.18 SCs and STs have Gross Enrolment Rates at primary level which are comparable with the general population (Table 4.7), as they have risen sharply for

TABLE 4.4
Land Owned per Household by Social Group, 2003

Characteristic	Rural				
	SC	ST	OBC	Others	All
Percentage of area of land owned	9.04	11.2	43.5	36.3	100
Average area (ha) owned per household	0.3	0.77	0.76	1.003	0.73
Percentage of households	21.6	10.6	41.6	26.26	100
	Urban				
	SC	ST	OBC	Others	All
Percentage of area of land owned	4.76	3.25	36.8	55.21	100
Average area (ha) owned per household	0.04	0.15	0.14	0.151	0.13
Percentage of households	15	2.91	34.5	47.57	100

Source: Household Ownership Holdings in India, Ministry of Statistics and Programme Implementation, GoI, NSS 59th Round, 2003.

TABLE 4.5
Incidence of Indebtedness by Social Group

Indicators	Rural				
	ST	SC	OBC	Others	All
Average debt per household (Rs)	3205	4641	8288	10437	7539
Debt asset ratio (%)	2.3	3.7	3.1	2.4	2.8
Incidence of indebtedness (%)	17.9	27.1	28.9	25.7	26.5
	Urban				
	ST	SC	OBC	Others	All
Average debt per household (Rs)	9233	7744	11200	13577	11771
Debt asset ratio (%)	3.8	4.2	3.4	2.4	2.8
Incidence of indebtedness (%)	12.2	19.2	21.2	15.3	17.8

Source: All-India debt and investment survey, Ministry of Statistics and Programme Implementation, GoI, NSS 59th Round, 2003.

TABLE 4.6
Health and Nutrition Indicators by Social Groups in 2005–06 (NFHS-3)

Indicators	Rural			
	SC	ST	OBC	Others
Infant Mortality	71.0	63.9	61.1	55.7
Under-five Mortality	94.7	99.8	78.7	68.2
	Urban			
	SC	ST	OBC	Others
Infant Mortality	50.7	43.8	42.2	36.1
Under-five Mortality	65.4	53.8	54.5	42.1
	Total (Combined)			
	SC	ST	OBC	Others
Fertility	2.92	3.12	2.75	2.35
Infant Mortality	66.4	62.1	56.6	48.9
Under-five Mortality	88.1	95.7	72.8	59.2
Nutritional Status				
Mean BMI for Men	19.7	19.3	20.2	20.9
Mean BMI for Women	19.9	19.1	20.4	21.3

Source: National Family Health Survey (NFHS-3), 2005–06, International Institute for Population Sciences, Mumbai.

TABLE 4.7
Gross Enrolment, Dropout at Primary Stage (I–V) by Social Groups, 2004–05

Indicators	SC		
	Boy's	Girl's	Total
Gross Enrolment Ratio (GER)	123.33	106.62	115.30
Dropout Rate	32.73	36.14	34.21
	ST		
	Boy's	Girl's	Total
Gross Enrolment Ratio (GER)	128.06	115.49	121.91
Dropout Rate	42.55	42.04	42.32
	General		
	Boy's	Girl's	Total
Gross Enrolment Ratio (GER)	110.70	104.70	107.80
Dropout Rate	31.81	25.42	29.00

Source: Selected Educational Statistics, Ministry of Human Resource Development (MHRD), GoI, 2007.

all sections of the population in the recent decade. However, their dropout rates, before they complete five years of schooling (a minimum if they are to retain literacy acquired during those five years), are higher than for the general population. ST children are dropping out far more. Thus, we have a serious situation, in that in 2004–05 not only were 29% of the entire nation's children dropping out before completing primary schooling, but the SCs and STs were doing even worse.

Poverty Among Women

4.19 The incidence of income poverty among females tended to be marginally higher in both rural and urban areas. The percentage of female persons living in poor households was 28% in rural and 26% in urban areas in 1993–94, and 29 and 23 respectively in 2004–05. In contrast, the percentage of male persons living in poverty was 27 in rural and 26 in urban areas in 1993–94, and 27 and 23 in 2004–05 . The lower percentage of female persons among the poor despite higher female poverty ratio was due to an adverse sex ratio—which itself is a reflection of the discrimination that women and girls face over their life-cycle. It should be noted that the above measure of gender poverty ignores intra-household inequalities in consumption. There are other dimensions of poverty such as food insecurity, malnutrition, and illness associated more with female members.

4.20 That women are much worse off in terms of most social indicators is quite well known. SC and ST girls are the worst off in terms of most educational outcome indicators. For instance, in the critical age-group of 15–49 years, when women are in their reproductive and most productive years, it is remarkable that 73% of SC women , 79% of ST women , and 61% of OBC women are illiterate. 61% of Muslim women were also illiterate; this percentage is relatively low, only because the rate of urbanization among Muslims is higher than for other social groups.

4.21 The nutritional status of SC and ST women remains a source of worry as well. A good 42% of SC women and 46% of ST women had a BMI less than 18.5, which is seen as the cut-off for malnutrition. The fact that as much as 30% of the 'Other' women were also malnourished clearly indicates that there is a serious problem of under-nutrition among most segments of the population, not just SCs and STs.

POVERTY AMONG CHILDREN

4.22 Child poverty is widespread in India both in rural and urban areas. The percentage of children below 15 years living in below poverty line (BPL) households constituted 39 in rural and 41 in urban areas in 1993–94 and 44 in rural and 32 in urban areas in 2004–05. Among the poor population, the percentage of children increased from 44 in rural and 39 in urban areas in 1993–94, to 46 and 42 respectively in 1999–2000. This rising tendency in the proportion of children among the poor contrasts with the proportion of children in the population which was a constant 44% in rural areas in 1993–94 as well as in 2004–05 and a marginal decline from 39% to 32% in urban areas during the same period. The high and rising level of child poverty is not only linked to a high incidence of child malnutrition, but also undermines their future capabilities and adversely affects equality of opportunity.

MEASURING AND IDENTIFYING THE POOR: A NOTE ON REVISION OF POVERTY LINES

4.23 There are two policy-relevant sets of issues about poverty in the country at present. First, there has been controversy around the measurement of poverty, as presented in the official statistics of the Planning Commission. Second, there are issues around the identification of the poor who are potential beneficiaries of government programmes, as carried out by the Union MoRD. The two are not unconnected, since for some programmes State Governments have to accept the HCR of poor as measured by the Planning Commission.

4.24 There are many unresolved issues regarding measurement of poverty in India and upon the question of poverty line itself, which necessitate a revisit of this entire question. Accordingly, an Expert Group has been constituted by the Planning Commission whose recommendations, hopefully, will provide acceptable measures of both poverty and the population below the poverty line.

4.25 The identification of the poor since 1992 has been done in quinquennial surveys carried by the MoRD. The first one (1992) used income to identify the poor, the second one (1997) used consumption. The third one (2002) adopted a 13-criteria questionnaire giving each criteria equal weightage. This survey has been questioned in the Supreme Court in Public Interest Litigation. Before commissioning a new BPL survey for identification of poor, which is due, there is need to constitute an Expert Group with representatives from States, academics, and civil society and evolve an acceptable criteria and methodology for the forthcoming BPL survey. Suitable adjustments of the district specific and State specific poverty population yielded from this survey should be negotiated with the State Governments so that this number is not out of sync excessively with the poverty as measured by Planning Commission based on National Sample Survey (NSS) data.

DIRECTLY TARGETED POVERTY REDUCTION PROGRAMMES AND THE STRATEGY FOR INCLUSIVE GROWTH

4.26 Given the chronic and multi-dimensional nature of poverty in India, it is imperative that the programmes to address poverty rely on a multi-pronged approach. The preceding analysis has identified that there is a geography of poverty, with poverty being concentrated in the rural areas of certain States. It also pointed out that there is a sociology of poverty, with certain social groups increasingly concentrated among those who are identified as poor. It also noted that there are identifiable occupational features of the poor: they are concentrated in agricultural labour and artisanal households in rural areas, and among casual labourers in urban areas. Casual labourers in urban areas are essentially distress migrants from rural areas in States where agricultural land-man ratio is very adverse, and where agricultural incomes have not been growing—reinforcing the need for both land reforms as well as measures to increase productivity. Accordingly, in the next section, the strategy and programmes directly relevant to the emerging features of poverty groups in India are discussed.

4.27 First, regions which have large number of chronic poor people include tribal in forests concentrated in arid, semi-arid, and sub-humid areas in central and eastern parts of the country. However, in many semi-arid regions, where agriculture is mainly rainfed rather than irrigated, located in the more industrial States of western and southern India, there has been more dynamism. Migration from semi-arid areas may result in improvement of economic conditions for people in the rainfed areas due to better investment opportunities and market functioning compared to the forest-based regions. In forest regions, poor people's access to the resources which are located there in those regions have been limited, and their own low human capital endowment (e.g., low literacy and poor health services) have resulted in their incorporation into labour markets at disadvantageous terms. It is for this reason that the strategies that are needed for each of these agro-climatic regions have to rely upon an area-development approach. This is particularly true of rain dependent water stressed areas, where watershed development has been neglected. Thus watershed development in rainfed agriculture has to take center-stage in the poverty reduction strategy for the Eleventh Plan. Watershed development is discussed in the chapter on Agriculture (Chapter 1, Volume III). Similar initiatives that hold promise to impart dynamism to Backward districts/regions are (i) the Backward Regions Grant Fund, (ii) Border Area Development Programme, and (iii) Hill Area Development Programme. These initiatives are discussed in the chapter on Spatial Development (Chapter 6, Volume I).

4.28 Second, the poor are geographically concentrated in India. They also happen to be in States where a significant proportion of agriculture is irrigated, and not rainfed (and where the land-man ratio is the lowest in the country). In other words, without effective (i) land reforms and (ii) agricultural services, none of these regions are likely to be able to reduce poverty. There is also a need for programmes to modernize land relations in an era of rapid industrialization. We discuss agricultural services in the chapter on Agriculture, as we do land reforms including issues related to alienation of tribal lands.

4.29 Third, dependence on casual labour has grown, and a large proportion of the chronic poor are dependent on wage labour. There has been a steady increase in the share of the Indian population working as hired labour. All of the increase in recent decades has been due to the expansion of the share of casual hired labour. Most of these are SCs and STs. While male rural casual labourers have increasingly worked in the non-farm sector over time, women have increasingly been concentrated in agricultural casual labour and have lost jobs overall, especially in the 1990s. Growth in casual labour was strong among the landless and especially rapid after the 1987 drought. In the 1990s there was an explosion of self-employed people choosing to do subsidiary work as casual labourers. The incidence of poverty among rural casual workers is greatest among non-workers who do occasional casual work and especially among women. Most ST and 40% of SC casual workers are poor, the landless casual workers being the poorest. On an average, women are poorer than men casual labourers. Clearly, this calls for an effective wage employment programme in rural areas, especially focusing on women, of the NREG kind.

4.30 Fourth, the poor have to be enabled to increase their incomes by diversifying away from agriculture, and relying on non-farm sources for at least a subsidiary income. Casual labourers and artisans, especially women, can be brought together through social mobilization to form SHGs, and with credit support, to diversify their sources of income. In certain parts of India (e.g., Kerala, Andhra Pradesh, Gujarat) the success of such efforts have already borne fruit, and it is essential to make sure that this programme goes to scale in the country in regions which need it most—in the eastern and northern parts—where it has hardly taken root.

4.31 Finally, the poor need a safety net, if they are to escape the cycle of inter-generational transfer of poverty. At least 18 million rural people do not have a home over their heads, and the rural housing programme needs to focus on giving a homestead to at least those who are houseless. Homesteads will not only give them a home, but also provide a small plot of land where they can diversify their income by rearing goats and poultry and growing vegetables on the family plot. Similarly, the elderly destitute, widows, and disabled among the rural poor, need social assistance.

4.32 The poor also suffer from low human capital. Household size is closely related to both malnutrition of adults and children, and to the inter-generational transfer of poverty. The directly-targeted poverty reduction efforts of the government will fail in the Eleventh Plan if the quality of public health services and the integrated child development services do not improve, and also if the universalization of elementary education with quality does not happen. However, an inclusive growth strategy that focuses only on human capital formation or directly targeted poverty reduction is likely to fail. The structure of growth and also the pattern of production have to be employment-generating, especially outside agriculture. In other words, the simultaneous focus on a three-legged strategy—economic growth, income-poverty reduction through targeted programmes, and human capital formation—will put India on a sustainable growth path, since there is a recognized synergy between these outcomes.

GUARANTEED WAGE EMPLOYMENT—NATIONAL RURAL EMPLOYMENT GUARANTEE ACT (NREGA)

4.33 Workfare programmes have been important programme interventions in India and elsewhere in developing countries since long. These programmes typically provide unskilled workers with short-term employment on public works. They provide income transfers to poor households during periods when they suffer on account of absence of opportunities of employment. In areas with high unemployment rates and under employment, transfer benefits from workfare programmes can prevent poverty from worsening, especially during lean periods. Durable assets that these programmes create have the potential to generate second-round employment benefits as requisite infrastructure is developed.

4.34 We have a long history and experience in implementing wage employment programmes. However, beginning with Jawahar Rojagar Yojana in 1989, the outreach of these programmes increased significantly as in the period 1989 to 2006, ultimately culminating in NREGA. These wage employment programmes implemented by State Governments with Central assistance were self-targeting, and the objective was to provide enhanced livelihood security, especially of those dependent on casual manual labour.

4.35 Based on the experience of these programmes the NREGA was enacted to reinforce the commitment towards livelihood security in rural areas. The Act was notified on 7 September 2005. The significance of NREGA lies in the fact that it creates a right based framework for wage employment programmes and makes the government legally bound to provide employment to those who seek it. In this way the legislation goes beyond providing a social safety net, and towards guaranteeing the right to employment. The experience with NREGA so far suggests that it is one of the main planks of rapid poverty reduction in the Eleventh Five Year Plan.

4.36 Starting with 200 districts across the country in Phase-I during 2006–07, NREGA was extended to additional 130 districts in Phase-II during 2007–08. From 1 April 2008 onwards the Act will cover the whole of rural India. As a district is notified under the Act, Sampoorna Grameen Rozgar Yojana (SGRY) is automatically merged in the NREGA and would therefore cease to exist with effect from 1 April 2008.

4.37 The objective of the NREGA is to enhance the livelihood security of the people in rural areas by guaranteeing 100 days of wage employment in a financial year to a rural household whose members volunteer to do unskilled manual work. The Act further aims at creating durable assets and strengthening the livelihood resource base of the rural poor. The choice of works suggested in the Act address causes of chronic poverty like drought, deforestation, soil erosion, etc., so that the process of employment generation is on a sustainable basis.

4.38 Employment is dependent upon the worker exercising the choice to apply for registration, obtain a job card, and then to seek employment through a written application for the time and duration chosen by her. The legal guarantee has to be fulfilled within the time limit prescribed and this mandate is underpinned by the provision of unemployment allowance. The Act is thus designed to offer an incentive structure to the States for providing employment as 90% of the cost for employment provided is borne by the Centre, and there is a concomitant disincentive for not providing employment, if demanded, as the States then bear the double indemnity of unemployment and the cost of unemployment allowance. Earlier wage employment programmes were allocation based.

However, NREGA is not supply driven but demand driven. Resource transfer under NREGA is based on the demand for employment and this provides another critical incentive to States to leverage the Act to meet the employment needs of the poor. The delivery system has been made accountable, as it envisages an Annual Report on the outcomes of NREGA to be presented by the Central Government to the Parliament and to the State Legislature by the State Government.

FUNDING

4.39 The Central Government bears the costs on the following items:

- The entire cost of wages of unskilled manual workers.
- 75% of the cost of material, wages of skilled and semi skilled workers.
- Administrative expenses as may be determined by the Central Government, which will include, inter alia, the salary and the allowances of the Programme Officer and his supporting staff and work site facilities.
- Expenses of the National Employment Guarantee Council.

4.40 The State Government bears the costs on the following items:

- 25% of the cost of material, wages of skilled and semi skilled workers (as a ratio of 60:40 is to be maintained for wages of the unskilled manual workers and the material, skilled/semi-skilled workers' wages, the State Government has to bear only 25% of the 40% component, which means a contribution of 10% of the expenditure).
- Unemployment allowance payable in case the State Government cannot provide wage employment on time.
- Administrative expenses of the State Employment Guarantee Council.

KEY ISSUES

4.41 The key issues that require focus in the Eleventh Plan so that NREGA can be optimally realized for supplementing wage employment opportunities are briefly highlighted here.

(i) Articulation of Demand for Employment

4.42 Since NREGA is a right-based programme, articulation of demand by the rural poor is the basic premise of its operation, especially if wage seekers are not literate and not organized. Generating awareness among local rural communities through Information, Education, and Communication becomes critical for enabling the rural poor to articulate demand. States have forged a variety of methods for communication and social mobilization that include preparation of communication material on NREGA processes in simple local language, one day orientations of sarpanches/ward members, convening gram sabhas, using district teams for village level interactions, local vernacular newspapers, TV and radio spots, pamphlets and brochures, local cultural forums, information counters on local market days, village information wall, fixing a Rozgar Day in a week, and establishing a helpline. Full knowledge of the rights that NREGA confers to the rural poor is the most important prerequisite to enable them to seek employment as per their choice of time and duration.

(ii) Preparing a Labour Budget, Annual Shelf of Projects, and Perspective Plan

4.43 The Act guarantees providing employment within 15 days of demand and the instrument for providing employment is unskilled manual work selected from the list of permissible works. This legal guarantee has implications for the way in which works have to be planned. A Labour Budget as stipulated under the Act is required to be prepared to facilitate advance planning, whereby districts estimate their labour demand for the ensuing financial year by December-end. The National Guidelines indicate the way in which the annual shelf of projects may be prepared to meet the estimated labour demand. Districts have attempted to prepare shelves of projects to keep a list of works ready to meet employment demand. Greater precision in planning works has been suggested through assigning a unique location code to each work and mentioning the plot numbers of the sites where works are to be executed. Estimated benefits in terms of person days need to be assessed, so that the employment expected to be generated through the works planned may be clearly matched with the estimated employment demand. Physical improvement envisaged (land/water conservation etc.) has to be quantified so that the focus remains on creating durable and productive assets that support further self sustaining employment. Displaying the list of approved works at the GP Office and the details of works taken up on the work site has been stipulated so that the workers know the work opportunities locally available.

4.44 National Guidelines lay down the broad principles of preparing a Five Year District Perspective Pan that must have the following components viz., village mapping of natural resources and social infrastructure, identification of gaps and works that can be taken up as per NREGA permissible list, assessment of works that respond to what local people want, what will build a livelihood base to enable them to move out of NREGA to sustainable employment, and assessment of labour demand.

4.45 The planning capacity of the PRIs and district level functionaries needs to be strengthened to infuse the Plans with a long term vision of sustainable livelihoods.

(iii) Record of Work Done and Payment of Wages

4.46 The legal guarantee of the Act mandates that wages due to workers be paid within 15 days of work completion. This requires that a fair record be maintained for the work done. To ensure that authentic muster rolls are used, numbered muster rolls are to be issued for each sanctioned work by Programme Officer and maintained on the work site by the executing agency. Muster rolls must mention Job Card numbers of workers, days worked, quantum of work done, amount paid and must have space for recording inspections. Muster rolls should be read out on the work site during measurement and wage payment to prevent bogus records. Entries of the muster roll should be correspondingly recorded in the job cards of the workers. Updating of muster roll data at the Block level computers in a 15-day cycle needs to be ensured. Regular measurement and supervision of works should be done by qualified technical personnel on time. There is a need for stricter compliance of all the provisions of the Act so that payment to the labourers can be made in time.

(iv) Vigilance and Transparency

4.47 NREGA places a strong emphasis on vigilance and transparency. A web enabled management information systems (MIS) *www.nrega.nic.in* has been developed that seeks to place all information in public domain. It is a household level database and has internal checks for ensuring consistency and conformity to normative processes. All critical parameters get monitored in the public domain.

4.48 The field verification of NREGA processes is through external and internal agencies and the feedback is shared with the States for follow up. Independent concurrent studies have also been taken up. Monitoring at the State level needs to be strengthened and States are expected to ensure 100% verification at block, 10% at district, and 2% at the State level especially of works muster rolls, and records. Guidelines for muster roll verification have been evolved and need to be rigorously followed. The setting up and training local vigilance and monitoring committees is also required for bringing in lateral transparency.

(v) Public Accountability

4.49 The Act contains specific provisions for public accountability. This has to be accomplished through the provisions made in the Act and guidelines regarding Right to Information, proactive disclosure of information, and a transparent social audit process.

4.50 The Right to Information should be followed in both letter and spirit in all matters relating to NREGA as stipulated in Section 4 and Schedule I, Para 17 of the Act.

4.51 The Section 17 of NREGA provides for social audit of all works in a GP by the Gram Sabha and the GP has to provide records for social audit. This necessitates a need for creating capacity for social audit among officials, GP members, and the Gram Sabha. A significant feature here is the active role played by civil society organizations in facilitating social audit processes in partnership with State Government as well as independently.

(vi) Grievance Redressal

4.52 Enforcement of the right to employment requires

setting up an effective grievance redressal system. The Act vests the responsibility for grievance redressal with the Programme Officer. To ensure prompt grievance redressal certain basic arrangements must be ensured, such as setting up a grievance redressal cell at the Programme Officer/District Programme Co-ordinator (DPC) offices, preferably with a toll free helpline. The Programme Officer and DPC must review the disposal of complaints on a monthly basis and the persons concerned must be informed.

(vii) Strengthening Administrative Systems

4.53 Technical Resource Support Groups are required to bring in multidisciplinary professional expertise in MoRD, to provide resource support in critical areas, inter alia, assisting the Ministry in formulating and codifying standard operating procedures for setting measurable outcomes, for laying down standards of programme delivery, for designing appropriate management information systems (MIS) for monitoring programme outcomes. They would also carry out training needs assessment for capacity building at the State, district, and sub-district level and formulate the framework for training and capacity building at various levels.

4.54 Another issue critical to strengthening administrative systems pertains to training of different stakeholders. The requirements of training are considerable at all levels and include functionaries, PRIs and the local vigilance committees. The challenge is to design training programmes calibrated in content and process according to different target groups and to manage large scale training needs without compromise on quality.

(viii) Financial Management

4.55 A non-lapsable Central Employment Guarantee Fund has been set up to ensure that availability of funds match working season demands. Districts have dedicated accounts for NREGA funds and submit their proposals based on clearly delineated guidelines so that funds may be devolved efficiently at each level, and adequate funds may be available to respond to demand.

4.56 The funds are released on the basis of demand for employment received in a district and are based on an appraisal of both financial and physical indicators of outcomes. To meet the norms for fund release, districts need to strengthen their capacity for both preparing a Labour Budget to project an annual requirement of funds based on an estimation of labour demand, and undertake rigorous monitoring of funds spent and the physical outcomes to track current trends of employment generation, so that adequate funds can be demanded and deployed efficiently.

ROAD AHEAD

(i) Empowering Workers

4.57 NREGA is a right-based statute and its effectiveness lies eventually in the extent to which wage seekers can exercise their choice and assert their rights to claim entitlements under the Act. The issues involved in empowering workers are in the range of enhancement of knowledge levels, development of literacy skills, organizing workers, and enhancing social security levels of workers. Opening savings accounts of workers' in banks and post offices that has been initiated needs to be supported on a larger scale so that thrift and small savings can be encouraged among workers. The inclusion of NREGA workers under the cover of various life and health insurance schemes will also raise their security thresholds.

(ii) Linkages with Other Development Programmes

4.58 Empowerment of workers and creation of durable assets depend to a great extent on the linkages between NREGA and other development programmes. Linkages with human development programmes such as National Rural Health Mission (NRHM), National Mission for Literacy and Elementary Education, and other livelihood and infrastructure initiatives are needed to ensure basic human entitlements to the workers and to strengthen the natural resource base of livelihoods. The full potential of the kind of works permissible under NREGA can be tapped if planning for these works is coordinated with other development projects, for example watershed management, agricultural pro-grammes, horticultural projects, etc. Initiatives for NRM also need to be dovetailed with income generation projects to enable workers to move from wage employment to self-sustaining employment.

(iii) Exploring the Possibility of Other Works

4.59 The list of permissible works under NREGA recognizes the possibility of a need arising for works other than those specifically indicated in Schedule I which may be notified by the Central Ministry in consultation with the States. The Ministry may consider formulating guidelines for the States that may enable them to identify other works in conformity with the general principles of the Act and the rationale for them.

4.60 The allocation for the Eleventh Plan (at current price) is tentatively provided at Rs 100000 crore. However, since NREGA is a demand driven programme and the government is legally bound to provide employment mandated under the act, this figure is only indicative.

SELF-EMPLOYMENT—SWARNJAYANTI GRAM SWAROZGAR YOJANA (SGSY)

Rationale

4.61 Persistent efforts made by the government to fine-tune the self employment programmes during various Plan periods, especially oriented towards improving the implementation quality, yielded some new concepts that emerged at various times and got consolidated. The need to integrate the cluster approach, capacity building, skill upgradation, infrastructure including marketing development and technology penetration were felt more acutely with every passing year. Emphasis also was necessary to be laid on micro enterprise development with effective forward and backward linkages, so as to ensure best returns on the investment. Therefore, the SGSY was launched with effect from 1 April 1999 to bring the assisted poor families above the poverty line by ensuring appreciable sustained level of income over a period of time. This objective was to be achieved by organizing the rural poor into SHGs through the process of social mobilization, their training and capacity building and provision of income generating assets. The SHG approach helps the poor to build their self-confidence through community action. Group processes and collective decision were to enable them in the identification and prioritization of their needs and resources. This process would ultimately lead to the strengthening and socio-economic empowerment of the rural poor as well as improve their collective bargaining power.

4.62 The SGSY is, by design, meant to create widespread income generating activities, through the empowering mechanism of SHGs, where group dynamics are expected to compensate for the basic weaknesses of the individual rural poor and present them as credit worthy and financially accountable units. The system of grading the SHGs through a rigorous process is expected to separate the more vibrant of the SHGs and eventually give them a capital subsidy assistance so that they undertake self-employment oriented livelihood opportunities.

4.63 The SGSY scheme has been successful in delivering the outcomes in terms of poverty alleviation wherever capacity building and beneficiary mobilization have been carried out. Thrift, multiple lending, participatory process of identification, and pursuit of economic activities have succeeded in States like Andhra Pradesh, Tamil Nadu, and Kerala substantially because the basic processes had been grounded.

4.64 The higher performance parameter of multiple lending and increased quantum of lending have been achieved in States like Andhra Pradesh due to the SHGs having been federated at different levels from the village to the district. With the emergence of a well federated organizational base, the SHG network has been observed to acquire dynamism and versatility in activities in States like Kerala and Andhra Pradesh. There have been diverse models of Self Help in various parts of the country, most important among them being the Kudumbashree in Kerala with active linkages with the PRIs, and the AP model that relies on the fulcrum of federations of SHGs that have grown into organizations of the poor. The NABARD also sponsors SHGs.

Key Issues

4.65 The SGSY is being implemented since 1999. Close to 2.6 million SHGs have been formed under the SGSY since its inception. Of these SHGs 16 lakh have already crossed the Grade-I stage. About 8 lakh SHGs have passed the Grade-II stage and of them, slightly less than five lakh SHGs have taken up economic activities. About 60% of the Grade-II SHGs have taken up economic activities, the balance number waiting for financial assistance. Of the nearly Rs 25000 crore credit flow targeted under the programme, less than 50% has been achieved. SHGs have several in-built strengths, most of which are intangible, such as group cohesion, enhanced ability for articulation of common demands, better and efficient use of available local resources, etc. While it would be necessary to work on the strengths of the SHGs, it is equally necessary to learn the lessons from the experience of implementing the SGSY over the past eight years. There are several issues—some conceptual ones pertaining to larger aspects of the programme, such as the role and utility of the subsidy component, and some programme specific second generation issues such as forming federations, provision of interest subsidy, social mobilization issues, etc. Some such issues are highlighted below:

- Diverse views are being expressed in various quarters about the relevance or otherwise of subsidy-driven programmes. A rational response would have to be found for such positions. Subsidy is a form of support to the poor and stopping it entirely would be unwarranted. However, the idea of directing the subsidy flows properly and to examine if there was any case for putting conditionalities to the system of subsidy flow so that the targeted populations are better served, merits examination.
- The number of SHGs formed under the SGSY is very large, but there is a feeling about whether such large numbers mean anything from the point of view of poverty alleviation. Agencies such as NABARD, Small Industries Development Bank of India (SIDBI), and Rashtriya Mahila Kosh (RMK), and Ministries such as Women and Child Development have their own models of SHG formation and their sustenance. Some State Governments such as Andhra Pradesh and Kerala have their own models. There is therefore, a need for placing the SGSY programme on this large canvas and fitting it in the broader context of the SHG movement of the country.
- There is tremendous shortage of manpower in the area of technical support for rural development. Andhra Pradesh continually engages about 6.00 lakh SHGs through a separate structure, Society for the Elimination of Rural Poverty that has independent units that deal with Risk Mitigation, Food Security, Micro Finance, Institution Building, Marketing, and Livelihood Promotion. At the district level too they have equivalent units that go upto the Mandal level. The dedicated institutional machinery seems to have made a difference. There is a case for similar efforts from other States as well.
- Going by the experience of the States like Andhra Pradesh, Kerala, and Tamil Nadu, federating the SHGs appears essential for improving the bargaining power of the SHGs and better sustainability of the SHG movement. Encouraging the inter-state, inter-district networking of the SHGs/SHG Federations for marketing of the SHG products would be the next step. Current institutional arrangements for social mobilization and livelihood generation are somewhat limited in scope. Therefore, a mission mode approach to enhance facilitation, institutional building, and hand holding support to SHG movement is required over a long period of time to secure sustainability of SHGs and their apex organizations. The social mobilization aspect of the SGSY programme has hitherto not been given due attention. Social mobilization is both a means and an end in itself. Expansion of political rights of the mobilized poor will have tremendous intrinsic value, not always measurable. A few of the SHGs that acquire the characteristics of good entrepreneurs may be encouraged to become entrepreneurs. SGSY is actually lagging behind in keeping pace with the SHG movement sweeping the country.
- Credit is a very important issue. It would be necessary to enhance the credit flow to the SHGs in a more creative manner than what has been possible so far. The credit achievement, in terms of the total volume as well as the rate of flow, in Andhra Pradesh model seems to be much higher than the national achievement. An issue that requires to be looked into is also the possibility of introducing interest subsidy as an alternative to the capital subsidy. There are no two opinions about the utility of financial intermediation for making the lending under the programme cost effective for the banks. Federations of SHGs having their own corpus can work as intermediaries. An investment on making the SHGs credit-worthy cannot be wished away. In terms of

priority, saving followed by risk mitigation and then credit would be the natural sequence for financial intervention. Federations acting as financial intermediaries is a high skill activity and it is essential that investments are made on enhancing the skill base of the Federations. There is a need to promote institutional partnerships between the SHGs/Federations with the bankers. Enhancing the credit flow to the poor may call for grounding several strategies and partnerships and not just one. The country is also on the threshold of a major initiative for micro finance. Again, there are diverse views on the role, utility, and relevance of micro finance in poverty alleviation. The issue of harmonizing the SGSY and the micro finance models also requires to be looked at.

- New areas are emerging in view of the changes in the economy due to liberalization, privatization, and globalization. It may not be possible for the SGSY, a pure self-employment programme to capture all the aspects of poverty. Purely from a family's economic security point of view, BPL families might want to have at least one wage earner among them, so as to provide the requisite certainty to their family incomes. In such a situation there may be a case for introducing a placement-oriented skill enhancement model for youth as a sub-set of the SGSY. This programme will be a hybrid of the wage-employment and self-employment programmes.
- Special projects of the SGSY, that were expected to ground innovative and alternative ways of reducing poverty do not seem to have actually made much difference. The higher quantum of subsidy available through special projects appeared to have driven large number of projects. Often activities proposed are eligible to be funded by different schemes of the line departments of the concerned sectors. Even then funds are sought in the project proposals through special projects. States and other agencies follow up proposals vigorously till the sanction of the project and thereafter virtually no monitoring of projects seemed to have been undertaken. Of the 231 special projects that have already been sanctioned, only about 29 have been completed. Due to the indifferent performance it does not appear that there is a case for continuing with the special project component under the SGSY. There have been very wide inequities in the sanction of special projects among the States so far.

THE WAY FORWARD—STRATEGY FOR THE ELEVENTH PLAN

4.66 Eleventh Plan strategy for SGSY would have to necessarily take the best out of what has evolved in the Self Help movement across the country over the last few years and integrate it with the programme. Likewise a few aspects of the SGSY programme that have failed to give the desired results require a fresh look and if necessary, dropped.

4.67 One of the most important aspects that requires examination is the institutional mechanism that had been erected to undertake the poverty alleviation programmes. The District Rural Development Agency (DRDAs) in their current form and content do not appear to have the requisite wherewithal to handle a complex issue such as poverty. The current administrative setup at the national level is unequal to a large task such as poverty elimination across the geographical and social complexity and it requires a different order of involvement of the MoRD. It is therefore, necessary to set up a National Agency outside the ministry to manage the National Rural Poverty Elimination Programme to achieve the objectives of the programme meaningfully and comprehensively. The need for setting up a national level agency with a flexible administrative structure, for better planning, organizing, and coordinating the poverty elimination effort cannot be overstated. The national level organization will be the intellectual backbone and provide requisite technical expertise and capacities, while the ones at the level of the State Governments will be the functional bodies. These organizations would have to be manned by people with an active commitment to poverty alleviation as well as an undertaking from the States to assure minimum tenures to the officials prior to making any funding arrangements, if necessary, through a MoU. The administrative set-up could essentially be a society attached to the MoRD. The national organization will co-ordinate with the poverty elimination agencies established by the State Governments for implementing the SGSY in its revised form. It will also be the agency to document and be the clearing house for the best practices with respect to the poverty elimination programmes and strategies of the country. It should devolve funds to the State Governments based on rational formulae, evolving and working out the MoUs with the State Governments for the implementation of the poverty elimination programmes. The national and State level organizations so created will systematically address the key subjects of poverty alleviation like livelihood generation, capacity building, skill upgradation, credit, and international assistance .

4.68 Considering the experiences and lessons learnt from various development projects, the revised SGSY programme should aim at promoting and strengthening member-owned, member-controlled, and member-managed institutions of the poor that enable them to secure sustainable livelihoods and better quality of life. These institutions should provide a wide range of services to their members as per their demand. The revised SGSY should promote and nurture a large cadre of activists and leaders from the poor for providing support services to the institutions of the poor on a sustainable basis. The approach for organizing the poor stems from the conviction that there is an immense desire and latent capability among the poor to come out of poverty. They have a tremendous potential to help themselves and the potential of each member can be harnessed by organizing them. Social mobilization enables the poor to build their own organizations in which they participate fully and directly and take decisions on all issues concerning poverty elimination.

4.69 The current mechanism of fund flow to the SHGs through a graded system requires a comprehensive review. The current scheme allows a Revolving Fund entitlement of upto Rs 10000 for the Grade-I SHGs, that will also entitle them to draw cash credit from a financial institution. The rate of attrition between the Grade-I and II indicates that a large number of SHGs fizzle out mid-way after availing the Revolving Fund. Further, the SHGs that have cleared the Grade-II stage seem to wait for long periods before getting an opportunity to avail the subsidy assistance. Close to 3 lakh such SHGs are waiting in the wings for such assistance. The overall credit achievement under the programme is abysmally low. The overall credit targets are achieved only by about 50%. More importantly in a capital subsidy mechanism there is little scope to leverage higher credit flow because of the subsidy entitlements. The volume of credit extended to SHGs in one State, Andhra Pradesh, alone is higher than the national credit achievement under the SGSY. This calls for serious scrutiny.

4.70 The SHGs can be further strengthened and stabilized by federating them at, say village or cluster of villages or block level depending upon the number of SHGs and their spatial distribution. The federations shall be formal organizations registered under the most appropriate Acts (Societies Registration Act, State Cooperative Act, Trust, Mutually Aided Cooperative Societies Act, or Mutual Benefit Trust) that exist in the State. The second tier of Institution Building phase is the federation of SHGs either at village or at cluster of villages' level. The Village Level Federations (VLFs) are vital for demonstrating solidarity, initiating collective action on various poverty related issues and reducing dependency on the external agency for information, technical support and resolving conflicts. The VLFs provide a forum to voice the problems of the poor in the village, exchange of experiences including flow of information from various government departments, and raises resources required to take up the appropriate development interventions in poverty reduction. It generates income by collecting share capital, membership fee, savings, interest margins and penalties, and become financially sustainable in a period of 3–4 years. Based on the proposals of the VLFs, the district level agency sanctions fund for on-lending to SHGs. Once the VLFs attain a certain level of maturity, the Block Level Federation is promoted. The Block Level Federation provides solidarity to all the VLFs and SHGs. It plays a vital role in bringing all the BPL families into the SHG fold, building the capacities of the SHGs and VLFs, framing required policies and ensuring the quality of institutions, etc.

4.71 However, in order to strengthen the existing programme an effort should be made to graduate the allocations in such a manner that all further increases in the allocations to the SGSY should be based on demand-driven model, with attendant commitments of the State with respect to erecting institutions of the poor, dedicated implementation machinery and adhering to the framework provided by the national level agency. The current allocations to the SGSY can taper off over the balance Plan period so that at the end of the Plan period the new model will be firmly in place.

4.72 To capture the opportunities that are emerging in the economy due to the processes of globalization and liberalization, it will be necessary to launch a new sub-set of the SGSY—that can be known as the placement-linked skill enhancement programme. The Ministry's experience of the Reddy's Labs initiative of the SGSY and more recently with the Infrastructure Leasing and Financial Services (IL&FS), are worthy models for institutionalization and systemic action. The sectors that can be looked at are Textiles, Leather, Gems and Jewellery, Retail Chains, etc., where there is a shortage of supply of trained labour. Skill formation, by use of in-house programmes, evolving specific curriculum, independent accreditation, and placement are the essential components of this process. It is suggested that a definite component of the skills programme be included in the revised SGSY programme.

Rural Housing for the Houseless

4.73 Housing is a basic human need. A roof over her head endows a shelterless person with an essential asset and improves her physical and mental well-being.

4.74 The importance of housing has been acknowledged and housing as a human right was recognized way back by the Universal Declaration of Human Rights adopted by the General Assembly of the United Nations on 10 December 1948. Article 25 of this declaration states: 'Everyone has the right to standard of living adequate for the health and well being of himself, and his family, including food, clothing, housing....'

4.75 Article 11 of the International Covenant on Economic, Social and Cultural Rights, 1966 also required the States Parties to the Covenant to recognize the right of everyone to an adequate standard of living for herself and her family, including adequate food, clothing, and housing and to the continuous improvement of living conditions. It further asked the States Parties to take appropriate steps to ensure the realization of this right.

4.76 India also embarked on the path of making 'housing for all' a reality. The conference of Chief Ministers, 1996 recommended the Basic Minimum Services (BMS) Programme. One of the seven BMS requiring priority attention was 'Provision of Public Housing Assistance to all shelterless poor families'. Consequently, the BMS programme became part of Ninth Five Year Plan and concerted efforts in a focused manner were initiated to make these basic services accessible to every one. Later, the National Housing and Habitat Policy, 1998 stated that the ultimate goal of the policy was to ensure 'Shelter to all' and better quality of life for all citizens.

Indira Awaas Yojana (IAY)

4.77 Though the earliest housing programme taken up by the GoI was for rehabilitation of refugees immediately after the partition of the country, the government started implementing its major housing scheme of IAY as an independent scheme only from 1 January 1996.

4.78 In the present form, IAY is one of the very popular schemes of the MoRD and has caught the imagination of the rural people. The popularity can be attributed to the fact that the scheme enables beneficiaries to participate and involve themselves in construction of their home. The role of the State Government is confined to mere facilitating use of local, low cost, environment-friendly, and disaster-resistant technology and also in encouraging construction of sanitary latrine and smokeless *chulha*. There is no prescribed design or technology and no contractors are involved. Funds are released in installments directly to the beneficiaries and there is no credit portion as part of the assistance which enable timely release of funds. The beneficiaries construct the houses as per their own choice of design, technology, and requirement. Not surprisingly, evaluation studies reveal high levels of occupancy and satisfaction.

4.79 In spite of criticism from certain quarters about IAY being a full subsidy scheme, experience reveals that houses get completed more or less on time which may not have been the case if credit was part of the assistance. Moreover the unit assistance of Rs 25000 per dwelling in the plain areas and Rs 27500 in the tribal and hilly areas is not adequate and beneficiaries have to contribute at least by way of their own labour for completion of the house. This participation makes the scheme even more meaningful.

4.80 The funds for the IAY scheme are shared between the Central and the State Government in the ratio of 75:25. The Central budget is allocated to the States based on a 75% weightage to housing shortage and 25% weightage to poverty ratio. Similarly the district allocation is based on a 75% weightage to housing shortage and 25% to the share of SC/ST population. To introduce transparency, the selection of beneficiaries which was being done through the gram sabhas is now expected to be from the permanent IAY waitlists. These lists are prepared based on the ranking given to families as part of the BPL Census 2002. Further, 60% of the IAY funds are earmarked for SC/STs, 3% for persons with disability, and 15% for minorities. It is expected that all houses will be sanctioned in the name of women or jointly with the husband. These provisions have enabled effective targeting of the weaker sections and the scheme has succeeded in empowering the poorest.

Adequacy of Houses and Tackling Shelterlessness

4.81 Based on building materials used for construction of structure, houses have been classified as per Census 2001 as *pucca* houses (the walls and roof of which are made of permanent materials), semi-*pucca* houses (either the wall or the roof is made of permanent material and the other is made of temporary material), temporary house (both walls and roof are made of materials which have to be replaced frequently), serviceable temporary houses (wall is made of mud, unburnt bricks, or wood), and non-serviceable temporary houses (wall is made of grass, thatch, bamboo, plastic etc).

4.82 Trends indicate that share of pucca houses has increased. However, *kutcha* houses account for 26.5 million, and the next important cause of shortage is congestion (10.18 million houses).

4.83 For the Eleventh Plan, however, focus could be on targeting the poorest of the poor as far as IAY is concerned while targeting the remaining shortage with other interventions. Hence for the purpose of IAY the shortage emerging due to factors of (i) houseless, and (ii) unserviceable kutcha house could be tackled. With these factors, the estimate of housing shortage for 2001 stands at 148.6 lakh houses and for 2007 at 159.5 lakh houses. Hence a target of constructing about 150 lakh houses under IAY needs to be fixed for the Eleventh Plan.

KEY ISSUES AND STRATEGIC INTERVENTIONS

IAY

(i) Selection of Beneficiaries

4.84 Though selection had to be done by the gram sabhas, studies have revealed that 25% to 50% of the beneficiaries are not being selected through the gram sabhas. Further, the selection as well as allocation among Panchayats has been influenced by the PRIs/ MLAs. The vocal and active segments of beneficiaries influence the selection process because of the limited allotment under IAY. In the process, the poorest among BPL households are left out, and non-BPL families also get selected for the IAY houses. Besides, collection of illegal gratification of selection by PRIs is a common complaint often heard at the field level, as brought to light by the several studies. Moreover, only beneficiaries who have house-sites are selected and thus, the very poor who do not have a plot of land get out from the purview of the scheme. This is a serious problem, since these are the people who are the most vulnerable. Some 8 million of the 14 million houseless are actually those who have no land, or live on homes located on land belonging to others (e.g., landlords, public land, etc.). The focus of the IAY programme must be on the houseless (e.g., such communities as the Saharyas, Musahars, the so called de-notified tribes, those living on canal bunds or roads, and other such who are seen to be at the bottom of the social ladder.

4.85 A more accurate targeting may result by the preparation of permanent IAY waitlists. These waitlists have to be based on scores given to families as part of

BPL Census 2002. This can bring about more transparency and tackle the problem of illegal gratification. Regarding provision of plots and homesteads for the landless both State Government and Panchayats have to be encouraged to play a major role. State government need to be incentivized and Panchayats have to be appropriately empowered.

(ii) Adequacy of Unit Cost

4.86 Inadequacy of cash assistance for construction has resulted in poor quality of house, non-fulfillment of requirements of the disaster-prone areas, and debt trap on account of the beneficiaries having to borrow funds to complete the construction of a pucca house. Several examples have been reported of poor quality of construction, sagging foundation, use of temporary materials for roofing or leaving the construction incomplete because of inadequate finance. Even after contributing their labour and borrowing from local sources, a significant number of families are not able to complete the house in all respects, and most houses remain without plastering or flooring.

4.87 There is an urgent need to increase the unit cost from the present level of Rs 25000 for plain areas and Rs 27500 for hilly areas.

(iii) Structural Facilities and Provision of Infrastructure

4.88 Studies have revealed that only about 50% of IAY houses have sanitary latrines and even a lesser percentage have installed smokeless chullas. This is a serious problem. Over a million women and children not only suffer from upper respiratory tract infections due to inhaling of indoor smoke but many die as a result. In addition, India is one of the countries in the world with much of its population not having access to sanitary means of excreta disposal (despite the existence of TSC, another CSS, which is part of the Bharat Nirman set of pro-grammes). Houses built as part of the Central Government's own programmes, like IAY, need to succeed in building of smokeless chulhas and of sanitary latrines.

4.89 The quality of life may not improve despite the construction of new houses unless there is provision for infrastructure. There is a need to provide a minimum level of infrastructure such as internal road, drainage, water supply stand post, along with the provision of houses by way of convergence of schemes.

(iv) Ownership Issues

4.90 It is found that the title of the house site tends to be in the name of the male member of the household. Hence the benefit to accrue to women by allotment of the scheme is restricted only for the purpose of the scheme sanction. Some effort to ensure clear cut ownership in the name of women needs to be made.

OTHER STRATEGIC INTERVENTIONS

4.91 Other than the IAY, the States have rural house construction programmes usually targeting the poor. While IAY can focus on eliminating the backlog of houselessness and temporary and unserviceable houses in rural India, the States should take responsibility for addressing any emerging needs. It is necessary to have the right kind of interventions so that the programme objective of tackling shelterlessness is achieved within the target time. Hence, the following strategic interventions are suggested:

- Encourage primary lending institutions to enhance their credit flow to the rural population and actively involve the existing institutional mechanisms of SHGs and micro finance institutions to extend loans to the rural population.
- Encourage new, flexible financial products through commercial banks geared to payback cycles of rural families to bring about a higher degree of inclusivity in institutional lending for rural housing.
- Encourage small and medium developers to take up housing in rural areas through a mix of fiscal incentives and business volumes after necessary environment and social impact assessments and clearances from the PRIs.
- Create institutional mechanisms to address the higher risk perception in rural areas.
- Consider housing at par with rural infrastructure as far as funding and concessions are concerned, in order to encourage investments in the sector.

4.92 Based on the aforementioned multidimensional approach and strategic interventions, specific initiatives can be taken up, as listed below.

- The IAY funds are being released directly to DRDAs for further disbursement. But it has been observed that there is no uniformity in disbursing the amount to the beneficiaries. To streamline the process as well as also speedy disbursement to the beneficiaries which may also speed up physical progress, implementing agencies of IAY at district level may be advised to disburse the amount directly to beneficiaries by depositing in bank accounts as far as possible.
- To ensure transparency and fair selection of beneficiaries, all State Governments have either finalized or are in the process of finalizing permanent IAY waitlist in such a manner that the poorest of the poor get the top slot. Further, implementing agencies should introduce the system of social audit to ensure proper utilization of funds and to make the system leakage proof. In addition to this the database of the IAY beneficiaries may also be prepared by the States and put on the website for information of IAY beneficiaries.
- It is gratifying to note that many State Governments are already implementing State-run schemes to supplement the efforts of the Central Government to provide houses to the poor. Still the gap between the demand and supply is huge. Hence to cover up the shortage of houses for the rural poor, the States which do not have State-run schemes may be incentivized to have their own State-run schemes.
- Even though 164.00 lakh houses have been constructed under IAY till date to provide shelter to the poor, still the poorest of the poor may fail to take benefit under the scheme because of their being landless people in the rural areas. To ensure social and economic equity, it is necessary to reach out to these people. State should acquire land and distribute homestead plots. Funds for this may be provided by the government.

National Rural Housing Consortium

4.93 A consortium could be created comprising nodal organizations such as National Housing Bank (NHB), NABARD, nationalized and premier commercial banks and apex microfinance institutions to provide equity and debt for rural housing for small and marginal farmers, small village artisans, self employed, etc. MoRD could play the role of a Key Facilitator.

Incentivizing Lending Institutions

4.94 Presently, Housing Finance Companies (HFCs) registered with NHB are allowed to create a Special Reserve to the extent of 40% income earned through long term mortgage financing (mortgage loans for more than 5 years) under Section 36(1) (vii) of the IT Act. This fiscal incentive is, however, not available to banks, who are presently the leaders in the housing finance market. At present, the rural housing loan portfolios of banks and HFCs, comprise only 10–12% of their total housing loans. There is need to incentivize these institutions to increase their lending in rural areas. It is, therefore, proposed that the limit under this provision should be increased from the present level of 40% to 60% for HFCs, banks, and NHB. The additional 20% provisions will exclusively be for lending in rural areas. It is proposed that banks may also be allowed to create the Special Reserves on the lines of HFCs for long term mortgage financing in rural areas. This will encourage banks and HFCs to aggressively lend for housing in rural areas. SHGs and micro finance institutions (MFIs)could also be encouraged to be actively involved in extending housing loans.

Role of HUDCO

4.95 Housing Urban Development Corporation (HUDCO) started its rural housing activity from 1977–78 by extending assistance for construction/ upgradation of rural houses. As part of its commitment to rural housing, HUDCO makes available financial assistance to State Governments and their agencies like Housing Boards, District Taluka, and Panchayat Development Boards nominated by the State Government for undertaking housing schemes with its assistance.

4.96 HUDCO's normal rural housing programme by and large caters to Economically Weaker Sections (EWS) (with a monthly household income less than Rs 2500). In rural areas, the three types of schemes financed by HUDCO include:

(i) EWS rural housing schemes for landless persons,
(ii) EWS rural housing schemes for land owning persons and,
(iii) The village abadi scheme including house repair.

4.97 Under the first two schemes, the cost ceiling per dwelling unit is Rs 60000. The maximum extent of finance is 90% of the project cost or Rs 40000, whichever is less. Under the first scheme HUDCO supplements effort of State Governments to provide free house sites by extending loans at low interest rates. The third scheme envisages improvement of existing houses as well as environmental improvement of surrounding areas by providing for sanitation, drainage, water supply, link roads, etc. Most of the HUDCO's sanctions pertain to the second scheme.

4.98 Over the last 28 years, HUDCO has sanctioned 2472 schemes with a loan amount of Rs 5807 crore for construction of 86.11 lakh dwelling units in various States in the country (as on 31 March 2006). There is an urgent need to strengthen the role of HUDCO and provision of its services to enhance construction activity in rural areas, especially to cater to EWS.

4.99 The allocation for the Eleventh Five Year Plan (at current price) is tentatively provided at Rs 26882 crore.

SOCIAL PROTECTION—NATIONAL SOCIAL ASSISTANCE PROGRAMME (NSAP) AND ASSOCIATED PROGRAMMES

4.100 The Constitution of India (Article 41) states: 'The State shall, within the limits of its economic capacity and development, make effective provision for securing the right to work, to education and to public assistance in cases of unemployment, old age, sickness and disablement, and in other cases of undeserved want'. Social protection refers to public assistance in all cases of underserved want. It provides human security to the poor and the destitute.

4.101 For the first time in India, the NSAP was launched on 15 August 1995. The basic aim of this programme was to provide social assistance benefit to the rural poor in case of old age, death of primary breadwinner, and for poor women during maternity. It aims at providing them with a modicum of dignity and support, thereby ensuring a minimum quality of care and attention from the community. It provides an opportunity for linking the social assistance package to schemes for poverty alleviation and provision of basic needs. It was a CSS with 100% Central assistance provided to States/UTs. This programme is implemented through a synergistic partnership with State Governments and under the direct supervision of DRDAs in close collaboration with the various PRIs. This programme included three schemes viz., National Old Age Pension Scheme (NOAPS), National Family Benefit Scheme (NFBS), and National Maternity Benefit Scheme (NMBS).

- Under NOAPS, old age pension of Rs 75 per month was provided to persons of 65 years and above who are destitute. This amount has since been enhanced to Rs 200 per month from the year 2006–07. The response for this scheme has been overwhelming from the poor as well as the State Governments. Many States are matching these pension amounts equally and many more are extending the coverage of this scheme to all those identified from among BPL families.
- The NFBS provides a lump sum family benefit of Rs 10000 to the bereaved household in case of the death (natural or accidental) of the primary breadwinner (male or female) whose earnings contribute substantially to the total household income. This scheme is applicable to all the eligible persons in the age group 18 to 64. The bereaved household should belong to BPL families to qualify for this benefit.
- Under the NMBS there is a provision for payment of Rs 500 per pregnancy to women belonging to poor households for pre-natal and post-natal maternity care upto the first two live births. This benefit is provided to eligible women of 19 years and above. The objective of the scheme is to extend financial assistance to pregnant women from BPL households, for the first two live births. To ensure better linkage with nutrition and national population control program-mes, NMBS was transferred to Department of Family Welfare and is renamed as Janani Suraksha Yojana in 2001–02. It is now part of the NRHM.

4.102 On the recommendations of the Group of Ministers (GoM) a new scheme called Annapurna was launched on 1 April 2000 as a CSS. It aims to providing food security to meet the requirement of those senior citizens who though eligible, have remained uncovered under the NOAPS. Under the Annapurna scheme the beneficiaries should be 65 years or above and must be destitute. The beneficiaries are entitled to 10 kg of food grains per month free of cost. The ceiling on the total number of Annapurna beneficiaries will be at least 20% of the persons eligible to receive pension under NOAPS.

4.103 These schemes continued to be administered by the MoRD upto 2001–02 as CSS, and during 2002–03 these schemes were transferred to Central Assistance for State Plans on the recommendation of the National Development Council (NDC) with the requisite flexibility in the choice of implementation.

KEY ISSUES

4.104 Various studies conducted in respect of the NOAPS indicate that the criteria of destitution are difficult to apply. Many States have adopted the poverty line itself to define destitution. This is, in fact, reasonable since a BPL family can hardly support itself and would not be in a position to support the aged. Therefore, the NOAPS has now been extended to all old persons above 65 years of age in BPL families with effect from 2007–08. Consequently the Annapurna Scheme which provides 10 kg of foodgrains to senior citizens uncovered under NOAPS would be discontinued soon after these beneficiaries are covered under NOAPS.

4.105 The National Policy for Older Persons, 1999 recognizes that a person becomes a senior citizen at the age of 60 and would be eligible for the facilities and concessions available to senior citizens. Indeed, the aged over 60 years, from among the poor families, can hardly participate in the workforce and support given to them will be more useful when above 60 years, than if given only after 65 years. Therefore, the scheme of NOAPS needs to be made applicable to persons of the age of 60 years or more.

4.106 The rate of pension under NOAPS has recently been enhanced to Rs 200 per month. The State Governments have been urged to top it up with another Rs 200 so that every pensioner would get a minimum of Rs 400 per month. Currently, ten States/UTs are already providing an additionality of Rs 200 per month or even more. Other States need to be encouraged to supplement the Central Government's Old Age Pension, so that a minimum of Rs 400 per month is provided to the deserving aged.

4.107 NSAP requires to be extended to two more categories of deserving poor in dire need of this assistance viz., persons with severe/multiple disabilities and widowed women. Similarly, national schemes for maintenance of orphans, street children, and other sections of the poor in distress are needed.

4.108 The scope of the NFBS needs to be extended to cover instances of death of any adult member of the family without limiting to the death of breadwinner.

4.109 At present, there are two life insurance schemes operated by Life Insurance Corporation (LIC) that are making headway among the people below and marginally above the poverty line viz., 'Janashree Bima Yojana' for the rural poor and the 'Aam Aadmi Insurance Scheme' for the landless agricultural labour. These two schemes under which the premium is contributed by the Centre and the State Governments in equal proportions provide significant supplementation to the Family Benefit Scheme with enhanced benefits on death, accidental death, and disability for the persons insured in the BPL families.

4.110 The poor require comprehensive access to strengthened public health system and facilities. In addition, they need suitable instruments in the form of health insurance in cases involving serious illness requiring hospitalization, which are not provided in institutions of public health.

4.111 In the execution of NSAP, greater professional support is needed for ensuring quality, delivery and for suitable monitoring and evaluation purposes, both at the Centre and State levels. Advisory Committees comprising of professionals and voluntary organizations should be set up at Central, State, and district levels for continuous review of policy and performance of NSAP. Technical support groups should also be established at all level to ensure smooth implementation and closer monitoring of NSAP.

ANNEXURE 4.1
Headcount Ratio and Number of Poor Persons Below Poverty Line in India (Combined)

States/UTs	Headcount Ratio				Number of Poor Persons (in Lakh)			
	1973–74	1983	1993–94	2004–05	1973–74	1983	1993–94	2004–05
Andhra Pradesh	48.9	28.9	22.2	15.8	225.7	164.6	154.0	126.1
Assam	51.2	40.5	40.9	19.7	81.8	77.7	96.4	55.8
Bihar	61.9	62.2	55.0	41.4	370.6	462.1	493.4	369.2
Delhi	49.6	26.2	14.7	14.7	22.8	18.4	15.5	22.9
Goa	44.3	18.9	14.9	13.8	4.2	2.2	1.9	2.0
Gujarat	48.2	32.8	24.2	16.8	138.4	117.9	105.2	90.7
Haryana	35.4	21.4	25.1	14.0	38.3	29.6	43.9	32.1
Himachal Pradesh	26.4	16.4	28.4	10.0	9.7	7.4	15.9	6.4
Karnataka	54.5	38.2	33.2	25.0	170.7	149.8	156.5	138.9
Kerala	59.8	40.4	25.4	15.0	135.5	106.8	76.4	49.6
Madhya Pradesh	61.8	49.8	42.5	38.3	276.3	278.0	298.5	249.7
Maharashtra	53.2	43.4	36.9	30.7	287.4	290.9	305.2	317.4
Orissa	66.2	65.3	48.6	46.4	154.5	181.3	160.6	178.5
Punjab	28.2	16.2	11.8	8.4	40.5	28.6	25.1	21.6
Rajasthan	46.1	34.5	27.4	22.1	128.5	126.8	128.5	134.9
Tamil Nadu	54.9	51.7	35.0	22.5	239.5	260.1	202.1	145.6
Uttar Pradesh	57.1	47.1	40.9	32.8	535.7	556.7	604.5	590.0
West Bengal	63.4	54.9	35.7	24.7	299.3	318.7	254.6	208.4
Chhattisgarh	–	–	–	40.9	–	–	–	91.0
Jharkhand	–	–	–	40.3	–	–	–	116.4
Uttarakhand	–	–	–	39.6	–	–	–	36.0
Chandigarh	28.0	23.8	11.4	7.1	0.8	1.2	0.8	0.7
Dandra & Nagar Haveli	46.6	15.7	50.8	33.2	0.4	0.2	0.8	0.8
J&K	40.8	24.2	25.2	5.4	20.5	15.6	20.9	5.9
All India	54.9	44.5	36.0	27.5	3213.4	3229.0	3203.7	3017.2

Note: 1. Poverty Ratio of Assam is used for Sikkim, Arunachal Pradesh, Meghalaya, Mizoram, Manipur, Nagaland, and Tripura.
2. Poverty Ratio of Tamil Nadu is used for Pondicherry and Andaman and Nicobar Islands (A&N Islands).
3. Poverty Ratio of Kerala is used for Lakshadweep.
4. Urban Poverty Ratio of Punjab is used for both rural and urban poverty of Chandigarh.
5. Poverty Line of Maharashtra and expenditure distribution of Goa is used to estimate poverty ratio of Goa.
6. Poverty Line of Maharashtra and expenditure distribution of Dadra & Nagar Haveli is used to estimate poverty ratio of Dadra & Nagar Haveli.

Source: Planning Commission.

ANNEXURE 4.2
Headcount Ratio and Number of Poor Persons Below Poverty Line in India (Rural)

States/UTs	Headcount Ratio				Number of Poor Persons (in Lakh)			
	1973–74	1983	1993–94	2004–05	1973–74	1983	1993–94	2004–05
Andhra Pradesh	48.4	26.5	15.9	11.2	178.2	114.3	79.5	64.7
Assam	52.7	42.6	45.0	22.3	76.4	73.4	94.3	54.5
Bihar	63.0	64.4	58.2	42.1	336.5	417.7	450.9	336.7
Delhi	24.4	7.7	1.9	6.9	1.1	0.4	0.2	0.6
Goa	46.9	14.8	5.3	5.4	3.2	1.2	0.4	0.4
Gujarat	46.4	29.8	22.2	19.1	94.6	72.9	62.2	63.5
Haryana	34.2	20.6	28.0	13.6	30.1	22.0	36.6	21.5
Himachal Pradesh	27.4	17.0	30.3	10.7	9.4	7.1	15.4	6.1
Karnataka	55.1	36.3	29.9	20.8	128.4	100.5	96.0	75.1
Kerala	59.2	39.0	25.8	13.2	111.4	81.6	56.0	32.4
Madhya Pradesh	62.7	48.9	40.6	36.9	231.2	215.5	216.2	175.7
Maharashtra	57.7	45.2	37.9	29.6	210.8	193.8	193.3	171.1
Orissa	67.3	67.5	49.7	46.8	142.2	164.7	140.9	151.8
Punjab	28.2	13.2	12.0	9.2	30.5	16.8	17.8	15.1
Rajasthan	44.8	33.5	26.5	18.7	101.4	96.8	94.7	87.4
Tamil Nadu	57.4	54.0	32.5	22.9	172.6	181.6	121.7	76.5
Uttar Pradesh	56.5	46.5	42.3	33.4	450.0	448.0	496.2	473.0
West Bengal	73.2	63.1	40.8	28.6	258.0	268.6	209.9	173.2
Chhattisgarh	–	–	–	40.8	–	–	–	71.5
Jharkhand	–	–	–	46.3	–	–	–	103.2
Uttarakhand	–	–	–	40.8	–	–	–	27.1
Chandigarh	28.0	23.8	11.4	7.1	0.1	0.1	0.1	0.1
Dadra & Nagar Haveli	46.9	14.8	52.0	39.8	0.4	0.2	0.7	0.7
J&K	45.5	26.0	30.3	4.6	18.4	13.1	19.1	3.7
All India	56.4	45.7	37.3	28.3	2612.9	2519.6	2440.3	2209.2

Note: 1. Poverty Ratio of Assam is used for Sikkim, Arunachal Pradesh, Meghalaya, Mizoram, Manipur, Nagaland, and Tripura.
2. Poverty Ratio of Tamil Nadu is used for Pondicherry and A&N Islands.
3. Poverty Ratio of Kerala is used for Lakshadweep.
4. Urban Poverty Ratio of Punjab is used for both rural and urban poverty of Chandigarh.
5. Poverty Line of Maharashtra and expenditure distribution of Goa is used to estimate poverty ratio of Goa.
6. Poverty Line of Maharashtra and expenditure distribution of Dadra & Nagar Haveli is used to estimate poverty ratio of Dadra & Nagar Haveli.

Source: Planning Commission.

ANNEXURE 4.3
Headcount Ratio and Number of Poor Persons Below Poverty Line in India (Urban)

States/UTs	Headcount Ratio				Number of Poor Persons (in Lakh)			
	1973–74	1983	1993–94	2004–05	1973–74	1983	1993–94	2004–05
Andhra Pradesh	50.6	36.3	38.3	28.0	47.5	50.2	74.5	61.4
Assam	36.9	21.7	7.7	3.3	5.5	4.3	2.0	1.3
Bihar	53.0	47.3	34.5	34.6	34.1	44.4	42.5	32.4
Delhi	52.2	27.9	16.0	15.2	21.8	18.0	15.3	22.3
Goa	37.7	27.0	27.0	21.3	1.0	1.1	1.5	1.6
Gujarat	52.6	39.1	27.9	13.0	43.8	45.0	43.0	27.2
Haryana	40.2	24.2	16.4	15.1	8.2	7.6	7.3	10.6
Himachal Pradesh	13.2	9.4	9.2	3.4	0.4	0.3	0.5	0.2
Karnataka	52.5	42.8	40.1	32.6	42.3	49.3	60.5	63.8
Kerala	62.7	45.7	24.6	20.2	24.2	25.2	20.5	17.2
Madhya Pradesh	57.7	53.1	48.4	42.1	45.1	62.5	82.3	74.0
Maharashtra	43.9	40.3	35.2	32.2	76.6	97.1	111.9	146.3
Orissa	55.6	49.2	41.6	44.3	12.2	16.7	19.7	26.7
Punjab	28.0	23.8	11.4	7.1	10.0	11.9	7.4	6.5
Rajasthan	52.1	37.9	30.5	32.9	27.1	30.1	33.8	47.5
Tamil Nadu	49.4	47.0	39.8	22.2	66.9	78.5	80.4	69.1
Uttar Pradesh	60.1	49.8	35.4	30.6	85.7	108.7	108.3	117.0
West Bengal	34.7	32.3	22.4	14.8	41.3	50.1	44.7	35.1
Chhattisgarh	–	–	–	41.2	–	–	–	19.5
Jharkhand	–	–	–	20.2	–	–	–	13.2
Uttarakhand	–	–	–	36.5	–	–	–	8.9
Chandigarh	28.0	23.8	11.4	7.1	0.8	1.1	0.7	0.7
Dadra & Nagar Haveli	37.7	27.0	39.9	19.1	0.0	0.0	0.1	0.2
J&K	21.3	17.8	9.2	7.9	2.1	2.5	1.9	2.2
All India	49.0	40.8	32.4	25.7	600.5	709.4	763.4	808.0

Note: 1. Poverty Ratio of Assam is used for Sikkim, Arunachal Pradesh, Meghalaya, Mizoram, Manipur, Nagaland, and Tripura.
2. Poverty Ratio of Tamil Nadu is used for Pondicherry and A&N Islands.
3. Poverty Ratio of Kerala is used for Lakshadweep.
4. Urban Poverty Ratio of Punjab is used for both rural and urban poverty of Chandigarh.
5. Poverty Line of Maharashtra and expenditure distribution of Goa is used to estimate poverty ratio of Goa.
6. Poverty Line of Maharashtra and expenditure distribution of Dadra & Nagar Haveli is used to estimate poverty ratio of Dadra & Nagar Haveli.

Source: Planning Commission.

ANNEXURE 4.4
Percentage of Population Below Poverty Line by Social Groups—2004–05

States	Rural			Urban		
	SC	ST	OBC	SC	ST	OBC
Andhra Pradesh	15.4	30.5	9.5	39.9	50.0	28.9
Assam	27.7	14.1	18.8	8.6	4.8	8.6
Bihar	64.0	53.3	37.8	67.2	57.2	41.4
Chhattisgarh	32.7	54.7	33.9	52.0	41.0	52.7
Delhi	0.0	0.0	0.0	35.8	9.4	18.3
Gujarat	21.8	34.7	19.1	16.0	21.4	22.9
Haryana	26.8	0.0	13.9	33.4	4.6	22.5
Himachal Pradesh	19.6	14.9	9.1	5.6	2.4	10.1
J&K	5.2	8.8	10.0	13.7	0.0	4.8
Jharkhand	57.9	54.2	40.2	47.2	45.1	19.1
Karnataka	31.8	23.5	20.9	50.6	58.3	39.1
Kerala	21.6	44.3	13.7	32.5	19.2	24.3
Madhya Pradesh	42.8	58.6	29.6	67.3	44.7	55.5
Maharashtra	44.8	56.6	23.9	43.2	40.4	35.6
Orissa	50.2	75.6	36.9	72.6	61.8	50.2
Punjab	14.6	30.7	10.6	16.1	2.1	8.4
Rajasthan	28.7	32.6	13.1	52.1	24.1	35.6
Tamil Nadu	31.2	32.1	19.8	40.2	32.5	20.9
Uttar Pradesh	44.8	32.4	32.9	44.9	37.4	36.6
Uttarakhand	54.2	43.2	44.8	65.7	64.4	46.5
West Bengal	29.5	42.4	18.3	28.5	25.7	10.4
All-India	36.8	47.3	26.7	39.9	33.3	31.4

Note: 1. Poverty Ratio of Assam is used for Sikkim, Arunachal Pradesh, Meghalaya, Mizoram, Manipur, Nagaland, and Tripura.
2. Poverty Ratio of Tamil Nadu is used for Pondicherry and A&N Islands.
3. Poverty Ratio of Kerala is used for Lakshadweep.
4. Poverty Ratio of Goa is used for Dadra & Nagar Haveli and Daman & Diu.
5. Urban Poverty Ratio of Punjab is used for both rural and urban poverty of Chandigarh.
6. Poverty Line of Maharashtra and expenditure distribution of Goa is used to estimate poverty ratio of Goa.
7. Poverty Line of Maharashtra and expenditure distribution of Dadra & Nagar Haveli is used to estimate poverty ratio of Dadra & Nagar Haveli.
8. The poverty ratio among the ST population in some States may be treated with caution due to the smallness of the sample household based on which the class distribution of persons have been obtained in the NSS. These States are: in the rural areas Haryana and Punjab, where the number of sample households among the STs is 10 or less. Similarly, in the urban areas, the States are: Bihar, Haryana, Himachal Pradesh, J&K, Kerala, and Punjab, where the number of sample households among the STs is 10 or less, and Delhi, Tamil Nadu and Uttarakhand, where the number of sample households is 20 or less.

Source: Planning Commission.

5

Ensuring Rural and Urban Livelihoods

INTRODUCTION

5.1 The dispersed, unorganized and often household-based micro and small enterprises are capital-saving, labour-intensive, and environment-friendly tools of inclusion. In India, they are the largest source of employment after agriculture and are found in both rural as well as urban areas.

5.2 In nearly three decades, the structure of rural employment has not changed much.[1] According to the latest NSS figures (61st Round), agriculture continues to employ 70% of our rural workforce, industry (14.4%), and services (14.8%) make up for the rest. However, in view of the decline in agriculture's contribution to GDP and the near constant proportion of workers dependent on it, there is need for rapid generation of off-farm employment. The chapter on Agriculture deals with diversification within agriculture (to sericulture, horticulture, pisciculture) to expand the scope of off-farm rural livelihoods. The real potential for employment generation, however, rests with the micro and small enterprises (MSEs) sector which comprises weavers, artisans, people engaged in food processing, hawkers, vendors, and carpenters.

5.3 In developing countries across Asia, small and medium enterprises (SMEs)[2] (i) make up 80%–90% of all enterprises, (ii) provide over 60% of the private sector jobs, (iii) generate over 30%–40% of total employment, and (iv) contribute about 50% of sales or value added. In India, they constitute[3] 95% of all enterprises. Labour productivity[4] of small-scale industries (SSIs) in India during 1990–98 at the compound growth rate was 8.5% whereas labour productivity of large-scale industries (LSIs) was 7.54%. However, recently in a study of 53 countries done by Fortune Small Business Survey, June 2007 on 'Most and Least Friendly Countries to Small Businesses', India ranked 46th, well behind the other neighbouring Asian countries such as Singapore (5th), Hong Kong (6th), Thailand (15th), Malaysia (28th), etc.

5.4 Inadequate working capital, lack of information to access markets and foreign business opportunities, lack of trained personnel, and obsolete technology are

[1] Male and female employment in industry in rural areas has risen from 8% and 6.7%, respectively, in 1977–78 to 15.5% and 10%, respectively, in 2004–05. Most of the employment in manufacturing is in textiles (4 million), wood products (3.7 million), non-metallic products (3.4 million), food products (3.1 million), tobacco (3.1 million), and wearing apparel 2.8 million) (NSS 2004–05, Report 515). In services, employment in rural areas has risen from 10.5% of male employment and 5.1% of female employment in 1977–78 to 18% and 6.6% respectively in 2004–05.

[2] Asian Association of Management Organization Report—SMEs in Asian Region: Harnessing the Growth Potential.

[3] UNCTAD-2003, OECD-2000, and Country reports.

[4] Asian Association of Management Organization Report—SMEs in Asian Region.

the major barriers to the growth of MSEs across the world in general and in India in particular.

5.5 Shortage of working capital is widely recognized as the biggest hurdle in the growth of unorganized and organized MSEs. Securing bank credits, difficulties in documentation for bank loans, and lack of collateral security are bigger problems in India than in majority of the other developing countries in Asia. It is estimated that less than 8% of the total bank credit finds its way to the MSE sector.

5.6 Unorganized sector enterprises generally suffer from weak marketing. They need better market infrastructure, professionally organized exhibition of products at the international level, efficient system of supply chain management, brand promotion, and standardization. Efforts are needed to establish better linkages with the industry.

5.7 In post-WTO agenda, domestic markets have been opened up for imports, creating severe competition for the local industries. At the same time, this has created opportunities for the small industries to export products to the developed countries. To gain from this opportunity, however, effort must be made in pushing for greater market access in the developed countries.

5.8 Technology is one of the most critical elements in the growth of the MSE sector. India is ranked at the top[5] in terms of availability of Science and Engineering personnel; however, MSEs in India are losing their competitive edge in the global markets due to lack of modern technology. Owing to obsolete technology, the cost of manufacturing is much higher in India compared to the other developing countries in Asia.

5.9 Addressing these problems to ensure a vibrant MSE sector is essential for sustained and inclusive growth.

Village and Cottage Industries, Handlooms, Handicrafts, and Food Processing and Agro Industries: Engines of Sustained and Inclusive Growth

5.10 The MSE sector provides livelihood, checks rural–urban migration, generates export earnings, and touches upon the lives of the remotest and most marginalized people. The needs, problems, and potential of this sector differ not just with the nature of activity (weaving, building components for big industries, etc.), but also with size, geographical location, and structure (organized/unorganized). The importance of this sector and the vision for it in the Eleventh Plan has been outlined in the chapter on Industries. The untapped domestic and international markets for traditional crafts has been indicated in Box 5.1.

5.11 This sector has been fragmented across various ministries and departments which have often been pitted against each other: powerloom versus handloom, anti-dumping duty on foreign silk yarn to protect interest of silk rearers versus removal of duty for handlooms and powerlooms, interest of petty traders versus greater control for home-based producers—these have been recurring debates. There is a need to move from competitive to complementary relationships by

Box 5.1
Untapped Domestic and International Markets for Traditional Crafts

In the small town of Chamba in Himachal Pradesh, over 500 artisans make sturdy and beautifully designed leather footwear. They sit inside homes or in tiny shops making one pair of *chappals* in approximately two hours. They earn Rs 30 per pair; each pair retails for anything between Rs 100 and Rs 500. At one time, Chamba made footwear for the entire Punjab. Chamba chappals have long been known for their durability and exclusive designs, many of which are now being developed and sold by big footwear manufacturers at exorbitant prices. These chappals have tremendous export potential and can take the domestic market by storm. Yet, in the absence of proper advertising and market linkages, the Chamba artisans are finding it increasingly difficult to make ends meet. Similarly, the bamboo products developed in North East India—in Meghalaya, Tripura, Manipur, Mizoram, even Assam, and Siliguri and Jalpaiguri (both in West Bengal)—have tremendous export potential. The range of products vary from picnic baskets to furniture, dinner sets, and even furnishing material.

[5] Global Competitive Index—2005; World Economic Forum.

making each sector a resource for the other. Encouraging this symbiotic relationship between different segments of the MSE sector will be the key Eleventh Plan strategy.

5.12 The Eleventh Plan will also move away from looking at certain sub-sectors of MSE as purely rural or urban sectors. Handlooms and handicrafts are often found in towns and cities (Benaras, Murshidabad, Berhampur, Jodhpur, Delhi, Jaipur, etc); powerloom units tend to be concentrated in urban areas but are also found in villages; food processing units and small industries involved in manufacturing of components, dyes, etc., are found in both urban and rural settings. Yet often, the traditional sectors are looked upon as rural livelihoods and the modern enterprises as urban livelihoods. Thus, urban planning that involves demolition of slums and street (flea) markets, widening of streets, or construction of apartments and flyovers fails to take into account the impact on the small and tiny sectors, robbing vendors, petty traders, weavers, artisans, rickshaw pullers, and small entrepreneurs of their source of livelihood. Similarly, rural planning often fails to meet the needs of the non-traditional small industries. In the Eleventh Plan concerted efforts will be made to ensure that the perceived locational distinctions do not hinder the progress of this sector.

5.13 The Eleventh Plan will use a two-pronged approach, focusing on both the lives and livelihoods of the people engaged in the MSE sector. Thus far, we have mostly concentrated on production. In the Eleventh Plan, both production and producer will receive attention as each is dependent on the other. Higher productivity and earnings cannot be achieved if the weaver, artisan, entrepreneur, or worker is starving, diseased, uneducated, and untrained. Similarly, the quality of life of the producer cannot improve until his/her productivity increases.

MSMEs AS INSTRUMENTS OF INCLUSION

NORTH EAST, J&K, AND OTHER DIFFICULT TERRAINS

5.14 Be it the desert sands of Rajasthan, the hills of Himachal Pradesh, North East, and Kashmir, or the islands of Lakshadweep and Andaman and Nicobar, the MSE sector is often the only source of livelihood in these ecologically fragile regions. According to a study sponsored by the North Eastern Development Finance Corporation Ltd (NEDFI, 2002), the North East accounts for 19.18% of the total number of handicrafts units in India and 21.71% of the artisans. The region also has a huge potential for the development of food processing and knowledge-based small industries. The situation in J&K, Himachal Pradesh, Rajasthan, and Kutch is similar. These areas are, however, also places[6] where infrastructure facilities are minimal, banking facilities are limited, and connectivity is poor, making access to markets difficult. The flow of credit to the NER is hampered due to adverse topography, problem of land collateralization (traditionally, in many parts of NER, land is owned by the community), lack of awareness about schemes, and poor recovery of loans.

WOMEN

5.15 While a gender-disaggregated, comprehensive database on the sector is not available, there is ample evidence to prove that a majority of women are engaged in the MSEs. In sectors such as handloom, over 60% of the workforce comprises women. Chemical and plastics, food processing, and village industries also employ a large number of women. The proportion of women entrepreneurs is, however, quite low. As per the Third All-India Census (2001–02), only 995141 (9.46%) MSEs are actually managed by women. As against this, in the US, women own 38% of the small enterprises,[7] which employ more than 50% of the private sector workforce. In countries such as Brazil, Ireland, Spain, and the US, women are creating new enterprises at a faster rate than men (OECD, 2001). The absence of property rights and the concomitant difficulty in accessing credit may be responsible for the low proportion of women entrepreneurs in India. Most women either do job work, assist their family members, or are employed as workers in small-scale units. They face widespread discrimination and exploitation. *Zari* workers, *agarbatti* and *bidi* rollers, embroidery workers make as little as Rs 10 for an eight-hour day. During the Eleventh Plan period, it is essential to

[6] Scheme for North East Handlooms and Handicrafts.

[7] Milken Institute, 2000.

provide a social security cover that is sensitive to women's special needs. Equal wages, adequate protection, provision of drinking water, toilets, crèche, and feeding facilities will be ensured in all small units and for every cluster. Women entrepreneurs will be provided easy access to credit and appropriate advisory and mentoring services.

MARGINALIZED GROUPS—SC/ST/MINORITIES

5.16 The MSE sector, especially traditional enterprises, provides livelihood to many marginalized groups. While the sector in general lacks access to marketing and credit, the problem is even more pronounced for people belonging to SC/ST and minorities. The Eleventh Plan, therefore, will introduce social security, training, and health insurance schemes for these vulnerable groups. Efforts will also be made to collect disaggregated data, set targets for credit availability, and ensure access to schemes for the people belonging to these communities.

DIFFERENT SEGMENTS, DIFFERENTIAL NEEDS

HANDLOOMS

5.17 As a metaphor for Indian culture and heritage, handlooms enable 65 lakh persons to earn a living by skilfully blending myths, faiths, symbols, and imagery. Today, the handloom industry directly and indirectly provides livelihood to 124 lakh people,[8] of which 60% are women, 12% SC, and 20% ST (Ministry of Textiles, 2001). While the exact numbers are not available, a chunk of the handloom weavers belong to minorities.

5.18 Indian handloom products range from coarse cloth to very fine fabrics from a variety of fibres such as cotton, silk, tasar, jute, wool, and synthetic blends. Each region has handcrafted textiles that are unique in design and style. What is woven is, however, inseparable from where and how it is woven, that is from the structure of production. There are independent weavers, weavers organized into co-operatives, and there are those working under master weavers. Often a combination of production types exists at one time in one area, even within a single household. Yet there is no data reflecting this diverse nature. We do not have updated figures on the number of looms or people. The last Census was carried out in 1995–96.

Current Situation

5.19 With the largest number of handlooms in the world, India produces approximately 6541 million sq m of handloom cloth annually. While the total production of cloth has increased by about 30% between 1996–97 and 2004–05, the production of handloom sector has declined by about 23%. Between 2000 and 2005, the average annual growth rate of handloom production has been 6.99%. This has hit the livelihoods of the handloom weavers. West Bengal, Tamil Nadu, Uttar Pradesh, Andhra Pradesh, Assam, and Manipur are the major handloom States accounting for 75% of handloom weaving in the country. As per the Second Handloom Census, Assam (10.97 lakh), West Bengal (2.22 lakh), and Manipur (2.15 lakh) together accounted for 64% of the handloom units. Almost all handloom production in India is for domestic markets. According to the Directorate General of Handlooms, though handlooms account for 10% of our textile exports, only 1.3% of working looms produce fabric[9] for export markets. Europe is the largest destination, accounting for nearly half of the total exports in 1999–2000.

5.20 In the terminal year of the Tenth Plan, handloom cloth production was 6541 million sq m with exports at Rs 4605 crore. The Tenth Plan performance is indicated in Table 5.1.

5.21 With the phasing out of quota and the opening up of markets, 'Handloom' cloth and designs are being produced cheaply by mills and powerlooms both in India and in China. As the market is shrinking, weavers are becoming manual labourers or in extreme cases committing suicide. This has led many to label this industry as a sunset sector. This, however, is far from

[8] India's Handloom Sector—K. Rajendran Nair (Former Development Commissioner for Handlooms).

[9] Handloom Mark Scheme—A Report on Diagnostic Survey and Business Plan for Handloom Sector in Bihar, submitted to Department of Industries, Government of Bihar by IL&FS.

TABLE 5.1
Performance of Handloom Sector during the Tenth Plan Period

Item	2002–03	2003–04	2004–05	2005–06	2006–07
Cloth production (million sq m)	5980	5493	5722	6108	6541
Employment(lakh persons)	65	65	65	65	65
Export (Rs crore)	na	na	na	na	4605

Source: Office of Development Commissioner (Handlooms), Ministry of Textiles.

the truth. Health- and environment-friendly hand-woven fabrics have a huge international demand and have the potential to generate domestic demand as well. In the post-Multi-Fibre Agreement era, weavers can capture new markets. Box 5.2 highlights the potential for this sector.

Box 5.2
Hope Looms

Though handloom is regarded by many as a sunset industry, there are enough success stories across the country—Self Employed Women's Association (SEWA) in Lucknow, Kutch Mahila Samiti in Gujarat, and Dastkar in Andhra which expose this myth and show the way forward for this sector. Maheshwar, a small town of Madhya Pradesh has been weaving for the last 250 years, ever since Rani Ahilyabai Holkar brought the profession to this town and etched a beautiful design palette in stones along the banks of the Narmada. Three decades ago the market for Maheshwari sarees started shrinking and there were less than 25 looms left in the town. Once again the Holkars intervened—this time in the form of REHWA society. Rehwa is another name for the Narmada. Through this society they carried out design interventions, moved from the '*nauwari*' to '*chhewari*' sarees, and organized exhibitions. They provided weavers with work, looms, health facilities, crèches and schools for their children, and even homes. Today, there are about 2500 looms creating poetry with silk and cotton yarn in Maheshwar and they have the potential to install more. The wages have gone up from Rs 9 per saree to Rs 150 per saree. Phalodi, in district Jaisalmer of Rajasthan, traditionally produced *Pattu*—two pieces of cloth woven in local wool, stitched together laterally, and enhanced by an extra weft ornamentation known as *Kashida*. Pattu weavers were disorganized and were dependent for sale on the intermediaries and fairs/exhibitions. In 1991, with the help of Urmul Trust, they organized themselves into a registered NGO, the Urmul Marusthali Bunkar Vikas Samiti (UMBVS). Today more than half of the weavers in Phalodi are its members. At the time of registration, a compulsory three-month training is imparted. For every group of 8–15 weavers, a commission-based *Vyavasthapak* (manager) delivers raw materials and designs; monitors quality during weaving; weighs, checks, and delivers products; and makes payments. UMBVS provides raw materials and markets products through fairs and exhibitions, websites, and its own showroom. It has managed to get financial support from banks and new designs from NIFT, NID, etc. Pochampally, a small town in Nalgonda district of Andhra Pradesh, is known for its unique *Ikat* design. About 50% of the population here depends on handlooms. In December 2003, Pochampally became the first traditional Indian craft to get a Geographical Indication (GI) registered. Less than two years later, the proprietors of the GI found that a retailer in Hyderabad was selling sarees produced by a Mumbai-based manufacturer under the false GI of 'Pochampally'. They immediately filed a case. Both the retailer and the manufacturer accepted the case of infringement and agreed to an out of court settlement. They also gave an undertaking not to sell any products in the name of Pochampally. 13 SHGs of weavers from Chanderi, Madhya Pradesh, have come together to form Chanderi Bunkar Vikas Samiti (CBVS). Quality control is emphasized and a mechanism has been devised to reject products that do not conform to specifications. The groups affiliated to the Samiti are heavily represented by women. The unique selling point (USP) of CBVS is its market linkage to Fab India. The weavers have regular work and they can sell their products to the Samiti and get timely payments. The Samiti has tried to become self-reliant by developing a common facility centre (CFC) for dyeing and a raw-material depot. This raw-material depot takes advantage of the Mill Gate Price Scheme and sells yarn with a 3% mark-up on the procurement price to Samiti members and with a 5% mark-up to non-members. For almost 80 years now, Nalli has monopolized the silk industry in India. From one loom in Kancheepuram and one shop in Chennai's T-Nagar set up in 1928, the Nallis today have 50 looms under their direct control and another 10000 looms working for them in Kancheepuram, Salem, and Kumbakonam. They have 14 shops including one each in Singapore, San Jose (California), and Toronto (Canada). Nalli manages over 5000 dedicated suppliers and has an annual turnover of Rs 325 crore. It has a range of products from Rs 80 to Rs 50000.

Challenges For the Eleventh Plan

5.22 Many challenges for the handloom sector have already been discussed in the chapter on Industry (see paragraphs 7.1.356 to 370, Chapter 7.1, Volume III). This section looks at some specific issues which will be tackled during the Eleventh Plan to ensure the vibrancy of this sector.

AVAILABILITY OF WORKING CAPITAL

5.23 Though NABARD provides refinance facilities to the State co-operative banks and RRBs for financing requirements of primary and apex weavers' co-operative societies, the service charges levied by these institutions result in the doubling of interest rates for the artisans and societies. Further, most State handloom co-operative societies lift stock and reimburse weavers only on sale of products. This blocks the working capital for the weavers.

AVAILABILITY OF QUALITY RAW MATERIALS:[10]

5.24 Despite the setting up of co-operative spinning mills and the hank yarn obligation, yarn shortages and steep prices are continuing problems. As early as in 1995, the gap between the supply and the demand for hank yarn used by the handloom sector was 150 million kg. The use of hank yarn by mills and powerlooms also diverts yarn meant for handlooms. The schemes ensuring availability of hank yarn at reasonable prices, usually only benefit the big weavers or the co-operative sector which covers 20.3% weavers.

TRAINING AND TECHNOLOGY

5.25 The Janata Cloth Scheme de-skilled weavers and we now have two categories of weavers—skilled and semi-skilled. The products manufactured by the latter are easily produced by mills and powerlooms at much cheaper rates. Their market is shrinking and there is little hope for its revival. Reskilling of semi-skilled weavers in handlooms or in any other field and skill upgradation for the skilled weavers are necessary. Currently, weaving has become a profession for the uneducated. People need to take up this profession out of choice, not necessity. Encouraging educated individuals to provide design inputs, marketing, etc., to this sector is a challenge.

MARKETING AND PUBLICITY

5.26 Primary producers have no direct access to either markets or market information. As a result, there is a mismatch between production and market demand. Markets today are created and captured through aggressive publicity campaigns using icons. The challenge in the Eleventh Plan is to create a demand for handloom products by flaunting their unique selling point (USP). Unfortunately, marketing efforts thus far have been limited to organizing buyer–seller meets and holding a few exhibitions where space is often provided to master weavers and *gaddidars*, not poor weavers. The challenge is to encourage market research and product diversification. The latter does not imply a rejection of the traditional designs. It means development of new products using the traditional designs adapted to modern tastes.

INFRASTRUCTURE DEVELOPMENT

5.27 Few clusters have organized dyeing centres with modern facilities such as water softening plants or dyeing chambers. Dyeing is unorganized and marked with low end applications. All this has a significant bearing on the quality of final products and the resultant poor earnings of weavers. It also harms the environment. Electricity, space to keep the looms, yarn banks, dyeing units, roads connecting weavers to markets, water supply, processing and packaging facilities are needed.

ENCOURAGING ORGANIZATION OF WEAVERS

5.28 Organizing weavers into SHGs or cluster committees to increase their bargaining power, enable them to access credit, design and common facilities centres, and undertake collective marketing is an important challenge.

SOCIAL SECURITY

5.29 Provision of a social security net that includes education, skill training, access to health facilities, and insurance is essential. Occupational health centres are needed to treat tuberculosis (TB) and silicosis. Moreover, in places like Varanasi, weavers have incurred huge electricity arrears; paying them off frees the weavers from the cycle of debt.

[10] *The Hindu*, 2005.

BETTER GOVERNANCE

5.30 Major institutions for providing inputs are centralized and hence are unable to reach the dispersed and largely home-based industry. Schemes run by the various Central and State bodies currently operate as silos with little convergence.

OTHER MEASURES

5.31 There are various other challenges during the Eleventh Plan: branding of handloom products, mapping of handloom clusters, development of design banks, and handloom research centres. The priority areas for research in the industry are energy conservation measures, improvement in the quality to boost exports, and providing cheaper and more durable fabrics for internal consumption.

The Way Forward

5.32 Government interventions for revival of handlooms during the Eleventh Plan will focus on two kinds of interventions: policy and programmatic. Policy interventions will include taking decisions on issues such as removal of anti-dumping duty on Chinese silk, specifying the policy on export of cotton yarn, availability of yarn, marketing as a value-added niche product, and preferential procurement by the government institutions. These will be backed by suitable programmatic interventions. For this, many of the existing Tenth Plan schemes such as workshed scheme, health insurance scheme, and *Deen Dayal Hathkargha Protsahan Yojana* (DDHPY) have been suitably restructured. To streamline the operations, various handloom schemes have been clubbed together under four major schemes—Integrated Handloom Cluster Development Scheme, Weavers Welfare Scheme, Marketing and Export Promotion, and Diversified Handloom Development Scheme. In the Eleventh Plan, schemes for the well being of weavers will include (i) Health Insurance Scheme, (ii) Mahatma Gandhi Bunkar Bima Yojana, (iii) Thrift Fund Scheme, (iv) Pension Scheme, and (v) Distress Relief Fund. The insurance schemes not only offer social security but also have a component for education of weavers' children. Under the new pension scheme, weavers aged 60 years or above will be provided Rs 200 every month. The Distress Relief Fund will provide immediate relief to weavers in distress situations and those affected by natural calamities, riots, floods, etc.

5.33 The Integrated Handloom Development Scheme is based on a cluster approach where basic inputs and worksheds are provided, training is imparted, and formation of SHGs is encouraged. In fact, a cluster-based approach would be a major thrust of Eleventh Plan in the case of all the sectors covered and discussed in this chapter. Annexure 5.1 provides a detailed note. Under this scheme, the committees of weavers, supported by an external cluster development agency, will be empowered to decide which interventions need to be carried out. Branding of cluster products, GI registration, and construction of CFC will be carried out. This will not only give greater power to weavers, but will also help in marketing products, quality control, and processing of bigger orders. Under DDHPY, financial assistance for design development, product diversification, publicity, CFCs, market survey, and market incentives will be encouraged. The workshed cum housing scheme will be extended to weavers outside the co-operative fold as well.

5.34 The Marketing Promotion Programme (MPP) will be restructured to focus on brand equity, providing market consultants, doubling market events—expos, melas, etc.—and building promotional websites. Urban *Haats* and market complexes will be set up at important places of tourism and business. Space on rent will be taken up at upcoming malls, marketing complexes, large retailing stores, etc. Private business houses will be requested to earmark outlets for handlooms. Fabric tourism, on the lines of vineyard tourism in France and glass tourism in Italy (Murano glass factories), will be promoted. Special expos will be organized to encourage big retail chains and hotels to use handloom furnishings. Exclusive fashion shows with the participation of National Institute of Fashion Technology (NIFT) and SHGs/co-operatives will be organized to reach the youth in schools and in college festivals. A huge publicity campaign backed by icons will be initiated. At the same time, measures will be taken for protection of traditional designs and patterns under the GI Act. Handloom Mark will be used to popularize handwoven products and guarantee to the buyer that the product being purchased is genuinely handwoven. To attract entrepreneurs and investors into the

Handloom Export Sector, Handloom Export Scheme will be subsumed under MPP. It is expected that exports will grow at 15% per annum and reach Rs 10000 crore by the end of the Eleventh Plan.

5.35 Under the Diversified Design Development Scheme, 20 design studios will be set up in handloom clusters for creating designs based on the client needs. The design studios may be a joint collaboration between the GoI and the industry/Handloom Export Promotion Council (75:25 ratio). A heritage library housing all the traditional designs will also be created. Inputs such as hank yarn will be provided at mill gate price.

5.36 A committee with Managing Director, NABARD as Convenor has suggested (i) cleansing of balance sheets of apex societies and primary societies, (ii) waiver of overdue loans and interest of primary weavers co-operative societies and apex societies, (iii) interest subvention—working capital, and (iv) contribution to Handloom Development and Equity Fund and Credit Guarantee Fund Scheme for handloom weavers. On the basis of this report and the Vaidyanathan Committee report, a Rs 1200 crore package for handlooms has been formulated.

5.37 For schemes to be effective, strengthening of the delivery mechanism with the help of an NGO/ voluntary sector is essential. All the schemes will be widely publicized in local and regional languages. A convergence between various schemes for health, nutrition, education, etc., will be ensured. A necessary step in this direction would be a mapping of weavers and artisans. The preservation of the rich handloom heritage can be achieved only through the socio-economic upliftment of the individuals who create the heritage.

HANDICRAFTS

5.38 Like handlooms, this sector also touches upon the lives of the most marginalized and has the potential to transform the economy of difficult areas such as the North East, border States, J&K, desert habitations, etc. It produces a range of items from utility goods to clothing and variety of lifestyle items.

Current Situation

5.39 The performance of handicrafts sub-sector during the Tenth Plan period is given in Table 5.2.

5.40 The current global handicraft market is valued at more than US$ 400 billion. China accounts for 30% of this and India's share is less than 2%. Over the last 10 years, the average annual rate of growth of our handicraft exports market has been 15%. During the next five years, it is projected to increase by 42% and generate an impressive US$ 9100 million. The US is the preferred destination for Indian handicrafts, accounting for 29.59% of our total exports. Europe accounted for 33.86% in 2004–05.[11]

5.41 Despite this, while some crafts such as woodwork, metal work, and carpets are flourishing, others are floundering. Even for the handicrafts that are doing well, increase in exports and demand has not led to a concomitant rise in the income. In places such as Rajsamund (silver *minakari*), Bhopal (zari work), Bhadohi (carpets), and Indore (sequins and embroidery), wages have not changed in the last two decades. In zari, gems, and jewellery units, often women and children are employed due to their deft fingers. The conditions of work are oppressive and workers earn wages as little as Rs 10–15 per day. The profit is taken over by the middlemen and the export houses. As in the case of handlooms, there is no database or mapping of crafts across the country.

TABLE 5.2
Performance of Handicraft Sector during the Tenth Plan Period

Item	2002–03	2003–04	2004–05	2005–06	2006–07	CAGR (%)
Production (Rs crore)	19565	24019	28936	29804	38660	14.5
Employment (lakh persons)	60.16	61.96	63.81	65.72	67.69	2.3
Export (Rs crore)	10934	12768	15616	17277	20963	14.0

Source: Office of Development Commissioner (Handicrafts), Ministry of Textiles.

[11] Confederation of Indian Industries (CII).

Challenges

5.42 The distinction between handlooms and handicrafts is often artificial and difficult to understand. For instance carpets, though hand-woven, are counted as handicrafts. This distinction limits the workers' access to schemes and in many cases results in a duplication of efforts. Resolving this will be a principal challenge for the Eleventh Plan. Apart from usual challenges mentioned in paragraphs 5.22 to 5.31, the specific challenges faced by the handicrafts sector are:

TECHNOLOGY UPGRADATION

- Use of old and obsolete technology increases drudgery, impacts on the health of the worker, reduces productivity, and in many cases even affects quality.

IMPACT ON ENVIRONMENT AND HEALTH

- Activities such as printing, metal works, use of dyes, and woodwork seriously impact the environment and the health of the workers. As most units are home-based or small-scale units, they do not have adequate safety arrangements or sewage treatment facilities. Thus, they get caught in non-tariff barriers. The challenge is to ensure occupational health for artisans and to develop simple, cheap technology for treatment of waste and pollution control.

SAFEGUARDING THE INTERESTS OF ARTISANS

- An ongoing debate in the handicrafts sector (particularly in areas such as carpet weaving) is about greater flexibility in labour laws to permit export houses to expand. The challenge in the Eleventh Plan is to balance productivity gains with the interests of the actual producers, the artisans. A recurring suggestion has been to allow firms some flexibility if the State Governments are willing to provide social security.

QUALITY CONTROL AND STANDARDIZATION

- Lack of standardization procedures and inadequate facilities for testing and certification of raw materials and products impacts the export potential.

The Way Forward

5.43 During the Eleventh Plan, it is proposed to more than double the production of handicrafts (from Rs 43600 crore in 2007–08 to Rs 90412 crore in 2011–12), double the exports (from Rs 23400 crore in 2007–08 to Rs 48522 crore in 2011–12), and create almost 11 lakh additional jobs. Special targets which include export turnover of Rs 500 crore and credit flow of Rs 150 crore have been set for the NER. For this, infrastructure is vital. In order to augment the government resources, schemes will be adopted in the PPP mode. The government will partner with good NGOs to ensure an effective implementation of the schemes and policies and to compile an accurate database of the artisans. In the Eleventh Plan, the existing Tenth Plan schemes have been modified and clubbed into seven schemes to improve the delivery of services and ensure effective and focused implementation. Eleventh Plan Schemes for handicrafts are indicated in Box 5.3.

Box 5.3
Eleventh Plan Schemes—Handicrafts

- Baba Saheb Ambedkar Hastshilp Yojana: Revised to a demand driven, needs-based scheme for integrated development of handicraft clusters. Setting up of CFCs and e-Kiosks, publicity, toolkits distribution will be included. Target: 375 new clusters in 322 districts covering four lakh artisans.
- Design and Technology Upgradation: Thrust on skill upgradation, new designs, technologies, innovative products, revival of languishing crafts, setting up of Design Bank. Target: 1000 Design Workshops and 400 Integrated Design Projects to benefit 38600 artisans.
- Marketing Support, Services, and Export Promotion: This scheme will continue. Target: 1.2 lakh artisans.
- R&D Scheme: The scheme includes conducting research studies, all-India census for handicrafts, setting up of six labs, technology development, transfer/adoption of technology.
- Handicraft Artisans Comprehensive Welfare Scheme: The scheme includes Bima Yojana and Rajiv Gandhi Shilpi Swasthya Bima Yojana. Target: Two lakh artisans per year for each scheme.
- Human Resource Development: Special Handicraft Training Programme (SHTP) implemented during Tenth Plan has been modified. Target: Capacity building of two lakh artisans and stakeholders.
- Infrastructure Projects for development of specific need-based infrastructure, building, haats, expo marts, etc.

5.44 To fulfil the commitment towards inclusive growth, at least 10% of all the schemes in the Eleventh Plan will be earmarked for the NER. In addition to this, special schemes will be introduced for women and for people belonging to SC/ST and minority groups. These include: (i) Scheme for skill upgradation under the Guru Shishya Pattern of the Special Handicrafts Training Project (SHTP) for women and artisans belonging to SC/ST community, and (ii) special components will be introduced in all the existing schemes of Office of Development Commissioner (Handicrafts), in association with the Ministry of Minorities Affairs to fulfil specific needs of minority artisans.

POWERLOOMS

5.45 Today, the decentralized powerlooms sector provides employment to 48.60 lakh persons and contributes 62% to the total cloth production in the country.

Current Situation

5.46 As on 31 March 2006, there were approximately 4.30 lakh powerloom units with 19.44 lakh looms. Of this, nearly 3.66 lakh looms employing 9.14 lakh people were in Tamil Nadu alone. The technology level of the powerloom sector varies from obsolete plain looms to high-tech shuttle-less looms. Most looms are old and archaic.

5.47 Not only do powerlooms meet most of the cloth requirement of the country, they also contribute more than 60% of the fabric meant for export. The US, France, Germany, Hong Kong, Italy, etc., are the major markets. Even within the country, the readymade garments and home textiles sectors are heavily dependent on the powerloom sector to meet their fabric requirements. The performance of the powerloom sector during the Tenth Plan are given in Table 5.3.

Challenges

5.48 The major challenge is to look at the powerloom sector as an important segment of the textile industry that can engage in bulk production, especially of everyday necessities. While selling of powerloom cloth as handloom and copying handloom designs on powerlooms will be checked, the poor powerloom weavers will not be penalized for the problems of the handloom industry. In fact, like handloom weavers, many powerloom weavers also suffer from lack of credit, absence of quality raw materials, poor quality dyes, absence of proper market linkages, and exploitation at the hands of the middlemen. Several powerloom weavers come from economically and socially marginalized groups. Fluctuation in yarn prices impacts them equally. The tax on cone yarn affects their profits. The challenges in the Eleventh Plan are:

- Ensuring uninterrupted power supply to powerloom centres and units is a big challenge. Without this, the looms fall silent and the weavers suffer from heavy losses.
- Powerloom weavers suffer from many health problems such as TB, silicosis, hearing impairment. The challenge is to provide occupational health facilities to the weavers and their families. Given the incessant din of the looms, it is essential to eventually move the looms out of homes and into common worksheds.
- Most powerlooms in the country are obsolete and need to be replaced immediately to increase productivity and profits. However, powerloom weavers in places such as Bhiwandi and Malegaon are too poor to benefit from Technology Upgradation Fund Scheme (TUFS) or to finance the upgradation. The challenge is to come up with schemes that enable poor powerloom weavers to upgrade their looms.

TABLE 5.3
Performance of Powerloom Sector during the Tenth Plan Period

Item	2002–03	2003–04	2004–05	2005–06	2006–07	CAGR (%)
Cloth production (million sq m)	25954	26947	28325	30626	33159	5.0
Employment (lakh persons)	42.32	45.92	47.57	48.60	49.76	3.2
Export (Rs crore)	6007.17	6201.72	6302.43	7562.08	na	6.0

Note: Export figures are for textile export including powerloom cloth and cloth used for readymade garments exported.
Source: Ministry of Textiles.

The Way Forward

5.49 It is proposed to increase production of powerloom cloth from 38138 million sq m in 2007–08 to 58437 million sq m and to raise exports to US$ 56.05 billion by the terminal year of the Eleventh Plan.

5.50 Like in the case of handlooms and handicrafts, two kinds of measures are essential for the powerloom sector. Policy interventions need to deal with issues such as yarn availability and pricing and to resolve the perceived 'conflict' between handlooms and powerlooms. Programmatic interventions will focus on research and technology upgradation, promotion of value-added textiles, strengthening of existing infrastructure facilities, creation of design banks and Computer Aided Design (CAD) centres, and easy access to credit and modernized workshed scheme. Here again, the cluster approach will be adopted and common facilities such as yarn depots, dyeing houses, quality testing labs, etc., will be provided. Weavers will be organized into SHGs and will be encouraged to move their looms into common worksheds. Clusters will be supported in setting up mini-power generation plants to ensure uninterrupted power supply. During the Eleventh Plan, cluster development activities will be undertaken in 50 powerloom clusters. Product innovation and diversification will be encouraged and weavers will be included in cluster development committees.

5.51 The TUFS will be modified and continued in the Eleventh Plan. Currently, powerloom units in places such as Sholapur, Surat, and Ichalkaranji are able to draw benefits from TUFS; however, small and weak units in backward clusters such as Malegaon, Burhanpur, and Mau are unable to do so due to their inability to provide collateral guarantees. For them, the National Climatic Data Centre co-operative funding route may be more useful. During the Eleventh Plan period, TUFS will be modified to enable the weak and small powerloom units to take the advantage of this scheme.

5.52 Besides this, a survey of the powerloom sector will be carried out to find out the profile of the people engaged in the sector, as well as the number and the type of looms. New CAD centres will be set up and existing powerloom service centres (PSCs) will be upgraded. Health insurance schemes that have been announced for BPL workers would be made available to the powerloom workers and their families.

5.53 Presently, there is only one State in the NER where powerlooms exist. In Guwahati (Assam), there are about 2700 conventional looms providing employment to approximately 7000 workers. Most of the looms are engaged in job work, producing acrylic shawls. The feasibility of setting up a new CAD centre in the Guwahati PSC will be examined.

SILK AND SERICULTURE

5.54 India is the only country producing all the four known commercial silks, namely, mulberry, tasar, eri, and muga. It is the second largest producer of raw silk in the world. At present, over 60 lakh families—mostly in the States of Karnataka, Andhra Pradesh, Tamil Nadu, West Bengal, Jammu and Kashmir, and Assam—are involved in this labour-intensive agro-based industry in activities such as food plant cultivation, silkworm rearing, silk reeling, twisting, de-gumming, weaving, dyeing, printing and finishing, and garment manufacturing. Sericulture is at various stages of development in Uttarakhand, Uttar Pradesh, Madhya Pradesh, Chhattisgarh, Orissa, Bihar, and the North East.

5.55 Sericulture in India is a sustainable farm-based economic enterprise that generates a steady stream of income (on average, a net income of up to Rs 45000 annually in about four to five splits, from one acre of irrigated mulberry). A large number of people in sericulture, especially in production of tasar, belong to tribal groups. It is estimated that every hectare of mulberry provides employment to about 16 persons. Besides the weaving industry, sericulture is beneficial to farmers as well. Today, of the 60 lakh people dependent on this industry, 47 lakh are agriculturists.

Current Situation

5.56 China, producing 102560 metric tonnes (81.65%) of raw silk is the largest exporter, whereas India, contributing about 13% of the world's raw silk production, is the largest consumer. According to the Mysore-based Central Sericulture Research and Training Institute, against an annual requirement of about 25000 metric tonnes of silk, India produces only about

15000 metric tonnes. The rest of the demand is met through imports. In 2006–07, around 9258 tonnes of silk, worth over Rs 600 crore, was imported from China. As a result, cocoon prices crashed and nearly 49000 ha of mulberry crop was uprooted in Karnataka causing a loss of 3000 tonnes to the country's overall silk production.[12] Thus, while productivity of silk has gone up from 16 kg to 85 kg raw silk per ha per year from the Ninth to the Tenth Plan, raw silk production has remained almost static. Against the total production target of 26450 metric tonnes of raw silk per year, achievement was just 15445 metric tonnes by 2005–06 and 16805 metric tonnes by the end of the Tenth Plan period (Table 5.4). This was due to shortfall in mulberry bivoltine raw silk production despite the addition of 17 new components targeting bivoltine production in the Catalytic Development Scheme. The physical achievements during the Tenth Plan are given in Table 5.4.

5.57 Indian silk exports are primarily in the form of finished goods and not silk yarn. Thus Indian exports are largely dependent on the import of quality silk from China. US, United Kingdom (UK), Italy, Germany, and Hong Kong together account for over 55% of India's total export earnings from silk. Estimates say that India requires 120000 metric tonnes of silk to meet the demand in world market. With better infrastructure facilities, the sericulture industry can improve its productivity to 15% as against the current 9%.

Challenges

5.58 The Indian sericulture industry, which provides livelihoods to not just farmers and reelers but also dyers and silk weavers, is currently grappling with many problems similar to those faced by other sectors. However, it faces some specific challenges such as

IMPROVING QUALITY OF SILK

- Indian silk yarn is of poor quality, especially in comparison to that of China. This not only affects our competitiveness in the world market, it also results in a preference for imported yarn in the domestic sector. Though Indian breeds have the potential to produce the same quality of bivoltine silk as China, there has been lack of sufficient thrust on the adoption of improved technologies, strict disease control measures, lack of quality leaf due to insufficient inputs to mulberry garden, use of young age silkworms, appropriate mountages, lack of grading system for cocoons, and quality-based pricing system.

ARRESTING FALL IN PRODUCTION

- The challenge is to initiate area-specific research to improve fertility of the soils, which will ultimately enhance soil productivity, mulberry and non-mulberry host plant leaf and silkworm cocoon production, and arrest decline in area under silk food plants.

MULTIVOLTINE VERSUS BIVOLTINE

- Bivoltine yarn is sturdier and is used by the powerloom industry. Yet only 5% of the silk produced in India is bivoltine because its production requires much more attention and resources. It also yields just two crops in a year, as against the yield of four to six crops by multi-voltine. Since the difference in the selling price of bivoltine and multivoltine silk is not much, farmers do not have any incentive to switch to bivoltine silk yarn production. Insufficient adoption and proliferation of technology packages developed through R&D efforts; no effort to increase the area under mulberry; fragmented and ad hoc approach; non-involvement of private partners in a big way in seed production;

TABLE 5.4
Performance of Sericulture Sector during the Tenth Plan

Item	2002–03	2003–04	2004–05	2005–06	2006–07
Raw silk production (metric tonnes)	14617	13970	14620	15445	16805
Employment (lakh persons)	56.00	56.50	58.00	59.50	60.03
Export (Rs crore)	2294.05	2779.19	2879.56	3194.20	3200.00

Source: Central Silk Board (CSB), Ministry of Textiles.

[12] Indian Silk Industry—Gaurav Doshi.

farming and reeling; non-penetration of the schemes; improper forward and backward linkages; and dumping of cheap Chinese raw silk and fabric are the other factors. The challenge in the Eleventh Plan period is to encourage farmers to move from production of multivoltine silk to bivoltine silk through proper incentives. Yet, care should be taken to ensure that adequate amount of multivoltine is available for the handloom sector to continue production.

ANTI-DUMPING DUTY ON SILK

- There has been a decline in the cultivated area and the raw silk production during 2002–04 due to drought and dumping of Chinese silk at cheap prices. The sericulturists want imports of raw silk to be restricted and the anti-dumping duty on yarn to remain in place. Exporters and weavers, on the other hand, want the anti- dumping duty to be withdrawn so that they get an assured supply of yarn and are able to export more silk products at competitive rates. The challenge is to balance the aspirations of farmers and weavers.

NON-MULBERRY SILK PRODUCTION

- Non-mulberry silk production in the country continues to be unsteady and fluctuates from year to year. With its uniqueness, non-mulberry silk production in India has a great potential for value-added exports.

NEED FOR QUALITY-BASED PRICING

- Reeling sector is an input-dependent activity and its operations are influenced heavily by three factors—cocoon quality, cocoon price, and cocoon supply. However, due to the absence of quality-based price fixation, there has been very little quality control.

The Way Forward

5.59 The CSB has set a target of 26000 tonnes of raw silk production by the year 2011–12 and it has also proposed to:

- Enlarge area under mulberry silkworm food plants to 2.5 lakh ha by adding 0.50 lakh ha. This will produce an additional 6400 metric tonnes of mulberry raw silk.
- Raise national mulberry silk productivity from 85 kg per ha to 100 kg per ha per year.
- To increase production of non-mulberry silks from 125 gm per person per day to 150 gm per person per day.
- Increase employment to 77.04 lakh and exports to Rs 4500 crores.

5.60 To achieve these targets, association of private sector and especially the major agro-based industries in both pre-cocoon and post-cocoon segments, will be encouraged. Medium and small corporate sectors will be supported for the production of cocoons by contract farming through a participatory (not subsidy oriented) approach. R&D in the areas of reeling, twisting, spinning, and blending for all varieties of silk will be carried out and exotic fabrics, which may be used for furnishing, carpets, and other dress material, will be created.

5.61 The reeling sector has seen poor growth during the Tenth Plan. There are around 182000 handlooms and 30000 powerlooms with an average age of 15–20 years. About 20% improvement in productivity in addition to yarn quality can be achieved by upgrading the old machines. Additional production of raw silk to the tune of 7000 metric tonne will feed 80000 handlooms and 20000 powerlooms/shuttle looms. Therefore there is a need to upgrade the handlooms, powerlooms, and wet processing sectors to support non-mulberry reeling/spinning activity to improve the productivity and reduce drudgery.

5.62 Recently, an amendment to the CSB Act by the Parliament was made providing a regulatory mechanism for production and sale of silkworm seed. It ensures: (i) production and sale of seed of authorized races only, (ii) control on unauthorized production and trade, (iii) control and prevention of entry of untried and untested hybrids from other countries likely to be carrying diseases and other unknown risks.

5.63 During the Eleventh Plan period, CSB will implement all schemes of pre- and post-cocoon sectors in the form of clusters. Village Panchayats, reputed voluntary service organizations, rural development agencies, and financing institutions will be involved in planning from the project formulation stage onwards to facilitate integration of producer groups into the production chain and develop a marketable product within the geographical niche. Large-scale bivoltine seed production; supply of *chawki* worms to all bivoltine farmers; setting up of infrastructure such as rearing house, grainages, and chawki rearing centres (CRCs), and improved rearing appliances will be adopted under the existing Catalytic Development Programme schemes. Extensive training and demonstrations with the active participation of SHGs and expert farmers will be undertaken; linkages between the grainages and CRCs, the farmers, and the reelers will be established. Important policy interventions providing incentives to farmers who undertake bivoltine production will be carried out, but without hurting the handloom sector. The import policy for raw silk will be reviewed periodically, balancing interests of the sericulturists as well as export manufacturers and weavers.

5.64 To meet international standards in quality, large investments in seed production, farming, reeling, and processing are needed. The Eleventh Plan proposes to link large number of small farmers to few large entrepreneurs capable of making huge investments as in the case of castor cultivation, sugarcane cultivation, etc. The Plan also proposes to launch a new scheme for establishment of large bivoltine grainages and to open it to State departments.

5.65 During the Eleventh Plan, efforts will be made to enable networking of various cocoon and silk markets to facilitate availability of real time information on the availability of raw materials and market trends on the Internet. Existing National Informatics Centre (NIC) infrastructure will be utilized and an NIC Cell will be started in CSB on the pattern of other government institutions. Pest and disease forecasting and forewarning system for mulberry and silkworms will be introduced to provide sericulture farmers and the State departments enough time to organize effective management of pests and diseases and minimize the crop losses. This programme will be linked to NRSA, Hyderabad and Indian Meteorological Departments in various States.

5.66 The existing Tenth Plan schemes that are doing well such as the Silk Mark will be continued in the Eleventh Plan.

5.67 The Eleventh Plan interventions will promote inclusive growth for regions and social groups. At least 30% of beneficiaries in all schemes will be women. A women's credit fund will be set up, women-friendly technologies will be developed, and appropriate training will be provided. For other marginalized groups such as SC/ST and minorities, concessions like reducing beneficiary share by 10% of the envisaged contribution will be provided. Special programmes will be taken up in areas dominated by the marginalized groups.

UNORGANIZED WOOL SECTOR

5.68 The wool sector plays an important role in linking the rural economy and shepherds with the small, medium, and large-scale manufacturing units. This sector also has a diverse product portfolio: from textile intermediates to finished textiles, garments, knitwear, blankets, carpets, and a nominal presence in technical textiles. India is the seventh largest producer of raw wool accounting for 1.8% of the world production. In 2003, it had 615 lakh sheep, that is about 4.2% of the world's total sheep population.

5.69 The wool industry is broadly divided between the organized and decentralized sectors. The organized industry comprises: (i) composite mills, (ii) combing units, (iii) worsted and non-worsted spinning units, (iv) knitwear and woven garment units, and (v) machine-made carpet manufacturing units. The decentralized industry is engaged in (i) hosiery and knitting, (ii) powerlooms, (iii) hand-knotted carpets, druggets, and namadahs, and (iv) independent dyeing and processing houses.

Current Situation

5.70 The wool industry currently employs 27.2 lakh people—12 lakh in the organized sector, 12 lakh in sheep rearing and farming, and 3.2 lakh weavers in the carpet sector. The productivity of this sector is low. The world average for wool productivity has been about 3.5 kg per sheep per year, while in India the average is 0.8 kg per sheep per year. The quality of domestic wool is also coarse and brittle. It is basically carpet grade wool and has an important role in the national economy: it is rural-based (sheep breeding), defence-oriented (blankets and made-ups), and contributes significantly to exports (carpets). About 80% of good quality Indian wool goes into the manufacturing of carpets. Of the remaining, 15% is very coarse grade and 5% is apparel grade but of shorter average fibre length. Rajasthan (44%), J&K (13%), Karnataka (12%) along with Gujarat, Uttar Pradesh, Andhra Pradesh, and Haryana (23%) are the major wool-producing States in the country.

5.71 As the production of fine apparel grade wool is not adequate in the country, a large quantity of wool is imported from Australia, New Zealand, China, Middle East, and other countries. In 2004–05, the total wool consumption at industry level in the country was 135 million kg. Of this, just 55 million kg was domestic wool; rest was imported. Of the total imported 80 million kg of wool, 47 million kg is apparel grade and the rest carpet grade. There has been a consistent increase in the quantity of imported raw wool in the Tenth Plan. But export of woollen items has also shown an increase from Rs 3597.31 crore in 2002–03 to Rs 4969.02 crore in 2005–06. This is mainly on account of the carpet industry which exports 95% of its output. There are 718 woollen units in the organized sector and many more in the small-scale sector. The wool-combing capacity of the sector is around 30 million kg and synthetic fibre combing is 3.57 million kg. Approximately 7228 powerlooms operate in this industry.

5.72 During the Tenth Plan, the Central Wool Development Board (CWDB), Jodhpur, implemented Integrated Wool Improvement Programme for the unorganized wool sector. The various components of the scheme were improvement of wool fibre and breed; product development; provision of quality-testing centres, provision of CFCs for scouring, drying, carding, design development, product diversification, training, improvement, and development of speciality fibre such as Angora and Pashmina. The CWDB programmes have covered 25.5 lakh sheep and benefited 55091 families upto the end of the Tenth Plan period.

5.73 The CWDB installed wool-testing centres at Bikaner and Beawar in Rajasthan to test the fibre supplied by growers, merchants, and industries. The Board has also implemented two R&D projects, and set up one CFC and two common facility-cum-training centres.

5.74 The growth of the production of woollen items displayed mixed trends during the Tenth Plan. Hand-made carpets recorded the highest growth, but there was nominal annual increase in the production of woollen yarn and worsted yarn production. Despite this, the woollen industry could not achieve the overall targets of wool production due to the fluctuations in the prices of Australian raw wool, lack of promotion, unfavourable climate, change in fashion trends in favour of cotton, lifestyle changes, weak participation by the State Governments, and inadequate infrastructure.

The Way Forward

5.75 The Tenth Plan achievements and targets for the terminal year of the Eleventh Plan are given in Table 5.5. Eleventh Plan Schemes for unorganized wool sector are indicated in Box 5.4.

5.76 During the Eleventh Plan period, the productivity per sheep will be increased from present 0.8 kg per sheep per year to 1.5 kg per sheep per year. During this Plan period, the effort will be to produce good

TABLE 5.5
Tenth Plan Achievements and Eleventh Plan Targets for Wool Sector

Item	Tenth Plan Achievements	Assumed Growth Rate during Eleventh Plan (%)	Terminal Year of Eleventh Plan
Wool production (million kg)	55.00	10	88.50
Employment (lakh persons)	27.00	17	60.00
Export (Rs crore)	5600	13	10000

Source: Central Wool Development Board, Ministry of Textiles.

Box 5.4
Eleventh Plan Schemes

- Integrated Wool Improvement and Development Programme: To increase production, ensure breed improvement, health care, marketing of wool, survey and study, training, processing, and strengthening of indigenous varieties of wool, establishing multi-purpose extension centre, etc. Target: 26 lakh new sheep, 26000 rams, and 15 farms, 400 families under Angora and 2400 families under Pashmina Wool Development.
- Quality Processing of Wool and Woollen Products: To help in provision of processing facilities with latest technology for improving the quality of yarn and its end products. Target: 14 CRCs and 4 finishing centres.

New Initiatives

- Social Security Scheme for Insurance of Sheep Breeders in case of natural as well as accidental death. Target: 93500 shepherds.
- Sheep Insurance to cover accidents including fire, flood, famine, storm, etc., and diseases. Target: 24 lakh sheep.

quality carpet wool. The Tenth Plan schemes will be continued after suitable modifications. Two new schemes will also be started—insurance for shepherds as well as insurance for sheep. A revolving fund for procurement of raw wool from shepherds to help them in getting remunerative prices will be set up as a pilot project. The State Governments of Rajasthan and Uttarakhand have already demonstrated good results with similar initiatives. The wool sector needs convergence between various departments such as animal husbandry and rural development. In the Eleventh Plan, a comprehensive policy for pasturelands and commons will be developed.

5.77 One of the major problems with the wool industry has been the virtual absence of a system of grading. This will be taken up on a priority basis in the Eleventh Plan.

5.78 Marketing of wool is critical; it is also a weak link in the sector. There should be project-based assistance with clear identifiable objectives. Processing and finishing of wool products requires huge capital investment for which common infrastructure facilities will be developed with assistance from the government. To improve the breed, there has to be import of high breed germ plasms. Legislative measures would need to be taken up for issues of grazing, routes through forests for migratory sheep. CFCs for finishing carpets and shawls are being set up in the PPP mode. Involvement of industry associations is being obtained with the government support and assistance.

Khadi and Village Industries (KVI)

5.79 The KVI sector comprises khadi manufacturing and production from village/rural industries spread all over the country. The KVI programmes have now reached over 2.61 lakh villages providing employment opportunities to the rural poor in remote and hilly areas, border, and tribal areas. SCs/STs artisans account for 32% and women for 46% of the total artisans.

Current Situation

5.80 A large part of the employment in the khadi segment is part-time (4.05 lakh part-time and 4.65 lakh full-time). Spinning activity is carried out almost entirely by women, mostly belonging to the disadvantaged sections of the society. KVI institutions provide '*charkhas*' to the spinners, usually at their homes and occasionally in common worksheds. These institutions are run by the office bearers of the societies. The wage payments are irregular and generally made only after the permanent employees of the society receive their salaries. The sale of khadi products is only through the 'departmental outlets' of either the institutions or those of the Khadi and Village Industries Commission (KVIC) or State KVI boards. The focus is on charity and appealing to the 'goodness of people's hearts', not on the value of the product itself.

5.81 Currently, more than 60 lakh artisans/entrepreneurs in villages are engaged in production/services such as of minerals, leather, bee-keeping, honey, polyvastra, shoe repairing and manufacturing, papad making, food processing, and repairing agricultural implements.

5.82 The NCMP declared that the KVIC (and the programmes implemented through the KVIC) would be 'revamped'. The Expert Committee (EC) set up for this purpose in its report recommended to: (i) make the Commission more professional, like a modern corporate body, (ii) introduce a permanent consultative mechanism at the zonal level, and (iii) include enabling provisions in the law to get the programmes and activities implemented through selected non-governmental professional agencies.

5.83 The performance of KVI sector during the Tenth Plan period is given in Table 5.6.

Challenges

5.84 There is an urgent need to change the mindset towards khadi products; to move away from the welfare approach and publicize their USP—handcrafted, hand-spun, energy saving, and healthy products. People should buy khadi not as a 'national duty' or 'act of charity' but because it is fashionable, admired the world over, and intrinsically of high value.

5.85 There is a need to rejuvenate the khadi programme and to enlist new khadi institutions by relaxing the restrictions on registration, particularly in general areas. Attempt should be made to revive the defunct/dormant societies under 'D' category. Raw material supply has to be strengthened and the existing infrastructure of six sliver plants expanded to meet raw material requirements. Old charkhas and looms require attention during the Eleventh Plan period. The shortage of working capital needs to be addressed by undertaking credit rating system for khadi institutions. A new scheme for khadi could be devised on the lines of handloom mark/silk mark for promotion and for establishing authenticity of products.

5.86 At the same time, it is necessary to assist traditional village industries by providing necessary loans to adopt modern manufacturing techniques. Village industries have an important role in generating employment at comparatively low cost, especially for socio-economically weaker sections and backward areas. The fund flow to KVI sector from budgetary resources is declining from one plan period to another in terms of percentage. After introduction of the value-added tax (VAT) system, the sales tax exemption enjoyed by village industries has been taken away, thereby affecting their competitiveness. Low quality standards and use of obsolete technology and tools are the most restricting problems for village industries.

The Way Forward

5.87 KVIC recently introduced the 'Product Development, Design Intervention, and Packaging (PRODIP)' scheme to provide incentives for development of new products, designs, and better packaging of both khadi and village industry products. Some designs developed under the scheme are already a big hit and have recorded big sales. The Rural Industries Service Centres (RISC) scheme was started in 2004–05 for establishing CFCs by providing grant up to Rs 5 lakh per RISC. Both these schemes have proved successful and will be carried forward into the Eleventh Plan.

5.88 Similarly, the Scheme of Fund for Regeneration of Traditional Industries (SFURTI) such as khadi, village, and coir industries approved in October 2005 will be continued in the Eleventh Plan. On the basis of the strategy for cluster development, this scheme ensures that the regeneration of employment-intensive industries is made sustainable through empowerment of the enterprises.

5.89 During the Eleventh Plan, 'Khadi' will be registered as a brand name as well as a domain name. New

TABLE 5.6
Performance of the KVI Sector during the Tenth Five Year Plan

Item	2002–03	2003–04	2004–05	2005–06	2006–07
Production (Rs crore)	8569.37	9681.77	10920.43	12383.84	14531.69
Employment (lakh persons)	66.45	71.19	76.78	82.77	88.52
Export (Rs crore)	45.94	52.00	39.08	40.41	52.90

Source: Khadi and Village Industries Commission, Ministry of MSME.

products and new designs will be developed with the help of National Institute of Design (NID) and NIFT. Packaging of khadi products will be improved. A mechanism to ensure the quality of khadi products will be evolved. Advertising campaigns in India and abroad will be carried out to make people aware of khadi and to project it as a fashion statement for the youth. Shops will be opened at all international airports in India and the possibility of marketing KVI products through e-commerce will be explored.

COIR INDUSTRY

5.90 The 150-year old coir industry is mostly concentrated in Kerala, Tamil Nadu, Andhra Pradesh, and Karnataka due to availability of coir husk, a by-product of coconut plantation. It has an annual turnover of Rs 1300 crore with a steady growth rate of 10%. India accounts for 90% of the world's coir production and our coir products are exported to approximately 90 countries across the world. The industry provides livelihood and/or additional income to more than 31.25 lakh people, mostly the disadvantaged sections of the population—SC, ST, and minorities. Women constitute 80% of its workforce.

Current Situation

5.91 The coir industry is highly decentralized, seasonal, and labour intensive. In 2006–07, coir exports amounted to Rs 605.17 crore, well above the Plan target. SFURTI has been taken up in 25 clusters selected in consultation with the principal coir-growing States such as Kerala, Andhra Pradesh, Tamil Nadu, Karnataka, etc.

5.92 The performance of the coir industry during the Tenth Plan period is given in Table 5.7.

Challenges

5.93 Though coir is found in many coastal areas, for historical reasons, coir products are primarily made in Kerala. There is an urgent need to promote and encourage healthy competition among the coconut-growing States to catalyse State/region—specific innovations for tapping the immense growth and employment potential of this versatile fibre. The challenge in the Eleventh Plan is to develop new market driven products, to explore new markets—both in India and abroad—and, most importantly, to ensure a rational growth of coir industry on the basis of mutual co-operation.

5.94 There has been no comprehensive study to assess the actual global demand for coir products and the demand–supply gap, if any. Though coir industry is capable of producing a range of products, the use of coir products has remained confined to floor-covering material. Apart from this, the sector also faces some specific challenges such as

TARIFF AND NON-TARIFF BARRIERS

- In the international market, the duty applicable on import of coir and coir products ranges between 4% and 35%.

DISEASE

- Production of coir fibre has been affected by disease, which reduces the size of the coconut husk, resulting in low yield and inferior quality fibre.

SCATTERED PRESENCE

- Barring a few natural clusters, the industry is dispersed. Even in these clusters, the industry is not well integrated to take advantage of the development and promotional efforts towards modernization.

TECHNOLOGICAL OBSOLESCENCE

- The method of production has not undergone any significant change. The cost of production has been progressively rising, rendering it non-competitive.

TABLE 5.7
Performance of Coir Industry during the Tenth Plan Period

Item	2002–03	2003–04	2004–05	2005–06	2006–07
Coir fibre production (metric tonnes)	353700	364000	385000	410000	430025
Employment (lakh persons)	5.79	5.86	6.06	6.22	6.40
Export (Rs crore)	352.71	407.50	473.40	508.44	605.17

Source: Coir Board, Ministry of MSME.

MARKETING NEW PRODUCTS

- There is a need to undertake product development in traditional and non-traditional applications. New products that have phenomenal applications, such as rubberized coir, needle felt, geo-textiles, and coir pith, could be promoted to increase the demand for coir.

The Way Forward

5.95 During the Eleventh Plan period, most of the Tenth Plan schemes will be continued to reduce drudgery and increase production and wage levels. A major cluster development project with an approved outlay of Rs 56.8 crore has been taken up, in association with the Department of Industrial Policy and Promotion (DIPP), for the development of coir industries in and around Alappuzha, Kerala, with a Central grant of Rs 42.6 crore.

5.96 It is proposed to increase the level of growth of the industry to 15% and achieve a turnover of Rs 2100 crore by the terminal year of the Plan. Approximately 176250 new jobs will be created in the coir sector during the Eleventh Plan. Of this, 1.41 lakh jobs will be for women.

5.97 In the Eleventh Plan there is a need to focus upon R&D for diversification and popularizing new coir products in the market. Rejuvenation, modernization, and technology upgradation schemes will be introduced in the Eleventh Plan period. Better conversion rate of husk-to-coir products as a result of this scheme will require 50000 additional coir workers. Five mega clusters, one each in Kerala, Tamil Nadu, Andhra Pradesh, Karnataka, and Orissa, with thrust on technology upgradation will be promoted.

FOOD PROCESSING INDUSTRIES

5.98 Traditionally, food processing has been an important part of the rural and semi-urban economy, with pickles, jams, chutneys, and papads being made by women at the household level. As an industry, however, the food processing sector is yet to realize its potential. India currently produces about 50 million tonnes of fruits, about 9% of the world's fruit production, and 90 million tonnes of vegetables, accounting for 11% of the world's vegetable production. Yet, only about 2% of these fruits and vegetables are processed as against 23% in China, 78% in Philippines, 83% in Malaysia, and 80% in South Africa. Within the country, share of fruits and vegetables processing is less than other products such as milk (35%) and marine products (26%). Lack of processing and storage capacities for fruits and vegetables results in about 35% waste in the annual production, the value being approximately Rs 54000 crore. A progressive and vibrant food processing industry (FPI) fetches more remunerative price for farmers and reduces waste.

Current Situation

5.99 There are three segments in the Indian food-processing industry—household, small, and large. Together they contribute 14% to the manufacturing GDP and employ about 130 lakh people directly and 350 lakh people indirectly. Of this 45.34 lakh people are employed in the MSME segment as indicated in Table 5.8. Then there are vendors, hawkers, people employed by large food processing industries, etc. For an investment of Rs 1 crore in organized and unorganized food processing sector, 140 and 1050 jobs are created, respectively. The multiplier effect of investment in food processing is 2.5 times in comparison to other industrial sectors.

5.100 In sectors such as marine products, cashew processing, and pickle manufacturing, the involvement of women is as high as 90%. Evaluation of schemes implemented by Ministry of Food Processing Industries (MFPI) in NER during the Tenth Plan show that 30% of permanent employment generated due to assistance provided under the programmes/schemes of MFPI was availed by women.

5.101 During the Tenth Plan, the schemes run by the MFPI were primarily for the small and large sectors of the industry. Little was done for the household sector, especially street food vendors who are present in large numbers in various cities (1 lakh in Ahmedabad, 2 lakh in Mumbai, and 1.5 lakh in Kolkata). While physical targets were met in some schemes, others such as food parks faced problems of gross underutilization. Most of the 54 food parks sanctioned since the Eighth Five Year Plan are yet to become operational. Currently only

28 units are running in eight parks. Similarly, though 18 projects were sanctioned under cold chain facilities and five under value-added centres, only four cold storages and two value added centres are currently operational.

5.102 The performance of FPI sector during the Tenth Plan period is given in Table 5.8.

5.103 To provide an impetus to food processing industries (FPIs), a number of policy measures were initiated during the Tenth Plan. Excise duty on fruit and vegetable processing was waived, Income tax holiday was provided, and customs duty reduced on freezer van from 20% to 10%.

5.104 Availability of raw materials for FPIs is a major strength of India. The growing middle-income and upper middle-income groups, increasing health consciousness, growing number of working women, time constraint, convenience, and need for hygienic food have also increased the demand for processed foods. Malls and departmental stores in metros, medium and small towns are providing better forward linkages.

Challenges

5.105 All three segments of the food processing sector face specific challenges. This section deals with the challenges faced by the dispersed small and household sector.

- Infrastructure Development: Since deterioration of agricultural produce starts within five hours of harvesting, much higher investments are required in pre-cooling and controlled atmosphere components at the farm level. Cold chain facilities also help in the decentralized distribution of processed food in small and medium-sized towns. Non-availability of adequate power of appropriate voltage is, however, a major hurdle.
- Investment and Credit Availability: Estimates indicate that more than 40% of the credit needs of small and marginal farmers are met by the traditional *arhtias* at very high interest rates. Similarly, more than 75% processors rely on informal credit. Development of a secondary market on the basis of financial instruments and negotiable warehouse receipt system is necessary for providing liquidity. The use of warehouse receipts as a financial instrument has not picked up. The Eleventh Plan will see a more secure system of accrediting warehouses so that they can provide certification about quality and quantity of the goods plus credits and standards of the goods stored. The Amendment to the Warehousing Act, pending in the Parliament will be expedited.
- Year Round Availability of Raw Materials: Non-availability of agriculture and horticulture surpluses in the required quantity and quality at the appropriate time is a major concern. To ensure the availability of varieties suitable for processing, a

TABLE 5.8
Performance of FPI Sector during the Tenth Plan Period

Item	2002–03	2003–04	2004–05	2005–06	2006–07	CAGR (%)
Production at current price#—(Rs crore) MSME sector CSO data	66472.05	76264.13	86128.19	94127.99	104758.54	9.5
FPI component of GDP*	45146.00	51846.00	55772.00	59281.00 (Prov.)	na	
Employment (lakh persons)**	38.30	39.97	41.74	43.51	45.34	3.4
Export***(Rs crore)	4727.57	5467.06	6154.77	8634.49	8493.40 (Prov.)	12.4

Note: # Data compiled on the basis of the Third Census results of MSME sector and growth rate estimated using Index of Industrial Production (MSME sector).

*Provided by Central Statistical Organization (CSO). These figures would be revised by the MFPI after compiling the data for FPI sector, which includes MSMEs and large industries.

**Estimated on the basis of the Third Census results of MSME sector.

***Agricultural and Processed Food Products Export Development Authority (APEDA) data.

Source: MFPI.

co-ordinated network of research and extension services is required.

- A significant challenge is the limited period of availability of products. Mango is available for three to four months; lychees for fifteen days in a year. Thus, units have to procure maximum crop during harvest time and process it throughout the year. Many units argue for flexibility in hiring, but workers' interests need to be ensured.
- Creating Markets: The high cost of transporting agricultural commodities and processed food affects efficiency. The challenge is to establish an integrated, comprehensive but simple system for the movement of commercial transport vehicles to increase efficiency, reduce delays, and make produce available on a timely basis. With rural connectivity, the country should become a single market.
- The complex tax structure and multiplicity of state-level taxes need to be rationalized. VAT should become uniform in all States/UTs. Abolition of all indirect taxes on agricultural/horticulture products could resolve the problem of border taxes.
- Farmers' associations, SHGs, and co-operatives as well as private companies need to be promoted so that they can bargain with the processors and retailers for better price. Realization of the economies of scale in procurement, technology, and market are also better ensured by producer's groups.
- The food supply chain is complex with perishable goods and numerous small stakeholders. Each stakeholder works in a silo. Demand forecasting is totally absent and the farmers try to push what they produce into the market. There is need for data integration, financial flow management, supply–demand matching, collaborative forecasting, information-sharing, and goods movement synchronization through efficient transport scheduling.
- Packaging has become the competitive tool to reach the consumer. Cost of packaging ranges from 10% to 64% of the production costs, and efforts are needed to reduce this.
- The expenditure on R&D is less than 1%. This needs to be enhanced for finding effective technologies for household and small units.
- Standardization is a powerful tool for improving the supply chain efficiency. There are two standards. The first is about content, manufacturing process, and packaging. The second one deals with logistics and IT systems such as standardization of cartons, pallets, and IT software so that seamless transfer of goods and information is possible. Both these standards need to be enforced so that the demand is not affected by the issue of quality control.
- The increase in world food trade and the advent of the SPS Agreement under the WTO have led to increasing recognition and adoption of food safety measures. Our ability to compete in world markets depends on our compliance with the increasingly stringent food safety standards, especially in view of the breakout of diseases such as Avian Influenza and Bird Flu.

5.106 The household sector of food processing faces another problem. Street vendors are increasingly being removed for urban planning and development. This not only robs many of their livelihoods, but also reduces the access of low-income groups to street food.

The Way Forward

5.107 Integration of the food processing infrastructure from farm to market, providing choice to consumers, assurance about safety and quality of food, setting up a transparent and industry-friendly food authority, and putting in place a transparent system of standards will be the thrust areas during the Eleventh Plan. For this purpose, certain targets have been set, for example: (i) increase the level of processing of perishables such as fruits and vegetables from 6% to 20%, (ii) enhance the value addition in food processing from the present 20% to 35%, and (iii) increase share in global food trade from 1.5% to 3% by 2015. The year-wise physical targets for the Eleventh Plan is given in Table 5.9.

5.108 A paradigm shift is required for the implementation of the various schemes. Management and implementation arrangements in the PPP mode and strong project implementation capabilities will be developed. The scheme for technology upgradation and modernization would be decentralized and operated through nodal banks in place of State nodal agencies to provide back-ended credit-linked subsidy. A new integrated approach would be adopted based on the strategy of (i) better project selection, development,

TABLE 5.9
Year-wise Physical Targets for the Eleventh Plan for FPI
(MSME Manufacturing Units)

Item	2007–08	2008–09	2009–10	2010–11	2011–12	CAGR (%)
Production at current prices (Rs crore)	120472.33	138543.18	159324.65	183223.35	210706.85	12
Employment (lakh persons)	47.61	49.99	52.49	55.11	57.87	4
Export (Rs crore)	11630.00	13185.00	14955.00	16970.00	19270.00	10.7

Source: MFPI.

Box 5.5
From Poverty to Prosperity

Shri Mahila Griha Udyog, the makers of the popular Lijjat Papad, started with a modest loan of Rs 80 and an annual turnover of Rs 6196. This triumphant journey began on 15 March 1959, when seven women inhabitants of South Bombay, without any seed money, gathered on the terrace of a building to prepare papad. Today, Lijjat Papad involves a workforce of more than 40000 women, has an annual turnover of Rs 300 crore, and an annual export of Rs 10 crore. Though Lijjat has achieved huge success, its annual expense on advertisements and promotions is Rs 60 lakh, a mere 0.2% of the total turnover. The co-operative believes in promotion by word of mouth and thus concentrate on cost effectiveness and quality rather than promotion through advertisements. Lijjat has now diversified into other products such as grounded spices, *khakhra*, black pepper powder, detergent powder, and cake, *vadi*, bakery products, etc. Kanjikuzhy GP in Allepuzha district of Kerala was one of the poorest and least-developed Panchayats of the State. Under the leadership of a dynamic woman *pradhan*, the village started vegetable gardens. They began making coir products and processing different varieties of food that they cultivated—*amla*, lime, garlic, ginger, bittergourd, and mango. Today the Panchayat has a turnover of over Rs 2 crore per month by selling its coir products, pickles, jams, squashes, etc. under its own brand. There are over 2000 women SHGs in five villages with a population of 1.6 lakh. Women earn Rs 60 per day as wage and get a share in profits.

and implementation, (ii) decentralized cluster-based development, particularly for creation of infrastructure and fostering linkages with the retail outlets, (iii) industry-led capacity building and upgradation of standards, (iv) an integrated food law and scientific food standards, and (v) strategic intervention with redesigned schemes and strong implementation arrangements.

5.109 The Eleventh Plan will see the development of carefully planned, cluster-based, privately driven food parks; publicly owned and privately managed abattoirs; integrated cold chain facilities and strategic distribution centres (SDCs); cluster-based preservation infrastructure (cold storages, reefer vans, etc.) and irradiation centres; public and private testing and certification labs; and a liberalized wine policy leveraging the agri/horticultural surpluses. Emphasis will be laid on upgrading the quality and hygiene of the street food. National Meat Board, Wine Board, and National Institute of Food Technology and Management will be set up and the Paddy Processing Research Centre, Thanjavur will be modernized. New markets will be tapped by creating the 'Halal Food Hub', the 'Organic Food Hub', the 'Vegetarian Food Hub', the 'Sea Food Hub' among others.

ELEVENTH PLAN SCHEMES

5.110 The scheme for infrastructure development aims to establish 30 mega food parks (new scheme), 50 abattoirs for modernization, and 30 cold chain infrastructure and value-added centres. The mega food parks would be set up with the objective of: (i) state-of-the-art infrastructure for food processing, (ii) ensuring value addition, (iii) inducting latest technology, (iv) fostering of inter-agency linkages for pooling of resources, and (v) quality assurance through better process control and capacity building. Integrated cold chain and SDCs would be set up in a network of towns in associations with private infrastructure companies. Local bodies would be encouraged to participate in setting up of modern abattoirs with a focus on capacity building and training for hygienic and scientific slaughtering.

5.111 The scheme for technology upgradation, establishment, and modernization of FPI will be decentralized and operated through nodal banks/financial institutions directly in place of State nodal agencies. The target under this scheme is 300–350 food processing units. With effect from 1 April 2007, the Ministry has decentralized the disbursement of grants to the applicants directly from the banks which have appraised their projects and provide term loan/working capital. This has resulted in increasing the outreach of the scheme. The new demand coupled with the outstanding applications implies that there will be greater allocation for this scheme during the Eleventh Plan.

5.112 The scheme for quality assurance, codex standards, and R&D and promotional activities provides financial assistance for total quality management, International Organization for Standardization (ISO) standards, bar coding, quality control labs, strengthening of codex cell, and R&D. The scheme also encourages promotional activities. The existing scheme is proposed to be modified for making it more attractive. Private parties will be encouraged to set up quality control/food testing laboratories. FPI units will be provided inputs for adopting modern practices such as HACCP, good manufacturing practice (GMP), good handling practice, ISO 9000, etc.

5.113 Four thousand programmes will be taken up under the scheme for HRD to provide assistance for skill development, strengthening of technical courses in food processing in universities, Entrepreneurship Development Programmes (EDPs), training centres, etc. Follow-up support would be provided to the trainees of EDPs as well as linkages for availing loans from banks/financial institutions would be provided.

5.114 A new scheme for upgradation of quality of street food will be introduced to provide assistance for upgrading and establishing safe food town/food street in 25 cities. This would play a major role in making available hygienically prepared food to *aam admi* (common man). Industry associations, NGOs, PRIs, municipal bodies, etc., would be involved to ensure safety and good quality of street food with the focus on value addition to augment the income levels of the food vendors.

5.115 The total projected GBS for the Eleventh Plan for the MFPI is Rs 3564 crore (2006–07 price) and Rs 4031 crore (current price). A matching private sector investment and a leveraging ratio of 2.5 would result in an investment of about Rs 20000 crore in the processing units. This will lead to creation of 28 lakh additional jobs in the organized sector during the Plan period. Further, assuming a reasonable investment turnover ratio of 2, a total investment of Rs 20000 crore would lead to an aggregate turnover of Rs 40000 crore over the Plan period. The income levels of the farmers are also expected to go up by 20% due to better realization, value addition, and integration of the supply chain. During the Plan period, supportive steps will be taken in a number of other sectors which have a direct or indirect impact on the agricultural/horticultural surpluses available for processing. These will include quality of the inputs, research, and institutional support to enable the farmer to generate surpluses, facilitating transportation of produce across State borders, formation of a national market, etc.

5.116 During the Eleventh Plan period, special programmes for capacity building of SCs, STs, minorities, and women will be formulated. Potential entrepreneurs belonging to these groups will be identified, and tailor-made EDPs, skill development programmes, study tours, etc., will be organized. Gender sensitization programmes for stakeholders including extension functionaries and other implementing agencies will be carried out. Training programmes for women will be redesigned to include technology, management, and micro credit and to promote rise of women entrepreneurs. R&D institutions will be encouraged to develop women-friendly technologies for post-harvest handling and processing, especially for drudgery reduction and providing ease of operation. Most importantly, provision of utilities, basic amenities, and crèches for women staff workers will be made mandatory in the infrastructure projects. An increased scale of assistance will be given for all the infrastructure projects to attract investment in the North East.

ANNEXURE 5.1

CLUSTER DEVELOPMENT IN INDIA—TOWARDS A REINVIGORATED CLUSTER APPROACH

Clusters are defined as a sectoral and geographical concentration of enterprises, institutions, service providers, and related regulatory bodies, engaged in the production of homogeneous or inter-related products and faced with common opportunities and threats.

TYPOLOGY OF CLUSTERS IN INDIA FROM A POLICY PERSPECTIVE

In India, as per the current estimates, there are over 6600 clusters. Agencies have come up with a range of definitions of clusters by specifying a minimum number of units in a given measured location. However, from a policy perspective, it makes sense to typify cluster by their broad challenges relevant for policy intervention. Accordingly, clusters in India can be classified into three broad categories, namely, (i) high-tech clusters (very few at present) targeting innovation for existence, (ii) traditional manufacturing clusters (around 400 plus) targeting competitiveness and consequent employment, and (iii) low-tech micro enterprise 'poverty-intensive' clusters (around 6000) that have both employment as well as poverty implications. Industry/region-wise overview of Indian clusters is indicated in Table A5.1.

A POLICY FRAMEWORK

Activation should be Preferred over Cluster Creation

Cluster-level support is required for both 'soft' [e.g., marketing, training, network creation, Business Development Service provision, benchmarking, productivity improvement areas] as well as 'hard' (cluster-specific infrastructure) interventions. Besides, support is also required for programme management for implementing agencies, resource organization, and cluster development executives.

Capacity Building for Creation of Cluster-related Institutional Infrastructure

Develop a cadre of human resources to initiate cluster development. Develop at least 8–10 national and 25–30 regional institutions to support the implementation of cluster-based development initiatives.

Policy institutions should set up cluster cells and either deploy adequately trained personnel or hire expert institutions for continuous monitoring and evaluation.

ACTIONS BY CENTRAL GOVERNMENT

- The National Commission for Enterprises in the Unorganized Sector (NCEUS) has recommended creation of a National Fund for the Unorganized Sector (NAFUS). NAFUS should be a statutory body funded by the Central Government, public sector banks, financial sector institutions, and other government agencies. The functions of the Fund would not be merely to enable better access of credit to farm and non-farm enterprises alone but to enable the unorganized sector to benefit in areas of marketing, technology, skill and entrepreneurship, guidance and counselling, and capacity

TABLE A5.1
Indian Clusters—An Overview

Region	Traditional Manufacturing		Micro Enterprise					
			Handicraft		Handloom		Others	
	No.	(%)	No.	(%)	No.	(%)	No.	(%)
North	123	31.7	716	25.75	140	23.56	698	24.11
East	36	9.28	645	23.19	43	7.24	464	16.02
West	140	36.09	764	27.47	134	22.57	787	27.17
South	89	22.95	502	18.05	214	36.02	858	29.62
North East	0	0	153	5.51	63	10.61	89	3.08
Total	388	100	2780	100	594	100	2896	100

Source: Compiled from DC (Handicrafts), DC (Handlooms), UNIDO, and the Third Census of SSI units, 2001–02.

building. The target group of the Fund should be the micro enterprises, with focus on those below an investment of Rs 0.5 million. These constitute 94% of the small enterprises in the country but receive about 2% of the net bank credit (NBC), despite providing employment to 70 million people and contributing 30% of industrial production. The Fund could ensure convergence among the various institutions and programmes, through refinancing and confidence schemes for the banks.

- The NCEUS has also piloted Growth Poles for the unorganized sector, based on a concept of developing a cluster of clusters in project mode with PPP. The Commission recommends that 25 Growth Poles (one in each State) be supported during the Eleventh Plan with incentives similar to those offered to SEZs.

ACTIONS BY STATE GOVERNMENTS

- State governments and institutions with specific areas of focus may draw up their own criteria to define clusters. In view of the huge employment potential of the services clusters, there is need for identifying such clusters and subsequent interventions in urban, semi-urban, and rural hubs.
- Although the international experience (especially in Italy and China) has been that local governments are the key players in promoting clusters, in India local governments currently lack this capacity. There is need to shift to a pattern of funding and support driven by State Governments.
- Targeting poverty reduction through cluster development calls for addressing the needs of an estimated 6000 clusters. While the handloom and handicrafts clusters are well-defined, micro clusters need to be further documented with respect to their products, marketability, and dispersion. Within those clusters, highest importance needs to be given to the presence of certain social groups such as higher presence of SCs, STs, and minority communities and those having higher involvement of women as entrepreneurs/workers.

ACTIONS BY PRIVATE ACTORS AND INDUSTRY ASSOCIATIONS

The international experience is that for co-operative action to take place within clusters, the enterprises within clusters should have an association. There are about 3000 associations in existence; however, nearly all these associations are for industrial clusters and not for artisanal clusters. In other words, the 400–500 odd industrial clusters are serviced by some 3000 associations, while the artisanal clusters have no more than 100 associations between them. Without such associations, the articulation of the demands and needs of such artisanal clusters is likely to remain inadequate, and the government programmes or cluster development agency efforts may be supply driven, as opposed to being demand driven and responding to the real felt needs of players involved.

6

Bharat Nirman and Flagship Programmes

INTRODUCTION

6.1 The development of rural India is an imperative for inclusive and equitable growth and to unlock the huge potential of the population that is presently trapped in poverty with its associated deprivations. The analysis of incidence of poverty across Indian States indicates that poverty is very closely linked to the absence of social infrastructure. The Eleventh Finance Commission had constructed an index of infrastructure which included economic, social, and administrative infrastructure indicators. These were (i) agriculture, (ii) banking, (iii) electricity, (iv) transport, (v) communication, (vi) health, and (vii) civil administration. If we juxtapose the index of infrastructure with incidence of poverty, we find that generally States with high infrastructure index have low incidence of poverty. This is reflected in Table 6.1.

6.2 Creation of infrastructure, both physical and social, has been given a greater thrust in the Tenth Five Year Plan. The Eleventh Plan would build on the foundations laid by the Bharat Nirman Programme and other flagship programmes to provide opportunities for improved living conditions as well as livelihoods.

6.3 This chapter, organized in two sections, provides a brief write-up on the Bharat Nirman Programme and on flagship programmes for rural areas. The detailed discussion on the schemes/programmes is contained in different chapters of the Plan document.

TABLE 6.1
Index of Social and Economic Infrastructure

State	Index of Infrastructure	HCR (2004)
Andhra Pradesh	103.30	11.17
Assam	77.72	22.33
Bihar	81.33	42.14
Gujarat	124.31(5)	19.08
Haryana	137.54(4)	13.57
Karnataka	104.88	20.85
Kerala	178.68(2)	13.25
Madhya Pradesh	76.79	36.87
Maharashtra	112.80	29.58
Orissa	81.00	46.76
Punjab	187.51(1)	9.15
Rajasthan	75.86	18.71
Tamil Nadu	149.10(3)	22.85
Uttar Pradesh	101.23	33.40
West Bengal	111.25	28.62

Source: Eleventh Finance Commission Report and Poverty Estimates by Planning Commission.

BHARAT NIRMAN

6.4 The GoI in recognition of the role played by infrastructure in poverty removal has taken up massive programmes for construction of rural infrastructure under different programmes in the past. The government launched a time-bound plan under Bharat Nirman in 2005 for implementation during the four-year period, 2005–09. The first half of the programme was in the Tenth Plan period and the second half coincides with the first two years of the Eleventh Plan period (2007–12). The six components included under the programme are irrigation, drinking water, electrification, roads, housing, and rural telephony.

6.5 Certain physical targets have been set under each of the components. These are indicated in Table 6.2.

6.6 The investment proposed to be made is of the order of Rs 174000 crore during the four-year period. The objective of the Bharat Nirman Programme is to impart a sense of urgency to create rural infrastructure by setting time-bound goals under various schemes which form a part of the Bharat Nirman Programme. The Programme imposes a responsibility on the State to create these facilities in a transparent and accountable manner.

IRRIGATION

6.7 Under the Bharat Nirman Programme, creation of average rate of irrigation potential creation is to be increased from 1.4 MH per annum (i.e., the average rate of creation from 1951–2002) to 2.5 MH per annum. With this objective, it is targeted to create 10 MH of irrigation potential through a combination of major and medium projects, minor irrigation, and restoration of water bodies. The year-wise physical details are given in Table 6.3.

6.8 The creation of additional irrigation potential of 4.30 MH was targeted in the first two years of the Bharat Nirman Programme against which the achievement reported up to March 2007 is 2.587 MH which is about half of the target. Clearly the acceleration of potential creation has not been as targeted.

TABLE 6.2
Targets under Bharat Nirman

Component	Targets to be Achieved by Year 2009
Irrigation	To create 10 million ha of additional irrigation capacity.
Roads	To provide all-weather roads to every habitation over a 1000 population and above (500 in hilly and tribal areas); remaining 66802 habitations to be covered.
Electricity	To provide electricity to remaining 125000 villages and to 23 million households.
Housing	To construct 60 lakh houses.
Drinking water	To provide drinking water to 55067 uncovered habitations by 2009. All habitations with failed sources and water quality problems will be addressed.
Telephone connectivity	To connect remaining 66822 villages with telephone by 2007.

Source: Booklet on Bharat Nirman.

TABLE 6.3
Irrigation Targets under Bharat Nirman

(Unit in Million Ha)

	Components	2005–06	2006–07	2007–08	2008–09	Total
I	Major and Medium Irrigation					
	Completion of ongoing projects	0.90	1.10	1.10	1.10	4.20
	Extension, renovation, modernization of MMI projects	0.25	0.25	0.25	0.25	1.00
	Major and medium irrigation total	1.15	1.35	1.35	1.35	5.20
II	MI					
	Surface water	0.25	0.25	0.25	0.25	1.00
	Ground water	0.45	0.75	0.80	0.80	2.80
	Repair, renovation, and restoration of water bodies/ERM of MI schemes	0.05	0.05	0.45	0.45	1.00
	MI total	0.75	1.05	1.50	1.50	4.80
	Grand total	1.90	2.40	2.85	2.85	10.00

Source: MoWR.

6.9 The Eleventh Five Year Plan would target to create 16 MH potential. During the first two years of the Eleventh Plan, it was proposed to create 5.7 MH irrigation potential through the Bharat Nirman Programme. This would call for higher outlays for irrigation from the States and liberal assistance under AIBP (which is now only a grant and available for surface MI schemes also) for completion of ongoing projects. External assistance for restoration of lost potential by restoring tank irrigation would be utilized. Groundwater potential would be utilized in the States where there is still scope for development. Close monitoring of the projects with remote sensing and completing the projects on a fixed cost turn key mode are required to achieve the targets of the Bharat Nirman Programme. (Details on the irrigation sector are given in Chapter 2, Volume III.)

ROADS

6.10 Rural connectivity is the key component of rural development and poverty alleviation in India. Rural roads (RRs) provide accessibility for the rural habitations to market and other facility centres. In order to give a boost to rural connectivity, a rural roads programme, Pradhan Mantri Gram Sadak Yojana (PMGSY) was launched as a 100% CSS in December 2000.

6.11 The Bharat Nirman Programme envisages a massive scaling up in terms of habitation connectivity coverage, construction targets, and financial investment. To achieve the targets of the Programme, 146185 km of RRs are proposed to be constructed to benefit 66802 unconnected eligible habitations in the country. It is also proposed to upgrade nearly 1.94 lakh km of the existing RRs which are identified through routes of the core network. The physical progress under the Bharat Nirman Program-me during its first two years, that is 2005–07 is given in Table 6.4.

6.12 The targets for new connectivity and upgradation for the remaining two years, that is 2007–09 are as under:

- New Connectivity:
  - Number of habitations to be covered under the Bharat Nirman Programme upto 2009: 43638 km.
  - Length of the road: 95510 km.
- Upgradation:
  - Length of upgradation: 128067 km.

6.13 The main objective of the Eleventh Five Year Plan is achieving the targets of the Bharat Nirman Programme by 2009. However, the physical targets set under the Bharat Nirman Programme till the end of 2008–09 are found to be beyond the capacity of the States. Therefore, the leftover targets of the Programme for 2007–09 will be completed only by the end of the financial year 2009–10. In order to augment funding for meeting the targets of rural connectivity under the Bharat Nirman Programme, it is proposed to borrow Rs 16500 crore from NABARD by leveraging the cess accruals. This would, however, entail setting aside substantial amounts that would accrue from cess from 2009–10 onwards for repayment of the NABARD loan. The outlay for Central sector RRs for the Eleventh Plan is Rs 43251.07 crore at current price, excluding the borrowing from NABARD. (For a detailed write-up see Chapter 9, Volume III.)

DRINKING WATER

6.14 The Bharat Nirman Programme envisages covering the 55067 habitations not covered, covering the slipped back habitations from not covered to partially

TABLE 6.4
Physical Progress of Bharat Nirman during 2005–07

Status		2005–06		2006–07		2005–07		Percentage
		Target	Achieved	Target	Achieved	Target	Achieved	Achieved
New connectivity	Length (in km)	15492.4	18053.7	35182.15	21422.85	50674.55	39476.55	77.90
	No. of habitations	7034	5552	16130	8279	23164	13831	59.71
Upgradation	Length (in km)	11394.4	3925.6	54669.26	46129.90	66063.66	50055.50	75.77

Source: MoRD.

covered status, and providing safe drinking water to water-quality-affected habitations. During the first two and half years there was an impressive achievement (63%) in covering the slipped back habitations as they are relatively easier (involves restoring the defunct bore pumps, carrying out repairs to water supply pipelines, augmentation wherever required, etc.) to execute. The coverage of not covered habitations has also progressed well with 48% of the targeted habitations being covered. However, there is a huge shortfall in covering the water-quality-affected habitations in which only 5% coverage is achieved.

6.15 Sustainability of water supply has become the focal point to avoid slipped back habitations. Convergence of various rural development programmes of the government (such as NREGP, BRGF, watershed development, restoration of water bodies, etc.) need to be vigorously pursued, supported by village-level planning. The issue of water quality has assumed serious proportions. While providing water supply from surface water sources and the conjunctive use of ground water, surface water, and rooftop rainwater harvesting would be ideal, in situ methods such as dilution of chemical contaminants through augmented groundwater recharge (aided through convergence of programmes), adopting cost-effective scientific water quality treatments on an individual village basis would go a long way to improve coverage of water in the water-quality-affected areas. (For a detailed discussion see Chapter 5, Volume II.)

RURAL ELECTRIFICATION

6.16 The rural electrification targets are set to be achieved under RGGVY. The twin objectives of electrification of 125000 villages and electrifying the 2.3 crore BPL households are proposed to be achieved under the Bharat Nirman Programme. During the first two years, the progress under both the objectives has registered an achievement of 34% and 6%, respectively. There are major shortfalls in this sector. Clearly there is a need for acceleration to achieve the target during the Eleventh Plan. Non-availability of electrification materials due to sudden demand is also a contributing factor for under achievement. Rural electrification assumes additional significance since enormous groundwater potential in eastern and north eastern parts of the country could be tapped for MI development. Electrification should trigger economic activity for rural development. Fully operationalizing the franchisee system for revenue collection and viable tariff are key to sustaining the power supply in rural areas. (For a detailed write-up see Chapter 10, Volume III.)

HOUSING

6.17 The Bharat Nirman Programme has recognized and accorded due priority to the need to end shelterlessness. The programme has set a target to construct 60 lakh houses from 2005 to 2009. In the first two years of the Bharat Nirman Programme, 28.69 lakh houses have been constructed. The housing component under the Programme is being implemented in parallel with IAY scheme. This scheme was launched as an independent and major housing scheme from 1 January 1996 to provide assistance for construction upgradation of dwelling units to the BPL rural households.

6.18 For the Eleventh Plan, the focus should be on targeting the poorest of the poor while targeting the remaining housing shortage with other interventions. Housing shortage for 2001 stands at 148.6 lakh houses and for 2007 at 159.5 lakh houses. Hence a target of constructing about 150 lakh houses under IAY needs to be fixed for the Eleventh Plan. This translates into an annual target of 30 lakh houses as against 15 lakh houses being constructed under IAY presently. The per unit cost is also proposed to be revised from the present level of Rs 25000 in the plain areas and Rs 27500 in the hilly and difficult areas. For more accurate targeting of beneficiaries, permanent IAY waitlists should be prepared on the basis of the scores given to families, as part of BPL Census 2002. For this, the State Governments need to be incentivized and Panchayats have to be appropriately empowered. Houses built as part of IAY should be with smokeless chulhas and sanitary latrines. The title of the house site/ownership should be in the name of female member of the household. While IAY can focus on eliminating the backlog of houselessness and temporary and unserviceable houses in rural India, the States should take responsibility for addressing any emerging needs. With the help of certain feasible interventions, the prime objective of tackling shelterlessness can be achieved within the stipulated time. (For details see Chapter 4, Volume III.)

Rural Telephony

6.19 Under the Bharat Nirman Programme, 66822 revenue villages not having telephone connectivity are to be provided with Village Public Telephone (VPT) facility. Out of these, 14183 remotely located villages are to be provided VPTs through digital satellite phone terminals, while the remaining 52639 villages are to be provided any other technology. An estimated sum of Rs 451 crore is likely to be disbursed as subsidy support towards these VPTs. The entire funding is to be met out of the Universal Service Obligation Fund (USOF). A total number of 48704 VPTs have been provided telephone connectivity and 18118 VPTs are likely to be provided by June 2008. It is important to improve the tele-density in rural areas and move to the next step of making every village a knowledge centre with telecommunication. For this high-speed Internet connection providing the necessary knowledge content relevant to the villages for the benefit of all sections of the society is required. (For details see Chapter 12, Volume III).

FLAGSHIP PROGRAMMES

6.20 The thrust of the Eleventh Five Year Plan is social inclusion coupled with provision of improved livelihood opportunities. This approach calls for renewed emphasis on education, health, and other basic public facilities. Inadequate access to these essential services directly limits the welfare of large sections of our population, and also denies them the opportunity to share fully in the growth process. Indeed, inadequate attention to human resource development limits the growth process itself. In the Tenth Plan, many schemes were either launched or revamped and strengthened to provide education, health care, nutrition, sanitation, and social security. Many of these programmes are implemented on an all-India basis, while some are implemented only in rural areas. Even the programmes that are implemented across the country tend to favour rural and backward areas in terms of resource allocation. These programmes, called flagship programmes, form the second strand for development of rural areas, the first being the Bharat Nirman Programme. The following flagship programmes are discussed in the ensuing paragraphs:

- NREGP.
- NRHM.
- Integrated Child Development Services (ICDS).
- Sarva Shiksha Abhiyan (SSA).
- MDM.
- TSC.
- NSAP.
- BRGF.

National Rural Employment Guarantee Programme (NREGP)

6.21 The NREGA has been enacted to reinforce the commitment towards livelihood security in rural areas. The Act was notified on 7 September 2005. The significance of NREGP lies in the fact that it creates a right-based framework for wage employment programmes and makes the government legally bound to provide employment to those who seek it. The NREGP marks a paradigm shift from the previous wage employment programmes by providing a statutory guarantee of wage employment and not being just a scheme. The objective of the NREGP is to enhance the livelihood security of the people in the rural areas by guaranteeing 100 days of wage employment in a financial year to a rural household whose members volunteer to do unskilled manual work. The Act further aims at creating durable assets and strengthening the livelihood resource base of the rural poor. The choice of works suggested in the Act address causes of chronic poverty such as drought, deforestation, soil erosion, etc., so that the process of employment generation is on a sustainable basis. The experience with NREGP so far suggests that it is one of the main planks of rapid poverty reduction in the Eleventh Five Year Plan.

6.22 Starting with 200 districts across the country in Phase-I during 2005–06, NREGA was extended to additional 130 districts in Phase-II during 2007–08. From 1 April 2008 onwards, the Act will cover the whole of rural area in the country. (For a detailed discussion see Chapter 4, Volume III.)

National Rural Health Mission (NRHM)

6.23 The main aim of NRHM is to provide accessible, affordable, accountable, effective, and reliable primary health care, especially to poor and vulnerable sections of the population. It also aims at bridging the gap in rural health care through creation of a cadre of accredited social health activists and improves hospital care, decentralization of programme to district level to improve intra- and inter-sectoral convergence, and effective utilization of resources. The programme sets standards for rural health care and provides financial resources to meet these standards. The programme is under implementation in 18 States which have poor health infrastructure.

6.24 As per Rural Health Bulletin (2006), it is noted that the number of sub-centres without regular water supply, electric supply, and all-weather motorable approach roads is very large in Bihar, Chhattisgarh, Maharashtra, Orissa, Uttar Pradesh, West Bengal, and other States. Similar position is noted regarding facilities at primary health centres also. Out of the six tasks to be completed under the Bharat Nirman Programme in a time-bound manner, five (namely electricity, all-weather roads, safe drinking water, telephone, and rural housing) have direct impact on the NRHM. (For details see Chapter 2, Volume II.)

INTEGRATED CHILD DEVELOPMENT SERVICES (ICDS)

6.25 The ICDS scheme is a child-focused intervention to address the inter-related needs of young children and pregnant and lactating mothers. The ultimate objective of the scheme is to reduce incidence of mortality, morbidity, malnutrition, and school dropouts and enhance the capability of the mother and family to look after the health, nutritional, and development needs of the child. It is now a nation-wide programme, which aims at promoting health and nutritional requirements of children up to six years and expectant and nursing mothers. As on 31 March 2007, there are 6284 sanctioned projects and 10.53 lakh *anganwadi* centres in the country. Out of these, 5672 projects are operational through 7.8 lakh anganwadi centres servicing 7.05 crore beneficiaries comprising 5.81 crore children below six years and 1.23 crore pregnant and lactating mothers. The ICDS would be one of the major programmes for achieving the following goals:

- Raising the sex ratio of the girl child in the age group of 0–6 years from 927 in 2001 to 935 by 2011–12 and to 950 by 2016.
- Reducing IMR to 28 and maternal mortality ratio to 1 per 1000 live births.
- Reducing malnutrition among children of age group of 0–3 years to half its present level and anemia among women and girls by 50% by the end of the Eleventh Plan.

(For a detailed discussion see Chapter 6, Volume II.)

SARVA SHIKSHA ABHIYAN (SSA)

6.26 SSA is the principal programme for universalization of elementary education. SSA aims to provide useful and relevant elementary education for all children in the age group of 6–14 years by 2010. The other significant objective is to bridge social, regional, and gender gaps with the active participation of the community in the management of schools, besides focusing on elementary education of satisfactory quality with emphasis on education for life. SSA addresses the needs of about 20 crore children in more than 12.37 lakh habitations covering 10.42 lakh existing primary and upper primary schools (SES, 2004–05; MHRD, 2007). SSA successfully ensured universal access to primary education. About 94% of Indian villages/habitations have access to schools within a distance of 1 km. In the remaining villages/habitations, alternative schooling arrangements have been made through Education Guarantee Scheme (EGS) and Alternative and Innovative Education (AIE) centres.

6.27 As a result of SSA interventions, between 2001–02 and 2004–05, total enrolment in primary classes has increased from 11.39 crore to 13.08 crore (14.84%) and in upper primary classes from 4.48 crore to 5.12 crore (14.29%). A remarkable feature has been the spurt in girls' enrolment in the corresponding period, from 5.03 crore to 6.11 crore in primary classes (21.47%) and from 1.87 crore to 2.27 crore (21.39%) in upper primary classes. (For details see Chapter 1, Volume II.)

MID-DAY MEAL (MDM)

6.28 The MDM Scheme launched in 1995 aims to give a boost to universalization of primary education by increasing enrolment, retention, and attendance and simultaneously impacting upon nutritional status of students in primary classes. The Scheme was revised in June 2006, provides for 450 calories, 12 gm of protein, and adequate quantities of micronutrients such as iron, folic acid, and vitamin A to the children. The cooking cost has been enhanced to Rs 2.00 per child per school day. All the States and UTs are providing cooked meal to the children in primary classes. The coverage of school children under the programme has risen to 12 crore in 9.5 lakh primary schools/EGS centres during 2006–07. With a proposed investment of Rs 48000 crore in the Eleventh Plan period, MDM is to be expanded in the Eleventh Plan to upper primary classes (VI–VIII) in 3479 educationally backward blocks in 2007–08 and universalized at elementary level by 2008–09. MDM will thus reach out to an additional 3 crore children at upper primary stage reaching out to a total of about 15 crore children at primary and upper primary level in 2007–08 and about 18.0 crore children by 2008–09.

- The nutrition value of the MDM for upper primary children has been fixed as 700 calories, derived from at least 150 gm of cereals and 20 gm of protein, with Central assistance for cooking cost going up to Rs 2.00 per child per school day (Re 0.50 from the States).
- Kitchen sheds to be built in 3.13 lakh primary and 3.0 lakh upper primary schools at a rate of Rs 60000 per unit, and kitchen devices to be provided at a rate of Rs 5000 per school.
- The programme is to be managed and implemented by the local community and PRIs and would not be contractor-driven.
- School health programme to be revived and best practices replicated.
  (For details see Chapter 1, Volume II.)

National Social Assistance Programme (NSAP)

6.29 The NSAP is a flagship programme of the government which aims to provide human security to the poor and the destitute. The programme was launched on 15 August 1995 as a wholly Centrally funded program to give financial assistance to families with little or no regular means of subsistence, living below the poverty line. NSAP presently consists of three components, namely, NOAPS, NFBS, and Annapurna Scheme. These schemes continued to be administered by the MoRD upto 2001–02 as CSS, until these schemes were transferred to Central assistance for State plans in 2002–03. The details of each component have been explained in Chapter 4, Volume III on Rural Poverty Reduction. Government of India has recently modified the criteria for grant of pension under NOAPS to all persons of 65 years or above and belonging to a household below the poverty line. With this modification, the pension under NOAPS which was restricted to only destitutes will now be universalized and approximately 1.57 crore beneficiaries will be covered against the present coverage of around 87 lakh.

6.30 During the Eleventh Plan it is proposed to extend the NOAPS to all old people above the age of 60 years (from the present 65 years) from among the BPL families with a minimum pension of Rs 400 per month funded by the Centre and the States. The Annapurna Scheme, targeted at senior citizens who remained uncovered under NOAPS, can be discontinued soon after these beneficiaries are covered under the NOAPS. The Scheme will include persons with severe/multiple disabilities from BPL families and widows. The NFBS would continue during the Eleventh Five Year Plan with the support enhanced from Rs 10000 to Rs 25000. This amount will be sufficient for meeting the funeral charges and other incidental expenditure. To ensure smooth implementation and closer monitoring of the Scheme, advisory committees comprising professionals and voluntary organizations along with technical support groups should be set up at Central, State, and district levels. (For details see Chapter 4, Volume III.)

Total Sanitation Campaign (TSC)

6.31 Provision of sanitation facilities in rural areas has been highly inadequate. Many programmes were initiated in the past to expand coverage but with little success. In 1999, the DoDWS launched 'Total Sanitation Campaign' (TSC) which is a demand-responsive, community-oriented, low-subsidy programme in a project mode. The performance of project mode TSC was very satisfactory and, therefore, from 2002–03, the entire Central Rural Sanitation Programme has been converted into TSC. The objective of TSC was attaining 100% sanitation coverage in terms of household, schools, and anganwadi toilets and also providing hygiene education to the people.

6.32 The target of the Millennium Development Goal is to cover 50% rural sanitation by 2015. Under TSC, the target is to achieve 100% coverage by the end of the Eleventh Plan (2012). This programme also includes funds for Nirmal Gram Puraskar which has helped in accelerating the pace of implementation of TSC since its inception in 2005. The approach of the Nirmal Gram Puraskar also helps in sustainability and maintenance of the sanitation programme. The outlay proposed for the Eleventh Plan is Rs 7816 crore (Rs 6910 crore at 2006–07 price). The allocation for AP 2007–08 is Rs 1060 crore. The physical target for the Eleventh Plan is to cover 69 million households, 25769 sanitary complexes, 133114 aganwadis, all the remaining schools (new schools will be covered under SSA) and Rural Sanitation Marts/Production Centres (figures will be finalized after the receipt of revised proposals from the districts). (For details see Chapter 5, Volume II.)

BACKWARD REGIONS GRANT FUND (BRGF)

6.33 The BRGF has replaced the Rashtriya Sam Vikas Yojana (RSVY) in order to provide a more participative approach through the involvement of PRIs. The spatial coverage was also expanded and it now covers 250 districts (RSVY covered 147 districts). The scheme aims to help converge and add value to other programmes such as the Bharat Nirman Programme, the NREGP, and other flagship programmes that are explicitly designed to meet rural infrastructural needs but that need supplementation to address critical gaps. It aims at catalysing development in backward areas by: (i) filling infrastructure gaps; (ii) promoting good governance and agrarian reforms; (iii) converging, through supplementary infrastructure and capacity building, the substantial existing development inflows into these districts.

6.34 The scheme has two components, namely, (i) the districts' component covering 250 districts which will be anchored on a well conceived, participatory district plan with schemes selected through peoples' participation for which PRIs from the village upto the district level will be the authorities for planning and implementation; and (ii) special plans for Bihar and the KBK districts of Orissa. The special plan for Bihar had been formulated, in consultation with the State Government of Bihar, to bring about improvement in sectors such as power, road connectivity, irrigation, forestry, and watershed development. The special plan for the KBK districts focuses on tackling the main problems of drought proofing, livelihood support, connectivity, health, education, etc., as per local priorities. (For details see Chapter 7, Volume II.)

III
Industry

7

Industry

7.1 INDUSTRY INCLUDING SMALL AND MEDIUM ENTERPRISES (SMEs)

INTRODUCTION

7.1.1 The Tenth Plan target of 10% industrial growth has not been met, but there was an acceleration in the industrial growth rate during the Plan period and the target was exceeded in the terminal year. The CAGR rose from 4.5% in the Ninth Five Year Plan to 8% in the Tenth Five Year Plan. Manufacturing showed particular dynamism, the CAGR rising from 3.8% in the Ninth Five Year Plan to 8.7% in the Tenth Five Year Plan. The annual growth rate of manufacturing rose consistently during the period, registering 12.3% in 2006–07. For the first time in many years, industrial growth at 11% equalled the growth rate in services, with manufacturing outstripping both (Table 7.1.1).

7.1.2 The rising demand in both domestic and external markets was a major contributory factor but the impressive performance of manufacturing was due in no small measure to the cumulative effect of industrial and fiscal policy changes carried out since the economic reforms of 1991–92. The competitive environment created by the reduction of external barriers to trade finally started to bear fruit. Against a CAGR of 6.3% in the Ninth Five Year Plan, exports of manufactures registered a CAGR of more than 19% during the Tenth Five Year Plan.

7.1.3 Going by the marked improvement in the GCF in manufacturing and the quantum jump in the values shown in the Industrial Entrepreneurs' Memoranda (IEM) filed with the DIPP, a continuation of the high growth rates of manufacturing is highly likely during the Eleventh Five Year Plan (Annexure 7.1.1).

TABLE 7.1.1
Growth Rates

	CAGR in Ninth Plan	2002–03	2003–04	2004–05	2005–06 (QE)	2006–07 (RE)	CAGR in Tenth Plan
GDP	5.5	3.8	8.5	7.5	9.0	9.4	7.6
Agriculture, forestry, and fishing	2.0	–7.2	10.0	0.0	6.0	2.7	2.1
Industry (manufacturing)	4.5	6.8	6.0	8.4	8.0	11.0	8.0
	(3.8)	(6.8)	(6.6)	(8.7)	(9.1)	(12.3)	(8.7)
Services#	8.1	7.4	8.9	10.0	10.3	11.0	9.5

Note: # Construction is included in Services; QE = Quarterly Estimates. Figures in parentheses relate to manufacturing.
Source: Central Statistical Organization.

Review of the Tenth Plan

7.1.4 During the Tenth Five Year Plan the sectoral share of industry in the GDP started rising after several years of decline. The share of manufacturing also maintained a rising trend after falling in the first year of the Tenth Plan (Table 7.1.2).

TABLE 7.1.2
Sectoral Share in GDP

(in %)

	Agriculture, Forestry, and Fishing	Industry (Manufacturing)	Services
2001–02	24.0	25.0 (14.8)	51.0
2002–03	21.5	25.8 (15.2)	52.7
2003–04	21.7	25.6 (15.0)	52.7
2004–05	20.2	26.1 (15.1)	53.7
2005–06 (QE)	19.7	26.2 (15.1)	54.1
2006–07 (RE)	18.5	26.6 (15.5)	54.9

Note: The data given here are not comparable with the data used in the Ninth Five Year Plan and MTA Documents as the base year has been changed by CSO from 1993–94 to 1999–2000.
Source: Press Note, 31 May 2007, National Accounts Statistics 2007, CSO.

Output of the Manufacturing Sector

7.1.5 The Annual Survey of Industries (ASI) is the basic source of data for the registered units and no reliable data are available for the unregistered ones. In this situation, the Central Statistics Organization (CSO) has been using the somewhat limited Index of Industrial Production (IIP) to project growth of both the registered and the unregistered units at a two-digit level for manufacturing. The data from the IIP shows that manufacturing posted a CAGR of 8.82% during the Tenth Five Year Plan in terms of the output (Table 7.1.3).

7.1.6 Cotton textiles, textile products, paper and paper products, basic metals and alloys, machinery and equipment, transport equipment, and other manufacturing industries scored substantial increases in the rate of growth, while beverages and tobacco as well as chemicals and chemical products maintained impressive rates of growth. After recording negative growth in the first two years of the Plan period, cotton textiles made remarkable progress in the last three years following the fiscal policy reforms in the 2004–05 Budget, which created a level playing field between the small-scale and other industries. The performance of the textile industries other than cotton was even more striking. The performance of the capital goods industry was another positive feature in view of the implication it has about the increasing investment in manufacturing. The production of metals surged ahead, with both steel and non-ferrous metals showing a good response to the worldwide buoyancy. Although paper and paper products showed good overall growth, the performance was uneven. Chemical products were lifted by the accelerating growth in the export of pharmaceutical products. Another major industry that seems to be on a high growth path is automobiles and auto products, in which both do mestic and export demand have been picking up. The three areas that showed negative growth are jute textiles, wood and wood products, and leather and leather products. In leather the negative growth in 2002–03, 2003–04, and 2005–06 is not consistent with the export data which show substantial increases in those years. The anomaly in data is due to fact that there is less than full coverage of the enterprises engaged in manufacturing in this sector in the collection of production data by the DIPP.

Capital Formation

7.1.7 After having reached a high of 13.53% in 1995–96, the rate of GCF in manufacturing as a percentage of GDP at market price showed a declining trend, bottoming out in the terminal year of the Ninth Plan. The Tenth Five Year Plan period saw a striking reversal of trend from the outset and in 2005–06 it had increased to 13.6%. Registered manufacturing showed a higher level of GCF rising from 3.8% in 2001–02 to 10.4% in 2005–06 (Table 7.1.4).

Industrial Investment Intentions

7.1.8 The optimistic outlook about future investment in manufacturing also emerges from the industrial investment intentions, as reflected in IEM, Letters of Intent (LOI), and Direct Industrial Licenses (DIL). There was a significant increase particularly between 2005 and 2006 in the value of proposed investment (Annexure 7.1.1).

TABLE 7.1.3
Trends in the Performance of Industrial Sub-Sectors— Annual Growth Rate

(in %)

Industry Code	Industry Name	Weight in IIP	CAGR 1997–2002	2001–02	2002–03	2003–04	2004–05	2005–06	2006–07	CAGR 2002–07
20–21	Food products	9.08	2.49	–1.68	11.0	–0.5	–0.4	2.0	8.7	4.05
22	Beverages and tobacco	2.38	11.17	12.18	27.9	8.5	10.8	15.7	11.3	14.67
23	Cotton textiles	5.52	0.29	–2.20	–2.7	–3.1	7.6	8.5	14.8	4.79
24	Wool, silk, and man-made fibre textiles (except cotton)	2.26	8.53	4.40	3.0	6.8	3.5	0.0	8.1	4.25
25	Jute textiles	0.59	0.37	–5.86	8.3	–4.2	3.7	0.5	–15.8	–1.85
26	Textile products	2.54	2.60	2.40	14.4	–3.2	19.2	16.3	11.5	11.38
27	Wood and wood products	2.70	–6.79	–11.03	–17.6	6.8	–8.4	–5.7	29.1	–0.39
28	Paper and paper products	2.65	4.29	2.99	6.8	15.6	10.5	–0.9	8.4	7.95
29	Leather and fur products	1.14	8.07	5.93	–3.2	–3.9	6.7	–4.8	0.4	–1.05
30	Chemical and chemical products	14.00	8.56	4.76	3.7	8.7	14.5	8.3	9.4	8.86
31	Rubber, plastic, petroleum	5.73	7.55	11.08	5.5	4.5	2.4	4.3	12.7	5.81
32	Non-metallic mineral products	4.39	8.89	1.37	5.1	3.7	1.5	11.0	12.9	6.75
33	Basic metals and alloys	7.45	2.16	4.01	9.2	9.2	5.4	15.8	22.9	12.32
34	Metal products and parts	2.81	5.34	–9.59	6.4	3.7	5.7	–1.1	11.4	5.14
35–36	Machinery and equipment	9.57	6.51	1.02	1.6	15.8	19.8	12.0	14.2	12.48
37	Transport equipment	3.98	6.40	6.83	14.6	17.0	4.1	12.7	15.0	12.58
38	Other manufacturing industries	2.56	0.35	8.86	0.1	7.7	18.5	25.2	7.7	11.49
	Manufacturing	79.36	5.27	2.86	6.0	7.4	9.2	9.1	12.5	8.82

Source: Central Statistical Organization.

TABLE 7.1.4
Gross Capital Formation and Capital Formation in Manufacturing

Year	Capital Formation as % of GDP (at Market Price)				Capital Formation in Registered and Unregistered Manufacturing as % of Respective GVA@	
	GDCF# at Current Price	Manufacturing GCF&	Registered Manufacturing	Unregistered Manufacturing	Registered	Unregistered
1999–2000	25.9	8.9	7.0	2.0	78.5	42.0
2000–01	24.3	6.9	4.6	2.4	48.0	49.5
2001–02	22.9	5.0	3.8	1.2	40.5	27.9
2002–03	25.2	7.1	4.9	2.3	51.0	50.2
2003–04	28.0	8.4	5.4	3.0	56.6	67.1
2004–05	31.5	11.6	8.1	3.4	81.4	76.2
2005–06 (P)	33.8	13.6	10.4	3.2	102.5	72.2

Note: @ Gross Value Added (GVA), #Gross Domestic Capital Formation (GDCF), & Gross Capital Formation (GCF).
Source: Central Statistical Organization.

7.1.9 The data on capital investments compiled by the RBI on the basis of the envisaged capital expenditure of companies that have been sanctioned assistance by the banks and the financial institutions during 2004–05, 2005–06, and 2006–07 reinforce the picture of increasing investment in the pipeline in the industry and some other sectors (Annexure 7.1.2).

7.1.10 In the last three years of the Tenth Five Year Plan, the investment in projects in the pipeline rose rapidly, not only in power, petroleum products, metal and metal products, textiles and cement but also in sugar, chemical and petrochemical products, electrical and non-electrical machinery, transport equipment, and construction.

Exports of Manufactured Products

7.1.11 A major feature of the performance of industry was the remarkable increase in the export share of manufacturing sustained during the entire Plan period. Against a CAGR of 6.3% achieved during the Ninth Plan, exports of manufactured products had a CAGR of 19.9% during the Tenth Five Year Plan (Annexure 7.1.3).

7.1.12 The export of engineering goods recorded the highest CAGR of 33.1% mainly on the basis of the increase in auto and auto components; the export of basic chemicals was not very far behind, with CAGR of 23.1% due to the growth recorded in pharmaceuticals. Among traditional products, textiles and readymade garments responded well to the dismantling of quotas that had restricted imports to the major developed economies until 1 January 2005, and gems and jewellery bettered the performance during the Tenth Plan. The share of manufactures in world exports also inched up.

Share in World Trade

7.1.13 Despite the recent impressive growth in exports, textiles and clothing, iron and steel, and chemical products are the only products in which India's share was 1% or more of the world exports in 2005. Taking manufactures as a whole, India's share in the world trade of manufactures is close to 1%. Apart from China, which has become the manufacturing powerhouse of the world, six developing countries and customs territories have a larger share in world exports of manufactured products (Figure 7.1.1).

7.1.14 The comparatively low share of India in the world export of manufacturers is reflected in its low share of manufacturing value added in GDP compared to countries in South East and East Asia [15.9% of

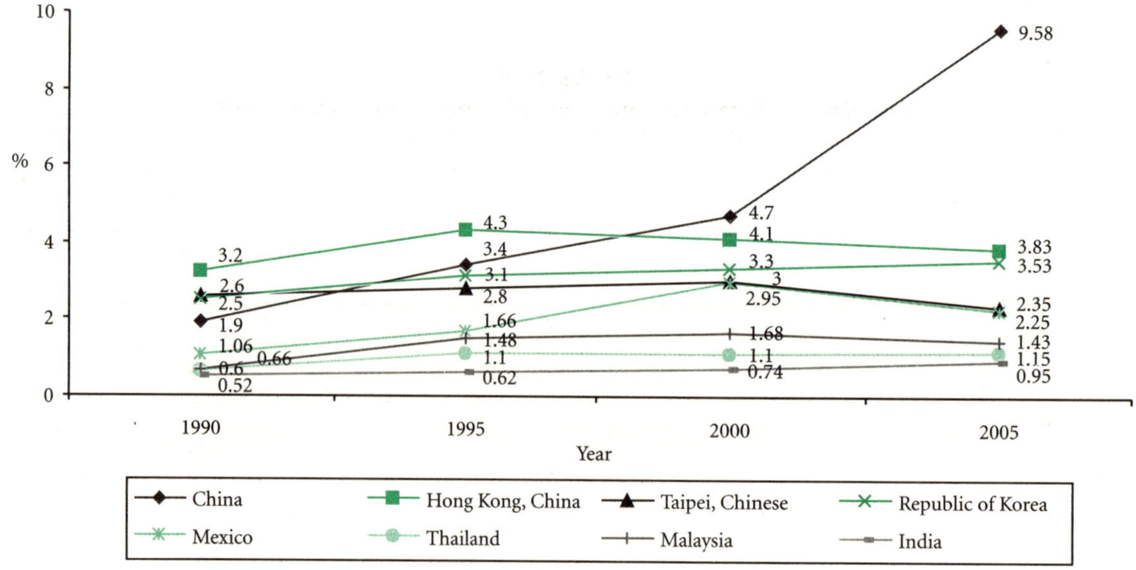

Source: International Trade Statistics, WTO.

FIGURE 7.1.1: Share in World Exports of Manufactured Goods

India against China (34.5%) in year 2000, Thailand (34.5%), and Malaysia (31.4%)].

Creation of Jobs in Manufacturing

7.1.15 The performance of the organized manufacturing sector continued to be a source of concern. There was a massive decline in employment in the public sector following the rationalization of staffing in some units and closure of the sick units. In the early post-reform years, the increase in private sector employment made good the decline in the public sector; however, the early years of the Tenth Five Year Plan saw a decline in the private sector employment as well, causing an absolute decline by as much as 5.40 lakh employees (Table 7.1.5).

7.1.16 The grim scenario reflected by the above data has, however, been considerably brightened by the release of findings of the Fifth Economic Census and the 61st Round of the NSS. Both the surveys found that accelerating output growth has been accompanied by the faster rate of job growth. The Fifth Economic Census has found that the employment in economic activities other than crop production and plantations increased by 2.49% annually between 1998 and 2005 (against the annual increase of 5% in workforce). Data from the latest NSS round for 2004–05 suggests that the non-agricultural employment expanded strongly at the annual rate of 4.7% during 1999–2005. Obviously this growth has come entirely from the unorganized sector in manufacturing and services, which accounts for about 71.6% of all non-agricultural workers in the unorganized sector. The slow growth of regular jobs and the intensification of duality in labour markets (formal versus informal) has become a serious issue.

INVESTMENT CLIMATE

7.1.17 A number of favourable factors have helped to improve the investment climate for the industry and to create considerable optimism on the manufacturing front. India maintained an upward climb in the global competitiveness indices drawn up by reputed bodies and business confidence was high at the end of the Tenth Five Year Plan.

Elimination of Entry Barriers

7.1.18 Entry barriers adversely affect the investment climate of the State. One of the determinants of the investment climate for an industry is the ease with which the firms are able to enter into the business activities. *Doing Business 2007: How to Reform*—a copublication of the World Bank and the International Finance Corporation (2007) shows that the average time spent in completing entry requirement in India is 35 days and the number of procedures is 11 compared to 35 days and 13 numbers of procedures in China. Figure 7.1.2 illustrates this point.

7.1.19 Industrial licensing had already been substantially dismantled and during the Tenth Five Year Plan period further measures were taken to pare it down. Drugs and pharmaceuticals including biotechnology were delicensed in 2005. At the end of the Tenth Five

TABLE 7.1.5
Employment in Organized Manufacturing

(in Lakh)

	Manufacturing (Private Sector)	Manufacturing (Public Sector)	Total Employment in Manufacturing	Employment (in Public Sector Industry)	Employment (in Private Sector Industry)	Total Employment Organized Sector
1991	44.81	18.52	63.33	190.57	76.77	267.34
1996	50.49	17.38	67.87	194.29	85.12	279.41
2000	50.85	15.31	66.16	193.14	86.46	279.60
2001	50.13	14.30	64.33	191.38	86.52	277.89
2002	48.68	13.50	62.18	187.73	84.32	272.06
2003	47.44	12.60	60.04	185.80	84.21	270.00
2004	44.89	11.89	56.78	181.97	82.46	264.43

Source: Economic Survey, 2006–07.

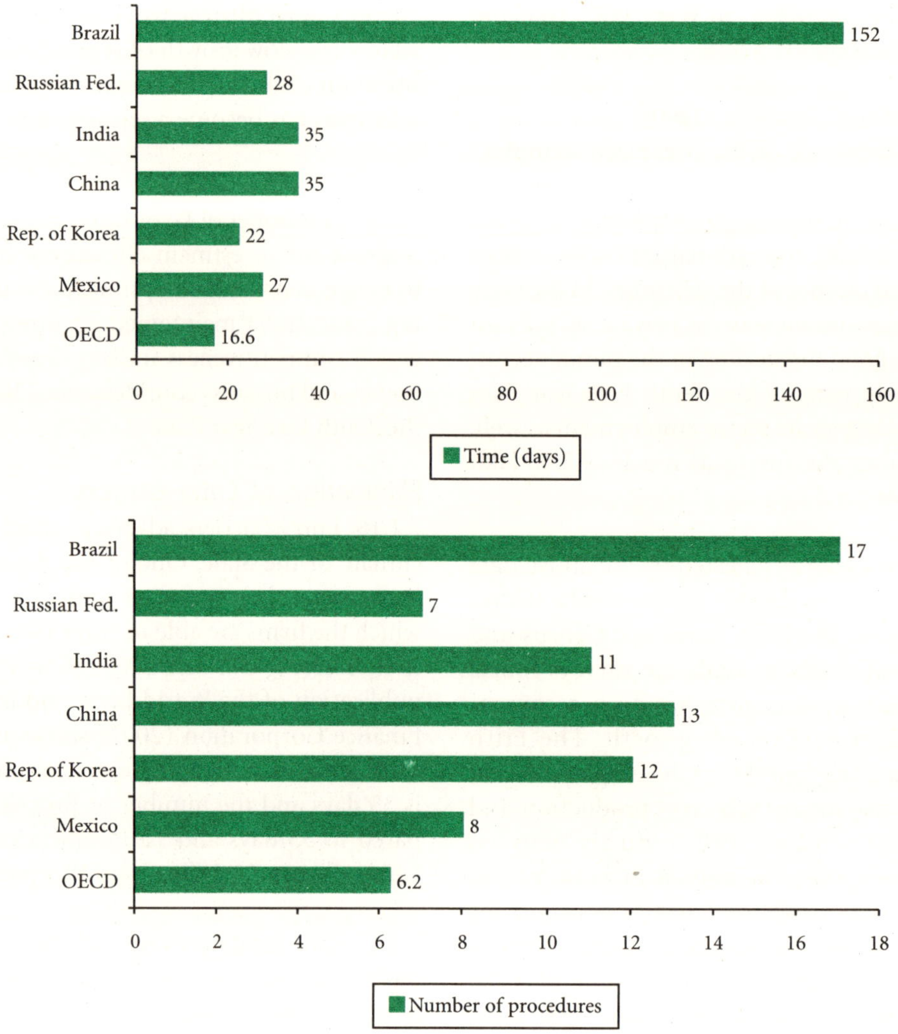

Source: Unleashing India's Innovation: Toward Sustainable and Inclusive Growth, Mark A. Dutz, World Bank Publication, 2007.

FIGURE 7.1.2: Starting a Business—Time, and Procedures

Year Plan period only the following manufacturing activities needed industrial license:

- distillation and brewing of alcoholic drinks;
- cigars and cigarettes of tobacco and manufactured tobacco substitutes;
- electronic aerospace and defence equipment;
- industrial explosives;
- specified hazardous chemicals.

7.1.20 Entrepreneurs are free to select the location for setting up industry. Approval is required from the government for locating an industrial unit within 25 km of the periphery of cities having a population of more than one million according to the 1991 census, provided that is not within an industrial area designated before 24 July 1991. However, these locational restrictions are not applicable for electronics, computer software, printing industries, and other non-polluting industries that may be designated from time to time.

7.1.21 Apart from the licensing restrictions, there are some restrictions arising from certain industries reserved for the public sector and for the small-scale sector. Reservation for the public sector is now very limited, covering only manufacturing involving certain substances relevant for atomic energy (as well as production of atomic energy and provision of railway transport). The list of items reserved for SSIs has been reduced to 114. Larger units are allowed to manufacture items reserved for the small-scale sector only if they undertake an export obligation of 50% of their industrial production.

7.1.22 The Foreign Direct Investment (FDI) policy was also successively liberalized during the Tenth Five Year Plan. Following a comprehensive review in 2006 it was further liberalized, particularly by allowing FDI under the automatic route for manufacture of industrial explosives and hazardous chemicals and making it easier for new investments by foreign investors who had entered into joint ventures with Indian partners earlier. At the end of the Plan period, FDI upto 100% was permitted in all manufacturing activities except where the foreign investor had an existing joint venture/technical collaboration/trademark agreement in the same field of activity.

7.1.23 There are caps on the foreign equity in certain service sectors, viz., 20% on FM radio broadcasting; 26% on insurance, defence production, print and electronic media covering news and current affairs; 49% on air transport services, asset reconstruction companies, cable network, direct to home (DTH), hardware for uplinking, HUB, etc.; 51% on single brand retailing of products; and 74% on atomic minerals, private sector banking, telecom services, and the establishment and operation of satellites. FDI is even prohibited in a few other services, viz., retail trading (except single brand product retailing), gambling and betting, lottery, and atomic energy. However, there is no foreign equity cap on any manufacturing activity other than in public sector undertakings (PSUs) for petroleum refining.

Elimination of Exit Barriers

7.1.24 Investment climate in the country is also affected by the exit barriers. Perhaps the most important exit barrier relates to Chapter V-B of the Industrial Disputes Act 1947 under which units with more than 100 employees cannot exit an unprofitable enterprise without the consent of the concerned State Government. This consent is often difficult and time consuming to obtain.

7.1.25 The other important exit barrier to the industries in India is the legal provision relating to insolvency, rehabilitation, liquidation, and winding up proceedings, which need to be simplified and be made time bound. The co-publication of the World Bank and the International Finance Corporation (2007) reports that resolving the insolvency cases takes upto 10 years in India against 2.4 years in China, 1.5 years in South Korea, and 3 years in the US. Similarly, the recovery rate of closing business is 13% in India compared to 82% in South Korea. Figure 7.1.3 illustrates this point.

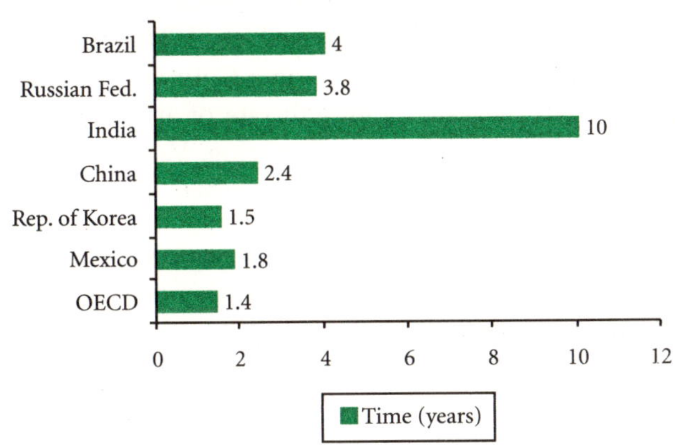

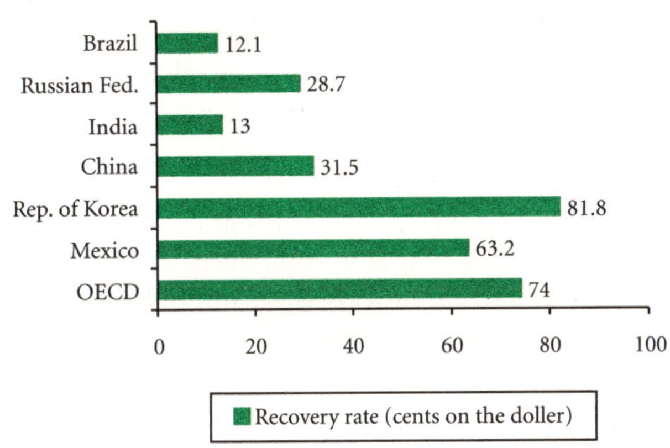

Source: Unleashing India's Innovation: Toward Sustainable and Inclusive Growth, Mark A. Dutz, World Bank Publication, 2007.

FIGURE 7.1.3: Closing a Business—Time, and Recovery Rate

7.1.26 A comprehensive draft of the new Companies Bill 2007 has been proposed by the Ministry of Corporate Affairs (MCA) to simplify the rules and procedures and to set up a quasi judicial fora such as the National Company Law Tribunal and the National Company Law Appellate Tribunal to deal with cases relating to insolvency, rehabilitation, liquidation, and winding up proceedings, taking over the related functions of Company Law Board, Bureau of Industrial and Financial Reconstruction (BIFR), and the judiciary in this respect. The actual setting up of such bodies can be done on the basis of the decision in a related matter pending before the Constitution Bench of the Supreme Court.

7.1.27 A major initiative taken during the Tenth Five Year Plan period, which would help to alleviate entry barriers, was the introduction of MCA 21 e-Governance Project' to computerize and speed up the process of registration of companies. The decision to introduce legislation for limited liability partnerships was another step forward.

Liberalization of Trade

7.1.28 Quantitative restrictions on trade had already been progressively eliminated before the Tenth Five Year Plan period and import tariffs on non-agricultural products drastically reduced after the introduction of economic reforms in 1991–92. The process was carried forward strongly and peak tariffs on non-agricultural products were brought down from 30% in 2002–03 to 10% in the Union Budget for 2007–08, although there are some exceptions. The liberalization of trade was one of the factors contributing to the impressive increase in manufacturing value added and increase in the GCF in manufacturing.

Rising Domestic Demand

7.1.29 India's growing competitiveness in skill-intensive segments such as auto components, fine chemicals, and pharmaceuticals is an important recent development. The sustained increase in merchandise exports at a rate above 20% over the last few years has established India's export competitiveness over a wide range of manufactured products. However, the future growth of India's manufacturing (as of services) will be stimulated increasingly by the domestic consumer demand. The research carried out by the National Council for Applied Economic Research (NCAER) (*The Great Indian Middle Class: Results from the NCAER Market Survey of Households*, NCAER in association with Business Standards, 2004) and McKinsey (*The 'Bird of Gold': the Rise of India's Consumer Market*, Mckinsey & Company, 2007) has brought out that the number of households with an income above Rs 2 lakh will rise from 14.4 million households in 2005 to 63.9 million in 2015 and 137.5 million in 2025. The aggregate disposable income in the hands of this class will rise by about four-fold by 2015 and more than 10-fold by 2025. Another factor influencing consumer demand will be the changing demographic profile of the country resulting in a drop in the dependency ratio from 60% in 2005 to 52% in 2015 and 48% in 2025. By 2025, India is expected to become the fifth largest market in the world, overtaking Germany's consumer market. 'Rising incomes will lift 291 million out of poverty and create a 583 million-strong middle class' (Mckinsey).

The Eleventh Plan Perspective on Industry

7.1.30 In order to achieve an average growth rate of 9% per annum in GDP during the Eleventh Plan, it has been projected that, individually, industry and manufacturing will have to grow at an average annual rate of 9.8%. However, if a number of issues are addressed as discussed below and particularly the plans for improvement of infrastructure (power and transport) fructify in full measure, and the recommended policies on mining (para 7.2.60) and construction (para 8.1.6) are implemented, a substantially higher industrial growth rate can be achieved. The National Manufacturing Competitiveness Council (NMCC) has, infact, suggested a growth rate of at least 12%–14% per annum for manufacturing. Various issues requiring urgent attention are discussed as under:

Issues in Industrial Growth

World-class Infrastructure

7.1.31 Investment in physical infrastructure was intensified during the Tenth Five Year Plan, and in other chapters we describe the investment plans and policies being adopted for the Eleventh Five Year Plan. However, despite substantial progress, the quality of infrastructure remained many notches below world class at the end of the Tenth Five Year Plan. Problems related to the availability and quality of electric power as well as roads, railways, ports, and airports have been highlighted in Chapter 1 of Volume I along with the outline of the new strategies adopted in the Eleventh Plan to tackle these problems.

Taxation

7.1.32 Tax policy is a very important determinant of the investment climate. The rates of direct taxes determine the structure of incentives to work, save, and invest, while the level and structure of indirect taxes influences the aggregate demand and thus the scale of operations on the one hand and relative prices of different goods and services on the other. Concerted efforts to simplify the tax system, moderate the rates of tax, and avoid cascading of taxes, which intensified since the 1991–92 reforms and were continued during the Tenth Five Year Plan, have improved the investment climate. But more needs to done.

DIRECT TAXES

7.1.33 The rate of Corporate Tax has been brought down to a level of 30%, which with surcharge and cess amounts to a maximum marginal rate of 33.99%. However, analysis has brought out two features of the direct taxation in the country arising from the regime of exemptions. First, the average effective rate of Corporate Tax paid in 2005–06 was 17% or about half of the statutory rate. Second, the range of incidence varied from 11.7% to 32.5%.

7.1.34 Different effective rates of direct taxes can cause misallocation of resources. Capital investment should be driven by efficiency considerations rather than by tax advantage. Withdrawal of industry-specific concessions will make it possible to consider the introduction of a flat rate without any exemptions. The desirability of a flat rate stems from the fact that it promises to introduce transparency and equity in taxation of different economic activities, reduces the incentive to evade or avoid tax, and minimizes the use of discretion of tax authorities (regarding eligibility for concessions). The Kelkar Task Force on direct taxes had recommended a similar regime of Corporate Tax at 25%.

INDIRECT TAXES

7.1.35 In indirect taxes great progress was made during the Tenth Five Year Plan in reducing the cascading effect of indirect taxes by the adoption of State VAT by almost all the States and UTs. However, the rates of indirect taxes in India remain among the highest in the world. Most industrial products are subject to Central value-added tax (CENVAT) on the manufactured value, at an average of 16% and a State VAT at a modal rate of 12.5% of retail value (though there are a number of goods that are exempt from State VAT and some are subject to lower rates of tax). At present the incidence of CENVAT and State VAT together is about 23%. In addition, States and local levels of government levy such taxes as octroi or entry tax, etc. The overall rate of indirect taxes compare unfavourably with those prevailing in Association of South-East Asian Nations countries, which are closer to 10%–12%.

7.1.36 High taxes raise the final price of products, reducing demand for specific products and dampening aggregate demand. Lower taxes lead to an increase in the aggregate demand, providing long-lasting incentive to investment, simultaneously increasing employment and incomes. If the buoyancy in tax collection seen in the recent years continues, it will provide an opportunity for making a beginning toward the gradual reduction of the combined incidence of CENVAT and State VAT.

INVERTED DUTY STRUCTURE

7.1.37 The customs duty in India on non-agricultural products has come down drastically since 1991–92, and during the past five years the peak duties (except for a handful of products) have fallen from 30% to 10% ad valorem (as on 1 March 2007). The vast majority of manufacturing industries have withstood increased competition from imports arising from the lowering of customs duties. However, what is affecting them adversely is the inverted duty structure arising from elimination or reduction of duty on value-added products, while higher duties apply on the raw material and intermediate products. In some cases, inverted duties are embedded in the Most-Favoured-Nation duties, as in the cases of Information Technology (IT) products and books. Although under the obligations of the

Information Technology Agreement, basic customs duty has been eliminated from almost all IT products including intermediate products, some basic raw materials that go into the production of these products still attract varying levels of customs duty. Similarly, paper is subject to excise duty (and when imported it is subject also to import duty), but import of printed books does not attract any basic customs duty or additional customs duty imposed in lieu of excise. The incidence of inverted duty structure has been considerably increased by the Regional Trading Arrangements (RTAs) that India has entered into, and exacerbated by selective preferences implemented at the outset through Early Harvest Lists. While measures have been taken to alleviate the problem of inverted duty structure arising from RTAs through specific interventions, more needs to be done.

7.1.38 It is also important to safeguard the domestic industry from possible disruption as a result of implementation of several free trade agreements (FTAs), the negotiations for which are in an advanced State with some of world's leading trading countries. Efficiency in manufacturing, in particular, is a function of the quality of physical infrastructure and of skill development, and our infrastructure, both social and physical, is at present not of world class. It is necessary to raise the level of education and skills and to improve power and transport infrastructure in the country even as we enter into FTAs, as otherwise there would be flight of capital from the country to the trading partners with superior infrastructure and level of skills. Furthermore, a level playing field must be created on the fiscal side. In order to ensure that our industries do not suffer a disadvantage in an FTA, the introduction of Goods and Service Tax (GST) must be firmly on course. There must be an understanding also on the exchange rate policy as well before we can have a soundly functioning FTA, because a market driven exchange rate policy in one partner country cannot co-exist with a substantially controlled exchange rate policy in another. These fundamental aspects need to be attended to first before the major FTAs, which we are negotiating, enter into force.

GOODS AND SERVICES TAX

7.1.39 Non-discretionary application of uniform taxes to all economic activities is among the most important desiderata of a tax system. The introduction of an integrated GST would go a long way in meeting this objective. The Report of the (Kelkar) Task Force on Implementation of the Fiscal Responsibility and Budget Management Act 2003 recommended the introduction of the GST. The government has agreed to introduce the GST and has set 2010 as the target year for its introduction. To prepare for this, it has also begun a phased reduction of Central Sales Tax (CST) to zero by 2010. This is because CST, which is an origin-based tax, is inconsistent with VAT, which are destination based—the two should not co-exist. As revenue from CST was transferred to the states, they are to be compensated by being given the right to levy service tax on certain commodities. A Group of State Finance Ministers has been constituted to work on the modalities for the introduction of GST on lines similar to the group that had been set up for the introduction of State VAT.

7.1.40 Once the integrated GST across the country is introduced, it will simplify tax administration and eliminate cascading of taxes. It will lead to a reduction in the distortions in the structure of production, consumption, and exports and further to a more efficient allocation of the resources. The demand for manufactured goods can be expected to grow significantly.

Structural Change in Manufacturing Sector

7.1.41 Review of data from the ASI, which covers all factories registered under Factories Act 1948, reveals that by 2004–05 a substantial change in the shares of different sectors of manufacturing had occurred since 1990–91. After accounting for the change in classification from National Industrial Classification (NIC) 87 prevalent in 1990–91 to NIC 2004 based on which the index of industrial production is computed in 2004–05, the main changes seen are increases in the shares of chemical and chemical products from 8.42% to 16.4% and basic metals and alloys industry from 12.9% to 19%, and reductions in the shares of machinery, machine tool, and electrical machinery (NIC 35–36) from 16.14% to 10% and of textile and textile products including apparel from 14.37% to 7.3%. Transport equipment and parts registered a small increase from 8.3% to 9.5% while food, beverages, and tobacco showed a decline from 11.9% to 8.8%.

7.1.42 The capital intensity of the manufacturing sector in terms of fixed capital per employee has increased at a CAGR of about 6.5% since 1990–91 at constant prices. Increase in outsourcing in manufacturing segment might have inflated the increase in capital intensity. The fixed capital to net value-added ratio decreased from 2.53 in 1980–81 to 1.85 in 1990–91 before rising marginally to 1.97 in 2004–05. The segments where capital intensity has increased are paper, basic metals, and non-metallic minerals and even large employment-generating sectors such as textile and food processing.

7.1.43 A recent study on India's pattern of development by Kalpana Kochhar et al.[1] has noted that 'The paradox of Indian manufacturing in the early 1980s is that a labor-rich, capital-poor economy using too little of the former, and using the latter very inefficiently'. It has further observed that little has changed since the economic reforms on account of the fact that the labour markets have not been touched and the education expenditure continues to be skewed toward tertiary education. If the structure of Indian industry is to be adapted to the factor endowments of the country, it is evident that the impediments in the way of labour-intensive industries must be removed and, while not relenting on the expenditure on higher education, emphasis must be also put on skill development for making the workforce employable in such industries.

Skill Development

7.1.44 A skill deficit in virtually all areas of manufacturing has emerged as one of the major impediments to growth in manufacturing. All areas of manufacturing are affected but the more dynamic areas such as pharmaceuticals, automobiles and auto parts, textiles and clothing, leather and leather manufactures are affected more severely. And the shortages are at all levels, from executives and designers at the top to the base level skilled workers such as tailors and machine operators. The shortage has led to a serious problem of poaching of skilled personnel being experienced by established industrial units.

7.1.45 Skills and knowledge are the driving force of the economic growth and social development of the country. Development of skills and knowledge is basic to enhancing employment opportunities and a comprehensive strategy to address this problem in the Eleventh Plan is outlined in Chapter 4 of Volume I.

Labour Flexibility

7.1.46 We need to recognize three influences that could work on firm behaviour in organized manufacturing in the future. First, in order to meet the pressures of increased competition resulting from global integration, firms have a need to build flexibility into their organizational structure, so that they can adjust to volatility in the international demand for their products. Enterprises are increasingly focusing on their core competence and outsourcing all other activities to specialist organizations, which can deliver better and at lower cost.

7.1.47 Second, the lack of flexibility in some of the labour laws, such as Chapter V-B of the Industrial Disputes Act 1947, and Contact Labour (Regulation and Abolition Act), which focus on job protection, inhibits employment. In the MTA it was recognized that these laws make it difficult for employers to flexibly respond to the changes in demand when necessary and have the net effect of discouraging the growth of strong labour absorbing sectors. It must be acknowledged here that the aforementioned provisions of the Industrial Dispute (ID) Act 1947 has not proved to be a major obstacle in downsizing by several manufacturing enterprises during the past few years with the aid of generous packages for voluntary retirement. Furthermore, in the context of severe shortages of skilled personnel being experienced by existing manufacturing enterprises, the need to reduce staff is not a current problem for many labour-intensive enterprises. Similarly, despite the provisions of the Contract Labour

[1] *India's Pattern of Development: What Happened, What Follows*, Kalpana Kochhar, Utsav Kumar, Raghuram Rajan, Arvind Subramanian, and Ioannis Tokatlidis, Working Paper 12023, National Bureau of Economic Research, Cambridge, February 2006.

(Regulation and Abolition) Act, the scope of prohibitions issued under Section 10 of the Act has not been very wide, being limited to specific processes, operation, or other work in particular establishments. However, Chapter V-B of the ID Act 1947 does create a psychological block in entrepreneurs against establishing new enterprises with a large workforce and impede attainment of economies of scale. As a result, firms prefer to set up enterprises with a smaller permanent workforce, and these enterprises are unable to cope with large size orders from retail market chains in garments and footwear for instance. Similarly the Contract (Regulation and Abolition) Act constrains seasonal employment because of the fear that work done by employees recruited to meet the temporary or seasonal demand would be declared to be work of perennial nature.

7.1.48 Third, while several fiscal incentives for corporate investment encourage capital, only one relates to labour use, and that too is of little practical value. This induces enterprises to give preference to capital-intensive over labour-intensive technology.

7.1.49 We have seen earlier that, according to the *Economic Survey*, employment in the organized manufacturing sector was on the decline up to 2004. The 61st Round (2004–05) NSS data has revealed that in manufacturing, employment growth was 3.9% per annum, raising the sectoral share of manufacturing in employment from 12.13% in 1999–2000 to 12.90% in 2004–05. The latest NSSO data implies that the increase in the manufacturing employment has come from the unorganized sector. The quality of employment in the unorganized sector is poor and the NSSO 61st Round shows that large numbers of such workers do not have written job contracts as well as are not eligible for paid leave and social security benefits. The need is to bring about an increase in quality employment, which only either the organized sector or the MSME's hiring workers on wage contract can provide. For this reason, it is necessary to consider during the Eleventh Five Year Plan practical ways of resolving the difficulties created by these laws. In addition, fiscal benefits related to employment objectives will have to be carefully designed and implemented.

Scarcity of Raw Materials

7.1.50 Scarcity of raw materials, feedstock, and fuels is another impediment limiting the growth of some industries. Coal, natural gas, and forestry resources are the main materials in short supply.

COAL

7.1.51 A number of industries, including steel and cement (which are essential inputs for building infrastructure) and electricity generation, use coal as the basic fuel in their production process. Adequate availability of the required grades of coal needs to be ensured for them if their supply is not to prove an obstacle to growth.

7.1.52 Since the nationalization of coal mines, the investment in coal mining for commercial sale has been determined by the availability of financial resources with Coal India Ltd. Only owners of captive coal mines could undertake production according to their demand perceptions. All other users have had to rely on the coal-linkage committee to allocate whatever coal was available in an equitable manner. The coal-linkage committee classified coal consumers as core and non-core. Initially the core sector included power utilities, independent power producers, cement, defence, railways, fertilizer, sponge iron, and steel plants. Subsequently, in 2004, aluminum, paper, Central public sector enterprises (CPSEs), and coal for export were also included in the core sector.

7.1.53 India has large reserves of coal, and there is a need to utilize coal in an optimal manner. As the public sector coal mining companies have, for various reasons, not increased their output to the desired level, there is a need to supplement their efforts by private participation in coal mining for merchant sale. The availability of adequate quantity of coal is as important as, and a pre-condition for, the availability of electric power, which is a basic requirement of growth.

7.1.54 Improvement in availability can come only when it is possible to increase production so that the need for coal linkages and allocation by government committees can be minimized. Until that becomes possible, merchant sales should be allowed not only to new players but also to captive mine owners.

FERTILIZER FEEDSTOCK/NATURAL GAS

7.1.55 The increased emphasis on the agriculture sector and agricultural productivity requires that all the inputs for agricultural production are made available in adequate measure and at affordable prices. One of the most important inputs for the agricultural production is fertilizer. The government recognizes this and has been providing fertilizer subsidy.

7.1.56 Urea is the most widely used fertilizer and the ideal feedstock for it is natural gas. Many urea units are producing urea using uneconomic feedstock such as naphtha and diesel oil. A decision has now been taken, in principle, to convert all these units into gas-based units. Assured supply of natural gas for the production of urea, the sources of supply, and the price at which such supplies would be made are unresolved issues. The most efficient use of gas is in the production of fertilizer (urea) that utilizes this as a feedstock using both its heat value and the chemical components. Therefore, the sectors where gas is utilized as feedstock should have priority in terms of allocation.

7.1.57 A lot of offshore gas has been discovered in the Krishna–Godavari (K–G) basin in fields allocated under the New Exploration Licensing Policy (NELP). There is a production sharing agreement in the NELP, according to which the government is entitled to an agreed share of the profit. One option that is often suggested is for the Central Government to provide gas from its share in the production sharing agreement to the urea-producing units. However, even when taken in kind it will be available in significant amount only after five to seven years of the start of production of gas. In any case, whether the government gives gas at a subsidized price or gives a subsidy for it makes no difference.

7.1.58 The pricing of gas is a contentious issue, as there is no properly functioning market for gas in India. Power plants and fertilizer units are entitled to a pass-through of the cost of gas and thus have no incentive to push for lower prices. Consequently, price bids by them cannot be accepted for price discovery of fair market value. As the government provides fertilizer subsidy, supplying gas at the cost of production could be considered until a fair market price has been determined. As in the case of gas produced by Oil and Natural Gas Corporation (ONGC) and by Oil India Ltd (OIL) the Tariff Commission could be asked to determine the cost of production/fair price for K–G basin gas as well.

RAW MATERIAL FOR PAPER

7.1.59 The growth of the paper industry has not been able to match the growth in the demand for paper as the industry has been acutely short of domestically available wood. The limitation on cutting trees and other forest produce has led it to depend on imported wood and wood-based materials. As there is a low import duty on paper, domestic production of paper is progressively becoming uncompetitive. For the industry to grow, it needs to have an assured source of supply of wood from domestic sources.

7.1.60 One way to achieve this and also improve the forest cover is to lease degraded forestland to the paper mills for development of captive plantations. They could thus grow trees to meet their raw material needs and in their self-interest they would need to do this on a sustainable basis.

7.1.61 The degraded forestland in the hands of the Forest Department has remained degraded owing to the other demands on the Department's resources and time. The land could benefit by grant of long-term lease to paper mills, which will devote the resources necessary to grow trees, as a matter of their own commercial viability. The lease agreement could have a condition that the lease is given on usufruct terms, that is, at the end of the lease period the lessee will return the land in a condition that is no worse than when the lease was awarded. Experience in some developed countries has shown that the generation of trees in captive plantations is more than the requirement of the paper mills and can provide additional forest cover.

7.1.62 In view of the accepted position that the first charge on natural resources should be of the local communities and the policy of JFM, an arrangement such has been advocated above has not been possible. This leaves the government with the possibility of allowing joint ventures with paper mills only on non-forest wasteland. Consent of the local communities in public hearing would be required here too, but this could be obtained if the paper mills agree to spend a part of their turnover in social infrastructure for their benefit. The other alternative is for the State Governments to facilitate linkages between paper mills and farmers for growing tree crops as suggested in Chapter 3, Volume III.

Fostering Innovation

7.1.63 For the growth of the Indian economy, the key driver has to be innovation. Innovation[2] is broadly defined to include 'new to the world' knowledge creation and commercialization as well as 'new to the market' knowledge diffusion and absorption. Although both types of innovation activities are essential, India stands to gain more from catching up to the global frontier of knowledge through increased absorption than from trying to push out the frontier through creation. An enormous amount of global knowledge is not fully utilized in India. Given the overriding need to better address the needs of the poor in India, innovation could be 'inclusive' by addressing knowledge creation and absorption efforts most relevant to the poor. For fostering innovation, sharpening competition by reducing entry and exit barriers is essential so that innovation becomes a necessity. Similarly, innovation-friendly socio-cultural norms could be strengthened by dissemination of success stories and provide high profile awards and prizes. For diffusing and absorbing knowledge, technology-support programmes could be taken at cluster level for the MSMEs and world-class demand responsive metrology, standards, testing, and quality infrastructure closely linked to innovation created for fostering inclusive innovation. Financial support for grassroot innovators could be increased and Intellectual Property Rights for traditional knowledge strengthened.

7.1.64 Innovation whether in goods and services or processes can be instrumental in increasing profitability by increasing competitiveness and market share. The national investment on R&D activities during 2002–03 as per the Ministry of Science and Technology was Rs 18000.16 crore, of which only about one-fourth could be attributed to the private sector (20.3%) and public sector (4.5%) enterprises. The ratio of R&D expenditure to the gross national product was only 0.80% in 2002–03 compared to 5.11% in Israel, 4.27% in Sweden, 3.11% in Japan, and 1.23% in China. Obviously, there is scope for considerable improvement on the R&D front in India for fostering innovation.

7.1.65 The National Knowledge Commission, set up by the Planning Commission, has highlighted the following aspects in its national survey on innovation:

- Innovation intensity (i.e., the percentage of revenue from products/service less than three years old) has increased for large firms and SMEs, with the SMEs registering a greater increase in innovation than large firms.
- About 7.3% of the large firms have achieved breakthrough in innovation while 76.4% have introduced incremental innovation.
- Internal processes for innovation such as maintaining a specific innovation department, allocating funds, rewarding innovative employees, maintaining physical locations for innovations, and constituting cross functional teams are all important factors which encourage firms to become more innovative.
- Firms with more patent filings and use of IPR consultants are more innovative.
- Firms partnering with government agencies, collaborating with universities and R&D labs also tend to be innovative.

7.1.66 However, the most important barrier to innovation is skill shortage and a lack of effective collaboration with the R&D institutions. NDC has recommended that there is a need for systematic reforms of the higher education system, including skill-based marketable vocational education in India which would facilitate the development of the required intellectual capital as well as enable more effective collaboration between industry, educational institutions, and the government. Apart from this, it is necessary to

[2] *Unleashing India's Innovation: Toward Sustainable and Inclusive Growth*, Mark A. Dutz, World Bank Publication, 2007.

encourage innovation through fiscal incentives on a continuing basis.

7.1.67 The NMCC was set up in September 2004 by the government to provide a continuing forum for policy dialogue to energize and sustain the growth of manufacturing industries in India. The NMCC presented its report 'The National Strategy for Manufacturing' to the government in March 2006 which has identified challenges being faced by Indian manufacturing and has recommended measures in consultation with different departments and industries. A High-Level Committee on Manufacturing under the Chairmanship of the Prime Minister has been constituted to ensure implementation of the recommendations. The analysis and policy recommendations in the sections that follow reflect, inter alia, the strategy drawn up by the NMCC as well as suggestions made in the 11 Working Groups set up by the Planning Commission for the Eleventh Five Year Plan.

PUBLIC SECTOR ENTERPRISES (PSES)

7.1.68 PSEs have made a notable contribution to the economic growth of the country, particularly by creating a diversified industrial base. After the introduction of economic reforms in 1991–92, a policy of disinvestments and privatization was adopted and upto 2001–02 equity had been sold in 123 enterprises and receipt of Rs 26012 crore realized. During the first two years of the Tenth Five Year Plan, the process intensified and a sum of Rs 18895 crore was realized from disinvestments. In 2004–05, there was a policy shift and the United Progressive Alliance (UPA) government, while expressing a commitment toward a strong and effective public sector, decided that 'generally profit making companies will not be privatized'. Residual disinvestments made in the last three years of the Plan brought in receipts of Rs 4335 crore.

Performance of Central Public Sector Undertakings

7.1.69 Despite the privatization accomplished upto the middle of the Tenth Five Year Plan, when the policy changed, the role of PSEs and their contribution to the GDP has not diminished. In fact, the GDP from non-departmental enterprises (NDEs) registered an increase during the first two years of the Tenth Five Year Plan as shown in the Table 7.1.6.

TABLE 7.1.6
Contribution of Non-departmental Enterprises to GDP at Factor Cost (Current Price)

Year	GDP from NDEs (Rs Crore)	GDP at Factor Cost (Rs Crore)	Share (%)
1996–97	141710	1260710	11.24
2001–02	244345	2100187	11.63
2002–03	282518	2265304	12.47
2003–04	312364	2549418	12.25
2004–05	338352	2855933	11.85

Source: National Accounts Statistics 2007 for 2001–02 onwards; for 1996–97 based on 'Back Series' information provided by CSO.

7.1.70 In 2004–05, the share of CPSEs in the GDP was 6.82% out of 11.85% for NDEs. The number of operational CPSEs has decreased from 231 in 2001–02, the last year of the Ninth Five Year Plan, to 225 in 2005–06. What is significant is that the number of profit-making CPSEs has gone up from 120 to 157 and the number of loss-making CPSEs has decreased from 109 to 58. The profits of profit-making CPSEs have increased from Rs 36432 crore to Rs 76240 crore and the losses of loss-making ones has come down from Rs 10454 crore to Rs 5752 crore during the same period. Table 7.1.7 gives the macro picture of CPSEs.

7.1.71 The net profits made by the CPSEs has led to the accumulation of large reserves which totalled as much as Rs 353641.62 crore for 157 profit-making enterprises at the end of the financial year 2006–07. Between 2002–03 and 2005–06, the cash and bank balances of all CPSEs rose from Rs 53453 crore to Rs 150680 crore. Thus, CPSEs have accumulated large amounts of investible funds, which are not being put to productive use.

7.1.72 The top 10 profit-making CPSEs made a net profit of Rs 47371 crore in 2005–06. The ONGC (Rs 14431 crore), Bharat Sanchar Nigam Ltd. (BSNL) (Rs 8940 crore), National Thermal Power Corporation (NTPC) (Rs 5820 crore) were the top three profit-making CPSEs. The top 10 loss-making CPSEs accounted for a net loss of Rs 4552 crore, the top three loss-making units being the Fertilizer Corporation

TABLE 7.1.7
Macro View of Central Public Sector Enterprises

(Rs Crore)

	2001–02	2002–03	2003–04	2004–05	2005–06	April–September 2005	April–September 2006
Number of operating CPSEs	231	226	230	227	225		
Profit before interest, tax, and EP (PBITEP)	63190	72539	95039	108420	106533	64962	73169
Capital employed	289934	417160	452336	504407	581250		
Turnover	478731	572833	630704	744307	832584	377370	468221
Net profit	25978	32344	52985	64963	70288	27235	35465
Net profit as % of turnover	5.4	5.6	8.4	8.7	8.4	7.2	7.6
Profit of profit-making CPSEs	36432	43316	61606	74433	76240		
Loss of loss-incurring CPSEs	10454	10972	8522	9356	5952		
Profit-making CPSEs (nos.)	120	119	139	138	157		
Loss-incurring CPSEs (nos.)	109	105	89	79	58		

Source: Public Enterprise Survey 2005–06 and Mid-Year Review of CPSEs for 2006–07, Department of Public Enterprises (DPE).

of India, Food Craft Institute (FCI) (Rs 1294 crore), Hindustan Fertilizer Corporation Limited, HFC (Rs 965 crore), and Hindustan Photo Films Co. Ltd, (Rs 561 crore). While the top 10 profit-making enterprises are diversified, the top 10 loss-making enterprises are largely concentrated in manufacturing.

7.1.73 Mid-year review (April–September 2006 against April–September 2005) showed that the turnover of 202 CPSEs (out of 225) for which data was available increased by 24.07% and the net profit increased by 18.18%. The performance of CPSEs in different industry sectors during the Tenth Five Year Plan is presented in Annexure 7.1.4.

Policies toward CPSEs and their Implementation

7.1.74 In accordance with the mandate in the NCMP the two main elements of the GoI policy have been devolution of full managerial and commercial autonomy to successful, profit-making companies and modernization and restructuring of sick PSUs (as well as sell-off or closure of chronically sick CPSEs).

7.1.75 Pursuant to the recommendations of an ad hoc group of experts under the chairmanship of Arjun Sengupta, the government introduced a series of measures for enhancement of financial delegation to *Navratnas*, *Miniratnas*, and profit-making CPSEs. These include measures for creation of and disinvestment in subsidiaries, transfer of assets to such subsidiaries, and floating of fresh equity.

7.1.76 Under the provisions of Sick Industrial Companies (Special Provisions) Act 1985, 62 CPSEs had already been referred to the BIFR earlier and during the Tenth Five Year Plan 12 more were referred to them for considering revival/restructuring/closure. A total of 28 of these had been recommended for winding up. Because of the delays inherent in the process of BIFR, the government has already sought to replace it by the National Company Law Tribunal (NCLT) but the creation of NCLT has been under dispute in the Honourable Supreme Court. Hearing in the special leave petition is already over and the final judgment has been reserved.

7.1.77 The government constituted a Board for Reconstruction of Public Sector Enterprises (BRPSE) in December 2004, as a part time advisory body to address the task of strengthening, modernization, revival, and restructuring of CPSEs. Until February 2007, the BRPSE had considered cases of 46 CPSEs received from 14 administrative ministries/departments and made recommendations in respect of 40 CPSEs. On the basis of the recommendations of BRPSE, the government has also approved the winding up of one CPSE, namely, Bharat Opthalmic Glass Limited. It has approved revival schemes in respect of 25 CPSEs, envisaging assistance of Rs 1951.30 crore in cash by way of equity/loan/grant and Rs 5709 crore by way of waiver of interest/loan/guarantee fees. Out of the 20 CPSEs for which the budgetary support has been sanctioned for revival, 13 had posted profits after tax in 2005–06 while the remaining have continued to incur losses. The data for 2006–07 that have been made available in respect of some CPSEs show that while some like the Cement Corporation of India, Heavy Engineering Corporation, Mineral Exploration Corporation Ltd (MECL), Bharat Compressors Ltd have shown better financial performance than projected in the revival proposal, others such as Hindustan Antibiotics Ltd and Andrew Yule & Company Ltd have been below the projected levels. Thus rehabilitation proposals have been effective in about 50% of the cases. However, it must be observed here that the improvement in market situation and hand-holding by the government in terms of price preference, placing of orders on nomination basis have also contributed to the success of the revival efforts of the government.

Performance of State-level Public Enterprises (SLPEs)

7.1.78 No regular survey is carried out for SLPEs. As on 31 March 2005, 1129 SLPEs were in operation (Table 7.1.8). The majority of SLPEs—about 50% in number—are in manufacturing followed by utilities, promotional, and welfare enterprises. The total investment in SLPEs increased every year in the post-economic reform period reaching a peak of Rs 285564 crore in 2002–03 before going into a declining trend ending up with Rs 259124 crore in 2004–05. The accumulated losses of SLPEs have been on the increase reaching a figure of Rs 60517 crore in 2004–05, with consequential adverse fiscal impact on the States. Table 7.1.8 gives the picture of the financial performance of SLPEs at the end of Seventh, Eighth, and Ninth Five Year Plan periods and in the first three years of the Tenth Five Year Plan. The overall financial health of SLPEs was very weak at the end of 2004–05.

7.1.79 A total of 579 manufacturing sector SLPEs constituted about 51% of the total number of 1129 SLPEs. Manufacturing SLPEs constituted a major share of the SLPEs portfolio in States such as Assam, Gujarat, Kerala, Maharashtra, Rajasthan, Tamil Nadu, Uttar Pradesh, and West Bengal. It is also noteworthy that a considerable number of these enterprises are taken over sick units. The investment in manufacturing enterprises increased from Rs 17099 crore in 1997–98 to Rs 23912 crore in 2004–05. The CAGR of investment was 4.2%. These enterprises incurred losses during all the years excluding 2003–04 and 2004–05. As a result of that their net worth in 2004–05 was Rs 12951 crore.

RESTRUCTURING OF SLPES

7.1.80 Some States have been active in restructuring sick PSEs. According to the information collected by Institute of Public Enterprises (IPE) Hyderabad upto 2004–05, 30 units including co-operatives had been privatized in Andhra, 3 in Gujarat, and 1 each in Haryana, Orissa, Punjab, and Rajasthan. West Bengal is another State which has shown substantial progress in the last two or three years. Out of 82 PSEs, 18 were profit making, and 63 loss making at the end of 2004–05. The Government of West Bengal has taken up restructuring of 34 units in the first phase, of which 4 have been successfully restructured under government ownership, 3 have been converted into joint ventures, and 21 units have been closed. The 34 units had about

TABLE 7.1.8
Performance Indicators of State-level Public Enterprises

(Rs Crore)

	1991–92	1996–97	2001–02	2002–03	2003–04	2004–05
Number of operating SLPEs						1129
Turnover	42986	86681	87375	86284	113208	127150
Total investment	90983	144471	280116	285564	247676	259184
Capital employed	83277	150291	179831	179627	232889	244770
Accumulated losses	8754	13122	22764	27353	64486	60517
Net worth	13248	35352	38429	44631		

Source: Study by IPE, Hyderabad.

11000 employees. With a view to reducing manpower these employees were offered compensation if they opted for early retirement. Insurance and retraining facilities were also given.

Future Strategies

7.1.81 In a globalized economy, cost-cutting strategic acquisitions and mergers are vital for facing international competition. CPSEs must have full autonomy and functional powers to take investment decisions to take advantage of the opportunities offered by the competitive international market. The informal levers of control from the ministries have no place in the competitive corporate world. Constitution of an independent Advisory Board to look after the government's interests in the CPSEs and leaving them to manage the corporation with the help of strong independent directors would be explored.

7.1.82 Substantial progress has been made in the revival of sick CPSEs, but close monitoring would be needed to ensure that the restructuring plans are successfully implemented. In considering the revival of the remaining sick CPSEs, greater caution is necessary as it has been seen that a few of the rehabilitated units are not performing in accordance with expectations.

7.1.83 The investment behaviour of the large profit-making CPSEs needs review. Many CPSEs appear to prefer investing in financial assets or reducing their debt burden in preference to investment which would contribute to capital formation. As on 31 March 2006, CPSEs have made financial investment to the tune of Rs 136558 crore. A substantial portion of this investment is by Navratna CPSEs. One reason for this phenomenon is the risk-averse nature of top management in CPSEs and the absence of institutional mechanisms which facilitate quick decision-making. The government has set up a special mechanism of an Empowered Committee of Secretaries in Ministries of Petroleum and Natural Gas, Ministry of Finance, and DPE for considering projects in the oil sector involving financial decisions above a certain threshold. The recommendations of this Empowered Committee are submitted to the CCEA directly for approval. Present mechanisms are inadequate to ensure optimum investment decisions. The supervisory body (that is, independent Advisory Board) suggested above could also be given the task of guiding and facilitating the investment decisions in all profit-making CPSEs.

7.1.84 The system of MoUs between CPSEs and the government has proved to be ineffective and dysfunctional. While the CPSEs are expected to perform in accordance with the norms, the government's commitments are marginal and not effectively monitored. There is a need to review and overhaul the system to ensure effective operational autonomy and functioning of the CPSEs. Financial delegations, particularly of the profit-making CPSEs, will have to be enhanced.

Autonomous Institutions in Industry Sector

7.1.85 Over the past Plans a number of autonomous institutions were set up to support the industry to meet various needs, such as technology transfer, skill development, and introduction of advanced technology. These institutions were designed to function in close coordination with industry and the governing bodies included all stakeholders. Some industry associations set up such institutes on their own initiative with initial government support. Some institutes such as the Central Pulp and Paper Research Institute (CPPRI) and Institute of Pesticides Formulation Technology (IPFT) were set up with assistance from international organizations such as United Nations Industrial Development Organization (UNIDO). Institutes such as the National Test House (NTH) have the backing of statutes for some of the activities although they work on a commercial basis also.

7.1.86 No systematic study has been carried out so far on a comprehensive basis on the functioning of these autonomous institutions. The Expenditure Reform Committee (ERC) in 2001 had recommended that budgetary support should be progressively reduced having regard to the scope for maximizing internal resources generation and restraining of expenditure growth. ERC also proposed greater autonomy to autonomous institutions whose performance had been outstanding and had received international acclaim and recommended that an MoU be entered into by autonomous institutions with the parent ministry/department, spelling out clearly not only the input but also more importantly the output targets.

7.1.87 There are about 24 institutions under the control of different ministries/departments concerning Industry Sector (see Box 7.1.1).

7.1.88 In the Tenth Plan, Budgetary support of about Rs 850 crore was provided to autonomous institutes for new infrastructure/modernization. Apart from institutes shown in the Box 7.1.1, there are a number of autonomous institutes providing services to small-scale industries, FPI, and handloom and handicraft industries. The emphasis in the Tenth Five Year Plan has been to enable the institutions to achieve higher levels of self-sufficiency and to provide only project-based support. An important new initiative during the Tenth Five Year Plan was to set up the National Automotive Testing and R&D Infrastructure Project (NATRIP) to meet the homologation and testing need of automotive industry. The seven centres of NATRIP in different locations in the country, mainly in the areas of concentration of manufacturing activity in automobiles and auto components, will be completed during the Eleventh Five Year Plan. Once completed, the individual centres will be managed by the industry with no recurring assistance from the government. During the Tenth Five Year Plan period new centres of NIFT, Central Institute of Plastics Engineering and Technology (CIPET), and NID were also set up.

7.1.89 The emphasis in the Eleventh Plan would continue to promote self-sufficiency in these institutions so that they can operate on a self-sustaining basis without the requirement of budgetary support. The government support will be limited to one time grants for the creation of new facilities, with recurring expenses being met from the revenues generated by them.

AREA DEVELOPMENT FOR INDUSTRY

7.1.90 Since the beginning of planned development, a policy has been followed for the development of industrial areas and industrial estates within such areas to facilitate the establishment of small and medium industrial units. Initiative has also been taken for improving the infrastructure of existing clusters outside of such areas. At the end of the Tenth Five Year Plan there were a multiplicity of schemes of cluster and area development established for the creation or upgradation of infrastructure as shown in Box 7.1.2.

Box 7.1.1
Autonomous Institutions in Industry Sector

- Quality Council of India (QCI).
- Central Manufacturing Technology Institute (CMTI), Bangalore.
- National Council for Cement and Building Materials.
- Indian Rubber Manufacturers Research Association (IRMRA).
- NID.
- National Productivity Council.
- Central Institute of Plastics Engineering and Technology (CIPET).
- National Institute of Pharmaceutical Education and Research (NIPER) and IPFT.
- Six Textiles Research Associations (TRAs).
- NIFT.
- Bureau of Indian Standards (BIS).
- NTH.
- Automotive Research Association of India (ARAI), Pune.
- NATRIP.
- Fluid Control Research Institute (FCRI).
- National Ship Design and Research Centre, Visakhapatnam.
- Biju Patnaik National Steel Institute.
- National Institute of Secondary Steel Technology.

Box 7.1.2
Industrial Area Development Schemes

- Growth Centre Scheme—announced in June 1988 and became operational from 1991—DIPP.
- Industrial Park Scheme 1999–2000, DIPP.
- IIUS 2003–04, DIPP.
- Apparel Parks for Exports 2001–02, Ministry of Textiles.
- Textile Centres Infrastructure Development Scheme (TCIDS) 2002–03, Ministry of Textiles.
- Scheme for Infrastructure Development 2002–03, MFPI.
- SEZs 2005–06, Department of Commerce.
- PURA—2004–05, Ministry of Rural Development.
- Scheme for Integrated Textile Parks (SITP) 2005–06, Ministry of Textiles.
- Petroleum, Chemicals, and Petrochemical Investment Regions (PCPIRs) 2006–07, Department of Chemicals and Petrochemicals.

7.1.91 Among the listed schemes the oldest is the Growth Centre Scheme of the DIPP, which was designed for promoting the development of manufacturing industries in industrially backward areas. Although as many as 52 growth centres were established, there was a weak response from the entrepreneurs to set up units within the centres, as a result of which large areas within the centres were lying vacant. The scheme was discontinued after the MTA of the Tenth Five Year Plan. The Industrial Parks Scheme, also of DIPP, envisaged the establishment of industrial parks for development of industrial infrastructure or built up space with common facilities in any area allotted or earmarked for the purposes of industrial development. Driven by the benefits available under Section 80 IA of the Income Tax Act 1961, as many as 270 industrial parks were set up. The objective of the Industrial Infrastructure Upgradation Scheme (IIUS) was to provide quality infrastructure facilities in existing functional clusters/industrial locations. Eligible activities included physical infrastructure such as water supply, effluent treatment, solid waste management, etc. A total of 26 industrial areas spread over 14 districts have been sanctioned assistance under the scheme. A feature of the IIUS is that it is based on PPP and the initiative has to come from the beneficiary units.

7.1.92 To improve the infrastructure facilities specifically for units in textiles and clothing, the Central Government initiated two CSS of the Ministry of Textiles in 2002, namely, (i) Textile Centres Infrastructure Development Scheme (TCIDS) with the objective of modernizing infrastructure facilities at major textiles centres in the country and (ii) Apparel Parks for Exports Scheme (APES) to promote setting up of modern apparel units at major growth centres. Although 19 TCIDS and 12 APES projects were taken up, the progress was slow and eventually none could be completed during the Tenth Five Year Plan. Consequently, the Scheme for Integrated Textile Parks (SITP) was introduced in 2005–06. As in the case of the IIUS, the SITP is based on PPP and is demand driven, and following a good response from the industry 30 SITP projects were taken up during the Tenth Five Year Plan.

7.1.93 The scheme for food parks was an element of the scheme for infrastructure development begun in 2002–03 by the MFPI. The scheme also envisaged the establishment of packaging centre, integrated cold chain facilities, value-added centre, and irradiation facilities. During the Tenth Five Year Plan, 18 food parks were approved, but progress was limited as only 8 were actually established with just 28 industrial units functioning within the parks. In 2004–05, the MoRD launched the scheme for Provision of Urban Amenities in Rural Areas (PURA) to encourage development of identified growth centres for the working population in the rural areas and prevent their migration to the urban areas. To start with, the development of clusters on a pilot basis has been envisaged at seven locations in the country.

7.1.94 A new scheme for SEZs has been launched by the Department of Commerce on the basis of the SEZ Act 2005. The objective of the scheme is to establish industrial townships divided into processing and non-processing areas. Apart from the existing export processing zones earlier set up by the Department of Commerce, which have been converted into SEZs, the establishment of new SEZs has been left to the initiative of private developers. The SEZs benefit from various tax incentives such as exemption from excise or customs duty, income tax exemption under Section 80-1AB of the Income Tax Act, exemption from minimum alternate tax, dividend distribution tax, CST, and Service Tax. Units in SEZs have access to the Domestic Tariff Area on payment of full customs duties on the finished product. The scheme has evoked a good response and up to the end of August 2007, 366 SEZs had been approved formally and 141 had been notified.

7.1.95 In 2006 another area development scheme known as the Petroleum, Chemicals, and Petrochemical Investment Regions (PCPIRs) was announced through a policy resolution of the Ministry of Chemicals and Petrochemicals. The PCPIR is a 'specifically delineated investment region/s with an area of around 250 sq km—including SEZ/s, Free Trade and Warehousing Zones, EOU units, and other existing industrial clusters—wherein is provided an internationally competitive and hassle-free environment with world-class infrastructure facilities to encourage global scale investments in petroleum, chemical, and petrochemical sectors to accelerate economic growth'. The policy provides for a duly notified SEZ to be set up within the PCPIR. Although a number of locations are under consideration, up to the end of August 2007, no State Government had initiated action for notifying a PCPIR.

7.1.96 Experience of establishing area development programmes up to the end of the Plan period seems to suggest that they can succeed only if they are demand driven and are so designed as to ensure that the initiative comes from entrepreneurs who are willing to commit not only to make a substantial initial capital investment on their part but also to run the programme on a self-sustaining basis.

7.1.97 The newly conceptualized Delhi–Mumbai Industry Corridor (DMIC) project is in partnership with Japan. An approximately 150 km wide band on either side of the proposed 1483 km long dedicated rail freight route is to be developed into a planned industrial belt. Several large hubs/nodes have been identified for development as large industrial regions in consultation with the government of the six States through which the corridor would pass. In the first phase (2008–09 to 2012–13), it will have six investment regions (about 200 sq km each) and six industrial areas (about 100 sq km each). The implementation would adopt a PPP approach.

Regional Development of Industry

7.1.98 The disparities in the performance on manufacturing output and employment of the States are reflected in Figure 7.1.4, which depicts the position as it stood in 2003–04.

7.1.99 The State-wise data on investment intentions notified to the DIPP during the Tenth Five Year Plan bring out some new trends (Annexure 7.1.5). While Gujarat, Karnataka, and Maharashtra continue to be in the forefront, Chhattisgarh, Jharkhand, Orissa, and West Bengal are getting increasing attention. The data on capital investments compiled by the RBI on the basis of the envisaged capital expenditure of companies that have been sanctioned assistance by banks and financial institutions show a different picture (Annexure 7.1.6). In 2006–07, Gujarat has emerged as the leading investment destination in the country, while Andhra Pradesh, Karnataka, Maharashtra, and Tamil Nadu are also attracting very substantial investments. Orissa too has come up, registering a substantial increase in projects in the pipeline during 2006–07. Jharkhand, Himachal Pradesh, and Uttarakhand have shown large increases in investment projects during the last two years of the Tenth Five Year Plan.

7.1.100 The most important determinant of the investment climate in the States is the state of physical infrastructure, particularly power and transport connectivity with the rest of the country. Although skilled personnel can move from other parts of the country, local availability of such personnel is an advantage. A fundamental requirement, however, is

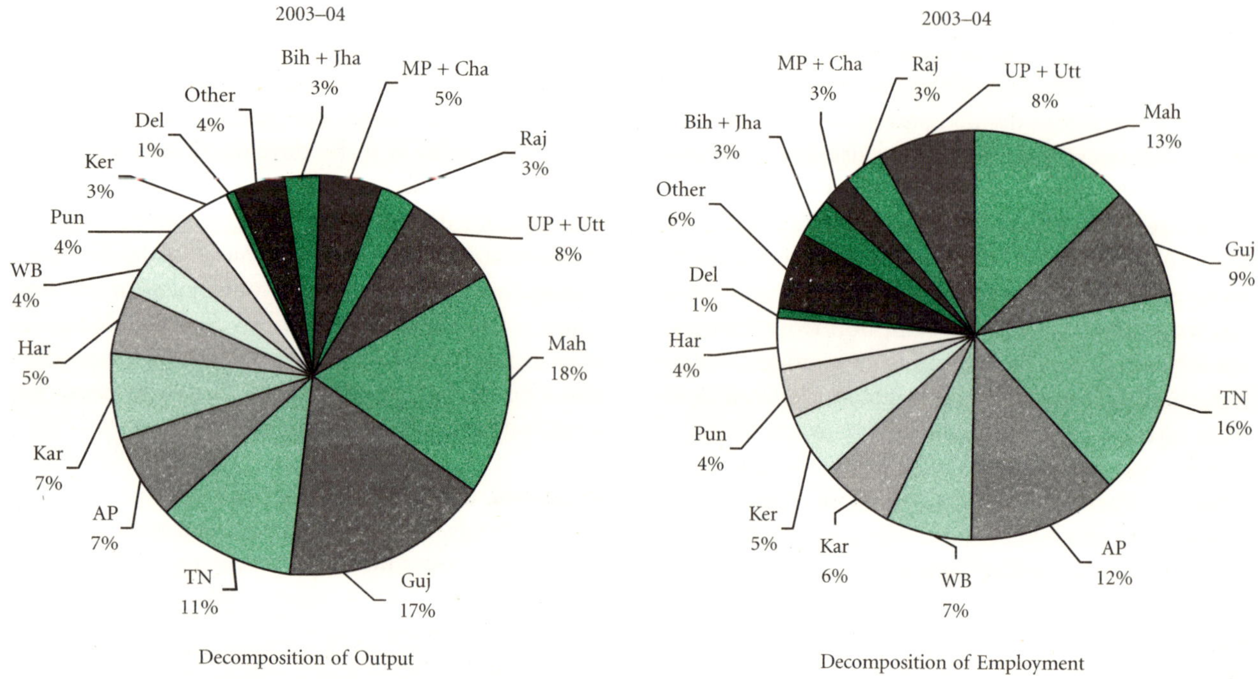

Source: 'Towards a Competitive Manufacturing Sector', ICRIER paper by Rajiv Kumar, Chief Executive and Director, ICRIER and Abhijit Sen Gupta, Fellow, ICRIER.

FIGURE 7.1.4: Contribution of States to Output and Employment in Manufacturing

social stability and the existence of the rule of law, giving confidence to the entrepreneurs that their life and property will be safeguarded. Efforts of the government have to address these prerequisites for fostering a more balanced industrial development of the country.

Central Government Initiatives for Balanced Industrial Development

7.1.101 On 24 December 1997, the Central Government notified the North East Industrial Policy (NEIP) providing a package of fiscal and other incentives aimed at facilitating the process of industrial development in the NER. During the Tenth Five Year Plan period, industrial incentives were extended to some other States. On 23 December 2002, similar incentives were extended to Sikkim, when it became a member of the North Eastern Council. A special package for J&K was announced on 14 June 2002. On 7 January 2003, the Central Government granted incentives for industrial investment to the States of Himachal Pradesh and Uttarakhand, which would remain for industries that are set up till 31 March 2010. The NEIP, which was originally valid until 31 March 2007, has been extended for another period of 10 years.

7.1.102 All the States covered by the incentive programmes benefit from full excise duty exemption on finished products as well as income tax exemption on profits as also from capital subsidy on investment in plant and machinery. The North Eastern States get additionally enhanced capital subsidy, interest subsidy on working capital loan, reimbursement of 100% premium under Comprehensive Insurance Schemes as well as transport subsidy of 50%–90% of the cost of transportation of raw materials and finished products to/from designated railheads. J&K also benefits from most of the additional incentives appli/cable to the North Eastern States. An evaluation report by a professional consultant in 2004 had brought that in the NER a total of 681 units had been set up from 1999 to September 2004, with an investment of Rs 1067.28 crore and employment generation of 20709. Assam accounted for about 49% of the investment and

Meghalaya for about 41%. The experience of other States is much better. According to the reports submitted by the State Governments concerned, the investment already made up to March 2007 was Rs 5902 crore in Uttarakhand, Rs 2884 crore in Himachal Pradesh, and Rs 3403 crore in J&K, the latter predominantly in the Jammu region. Data compilation from IEMs and RBI of the investment envisaged in projects receiving financial assistance from banks and financial institutions also suggest that the incentives have stimulated industrial activity in Himachal Pradesh and Uttarakhand significantly.

7.1.103 There have been complaints from not only the adjoining States but also from the States in the south of flight of capital induced by excise duty exemptions in Himachal Pradesh and Uttarakhand. Some other States with hilly regions such as West Bengal have raised questions of equity. During the Eleventh Five Year Plan, the industrial incentives would have to be closely monitored. Because of the distortions introduced by excise duty exemptions in particular, consideration would have to be given to replacing the incentives, fully or partly, by an accelerated programme for infrastructure improvement.

INTELLECTUAL PROPERTY RIGHTS (IPRS)

7.1.104 Recognizing the importance of the IPRs as a means for fostering innovation and contributing to enhanced economic growth and competitiveness, India has adopted a four-pronged strategy to strengthen its IPR regime: (i) to meet international obligations, (ii) to safeguard national interests, (iii) to modernize the IPR administration, and (iv) to create awareness regarding IPRs.

Legislation

7.1.105 In keeping with the above strategy, India has updated its Intellectual Property related legislation, that is, patents, trade marks, geographical indications, industrial designs, copyrights, biodiversity, semiconductor integrated circuits layout design, etc., so as meet its international obligations. At the same time, necessary safeguards to protect public interest have also been suitably incorporated in the Patents Act to ensure availability of patented products, including pharmaceuticals, at reasonably affordable price. The law also contains provisions which ensure that grant of patents for frivolous innovations resulting in 'evergreening' of patents would not be possible. 'Evergreening' of patents could have adverse consequences on both the availability as well as the prices of essential medicines impacting the health and lives of millions of people. The law thus encourages substantive R&D.

7.1.106 The legislative modernization exercise has also been utilized to streamline and rationalize the procedural aspects so as to make the system more efficient and user-friendly. Definitive timeframes have been prescribed for various activities by the Patent Offices. At the same time, the time lines available for the applicants and the public have been extended. In addition, the maximum time period for grant of patent has been reduced from 104 months to 52 months. A patent can be obtained in a shorter period depending upon the initiatives taken by the applicant.

Modernization of Infrastructure

7.1.107 As a part of improving and strengthening the infrastructure, the government has implemented modernization of IP Offices at a cost of Rs 153 crore in the Ninth and the Tenth Five Year Plans. This included: new, integrated IP offices in the four metros; strengthening of library and novelty search facilities by acquiring books, journals, and CD-ROMs of patents, designs, trademarks, and geographical indications granted or registered; and making operations in the IP offices IT enabled.

Impact

7.1.108 The legislative and administrative initiatives taken during the last few years have had a very positive impact on the creation and securing of IP in India during the Tenth Five Year Plan period. Patent filing which was a mere 11466 in 2002–03 has gone up by two and a half times to 28882 in 2006–07. The patents granted also registered a five-fold growth from 1379 to 7559 during the same period. The number of trademarks registered increased phenomenally from 11190 in 2002–03 to 109361 in 2006–07.

7.1.109 The Geographical Indications of Goods (Registration and Protection) Act 1999 was an entirely new legislation for India. This was brought into force on 15 September 2003 and with the initiatives taken by the government, it has been possible to generate 97 applications out of which 37 products have already been registered including Darjeeling tea, Chanderi saree, Pochampally ikat, etc.

7.1.110 A major initiative taken recently has been the announcement of a National Design Policy. This is expected to give a boost to the design sector in India where the country with its diversity and long cultural traditions has an edge over others.

7.1.111 The increase in the activities in the IP offices has also resulted in substantial growth in revenue generation. The income of the Patent and Trademark Offices, which was a mere Rs 17.06 crore in 2002–03 has gone up to Rs 163.67 crore in 2006–07. This has been possible because of the trust and confidence that the IP creators and owners developed in the services provided by these offices, particularly in clearing huge backlogs.

Second Phase of Modernization

7.1.112 Further modernization of IP offices has also been planned in the Eleventh Five Year Plan. This would address the needs of human resource development, training, and awareness and also infrastructure besides regular updating of the IT facilities.

7.1.113 The second phase of modernization would contribute toward making the Indian Intellectual Property Office (IPO) a front ranking IPO. The Indian IPO would be made an International Searching Authority (ISA) and an International Preliminary Examining Authority (IPEA) under the Patent Cooperation Treaty of World Intellectual Property Organization, placing it in an exclusive group of 12 countries currently recognized as ISA/IPEA. Accession to the Madrid Protocol, a facilitation system for international registration of trademarks, will also be considered. A National Institute for Intellectual Property Management will be established at Nagpur. The Institute will cater to the requirements of training and awareness and also act as a centre for policy, research, and IP think tank.

Plan Outlays and Expenditure in the Tenth Plan

7.1.114 The Industry and Mineral Sector spans 11 departments and ministries. The actual expenditure on the schemes in the industry sector was about Rs 25000 crore during the Tenth Five Year Plan period, which is 65% of the original outlay and 75% of the outlay as revised after the MTA. A summary of the Plan outlay and expenditure on major schemes in the industry sector during the Tenth Plan is given in Annexure 7.1.19. A review of the major schemes implemented during the Tenth Five Year Plan is given in the following paragraphs.

7.1.115 With a view to enhancing competitiveness by providing quality infrastructure in existing clusters, IIUS was launched in 2003 with an outlay of Rs 675 crore for assisting 20–25 clusters. The IIUS was envisaged as a user-driven scheme, based on PPP, implemented through a Special Purpose Vehicle (SPV) formed by the users, and administered by the Apex Committee in the DIPP. During the Tenth Five Year Plan, the Apex Committee sanctioned 26 projects with total cost of Rs 1766.18 crore and a GoI grant component of Rs 952.10 crore. A sum of Rs 437.38 crore was released up to the end of 2006–07. Evaluation has not been possible, as none of the schemes have been completed although several are in an advanced state of completion. However, since the design of the scheme ensures that the schemes are taken up only after the users have taken initiative and made investments, and several schemes are in an advanced state of completion, it will be useful to continue with the scheme in the Eleventh Five Year Plan. The scheme would need to undergo a mid-term review on the basis of the progress made.

7.1.116 A programme focused on tannery modernization in a small way was initiated in 1999 and during the Tenth Five Year Plan it was subsumed in an enlarged Indian Leather Development Programme (ILDP) with an approved outlay of Rs 400 crore, comprising two separate components, viz., Integrated Development of Leather Sector (IDLS) and Infrastructure Strengthening of Leather Sector with outlays of Rs 290 crore and Rs 110 crore, respectively. Owing to late sanction on the account of procedural delays in the GoI the scheme could not take off during the Tenth Five Year Plan and will spill over into the Eleventh Five Year Plan.

7.1.117 The major schemes implemented by the Ministry of Textiles are the TUFS, Technology Mission on Cotton (TMC), APES, and TCIDS.

7.1.118 The TUFS was initially introduced in 1999 with the objective to provide adequate impetus to all the sub-sectors of textiles and jute industry by way of 5% interest reimbursement so as to reduce the cost of capital for modernization. Small-scale textile and jute industrial units were given an option either to avail Credit-linked Capital Subsidy (CLCS) or interest reimbursement. An additional option of credit linked 20% capital subsidy for small-scale powerloom and weaving preparatory machinery, with the option to obtain credit from an enlarged credit network, was also introduced. Besides, an additional capital subsidy of 10% for benchmarked processing machinery over and above the extant 5% interest reimbursement was started in April 2005. In the Tenth Plan, as against the loan disbursed by the banks and financial institutes of Rs 18506 crore, subsidy amount of Rs 2043.66 crore was granted under the scheme. In the Eleventh Plan period, there is a spillover liability of Rs 984 crore relating to the subsidy for the projects sanctioned during the Tenth Plan period. Preliminary findings of the evaluation of the scheme by a professional consultant reveal an improvement in profitability and productivity. However, substantial dependence on import of second-hand machinery and low share of powerloom and processing sector have emerged as areas of concern. In view of the continuing need to stimulate investment and the positive response of the industry to the scheme, the TUFS would need to be continued during the Eleventh Five Year Plan.

7.1.119 The SITP was launched in August 2005. The primary objective of the scheme is to provide the industry with world-class infrastructure facilities for setting up of textile units in clusters. As in the case of IIUS, the scheme is being implemented through SPVs with industry associations/groups of entrepreneurs as the main promoters of the integrated textile parks. GoI's support under the scheme by way of grant or equity is limited to 40% of the project cost, subject to a ceiling of Rs 40.00 crore. The SITP envisaged creation of 30 new textile parks of international standards in potential growth centres before 2007–08. An amount of Rs 625.00 crore was allocated for the development of these parks against which Rs 88.27 crore of GoI grant was released till the end of the Tenth Five Year Plan. In all the 30 schemes, the SPV has been formed and land has been acquired. Since 9 schemes were sanctioned late in 2005–06 and the remaining 21 in the period after July 2006, none of the projects has been completed. A major factor has been that the industry is awaiting the issuance of the guidelines for the revised TUFS before moving for bank loans for the units within the parks. During the Eleventh Five Year Plan the first priority will have to be completion of the 30 projects already taken in hand but provision will have to be made for additional projects within the available plan allocation.

7.1.120 In addition to the SITP there were two pre-existing schemes, the APES and the TCIDS, which were commenced in 2002. A total of 18 projects were sanctioned under TCIDS and 12 under APES, with a GoI assistance of Rs 271.06 crore and Rs 191.70 crore, respectively. An amount of Rs 172.50 crore is estimated to have been spent by the end of the Tenth Five Year Plan under APES and TCIDS. There was a design defect in these schemes in as much as the schemes were implemented on the initiative of the State Governments without the assurance of interest among the entrepreneurs. As a result, these schemes have been languishing. An assessment would need to be made on the sustainability of these schemes, and during the Eleventh Five Year Plan only those would need to be assisted in which there is an interest among the entrepreneurs.

7.1.121 The Technology Mission on Cotton (TMC) was launched in February 2000, with the objective of bringing tangible improvement in the productivity and quality of cotton. An evaluation of the scheme by a professional consultant has indicated marked improvement by way of reduced contamination levels in cotton processed by the modernized Ginning and Pressing (G&P) factories matching to international levels. It is expected that 80% of the cotton produced in the country would be able to meet the higher standards of international markets on completion of modernization of 1000 G&P factories. This scheme too will need to be continued during the Eleventh Five Year Plan.

7.1.122 The Consumer Protection Act has been in operation for about 20 years. The objective of the Central Consumer Protection Council established under the Act is to promote and protect consumer rights that include the right to be informed and the right to consumer education. The consumer movement is still in infancy in the country. One of the reasons for the slow progress is lack of consumer awareness especially in the rural areas. The National Action Plan taken up by the Department of Consumer Affairs envisages a two-pronged approach, that is creating consumer awareness and strengthening grievance readressal machinery for consumer protection. A new service, National Consumer Helpline, was launched during 2004–05. From the expenditure level of Rs 9.12 crore in the first three years of the Tenth Five Year Plan, the allocation was stepped up significantly to Rs 67.49 crore and Rs 69.40 crore during 2005–06 and 2006–07, respectively. The multimedia campaign covered topics such as maximum retail price (MRP), gold hallmarking, ISI mark on products, expiry dates, and consumer rights. About Rs 70.00 crore was utilized on consumer awareness *'Jago Grahak Jago'* campaign during each of the years 2005–06 and 2006–07. An evaluation of the scheme carried out by the Indian Institute of Mass Communication (IIMC) in August 2006 has shown that the percentage of recall of the campaign among the consumers was 65% in the sample states.

7.1.123 The industry programmes run by the Department of Atomic Energy (DAE) provide inputs such as structural materials, fuels, heavy water, and electronics and instrumentation to the nuclear power plants. The Department is also engaged in activities pertaining to fuel reprocessing, waste management, and thermal and fast reactor technology. The industry programmes were allocated Rs 818.93 crore but the expenditure was higher at Rs 1280.88 crore. Some of the developments during the Tenth Plan were the following: augmentation of existing zirconium sponge plant and capacity expansion of zirconium oxide plant, modification of heavy water plant, tube bundle for condensers, heavy water clean up facility, boron exchange distillation facility, advanced vetrification system, large capacity spent fuel storage facilities, fabrication of fuel and structural materials, and Instrumentation packages for nuclear power plants.

7.1.124 The ship-building sector of the Department of Shipping was allocated Rs 1047.86 crore against which the actual expenditure has been Rs 282.45 crore. The shortfall in expenditure was on account of the fact that the expansion plans of Cochin Shipyard Ltd and the revival plan of Hindustan Shipyard Ltd (HSL) did not materialize.

7.1.125 The outlay of the Ministry of Steel was revised from Rs 11044 crore to Rs 8477 crore at MTA stage, mainly financed by Internal and Extra Budgetary Resources (IEBR), except for Rs 65 crore. The actual expenditure on steel sector schemes was Rs 4119 crore out of total expenditure of Rs 4825 crore in the Industry and Minerals (I&M) sector. Implementation of the modernization and expansion programmes of Steel Authority of India Ltd (SAIL) was sluggish in the first three years of the plan. The expansion plan of Rashtriya Ispat Nigam Ltd (RINL) from 3.5 million per year hot metal capacity to 6.3 million per year hot metal capacity, which was approved in 2005, also remained behind schedule.

7.1.126 The outlay of the Department of Heavy Industry was increased in the later half of the Tenth Five Year Plan with the new emphasis in the government policy on restructuring of sick PSEs. The overall expenditure was Rs 2606 crore. The expenditure on 'support to existing public sector undertakings' and 'restructuring of CPSEs' was increased considerably. The progress of expenditure in respect of the NATRIP scheme was satisfactory. Revival and restructuring of the Nagaland Pulp and Paper Company Ltd at Tuli, Nagaland and expansion of the Hindustan Newsprint Ltd, Kerala were taken up during the Tenth Plan in addition to restructuring of 14 sick CPSEs based on the recommendation of BRPSE.

7.1.127 The DBT took up a new scheme for setting up of biotechnology incubators, pilot-level facilities, and biotech parks. Subsequently, a new scheme under the PPP mode to promote Small Business Innovation Research Initiative (SBIRI) towards development of new technologies/products through industry academia interaction was also started. Under the Biotech Park Scheme two projects were taken up for implementation: setting up of the Biotechnology Park at Lucknow and establishment of Biotechnology Incubators Centre at Shapoorji Pallonji Biotech Park at Hyderabad. Financial support for another four incubation centres was also provided. The actual implementation of SIBRI scheme commenced in 2005–06 and some research projects have been supported. The schemes were initially allocated Rs 30 crore in the Tenth Five Year Plan but the expenditure was higher at Rs 102 crore.

Eleventh Plan Outlays and Major Schemes

7.1.128 Eleventh Plan outlays of various ministries/departments concerning the industry sector are indicated in Annexure 7.1.19. The scheme-wise break-up is indicated in the Appendix, Volume III. Major ongoing and new schemes are as follows.

Ongoing Schemes

- TUFS
- SITP
- TMC
- Second phase of NATRIP
- Modernization and strengthening of Intellectual Property offices
- IIUS
- Setting up of Biotechnology Incubators, Biotech parks and SBIRI
- Industry segment of DAE
- Strengthening, reviving, and restructuring of PSEs
- North East Industrial and Investment Promotion Policy, and package for special category states

New Schemes

- ILDP (modified and increased coverage)
- Scheme for enhancement of competitiveness in capital goods sector
- Setting up of National Institute of Pharmaceutical Education and Research (NIPER) like institutes for pharmaceutical sector
- Schedule M compliance by SMEs in Drugs and Pharmaceuticals
- Capital Subsidy for conversion of existing Furnace Oil (FO)/Low Sulphur Heavy Stock based fertilizer plants to NG/liquefied natural gas (LNG)
- DMIC
- R&D in ship-building sector

Sectoral Profiles

The Automotive Industry

7.1.129 If there is one manufacturing industry in India that has moved from strength to strength after the economic reforms of 1991–92, it is the automotive sector. It has grown at the spectacular rate of 17% over the last few years, with an investment of Rs 50000 crore in 2005–06 (and another Rs 30000 crore in the pipeline), attaining a turnover of Rs 165000 crore. In 2005–06, the passenger car segment crossed the one million mark.

7.1.130 At present the direct employment in the industry is 2 lakh in vehicle manufacturing and 2.8 lakh in component companies. With the additional investment and increase in production, it is expected that the direct employment in the sector will double in the next five years. In 2005–06, the component manufacturers added investment worth US$ 1 billion (Rs 4500 crore) in new capacity. In 2006–07, the automobile manufacturers have announced investment of Rs 60380 crore and the component manufacturers have announced investment of Rs 2523 crore so far.

Production and Exports of Vehicles

7.1.131 The production of various categories of automobiles in the Tenth Five Year Plan period grew at a CAGR of 16% crossing the 10 million mark in 2006–07, as shown in the Annexure 7.1.7.

7.1.132 The industry proved its international competitiveness in all categories of vehicles by achieving a CAGR of 35% in exports during the Tenth Five Year Plan period (Annexure 7.1.7). The segments that have shown particular buoyancy are passenger vehicles, two wheelers, and three wheelers, which have risen four-fold, six-fold, and ten-fold, respectively, during the Tenth Five Year Plan period as compared to the last year of the Ninth Five Year Plan. About 2 lakh passenger vehicles and 6 lakh two wheelers were exported in 2006–07.

AUTO COMPONENTS

7.1.133 The performance of the Indian auto components industry has been even more impressive. Around 500 manufacturers in the organized sector and more than 10000 in the small-scale sector had a turnover of about Rs 54000 crore (US$ 12 billion) in 2005–06. The auto components industry now has holistic capability, manufacturing the entire range of components. The share of different segments in the industry are engine parts (31%), transmission parts (19%), suspension and braking parts (12%), electrical parts (9%), body and chassis parts (12%), equipment (10%), and others (7%). This has enabled the wholly Indian producers to achieve full indigenization in popular makes such as Tata Indica, Tata Indigo, Mahindra Scorpio, Bajaj Pulsar, TVS Victor, etc. The fact that nine manufacturers are Deming Prize winners, four are Japan Institute of Plant Maintenance award winners, and one is a Japan Quality Medal winner bear testimony to quality of the auto components produced in India.

7.1.134 One of the biggest auto ancillary industries in the country is the tyre industry. The total installed capacity is 850 lakh units against which 660 lakh units were produced and 620 lakh units were consumed within the country in 2005–06. All types of tyres barring some specialized ones such as aircraft tyres and snow tyres are now manufactured in the country.

7.1.135 India's exports of auto components have been growing even faster than of complete vehicles. During the last three years of the Tenth Five Year Plan period exports have grown by 40%, 50%, and 33%, respectively, and annual exports crossed Rs 11000 crore in 2006–07. A quantum forward leap in the quality of Indian auto components has brought about a major change in the customer base in global markets. In the 1990s, more than 80% of the exports were to the international after-market. In the year 2005–06, more than 70% of the exports were to the global original equipment manufacturers (OEMs) and Tier 1 companies.

PROJECTION OF GROWTH IN PRODUCTION AND EXPORTS OF VEHICLES AND COMPONENTS

7.1.136 The inherent strength of the Indian automotive industry has given it the confidence to make a bold projection of growth in production and exports of vehicles during the Eleventh Five Year Plan. Table 7.1.9 gives the projections for the last year of the Eleventh Five Year Plan as compared to the achievement in the last year of the Tenth Five Year Plan.

TABLE 7.1.9
Projection of Growth in Vehicle Production and Exports in the Eleventh Five Year Plan

(In Thousand)

Category	Production		Export	
	2006–07	2011–12	2006–07	2011–12
Passenger Vehicles	1238	1850	192	462
Multi-utility Vehicles (MUVs)	306	321	6	12
Commercial Vehicles (CVs)	520	604	50	71
Two wheelers	8444	18934	619	1634
Three wheelers	556	903	144	229
Total	11065	22612	1011	2408

Source: Report of the Eleventh Five Year Plan Working Group on Automotive Industry.

7.1.137 The projections of auto component exports are even more ambitious. The projection made by the Eleventh Five Year Plan Working Group on Automotive Industry is given in Figure 7.1.5.

CHALLENGES

7.1.138 Improvement of infrastructure to lower logistical cost is the most critical requirement of the auto and auto components industry. The major clusters of the auto industry are in and around Gurgaon and Manesar in the north, Pune in the west, Chennai and Bangalore in the south, Jamshedpur and Kolkata in the east, and Indore in central India. However, industry depends upon movement of large volumes of raw materials and finished products by surface transport to and from every part of the country. Speedy transport of goods can contribute considerably to increasing its competitiveness. At present transport of auto components from Ludhiana to assembly plants in Kolkata takes as many as five days, thereby increasing

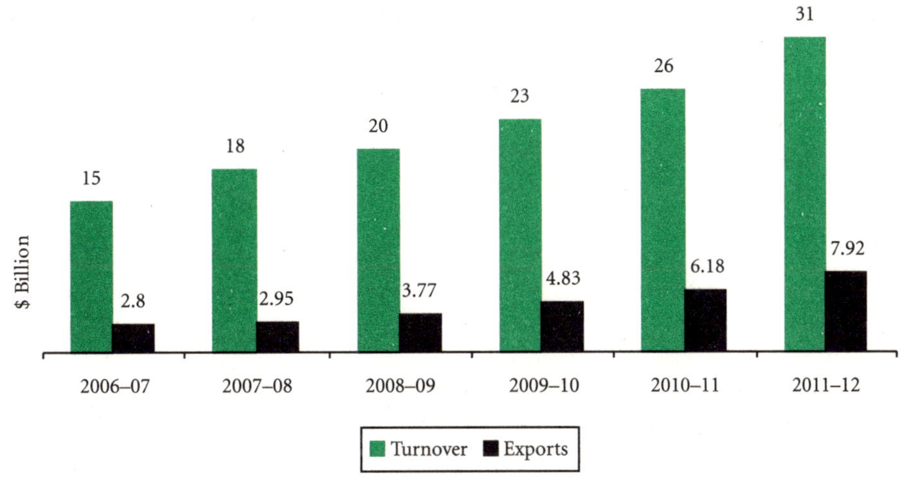

Source: Working Group on Automotive Industry for Eleventh Five Year Plan.

FIGURE 7.1.5: Auto Components—Projection of Turnover and Exports

the working capital requirement and making the adoption of just-in-time manufacturing impossible.

7.1.139 Since the industry will become increasingly export-oriented, the port infrastructure is also crucial for its development. Chennai and Mumbai ports, which handle the bulk of the exports of vehicles, lack space for parking and repair of vehicles damaged in transit. The longer turnaround time and poor port connectivity are also impediments that need to be addressed.

7.1.140 Adequate and supply of quality power is another infrastructure requirement. It is estimated that the industry will need an incremental supply of 12000 MW of power during the Eleventh Five Year Plan period.

7.1.141 Harmonization of emission norms as per Economic Commission for Europe (ECE) guidelines, measures to increase road safety, computerization and interconnection of Regional Transport Authorities (RTOs) to enable recall of vehicle in case of defects, mandatory inspection and certification of vehicles in use are other suggestions that have been made for the benefit of the vehicle users as well as the industry.

7.1.142 The industry needs to strive continuously for innovation and upgradation for increasing its productivity, and for this the industry has to carry out R&D activities. The government encourages research by giving weighted reduction in corporate tax for expenditure incurred on R&D, but the provision is renewed for short periods, discouraging long-term commitment to R&D. In addition to the fiscal benefits, the government's assistance is needed for setting up world-class automotive testing and R&D infrastructure.

STRATEGIES

7.1.143 The substantial programme for improvement of transport infrastructure and power being undertaken during the Eleventh Five Year Plan and described elsewhere in this document will go a long way toward alleviating the problems faced by the automotive industry. Of special relevance to the automotive industry will be the Dedicated Freight Corridor (DFC) of the railways, the expressways, and the port modernization programme. With the expected increase in exports of completed vehicles, it is necessary to consider dedicating existing or new berths for export of vehicles, at Mumbai, Chennai, and Kolkata, with provision for ample parking space.

7.1.144 An ambitious NATRIP has already been commenced in the Tenth Five Year Plan, for full-fledged testing and homologation centres in Manesar and Chennai, upgradation of existing testing and homologation centre at Pune and Ahmednagar, world-class testing tracks at Nagpur, facilities for testing of tractors and off-road vehicles at Rae Bareilly, and hill area driving training centre at Silchar. Substantial work remains to be done to complete the initiative.

7.1.145 Concessions in corporate taxes for R&D expenditure must be made a permanent feature of our corporate tax laws.

7.1.146 A National Road Safety Board needs to be established at an early date as recommended by the Sunder Committee set up by the Ministry of Roads, Transport, and Highways. Mandatory inspection and certification of in-use vehicles is also a pre-requisite for improving road safety. Computerization of RTOs and their interconnection is also a desirable course of action from the point of view of effective regulation of transport services and also for facilitating recall if a manufacturing defect is detected.

7.1.147 It is necessary for the industry to achieve international safety and pollution standards by 2015 by aligning the domestic standards with the ECE regulations.

7.1.148 In order to meet the growing scarcity of trained human resources there is need to consider the setting up of a National Level Automotive Institute for running training courses in the automobile sector and formulating courses and modules for training in the automobile sector to be imparted by various Industrial Training Institutes (ITIs) and Automotive Training Institutes (ATIs). It is also necessary to create centres of automotive manufacturing excellence in four IITs and open an auto design centre at NID Ahmedabad. The OEMs and Tier 1 component manufacturers could be encouraged to adopt ITIs and ATIs.

7.1.149 Encouragement through suitable fiscal concessions should be provided for manufacture and assembly of fuel-efficient and hybrid vehicles and for use of alternative fuels for promoting energy conservation and environmental protection.

7.1.150 The main ongoing Plan scheme is setting-up of NATRIP. In the Eleventh Plan an outlay of Rs 1407 crore has been made to complete the second phase of the project.

Capital Goods and Engineering Industry

7.1.151 The Indian engineering industry has emerged as a dynamic sector in the country's industrial economy and has made the country self-reliant in key areas. The capital goods value addition contributes about 9%–12% to the total manufacturing. The annual production of the capital goods industry stood at Rs 50000 crore as of 2003–04. The capital investments made in this sector have registered a healthy CAGR of close to 10% during the period from 1995 to 2005, the investment picking up from 2001–02.

7.1.152 The five major sectors in the capital goods industry, viz., electrical machinery, process plant equipment, mining and construction machinery, machine tools, and textile machinery contribute nearly 57% of the total sector. The production, export, and import in these five sectors are presented in Annexure 7.1.8. Production of the five segments grew at rates ranging between 12% and 32%. Exports of machine tools, mining and construction machinery, and process plant equipment grew impressively and export of textile machinery grew modestly. Exports of electrical machinery fell during the Tenth Five Year Plan.

MACHINE TOOLS SECTOR

7.1.153 The industry constitutes 450 manufacturing units of which nearly 33% are in the organized sector. Top 10 companies in the sector contribute to almost 73% of the total production in the sector. Since 2002, the industry has shown a healthy growth and as in 2006, production in the sector has been growing at 12% and export at 17%. The industry's turnover in 2006–07 was Rs 2900 crore and it is estimated that the industry's turnover would be Rs 6000 crore by 2011–12.

7.1.154 During the Tenth Plan, the support measures by the government were in the form of machine tool cluster under IIUS Scheme, UNIDO-sponsored Bangalore Machine Tool Cluster and support for infrastructure and technology development to CMTI, Bangalore.

TEXTILE MACHINERY

7.1.155 The textile engineering industry currently has an annual installed capacity to the tune of Rs 3800 crore per annum and the capacity utilization has gone up from 55% to 67% during 2005–06 over its preceding year. The size of the industry is likely to grow up to Rs 10000 crore by 2010. The industry is unable to cope with the demand of domestic textile and clothing units and at present it is estimated that 80% of the requirement is being imported. The liberal policy of import of second-hand textile machinery promoted in the sector has affected the prospect of fresh investment in the sector.

INDIAN HEAVY ELECTRICAL INDUSTRY

7.1.156 The Indian heavy electrical industry has registered a growth of almost 20% during 2004–05 over its preceding year. The fortune of the industry is closely linked to the development of power sector in the country. A capacity addition of 78000 MW is planned in the Eleventh Five Year Plan. There is a substantial order backlog in the industry that is to be completed over a span of two years. Capacity addition in the country, particularly for the manufacture of boilers, has become imperative. The sector is experiencing difficulties in technology transfer since foreign companies can now directly participate in the infrastructure projects. The level of R&D and technology innovation within the country is low by international standards.

MINING AND CONSTRUCTION EQUIPMENT SECTOR

7.1.157 The mining and construction equipment industry is dominated by a few large manufacturers in each product segment. Bharat Earth Movers Limited supplies to nearly half of the total market. The mining and construction equipment sector registered a healthy growth in its output and exports over the last two years. The domestic demand has increased from a level of Rs 6300 crore in 2004–05 to Rs 8400 crore in 2006–07.

PROCESS PLANT EQUIPMENT INDUSTRY

7.1.158 The process plant machinery and componenet industry in India is a very heterogeneous industry with a turnover of Rs 10000 crore per annum as of 2004–05. The growth projection for 2005–06 manufacturing total equipment in the process industry was Rs 6000 crore, a jump of 15% on an average. Owing to the fragmented nature of the industry and the small size of the players, most of them have not implemented any of the latest soft technologies.

CHALLENGES

7.1.159 The Indian Capital Goods Industry shares with other industries the major hindrances to growth in the country, which are low scale of operation, technological dependence, high input costs (raw materials, power, fuel, and high rates of interest on term loan and working capital), lack of world-class infrastructure, and stringent labour laws.

7.1.160 Some of the problems specific to the sector are purchase preference to CPSEs and unimpeded imports of second-hand machinery.

STRATEGIES

7.1.161 To encourage investment, assistance would need to be provided for setting up of sector-specific parks in machine tools, textiles machinery, and heavy electricals. Apart from general infrastructure, the parks could also have CFCs such as testing laboratories and R&D centres. But the process would have to be demand driven and the initiative would have to come from the industry.

7.1.162 On the same pattern as sector-specific parks, CFCs for existing clusters could be set up with facilities for testing, R&D, heat treatment, etc., on the model of the IIUS scheme of the DIPP.

7.1.163 To bring some level playing between private sector and CPSEs, the purchase preference policy for CPSEs would need to be discontinued.

7.1.164 The policy for import of second-hand capital goods in textiles and other areas should be reviewed and government assistance by way of interest subsidy on bank finance should not be provided for imports of such capital goods.

7.1.165 For attracting investors from abroad who have the necessary technology in textile machinery, it is necessary to mount a campaign. It is also necessary to induce foreign companies manufacturing electrical generation equipment to set up manufacturing facilities in the country by introducing an offset clause in the procurement of generation units for PSUs.

Cement

7.1.166 Although India is the second largest cement producer in the world, it is way behind China, where the capacity is more than five times larger. The industry provides direct employment to 70000 people and has the capability to create huge indirect employment downstream. It has a high rate of excise duty and accounts for 5% of total excise collection.

CAPACITY, PRODUCTION, AND EXPORTS OF CEMENT

7.1.167 During the Tenth Plan, cement production grew at a healthy CAGR of 8.67% while the installed capacity showed modest CAGR of 3.69%. Exports too showed an upward trend. The growth in capacity, production, and export are given in Table 7.1.10.

TABLE 7.1.10
Capacity, Production, and Export of Cement

(Million mt)

Year	Capacity	Production	Exports
2002–03	151.17	116.35	6.92
2003–04	157.74	123.50	9.00
2004–05	165.39	133.57	10.06
2005–06	171.34	147.81	9.19
2006–07	174.99#	162.00*	10.00
CAGR%	3.69	8.67	14.24

Note: #Capacity: As in June 2006; *Estimated.
Source: Report of the Working Group on Cement Industry for the Eleventh Five Year Plan.

7.1.168 The industry has been modernizing and some units can now boast of having the state-of-the-art technology plants with energy consumption comparable with the best in the world. Till the late 1970s, a major share of production relied on the inefficient wet process technology. By 2006, 96% of the production had shifted to the dry process. The average consumption of energy in domestic industry hovers around 725 kcal per kg of clinker (thermal energy) and 82 kWh per tonne of cement (electrical energy). The best thermal and electrical energy consumption is as low as 667 kcal per kg of clinker and 68 kWh per mt of cement, which are comparable to the best global figures of 650 kcal per kg of clinker and 65 kWh per mt of cement.

DEMAND FORECAST AND INVESTMENT REQUIREMENT FOR THE ELEVENTH PLAN

7.1.169 Cement consumption has generally grown at 2%–3% higher than growth of GDP. Keeping the past trends in view and taking into consideration the renewed emphasis on infrastructure, the cement industry can be expected to grow at about 11.5% corresponding to the GDP growth of 9%. The demand projections in 2011–12 are given in Figure 7.1.6.

7.1.170 Realization of capacity projection of 298 million tonnes would imply a capacity addition of 118 million mt during the Eleventh Plan period. Of the total capacity addition required for the Eleventh Plan, 86 million mt would come from new greenfield units requiring an investment of Rs 34400 crore and 32 million tonnes through brown field expansions/de-bottlenecking requiring investment of Rs 6400 crore. Thus the total investment requirement during the Eleventh Plan works out to Rs 52400 crore together with Rs 1100 crore and Rs 500 crore required for conversion of existing wet process plants to dry process technology and setting up of coal washeries.

ISSUES AND CHALLENGES

7.1.171 Achievement of growth and targets for the cement industry is crucially dependent on various inputs such as limestone, coal, power, and last but not the least, on transportation of limestone. Coal

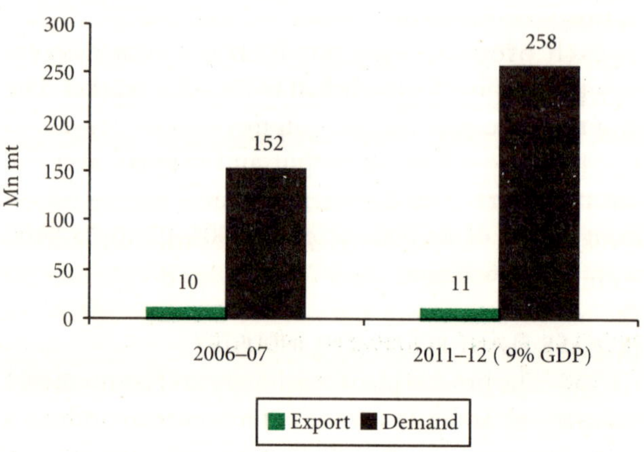

Source: Report of the Working Group on Cement Industry for the Eleventh Five Year Plan.

FIGURE 7.1.6: Cement—Export, Project Demand and Capacity needed by 2011–12

continues to be the main fuel for the cement industry and will remain so in the near future. At present, 60% of coal requirement of the cement industry is met through linkages and fuel supply agreements, while the remaining requirement is met from open-market purchases, import, and use of petroleum coke. With the capacity addition projected for the Eleventh Plan, the annual requirement of coal would substantially go up from the current level of 28.68 million tonnes to 57.97 million tonnes by the end of the Eleventh Plan. Side-by-side depletion of higher quality of coal reserves and increasing open cast mine would call for increasing beneficiation of coal in the regional washeries.

7.1.172 The production of cement is a continuous process requiring uninterrupted power supply. Since the availability and quality of grid power supply continue to be a problem, the use of captive power has been increasing. Most of the cement units have installed captive power generation capacities to the extent of 60% to 100% of their requirement. The captive power generation capacity of cement industry is estimated to be 1825 MW at present, of which 61% is based on diesel and the rest 39% on coal. With growing uncertainties of grid power availability, it is estimated that 2000 MW captive power would be required during Eleventh Plan.

7.1.173 Cement is a low-value and high-volume commodity mainly concentrated near limestone deposits available in a few States. The main input coal is also available in a few States. In view of this, long leads of movement both for inputs and for outputs are required and the railways remain the only economical mode for such transportation. Against the envisaged level of 60% movement of cement production by rail on macro level, the current share of dispatches through rail accounts for 39%–45% after continuous decline during the past decade. With the intended capacity addition in the Eleventh Plan, requirement of rail facilities for movement of cement and clinker as well as other inputs such as coal, granulated slag, and fly ash would increase substantially.

7.1.174 The availability of cement grade limestone is essential for making technological and financial decisions of the entrepreneurs for capacity addition projected for the Eleventh Plan. The gross reserves of cement grade limestone stood at 97430 million tonnes as on 31 March 2006 as under.

7.1.175 Out of 97430 million tonnes of gross reserves as on 31 March 2006, proven reserves are only 22931 million tonnes. Since 50% of the proven reserves are located in inaccessible or ecologically sensitive areas, these would suffice only for the lifecycle of cement plant that would be existing at the end of the Eleventh Plan period.

7.1.176 Modernization of the construction industry is heavily dependent on the availability of cement in bulk and ready-mix concrete (RMC) usage. However, bulk transportation of cement in our country accounts for only 5% as against the global average of 70%. Likewise use of RMC in construction activity is only 10% in India. RMC usage and bulk transportation of cement complement each other with inherent advantages of lower pilferage, higher consistency, and environment-friendly application. A major limiting factor in bulk handling of cement is the small number of bulk cement terminals in the country. There are only two rail bulk cement terminals and three port-based bulk cement terminals in the country.

7.1.177 Ordinary Portland Cement is currently used in the government/public sector for most of the construction activities. However, the performance requirement of most constructions could be met by the use of Portland Pozzolana Cement/slag cement, and in fact these types should be preferred as they conserve non-renewable resources.

STRATEGIES

7.1.178 Additions to capacity to the tune of 118 million mt projected for the Eleventh Plan would be critically dependent on the measures adopted to mitigate logistics-related issues. Substantial augmentation of railway capacity being envisaged in the Eleventh Five Year Plan will help in meeting the requirements of the cement industry. However, to facilitate long-term planning and to ensure that adequate handling and storage facilities and wagon capacity are created, the railways should set up a consultative process with the industry.

7.1.179 Bulk cement transportation in specialized tankers, viz., railway wagons, trucks, or ships provide business opportunities to railways, truck, and cargo operators. Setting up bulk cement terminals would help in attracting huge investments. Wherever possible the railways could provide land on long-term lease for the purpose.

7.1.180 Concerted efforts would be required to identify new commercially exploitable limestone deposits. Joint exploration should be intensified by various State departments of mines and geology in association with the Indian Bureau of Mines (IBM), MECL, etc., for exploring and identification of new limestone deposit.

7.1.181 With a view to promoting the use of PPC and slag cement, construction codes of the Central and State Governments need to be appropriately modified to allow their use. Furthermore, in addition to standards for slag and fly ash based cement, Bureau of Industrial Standards should work for setting standards of cement using more than one waste material.

7.1.182 Installation of greenfield mini-cement plants should not be encouraged except in deficient far-flung areas, that is North Eastern States, J&K, etc. The ceiling on the capacity of a mini-cement plant should be removed and they should be set free to use the most economically viable technology.

Chemical Industry

7.1.183 The chemical industry is an important constituent of the Indian economy with an estimated turnover at around US$ 35 billion, constituting 1.5% of the global chemical industry estimated at US$ 2400 billion. The total investment in the sector is nearly US$ 60 billion and the employment is about one million. It accounts for 13%–14% of total exports and 8%–9% of total imports of the country. Gujarat dominates with 51% of the total share of major chemicals produced in the country. Various sub-sectors such as chloralkali, inorganic chemicals, organic chemicals, dyestuffs and dye intermediates, and agrochemicals grew at varying rates during the Tenth Five Year Plan, with inorganic chemicals recording the highest CAGR at 10% and agro-chemicals the lowest CAGR at 0.7%. The chemicals industry as a whole grew at an average of 4.7% during the Tenth Five Year Plan. The industry expectation is that the sector may grow in the range of 5%–8% during the Eleventh Plan (Annexure 7.1.9).

7.1.184 Increased competition resulting from globalization is driving the chemical industry towards consolidation, cost reduction, location of manufacturing bases close to raw materials, cheaper energy sources, lower tax regimes, increased use of information technology (IT), and intensification of R&D activities. At the same time the industry is responding to the increased environment consciousness worldwide. Consolidation has become imperative as the industry seeks economies of scale in manufacturing, logistics, and R&D. Cost reduction is being aggressively attempted through improved operating norms and financial restructuring. Enhanced worldwide concern for the protection of the environment has been forcing the industry to modernize and innovate.

7.1.185 Over the last decade, the Indian chemical industry has evolved from being a basic chemical producer to becoming an innovative industry. With increasing investments in R&D, the industry is registering significant growth in the knowledge sector comprising specialty chemicals, fine chemicals, and pharmaceuticals. Broadly, the share of basic, knowledge, and specialty chemicals is 57%, 18%, and 25%, respectively. Share of different segments of Chemical Industry in India is shown in Figure 7.1.7.

CHALLENGES

7.1.186 The major hindrances for a double-digit growth of the Indian chemical industry are suboptimal size of plants, higher input costs (raw materials, power, fuel, etc.), lack of world-class infrastructure (roads, ports, and power supply), lack of competitiveness, and stringent labour laws. Without addressing these issues it would be very difficult for the industry to compete globally with rapidly declining duty differentials and appreciation in the value of rupee. Some of the sector-specific challenges are:

- While peak duties on non-agricultural products have been reduced from year to year, commensurate

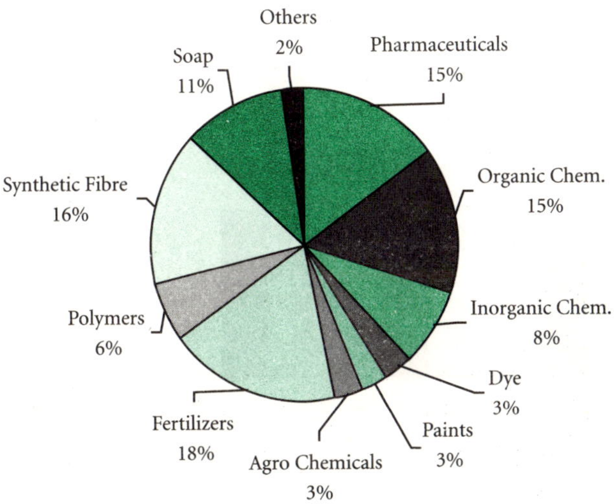

Source: Report of the Task Force on Chemicals, 2002, Department of Chemicals and Petrochemicals.

FIGURE 7.1.7: Share (Value of Output) of Different Segments of Chemical Industry in India

reduction has not taken place on fuels, raw materials, building blocks, and feedstock, such as denatured ethyl alcohol, flourspar, carbon black feedstock, and molasses, that go into the production of various downstream value-added chemicals.

- Tank terminals for such chemicals as methanol, ammonia, benzene have not been provided at critical railway junctions.
- Although various laws have been enacted by the government relating to air and water pollution, environment protection in general, hazardous waste management, and product liability insurance, and the government is a signatory to international treaties, conventions, protocols, and codes of conduct, there is lack of awareness in the industry about these laws and international agreements.
- In 2007, the European Union had passed legislation on registration, evaluation, and authorization of chemicals (REACH). For compliance with the provisions of this legislation it would be necessary for exporters to submit test data from accredited laboratories following good laboratory practices (GLP). Until Indian laboratories are so accredited the exporters would have to get the test data generated in foreign laboratories, which will be costly.
- The levels of R&D expenditure by the chemical industry in India are very low by international standards.

STRATEGIES

7.1.187 Duty structure on building blocks for the chemical industries needs to be reviewed with a view to considering how far these can be brought on par with those prevailing in the other emerging economies.

7.1.188 Railways should consult with the chemicals industry with a view to determining the locations in which it would be in their mutual interest to establish infrastructure at ports to handle bulk chemicals and Petroleum, Oil, and Lubricants (POL) products.

7.1.189 Creation of R&D hubs with state-of-the-art testing needs to be initiated in the PPP mode in the line of NATRIP.

7.1.190 The government should consider upgrading the national laboratories such as the Indian Institute of Chemical Technology, Hyderabad and the Central Drug Research Institute, Lucknow to GLP standards so that they can obtain accreditation from the European Union (EU) bodies to enable them to generate test data for compliance with REACH.

7.1.191 The government should regularly hold workshops and seminars to disseminate knowledge relating to environmental laws and related international treaties and negotiations.

Drugs and Pharmaceuticals

OVERVIEW

7.1.192 The Indian pharmaceutical industry registered strong growth during the Ninth and Tenth Five Year Plan periods and has emerged as an area of strength especially in generics. The adoption of world-class patent laws for pharmaceutical products w.e.f. 1 January 2005, pursuant to obligations under the WTO Agreement, has not dampened the robust growth but has improved the overall IPR environment. The turnover of the industry was Rs 72000 crore during 2006–07, having risen by more than 12 times since 1990. India has become one of the leading global

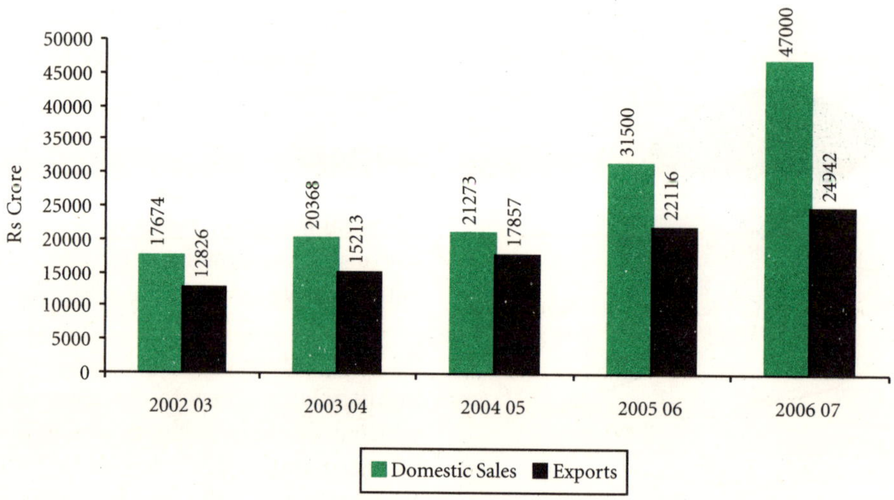

Note: Estimated retail market in 2005–06 is based on ORG-IMS, for 2006–07 retail market includes institutional sales.

Sources: Export: actual—DGCI&S; estimate—Indian Pharmaceuticals Alliance; Domestic sales actual/estimated—ORG-IMS.

FIGURE 7.1.8: Domestic Sales and Exports of Pharmaceuticals (Rs Crore)

players, holding fourth position in terms of volume and thirteenth position in terms of value of production. Exports have also grown significantly to over Rs 24942 crore in 2006–07, accounting for as much as 34% of the turnover (Figure 7.1.8).

PRODUCTION AND EXPORTS OF PHARMACEUTICALS

7.1.193 According to the report submitted in 2003 by the committee headed by R.A. Mashelkar, the number of drug manufacturing licenses issued was as follows: bulk drugs (1333), formulations (4534), large volume parenterals (134), and vaccines (56) making the total of 6057 manufacturing units. About 300 of these pharmaceutical units are large units.

7.1.194 India is one of the signatories of the World Health Organization (WHO) certification scheme on the quality of pharmaceutical products moving in international commerce. WHO GMP certificate is granted after inspection by the Central Drugs Standard Control Organization and the State Licensing Authorities. The GMP, which involve both the premises and the plants, are laid down in Schedule M of the Drugs and Cosmetics Rules 1945. The present Schedule 'M' provisions, which have become mandatory since 1 July 2005, conform to international standards and have a higher level of GMP that can lead to better quality of products destined for both domestic and international markets. Another important development is that the manufacturers and exporters are going beyond the WHO GMP and accepting regulatory approvals from national agencies of important foreign markets such as United States Food and Drug Administration (USFDA), UK Medicines and Healthcare Products Regulatory Agency, Australia Therapeutic Goods Administration, and South Africa Medicines Control Council. With about 100 USFDA approvals, India has the largest USFDA approved plants outside the US. As the US is the largest market for pharmaceuticals, accounting for half of the world's generics market, the focus of many Indian companies has remained on the US generics market, with India accounting for almost half of Drug Master File (DMF) filings and one-fourth of Abbreviated New Drug Application (ANDA) in the US in 2006. DMF is a document filed with the USFDA by a manufacturer of bulk drug (Active Pharmaceutical Ingredient, API) offering API in the US market. ANDA is a document filed by a manufacturer of generic formulations (finished dosage form). Regulatory approval of DMF takes two years and that of ANDA 30 months.

7.1.195 Production, domestic sales, and exports rose rapidly during the Tenth Five Year Plan period. During the Tenth Five Year Plan domestic sales grew generally at the rate of 11%–15% and exports at the rate of 20%–26%. Industry estimates are that domestic sales will grow at the rate of 16% and exports at the rate of 30%–35% during the Eleventh Five Year Plan, so that by the terminal year exports will constitute close to 60% of the domestic production. The optimism about increase in the export growth rates is based on the fact that the sharp increase in DMF and ANDA filings by Indian manufacturers in the US during the years 2004–06 will begin showing its effect only from the year 2007–08, because of the time taken for regulatory approvals. Projections for 2011–12 are given shown in Figure 7.1.9.

7.1.196 India's rich human capital is its greatest asset for this knowledge-led industry. With US$ 60 billion worth of medicines coming off patents in the next few years, India is poised to emerge as one of the biggest player in the area of generics. The biopharmaceuticals market is also evolving very fast and India could emerge as the largest vaccine producer in the world. Other favourable factors are the growing dependence on generics across the world, wide acceptance of Indian generic products as safe and effective, aggressive thrust of Indian companies for building and acquiring sales, and marketing network abroad, entry of third and second tier Indian companies in the international market. The industry projection is that by the end of the Plan period the domestic sales will increase to Rs 78000 crore (about US$ 19.5 billion) and exports to Rs 112000 crore (US$ 28 billion).

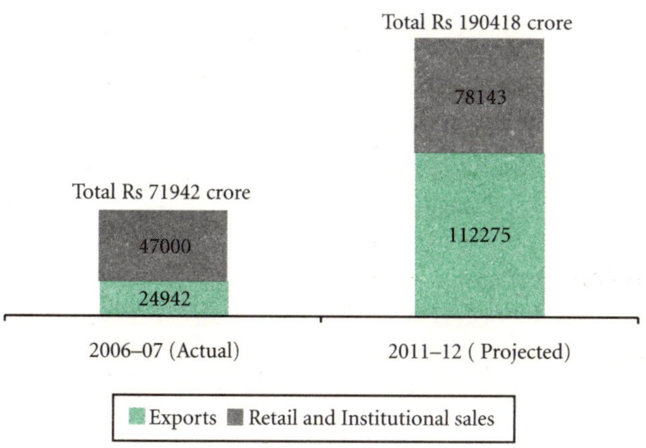

Source: Report of the Working Group on Drugs and Pharmaceuticals for the Eleventh Five Year Plan (2007–12).

FIGURE 7.1.9: Pharmaceuticals—Exports, Retail Sale and Institutional Sale by 2011–12

RESEARCH AND DEVELOPMENT (R&D)

7.1.197 Internationally, pharmaceutical companies spend 15%–20% of their sales revenue on R&D, particularly for the discovery and development of new chemical entities. In the absence of the law for product patents before 2005, Indian pharmaceutical companies had traditionally confined their research activities to processes rather than to products. The law for grant of product patents on pharmaceutical products has now been enacted. But few Indian company has the resources to pursue the cutting edge research and take a new compound through all stages up to marketing. However, Indian companies are adopting one of the following options to lower costs and mitigate risks:

- Collaboration with large R&D based MNCs either for co-development or through the co-licensing route.
- Work on existing molecules with proven market by developing chiral molecules or race-mates currently marketed, or through new formulations of existing drugs with beneficial characteristics of increased efficacy and safety.
- Identify through clinical trials new indications for marketed drugs.
- Develop traditional medicines acceptable to global markets.

7.1.198 Apart from the Indian companies investing in R&D, MNCs are setting up research facilities in India or entering into tie-ups with Indian companies. Astra-Zeneca of the UK, Altan Pharma of Germany, Eisai of Japan, and Ethy Pharma of France have set up R&D centres and wholly owned sub-sidiaries and Eli Lily has entered into collaboration with Jubilant. More importantly, nine Indian companies (three in Hyderabad, two each in Mumbai and Chennai, and one each in Bangalore and Vadodra) have entered business to exploit the outsourcing opportunities in drug discovery services and their clients include MNCs. International drug discovery companies are also in the process of setting up their presence in India.

7.1.199 Cost advantage has also resulted in the country becoming a hub for clinical trials and MNCs such as Pfizer, Johnson & Johnson, GSK, Merck, Eli

Liliy, Novartis, and Novo Nordisk are using India as a base for running their Phase II and Phase III clinical trials. Quintiles, Icon Clinical, and Pharmaolam are some of the foreign clinical research organizations working in India.

7.1.200 The enactment by the Parliament of world-class IPR laws has created the environment conducive to the outsourcing of drug discovery and clinical research to India. Apart from this, the adoption of GLP and Good Clinical Practices by Indian companies has also induced the outsourcing of these services. By some estimates, the global R&D expenditure on pharmaceuticals may touch US$ 100 billion by 2011–12 and if outsourcing is done from Indian companies. India's share at the end of the current Plan could be in the range of US$ 1–3 billion. Estimate from industry puts the Indian Clinical Trial market at present at US$ 100 million, which may increase to US$ 300 million in two or three years.

PRODUCT PATENTS AND DRUG PRICES

7.1.201 At the time of India's decision to accept the WTO Agreement, there was a fear that the introduction of product patents in pharmaceuticals in the country would lead to the price of drugs becoming unaffordable for the poor people. This has not happened and is not likely to happen on account of several factors. First, all the drugs included in the list of essential drugs published by the Ministry of Health are already in the public domain. Second, most of the patented medicines introduced from time to time usually bring about some improvement over the previous generation and their price cannot be far out of line with that of the existing drugs. At any point of time there are more than half a dozen patent expired therapeutic equivalents available. Thus the price competition among drugs in the same therapeutic group will automatically keep the prices of new entities under control. The limited purchasing power of the Indian public will also act as a check on any dramatic rise in price. And ultimately recourse can be always had to the provisions on compulsory licensing and government use for non-voluntary licensing of patented drugs.

7.1.202 India has had price control on drugs for a long time but the span of control has been progressively reduced. If the promise shown by this dynamic industry is to be realized and the figures of production and export projected above are to be achieved, it would be important to maintain this trend even though the price control is consistent with WTO obligations. Concerns for making medicines available at affordable prices must be met through alternatives other than by means of control on the basis of cost plus pricing. The route to lower prices is greater competition and that will happen if new manufacturers find it attractive to enter the sector. Price control will diminish profits and turn entrepreneurs away from the sector and lower the competition. Furthermore, diminishing profits will limit the capacity of firms to invest in R&D, which is the soul of a vibrant pharmaceutical sector.

CHALLENGES

7.1.203 According to a survey of the small-scale pharmaceutical companies in 2001–02, as many as 327 units had been closed or had their licenses suspended or may have shifted to some other States and another 370 units were not in a position to comply with the GMP norms. Since the GMP norms have been made mandatory with effect from 1 July 2005, these units have been closed.

7.1.204 If the Indian pharmaceutical sector is to live up to the promise in both manufacturing and R&D services, the supply of science and pharmacy graduates with quality education has to be substantially raised. In order to double the exports, the pharmaceutical industry requires 1000 highly trained manpower every year for the next 10 years.

7.1.205 Since R&D in pharmaceuticals is a highly risky venture, there is need to incentivize it through tax concessions on a permanent basis.

INTERVENTIONS

7.1.206 In order to enable the small-scale sector to acquire GMP compliant facilities, it is necessary to provide financial assistance to them through interest subsidies.

7.1.207 The NIPER at Mohali has made a significant contribution in providing human resources of the right calibre needed by the industry, academia, and regulatory bodies. To meet the future demand of the industry, it is necessary to replicate NIPER through five more institutes in different parts of the country.

7.1.208 The provision for weighted reduction of R&D expenses for corporate tax purposes should be made permanent after the current validity expires.

7.1.209 The main Eleventh Plan Scheme is setting-up of five new NIPER like institutes in the PPP mode. An allocation of Rs 514 crore has been made for these new institutes. The existing NIPER has been provided an allocation of Rs 164 crore for modernization and expansion. An allocation of Rs 340 crore has been made for a new scheme to support Schedule M compliance by SMEs in drugs and pharmaceutical sector by providing interest subsidy to these units in Eleventh Plan. A new scheme with an allocation of Rs 75 crore has been envisaged to assist the Pharma CPSEs to meet WHO pre-qualification.

Fertilizer Industry

7.1.210 India is the fourth largest producer of fertilizers in the world after China, the US, and Russia. It meets the bulk of its substantial needs for nitrogenous and phosphatic fertilizers from domestic production but potassic fertilizers' needs are met through imports. For the production of phosphatic fertilizers, the country relies on imports of raw materials.

7.1.211 During the Tenth Plan the increase in consumption outstripped the slow growth in production, with the result that in the later years of the Plan period, imports registered strong increases (Annexure 7.1.10).

7.1.212 During the terminal year of the Ninth Five Year Plan (2001–02), the installed capacity of the domestic fertilizer industry was 120.58 lakh metric tonnes (LMT) of nitrogen and 53.87 LMT of P_2O_5 (phosphate) per annum. In the absence of fresh investment, the capacity of the fertilizer industry remained by and large stagnant during the Tenth Plan period. The actual domestic production of urea in 2005–06 was 200.98 LMT from 28 functional units and 13.25 LMT from the Joint Venture (JV) Oman India Fertilizer Company (OMIFCO) against the projected demand of 242.14 LMT per annum urea by the terminal year (2006–07). During the Tenth Five Year Plan various capacity additions such as Brahmaputra Valley Fertilizer Corporation Limited revamp project, OMIFCO materialized. Thal III expansion of Rashtriya Chemicals and Fertilizers Ltd (RCF) (11.55 LMT) and Krishak Bharati Co-operative Limited (KRIBHCO)-Hazira expansion Projects (10.56 LMT) could not be taken up due to lack of availability of natural gas/LNG.

7.1.213 There has been a significant growth in fertilizer consumption over the years. The per hectare consumption of NPK (nutrients) increased from less than 1 kg in 1951–52 to 106.7 kg in 2005–06. However, the consumption is still much lower than the levels achieved even in China and Pakistan. With a growth rate of 4.1 per annum on the estimated base level consumption of 220 LMT in 2006–07, the total nutrient consumption for 2011–12 is envisaged at 269 LMT. The demand forecasts for 'N', 'P', and 'K' are estimated at 163.10 LMT, 72.90 LMT, and 33 LMT, respectively, in the terminal year of the Eleventh Five Year Plan. This corresponds to a demand of 287.55 LMT for urea, 95.10 LMT for di-ammonium phosphate (DAP), 37.40 LMT for muriate of potash (MOP), 93.30 LMT for complex fertilizers, and 36.45 LMT for SSP (Figure 7.1.10).

7.1.214 The Working Group on Fertilizer for the Eleventh Plan has estimated that over and above the present installed capacity of 213.52 LMT of urea, a total of 128 LMT of additional urea capacity can come up through revamp of existing gas-based units; new Brownfield expansion of plants such as Indo Gulf, RCF, KRIBHCO, and Indian Farmers Fertilizer Cooperative Ltd (IFFCO); JV abroad on the basis of cheap gas/LNG and revival of seven FCI and HFC plants by joint venture or any other suitable model. Investment of Rs 36000 crore may be required to increase the capacity of urea by about 12 million mt by expanding domestic units and reviving sick ones.

CHALLENGES

7.1.215 The production of urea in the country is still saddled with the legacy of the era of import substitution policies, when pursuit of self-sufficiency led to the establishment of units based on inefficient feedstock/fuel such as naphtha and fuel oils. Since the

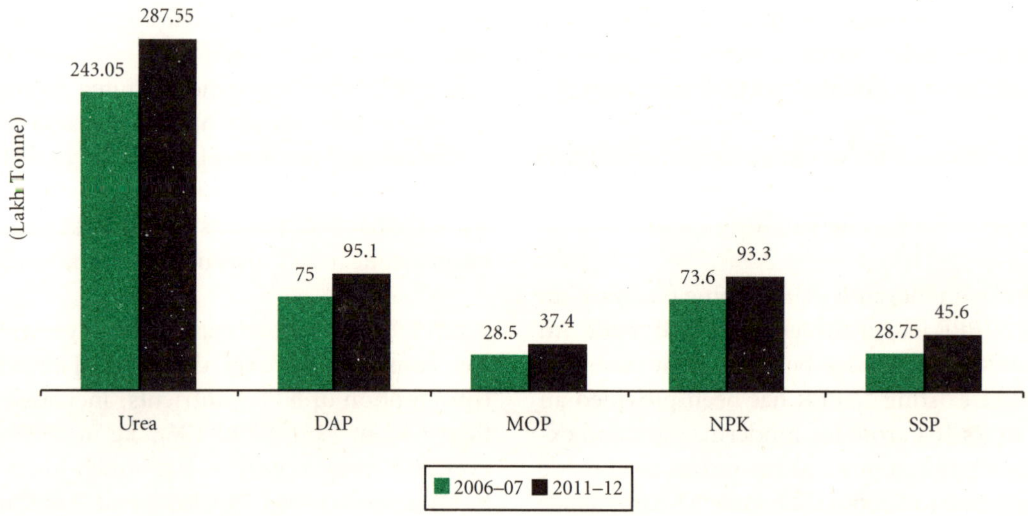

Source: Report of the Working Group on Fertilizers for the Eleventh Plan.

FIGURE 7.1.10: Demand of Fertilizer by 2011–12.

costs of production of these units were much higher than those of units based on natural gas, the GoI introduced the Retention Price Scheme (RPS). Each urea unit had a unique retention price depending upon the technology, feedstock used, capacity utilization, energy consumption, distance from the source of feedstock, etc., and the government paid to them the difference between the retention price and the MRP fixed by the government for sale of urea to farmers. As the RPS was cost plus in nature and encouraged gold plating, it was replaced by the New Pricing Scheme (NPS) on the recommendations of the Expenditure Reforms Commission in 2000, to be implemented in three stages: Stage I (1 April 2003 to 31 March 2004), Stage II (1 April 2004 to 31 March 2006), and Stage III. Under the NPS, the existing units have been divided into six groups on the basis of vintage and feedstock for determining the group-based concession. Stage III has commenced on 1 October 2006, with some policy changes to encourage additions to capacity. An important decision taken is that the non-natural-gas-based units would have three years to convert into NG/LNG units. But to make such conversion possible, issues have to be resolved relating to connectivity, supply, and price of gas.

7.1.216 While there is an increasing gap between supply and demand, a number of sick PSE units are lying closed. Most of these units have excellent infrastructure in the shape of residential colonies, coal and electricity tie-ups, railway sidings, etc., and revival of these units is a major issue that needs to be tackled.

7.1.217 Fertilizer use in India is inadequate, imbalanced, and skewed in favour of nitrogen, which has resulted in the emergence of nutrient deficiencies in Indian soils. As against the recommended N:P:K ratio of 4:2:1, the average for the country was 5.3:2.2:1 in 2005–06. However, the average conceals variation within the States and the actual ratio in Punjab in the same year was 20:6:1 and in Haryana 30:9:1. Balanced use of fertilizers will have implications for the demand for production and import of fertilizers.

7.1.218 India does not have sufficient quantities of known reserves of rock phosphates, and where available these are of low quality. As a result, India has to import large quantities of rock phosphates or phosphoric acid.

7.1.219 Large quantities of urea, DAP, rock phosphates, and MOP are being imported and the ports are not sufficiently equipped to deal with such large volumes of imports. Absence of railway wagons designed for the bulk movement of fertilizers is another impediment that the industry faces.

STRATEGIES

7.1.220 The most important element of future strategies relating to the urea industry is to establish a single producer price, and with this end in view, the GoI has already decided on a sunset for non-gas-based units. For implementation of the decision, the issues of connectivity, supply, and price has to be resolved. Pipeline connectivity already exists in respect of 22 units and it is likely to become available to others in the next few years. The units at Goa, Mangalore, and Tuticorin are expected to be serviced by the Reliance Gas Transportation Infrastructure Limited Chennai–Tuticorin pipeline and Chennai–Mangalore pipeline. Although in the past natural gas has been in short supply even for gas-based units, it is expected that the new discoveries will make it possible to supply gas not only to them but also to the newly converted units. As for price, a single producer price policy will necessitate that the government ensures gas supplies to all urea producers at the same price.

7.1.221 Although currently the import parity prices for urea are ruling high, the fact remains that natural gas is available in oil-rich countries at a much lower price than in India; an appropriate long-term policy should be announced so that more joint ventures are set up such as the one in Oman.

7.1.222 Effort should be made to revive those units that are revivable, including setting up of joint ventures with private sector participation.

7.1.223 Efficient use of fertilizers can be promoted by extension for adoption of better agronomic practices. However, the single most effective way for achieving efficient use of fertilizers will be to make subsidies for agriculture nutrient-based.

7.1.224 In order to ensure sufficient supplies of raw materials for phosphatic fertilizers, it is necessary to intensify exploration activities in India. Additionally, Indian companies must be encouraged to invest in mining and production of intermediates in resource-rich countries.

7.1.225 Port facilities need to be enhanced to enable efficient handling of imported fertilizers and fertilizer material. The railways should also introduce specially designed wagons for handling of fertilizers.

7.1.226 An outlay of Rs 20628 crore including a budgetary support of Rs 1492 crore has been made in the Eleventh Plan, mainly to support conversion of old fuel oil-based fertilizer units to gas-based ones and restructuring of the CPSEs.

Leather and Leather Goods

7.1.227 The importance of the Indian leather industry is derived from the fact that it is labour-intensive and contributes substantially to exports. Artisans, micro enterprises, and SSIs account for 60% to 65% of the total production. The manufacturing activity provides full-time employment to 1 million persons and activities connected with the recovery of hides from carcasses provides part-time employment to another 0.8 million. The turnover of the industry was Rs 25000 crore in 2004–05, out of which Rs 10800 crore (43%) was exported. Exports have risen in recent years from US$ 1.9 billion in 2000–01 to US$ 2.9 billion in 2006–07. The composition of exports of leather and leather goods has been moving increasingly toward leather footwear, but the share (32% in 2006–07) still falls far short of the 65% share of footwear in the world export of leather and leather products (Figure 7.1.11).

7.1.228 The Inter-Ministerial Group constituted to evolve a comprehensive strategy for the development of the leather sector has assessed that India has the potential to expand exports from the level of US$ 2.7 billion in 2005–06 to US$ 7 billion in 2011–12. The break-up of the projections is given in the Figure 7.1.12.

7.1.229 Footwear is the component accounting for the largest growth. In quantitative terms, the exports of footwear translate into 300 million pairs in the last year of the Eleventh Five Year Plan period against 92 million pairs in 2005–06. This would require the creation of capacity of 750000 pairs a day against the capacity of 250000 pairs a day in 2005–06. If non-leather footwear is added, the required capacity for exports alone will be 1 million pairs. Similarly the production of leather garments would need to grow from 24 million

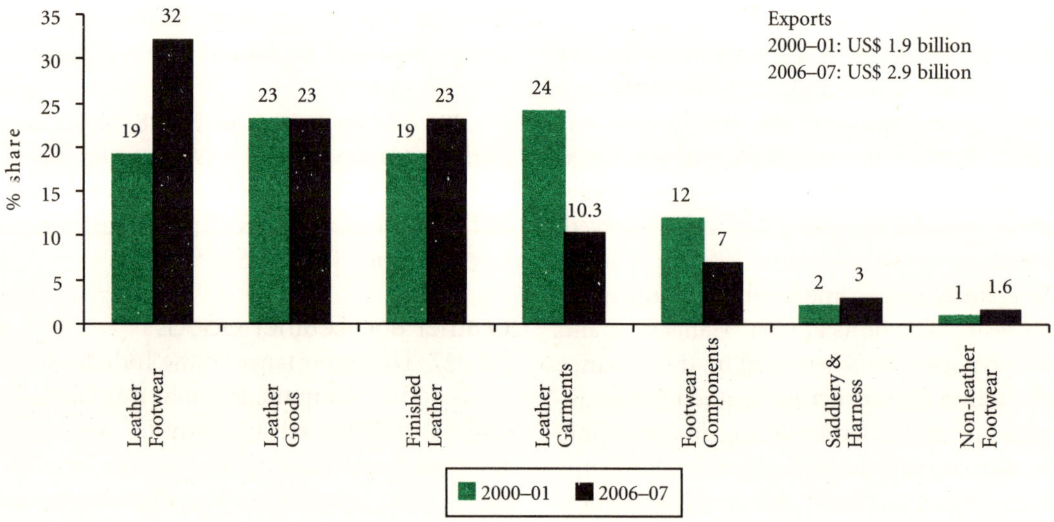

Source: Council for Leather Exports, India.

FIGURE 7.1.11: Indian Leather Exports—Changing Structure

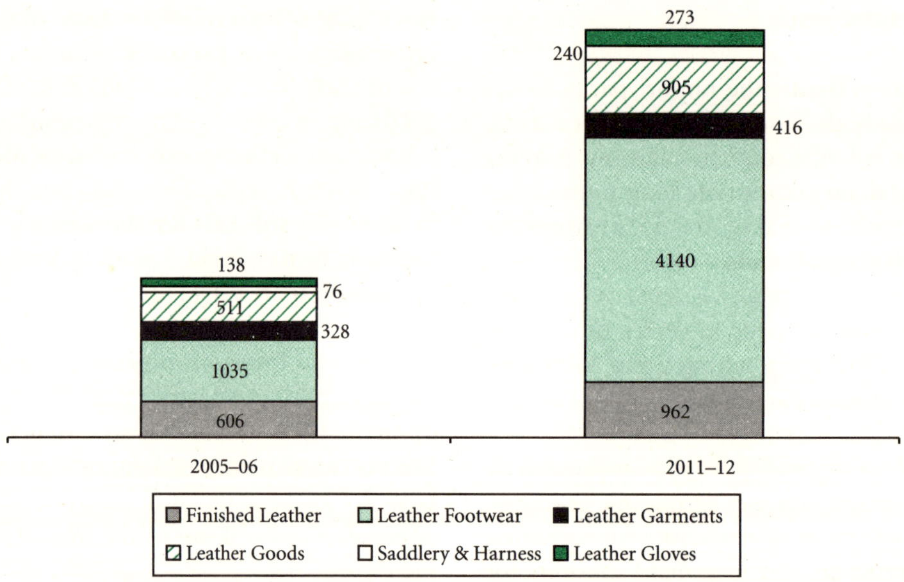

Source: Inter-Ministerial Committee on Enhancement of the Competitiveness of Leather Industry, 2008.

FIGURE 7.1.12: Projected Growth of India's Exports of Leather and Leather Products (in US$ Million)

pieces in 2005–06 to 72 million pieces in 2011–12, and of leather goods from 6 million pieces to 18 million pieces in the same period.

7.1.230 However, before the above potential can be realized a number of challenges would need to be addressed.

CHALLENGES

- The indigenous raw material base of the industry is deficient. As of now about 90% (1.8 billion sq ft) of leather is produced in the country from indigenous hides and skins. To achieve exports of US$ 7 billion, 4 billion sq ft will be needed in 2012.

- The tanneries in the country have low capacities and outdated technologies with a majority of tanneries still using manual systems. During the Tenth Five Year Plan, the scheme for IDLS under ILDP was launched for technology upgradation and modernization, but the funds could be utilized only to a small extent because of delay in the finalization of the scheme.
- Another problem faced by the existing tanning units (in Tamil Nadu) has been the imposition of rigorous environmental requirement (Zero Liquid Discharge) by the State Pollution Control Board under the directions of the Honourable High Court. While the large units have been able to make additional investment needed to comply with the requirement, the small-scale units do not have the financial strength to do so without the government assistance.
- There is acute shortage of skilled and semi-skilled workforce and it is estimated that if the full potential is to be realized 0.5 million workers would need to be trained.
- A large majority of the manufacturers produce small quantities and are unable to meet the large volume orders from the US, which accounts for a large share of world imports. Also much of the footwear production in India is of dress shoes for men, while there is increasing requirement for comfort shoes. Ladies shoes are also not being manufactured for exports. What is needed is to scale up the production and diversify the product mix.
- The competitiveness of Indian exporters of leather products suffers on account of bad roads, delays in Inland Container Depots, and the fact that a large part of Indian cargo from the eastern seaboard, where the production is concentrated, is transshipped at Colombo and Singapore. This is due mainly to the fact that the channels in the ports on the eastern coast lack the depth necessary to allow large ships to come to these ports.

STRATEGIES

7.1.231 In order to address the above challenges the following significant interventions are proposed.

7.1.232 For augmenting the raw material base, rearing of male buffalo calves would be encouraged as also scheme for modernization of slaughter launched under PPP. For the better utilization of the skins of fallen animals, a scheme will be launched in the Department of Animal Husbandry for establishing 50 carcass centres, 20 bone-crushing plants, and 5000 hide-flaying units.

7.1.233 In order to stimulate fresh investment in new tanning units as well as in leather products, it is proposed that at least 10 leather parks/complexes would be established on the pattern of the SITP scheme of the Ministry of Textiles.

7.1.234 The Tenth Five Year Plan schemes, Leather Tanning Complex at Nellore (which did not take off during the Plan period but in which the State Government has recently taken positive steps) and the Footwear Complex in Tamil Nadu (which has been substantially completed) need to be carried forward into the Eleventh Five Year Plan. It is also proposed to continue the Tenth Five Year Plan scheme for the IDLS but the expenditure would be limited to the extent that the allocations remained unutilized in the Tenth Five Year Plan.

7.1.235 The small and medium tanning units in Tamil Nadu and elsewhere would be assisted for making investment to enable them to comply with rigorous environment norms imposed by the Pollution Control Boards. The GoI will provide 60% assistance, the remaining amount coming from the State Government and the units themselves.

7.1.236 A large Human Resource Development Mission will be launched for onsite training of workers and artisans in the unorganized sector and also for entrepreneurship development. The Mission will also cover the development of skilled manpower by the existing institutions, which offer courses at the degree level. The Footwear Design and Development Institute (FDDI), Noida, will be provided with additional machinery, equipment, workshops, and laboratory facilities for running courses on design and technology with increased intake and a new branch of the FDDI will be set up at Fursatganj. Consideration will be given to setting up more branches of FDDI in other parts of the country with concentrations of leather manufacturing units.

7.1.237 In the Eleventh Plan an allocation of Rs 1300 crore has been made for the ILDP.

Paper Industry

OVERVIEW

7.1.238 Paper industry is one of the 35 high-priority industries in India and is presently growing at a rate of 6.3% per annum. The turnover is nearly Rs 17000 crore per annum and its contribution to the national exchequer is around Rs 2500 crore. The industry employs 0.3 million people directly and is estimated to employ 1 million people indirectly. The per capital consumption of paper in India is 7.2 kg, which is far lower than in other emerging economies, for example 45 kg in China, 15–20 kg in other East Asian countries, and much higher level that exists in the US and Europe. The consumption of paper is likely to increase manifold with the growth in the economy and the rise in literacy.

7.1.239 At the end of the Tenth Five Year Plan there were about 666 industrial units with the total installed capacity of 8.50 million mt for paper and paperboard. However, 98 units with a capacity of 1.1 million mt are closed due to environmental problems. The industry produces 5.80 million mt of paper and paperboard. It has made significant progress after independence with government support and fiscal incentives. The country is almost self-sufficient in most varieties of paper and paperboard, and imports are taking place only of certain specialty items such as coated paper, cheque paper, etc. However, the industry has failed to keep pace with the technological advances and is beset with major difficulties such as high production cost, pollution problems, and finished paper quality not conforming to international standards.

7.1.240 The Indian paper industry is highly fragmented and 458 mills are of capacities less than 60 tonnes per day (tpd), 48 are of capacities ranging from 60 tpd to 100 tpd, and 62 are of capacities above 100 tpd. A variety of fibrous raw materials, viz., bamboo, hardwoods, agricultural residues, and waste paper are being used for paper-making in the country.

7.1.241 From the raw material perspective, the industry can broadly be divided into three segments, namely, wood based, agro based, and recycled fibre based. The contribution of these towards production is 30%, 32%, and 38%, respectively. The industry lacks abundant raw material here in the country and increasing quantities of waste paper and wood pulp are being imported. The imports of waste paper increased from about 1.4 million mt in 2004–05 to about 1.8 million mt in 2005–06. During the same period, the import of wood pulp increased from 378432 mt to 472391 mt. The production, import, and export of paper and paperboard are given in Annexure 7.1.11. The production has shown a slow increase during the Tenth Five Year Plan.

NEWSPRINT INDUSTRY

7.1.242 The paper mills producing newsprint conforming to BIS and supplying to newspaper publishers are considered for inclusion in Schedule of Newsprint Control Order 2004, enabling them to avail exemption of the excise duty. There are at present 77 mills including 2 Central public sector units and 2 State public sector units which are manufacturing newsprint paper with a total installed capacity of 15.9 lakh mt. The domestic production was 9.1 lakh mt in the year 2005–06 and 10.3 lakh mt in 2006–07.

7.1.243 The production, import, and export of newsprint during the last four years are as given in Annexure 7.1.12.

ISSUES AND CHALLENGES

7.1.244 The paper industry uses wood, agri-residue, and waste paper as raw materials with all the three segments contributing equally to the production. The use of non-wood raw material and waste paper has increased over the years and accounted for about 70% of total production at the end of the Tenth Five Year Plan period. With the liberalization of trade, the domestic industry has been exposed to increasing competition, and both product quality and price have come under pressure. While production has been increasing gradually, growth of the industry is hamstrung by the non-availability of particularly forest-based raw material. From the angle of this important industry, it has become imperative that there is a paradigm shift in the management of forest from a 'conservation-centred' to a 'production-centred' approach.

7.1.245 No major greenfield integrated pulp and paper mill has come up in a decade. Raw material shortage is undoubtedly a major factor contributing to the stagnation of production capacity. Low per capita consumption of paper in the country and rising literacy levels present opportunities for growth of this industry. Steps are required to improve competitiveness of the industry which should specifically focus on the problems of technological obsolescence and economic use of water and energy as well effluent treatment to mitigate environmental problems.

STRATEGIES

7.1.246 The foremost problem that needs to be addressed is increasing the raw material base of the industry. Vast opportunities exist on degraded forest land but the rights of local communities and the principle of JFM constitute an insurmountable obstacle in leasing out such land to paper mills. If these lands remain bereft of forests for prolonged periods, the issue would need to be revisited. In the meantime, wastelands should be considered for developing forests under appropriate PPP arrangements, with the participation of local communities. The State Governments also need to consider ways of stimulating agro-forestry.

7.1.247 A programme should be put in place for incentivizing the SMEs to adopt energy-reducing and less water-intensive technologies and to take adequate steps for effluent treatment.

Petrochemical Industry

7.1.248 Internationally the petrochemical industry has been one of the drivers of industrial development, constituting 40% of the global chemical market. During 1950–90 countries West of Suez were dominating in the manufacture of petrochemicals but after that the global epicentre shifted to East of Suez, largely due to the availability of crude oil and natural gas in the Middle East and the growth of consumption centres in Asia, which has a large population base.

7.1.249 With 15 raw material producers and more than 50000 downstream processing units, the Indian petrochemical industry has a share of about 2.5% of the global petrochemicals production capacity. The Indian petrochemical industry consists of building blocks, commodity polymers, performance plastics, synthetic fibre, synthetic rubber, surfactants, and downstream plastic processing industry. Domestic demand growth for petrochemicals has slowed down during the Tenth Five Year Plan as compared to the previous Plan period. The production of commodity polymers and synthetic fibre which grew modestly during the Tenth Plan is presented in Annexure 7.1.13.

7.1.250 The downstream plastic processing sector is highly labour-intensive, currently providing employment to 3.3 million people but having the potential to generate 3.7 million new jobs by 2011–12. Domestic industry is extremely fragmented and operating with sub-optimal scale of operation, which is inhibiting its international competitiveness. This is mainly due to the government's past policy of reservation of various plastic products for exclusive manufacture in small-scale units and excise duty exemptions for them. The scale of operation in downstream plastic processing industry is sub-optimal in the country as can be seen from Figure 7.1.13.

7.1.251 Imports of plastic products from China and Thailand into India have increased rapidly in the recent years due to non-availability of quality plastic products in the country. Recognizing the economic

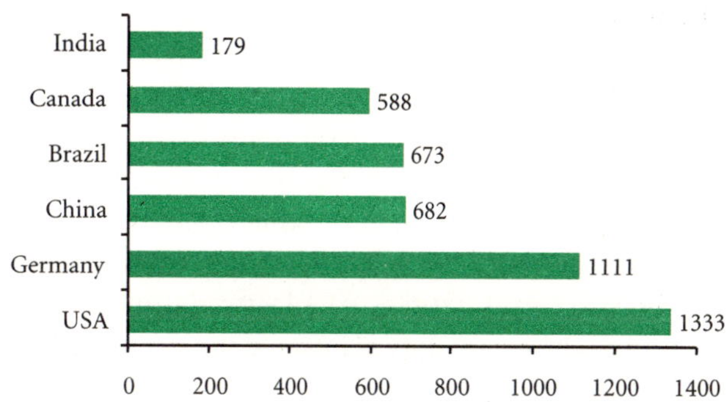

Source: Industry Association, Report of the Working Group on Petrochemicals Sector, Eleventh Five Year Plan.

FIGURE 7.1.13: Relative Scale of Operation of Plastic Processing Industry (unit size in tons per unit)

benefits and employment potential of the downstream sector, China had first developed the plastic processing sector and is the largest global exporter of plastic goods worth of US$ 18 billion compared to India's US$ 1 billion. After establishing globally competitive downstream processing industry, China started focusing on upstream cracker investments to increase their raw material and intermediate security.

7.1.252 India's competitiveness in the plastic processing industry is likely to improve in the future because in January 2007 and March 2007 the government has de-reserved 70 out of 84 items. Further the Micro, Small, and Medium Enterprises Act 2006 has raised the limit on investment in plant and machinery for SSIs from Rs 1 crore to Rs 5 crore.

7.1.253 According to the assessment of the Working Group on the Petrochemical Sector for the Eleventh Plan, the demand for polymers in the country has the potential to reach 12.5 million mt by the end of the Eleventh Five Year Plan growing at a CAGR of 18% necessitating commissioning of 5 additional crackers of 1 million mt average size with investments of US$ 8 billion and US$ 6 billion investments in the downstream plastic processing sector by 2011–12. The existing naphtha and gas cracker plants at Pata and Haldia are under expansion and new upcoming investments are in the Crackers at Panipat and Jamnagar and Assam with an investment of Rs 32000 crore.

CHALLENGES

7.1.254 The polymer industry has not grown because of stagnation in the processing industry on account of structural factors, viz., fragmentation of the industry on account of reservation of manufacturing for SSIs. Now that this problem has been resolved, modernization and achievement of scale economies need to be incentivized. The high level of 16% excise duties on polymers and articles of plastic dampens the demand. If the excise duty is lowered the demand will be stimulated.

7.1.255 At a time when growth in the processing industry is likely, it would be important to ensure that the industry adopts the highest quality standards. Although India is late in making its presence felt in the international markets in plastic products, high quality products can enable the industry to make up for the lost time.

7.1.256 To facilitate modernization, special effort will be needed for improvement of infrastructure in the vicinity of existing and proposed industrial units.

7.1.257 If expansion of the industry takes place at the scale that is envisaged, additional manpower requirement will be of 6 lakh including 1.4 lakh skilled workers. The training arrangements will have to be stepped up.

7.1.258 The use of plastic conserves natural reserves such as wood, metals, etc., for better productive use.Plastics can boost agricultural growth through plasticulture, better access to potable water, laying durable roads based on polymer-modified bitumen, and can save precious materials currently used in construction industry. The challenge is to persuade the users to use plastics in preference to more scarce alternatives derived from natural resources.

STRATEGIES

7.1.259 Consideration should be given to the reduction of excise duties on polymers and plastic products in order to stimulate demand.

7.1.260 The use of BIS specifications should be made mandatory for both domestically produced and imported articles of plastic for identified areas.

7.1.261 Since with enhanced demand both petrochemical producers and processing industry will be benefited, a joint effort of promoting polymer application in non-traditional areas should be initiated through their associations.

7.1.262 At present, CIPET is entrusted with providing the middle-level manpower requirement of the process industry. CIPET is creating technical manpower for the process industry in its 15 branches at different parts of the country and till date it has created 27000 professionals since its inception 40 years ago. In view of the projected demand of 1.4 lakh skilled plastic professionals during the Eleventh Plan, the intake capacity of each centre may be enhanced.

7.1.263 PCPIRs should be established with dedicated plastic parks to stimulate new investment activity in the sector. Cluster development programmes such as in the IIUS of DIPP also need to be undertaken for the existing clusters.

7.1.264 The Eleventh Plan allocation for CIPET is Rs 136.50 crore including an Organization of the Petroleum Exporting Countries (OPEC) loan of Rs 55 crore. The Assam Gas Cracker Project has been approved by the government in 2006. The project is being implemented by a joint venture company, with Gas Authority of India Ltd (GAIL) having 70% equity participation. The joint venture company namely M/s Brahmaputra Cracker and Polymer Ltd (BCPL) was incorporated during January 2007 for implementation of this project.

Shipbuilding and Ship-repair Industry

SHIPBUILDING

Overview

7.1.265 The Indian shipbuilding is mainly centred around 27 shipyards comprising 8 public sector (6 yards under Central Government and 2 under State Governments) and 19 private sector shipyards. The shipyards between them have 20 dry docks and 40 slipways with an estimated capacity of 281200 Dead Weight Tonnage (DWT). A major share of this capacity is held by the 8 public sector yards and only Cochin Shipyard Limited (110000 DWT) and HSL (80000 DWT) have the required infrastructure and graving dock to build large vessels.

7.1.266 After a pronounced boom in the mid-1970s, the global shipbuilding industry experienced a prolonged depression for more than 20 years, which lasted until the end of the Tenth Five Year Plan. Since then another boom has set in and the outlook of the shipbuilding industry has been transformed. At the beginning of the Eleventh Five Year Plan, the order book position of Indian shipyards was very healthy. Private shipyards are severely limited by capacity and the size of ship they can build. However, five of them are in the process of expanding or setting up new capacities, including for building Very Large Crude Carrier (VLCC) size ships, with an investment in the region of Rs 4000 crore.

Production and Export

7.1.267 The growth of shipbuilding in India has gone up from 4.5% in the Ninth Five Year Plan period to 15% per year in the Tenth Five Year Plan period, and India's share in the world market from an insignificant 0.1% in the beginning of Tenth Plan to 1.3% in 2006. On the export front, one public sector shipyard, that is Cochin Shipyard Ltd (CSL), and three private sector shipyards, viz., ABG, Bharati, and Chowgule, performed remarkably well during the Tenth Five Year Plan period and were able to get export orders. The Indian ship-repair industry is having an average turnover of around US$ 76 million. The ship-repair market potential is much more than what is presently being undertaken.

7.1.268 A meagre six ships were exported in the Ninth Five Year Plan but orders for export of more than 50 ships have been taken by Indian yards in the Tenth Five Year Plan. Against 0.3 million DWT exported during the Ninth Five Year Plan, the order book for export is more than 1.0 million DWT and the projections for the Eleventh Five Year Plan are about 4.00 million DWT. The bulk of the export is in the small-ship segment where India has emerged as a major supplier, and for the construction of offshore and oil industry ships such as Offshore Supply Vessels (OSVs) and anchor handling tugs. From an inward-looking industry dependent on government orders, the Indian shipbuilding industry has emerged as a competitive export-led industry.

Market Potential

7.1.269 As per Indian National Shipowners Association (INSA), the total tonnage required to be added in the Eleventh Plan will be around 5.33 million GT involving about 455 vessels, and the investment required will be Rs 55000 crore.

7.1.270 The annual average global order book grew by 78.86 million DWT in the period 2001–05 and in excess of 100 million DWT in the last two years. Of the Rs 14000 crore worth vessels on order in the Indian yards, nearly 68% are for foreign buyers. Clearly the outlook for the Indian shipbuilding industry is very bright and a faster growth of shipbuilding capacity is imperative for seizing the opportunity presented by the current boom. Projected shipbuilding order book turnover in Eleventh Five Year Plan is given in Table 7.1.11.

TABLE 7.1.11
Projected Shipbuilding Order Book Turnover

	2006–07	2007–12
Order book (Mn DWT)	1.3	5.00
Global order book (Mn DWT)	231.2	231.2
India's share of global order book	0.4%	2.2%
Delivery (Mn DWT)	0.65	2.50
Turnover (US$ Billion)	0.65	2.50
Shipbuilding industry % of GDP	0.04%	0.16%
Total employment	12000	78000

Source: DIPP.

Investment

7.1.271 The Indian Shipbuilders Association has estimated that the industry can grow at a rate of more than 30% and this momentum can be maintained for the next 10 years to reach a level of 5 million DWT order book for the Eleventh Five Year Plan as against 1.3 million for the Tenth Five Year Plan.

Challenges

7.1.272 Shipyards get orders only if they are credible (i.e., deliver quality ships on time) and it can be credible only after successfully executing consistently under international competition. During the Tenth Five Year Plan the industry has demonstrated its international competitiveness and the ability to respond to a buoyant market. The main challenges are removing the policy impediments, ensuring a stable environment, and encouraging R&D, design, and productivity improvement.

7.1.273 The Working Group has highlighted that cost competitiveness of Indian yards was affected on account of service tax, custom duty on ships manufactured in Indian yards, high excise duty on raw materials and capital goods required for manufacturing ships, etc. While foreign shipping companies are building their medium and small merchant ships in India, Indian shipping companies are purchasing their ships from abroad, both big and small but more big than small. The present fiscal and statutory rules on shipbuilding in the country are heavily loaded in favour of export and discourage construction of ships by Indian yards for the Indian flag.

7.1.274 The shipbuilding subsidy has been the main promotional instrument for the shipbuilding industry. The shipbuilding subsidy scheme has been operating since 1971 for Central public sector shipyards. The scheme was discontinued in 1975, was later re-introduced in 1977, and was modified in August 2000. The shipbuilding subsidy up to 2002 has been used as a measure for revival of public sector shipbuilding. Re-modified subsidy scheme introduced in 2002 discontinued Interest Differential Subsidy upto 5% and extended the benefits to 30% subsidy on the price of the ship to private sector yards also. The subsidy has clearly been a major contributing factor in enabling the industry to get a foothold in the international market. It is also a fact that the major shipbuilding nations of the world have been granting shipbuilding subsidies in the past.

7.1.275 In order to be able to join the league of major shipbuilding nations, the industry needs to undertake design development and R&D. With the changing technological environment, increasing application of information technology, and changes in safety norms, it is imperative for shipyards to keep pace with such developments to meet emerging classification standards.

Strategies

7.1.276 It is necessary to examine in depth the impact of the fiscal regime on the Indian shipbuilding industry to see if any corrective measures need to be taken. In particular, the reasons have to be ascertained for the preference of the Indian shipping industry to purchase from foreign sources and remedial measures taken.

7.1.277 It has become apparent that the existing shipbuilding subsidy scheme cannot be continued indefinitely when boom conditions are prevailing in the international market. However, a gradual phase down rather than sudden termination may seem to be called for.

7.1.278 The R&D institutional set up serving the shipbuilding sector needs to be reviewed and strengthened. The R&D scheme in the shipbuilding sector will have to cover projects for industry-wide improvement in knowledge base, standardization, and skill development. The government should extend budgetary support for R&D in shipbuilding.

7.1.279 An allocation of Rs 170 crore has been made in the Eleventh Plan for R&D in the shipbuilding sector.

SHIP-REPAIR INDUSTRY

Overview

7.1.280 Unlike the shipbuilding industry, which experiences cyclical downturns and upturns, the ship-repair industry is evergreen. Ship-repair yards generally have a continuous and consistent flow of business and revenue generation is more predictable. Another attractive feature of the ship-repair industry from the Indian perspective is its job-creating potential on the one hand and the availability of skilled personnel on the other.

7.1.281 Unlike in some other countries where ship repairs are done mainly in dedicated units, in India there is only one dedicated unit and all the other yards carry out ship repairs and shipbuilding side by side. Ship repairs are also carried out in dry docks and floating docks. The Indian ship-repair industry is regulated through ship-repair units (SRUs), which are registered and licensed by the Director General of Shipping to enable them to avail customs duty and other concessions. There are 35 SRUs of which only 7 SRUs have been registered on a permanent basis.

PERFORMANCE AND MARKET POTENTIAL

7.1.282 During the Tenth Five Year Plan the industry achieved an annual turnover of about Rs 436 crore. The Tenth Five Year Plan had envisaged that India would emerge as a dominant ship-repair centre challenging Dubai, Singapore, and Bahrain. This did not happen because, inter alia, the industry turned its attention to shipbuilding in response to the prevailing boom conditions. The Working Group has assessed the annual market potential for ship repairs in India to be between Rs 2440 crore and Rs 2790 crore. Of this almost 50% will be accounted for by foreign ships on overseas trade visiting Indian ports, and the remaining by domestic ships engaged in overseas trade, coastal/service vessels, offshore rig repairs, navy and coast guard vessels, and other merchant vessels in the region.

Challenges

7.1.283 While the Indian shipbuilding industry is benefiting from an unprecedented boom, the ship-repair industry is in the doldrums. One of the reasons is poor productivity. The Yiu Lian Dockyard Ltd, the biggest shipyard in China, has steel renewal capacity of 250 mt per day as against 5 mt per day at best in India, and sand/grit blasting capacity of over 15000 sq m per day against around 1000 sq m per day in India. It takes 6 to 7 days in India to blast the outer hull of a 30000–40000 DWT ship and 50 days to replace 250 mt of steel in India against just one day in China for each of these operations. Since the time taken for ship repair of the essence for competitiveness, the longer time taken by the Indian ship-repair industry makes it less competitive.

7.1.284 The existing docking facilities in India have not grown to meet the requirements of the modern tonnage with only the two CPSEs, Cochin Shipyards Ltd and Hindustan Shipyards Ltd, able to provide dry dock and repair facilities for large size vessels. There is no dry dock facility for VLCC class of vessels, which are bound to increase in number on the west coast with the commencement of new refineries in Gujarat. Even Suezmax size vessels do not have dry docking facilities in the country. Further, the 13 dry docks and 1 floating dock in existence in the major port trusts are underutilized for the repair business.

7.1.285 While exemption is available to SRUs from both customs duty and excise duty, no such exemption is available in respect of service tax. The service tax of 12.24% has made the industry uncompetitive vis-à-vis ship repairers in Bahrain, Dubai, and Singapore.

Customs clearance procedures also are time consuming and impose costs on the industry.

Strategies

7.1.286 The CPSEs are the engines of growth in ship repairs. While the private sector units will no doubt respond to market demands by creating the capacity for repair of large size ships and to improve productivity, it is also necessary to make additional investments toward this end in the CPSEs, particularly the CSL and HSL. Further the reasons for underutilization of dry dock and floating dock facilities in major ports need to be examined and corrective measures taken.

7.1.287 The possibility of exemption of the ship-repair industry from service tax and improvement of customs procedures for speedy clearance of import consignments of spare parts needed for ship repairs need to be examined.

Steel Industry

OVERVIEW: PRODUCTION, IMPORT, AND EXPORT

7.1.288 The Tenth Five Year Plan has seen robust growth of the steel industry with significant increases in both production and consumption. Crude steel production grew at the rate of 9.8% annually from 34.83 million tonnes in 2002–03 to 50.88 million tonnes in 2006–07 (provisional). This growth was driven by both capacity expansion (from 40.41 million tonnes in 2002–03 to 56.84 million tonnes in 2006–07) and improved capacity utilization (from 86% in 2002–03 to 89% in 2006–07). The year-wise production, availability, consumption, export, and import of finished steel in the Tenth Plan are presented in Annexure 7.1.14.

7.1.289 The average increase in production during the Tenth Five Year Plan was 3.7 million tonnes per annum compared to just 1.1 million tonnes per annum in the Ninth Five Year Plan (1997–2002), and the annual growth rate of steel consumption doubled to 9.8% in the Tenth Five Year Plan compared to only 3.8% in the Ninth Five Year Plan. Capacity creation during the last decade after deregulation has taken place entirely in the private sector. As a result, there has been a noticeable shift towards the private sector both at the crude and finished steel stages. Private sector during 2006–07 accounted for 67% of the total crude steel output compared to 41% in 1992–93 and 74% of the total finished steel output compared to 54% in 1992–93.

7.1.290 The National Steel Policy 2005 has projected consumption to grow at 7% based on GDP growth of 7%–7.5% and production capacity of 110 million tonnes by 2019–20. The estimates have been revised upward by the Working Group. In the 'Most Likely' scenario of 9% GDP growth, demand for steel is projected to be 70 million tonnes by 2011–12. Therefore, it is envisaged that in the next five years, the demand will grow at a considerably higher annual average rate of 10.2% as compared to around 7% growth achieved between 1991–92 and 2005–06.

7.1.291 Several existing steel mills have planned expansion of capacity and there are new investments including foreign investment in the pipeline. The public sector units, namely, SAIL and RINL, are planning to increase production of crude steel from a level of 16 million tonnes per annum in 2006–07 to 30 million tonnes per annum by 2011–12. The Eleventh Five Year Plan Working Group on the steel industry has estimated that the capacity that will actually come up by the terminal year will be 80 million tonnes per annum of crude steel.

7.1.292 The world steel industry has been buoyed up by the frenetic pace of growth in the consumption and production of steel in China. The world crude steel production grew from 0.850 billion tonnes in 2001 to approximately 1.24 billion tonnes in 2006 recording a growth of 7.9% per annum compared to a mere 2% annual growth recorded between 1995 and 2001. China's steel production rose by more than 210 million tonnes since 2001 to reach a level of 423 million tonnes in 2006. Today more than 34% of the global steel production is attributed to the Chinese economy. The World Steel Dynamics in its latest forecast for next 15 years (June 2006) projects global steel demand at least at a rate of 3.1% per year till 2015. The impetus for expansion of steel capacity in India has come from the expected expansion of the domestic demand.

7.1.293 The Indian steel industry has withstood international competition despite the reduction of basic customs duty on steel from 25%–30% in 2002–03 to 5% in 2006–07. By the end of the Tenth Five Year Plan the industry was fully geared to operate in an open economy where exports and imports respond to increases or decreases in the domestic demand driven primarily by market signals. While exports of finished carbon steel were sustained at a level of 4–5 million mt per annum during the Tenth Five Year Plan imports increased sharply from about 1.5 million mt in 2002–03 to 4.10 million mt in 2006–07 (provisional), it was not because of fall in competitiveness but rather to fill up supply–demand gap in the domestic market.

CHALLENGES

7.1.294 If steel production is to increase to the projected levels by the end of the Eleventh Five Year Plan, there would be a large requirement of raw materials and other inputs. The indicative requirements that have been worked out by the Eleventh Five Year Plan Working Group are presented in Annexure 7.1.15.

7.1.295 The challenge arises from the fact that iron ore resources in the country are depleting, aided by the rapid growth of exports, and high grade coking coal needed by the industry which is in short supply, globally leading to hardening of prices from US$ 48 per mt FOB Australian ports in 2003 to US$ 115 per mt in 2006. Although non-coking coal reserves in the country are adequate, the production of the raw material is constrained by low investment by Coal India Ltd. An added problem of the Indian steel industry is that adequate sintering and pelletization capacities do not exist in the country as a result of which steel mills rely on lump ores and fines have to be necessarily exported.

7.1.296 A related problem is that of movement of raw materials such as iron ore, non-coking coal, and limestone from the mines to the plants. Large volumes of coking coal would have to be moved from the ports to the plants, which are mostly situated inland. The quality of transport infrastructure in the country imposes huge costs on the steel industry and with increased quantities needed to be moved the problem will increase.

STRATEGIES

7.1.297 It would be necessary to monitor the exports of iron ore from the country with a view to ensuring that supplies to the Indian steel plants are not affected. Export duty has already been imposed and it is expected that the exports would come down. At the same time, for assured metallurgical coke supplies, the possibility should be explored of an arrangement with China to swap iron ore for metallurgical coke. To incentivize the development of sintering and pelletization capacities consideration should be given for fiscal concessions to the industry.

7.1.298 Increased movement of input and output from the steel industry will be considerably facilitated by the investment envisaged in the Eleventh Five Year Plan in road, rail, and ports. The financing plan of ports already takes into consideration the likely increase in imports of coking coal. Since the internal movement of bulk raw materials will be largely by rail, and projected increases of movement are very large, the railways should set up joint consultative machinery with the industry to ensure that the requirements of the industry are fully factored into the plans of the railways.

7.1.299 In steel sector, in the Eleventh Plan, the outlay of Rs 37318.18 crore includes the budgetary Rs 216 crore only. Out of total allocation of Rs 37318.18 crore, SAIL and RINL account for Rs 27409 crore and Rs 9569.18 crore, respectively. The budgetary support is for the restructuring of CPSEs in steel sector and for some of the ongoing and new R&D schemes.

Sugar Industry

7.1.300 India is the largest producer–consumer of sugar in the world. The sugar industry is the second largest agro-based industry, next to textiles in the country. About five lakh workers are directly employed in the sugar industry besides many more in industries, which utilize by-products of sugar industry as raw material. The country has 582 sugar factories with an aggregate capacity of 197.97 lakh tonnes. The ownership-wise break up is given in Figure 7.1.14.

7.1.301 As a result of a conducive policy environment resulting from progressive decontrol and favourable

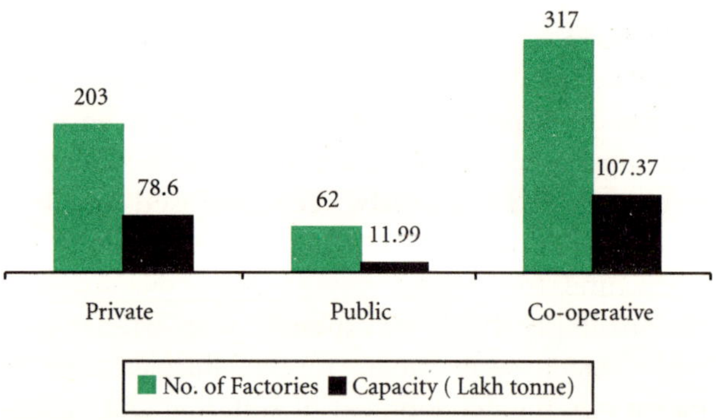

Source: Annual Plan 2007–08, Department of Food and Public Distribution (DFPD).

FIGURE 7.1.14: Ownership-wise Distribution

monsoon, sugar production in the country experienced strong growth in the last four years of the Ninth Plan to reach an all time high level of 201.32 lakh tonnes in 2002–03. After a decline due to failure of monsoon in some States during 2003–04 and 2004–05 seasons, domestic production again picked up, achieving the estimated level of 283 lakh tonnes in 2006–07.

7.1.302 Out of 582 sugar-producing units in the country, 410 are in the small segment, with 228 having a capacity of 2500 Metric Tonnes Crushed per day (TCD) and 282 having a capacity of 2500 to 5000 TCD. Mid-size segment has 64 units with capacities higher than 5000 TCD but below 10000 TCD, while only 8 units are large, having capacities of 10000 TCD and above. The position regarding production, internal consumption, and export of sugar during 2002–03 to 2005–06 are given in the Annexure 7.1.16.

POLICY INTERVENTIONS

7.1.303 While the sugar industry has benefited from the withdrawal of industrial licensing under the Industries Development and Regulation Act 1951 and the abolition of stockholding and turnover limits on wholesalers/dealers, it is still subject to a number of policy interventions as described below:

- The industry is subject to statutory minimum price (SMP) for sugarcane fixed by the Central Government from year to year on the basis of the recommendations of the CACP taking into account cost of production of sugarcane, return to growers from alternative crops, fair consumer price of sugar, etc. SMP is fixed after consulting the State Governments and associations of sugar industry and cane growers.
- While the policy of blanket control on sugar under Essential Commodities Act 1955 has been discontinued, a policy of partial control and dual pricing is still in operation. Under this policy, a certain percentage of sugar production in factories is levied by the government on a pre-fixed price for distribution under PDS and the remaining production goes for free sale. The proportion of levy sugar has however been reduced from 40% to 10%. The Sugarcane Control Order stipulates that a new mill cannot be established within a distance of less than 1 km from an existing mill.
- While the erstwhile Sugar Export Promotion Act 1958 was repealed and export of sugar decanalized, the level of exports is regulated through several measures such as system of advance licensing, periodic ban, etc.

SUGAR DEVELOPMENT FUND (SDF)

7.1.304 Under the Sugar Cess Act 1982, a cess of Rs 14.00 per quintal is collected on all sugar produced in the country and an amount equivalent to the same is credited in the SDF created under the SDF Act 1982. The Fund has benefited the domestic industry by providing loans at concessional rates to sugar factories for modernization and expansion of capacities, rehabilitation, development of sugarcane, setting up facilities for internal transportation for export obligation, setting up of bagasse-based co-generation units, production of ethanol from molasses, and maintenance of buffer stock as well as providing grant for industrial research. Commensurate with the technology upgradation and price escalation, normative project costs of various components, especially, bagasse-based co-generation, etc., are being revised from time to time. In an amendment dated 15 September 2006 the normative project cost for bagasse-based co-generation unit has been revised upwards and the SDF loan component raised to 40% of the project cost from 30% earlier. The amendment also relaxed the earlier requirement of bank guarantee for SDF loans to set up ethanol units by sugar factories.

BUFFER STOCKS

7.1.305 In order to alleviate the difficulties of the mills in times of surplus production, the Central Government undertakes buffer stock operations from time to time. In August 2007 the government decided to create a buffer stock of 30 lakh mt for a period of one year.

CHALLENGES

7.1.306 While international prices have been fluctuating, the SMP fixed by the Central Government has been raised gradually from Rs 62.05 per quintal in 2001–002 to Rs 81.18 per quintal in 2007–08. Additionally some of the State Governments have been advising sugar factories to pay cane price at a higher level than the SMP. The sugar industry thus faces a predicament in which it is asked to pay more for the raw materials even as it gets less for its produce in the market.

7.1.307 Indian sugar exports experience wide fluctuations from year to year. While exports are restricted in the years when international prices are high, they need to be subsidized in years in which such prices are low. Export subsidies have become inconsistent with India's obligations under the WTO Agreement from 2004 after the expiry of the validity of the WTO provision which gave special dispensation to the developing countries in respect of subsidies on market promotion expenses including international freight as well as on concessions on internal freight on export shipments.

7.1.308 Indian sugar industry is amongst the most diversified industry in the world, with an installed capacity to produce 1000 MW co-generated power against a potential of 7500 MW. An addition of 1000 MW is under implementation. Despite emphasis laid by the GoI to harness the growth potential further, the progress as co-generation of power is sapped by problems with regard to tariff fixation, third-party sale, and timely payments by State Electricity Boards (SEBs).

7.1.309 The economics of sugar production are crucially dependent on the production of by-product ethanol. Recently, the 5% ethanol-doping programme has been extended to the country as a whole, with the annual doping requirement estimated at 550 million litres of ethanol. With further increase in the ethanol doping to 10% from June 2007, the annual demand would rise up to about 1100 million litres. Already a capacity of about 1550 million litres has been established in major sugarcane-producing States, which is sufficient to meet this scale of ethanol-doping requirement. However, the oil companies are going slow. Further, in as many as seven States, the EDP has not been implemented due to taxation problem by the State Governments. It may be noted that in Brazil, doping has been mandated by the government at 24%.

STRATEGIES

7.1.310 Since fluctuation in international prices is a feature of international commodity markets, it needs to be examined how the fall in sales realization in certain years can be taken into account in fixing the SMP for sugarcane or in considering additional payments sometimes mandated by the State Governments.

7.1.311 The evolution of the WTO rules has made export subsidies by India in sugar (or any agricultural products) arguably inconsistent with the WTO obligations. The developing countries are likely to get a time-limited window for such subsidies once the Doha Round concludes. In the meantime, it needs to be examined how the government can assist the industry in a WTO-consistent manner to deal with surplus production.

7.1.312 The difficulties of sugar mills in the sale of additional power from co-generation need to be resolved.

7.1.313 A long-term policy needs to be devised on the mixing requirements for petroleum fuel with ethanol.

Textiles and Jute

7.1.314 The strength of the Indian textiles and clothing industry is based on the long tradition of manufacturing, strong raw material base, indigenous design capabilities, presence in the entire value chain, large and growing domestic demand, and the availability of trained manpower at internationally competitive rates. The Indian textile and clothing industry consumes a diverse range of fibres and yarns but is predominantly cotton based. At current price, the total market size of the Indian textiles industry is approximately US$ 47 billion. The industry contributes 14% to the total industrial production and directly employs 35 million people. It accounted for 17% of India's export earnings, 3.37% share in international merchandise, and 18% of industrial employment in 2006.

7.1.315 During the Tenth Five Year Plan period, the growth rate of the industry accelerated under the twin stimuli of domestic policy reforms and the end of the quota regime with effect from 1 January 2005 in major industrialized countries following agreement in the WTO. The excise duty structure was streamlined and rationalized, customs duty on machinery reduced, and the reservation for SSI units for garments eliminated. Removal of the policy tilt towards the SSI units had a significantly positive effect on the industry. The TUFS and the cotton technology mission also boosted the industry. The production of cloth increased strongly in the last three years of the Plan period after stagnating in the first two years. During the first two years of the Tenth Five Year Plan, the total production of cloth hovered around 42 million sq m but rose to 49.5 million sq m in 2005–06, and is estimated to have reached a figure of 53.7 million sq m in 2006–07 (Annexure 7.1.17).

7.1.316 Following the end of textile quotas, exports registered a strong increase in the year 2005–06 but there was a deceleration in the subsequent year. Export of textiles and clothing during the Tenth Five Year Plan is presented in Annexure 7.1.18.

7.1.317 The available export data (April 2006–February 2007) seem to suggest that the growth of exports decelerated sharply (to about 7.75%) as compared to 25.9% during April 2005–February 2006. Even in 2005–06, when exports had risen overall, man-made textiles had shown a decline, indicating lack of competitiveness in a quota-free regime. Clearly, despite the progress in the latter half of the Tenth Five Year Plan, the well-known constraints, which are indicated later, are still affecting competitiveness in man-made textiles. Overall, however, at the end of the Tenth Five Year Plan period there was considerable vibrancy in the textile industry and confidence that it was poised for significant growth during the Eleventh Five Year Plan. The vision projected by the industry envisages that cloth production would grow at 12% and the total turnover at 16% during the Eleventh Five Year Plan. The turnover will rise from US$ 47 billion to US$ 115 billion and the exports from US$ 17 billion to US$ 55 billion. The industry expectation is that the incremental investment of Rs 30000 crore would be replicated during each of the five years of the Eleventh Five Year Plan. The industry also projects an increase in employment by 6.5 million, of which almost 2 million will be in the skilled and managerial categories.

TEXTILES MACHINERY INDUSTRY

7.1.318 The fortunes of the textiles engineering industry are linked with textiles industry. The performance of textiles engineering industry has shown significant improvement during the last—two to three years in line with the textiles industry. The production of textiles machinery has been steadily increasing over the last five years and a significant increase of 28% has been recorded during the year 2005–06. The capacity utilization of the industry has also been gradually increasing. It has increased from 28% in 2001–02 to 57% in 2005–06. In terms of value, the production of textiles machinery has increased from Rs 1072.46 crore in 2001–02 to Rs 2151.10 crore during 2005–06.

JUTE INDUSTRY

7.1.319 The jute industry occupies an important place in the national economy. It is one of the major industries in the eastern region, particularly in West Bengal. It supports nearly four million farm families, besides providing direct employment to about 2.6 lakh industrial workers and livelihood to another 1.4 lakh people in the tertiary and allied sectors. The target for raw jute production in the Tenth Plan is likely to be achieved in 2006–07. Against the production target of 110 lakh bales for the terminal year 2006–07 of the Tenth Five Year Plan, the achievement in 2005–06 was 85 lakh bales and the expectation is that the target would have been achieved in 2006–07. The average of jute and mesta produced during 2002–03 to 2005–06 was 91.25 lakh bales. Jute goods production, however, will fall short of the Plan target by 18%: against the target of 19.50 lakh mt for terminal year 2006–07, the achievement during 2005–06 was 15.82 lakh mt and the average production of jute goods from 2002–03 to

2005–06 was 15.96 lakh mt. In contrast, export targets had been met and exceeded. Against the export target for jute goods of US$ 154.36 million for the terminal year 2006–07, the achievement in 2005–06 was US$ 276 million. The average exports of jute goods from 2002–03 to 2005–06 was US$ 240 million.

REVIEW OF MAJOR TENTH PLAN SCHEMES

7.1.320 We review below the three major Plan schemes that were in operation during the Tenth Five Year Plan.

Technology Upgradation Fund Scheme (TUFS)

7.1.321 Investments in the textiles sector, which was being incentivized by the TUFS, picked up steam from 2004–05 after the major steps taken by the Central Government for rationalizing the excise duty structure in that year. Another reason for the spurt was the implementation of the WTO Agreement for the elimination of quotas. Figure 7.1.15 shows the growth of investment stimulated by the TUFS.

Technology Mission on Cotton (TMC)

7.1.322 TMC, which commenced during the Ninth Plan, had four mini-missions, the first two for increasing agricultural productivity, implemented by the Ministry of Agriculture, and the other two for the development of marketing yards and modernization of G&P units, implemented by the Ministry of Textiles. The missions implemented by the Ministry of Agriculture have contributed to an increase in the productivity from 308 kg per ha in 2002 to 467 kg per ha in 2005 (world average: 680 kg per ha; US: 830 kg per ha; Brazil: 1180 kg per ha; China: 1140 kg per ha).

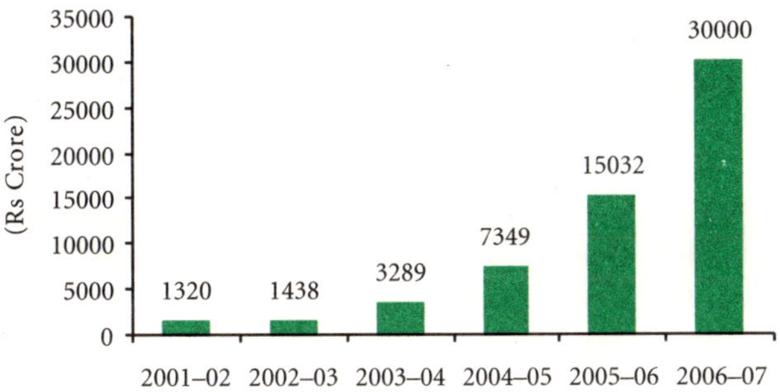

Source: Report of the Working Group on Textiles and Jute Industry for Eleventh Plan.

FIGURE 7.1.15: Project Cost Sanctioned under TUFS

Under mini-mission III 250 marketing yards were sanctioned for development against which 225 are expected to have been sanctioned until the end of the Tenth Five Year Plan. Under mini-mission IV, modernization of about 900 Ginning and Pressing units is expected to have been sanctioned against a target of 1000. Some of the ginners have availed of the TUFS for modernization, making the total number 1500. With the completion of these programmes the industry will have the capability to process about 325000 bales of cotton, which is expected to be clean and contamination free.

Scheme for Integrated Textile Parks (SITP)

7.1.323 The SITP was launched in 2005 to neutralize the weakness of fragmentation in the various subsectors of textiles value chain and the non-availability of quality infrastructure. The aim was to consolidate individual units in a cluster, and also to provide the industry with world-class infrastructure facilities on a PPP model to set up their textile units. A total of 26 parks have already been approved and these are expected to be developed by March 2008. These parks would incorporate facilities for spinning, sizing, texturizing, weaving, processing, apparels, and embellishments. The estimated project cost (for common infrastructure and common facilities) is Rs 2428.33 crore of which the GoI assistance under the scheme would be Rs 866 crore. (The estimated investment in these parks would be Rs 13445 crore and the estimated annual production would be Rs 19200 crore.) A total of 2219 entrepreneurs will put up their units in these parks. The estimated employment generation would be around five lakh (direct/indirect).

CHALLENGES

7.1.324 The Indian textiles industry suffers from all the handicaps of the manufacturing sector mentioned earlier, viz., deficiencies in the transport infrastructure, shortcomings in the quantity and quality of supply of electricity, lack of adequate flexibility in the labour laws, high transaction cost, and direct and indirect taxes that are short of world standards. Although much has been done during the Tenth Five Year Plan in particular, the task remains formidable. We consider some of these problems in the context of the textiles industry.

7.1.325 The main reason for India to be well behind China in textiles and clothing is the absence of economies of scale in the manufacturing enterprises in the country. While many units in China have tens of thousands of workers, the industrial units in India are discouraged by the requirements of Chapter V-B of the Industrial Disputes Act 1956 from employing more than 100 workers. The result is that the industry is fragmented and is unable to respond to the large volumes of orders that are placed by the retail chains in the industrial economies. The Contract Labour (Regulation and Abolition) Act 1970 is another hurdle in these enterprises being able to respond to enquiries for supply of large volumes of goods unless they are assured of long-term demand, which is seldom the case. This is the main reason behind the fact that the share of textiles in the FDI flows into the country so far has been about 1% against 10% in China.

7.1.326 Technologically, our textiles industry is still backward and the modernization process that began during the Ninth Five Year Plan and accelerated midway through the Tenth Five Year Plan has not made enough progress. To give one example, only 2% shuttleless looms are in place as against the world average of 16%. Another segment that has not made progress is processing. A big handicap is that the order books of the textile machinery industry are full and the industry is not able to get delivery in quick time. As a result the enterprises are purchasing second-hand equipment, which costs a fraction of the new equipment. Large-scale purchase of the used machinery, with a limited life, cannot be really called modernization.

7.1.327 The technical textile is an upcoming area in the textile sector which is primarily textile materials and products with specific physical and functional properties, mostly used as component/part of another product to improve the performance of the product. These include spun-bonded geo-textiles, needle-punched geo-textiles, woven geo-textiles, geo-grids, woven narrow fabrics, and non-woven for disposables healthcare textiles, sanitary napkins, incontinence diapers, and diapers. The domestic market in 2005 was worth US$ 6.7 billion as against the size of US$ 107 billion. The global market is expected to grow to US$ 127 billion by 2010. The challenge for the Indian textile sector is to increase its share of the global market during the Eleventh Five Year Plan.

7.1.328 A related problem is that modernization is based on the government support through the TUFS, which was made operational in the Ninth Five Year Plan. The financial assistance being given by the Central Government under the programme is not inconsistent with WTO obligations, but the problem is that it renders our exports vulnerable to countervailing duties being imposed by importing countries if these exports are assessed by them to be causing material injury to their domestic industry. Since the subsidy is on capital goods, the vulnerability will remain for the entire period of the useful life of the machinery. If the SEZ benefit of income tax concession on profits from export income and/or the benefits of the SITP are added, the importing countries could impose high countervailing duties. Furthermore, the requirement of funds for continuing the TUFS is likely to be very high if the scheme is rolled over into the Eleventh Five Year Plan.

7.1.329 As mentioned earlier, it is expected that during the Eleventh Five Year Plan period there would be a large requirement of additional workforce in the industry. The Working Group for Textiles and Clothing for the Eleventh Five Year Plan has identified category-wise requirement (in lakh) of workforce as managerial, technical, and administration (6.5); skilled, ITIs and Certificate courses (13); semi-skilled machine operators (32.5); and unskilled (13). In the absence of organized effort the requirement is not likely to be met.

STRATEGIES

7.1.330 It has been difficult to achieve consensus on proposals for changes in labour laws, particularly Chapter V-B of the Industrial Disputes Act 1956 and the Contract Labour (Regulation and Abolition) Act 1970, but given the potential for unlocking substantial additional employment in the textile and clothing industry if these changes are carried out, consideration of such changes and consultations for the same would have to continue so that early action is taken during the Plan period. In the absence of any change, the ambitious programmes of the industry are likely to remain unrealized.

7.1.331 In order to continue the stimulus for investment for modernization, upgradation, and additional capacity creation, the TUFS, SITP and TMC would have to be continued during the Eleventh Five Year Plan. However, it would be necessary to limit the TUFS, either in time or scope, in order to ensure that the financial commitment of the Central Government does not cross the allocation available for the programme. Furthermore, in order to ensure that the industry modernizes, the assistance should be restricted only to the purchase of new machinery.

7.1.332 It has become apparent that substantial additional effort would be needed for skill upgradation and training of managerial, skilled, and semi-skilled manpower. In order to ensure that the effort is demand driven, the individual initiatives must come from the industry, which should be willing to take complete responsibility for running the additional programmes. The government's contribution could come as a one-time assistance for developing the needed infrastructure, by way of buildings and equipment needed for the creation of new facilities or expansion of existing ones.

7.1.333 The total outlay for the industry segment of the textile sector is Rs 11000 crore. In the Eleventh Plan the TUFS would continue for two years. Other main continuing schemes are SITP and TMC. Jute Technology Mission has already been revised by bringing all components together in Mission Mode in 2006. For skill upgradation, a 'Human Resource Development Scheme' is proposed in the Eleventh Plan.

MICRO AND SMALL ENTERPRISES (MSEs)

Introduction

7.1.334 Worldwide, MSMEs[3] have been recognized as engines of economic growth. In India, MSEs (till recently, known as village and small enterprises) account for almost 40% of the total industrial production, 95% of the industrial units (along with medium industries), and 34% of the exports. They manufacture over 6000 products ranging from handloom sarees, carpets, and soaps to pickles, papads, and machine parts for large industries.

7.1.335 It is estimated that an investment of Rs 10 lakh in fixed assets in the small sector produces goods or services worth Rs 46.2 lakh with an approximate value addition of 10 percentage points. In 2003–04, the contribution of SSI sector alone to the GDP was 6.71%. In the last decade, the growth rate of MSEs has been consistently higher than the overall growth rate of the industrial sector, crossing the 12% mark in the terminal year of the Tenth Plan.

7.1.336 The MSEs are, however, more than just GDP earners; they are instruments of inclusive growth which touch upon the lives of the most vulnerable, the most marginalized—women, Muslims, SCs, and STs—and the most skilled. Being the largest source of employment after agriculture, the MSE sector in India enables 650 lakh men, women, and children living in urban slums, upcoming towns, remote villages and isolated hamlets to use indigenous knowledge, cultural wisdom, dextrous hands, and entrepreneurial skills for the sustenance of their lives and livelihoods. Yet, in successive Five Year Plans this sector has not received its due. A subset of the MSE sector is what can be termed as 'cultural and creative industries'. India's cultural diversity and heritage is capable of giving the country a strong presence in the global market for products from such industries. The Planning Commission had constituted a Task Force with a view to integrate production by cultural and creative industries with our development strategy. The recommendations of the Task Force will be examined for implementation in the Eleventh Plan.Table 7.1.12 indicates the allocation for Village and Small Enterprises (VSE) in the past three Plan periods.

TABLE 7.1.12
Plan Outlays for the Last Three Five Year Plans for VSE Sector

(Rs Crore)

Sector	Eighth Plan Period	Ninth Plan Period	Tenth Plan Period
MSME	1629.55	4303.85	5534.00
Textiles	1157.00	1270.00	1600.00
FPI	146.00	235.04	650.00

Source: Ninth and Tenth Plan, Planning Commission.

[3] In this chapter, MSME means micro, small, and medium enterprises; SME means small and medium enterprises; while MSE means micro and small enterprises.

7.1.337 TThe MSME sector has been artificially fragmented across various ministries, such as MSME, textiles, and FPI to name a few. As a result, sectors such as handloom, powerloom, handicrafts, khadi, and coir have suffered greater neglect than other manufacturing and service based MSEs.

7.1.338 In an attempt to correct these discrepancies and neglect, the Micro, Small and Medium Enterprises Development Act was enacted on 16 June 2006. This Act provides the first-ever legal framework recognizing the concept of 'enterprise' (comprising both manufacturing and service entities), defining medium enterprises and integrating the three tiers of these enterprises, namely, micro, small and medium. Carrying forward the vision behind this Act, the Eleventh Plan recognizes the MSE sector as an important component of the industry that needs infrastructure, credit, and policy support. During this Plan period, the endeavour would be to recognize the heterogeneity of the MSE sector and at the same time remove artificial distinctions within the sector to ensure that the unorganized, home-based industries such as handlooms and food processing are able to avail the benefits and schemes launched for the industry in general and the MSE in particular.

Role of SMEs in Global Economy: International Scenario

7.1.339 The overall contribution of small firms—formal and informal—to the GDP and employment remain about the same across low, middle, and high-income group countries. As income increases, the share of the informal sector decreases and that of the formal SME sector increases.[4]

7.1.340 In Brazil, MSEs represent 20% of the total GDP. Of the country's 4.7 million registered businesses, 96.8% are MSEs and–along with the other 9.5 million informal enterprises—they employ 59% of the economically active population.[5] Similarly, informal and micro enterprises account for 39% of labour force and contribute to 24% of the GDP in South Africa; SMEs employ 27% of the labour force and contribute 32% to the GDP; while large enterprises employ 34% people and account for 44% of GDP. (Stats SA 2000 and Abedian 2001).[6] SMEs comprise over 90% of all industrial units in Bangladesh contributing between 80% and 85% of the industrial employment and 23% of the total civilian employment (SEDF, 2003).[7] They contribute three-quarters of the household income in both the urban and the rural areas. In Japan, SMEs employ more than 70% of the wage earners, contributing over 55% of value added in the manufacturing sector.[8] In Thailand in 2003, there were 2006528 enterprises of which 99.5% were SMEs. These SMEs generated products worth 38.1% of GDP and in 2003 they employed 60.7% of Thailand's working population.[9]

7.1.341 The real importance of the SMEs, however, can be seen in China where over 68% of the exports come from the SMEs (Table 7.1.13). China has created more SMEs in the last 20 years than the total number of SMEs in Europe and the US combined. Their numbers have

TABLE 7.1.13
Chinese Town and Village Enterprises (TVEs) Exports
(in Billion US$)

	Total Exports	SME Exports	SME Exports as % of Total
2002	438.23	272.48	62.3
2003	593.32	390.44	65.8
2004	761.99	518.16	68.0

Source: SME Briefing, Vol. 91, by SME Division of National Development and Reform Commission on 28 November 2006.

[4] *http://www.worldbank.org/research/projects/sme/abd.pdf*
Small and Medium Enterprises across the Globe: A new Database, Meghana Ayyagari, Thorsten Beck, and Asli Demirgüç-Kunt, August 2003.

[5] *http://www.dai.com/pdf/developments/developments_ fall_2005.pdf*

[6] *http://www.ciionline.org/services/112/Images/defsme.pdf*

[7] SEDF: South Asia Enterprise Development Facility *http://www.bei-bd.org/beireport/sme/The%%20Small%% 20and%%% 20Medium% 20Enterprises %%20(SME) %%20in %%20Bangladesh.pdf*

[8] *http://www.mofa.go.jp/region/asia-paci/thailand/joint0312.pdf*

[9] *http://www.jetro.go.jp/thailand/e/data/smesupport.htm*

increased from about 1 million private sector SMEs in the 1990s to 40 million in 2004. In China, an industrial SME is defined as having up to 2000 employees, while a small business has less than 300 employees and a medium-size business has employees between 301 and 2000.

Defining MSEs—MSMED Act, 2006

7.1.342 There is no globally accepted definition of MSMEs. Different countries use different criterion; most of the definitions are based on investment ceiling and number of people employed.[10] In India, the Micro, Small, and Medium Enterprises Development (MSMED) Act 2006 defines MSMEs. It introduces the concept of 'enterprise' as opposed to the earlier concept of industry. According to the Act, MSMEs are classified into the following: (i) enterprises engaged in the manufacture or production of goods pertaining to any industry specified in the first schedule to the Industries (Development and Regulation Act 1951) and (ii) enterprises engaged in providing or rendering services. Table 7.1.14 defines the MSMEs in both these sectors:

TABLE 7.1.14
Definition of MSMEs

	Manufacturing Sector
Enterprises	Investment in plant and machinery (original cost excluding land and building and the items specified by the then ministry of small scale industries, vide its notification No. S.O.1722(E) dated 5 October 2006)
Micro enterprises	Does not exceed Rs 25 lakh
Small enterprises	More than Rs 25 lakh and less than Rs 5 crore
Medium enterprises	More than Rs 5 crore and less than Rs 10 crore
	Service Sector
Enterprises	Investment in equipments
Micro enterprises	Does not exceed Rs 10 lakh
Small enterprises	More than Rs 10 lakh and less than Rs 2 crore
Medium enterprises	More than Rs 2 crore and less than Rs 5 crore

Source: Micro, Small, and Medium Enterprises Development Act, 2006.

7.1.343 The Act also provides for a statutory consultative mechanism at the national level with a balanced representation of all the sections of stakeholders and with a wide range of advisory functions. Establishment of specific funds for promotion, development, and enhancement of the competitiveness of these enterprises; notification of schemes/programmes, progressive credit policies and practices; preference to products and services of MSEs in the government procurement; more effective mechanisms for mitigating the problems of delayed payments; and a scheme for easing the closure of business by these enterprises are some features of the Act.

Need for Greater Engagement with MSEs

TO GENERATE LARGE-SCALE EMPLOYMENT

7.1.344 As countries develop, the share of agriculture in providing employment and in GDP decreases. According to the Australian Economist Chris Hall, the SMEs contribute about 70% of net new jobs across the globe, while larger firms tend to be job destroyers.[11]

7.1.345 The MSE sector in India has grown significantly since 1960, when there were only 12376 MSEs providing employment to 10 lakh people—of which, direct employment was 1.85 lakh; annual production level was Rs 875 crore. At the beginning of the Tenth Plan, 249 lakh people in the rural and urban areas were employed in 105.21 lakh MSEs. This has increased to 295 lakh people in 128 lakh units now; an average annual growth rate of 4.4% in the number of these units and 4.62% in employment. If the units in the khadi industries, village industries, and coir industries are taken into account, the employment is estimated to be over 332 lakh. With the inclusion of handlooms, handicrafts, wool, and sericulture, the total job in the MSE sector in India goes up to 650 lakh. The employment intensity of the registered units indicates that an investment of Rs 0.72 lakh is required for creating one employment in MSME sector as against Rs 5.56 lakh in the large organized sector.

[10] *http://www.worldbank.org/research/projects/sme/abd.pdf.* According to a World Bank research paper, 54 countries define SMEs as enterprises employing no more than 200–300 people. These include 13 low-income, 24 middle-income, and 17 high-income countries. Most African countries use a cut-off of 200 employees; Japan uses 300 employees.

[11] *http://www.cesifo-group.de/pls/guestci/download/CESifo%20Forum%202007/CESifo%20Forum%202/2007/forum 2-07-focus5.pdf*

7.1.346 Not only do MSEs generate the highest employment per capita investment, they also go a long way in checking rural–urban migration by providing villagers and people living in isolated areas with a sustainable source of employment. Among the MSEs in India, the dispersed food products sector generates maximum employment (13.7% of total employment in the MSE sector), followed by non-metallic mineral products (10.9%) and metal products (10.2%). In chemicals and chemical products, machinery parts except electrical parts, wood products, basic metal industries, paper products and printing, hosiery and garments, repair services, and rubber and plastic products, the contribution ranges from 9% to 5%. In all other industries the contribution is less than 5%.

7.1.347 Per unit employment is highest (20) in units engaged in beverages, tobacco, and tobacco products. Next come cotton textile products (17), non-metallic mineral products (14.1), basic metal industries (13.6), and electrical machinery and parts (11.2). Per unit employment is highest (10) in the metropolitan areas and lowest (5) in the rural areas. Non-metallic products contribute 22.7% to the employment generated in the rural areas, followed by food products (21.1%), wood products, and chemicals and chemical products. As for the urban areas, food products and metal products almost equally share 22.8% employment. Machinery parts except electrical, non-metallic mineral products, and chemicals and chemical products between them account for another 26.2% employment. Metal products, machinery and parts except electrical, and paper products and printing (total share being 33.6%) are the leading industries in metropolitan areas.

7.1.348 The presence of MSEs across States is not uniform. Tamil Nadu (14.5%) makes the maximum contribution to employment followed by Maharashtra (9.7%), Uttar Pradesh (9.5%), and West Bengal (8.5%). Per unit employment is high—17, 16, and 14, respectively—in Nagaland, Sikkim, and Dadar & Nagar Haveli; Madhya Pradesh has the lowest figure of 2. In all other cases it is around 6.

TO SUSTAIN ECONOMIC GROWTH AND INCREASE EXPORTS

7.1.349 Estimates say that in order to achieve the target of 10% growth in the Eleventh Plan, the MSE sector needs to grow at 12%.

7.1.350 Figure 7.1.16 indicates the growth of the SME sector in terms of number of units, employment, and production.

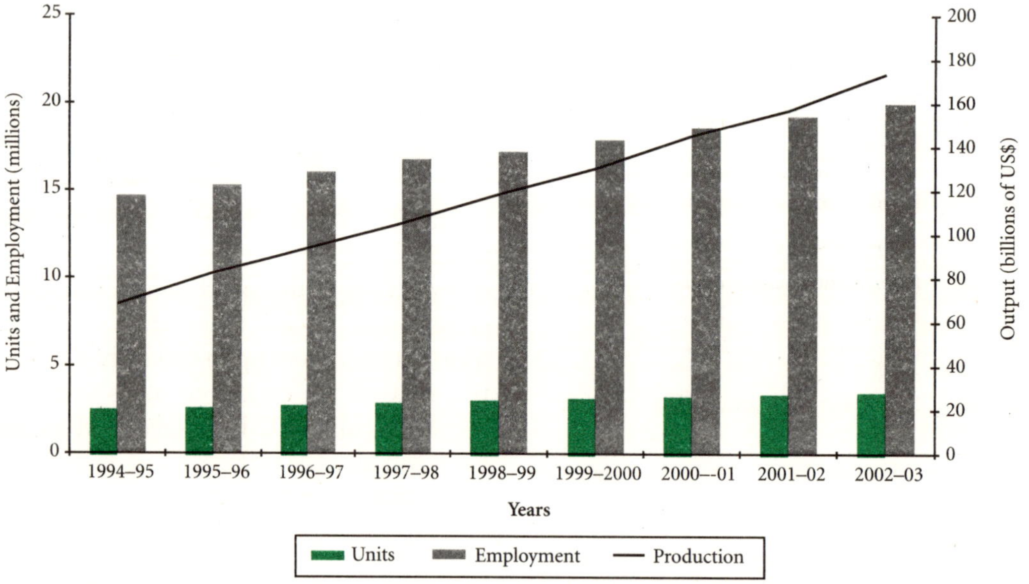

Source: CII Website.

FIGURE 7.1.16: Growth of the SME Sector in India

7.1.351 Non-traditional products account for more than 95% of the SSI exports. The performance of garments, leather, and gems and jewellery units has been remarkable in the last decade. The SSI sector dominates in export of sports goods, readymade garments, woollen garments and knitwear, plastic products, processed food, and leather products. Annexure 7.1.20 indicates performance of SSIs from 2000–01 to 2006–07. The US, Europe, and West Asia are the major export destinations as indicated as Annexure 7.1.21.

7.1.352 There is tremendous potential to expand the quantum of exports from traditional MSEs because they are handcrafted and hence eco-friendly and exclusive. Further, while MSEs are unable to take advantage of economies of scale, they are ideal for meeting small order quantities—a bonus in industries such as readymade garments, home furnishings, etc.

7.1.353 MSEs often act as ancillary industries for LSIs providing them with raw materials, vital components, and backward linkages. For instance, large cycle manufacturers of Ludhiana rely heavily on the small MSEs of Maler Kotla which produce cycle parts. MSEs also promote eco-friendly growth, especially in difficult terrains and the ecologically sensitive areas. In large tracts of barren desert land in Barmer and Kutch, in the scattered *dhanis* of Udaipur, in the hilly hamlets of J&K, Ladakh, Himachal, and the North East, in the tribal hinterlands of central India, they are the only source of livelihood.

FOR MAKING GROWTH INCLUSIVE

7.1.354 The MSE sector is a microcosm of all vulnerabilities—it touches upon the lives of women, children, minorities, SCs, and STs in the villages, in the urban slums, and in the deprived pockets of flourishing towns and cities. For many families, it is the only source of livelihood. For others, it supplements the family income. Thus, instead of taking a welfare approach, this sector seeks to empower people to break the cycle of poverty and deprivation. It focuses on people's skills and agency.

7.1.355 Different segments of the MSE sector are dominated by different social groups. Women are mostly found in the unregistered sector—food processing enterprises, manufacturing enterprises, and weaving—and often work part time in the family enterprises. Women and small children roll bidis, make agarbattis, do zari and sequin work for meagre wages. Annexure 7.1.22 gives state-wise figures for women employed in MSMEs.

7.1.356 Large number of Muslims are found in the unorganized weaving sector and in powerlooms. STs produce wonderful handcrafted articles and are involved in sericulture. In the North East, most women weave. In States like Tripura, 50% of rural men and 35% rural women are engaged in MSEs. In Nagaland and Mizoram over 68% of urban men are with MSEs.

Challenges

AN OVERVIEW

7.1.357 The MSE sector in India is heterogeneous, dispersed, and mostly unorganized. It includes diverse types of production units ranging from traditional crafts to high-tech industries. Yet, it is often considered to be limited to large units among the SSIs which deal with high-tech industries or serve as ancillaries to large industries. Segments such as powerlooms, handlooms, handicrafts, food processing, coir, sericulture, khadi, village industries, and wool, which are mostly unorganized, are fragmented across various ministries and often seen only as rural livelihoods. This is, however, far from the truth. Towns and cities such as Benaras, Berhampur, etc., are big handloom centres; Lucknow, Bhopal, Delhi, and Jaipur are famous for their handicraft products while powerlooms are normally only found in urban areas. The artificial fragmentation of the sector often pits the traditional MSEs against each other and against non-traditional ventures. It also limits their access to capital, infrastructure, and support policies.

7.1.358 Due to the unorganized nature of the sector, entrepreneurs and artisans/workers face difficulties in accessing government schemes. Consequently, the workers engaged in the MSE sector—and these are often the most vulnerable and poor—have very little bargaining power and are exploited by the middlemen, unit owners, and big business houses. Unable to take up aggressive marketing, like big industries, they cannot find markets despite good quality and competent prices (Box 7.1.3)

7.1.359 The dispersed, unorganized nature of the industry also raises issues of quality, bulk production, and inability of meeting big orders. Often individual units lack packaging facilities.[12] As a result, markets, especially for traditional MSEs, are shrinking and workers are experiencing a dip in wages. Moreover, as most non-traditional MSEs serve as 'captive units' for big industries, often workers, especially women do not get paid until the product is picked up. The situation is same for the traditional sector where payments are made by traders and even government corporations only after the stock is sold. Thus money is held up, further impoverishing the workers.

7.1.360 The MSEs engaged in manufacturing of products such as paints, dyes and chemicals, explosives, minerals, leather and leather goods, etc., pollute the environment. These units have to obtain non-pollution certification from the concerned pollution control agencies of the State.

INADEQUATE ACCESS TO CREDIT AND WORKING CAPITAL

7.1.361 Though most sub-sectors of the MSE under different ministries have a scheme for credit availability, everywhere across the country—from the iron mongers of Jodhpur to powerloom units of Malegaon, from young entrepreneurs trying to set up food processing units in Kargil to handloom weavers of Kaithun, Berhampur, and Pochampally—artisans, weavers, and entrepreneurs rue the non-availability of the working capital. The percentage share of the MSEs (erstwhile SSI) in non-food Bank Credit declined from 15.1% in 1990–91 to 8.0% in March 2007. The fall in the percentage share of credit to MSEs under priority sector can, in part, be attributed to the expanding scope of the priority sector lending to accommodate fast-growing areas such as housing, exports, etc. As per the Third All-India SSI Census (2001–02), only 14.2% of the registered and 3.09% of the unregistered MSEs availed of bank finance. Though the Nayak Committee (set up by RBI in 1991–92) had recommended working capital to the SSEs at 20% of their annual turnover, SSI and KVI units together received only 13.3% of their production value from scheduled commercial banks (SCBs) in 2005–06.

7.1.362 Lending to micro enterprises, which is stipulated at 60% of the total credit to MSE sector, has fallen from 51.2% in 2002–03 to 45.1% at the end of 2005–06. Moreover, difficulty in arranging collaterals or third-party guarantees continues to be a problem. Though the RBI had issued instructions to advance collateral free loans up to Rs 5 lakh, at the end of 2005–06, only 24% of the total outstanding loans under Rs 5

Box 7.1.3
Dwindling of a Vibrant Sector

People working in MSEs, especially in the traditional sector, are being increasingly impoverished. In Tantol village (Rajsamand district, Rajasthan), the silver minakari workers have not received a hike in wages for the last 60 years. As the markets are flooded by cheap machine-made and Chinese goods, weavers of Barabanki, Uttar Pradesh, have experienced a fall in wages. So while the trendy stoles, shawls, and *duppattas* they make are sold at upmarket stores for Rs 300 onwards, they get only Rs 5–10 a piece.The powerloom weavers of Bhiwandi and Malegaon and the handloom weavers of Benaras have no civic amenities. In Malegaon, powerloom weavers say that every day they suffer a loss of Rs 1 crore due to power cuts. Most of the looms in both Malegaon and Bhiwandi are old. Hence productivity is very low. The Bhairongarh print from district Ujjain, Madhya Pradesh is one of the many crafts which have become extinct. Handloom Himroo Shawl from Aurangabad is on the verge of exitinction. The Langas and Manganiyars of Rajasthan who have long entertained people with their music are now finding it difficult to survive. Leh and Kargil cannot sustain big industries but have a huge tourist market where their handlooms, handicrafts, processed apricots plus Leh berry juice can be sold. Yet in the absence of packaging facilities and credit, small entrepreneurs are unable to set up food processing units.

[12] Specific challenges faced by different segments of the MSE sector will be discussed separately in the chapter on MSEs and Rural Livelihoods (Chapter 5, Volume III).

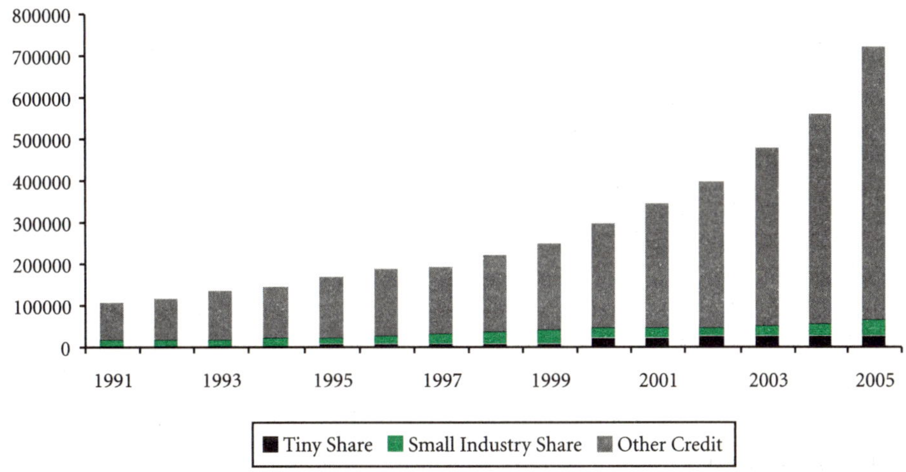

Source: RBI and Ministry of SSI, GoI, Annual Report 2005–06.

FIGURE 7.1.17—Availability of Credit for SSI and Tiny Units

lakh were without collaterals. The high cost of credit to MSEs also impacts the competitiveness of their products. The Figure 7.1.17 indicates availability of credit for the SSI and tiny units.

7.1.363 Though the percentage of NBC available to MSEs has been declining, the absolute amount of credit to this sector has been increasing. Since the Union Budget 2003–04, Indian Banks' Association has advised banks to adopt the interest rate band of 2% above and below their prime lending rates (PLRs) for advances to SSI. In order to ensure that credit is available to all segments of SSI sector, RBI has issued instructions that 40% of funds available to MSE sector be given to units with investment in plant and machinery up to Rs 5 lakh, 20% for units with investment between Rs 5 lakh to Rs 25 lakh, and remaining 40% for other units. As on March 2002, 391 specialized SSI branches were working in the country. Laghu Udyami Credit Card Scheme was also launched by public sector banks for providing simplified and borrower-friendly credit facilities to SSI, tiny enterprises, retail traders, and artisans.

7.1.364 The Credit Guarantee Cover Fund Scheme for Small Industries was launched jointly by the GoI and SIDBI (on a 4:1 contribution basis) in August 2000, with a view to ensure greater flow of credit to the MSE sector without collateral security. It picked up during the last two years of the Tenth Plan and till the end of March 2007, 68062 proposals were approved and guarantee covers for Rs 1705 crore were issued.

NON-AVAILABILITY OF QUALITY RAW MATERIALS AND PACKAGING FACILITIES ON A TIMELY BASIS

7.1.365 Non-availability of quality raw materials such as dyes and yarn (especially for handlooms and powerlooms); vital inputs such as power (for powerlooms, handicrafts, other industrial MSEs); and proper packaging facilities continue to be a major bottleneck. Lack of credit combined with inadequate raw materials often forces weavers, artisans, and entrepreneurs into the clutches of loan sharks and middlemen. The modern manufacturing MSE units are also constrained due to non-availability of quality raw materials in adequate quantity. Though the National Small Industries Corporation (NSIC) and State Small Scale Industries Development Corporations are providing some raw materials, their efforts are not in consonance with the requirements.

INSUFFICIENT MARKET RESEARCH, LINKAGES, AND DESIGN INPUTS

7.1.366 Most MSEs do not have money to invest in market research and are unable to carry out design and technical improvements to keep up with market demands. Unlike big businesses, they cannot invest in advertising and packaging. This limits their ability to tap markets and attract consumers. Most people are unaware of *Chamba Chugh*, natural fibre purses and cushion covers, passion fruit pickles, *Bhuvastra* (garment of the Earth—made in coir), *Chamba Chappals*, Camel Hair Carpets (which do not burn) of Jodhpur, and the intricately carved tables of Ladakh. MSEs, especially those pertaining to traditional livelihoods, are therefore, increasingly being forced to rely on middlemen, petty traders, and big businesses to market their products. This has reduced many to the status of daily workers, earning less than the minimum wages.

REHABILITATION OF SICK SSI UNITS

7.1.367 The major causes of sickness in the SSI sector, as per the Third Census of SSI (2001–02), were lack of demand, shortage of working capital, non-availability of raw material, power shortage, marketing problems, etc. Combining the three yardsticks used to measure sickness, viz., (i) delay in repayment of loan over one year, (ii) decline in net worth by 50%, and (iii) decline in output in last three years, 13.98% of the units in the registered SSI sector and 6.89% in the unregistered sector were either sick or incipiently sick. In the total SSI sector, this percentage was 7.82%.[13] The five States of Kerala, Tamil Nadu, Andhra Pradesh, Karnataka, and Maharashtra together accounted for 54.28% of the sick/incipiently sick SSI units in the country.

GLOBALIZATION

7.1.368 Many segments of MSE, especially the traditional sectors, find it difficult to compete against aggressive marketing by the big domestic and multinational players. Street vendors, petty traders, handloom and powerloom weavers, home-based food processing units, khadi institutions, *attar* (perfumers), zari workers, and rural artisans, many of whom have even lost livelihoods and places of work due to developmental works, are the worst affected. There is a need to evolve a constructive response to this situation. As these sectors employ the most marginalized, our indigenous/traditional industries should be given opportunities to tap both the domestic and international markets. Most important, however, is that the license raj and redtapism, which is being minimized in other sectors, needs to wither away from the micro sector as well.

7.1.369 As in other countries, globalization can also act as a tool for development of the MSE sector. MSEs engaged in the manufacturing of engineering and automobile products have shown excellent growth in the past decade due to their expertise in supplying OEM assemblies and sub-assemblies, components, etc. What is needed is a rational policy which offers adequate support and protection to this sector, enabling it to reach Indian markets. MSEs have many inherent advantages such as exclusivity, ability to produce small order quantities, etc. In a globalized world, they can tap new markets, especially in the West where there is a big demand for handcrafted products. Information technology can be used as a tool to provide online information on indigenous products and producers, while the GI Act and patents can be used to prevent cheap imitations of our designs and products by other countries.

TECHNOLOGY UPGRADATION AND ACHIEVING 'ECONOMIES OF SCALE'

7.1.370 The investment ceiling on plant and machinery used for defining the small-scale units create problems. Efforts such as raising investment ceiling to Rs 5 crore for micro and small-scale units will help these units to graduate to medium-scale enterprises. The Tenth Plan schemes such as TUFS and SITP, which have helped some units to modernize, will be continued in the Eleventh Plan as well. There is an urgent need to devise measures to tackle the problem of loss of fiscal benefits when the micro and small-scale units graduate into larger units. The general excise duty exemption, which was traditionally available to the SSIs, is now restricted to Rs 1.5 crore of the transactions, a figure which is largely insignificant for many of the larger SSEs. As has been demonstrated by units such as Hero Cycles, Nirma detergents, Videocon, and Onida electronics, and vertical expansion and upward movement of MSEs to the medium and large sector enables them to achieve economies of scale. But today MSEs are encouraged to go for horizontal expansion and deliberate fragmentation, mainly to stay within the

[13] *http://www.smallindustryindia.com/ssiindia/performance.htm*

limits of excise exemptions. During the Eleventh Plan it would be necessary to consider policy initiatives to incentivize MSEs to achieve economies of scale by expanding production. One possibility could be to allow them to retain the benefit of excise duty exemption up to the prescribed limit even after they graduate into medium-scale enterprises. Measures would also need to be taken to deal with the problems arising from Chapter V-B of the Industrial Dispute Act to facilitate the MSEs to overcome fragmentation and inefficiency. While doing all this, however, it is imperative to ensure that the small, household based units are not neglected.

7.1.371 Owing to liberalization and opening up of the economy, the MSEs are facing stiff competition from imports and need technological upgradation to produce better quality products at cheap rates. They should be able to access production supply units around the world through the Internet. Information dissemination about availability of recent technologies, literature on modern machinery, contact details of suppliers, etc., is essential. A Technology Bank could be set up for this purpose. There is a need to intensify implementation of the Credit Linked Capital Subsidy Scheme (CLCSS) along with ready availability of model modernization projects for manufacturing industries.

Potential of MSE Sector in Eleventh Plan: Monitorable Targets

7.1.372 Monitorable targets for the MSE sector (excluding khadi, village industries, handicrafts, handloom, and food processing) for the Eleventh Plan are given in the following Table 7.1.15.

ELEVENTH PLAN STRATEGIES FOR PROMOTION OF MSEs

7.1.373 The Eleventh Plan approach to the MSE sector marks a shift from the welfare approach to that of empowerment. The Plan looks at this sector as an engine for sustained and inclusive economic growth and employment. The strategy is two-pronged—it focuses on livelihood and social security. This is not just a rights issue but also makes economic common sense—artisans and entrepreneurs can be most productive only when they are physically and mentally fit.

7.1.374 The Eleventh Plan considers the MSE sector as an important segment of industry which is unorganized and hence needs support and access to all schemes of industry with special enabling provisions. As it is, Tribal Sub-Plan (TSP) and Special Component Plan (SCP) are constitutional requirements. Support for women's empowerment and minority development has been stressed upon in the Prime Minister's 15-point programme and in other flagship schemes of the government. We know that it is mostly the tribes, SCs, minorities, and women who are engaged in traditional livelihoods and in the small and micro sector. In the handloom sector alone, 60.6% weavers are women, 10.76% belong to SCs, 25.5% to STs, and 42.65% to OBCs.[14]

7.1.375 Thus providing enabling provisions for artisans, weavers, and small entrepreneurs within industrial policies and schemes will automatically fulfil the constitutional requirement and the commitments made by various Plans. While planning infrastructure development for industries, the needs of the micro and small sector would be kept in mind. There is need to move from adversarial to complementary relationships between various segments of industry and MSE. For instance, handlooms can target hi-end exclusive products—stoles, shawls, sarees, and furnishings—while powerloom mills do bulk production for *gamcha*s, *dhoti*s, towels, bed and table linen, etc. Big

TABLE 7.1.15
Year-wise Physical Targets for the Eleventh Plan

Item	2007–08	2008–09	2009–10	2010–11	2011–12	CAGR
Production at current price (Rs crore)	682613	816705	977144	1169112	1398803	15.4%
Employment (lakh persons)	322.28	338.39	355.31	373.08	391.73	4%

Source: Ministry of MSME.

[14] Joint handloom and powerloom census conducted in 1995–96.

brands can continue to develop products such as suitings, shirtings, t-shirts, etc.

7.1.376 The MSE sector, including handlooms and handicrafts, presents an opportunity for exports. Exclusivity, which stems from the dispersed nature of this sector, is its biggest strength (Box 7.1.4). And yet, the dispersed nature of the sector makes it difficult to meet bulk orders, raises quality control issues, robs the workers of bargaining power, limits access to credit and markets, results in absence of social security, and prevents enterprises from benefiting from economies of scale. The effort during the Plan period will therefore be to organize this sector, to create clusters and SHGs of weavers/artisans to improve their bargaining power and to enable them to pool resources. These groups, comprising weavers, artisans, and entrepreneurs, will be given full control over cluster decisions and will be provided support in the form of credit, inputs, expertise, and marketing links.

7.1.377 The Working Group on MSMEs for the Eleventh Plan had projected the need for Rs 296400 crore as the working capital and term loans for MSEs during the Eleventh Plan. At present, there is no sub-sector target for the MSE sector within the overall stipulated 40% ceiling for the priority sector lending. Since sub-targets have already been fixed at 18% for agriculture and at 10% for the weaker sectors, the MSE sector has to compete with real estate, housing, education, retail, etc. for the remaining 12%. Considering the vital role of the MSE sector in generation of large-scale employment opportunities, consideration should be given to whether a separate sub-target for the MSE sector can be effectively introduced in all SCBs. If this is not possible then other means must be found to incentivize lending to this sector.

7.1.378 For micro and small entrepreneurs who cannot bring in sufficient equity/promoter's contribution, a flexible debt–equity ratio may need to be adopted while sanctioning export credit. Banks will be encouraged to ensure that all loans upto Rs 5 lakh to MSEs (excluding credit from MFIs) are given free of collateral at the interest rate of 8%. Coverage under the Credit Guarantee Trust Fund will be increased. As international experience indicates cluster based financing is the most effective way of providing credit to MSEs, 100 MSE clusters based on the PPP model will be adopted on a pilot basis.

7.1.379 During the Eleventh Plan period, an aggressive marketing campaign using the media and icons will be launched. Handlooms, handicrafts, food

Box 7.1.4
Small Success

Individual success stories in various nooks and corners of the country have demonstrated the potential of MSEs. Kolkata-based Mallika's *Kantha* has rejuvenated the traditional Kantha weave. Today, hundreds of women sit at their village homes in West Bengal, making stoles, shawls, sarees, dupattas, table covers, cushion covers, etc., which sell for anything between Rs 5000 to Rs 50000. From the Pope to the Prime Minister, everyone appreciates the art of Kantha.Fab India has shown the tremendous appeal of Indian handlooms and handprints, especially for the young, college-going crowd. Even brands like Pantaloons are starting handloom ranges for both men and women. In Andhra, designer shirts and *kurtas* of khadi made under the PRODIP scheme are a big success. Hotels like the Jahanuma Palace in Bhopal use handlooms and other handcrafted products for interior decoration. This experience is cherished by tourists. Tourists pick up a large number of products, chappals, bags, masks, papier mâché etc., from small shops allotted to artisans inside the Mehrangarh Fort in Jodhpur. The artisans on their part get a steady source of income.Chizami is a small village in the Phek district of Nagaland. Here, an NGO, North East Network, has provided the local youth with a source of livelihood. They make passion fruit, guava, and ginger jams, pickles, and squashes. India has many natural fibres such as banana, *khus*, sisal, korai grass, talipot, palm leaf, coconut, pineapple, screwpine, golden grass, jute, sabai, etc. Not-for-profit organizations such as Industree Crafts are encouraging rural artisans to convert these fibres into value-added finished products such as bags, table mats, cushion covers, hats, floor coverings, curtains, office and home accessories, etc. These products are now being marketed in top stores across the country. Likewise, natural soaps, shampoos, and cosmetics produced by various small units under the brand name of Khadi are already catching on in the domestic market and have tremendous scope for exports.

processing, and other cultural industries will be linked to tourism; circuits for heritage and fabric tourism will be developed. In the West, the cultural industries have become the most rapidly growing sector in the world, contributing over 7% of the world's GDP. Giving an 'industry' status to craftspersons is important because it entitles them to tax benefits and export promotion schemes, makes them eligible for banking and credit support, and helps them lobby for protection of intellectual property.[15]

7.1.380 Mapping of the MSE sector will be carried out and registration of products under the GI Act will be encouraged and supported. Strict enforcement of laws relating to reservation will be carried out. Neglected areas such as occupational health, insurance, and so on will be taken up as an integral part of the MSE policy. Special emphasis will be laid on skill development and upgradation across all sectors.

7.1.381 An effective preference policy for procurement of goods and services produced by MSEs both at Central and State levels will be developed. A policy for women in the micro and small sector, particularly in the unorganized segments, will also be formulated to ensure that women get their rights and that their special needs are catered to.

ELEVENTH PLAN SCHEMES OF MINISTRY OF MSME

7.1.382 Most of the existing schemes for the MSME sector have been evaluated by independent organizations and suitably modified and reorganized. These will be continued during the Eleventh Plan period along with addition of some new schemes. The schemes which will be carried forward in the Eleventh Plan are given in Annexure 7.1.23.

NEW INITIATIVES

7.1.383 The Small Industries Development Organization (now called Micro, Small, and Medium Enterprises Development Organization) has a network of more than 3000 technically qualified personnel working through its Small Industries Service Institutes (and Branch SISIs), testing centres, and autonomous organizations such as the Tool Room, Product and Process Development Centres, etc. In the Eleventh Plan, the Ministry of MSME will establish a Technology Mission to promote new and emerging technologies, assess present levels of technology and their upgrdation, set up technology information centres/data banks and an IT portal for information dissemination to carry out detailed technology audits.

7.1.384 In 2006, the government launched the National Manufacturing Competitiveness Programme. The NMCC and the Ministry of MSME chalked out a five-year programme with a projected expenditure of Rs 850 crore. The programmes include: setting up of design clinics, application of lean manufacturing technologies for increasing competitiveness of firms by systematically identifying and eliminating waste throughout the business cycle. These programmes will be demand driven and will be implemented in the PPP mode in selected industrial clusters.

7.1.385 Infrastructural constraints, notably the power outages, affect the MSEs much more than the larger enterprises. Although some States do offer differential power tariffs in favour of the MSEs, the real deficiency is the quality and quantity of power supply. During the Eleventh Plan, group/associations of the MSEs will be incentivized to establish captive power plants as enjoined in the Electricity Act 2003 or to set up common large-scale generation facilities with dedicated feeder lines. Roads, transport, water, and other infrastructure problems, or their total absence, push up operating costs of MSEs as against goods produced in more favourable conditions in other countries and it is, therefore, imperative for the government to develop adequate infrastructure.

7.1.386 Labour Laws and Factory Laws have created problems for MSE units in terms of number of inspections. The committee set up under Member (Industry) Planning Commission recommended a system of third-party inspection to give enterprises an option to get their regulatory compliance certified by accredited agencies. Once such certification has been obtained the unit would be exempted from routine inspection. Special inspections would be

[15] InfoChange News and Features, September 2006.

authorized only on receipt of credible complaints. Early implementation of this recommendation during the Eleventh Plan will provide relief to the MSMEs.

7.1.387 A proper database is critical for formulation of appropriate schemes for the MSE sector. The recently announced 'Package for Promotion of Micro and Small Enterprises (SMEs)' contains a proposal for providing financial support to the MSE Associations for their capacity building and for strengthening the database and contacts with the grassroots. This initiative would be carried forward during the Eleventh Five Year Plan.

7.1.388 An outlay of Rs 11500 crore has been allocated to Ministry of MSME, out of which Rs 4000 crore is for DC (MSME) and Rs 7500 crore is for agro and rural industries.

7.2 MINERALS

INTRODUCTION

7.2.1 Accelerated growth rate of the Indian economy needs rapid development of the mining sector, on which most of the basic industries depend. The efforts for locating minerals over the last 55 years have enhanced reserves for various minerals such as mica, barites, chromite (metallurgical), coal (thermal), lignite, bauxite (metallurgical), manganese ore, and iron ore, and have placed the country among top 10 producers of these minerals. However, in respect of fertilizer minerals, diamond, gold, nickel, copper, lead, zinc, platinum group of metals, and rare metals, there has hardly been any discovery despite an extremely favourable geological environment.

7.2.2 With the surge in the demand for metals in response to strong economic growth, it has become necessary to mount a well-planned, comprehensive, and time-bound programme for regional and detailed exploration for locating and delineating the country's hidden mineral deposits, which are likely to be considerable.

7.2.3 The mining sector was opened to FDI in 1993 and 100% FDI has been allowed since 2000. However, the actual flows have been minimal in the absence of policies conducive to FDI for prospecting. Attracting the FDI into exploration and prospecting will require a revision of the current non-investor-friendly mining regime and adoption of a multi-disciplinary approach, embracing the legal framework, technology, sustainability, infrastructure, and procedural streamlining.

REVIEW OF THE TENTH PLAN

7.2.4 The Offshore Areas Mineral (Development and Regulation) Act 2002 providing for the development and regulation of mineral resources in the territorial waters, continental shelf, and the exclusive economic zone was notified on 31 January 2003. The legislation would enable the streamlining of mineral exploration and development in the offshore areas and ensure systematic and scientific exploitation of mineral reserves (except petroleum, natural gas, and hydrocarbon resources) for attracting private investment in the offshore mineral sector.

7.2.5 In 2000, the ceiling of 74% on FDI in exploration and mining of diamonds and precious stones was removed though it continued to require Foreign Investment Promotion Board approval. In 2006, this restriction too was removed and all FDI in the mining sector, including FDI above 74% in mining of diamonds and precious stones, is now on the automatic route.

7.2.6 For a comprehensive review of the National Mineral Policy and for suggesting possible amendments to the MMDR Act 1957, the Planning Commission constituted a high-level committee under the Chairmanship of Member (Industry), Planning Commission. The high-level committee submitted its report to the government on 19 July 2006. The committee recommended a number of changes in the National Mineral Policy and in the relevant laws and rules to stimulate mineral exploration activities and promote the development of a vibrant mining and mineral sector in the country. For augmenting state revenues from the mineral sector, the committee recommended that the method of fixation of royalty should move decisively toward ad valorem rates, away from the tonnage system currently prevailing for a number of economically important minerals. Based on the recommendations of the high-level committee, the government approved the National Mineral Policy 2008, and the next task is to introduce a Bill in the Parliament for amendment to the MMDR Act 1957 and further appropriately amend Mineral concession Rules, 1960 and Mineral Conservation and Development Rules (MCDR), 1988.

7.2.7 The Ministry of Mines constituted a study group in August 2006 for revision of the rates of royalty and dead rent on major minerals (other than coal, lignite, and sand for stowing), and to make appropriate recommendations to the government. The terms of reference of the group are in line with the recommendations of the high-level committee on National Mineral Policy.

7.2.8 The concept of reconnaissance permit (RP) was introduced in 1999 and until 31 December 2006, 205 RPs covering an area of 282908.50 sq km were granted prior approval. However, during the Tenth Five Year Plan there was a declining trend in the number of RP approvals as shown in Figure 7.2.1.

7.2.9 The RP instrument resulted in the mining companies blocking up large areas while actually undertaking exploration over very small areas. It is in this context that the high-level committee has recommended the introduction of Large Area Prospecting License.

THE SUB-SECTOR PROFILE DURING THE TENTH PLAN

Iron Ore

7.2.10 Owing to the increase in the demand and production of steel worldwide and particularly in China, there was considerable buoyancy in the production and exports of iron ore during the Tenth Five Year Plan period. The production of iron increased from 86.23 million mt in 2001–02 to 172.30 million mt in 2006–07 and the exports increased from 23.09 million mt in 2001–02 to 84.05 million mt in 2005–06.

Non-ferrous Metals

ALUMINUM

7.2.11 The production of bauxite increased from 8.60 million tonnes in 2001–02 to 13.075 (P) million tonnes in 2006–07. Panchpatmali bauxite mine of National Aluminium Company Ltd. (NALCO) in Orissa accounts for about 40% of the country's production. It is a world-class, fully mechanized mine with an existing capacity of 4.8 million tonnes per annum. There are six alumina refineries owned by five aluminium companies in the country, namely NALCO, HINDALCO, Indian Aluminium Company Limited (Indal), Bharat Aluminium Co. Ltd (BALCO), and Madras Aluminium Company Ltd.

7.2.12 The total alumina capacity increased from 2.72 million tonnes in 2001–02 to 4.24 million tonnes in 2006–07, which is very small considering the prospect

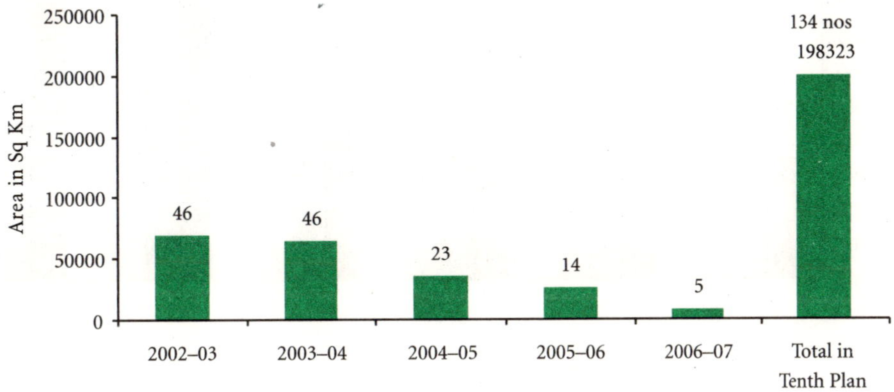

Source: Ministry of Mines.

FIGURE 7.2.1: Approvals of Reconnaissance Permit

for producing and exporting this product in which India is internationally very competitive.

7.2.13 Despite the limitation imposed by the high energy cost, there was a substantial increase in the capacity, production, and export of aluminum in the country during the Tenth Five Year Plan as shown in Figure 7.2.2.

7.2.14 Production of aluminum is estimated to have increased by 65% during the Plan period, the bulk of the increase being absorbed domestically. NALCO, a CPSE, has about 35% share of production.

COPPER

7.2.15 India has a substantial capacity for the production of primary copper metal but is significantly

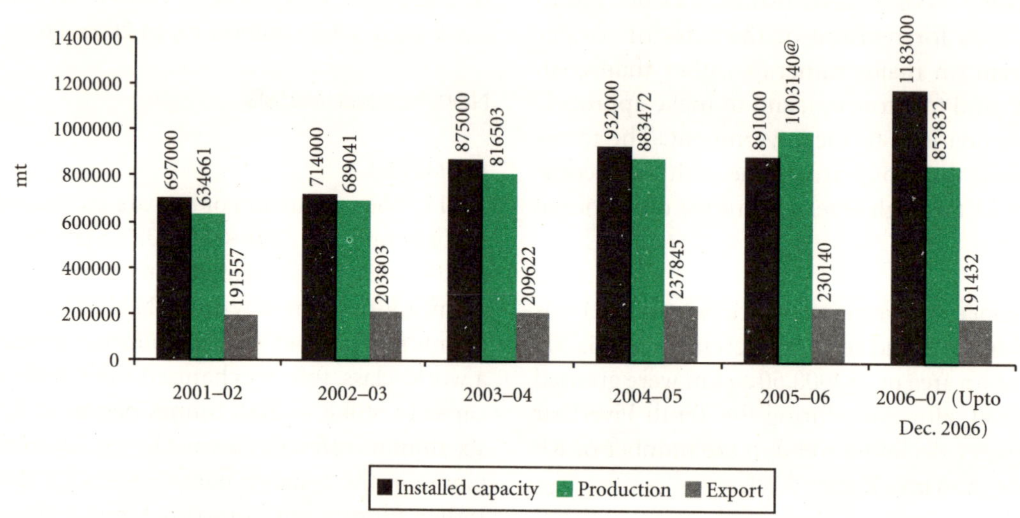

Note: @ In 2005–06, additional production of aluminum is due to capacity expansion in BALCO.
Source: Annual Reports, Ministry of Mines and Department of Commerce.

FIGURE 7.2.2: Production and Export of Aluminium

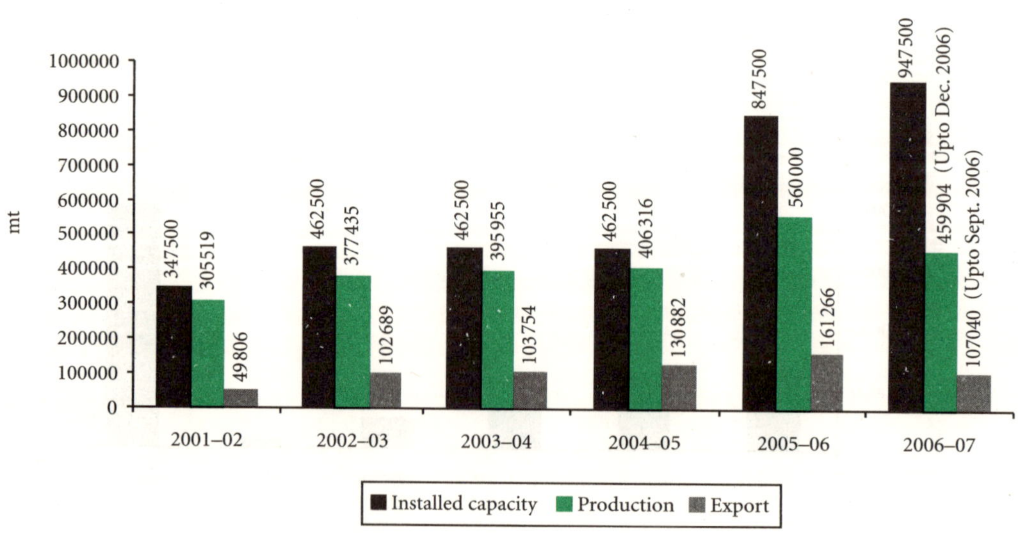

Source: Annual Reports, Ministry of Mines and Department of Commerce.

FIGURE 7.2.3: Capacity, Production and Export of Copper

dependent on the import of copper metal-in-concentrates. The production and import of copper concentrate in 2005–06 was 22984 mt and 1072905 mt, respectively. Figure 7.2.3 gives the figures of capacity, production, and export of primary copper during the Tenth Five Year Plan period.

7.2.16 Although India is dependent on imports of copper concentrate, its smelting capacity in the metal grew almost three-fold and the production by about 60% during the Tenth Five Year Plan period. The share of the public sector (HCL) in the production fell from about 13% in 2001–02 to about 6% in 2005–06.

ZINC AND LEAD

7.2.17 The capacity expansion and growth of production of zinc and lead were also impressive, almost doubling for both metals as shown in Figure 7.2.4.

7.2.18 After privatization, Hindustan Zinc Ltd (HZL) expanded its zinc mining and used the mineral from its captive Rampura Agucha mines to expand smelting. The capacity and production of lead during the Tenth Five Year Plan are shown in Figure 7.2.5.

PLAN OUTLAY AND EXPENDITURE DURING THE TENTH PLAN

7.2.19 An outlay of Rs 8344.50 crore was approved for the Tenth Five Year Plan (2002–07) for the Ministry of Mines with gross budgetary support of Rs 1271.00 crore, net budgetary support of Rs 1021.00 crore, and (IEBR) of Rs 7073.50 crore. There was a provision of Rs 250 crore [Geological Survey of India (GSI) Rs 200.00 crore and IBM Rs 50.00 crore] for external aid through the Budget in the Tenth Plan. However, during the MTA of the plan, the outlay was reduced to Rs 4485.28 crore against which the expenditure was of the order of Rs 2856.29 crore. The shortfalls were mainly on account of delay in the approval of second phase expansion of NALCO and slow progress in the modernization and replacement scheme of the GSI. (The details are given in Annexure 7.2.1).

ELEVENTH PLAN OBJECTIVES

7.2.20 The following are the main objectives of the Eleventh Five Year Plan in the mining sector:

- Intensification of exploration for low-volume high-value minerals such as gold, diamond, base metals, and platinum group of minerals and efforts towards augmentation of the existing resources in respect of ferrous and non-ferrous minerals and industrial minerals.
- Improvement of the National Mineral Inventory, particularly for those minerals in which reserves are low such as base metals, nickel, tin, graphite, noble metals, precious stones, and rock phosphate.
- Restructuring and modernization of the GSI in the

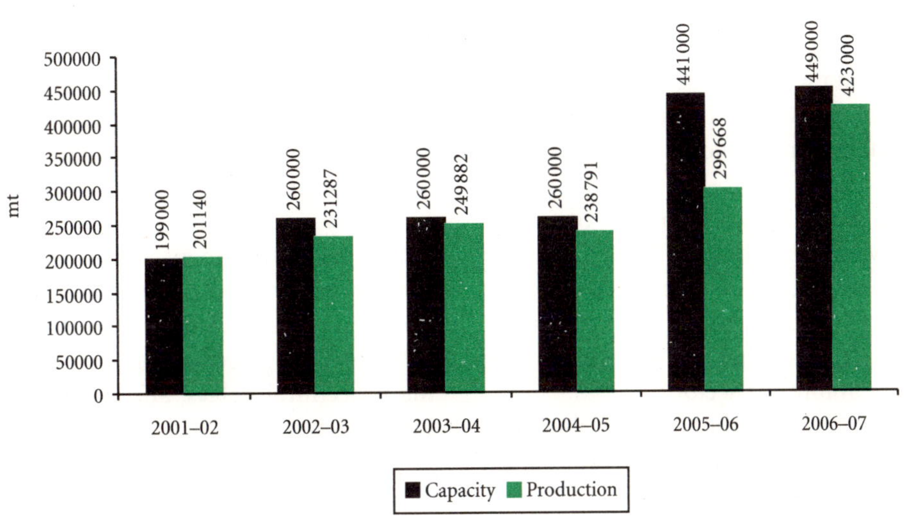

Source: Working Group Report on Mineral Exploration and Development (Other than coal and lignite), Eleventh Five Year Plan, Volume III.

FIGURE 7.2.4: Capacity and Production of Zinc

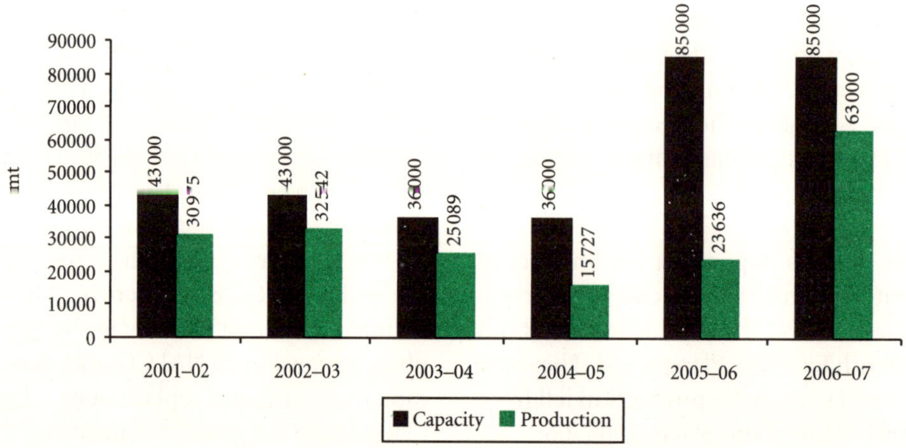

Source: Working Group Report on Mineral Exploration and Development (Other than coal and lignite), Eleventh Five Year Plan, Volume III.

FIGURE 7.2.5: Capacity and Production of Lead

areas of instrumentation for both ground and airborne surveys, and acquisition of state-of-the-art laboratory facilities with high-precision capabilities. Establishment of a comprehensive portal giving meta-data in respect of regional exploration work done by GSI and the scope for investment based on such work.

- Modernization of the IBM and the State directorates for establishment of a national registry (Cadastre) and a mineral atlas. The database would comprise both physical and resource inventory and include a Tenement Registry with details of green field areas, brown field areas, and relinquished areas including areas identified by the GSI as not worth pursuing. The data would be maintained online giving instant information to prospective investors on what is available for reconnaissance, prospecting, and mining.
- Acceleration of the process of adoption of United Nations Framework Classification (UNFC) system of classification of mineral resources so as to present reserves/resources of minerals on an internationally uniform system and help in attracting more private investment into the sector.
- Development of minerals in the NER with the States of this region playing a major role and the Central Government agencies facilitating their initiatives with specific interventions.
- Strengthening R&D activities in all aspects of mining.

Eleventh Plan Strategy

7.2.21 Given the technology and resource limitations of GSI, it would be necessary to encourage private sector initiative as the main driver of investment in exploration even as the GSI is strengthened to access the latest technologies such as deep imaging and electromagnetic probing.

7.2.22 In line with the current economic policy, in future the core functions of the State in mining will be facilitation of the exploration and mining activities of investors and entrepreneurs, provision of infrastructure, regulation, and tax collection. Where it is deemed necessary for the State to continue the mining activities, there will be arm's length between State agencies that explore and mine and those that regulate. Transparency would be maintained in the allocation of ore bodies for mining.

7.2.23 An environment conducive for private sector investment will be promoted by streamlining the licensing procedures, granting security of tenure to the RP/prospecting license (PL)/ML holders, minimizing the procedural delays, and improving the transport infrastructure.

7.2.24 It would be ensured that mining is done in a sustainable manner, without any adverse effect on the environment, by effective enforcement of the laws and by developing a Sustainable Development Framework

(SDF), especially tailored to the context of India's mining environment, to be adhered to voluntarily by the mining firms.

7.2.25 New relief and rehabilitation norms (to be adhered to on a voluntary basis) will be developed building on the existing packages announced by the States for compensation to the PAPs as well as for the benefit that must accrue to the communities living in the villages around the mining area.

STRUCTURE OF OUTPUT

7.2.26 In all, about 90 minerals are produced in the country, which include 4 fuel minerals, 10 metallic minerals, 50 non-metallic minerals, 3 atomic minerals, and 23 minor minerals. The total value of mineral production (excluding atomic minerals) during the year 2006–07 is estimated at Rs 87866.35 crore. During the year 2006–07, the provisional value of fuel minerals was put at Rs 63938.76 crore (73% of total value), metallic minerals at Rs 12858.71 crore (15% of the total value), and non-metallic minerals including minor minerals at Rs 11068.88 crore (12% of the total value).

Life Indices of Principal Minerals

7.2.27 The life indices as at the end of the Tenth Plan of important minerals such as bauxite, copper ore, chromite, lead–zinc ore, iron ore (haematite and magnetite) are given in Annexure 7.2.2. The life indices beyond 1 April 2007 estimated at the current level of production for important minerals are: bauxite (166 years); copper (200 years); chromite (33 years); lead–zinc ore (69 years); and iron ore (97 years).

7.2.28 The estimated apparent consumption, domestic production, resource situation, and life indices of some selected minerals in the terminal years of the Tenth and Eleventh Plans are given in Annexure 7.2.3. The life indices in years at the end of the Eleventh Five Year Plan of some of the important minerals are estimated as follows: bauxite—refractory grade (96 years); chromite (16 years); graphite (58 years); gypsum (125 years); and rock phosphate (68 years).

Material Balance of Principal Non-ferrous Metals

7.2.29 The projections of production, import, export, and domestic demand up to 2011–12 of principal non-ferrous metals—such as aluminum, copper, zinc, and lead—based on the Eleventh Five Year Plan Working Group Report on Mineral Exploration and Development are given in Annexure 7.2.4. Strong growth in domestic demand is expected in all non-ferrous metals, but the country will remain a net exporter of aluminum and copper (based largely on imported mineral concentrate). It will become self-sufficient in zinc but will be a net importer in lead.

Sectoral Profile

IRON ORE RESOURCES

7.2.30 The iron ore resources identified so far and estimated on the UNFC basis as on 1 April 2005 are about 14630 million tonnes of haematite ore and about 10619 million tonnes of magnetite ores. Unlike haematite, almost the entire magnetite resource is still to be converted to reserves. Even the small proportion, which has been converted so far by the National Mineral Development Corporation Limited, is in the Western Ghats biodiversity area and is presently not available for extraction because of the ban imposed by the Supreme Court for reasons of environmental protection. Of the haematite resources, high-quality reserves above 65% Fe content constitute only about 1.3 billion tonnes. The details are given in Annexures 7.2.5 and 7.2.6.

MANGANESE ORE

7.2.31 The all-India total resources of manganese ore as on 1 April 2005 are 380 million tonnes. Out of these, 37.29% are in the reserve category and balance 62.71% in the remaining resource category. Of the total resources, the blast furnace grade constituted 130.2 million tonnes, medium grade 31.63 million tonnes, and ferro–manganese grade 25.3 million tonnes.

CHROMITE

7.2.32 The all-India total resources of chromite are 232.12 million tonnes as on 1 April 2005 (provisional). Out of these 28.48% are in the reserve category and 71.52% are in the remaining resource category. Grade wise, 18% are metallurgical, 1.79% are refractory, 23.69% are charge chrome, 18.28% are beneficiated, and the balance 38.24% are low-grade ferrochrome, other unclassified and undefined grades. The bulk of the resources, that is 93.38%, is located in Orissa. Out of the 161 million tonnes of resources in leasehold, 33.67% are in the public sector and 66.33% in the private sector. Chromite deposits associated with Iron Ore Group are the most important. Among them, two belts, namely, Sukinda Ultramafic Belt and Nausahi Ultramafic Belt of Orissa, contain about 97% of the total Indian resources of chromite.

BAUXITE

7.2.33 The all-India total resources of bauxite as on 1 April 2005 (provisional) are 3306 million tonnes. Out of these, 915 million tonnes are under the reserve category and the balance 2392 million tonnes under the remaining resource category. Grade wise, 0.4% are chemical, 2.1% are refractory, 83.39% are metallurgical, and the balance 14.1% are unclassified and other mixed grades. Out of the leasehold resources of 1079 million tonnes, 41.94% are in the public sector and 49.06% in the private sector. Out of the total resources, 54.35% are in the captive sector and 45.65% are in the non-captive sector. Out of the public sector resources of 453 million tonnes, 300 million tonnes are in the captive area.

COPPER ORE

7.2.34 The all-India total resources of copper ore as on 1 April 2005 (provisional) are 1394 million tonnes, with a metal content of 11.41 million tonnes. Out of these, 369.5 million tonnes of ore with a metal content of 4.4 million tonnes is under the reserve category and the balance under the remaining resource category. Grade wise, 28.031 million tonnes are with +1.85% copper, 622 million tonnes are with 1.0%–1.85% copper; 604 million tonnes are with 0.5%–1.0% copper, and 140 million tonnes are with less than 0.5% copper.

7.2.35 HCL, a CPSE, is the only undertaking mining copper ore in the country. Most of the copper deposits under mining have been explored in detail. Exploration activities have also led to discovery of small deposits in the western, eastern, southern, and central Precambrian shield areas of the country. It is necessary to intensify exploration activities for copper and for this HCL could enter into joint ventures with specialized companies abroad that have the latest technologies to undertake the exploration activity.

LEAD–ZINC ORE

7.2.36 The all-India total resources of lead–zinc ore are 522 million tonnes with 7.2 million tonnes of lead metal and 24.25 million tonnes of zinc metal. Out of the total resources, 126 million tonnes with 2.6 million tonnes of lead metal and 11.0 million tonnes of zinc metal are under reserve category. Grade wise, 86.82 million tonnes are with +10% lead and zinc, 144.67 million tonnes are with 5%–10% lead and zinc, and 291 million tonnes are with less than 5% lead and zinc metal. Out of the total resources, 352.82 million tonnes with 3.7 million tonnes of lead metal and 8.99 million tonnes of zinc metal are in the freehold sector. In the leasehold, the total resources are 169.7 million tonnes with 3.5 million tonnes of lead metal and 15.26 million tonnes of zinc metal. Table 7.2.1 gives the production and import figures for lead–zinc ores.

TABLE 7.2.1
Production and Imports of Lead–Zinc Concentrate
(Million Tonnes)

Year	Production	Imports
2001–02	450438	68148
2002–03	544986	37550
2003–04	663234	103007
2004–05	750675	81547
2005–06	984745	40187

Source: Annual Reports—Ministry of Mines.

GLOBAL SCENARIO VIS-À-VIS INDIAN MINERAL SECTOR

7.2.37 Mineral exploration activities are risky ventures with long gestation period and requiring huge investment. During the first half of the last decade (1991–95), the global spending on mineral exploration was US$ 18500 million, which declined to US$ 14900 million in the second half (1996–2000). Indian spending on mineral exploration is hovering around 0.7%–0.8% of the total global expenditure. Low spending on the exploration activities has resulted in non-realization of the mineral potential in the country. The following data of some important minerals suggest that there is need for accelerating exploration activities for converting resources into reserves (Table 7.2.2). Reserve-to-resource ratio is lower in the case of India as compared with global reserve-to-resources ratio except for lead and zinc.

TABLE 7.2.2
Minerals—Unrealized Potential

(in Million Tonnes)

Commodity	Global		India	
	Resources	Reserves	Resources	Reserves
Copper	1600	940	11.4	4.4
Zinc	1900	460	24.2	11.0
Lead	1500	140	7.2	2.6
Nickel	140	140	1.9	0.0
Gold#	90000	90000	497	85.0
Diamonds*	1250	1250	4.6	1.2

Note: # in tonnes, * in million carats.
Source: Indian Mineral Year Book 2004, IBM.

MAIN ACTIVITIES OF GOVERNMENT AGENCIES AND CPSEs PROPOSED FOR THE ELEVENTH PLAN

Geological Survey of India (GSI)

7.2.38 During the Eleventh Five Year Plan, the GSI will be undertaking seven schemes namely, Survey and Mapping, Mineral Exploration, Specialized Investigation, R&D and other Exploration, Map and Publication and Information Dissemination, Human Resource Development, and Modernization and Replacement. Under the Mineral Exploration programme, the GSI would be undertaking activities for augmentation of resources of such minerals in which the country is deficient and also for high-value minerals such as gold, diamond, platinum group of elements (PGE); other minerals such as copper, lead, zinc, iron ore, manganese ore, chromite, bauxite, and limestone; and strategic minerals such as tungsten, nickel, fertilizers minerals, etc. The GSI will also undertake the procurement of laboratory equipments and replacement of blue water research vessel for the aging RV Samudra Manthan for carrying out sea-bed survey and exploration. It will also acquire a geo-technical vessel and a Heli-borne geophysical survey system. The process for procurement of these items was initiated in the Tenth Five Year Plan and is programmed to be completed in the Eleventh Five Year Plan. Details of physical programmes proposed for the Eleventh Five Year Plan by GSI are given in Annexure 7.2.7.

7.2.39 Two issues that need to be tackled quickly vis-à-vis the GSI are the separation of earth science activity from the mineral search activity and out-sourcing the search for coal and lignite to Coal India Limited which should undertake such search on a commercial basis.

Indian Bureau of Mines (IBM)

7.2.40 In accordance with its charter of function, the activities of IBM have been grouped into four broad schemes, namely, Inspection of Mines for Scientific and Systematic Mining; Mineral Conservation and Mines Environment, Mineral Beneficiation Studies—Utilization of low grade and sub-grade ores and analysis of environmental samples; Technological Upgradation and Modernization; and Collection, Processing, Dissemination of data on mines and minerals through various publications. It is imperative that the budgetary resources of IBM are augmented in order to strengthen it with manpower and equipment so that it can effectively tackle the problem of bad mining practices in the country. IBM will be taking two new projects, namely, (i) computerized online register of mining tenements system and (ii) management of solid waste from mining in India. The details of physical targets proposed for Eleventh Five Year Plan by the IBM are given in Annexure 7.2.8.

Mineral Exploration Corporation Ltd (MECL)

7.2.41 During the Eleventh Five Year Plan, MECL will undertake detailed exploration work under the promotional scheme and procurement of equipments under the capital scheme. MECL needs funds for undertaking development (promotional) and exploration in areas which the private sector finds unattractive. It also needs to enter into joint ventures with specialized exploration companies abroad for undertaking commercial exploration for RP and PL holders.

7.2.42 The company will make concerted efforts on improving the mineral inventory, particularly of ferrous and non-ferrous minerals, and will endeavour to improve its competitiveness so that it can secure work orders from mineral-rich States. Details of the physical targets proposed for the IBM and MECL for the Eleventh Five Year Plan are given in Annexure 7.2.8.

National Aluminium Company Ltd (NALCO)

7.2.43 NALCO is a profit-making CPSE with a share of 35% of the domestic production of the metal. Its second phase expansion scheme, which was approved by the GoI in October 2004 at an estimated cost of Rs 4091.51 crore, is likely to be completed by December 2008. The capacity of various project segments being expanded is given in Annexure 7.2.9. NALCO will also initiate action for setting up green field projects and diversifying its activities.

Hindustan Copper Ltd (HCL)

7.2.44 HCL, which was earlier a sick CPSE, has been making profits over the past three years. During the Eleventh Five Year Plan, HCL will be undertaking replacement and renewal of equipments to be funded through their internal resources for maintaining the existing level of production and for planning enhanced production in the future.

Research and Development (R&D)

7.2.45 Research work is being undertaken by the National Institute of Rock Mechanics, Jawaharlal Nehru Aluminium Research, Development, and Design Centre, the National Institute of Miners' Health, and other educational institutions. The funds for research are being provided to these institutions by the Ministry of Mines on approval of research projects by the Standing Advisory Group in the Ministry.

7.2.46 The major thrust areas identified for R&D in the mineral sector include: exploration, mining technology, mineral processing and value addition, metal extraction, alloys and product development, and environment management for ensuring sustainable development of the sector.

7.2.47 There is need for a focused approach in the field of R&D in the mineral sector. Some of the specific projects identified for the Eleventh Plan are as follows:

- Study of greenstone belts and their associated minerals, especially gold (Au) and PGE mineralization.
- The by-products and wastes that are available are valuable products for the future. With metal prices for titanium (Ti), vanadium (V), and gallium (Ga) scaling new highs, an integrated approach to win many materials from the same source has become imperative. Red mud requires a serious second look as it is possible to recover the above-mentioned metals. Similarly, a re-look at various slags and anode slimes for high-value trace metals for PGE metals is needed and specific R&D programmes should be taken up for secondaries and wastes.
- Multi-material extraction technology for extraction of metals such as tungsten, molybdenum, vanadium, chromium, nickel, etc., on the one hand, and value-added trace elements such as gallium, indium, tellurium, etc., on the other hand, needs to be developed.

7.2.48 For strengthening R&D activities in mining, consideration needs to be given to the proposal to set up a centralized R&D institution for undertaking research on all aspects of mining.

Human Resource Development

7.2.49 GSI, IBM, State Directorates of Mines and Geology, State Mining Corporations, Central Public Sector Undertakings (CPSUs), private and joint venture exploration and mining companies, research institutions, and academic institutions are the key players which recruit competent and trained manpower in the mineral sector. Organizations such as GSI and IBM are facing problems of shortage of trained manpower. The best talents are being attracted by areas such as IT and business management and there is little demand among students for taking up mining engineering and geology as courses of study. Non-induction of officers at the entry level in the GSI and IBM has compounded the problem. In order to remedy the situation, it is necessary to make an assessment of the future requirement of geologists and mining engineers in the GSI and IBM and announce a long-term programme of recruitment.

Sustainability of Mineral Development

7.2.50 Mineral development faces opposition in the country on two accounts. First, there is scepticism about mining operations being done in a manner that does not have an adverse impact on the environment. Second, there is a feeling among PAPs that they have not received enough compensation. More importantly, there are unfulfilled expectations from mining companies for providing development services in return for the social license to operate the mines.

7.2.51 There are two statutes, viz., the Forest (Conservation) Act 1980 and the Environment (Protection)

Act 1986, which lay down the law that must be followed in the development of mines. A criticism that has been made is that the two statutes have a preoccupation with two concerns, namely, compensation for diversion of forest land to non-forest use in various forms (including compensatory afforestation) and the need for environment impact studies prior to the grant of environmental clearances. The best practice internationally goes much beyond these concerns. Worldwide, mining interventions are becoming increasingly sophisticated and the objective is 'to ensure that the critical natural capital is maintained, that ecosystems are enhanced where possible, and that mineral wealth contributes to net environmental continuity.' (National Mineral Policy: Report of the High Level Committee, 2006).

7.2.52 As for relief and rehabilitation, various mineral-rich States already have in position policies and executive orders that lay down the entitlements of the PAPs. But the practice in the country falls short of that prevailing internationally in mining sector interventions. The international best practices include 2%–3% of the turnover of mining companies being expended on social infrastructure in the region, a direct financial stake in the mining venture to indigenous communities (e.g., tribals) in the form of equity, and all this is in addition to fair compensation to PAPs by way of cash, housing, and jobs. Mining companies in India now under statutory obligations, routinely undertake welfare measures for the development of entire local communities. However, as observed by the high-level committee, 'these are unorganized ad hoc initiatives that are voluntary in nature and for which there is no accountability to outside agencies'. It is necessary to have a formalized framework so that standards are laid down and adherence to the standards is ensured.

7.2.53 In order to enhance the contribution of mining to the enrichment of the environment and improve the well being of the indigenous communities beyond what the current law and policy provides, the high-level committee on the Mineral Policy has recommended that a framework should be prepared and adapted to the Indian mining context on the basis of the SDF developed by the International Council of Mining and Metals and the International Union for the Conservation of Nature and Natural Resources. Once such a framework has been prepared, all mining leaseholders would be required to adhere to it as a condition of their lease. The government would establish a mechanism for monitoring such adherence in a participative mode along with the NGOs and PAPs.

Impediments to Investment in Mining

7.2.54 The main reason for the lack of private sector investment in exploration and mining activity is that there is no assurance that the RP holder will get the prospecting license and the PL holder will get the ML. Further, even after an entrepreneur gets the ML, several discretionary provisions in the statutes pose a threat to the ML holder's security of tenure.

7.2.55 At present, the system of exclusive RPs contains no incentive for the RP holder to expedite reconnaissance work. Furthermore, the lack of clarity on the right to transfer PLs limits the applications for RP only to large companies, which have the ability to take up reconnaissance, prospecting, as well as mining activity. Without a guaranteed and explicit right to transfer the PLs, standalone exploration companies, which have the ability to do reconnaissance and prospecting on the basis of state-of-the-art techniques, but do not undertake mining as this is a separate activity, are discouraged from making an application for RP. This is the single most vital issue for attracting investment in exploration and it lies at the core of the recommendation for 'unbundling' made by the high-level committee on the National Mineral Policy.

7.2.56 Even though the regulations contain time limits for the State Government in disposing of applications, they may defer indefinitely a decision on an application for RP/PL/ML in the hope that applications would come in future from value-adders.

7.2.57 Procedural delays in the disposal of applications occur for a number of reasons. One of them is that a great deal of time is taken for the verification of mineral titles. The availability of a spatially represented, easily accessible registry of all pending and granted exploration titles is a key part of a modern regulatory system.

7.2.58 Several State Government undertakings are involved in mining activity and since the State is also a regulator the State's involvement in mining, in competition with private mining companies it can become a disincentive for the private sector investment.

MINERAL DEVELOPMENT IN THE STATES

7.2.59 In line with the current economic and new mineral policy, the core functions of the State in mining will be facilitation of exploration and mining activities of investors and entrepreneurs, provision of infrastructure, and regulation and tax collection. The mineral-producing States need to update their mineral policy in line with the National Mineral Policy.

INFRASTRUCTURE IN MINING AREAS

7.2.60 While deficiencies in arterial roadways, railways, and port infrastructure need to be addressed by the Central Government, equally crucial for the development of mining is the infrastructure that links mines to the arterial routes. While the Central Government is providing funds for arterial routes, there is a need for funds for linking infrastructure as well. This is particularly important in our country where non-captive mining is mainly an SME sector activity.

STRATEGIES TO MEET THE CHALLENGES

7.2.61 At the end of the Tenth Five Year Plan, the potential of the mineral sector in the country remains largely unrealized in the absence of exploration activities on the scale needed. The public sector bodies are hamstrung by the lack of financial resources and the private sector does not find the legal framework and the procedures to be conducive for the enterprise. There are other challenges as well, particularly those relating to the transport infrastructure, the protection of the environment, rehabilitation of the people displaced by the mining activity, and increasing the revenue for the State Governments from mining activity. We give below the more important strategies for tackling them, based largely on the recommendations of the high-level committee on National Mineral Policy referred to earlier.

- It is necessary to effect changes in law so that the transition from RP to PL and further to ML is made seamless. Discretionary powers of the government, which affect the security of tenure of the holders of RP/PL/ML, should be eliminated or at least substantially curtailed.
- For maximizing the investment in exploration, RPs should be made non-exclusive and prospecting companies should be given explicitly a guaranteed right to transfer the PL with the accompanying right to be granted the ML.
- The present registry system should be modernized by creating a digitized online mineral atlas, which would show the mineral titles clearly. This will make it feasible for applicants to ascertain the availability of areas before applications and to apply online, which should be allowed.
- Co-ordination-cum-empowered committees need to be established in the Centre as well as in the States to monitor the clearances and to serve as a pressure point to ensure speedy clearance by different departments and agencies.
- In line with the current economic policy, the core functions of the State in mining should be facilitation of exploration and mining activities of private sector investors and entrepreneurs, provision of infrastructure, and regulation and tax collection.
- To facilitate the provision of infrastructure linking the mines to the arterial routes, each State Government with major mining activity should set up a mineral development fund (MDF) by earmarking 15% of the annual royalty collections for the fund. The GoI should also make matching contribution to the MDF of each State every year for the duration of the Eleventh Plan.

PLAN OUTLAY IN THE ELEVENTH PLAN

7.2.62 The scheme-wise break up of the Eleventh Plan outlay is given in Annexure 7.2.10. The total projected outlay for the Eleventh Five Year Plan for Ministry of Mines is Rs 7430 crore at 2006–07 price (Rs 8404 crore at current price) which includes Rs 1043 crore of GBS at 2006–07 price (Rs 1180 crore at current price) and Rs 6387 crore of IEBR at 2006–07price (Rs 7224 at current price).

ANNEXURE 7.1.1
Industrial Investment Proposals

Year	Industrial Entrepreneur Memoranda (IEM)		Letter of Intents (LOIs)		Direct Industrial Licenses (DILs)	
	No. of Proposals	Proposed Investment (Rs Crore)	No. of Proposals	Proposed Investment (Rs Crore)	No. of Proposals	Proposed Investment (Rs Crore)
2001	2981	91234	117	1318		
2002	3172	91291	89	649		
2003	3875	118612	116	1395	14	
2004	5118	267069	39	381	61	4884
2005	6203	353956	24	333	111	2657
2006	6260	588271	20	137	90	4693
2007 (up to March 2007)	1030	204517	1	37	6	886

Source: SIA Statistics, April 2007, DIPP.

ANNEXURE 7.1.2
Investment Projects Benefiting from Loans from Banks/FIs in 2004–05, 2005–06 and 2006–07

	2004–05			2005–06			2006–07		
	Number of Projects	Project Cost Amount (Rs Crore)	% Share	Number of Projects	Projects Cost Amount (Rs Crore)	% Share	Number of Projects	Project Cost Amount (Rs Crore)	% Share
1 Industry				2	3	4	5	6	7
1. Infrastructure	75	31294	33.3	109	44541	33.9	125	101744	35.9
(i) Power	60	12419	13.2	66	35358	26.9	64	51451	18.2
(ii) Telecom	4	15832	16.9	5	2639	2.0	9	17950	6.3
(iii) Ports and airports	11	3043	3.2	3	2295	1.8	7	10745	3.8
(iv) Roads, storage, and water management				22	2386	1.8	8	13083	4.6
(v) SEZ, industrial, biotech, and IT parks				13	1864	1.4	37	8515	3.0
2. Sugar	14	763	0.8	20	2857	2.2	33	8867	3.1
3. Textiles	126	7458	8.0	158	14128	10.8	258	25933	9.2
4. Paper and paper products	17	2330	2.5	23	2397	1.8	24	2915	1.0
5. Coke and petroleum products				2	1107	0.8	11	44083	15.5
6. Chemicals and petrochemicals	38	2822	3.0	26	3021	2.3	35	4136	1.5
7. Cement	14	3642	3.9	13	1945	1.5	27	10567	3.7
8. Metal and metal products	141	27331	29.1	126	21799	16.6	130	39876	14.1
9. Electrical and non-electrical machinery	23	671	0.7	22	384	0.3	20	4486	1.6
10. Transport equipments	25	1289	1.4	13	988	0.8	29	5174	1.8
11. Construction	8	275	0.3	33	4700	3.6	34	9277	3.3
12. Hotels and restaurants	20	2254	2.4	37	4454	3.4	74	11122	3.9
13. Transport services	45	4201	4.5	21	16947	12.9	17	1561	0.5
14. Entertainment				9	1807	1.4	20	761	0.3
15. IT	16	974	1.0	7	2683	2.0	8	228	0.1
16 Food products/processing	47	1754	1.9						
17. Others*	81	3401	3.6	193	7540	5.7	209	12710	4.5
Total	720	93859	100.00	812	131299	100.0	1054	283440	100.0

Note: *Comprise industries, each with a share of less than 1% in total cost of projects in 2005–06 and 2006–07.
Source: RBI, Bulletin, August 2006 and August 2007.

ANNEXURE 7.1.3
Composition of Exports and Growth Rates

Commodity	Exports 2006–07 P (US$ Million)	% Share of Exports		Compound Annual Growth Rate (CAGR) in Ninth Plan	Growth Rate over Previous Year					CAGR in Tenth Plan
		Ninth Plan	2006–07		2002–03	2003–04	2004–05	2005–06	2006–07	
I. Primary Products	19547.8	18.3	15.5	–2.3	21.5	13.7	36.9	20.9	19.4	22.2
A. Agriculture and allied products	12514.6	15.6	9.9	–3.0	13.7	12.3	12.5	20.3	22.5	16.2
B. Ores and minerals	7033.1	2.7	5.6	1.5	58.1	18.7	114.4	21.9	14.1	41.0
II. Manufactured Goods	82817.8	77.4	65.6	6.3	20.6	20.5	25.2	18.3	14.1	19.9
A. Leather and manufactures	2933.1	4.5	2.3	3.5	–3.2	17.0	12.0	8.4	8.7	9.0
B. Chemicals and related products	16727.1	12.9	13.2	9.1	23.2	26.7	31.7	16.6	13.3	22.5
1. Basic chemicals, pharmaceuticals, and cosmetics	10445.8	8.2	8.2	8.2	26.0	25.5	22.1	25.2	14.4	23.1
2. Others	6281.3	4.7	5.0	10.7	18.8	28.7	47.3	5.1	11.3	21.7
C. Engineering goods	29079.1	14.9	23.0	7.0	29.8	37.3	39.8	24.2	33.9	33.1
D. Textile and textile products	17009.7	25.5	13.5	3.4	13.8	10.1	6.0	18.3	3.7	10.8
1. Cotton yarn, fabrics, madeups, etc.	4136.6	8.1	3.3	–0.3	9.1	1.3	1.6	12.0	4.9	6.1
2. Readymade garments	8694.7	12.2	6.9	5.9	13.6	9.5	5.3	28.1	0.9	11.7
3. Man-made yarn, fabrics, madeups, etc.	2164.6	2.3	1.7	8.7	28.8	28.4	11.4	–2.2	10.6	15.2
4. Other (silk, jute, coir, woolen products, and carpets)	2013.8	2.9	1.6	0.1	13.4	16.6	12.6	17.2	7.0	13.7
E. Gems and jewellery	15585.7	17.3	12.3	9.0	23.6	17.1	30.2	13.0	0.4	16.4
F. Handicrafts (excluding hand-made carpets)	371.7	1.6	0.3	2.9	43.0	–36.4	–24.5	8.7	–19.5	–7.5
G. Other manufactured goods	1111.4	0.8	0.9	7.7	22.5	29.0	34.1	37.7	13.0	23.4
III. Petroleum Products	18551.9	2.3	14.7	34.5	21.6	38.5	95.9	64.7	59.4	54.3
IV. Others	5413.7	2.0	4.3	28.2	1.5	57.7	20.3	32.9	115.6	35.8
Total Exports	126331.1	100.0	100.0	5.5	20.3	21.1	30.8	23.0	22.5	23.6

Note: P = Provisional.
Source: Handbook of Statistics on Indian Economy, RBI, 2007.

ANNEXURE 7.1.4
Performance of CPSEs during the Tenth Five Year Plan

(Rs Crore)

	Turnover					Net Profit/Loss (–)				
Industry	2001–02	2002–03	2003–04	2004–05	2005–06	2001–02	2002–03	2003–04	2004–05	2005–06
Steel	20135	24885	31008	40820	41742	–1781	229	4091	8893	5307
Minerals and non-ferrous metals	5461	5846	7160	10153	12384	568	755	1467	2876	4039
Coal and lignite	22001	26920	29048	33698	34489	2158	3035	5238	4826	8216
Power	23977	25271	25321	30010	34306	5613	5219	8605	8730	9082
Petroleum	253012	305335	330074	406247	499555	12639	22322	23819	25959	26181
Fertilizers	7429	8280	8017	8999	9364	–1796	–2329	–2128	–2104	–1990
Chemicals and pharmaceuticals	810	981	1005	1298	976	–388	–253	–376	–557	–74
Heavy engineering	7892	7973	9041	10823	15042	144	–6	43	313	977
Medium and light engineering	7808	7946	7864	8443	9559	–191	–687	–977	–450	–25
Transportation equipment	6112	6505	6962	8198	9619	776	388	293	679	1045
Consumer goods	1241	1241	1311	1325	1606	–306	–721	–575	–848	225
Agro-based industries	129	142	158	150	173	–14	–14	–11	–26	–21
Textiles	753	940	825	875	856	–1032	–1961	425	–1479	1211
Total industry	356759	422264	457793	561039	669672	16390	25978	39914	46815	54172
Enterprises rendering services	107174	138930	160064	166302	162912	10003	6199	12576	17269	16117
Total CPSEs	463934	561194	617857	727341	832584	26393	32176	52490	64083	70288

Note: The data is in respect of 225 CPSEs in operation in 2005–06 for 2001–02 to 2004–05. In 2005–06, 10 CPSEs did not report the data to DPE and therefore data for 2005–06 pertains to 215 CPSEs.

Source: DPE, 2007, Public Enterprises Survey 2005-06, Volume–I.

ANNEXURE 7.1.5
State-wise and Year-wise Investment Intentions (IEMs + LOIs + DILs)

(in Rs Crore)

S. No.	Name of the State	2003–04	2004–05	2005–06	2006–07	2007–08 (April–May)
1.	Andhra Pradesh	16527	16596	19001	48660	2577
2.	Assam	163	430	809	2044	169
3.	Bihar	27	314	3913	4850	308
4.	Chhattisgarh	16155	47602	39914	118737	17559
5.	Dadra and Nagar Haveli	4137	834	2374	2794	431
6.	Gujarat	32341	29695	82901	72283	7946
7.	Haryana	8372	2737	5578	16095	769
8.	Himachal Pradesh	1126	3384	1774	1906	254
9.	Jammu and Kashmir	774	2719	2058	2306	400
10.	Jharkhand	1861	10539	54089	35257	17969
11.	Karnataka	14074	10969	15353	72250	7059
12.	Madhya Pradesh	1616	8538	18782	12537	1963
13.	Maharashtra	8878	13256	24694	62191	6907
14.	Orissa	17718	45565	38255	96869	5997
15.	Punjab	1844	4190	7127	10128	544
16.	Rajasthan	1096	2162	5077	10040	1768
17.	Tamil Nadu	2898	54481	11841	20377	5373
18.	Uttar Pradesh	2179	21633	31710	33745	1823
19.	Uttarakhand	1334	2441	5706	14887	968
20.	West Bengal	7637	14078	12047	51836	9410
21.	Others	17628	1931	3378	6574	1857
	Total	158385	294094	386381	696366	92051

Note: Investment in terms of IEMs filed, Letters of Intent (LOIs) issued, and DILs.
Source: SIA Statistics, June 2007.

ANNEXURE 7.1.6

State-wise Investment Projects Benefiting from Loans from Banks/FIs during 2004–05, 2005–06 and 2006–07

State	2004–05			2005–06			2006–07		
	Number of Projects	Project Cost		Number of Projects	Project Cost		Number of Projects	Project Cost	
		Amount (Rs Crore)	% Share		Amount (Rs Crore)	% Share		Amount (Rs Crore)	% Share
1	2	3	4	5	6	7	8	9	10
Andhra Pradesh	38	3330	3.6	76	11254	8.6	105	25173	8.9
Chhattisgarh	40	8620	9.2	19	5162	3.9	13	2365	0.8
Delhi	12	1471	1.6	24	2127	1.6	19	6359	2.2
Gujarat	81	10983	11.7	95	24531	18.7	86	73170	25.8
Haryana	21	1440	1.5	29	1805	1.4	42	3897	1.4
Himachal Pradesh	17	1358	1.4	19	9325	7.1	30	2644	0.9
Jharkhand	–	–	–	8	367	0.3	13	7174	2.5
Karnataka	50	6641	7.1	51	4537	3.5	91	19930	7.0
Madhya Pradesh	19	766	0.1	12	2514	1.9	23	4878	1.7
Maharashtra	102	9808	10.4	121	24828	18.9	142	24330	8.6
Orissa	30	9256	9.9	20	4525	3.5	23	14806	5.2
Punjab	32	2609	2.8	27	2041	1.5	48	5902	2.1
Rajasthan	26	1587	1.7	27	2466	1.9	38	9806	3.5
Sikkim	–	–	–	–	–	–	3	9418	3.3
Tamil Nadu	110	9929	10.6	124	12160	9.3	157	24299	8.6
Uttar Pradesh	23	1348	1.4	50	10415	7.9	60	9836	3.5
Uttarakhand	10	599	0.6	24	2959	2.2	31	5633	2.0
West Bengal	40	2324	2.5	27	2548	1.9	37	3404	1.2
Multi-State	33	18893	20.1	29	5730	4.4	46	25428	9.0
Others*	36	2898	3.1	30	2005	1.5	47	4988	1.8
Total	720	93859	100.0	812	131299	100.0	1054	283440	100.0

Note: *Comprise States/UTs, each with share of less than 1% in aggregate cost of projects in 2005–06 and 2006–07.
Source: RBI Bulletin August 2006 and August 2007.

ANNEXURE 7.1.7
Production and Export of Vehicles

Category	2001–02	2002–03	2003–04	2004–05	2005–06	2006–07
			Production of Vehicles (in thousands)			
PVs	564	609	842	960	1046	1238
MUVs	106	114	146	249	263	306
CVs	163	203	275	350	391	520
Two-wheelers	4271	5076	5625	6527	7600	8444
Three-wheelers	213	277	341	374	434	556
Total	5316	6280	7229	8461	9735	11065
			Exports of Vehicles (in thousands)			
PVs	50	71	126	161	170	192
MUVs	3	1	3	6	6	6
CVs	12	12	17	30	40	50
Two-wheelers	104	180	265	367	513	619
Three-wheelers	15	43	68	67	77	144
Total	183	307	479	630	806	1011

Note: PVs = Passenger Vehicles.
Source: Society of Indian Automobile Manufacturers.

ANNEXURE 7.1.8
Production and Export Performance in Capital Goods Sector

(Rs in Crore)

Category	2002	2003	2004	2005	2006	CAGR (%)
			Production Performance in Capital Goods Sector			
Machine tools	1835	2371	2457	2645	2899	12
Textile machinery	1073	1175	1256	1668	2151	19
Heavy electrical equipments			16500	21000		27
Mining and construction equipments		4150	4750	6300		23
Process plant equipments		2850	3560	5000		32
			Export Performance			
Machine tools	436	568	628	686	819	17
Textile machinery	427	406	535	457	516	5
Heavy electrical equipments			3075	2700		–12
Mining and construction equipments		216	280	330		24
Process plant equipments		630	860	1150		35

Source: Department of Heavy Industry.

ANNEXURE 7.1.9
Production of Chemicals

(Thousand Tonnes)

Category	Installed Capacity (as on March 2007)	2001–02	2002–03	2003–04	2004–05	2005–06	2006–07	CAGR
Alkali	7072	4342	4792	5070	5272	5475	5269	3.9
Inorganic chemicals	748	374	404	441	508	544	602	10
Dyestuffs and dye intermediates	52	24.8	26.2	25.9	28.5	29.5	32.5	5.6
Agro chemicals	145	81.8	69.56	85.12	93.97	82.24	84.7	0.7
Organic chemicals	1889	1166	1353	1473	1506	1545	1545	5.8
Total chemicals	9908	5990	6645	7096	7408	7676	7534	4.7

Source: Department of Chemicals and Petrochemicals.

Foreign Trade in Chemicals

(in Rs Crore)

	Inorganic Chemicals		Organic Chemicals		Pesticides		Dye and Dyestuff	
Year	Export	Import	Export	Import	Export	Import	Export	Import
2001–02	1259	5730	7624	8795	1356	362	2436	1138
2002–03	1946	5579	10190	10695	1487	287	2943	1344
2003–04	1949	5916	12975	14363	1746	501	3112	1617
2004–05	2872	8130	16269	18785	2096	712	3111	1878
2005–06	3431	10446	21504	22775	2791	754	3750	2245
2005–06 (April–December)	2638	8531	19080	20451	2001	656	3366	2072

Source: Department of Chemicals and Petrochemicals.

ANNEXURE 7.1.10
Production, Consumption and Import of Fertilizers

(Lakh Tonnes)

	2001–02	2002–03	2003–04	2004–05	2005–06	2006–07 (Est.)
Production						
Urea	190.03	186.21	190.38	202.39	200.85	203.08
DAP	50.91	52.36	47.09	51.84	46.28	48.51
MOP	0	0	0	0	0	0
NPK (Complex Fert.)	49.66	48.16	47.59	55.08	66.94	74.44
Consumption						
Urea	199.17	184.93	197.67	206.65	222.98	244.85
DAP	61.81	54.73	56.25	62.56	67.64	69.24
MOP	19.92	19.73	20.13	23.10	27.31	24.50
NPK	49.63	50.67	51.20	53.63	66.94	74.44
SSP	26.05	24.99	25.44	25.49	27.56	30.57
Import of Fertilizers						
Urea	2.20	1.19	1.43	6.41	20.57	47.18
DAP	9.33	3.83	7.34	6.44	24.36	28.41
MOP	28.3	25.33	25.83	34.09	45.78	–

Note: Est = Estimate.
Source: Department of Fertilizers.

ANNEXURE 7.1.11
Production, Import and Export of Paper and Paperboard

(Lakh Tonnes)

Year	Production	Imports	Exports
2003–04	55.57	3.15	2.32
2004–05	57.93	1.95	2.70
2005–06	58.70	2.85	2.29
2006–07	61.28	3.10 (April 2006–February 2007)	2.6 (April–Dec 2006)

Source: Annual Reports, DIPP.

ANNEXURE 7.1.12
Production, Import and Export of Newsprint

(Lakh Tonnes)

Year	Production	Imports	Exports
2003–04	6.8	7.5	0.03
2004–05	7.6	6.7	0.05
2005–06	9.1	6.8	0.10
2006–07	10.3	7.9	0.04

Source: Annual Reports, DIPP.

ANNEXURE 7.1.13
Performance of Commodity Polymers and Synthetic Fibres

(Kilo Tonnes)

	2001–02	2002–03	2003–04	2004–05	2005–06	2006–07
Performance of Commodity Polymers						
Capacity	4252	4316	4431	4614	4710	5187
Production	3974	4175	4499	4776	4768	5183
Consumption	3826	3795	4107	4177	4795	na
Imports	420	381	450	416	722	na
Exports	568	761	843	1015	695	na
Net trade	148	380	393	599	(–) 27	
Performance of Synthetic Fibre						
Capacity	2071	2113	2204	2341	2413	3246
Production	1669	1755	1868	1875	1906	2244
Consumption	1718	1800	1882	1890	1893	na
Imports	147	189	155	193	162	na
Exports	98	144	141	178	175	na
Net trade	(–) 49	(–) 45	(–) 14	(–) 14	13	

Source: Department of Chemicals and Petrochemicals.

ANNEXURE 7.1.14
Production, Import and Export of Finished Steel

(Million Tonnes)

	2002–03	2003–04	2004–05	2005–06	2006–07(P)
Production for sale	35.41	38.58	41.32	44.39	49.58
Domestic availability	28.6	31.2	34.5	39.4	43.7
Consumption (apparent)	28.7	31.1	34.3	39.1	43.7
Import	1.51	1.54	2.11	3.85	4.10
Export	4.51	4.84	4.38	4.48	4.75

Source: Joint Plant Committee.

ANNEXURE 7.1.15
Estimated Requirement of Raw Material and Other Inputs in Steel Production by 2011–12

Input	Unit	Estimated Consumption 2005–06	Estimated Consumption 2011–12
Coking coal	Million mt	31.5	46.0
Non-coking coal	Million mt	15	24.5
Coal dust injection	Million mt	Negligible	3.00
Iron Ore	Million mt	66.9	130
Scrap Steel	Million mt	10.2	18.0
Limestone	Million mt	11	19.5
Dolomite	Million mt	4.0	7.4
Natural Gas	Mcal	10000	15000
Ferro Alloys	Million mt	0.85	1.5
Power	MW	4120	7700

Source: Report of the Working Group on Steel for the Eleventh Five Year Plan.

ANNEXURE 7.1.16
Production, Consumption and Export of Sugar during 2002–03 to 2006–07

(Lakh Tonnes)

S. No.	Particulars	2002–03	2003–04	2004–05	2005–06	2006–07
1.	Carryover stock	113.19	116.16	85.00	40.00#	
2.	Production	201.32	198.58	130.00	189.59	283.0
3.	Import	0.41	5.53	20.74	3.62	
4.	Internal consumption	183.76	175.00	171.44	183.21	
5.	Exports	15.00	2.94	0.98	13.68	
6.	Closing stock	116.16	85.00*	57.00*	36.32	

Note: #After excluding damaged sugar; * as indicated by Central Excise Authority.

Source: Annual Plan 2007–08 of DFPD, GoI, 2006–07 statistics from Indian Sugar, August 2007.

ANNEXURE 7.1.17
Production of Cloth—Year on Year Growth

	2001–02	2002–03	2003–04	2004–05	2005–06	2006–07#
Cotton	0.26	–2.37	–6.53	14.50	15.13	9.67
Blended	–1.01	–6.54	3.27	–0.59	3.48	8.34
100% non-cotton	12.70	5.22	9.16	2.19	4.16	7.07
Khadi, etc.	15.41	2.80	0.00	4.68	0.00	0.00
Total cloth	4.48	–0.15	0.98	7.07	9.00	8.37

Note: # Provisional, Confederation of Indian Textile Industry.
Source: Report of the Working Group on Textiles and Jute Industry for the Eleventh Five Year Plan.

ANNEXURE 7.1.18
Exports of Textiles and Clothing during the Tenth Five Year Plan

(US$ Million)

	2001–02	2002–03	2003–04	2004–05	2005–06	April 2005–February 2006#	April 2006–February 2007#	Y-o-Y Growth (%)
Cotton textiles	3092	3370	3609	3543	4493	4038.0	4781.90	18.40
Man-made textiles	1092	1421	1826	2050	2000	1813.70	2104.70	16.00
Silk textiles	287	315	381	405	430	631.50	634.30	0.50
Woolen textiles	52	51	58	70	84	418.10	412.50	–1.30
Clothing	5024	5705	6248	6559	8403	7051.40	7273.40	3.10
Total	9547	10862	12122	12627	15410	13952.70	15206.80	9.0
Jute, coir, and handicrafts	1254	1583	1409	1394	1668	1574.80	1524.70	–3.18
Grand Total	10801	12445	13531	14021	17078	15527.50	16731.50	7.75
Percentage growth		15.22	8.73	3.62	21.80			7.75

Note: # DGCI&S, Kolkata.
Source: Report of the Working Group on Textiles and Jute Industry for the Eleventh Plan.

ANNEXURE 7.1.19

The Tenth Plan Outlay and Anticipated Expenditure and the Eleventh Plan Outlay

(Rs Crore)

Ministry/Department	Tenth Plan						Eleventh Plan (at Current Price)		
	Outlays			Anticipated Expenditure					
	BS	IEBR	Outlay	BS	IEBR	Expenditure	BS	IEBR	Outlay
1. Steel	65	10979	11044	106	4708	4814	217.00	45390.08	45607.08
Iron and Steel	60	6039	6099	103	3994	4097	216.00	37102.18	37318.18
Minerals	5	4940	4945	3	714	717	1.00	8287.90	2288.90
2. Fertilizer	1050	4850	5900	657.36	1893.74	2551.10	1492.06	19135.87	20627.93
3. Chemicals and Petrochemicals	300	2744	3044	574.91	0	574.91	1960.00	296.36	2256.36
4. Industrial Policy and Promotion	2000	0	2000	1779	0	1779	4183.00	0.00	4183.00
5. Heavy Industry	700	1363	2063	1351	1255	2606	4093.00	7208.67	11301.67
6. Public Enterprises	50	0	50	94	0	94	54.00	0.00	54.00
7. Textiles	3500	80	3580	4504.48	0	4504.48	14000.00	0.00	14000.00
Industry segment	1900	80	1980	2686.63	0	2686.63	11000.00	0.00	11000.00
VSE segment	1600	0	1600	1817.85	0	1817.85	3000.00	0.00	3000.00
8. Consumer Affairs	55	0	55	280.24	0	280.24	1083.00	0.00	1083.00
9. Company Affairs (Corporate Affairs)	50	0	50	0	0	0	211.00	0.00	211.00
Industry Segment Outlay in other Ministries/Departments									
10. Petroleum (Petrochemicals and Engineering)	0	7614.81	7614.81	0	6824	6824	0.00	15557.00	15557.00
11. Ship Building	242.86	805	1047.86	156	127	282	170.00	550.00	720.00
12. Atomic Energy (I&M)	2270	1079.5	3349.5	1645.53	392.44	2037.97	8425	2554.12	10979.12
Industry	1811	90.0	1901.0	1241.23	39.65	1280.88	6975	160.00	7135.00
Minerals	459	989.5	1448.5	404.30	352.79	757.09	1450	2394.12	3844.12
13. Biotechnology	30	0	30	102	0	102	750.00	0.00	750.00
14. DSIR	25	0	25	25	0	25	150.00	0.00	150.00
15. Earth Sciences (Ocean Development)	100	0	100	93	0	93	319.00	0.00	319.00

Source: Planning Commission.

ANNEXURE 7.1.20
Performance of SSIs, Year 2000–01 to 2006–07

Year	Total SSI Units (Lakhs)	Fixed Investment (Rs Crore)	Production		Employment (In Lakh Persons)	Exports (Rs Crore)
			Current Price (Rs Crore)	Constant Price (1993–94 in Rs Crore)		
2000–01	101.1	151527	261297	184401.4	240.94	69797
	(4.07)	(8.25)	(11.78)	(8.23)	(5.17)	(28.78)
2001–02	105.21	160673	282270	195613	252.29	71244
	(4.07)	(6.04)	(8.03)	(8.00)	(4.71)	(2.07)
			At 2001–02 Price			
2002–03	109.49	169579	314850	306771	263.68	86013
	(4.07)	(5.54)	(11.54)	(8.68)	(4.51)	(20.73)
2003–04	113.95	178269	364547	336344	275.30	97644
	(4.07)	(5.12)	(15.78)	(9.64)	(4.41)	(13.52)
2004–05	118.59	188793	429796	372938	287.55	124417
	(4.07)	(5.90)	(17.90)	(10.88)	(4.45)	(27.42)
2005–06	123.42	198050	497842	418884	295.85	150242
	(4.07)	(4.90)	(15.83)	(12.32)	(4.28)	20.76
2006–07 (Prov.)	128.44	207307	585112	471663	312.52	–
	(4.07)	(4.67)	(17.53)	(12.60)	(4.23)	–

Note: Figures in brackets indicate increase in the percentage over the last year.
Source: Ministry of SSI, GoI, Annual Report 2005–06.

ANNEXURE 7.1.21
Export Destination (Country) of SSI Products

S. No.	Product Group	Main Destination (Countries)
1.	Readymade garments	USA, Europe, Canada, West Asia, and North Africa.
2.	Plastic items	UAE, China, Italy, Saudi Arabia, and Oman.
3.	Marine products	Japan, USA, European Union, China, and South East Asia.
4.	Sports goods	UK, USA, Australia, Germany, and South Africa.
5.	Spices	East Asia, European Union, North African Zone, and American Zone.
6.	Cashew items	USA, Netherlands, UK, Japan, and UAE.
7.	Shellac items	Indonesia, Germany, UAE, USA, and Italy.
8.	Synthetic items (Madeups)	UAE, UK, Turkey, USA, and Italy.
9.	Leather and leather items	Germany, UK, Italy, USA, and France.
10.	Engineering and electronic items	USA, Europe, Japan, Hong Kong, UAE, Germany, Belgium, and France.
11.	Basic chemical and cosmetic products	USA, Japan, Saudi Arabia, China, Singapore, and Netherlands.
12.	Chemical and allied products	Japan, Belgium, Italy, France, Bangladesh, USA, and UK.
13.	Wool and woollen (Madeups) knitted garments, etc.	Europe, Japan, and Bangladesh.
14.	Processed food items	USA, Europe, and Japan.
15.	Electronic items and computer software	USA, Hong Kong, UAE, UK, Germany, and Japan.
16.	Tobacco and tobacco items	East Europe.

Source: http://www.laghu-udyog.com/ssiindia exportdest.htm

ANNEXURE 7.1.22
Participation of Women in SSI Sector, State-wise

Name of State/UT	No. of Female Employees			No. of Enterprises Managed by Women	No. of Women Enterprises
	Regd. SSI Sector	Unregd. SSI Sector	Total		
Jammu & Kashmir	3313	8153	11466	5640	5742
Himachal Pradesh	4016	4134	8150	3515	3722
Punjab	11757	36013	47770	30190	29068
Chandigarh	659	1975	2634	2059	2243
Uttarakhand	2940	13240	16180	8706	8804
Haryana	15651	14889	30540	10087	9620
Delhi	6306	35798	42104	13368	14383
Rajasthan	15003	46065	61068	29785	36371
Uttar Pradesh	23506	180918	204424	54491	72667
Bihar	8353	68908	77261	38170	49443
Sikkim	212	9	221	30	98
Arunachal Pradesh	342	104	446	131	150
Nagaland	637	2574	3211	207	179
Manipur	3853	19485	23338	9168	10745
Mizoram	2188	4636	6824	3076	3700
Tripura	4294	3325	7619	631	863
Meghalaya	3139	5664	8803	3658	3580
Assam	9077	16988	26065	11189	11757
West Bengal	26549	304969	331518	71847	69625
Jharkhand	5105	8907	14012	7271	7865
Orissa	11723	213123	224846	33274	38233
Chhattisgarh	10177	52476	62653	11766	10034
Madhya Pradesh	29612	111703	141315	62351	68823
Gujarat	41189	79990	121179	55361	53703
Daman & Diu and Dadra & Nagar Haveli	6106	126	6232	167	213
Maharashtra	78731	162700	241431	80662	100670
Andhra Pradesh	60693	270026	330719	77347	77166
Karnataka	117934	223142	341076	101264	103169
Goa	5309	1833	7142	677	810
Lakshadweep	26	405	431	61	67
Kerala	189640	224491	414131	137561	139225
Tamil Nadu	270936	223050	493986	130289	129808
Pondicherry	5613	2670	8283	1089	1065
Andaman & Nicobar Islands	124	294	418	53	110
	974713	2342783	3317496	995141	1063721

Note: Regd. = Registered; Unregd. = Unregistered.
Source: 3rd SSI Census 2001–02– Ministry of MSME.

ANNEXURE 7.1.23
Schemes for MSME

Scheme/Goal	Eligibility	Description
	Fiscal Incentives/Subsidies	
Central excise duty exemption to make MSE products price competitive	All MSEs (manufacturing), including khadi and village industry units	Exemption up to Rs 100 lakh from excise duty, if total annual clearances or sales do not exceed Rs 400 lakh.
	Credit (Grants and Loans)	
Priority-sector lending to facilitate lending to MSEs	All MSEs	10% of all NBC by foreign banks to go to the MSE sector; no specific sub-target for domestic banks, which have to provide 40% of NBC to the priority sector as a whole.
CLCSS for Technology Upgradation	All (manufacturing) MSEs, including khadi and village industry units	Subsidy of 15% (12% prior to 29 September 2005) of capital acquired for upgrading technology or techniques for sub-sectors/products approved under the scheme upto a limit of Rs 100 lakh (Rs 40 lakh prior to 29 September 2005).
Credit Guarantee Scheme, to banks lending to MSEs	All (manufacturing) MSEs, including khadi and village industry units	Guarantee of 75% for loans up to Rs 25 lakh extended by member lending institutions of the Credit Guarantee Fund Trust, guarantee fee being borne by the borrower.
Prime Minister's Rozgar Yojana for employment generation	Educated (VIII standard pass) unemployed youth with family income up to Rs 40000 per annum	Loans of up to Rs 2 lakh for self-employment projects each case (Rs 1 lakh for business/service activities). Subsidy is released as a grant by the government, through the RBI, to the participating banks for crediting to the account of beneficiary, and adjusted against the repayment of last installment of loan by the beneficiary. The subsidy is 15% of the project cost or Rs 7500 per entrepreneur, whichever is less. The bank charges interest (not exceeding PLR) on the loan amount minus subsidy.
ISO 9000/ISO 14001 Certification Fee Reimbursement Scheme for improving quality and business processes	Individual MSEs, including those engaged in business/service	Reimbursement of expenses incurred in acquiring Quality Management System ISO 9000 certification/ environment management ISO 14001 certification, at 75% of the cost or Rs 75000, whichever is less.
Participation in international fairs for export promotion	Individual MSEs	Subsidy for renting space and partial reimbursement of air fare.
	Other Schemes	
Credit Appraisal and Rating Tool (CART)		Scheme for reimbursement of performance and credit rating of MSMEs through reputed Credit Rating agencies. To rationalize the pricing of credit, SIDBI has developed an advanced but simplified, technology-based rating model for MSEs called CART.
Reservation of products for exclusive mfg. by MSEs	All MSEs	114 items at present.
Purchase and price preference in government procurement to help improve marketing	MSEs registered with NSIC	358 items are currently reserved for exclusive purchase by the Central Government and its PSUs from the MSEs. 15% price preference for Central Government purchases, i.e. a micro/small enterprise quoting up to 15% above the quote of a non-MSE bidder would be eligible to get the order, other

Annexure 7.1.23 (contd.)

Annexure 7.1.23 (contd.)

Scheme/Goal	Eligibility	Description
		conditions of quality, terms of supply being met. Tender document is also provided free of charge and exemption from earnest money/security deposits.
Small Industry Cluster Development Programme (renamed as Micro and Small Enterprises Cluster Development Programme) to enhance the productivity, and competitiveness, as well as capacity building of micro and small enterprises	Micro and small (MSE) clusters	Implemented in PPP mode, GoI assistance varies from 30% to 80% of the project cost depending on the average investment in plant and machinery, location of the cluster, level of commercial self-sufficiency, etc.
Integrated Infrastructure Development (IID) Scheme, to facilitate provision of built-up infrastructure with necessary facilities for manufacturing and related service enterprises, with reservation of 50% for rural areas	State governments, industry associations, and NGOs for development/disposal of plots/ sheds on commercial basis	Central Government grants assistance of up to Rs 200 lakh or 40% of the project cost, whichever is less, for setting up new industrial estates for MSEs (up to 80% or Rs 40 million for the NER, including Sikkim, Himachal Pradesh, Jammu & Kashmir, and Uttarakhand). Also available for improvements in existing estates.
Mini Tool Rooms to improve availability of quality equipment, machines, and tooling facilities, necessary for manufacturing, on payment of user charges	State Governments/State Government agencies	Assistance up to 90% of the cost of plant and machinery or Rs 900 lakh, whichever is less, for setting up new mini tool rooms (75% of the cost of plant and machinery or Rs 750 lakh for upgrading existing tool rooms).
Testing centres to improve availability of quality test equipment, machines and other facilities, necessary for testing of raw material, intermediates, and finished products on payment of user charges	Industry associations	Assistance up to 50% of the cost of testing equipment and machinery or Rs 50 lakh, whichever is less, for setting up testing centres.
Sub-contracting exchanges to assist associations of MSEs track bulk orders/ tenders for bulk supplies by large industries to enable member MSEs to bid for parts of these orders	Industry associations	One time grant upto Rs 4 lakh for procurement of hardware such as plain paper copier, telex, fax machine, computer, furniture. Grant paid on reimbursement basis and provides a matching grant on a tapering basis at 50%, 30%, and 10% for running expenses, not exceeding Rs 125000, Rs 75000, and Rs 25000, respectively, during the first three years, subject to a ceiling of Rs 157000 per exchange.
SSI Market Development Assistance for export promotion	MSEs and their associations	Partial subsidization of costs of air fare, space rental, publicity, etc., to MSEs at varying rates, with preferential terms to the micro enterprises, partial financial assistance to contest anti-dumping cases, undertaking market studies, etc. Provision for reimbursement of 75% of one-time registration fee or Rs 15000, whichever is less for adoption of bar coding.
Assistance to Entrepreneurship Development Institutes	State/UT governments and other agencies involved in entrepreneurship development	Financial assistance in the form of non-recurring grant for strengthening infrastructure like building, training aids/equipment, and other support services on matching (50:50 basis) of the cost or Rs 100 lakh whichever is less.
Micro Finance Programme	Micro finance institutions (MFIs)	Portfolio Risk Fund provided to SIDBI for security deposit requirements of the loan amount from the MFIs.

Source: SIDO online information, viewed at *http://www.smallindustry.india.com* [4 July 2006]; RBI online information, viewed at *http://www.rbi.org.in/scripts/FAQView.aspx?Id=8*; and Ministry of Finance (2006), *Economic Survey 2005–06*.

ANNEXURE 7.2.1

Organization/Company-wise Actual Expenditure in the Tenth Five Year Plan—Ministry of Mines

(Rs Crore)

Organization	Approved Tenth Plan	Revised Tenth Plan (Mid-term)	Actual Tenth Plan
National Aluminium Co. Ltd	7056.00	2864.25	1840.27
Hindustan Copper Ltd	50.00	326.16	266.34
Mineral Exploration Corp. Ltd	50.00	73.75	66.45
Geological Survey of India	1000.00	998.56	537.54
Indian Bureau of Mines	103.00	136.08	84.88
S&T Programmes	57.50	52.48	32.95
Construction#	28.00	34.00	27.86
Total	8344.50@	4485.28	2856.29
GBS	1271.00	2881.75	986.27
IEBR	7073.50	1603.53	1870.02

Note: @ excluding outlay for HZL since disinvested; # construction in GSI and IBM.

Source: Tenth Five Year Document, Planning Commission, and Ministry of Mines.

ANNEXURE 7.2.2

Life Indices of Important Minerals

(in Million Tonnes)

S. No.	Mineral	Total Resources as on 1 April 2000	Total Balance Resources as on 1 April 2007	Estimated Domestic Production during 2006–07	Life Index Beyond 1 April 2007 at 2006–07 Production Level
1.	Bauxite	3306.763 (2221.549)	3269.525 (2184.311)	13.142	166
2.	Copper ore	1394.425 (659.789)	1385.094 (650.458)	3.293	200
3.	Chromite	232.120 (146.483)	220.532 (134.895)	4.090	33
4.	Lead–zinc ore	522.579 (316.879)	510.072 (304.372)	4.414	69
5.	Iron ore (haematite and magnetite)	25250 (15946)	24795 (15432)	160.33	97

Note: Figures in parentheses (of proved and probable reserves) have been considered for life index.

Source: Working Group Report on Mineral Exploration and Development (Other than coal and lignite) for Eleventh Five Year Plan, Volume II.

ANNEXURE 7.2.3
Estimated Apparent Consumption, Domestic Production, Resource Situation and Life Index of Selected Minerals

(Thousand Tonnes)

Minerals	Estimated Apparent Consumption in Terminal Year of		Estimated Production for Terminal Year of		Total Estimated Balance of Resources as on 1 April 2012	Life Index beyond 2012
	Tenth Five Year Plan 2006–07	Eleventh Five Year Plan 2011–12	Tenth Five Year Plan 2006–07	Eleventh Five Year Plan 2011–12		
A Refractory minerals						
1. Bauxite	12934	19900	14214	21875	3176799 (2091585)	96
2. Chromite	2978	4583	4302	6619	192569 (106932)	16
3. Graphite	113	174	113	174	157788 (10087)	58
4. Ball clay	2045	3147	1610	2477	52493 (13335)	5
5. Wollastonite	170	262	194	298	18429 (14255)	48
B Flux and construction minerals						
1. Gypsum	3437	5289	3994	6145	1194934 (767507)	125
2. Asbestos	227	349	6	9	21724 (11228)	Very large
C Fertilizer and chemical minerals						
1. Rock phosphate	4475	6695	1340	2061	383547 (139631)	68
2. Sulphur (by-product)	1320	2031	128	197	–	–
3. Fluorspar	126	194	12.86	20	12591 (10765)	538

Note: Figures in parenthesis (proved and probable reserves) considered for life indices.

Source: Working Group Report on Mineral Exploration and Development (other than coal and lignite) for Eleventh Five Year Plan, Volume II.

ANNEXURE 7.2.4
Material Balance of Principal Non-ferrous Metals

(Thousand mt)

	Aluminium			Copper			Zinc			Lead		
	2001–02	2006–07	2011–12	2001–02	2006–07	2011–12	2001–02	2006–07	2011–12	2001–02	2006–07	2011–12
Production (Primary)	660	950	1250	390	740	808	201	423	638	31	63	95
Secondary	40	50	60	–	–	–	25	30	40	40	60	75
Total Production	700	1000	1310	390	740	808	226	453	678	71	123	170
Import	150	120	270	45	–	–	71	2	–	61	152	273
Export	150	200	300	61	300	219	–	–	11	–	–	–
Domestic Demand	700	920	1280	374	440	589	297	455	667	132	275	443

Note: Demand for copper for 2011–12 has been projected at 6% compound growth rate per annum and production at 90% capacity utilization of existing installed capacity of 897500 tonnes.

Source: Working Group Report on Mineral Exploration and Development (other than coal and lignite), Eleventh Five Year Plan, Volume III.

ANNEXURE 7.2.5
Iron Ore Availability—Haematite (as on 1 April 2005)

(Qty in Million Tonnes)

Grade	Reserves	Remaining Resources	Total
High grade (Fe +65%)	1304.3	629.03	1933.33
Medium grade (Fe 62%–65%)	3544.03	3062.02	6606.05
Low grade (Fe below 62%)	1989.75	1686.94	3676.69
Unclassified	159.23	743.67	902.90
Black iron ore	2.52	12.72	15.24
Others	1.62	5.05	6.67
Unclassified	1.98	0	1.98
Not known	0.73	1486.79	1487.52
Grand Total	7004.17	7626.22	14630.39

Source: IBM.

ANNEXURE 7.2.6
Iron Ore Availability—Magnetite (as on 1 April 2005)

(Qty in Million Tonnes)

Grade	Reserves	Remaining Resources	Total
Metallurgical	0.67	2185.05	2185.74
Coal washery	3.33	5.00	8.33
Foundry	0.46	0.30	0.76
Others	0.97	24.16	25.13
Unclassified	52.64	8060.34	8112.98
Not known	0.43	286.12	286.55
Grand total	58.50	10560.98	10619.48

Source: IBM.

ANNEXURE 7.2.7

Physical Targets Proposed by GSI for some Important Activities for the Eleventh Plan (2007–12)

Schemes	Physical Target
1. Survey and Mapping	
Specialized thematic mapping	35000 sq km
Geochemical mapping	180000 sq km
Geophysical mapping	240000 sq km
Air-borne geophysical survey	76000 sq km
Marine surveys	12 cruises with RV Samudra Manthan, 13 cruises with new blue water research vessel, 70 cruises by coastal launches, that is RV Samudra Kaustubh and RV Samudra Saudhikama.
2. Mineral Exploration	226 items out of which 154 items on non-coal minerals and 72 items on coal and lignite (coal 66 items and lignite 6 items). Large scale: mapping 13530 sq km, Drilling: 429000 m
3. Specialized Investigations	Land slide hazard zonation on 1:50000/25000 scale of about 10000 line km through land slide prone hilly terrains; on 1:10000/5000 scale in thickly populated localities. In 20 sites, development of early warning system in 3 problematic land slides. Other specialized investigations include earthquake geology and seismology, environmental geology, geotechnical studies, glaciological and geothermal studies.
4. R&D and Antarctica Studies	202 items covering geochronology and isotope geology, petrology, photo-geology, and remote sensing, etc.
5. Publication and dissemination of information	Transformation of 3892 maps of 1:50000 scale geological maps into uniform .COOF format under GIS platform out of total 4306 maps digitized so far and digitization of 118 mineral belt maps; 130 district resource maps to be placed in public domain after completing them; completion of 1:0.5 M scale maps of 14 States; departmental publication: 100.
6. Human Resource Development	177 in house training courses.
7. Modernization and Replacement	Procurement of laboratory equipment, replacement of RV Samudra Manthan, Geotechnical vessel, and Heli-borne Geophysical Survey System.

Note: M scale = Million scale.
Source: Ministry of Mines.

ANNEXURE 7.2.8

Physical Targets Proposed by IBM and MECL for some Important Activities for the Eleventh Plan (2007–12)

Schemes	Target
Indian Bureau of Mines	
Inspection of mines for enforcement of provision of MCDR 1988.	2500 mines per annum.
Mineral beneficiation studies	Ore dressing investigations: 70 and chemical analysis of 50000 radicals annually; mineralogical studies: 2300.
Technological upgradation and modernization	Management of solid waste from mining in India.
Collection, processing, dissemination of data on mines and minerals	Adoption of UNFC system, 100 multi-mineral maps with corresponding forest overlays on yearly basis. Computerized online register of mining tenements system.
Mineral Exploration Corporation Limited	
Remote Sensing studies	23 items
Environmental studies	75 items
Geophysical surveys	1535 sq km
Geophysical logging	557462 sq m
Geological mapping	4655 sq km
Drilling	1066325 m
Exploratory mining	17500 m
Sampling and analysis	358250 nos

Source: Ministry of Mines.

ANNEXURE 7.2.9
Expansion Projects of NALCO—Capacity Additions

	Product	Unit	Existing Capacity	Expanded Capacity	Increase Capacity
Mine	Bauxite	Lakh TPY	48.00	63.00	15.00
Alumina Plant	Alumina Hydrate	Lakh TPY	15.75	21.00	5.25
Smelter	Aluminium	Lakh TPY	3.45	4.60	1.15
CPP	Power	MW	960 (120 × 8)MW	1200 (120 × 10) MW	240 (120 × 2) MW

Note: TPY = Tonne per Year; CPP = Captive Power Plant.
Source: Ministry of Mines.

ANNEXURE 7.2.10
Scheme-wise Break-up of the Eleventh Plan Outlays at Current Price—Ministry of Mines

(Rs Crore)

S. No.	Organization/Company	Outlay	IR	EBR	GBS	NBS
1.	NALCO	6927.08	6927.08	0.00	–	–
2.	HCL	223.00	223.00	–	–	–
3.	MECL					
	Promotional	50.00	–	–	50.00	50.00
	Capital	44.00	44.00	–	–	–
4.	GSI (including construction)	1020.00	–	–	1020.00	1020.00
5.	IBM (including construction)	90.00	–	–	90.00	90.00
6.	S&T	49.92	26.97	2.95	20.00	20.00
	Total	8404.00	7221.05	2.95	1180.00	1180.00

Note: NBS = Net Budgetary Support.
Source: Planning Commission.

IV
Services

8

Services

8.1 CONSTRUCTION

Background

8.1.1 The development of physical infrastructure in the country and, consequently, the construction sector has been in focus during the last decade. The increasing significance of construction activities in the growth of the economy was also evident during the course of implementation of the Tenth Plan with areas such as transportation, irrigation, housing, urban development, and civil aviation having received greater importance. It is well established that the influence of the construction industry spans across several sub-sectors of the economy as well as the infrastructure development, such as industrial and mining infrastructure, highways, roads, ports, railways, airports, power systems, irrigation and agriculture systems, telecommunication systems, hospitals, schools, townships, offices, houses and other buildings; urban infrastructure, including water supply, sewerage, and drainage, and rural infrastructure. Thus, it becomes the basic input for socio-economic development.

Criticality to Economy

8.1.2 The contribution of construction to the GDP at factor cost in 2006–07 was Rs 196555 crore, registering an increase of 10.7% from the previous year. The share of construction in GDP has increased from 6.1% in 2002–03 to 6.9% in 2006–07. The increase in the share of construction sector in GDP has primarily been on the account of increased government spending on physical infrastructure in the last few years, with programmes such as National Highway Development Programme (NHDP) and PMGSY/Bharat Nirman Programme receiving a major fillip of late. The construction industry is experiencing a great upsurge in the quantum of the work load, and has grown at the rate of over 10% annually during the last five years. Although various steps have been taken to strengthen the construction industry, it is crucial to take necessary measures in order to prepare the industry to meet the challenges of growth.

8.1.3 The importance of construction activity in infrastructure, housing, and other asset-building activities can be seen from the fact that the component of construction comprises nearly 60%–80% of the project cost of certain infrastructure projects such as roads, housing, etc. In projects such as power plants, industrial plants, etc., though the share is lower but it still remains critical. In terms of magnitude, construction activity is second only to agriculture. The construction industry also has major linkages with the building material manufacturing industry including cement and steel, bricks and tiles, sand and aggregates, fixtures and fittings, paints and chemicals, construction equipment, petrol and other petro-products, timber, mineral products, aluminum, glass, and plastics. Construction materials account for nearly two-third of the average construction costs. On the basis of an analysis of the forward and backward linkages of construction, the multiplier effect for construction on the economy is estimated to be significant.

Employment in the Construction Industry

8.1.4 With around 27770 enterprises involved directly in the activity of construction in 2005, the industry is one of the largest employers in the country and is characterized by a mix of both organized and unorganized entities. The employment figures have shown a steady rise from 14.6 million in 1995 to more than double in 2005, that is 31.46 million personnel comprising engineers, technicians, foremen, clerical staff, and skilled and unskilled workers. Larger investments in infrastructure have resulted in an increased demand for construction and, consequently, for construction engineers and technicians. However, due to the limited availability of engineers and technicians in general and the greater demand in sectors such as IT, there is a substantial drop in the percentage of qualified engineers employed at the work sites from 4.71% in 1995 to 2.65% in 2005, and similarly at sub-engineering levels from 2.46% in 1995 to 1.85% in 2005. The strength of skilled workforce has also been consistently and substantially going down from 15.34% in 1995 to 10.57% in 2005, whereas relative proportions of unskilled workers have gone up from 73.08% in 1995 to 82.45% in 2005. The workers community accounted for 93% of the total employment in the construction sector in 2005, with a predominance of migrant labour workforce. It is important to create a reliable information system for labour migration both at the destination as well as at the point of origin of migration to reduce vulnerability. As macro level data is often inadequate to capture the flow and pattern of migration, state-centric surveys are required to fill in this gap. With several ambitious projects on anvil during the Eleventh Plan, the demand for construction manpower is going to grow at a consistent pace of at least 8%–9%, thereby resulting in an annual accretion of around 25 lakh persons to the existing stock.

Developments during the Tenth Plan

8.1.5 During 2002–07, many milestones were achieved by the Indian construction industry in the areas of institutional finance, human resource development, dispute resolution, procurement procedures, safety and quality in the construction industry, and disaster mitigation initiatives. The construction industry was accorded Industrial Concern Status under the Industrial Development Bank of India (Amendment) Act, thereby providing the much-needed impetus in terms of availability of finance to the construction industry. Many national initiatives in human resource management were implemented for the non-formal construction sector, addressing workers as well as engineers and management professionals in the industry. Other major initiatives included, inter alia, the establishment of arbitral institutions for dispute resolution, development of institutions for safety and quality aspects, setting up of disaster mitigation and Retrofitting Clinics along with the training of professionals in disaster mitigation, improvement in procurement practices in public sector, development of regulatory manuals for procurement procedures, as well as dissemination of information regarding good practices and development of action framework for quality and safety audits, certification, and training of manpower.

Strategies for the Eleventh Plan

8.1.6 The major challenge that the construction industry faces during the Eleventh Plan is to raise its delivery capabilities commensurate with the Plan targets for sectors such as transportation, housing, and urban development. The planned development of infrastructure would face constraints, unless the construction industry improves the delivery potentials by addressing crucial issues and impediments by bringing in systemic changes. The major issues in the construction industry have been detailed in the following sections.

Productivity in the Construction Industry

8.1.7 Since capacity building for the construction industry to achieve expected delivery capabilities is the key focus area, introduction of efficient technologies and modern management techniques to raise the productivity of the industry are vital. R&D in the construction industry should be seen as a continuing activity, because the scientific and technological advancements are needed to strengthen and raise the technological base of the construction industry. Recognizing this, support to the national institutions engaged in scientific research and incentives for private sector players to undertake in-house R&D need to be provided.

8.1.8 The low technological level of Indian construction leads to low value addition, productivity, quality, and high time and cost overruns. A national strategy and policy framework, focusing particularly on productivity enhancement and cost reduction, is required to be developed to match the envisaged work load and delivery targets. Introduction of new technologies, construction systems, and energy-efficient materials (preferably based on waste recycling) needs to be adequately emphasized in the national strategy. For RR sector, there is a need for developing and introducing use of 'marginal materials' to enhance the cost effectiveness of works. Adequate funds should be earmarked in the field of R&D for identification of appropriate and alternate materials to reduce the cost of construction.

8.1.9 Management of information in contemporary construction projects is one of the biggest challenges that project teams face in the upgradation of productivity levels. Information technology can be leveraged to address issues related to tendering, bidding, bid evaluation, grading of construction entities, project execution logistics, project management, as well as financial accounting and reporting for the construction industry. An appropriate MIS should be developed and implemented at the national, district, and local levels. Further, an institution needs to be nominated as the repository of National Database for construction industry.

Human Resource and Entrepreneurial Development Framework

8.1.10 The major impediments faced by the construction industry in raising the levels of productivity are the acute shortage of skilled manpower, both at worker and supervisory levels, as well as the lack of experienced construction engineers. The construction industry, particularly the highway and road construction sectors, is facing acute shortages of contracting agencies. The present situation is marked by lack of a harmonized skill upgradation and certification programme for construction workers and lack of incentives and regulatory framework to prescribe a certain percentage of trained and certified manpower by the contractors. There is also a need to encourage adequate intake of civil engineers in engineering institutions to mitigate the existing shortage.

8.1.11 One of the initiatives undertaken by Construction Industry Development Council (CIDC) is the training, testing, and certification programme of the construction workers. This initiative has resulted in successfully upgrading the skills of construction workers in 47 designated trades through training, testing, and certification of the construction workers (see Box 8.1.1).

8.1.12 A National Plan for training and certification of construction personnel at all levels needs to be developed and implemented. The Plan should include

Box 8.1.1

Holistic Human Resource Development (HRD)—Construction Industry Development Council (CIDC)

- CIDC, in association with several universities and industry constituents, has offered an HRD Programme for the workers from construction industry for last three years. The programme, based on an open learning and distant mode of education, offers 38 trades through 19 centres situated in various parts of the country. A number of PSUs, SPVs, and State Governments have also been actively participating.
- CIDC conducts programmes in 29 ITIs across four States—Madhya Pradesh, Rajasthan, Haryana, and Bihar. As of date, more than 100000 workers have been tested and certified under this programme and have found gainful employment with construction companies.
- Initiative has been taken by NHAI and the State Government of Madhya Pradesh for the inclusion of a prequalification condition in NHAI's tender document that a minimum of 5% of trained and certified workers should be employed, to become eligible for any of the bid from NHAI. Such practices need to be replicated by other States.
- CIDC is also actively designing, developing, and disseminating Management Development Programmes for supervisors, managers, and senior officers in Construction Management, Project Management, Emerging Technologies, and other related issues. CIDC's Diploma Programme in Civil, Mechanical, and Electrical Engineering for Army personnel is field tested and finds increased favour with the armed forces.

initiating a system of 'Graded Certification' depending upon the levels of proficiency achieved. In order to meet the shortage of trained manpower, short-term courses in certain important trades may be introduced. The role of advisory and consultancy services in strengthening the stature of construction industry is vital. However, presently these services are only a small part of the overall construction services and need to be suitably upgraded.

Need to Reduce Construction Cost

8.1.13 It is estimated that the total cost of procuring, monitoring, and supervising and other indirect costs of construction projects consists of about 22% of the cost of the asset that is created. The reduction of these and other transaction-related costs would be decisive in improving the profitability of the Indian construction industry. Apart from the measures to improve productivity, as discussed in the earlier sections, efforts are also required to streamline procedures and mechanisms within the industry as well as enhance the levels of quality for the sector as a whole.

Contract Procedures

8.1.14 The present contract conditions, procedures of procurement of projects, and services being used by various project authorities in the country, both in the public and private sector, need to be reviewed and harmonized. According to some estimates, the cost of procuring comprises 16% of the total construction cost for certain projects. Development of standard contract procedure, documents, and the evaluation criteria would lead to significant reduction in the transaction cost and time. In order to enable fair competition as well as maintain the quality of the output, the system of pre-qualification should be adopted for large PPP projects, whereby only those companies that meet the stringent qualification criteria would be shortlisted and invited to make a bid. For smaller projects, especially those involving repair and maintenance, pre-qualification should be done periodically and bidding should be made on the basis of limited circulation. The guidelines issued by the Ministry of Statistics and Programme Implementation in the form of a set of Uniform Contract Conditions may be taken as a basis for further consultation with experts and stakeholders with a view to formulating standard contract and bidding documents. A shift from the current practices towards electronic tendering process, online publishing of tender notices, online contract bidding documents, and reverse bidding would eliminate unfair competition and make the bidding process transparent.

Dispute Resolution

8.1.15 In the absence of institutionalized procedures and practices, arbitration continues to be costly and time consuming. As per a survey conducted in 2001 by the CIDC, the amount of capital blocked in the construction sector disputes was over Rs 54000 crore. To minimize disputes leading to time and cost overruns, proper project planning process should be encouraged and DPRs may be completed before technical sanction. After the Arbitration and Conciliation Act 1996 came into force, there has been an improvement in the number of disputes resolved. However, certain shortcomings remain to be addressed in the ad hoc arbitration process in terms of defined selection procedures and working ethics of arbitrators, absence of specific rules for agreement, and provision of a neutral body to administer and supervise arbitration. In view of these deficiencies, there is a need to introduce new measures to resolve disputes in a fair, speedy, transparent, and cost-effective manner.

8.1.16 A procedure involving the amicable resolution by conciliation should be followed, failing which reference to arbitration by a Board of Arbitrators in accordance with the Rules of Arbitration of the International Center for Alternate Dispute Resolution, New Delhi should be made. Moreover, institutional arbitration rules, a panel of accredited arbitrators based on selection criteria to maintain the quality, standards, and code of ethics/conduct, norms for negotiable terms of appointment, management of arbitrator's fees, monitoring and supervision of progress of case, etc., should be developed and institutionalized in line with Indian Arbitration and Conciliation Act 1996, after consultation with experts and stakeholders.

Quality and Standards

8.1.17 To make the Indian construction industry more competitive, aspects related to enhanced quality in construction products should be accorded attention at all levels. The inadequate quality in construction works emanates from lack of incentives for inducting new technology, lack of pre-qualification requirements for trained and certified workmen, lack of appreciation for lifecycle costing approach, and lack of adequate R&D. In order to enhance the technological capabilities of the industry, all stakeholders would be required to actively support training and certification levels for skilled workers, supervisors, and managers, and promote construction techniques (such as ready-mixed concrete, pre-fab techniques) that use information technology.

8.1.18 The Performance Appraisal Certificate Scheme is being implemented for the development and promotion of materials, products, and systems under the joint initiatives of Building Materials and Technology Promotion Council (BMPTC), CIDC, BIS, and other agencies. Further, in view of the widespread infrastructural development programmes, covering both urban and rural areas, particularly for roads, highways, and rural connectivity schemes, district-level testing laboratories should be established for testing and quality evaluation of materials.

8.1.19 The importance and benefit of adhering to performance standards, both in inviting tenders and in implementation, are being increasingly realized by construction entities and procurement agencies. BIS is formulating a performance standard for special jobs requiring high-quality levels. Another development, aimed at enhancing quality in construction works, is that a large number of construction companies are working to obtain ISO 9000 series certification.

Construction Finance

8.1.20 The Indian construction industry is faced with high operation, maintenance, and financial costs. This aspect is further exacerbated by inadequate access to institutional finance, especially for small contractors who execute over 90% of the total construction works. Moreover, subsequent to the conferring of Industrial Concern Status on the construction industry, existing financial institutions, and banks should adopt construction industry-specific lending norms and eligibility criteria for the borrowers from the construction sector as well as introduce special incentives or schemes for financing import of hi-tech construction equipment for infrastructure projects.

Other Important Issues

Safety and Related Issues of Construction Workers

8.1.21 Workers employed in construction activity are highly vulnerable segments of the labour force particularly because of its unorganized nature. The workers in construction industry are vulnerable to the inherent risk to their life and limbs. Construction activities are also characterized by poor training, temporary relationships between the employer and the employee, uncertain working hours, lack of basic amenities, inadequacy of welfare facilities, and casual approach of employers towards the problems of employees. In the absence of adequate statutory provisions, the requisite information regarding the nature and number of accidents is also not generally available.

8.1.22 In the recent past, several initiatives have been taken for the improvement of working conditions of the construction workers through the mandatory provision for instituting the Provident Fund Scheme among casual workers and the introduction of the Workers Welfare Cess. The Building and other Construction Workers (Regulation of Employment and Conditions of Service) Act 1996 was also enacted recognizing the need for a comprehensive Central legislation for regulating the safety, health, welfare, and other conditions of service for construction workers. However, only a few States have implemented the provisions of the Act, such as setting up welfare boards, and efforts need to be renewed to speed up the implementation of the Act.

8.1.23 Along with the provision of appropriate training facilities for safety aspects related to construction, vigilant Safety Management Teams adequately trained in compliance procedures, hazard and risk assessment, and documentation of inspections of stipulated measures for safety of workers are required to be put in place. As a substantial segment of the construction industry workforce, women workers need to be accorded special focus in terms of vocational training and skill upgradation as well as the provision of stipulated social benefits.

Asset Management and Maintenance

8.1.24 Although the construction of physical infrastructure has been receiving emphasis in the successive Five Year Plans, the maintenance of the assets that are created has not been accorded similar importance due to the absence of necessary framework, planning, and professionals for asset maintenance. The present system of asset management needs to be reviewed and strengthened at the local, State, and Central Government levels. A policy framework for ensuring mandatory provision for maintenance of assets needs to be evolved.

Environmental Issues

8.1.25 Sustainable development concepts applied to the design, construction, and operation of construction projects can enhance both the economic well-being and the environmental health of communities. Environmental Impact Assessment (EIA) is recognized as an important tool for integrating these objectives, wherein EIA should be a necessary pre-condition before construction projects beyond stipulated size are approved. Further, initiatives for ensuring adherence to international standards and regulations, such as the Environment Protection Act 2006 and the Energy Conservation Act of 2001 are also required. Various interdisciplinary organizations such as CIDC and Building Materials and Technology Promotion Council (BMTPC) have been set up to address the issues of environment-friendly technologies and energy efficiency in building materials, along with Central and State Pollution Control Boards to approve, monitor, and regulate projects from all sectors including construction, keeping in view their impact on environment.

Construction Law

8.1.26 As per the prevailing scenario, any organization engaged in construction activity requires registration under five different legislations, apart from obtaining licenses under three enactments and being subject to inspection under 12 laws. Further, there are 27 statutes pertaining only to labour. The multiplicity of laws and authorities, anomalies in the existing legal systems, and the complexities thereof suggest the need for a Unified Construction Law along with the formulation of a single window arrangement. The Unified Construction Law should have chapters pertaining to national construction policy and plan; constitution and functions of Central and State construction authorities; dispute resolution and arbitration; grants, funds, accounts, audit, and report; registration and other provisions.

Taxation

8.1.27 The construction sector experiences a very high incidence of direct and indirect taxes for construction and construction-related activities as compared to other sectors. The taxation and regulatory systems pertaining to construction should be reviewed with a view to rationalize the same and eliminate multi-source taxation. Greater clarity needs to be brought out on the treatment of the sector as 'Industry' or 'Service' for taxation purposes.

Combating Natural Disasters

8.1.28 There is an increasing realization that the problem of natural disasters is grave because their frequency has recorded more than a five-fold increase in the last two decades. Institutional arrangements are required to identify, prevent, and mitigate the effects of natural disasters. New programmes need to be taken as per the guidelines and programmes announced by the NDMA. The development of human resources and training of professionals in disaster mitigation, disaster-resistant construction technologies, and setting up of Retrofitting Clinics and Disaster Identification Centres in all major districts falling in disaster-prone regions is also recommended.

8.1.29 Substantial national resources are being spent on building assets and the pace of investment is going to enhance considerably during the Eleventh Plan, with several new projects related to transportation including RRs, housing, industrial infrastructure, energy, and agriculture slated for time-bound implementation. Necessary modifications, amplifications, and introduction of good practices need to be adopted to achieve the desired growth in the construction sector and to align it with global trends in terms of growth, quality, and competitiveness.

PATH AHEAD

- Enhance capacity building in the construction sector by improving productivity through introduction of efficient technologies and modern management techniques.
- Reduce transactional costs by reviewing contract procedures and dispute resolution mechanisms.
- Enhance quality standards and provision of adequate institutional finance to the construction sector.
- Develop a National Plan for human resource development through training and certification of construction personnel.
- Accord greater importance to safety in construction activities by establishing trained and certified Safety Management Teams.
- Earmark funds in the field of R&D for identification of appropriate and alternate materials to reduce the cost of construction.

8.2 TOURISM

OVERVIEW

8.2.1 Tourism is a multi-sectoral activity characterized by multiple services provided by a range of suppliers. It is the largest service industry in the country. Its importance lies in being an instrument for economic development and employment generation, particularly in remote and backward areas. It is contributing towards overall socio-economic improvement and accelerated growth in the economy. The economic benefits flow into the economy through growth of tourism in the shape of increased national and State revenues, business income, employment, wages, and salary income. Tourism is overwhelmingly an industry of private sector providers and the public sector has a significant role to play in infrastructure areas either directly or through Public Private Partnership mode.

8.2.2 Tourism is one economic sector in India that has the potential to grow at a high rate and can ensure consequential development of the infrastructure of the destinations. It has the potential to stimulate other economic sectors through its backward and forward linkages and cross-sectoral synergies with sectors like agriculture, horticulture, handicrafts, transport, construction, etc. The particular significance of tourism industry in India is its contribution to national integration and preservation of natural as well as cultural environments and enrichment of the social and cultural lives of people like preservation of monuments and heritage properties.This sector is also helping the traditional art forms, crafts, and culture.

GLOBAL STATUS AND TRENDS

8.2.3 Over the past few years, the Travel and Tourism (T&T) industry has had to contend with a series of unprecedented challenges. International events, such as terrorism and SARS, and economic turbulence have led to significant changes in T&T demand. At the same time, international events such as an increase in information and booking facilities made available over the Internet; an ongoing desire by consumers to travel more frequently; stronger branding and globalization by companies; and the expansion of low-cost carriers have acted as a catalyst, accelerating fundamental changes in market behaviour and travel patterns that have been slowly emerging over the past decade. While business plans have become increasingly short term, more and more governments are starting to realize that they cannot leave the growth of T&T to chance. This emerging global consciousness represents a great opportunity for this industry.

8.2.4 As per the estimates of World Travel and Tourism Council (Table 8.2.1), the worldwide travel and

TABLE 8.2.1
Contribution of Travel and Tourism (T&T) in GDP and Employment in 2007

	India (%) 2007	World average % during 2007	World average % Estimated in 2017
Contribution of T&T Economy to GDP	5.4	10.4	10.7
Contribution of T&T Industry to GDP	2.0	3.6	3.4
Contribution of T&T Economy employment	5.5	8.3	8.3
Contribution of T&T Industry Employment	2.3	2.7	2.8

Source: WTTC (World Travel and Tourism Council).

tourism is expected to grow by 4.3% per annum between 2008–17. The industry is expected to post US$ 7060.3 billion of economic activity (total demand) in 2007, which will increase to US$ 13231.6 billion by 2017. The industry is expected to contribute 3.6% to GDP in 2007 (US$ 1851.1 billion), which is expected to rise to US$ 3121.7 billion in absolute terms but percentage wise it will decrease to 3.4% by 2017. The earnings from T&T have made it one of the largest industries in the world and the fastest growing sector of global trade accounting for 10.4% of global GDP, 12.2% of global exports, 8.3% of global employment, and 9.5% of global capital investment.

INDIA'S TOURIST PROFILE

8.2.5 Tourist growth in India has undergone a remarkable change during the Tenth Plan. Table 8.2.2 shows that foreign tourist arrival has increased by about 87% from a level of 2.38 million in 2002 to 4.45 million in 2006. Share of India in world tourist arrivals has increased from 0.34% to 0.52% during this period.

TABLE 8.2.2
Tourists Arrivals in India

(in Million)

Year	World Tourist Arrivals	Foreign Tourist Arrivals (In India)	Domestic Tourist Visits	Share of India in World Arrivals (%)
2002	706.4	2.38	269.6	0.34
2003	693.2	2.73	309.0	0.39
2004	761.0	3.46	366.2	0.46
2005	802.0	3.92	390.5	0.49
2006	842.0	4.45	461.2	0.52

Source: Ministry of Tourism (MoT).

8.2.6 Similarly, it is evident from the Table 8.2.3 that the foreign exchange earnings have grown by about 147% during the same period (US$ 2923 million to US$ 6569 million), 0.9% of the international tourist receipts. The average per tourist earnings in India was about US$ 1476 against the world average of US$ 872 during 2006.

8.2.7 Domestic tourist visits has also grown rapidly during the Tenth Five Year Plan from 269.6 million in 2002 to 461.2 million in 2006. According to the Tourism Satellite Account for India prepared by the MoT, the contribution of tourism sector, including both direct and indirect to GDP and employment was 5.83% and 8.27% respectively during 2002–03.

TABLE 8.2.3
Tourism Receipts

(in Billion US$)

Year	World Earnings	Earnings by India	Share of India in World Earnings
2002	487.0	2.9	0.60
2003	533.1	3.5	0.66
2004	633.0	4.8	0.75
2005	678.0	5.7	0.85
2006	735.0	6.6	0.89

Source: MoT.

8.2.8 It is universally acknowledged that the tourism resources in the country have the potential to generate significantly higher levels of demand from the domestic and international markets, which if exploited intelligently in a sustainable manner, can prove to be the proverbial engine of growth for the economy.

REVIEW OF THE TENTH FIVE YEAR PLAN

8.2.9 Against an outlay of Rs 2900 crore in the Tenth Five Year Plan (Central sector) an expenditure of Rs 2635.67 crore (91%) has been incurred. The scheme-wise financial performance during the Tenth Five Year Plan is given at Annexure 8.2.1. In the Tenth Five Year Plan period an emphasis was laid on positioning and maintaining tourism development as a national priority activity by enhancing and maintaining the competitiveness of India as a tourist destination and improving existing tourism products and expanding these to meet new market requirements by creating world class infrastructure, developing sustained and effective market plans and programmes and giving special thrust to rural and small segment tourism. Through broad fields of development, the MoT focused on infrastructure development in five key destinations like Ajanta-Ellora, Bodhgaya, Rajgiri-Nalanda, Kurukshetra, and Mahabalipuram. Information and technology was also given a major thrust to promote Indian tourism products in the country and abroad. Human resource development and capacity building for service providers were given more importance. As a result more than 40000 persons were given training through 24 Institutes of Hotel Management (IHM) and 12 Food Craft Institutions. In addition to these, large revenue generating products like convention centers at Suraj Kund, Haryana, luxury trains in Karnataka, Night Safari Park at Jorepokhari in Darjeeling, West Bengal were developed through PPP mode.

Objective and Strategy for the Eleventh Five Year Plan

8.2.10 Though the Working Group on Tourism for Eleventh Five Year Plan has recommended a target of 10 million international tourist arrivals by 2011, the Vision Document presently being drafted by MoT envisages achievement of this target by 2010. As per this strategy, target for the year 2011 will be 10.25 million. This target is proposed to be achieved through diversification of principal source markets, improving the infrastructural facilities such as airports, roads, civic amenities at the tourist destinations, increasing the air seat capacity and connectivity, vigorous publicity, etc. For domestic tourism, the target to be achieved in 2010 and 2011 will be 725 million and 812 million respectively assuming an annual growth rate of about 12% over the level of 461 million domestic tourist visits in 2006.

8.2.11 In order to achieve international visitor levels of 10 million by the end of the Eleventh Five Year Plan, the emphasis would be on diversification of principal source markets to include countries such as South Africa, Israel, Spain, China, Japan, South Korea, Australia, Brazil, Argentina, etc., which offer high growth potential and from where present level of inbound tourist is low. There is also a need to concentrate on countries like South Africa, Mauritius, Kenya, Malaysia, Fiji, etc., with a large Indian diaspora for higher tourist arrivals from those countries. Similarly, greater resonance needs to be created in NRIs and persons of Indian origin to visit the country of their origin and discover their roots. The 'Baby-Boomers' group in North America and Europe would be encouraged to visit India by creating in them the desire to discover one of the oldest civilizations of the world to enjoy the plurality of cultural enjoyment, offered by this country.

8.2.12 In order to meet the requirement of growth in traffic, there would be further creation of quality accommodation. It is estimated that 200000 approved quality accommodation rooms would be required in 2011 against the current level of about 100000 rooms. Domestic travel must complement international travel. This would help in optimizing the utilization of infrastructural facilities and also make the future investment viable. The possibility of constructing hotels on surplus land with Airport Authority of India near international airports needs to be considered. The surplus railway land at specified railway stations may also be utilized for constructing budget hotels. New forms of tourism like rural tourism, cultural tourism, adventure tourism, cruise tourism, MICE tourism, and medical tourism need to be taken up with renewed zeal and efforts.

8.2.13 To achieve the above goals, suitable measures would be taken for:

- Positioning and maintaining tourism development as a national priority activity.
- Enhancing and maintaining the competitiveness of India as a tourist destination.
- Improving India's existing tourism products further and expanding these to meet new market requirements.
- Creation of world-class infrastructure.
- Developing strategies for sustained and effective marketing plans and programmes.
- Developing human resources and capacity building of service providers.

Positioning and Maintaining Tourism as a National Priority

8.2.14 Effective linkages and close coordination among various departments and ministries of government will be established to plan and implement a professionally managed and integrated communications strategy to increase awareness about tourism and its social and economic impact on the society. State governments would be encouraged to set up land banks and streamline procedure and practices to facilitate investment in the tourism sector.

Enhancing and Maintaining the Competitiveness of India as a Tourist Destination

8.2.15 Effective steps for easier and faster availability of visas, increasing air connectivity and seat capacity from overseas markets, improving facilities and quality of services at international and major domestic airports, rationalization of taxes, and removing restrictions like Restricted Area Permit/Protected Area Permit/Inner Line Permit would facilitate tourist flow to the country.

8.2.16 Connectivity has been one of the impediments for the growth of tourism in India. Steps taken during the Tenth Five Year Plan to liberalize civil aviation sector to a large extent eased the position with regard to the availability of seats. While international airlines inducted more capacity, there is a growth in the number of carriers providing domestic air services. The increase in capacity has not only resulted in meeting the demand of the air travel but also in lowering the airfares. The infrastructure facilities at the airports would be developed to meet the rising air traffic requirements. For the promotion of tourism in the country, trained personnel and workforce need to be provided at airports for increasing the quality of service at the airports. The possibility of extending facilities of visa on arrival would be considered for tourist originating from selected countries.

8.2.17 Quality of rail services would be improved to encourage tourists to travel by train. Budget hotels may be provided by railways in all metro cities within the realm of PPP. Well maintained clean waiting rooms, basic amenities like drinking water, toilets, tea/coffee facilities, parking facilities for tourist vehicles may be available at railway stations.

8.2.18 All major tourist destinations/heritage sites should be well connected with the highways. Tourist coaches have to queue up at the border for paying toll tax and transport tax at every barrier, which is a harassment for the tourists. The respective State Governments may introduce a single toll collection point for free movement of tourist transport. Tourist transport vehicles may also be given separate identification under Motor Vehicles Act to allow free movement between States. Oil companies on the highways may be encouraged to provide basic amenities at petrol pumps.

Improving India's Existing Tourism Products Further and Expanding these to Meet New Market Requirements

8.2.19 India has a rich resource of both tangible cultural heritage in its monuments and sites and also an intangible cultural heritage in the form of its architecture, music, dance/drama, local rituals and traditions, and other folk arts. Cultural and heritage tourism will be expanded to tap rich resources of cultural heritage in its monuments and sites. An integrated circuit linking heritage monuments, with culturally rich villages and towns around them are to be formed to enable and strengthen the development of cultural tourism in India. The National Highways Authority may consider facilitating provision of suitable tourism facilities on their routes such as budget tourist accommodation and improvements in wayside amenities on roadsides and highways. Beach and coastal tourism on the beaches of Goa, Kerala, and North Karnataka may be considered for development due to easier accessibility of these places by air. Kerala and the Andaman and Nicobar Islands have already been developed as international cruise destinations. Riverine tourism may be developed along traditional routes, which may have an exotic appeal and also help sustain villages and settlement along the routes. In this way, village tourism would also be promoted. Indian cuisine has caught the fancy of people across the globe. This can be capitalized by developing culinary tour routes into different regions for enthusiasts to taste and learn the authentic way. This will create a highly skilled workforce of culinary professionals not only for India but also to promote Indian cuisine internationally. Wild Life Sanctuaries and National Parks would also be made an integral part of the Indian tourism product. For sustainable tourism, the facilities at the parks may be enhanced and proper site and visitor management plans need to be prepared so as not to disturb the ecological balance and the local habitat.

8.2.20 India offers the best mountain-based adventure tourism in the world in the Himalayas. Already a lot of work has been initiated in this segment but they have to be made comparable to or better than what is being offered in the Alpine countries. India's medical expertise has been gaining popularity in the West where the costs are prohibitive. The development of special interest tourism segment will accrue greater socio-economic benefits.

8.2.21 Indian textiles, handlooms, and handicrafts, its furniture and jewellery are already popular abroad. Now with Indian designers also receiving global recognition, shopping has become an integral part of a tourist's itinerary. Hence the development of dedicated shopping centers and the flow of special interest shopping tourists may be encouraged as it will help revive traditional crafts and craftsmen, textiles and weavers, and give these families a means of livelihood.

8.2.22 Domestic tourism in India is mainly pilgrimage related. Travel facilities as well as facilities at pilgrimage centers need to be strengthened and made more tourist-friendly. Pilgrimage centers may be identified and integrated with new domestic tourist circuits wherein transport, accommodation, catering, and darshan are all synergized to make pilgrimage tourism into a popular and comfortable mode.

Creation of World-class Infrastructure

8.2.23 Quality infrastructure may be created for developing tourist products and for providing better services to both domestic and international tourists. Creation of tourism infrastructure has favorable impact on overall economic growth and employment and on the preservation of art, culture, and heritage. Tourism projects like Destination Development are capital intensive, commercially unviable, and require financial support from the government. At the same time, it is necessary that such infrastructure is created with professional expertise of architects and landscaping experts and is then privately managed through a transparent process. Large revenue projects such as setting up of hotels, convention centers, golf courses, tourist trains, etc., normally have substantial gestation periods. These facilities may be created by private initiative with the government acting as a facilitator and catalyst.

8.2.24 Tourist sites and destinations need to be carefully selected on the basis of their potential to provide all infrastructure facilities required by the tourists within such destinations and circuits. Master planning of destinations and circuits will be done by outstanding architects/consulting agencies with sensitivity towards conservation, preservation, and aesthetic aspects to enable their development in an integrated holistic manner.

8.2.25 During the Eleventh Five Year Plan, the strategy for infrastructure development should be to select only 10 major Destinations and 6 Circuits on an annual basis. Destination Management needs attention and coordination at the 27 World Heritage Sites in the country, which are impacted by increasing number of visitors and are also subject to a number of regulatory authorities. For the development of rural tourism, a panel of professionals may be identified for selecting the rural sites, interacting with the community, and preparing projects based on tourism potential of the site.

8.2.26 One of the major bottlenecks in creation of hotel infrastructure is non-availability of land for the purpose. The steps that may be taken are: (i) Master Plan of major cities should mark commercial sites for construction of hotels, convention and exhibition centers; (ii) the hotel sites should be allotted on long-term lease basis or could be allotted under the PPP mode through joint venture, revenue sharing, etc.; (iii) our endeavor should be that the hotels are allowed higher Floor Area Ratio/Floor Space Index (FAR/FSI) so that more rooms and commercial spaces are created out of the same space and it also helps in generating sustainable revenues; (iv) the land should also be allotted for building of guest houses in all major cities and tourist destinations, if possible; (v) home stay programme under the Government of India Scheme of 'Incredible India Bed & Breakfast' needs to be promoted by all State Governments by allowing such establishments to be treated as non-commercial.

8.2.27 Rural villages, which have immense cultural heritage potential, need to be developed to showcase India's vast heritage. Infrastructure and other tourist facilities should be developed and local community involved in the management so as to percolate tourism and its socio-economic benefits to rural areas. The focus would be on both tangible heritage and intangible heritage. The tangible heritage represents the 'hard' culture of a community, whereas intangible heritage represents the 'soft' culture—the people, traditions, folklore, music, dance, traditional games, mythology, rituals, customs, handicrafts, arts, festivals, events, storytellers, local markets, and also living human treasures.

Developing Strategies for Sustained and Effective Marketing Plans and Programmes

8.2.28 This objective can be achieved by evolving and maintaining a system of market research activities in India's major source markets to continuously receive, analyse, and respond to information on pricing, security issues, health, safety, quality of tourism services and products, etc., and making use of various technological tools, including the Internet, for advertising for greater and wider impact. Besides, it is necessary to encourage e-commerce portals to extend effective marketing support to SMEs and also offer competitive packages.

Developing Human Resources and Capacity Building of Service Providers

8.2.29 Tourism sector in the country is witnessing a boom that may bring an exponential demand for the workforce at managerial, supervisory, skilled and semi-skill levels. This increase in growth will have a direct impact on the demand and supply mismatch that the country is already passing through and trying to correct for providing of satisfactory service to visiting tourists. To bridge the widening gap at skill-level, the existing Food Craft Institutes (FCIs) are required to be strengthened and new ones opened. To enlarge the scope, hospitality education needs to be imparted through the network of ITIs, Polytechnics and at the +2 stage as a vocational stream of the school system. IHMs, which are processing the bulk of manpower at managerial and skill level, need to be strengthened and capacities augmented, with international linkages for quality and quantity output of human resources. New IHMs in the States/regions that have not been covered as yet should be established for proper distribution of government resources. Through integrated efforts with States, IHMs under PPP should be encouraged. For the young untrained staff who continue to join the industry, the government should through short-term training programmes build capacities in order to provide quality service. A scheme is required to be mooted to examine and certify the large number of industry/conventional trained skilled manpower available in the country. The existing scheme of 'Train the Trainer' should be strengthened and implemented countrywide for boosting availability of adequate trainers for training.

8.2.30 Capacity building of the service providers through shorter training courses should be taken up as an integral effort to strengthen/enlarge the manpower required by the hospitality industry. More FCIs need to be opened to meet the demand for skilled personnel in food crafts. The training programmes must cover the skill development in general for fresh candidates, specialized skill development including language courses, for fresh as well as existing service providers, basic skill upgradation in general for existing service providers, training of trainers programme, and creating awareness of tourism benefits/knowledge in rural areas.

PROMOTION AND PUBLICITY

8.2.31 The MoT is carrying out its promotion and publicity in both overseas and domestic market vigorously. The strategy to be adopted for the Eleventh Plan on publicity and marketing is to promote Indian tourism in the European markets like Italy, Spain, France, and Germany in the regional languages and in the Korean and Japanese markets in a focused manner. India should be promoted as a summer retreat in the months of July, August, and September when many European and North American schools and colleges have their holiday breaks. The campaign should convey India as a 'Year Round' Destination. 2009 should be declared as 'Visit India Year' as this will be very close to the Commonwealth Games in 2010, and would enable a boost to inbound tourism. While producing publicity material like brochures, etc., the key areas should be identified and a balance needs to be established between the print collaterals and the digital formats. While producing tourist literature, the availability of infrastructure and connectivity of the areas being marketed through the collaterals also needs to be taken into account.

Taxation, Incentives, and Concessions

8.2.32 Provision of tax holiday to the T&T industry may be considered to encourage investments from non-tourism sectors into the tourism sector. The Ministry of Finance (Budget 2007–08) has accorded Tax holiday for 5 years for 2-star, 3-star, and 4-star, category of hotels in and around the adjoining districts of Delhi for the Commonwealth Games. This needs to be extended if possible, throughout the country and for all categories of hotels. Special incentives may be considered for the hilly areas, rural areas and places of pilgrimage, the NER including Sikkm, J&K, Uttaranchal, and Himachal Pradesh. Each State Government has its own criteria for Luxury Tax varying from 5% to 20%. Rationalization of Luxury Tax and other tourism related taxes and levies may be considered by all the States. The tax structure should not be based on announced tariff; rather it should be on the basis of actual payment made by the clients. There is acute shortage of hotel accommodation and in particular budget accommodation all over the country. The MoT has estimated that there is a shortage of 150000 hotel rooms all over the country. Out of this, 110000 rooms are in the budget category. The subsidy/incentives should be on the room created basis and should be also applicable in metro towns and the procedure of disbursement of subsidy should be simple. In order to create standard budget accommodation, incentives may be given to guest houses and accommodation under the Home Stay programme of the government also.

Outlay for the Eleventh Plan

8.2.33 The total projected GBS for the Eleventh Plan for the MoT is Rs 4558 crore (2006–07 price) and Rs 5156 crore (current price). The scheme-wise details are given in Appendix (Volume III).

8.3 IT AND IT-ENABLED SERVICES

Overview

8.3.1 Information Technology has marked a turning point in the history of global trade and services. With ever increasing availability of international bandwidth and powerful workflow management software, it is now possible to disaggregate any business process, execute the sub-processes in multiple locations around the world, and reassemble it, in near-real time, at another location. This is driving fundamental changes in the global IT services landscape. The vendors and customers are redefining the levels of value creation in the industry. IT also makes significant contribution in increasing productivity in various sectors of the economy. Indeed, the phenomenal growth of the Indian IT Software and Services and IT-enabled Services-Business Process Outsourcing (ITES-BPO) sector has had a perceptible multiplier effect on the Indian economy as a whole. In addition to the direct positive impact on the national income and employment generation, it has triggered a rise in direct-tax collections and propelled an increase in consumer spending, thanks to the significantly higher disposable incomes. Today, India has found its niche in the IT world and is regarded as the premier destination for the global sourcing of IT and IT-enabled Services (ITES). ITES like Medical Transcription, Call Centers, Data Processing, Back-Office Operations, GIS, Revenue Accounting, etc., are considered as niche areas of the country and the IT industry is now getting involved in providing end to end business solutions, system integration, remote management, etc.

Review of the Tenth Plan

8.3.2 The IT and ITES fall into two segments: (i) Exports and (ii) Domestic, as described below.

IT-ITES (Exports Segment)

8.3.3 India's success in the export of IT Software and Related Services over the past decade remains unparalleled. Total export revenues earned by this sector have grown from US$ 7.7 billion in 2001–02 to US$ 31.3 billion in 2006–07, thus showing a near 32% compound growth rate. India now accounts for 65% of the global market in offshore IT and 46% of the ITES market. A majority of the Fortune 500 and Global 2000 corporations are sourcing IT and ITES from India. While the US and the UK remain the dominant markets, contributing to 67% and 15% of total exports respectively, Indian firms are also keenly exploring new geographies for business development, and to strengthen their global delivery footprint.

8.3.4 Since the inception of IT industry in India, companies have been focusing on quality initiatives to align themselves with international standards. Over the years, the industry has built robust processes and procedures to offer world class IT software and technology related services. Today, India-based centers (both Indian firms as well as MNC-owned captives) constitute the largest number of quality certifications achieved by any single country. As of December 2006, over 440 Indian companies had acquired quality certifications with 90 companies certified at Software Engineering Institute–Capacity Maturity Model (SEI–CMM) Level 5—higher than any other country in the world.

8.3.5 The growth of the sector has led to tremendous payoffs in terms of wealth creation and generation of high quality employment. Market capitalization values of leading Indian IT companies now exceed those of global competitors, and the exports segment of the Indian IT-ITES sector directly employed over 920000 people in 2005–06.

8.3.6 With only 10% of the US$ 300 billion market potential accessed so far, there is significant headroom for growth. Further, with the global offshoring market continuing to grow rapidly, as the proven benefits of offshoring (also termed global sourcing or global delivery) induce more companies to adopt these practices and develop the capabilities to offer more sophisticated products and services—the size of the overall pie is also expanding.

8.3.7 Key service lines and vertical markets including newly emerging sectors for the ITES industry are listed below:

SERVICE LINES
- R&D and engineering services
- Consulting services
- System integration
- Application development and maintenance
- Traditional IT outsourcing
- Horizontal services (finance accounting and administration, customer interaction services, human resource administration, research, etc.)

VERTICALS (INCLUDING NEWLY EMERGING SECTORS)
- Agriculture
- Banking
- Insurance
- Manufacturing
- Health Care and pharmaceuticals
- Travel and hospitality
- Animation, media, and entertainment
- Biotechnology and life sciences
- Nanotechnology
- Judiciary
- Power and energy
- Very Large Scale Integration (VLSI) and CAD
- Automobile and transportation
- Smart governance

8.3.8 This represents a 'make or break' opportunity, capable of catapulting India into a high growth orbit and on a fast track to becoming a developed nation. Given that we are closely chased by other aspiring countries to grab a share of this pie, there has to be a concerted effort by the government and industry to maintain the lead position thus created and expand it further. The benefits of global leadership in these knowledge industries go far beyond the economic dimensions. As major global companies offshore more mission-critical work to India, their dependence on India increases, thus providing significant strategic advantage.

Domestic IT/ITES-BPO Segment

8.3.9 The Banking and Financial Services, Communications and Media, Manufacturing (Consumer Durables/Automobile), Aviation, Hospitality, and Retail are some of the key verticals that primarily benefit from the ITES-BPO services in the domestic market in India. While cost savings have been the primary driver of offshore outsourcing, vendors do not have comparable differences in labour costs to leverage while serving the domestic market. As a result, the primary motivation for the domestic market, in its early years of evolution are not cost savings but access to specialist skills and freeing client resources to focus on the core business. Scalability and process efficiency are expected to result in some degree of cost savings in the domestic market as well. Notwithstanding its relatively smaller contribution to the industry revenues, this segment is witnessing a noticeable increase in interest and activity on the part of customer organizations as well as service providers. However, the total size of the domestic market is expected to cross US$ 8.335 billion in financial year 2006–07, a growth of 28% over financial year 2005–06. Although this segment has been led by MNCs in the past few years, Indian firms are gradually gaining ground. Over time, this segment would provide significant space for larger SMEs, as the mid-sized firms increase their levels of IT adoption. Table 8.3.1 depicts the growth of IT-ITES professionals in India during the Tenth Five Year Plan period.

VISION AND STRATEGY FOR THE ELEVENTH PLAN

Vision

8.3.10 Our vision is to make India the most preferred destination for providing IT and IT-enabled services and creating the required eco-system to demonstrate the full potential of Indian skills and enterprise in this vital sector. The objective during the Eleventh Plan would be to make an effective and maximal utilization of ICT to improve the quality of life of the common man and promote inclusive growth, increase productivity and competitiveness and generate wealth and strength so that India emerges as a knowledge superpower in the comity of developed nations.

Strategy

8.3.11 India's performance in IT-enabled and other high end services is clearly a source of strength that we must build upon. Our strategy is to identify gaps, if any, in existing skill sets in different ITES-BPO/ Knowledge Process Outsourcing (KPO) verticals and suggest programmes for bridging them through formal and non-formal sectors so that India becomes a leading software developer in the world. Besides, the thrust areas need to be identified where the country has potential to become internationally competitive for achieving significant exports in the field of electronics hardware manufacturing.

POLICY ISSUES, PROGRAMME REFORMS, AND NEW INITIATIVES IN THE ELEVENTH PLAN

8.3.12 Some of the policy issues which need to be addressed in a focused manner in the IT and ITES sector in the country are elaborated hereunder.

Improving the Supply of Suitable Talent

8.3.13 Table 8.3.2 shows the manpower requirements for IT-ITES in India, which is self-explanatory. Our biggest challenge is, of course, in relation to human resources. While we produce a large number of graduates and technologists, the demand of the IT industry is growing and is becoming more discerning. There are problems of quantity and quality in this regard. These problems have to be tackled in different time frames: the short-term, medium-term, and long-term.

8.3.14 In the short term, we need programmes to top up the skill level of graduating students through 'finishing schools' and 'finishing programmes' which will help resolve the quality problem. As the quality of talent pool is not industry ready, implementation of finishing school concept ensures that the right talent is available for immediate deployment. To enhance the

TABLE 8.3.1
Growth of IT-ITES Professionals in India—Indian IT Sector: Knowledge Professionals Employed*

(Nos)

	1999–2000	2000–01	2001–02	2002–03	2003–04E	2004–05E	2005–06E
IT, Engineering and R&D, Software Products Exports	110000	162000	170000	205000	296000	390000	513000
ITES Exports	42000	70000	106000	180000	216000	316000	409000
Domestic Sector	132000	198114	246250	285000	318000	352000	365000
Total	284000	430114	522250	670000	830000	1058000	1287000

Note: *Does not include employee numbers in the hardware sector; E = Estimated.
Source: National Association of Software and Service Companies (NASSCOM).

TABLE 8.3.2
Manpower Requirements for IT-ITES in India

(Million)

	2002	2003	2006	2009	2012
IT export services					
Consulting, Integration, Installation	0.01	0.02	0.03	0.09	0.27
IT Development	0.07	0.08	0.08	0.08	0.11
Outsourced IT Support	0.09	0.11	0.17	0.28	0.53
Training and Education	0.00	0.00	0.00	0.02	0.06
Total	0.17	0.21	0.29	0.48	0.97
IT-enabled services					
Customer Care	0.03	0.05	0.15	0.42	1.03
Finance	0.02	0.03	0.05	0.09	0.21
Human Resource	0.00	0.00	0.02	0.15	0.69
Payment Services	0.00	0.1	0.05	0.14	0.45
Administration	0.2	0.3	0.5	0.15	0.15
Content Development	0.03	0.04	0.07	0.09	0.20
Total	0.11	0.16	0.38	1.0	2.72

Source: ITD, NASSCOM-Mckinsey Manpower Profile of India, KPMG, 2003.

pool of experienced, mid-level managers, that is willing and suitable to work in the IT-ITES sectors, a 'bridge course' could be introduced to equip professionals who may not have read for a course in IT. In the medium term, this kind of training needs to be back-ended into the formal system itself by improving the quality of our technical and general education programmes at the graduate level. This will make graduates far more employable. In the long term, we need to address the quantity problem. The education system needs to be expanded rapidly at all levels. This would also require a huge expansion in our Masters and Doctoral programmes. Easing the supply constraint requires more investment as well as a radical reform of our education system. There is also a need for starting academic programmes for developing manpower in some of the niche areas like IT in health care, transportation, manufacturing, nanotechnology, animation and entertainment, etc. Faculty development is another major issue which needs focus. For this purpose, a national programme on faculty development in niche areas would be required. During the Eleventh Plan period, the above important issues need to be tackled and the government needs to provide the necessary resources and policy framework for achieving the desired objectives. In this national endeavour, industry and government need to work together in close unison. Some of the other measures that need to be introduced in order to maintain and improve the quality of manpower are:

- Introduction of standardized national level tests similar to Scholastic Aptitude Test (SAT), Graduate Record Examination (GRE), Management Aptitude Test (MAT) etc., for benchmarking of students seeking admissions in undergraduate and postgraduate institutes in India.
- Rating and accreditation of all educational institutions by an independent agency.
- Introduction of a common nation-wide benchmark for assessing graduating students and inclusion of industry needs in this assessment process.
- Making the teaching/academic profession more attractive and respectable.
- Encouraging students and working professionals to pursue further education for skill enhancement.
- Periodic review and updation of curriculum to make it more industry oriented and encouraging faculty to constantly upgrade skills.

Building Adequate Basic, Business, and Social Infrastructure

8.3.15 The growth of IT and ITES industry requires building and strengthening of basic, business, and social infrastructure. The incremental infrastructure required to support the projected growth is unlikely to be absorbed into the existing city centres (Tier I/II), which are already witnessing signs of strain. With Tier III/IV cities lacking important elements of business and social infrastructure, decentralized growth of the IT and ITES sector will require a coordinated, large scale (distributed) urban planning exercise. Some of the important initiatives required to be taken include:

- Strengthening of the intra-city road network and public transport infrastructure to decongest existing hubs.
- Decentralization of the industry beyond existing hubs by developing new townships.
- Introduction of faster public transport (high speed trains similar to Train à Grande Vitesse of France and Bullet of Japan) between important cities.

Ensuring a Favourable Business Policy and Regulatory Environment with Special Focus on Encouraging Small and Medium Enterprieses (SMEs) and New Ventures

8.3.16 A favourable business policy and a regulatory environment are critical for the success of any sector. The example set by the Software Technology Parks of India (STPI) scheme stands testament to this fact. In order to strengthen India's proposition for sustained leadership in the IT and ITES space, it is essential to actively support the SME sector. In addition, the issue of intellectual property protection, data and information security is a key risk to the sector. Hence, it is essential for India to proactively formulate a robust policy framework to address this challenge. This calls for: (i) Continuation of the benefits provided by the STPI scheme, (ii) strengthening the IP protection, data privacy, and information security environment in the country, (iii) providing support for SME segment growth to ensure that SMEs can continue to leverage the benefits offered under the STP/SEZ scheme without constraints on where they may be located, and (iv) ensuring adequate access to venture capital and angel funding for start-ups.

Global Trade Development and Promotion of Global Free Trade in Services

8.3.17 Expansion of the global IT-BPO market opportunity is directly influenced by the policy and regulatory frameworks governing cross-border trade in services. Growth of cross-border trade in services is constrained not only by tariff barriers—but more so by non-tariff barriers (e.g., national treatment in cross-border supply and movement of people). India must continue to work proactively with its trading partners (through the WTO and other trade promotion agencies) to streamline trade in professional services. India must push for the free movement of professionals engaged in delivering services on the basis of formal contracts, through a global General Agreement on Trade in Services or professional services visa. At the same time, it must engage in bilateral or multilateral negotiations on these issues with countries of specific interest to us. Negotiations are also needed to conclude agreements relating to exemption or refund of social security taxes paid by Indian professionals working abroad.

Fostering a Sustainable Ecosystem for Innovation and Research and Development (R&D)

8.3.18 In order to structurally strengthen India's proposition and ensure its long-term leadership, it is essential to nurture a sustainable ecosystem for innovation and R&D in the country. This will require a multifaceted approach comprising (i) developing core capabilities at the academic level in identified focus areas, (ii) encouraging industry–academia participation in R&D, and (iii) facilitating the incubation/commercialization of innovations. IPR awareness should be increased in institutes and industries. With a view to encourage and reward innovation, there is a need to ensure availability and access to adequate funding for technology entrepreneurs and commercialization of innovation. Research and training should go hand in hand. This is the practice worldwide. The CSIR laboratories should pair with universities and targeted R&D should be undertaken.

The Transformation of the Industry from BPO to KPO and Related Human Resource (HR) Issues

8.3.19 The society is shifting from an era of industrial society into 'knowledge society'. Knowledge creation and its applications are primary features of this change in today's networked society. In any industrial society, the growth rate in the services sector is higher than that of the manufacturing sector. Services themselves are also becoming an increasingly integral part of all production businesses and there are relatively more people working in this sector now. This trend is ultimately leading to an increased emphasis on intangible products, which is also called service concepts. Providing services is a much more challenging task than just delivering goods, and, therefore, there will be an increasing focus on making optimal use of resources for maximizing their competitiveness.

8.3.20 The IT and ITES-BPO sector should continuously identify the emerging verticals, which have the potential to grow and generate revenues keeping the dynamic nature of this sector in view. Generating the right kind of manpower with skill-sets requirement for each of the potential vertical is so diverse that it becomes a challenge for the HR function of a company to continuously evolve vertical specific training methodologies and design suitable training modules. Further, the HR companies will have to continuously scan the horizon for the emergence of newer technologies and knowledge areas. The situation will become more complex as the transition from BPO to KPO takes place. Intuitively, one can say that the transition is likely to be very crucial for sustenance of the industry's growth and subsequent establishment in the market place.

8.3.21 It will be essential for each company to build internal capabilities to manage knowledge effectively and also the collective competence building for the IT sector. Managing knowledge is a process which involves multi-period decision framework, starting from investment in R&D to diffusion of knowledge to creation of innovation and ultimately realizing the value through commercialization of innovation and inventions.

Software Technology Parks (STPI) Scheme

8.3.22 A favourable business policy and a regulatory environment are critical for the success of any sector and the STPI scheme stands testament to this fact. STPs were set up in various parts of the country as per the Resolution issued by the government in 1993. Over the last few years, it has played a seminal role in placing India on the global map as an IT superpower. In fact, significant credit for the record growth in exports, foreign exchange earnings, employment generation, and the development of the Indian IT-ITES sector is attributed to this scheme. Under the STP scheme, units engaged in the export of IT-ITES are entitled to tax benefits under section 10A and 10B of Income Tax Act 1961. However, these benefits under the scheme are scheduled to lapse post assessment year 2009–10.

IT in School Education

8.3.23 Technology could be effectively used for digital delivery of high quality lectures and course material to other institutions and embellish the same with class room teaching for enhancing the learning. ICT tools can make it easier to monitor not only the attendance and performance of the students but also that of the teachers as well. The MIS also needs to be developed to monitor national projects such as SSA, MDM, ICDS, etc.

Gender Empowerment through ICT

8.3.24 The Indian IT-ITES industry with revenues of US$ 39.6 billion has emerged as the largest private sector employer in the country with direct employment of 1.6 million professionals, and indirect employment for over 6 million people in different sectors. This fast expanding IT and ITES sector in India has opened new doors of opportunity for women. The participation of women in the IT-BPO workforce is seen as a critical enabling factor for continued growth of the industry. While the percentage of women in the IT-BPO workforce at an entry level is commensurate with their proportion amongst graduating students, anecdotal evidence suggests that this is not so at the middle and senior management positions. However, companies are recognizing that having women on board at all levels in the organization makes good business sense. IT-BPO companies are, therefore, considering ways to involve and develop women for higher roles and functions. Their increased professional participation will result in changing the socio-economic status of women within the employing organization and will also contribute towards the breakdown of gender disparity. In a study conducted by NASSCOM in 2006, 76% of software professionals in IT companies are men, whereas

24% are women. However, NASSCOM says this ratio is likely to be 65:35 (men:women) by the year 2007. Interestingly, this ratio is reversed in the ITES-BPO sector where the ratio of men to women is 31:69. In line with the basic principles of governance to which the government is committed under the NCMP, which includes empowerment of women, the government has introduced gender budgeting. In accordance with this, gender empowerment through ICT should be a regular feature during the Eleventh Plan and efforts should be made to support schemes of gender empowerment through ICT for reducing digital divide.

Faculty Development in IT

8.3.25 The prevailing system of education in India is constrained by several factors. The government needs to strengthen the education system structurally with a number of strategies. There is a dire need for continuously updating the course content, curriculum, and pedagogic methods to make them more relevant to the needs of the industry. Additionally there is a need to take up specific programmes for the development of faculty and provide adequate incentives for making teaching an attractive career option. Some of the policy issues in this regard which need immediate attention are the following:

- Make teaching/academics as attractive a career option as working in the industry. The academic institutes need to provide suitable faculty remuneration as there is a large gap between the salary structures in the industry and in academics. The industry needs to come forward and supplement government efforts through establishment of Chairs for professors, incentives, sponsored research, and the like.
- Need to increase the number of faculty positions in the Indian universities and technical institutions as well as creation of adjunct faculty from the industry to address the twin issue of quantity and quality and R&D activities.
- Need to tie up with institutions abroad for professors to come here on sabbatical.
- Need to train the ICT faculty of both the formal and the non-formal sector of education to keep pace with the demands of the industry as well as the technological changes.
- Develop a mechanism to encourage migration of students between formal and non-formal streams to address the issue of quantity. Also introduce a credit system whereby the students can accumulate and carry forward their credits and complete their education at their own pace. This would particularly help the in-service personnel.
- Evolve National Mission for faculty development in general and faculty development in niche ITES areas such as IT in tourism, health, medical, and legal services and finance in particular.

IT in Health Sector

8.3.26 The importance of Health in the process of economic and social development and improving the quality of life of our citizens has been well recognized. The government has identified Health as one of the seven Thrust Areas and has given focused attention to it. Since independence, a vast public health infrastructure has been created comprising Public Health Centres and Community Health Centres (CHCs) and District/State and Super Specialty hospitals. In rural areas especially, there are pockets of under-served populations where the vicious circle of poverty, malnutrition, and poor health reinforce each other. There is an urgent need to reach out to the un-reached especially in the remote areas. This can effectively be done with the infusion of technology into the Health sector.

8.3.27 Integrated disease surveillance projects, creation of district and State Health Data Centres for the surveillance units, networking and operating of district health centres through video based distance communications, early warning system for disease incidence and collection of call centre based information, web-based health MIS, and telemedicine are some of the important areas that need to be operationalized. Electronic health—or e-health is one of the next frontiers of ICT innovations. Some of the well known hospitals in the country have developed MIS for health which is also known as Medical Information System, which would go a long way in creation and adoption of nationwide electronic medical records for all patients treated at various hospitals in the country. The issues like data privacy, security, and interoperability of systems are to be dealt with properly from an e-health perspective.

IT in Agriculture Sector

8.3.28 Agriculture continues to be one of the mainstays of Indian economy. Increased agricultural production and incomes would put more money in the hands of the people living in the rural areas. Keeping in view the important role that IT can play in boosting productivity and incomes of farmers and reducing the cost of operations, agriculture has been identified as one of the Mission Mode Projects (MMPs) under the National e-Governance Plan (NeGP), a nationwide initiative for promoting e-governance in the country.

8.3.29 By means of IT, the agriculture sector would achieve higher efficiencies to redefine the way in dealing with the production and post harvest losses. The Agricultural Resources Information System is envisaged to create a comprehensive database on various parameters related to land use, water use, and a system for strengthening advisory services to farmers in adopting the latest agricultural production practices. The portal AGMARKNET which provides daily market information on commodity prices in respect of about 300 commodities and 2000 varieties from over 2700 markets is a Sunshine Portal for farmers to bargain better prices for their produce. Similarly, the 'Gyandoot' portal of the State of Madhya Pradesh provides information regarding rates of grains and vegetables, dispenses land records and issues income, domicile, and caste certificates. Further attempts need to be made in providing the latest information on real time basis to the farmers and other rural population in the remotest parts of the country. Market is now the driver for agricultural growth and efficiency of the market depends on effective dissemination of information. IT has the potential to help the agriculture sector to overcome some of the traditional barriers to development by improving access to information, expanding the market base, enhancing employment opportunities, and making government services work better. Decision Support System on agricultural production and marketing, water allocation in an irrigation system, and cattle farming system in livestock are required to be developed aggressively.

8.3.30 In the private sector also several initiatives have been taken to optimize the supply chain. 'e-Choupal' has been conceived as a more efficient supply chain aimed at delivering value to its customers around the world on a sustainable basis. The e-Choupal model has been specifically designed to tackle the challenges posed by the unique problems of Indian agriculture, characterized by fragmented farms, weak infrastructure, and the involvement of numerous intermediaries, among others.

IT in Rural Sector

8.3.31 Rural Content Providers: The creation of local/rural content is of utmost importance in order to make the PCs and Internet an attractive proposition to a much larger number of people. Involving the private sector in this regard would also be essential. Therefore, it is felt that a new entrepreneurial category of Rural Content Providers would give a further boost to and drive the demand, both for PCs and Internet access as well as for rural connectivity. It will also help in better utilization of the cable/wireless network already laid, or being planned in the rural areas by the bandwidth providers. The Rural Content Providers would provide content and other facilities, including entertainment, which will be of interest to the rural population.

8.3.32 Content creation would be a specialized area requiring thorough understanding of the local requirements and language which can only be done through local entrepreneurs. The business model of such a Rural Content Provider would vary from region to region and would be driven by the market. The Department of IT and the Department of Telecommunications (DoT) need to evolve a suitable strategy to encourage such Rural Content Providers. The IT revolution would remain incomplete unless the benefit of this revolution reaches rural masses.

Targets of IT-ITES Sector for the Eleventh Five Year Plan

8.3.33 Given the backdrop of large untapped demand potential and strong fundamentals, India is uniquely positioned to secure global leadership. Table 8.3.3 shows the exports forecast for the Eleventh Plan period as estimated by NASSCOM-McKinsey Report 2005.

TABLE 8.3.3
Indian IT-ITES Exports Forecast 2007–12

Year	IT-ITES Exports (US$ billion)
2007–08	37.6
2008–09	47.5
2009–10	60.0
2010–11	72.1
2011–12	86.6

Source: NASSCOM-McKinsey Report 2005.

8.3.34 Additionally, Indian IT-ITES export growth can be further accelerated through deep and enduring innovation by industry participants. Such extensive innovation could generate an additional US$ 15–20 billion in export revenue over the next five to ten years.

8.3.35 Further, establishing India's leadership in the global IT-ITES sector will mean more than achieving a targeted growth in exports. Attaining these ambitious outcomes will require breakthrough collaboration amongst industry players, Central and State Governments, and NASSCOM—to ensure that appropriate actions required to maximize the global sourcing market potential and sustain India's superiority as the preferred sourcing destination are executed in a timely manner.

8.3.36 Achieving these growth targets will entail a significant demand for incremental human and financial capital in the country. US$ 86 billion in IT-ITES exports by 2012 translates to incremental direct employment of about 2.5 million people and capital investment of approximately US$ 20 billion.

The Path Ahead

8.3.37 The outlook for Indian IT/ITES-BPO remains bright and the sector is poised to achieve its target of US$ 86.6 billion in export revenues by financial year 2011–12. In order to achieve these targets, both the GoI as well as the industry need to work in unison. While the basic policy framework and fiscal incentives as enumerated above need to be put in place by the government, the industry associations and industries need to actively support the initiatives.

8.4 FINANCIAL SERVICES

Introduction

8.4.1 The financial services sector in the country has been displaying a varying growth rate in the recent past. The annual growth rates since 2000–01 are given in Table 8.4.1.

TABLE 8.4.1
Growth Rate (Real) of Financial Services (Banking and Insurance)

S No.	Year	Rate of Growth	Percentage Share in the GDP
1.	2000–01	–2.0	5.5
2.	2001–02	9.1	5.7
3.	2002–03	11.3	6.1
4.	2003–04	2.2	5.8
5.	2004–05	8.8	5.9
6.	2005–06	14.0	6.1
7.	2006–07	13.0	6.3
8.	2000–01 to 2006–07 (Average)	8.1	5.9

Source: CSO.

8.4.2 The financial sector as a whole is estimated to employ between 3.5 million to 4.0 million people, including direct employees and agency forces. To support the GDP growth aspiration of 9%–10%, the financial sector would need to grow by 25%–30% annually over the next five years. The penetration of the financial sector in India remains low relative to many markets, with bank credit/GDP at under 50.0%, overall insurance premium/GDP at under 5.0%, and general insurance premium/GDP at under 1.0%. The underlying GDP growth and higher penetration potential offer strong growth opportunities for the financial sector. The financial sector also has substantial potential for employment creation.

8.4.3 This sector performs the vital functions of enabling productivity and income growth in the economy as a whole, and has an equally important part to play in making this growth more inclusive. The sector has to be enabled to attain an increasing level of sophistication so as to meet the requirements of globalizing trade and industry and the increasing engagement of the Indian economy with the rest of the world, both on the current as well as on the capital accounts. The government has recently received the report of the EC on making Mumbai an International Financial Centre. This report has made very far reaching recommendations on the fiscal and monetary policies, financial sector regulation and supervision, as well as on the development of various financial markets. While these recommendations would be relevant to the needs of medium- and large-scale industry and commerce, it would be necessary to look at certain further policy measures in order to ensure that small and marginal farmers, micro enterprises in the unorganized sector, the weaker and disadvantaged sections of society, and the relatively backward regions and States are enabled to participate more fully in the growth process.

8.4.4 This chapter outlines some of the major issues that the financial services sector needs to address in this task of facilitating inclusive growth and suggest some necessary steps in the way forward.

Financial Inclusion

8.4.5 Financial inclusion can be described as the delivery of banking and other financial services at affordable costs to the vast sections of the disadvantaged and low-income groups. To bring the 'financially excluded' population within the formal financial system, many policy initiatives have been taken, such as making available a basic banking 'no frills' account either with 'nil' or very low minimum balances, issuing of General Credit Cards to eligible beneficiaries without insistence on security, purpose, or end use of credit; introduction of KCCs, allowing banks to utilize the services of NGOs, SHGs, MFIs, and other civil society organizations as intermediaries in providing financial services; credit linking of SHGs, support to MFIs; introduction of Financial Sector (Regulation and Development) Bill 2007 to develop and regulate the MFIs; and constitution of Financial Inclusion Fund and Financial Inclusion Technology Fund of Rs 500 crore each to strengthen the institutional and technological infrastructure for greater financial inclusion. We have to introduce suitable policy interventions and technological innovations to maximize the financial inclusion during the Eleventh Plan period.

Extent and Causes of Financial Exclusion

8.4.6 Lack of access to financial services such as credit, savings, and insurance at an affordable cost not only results in exclusion but also acts as a constraint to growth impetus in the rural and unorganized sectors. Despite years of policies aimed at the financial inclusion, a large number of households do not have access to formal financial services even today.

8.4.7 The financial exclusion covers exclusion from any or all of the financial services necessary for participating in a modern market economy. Nevertheless, exclusion from credit provision has been looked at as being more significant than that from other services. There is a rural–urban divide and a regional skew to the financial exclusion. Table 8.4.2 presents the prevailing situation:

TABLE 8.4.2
Savings and Loan Accounts

S. No.	Regions	No. of Savings Accounts to Adult Population (2005) (%)	No. of Loan Accounts to Adult Population (2005) (%)
1.	North	80	12
2.	North East	37	7
3.	East	34	8
4.	Central	52	9
5.	West	60	13
6.	South	66	25
7.	All-India	59	14
7a	Rural	39	9.5
7b	Urban	60	14

Source: Speech of Usha Thorat, Dy Governor, RBI (19 June 2007).

8.4.8 The NSSO Situation Assessment Survey on 'Indebtedness of Farmer Households' (2003) reveals that 51.4% of farmer households do not access credit either from formal or non-formal sources. The region-wise position of the level of indebtedness is indicated in Table 8.4.3.

8.4.9 There are several reasons for financial exclusion: lack of awareness, low income/assets, social exclusion, and illiteracy are the demand side factors. On the supply side, distance from branches, branch timings, cumbersome documentation and procedures, unsuit-

TABLE 8.4.3
Credit Access of Farmer Households

Region	Farmer Households (HHs) Borrowing from both Formal and Non-formal Sources		Farmer Households (HHs) not Accessing Credit from either Formal or Non-formal Sources	
	No. (Lakh)	Percentage of total HHs	No. (Lakh)	Percentage of total HHs
Northern	56.26	51.40	53.20	48.60
North Eastern	7.04	19.90	28.36	80.10
Eastern	84.22	40.00	126.39	60.00
Central	113.04	41.66	158.29	58.34
Western	55.74	53.77	47.92	46.23
Southern	117.45	72.70	44.11	27.30
Group of UTs	0.49	33.10	0.99	66.90
All-India	434.24	48.6	459.26	51.4

able products, language, and staff attitudes are the reasons for exclusion.

8.4.10 While steps need to be taken to improve the access to and the supply of credit and other financial services, there can be no overemphasis of the importance of building up the capacity of the weaker sections to use the financial services. To some extent, a financial service such as insurance would be necessary to use another financial service such as credit; financial literacy would help in using savings, credit, and insurance services, etc., but there remain several other very important factors outside of the financial sector that are complementary to financial services and need to considered as an integrated package.

8.4.11 On the supply side, the post-1991 period has also seen significant changes in the credit provision for the weaker sections. Despite emphasis on increasing the credit penetration and outreach of institutional sources of credit, the number of rural bank branches has declined from 35134 in March 1991 to 30572 in March 2006. Even the number of small borrowers' accounts (less than Rs 25000) has declined from 625.48 lakh to 387.33 lakh. The result has been that the share of money lenders in the total dues of rural households has increased from 17.5% in 1991 to 29.6% in 2002. (All-India Debt and Investment Survey as on 30 June 2002, NSS 59th Round Released in December 2005.)

8.4.12 A continuing policy measure is the stipulation of priority sector lending. However, this has got diluted in the last 10 years by a shift in the focus to better creditworthy activities such as housing, transport, professional activities, etc.

8.4.13 The priority sector now comprises agriculture (both direct and indirect), SSIs, small road and water transport operators, small business, retail trade, professional and self-employed persons, State-sponsored organizations for SC/ST, education, housing loans, micro credit, loans to software, and food, and agro-processing sectors.

8.4.14 The share of agriculture in total bank credit declined sharply from 15.9% at end-March 1990 to 9.6% by end-March 2001. During this period, however, the share of agriculture in GDP also declined significantly. As a result, the credit intensity of the agriculture sector (credit to agriculture sector as percentage of sectoral GDP) remained broadly at the same level. Credit to agriculture picked up significantly from 2004–05 onwards. The government announced on 18 June 2004 a package for doubling the flow of credit to agriculture and allied activities in a period of three years commencing from 2004–05 over the amount disbursed during the year 2003–04. Table 8.4.4 indicates the target and achievement of the agricultural credit flow during 2004–05, 2005–06, and 2006–07.

8.4.15 The credit intensity of the sector increased sharply from 11.1% in 2001–02 to 27% in 2005–06. The number of borrowal accounts in the agriculture sector also increased from 19.84 million in 2000–01

TABLE 8.4.4
Flow of Credit to Agriculture

(Rs Crore)

Year	Target	Achievement
2004–05	105000	125309
2005–06	141000	180486
2006–07	175000	203296
2007–08	225000	66888#

Note: # Upto July 2007.

to 26.66 million in 2004–05. Within the overall minimum priority sector target of 40% of NBC, the share of agriculture is 18%. The share of agricultural loans as a percentage of NBC for public sector banks was 15.3% at end-March 2005 and 15.2% at end-March 2006. Private sector banks were at 13.5% as at both end-March 2005 and 2006. While commercial banks have taken care of the needs of the small farmers, they have not done so in respect of the marginal/sub-marginal farmers, tenants/share croppers, oral lessees, non-cultivator households, etc.

8.4.16 The distribution of credit upto Rs 2 lakh by SCBs over the last 10 years reveals a disturbing trend (see Table 8.4.5). The number of loan accounts for availing credit upto Rs 25000 has declined from 5.19 crore in 1996 to 3.84 crore in 2006. As a proportion of total loan accounts, it has declined from 91.6% to 45% during the same period. Similarly, the outstanding credit has reduced drastically from about 14.2% of total bank credit in 1996 to 3% in 2006. However, the average outstanding has increased from Rs 6985 to Rs 11769.

8.4.17 For credit disbursed above Rs 25000 and upto Rs 2 lakh, the number of loan accounts has increased nearly 10-fold and credit outstanding has multiplied over seven times. Consequently, the average loan outstanding has declined from about Rs 70000 in 1996 to Rs 52500 in 2006.

8.4.18 Disbursal of credit displays the rural–urban divide (see Table 8.4.6). Rural and semi-urban loan accounts, as a proportion of total loan accounts, have declined from about 79% in 1996 to about 59% in 2006. The fall has been sharper in the rural segment. The credit outstanding in this category has declined by about five percentage points from 29.64% of bank credit to 24.72% during the same period. On the contrary, the urban and metro segments reflect the opposite trend. The number of loan accounts in the urban and metro areas has multiplied about two and

TABLE 8.4.5
Distribution of Outstanding Credit of SCBs according to the Size of the Credit Limit

S. No.	Year	Credit upto Rs 25000			Credit above Rs 25000 and upto Rs 2 lakh		
		No. of Accounts	Amount Outstanding (Lakh)	Average Outstanding	No. of Accounts	Amount Outstanding (Lakh)	Average Outstanding
1.	1996	51904658 (91.59)	3625319 (14.23)	6985	3991468 (7.04)	2808470 (11.03)	70362
2.	1999	42747346 (81.73)	3828497 (10.01)	8956	8249220 (15.77)	4999659 (13.07)	60608
3.	2001	37252319 (71.14)	3781632 (7.02)	10151	13203909 (25.22)	6847786 (12.72)	51862
4.	2004	36766092 (55.38)	3855543 (4.38)	10487	25133746 (37.86)	12414438 (14.10)	49394
5.	2005	38732564 (50.20)	4299179 (3.73)	11100	32373797 (41.96)	15688824 (13.61)	48461
6.	2006	38419104 (44.97)	4521734 (2.99)	11769	38703221 (45.30)	20328082 (13.43)	52523

Note: Figures in brackets are percentages.

Source: Basic Statistical Returns, RBI.

TABLE 8.4.6
Sector-wise Distribution of Outstanding Credit of SCBs

S. No.	Year	Rural		Semi-urban		Urban		Metro	
		Accounts	Outstanding	Accounts	Outstanding	Accounts	Outstanding	Accounts	Outstanding
1.	1996	28795008 (50.8)	3861351 (15.2)	15907178 (28.1)	3689050 (14.5)	7034553 (12.4)	4439731 (17.4)	4935690 (8.7)	13479079 (52.9)
2.	1999	24473040 (46.8)	5390862 (14.1)	14457568 (27.6)	5482002 (14.3)	6992485 (13.4)	7071668 (18.5)	6382363 (12.2)	20297971 (53.1)
3.	2001	22510707 (43.0)	6888194 (12.8)	14046994 (26.8)	7110588 (13.2)	7933614 (15.2)	9530289 (10.8)	7873080 (15.0)	30314307 (56.3)
4.	2004	25564806 (38.5)	10990745 (12.5)	16108316 (24.3)	11487098 (13.0)	8931305 (13.5)	16997379 (14.7)	15785863 (23.8)	48555981 (55.2)
5.	2005	29357131 (38.1)	16047938 (13.9)	18225926 (23.6)	14283629 (12.4)	10176816 (13.2)	21229977 (18.4)	19390921 (25.1)	63685248 (55.3)
6.	2006	29053685 (34.0)	19942287 (13.2)	21474702 (25.1)	17479436 (11.5)	12918689 (15.1)	27636541 (18.3)	21988305 (25.7)	86325949 (57.0)

Note: Figures in brackets are percentages.
Source: Basic Statistical Returns, RBI.

four times, respectively. As a proportion of the total loan accounts, it increased from about 21% in 1996 to about 41% in 2006. The loan outstanding has increased by about five percentage points from 70% in 1996 to 75% in 2006.

8.4.19 Artisan, village, and tiny (AVT) industries and other SSIs have received insufficient credit. The number of AVT and other SSIs loan accounts, as a percentage of total bank accounts, has declined by 4.6 percentage points from 7.2% in 1996 to 2.6% in 2006 (see Table 8.4.7). In absolute terms, it declined from 40.9 lakh to 21.8 lakh. The loan accounts have declined secularly during the period in rural, semi-urban, and urban areas. However, in the metros it has increased. The outstanding credit has also declined by 6.6 percentage points from 10.7% of bank credit in 1996 to 4.1% in 2006. The decline across the rural and

TABLE 8.4.7
Artisan and Village Industries and Other Small-scale Industries

Year	No. of Accounts					Amount Outstanding (Rs lakh)				
	Rural	Semi-urban	Urban	Metro	Total	Rural	Semi-urban	Urban	Metro	Total
1996	2306666 (8.01)	1022012 (6.42)	537760 (7.64)	227208 (4.60)	4093646 (7.22)	333261 (8.63)	503052 (13.64)	740522 (16.68)	1155699 (8.57)	2732534 (10.73)
1999	1894551 (7.74)	1069453 (7.40)	616374 (8.81)	347256 (5.44)	3927634 (7.51)	414597 (7.69)	592352 (10.81)	985547 (13.94)	1342224 (6.61)	3334720 (8.72)
2001	1340518 (5.96)	715700 (5.10)	588912 (7.42)	442582 (5.62)	3087712 (5.90)	373850 (5.43)	716957 (10.08)	1105629 (11.60)	1701256 (5.61)	3897692 (7.24)
2004	1134176 (4.44)	480711 (2.98)	258361 (2.89)	138583 (0.88)	2011831 (3.03)	489411 (4.45)	809427 (7.05)	1247847 (7.34)	1787782 (3.68)	4334467 (4.92)
2005	1213263 (4.13)	555214 (3.05)	287666 (2.83)	171364 (0.88)	2227507 (2.89)	601963 (3.75)	977442 (6.84)	1558533 (7.34)	2184599 (3.43)	5322537 (4.62)
2006	1000377 (3.44)	550984 (2.57)	352933 (2.73)	279702 (1.27)	2183996 (2.56)	711926 (3.57)	1156510 (6.62)	1834442 (6.64)	2532432 (2.93)	6235310 (4.12)

Note: Figures in brackets are percentages.
Source: Basic Statistical Returns, RBI.

urban areas is, however, more pronounced in the metros. Though the loan accounts during the period have nearly halved, the average outstanding credit has increased more than four-fold from Rs 66750 in 1996 to Rs 285500 in 2006. While AVT industries are concentrated predominantly in the rural areas, other SSIs are dominant in the urban areas and the metros. This reflects that the AVT industries, which are relatively less credit worthy, have been credit starved.

8.4.20 The share of credit to SSIs has declined from 15% of NBC in 1998 to 6.4% of NBC in 2005–06. Including small business, retail trade, etc., the total share is less than 10% of NBC. Housing has gone up from 2.9% to 9.23%.

8.4.21 SHGs and their linking up to the banking system has been a very notable feature of the provision of the financial services to the weaker sections in the recent years. However, apart from the fact that this has been largely in the south, the overall quantum of credit extended is still quite small. As at end-March 2006, 22.39 lakh SHGs were linked to banks. Cumulative lending amounted to Rs 11398 crore. The current outstanding credit is around Rs 4000 crore which is a very small fraction of the NBC. About 24 million families have been assisted. The average bank loan per SHG has increased from Rs 18227 in 2001 to Rs 32012 in 2005.

Policy Issues

8.4.22 A number of committees have provided guidance on improving the financial inclusion. The Sub-Group on Financial Services headed by K.V. Kamath (2007) is the most recent one. The C. Rangarajan Committee on Financial Inclusion (2007) has, in its Interim Report, made detailed recommendations on the supply side solutions to improve the delivery of financial services through traditional and non-conventional channels. It has also laid emphasis on the complementary demand side measures that are necessary. The Vaidyanathan Committee on Restructuring of Co-operatives (2004) and the Committee on Moneylender Legislation (2006) have recommended policy measures to improve the financial inclusion.

8.4.23 Some of the key policy issues emerging out of these and the other reports for extending the outreach and depth of the financial inclusion are discussed in the succeeding paragraphs.

Interest Rate Caps

8.4.24 Interest rates on loans made by the banks have been deregulated from 1994, with the exception of export credit and loans upto Rs 2 lakh. In the latter case, the interest rate cannot exceed the bank's notified benchmark PLR. Recently, the government has announced a subsidy of 2% to the banks for extending the production credit upto Rs 3 lakh for agriculture at 7%. However, as the Report on Currency and Finance 2005–06 States, 'although the supply-led approach to rural credit prior to the 1990s ensured availability of credit at a subsidized rate, it turned out to be financially unsustainable as it impacted on the health of credit institutions adversely'.

8.4.25 The entire issue of deregulating/regulating the interest rate is embedded in the question of whether access and timely availability of credit should be an overriding concern rather than the cost of credit per se.

8.4.26 The Working Group on Outreach of Institutional Finance and Co-operative Reforms examined this issue and also conducted studies, through its sub-groups, on the actual costs incurred in financing small borrowers in the rural areas. A sample study of lending by a public sector bank showed that the all-inclusive cost of loans of Rs 25000 and less is 21%. In the case of a private sector bank, it was found that the cost of direct lending was much more than when the lending was through an intermediary MFI. However, the cost difference declines as the size of the loans increases. The all-inclusive cost, as per this study, works out to as much as 33.1% for the direct lending of loan of Rs 10000 while this is 17.5% for a loan of Rs 25000 through an MFI. The overall balance sheet analysis of RRBs and Central Co-operative Banks (CCBs) produced a cost of 7.75% on earning assets for RRBs and 10.16% for CCBs. Commercial banks estimates range from 7.5% to 13.5%. A College of Agricultural Banking study of 22 MFIs showed an average cost of 30.2%.

8.4.27 There is clearly a need for carrying out periodic studies based on scientifically selected samples and factoring in all costs to arrive at the actual cost of lending to small borrowers in the rural areas.

8.4.28 In addition to the interest rates charged, the borrowers have to incur other costs, such as submitting certificates/documents (land documents, search reports by lawyers, 'no dues' certificate from other bank branches, valuation certificates, etc.), and often bribes. Taking all these into account, the total cost of borrowing through the formal institutional channels may not be less than the rates charged by the formal credit channels.

8.4.29 If documentation and other procedures are simplified, thereby reducing the transaction costs of the farmers significantly, the farmers may not mind paying market driven rates of interests, covering the costs of funds, and the transaction costs and risk costs of the banks. Allowing the interest rates to be market driven and taking into account the risk perceptions of the banks would lead to the banks considering agricultural lending as a viable business proposition.

8.4.30 The Report on Currency and Finance itself quotes the Prime Minister to raise significant questions relating to credit to the weaker sections. It raises the fundamental issue of whether farmers need reliable access to credit at reasonable rates or a lower rate of interest, whether we need to create new institutional structures, etc.

8.4.31 There appears to exist an element of inconsistency in the stipulations relating to the interest rates. While the interest rate on direct lending by the banks upto a limit of Rs 2 lakh cannot be at a rate higher than the bank's PLR, there is no such restriction if the lending is to an ultimate borrower through the intermediation of an MFI. The RBI in 2000 deregulated the interest rates on loans made by the commercial banks to the MFIs, and interest rates on loans made by the MFIs to the borrowers. Micro credit extended by the commercial banks either directly or through an intermediary was to be considered as part of the bank's priority sector lending. Again in 2006, the RBI emphasized that the interest rates applicable to loans given by banks to MFIs or by MFIs to SHGs/member beneficiary would be left to their discretion. This leads to an anomalous situation where loans to the same beneficiaries if dispensed through alternate channels of financing are priced differently. In order to remove this anomaly, no interest rate ceilings should be imposed on the banks by the government.

8.4.32 The available data show that around 82% of the lending by the banks is taking place at sub-PLR rates. While better creditworthy corporates are getting credit at sub-PLR rates, the agriculture and SSI sectors and others are charged PLR or even higher rates. This would again point out to the need to carry out proper costing studies for credit provision to different classes of customers. It must be recognized that if the effort for financial inclusion of the underprivileged is to be sustained, the cost of providing such services should invariably be met. However, the model should, at the same time, penalize inefficiencies in providing credit. Therefore, the costs should be appropriately benchmarked in accordance with the best practices. A free interest rate regime and competition should be recognized as the primary means of ensuring reasonable rates; this should be supplemented by the publication of the results of such studies.

8.4.33 It is necessary to recognize that there are limitations beyond which the institutional credit system will not be able to provide services inspite of the adoption of technology, especially when it pertains to the disadvantaged groups. Experience through case studies shows that the expansion of micro finance has helped in smoothening of the interest rates charged by the informal sector.

8.4.34 While the approach of the RBI has been very open and driven by the larger interest for the development of the micro finance sector, there have been instances of the State Governments regulating the interest rate. The State Governments have taken the plea that MFIs charge usurious rates of interest and this increases the indebtedness of the usually poor borrowers.

8.4.35 Consultative Group to Assist the Poor guiding principles on regulation and supervision of micro finance state that interest rate caps, where they are in force, almost always hurt the poor by limiting the services, far more than they help the poor by lowering the rates. The Report of the Internal Group to Examine Issues relating to Rural Credit and Micro Finance (Khan Committee) of the RBI has also deliberated on this issue. The Report mentions that the empirical data in respect of several micro finance projects being carried out in different parts of the world prove that timely availability and right quantity of credit, and not the interest rate, are crucial to the success of the micro finance programmes. Since the method of costing applied by the MFIs is fundamentally different from that followed by the banks, the methodology for applying interest rates for them would be different from the methodology for the banks. Since providing services at the doorstep of the customer has a cost, no undue intervention is required to set the interest rates charged to the ultimate borrower through the financial intermediation route. This is best left to the commercial judgment of the borrowing MFIs and the lending institutions.

8.4.36 It has been argued that both the Central Government and State Government can play a central role in reducing the interest rates without introducing rate caps. This can be done by creating a database and monitoring system for interest rates being charged by the MFIs. Under the system, it would be mandatory for the MFIs to report the effective interest rate offerings periodically. However, transparency in the fixation of interest rates is the major bottleneck. At present, there is no uniform agreed methodology followed by the MFIs for disclosing effective interest rate charged including loan processing fees, bad debt provisions, and other ancillary charges. This makes it difficult to compare interest rates across all MFIs. One of the options could be self-regulation, that is associations of the MFIs themselves voluntarily adopt and enforce a code of conduct including disclosure norms. As self-regulatory organizations have serious limitations to enforcing their rules, the other option is formal regulation of the sector. This would include formulation and enforcement of uniform financial reporting guidelines including norms for treatment of non-performing assets; unambiguous interest rate disclosure guidelines including norms for disclosing loan processing fees, bad debt provisions, and other hidden charges; clear conduct codes for behaviour of the MFI staff with penalty for breach of conduct rules; and audit provision for the MFIs above a certain level of portfolio.

8.4.37 Ratings of MFIs by external agencies such as SIDBI could also be thought of to promote transparency in the operations of the MFIs.

8.4.38 With the use of IT solutions and transparency in pricing coupled with growing competition amongst MFIs, it is expected that the interest rate charged by the MFIs would come down. Credit dispensation through alternate channels, namely, MFIs, SHGs, Non-banking Financial Companies (NBFCs), HFCs, and post offices would be effective in increasing access, reducing transaction costs, as also in improving recovery.

Modes of Extending Outreach

UP-SCALING SHGs–BANK LINKAGE PROGRAMME (SBLP)

8.4.39 Essentially, two forms of providing micro credit are being followed, namely SBLP and MFIs. Within the SHG–bank linkage model, SHGs are formed by NGOs and SHG Promoting Institutions (SHPIs) and credit is extended by the banks to the SHGs directly. This is the predominant form of disbursement of credit within the SBLP model.

8.4.40 The geographical distribution of both the SHGs–bank linkage and the MFIs is highly skewed. The southern States account for the bulk of SHGs. However, in the recent years, SBLP has been making inroads into the regions with a large percentage of rural poor. About 90% of the SHGs that are linked to the banks are of women.

8.4.41 SBLP has registered an impressive growth during the last five to seven years. At present, 90% of the micro credit is being disbursed through the SHGs–bank linkage model. The SHGs linked to banks have increased from 2.64 lakh in 2000–01 to 22.39 lakh in 2005–06. Despite such an impressive growth, a vast gap between the demand and supply of micro credit exists. As per the estimate by the Task Force headed by V.S. Vyas (2007), the minimum requirement of the micro credit is Rs 70000 crore as against the supply of Rs 11378 crore. This programme is also concentrated in the southern States. However, in 2005, NABARD had identified 13 priority States accounting for the bulk of India's poor for special efforts and location-specific strategies.

8.4.42 Under the SBLP, the average loan per member is less than Rs 4000. This is grossly insufficient for financing income-generating activities. The interest rate charged from members has been reported to be 15%–24% per annum. The cost of forming and nurturing the group up to the stage of credit linkage is borne by NABARD. The norms of the MoRD provide for Rs 10000 per group as the cost of formation of the groups.

8.4.43 The binding constraint in the SBLP is the ability to form groups and to build up their capacities. This, in turn, is strongly dependent on the availability of committed NGOs and SHPIs. The Rangarajan Committee has identified the SBLP as one of the two main instruments for achieving financial inclusion and has suggested that the Department of Women and Child Development should be actively involved in this process. Upon the recommendation of this Committee, a Financial Inclusion Fund has been set up by NABARD for promotional activities. NABARD is already engaged in a variety of capacity-building efforts in this area. NABARD's programme needs to be more closely integrated with those of the State Governments, especially in the 13 priority States. It is to be noted that the NCEUS has also made a similar recommendation for a fund to be used for promotional activities.

8.4.44 At the same time, it has been suggested by some that this model may be allowed to grow organically in response to needs and capabilities and there should be emphasis on quality rather than quantity. SHGs should not be allowed to go the co-operatives way. Co-operatives were burdened with non-credit business that is used as a mechanism to deliver government programmes such as PDS, sale of fertilizer, etc. They subsequently became politicized. SHGs being such a large-scale movement are also susceptible to politicization. It needs to be ensured that SHGs retain their character as a peoples' movement and do not become a tool in power politics.

8.4.45 Interestingly, the Vaidyanathan Committee States that co-operatives, of the mutual thrift and credit type, are the only form of organization by which economically disadvantaged individuals and groups, through voluntary collective action, overcome their disadvantageous position in an unequal market and promote their well being. It further adds that the credit would be put to good use in the organizations in which the members know each other first hand, are closely linked through kinship and social relations, and have a strong mutual stake in the proper use of the common credit pool. One would not be mistaken if this description were understood as being one of SHGs. In fact, there is nothing new in the SHG concept that has not been embedded in that of the co-operatives earlier. That the co-operatives have reached their present state should serve as a serious warning to the SHG movement as well.

THE MFI SECTOR

8.4.46 In the MFI model, the MFIs both form the groups and provide credit to SHGs and individuals. MFIs raise funds from the banks and financial institutions for on-lending to SHGs and individuals.

8.4.47 MFIs are an amorphous collection of legal entities, both for-profit and not-for-profit institutions. Amongst not-for-profit institutions are included NGOs incorporated as trusts/societies, co-operatives set up under the Co-operative Acts, and Section 25 companies under the Companies Act. For-profit MFIs include NBFCs incorporated under the Companies Act and regulated by the RBI.

8.4.48 In the MFI model, the rate of interest charged is higher (at about 20%–24%) than the SBLP model as the MFIs have to charge a rate of interest that recovers cost of funds as well as the cost of formation of groups. Sa-Dhan's voluntary code of conduct lays down that the MFIs will charge reasonable rate of interest, that is 21%– 24% per annum. This is comparable to the rate of interest charged by SHGs from their members. Even the cost of formation and nurturing the groups is borne by the MFIs themselves. The cost of funds to MFIs is higher than the rate at which the banks lend to SHGs under the SBLP. Transaction costs are also higher owing to weekly collections and delivery of services at the doorstep. On the flip side, transparency in fixation of the rate of interest and disclosure norms, consumer protection, and coercive practices of MFIs have emerged as the major concerns.

8.4.49 MFIs require funds for credit expansion and on-lending to the SHGs and individual members. As of now, studies reveal that the Indian MFIs are very highly leveraged compared to those of the rest of the world. With a low equity base, the ability of MFIs to raise debt resources from the banks and other financial institutions is limited. Several measures to enlarge equity capital of MFIs include relaxing the constraint on equity investment by venture capital into MFIs, lowering the minimum capital requirement for foreign equity participation, and enhancing the corpus of equity support from NABARD.

REVITALIZATION OF CO-OPERATIVES

8.4.50 Co-operatives have the largest nominal outreach amongst the rural financial institutions including the commercial banks. Presently, they are at a crossroads owing to resource constraints, poor governance, bad management, and inefficiency. On the basis of the recommendations of the Vaidyanathan Committee, the GoI has formulated a revival package for restructuring and strengthening of the rural co-operative credit institutions. A total of 17 States have accepted 'in-principle' the revised revival package as formulated by the GoI. Of the 17 States, 12 States have executed an MoU with the GoI and NABARD. The conditionalities free the societies from the necessity of being a part of the three-tier structure. Individual societies would also be free to establish business contact with the commercial banks and borrow from any RBI regulated institution. Freedom from compulsory federation would help in reducing unnecessary tiers in financing which add to costs. The co-operatives are also to be free to decide interest rates on deposits and advances subject to RBI regulations. These reforms are salutary and will enable the co-operatives to function on sound commercial lines. The insistence on signing the MoU with its conditionalities and acceptance of guidelines prescribed by RBI for ensuring 'fit and proper' criteria for Directors in the Boards and Chief Executive Officers of rural co-operatives are apparently some of the reasons for the slow pace of implementation of the revival package.

8.4.51 It is imperative that the revival package is implemented in toto, without diluting the contingent legal, financial, regulatory, and institutional reforms. This would have the effect of cleansing the balance sheets and strengthening the capital base of rural co-operatives so that they begin on a clean slate and are at par with other rural financial institutions. However, there are several valid concerns that need to be addressed so that the financial and institutional sustainability of the rural co-operatives is not impaired.

8.4.52 The Vaidyanathan Committee states that, co-operative societies in India, unlike the world over, have not been mutual, but only agencies for credit dispensation. Upper tiers were created to provide refinance for the lower tiers. This resulted in a structure driven by borrowers at all levels. The Committee, therefore, recommended that there should be an aggressive effort to convert pure credit to thrift-cum-credit societies. In this form, it is expected that there would be natural incentives for good governance. This vision has been largely preserved in the reform package that has now been worked out. However, the process of organic growth that this entails is likely to constrain the ability of the co-operatives to quickly scale up their operations.

8.4.53 The Vaidyanathan Committee has recommended liquidation of the non-viable and defunct Primary Agricultural Co-operatives (PACs). The exact modality of liquidation, however, has not been spelt out. As the number of PACs to be liquidated is quite large, transitional arrangements need to be put in place to maintain the ground-level credit flow. Mergers with healthy PACs or take-over by neighbouring PACs may adversely affect the financial performance and burden the functioning of the taking-over PACs. A better solution lies in development of new PACs under the Model Act suggested by the Vaidyanathan Committee. However, this would be a time-taking but a sustainable option in the long run.

8.4.54 Co-operatives offer high rates of interest on deposits. Co-operatives also suffer from high transaction costs owing to over-staffing and salaries unrelated to the magnitude of business. High-risk costs arise on account of low recovery levels, lack of adequate risk mitigation systems and procedures, absence of appropriate credit appraisal and monitoring, and over-exposure to agricultural lending. Actual repayments are influenced by ad hoc government decisions to suspend, delay, or even waive recovery. The revival package, significantly, does not disempower the State Governments from giving directives to the credit co-operatives. These powers have been used often in the past to subject the co-operatives to commercially unsound decisions. The costs of funds are also high as PACs depend on borrowings from the upper tier co-operatives. Lack of information about credit worthiness of the clients further compounds the problem. The lending rates need to cover cost of funds, transaction costs, and risk costs. While the Vaidyanathan Committee has identified these factors that increase the cost of co-operative credit operations, it has not adequately suggested mechanisms to reduce the associated transactions and risk costs.

8.4.55 The apprehension, therefore, is that the implementation of the revival package is unlikely to provide any substantial remedy to the problem of financial exclusion. This would be even truer of the production and investment financing needs of agriculture. There appears to be no alternative to a vigorous increase in the outreach and the scale of rural operations of the commercial banks.

SCHEDULED COMMERCIAL BANKS (SCBs)/ REGIONAL RURAL BANKS (RRBs)

8.4.56 While the rural branch network of commercial banks had steadily grown in the years following nationalization in 1969, there has been a rollback since 1991. The average rural population served by a bank branch has therefore gone up, as shown by the following numbers (see Table 8.4.8).

TABLE 8.4.8
Average Population per Branch Office

	1991	2005
Population per branch	13711	15680
Population per rural branch	13462	16650
Population per urban branch	14484	13619

8.4.57 However, there is an opinion that the existing rural branch infrastructure can be more intensively used so as to service a much larger customer base. A major recommendation of the Rangarajan Committee is that the banks be given targets to add at least 250 farmer accounts per year per branch. This, the Committee feels, will enable covering all the unbanked farmer households in the next five years. Prescribing a target-based approach for the commercial banks to extend their outreach in rural areas may not be a viable option until and unless banks are allowed to charge a rate of interest that covers their cost of funds, transaction costs, and risk costs.

8.4.58 While several policy measures have been initiated to augment the credit flow to small and marginal borrowers, the results speak differently. During 1996 and 2006, the loan outstanding for accounts upto Rs 2 lakh credit has declined from 25.3% to 16.4% of bank credit. These loans are disbursed at or below PLR. Sub-PLR lending has increased from 39% in September 2004 to 82% in March 2007. These loans are essentially disbursed to better creditworthy corporates. However, agriculture and SSI sectors, in particular AVT and other SSIs whose loan outstanding is more than Rs 2 lakh, are charged interest rates above PLR. This has several implications. First, lending at below PLR lacks transparency and affects both lenders and borrowers. Second, to compensate for the sub-PLR lending, other segments are charged higher rates of interest thus leading to cross-subsidization of the economically well-off borrowers by the economically poor borrowers.

8.4.59 The employment intensive and greater regional spread of AVT and other SSIs make them an engine of inclusive growth. However, they are considered more risky by the banks and collaterals are insisted upon. This has been partly addressed by setting up of a Credit Guarantee Fund Trust for SSIs. This fund guarantees upto 75% of the credit risk subject to loan cap of Rs 50 lakh per borrower. The other option to obviate the need for collateral could be introducing independent rating of the borrowers and generating their credit history.

8.4.60 Today's small entrepreneur is tomorrow's big businessman, if provided appropriate financial support. The banks have to be proactive and gear up their risk assessment and management capacities. They have to finance the first-time entrepreneurs, notwithstanding the risk, if financial inclusion is to become a reality. The inevitability of some degree of failed ventures should not lead to unreasonable attachment of accountability which otherwise leads to risk aversion amongst lenders. Prudential norms need to be laid down by the regulator to provide this comfort.

8.4.61 Along with the above, it may be necessary to modify the priority sector lending guidelines by creating sub-limits for lending to the weaker sections. As suggested by the NCEUS, a sub-target of 10% should be reserved for marginal and small farmers within the 18% reserved for agriculture. The flow of credit against this sub-target should be separately monitored. Similarly, a separate target of 10% for small and micro enterprises, of which again 4% is reserved for micro enterprises with a capital investment of less than Rs 5 lakh, should be imposed and enforced. Along with the freeing of interest rate that has been recommended above, this would help in credit reaching the needy sections.

8.4.62 There have been some suggestions made that the priority sector targets should be enforced in a different fashion than hitherto. A suggestion that merits consideration is that the targets be made tradeable amongst banks. This would have the merit of acting as means of achieving the targets at the lowest possible cost.

8.4.63 A major step taken recently is to permit the banks to extend their outreach through engaging business facilitators and business correspondents (BC). The banks are required to formulate their own schemes in line with the guidelines of the RBI to operationalize these mechanisms. Though these guidelines were brought out more than one and a half years ago, the NCEUS notes that the banks are not inclined to adopt this model because of cost considerations. They, therefore, suggest that some incentives may be provided to the banks, in the form of tax or other benefits, to adopt this model. The Rangarajan Committee says that the banking system has not yet been able to fully appreciate the business gains that could accrue from adopting the model. It adds that discussions with a cross-section of bankers reveals that the muted response is, in part, due to disinclination on the part of the banks to absorb the costs involved on grounds of its impact on the viability of operations.

8.4.64 Prohibition on banks to charge more than the PLR on loans less than Rs 2 lakh has made the BC model unworkable for provision of micro credit. Even if the banks were willing to absorb the difference between their PLR and their cost of funds, margins would not be adequate to compensate the BCs to cover the costs of originating, monitoring, and collecting loans. Second, under the model, the bank is responsible for omissions and commissions of the BC. Third, the lack of IT connectivity (owing to cost considerations) would make it difficult to report and incorporate the BC's transactions in the books of the bank by the end of the next working day. Due to these reasons, the BC model has received a rather lukewarm response from the banks. However, this seems to be the best available option for increasing financial inclusion. Apart from removing interest rate controls, a systematic programme for capacity building for the BCs, establishing robust procedures for monitoring their performance and rating them, and the building up of IT connectivity, perhaps even by sharing it amongst banks so as to reduce costs, are all essential for this model to succeed.

8.4.65 The industry feels that the financial sector participants would find it difficult to expand into underserved areas in the absence of appropriate payment processing infrastructure. More than 80% of India's financial transactions are processed in physical cash. Cash as means of payment has a large cost in terms of handling, transaction processing, holding, and risk of loss. Looking ahead, card-based solutions are likely to emerge as the key mechanism for delivering financial services to the unbanked. There is therefore a need to create a national payments system with participation by all banks, reduce transaction costs, and substantially increase the deployment for Point of Sales terminals and their utilization for both high- and small-value payments.

8.4.66 India has achieved good mobile penetration both geographically and in terms of socio-economic classes. The total number of mobile phone connections has already greatly exceeded the number of bank accounts. South Africa has reportedly pioneered the large-scale use of mobiles for payment. Japan, South Korea, and other countries also are said to be using this method. Enabling mobile payments would facilitate cheaper payment processing, wide geographic coverage, online payments straight through processing, and financial inclusion. The mobile phone can be used as a device to transfer funds and make payments from a bank account using appropriate authentication protocols.

TRADITIONAL MONEYLENDERS

8.4.67 The All-India Debt and Investment Survey (NSS 59th Round) has revealed that the share of institutional agencies in the total cash dues of urban households had increased from 72% in 1991 to 75.1% in 2002 and that of moneylenders had also increased during the period from 10.2% to 14.1%. In the case of rural households on the other hand, the share of institutional agencies had in fact declined from 64% in 1991 to 57.1% in 2002. And more significantly, the share of moneylenders had increased in the same period from 17.5% to 29.6% in the case of rural households.

8.4.68 Despite measures to extend institutional credit especially in the rural areas, the dependence on moneylenders has only increased. Thus there is a case to look at the possibility of using moneylenders for providing credit within a regulated framework. Usurious rates of interest and coercive practices are a reality that needs to be appropriately addressed.

8.4.69 International experience also suggests that moneylenders perform similar activities all over the world both in developed and developing countries. Internationally, the nature of moneylending laws is regulatory. The emphasis of such laws is on protecting the interests of the borrowers by capping the rate of interest and curbing coercive recovery practices.

8.4.70 The technical group of the RBI to review the legislations on moneylending in its report has also recommended that registration of the moneylenders should be made compulsory and a penalty should be imposed on those conducting business without registration. It has also recommended that the State Governments should stipulate the maximum rate of interest that could be charged by the moneylenders. The group has also recommended a model legislation for adoption by the State Government to regulate the moneylenders. The legislation provides incentives for registration and mainstreaming the activity of moneylending. It also provides for penalties for violation of its provisions as well as disincentives to those who circumvent the law in the form of more stringent action against unregistered lenders.

8.4.71 A major issue that needs to be resolved here is the regulatory capacity of State Governments, who are the competent authorities for this purpose. A possible solution could be to outsource the regulatory function to the banking system. The incentive of obtaining credit from banks to enlarge their businesses could be used to overcome the fear of costs associated with registration. The government could consider mainstreaming moneylending by instituting an effective regulatory framework as has been done worldwide.

Building up the Demand Side

8.4.72 Perhaps the greatest benefits of public policy initiatives towards the financial inclusion are in the area of creating systemic infrastructure for provision of credit and other financial services. Specific measures include creating credit registries, national identification numbers, payment systems, electronic commodity and auction markets, and weather measurement systems—all of which are public goods which would help stimulate economic activity. Other measures that would help generate demand for financial services include public investment in rural infrastructure programmes, vocational training programmes, and measures to improve market linkages that help micro entrepreneurs find reliable channels for marketing their products and services.

New Initiatives

8.4.73 There are certain NGOs, societies, trusts, and co-operative societies operating in the micro financial sector that are engaged in providing credit and other financial services to the economically active low-income people especially women, poor households, and their micro enterprises. However, the financial activities undertaken by such organizations lack a formal statutory framework. It was, therefore, considered expedient to provide a formal statutory framework for the promotion, development, and orderly growth of the micro credit sector. Accordingly, the Micro Financial Sector (Development and Regulation) Bill 2007 was introduced in the Lok Sabha on 20 March 2007. Some of the important features of the Bill are given below:

- Entrust the function of development and regulation of the micro financial sector to the NABARD.
- Define various entities engaged in the activity of micro finance such as co-operative societies, mutual benefit societies, or mutually aided societies registered under any State enactments or multi-State co-operative societies registered under the Multi-State Co-operative Societies Act, 2002; societies registered under the Societies Registration Act 1860; or any other State enactments governing such societies and a trust created under the Indian Trust Act, 1882 or public trust registered under any State enactments, that will be governed by the regulatory framework that is proposed to be set up.
- Define various categories of beneficiaries of micro financial services as eligible clients including SHGs or joint liability groups of such eligible clients.
- Provide for extending micro financial services to eligible clients by way of financial assistance subject to ceilings to be prescribed and such other financial services as may be specified by NABARD.
- Provide for constitution of Micro Finance Development Council to advise the NABARD on formulation on policies, schemes, and other measures required in the interest of orderly growth and development of the micro finance sector.
- Provide for constitution of Micro Finance Development and Equity Fund to be utilized for the development of the micro finance sector.

8.4.74 The Bill is currently under examination with the Standing Committee on Finance.

ANNEXURE 8.2.1
Financial and Physical Performance of Tourism during the Tenth Five Year Plan

(Rs in crore)

S. No.	Schemes/ Programmes	Financial Performance Tenth Plan				Physical Performance Tenth Plan	
		Outlay	BE	RE	Actual Exp.	Targets	Achievements
I	Central Sector Schemes						
1	Externally Aided Projects	50.00	40.50	40.50	31.24	To ensure effective plan preparation and supervision on execution of Ajanta-Ellora Conservation and Tourism Development Project Phase-II and Development of Buddhist Circuit projects in UP with the assistance of Japan Bank for International Cooperation (JBIC).	Infrastructure upgradation of Buddhist circuits has been taken in a big way through identification of 22 important Buddhist sites throughout the country. MoT has entered into an agreement for undertaking infrastructure development at Buddhist sites of Sarnath, Kushinagar, Kapilvastu, Shravasti, and Sankisa in UP, with JBIC for a loan assistance of Rs 395.63 crore for total project of Rs 680 crore.
2	Assistance to IHMs/FCIs etc.	110.00	127.50	127.50	135.43	To provide financial assistance for improving and upgrading of existing infrastructure of IHMs/FCIs/Indian Institute of Tourism and Travel Management (IITTMs).	Assistance was extended to 22 IHMs and 7 FCIs following National Council's curriculum.
3	Capacity Building for service providers	24.00	31.50	31.50	12.25	To conduct training programmes for participants thereby qualitatively improving tourism manpower in the country.	Conducted training to the persons who are engaged in the unorganized sectors and come in contact with a major segment of the tourists. More than 40000 persons were given training under this CBSP scheme.
4	Overseas promotion and Publicity including Market Development Assistance (MDA)	500.00	485.00	485.00	509.34	To promote tourism across the globe through global campaigns, fairs and festivals, road shows etc.	Global campaigns and market specific campaigns as a part of the 'Incredible India' campaign in the overseas markets were carried out. Participated in international trade fairs and exhibitions and organized road shows/ India Presentations in important overseas markets to showcase the varied Indian tourism products.

(Annexure 8.2.1 contd.)

(*Annexure 8.2.1 contd.*)

S. No.	Schemes/ Programmes	Financial Performance Tenth Plan				Physical Performance Tenth Plan	
		Outlay	BE	RE	Actual Exp.	Targets	Achievements
5	Domestic promotion and publicity including hospitality	230.00	172.00	172.00	173.40	To popularize the culture and natural beauty of different regions, pilgrim sites, and new tourism products like Eco-tourism, Adventure and Rural Tourism, etc.	Theme-based domestic media campaigns, mass social awareness programmes, production of publicity material and collaterals, were carried out and central financial assistance was extended to States/UTs for fairs & festivals.
6	Incentive to accommodation infrastructure	45.00	47.00	47.00	47.50	To create budget accommodation in the country by providing subsidies/incentives.	Provided subsidy on the loan taken by the entrepreneurs for construction of budget category hotels.
7	Construction of building for IISM at Gulmarg, Kashmir.	0.00	16.00	16.50	13.80	To upgrade the Institute with construction of building and providing machinery and other equipments.	The construction of building is near completion.
8	Market research including 20 years perspective plan.	20.00	15.50	15.50	32.22	To conduct Master Plans/DPRs (Detailed Project Report), Survey/Study reports and tourism statistics publications supported on different aspects of tourism to provide inputs to policymakers.	24 Master Plans/DPRs, 14 Survey/Study reports, and 2 tourism statistics publications were published in different aspects of tourism to provide inputs to policymakers.
9	Assistance for Large Revenue Generating Projects	98.00	122.00	92.00	34.96	To promote large revenue generating tourism projects in PPPs and in partnerships with other government/semi-government agencies.	21 Large Revenue Generating Projects were sanctioned.
10	Computerization and IT	100.00	72.00	72.00	52.33	Effective use of IT for exclusive promotion and publicity, and streamlining data collection and updating through appropriate hardware and software.	Emphasis has been given on maximum use of IT to promote 'Incredible India' more aggressively through OnLine Campaign on World Wide Web to drive traffic to the official website of the MoT.
11	Tourism Infrastructure Development Fund	0.00	30.00	30.00	0.00		The Scheme was dropped
12	Revival of Tourism in J&K	0.00	9.00	16.00	16.00	To create employment, self employment, and revival of economic activities.	Ministry had extended a package for financial assistance and subsidy to the service providers

(*Annexure 8.2.1 contd.*)

(Annexure 8.2.1 contd.)

S. No.	Schemes/ Programmes	Financial Performance Tenth Plan				Physical Performance Tenth Plan	
		Outlay	BE	RE	Actual Exp.	Targets	Achievements
							viz., Houseboat Owners, Hotels and Guest Houses, Shikara owners, and Ponywalas. An amount of Rs 7.00 crore was sanctioned and released to the Government of Jammu and Kashmir during the year 2003–04 and Rs 9.00 crore in the year 2004–05.
13	Ongoing Ninth Plan Schemes	71.50	71.50	71.50	78.88		The amount was utilized for the schemes which were continued from Ninth to Tenth Five Year Plan.
II	Centrally Sponsored Schemes						
1	Product/Infrastructure Development for Destinations and Circuits	1361.50	1242.50	1260.00	1498.21	To create tourism infrastructure facilities at circuits and destinations in various States/ UTs in consultation with the concerned State/UT governments.	The MoT sanctioned 1160 projects comprising a major part of infrastructure projects.
III	10% lump sum provision for NE States including Sikkim	290.00	184.00	184.00	0.00	As per specific schemes mentioned above.	As per specific schemes mentioned above
	Total (I+II+III)	2900.00	2666.00	2661.00	2635.67		

Note: BE = Budget Estimate, RE = Revised Estimate, Exp. = Expenditure.

V
Physical Infrastructure

9

Transport

9.1 INTEGRATED TRANSPORT SYSTEM

9.1.1 The transport system in India comprises a number of distinct modes and services, notably railways, roads, road transport, ports, inland water transport, coastal shipping, airports, and airlines. Railways and roads are the dominant means of transport carrying more than 95% of total traffic generated in the country. Although other modes such as coastal shipping and inland water transport would play a greater role, the railways and roads would continue to dominate the transport landscape in the foreseeable future.

9.1.2 It is necessary to foster the development of the various transport modes in an integrated manner that will lead to the realization of an efficient, sustainable, safe, and regionally balanced transportation system, where each mode of transport operates in its field of economy and usefulness, with competitive and non-discriminatory prices that are adequate to support progressive development of transport infrastructure and services. This would also enable the comparative advantages and economic efficiencies to be properly reflected in the user costs.

9.1.3 The liberalization of our economy has brought home the urgency of recognizing that an efficient transportation system is necessary for increasing productivity and enabling the country to compete effectively in the world market. Adequacy and reliability of transport infrastructure and services are important factors that contribute towards the ability of the country to compete in the field of international trade and attract foreign direct investment. The government has a major role to play in this sphere. Even in a market economy, the framework that national governments provide for the transport sector largely determines the level of cost and transport operations. It is, therefore, necessary to create a policy environment that encourages competitive pricing and co-ordination between alternative modes in order to provide an integrated transport system that assures the mobility of goods and people at maximum efficiency and minimum cost.

9.1.4 With the vision of formulating an integrated policy and long-term investment planning, the Planning Commission has undertaken a project of conducting a Total Transport System Study with the help of M/s Rail India Technical and Economic Services. This study will generate traffic flows covering the four major mechanized modes of transport—railways, highways, airways, and shipping—and also forecast mode-wise traffic demand for specified horizon years upto 2025–26. The study will also help to analyse inter-modal transport resource costs and determine optimal inter-modal mix.

9.2 RAILWAYS

9.2.1 Indian Railways is often referred to as the lifeline of the Indian economy because of its predominance in transportation of bulk freight and long-distance passenger traffic. The network criss-crosses the nation, binding it together by ferrying freight and passengers across the length and breadth of the country. As the Indian economy moves into a higher growth trajectory, Indian Railways has also stepped up developmental efforts and is preparing itself for an even bigger role in the future.

REVIEW OF THE TENTH PLAN

9.2.2 The Tenth Plan has seen a remarkable turnaround in the financial performance of the Indian Railways, making it possible for it to place increased reliance on internal resources and market borrowings for development. The actual mobilization of internal resources went up from a meagre Rs 3113 crore or 27% of the total resource mobilization in its first year to a sizeable contribution of more than Rs 12000 crore or nearly 50% of the total resource mobilization in its final year. The table in Annexure 9.2.1 also shows the marked step up in internal resource generation in the last two years of the Tenth Plan, with commensurate decrease in the contribution of GBS during this period. Notably, the bulk of the contribution to the GBS has been on account of the Special Railway Safety Fund (SRSF), as brought out in the table in Annexure 9.2.2. Additional GBS provided through SRSF has helped the Railways in wiping out arrears in renewal of critical assets that enabled improvement in availability as well as utilization of assets, which has eventually contributed to the turnaround in the performance of the Railways.

Physical Targets and Achievements

9.2.3 The Tenth Plan targets and achievements are summarized in Table 9.2.1. Indian Railways have far exceeded the Tenth Plan projections both in passenger and freight traffic. Originating freight has shown an average annual growth of 8.1% over the Tenth Plan period as against 3.8% in the Ninth Plan period. Similarly, in BTKM, the corresponding growth in freight was 7.4% and 3.7%. The average annual passenger growth in the Tenth Plan was no less impressive, at 4.2% in terms of the number of originating passengers and 7.4% in terms of the passenger kilometre as compared to respective figures of 4.2% and 6.7% in the Ninth Plan.

A Remarkable Performance

9.2.4 The impressive achievement in freight loading and movement—exceeding the target by 16.7%/20%—was the result of a market-focused strategy aimed at capturing large volumes of traffic along with efficient utilization of assets and resources with associated reductions in unit costs despite rising input costs. The major initiatives that contributed to enhancing the competitive advantage included the decision to use the carrying capacity of the wagons optimally by increasing the loadability of the wagons on selected routes up to 15%, realignment of tariffs to the competitive conditions in the market, and incentivization of loading in the lean season and in the empty flow direction. Incremental loading has come across-the-board from all commodity groups, barring the expected decline in petroleum products. Major increases were seen in coal, iron ore for export and steel plants, cement, and other commodities (which include containers). The Railways' share in respect of commodities such as cement and steel has increased despite stiff competition from roadways. This praise-worthy performance needs to be sustained, consolidated, and carried forward with outcome-based enhancements in the Eleventh Plan.

TABLE 9.2.1
Physical Targets and Achievements

	Ninth Plan	Tenth Plan					
	(2001–02)	Target for Terminal Year (2006–07)	2002–03	2003–04	2004–05	2005–06	2006–07
Originating freight (mt)	492.5	624	518.7	557.4	602.1	666.5	728.4
Freight net tonne km(billion)	333.2	396	353.2	381.2	407.4	439.6	475
Originating Passengers(million)	5169.3	5885	5048.2	5202.9	5475.5	5832.4	6352.1
Passenger km (billion)	494.2	625	515.4	542.1	576.6	616.6	691.8

Productivity

9.2.5 The spurt in traffic has been supported by a concomitant increase in the productivity of the assets. This quantum jump in the productivity of assets, including wagon and track utilization, has come about as a result of various initiatives. The increase in axle load on mineral routes, improved maintenance practices, and reduced detentions at terminals have all contributed significantly to higher wagon productivity. With the growth in volumes and the improved productivity, the unit cost of operations has been brought down. Improved productivity of assets over the Plan period is summarized below in Table 9.2.2.

9.2.6 There is a sustained improvement in wagon utilization from 2468 net tonne kilometre (NTKM) per wagon per day in the first year of the Tenth Plan to 2963 NTKM in its final year. The wagon turnround has come down to six days from seven days in the beginning of the Tenth Plan and eight and a half days in 1996–97. Track utilization improved markedly from 7.74 million NTKM per route km to 9.05 million NTKM per route km.

9.2.7 Significant improvements in managerial practices have underpinned the improvements in the productivity of human resources during the Tenth Plan, which increased from 0.26 million NTKM per employee to 0.33 million NTKM per employee by the fourth year of the Tenth Plan while passenger km per employee increased from 0.37 million to 0.47 million during the same period.

POLICY ISSUES AND STRATEGIES FOR THE ELEVENTH PLAN

9.2.8 Indian Railways is at the threshold of a major change at the beginning of the Eleventh Plan. The key challenge before it is not attracting additional traffic, but rather meeting the accelerating demand for high-quality services imposed by a vibrant economy for which it has to take immediate and appropriate steps to augment capacity and deploy it optimally through new investment and tariff policies. The Railways also has to execute projects speedily and procure assets at a rapid pace by incorporating best practices in project implementation, production, and procurement of new assets.

9.2.9 The mid-term appraisal of the Tenth Plan document had noted that the Chinese Railways is carrying 4.5 times more freight than the Indian Railways, mainly due to the larger investments made in the Chinese Railways in expanding and strengthening the infrastructure which also contributed towards improvements in the productivity of the Chinese Railways. Indian Railways carries more passengers than Chinese Railways, but the longer term development of the Railways in India depends crucially upon its ability to

TABLE 9.2.2
Productivity Performance

Productivity Indicator	Ninth Plan	Tenth Plan			
	(2001–02)	2002–03	2003–04	2004–05	2005–06
Wagon Utilization					
NTKM/wagon/day (Broad Gauge [BG])	2223	2468	2574	2617	2872
Wagon km/wagon/day (BG)	191.6	204.6	187.8	204.5	211
Wagon turnround (in days) (BG)	7.2	7.0	6.7	6.4	6.1
Track Utilization					
NTKM/route km (million)	7.38	7.74	8.14	8.57	9.05
Passenger km/route km (million)	10.1	10.5	10.8	11.5	12.2
NTKM/Engine Day Online (Goods-BG)					
Diesel	167163	164713	199958	218045	279066
Electric	311061	326798	352669	415244	465375
Human Resources Productivity					
NTKM/employee (million)	0.24	0.26	0.28	0.31	0.33
PKM/employee (million)	0.35	0.37	0.40	0.43	0.47

move freight, in keeping with the needs of the growing economy, and at speeds and reliability determined by the need to be competitive. This is especially important given the greater energy efficiency of the Railways in the long-distance freight (Box 9.2.1).

Box 9.2.1
Expansion of Chinese and Indian Railways (1992–2002)— A Comparison

	China	India
New track (RKM)	13797	682
Track doubling (Kilometres)	9400	1519
Electrification (RKM)	8975	5192
Investment (billion $)	85	17.3
Freight (2003–04) (billion Net Ton Kilometres)	1724	381
Passenger (2003–04) (billion Passenger Kilometres)	478	541

Investments

9.2.10 In light of the huge arrears in replacement of over-aged assets in the early part of the Tenth Plan, a decision was taken to create a Rs 17000 crore SRSF of which Rs 12000 crore was to come from general revenues. As a result, the proportion of GBS had increased to 45% during the Tenth Plan as compared to 34% in the Ninth Plan and 23% in the Eighth Plan. With SRSF coming to a closure, the GBS would normally be expected to decline from this level in the Eleventh Plan. However, the projected levels of economic growth and the sharp rise in manufacturing output would necessitate that capacity augmentation of the Railways is supported by GBS to the maximum extent possible. Even so, the trend of increased reliance on internal resources (IR) and extra budgetary resources (EBR) witnessed in the last two years of the Tenth Plan would need to continue in the Eleventh Plan. For this to happen, innovative, non-traditional strategies and methods have to be adopted for garnering the resources to fund the higher levels of investment required for capacity augmentation of the system to meet the heightened demand for railways' services. The situation calls for concerted efforts to generate IR and EBR in light of the possibility that a significant proportion of the surpluses generated may have to be set aside for implementation of the Sixth Pay Commission recommendations, to meet the increased requirement of replacements and renewals, as well as the payment of increased dividend liability.

9.2.11 The scope for resource mobilization also needs to be enlarged by rationalizing the tariff structure of freight and passengers with a view to reducing the present cross-subsidization both within the passenger segment and also from the freight to the passenger segment. At present, there is excessive cross-subsidization from freight to passenger services. Specific areas have to be thrown open for private sector participation, including those through PPPs. The PPPs are projected to contribute over 9% of the total required investment of around Rs 215000 crore in the Railways during the Eleventh Plan, a sharp increase from the 0.4% private sector share in the Tenth Plan.

Renewals, Rehabilitation, and Replacements

9.2.12 A clear priority is achieving higher maintenance standards of the existing assets to sustain the 2006–07 levels of traffic of about 730 million tonnes. Renewals, rehabilitation, and replacements have to be accomplished with an overall objective of reduced asset failures and, even more importantly, improved safety. An investment of over Rs 60000 crore (at constant 2006–07 price) will be required during the Eleventh Plan to maintain existing assets by timely rehabilitation and replacements, as well as for modernization to improve their utilization levels. Such a strategy would enable the Railways to increase throughput from the existing level of assets.

Capacity Enhancement

9.2.13 Another key priority is to achieve a significant enhancement of the capacity given the expected growth in traffic. Until now the emphasis has been on incremental capacity augmentation. Recognizing the need for a major shift in the strategy for capacity augmentation, the mid-term appraisal of the Tenth Plan document had envisaged construction of Dedicated Freight Corridors (DFCs) on selected trunk routes. This has since been given effect to with the announcement of construction of DFCs separating freight traffic from passenger traffic on trunk routes. The proposal for capacity augmentation through construction of DFCs along the highly saturated freight routes is a major prong of the new long-term strategy to provide premium services in freight and passenger. Passenger services on the existing trunk routes along these DFCs will also benefit from the release of capacity by freight movement but would require investments to improve speeds and capacity so that both quantum availability and quality of passenger services offered can be significantly enhanced (Box 9.2.2).

9.2.14 Additional capacity on other routes based on a route-wise planning and low-cost capacity improvements will be another prong of the Eleventh Plan strategy. Route-wise planning will enhance line and terminal capacity simultaneously, since inadequate terminals often are the binding constraints affecting the seamlessness of train movement.

9.2.15 With the quantum increase in both passenger and freight traffic during the last three years of the Tenth Plan and the projected increase in the Eleventh Plan, rolling stock availability will be a key factor. In addition to augmenting the existing production capacities, new production facilities for coaches, locomotives, and wagons would be required. These new production facilities would have to be capable of producing superior locomotives, coaches, wagons, and other rolling stock.

9.2.16 For successful implementation of all the capacity-enhancement projects, including DFCs, a crucial input is availability of sufficient capacity in terms of construction agencies and qualified human resources. Adequate awareness has to be created in the country so that appropriate agencies, namely, the technical institutions and the construction industry, prepare for the task of making available necessary technical human resources and acquire necessary capabilities through joint ventures, etc. Identification of financially viable 'bankable' projects with acceptable risk profiles would need to be coupled with a cogent and comprehensive approach to regulation that establishes the role and scope of regulatory institutions, and their relationship with the legislative and executive branches of the government and the consumers at large.

Strategy for Capacity Enhancement in the Short Term

9.2.17 The strategy in the short run should be focused on maximum utilization of the existing capacity by addressing the directional and seasonal variations in demand. Initiatives taken in the recent years for generating traffic in the traditional empty flow direction and managing seasonal fluctuations in demand using a system of differential pricing should be further strengthened and the response mechanism

Box 9.2.2
Dedicated Freight Corridors (DFCs)

In order to create capacity and improve quality of services, Dedicated Railway Freight Corridor Projects on Western and Eastern Routes were included in the Rail Budget of 2006–07. The Western corridor of 1469 km will connect Jawaharlal Nehru Port to Dadri and Tughlakabad in the North. The Eastern corridor of 1232 km will connect Ludhiana to Sonnagar via Dadri and Khurja, thus facilitating transfer from one corridor to another. The Eastern corridor will further get extended to Kolkata region to connect the proposed deep-sea port. The estimated cost of construction of both these corridors is expected to be around Rs 28000 crore and it is likely to take about five years for completion of these corridors and have a spill-over beyond the Eleventh Plan.

In order to obtain increased throughput and reduce the cost of operations, DFCs are designed to run double stack container trains with 25 tonne axle load running at a maximum speed of 100 km per hour.

An SPV (Dedicated Freight Corridor Corporation of India Ltd) has been formed to implement the DFCs Project. The SPV will plan, construct, and maintain infrastructure. It will also be responsible for operation of trains. The relationship between the Ministry of Railways and the SPV will be codified in a Concession Agreement which draws upon best practices worldwide. Feasibility studies and detailed planning for DFCs on the North–South, East–West, East–South, and South–South routes would also be taken up.

Construction of DFCs would reduce unit cost of transportation with substantial savings in operations and by increasing throughput for infrastructure. Coupled with improved reliability and quality of service, including more efficient inventory management, competitive advantage of Indian goods in the international market is expected to improve significantly.

The Western DFC is expected to also service an Industrial Corridor, for which necessary initiatives are being planned.

institutionalized, so that policy and operations' responses are dynamic and flexible.

9.2.18 The second important strategy would be investments in identified mineral routes and feeder routes to DFCs. It is envisaged that the entire 6973 km of iron ore route will be upgraded for running 25 tonne axle load trains during the Eleventh Plan period. This has already started in the terminal year of the Tenth Plan. Track and bridge structures will be strengthened concomitantly. It is also envisaged that 4220 km of existing feeder routes joining the DFC will be upgraded to 25 tonne axle load. With investments directed into identified mineral routes, it should be possible to switch over to 25 tonne axle load concurrently with availability of requisite rolling stock.

9.2.19 Finally, the investments in signalling improvements such as automatic signalling, introduction of intermediate block sections, block-proving axle counters, track circuiting, etc. coupled with induction of high power locomotives should also create additional capacity in the short run at low cost. Further, the improved wagons with the higher pay-load to tare ratio of around 4, as against the extant 2.6, should be inducted expeditiously to obtain the much needed additional capacity. Switching over to mechanized maintenance of track by investing in track machines would also free some of the capacity locked up in manual maintenance of the track. Reduction in asset failures would also be a part of the strategy to improve line capacity in the interim period.

Technology Upgradation

9.2.20 To keep pace with the technological developments in various aspects of the Railways sector, it is necessary to continuously upgrade the technology. In addition to pursuing the measures indicated above, measures such as introducing longer trains and optimization of coach capacities have to be fully explored.

9.2.21 Speed differential between the freight and passenger trains has to be narrowed down by inducting high-speed freight stock and upgrading freight terminals and their approaches to obtain additional capacity in the medium term as well as to increase the reliability of service in freight business.

9.2.22 Information technology applications hold the key to the Railways' sustained improvement in services and efficiency. Internet ticketing was introduced in August 2002 with the objective of providing tickets at the doorstep of the customer. Initially it was started in Delhi, which is now extended to over 200 cities. Further, in September 2005, e-ticketing was started as a pilot project in two trains, which is now extended to all trains. Booking of *Tatkal* tickets was also started through Internet in December 2005.The concept of 'ticket at doorstep' will have to be further developed for reserved, unreserved, and sub-urban tickets. An integrated Railway information system on real-time basis would be developed and implemented to provide information of train movement, ticketing, facilities on display systems on stations and trains, as well as through diversified media.

9.2.23 Freight Operation Information System (FOIS) which was sanctioned initially in 1984 was taken up in right earnest after detailed scrutiny in 1998–2003 and the first module of the two modules identified, that is, Rake Management System, is fully implemented and commissioned. Implementation of the FOIS has reached the next stage with the implementation of the second module, that is, Terminal Management System, in 489 locations and benefits will now begin to accrue to customers. FOIS will have to be extended to all loading points and be interfaced with customers' information systems, weigh bridges, etc. This is expected to be over during this Plan period.

9.2.24 Coach toilets are the main source of poor sanitation in railway premises. In order to prevent discharge from the toilets while the train is in railway station premises, speed actuated controlled discharge toilets and biodegradable toilets will be introduced in passenger coaches. In collaboration with IIT, Kanpur, efforts are already on to develop indigenous technology to produce fully environment-friendly toilets to suit Indian conditions, so that the discharge from coach toilets does not create unhygienic conditions all along the railway track.

Throw Forward

9.2.25 The Railways has a large number of ongoing projects, which require very large funds for completion

(Box 9.2.3). The requirement of fund for completing these projects under various categories is as shown in Table 9.2.3. At current prices, the total throw forward would be around Rs 65000 crore. In comparison with the position at the beginning of Tenth Plan, the maximum increase has been in the areas of new lines and doubling.

Box 9.2.3
Throw Forward—A Way Forward

Arising from operational necessity, works on doubling, electrification, and gauge conversion are to be completed in a time-bound manner. Due to scarcity of the available resources it is not possible to fix time frames for the completion of other throw forward works. However, works on new lines, accounting for almost 60% of throw forward's value, have been accorded priority gradings as a part of the mid-term review of the Tenth Plan in order to focus the available resources on such works which give immediate benefits and also meet national priorities. All pending works were, thus, categorized in order of their importance into four categories, and higher outlays are being provided to 'last mile' projects, 'operationally required' projects, projects of strategic importance, and projects taken up on cost-sharing basis. This has already started showing results with physical achievements matching the financial outlays, especially in respect of gauge conversion works.

TABLE 9.2.3
Throw Forward of Projects

Type of Projects	Estimated Throw Forward	
	Km	Rs Crore
New lines	8132	31519
Gauge conversion	7148	10417
Doubling	3213	7314
Electrification	1952	1080
Traffic facility works	325 (nos)	2044
Metropolitan transport projects	–	3820
Total		56194

Tariff Regulating Mechanism

9.2.26 The Indian Railways has embarked upon a review of its accounting policies and practices to introduce a fully computerized accounting and MIS so as to generate costing data on commercial lines. The objective is to enable assessment of profitability of different operations and routes, provide specific cost information to be used for marketing purposes, and facilitate indexing of tariffs to input costs.

9.2.27 The fare–freight ratio, that is the ratio of passenger fare per km and freight rate per tonne km, in India is among the lowest in the world, indicating the extent of cross-subsidization from freight to passenger (Box 9.2.4). In addition, premium passenger services are priced very high vis-à-vis second class. This is not a viable strategy since the Railways are competing with air traffic for premier segment and the airline sector is strongly competitive. Reducing cross-subsidization within passenger fares and between the fares of passenger and freight is now an urgent necessity. In any case, Railways have to move towards aligning the fares with the costs in all modes and classes of traffic.

9.2.28 With the availability of more reliable and scientific data on costs, there will be a rational basis for arriving at costs for individual services within the passenger services as also for freight services. Therefore, the next logical step is to have a Tariff Regulating Authority to determine rail fares on a rational basis, after factoring in relevant issues of unavoidable losses on account of uneconomic lines and sub-urban services.

Box 9.2.4
Fare–Freight Ratio of World Railways

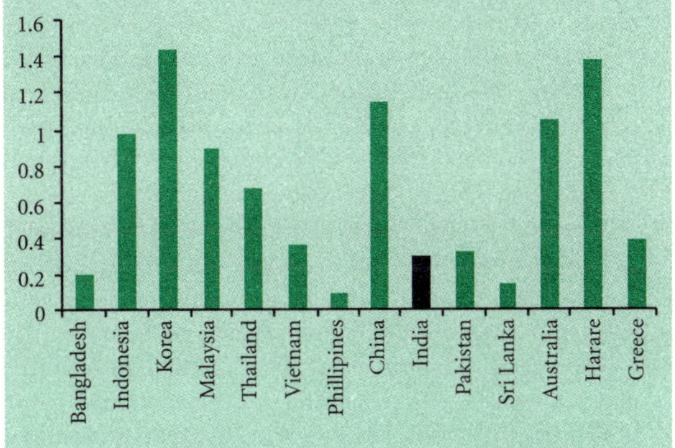

Source: World Bank Study.

Logistic Solutions

9.2.29 Railways have to play an increasing role in the integrated multi-modal transport system to capture the new traffic thrown up by the growing Indian economy. To realize this, Railways needs to seriously consider provision of complete logistic solutions to its freight customers, in addition to decreasing unit costs and providing superior services. It is proposed to develop logistic parks integrating bonded warehousing, logistic processing, commodity exposition, and logistic distribution. The key development is targeted at import/export logistic distribution facilitating international purchasers, third-party and fourth-party logistic companies, and logistic agencies.

9.2.30 Further, logistic hubs can be developed along or near important railheads through joint ventures between State Governments and Railways, through PPPs and direct private sector participation. These hubs will be strategically located to capture agro-industrial produce in the hinterland and to provide competitive transport to expand access to markets for industries in the covered areas. These hubs could be developed as mini-freight villages or as logistics parks depending on the turnover. In the event of a large turnover, there is scope for accommodating a gamut of value-added facilities such as warehousing, refrigerated store houses, cranes and other handling facilities, packing/repacking, assemble, repairs, maintenance, financial services, agro-marts, and electronic centres. These hubs can be developed through PPPs on Build–Own–Operate (BOO) basis as 24 × 7 service centres. For the promotion and development of logistical hubs, Railways should assume a central role and establish consultative machinery involving the major user industries and logistical service providers. Such a forum would also help the Railways to plan for capacity augmentation on a long-term basis.

High-speed Passenger Services

9.2.31 The Eleventh Plan strategy is to consolidate the share of Railways in passenger business, particularly, in long-distance and medium-distance segment by increasing the commercial speed of passenger trains, and introduction of fast services between metropolitan cities with peak speeds up to 150 km per hour from the present speed of 110–130 km per hour. The development of high-speed corridors, which are an

Box 9.2.5
Public–Private Partnership (PPP)

As on date, the Indian Railways have a large shelf of uncompleted projects whose completion would require about Rs 65000 crore. To meet the requirement of future growth of the Indian Railways, further new investment projects are required for which very large funds are needed. The magnitude of the task is huge and any neglect of the same is bound to lead to severe capacity limitations adversely affecting the competitiveness and growth of the economy.

It is estimated that the Indian Railways would not be able to generate sufficient funds internally, through borrowings and from budgetary support for meeting the investment requirements of the Eleventh Five Year Plan. The shortfall would be met through private investments in PPP projects. Additional investment from private sector is also expected through their investments in manufacturing facilities created as a consequence of partnerships with IR. Together it is expected that about Rs 20000 crore worth of investments would be done by private sector during the Eleventh Five Year Plan.

Private sector participation in container movement is already unfolding on a large scale after it was decided to introduce competition in this segment. Necessary Model Concession Agreement (MCA) has been finalized, agreements signed with 15 parties in January 2007, and the scheme has since been operationalized with seven new operators, excluding CONCOR, commencing operations by utilizing about 30 new rakes.

This policy is required to be taken forward by building in suitable guarantees and commitments from railways in order to enable the private operator to provide value-added container services and make investments in container handling facilities such as Inland Container Depots and Container Freight Stations (CFSs). Long-term commitments on transit time and access charges on the part of Railways would be necessary for stimulating private investments in the container logistics sector.

A range of PPP models have been identified which need further fine tuning. These include multi-modal logistics parks, upgradation of major freight and passenger terminal, construction of road over bridges (ROBs), Railway Optical Fibre Cable (OFC) network, consolidation of piece meal parcels into wagons and train loads, etc. A programme for re-development of 22 railway stations into world-class stations through the PPPs has already been initiated.

environment-friendly solution for high-speed passenger transport, will be explored on selected routes. This will be done through PPP route. Speeding up delivery of passenger services by utilizing Mainline Electric Multiple Unit (MEMU) and Diesel Electric Multiple Unit rakes would also be pursued with greater vigour. Trains would be augmented to 24 coaches on all important sectors.

Terminal Facilities

9.2.32 Terminal capacity is an important determinant of the carrying capacity affecting the flow of passenger and freight trains. Full benefits of the line capacity works cannot be derived until terminal constraints are removed. In order to make Indian Railways a world-class railway system, substantial improvements to the terminal facilities are required.

World-class Stations

9.2.33 Most of the railway stations and passenger terminals on the Indian Railway network were built several years back and are suffering from severe infrastructural inadequacies in handling the passengers. As the stations occupy the prime land in the heart of cities, they offer promising possibilities for their re-development by leveraging a part of the real estate development potential. A total of 22 stations have been identified which are located in metropolitan cities and major tourist centres for development through PPP route. The preparatory work for New Delhi and Patna stations through appointment of consultants has already been taken in hand.

Safety and Security

9.2.34 Improved safety is best achieved by upgrading technological aids together with improving reliability of assets, while minimizing human dependence. Elimination of collision through use of anti-collision devices, adoption of fire-proof coaches to reduce fire accidents, crash worthy coaches to reduce fatalities in case of accidents, and reducing level crossing accidents are all part of this Plan. Enhanced training to impart better skills in O&M of assets will also be the focus during the Plan. In order to improve the security of the passengers in general, and women and children in particular, efforts will be made to empower the Railway Protection Force by providing them modern equipment and weaponry as also through better training facilities and upgrading the information system.

PHYSICAL TARGETS FOR THE ELEVENTH PLAN

Freight Traffic

9.2.35 The freight traffic projections for the terminal year of the Eleventh Plan have been pegged at 1100 million tonnes of originating freight and 702 billion tonne km (BTKM) of transportation output. The projections for freight traffic are given in Table 9.2.4.

TABLE 9.2.4
Projection of Freight Traffic in the Eleventh Five Year Plan vis-à-vis Achievements in the Ninth and Tenth Plans

	2001–02	2006–07	2011–12
Originating freight (million tonnes)	492.5	728.4 (47.9)#	1100 (51.0)#
Freight tonne km	332.2	475 (43.0)#	702 (47.8)#

Note: # % increase over the previous Plan.

Passenger Traffic

9.2.36 Passenger traffic is expected to grow at a rate of about 5.5%. The projections for passenger traffic are given in Table 9.2.5. The Eleventh Plan will focus on reducing the cost of operations, developing attractive service packages, and adopting competitive pricing to safeguard the market share of upper-class rail travel against airlines.

TABLE 9.2.5
Projection of Passenger Traffic in the Eleventh Five Year Plan vis-à-vis Achievements in the Ninth and Tenth Plans

	2001–02	2006–07	2011–12
Originating passengers (million)	5169.3	6352.1 (22.9)#	8400 (32.2)#
Passenger km (billion)	494.2	691.8 (40.0)#	942 (36.2)#

Note: # % increase over the previous Plan.

9.2.37 To cater to the projected annual growth of non-sub-urban traffic at 8%–9%, it would be necessary to expand supply by increase in train services and augmentation of seating capacity of trains. Augmentation of train composition to 24 coaches, started in the Tenth Plan, would be continued and extended to other sectors.

Bridges

9.2.38 There are 127768 bridges of Indian Railways. Of these, 44% are more than 100 years old. Railways will undertake repair, rehabilitation, and rebuilding of bridges on the basis of their physical condition as ascertained during annual inspections.

Signalling and Telecommunication

9.2.39 More than 10000 Route Kilometres (RKM) still has obsolete overhead alignment-based communication system on certain routes. It is planned to speedily replace it with an Optical Fibre Cable (OFC) and quad cable-based communication system.

Electrification

9.2.40 During the Eleventh Plan about 3500 km of track will be electrified which is nearly double the Tenth Plan achievement of about 1800 km.

Energy Management

9.2.41 For the first time in the history of Indian Railways, direct power supply from the NTPC has been obtained for the Ghaziabad–Kanpur section yielding substantial savings of about Rs 50 crore per annum with relatively small investment of Rs 68 crore. Further, Railways is also exploring the possibility of buying power from NTPC or from other power utilities, through tariff-based competitive bidding, under Open Access System. Setting up of a 1000 MW captive generation power plant at Nabinagar in Bihar, a joint venture with NTPC, is also approved which is expected to be commissioned during this Plan period. To further the cause of clean and green energy, a 10 MW wind energy plant is being set up at Chennai to provide captive power to a Railway production unit.

Rolling Assets

9.2.42 Technological upgradation and modernization of rolling stock is a key element of the plan for rolling assets. Universal switch-over to 22.9 tonne axle load wagons from the present axle load of 21.3 tonne will lead to improved loadability of the wagons. Efforts will be directed to bring lighter and corrosion-resistant material to improve the payload to the tare ratio of wagons. Railways are also planning to introduce special types of wagons for movement of automobiles, bulk cement, fly ash, and hazardous chemicals. During the Eleventh Plan the proportion of high horsepower locomotives will be increased. The requirements are shown in Table 9.2.6.

TABLE 9.2.6
Eleventh Five Year Plan—Requirement for Rolling Stock

	Tenth Plan		Eleventh
	Target	Actual	Plan Target
Wagons (nos in FWUs)	65000	90554	155000
Electric locos (nos)	343	524	1800
Diesel locos (nos)	444	622	1800
BG conventional Coaches (VUs)	9160	10789	17500
EMUs/DEMUs/MEMUs (VUs)	2715	1413	5000

Note: EMUs = Electric Multiple Units; FWUs = Four Wheeler Units; VUs = Vehicle Units.

Metropolitan Transport Projects

9.2.43 The sub-urban services would require separation from main line systems in places like Mumbai. The emphasis in sub-urban services would be to increase peak time services and augment trains to 12 car rakes.

9.2.44 The Mumbai sub-urban services are severely strained and will be augmented with the capacity additions as part of the Mumbai Urban Transport Project (MUTP) works. The introduction of air-conditioned sub-urban coaches/trains will also be considered, if possible, through PPPs.

9.2.45 Mumbai Rail Vikas Corporation Ltd type model which is implemented for rail component of Phase II of the MUTP, wherein the State Government of Maharashtra has agreed for financing on the basis of Peak Cash Deficit Funding (a kind of viability gap funding [VGF] wherein the gap in debt service liability and the surcharge collection levied for servicing the debt is met by the concerned State Government) should be tried out for other sub-urban systems in Chennai, Kolkata, and Delhi. The first step would be to form a separate SPV for each of these sub-urban systems with the necessary mandate for modernization and upgradation of the existing system.

Physically Challenged and Senior Citizens

9.2.46 All mail and express trains would be provided with specially designed coaches which have separate compartments and suitably designed toilets for the physically challenged and senior citizens. In addition, trains having air-conditioned accommodation would also be provided with air-conditioned compartments for physically challenged persons.

North East Region (NER)

9.2.47 Providing rail connectivity to all States in the NER is a national priority. It has been decided to create a dedicated fund for the National Projects of North East with 25% contribution from the GBS of Railways and the remaining 75% to be provided as additionality from the general revenues. With these scaled-up funds, Railways has been directed to ensure completion of all the sanctioned works within the Eleventh Plan period.

RESOURCE MOBILIZATION

9.2.48 For the economy to grow at 9% per annum over the Eleventh Plan period, it is targeted to increase the GCF in the infrastructure from 5% of GDP at the start of the Tenth Plan to around 9% at the end of the Eleventh Plan. For this to be achieved, private sector participation in a big way is imperative. The areas identified for private sector participation include new manufacturing units, multi-modal logistics parks, construction of high-speed passenger corridors, induction of privately owned rolling stock of container operators, commercial development of land and air spaces, port connectivity works of the private ports, ore lines for steel plants, upgradation of major freight and passenger terminals, construction of road over bridges (ROBs), and railway OFC network.

9.2.49 To garner additional internal resources for bridging the gap between the projected requirement and the availability of resources, Railways may consider levying a 'developmental surcharge' on passenger as well as freight traffic to fund the DFCs as also upgradation of existing network to run high-speed passenger trains.

9.2.50 The total projected outlay for the Eleventh Plan for the Ministry of Railways is Rs 194263 crore at 2006–07 price (Rs 219717.36 crore at current price) which includes Rs 44263 crore of GBS at 2006–07 price (Rs 50063.36 crore at current price) including Rs 3750 crore at 2006–07 price (Rs 4241.36 crore at current price) of cess accruals. The scheme-wise break up of the GBS at current prices is given in the Appendix (Volume III). In addition, the sector is expected to generate private sector investment of Rs 20000 crore during this period. Further, the additional GBS needed for the National Projects of J&K and North East during the Eleventh Plan period would be of the order of Rs 12000 crore and this would be made available during the course of the year, as in the past. This should meet the requirement of Railways. However, if there is a need to further enlarge the Plan size, this would be accomplished by mobilizing necessary additional IEBR and private investments during the course of implementation of the Plan.

9.3 ROADS

9.3.1 A good road network is a critical infrastructure requirement for rapid growth. It provides connectivity to remote areas; provides accessibility to markets, schools, and hospitals; and opens up backward regions to trade and investment. Roads also play an important role in inter-modal transport development, establishing links with airports, railway stations, and ports.

9.3.2 India has one of the largest road networks in the world, of 33.14 lakh km, consisting of (i) national highways (NHs), (ii) State highways (SHs), (iii) major district roads (MDRs), and (iv) RRs that include other district roads and village roads. NHs with a length of 66590 km comprise only 2.0% of the road network but carry 40% of the road-based traffic. SHs with a length of about 137000 km and MDRs with a length of 300000 km together constitute the secondary system of road transportation which contributes significantly to the development of the rural economy and industrial growth of the country. The secondary system also carries about 40% of the total road traffic, although it constitutes about 13% of the total road length. RRs, once adequately developed and maintained, hold the potential to provide rural connectivity vital for generating higher agricultural incomes and productive employment opportunities besides promoting access to economic and social services.

9.3.3 Despite its importance to the national economy, the road network is grossly inadequate in various respects. It is unable to handle high traffic density and high speeds at many places and has poor riding quality. Besides speedy implementation of the Golden Quadrilateral (GQ) and the North–South and East–West (NS–EW) corridors, addressing the deterioration of large stretches of NHs and other improvements in the road network are, therefore, to be accorded high priority in the planning process.

REVIEW OF THE TENTH PLAN

9.3.4 Against an outlay of Rs 59490 crore in the Tenth Plan for the road sector, the expenditure was Rs 42577.43 crore (Rs 48593.95 crore at current price). The overall financial and physical performance is given in Annexure 9.3.1. The scheme-wise and year-wise outlay and expenditure are given in Annexure 9.3.2.

NATIONAL HIGHWAYS (NHS)

9.3.5 In absolute terms, there has been considerable growth in the NHs network since Independence. Table 9.3.1 details the various achievements over select periods and Annexure 9.3.3 provides Plan-wise details of increase in the NHs network.

9.3.6 The progress of four-laning, two-laning, strengthening of roads, and construction of bridges during the Tenth Plan period has been satisfactory, keeping in view the availability of funds. There has, however, been some shortfall in construction of bypasses, primarily due to the time-consuming process of land acquisition and shifting of utilities in the case of bypasses. A large number of deficiencies, however, remain in the network, in terms of inadequate capacity, insufficient pavement thickness, weak, narrow and distressed bridges/culverts, ROBs, etc. Annexure 9.3.1 provides an overview of the physical targets and achievements of normal NH works, Border Roads Development Board (BRDB) works, and works by the NHAI during the Tenth Plan period.

9.3.7 Despite the progress reported above, the NHs are not what they should be. Only 12.5% of their total length is wider than two lanes (as on 31 March 2007), leading to heavy congestion. Shortfall in construction of bypasses, inadequate capacity, insufficient pavement thickness, and weak, narrow, and distressed bridges/culverts as well as ROBs are some of the other deficiencies. Upgradation of large segments of SHs to NHs under the NHDP during the Ninth and Tenth Plans, although impressive, has not kept pace with the demand for road transportation, besides spreading available resources too thinly across competing projects. The result is poor maintenance and riding quality of NHs network, particularly of the non-NHDP section. Also many of the NHs declared during the last two Plan periods were substandard, resulting in further aggravation of the problem.

NATIONAL HIGHWAY DEVELOPMENT PROGRAMME (NHDP)

9.3.8 The Committee on Infrastructure (CoI) has approved a massive phased programme for the improvement and development of NHs during the period 2005–12. This programme envisages an investment of Rs 236247 crore. Although, the NHDP envisages award of concessions/contracts by 2012, the completion of

TABLE 9.3.1
Achievements on National Highways

Period	Total Length# (km)	Widening to Two Lanes (km)	Widening to Four Lanes (km)	Strengthening of Pavement (km)	Major Bridges (nos)
1947–69	24000	14000*	Nil	Nil	169
1969–90	33612	16000	267	9000	302
1990–2002	58112	3457	1276	7000	87
Tenth Plan (2002–07)	66590	4177	6769**	8377	611***
Total	–	37634	8312	24377	1169

Note: # Length at the end of the period.
* Includes 6000 km which were already two-lane at the time of designation as NHs.
** Includes 216.62 km which have been six- or eight-laned upto the Tenth Plan.
*** This does not include the bridges constructed/rehabilitated by NHAI under the stretches of NHDP.

part of Phase III and Phases IV, V, VI, and VII is expected to be accomplished only by the middle of the Twelfth Plan.

9.3.9 NHDP Phase I consists of the GQ, port connectivity, and 962 km of NHs covered under NS–EW corridor of NHDP Phase II. All works on GQ have been awarded, but there have been some slippages in its completion. Against the total length of 5846 km of GQ, 5602 km, that is 95.82%, have been four-laned, thereby leaving a balance of 244 km for completion. Progress of various segments of the GQ is given in Table 9.3.2.

9.3.10 The port connectivity project envisages improvement of 380 km of NHs connecting 10 major ports. Till date, the works on Kandla, Mormugoa, Phase I; JNPT, Phase I; and Vizag ports have been completed. By end-August 2007, four-laning of about 159 km roads of port connectivity and 322 km of other NH had been completed. Improvement of about 215 km roads of port connectivity and 620 km of other NH is under implementation and the balance length of 6 km of port connectivity and 20 km of other NHs is yet to be awarded.

9.3.11 Under NHDP II, by end-August 2007, 1418 km of the NS–EW corridors had been four-laned out of a total length of 7300 km (7200 km at present), that is 19.42% of the total. Work is in progress over a length of 4903 km, while work for the balance 821 km is still to be awarded. The target for substantially completing the NS–EW corridor project is December 2009.

9.3.12 The major reasons for shortfalls in fulfilling the targets fixed during the Tenth Plan period include, inter alia, delay in land acquisition, obtaining environment and forest clearances, getting clearance of Railways for ROB designs, shifting of utilities, local law and order problems, and poor performance by some contractors.

9.3.13 In respect of NHDP III, which initially envisaged four-/six-laning of about 10000 km (subsequently enhanced to 12109 km) on build, operate, and transfer (BOT) basis, the first phase covering 4815 km is expected to be completed in December 2009. Four-laning in a total length of 126 km road length has been completed in NHDP III, the work is in various stages of progress over an aggregate length of 1866 km, and work aggregating to 2823 km is yet to be awarded. The second phase of NHDP III, which has also been approved, involves preparation of DPR for the balance length of about 7294 km and is targeted for completion by December 2013.

9.3.14 Approval of NHDP IV for widening of 20000 km to two lanes with paved shoulders as well as for NHDP VII comprising construction of ring roads of major towns, bypasses, flyovers, etc. is pending.

TABLE 9.3.2
Corridor-wise Details of Progress on the Golden Quadrilateral as on 31 August 2007

Corridor	Four-laned	Under Implementation		Total Length (km)
	Length (km)	Length (km)	No. of Contracts	
Delhi–Kolkata (NH-2)	1364 (92.15)*	89	13	1453
Kolkata–Chennai (NH-5, 6, and 60)	1568 (93.11)	116	6	1684
Mumbai–Chennai (NH-4, 7, and 46)	1251 (96.97)	39	6	1290
Delhi–Mumbai (NH-8, 76, and 79)	1419 (100)	–	–	1419
Total	5602 (95.82)	244	25	5846

Note: Figures in parenthesis denote percentages.

9.3.15 Under NHDP V, out of 6500 km to be six-laned, two projects covering 148 km have already been awarded, leaving a length of 6352 km still to be awarded as on 31 August 2007.

9.3.16 NHDP VI which has also been approved relates to construction of 1000 km of expressways with full access control on new alignment. The Vadodara–Mumbai corridor (400 km) on NH-8, the highest density corridor, has been prioritized and is likely to be awarded by 2008–09. The balance 600 km will be selected out of the other high density corridor routes identified on the basis of traffic volume. The status of physical parameters of NHDP and other roads, including port connectivity projects, is given in Table 9.3.3.

9.3.17 The approved Special Accelerated Road Development Programme for the North Eastern (SARDP-NE) Region, which envisaged improvement of about 7616 km of road length (3251 km NH and 4365 km of State roads (SRs)/roads of strategic importance), has been subsequently enhanced to 8737 km of road length (3846 km of NHs and 4891 km of SRs/roads of strategic importance). This is to be undertaken in two phases. Implementation of Phase A of SARDP-NE aggregating to 2304 km as also initiating action for preparation of DPRs under Phase B for 6433 km has been approved. A High Powered Inter-Ministerial Committee (HPC) has been set up for co-ordinating the programme, ensuring avoidance of overlapping of various proposals, and sanctioning of individual sub-projects under SARDP-NE. The HPC has so far approved proposals in an aggregate length of 571 km at an estimated cost of Rs 1424 crore covering mainly Assam, Manipur, and Sikkim. The DPRs for the other stretches are under preparation. A provision of Rs 9562 crore (Rs 10814.83 crore at current price) has been made during the Eleventh Plan for this important initiative of road connectivity in the North East.

9.3.18 Regular monitoring of financial and physical progress of works is carried out at various levels with a view to removing bottlenecks. Several initiatives have been undertaken to expedite the implementation of contracts and make improvements in its internal processes, some of which are detailed in Box 9.3.1.

State Highways (SHs) and Major District Roads (MDRs)

9.3.19 The present condition and stage of development of the secondary network varies widely across States. Though reasonable in terms of size, the quality of SHs and MDRs is particularly worrisome. This is mainly because the funds for the development of this secondary system are very inadequate. The NHs and RRs are provided with reasonable funds for their development at the Central level, while the RRs also receive some share at the State level. In the process, the secondary system of roads is neglected.

9.3.20 The result is that there are several deficiencies in the existing SHs and MDRs as a result of (i) inadequate width of carriageway in relation to traffic demand; (ii) weak pavement and bridges; (iii) congested stretches of SHs and MDRs passing through cities/towns; (iv) poor safety features and road geometrics, and inadequate formation width in hilly and mountainous region; (v) missing links and bridges, and (vi) several railway level crossings requiring urgent replacement with ROB/road under bridge (RUB).

TABLE 9.3.3
Status of NHDP and Other NHAI Projects as on 31 August 2007

Project	Length (km)	Already Four-laned (km)	Under Implementation		Yet to be Awarded
			Length (km)	No. of Contracts	
Golden Quadrilateral	5846	5602	244	25	–
North–South/East–West	7300	1418	4903	148	821
Port Connectivity	380	159	215	8	6
Others	962	322	620	16	20
NHDP IIIA	4000	126	1866	31	2008
NHDP V	6500	–	148	2	6352
Total	24988	7627	7996	230	9207

Box 9.3.1
Initiatives taken to Expedite Completion of Quality Road Projects

- Standard format for acquisition of land approved by Ministry of Law, based on which Department of Road Transport and Highways (DoRTH) are to take action on specific proposals for land acquisition.
- For resolving problems in pre-construction activities, regular follow-up meetings are being held with senior officials and specifically designated nodal officers of State Governments.
- In pursuance of decision of CoI, an Empowered Committee of Secretaries has been constituted under the Cabinet Secretary to address Inter-Ministerial and Centre–State issues regarding land acquisition, utility shifting, environmental clearance, etc.
- MOU signed with M/s IRCON for speedy construction of ROBs.
- Works Manual incorporating the Guidelines for procurement of works and consultancy services, compiled by NHAI in July 2006, will guide procurements and management of contracts, including under PPP Projects.
- Action has been taken against defaulting civil contractors: 14 contracts terminated and 17 contractors declared non-performers.
- For ensuring preparation of quality DPRs for civil works, provisions made for peer review, 10% performance guarantee, and penalty for delays and variation of quantities of more than 15%.
- DPR Consultants are now required to co-ordinate at field level with Project Implementation Units (PIUs), NHAI, local officers, and local residents at every stage of preparation of DPR. Proof Consultants are to review the DPR to ensure full compatibility with project requirements, timelines, and detailed guidelines.
- DPR contracts to provide for mandatory continuation of certain key personnel of DPR consultants for a period of at least three to four months after award of civil contracts for technical co-ordination.
- JV partners to compulsorily submit performance security separately from each partner's bank account to the extent of their participation in JV.
- Steps taken to improve cash flow problems of contractors by granting interest bearing discretionary advance at the request of contractor, release of retention money against bank guarantee of equal amount, deferment of recovery of advances (on interest basis), and relaxation in minimum Interim Payment Certificate amount.

9.3.21 The existing road network is under severe strain due to traffic growth, overloading of vehicles, and paucity of funds for road maintenance. A broad assessment shows that over 50% of SHs and MDRs network have poor riding quality. According to one assessment, losses due to poor condition of these roads would be around Rs 6000 crore per annum.

9.3.22 Although, efforts have been made by several States to encourage and attract private sector financing in augmenting capacity of roads and provision of bridges, ROBs, and bypasses, the resources have remained a major constraint in the execution of the programmes for SRs during the Tenth Plan. Other constraints include, inter alia:

Thin Spreading of Resources

- More projects are sanctioned than can be undertaken within the available resources, leading to spreading of available funds thinly and resulting in time and cost overruns.

Delay in Pre-construction Activities

- Work has at times been awarded without acquiring full land for the project. This has affected obtaining the environmental clearance and shifting/removal of utilities.

Weak Management by Contractors

- Although, several measures have been taken by the contracting industry to acquire state-of-art equipment and procure good technical and managerial staff, considerable scope exists for improvement in achieving project management excellence, proper scheduling of human resources, and equipment resources.

Poor Implementation Capacities

- The State Public Works Departments (PWDs) are required to be reoriented for the current needs of modern technology and commercial management principles. There is a need to improve the capacity for planning, designing, and execution of works to meet the transport demand of users in many States. Considerable scope also exists for enhancing the training arrangements of engineering personnel. Side-by-side contracting industry and consultancy sector also need to grow on healthy lines.

RURAL ROADS (RRS)

9.3.23 To boost the rural connectivity, a rural roads programme, the PMGSY was launched as a 100% CSS. It aims to provide all-weather roads by 2003 to habitations with a population of 1000 and above, and by 2007 to those with a population of 500 and above. In respect of hilly/desert/tribal areas, it aims to link habitations with a population of 250 and above.

9.3.24 However, despite all efforts about 35% of all habitations still remain to be connected by all-weather roads. Table 9.3.4 details the progress made in physical parameters of PMGSY by end-March 2007. As may be seen, only 21% of the habitations have been actually connected so far, although 24% were targeted during the Tenth Plan period. To address this slippage, the PMGSY has been re-phased to achieve time-bound targets of rural connectivity by folding it into the Bharat Nirman Programme (initiated in 2005–06). It aims to connect all 1000-plus habitations in rural areas (500-plus for hilly and tribal areas) by 2009. The Bharat Nirman Programme also envisages a massive scaling up of the programme in terms of habitation, connectivity coverage, construction targets, and financial investment.

TABLE 9.3.4
Connectivity Status under PMGSY
(as on 31 March 2007)—Targets versus Achievements

Population Category	No. of Eligible Habitations	Target up to Tenth Plan	No. of Habitations Connected
1000 and above	60030	25371	20478
500 and above	79208	14854	13193
250 and above	39530	2511	3816
Total	178768	42736	37487

Issues in the Construction and Maintenance of Roads

ROAD MAINTENANCE

9.3.25 The road network built at a huge cost needs to be maintained properly to prevent disintegration and deterioration, ensure its continuous utilization in an optimum manner, and ensure road safety to users. However, maintenance of roads, being a non-plan activity, has tended to be neglected in the face of available financial resources. A study by the World Bank estimated that US$ 45 billion invested in main roads in 85 countries had been eroded over the previous 20 years. In India too, some of the excellent roads, constructed with International Development Association loan four decades back, have been reduced to a very poor condition. As the Twelfth Finance Commission has observed, '...it is far more important to ensure that assets already created are maintained and yield services as originally envisaged than to go on undertaking commitments for creating more assets....'. What is important is that repair activities, if required, on the road are to be taken up at an appropriate time, as the rate of progression of deterioration of roads increases rapidly once the deterioration starts. The vehicle operating cost on highways, which is a major component of the total transport cost, is entirely dependent on the condition of the roads. A rupee spent on maintenance saves two to three rupees in vehicle operating cost, besides providing a very cost-effective option to improving traffic flow. Although attention has been given to maintenance work in the Tenth Plan period, there is compelling need to give it overriding priority with increased emphasis on higher standards so as to reduce the frequency of reconstruction.

9.3.26 The maintenance requirement of the high density corridor of NHs under construction and post-implementation is provided by NHAI. However, the non-NHDP NH sections, which are maintained by State PWDs, are poorly managed, primarily because the funds made available to them for maintenance are well short of the requirement as per norms. For NHs, the DoRTH gets only 40% of the total funds required for maintenance of NHs, as per the specified norms. The year-wise details of shortfall are given in Table 9.3.5.

9.3.27 Maintenance of SHs and MDRs has also been suffering from paucity of resources made available for the purpose. Keeping this in view, the Twelfth Finance Commission allocated Rs 15000 crore for maintenance of roads and bridges in the entire country during the period 2006–10. This amount is distributed to the

TABLE 9.3.5
Shortfall in Funds for Road Maintenance in the Tenth Plan

(in Rs Crore)

Year	Requirement as per Norms	Amount Provided	Shortfall	Shortfall (%)
2002–03	2200.00	800.00	1400.00	63.64
2003–04	2200.00	731.74	1468.26	66.74
2004–05	2480.00	745.56	1734.44	69.94
2005–06	2480.00	868.10	1611.90	65.00
2006–07	2480.00	814.38	1665.62	67.16

States on the basis of their road length, with appropriate weights being assigned to different type of roads. For rural roads under PMGSY, there is provision for maintenance for five years following the completion of a project although the long-term issue of maintenance has not been addressed so far.

9.3.28 Besides inadequacy of resources, management of roads is unsystematic and inspections irregular. Maintenance work is done departmentally with disproportionate allocation spent towards the gang establishment. Modern mechanized equipments for road maintenance are not used to the desired degree. There is weak accountability and poor monitoring of the maintenance activities.

9.3.29 The first task is to ensure that the allocation for repair and maintenance is adequate. The Central Road Fund Act 2000, which gave statutory status to the Central Road Fund (CRF), clearly specifies that the fund be meant, inter alia, for development and maintenance of NHs. Despite the clarity in the statutory provision, the entire share meant for the NHs has been appropriated for the NHDP programmes for development and further upgradation of roads. Since maintenance of existing assets is more important than the creation of new ones, all alternatives for making resources available for maintenance must be considered, including possible earmarking of a fixed proportion, say one-third, of the NH share of road cess for maintenance. Likewise, State Governments may have to consider supplementing the allocation for road maintenance from the Twelfth Finance Commission with the State share of road cess. Beginning with the Eleventh Plan, but increasingly in future Plans, resources will have to be found for maintaining the substantial road assets being created in the PMGSY, bearing in mind that the road cess share for rural roads has already been pre-empted for original construction for many years.

9.3.30 Additionally, in NH projects under BOT mode, maintenance is taken care of during the period of concession. For other tollable roads, the Model Concession Agreement (MCA) for Operation, Maintenance, and Tolling (OMT), published by Planning Commission, should be adopted. For non-tollable roads on NHs, SHs, and MDRs, long-term maintenance contracts should be introduced. Other steps to be taken include adoption of Pavement Management Systems (PMS), outsourcing of work, increased mechanization, corridor management, and enforcement of the Control of National Highways (Land and Traffic) Act 2002 (Box 9.3.2).

Modalities for Execution of a Road Project

9.3.31 The problems of development of road networks are diverse and future requirements are of a formidable magnitude. Therefore, the strategy for development of roads would have to vary keeping in view the nature of problem and the development. It has been decided to award all contracts for high-density corridors under NHDP III onwards only on BOT basis, with traditional construction contracts awarded only in specified exceptional cases. However, NHs characterized by low density of traffic and passing through far flung, remote, or strategically important areas would be developed primarily through budgetary resources.

9.3.32 During the Tenth Plan, the total quantum of private sector investment on NHDP has been Rs 6367.25 crore, as against a target of Rs 7580.27 crore. The shortfall in its achievement, especially during 2006–07 (Rs 1578 crore against a target of Rs 2243 crore) is attributable mainly to the teething problems encountered while establishing an appropriate policy and regulatory framework for the PPPs, including their institutional mechanism. However, given the complexity of the PPP contracts and the exposure of the government in such contracts, some standardized structures that provide predictability and mitigate risk to private capital have been put in place. Thus, MCA for BOT projects has been developed to facilitate

Box 9.3.2
Modernization of Maintenance Management

- PMS incorporating a rational method of assessment of distress and decision support system for maintenance activities needs to be introduced for productive use of limited resources. Inventorization programme, including the Road Information System, may be used for PMS.
- Use of machines for repair of distress in pavements and mobile inspection units for proper inspection/distress in bridges to improve maintenance culture should be encouraged.
- Maintenance works hitherto being done departmentally should be outsourced to the private sector to enhance efficiency. Concepts involving OMT contracts need to be extended to NHs with State PWDs.
- Corridor management, including engineering and non-engineering experts, is needed for the proper management and maintenance of NHs section. This would include:
  - Maintenance of roads and bridges to the desired standard.
  - Tackling safety hazards and traffic bottlenecks.
  - Traffic management.
  - Collection of users' fee.
  - Incidence management.
  - Land management.
- Steps need to be taken for enforcing the necessary provision of the Control of National Highways (Land and Traffic) Act 2002, which came into force from January 2005 for safe and speedy movement of traffic on NHs. The Highways Administration has already been established for its enforcement.

speedy award of contracts and the roll out of projects are being accelerated. Besides, MCA for OMT has been published by the Planning Commission. The MCA for Annuity Projects is presently under finalization. The initiatives taken in order to facilitate private sector investment are given in Box 9.3.3.

9.3.33 Although, private sector investment would show an increase during the Eleventh Plan, there would undoubtedly be a limit to road stretches that can be awarded on BOT (Toll) basis. In this mode of delivery, the private sector takes a market risk as the concessionaire not only builds the road and maintains it during the concession period, but also charges toll to recover the cost of construction and maintenance. In view of the uncertainty of future traffic flows and in the cases where toll earning may not fully cover the capital cost, the concessionaire is allowed a VGF of upto

Box 9.3.3
Initiatives taken to Facilitate Private Sector Investment

- In order to maximize the volume of investments in the road sector, given the limited availability of public resources or the need to use them for development of roads in backward/remote areas, it has been decided that all the sub-projects in NHDP Phase III to Phase VII would be taken up on the basis of PPP on BOT mode.
- The government has announced several incentives such as tax exemptions and duty-free import of road-building equipment and machinery to encourage private sector participation.
- The MCA for NHs, which was approved by CoI in 2005, has now been adopted for implementation of PPP projects by Ministry of Shipping, Road Transport, and Highways (MoSRTH)/NHAI; the MCA for SHs has been published by the Planning Commission.
- A review of tolling policy in respect of NHs has been concluded and the report, once finalized, would serve to impart greater certainty in revenue projections for concessionaires.
- Manuals of Standards and Specifications for four-laning and six-laning of NHs through PPPs are under finalization by DoRTH. Adoption of these manuals would reduce project preparation time as project specific manuals would no longer be needed.
- The substantial completion of NHDP Phase I, that is GQ, has called for a shift in emphasis to corridor management so as to deliver maximum throughput in terms of speed and traffic volume, while minimizing operational cost and enhancing road safety. In this regard, an MCA for O&M of Highways has been published by the Planning Commission.

40% of the project cost based on competitive bid for the lowest subsidy. Some projects can also be taken up on BOT (Annuity) mode of delivery basis, wherein tolling is not an integral part of the project and the project is, therefore, essentially a road construction and maintenance arrangement that involves deferred payment by the government. It may not be difficult to find concessionaires willing to take up the project on BOT (Annuity) basis. This mode of delivery, which is not classical PPP, is costlier, and should be the least preferred option.

EXPRESSWAYS

9.3.34 Traffic conditions on the stretches other than those that would be taken up under NHDP VI, whether of two-lane, four-lane, or six-lane, are substantially short of world standards. The mix of motorized and non-motorized traffic on these roads is a huge hurdle. These roads pass through habitations and pedestrians' traffic impedes vehicular traffic flow. Bypasses have been built for some cities but ribbon development and roadside eating establishments abound. In the absence of adequate roadside amenities, roads are also used for parking by trucks encroaching upon the ROW. Intersections have been provided on these highways to enable vehicles to take a U-turn at different places. Vehicles standing in the middle of the road, waiting for the oncoming traffic to stop before turning around constrain the traffic flow. Worse, since there is no restriction on access, it is a common practice all over the country for vehicles to move in the wrong direction in order to avoid driving to the next intersection and coming back.

9.3.35 Another impediment is the stoppage of vehicles at the check posts at State borders even when the vehicle is merely transiting the State. Vehicles moving on inter-state routes remain stationary about 40% of the time in the process of being thus inspected. The World Bank has estimated that truck delays at checkpoints costs the Indian economy anywhere between Rs 900 crore to Rs 2300 crore.[1]

9.3.36 The cumulative result of all deficiencies is that even when the road surface is good and has adequate width, vehicles move at a slow speed. Trucks (with one or two drivers and one helper) travelling from Delhi to Mumbai (1419 km) take three days and those from Delhi to Bangalore (2019 km) four to five days. According to the same World Bank study, 'US equivalent transit times, with one driver operating legally would be two and three days (actually second and third morning), respectively. If the US carrier used two-driver teams, a day would be cut from each movement.' On the average, Indian trucks are used for 60000 km to 100000 km a year, which is less than a quarter of those in developed countries.

9.3.37 A study group of the Ministry of Shipping, Road Transport, and Highways (MoSRTH) set up during the Ninth Plan proposed a total expressways network of about 15600 km by the year 2020 with broad phasing as shown in Table 9.3.6.

TABLE 9.3.6
Phasing of Expressway by the Study Group of MoSRTH

Year	Cumulative Length (km)
2005	4900
2010	10500
2015	14100
2020	15600

More recently, the Tenth Plan Working Group on the road sector had observed 'It is strongly felt that segments of highways where traffic levels in the next five to seven years are assessed to be justifying a six-lane facility (considering both local and long distance inter-city traffic) say traffic exceeding 60,000 PCUs [Passenger Car Units] per day, it would be more prudent to think in terms of an Expressway than opting for widening of existing highway. The need of traffic in the interim period should be met by provision of paved shoulders along existing roads. Maharashtra State provides a good example of the initiative taken by them in going ahead with the construction of Mumbai-Pune expressway.' In 2005, the CoI approved a plan for the construction of NHs during the period 2005–12, which included the construction of 1000 km of expressways under NHDP Phase VI.

[1] *India Road Transport Service Efficiency Study*, World Bank, 2005.

9.3.38 In order to provide world-class road infrastructure during the Eleventh and Twelfth Plans, the NHDP Phase VI would need to be substantially scaled up. Access-controlled expressways best serve to overcome the deficiencies of NHs. Even checking on inter-state traffic can be minimized by requiring that the checks be carried out only at the time of entry into or exit from the expressway network. It is, therefore, necessary to formulate a comprehensive Master Plan for the construction of access-controlled expressways on new alignments and then proceed with land acquisition. Active participation and necessary financial support, especially for acquisition of land by the State Governments, would be essential for developing such expressways. A blueprint for the development of 15600 km of expressways, which may include the GQ and NS–EW corridors is required, using modern scientific methods to determine alignments and avoid habitations as far as possible. The establishment of an Expressways Authority of India to implement the scheme should be considered by the Ministry.

Need for Studying the Capacity of Existing Roads and Revision of Capacity Norms

9.3.39 The design service volume norms that have been developed quite some time back have been used for the purpose of planning. A study on updating of road user cost data (July 2001) carried out by Central Road Research Institute (CRRT) indicates that these norms, particularly those relating to four-lane, may be under-estimated. As a matter of fact, no systematic study has ever been undertaken to determine the capacity of multi-laned roads. The reduction in the difference of speed of various vehicles, change in the mix of traffic as well its pattern, etc., may also have favourable impact on the capacity of various categories of roads. Thus, there is a need to initiate a study on the capacity of highways depending upon the carriageway/roadway widths, etc.

Supply Side Constraints

9.3.40 Apart from the resource constraints, the limited absorptive capacity of certain States, inadequate institutional and implementing capacities, availability/capacity of local contracting and consulting services, and availability of raw materials and human resources are some of the important supply side constraints, especially when a number of competing road projects are under implementation under various initiatives such as the Bharat Nirman Programme, RSVY, etc. The State Government may depute a dedicated team of officials to strengthen and expedite the land acquisition process for projects under NHDP.

9.3.41 The measures to strengthen institutions responsible for developing and maintaining roads, such as NHAI, State PWDs, and Border Roads Organization (BRO), are underway. These include restructuring the NHAI and training technical officers in BRO in project preparation, new specifications, and construction and maintenance technologies. State PWDs need to reorient themselves to meet the challenges from heightened emphasis on private sector participation and large-scale projects funded by multi-lateral agencies. Although, the account codes and works manuals in the State PWDs are well developed, these need to be reviewed and synchronized with upgraded systems adopted at the Central level.

9.3.42 Although, Programme Implementation Units (PIUs) have been established at the district level under PMGSY for planning and executing rural road projects, a single specialized nodal agency, for State-level co-ordination, with responsibility for overall policy, planning, and management of RRs is desirable. As ownership of RRs will rest with the PRIs eventually, capacity is required to be built at the grass-root level by qualified manpower and training.

9.3.43 For RRs, which are essentially low cost roads, use of local materials which are cheap and involve minimum haulage should be maximized. The use of non-conventional road construction material such as industrial wastes and by-products should also be promoted.

Integrated Development of Road Network

9.3.44 The State Governments should consider formulation of an integrated transport plan for development of their road network. The Centre is providing funds for the balanced development of the SRs from the CRF. In this context, it may be mentioned that the SARDP-NE is a major initiative, not only for improving connectivity in hilly/remote areas but also for ensuring integrated development of road works.

Goals and Objectives for the Eleventh Plan

9.3.45 The main thrust is to create world-class road infrastructure, with the objective of improving mobility and accessibility while reducing the cost of transportation. The expanded NHDP when implemented will bring about a major improvement in the riding quality and capacity of around 46000 km of arterial roads out of a total of 66590 km of NHs, which carry around 40% of the road traffic. Some adjustment may be necessary in the NHDP programmes keeping in view the availability of resources. Out of the 20000 km originally envisaged under NHDP Phase IV, it may be possible to take up 6800 km through the BOT route during the Eleventh Plan. The remaining length of roads of 13200 km would be taken up in stretches, which have deteriorated so much that they have become virtually impassable, for Improvement of Riding Quality Programme (IRQP) and strengthening at the estimated cost ranging from Rs 50 lakh per km to Rs 1.75 crore per km. Furthermore, it is necessary to significantly up-scale the expressways project, initially by preparing a blueprint for 15600 km of access-controlled expressways, determining the alignments, and completing the acquisition of land for 6000 km within the Eleventh Plan period. Strict monitoring would be required in order to ensure that construction of 1000 km of expressways is expedited during the Eleventh Plan.

9.3.46 Ensuring a balanced development of the total road network across the country would continue to be an important objective of the Eleventh Plan, including thorough widening of roads, improvement in riding quality and strengthening, road safety measures, and providing world-class wayside amenities to cater to the growing demand for road services. In particular, 100% rural connectivity with all-weather roads to habitations with a population of 1000-plus (500-plus in hilly/tribal areas) is a priority objective under the Bharat Nirman Programme. Inter-modal issues such as road connectivity with airports, railways, ports, etc. are also crucial issues. The broad goals and objectives for road sector development in the Eleventh Plan are given in Box 9.3.4.

Mobilizing Resources

FUNDING FOR NHs

9.3.47 In the past, funds for development of NHs have essentially been provided through the Central Government budget. Fees/tolls levied by the Central Government on bridges on NHs and selected stretches are utilized for upgradation and improvement of roads. Of the Rs 2 per litre cess on petrol and high-speed diesel oil collected by the Central Government and accredited to the Central Road Fund, the cess amount of Rs 1.50 per litre is distributed for development and maintenance of NHs, SRs, RRs, and for the construction and development of ROB/RUB and other safety features, as provided in the CRF Act 2000, in accordance with the prescribed formula. The remaining cess of Rs 0.50 per litre is allocated solely for development and maintenance of NHs. The multilateral financing agencies such as the World Bank and the ADB have been providing loan assistance for highway projects and efforts need to be made to continue tapping this source.

9.3.48 Implementation of NHDP would leave a substantial part of non-NHDP NH network, which would also require development in the Eleventh Plan period. These sections are characterized by low density of traffic. Some of these stretches fall in backward and inaccessible areas, while others are of strategic importance. In fact, the substantial addition made to NH network during the last two Plan periods has led to an increased gap between availability of resources and requirements and thus contributed to poor maintenance and riding quality of the non-NHDP network. The development of these stretches of NHs would be financed primarily through budgetary resources. However, it would be essential to prioritize them in order to ensure that resources are not spread thinly among competing projects, which are responsible for time and cost overruns.

FUNDING FOR SHs

9.3.49 Although State Governments provide funds for SHs, besides allocations from the CRF (of, for instance, Rs 1566 crore during 2007–08), BOT projects are also being encouraged to meet the large financing requirements of SHs in the Eleventh Plan. For this purpose

Box 9.3.4
Road Sector Objectives for the Eleventh Plan

- Develop roads as an integral part of transport system, supplementing other modes, with high priority being accorded to balanced development of road network (primary, secondary and tertiary systems).
- Expedite implementation of enhanced NHDP.
  - Completion of balance work of GQ and North–South and East–West corridors.
  - NHDP Phases III through VII, with reduction in scope of NHDP IV from 20000 km to 6800 km.
  - Restructure NHAI, the main implementing agency of NHDP.
- Phased removal of deficiencies in existing NHs concomitant with development of traffic over the next 10–15 years:
  - Emphasis on augmentation of capacity of high-density corridors.
  - Greater attention to construction of missing links and missing bridges, rehabilitation and reconstruction of weak/dilapidated bridges for traffic safety.
- Formulate comprehensive Master Plan for development of 15600 km of access-controlled expressways:
  - Determine alignments.
  - Acquire land for about 6000 km.
  - Expedite and complete construction of 1000 km.
  - Consider establishing an 'Expressways Authority of India' to implement the Master Plan.
- Prioritize SARDP-NE:
  - Improve connectivity of all State capitals in North East with two- or four-lane NHs with paved shoulders.
  - Connect all district headquarters with two-lane NHs/SHs.
- Prioritize development of high-density corridors in SHs/MDRs.
- Promote private sector participation for development of the national and State roads networks:
  - Adopt BOT (Toll) for construction.
  - Adopt MCA for OMT for tollable roads.
  - Earmark sufficient funds for maintenance for non-tollable roads;
  - Adopt improved maintenance practices NHs/SHs/MDRs.
- Achieve Bharat Nirman time target of providing rural connectivity through all-weather roads to all habitations with a population of 1000-plus persons (500-plus in hilly/tribal areas) by 2009 and thereby improve the quality of life in rural areas and ensure balanced regional development.
- Focus on proper upkeep and maintenance of the existing road network and on attaining higher maintenance standards for optimum utilization of existing network capacity and preserving road assets already created. Adopt modern management techniques for scientific assessment of maintenance strategies/priorities.
- Improve capacities of implementing agencies: NHAI, State PWDs, and BRO.
- Prioritize road safety: prevent overloading of trucks, encroachments, unplanned ribbon development, etc. Focus on issues like energy conservation and environment protection.
- Provide world-class wayside amenities along highways.
- Reduce transportation costs: better riding surface, use of containers, multi-axle vehicles in the haulage of goods, etc.
- Ensure road connectivity where rail link is not possible.
- Integrate road development with railways and other modes of transport.
  - Identify feeder roads to important railway routes and undertake needed improvement including periodic maintenance.
  - Link minor important ports with minimum two-lane NHs/SHs/SRs.
  - Link all inland container depots/CFSs with minimum two-lane NHs/SHs.
- Develop a road data bank, computerize project monitoring system, promote use of information technology in the roads sector.

an MCA for the PPPs in SHs has been published by the Planning Commission and State Governments have been recommended to use it. Further, opportunities for providing VGF of up to 20% of project cost for financing State sector schemes have been made available by the Central Government. Specific initiatives have been taken by some State Governments, in particular, State Governments of Gujarat, Rajasthan, and

Punjab in order to strengthen and upgrade SRs (Box 9.3.5). The possibility of tolling ROBs, constructed at level crossings where heavy traffic crosses the railway line, could be explored and success stories replicated across States. External funding could also be explored as a possible source of finance for the development of selected highways. Some States have established Road Construction Corporations which augment resources through market borrowings.

FUNDING FOR RURAL ROADS (RRS)

9.3.50 In order to augment funding for meeting the time targets of rural connectivity under the Bharat Nirman Programme, it is proposed to borrow Rs 16500 crore from the NABARD by leveraging cess accruals. However, with loan repayments commencing in 2009–10, the amount of cess available (net of repayments) to finance the rural roads programme would be limited in the last two years of the Eleventh Plan. Options to continue leveraging cess, to increase budgetary support and various other strategies for mobilizing funds could be explored (Box 9.3.6).

PHYSICAL TARGETS FOR THE ELEVENTH PLAN

National Highways

9.3.51 High priority is accorded to expeditious completion of the balance works under NHDP Phases I and II and first phase of NHDP Phase III. The GQ is scheduled for substantial completion by December

Box 9.3.5
Innovations by some State Governments

- Crucial role being played by Madhya Pradesh Road Development Corporation and Gujarat State Road Development Corporation (GSRDC) in upgrading SRs using Central Government's VGF which extends subsidy of up to 20% of total project cost and an additional up to 20% financed by State Government. Contribution to GSRDC is also kept to defray expenditure on pre-construction activities.
- PPP (Annuity) model adopted by Gujarat since strengthening/widening of SRs does generate a commercially viable return despite 40% upfront subsidy.
- Adoption of a plan scheme for land acquisition for identified corridors by Punjab to reduce traffic congestion on major highways, with funds proposed to be released on the condition that these shall be recovered by PWD by imposing a cess on sale/purchase and any development activity carried out by the private parties on lands adjoining PWD roads.
- Creation of a Rajasthan State Road Development Fund, through a cess on sale of petrol and high speed diesel, towards extending interest free loan and share capital to the Road Infrastructure Development Company of Rajasthan for projects to upgrade SHs.

Box 9.3.6
Some Options of Resource Mobilization for Rural Roads

Independent Road Fund: There is practically no scope for private sector financing of rural roads since they carry very low volumes of traffic. Creation of an independent road fund in various States, as has been done by a few States such as Uttar Pradesh and Karnataka for maintenance, needs to be explored.

Market Committee Funds: Extension of the scheme of levying marketing fee and rural development cess on agriculture produce to all States with the support of the farmers' community could be explored.

Vehicle Fees: In addition to taxes on fuels, additional funds should be generated through special purchase tax on two wheelers, cars, and agricultural tractors. Part or whole of such funds so collected may be allocated for rural roads and provision of road transport services in rural areas.

Domestic Borrowings: Recently, NABARD in India has come up in a significant way to provide loan assistance for construction of rural roads in several States under RIDF programme. As the financial institution like NABARD may not have the requisite technical expertise, it may be worthwhile to consider providing NABARD loans with technical and management inputs of NRRDA. This would enhance the financial and technical discipline, as well as help in adoption of uniform standards for these roads, on the lines of the PMGSY. This can be channelized by transferring the total loan amount to a pool to be availed of by the States under guidelines similar to that of PMGSY.

2007. North–South, East–West corridors are expected to be substantially completed by December 2009. The other priorities include:

- Complete the first phase of NHDP Phase III by December 2009. Although, the second phase of NHDP Phases III, V (six-laning of 6500 km), and VI (expressways of 1000 km) are scheduled for completion in the Twelfth Plan, their implementation must be strictly monitored in the Eleventh Plan.
- Initiate work for two-laning 6800 km of identified stretches under NHDP Phase IV through the BOT (Toll) mode and construct ring roads of major towns and bypasses and flyovers under NHDP Phase VII.
- Consider establishing an Expressways Authority of India to formulate and implement a Master Plan for 15600 km of access-controlled expressways for high-density corridors and initiate action for determining the alignment and acquiring the land for 6000 km; simultaneously expedite construction of 1000 km of expressways under NHDP Phase VI to provide unhindered, high-speed, and safe movement of traffic.
- Complete SARDP-NE (Phase A) and initiate action to implement Phase B to catalyse development of the NER.
- To keep the balance non-NHDP section in reasonably good shape, earmark a proportion of the cess available for NH exclusively for maintenance.

9.3.52 The targets for stretches other than NHDP have to be prioritized according to their importance to the national economy so that the available resources are not spread thinly among competing projects. The major targets for non-NHDP components include:

- Accelerated efforts to bring NHs network (presently, 20644 km is single lane/intermediate lane) to a minimum of two-lane standard within the next 10 years and four-laning small segments of non-NHDP stretches.
- Removing existing deficiencies, such as inadequate capacity, insufficient pavement thickness, etc., in the road network by strengthening the NH network/improving riding quality.

State Roads (SRs)

9.3.53 Greater focus should be given to augment the capacity and quality of SRs rather than any large-scale expansion. There is a need to identify and develop a core network of major arterial routes covering SHs/MDRs, which are either already experiencing high volumes of traffic or have such potential in the light of industrial and other growth strategies by the public and/or the private sector.

9.3.54 The core network would include expressways, four-laned roads, strengthened pavements, and pavements with good riding quality, bypasses, bridges, etc. for a length of about 71500 km, with a financial outlay of about Rs 80000 crore covering the States. This network could be based on the 'corridor concept', such that a commercial vehicle can cover about 500 km on this network in one day (800 km or more on expressways) with adequate road safety.

9.3.55 Although, it is difficult to precisely estimate physical and financial requirements for upgrading SHs and MDRs without a detailed study of traffic forecasts and their existing conditions by concerned States, it is broadly estimated to amount to Rs 100000 crore for the construction of 300 km of expressways, four-laning 5000 km, and widening to two lanes 40000 km of the core network. For the non-core network in the NER, 2500 km length is to be upgraded for two-laning, and for the other States 10000 km length is to be upgraded to two lanes.

Rural Roads (RRs)

9.3.56 The physical targets set under the Bharat Nirman Programme till the end of 2008–09 are generally found to be beyond the capacity of the States to achieve them. Therefore, the leftover targets of the Bharat Nirman Programme (that is, about 33%) will be completed only in 2009–10. To achieve the targets of the Bharat Nirman Programme, 146185 km of rural roads are proposed to be constructed to benefit 66802 unconnected eligible habitations in the country. It is also proposed to upgrade nearly 1.94 lakh km of the existing rural roads which are identified in the core network. State-wise and year-wise targets for new connectivity, number of new habitations to be connected, and length to be upgraded under the

Bharat Nirman Programme are given in Annexure 9.3.4.

9.3.57 For the remaining two years of the Eleventh Plan, that is 2010–12, targets, both for new connectivity and upgradation, have been specified, leaving 42% of the balance PMGSY works to be completed in the Twelfth Plan, as given in Table 9.3.7.

9.3.58 As per the programme guidelines currently applicable in the plain areas, the eligibility of the habitations getting connected varies from 19% to almost 100% in different States. However, in some hilly States, for instance in Arunachal Pradesh, only 17% of the habitations (466 out of 2741) is eligible for new connectivity under PMGSY because of the very wide spread of smaller habitations. Efforts would, nevertheless, be made to initiate provision of connectivity to even lower order settlements as even such habitations need to have primary access to health, education, and market facilities. The issue of connecting habitations which are not eligible according to the current norms of PMGSY, therefore, will be tackled during the Eleventh Five Year Plan.

OUTLAY FOR THE ELEVENTH PLAN

9.3.59 The Eleventh Plan budgetary support for central sector roads is Rs 72530 crore (Rs 82032.97 crore at current price). The scheme-wise break up GBS at current prices for road sector is given in Appendix (Volume III). In addition, the sector is expected to generate IEBR amounting to Rs 34829 crore and private sector investment of Rs 86792 crore during this period.

ROAD TRANSPORT

Overview

9.3.60 The transport demand for freight and passenger movement within the country is met mainly through road transport and railways. Between these two modes, road transport has steadily expanded its scope of operation and is now not merely a mode for the last haul but is also handling freight over long distances. It also plays a complementary role to railways in moving freight from and to railheads vis-à-vis the Origin-Destination movements of cargo. Its intermodal share in carrying freight, which was around 14% in 1950–51, had increased to around 61% in 2004–05. The share of road transport in passenger movement has also witnessed a quantum jump from 15% in 1950–51 to an estimated 87% of the total traffic by the end of the Tenth Plan.

9.3.61 However, the growth of vehicular traffic on roads has been greater than the growth of the highways, with capacity saturation in the main arteries. Between 1951 and 2004, the vehicle population grew at a CAGR of 10% compared to CAGR of 4.3% in the total road length.

REVIEW OF TENTH FIVE YEAR PLAN

9.3.62 The approved outlay for the Tenth Plan for Central Road Transport Sector was Rs 210 crore, out of which 73% was for road safety and the balance 27% for the Model Driving Training School, pollution testing equipment, and National Database Network. Against this, the total expenditure incurred was 85.41% of the total allocation for the Tenth Plan. Scheme-wise

TABLE 9.3.7
Estimated Targets for the Eleventh Five Year Plan

Period	No. of Habitations to be Covered	Length for New Connectivity (km)	Length for Upgradation (Funded under PMGSY) (km)	Length (km) for Renewal (to be borne by the State Governments)
Target up to the year 2009 as per the Bharat Nirman Programme	30200	62720	43220	51227
Target for 2010–12#	30438	66987	57520	25759
Overall target for the Eleventh Plan	60638	129707	100740	76986

Note: # includes spill-over targets of the Bharat Nirman Programme.

financial and physical performance for the Tenth Plan is given in Annexure 9.3.5.

MODEL DRIVING TRAINING SCHOOL AS CENTRALLY SPONSORED SCHEME

9.3.63 The scheme, started in the Tenth Plan with the objective of imparting training to drivers in order to reduce the rate of accidents, envisages the Central Government assistance in the form of a one-time capital grant for building and other infrastructure of up to 70% of the project cost. The remaining cost, including maintenance and operational cost, is borne by the State Government. During the Tenth Plan, 11 such schools were sanctioned. Although the scheme has been dropped in the Eleventh Five Year Plan, it will need to be replaced by a more broad-based action plan. The State-wise and year-wise allocation and releases are given in Annexure 9.3.6.

PASSENGER SERVICES

9.3.64 Passenger road transport services in India are met by personalized and public transportation. Public transport is provided by the State Road Transport Undertakings (SRTUs) and by private operators. At the end of 2003–04, the country had about 73 million registered automobiles. The composition reveals a dominance of two-wheelers, with a share of more than 71%, followed by cars with 13%, and other vehicles (a heterogeneous category which includes three-wheelers, trailers, tractors, etc.) with 9.4%. The share of buses and trucks in the vehicle population is 1% and 5%, respectively. The share of the personalized modes of transport, viz. two-wheelers, cars, and jeeps increased from 60% in 1951 to 84% in 2004, at the expense of public transport, notably buses, whose share declined from 11.1% in 1951 to 1.1% by the end of 2003–04. Within the buses category, the share of SRTUs in total buses has declined from 37% in 1985–86 to 15.8% in 2002–03 and the share of private buses has risen from 63% in 1985–86 to a lion's share of 84.2% in 2002–03.

STATE ROAD TRANSPORT UNDERTAKINGS (SRTUS)

9.3.65 Of the 53 SRTUs operating in the country, 15 are operated by local bodies and 38 have been established by State Governments under the Road Transport Corporation Act 1950. These 38 SRTUs are estimated to have a total of 1.13 lakh buses, with a total investment of Rs 18669.19 crore, and they provided direct employment to about 7.09 lakh workers during 2006–07.

Physical Performance of SRTUs

9.3.66 The overall productivity of SRTUs improved in the Tenth Plan. Fleet utilization improved from 78.72% in 2002–03 to 82.50% in 2006–07, while vehicle productivity increased from 210 km per bus per day to 229 km per bus per day, staff productivity from Rs 39.23 per worker per day to Rs 39.39 per worker per day, and fuel efficiency from 4.11 km per litre to 4.31 km per litre during the same period.

9.3.67 However, there is wide variation in the performance of physical parameters of various SRTUs. Efficiently run undertakings include those in Haryana, Tamil Nadu, Andhra Pradesh, Rajasthan, Maharashtra, and Karnataka, while the undertakings in Bihar, Jammu and Kashmir, North Eastern States, Punjab Roadways, and Delhi Transport Corporation have considerable scope for improvement. An action plan on Management Monitoring needs to be worked out by these undertakings for speedy improvement in performance of their physical parameters. The State-wise physical performance of SRTUs is given in Annexure 9.3.7.

Financial Performance of SRTUs

9.3.68 The financial performance of the SRTUs has been deteriorating year after year, with their net loss of Rs 1503.02 crore in 2002–03 having increased to Rs 2137.66 crore in 2006–07. Uneconomic passenger fares, high burden of taxes, operations on uneconomic but obligatory routes, concessions in fares provided to certain category of commuters, and high bus staff ratio, and of late, increase in interest burden due to larger institutional borrowings have all contributed to the losses.

9.3.69 Various initiatives taken by SRTUs to improve their physical and financial parameters include route rationalization, introduction of special services such as deluxe buses and night time services, better maintenance practices at depot level, introduction of electronic ticketing, and outsourcing of staff and services. However certain other measures such as providing SRTUs with full reimbursement of cost concessions, allowing SRTUs to make required commercial fare adjustments, rationalization of motor vehicle and related taxes also need to be taken. It is also necessary to rationalize the procedures for award of transport routes to private operators. For commercial routes the private operator should be selected through the process of competitive tendering. As for non-commercial routes, instead of burdening the SRTUs with them, these too should be subjected to the competitive bidding process on the basis of alternatives such as universal service obligation (USO) or VGF models.

Freight Services

9.3.70 Freight movement on the road is predominantly carried out by the private sector truck operators. The volume of freight in BTKM carried by road grew annually at an average rate of 6.5% as compared to 3.6% for railway freight during the last 10 years. The road freight industry is mostly unorganized and highly fragmented with more than 85% of the truck operators owning less than five trucks. The population of goods vehicles has burgeoned from 82000 in 1951 to 8.63 lakh in 1986 (over 10-fold increase), and further to 37.49 lakh in 2004 (increase of 46 times from the 1951 level). This increase signifies the accelerating increase in the demand for road freight services faced by the industry and the subsequent challenges of improving service standards, rationalizing costs, enhancing productivity, and reorganizing the road freight services industry.

Policy Issues

9.3.71 The expected future growth of road transportation for both passengers as well as freight movement is tremendous, due to substantial investments in improvement of reach, capacity, and quality of the NH network. However the sector is beset with low technology, low energy efficiency, high pollution, poor quality roads, and hindered movement of goods and passenger traffic. A number of policy aspects are to be addressed for gearing up the Indian road transport sector to meet the challenges of further growth.

Need to Strengthen the Public Transport System

9.3.72 Public transport causes lesser environmental damage in terms of air and noise pollution, optimization of road space, increased per unit throughput, and reduction in traffic congestion, as compared to personalized vehicles. However, the composition of vehicle population in India is skewed towards personalized transport. The role of both public and private sector is crucial. Considering the advantage of public transport there is a need to strengthen the public transportation services through a policy regime, which fosters their financial viability and grants them more functional autonomy. They may be allowed to fix commercial fares based on a formula approved by the respective State Governments. The PSUs may also be reimbursed full cost of concessions provided to various categories of passengers.

Private Sector Participation

9.3.73 Almost all State Governments have facilitated entry of private sector in providing passenger transport services to ease pressure on the public sector. As on 31 March 2004, the share of private buses was 85%. Private bus operators have, however, exhibited deplorable quality of service, with disregard to traffic rules, unsafe driving practices, unscheduled operation, and usage of irrational cost cutting measures and tax evasion. The private sector has also adversely affected the performance of public sector by resorting to unfair competition.

9.3.74 A prerequisite is, therefore, to strictly enforce rules, for which specially designated regulatory bodies need to be set up, with powers to lay down minimum basic service standards, impose heavy fines, suspend or even cancel licenses, and launch and pursue prosecutions for accidents vigorously.

Pollution Control and Energy Conservation

9.3.75 Rapid growth of motorized vehicles in the country over last one decade has raised the demand for petroleum fuel, resulting in increased vehicle pollution. The Central Government has taken measures to bring down the existing sulphur content level of 0.5% in diesel to 0.10% in phases by introducing the following emission norms during the Tenth Plan:

- Bharat Stage II emission norms extended to entire country in respect of all categories of motor vehicles w.e.f. 1 April 2005 in respect of vehicles manufactured after 1 April 2005.

- Bharat Stage III emission norms have been introduced w.e.f. 1 April 2005 in respect of four-wheeled vehicles manufactured on and from 1 April 2005 in the National Capital Region (NCR) and cities of Mumbai, Kolkata, Chennai, Bangalore, Hyderabad, including Secundarabad, Ahmedabad, Pune, Surat, Kanpur, and Agra except for four-wheeled transport vehicles plying on interstate permits, national permits, or all-India tourist permits within the jurisdiction of these cities. The emission norms for tractors have also been upgraded. While Bharat (Trem) Stage II norms have come into force from 1 June 2003, the Bharat (Trem) Stage III norms have come into force from 1 October 2005.

9.3.76 The emission norms are being revised apace with international emission norms. Enforcement, however, is sadly lacking, and there may be improvements by accrediting private sector institutions to complement the responsible governmental agencies. Under the Motor Vehicles Act, the authorized testing stations issue certificate of fitness for transport vehicles. The State Governments are empowered to authorize any agency through a notification.

Barrier Free Movement of Freight and Passengers

9.3.77 Barriers to inter-state movement, through multiple checking by the police, sales tax department, transport department, and excise and custom, entailed huge economic costs in the range of Rs 3200 crore to Rs 4300 crore in 2004 which are estimated to progressively increase to Rs 60168 crore by 2017.

9.3.78 By way of remedy, apart from introducing online information network for registration and tax administration at national, regional, and local level, and different colour-codes for the number plate of trucks that move inter-state, the concept of 'Green Channel' may also be promoted, initially for high-value freight and perishable commodities, by certifying the consignment at the origin and transmitting the required documents to the authorities for an unhindered journey to their destination.

Motor Vehicle Taxation

9.3.79 The existing tax structure for CVs shows wide variations across States due to different classification principles for the taxation of vehicles, variations in the application of lifetime and annual tax rates to vehicle categories, use of specific and ad valorem rates, and the multiplicity of rates. There is a need to study the economic implications of rationalization of the tax structure across the country in terms of its impact on the reduction of transaction costs. Vehicle taxation is road damage related, but levied on the basis of gross vehicle weight rather than on potential axle loads, resulting in under-taxation of two-axle trucks compared to multi-axle vehicles, and should be changed for goods vehicles from gross vehicle weight to axel loads.

Overloading

9.3.80 To check overloading, Weigh in Motion (WIM) bridges need to be installed at selected points on NHs, inter-state check posts, industrial areas, etc., with facilities for unloading and temporary warehousing of excess loads. The Honourable Supreme Court has held that the excess load needs to be variably off-loaded even if the offence is compounded. The Government of India has recently proposed to expand the area of overloading offence of the Motor Vehicles Act 1988 by introducing the Motor Vehicle Bill 2007. The proposed extension makes the common carrier and consignor also liable for overloading along with vehicle owner (who is already covered under the present Act) and would therefore discourage the extensive operation of illegal overloading on goods.

Road Safety

9.3.81 The number of accidents has quadrupled from 1.1 lakh in 1970 to 4.3 lakh in 2004, with 92618 persons killed in accidents (one fatality per 4.6 accidents) and 464521 persons injured in 2004. The social cost impact of road accidents is 3% of the GDP.

9.3.82 Road safety is a multi-dimensional issue, incorporating development and management of road infrastructure, provision of safer vehicles, legislation and law enforcement, mobility planning, provision of health and hospital services, child safety, and urban land use planning. The success of road safety strategies also depends upon a broad base of support and common action from all stakeholders. Its existing institutional set up is multi-tier, with MoSRTH, National Road Safety Council, and the Transport Development

Council at the Centre, State Transport Department and State Road Safety Councils at the State level, and finally, organizations and agencies involved including the police, Indian Road Congress, CRRI, Central Institute of Road Transport (CIRT), NGOs, and academic institutes.

9.3.83 In order to assess the magnitude of road traffic injuries and fatalities in India and to suggest measures for rescue and relief of accident victims, an EC of India was constituted. The Committee has recommended setting up of a National Road Safety and Traffic Management Board to lay down standards and guidelines as well as to oversee and coordinate all activities pertaining to road safety at Centre as well as State level for promoting and improving traffic management in India. The Report is under active consideration.

9.3.84 With a view to reducing accidents, injuries, and deaths during the Eleventh Five Year Plan, some more measures need to be taken. Road safety audit on all NHs should be made mandatory at different stages of the projects, coupled with a stringent highway patrolling system. Trauma care centres need to be established, accident-prone spots need to be identified, and their road geometry improved. There is a need to upgrade all urban and rural roadside furniture standards to international best practices, coupled with review of road design, road maintenance, and traffic management. Strict enforcement of the Motor Vehicle Act to ensure adherence of traffic rules is vital.

Human Resource Development

9.3.85 The human resources requirement is estimated to grow from 12.83 million in 2007 to 17.64 million in 2012, out of which 66% will be drivers, four-fifth of which in turn would be absorbed in goods vehicle category. To substantially improve driving skills and enlarge the pool of drivers, institutions such as the ITIs and CIRT need to create competent driver training instructors with training of trainers by accredited institutions. Adequate infrastructure facility including driving tracks needs to be provided near the cities for use by driving schools. Many initiatives have been taken up both by the government and the private sector to promote road safety education and driving training facility in India, which include the Institute of Driving Training and Research (IDTR) which is a joint venture between the Department of Transport, Government of Delhi, and Maruti Udyog Limited; Automobile Association of Upper India (AAUI) Driving School (which also provides electronic simulator based training facilities); Institute of Road Traffic Education and Driver Training Institute by Ashok Leyland in Burari, near Delhi, in partnership with the Government of Delhi. Such initiatives inviting automobile manufacturers and insurance companies for providing training to drivers of automobiles need to be encouraged. The minimum educational qualification for obtaining a driving license needs to be increased from the passing certificate of Class VIII to Class XII in the future.

Research and Development (R&D) to Improve Vehicle Efficiency

9.3.86 R&D efforts should be focused on bus body design, with emphasis on energy conservation and eco friendliness; propulsion technology for use of hybrid cells, bio fuels, etc.; and developing appropriate transmission systems for urban driving conditions.

Database

9.3.87 Motor Vehicles Act provides for maintenance of State registers of motor vehicles. An IT-based centralized vehicle registration system; depository of motor vehicle registration by assigning unique number similar to permanent account number; data on tax paying and non-tax paying vehicles; public surveys to measure freight/passenger movement by road, with time motion surveys of trucks to assess transaction costs are required to be established.

Non-motorized Transport (NMT)

9.3.88 The status of NMT needs to be studied and appropriate infrastructure created coupled with enactment of safety code for NMT to reduce the risks borne by cycles, walk trips, and the like. This will also help to free road space for motorized transport.

OUTLAY FOR THE ELEVENTH PLAN

9.3.89 The Central Sector outlay for road transport sector for the Eleventh Five Year Plan at current price is Rs 1131.00 crore, which would be budgetary support.

The scheme-wise details are given in the Appendix (Volume III).

9.3.90 The total projected outlay for the Eleventh Plan outlay for DoRTH is Rs 108359 crore at 2006–07 price (Rs 122557 crore at current price) which includes Rs 73530 of GBS at 2006–07 price (Rs 83164 crore at current price) and Rs 34829 crore of IEBR at 2006–07 price (Rs 39393 crore at current price).

9.4 SHIPPING

SIGNIFICANCE OF SHIPPING

9.4.1 The recent accelerated growth in Indian economy and trade underscores the increasing criticality of the shipping sector for India, as the bulk of the country's Export-Import trade takes place through the maritime route. One of the objectives of the Foreign Trade Policy 2004–09 is 'to double our percentage share of global merchandise trade within the next five years' taking it to 1.5%. With 8.42 million gross tonnages (GT), India stands at the 20th rank among maritime nations, in terms of fleet size, with a share of 1.19% of the world fleet.

9.4.2 Indian tonnage was practically stagnant till 2004–05, but reforms introduced in that year stimulated a burst of growth in 2005–06. The Shipping Corporation of India (SCI), a PSU under the Department of Shipping, has a major share in India's shipping tonnage. A feature of recent experience in India's shipping sector is the sharp decline in the share of Indian ships in the carriage of India's overseas trade from 31.5% in 1999–2000 to 13.7% in 2004–05. Indian shipping fleet is characterized by the predominance of oil tankers and bulk carriers. While oil tankers account for 60.6% of the total tonnage, bulk carriers account for 29.6%, with the other vessel types such as liner vessels, OSVs accounting for a mere 9.8%.

REVIEW OF THE TENTH PLAN

9.4.3 During the Tenth Plan, shipping tonnage witnessed a rise from 560 vessels carrying 6.82 million GT to 787 vessels amounting to 8.60 million GT. A total of 227 vessels of 1.78 million GT were added to the fleet as against a target of 156 vessels of 3.26 million GT.

9.4.4 The main reason for the fleet growth in 2005–06 was the change in fiscal regime applicable to the sector. Tonnage Tax was introduced in 2004–05 and was further extended to dredgers in 2005, as an alternative to regular corporate tax, thereby reducing tax to a nominal rate and making profits from shipping exempt from tax if they were used for creating an investment fund for acquisition of new tonnage. Expansion of cargo volumes due to rapid growth of the economy and the increased availability of low cost capital due to liberalized policy governing external commercial borrowings also boosted acquisitions.

9.4.5 An outlay of Rs 7753.85 crore was provided in the Tenth Plan for the shipping sector. Against this, the expenditure was Rs 2991.62 crore, accounting for 38.6 % of the total outlay. The scheme-wise details are given in Table 9.4.1.

TABLE 9.4.1
Financial Performance of the Shipping Sector in the Tenth Plan

(In Rs Crore)

S No.	Scheme/Programme	Financial Performance—Tenth Plan		
		Approved Tenth Plan Outlays	Approved Annual Plan Outlays	Actual Expd.
1.	SCI	5800.00	6378.95	2380.94
2.	DG (S)	288.84	58.03	59.91
3.	DG (LL)	185.00	132.00	67.41
4.	IWT	903.00	615.57	475.87
5.	Information Technology	–	7.49	7.49
6.	Unallocated	577.01	–	–
	Total	7753.85	7192.04	2991.62

Note: Expd.= Expenditure

STRATEGIES FOR ELEVENTH PLAN

9.4.6 As recognized in the Report of the EC to Review Indian Shipping headed by Dr Rakesh Mohan (2002), 'Shipping is not a stand-alone industry and has got collateral linkages with several other industrial activities of considerable economic consequence', the Report goes on to give the assessment, 'Having regard to the combined impact of the mother industry i.e. Shipping and its satellites, the net aggregate contribution to the national economy could well be of the order of 2.5–3% of the national GDP.' In light of this and in order to maximize gains from the growth of merchandise trade, it is imperative that the shipping tonnage grows steadily along with trade. Retained earnings from the shipping sector are as important as export earnings from important service sectors such as IT and ITES.

9.4.7 A national shipping fleet commensurate with our overseas cargo needs would help in reducing the freight costs of Indian cargo. Transchart and 'right of first refusal' policy also help to discourage undue freight increases. A thriving shipping sector encourages the growth of associated industry and services providers required for servicing this industry, accounting to over 75% of the shipping sector's national contribution. Most importantly, national tonnage is decisive in maintaining the supply line of essential cargo during international emergencies, as was also demonstrated during the Iraq war, when every drop of crude imports from the Middle East came on Indian Ships.

Increase in Tonnage

9.4.8 During the Eleventh Plan, it would be possible to achieve a tonnage target of 10 million GT. An environment conducive to the growth of Indian shipping can be fostered by fiscal rationalization, strengthening of regulatory mechanism, and increased focus on maritime training. If supportive policy measures as detailed below are taken, acquisition of vessels up to 12 million GT and 15 million GT may be achieved. These scenarios are given in Table 9.4.2, along with their required investments.

TABLE 9.4.2
Increase in Tonnage

	Tonnage Target	Additional Ships		Investment (in Rs Crore)
		Numbers	Tonnage	
Scenario 1	10 m GT	279	4.6 m GT	35000
Scenario 2	12 m GT	404	6.2 m GT	55000
Scenario 3	15 m GT	609	9.2 m GT	80000

Fiscal Regime Rationalization

9.4.9 Ship owners can shift registrations easily and consequently they move to regimes where the tax regime is least onerous. The favourable effect in India of the introduction of the Tonnage Tax as seen initially, quickly evaporated because of the lower taxation in other regimes, estimated by the industry to be of the order of 5%–6%. There is an urgent need to study the cumulative incidence of taxes on ships registered in India vis-à-vis the incidence in other jurisdictions so that necessary measures can be taken to reduce or eliminate the disparity in tax treatment. Another aspect, which translates itself into a tax-related disadvantage for the ships with Indian flags, is that national manning is compulsory for them. The company has to make withholding tax payments for Indian seafarers since they are not exempt from income tax. As this obligation does not devolve on ships registered in other jurisdictions and employing Indian seafarers, the result is that the Indian ships have to pay a higher salary. It is critical for the growth of shipping in India that a level playing field is created as compared to other regimes in respect of taxes.

Cargo Support

9.4.10 The continuation of the policy with respect to government owned and controlled cargo to be imported on FOB basis and shipping arrangements to be channelized through the Department of Shipping's Chartering Wing, Transchart would be advisable. This policy, which is similar to that followed in some developing countries, has proved to be advantageous not only by providing cargo support to Indian ships, but also by enabling the buyers/receivers to retain control over shipping arrangements and shipment schedules according to their import requirements. The assurance of cargo support encourages new entrants and mitigates the risks of tonnage and fleet expansion for existing companies.

Maritime Human Resource Development and Training

9.4.11 India has positioned herself as a major human resources-supplying nation to the maritime industry. As a result of the initiatives taken by the government in encouraging private participation in maritime training, the number of maritime training institutes under the assurance of quality training by the Directorate General of Shipping DG(S) rose to 128 in 2005. India's share of global maritime human resources rose to 26950 officers and 75650 ratings, comprising an estimated 6% of the world's seafarers. The Eleventh Plan target for the marine training programme is to retain our 6% share of the global workforce and additionally supplying 20% of the current estimated shortages.

9.4.12 By virtue of income tax applicable to Indian seafarers, Indian ship owners are at an inherent disadvantage as foreign flag vessels become the first choice for Indian seafarers and the best talent is denied to the local shipping industry. Moreover, it is mandatory for Indian ships to employ Indian seafarers compounding the problem further. It would be necessary to review this restriction so that the Indian shipping industry may not face human resources shortage.

9.4.13 Policy initiatives are required to retain and build talent. In the area of maritime training, although the intake capacities at all training institutes for officers have risen from 2185 in 2000 to 5263 in 2006 and for ratings to 4726 in 2006 to reach the necessary targets, there is a shortage of sea-time berths to absorb the number of pre-sea officers and ratings trainees. Thus, there is a need to shift the focus in strategy from increasing cadet intake at pre-sea levels to more sea-time training slots. Initiatives for this could include the co-option of the member lines of the INSA into allocating 10% of each ship's manning scales exclusively for sea training berths at the cost of these future employers.

9.4.14 With the objective of providing world-class training opportunities for the shipping sector, the government would be establishing an Indian Maritime University (IMU) at Chennai, with campuses at Kolkata, Mumbai, and Vishakhapatnam, through an Act of Parliament. IMU would play the role of a centralized nodal agency for co-ordinating, monitoring, and controlling maritime training in India, through nation-wide rating, consolidation, and reorganization of training systems under IMU. This would facilitate and promote maritime studies and research in emerging areas such as marine science and technology and marine environment. The aim of IMU would be to become a centre of excellence in the content and quality of maritime training and also seek affiliation to the World Maritime University.

9.4.15 There is also a need for capacity building in the DG(S), with greater technological tools, training, human resources availability, and greater autonomy for authorizing surveyor movement to ships on foreign shores and deciding on the delegation of powers to Mercantile Marine Department.

Other Issues

9.4.16 In view of the increasing traffic in territorial waters, and with a growing fleet, marine disaster and emergency response system should be established. For the protection of the environment, it is also necessary to develop a 'Ballast Water Management System' in accordance with the requirements of International Convention for the Control and Management of Ships as adopted by the IMO in 2004, along with the development of waste disposal facilities in ports. Further, in the interest of safe operations of OSVs, a regulatory mechanism should be developed for this sector.

COASTAL SHIPPING

9.4.17 Coastal shipping serves as an integral part of the supply chain in the domestic and overseas trade of merchandise. It is a viable, eco-friendly alternative to the already stretched rail and road infrastructure with low socio-economic cost. Apart from their substantial contribution to the nation's trade and economy, shipping services also play a crucial role as the major source of income for the population in many of the coastal States and act as the lifeline especially for places such as Andaman & Nicobar Islands and Lakshadweep Islands. During 2004–05, the coastal traffic at major ports was 109.80 mt, accounting for 28.6% of the total major ports traffic and growing at 5.81% CAGR. India's coastal traffic is estimated to increase from 116 mt in

2002–03 to 220 mt by the end of the Eleventh Plan period (2012). A total of 497 vessels of 8.17 lakh GT comprised the Indian coastal vessels tonnage as on 31 March 2006. During the last decade, coastal shipping has exhibited significant growth in smaller size vessels such as liners, passenger-cum-cargo launches, tugs, ro-ros, dredgers, pilot/survey launches, etc. At present, coastal shipping also includes activities like offshore supply and multi-purpose support for the oil and gas exploration and production, port and harbour services, and dredging.

9.4.18 With a view to encouraging the growth of Indian coastal shipping, during the Plan period the government had accorded various concessions and initiatives to this sector such as certain relaxations in customs procedures, benefit of tonnage tax, lower vessel and cargo related charges at ports, and provision of dedicated terminals for coastal shipping. In addition to its economic advantages coastal shipping also eases traffic congestions which occur frequently in road transport. Despite the inherent advantages, coastal shipping is hampered by inadequate port and landside infrastructure, the burden of customs duties, cumbersome procedures, and poor port productivity. Considering the positive externalities of coastal shipping, there is a need to consider fiscal incentives for registered multi-modal transport operators, shippers, trade/industries that prefer transporting sizeable domestic cargoes through coastal shipping.

9.4.19 For improving infrastructure facilities for coastal shipping, it is important to provide adequate rail and road connectivity to each port along with the development of required infrastructure for encouraging emerging areas with promising potential in coastal shipping sector. Berthing capacities at Indian ports may be developed to address the needs of coastal shipping and berth space at all terminals may be reserved for coastal shipping vessels, if so required.

9.4.20 Other policy initiatives relate to manning requirements, training initiatives, and surveying. Although the manning scale of coastal vessels has been reviewed in the last few years with an objective to simplifying the same, yet it requires further rationalization. Adequate facilities may be instituted for training the floating staff to ensure that the operating standards are upheld and adequately trained hands are available. It is suggested that a Special Training Programme may be designed specifically for coastal shipping to produce and retain more cadet officers for employment only on Near Coastal Voyages. Since there is a shortage of surveyors, with a view to avoiding delays to vessels, the work of surveying may be assigned to classified surveyors.

Multi-modal Transportation

9.4.21 The growth of multi-modalism globally, fuelled by increasing trade, containerization, and reducing logistics costs, has impacted the Indian shipping scenario. The physical infrastructure required to propel the multi-modal movement in India is being addressed in terms of investments in port capacities and infrastructures, port to hinterland connectivity, and port–rail–road interfaces. However, there is also a need to simultaneously address policy issues such as regulation of services, co-ordination in planning, and simplification of processes and procedures in customs. The multi-modal transportation in India is governed by the Multimodal Transportation of Goods Act 1993 which needs to be strengthened in order to address issues such as liability regime, setting of service standards, registration of service providers, etc. in order to provide transparency in operations.

Shipping Corporation of India (SCI)

9.4.22 An outlay of Rs 5800 crore was provided in the Tenth Plan for SCI. This included a sum of Rs 1290 crore as internal resources and Rs 4510 crore as external borrowings. Against this outlay, the expenditure was Rs 2381 crore or 41.1% of the total outlay. Due to the speculation regarding its disinvestment, the SCI could only acquire 9 vessels of 0.79 million GT against the target of acquisition of 39 vessels of 2.10 million GT.

9.4.23 The profitability of SCI increased during the Plan. The net profit increased from Rs 241.6 crore to Rs 1042.2 crore and the fixed assets increased from Rs 3463.6 crore to Rs 5729.8 crore. As a result, net worth of the SCI rose from Rs 2095.6 crore to Rs 4355.4 crore during the same period, reflecting a rise in the level of reserves and surplus from Rs 1852.1 crore to Rs 4077.8

crore. The dividend payment also increased from Rs 98.8 crore in 2001–02 to Rs 239.9 crore in 2005–06.

9.4.24 The SCI plans to acquire 62 vessels of various categories during the Eleventh Plan period.

Directorate General of Shipping, DG(S)

9.4.25 The DG(S), a statutory authority under the Merchant Shipping Act 1958, is responsible for implementing the Act. During the Tenth Plan, the approved outlay for DG(S) was Rs 288.84 crore for the implementation of e-governance, execution of civil works, etc., including an IEBR component of Rs 200 crore for acquisition of simulators under grant-in-aid from the Government of Japan for the maritime training institutes under Indian Institute of Maritime Studies. However, this did not materialize and against the remaining amount of Rs 88.84 crore under GBS, the total anticipated expenditure is Rs 63.94 crore.

9.4.26 In the Eleventh Plan period, DG(S) proposes to carry out activities for strengthening the Mercantile Marine Department, procuring modern survey instruments for Minor Ports Survey Organization (MPSO), and establishing the IMU.

Lighthouses and Lightships

9.4.27 The Directorate General of Lighthouses and Lightships, DG(LL) provides marine aids to navigation along the Indian coast. At present, there are 169 lighthouses, 1 lightship, 22 differential global positioning systems (DGPS), 48 racons, and 22 deep sea lighted buoys available as aids to marine navigation. DGLL also earns revenue, deriving its income from light dues from ships entering and leaving Indian ports.

9.4.28 During the Tenth Plan, the anticipated revenue earning by DGLL is Rs 507 crore. Against the Plan outlay of Rs 185 crore, the expenditure in this sector is expected to about 45.9% of the outlay at Rs 85 crore. The major achievements are placement of work order for establishment of Vessel Traffic Service for Gulf of Kachch, installation of racons, and introduction of DGPS. To a certain extent, the progress of projects got affected due to tsunami damages along the East Coast and Andaman and Nicobar Islands, entailing priority restoration work.

9.4.29 In the Eleventh Plan, the Directorate would be taking up new projects such as visual aids, radio aids, development of information technology, replacement of assets and flotilla, along with new initiatives such as rendering assistance for improvement of local lights, beautification of lighthouses for attracting tourists, establishment of the National Automatic Identification System network, and the Vessel Traffic Service in the Gulf of Khambat.

Inland Water Transport (IWT)

9.4.30 India has about 14500 km of navigable waterways which comprises rivers, canals, backwaters, creeks etc. About 45 million tons of cargo (2.5 BTKM) is being moved annually by IWT. Inland Waterways Authority of India (IWAI) was constituted in 1986 for the development and regulation of inland waterways for shipping and navigation. However, most waterways suffer from navigational inadequacies such as shallow waters, narrow width, siltation, and bank erosion. Consequently, its operations are currently restricted to about 5200 km of major rivers and 485 km of canals suitable for mechanized craft operations. Today, there are three waterways that have been declared as National Waterways (NWs), namely Ganga from Haldia to Allahabad (1620 km); Brahmaputra from Dhubri to Dadiya (891 km); and West Coast Canal from Kottapuram to Kollam, including Champakara and Udyogmandal canals (205 km), with the declaration of three more waterways being considered. At present, organized cargo transportation is spread over the Ganga river in NW-I, the Brahmaputra river in NW-II, West Coast Canal in NW-III, and Goa and Mumbai waterways. The States covered are Uttar Pradesh, Bihar, Jharkhand, and West Bengal under NW-I; Assam under NW-II; and Kerala under NW-III. A number of private operators provide their services in all the three NWs whereas the public sector Central Inland Water Transport Corporation operates on NWs I and II.

9.4.31 The cargo movement by IWT increased from 197.65 lakh tonnes (1 BTKM) in the Ninth Plan to 504.13 lakh tonnes (2.82 BTKM) by 2005–06. An outlay of Rs 903 crore was approved for IWT in the Tenth Plan, against which an expenditure of Rs 275 crore or 30% of the outlay has been made. The approved Plan outlay for IWAI was Rs 626.73 crore against which an expenditure of Rs 386.74 crore or 62% of the outlay was made. The expenditure was mainly incurred on the maintenance of fairway including procurement of vessels for channel development (dredgers, survey launches, etc.), setting up of terminals, provision of navigational aids, procurement of cargo vessels for demonstration purpose, techno-economic feasibility studies on other waterways, assistance to States under CSS, and Inland Vessel Building Subsidy Scheme to entrepreneurs for procurement of IWT vessels.

9.4.32 With a view to providing an impetuous to the development of IWT mode, the Government of India had approved the Inland Water Transport Policy which includes several fiscal concessions and policy guidelines for the development of IWT, including encouraging private sector participation in the development of infrastructure and ownership and operation of inland vessels. IWAI is also authorized for establishing joint ventures and undertaking equity participation in BOT projects.

9.4.33 The CIWTC was earlier also engaged in activities of ship-building and ship repair, apart from operating a fleet of vessels. Following continuous losses since its inception and the decision to restructure CIWTC, Rajabagan Dockyard has been transferred to Garden Reach Ship Builders and Engineers on 1 July 2006 on outright sales basis. In respect of decision on writing off interest and conversion of outstanding principal amount into equity, a suitable provision has been made in the Supplementary Budget 2006–07 by the Minister of Finance. Regarding disinvestment of CIWTC and Voluntary Retirement Scheme (VRS), the government is in the process of assessing viability of disinvestment with different sets of employee number.

POLICIES AND PROGRAMMES IN THE ELEVENTH PLAN

9.4.34 The focus in the Eleventh Plan would be to put requisite infrastructure on the existing waterways to make them fully functional, along with the development of new waterways. By the end of the Eleventh Plan, three waterways, namely, canal system from Kakinada to Pondicherry integrated with Godavari and Krishna rivers (1095 km), East Coast Canal integrated with Brahmani river and Delta of Mahanadi river (623 km), and Barak river in Assam (152 km) are to be added to the existing three NWs, taking the coverage up to 4500 km.

9.4.35 For IWT to play a more meaningful role in multi-modal transportation, the planning and development process for IWT requires a structured and scientific approach. The investments required for augmenting the existing IWT infrastructure need to consider overall, end-to-end traffic movement and the requisite phasing of the project for holistic growth. The entire process of project formulation and approvals need to be systemized. IWAI may prepare a comprehensive proposal for each waterway for approval of Expenditure Finance Committee/Public Investment Board (EFC/PIB) and funds may be released according to the phasing as approved for these projects. The IWAI needs to identify some viable stretches and their development may be accorded high priority. Ministry of Shipping needs to formulate the development programme on the above lines.

9.4.36 During the Eleventh Plan, emphasis would be laid on co-operation with Bangladesh for achieving higher exports and better connectivity to NER, by adding more protocol routes, more ports of call, and improved cargo handling facilities on protocol routes. Uniformity in the legal regime and conducive, hassle-free inter-state IWT operations must also be fostered. Amendments in the Indian Vessels (I.V.) Act 1917 may be considered along with formulation of model IV rules framed by IWAI, for State Governments to follow.

OUTLAY FOR THE ELEVENTH PLAN

9.4.37 The Eleventh Plan outlay for the shipping sector is Rs 1000 crore at 2006–07 price (Rs 1131 crore at current price). The scheme-wise break-up of GBS at current prices is given in the Appendix (Volume III). The sector is also expected to generate IEBR amounting to Rs 12285 crore at 2006–07 price. In addition, the budgetary support for ship-building and repairs is Rs 150 crore (Rs 170 crore at current price). The IEBR for this sector is Rs 550 crore at 2006–07 price.

9.5 PORTS

9.5.1 Ports constitute the inter-modal interface between maritime and road and rail transport. India has a coast line of around 7517 km with 12 major ports and 187 notified non-major (minor/intermediate) ports along the coast line and sea islands. Almost 95% by volume and 70% by value of India's global merchandise trade is carried through the sea route. In 2006–07, the 12 major ports handled about 73% of the maritime cargo of the country. The balance 27% was handled by the non-major ports. Overseas cargo accounts for about 77% of the total cargo handled at Indian ports. Of the 12 major ports, 11 are administered by the respective Port Trusts and Ennore Port, the 12th major port, which started functioning in February 2001, is corporatized.

REVIEW OF THE TENTH PLAN

Traffic and Capacities

9.5.2 The projected traffic for the Tenth Plan period was 415 million tonnes for the major ports and 150 million tonnes for the minor ports, making an overall target of 565 million tonnes. The achievements have been more than the targets in the case of major ports and are likely to exceed the targets in the case of non-major ports also. Major ports have handled 463.84 million tonnes and non-major ports are expected to have handled around 171.92 million tonnes during 2006–07. The actual traffic handled as on 31 March 2006 is 423.42 million tonnes at major ports and 151.14 million tonnes at non-major ports. The commodity-wise traffic handled in the terminal year of the Tenth Plan is given in Table 9.5.1 and year-wise details are given in Annexure 9.5.1. Year-wise and port-wise (major ports) physical achievements are given in Annexure 9.5.2.

9.5.3 The increase of about 70 million tonnes over the target is primarily due to the increase in quantum of iron ore exports to countries such as China, Japan, and South Korea. The traffic in fertilizer (including FRM), break bulk cargo, and containers also exceeded the projections. On the other hand, there was a shortfall in POL, since the port facilities of Nagarjuna Oil Refineries Ltd and LNG handling facilities at Ennore and Cochin expected to be commissioned during the Plan period did not materialize. There is also a shortfall in coal traffic against the projections as the new power plants expected to come up at New Mangalore and Mumbai have not materialized.

9.5.4 The actual capacity of major ports at the start of the Tenth Plan was 343.95 million tonnes which was targeted to go upto 470.60 million tonnes by the end of the Tenth Plan. However, the actual capacity of major ports at the end of the Tenth Plan is likely to have gone upto 504.75 million tonnes by 31 March 2007, showing an increase of 160.80 million tonnes during the Plan period. Such capacity addition was achieved as a result of implementation of spill-over schemes of the Ninth Plan as well as new schemes during the Tenth Plan and improvement in productivity. Thus, the capacity of 504.75 million tonnes of major ports at the end of the Tenth Plan was a little over the actual traffic of 463.84 million tonnes. There has to be

TABLE 9.5.1
Tenth Plan Cargo Traffic Targets and Achievements

(Million Metric Tonnes)

Commodity	Tenth Plan Target	Actual in 2006–07		
		Major Ports	Non-major Ports (Prov.)	Total
POL	235.30	154.35	81.87	236.22
Iron ore	65.50	80.56	29.21	109.77
Coal	88.30	60.22	14.05	74.27
Fertilizers, incl. FRM	18.45	14.11	7.05	21.16
Containers	66.10	73.47	5.0	78.47
Other cargo	91.35	81.13	34.74	115.87
Total	565.00	463.84	171.92	635.76

Note: Prov.= Provisional.

greater cushion for making allowance for bunching of traffic. The details of the capacity addition of 160.80 million tonnes are given in Table 9.5.2.

TABLE 9.5.2
Tenth Plan—Capacity Added to Major Ports

(Million Metric Tonnes)

Commodity	Capacity as on 31 March 2002	Addition during the Tenth Plan	Capacity as on 31 March 2007
POL	135.35	39.35	174.70
Iron ore	43.60	13.90	57.50
Coal	44.20	2.05	46.25
Containers	37.00	51.08	88.08
Other cargo	83.80	54.48	138.22
Total	343.95	160.86	504.75

Productivity

9.5.5 The average turnaround time for all major ports has improved from 4.24 days during the last year of the Ninth Plan to 2.58 days during the last year of the Tenth Plan. Among the ports, Chennai, Tuticorin, Mumbai, Jawaharlal Nehru Port Trust (JNPT), and Kandla have shown appreciable improvement. The pre-berthing detention, which showed substantial improvement and reduced to 4.9 hours in 2003–04 as compared to 11.5 hours during the last year of the Ninth Plan, slipped down slightly in the last two years of the Tenth Plan (but was still better than the Ninth Plan performance). Among the ports, improvement has been noticed in Paradeep, Chennai, Tuticorin, Ennore, and New Mangalore. The output per ship berth day has also shown consistent improvement during the Plan period as detailed in Table 9.5.3.

9.5.6 The major factors contributing to deterioration in average pre-berthing retention time in the last two years were priority berthing and ousting priority to vessels carrying foodgrains and fertilizers notably in the ports of Kandla, Haldia Dock System in Kolkata Port, and Vishakhapatanam Port; bunching of vessels; and lack of mechanized cargo handling equipment for certain dry bulk commodities. Though the cargo handled was within the total capacity of the ports, there was shortfall in the capacity of certain commodities in some specific ports. Inadequate port capacity leads to congestion, thereby leading to ship detention, etc. Most of the ports are not equipped with latest navigational aides and facilities such as Vessel Traffic Management System, sophisticated marine crafts, etc., channel restrictions in width leading to unidirectional movements, number of dedicated berths available being limited leading to bunching of vessels and calling of larger vessels combined with inadequate cargo handling equipments are the other factors contributing to increase in detentions.

Private Sector Participation

9.5.7 The government has put in place a scheme for private participation in major ports mainly in container terminals, specialized cargo berths, warehousing/storage facilities, etc. on BOT basis with a concession period not exceeding 30 years. The scheme also includes formation of joint venture by the ports with the private operators selected on the basis of competitive bidding. The scheme did not take off as expected during the Tenth Plan. Necessary policy initiatives in respect of management control, etc., are required to be evolved for facilitating the formation of joint ventures. In case of non-major ports, the VGF

TABLE 9.5.3
Tenth Plan—Productivity Parameters of Major Ports

Year	Average Turnaround Time (Days)	Average Pre-berthing Detention (Hours)	Average Output per Ship Berth Day (Tonnes)
2001–02 (Ninth Plan)	4.24	11.53	7158
2002–03	3.69	6.90	8455
2003–04	3.45	4.90	9079
2004–05	3.41	6.03	9298
2005–06	3.41	8.73	9586
2006–07	2.58	9.94	12612

scheme of the GoI will have to be made compatible with the requirements and the operational imperatives of the sector so as to enable the non-major ports to access these funds. During the Tenth Plan period, private sector schemes costing Rs 11257 crore were identified, eight schemes costing Rs 2435 crore have been completed with incremental capacity addition of 44.40 million mt, another six schemes costing Rs 3818 crore have already been awarded to private operators which are expected to create an additional capacity of 45.50 million mt.

Sethusamudram Channel Project (SSCP)

9.5.8 SSCP, sanctioned in June 2005 with the objective of creating a navigable channel from Gulf of Munnar to Bay of Bengal/Palk Bay, would save up to 424 nautical miles of navigation and up to 30 hours sailing time for ships plying between the east and west coasts. For the project with an estimated cost of Rs 2427.40 crore, an SPV, the Sethusamudram Corporation Ltd was formed with equity participation of Rs 495 crore by the government.

Tsunami Rehabilitation Programme

9.5.9 The Tsunami Rehabilitation Programme initiated after the severe earthquake and tsunami waves severely damaged the 56 ports, harbours, jetties, wharfs, and allied structures, especially in the southern islands of Hut Bay, Car Nicobar, Nan Cowry group of islands, and Great Nicobar, at an estimated cost of Rs 897.31 crore, is to be completed by March 2009.

Tenth Plan Outlay and Expenditure

9.5.10 An outlay of Rs 5418.29 crore had been approved for the port sector, comprising Rs 972 crore as GBS and Rs 4446.29 crore through IEBR. However, year-wise allocations were aggregated to Rs 5954.84 crore (details are given in Annexure 9.5.3) of which Rs 2892.65 crore or 48.58% was utilized. The acute shortfall in expenditure, particularly in respect of major ports, is due to failure of project formulation leading to delays in implementation and savings on account of schemes dropped/deferred.

EMERGING SCENARIO IMPACTING THE PORT SECTOR

9.5.11 In the backdrop of doubling of India's share in the world trade in the next five years, efficiency and speed in the movement of cargo through ports are vital. Shipping and cargo technologies are changing rapidly; ships are bigger and faster with large-sized container vessels drawing 14.5 m draft and moving at speeds of 25 knots; and containerization of traffic is growing steadily and significantly.

9.5.12 To meet such challenges, initiatives taken include Electronic Data Interchange (EDI)-based single window clearance in many ports and development of an International Container Transshipment Terminal at Cochin. Non-major and private ports have seen spectacular growth. Notably, non-major ports increased their share of cargo traffic from 23.58% in 2000–01 to 27% in 2006–07 while their traffic volume grew by 11.74% (CAGR) in the last five years against 8.54% for major ports. However, the growth of traffic in non-major ports was skewed across coastal States, with Gujarat handling more than 60%.

9.5.13 Nevertheless, much more needs to be done by the Indian ports to improve their operational efficiency through enabling policies, regulatory and institutional mechanisms adopted to raise port efficiency, productivity, human resource planning, and equipment, initially to achieve the benchmarks of efficient ports in the region and to eventually become world class.

ISSUES AND STRATEGIES FOR THE ELEVENTH PLAN

Capacity Augmentation

9.5.14 To meet the overall projected traffic of 1008.95 million tonnes by 2011–12, of which the share of major ports would be 708.09 million tonnes, adequate port capacity is required to be created, the details of which are given in Table 9.5.4.

Dredging

9.5.15 In this crucial component of port capacity, only 11% of the target for capital dredging could be achieved during the Tenth Plan period. The requirement of capital dredging in the Eleventh Plan has increased more than two-fold, to 298.28 million cubic metres (MCuM) for major ports and SSCP and 367.18 MCuM for non-major ports, besides maintenance dredging of 380.06 MCuM and 33.89 MCuM, respectively. During the Eleventh Plan, dredging capacity of ports would

TABLE 9.5.4
Capacity Creation and Projected Traffic in Major Ports in the Eleventh Plan

(Million Metric Tonnes)

Port	Projected Traffic in 2011–12	Existing Capacity 2006–07	Capacity Addition by 2011–12	Total Capacity in 2011–12
Kolkata	13.43	13.40	18.85	32.25
Haldia	44.50	43.50	21.20	64.70
Paradeep	76.40	56.00	55.00	111.00
Vishakhapatnam	82.20	58.50	52.40	110.90
Ennore	47.00	13.00	51.20	64.20
Chennai	57.50	50.00	23.50	73.50
Tuticorin	31.72	20.55	43.43	63.98
Cochin	38.17	20.15	35.40	55.55
New Mangalore	48.81	41.30	22.50	63.80
Mormugao	44.55	30.00	37.46	67.46
Mumbai	71.05	44.65	48.16	92.81
JNPT	66.04	52.40	43.90	96.30
Kandla	86.72	61.30	58.80	120.10
Total	708.09	504.75	511.80	1016.55

be 29.73 MCuM per annum and that of the Dredging Corporation of India (DCI) 168 MCuM per annum.

9.5.16 To enable this capacity creation, a more liberal dredging policy has been brought into force which allows ports to charter foreign flag dredgers after granting the Indian companies the 'first right of refusal'. It is necessary to consider the policy option of procuring the required dredgers from private dredging companies on a long-term basis, with appropriate guarantees and risk-sharing with the terminal operator incorporated in the concession agreement. Joint Ventures should be preferred for projects with a substantial dredging component.

9.5.17 Cargo traffic in general and container traffic in particular is concentrated in western ports leading to congestion and delays. Western ports are typically used even for much of the East Sea lane traffic, which is about 40% of total container traffic. The development of dredging facilities to handle container vessels requiring deeper drafts at the eastern ports should be prioritized in the Eleventh Plan.

Dredging Corporation of India (DCI)

9.5.18 The capacity of the DCI, established in 1976, to provide integrated dredging services to major and minor ports at the beginning of the Tenth Plan was 73.60 MCuM of Trailer Suction Dredgers (TSDs) and 6.25 MCuM of Cutter Suction Dredgers (CSDs). Due to delays in finalization of procurement orders for the dredgers, there was no capacity addition during the Tenth Plan. The expenditure for the Tenth Plan is Rs 206.12 crore as against the outlay of Rs 365 crore.

9.5.19 During the Eleventh Plan, DCI proposes to acquire 10 TSDs of 5000–9000 CuM hopper capacity and 5 CSDs of 2000–3000 CuM hopper capacity in addition to other auxiliary equipment.

Development of New Deep Draft Ports

9.5.20 In order to meet the expected growth in traffic at ports of 10% and more, necessary feasibility and locational studies for developing some more ports, especially on the East Coast, are being undertaken.

Productivity

9.5.21 Improvement of labour productivity through enhanced training and redeployment of surplus human resources is a major area to be addressed during the Eleventh Plan. Equally important, ports would need to pay greater attention to selection, deployment, and operation as well as maintenance of the cargo handling equipment, with on-time replacement of obsolete equipment with state-of-art multi-tasking flexible equipment guided by specified procedures for disposal of surplus/obsolete equipment. Competition from private operators is already showing some improvements in productivity of public berths.

Dwell Time

9.5.22 The dwell time of cargo in Indian ports is high on account of many constraints. The workflow in Indian ports is manual with low level of IT penetration. For container handling, adequate electronic environment with Enterprise Resource Planning (ERP), which enables the resources of ports to be used in an even and efficient manner, is yet to be established in a full-fledged manner. The EDI, which ensures flow of data electronically between port, customs, shipping lines, and users, resulting in greater accuracy, speed, and efficiency of the total maritime logistic chain, is yet to be commissioned on a common platform. This information bottleneck is estimated to contribute to about 40% of the documentation. At present, EDI is minimal and consists of the proprietary message exchange format formulated by customs. To maximize the benefits of EDI and move towards a paperless regime, necessary steps have been already initiated to implement centralized web-based Port Community System (PCS), which would ultimately achieve seamless integration of the port community. Besides the above, there are other constraints such as inadequate infrastructure, absence of seamless connectivity with other modes, etc. A Committee of Secretaries has gone into these issues and made suitable recommendations indicating time frames ranging from December 2007 to June 2010. After implementation of these recommendations, the expected reduction in terminal dwell time for dry bulk, break bulk, and containers, respectively, would go down from the existing 3.23, 5.62, and 1.88 days to 1.60, 1.50, and 1.00 days in the case of imports and from 3.57, 6.60, and 3.78 days to 1.70, 3.30, and 1.50 days in the case of exports.

Risk Management System (RMS) of Customs

9.5.23 Two main customs components of detention of cargo at ports are assessment and examination at ports. Implementation of RMS is expected to bring about significant reduction in detention to cargo at ports. The basic approach of the RMS is to 'trust the accredited trade partners' and involves self-appraisal and use of minimal and appropriate intervention to address perceived risks. The scheme of the RMS incorporates an Accredited Clients Programme which envisages assured facilitation to clients who meet specified criteria in terms of amount of duty paid, volume of imports, and a clean compliance record. Their imports will be subject to a small percentage of system-generated random checks in order to monitor their continuing compliance and to retain an element of surprise. In respect of non-accredited clients' imports, the RMS will determine the treatment to be given to individual transactions on the basis of an assessment of risks associated with such transactions. The purpose is to ensure that the department's resources are focused on high risk areas so that the threats to revenue and restriction/prohibitions on imports are effectively tackled. A large number of low risk bills of entry are cleared on the basis of self-appraisal mode, without any assessment and examination by officers.

Private Sector Participation

9.5.24 The bulk of capacity augmentation would be undertaken through the PPPs and captive users. New berths at major ports would be constructed through PPP mode, except where operational exigencies necessitate taking up development of new berths through the ports' own resources. In addition to the areas already identified, possibilities for inviting private investment in maintenance dredging operations and pilotage would also be explored during the Eleventh Plan period. For providing stable policy and regulatory framework, the existing model bid documents including the concessions agreement are being refined on the basis of the experiences gathered from the existing PPP projects. A new MCA is being developed taking into account all the experience from existing private terminals and the concerns of all stakeholders.

Non-Major Ports

9.5.25 Traffic at non-major ports and private ports is growing at 11.74% (CAGR) and its share is expected to grow from 26.30% in 2005–06 to 30% in 2011–12. During the Eleventh Plan, non-major ports are expected to more than double their capacity, from 228.31 million tonnes upwards to 575 million tonnes. The total value of the developmental schemes to be taken up during the Eleventh Plan amounts to around Rs 36000 crore, with contribution predominantly from private entities.

9.5.26 A holistic and integrated development perspective of major and non-major ports is necessary as they would complement and compete with each other. Suitable policies need to be devised so that non-major ports also act as centres of growth with appropriate coordination among the maritime States and the Central agencies.

Tariff Regulation

9.5.27 Increasing induction of private players in port operations is resulting in the gradual emergence of a competitive environment. The multiplicity of port operators has brought into focus the pressing need for an institutional mechanism that provides a level playing field for all port operators. Areas such as navigational safety, security, and conservancy in ports; safety and occupational health; disaster management; and pollution control measures would also need to be regulated by a national authority. The jurisdiction of Tariff Authority for Major Ports is restricted to the levy of tariffs for services rendered by major ports or by private operators authorized by them. A suitable regulator and a regulatory framework to address issues specific to the ports should be put in place.

Institutional Reforms

9.5.28 To make port management more responsive to the dynamic and growing needs of port users, it would be necessary to impart (i) financial and operational autonomy to them, (ii) separate regulatory and management functions with a view to commercialize the latter, (iii) improve access to long-term capital and project finance, and (iv) unbundle various services and privatize identified areas.

Box 9.5.1
Tariff Setting Mechanism

The present 'cost plus' tariff setting mechanism combined with the revenue sharing model for the PPP projects has certain inconsistencies. The Task Force, set up under the chairmanship of Anwarul Hoda, Member, Planning Commission, to examine the tariff setting mechanism and bidding parameters for PPP projects has noted that tariffs to be charged by port operators would be determined by market forces once adequate capacity is developed and sufficient competition introduced. However, in the interim the berths should be bid out after determining the tariff caps up front on the basis of norms to be developed for the purpose. As at present the revenue share would continue to be the sole bidding parameter.

Corporatization

9.5.29 Corporatization of Ports Trusts would provide better accessibility to funds, create a board-managed corporate entity, and facilitate disinvestment. On the other hand, corporatization with revaluation of assets could merely push up tariffs without the port users seeing any change in the quality of service, if such a move is not supported by other reforms. The provisions of the Major Port Trusts Act can be purposefully invoked to serve the desired purpose in tandem with judicious privatization of the port services with the Ports Trusts playing a landlord's role. Where a particular service does not generate a sufficient stream of revenue and is thus non-viable for total privatization, the JV route for attracting private investment and management expertise should be encouraged.

9.5.30 For improving productivity, quality of service, and enhancing their competitiveness, the existing structure in the major ports would be reoriented for rendering port services, consistent with the practices followed in the Landlord Port Model.

IT in Ports

9.5.31 So far, from amongst the two basic IT systems, namely, Application Software to manage the operation of ports and EDI to facilitate appraisal and payment of duty without any human interface, the port–user interface has been achieved in some of the ports, while EDI has been introduced and port–customs interface achieved in all major ports, except Paradeep. Now, all activities across the maritime transport chain have to be integrated through one common standard PCS. It is expected that PCS in major ports would be implemented in the first year of the Eleventh Plan. The ports should draw up their IT Policy with the objective to develop and deploy state-of-art information and communication technologies to maximize the port's efficiency and effectiveness.

9.5.32 In sum, the thrust of IT in port sector in the Eleventh Plan would be: (i) to implement centralized web-based EDI-PCS at major ports and to further extend this to supply chain management system and to bring other ports into its ambit, (ii) to gear up ports to have Radio Frequency Identification (RFI) device reader to capture the data from RFI device tags on shipments, and (iii) to implement centralized ERP covering all major ports.

HINTERLAND CONNECTIVITY

9.5.33 Apart from other deficiencies, port efficiency is impeded owing to the port's inability to handle additional traffic because of slow evacuation of cargo from ports or slow turnaround of ships. This undermines the competitiveness of Indian ports vis-à-vis other ports in the region, and vitiates the environment for investment in manufacturing in the country. Therefore, it is important that connectivity of major ports with the hinterland is augmented not only to ensure smooth flow of traffic at the present level but also to meet the requirements of projected increase in traffic.

9.5.34 The recommendations of the Committee of Secretaries constituted to address hinterland connectivity include construction of a four-lane road as well as double railway line connectivity for each major port, consideration of projects less than minimum prescribed IRR on case to case basis, and consideration of budgetary assistance and also the assistance under VGF scheme for such projects. The Committee further recommended that 10 road projects of value Rs 2036 crore and 8 rail projects of value Rs 2014 crore, which had already been sanctioned, should be completed in a time-bound manner. All approved recommendations are to be implemented within a period of three years, that is, by 2009.

ANDAMAN LAKSHADWEEP HARBOUR WORKS (ALHW)

9.5.35 ALHW was set up in 1965 for planning, execution, and maintenance of port and harbour facilities in the Andaman and Nicobar Islands and Lakshadweep Islands. During the Tenth Plan, construction of breakwaters at Mus in Car Nicobar and extension of wharf at Hut Bay in Little Andamans were completed. Embanking facilities at Agathi, Amini, and Minicoy and Kawaratti in Lakshadweep, and development works of Junglighat Harbour in Port Blair and deep water wharf in Campbel Bay have been taken up. Against the Tenth Plan outlay of Rs 200 crore, expenditure incurred till 31 March 2007 was Rs 144.20 crore.

OUTLAY FOR THE ELEVENTH PLAN

9.5.36 The Eleventh Plan budgetary support for Central sector ports is Rs 3315 crore at 2006–07 price (Rs 3749 crore at current price). The scheme-wise break up of GBS at current prices is given in the Appendix (Volume III). In addition, the sector is expected to generate IEBR of Rs 26574.11 crore at 2006–07 price and private sector investment of Rs 36868.00 crore during this period. Further, a public investment of Rs 3627.00 crore is expected in the State sector.

9.5.37 The total projected outlay for the Eleventh Plan for the Department of Shipping (including Ports) is Rs 43874 crore at 2006–07 price (Rs 49623 crore at current price) which includes Rs 4465 crore of GBS at 2006–07 price (Rs 5050 crore at current price) and Rs 39409 crore of IEBR at 2006–07 price (Rs 44573 crore at current price).

9.6 CIVIL AVIATION

OVERVIEW

9.6.1 Air transport is the preferred mode of transport especially for long-distance travel, business travel, accessing difficult terrains, and for transporting high-value and perishable commodities mainly on account of the speed of travel and saving of time. With the opening up of domestic skies to private carriers in the second half of the Tenth Plan, air services have become affordable and are now effectively competing with other modes of transport. Propelled by growth of the economy and liberalization, the sector experienced an unprecedented growth during the Tenth Plan, accelerating particularly in its last three years.

REVIEW OF THE TENTH PLAN

9.6.2 During the Tenth Plan an outlay of Rs 12928.00 crore was provided to the Ministry of Civil Aviation (MoCA), out of which Rs 7792.09 crore or 60% of the outlay was spent by them. However, against a sum of Rs 672.73 crore provided as GBS, the expenditure incurred was to the tune of Rs 546.10 crore or 81%. Details of outlay and anticipated expenditure are given in Annexure 9.6.1.

9.6.3 Important developments in the airline and airport sector included: (i) modernization and restructuring of Delhi and Mumbai airports launched through JV companies; (ii) development of greenfield air-ports at Bangalore and Hyderabad on a Build–Own–Operate–Transfer basis with PPP; (iii) approval of modernization of 35 non-metro airports and 13 other airports to world-class standards in phases; (iv) liberalization of FDI limit upto 100% through automatic route for setting up greenfield airports; (v) acquisition of modern and technologically advanced aircraft for Air India (AI) Ltd, Air India Charters Ltd (AICL), and Indian Airlines Ltd; (vi) liberalization of bilateral air services agreement in line with the contemporary developments in international civil aviation sector; (vii) adoption of a limited Open Sky Policy in international travel to meet the traffic demand during peak season; and (viii) adoption of trade facilitation measures in custom procedures to facilitate speedy clearance of air cargo.

ELEVENTH PLAN

Objectives

9.6.4 The main objectives of the Civil Aviation Sector for the Eleventh Plan would be to provide (i) world-class infrastructure facilities; (ii) safe, reliable, and affordable air services so as to encourage growth in passenger and cargo traffic; and (iii) air connectivity to remote and inaccessible areas with special reference to north eastern part of the country.

Strategies

9.6.5 The realization of above objectives would call for capacity building that will include modernization and expansion of major international and domestic airports, construction of new greenfield airports including that of the NER, enhancement of cargo handling facilities at all airports, and upgradation/modernization of Air Traffic Management (ATM) System.

9.6.6 Similarly, in the airline sector, acquisition of modern fuel-efficient aircraft fitted with the latest equipment would be encouraged. The capacity building process in both airlines and airports would be mainly through increased private sector participation. While a decision has been taken to modernize the non-metro airports through the Airports Authority of India (AAI), the city side development at these airports would be done through PPP. Two major metro airports (Delhi and Mumbai) and two greenfield airports (Bangalore and Hyderabad), which would be completed during the Eleventh Plan, are already being developed through PPP. A similar strategy is envisaged for the Navi Mumbai airport for which in-principle clearance has been given. While the existing airports at Kolkata and Chennai would be developed by AAI, the greenfield airports at these locations will need to be taken up through PPP.

9.6.7 Acute shortage of technical and operating manpower would be addressed by upgrading the existing training institutes and opening new world-class flying training institutes.

Traffic Projections

9.6.8 Both domestic and international traffic witnessed a boom during the last three years of the Tenth Plan, that is 2004–05, 2005–06, and 2006–07, with growth in passenger traffic of 21.5%, 23.7%, and 31.38%, respectively, resulting in overall growth (CAGR) of 19.23% (13.58% in international passenger and 21.78% in domestic traffic) during the Tenth Plan. The main factors contributing to this growth include the growth of the economy, falling fares, and increasing capacities of domestic private airlines. It is estimated that international and domestic passengers are forecast to grow at the rate of 15.9% and 19.9%, respectively, resulting in overall increase of 18.8% during the Eleventh Plan. All the Indian airports taken together, passenger traffic is forecasted at 2054.00 lakh (540.37 lakh international and 1513.63 lakh domestic passengers) and cargo traffic at 2683.47 thousand metric tonnes (TMTs) (1822.69 TMTs international and 860.78 TMTs domestic cargo) by 2011–12.

9.6.9 Additional capacities of about 296.95 lakh international and 1035.74 lakh domestic passengers would require to be created at 45 major airports by 2011–12, as the total international passengers and domestic passengers projected would be 539.39 lakh and 1489.70 lakh, respectively.

9.6.10 Similarly, during the Tenth Plan, cargo traffic grew (CAGR) by 12.70% (12.75% international and 12.61% domestic cargo). During the Eleventh Plan, international and domestic cargo traffic is expected to grow at the rate of 12.1% and 10.1%, respectively, resulting in overall increase of 11.4%.

9.6.11 To take care of above growth in respect of cargo terminal, additional capacity would require to be created to the tune of 800.00 TMTs of international cargo traffic and about 300.00 TMTs of domestic cargo traffic by 2011–12.

POLICY FRAMEWORK

Air Transport

9.6.12 The main advantage of civil aviation lies in its speed particularly over long distances and difficult terrain. A major disadvantage is the high cost of transportation on account of high Aviation Turbine Fuel (ATF) cost, which is further aggravated by taxes. Viewed in inter-modal context, it is desirable to rationalize ATF pricing and to review the tax structure.

Multi-modal Connectivity

9.6.13 The major airports in India are mostly at considerable distance from the city centre. Apart from causing inconvenience to the passengers, this also adversely affects the comparative advantage in terms of saving in time otherwise enjoyed by air transport vis-à-vis other modes of transport. These airports need to be connected to cities by metros and expressways to get full advantage of air transportation by reducing the total travel time.

Foreign Equity Participation

9.6.14 The Domestic Air Transport Policy approved by the government provides for foreign equity participation up to 49% and investment by non-resident Indians (NRIs) up to 100% in the domestic air transport services. Foreign airlines are, however, not permitted to participate in equity directly or indirectly. With a view to attracting new technology and management expertise, this policy needs to be reviewed.

Air Cargo

9.6.15 Today, about 40% of the world's cargo business, in terms of value, moves by air. Although cargo traffic is growing steadily in recent years it has not kept pace with the passenger traffic growth because of shortcomings such as lack of facilities for transhipment of imports and exports; absence of integrated cargo infrastructure; deficiencies in gateway and hinterland connectivity through rail and road; complexities in custom procedures in air cargo; and need for technological upgradation and performance-based service standards. To address these shortcomings, during the Eleventh Plan, steps will be taken including (i) streamlining/simplification of procedures by various regulatory agencies; (ii) provision of infrastructural facilities relating to cargo handling; (iii) promoting and developing India as a Regional Air Cargo Hub; and (iv) setting up of 'Cargo Villages' at key international airports.

Maintenance, Repair, and Overhaul (MRO)

9.6.16 Owing to the availability of skilled manpower, India has the potential to emerge as an MRO hub in Asia Pacific region. Currently, the two merged National Airlines, viz., Indian Airlines and AI, have in-house aircraft maintenance facilities, but at times they too have to outsource maintenance to foreign companies. At present, there is virtually no credible third-party MRO facility in India to support the requirements of the rapidly expanding aircraft fleets of private operators. The current growth phase provides India an ideal opportunity to develop into an MRO hub. Investment by the private sector including foreign direct investment would be encouraged to this end.

Regional Airlines

9.6.17 In order to tap the vast potential of growth of traffic and to encourage balanced growth of civil aviation, regional airlines need to be promoted. The promotion of regional airlines would, however, be through more liberal policy and provision of better infrastructure facilities. The rules and procedures governing the entry may also be simplified.

Route Dispersal Guidelines (RDG)

9.6.18 According to the RDG laid down in 1994, all scheduled operators are required to deploy a certain percentage of their capacity on trunk routes (Category-I routes) to the North Eastern and other inaccessible areas (Category-II) and within Category-II regions. In view of the vital changes that have taken place in civil aviation sector since the policy was laid down, it is desirable to review the RDG to bring them in line with these developments. One way to make the RDG workable will be to make the obligation tradable. Another alternative could be to provide direct subsidies to operators willing to operate in inaccessible and isolated areas and require the operators on trunk routes to contribute towards the subsidy.

Air Connectivity in NER and Other Remote/Inaccessible Areas

9.6.19 In view of the hilly terrain with uneasy access through the land link, improvement of air connectivity and development of airport infrastructure in NER and other remote areas such as the hill States of Jammu and Kashmir, Himachal Pradesh, Uttarakhand, and island territories of Andaman and Nicobar and Lakshadweep need to be accorded top priority.

9.6.20 During the Eleventh Plan, three greenfield airports, one each at Pakyong in Sikkim, Itanagar in Arunachal Pradesh, and Chiethu in Nagaland, would be constructed. In addition, some existing airports in NER would also be taken up for expansion/modification so as to make them operational for scheduled flights. Airports in other crucial areas such as Jammu, Dehradun, Agatti, and Port Blair would be taken up under the scheme for modernization and upgradation of 35 non-metro airports.

Air Transport Security

9.6.21 Security issues, particularly arising out of the terrorist-related activities, have assumed even greater importance in the international environment in recent decades. The legal and institutional framework for civil aviation security needs to be strengthened by evolving appropriate technology, training, and equipments.

Role of the Private Sector

9.6.22 The private sector is now playing a crucial role in the development of both airline and airport sector. Its market share in the domestic traffic during 2006 reached 78.5%, which includes the 29% traffic of low cost airlines. Jet Airways has emerged as the market leader with a share of 31.2%, followed by Indian Airlines (21.5%), Air Deccan (18.3%), Air Sahara (8.8%), Kingfisher (8.7%), Spice Jet (6.9%), Go Air (2.8%), Indigo (1.3%), and Paramount (0.7%). The private sector share is likely to increase during the Eleventh Plan with an estimated further acquisition of additional fleet by them of about 258 aircraft through a mix of lease/purchase involving an investment of as much as Rs 71863.00 crore.

9.6.23 The total private investment envisaged for this sector, including Rs 1500.00 crore for city side development 35 non-metro airports, would be to the tune of Rs 93493.00 crore during the Eleventh Plan.

New Initiatives

9.6.24 In order to sustain the spectacular growth registered by the civil aviation sector in the last few years through the Eleventh Plan, the following initiatives have been taken:

- Model Concession Agreement (MCA) is being evolved to help attract private investments and also facilitate smooth execution of air transport projects.
- Airports Economic Regulatory Authority (AERA) is being established in order to create a level playing field and healthy competition amongst all major airports (handling more than 1.5 million passenger per annum); encourage investment in airport facilities; regulate tariffs of aeronautical services; protect reasonable interest of users; and operate efficient, economic, and viable airports.
- Merger of AI and Indian Airlines to optimize fleet acquisition, to leverage the asset base, to strengthen the network, and to achieve economy of scale, with estimated cost and synergy benefits (net) of Rs 600.00 crore at the end of the third year of merger.
- Human Resource Development (HRD) to mitigate the acute shortage of qualified personnel, especially pilots and flying instructors. The following steps are being taken in this regard:
  - Training facilities at Indira Gandhi Rashtriya Uran Akademi (IGRUA) would be upgraded/augmented.
  - A new Flying Training Institute would be set up at Gondia, Maharashtra.

- Flying clubs and schools would be encouraged to improve equipment and infrastructure.

• Revamping of AAI in light of the strain on aviation infrastructure resulting in traffic congestions and delays at some of the airports resulting from the high growth in the sector. It would be revamped with multidisciplinary staff and expertise along with independent directors. The framework for revamp of AAI would be worked out during the Eleventh Plan.

ORGANIZATIONS OF MINISTRY OF CIVIL AVIATION (MOCA)

Air India (AI)

9.6.25 During the Tenth Plan, AI Ltd has incurred an expenditure of Rs 2388.27 crore as against the approved outlay of Rs 2661.39 crore, which works out to about 90% of the approved outlay. The shortfall was mainly due to appreciation of Indian rupee and deferment of non-aircraft capital expenditure to subsequent years due to resource constraints. The financial performance of AI during the Tenth Plan is given in Table 9.6.1.

9.6.26 The net profit of AI Ltd has declined from Rs 133.86 crore during 2002–03 to Rs 12.50 crore during 2006–07 due to its fall in share of the traffic due to increased competition. Absence of an adequate fleet of new aircrafts was a major contributory factor for the decline in competitiveness of the airline.

9.6.27 AI has been successful in increasing its capacity as is evident from Table 9.6.2. During the Eleventh Plan, AI Ltd would acquire 50 new long-range aircrafts comprising 8 Boeing 777–2000 LR, 15 Boeing 777–300 ER, and 27 Boeing 787 aircraft. With these acquisitions, its targeted capacity would increase to 10484 million in terms of available tonne kilometres (ATKMs) and 7092 million in terms of revenue tonne kilometres (RTKMs) by the end of the Eleventh Plan.

Indian Airlines

9.6.28 During the Tenth Plan, Indian Airlines could spend only Rs 1431.54 crore as against the approved outlay of Rs 4240.50 crore, a shortfall of 66%, mainly attributed to the appreciation of Indian rupee, less outgo towards new aircraft project, and taking up of operationally essential projects only under 'other supporting facilities' on account of resource constraint. Indian Airlines has improved its financial performance as given in Table 9.6.3.

TABLE 9.6.1
Financial Performance of Air India

(Rs in Crore)

S. No.		2002–03	2003–04	2004–05	2005–06	2006–07
1.	Total revenue	5689.88	6331.78	7676.39	9251.02	8887.00
2.	Total expenses	5545.87	6238.07	7579.85	9232.52	8874.50
3.	Net profit/loss before tax	144.01	93.71	96.54	18.50	12.50
4.	Net profit/loss after tax	133.86	92.33	96.36	14.94	12.50

TABLE 9.6.2
Growth in Capacity and Traffic during the Tenth Plan

(in Million)

Year	Capacity Available (ATKMs)	Capacity Utilized (RTKMs)	Load Factor (%)
2002–03	2415.9	1561.0	64.6
2003–04	2897.5	1774.0	61.2
2004–05	3600.4	2218.0	61.6
2005–06	4193.2	2363.7	56.4
2006–07 (Prov.)	4152.9	2204.20	53.1
Total	17259.9 (13711.00)#	10120.90 (9185.80)#	58.6 (67.0)#

Note: # Targets for the Tenth Plan.

TABLE 9.6.3
Financial Performance of Indian Airlines

(Rs Crore)

S. No.		2002–03	2003–04	2004–05	2005–06	2006–07 (BE)
1.	Total revenue	4173.51	4725.67	5362.57	5788.82	7944.00
2.	Total expenses	4370.07	4677.50	5290.96	5725.82	7847.50
3.	Net profit/(loss) before tax	(–)196.56	48.17	71.61	63.00	96.50
4.	Profit/(loss) after tax	(–)196.56	44.17	65.61	49.50	43.00

Note: BE= Budget Estimate.

9.6.29 Indian Airlines started earning net profit of Rs 44.17 crore in 2003–04, mainly due to increase in domestic fares and various cost-cutting measures initiated by the company. However, increase in ATF price and fall in passenger yields as a result of intense competition in domestic aviation market made the financial performance erratic.

9.6.30 During the Tenth Plan, the physical performance of Indian Airlines, in terms of capacity produced and utilized, indicates that it has not been able to achieve the targets, mainly due to delay in acquisition of aircrafts and intense competition from other domestic airlines, as given in Table 9.6.4. In order to increase its capacity and expand network during the Eleventh Plan, Indian Airlines would acquire 43 new Airbus aircrafts, the order for which was placed during the Tenth Plan. In addition to these aircrafts, Indian Airlines proposes to lease 12 wide-body aircrafts and 8 Turbo Prop aircrafts (50-seater), among others, thereby enlarging the total fleet size to 117 by the end of the Eleventh Plan. At the same time, it proposes to phase out 11 Boeing 737–200, 3 Airbus A 300, and 2 Dornier. As a result, the capacity of Indian Airlines is expected to grow from 1686 million ATKMs to 4238 million ATKMs by the end of the Eleventh Plan. Similarly, the capacity in terms of RTKMs is expected to grow from 1233 million RTKMs during 2006–07 to 3093 million RTKMs during the same period.

Airports Authority of India (AAI)

9.6.31 Against the approved budget of Rs 5404.21 crore including budgetary support of Rs 250 crore, AAI spent Rs 3534.62 crore including budgetary support of Rs 150.67 crore during the Tenth Plan. The shortfall in expenditure of 35% was mainly due to deferment of projects at Delhi and Mumbai airports due to their restructuring through PPP, delay in finalization of certain projects for non-metro airports, and delay in procurement of communication/surveillance and distance measuring equipment.

9.6.32 The net profit of AAI has increased from Rs 282.05 crore during 2002–03 to Rs 793.71 crore during 2006–07, thus earning an appreciable total profit of Rs 2433.71 crore during the Tenth Plan, as indicated in Table 9.6.5.

9.6.33 During the Eleventh Plan, AAI would be undertaking development of 35 non-metro airports and 13

TABLE 9.6.4
Growth in Capacity and Traffic during the Tenth Plan

(In Million)

Year	Capacity Available (ATKMs)	Capacity Utilized (RTKMs)	Load Factor (%)
2002–03	1308.018	845.097	64.6
2003–04	1334.069	877.475	65.8
2004–05	1472.062	1017.284	69.1
2005–06	1592.642	1140.947	71.6
2006–07 (Prov.)	1686.29	1232.67	73.1
Total	7393.081 (8384.00)#	5113.473 (5793.00)#	69.2 (69.1)#

Note: # Targets for the Tenth Plan.

TABLE 9.6.5
Financial Performance of Airports Authority of India

(Rs Crore)

S. No.		2002–03	2003–04	2004–05	2005–06	2006–07
1.	Total revenue	2384.49	2630.59	2999.65	3490.46	3431.86
2.	Total expenses	1887.44	2086.63	2314.83	2281.85	1948.15
3.	Net profit/loss before tax	497.05	543.96	684.82	1208.61	1483.71
4.	Provision for tax	215.00	229.00	359.45	490.99	690.00
5.	Profit after tax	282.05	314.96	325.37	717.62	793.71

other airports; development of Chennai and Kolkata airports; construction of new greenfield airports, including three in NER; expansion of five airports in NER and other crucial areas; up-gradation of technology from ground-based Communication, Navigation, and Surveillance-Air Traffic Management (CNS-ATM) to satellite-based CNS-ATM facilities; installation of new facilities including security equipment at various airports; installation of safety and facilitation equipment; development of airspace capacity enhancement; and development of IT.

Pawan Hans Helicopters Ltd (PHHL)

9.6.34 PHHL has incurred an expenditure of Rs 281.95 crore as against an approved outlay of Rs 458.90 crore, which is 61% of approved outlay for the Tenth Plan. The shortfall was due to delay in acquisition of new helicopters.

9.6.35 In spite of ever increasing ATF price, PHHL could increase its profit to Rs 49.00 crore in 2006–07 from Rs 15.39 crore during 2002–03, as per the details given in Table 9.6.6.

9.6.36 During the Eleventh Plan, PHHL would add 20 more helicopters to expand its present fleet including five medium class helicopters with longer range and higher pay-load capabilities for deep water exploration. The provision of helicopter support services would also be extended, beyond servicing ONGC, National Hydroelectric Power Corporation Ltd (NHPC), Ministry of Home Affairs, and State Governments, especially of North Eastern States and other remote and inaccessible States/UTs, to new areas such as tourism, medical evacuation, law enforcement, news gathering, intra-city transportation, and corporate travel. Besides, possibility would also be explored to expand its repair and overhaul business by offering repair services to other operators as well as by creating a new state-of-art maintenance centre at Mumbai.

Hotel Corporation of India (HCI)

9.6.37 An outlay of Rs 15.00 crore was approved for HCI during the Tenth Plan, against which the expenditure incurred was Rs 26.27 crore, or 75% more than the allocation, mainly on the maintenance and operation of hotels due to delay in their disinvestment.

9.6.38 HCI is expected to earn a profit of Rs 2.19 crore during 2006–07 after incurring losses for the first four years of the Tenth Plan.

9.6.39 The hotels of HCI were recommended for disinvestment and, accordingly, the disinvestment in two hotels, viz., Centaur Hotels at Mumbai airport and Juhu Beach in Mumbai, was completed during 2002–03. The

TABLE 9.6.6
Financial Performance of Pawan Hans Helicopters Ltd

(Rs Crore)

S. No.		2002–03	2003–04	2004–05	2005–06	2006–07(RE)
1.	Total revenue	205.02	224.00	241.85	199.08	211.50
2.	Total expenses	145.54	158.78	173.90	163.98	177.86
3.	Net profit/loss before tax	24.37	77.84	83.86	64.60	40.30
4.	Profit after tax	15.39	52.69	49.58	47.39	49.00

Note: RE= Revised Estimate.

process of disinvestment was, however, discontinued following a change in the government policy under which it has been decided to run Centaur Hotel at Srinagar and Flight Kitchens at Mumbai on a long-term management contract. The two other hotels, viz., Centaur Hotel and Flight Kitchen at Delhi airport will be run by the HCI till the Commonwealth Games and a decision would be taken thereafter. During the Eleventh Plan these hotels would need renovation so as to make them competitive.

Air India Charters Limited (AICL)

9.6.40 AICL is a subsidiary of AI Ltd. It used to provide manpower for allied services at airports. However, there has been a metamorphosis in the role of the company from being merely a service provider of ground handling and security to the first international low cost, no frill 'budget' airline from India. Its low cost airline, viz., AI Express has commenced operations on 29 April 2005. Since then it has incurred plan expenditure of Rs 59.01 crore. The net profit earned by AICL has increased to Rs 2.50 crore in 2006–07 showing an increase of about 85% over the net profit of Rs 1.35 crore earned during 2005–06, as per the details given in Table 9.6.7.

9.6.41 With the objective of increasing capacity and modernizing its fleet, it had placed an order for 18 Boeing 737–800 aircrafts during the Tenth Plan, of which 6 were delivered. The remaining 12 would be delivered during the Eleventh Plan period. With these acquisitions, capacity enhancement in terms of ATKMs and RTKMs would be 1107.00 million and 883.00 million, respectively, by 2011–12.

Indira Gandhi Rashtriya Uran Akademi (IGRUA)

9.6.42 The approved outlay of IGRUA during the Tenth Plan was Rs 10.00 crore, against which an expenditure of Rs 37.88 crore was incurred mainly on account of upgradation/modernization of the institute to increase its capacity to meet the growing demand for pilots due to entry of new airlines and expansion of fleet by the existing airlines.

9.6.43 IGRUA, as the premier institute for imparting flying training to commercial pilots, would need to increase its capacity during the Eleventh Plan by upgrading and augmenting its existing facilities so as to increase the number of pilots to be trained from the existing capacity of 30 pilots per annum to 100 pilots per annum. A project for upgradation/strengthening of IGRUA including augmentation of training facilities such as acquisition of 11 aircrafts (10 single engine and 1 multi-engine aircraft) was approved during the Tenth Plan. However, during the Eleventh Plan two more aircrafts, one King Air Simulator (Glass Cockpit) and one TB-20 CPT (Glass Cockpit) would be acquired. Further, in order to bring professionalism in the management of the Akademi and to make the institute self-sustaining, the possibility of entrusting the management of IGRUA to a private sector partner on a management lease basis would be explored.

Aero Club of India (ACI)

9.6.44 During the Tenth Plan, ACI spent Rs 11.00 crore as against the approved outlay of Rs 5.00 crore which is 120% more than the approved outlay.

9.6.45 ACI being the apex body of all the flying clubs, gliding clubs, and aero sports organizations in India encourages them to improve equipment and infrastructure by providing support to them. During the Eleventh Plan, ACI would acquire trainer aircraft, simulator, and training aids for distribution among the member flying clubs. Besides, it would also explore the possibility to develop aero-sports facilities including an aero-sports complex.

TABLE 9.6.7
Financial Performance of Air India Charters Ltd

(Rs Crore)

S. No.	Particulars	2002–03	2003–04	2004–05	2005–06	2006–07 (RE)
1.	Revenue	–	–	–	432.38	736.50
2.	Expenses	–	–	–	427.54	734.00
3.	Net profit/(loss) before Tax	–	–	–	4.84	2.50
4.	Net profit/(loss) after Tax	–	–	–	1.35	2.50

Directorate General of Civil Aviation (DGCA)

9.6.46 During the Tenth Plan, an outlay of Rs 19.00 crore was provided to DGCA, against which it could spend only Rs 12.03 crore. The shortfall was due to the acquisition of lesser number of trainer aircrafts from National Aerospace Laboratories (NAL).

9.6.47 With the objective of ensuring safety in air transport, the existing training programmes of DGCA such as Safety Oversight Programme of ICAO, Co-operative Development of Operational Safety and Continuing Airworthiness Programme (COSCAP) and European Union Training Programme will be continued during the Eleventh Plan. The other programmes which DGCA would be taking up will be procurement of trainer aircrafts (light helicopters/simulators for restructuring of flying/gliding clubs/institutions), purchase of machinery and equipment for aircraft accident investigation laboratories, and modernization of examination system and civil works at DGCA headquarters and their field offices.

9.6.48 Keeping in view the acute shortage of technical and operating manpower, it is proposed to establish a new world-class state-of-the-art National Flying Training Institute at Gondia, Maharashtra. The main objective of the institute is to provide flying training to trainees for acquiring Private Pilot Licence, Commercial Pilot Licence, Airline Transport Pilot Licence, Micro Pilot Licence, etc. The institute would also be utilized for R&D in the field of flying training, aviation-related innovative and practical courses.

Bureau of Civil Aviation Security (BCAS)

9.6.49 During the Tenth Plan, BCAS could spend only Rs 9.52 crore as against the approved outlay of Rs 114.00 crore, which works out to about 8%. The huge shortfall in utilization of funds was mainly due to non-finalization of schemes, such as restructuring of BCAS, construction of additional Regional Deputy Commissioner of Security Office, setting up of additional Bomb Detection and Disposal Squad (BDDS)/dog squads, and also due to delay in commencing work on setting up the Civil Aviation Security Academy.

9.6.50 Security in airlines operations has assumed greater importance especially after the incident of 9/11 and threats arising out of other terrorist-related activities. It would be necessary to undertake measures to strengthen and restructure BCAS, its training methods and training infrastructure, etc. Other measures would include electronic perimeter surveillance and protection, automated smart card access control at airports, setting up of additional BDDS and dog squads at the identified hyper-sensitive airports, and setting up of Civil Aviation Security Training Academy during the Eleventh Plan period.

OUTLAY FOR THE ELEVENTH PLAN

9.6.51 The total projected outlay for the Eleventh Plan for MoCA is Rs 43560 crore at 2006–07 price (Rs 49267 crore at current price) which includes Rs 1680 crore of GBS at 2006–07 price (Rs 1900 crore at current price). The scheme-wise break up of GBS at current prices is given in the Appendix (Volume III). In addition, the sector is expected to generate private sector investment of Rs 93493 crore during this period. The IEBR may go up by Rs 2226.68 crore at 2006–07 price on account of higher generation and utilization by AAI to fund their projects.

ANNEXURE 9.2.1
Resource Mobilization for the Tenth Five Year Plan

(In Rs Crore at Current Price)

Year	Internal Resources		Market Borrowings		Gross Budgetary Support		Total
	Amount (Rs crore)	Share (%)	Amount (Rs crore)	Share (%)	Amount (Rs crore)	Share (%)	Amount (Rs crore)
2002–03	3113	27	2517	22	5778	51	11408
2003–04	3475	26	2837	21	7081	53	13393
2004–05	3712	24	3041	20	8669	56	15422
2005–06	7033	37	3731	20	8074	43	18838
2006–07 (RE)	12233	49	4794	19	7914	32	24941
Total (Provisional)	29567	35	16920	20	37516	45	84003
Tenth Plan Outlay			33000 (54.5%)		27600	45.5	60600

ANNEXURE 9.2.2
Gross Budgetary Support

(In Rs Crore at Current Price)

Year	Capital		Special Railway Safety Fund		Diesel Cess		Total	
	Amount (Rs Crore)	Share (%)	Amount (Rs Crore)	Share (%)	Amount (Rs Crore)	Share (%)	Amount (Rs Crore)	Share (%)
2002–03	4264	37.6	1350	11.9	164	1.5	5778	51
2003–04	5315	39.8	1600	12.0	166	1.2	7081	53
2004–05	5493	35.5	2975	19.2	201	1.3	8669	56
2005–06	5312	28.3	2499	13.3	262	1.4	8073	43
2006–07	6189	24.8	1365	5.5	360	1.4	7914	33
Total (Provisional)	26573	31.6	9789	11.5	1154	1.4	37516	45

ANNEXURE 9.3.1
Financial and Physical Performance

(In Rs Crore)

S. No.	Schemes/Programmes	Financial Performance Tenth Plan			
		Outlay	BE	RE	Actual Exp.
1	2	3	4	5	6
1.	Externally aided projects	13990.00	13050.70	10007.90	9495.18
	(i) Externally aided (RW)	2560.00	403.10	99.16	7.53
	(ii) Counterpart funds (RW)	640.00	126.00	28.54	4.66
	EAP Ministry	3200.00	529.10	128.00	15.53
	(iii) Externally aided (NHAI)	8712.00	10015.72	7893.62	5182.70
	(iv) Counterpart funds (NHAI)	49.50	0.00	0.00	0.00
	(v) Loan to NHAI	2028.00	2504.88	1986.28	1346.78
	EAP—NHAI	10789.50	12520.90	9879.98	9479.48
	(vi) Strengthening of PIC	0.50	1.00	0.85	0.47
2.	Other schemes—NH (O)	8664.00	7443.60	7789.67	7560.85
3.	Works under BRDB	950.00	1564.00	1508.00	1525.43
4.	Travel expenses (domestic)	20.00	5.27	3.47	3.05
5.	Other charges		2.90	1.18	0.53
6.	Development of Information Technology	20.00	24.00	14.50	9.44
7.	Strategic roads under RW	50.00	1.50	1.50	0.00
8.	Strategic roads under BRDB		192.17	202.42	178.30
9.	R&D Plg. studies	20.00	24.75	22.75	11.50
10.	Training	10.50	17.50	15.50	13.60
11.	Machinery and equipment	15.00	37.72	37.72	34.67
12.	Charged expenditure	50.00	25.00	25.00	17.79
13.	NHAI (investment)	10500.00	15518.19	15518.19	15518.19
14.	E&I for States from CRF	500.00	716.11	626.11	374.55
15.	E&I for UTs from CRF		31.09	31.09	8.55
16.	NHDP-III, two-laning expressways and six-laning		1510.00	810.00	810.00
17.	SARDP-NE		1000.00	1000.01	550.01
18.	Strategic Roads in Arunachal Pradesh under Ministry of Defence		100.00	100.00	0.00
19.	Provision for NER		0.00	0.00	0.00
	Total (BS)	34790.00	41264.70	37715.00	36112.05
20.	IEBR	24700.00	25500.00	17782.00	12481.90
	Grand Total	59490.00	66764.70	55497.00	48593.95

Note: The outlays include provisions for NER also whereas in BE and RE figures the provisions for NER have been segregated and shown separately under item no. 19; Exp. = Expenditure; RW = Road Wing; Plg. = Planning; E&I = Roads of Economic and Interstate Importance; NH (O) = National Highways (Original); BS = Budgetary Support.

(Annexure 9.3.1 contd.)

(Annexure 9.3.1 contd.)

NH (O)

S. No.	Schemes/Programmes (Normal NH Works)	Physical Performance Tenth Plan	
		Targets	Achievements
1.	Widening to two lanes (km)	4000	3420.88
2.	Widening to four lanes (km)	800	157.01
3.	Strengthening of weak two lanes (km)	2000	3346.14
4.	Bypasses (nos)	25	13
5.	Major bridges/minor bridges including ROBs (nos)	300	548
6.	IRQP	10000	15326.62

BRDB

S. No.	Schemes/Programmes (Normal NH Works)	Physical Performance Tenth Plan	
		Targets	Achievements
1.	Widening to two lanes (km)	528.92	755.94
2.	Widening to four lanes (km)	0.00	0.00
3.	Strengthening of weak two lanes (Kms)	200.82	164.12
4.	Bypasses (nos)	LS	3
5.	Major bridges/minor bridges including ROBs (nos)	LS	56
6.	IRQP	613.03	923.70

NHAI

S. No.	Schemes/Programmes (Normal NH Works)	Physical Performance Tenth Plan	
		Targets	Achievements
1.	Widening to two lanes (km)	Completion of GQ	
2.	Widening to four lanes (km)		6612.00
3.	Strengthening of weak two lanes (km)		4867.00
4.	Bypasses (nos)		10
5.	Major bridges/minor bridges including ROBs (nos)		7
6.	IRQP		

ANNEXURE 9.3.2

Central Road Sector Outlay and Expenditure—At Current and Constant Price for the Tenth Plan

(In Rs Crore)

S. No.	Schemes	Tenth Plan (2002–07)	AP (2002–03)		AP (2003–04)		AP (2004–05)		AP (2005–06)		AF (2006–07)		Total Outlay for Tenth Plan	Total Exp. at Current Prices
		Outlay	Outlay	Exp.	Outlay	Exp.	Outlay	Exp.	Outlay	Exp.	Outlay	RE		
1	2	3	4	5	6	7	8	9	10	11	12	13	14	15
1.	Externally aided projects	13990.00	2158.00	1512.64	2390.90	1448.90	3323.70	1602.30	3200.30	2953.34	1978.00	978.00	13050.70	9495.18
	(i) Externally aided (RW)	2560.00	123.80	4.88	39.30	0.00	80.00	2.65	160.00	0.00	0.00	0.00	403.10	7.53
	(ii) Counterpart funds (RW)	640.00	31.00	4.66	21.50	0.00	33.50	0.00	40.00	0.00	0.00	0.00	126.00	4.66
	EAP Ministry	3200.00	154.80	9.54	60.80	0.00	113.50	2.65	200.00	3.34	0.00	0.00	529.10	15.53
	(iii) Externally aided (NHAI)	8712.00	1602.00	1202.00	1863.52	1159.12	2568.00	1239.08	2400.00	0.00	1582.20	582.50	10015.72	5182.70
	(iv) Counterpart funds (NHAI)	49.50	0.00	0.00		0.00	0.00	0.00	0.00	0.00	0.00	0.00	0.00	0.00
	(v) Loan to NHAI	2028.00	401.00	301.00	466.38	289.78	642.00	360.50	600.00		395.50	395.50	2504.88	1346.78
	EAP—NHAI	10789.50	2003.00	1503.00	2329.90	1448.90	3210.00	1599.58	3000.00	2950.00	1978.00	978.00	12520.90	9479.48
	(vi) Strengthening of PIC	0.50	0.10	0.10	0.10	0.00	0.20	0.07	0.30	0.00	0.30	0.30	1.00	0.47
2.	Other Schemes—NH (O)	8664.00	1440.00	1425.17	1544.00	1474.57	1482.00	1503.88	1427.30	1570.34	1550.30	586.89	7443.60	7560.85
3.	Works under BRDB	950.00	145.00	210.04	210.00	256.00	210.00	210.00	415.00	321.39	584.00	528.00	1564.00	1525.43
4.	Travel expenses (domestic)	20.00	1.00	0.40	1.02	0.33	0.50	0.37	1.00	0.70	1.75	1.25	5.27	3.05
5.	Other charges		1.00	0.03	0.50	0.0045	0.40	0.00	1.00	0.00		0.50	2.90	0.53
6.	Dev. of Information Technology	20.00	4.00	2.48	5.00	1.81	3.00	0.29	6.00	1.86	6.00	3.00	24.00	9.44
7.	Strategic roads under RW	50.00	1.00	0.00	0.50	0.00	0.00	0.00	0.00	0.00	0.00		1.50	0.00
8.	Strategic roads under BRDB		8.50	10.25	19.00	24.50	19.50	19.50	71.00	49.88	74.17	74.17	192.17	178.30
9.	R&D Plg. studies	20.00	3.00	1.75	3.00	0.19	7.90	0.61	4.85	2.95	6.00	6.00	24.75	11.50
10.	Training	10.50	1.50	0.43	12.00	10.61	1.00		1.50	1.06	1.50	1.50	17.50	13.60
11.	Machinery and equipment	15.00	2.00	1.50	7.00	6.29	3.00	3.00	15.72	13.88	10.00	10.00	37.72	34.67
12.	Charged expenditure	50.00	5.00	5.00	5.00	3.71	5.00	0.03	5.00	4.05	5.00	5.00	25.00	17.79
13.	NHAI (investment)	10500.00	2000.00	2000.00	1993.00	1993.00	1848.00	1848.00	3269.74	3269.74	6407.45	6[illegible]07.45	15518.19	15518.19
14.	E&I for States from CRF	500.00	95.00	25.00	95.00	64.52	92.00	16.88	162.05	86.09	272.06	82.06	716.11	374.55
15.	E&I for UTs from CRF	0.00	5.00	0.00	5.00	0.00	4.00	0.00	8.54	0.00	8.55	8.55	31.09	8.55
16.	NHDP-III, two-laning expressways and six-laning								1400.00	700.00	110.00	10.00	1510.00	810.00
17.	SARDP-NE								450.00	0.00	550.00	50.01	1000.00	550.01
18.	Strategic Roads in Arunachal Pradesh under Min. of Defence								100.00	0.00	0.00	0.00	100.00	0.00
	Total (BS)	34790.00	5870.00	5194.79	6290.92	5284.44	7000.00	5204.86	10539.00	8975.28	11564.78	11-52.68	41264.70	36112.05
19.	IEBR	24700.00	6200.00	5592.90	4000.00	0.00	3300.00	0.00	8500.00	3389.00	3500.00	3[illegible]00.00	25500.00	12481.90
	Grand Total	59490.00	12070.00	10787.69	10290.92	5284.44	10300.00	5204.86	19039.00	12364.28	15064.78	14[illegible]52.68	66764.70	48593.95

ANNEXURE 9.3.3
Plan-wise Addition to NH Length

Period	Length Added in km	Total Length in km
As on 1 April 1947		21440
Pre First Plan (1947–51)	815	22255
First Plan (1951–56)	–	22255
Second Plan (1956–61)	1514	23769
Third Plan (1961–66)	179	23948
Interregnum Period (1966–69)	52	24000
Fourth Plan (1969–74)	4819	28819
Fifth Plan (1974–78)	158	28977
Interregnum Period (1978–80)	46	29023
Sixth Plan (1980–85)	2687	31710
Seventh Plan (1985–90)	1902	33612
Interregnum Period (1990–92)	77	33689
Eighth Plan (1992–97)	609	34298
Ninth Plan (1997–2002)	23814	58112
Tenth Plan (2002–07)	9008#	66590
	Tenth Plan (2002–07)	
2002–03	–	58112
2003–04	7457	65569
2004–05	–	65569
2005–06	556#	66125
2006–07	995	66590

Note: # Excluding 530 km of NHs denotified in 2006.

ANNEXURE 9.3.4
Bharat Nirman—Targets for New Connectivity

(Length in km, Habitations in Numbers)

S. No	Name of the State	2005–06		2006–07		2007–08		2008–09		Total	
		Length	Habs	Length	Habs	Length	Habs	Length	Habs	Length	Habs
1.	Andhra Pradesh	0	0	0	0	0	0	0	0	0	0
2.	Arunachal Pradesh	162.5	22	637.5	85	646.875	86	671.875	105	2118.75	298
3.	Assam	605.852	421	2864.063	1988	3889.845	2701	5793.46	4022	13153.22	9132
4.	Bihar	1665.831	896	3928.75	2062	6121.425	3214	7230.306	3784	18946.312	9956
5.	Chhattisgarh	1501.365	478	4367.606	1310	6450.644	2007	8255.181	2514	20574.796	6309
6.	Goa	0	0	0	0	0	0	0	0	0	0
7.	Gujarat	402.955	230	429.723	246	438.675	251	438.675	251	1710.028	978
8.	Haryana	0	0	0	0	0	0	0	0	0	0
9.	Himachal Pradesh	464.583	127	795.833	209	638.542	166	479.167	123	2378.125	625
10.	Jammu and Kashmir	169.972	57	1059.49	352	1781.869	593	1405.099	466	4416.43	1468
11.	Jharkhand	1051.779	526	2594.39	1295	1812.298	901	2319.31	1155	7777.777	3877
12.	Karnataka	0	0	0	0	0	0	0	0	0	0
13.	Kerala	0	0	0	0	0	0	0	0	0	0
14.	Madhya Pradesh	2602.139	768	6162.451	1760	8326.848	2399	10470.17	2905	27561.608	7832
15.	Maharashtra	0	0	0	0	0	0	0	0	0	0
16.	Manipur	100	11	460.714	48	464.286	48	719.048	74	1744.048	181
17.	Meghalaya	123.609	35	135.971	39	140.091	40	144.211	41	543.882	155
18.	Mizoram	82.746	12	274.819	39	277.884	39	306.498	43	941.947	133
19.	Nagaland	93.318	9	104.529	10	109.507	10	114.485	11	421.839	40
20.	Orissa	1055.95	493	1985.609	874	2524.021	1087	4427.774	1993	9993.354	4447
21.	Punjab	0	0	0	0	0	0	0	0	0	0
22.	Rajasthan	2153.615	743	3629.519	1252	3554.217	1225	2123.494	732	11460.845	3952
23.	Sikkim	75.031	22	104.042	30	108.043	31	132.053	37	419.169	120
24.	Tamil Nadu	0	0	0	0	0	0	0	0	0	0
25.	Tripura	94.774	66	261.74	183	354.701	248	447.661	313	1158.876	810
26.	Uttar Pradesh	1966.416	1236	2390.632	1504	2059.213	1295	1378.701	867	7794.962	4902
27.	Uttarakhand	380.609	95	422.008	106	1025.641	257	1020.299	255	2848.557	713
28.	West Bengal	739.378	787	2572.767	2738	3265.307	3473	3643.359	3876	10220.811	10874
	Total	15492.42	7034	35182.16	16130	43989.93	20071	51520.83	23567	146185.34	66802

(Annexure 9.3.4 contd.)

(Annexure 9.3.4 contd.)

(Length in km)

S. No	Name of the State	2005–06 Length	2006–07 Length	2007–08 Length	2008–09 Length	Total Length
1	2	3	4	5	6	7
1.	Andhra Pradesh	1821.494	2258.652	2258.652	2258.652	8597.45
2.	Arunachal Pradesh	0	0	0	0	0
3.	Assam	0	2005.71	2269.808	2219.843	6495.361
4.	Bihar	0	2393.617	3510.638	3390.958	9295.213
5.	Chhattisgarh	0	1986.063	3240.418	3222.996	8449.477
6.	Goa	190.114	190.114	190.114	190.114	760.456
7.	Gujarat	0	1557.971	1557.971	1413.043	4528.985
8.	Haryana	229.358	1146.789	1146.789	1238.532	3761.468
9.	Himachal Pradesh	0	1515.923	1694.268	1503.185	4713.376
10.	Jammu and Kashmir	0	1007.584	920.91	1007.584	2936.078
11.	Jharkhand	0	2108.433	2123.494	1987.952	6219.879
12.	Karnataka	2573.529	2573.529	2573.529	2573.529	10294.116
13.	Kerala	524.109	628.931	524.109	524.109	2201.258
14.	Madhya Pradesh	0	5189.543	6614.379	6823.53	18627.452
15.	Maharashtra	4334.365	4334.365	4334.365	4334.365	17337.46
16.	Manipur	0	0	0	0	0
17.	Meghalaya	0	587.583	587.583	665.189	1840.355
18.	Mizoram	0	257.998	257.998	216.718	732.714
19.	Nagaland	0	246.914	246.914	370.371	864.199
20.	Orissa	0	4438.574	4663.144	5059.445	14161.163
21.	Punjab	423.729	1483.051	1483.051	1680.791	5070.622
22.	Rajasthan	0	4764.543	4653.74	3656.51	13074.793
23.	Sikkim	0	196.85	137.795	98.425	433.07
24.	Tamil Nadu	1297.71	2824.427	2824.427	4167.939	11114.503
25.	Tripura	0	373.737	383.838	414.141	1171.716
26.	Uttar Pradesh	0	7158.962	6956.031	14408.12	28523.113
27.	Uttarakhand	0	889.454	1283.354	1270.648	3443.456
28.	West Bengal	0	2549.942	2878.965	4054.053	9482.96
	Total	11394.408	54669.259	59316.284	68750.742	194130.693

ANNEXURE 9.3.5

Tenth Five Year Plan (2002–07)—Financial and Physical Performance of Road Transport

S. No.	Schemes/Programmes	Financial Achievement (in Rs crore)				Physical Achievement
		Outlay	BE	RE	Actual Exp.	Achievements
1	Road Safety	153.00	156.95	154.16	137.19	
(i)	Refresher training to drivers in unorganized sector	12.00	15.85	15.55	13.81	192218 drivers trained.
(ii)	Publicity measures and awareness campaigns	60.00	59.80	62.35	59.97	686 video spots and 4326 radio spots were broadcast/telecast. Publicity material on road safety printed and distributed to States/UTs. Funds released to 499 NGOs for road safety awareness programme.
(iii)	Human Resource Development including training	2.00	1.40#	1.40#	1.38#	75 training programmes for State Transport Department Personnel conducted at ARAI, CIRT, Pune, IIP Dehradun, and ESCI Hyderabad.#
(iv)	Road Safety Equipment and Programme Implementation	10.00	8.60	8.56	5.14	22 interceptors provided to States of Uttarakhand, MP, Sikkim, Haryana, UP, Kerala, Rajasthan, Himachal Pradesh, Punjab, Chhattisgarh, Gujarat, and Karnataka.
(v)	National Highway Accident Relief Service Scheme	69.00	71.30	66.30	56.89	268 ambulances and 200 cranes were provided to States/NGOs.
2	Pollution Testing and Control	10.00	6.55*	4.05	3.32*	*
3	National Database Network	13.00	12.61	11.28	9.41	Physical progress cannot be quantified.
(i)	Computer Systems and National Database	8.00	7.70	7.59	7.58	
(ii)	Data Collection Research and Development transportation studies	5.00	4.91	3.69	1.83	
4	Model Driving Training School and Public Transport System	34.00	33.89	35.26	29.45	Against the target of 4, 13 schools have been sanctioned, and out of these 2 are operational.
	Grand Total	210.00	210.00	204.75	179.37	

Note: # During 2006–07, HRD has been merged with refresher training to drivers. Therefore, actual expenditure is for first four years of the Tenth Plan. * During 2006–07, Pollution Testing and Control has been merged with Road Safety Equipment and Programme Implementation. Therefore, actual expenditure is for first four years of the Tenth Plan.

ANNEXURE 9.3.6

State-wise Sanctions and Releases of Central Share in Respect of Model Driving Training School—Status as on 31 March 2007

(in Rs Lakh)

S. No.	Name of the State/NGO	Central Assistance	Amount Sanctioned					Total Amount Released	Balance
			2002–03	2003–04	2004–05	2005–06	2006–07		
1	2	3	4	5	6	10	8	9	10
1.	Assam (Betkuchi) RT-25036/2/2001-RSC	394.00	45.00 (25.3.03)	150.00 (11.3.04) 25.00 (31.3.04)	–	150.00 (19.05.05)	20.00 (14.02.07)	390.00	4.00
2.	M/s KDLOA (Vijayawada) RT-25036/2/2001-RSC	400.00	50.00 (25.3.03)	125.00 (18.3.04)	150.00 (14.10.04)	60.00 (20.6.05)	12.81 (30.3.07)	397.81	NIL [Out of 15.00 (Interest Rs 2.19 Lakhs on Rs 385 Lakhs)]
3.	Karnataka (Hagaribommanahalli) RT-25036/2/2001-RSC	269.00	100.00 (25.3.03)	–	100.00 (28.6.04)	50.00 (20.6.05)	15.00 (30.3.07)	265.00	4.00
4.	West Bengal (Jessore Road) RT-25036/2/2001-RSC	328.00	100.00 (25.3.03)	50.00 (11.12.03) 125.00 (31.3.04)	–	–	–	275.00	53.00
5.	Himachal Pradesh (Jassur) RT-25036/2/2004-RSC	181.00	–	–	75.00 (6.8.04)	80.00 (31.3.06)	–	155.00	26.00
6.	Kerala (Edappal) RT-25036/2/2004-RSC	299.00	–	–	100.00 (6.8.04)	–	–	100.00	199.00
7.	IDTR (Sarai Kale Khan) RT-25036/2/2004-RSC	325.00	–	–	100.00 (6.8.04)	150.00 (14.11.05)	40.00 (24.08.06)	290.00	35.00
8.	Uttrakhand (Dehradun) RT-25036/2/2004-RSC	325.00	–	–	125.00 (17.2.05)	–	–	125.00	200.00
9.	Uttar Pradesh (Allen forest at Kanpur) RT-25036/2/2004-RSC	339.00	–	–	–	101.70 (27.03.06)	–	101.70	237.30
10.	Orissa (Chandikhole) (joint venture with TATA Motors and All Orissa Truck Owners Federation) RT-25036/2/2004-RSC	336.00	–	–	–	100.80 (27.03.06)	200.00 (30.3.07)	300.80	35.20
11.	Nagaland at Dimapur RT-25036/2/2005-RS	354.00	–	–	–	–	106.20 (23.10.06) 200.00 (30.3.07)	306.20	47.80
12.	Madhya Pradesh (Indore) RT-25036/2/2006-RS	393.96	–	–	–	–	118.18 (13.2.07)	118.18	275.78
13.	Haryana at Bahadurgarh RT-25036/5/2007-RS	400.00	–	–	–	–	120.00 (30.3.07)	120.00	280.00
	Grand Total (As on 31 March 2007)	4343.96	295.00	475.00	650.00	692.50	832.19	2944.69	(Rs 1397.08 + Interest Rs 2.19) Rs 1399.27

ANNEXURE 9.3.7
Physical Performance of State Road Transport Corporations/Undertakings

SRTU	% Fleet Utilization		Vehicle Productivity— Rev. Earning per bus per km		Staff Productivity— Rev. Earning km per worker per day		Fuel Efficiency KMPL	
	2002–03	2006–07	2002–03	2006–07	2002–03	2006–07	2002–03	2006–07
Andhra Pradesh	99.24	99.50	320	339	48.00	55.00	5.24	5.27
Arunachal Pradesh	65.00	77.00	125	99	24.56	25.51	3.1	3.10
Assam	68.00	78.00	123	141	13.00	14.00	4	4.00
Bihar	12.00	67.00	29	176	7.52	30.83	4.1	4.03
DTC (Delhi)	79.85	85.65	171	179	17.99	27.48	3.78	3.96
Goa (Kadamba)	79.00	83.00	206	214	39.00	44.00	4.26	5.1
Gujarat	83.50	84.50	302	313	47.91	57.02	5.3	5.25
Haryana	97.00	96.00	311	338	57.50	62.79	4.54	4.93
Himachal Pradesh	97.00	98.00	223	235	45.79	46.95	3.57	3.64
Jammu and Kashmir	64.00	75.00	95	112	15.14	23.90	3.81	4.2
Karnataka								
KSRTC	95.30	95.00	343	368	62.20	57.30	4.97	5.22
NWKRTC	96.10	95.00	336	333	57.54	55.13	4.97	5.6
BMTC	95.00	95.00	216	218	42.20	37.10	4.6	4.75
NEKRTC	92.30	96.00	285	315	56.70	58.00	4.97	5.55
Kerala	78.00	82.00	335	329	45.66	52.96	3.89	4
Madhya Pradesh	83.00	0.00	245	0	42.00	0.00	4.06	0
Maharashtra	93.96	95.00	293	309	45.32	48.79	4.76	4.9
Meghalaya	72.00	68.00	85	154	7.45	3.67	3.66	3.67
Mizoram	53.00	63.00	60	138	5.92	6.26	3	3
Nagaland	61.00	63.00	90	89	13.61	19.84	3.5	3.7
Orissa	91.00	90.00	275	230	45.50	57.24	4.2	4.45
Punjab Roadways	85.10	88.40	238	206	41.40	47.80	4.29	4.42
PEPSURTC	95.00	95.00	267	318	57.90	60.82	4.39	5.12
Rajasthan	93.00	96.00	319	364	63.37	75.25	4.94	5.12
Sikkim	80.00	68.00	67	65	17.53	10.56	3.25	2.8
Tamil Nadu	91.72	93.02	379	404	52.06	58.31	4.37	4.8
Tripura	61.00	55.00	76	79	9.27	12.52	3.57	3.63
Uttar Pradesh	90.00	97.00	262	322	42.79	62.61	4.79	5.2
Calcutta STC	66.88	59.00	150	128	20.77	22.26	3.7	3.9
North Bengal STC	61.00	57.00	147	141	21.19	22.61	3.94	3.95
South Bengal STC	77.00	85.00	206	222	34.54	38.41	3.85	4.3
Calcutta Tramways	63.00	67.00	136	157	20.20	22.70	3.3	3.5
Uttarakhand	0.00	94.00	0	300	0.00	43.00	0	4.79
All-India Average	78.72	82.50	210	229	39.23	39.39	4.11	4.31

ANNEXURE 9.5.1

Year-wise Physical Targets and Achievements during the Tenth Plan—Major Ports (Commodity-wise)

(Million Metric Tonnes)

S. No.	Name of Commodity	Tenth Plan Target	2002–03 Ach.	2003–04 Ach.	2004–05 Ach.	2005–06 Ach.	2006–07 Ach.
1.	POL	154.30	109.63	122.16	126.44	142.09	154.35
2.	Iron ore	52.50	50.56	58.81	76.20	79.17	80.56
3.	Fertilizers and Fertilizer Raw Material (FRM)	13.45	8.55	7.54	9.68	12.19	14.11
4.	Thermal and Coking Coal	71.30	48.19	48.80	52.56	58.76	60.21
5.	Container	61.10	43.67	51.00	54.76	61.98	73.48
6.	Other cargo	62.35	52.95	56.49	64.11	69.38	81.13
	Total	415.00	313.55	344.80	383.75	423.57	463.84

Note: Ach. = Achievement.

ANNEXURE 9.5.2

Year-wise Physical Targets and Achievements during the Tenth Plan—Major Ports (Port-wise)

(Million Metric Tonnes)

S. No.	Port/Organization	Tenth Plan Target	2002–03 Ach.	2003–04 Ach.	2004–05 Ach.	2005–06 Ach.	2006–07 Ach.
1.	Kolkata	21.40	7.20	8.69	9.95	10.81	12.60
2.	Haldia	33.40	28.60	32.56	36.26	42.33	42.45
3.	Paradeep	28.90	23.90	25.31	30.10	33.11	38.52
4.	Vizag	60.00	46.01	47.74	50.15	55.80	56.39
5.	Chennai	40.00	33.69	36.71	43.81	47.25	53.41
6.	Tuticorin	18.70	13.29	13.68	15.81	17.14	18.00
7.	Cochin	17.20	13.02	13.57	14.09	13.89	15.31
8.	New Mangalore	32.70	21.43	26.67	33.89	34.45	32.04
9.	Mormugao	26.30	23.65	27.87	30.66	31.69	34.24
10.	Mumbai	30.40	26.80	30.00	35.19	44.19	52.36
11.	JL Nehru	34.50	26.84	31.19	32.81	37.83	44.82
12.	Kandla	51.00	40.63	41.52	41.55	45.91	52.99
13.	Ennore Port Ltd	20.50	8.49	9.28	9.48	9.17	10.71
	Grand Total	415.00	313.55	344.79	383.75	423.57	463.84

ANNEXURE 9.5.3
Tenth Plan—Outlays and Expenditure in Ports Sector

(in Rs crore)

S. No	Name of the Port/Organization	Tenth Plan Outlay	2002–03		2003–04		2004–05		2005–06		2006–07		Tenth Plan Act. Exp
			Approved Outlay	Actual Exp.	Approved Outlay	Actual Exp.	Approved Outlay	Actual Exp.	Approved Outlay	Actual Exp.	Approved Outlay	Actual Exp.	
1.	Kolkata#	789.42	199.92	6.85	210.30	10.48	46.22	47.55	54.04	59.66	50.04	71.99	196.53
2.	Mumbai	880.20	109.05	100.76	54.21	57.81	56.15	44.49	74.53	19.23	59.36	14.55	236.84
3.	JNPT	262.75	146.36	40.26	143.02	12.73	102.14	58.85	96.84	65.77	106.14	40.74	218.35
4.	Chennai	326.70	95.99	85.50	36.69	29.21	16.75	22.68	46.71	25.11	35.00	26.07	188.57
5.	Cochin	366.51	–	10.02	18.88	10.86	85.41	9.52	53.12	24.76	73.34	72.89	128.05
6.	Vizag	240.84	49.06	51.30	51.00	55.65	54.44	27.68	27.00	17.68	27.33	43.79	196.10
7.	Kandla	416.71	94.78	55.89	66.71	41.50	92.98	52.89	93.30	91.29	94.56	80.19	321.76
8.	Mormugao	348.06	30.86	26.53	87.14	43.06	53.85	11.05	33.50	17.92	28.06	20.77	119.33
9.	Paradip	222.70	59.00	41.42	53.40	14.56	87.16	28.99	116.00	44.02	83.40	23.15	152.14
10.	New Mangalore	147.40	37.00	24.41	25.00	5.14	20.00	29.60	26.00	18.09	18.00	18.02	95.26
11.	Tuticorin	230.0	76.10	36.02	17.54	21.84	25.81	5.48	43.67	13.56	52.31	29.12	106.04
12.	Ennore Port Ltd	300.00	1.00	-	150.00	0.99	95.00	2.32	76.00	13.40	70.00	9.57	26.28
	Total (A)	4531.29	899.12	478.96	913.89	303.83	735.91	341.1	740.71	410.49	698.54	450.85	1985.25
13.	Sethusamudram	–	–	–	–	–	10.00	–	107.00	150.00	304.00	334.66	484.66
14.	Web-based EDI PCS	–	–	–	–	–	–	–	6.00	0.34	7.33	1.66	2.00
15.	Others*	587.00	214.88	53.98	237.00	44.06	221.04	19.87	260.04	79.13	333.78	214.77	411.81
	Total (B)	587.00	214.88	53.98	237.00	44.06	231.04	19.87	373.04	229.47	645.51	551.09	898.47
	Total (A+B)	5118.29	1114.00	532.94	1150.89	347.89	966.95	360.97	1113.75	639.96	1344.25	1001.94	2883.70
16.	Survey Vessels	300.00	45.00	8.95	50.00	–	100.00	–	50.00	0.00	20.00	0.00	8.95
	Grand Total	5418.29	1159.00	541.89	1200.89	347.89	1066.95	360.97	1163.75	639.96	1364.25	1001.94	2892.65

Note: # includes Haldia and RR Schemes. * includes DCI, ALHW, R&D studies, Post-tsunami works, and Minor Port studies.

ANNEXURE 9.6.1
Financial Progress of the Civil Aviation Sector during the Tenth Plan

(in Rs crore)

S. No.	Organization	Tenth Plan Outlay	2002–03 Outlay	2002–03 Exp.	2003–04 Outlay	2003–04 Exp.	2004–05 Outlay	2004–05 Exp.	2005–06 Outlay	2005–06 Exp.	2006–07 Outlay	2006–07 Exp.	Tenth Plan Total Exp.
1	2	3	4	5	6	7	8	9	10	11	12	13	14
1.	Air India Ltd	2661.39 (1.00)	858.70 (1.00)	743.07	600.81 (1.00)	479.57	471.40 (1.00)	358.07	468.74 (1.00)	443.33	486.70	364.23	2388.27
2.	Indian Airlines Ltd	4240.50 (1.00)	510.00 (1.00)	418.93	280.00 (1.00)	248.78	226.00 (1.00)	221.70	911.73 (325.00)*	192.13 (325.00)*	706.00	350.00	1431.54 (325.00)
3.	Airports Authority of India	5404.21 (250.00)	996.05 (53.12)	445.66 (33.59)	800.00 (34.96)	566.22 (22.08)	795.08 (30.00)	606.49 (30.00)	892.30 (30.00)	876.08 (36.00)	1506.44 (42.91)	1040.17 (29.00)	3534.62 (150.67)
4.	PHHL	458.90	133.80	53.01	81.45	19.60	109.50	60.92	90.70	41.52	175.00	106.90	281.95
5.	Indira Gandhi Rashtriya Uran Academy	10.00 (10.00)	2.09 (2.09)	0.98 (0.98)	3.50 (3.50)	0.50 (0.50)	3.00 (3.00)	3.00 (3.00)	3.85 (3.85)	2.30 (2.30)	40.30 (40.30)	31.10 (31.10)	37.88 (37.88)
6.	Directorate General of Civil Aviation	19.00 (19.00)	3.10 (3.10)	2.54 (2.54)	4.15 (4.15)	2.86 (2.86)	4.00 (4.00)	3.06 (3.06)	5.00 (5.00)	1.83 (1.83)	29.00 (29.00)	1.74 (1.74)	12.03 (12.03)
7.	Bureau of Civil Aviation Security	114.00 (114.00)	7.69 (7.69)	3.87 (3.87)	7.00 (7.00)	4.24 (4.24)	10.00 (10.00)	0.28 (0.28)	5.00 (5.00)	0.98 (0.98)	5.00 (5.00)	0.15 (0.15)	9.52 (9.52)
8.	Hotel Corporation of India Ltd	15.00	8.76	8.76	1.00	0.51	1.00	1.00	1.00	1.00	15.00	15.00	26.27
9.	Air India Charters Ltd	0.00	0.00	0.00	0.00	0.00	0.00	0.00	0.00	16.83	70.70	42.18	59.01
10.	Aero Club of India	5.00 (5.00)	1.00 (1.00)	0.00 (0.00)	1.27 (1.27)	1.00 (1.00)	1.00 (1.00)	1.00 (1.00)	1.00 (1.00)	0.00 (0.00)	12.79 (12.79)	9.00 (9.00)	11.00 (11.00)
	Total	12928.00 (400.00)	2521.19 (69.00)	1676.82 (40.98)	1779.18 (52.88)	1323.28 (30.68)	1620.98 (50.00)	1255.52 (37.34)	2379.32 (370.85)	1576.00 (366.11)	3046.93 (130.00)	1960.47 (70.99)	7792.09 (546.10)

Note: Figures in brackets indicate Gross Budgetary Support.

* During 2005–06, budgetary support of Rs 325 crore was released to Indian Airlines for purchase of new aircrafts, out of which the company utilized Rs 47.61 crore during 2005–06 and balance amount of Rs 277.39 crore was utilized in April 2006.

10

Energy

ENERGY SECTOR

ISSUES AND CHALLENGES

10.1 Availability and access to energy are considered as catalysts for economic growth. The envisaged growth of the economy at 9% in the Eleventh Plan cannot be achieved without a commensurate increase in the availability of energy. Over half of the country's population does not have access to electricity or any other form of commercial energy. Meeting the energy access challenges and ensuring lifeline supply of clean energy to all is essential for empowering individuals, especially women and girls, who have the task of collecting and using non-commercial fuels such as fire wood, crop residues, and dung cakes that remain the primary energy source for cooking in over two-thirds of the households. Provision of clean fuels or at least wood plantation within one km of habitation and dissemination of technology for use of clean fuels is vital for good health. This is essential if growth is to be inclusive.

10.2 India is both a major energy producer and a consumer. India currently ranks as the world's seventh largest energy producer, accounting for about 2.49% of the world's total annual energy production. It is also the world's fifth largest energy consumer, accounting for about 3.45% of the world's total annual energy consumption in 2004. Since independence, the country has seen significant expansion in the total energy use in the country with a shift from non-commercial to commercial sources. The share of commercial energy in total primary energy consumption rose from 59.7% in 1980–81 to 72.6% in 2006–07. It must be noted, however, that India's per capita energy consumption is one of the lowest in the world. India consumed 455 kilogram of oil equivalent (kgoe) per person of primary energy in 2004, which is around 26% of world average of 1750 kgoe in that year. As compared to this, per capita energy consumption in China and Brazil was 1147 kgoe and 1232 kgoe, respectively.

10.3 The main challenge before the energy sector for fuelling the proposed growth in the Eleventh Plan is to enhance energy supply in cost-effective ways. The persistent shortages of electricity both for peak power and energy indicate the magnitude of the problem. Average peak shortages are estimated to be 12% in 2006–07 which is an underestimate as scheduled load shedding is not included in it. The very high load factor of 76.8% for the system indicates that the system is operating under strain or has limited reserve. At the same time, for want of natural gas, some gas-based power plants are kept idle. Nuclear plants are also operated at lower load factors for want of adequate uranium. Power shortages are an indication of insufficient generating capacity and inadequate transmission and distribution (T&D) networks. To a great extent this is the outcome of poor financial health of the State Electricity Utilities having high levels of Aggregate Technical and Commercial (AT&C) losses.

10.4 The task of meeting the energy needs of development has become more complex in recent times due to the imminent threat of global warming. This poses a challenge to the world as a whole including India and points to the need for an acceptable international approach to deal with the problem. India's energy strategy has, therefore, to bear in mind the need for action as part of a reasonable international agreement which is consistent with India's development objectives.

LONG-TERM REQUIREMENT

10.5 Since energy sector involves large gestation lags, we also need to look at the long-term requirement. The rate of growth and, therefore, the energy intensity are the key factors which impact the projections of future energy demand. The Expert Committee (EC) on Integrated Energy Policy, Planning Commission (Box 10.1) has projected primary energy demand for 2031–32 for India. Table 10.1 summarizes the range of projected requirement and supply. The projected requirement of coal has been estimated assuming its calorie content to be 4000 kcal per kg and 2865 kcal per kg for lignite.

AVAILABILITY OF ENERGY RESOURCE

10.6 India is not endowed with large primary energy reserves in keeping with her vast geographical area, growing population, and increasing final energy needs. The distribution of primary commercial energy resources in the country is quite skewed. Whereas coal is abundant and is mostly concentrated in the eastern region, which accounts for nearly 70% of the total coal reserves, the western region has over 70% of the hydrocarbons reserves in the country. Similarly, more than 70% of the total hydro potential in the country is located in the northern and the north eastern regions. The southern region, which has only 6% of the coal reserves and 10% of the total hydro potential, has most of the lignite deposits occurring in the country.

Box 10.1
Integrated Energy Policy

The Planning Commission had set up an expert group to recommend integrated energy policy. Its report submitted in 2006 (*http://planningcommission.nic.in/reports/genrep/rep_intengy.pdf*) deals with various sources and forms of energy (electricity, coal, oil, gas, nuclear, hydel energy, renewables including wind energy, solar energy, biofuels, wood plantations), the country's projected requirement and availability of resources, energy security, energy efficiency as well as R&D priorities.

The report lays strong emphasis on making the energy sector efficient and competitive. It argues for relative prices and taxes that reflect the true social cost of different fuels and forms of energy as the best way to encourage right choice of fuels and techniques; for competitive markets wherever possible; transparent and target subsidies when needed; policies that rely on incentives and disincentives; and policies that are implementable. The recommendations are being discussed with various ministries for implementation. Many of the policies recommended for the coal sector have already been implemented. Progress has also been made in policies concerning energy efficiency and renewable energy. Progress in the power sector has yet to show results. The oil and gas sector continues with an unsustainable pricing policy.

TABLE 10.1
Projected Primary Energy Requirement for India, 2030

(All in Mtoe)

Fuel	Range of Requirements	Assumed Domestic Production	Range of Imports#	Import (%)
Coal including lignite	632–1022	560	72–462	11–45
Oil	350–486	35	315–451	90–93
Natural gas including coal bed methane (CBM)	100–197	100	0–97	0–49
Total commercial primary energy	1351–1702	–	387–1010	29–59

Note: # Range of imports is calculated across all scenarios by taking the minimum requirement and maximum domestic production as the lower bound and maximum requirement and minimum domestic production as the upper bound.
Source: Integrated Energy Policy Report (IEPR), 2006.

COAL AND LIGNITE

10.7 Coal continues to be the major energy resource of the country. As on January 2007, the coal reserves were 253.3 billion tonnes (bt), out of which 97.92 bt are in the 'proved' category. The lignite reserves as on April 2006 were estimated at 38.27 bt, out of which 4.5 bt is in the proved category. If all the inferred reserves materialize, these reserves can sustain current level of production for 140 years.

PETROLEUM AND NATURAL GAS

10.8 The balance of recoverable oil reserves as on 1 April 2006 is around 1653 mt (Directorate General of Hydrocarbon, DGH 2005–06 report), which can sustain the current level of production for the next 35 years. The current level of production barely caters to 26% of the petroleum products demand and the balance oil requirements are met by importing the crude. The current level of natural gas production in the country is inadequate to meet the industrial demand, particularly of the power and fertilizer industries. LNG imports since 2004–05 have been able to bridge the gap partially. The situation is likely to improve once production starts from Krishna–Godavari (K–G) basin reserves in a couple of years.

10.9 Besides natural gas, the country has significant CBM and underground coal gasification (UCG) resources. Coal India Limited (CIL) and ONGC are already implementing two CBM projects. Blocks have also been allocated through competitive bidding process to private companies for exploration and exploitation of CBM. Production of 3.78 bcm from CBM and 2.99 bcm from UCG are included in the Eleventh Plan targets.

NUCLEAR ENERGY

10.10 At present, nuclear energy installed capacity is 3900 MW_e which is 3.1% of total installed power generation capacity and the Plant Load Factor (PLF) of Nuclear Power stations is 57%. India's long-term nuclear power programme is based on utilizing the vast indigenous resources of thorium for electricity generation. The three-stage nuclear power development programme in India is aimed at converting thorium to fissile material. India is poorly endowed with uranium and available uranium resources can support 10000 MW_e electricity generation programme based on pressurized heavy water reactors (PHWRs) using natural uranium as fuel and heavy water as moderator and coolant. The energy potential of natural uranium can be increased to about 300000 MW_e in the second stage through fast breeder reactors (FBRs) which utilize plutonium obtained from the recycled spent fuel of the first stage along with thorium as blanket to produce U_{233}. With the deployment of thorium in the third stage using U_{233} as fuel, the energy potential for electricity generation is large and substantial.

RENEWABLE SOURCES OF ENERGY

10.11 Projections made in the IEPR reveal that to achieve its development goals, India would need to rely increasingly on imported oil, gas, and coal in the medium term (2032). Against this backdrop, the role of new and renewable energy assumes added significance, irrespective of whether it replaces coal or oil. In this regard, IEPR recognizes 'the need to maximally develop domestic supply options as well as the need to diversify energy sources…', although renewables are likely to account for only around 5%–6% of the primary commercial energy-mix by 2032. Given the growing concerns for climate change and energy security, it is imperative that this energy in the longer term will substantially increase its share in the fuel-mix. Continuing to support the growth of new and renewable energy is in the country's long-term interest, even though in the medium term this option might appear somewhat costlier. Thus, a balanced approach for new and renewable energy that factors in the need to develop domestic and renewable sources of energy has to be adopted.

TRENDS IN PRIMARY ENERGY DEMAND AND SUPPLY

10.12 The demand for energy, particularly for commercial energy, has been growing rapidly with the growth of the economy, changes in the demographic structure, rising urbanization, socio-economic development, and the desire for attaining and sustaining self-reliance in some sectors of the economy. Table 10.2 gives the trend of primary commercial energy demand and supply between 1960–61 and 2006–07 and projected requirement for 2011–12.

Box 10.2
Energy Equivalence

The energy labeled as 'final energy' such as electricity, petrol, gas, coal, firewood, etc. is obtained from the sources available in nature, labeled as 'primary energy', and includes hydrocarbons (coal, oil, and natural gas), fissile or fertile elements primarily uranium, the kinetic energy of natural elements (wind, water, etc.), and the electromagnetic rays of the sun and the natural heat of the Earth (geothermal energy). As per convention, final energy consumption is generally expressed as weights of fuels burnt, or from kWh consumed if it is electricity. Each fuel, while burning, produces certain amount of energy in the form of heat that can be measured in standard units such as kilocalories or Joules. Fuels are compared using their calorie content with that of oil in tonnes or million tonnes of oil equivalent (mtoe). One tonne of oil is worth 42 billion Joules or 10 billion calories whereas one million tonne of Indian coal has 4.1 billion calories. Thus 1 mt of coal is 4.1/10 mtoe or 0.41 mtoe. Electrical energy measured in kWh is also converted into the thermal energy kcal or kJ using the definition and finally expressed as mtoe (1 billion kWh = 0.86 billion calorie). Taking the thermal efficiency of the power plant and other losses in the system, the equivalence between electricity and fossil fuels would be 1billion kWh = 0.28 mtoe (in case of coal-fired boilers) and 0.261 mtoe (in case of nuclear electricity). 1 billion kWh generated from hydroelectricity or wind power, however, are considered as equivalent to 0.086 mtoe since there is no intermediate stage of heat production while using these primary energies. It is possible to argue that the efficiency of thermal power plant should be used to convert hydroelectricity and wind power also. In this case, 1 billion kWh of hydroelectricity would be equivalent to 0.28 mtoe. This has an important bearing when one considers how much renewable energy is renewable. Thus in 2006–07 renewable energy was 2.8% or 8.3% of India's total primary commercial energy depending on the conversion factor used.

TABLE 10.2
Trends in Demand and Supply of Primary Energy

(All in Mtoe#)

	1960–61	1970–71	1980–81	1990–91	2000–01	2006–07	2011–12*
Domestic production of commercial energy	36.78	47.67	75.19	150.01	207.08	259.56	435
Net imports	6.04	12.66	24.63	31.07	89.03	131.97	111
Total commercial energy	42.82	60.33	99.82	181.08	296.11	391.53	546
Non-commercial energy	74.38	86.72	108.48	122.07	136.64	147.56	169
Total primary energy demand	117.20	147.05	208.30	303.15	432.75	539.09	715

Note: # Mtoe = million tonne of oil equivalent. For details see Annexure 10.3.

* Projected requirement at the end of the Eleventh Plan is as per the Report of the EC on Integrated Energy Policy and projection of domestic supply is as per the Working Group Reports. Import requirement is the difference between projected requirement and domestic supply projections.

(i) Domestic production of commercial energy includes coal, lignite, oil, natural gas, hydro power, nuclear power, and wind power.

(ii) Net imports include coal, oil, and LNG imports.

Source: IEPR.

10.13 While total primary energy requirement registered an average annual growth rate of 3.67% between 1990–91 and 2006–07, the primary commercial energy requirement registered an average annual growth rate of 4.93% during the same period. The Tenth Plan had envisaged a declining primary commercial energy intensity of GDP reflected in growth of 6.64% in primary commercial energy supply by the end of 2006–07 over the 2001–02 level while GDP grew at 8% implying an energy elasticity of 0.83. However, the primary commercial energy consumption actually registered a growth rate of 5.51% over the consumption level in 2001–02, whereas the economy registered an average growth rate of 7.8% during the Tenth Plan period yielding an elasticity of primary commercial energy consumption with respect to the GDP of only about 0.71%.

10.14 Non-commercial energy resources include the traditional fuels such as wood, cow dung, crop residue, and biogas and constitute a significant percentage of total primary energy consumption in the country. A larger share of these fuels is used by the households, particularly in rural areas, for meeting their cooking and heating needs. The consumption of 147.56 mtoe of traditional fuels in 2006–07 includes consumption of 238 mt of fuel wood, 98 mt of dung, and 38 mt of agricultural waste. Around 80% of the fuel wood is used for household consumption and the balance is used by the cottage industry, hotels, etc.

10.15 The total energy needs are met by different energy sources. Table 10.3 gives the source-wise breakup of the energy demand and Table 10.4 gives the percentages of these met from domestic production, the rest coming from imports.

10.16 Though the share of oil and gas has been progressively increasing over the years, coal continues to be the dominant fuel in the total energy use in the country. Imports constituted about 33.70% of the total primary commercial energy consumption in 2006–07.

10.17 While production of coal in 2006–07 has increased about three times the level of production in 1980–81, the share of coal and lignite in total primary commercial energy supply has been declining progressively over the years. On the other hand, share of oil and natural gas in the total primary commercial energy supply has been rising progressively. While the share of oil and natural gas rose from 37.89% in 1980–81 to 42.93% in 2006–07, the share of coal and lignite declined from 56.83% in 1980–81 to 53.11% in 2006–07.

10.18 Our dependence on imports is growing. Table 10.4 shows that we imported 13.4% of our coal requirement, 73.4% of oil and product needs, and 1.6% of gas requirement. Net imports of 131.97 mtoe in 2006–07 covers import of 95.43 mt of crude oil and petroleum products, 44.29 mt of coal, and 5 mt of LNG.

10.19 India needs to eliminate shortage of energy supply and enhance the availability of commercial energy resources if it has to sustain the projected 9% economic growth in the Eleventh Plan period. Table 10.5 shows projected commercial energy requirement of all the

TABLE 10.3
Source-wise Energy Demand

(All in mtoe)

	1960–61	1970–71	1980–81	1990–91	2000–01	2006–07	2011–12#
Coal	35.64	36.48	56.96	94.15	131.52	200.02	270
Lignite	0.01	0.81	1.23	3.58	6.43	8.72	13
Oil	8.29	19.14	32.26	57.75	106.97	132.75	186
Natural gas	–	0.60	1.41	11.49	25.07	34.60	48
Hydro power	0.67	2.17	4.00	6.16	6.40	9.75	12
Nuclear power	–	0.63	0.78	1.60	4.41	4.86	17
Wind power	–	–	–	–	0.13	0.83	<1
Total	44.61	59.83	96.73	174.73	280.93	391.53	546

Note: # Projected requirement at the end of the Eleventh Plan as per the IEPC report.
Source: Planning Commission.

TABLE 10.4
Percentage Demand met from Domestic Sources

(All in %)

	1960–61	1970–71	1980–81	1990–91	2000–01	2006–07	2011–12#
Coal	100	100	99.7	97.8	96.1	90.33	93.02
Lignite	100	100	100	100	100	100	100
Oil	5.4	35.6	32.6	42.8	30.3	26.6	27.59
Natural gas/LNG	–	100	100	100	100	82.08	69.30
Hydro power	100	100	100	99.93	99.96	99.74	95.94

Note: # Projections from various Working Group Reports.
Source: Planning Commission.

TABLE 10.5
Projected Commercial Energy Requirement for 2011–12 at the Rate of 9% Growth

Primary Fuel	Unit	Quantity
Coal	mt	731
Lignite	mt	55.59
Oil	mt	145
Natural gas	bcm	106
Hydro power	BkWh	165
Nuclear power	BkWh	44.64
Wind power	BkWh	7

Source: Working Group Reports of various sectors.

available resources in the terminal year of the Eleventh Plan period in physical units. Coal demand of 731 mt covers 51 mt of imports. 74% of this is expected to be consumed by the power sector including captive plants. Out of the oil demand of 145 mt, domestic production will be around 40 mt and the balance would be imported. Domestic availability of natural gas in the terminal year of the Eleventh Plan is expected to be about 47 bcm. An import of 23.75 mt of LNG would augment the supplies to meet the demand shortfall. There will be a gap of around 32 bcm between availability and demand if no addition by the private sector is achieved. The shortfall in availability will adversely affect the power sector and fertilizer industry, which consume around 70% of the current gas demand.

10.20 Availability of hydro, wind, and nuclear energy is estimated assuming a capacity factor of 37% for hydro, 20% for wind, and 70% for nuclear for taking into account the likely capacity additions during the Plan period.

10.21 Table 10.6 shows the realized growth rates of domestic supply of different fuels in the past as also those projected for the Eleventh Plan.

SUPPLY OPTIONS

10.22 Coal production in the terminal year of the Eleventh Plan period is projected to increase more than one and half times the production level in 2006–07. In spite of the significant increase in domestic coal production, around 51 mt coal is required to be imported to meet the gap between demand and supply. Domestic production is likely to reach 680 mt level in the terminal year of the Eleventh Plan registering an average annual growth rate of 9.37% as compared to a growth rate of 5.8% achieved during the Tenth Plan period. Power sector alone will consume more than 70% of the projected demand.

10.23 Domestic production of crude is likely to increase to around 40 mt in the terminal year of the Eleventh Plan representing a modest increase from the current level of about 34 mt. By the end of the Eleventh Plan, the domestic production will cater to only around 28% of the projected petroleum products demand of 145 mt.

10.24 Domestic production of natural gas in the terminal year of the Eleventh Plan is likely to be 63.23 bcm, which will be around 100% higher than the current level of production. This increase in gas production will be mainly from K–G basin production of 40 million standard cubic metres per day (MMSCMD). The level of production may go further up if the Gujarat State Petroleum Corporation Limited is able to develop its resources in K–G basin in the Eleventh Plan period itself.

TABLE 10.6
Growth Rates of Domestic Supply

(All in %)

	1960–70	1970–80	1980–90	1990–2000	2002–07#	2007–12*
Coal	2.74	4.57	6.39	3.87	5.80	9.37
Lignite	–	4.18	10.42	5.24	4.64	11.72
Oil	31.23	4.42	12.1	–0.18	0.56	3.31
Natural gas	–	5.50	22.32	5.06	0.09	18.53
Hydro power	12.61	7.03	3.17	2.66	9.02	7.87
Nuclear power	–	7.95	4.86	11.10	(–) 9.18	19.13

Note: # The Tenth Plan period; * projected for the Eleventh Plan as per various Working Group Reports.
Source: Planning Commission.

10.25 Ministry of Power's (MoP) proposal of 78577 MW during the Eleventh Plan includes addition of 16553 MW of hydro capacity and 3380 MW from nuclear reactors. Taking into account this capacity addition, projected energy generation from both hydro and nuclear plants will be 165 Trillion Watt hour (TWh) and 44.6 TWh, respectively.

ENERGY IMPORTS

10.26 Traditionally, India has remained supply constrained in energy and the country is forced to resort to imports to bridge the gap between demand and supply. With the rising demand of natural gas in the power and fertilizer sectors, LNG imports were started in 2004–05. Though LNG imports have augmented the demand to some extent, still there is a considerable shortfall. Oil imports also continue to grow every year to meet the petroleum products demand. Of late, import of non-coking coal by the power utilities and cement industry also started increasing besides the coking coal imports by steel industry to meet the growing demand. As a result of this, the share of imports in the total primary energy supply is progressively rising. The GoI is making efforts to import nuclear fuel from the US which is expected to improve the supply of nuclear fuel for nuclear power plants.

THE WAY FORWARD

10.27 It is evident from the discussions above that India is short of all energy resources and that coal will dominate India's energy basket. We need to expand resources through exploration, energy efficiency, renewables, and R&D. The environmental impact of various energy options is of growing concern owing to widespread use of energy. It is necessary that the demand of energy in the country is met in an environment-friendly and sustainable manner.

10.28 Available fossil energy resources must be optimally exploited using enhanced recovery techniques. Additional sources of energy such as CBM must be fully exploited and fossil fuel reserves advanced through more intensive exploration. Though the renewable energy sources such as wind energy, biomass, and biofuels account for a small percentage in the total energy, their contribution must increase by 2%–3% in the Eleventh Plan. Accordingly, a roadmap with detailed policy initiatives is necessary in all the subsectors of the energy sector for achieving the desired growth. While the Central and State sectors will continue to dominate the energy sector in the Eleventh Plan, energy policy should not be determined sector by sector where the dominant public sector players often have significant vested interests. We need to move towards a more transparent policy framework that treats different sources of energy in a similar fashion. Such a framework must be able to meet the energy requirements cost effectively by introducing competition for minimizing distortions across sectors and maximizing efficiency gains. Further, availability of clean, modern fuel to all households should be our guiding concern. This would require removal of barriers to entry at all stages and an optimal pricing and tax strategy so that resource allocation takes place based on market forces operating under a credible regulatory regime that also ensures a level playing field to public and private players.

10.29 Institutions for promoting and forcing the pace of energy conservation and improvement in energy efficiency need strengthening. Restructuring incentives and support by shifting from supply driven programmes to demand driven programmes and technologies would assist development and use of new and renewable energy sources. The subsidies and support need to be linked to the outcomes in terms of renewable energy generated rather than to capital investments. There is need for meeting social objectives as far as possible through direct and tradable entitlements offered to those in genuine need. The renewables may be given appropriate incentives for the environmental externalities.

10.30 It is also necessary to set up a robust energy R&D system for developing relevant technology and energy sources that enhance energy security and lead to energy independence in a cost-effective way in the long run. A number of technology missions covering areas such as in situ gasification, integrated gasification combined cycle (IGCC), solar energy, energy storage, etc. are proposed to be launched. The scope for biofuels including extraction of ethanol from agricultural waste using reported advances in technology needs to be pursued.

10.31 Sector-wise programmes and financial requirement for the Eleventh Plan are given in the following section.

POWER SECTOR

ISSUES AND CHALLENGES

10.32 Rapid growth of the economy will place a heavy demand on electric power. Reforms in this sector, for making the power sector efficient and more competitive, have been under way for several years and while there has been some progress, shortage of power and lack of access continues to be a major constraint on the economic growth. The greatest weakness is on the distribution front which is entirely the domain of the States. AT&C losses of most of the State Power Utilities (SPUs) remain as high as 40% and this has made them financially sick and unable to invest adequately in additional generating capacity. For the same reason, these utilities have had only limited success in attracting private investors to set up power plants.

10.33 The Eleventh Plan must ensure substantial expansion in order to move to a comfortable situation consistent with a growth rate between 9% and 10% per annum. Policies must be evolved that would ensure completion of on-going projects quickly and add new capacity in an efficient, least cost manner, while emphasizing exploitation of India's hydro potential and nuclear capabilities especially in the field of FBRs. Renewables such as wind power, which can be set up in a short time, play a useful role. One of the main challenges is a major step-up in investment in distribution infrastructure and a restructuring of the Accelerated Power Development and Reforms Programme (APDRP), using technological and managerial tools such as smart metering and GIS mapping for real time, monitoring and accountability at each distribution transformer with a goal set for the State Governments to bring down AT&C losses from the current level of around 40% to at least 15% by the end of the Eleventh Plan. Given the high level of such losses at present, it may be difficult for some States to attain these targets. Another challenge is to provide electricity access to all households and actually connect all BPL households under the RGGVY.

10.34 Establishment of new generation capacity and reducing cost of power will require action on many fronts:

- Availability of fuel such as coal or natural gas for new power plants must be assured.
- Long-term finance should be made available to lower the capital charge.
- The presently provided guaranteed rate of post tax returns for CPSUs, the rate of return to the utilities, needs to be realigned by Central Electricity Regulatory Commission (CERC) keeping in view the assessments of overall risks and prevalent cost of capital.
- Inter-state and intra-state transmission system of adequate capacity needs to be built that is capable of transferring power efficiently from one region to another.
- Distribution system must be made efficient which alone can ensure financially viable expansion.
- Thermal stations should be rehabilitated through Renovation and Modernization (R&M) to augment generating capacity and improve PLF.
- Hydro stations should be rehabilitated to yield additional peaking capacity.
- Supply side and demand side efficiencies should be improved to effectively lower primary energy demand by 5%–7% during the Eleventh Plan period.
- Use of washed coal should be ensured for power generation.
- Captive capacity should be harnessed to meet the power deficit.

REVIEW OF THE TENTH PLAN

Power Sector Reforms

10.35 Power sector reforms have been underway for over a decade. Enactment of 'Electricity Act 2003' during the Tenth Plan was an important step towards reforms in the power sector. The objectives of the Act are 'to consolidate the laws relating to generation, transmission, distribution, trading and use of electricity and taking measures conducive for the development of electrical industry, protecting interests of consumers and supply of electricity to all areas, rationalization of electricity tariffs, ensuring transparent policies regarding subsidies, promotion of efficient and environmentally benign policies, constitution of Regulatory Commissions and establishment of Appellate Tribunal for matters connected therewith or incidental thereto'.

10.36 The following milestones were achieved in the power sector during the Tenth Plan:

- As many as 14 States have restructured or corporatized their power sector and unbundled their boards into separate entities for transmission, distribution, and generation.
- Distribution has been privatized in Orissa and Delhi.
- Setting up of State Electricity Regulatory Commissions (SERCs) has become mandatory. A total of 25 States have either constituted or notified the constitution of SERC and 21 SERCs have issued tariff orders.
- A total of 26 States have notified rural areas under Section 14 of the Act, permits have been taken of composite schemes of generation and distribution without any license.
- In compliance with Section 3 of the Electricity Act 2003, the Central Government notified the National Electricity Policy in 2005. Similarly, National Tariff Policy was also notified in 2006. Further, in compliance with Sections 4 and 5 of the Electricity Act 2003, the Central Government notified the Rural Electrification Policy on 28 August 2006.
- The Central Government constituted the Appellate Tribunal for Electricity and the same became operational in July 2005. The Tribunal has started hearing appeals against orders of the Regulatory Commissions/Adjudicating Officers.
- Open access has been technically allowed and also made functional for inter-state transmission; however it has, in fact, been hindered by the high cross-subsidy surcharge set by many SERCs.
- Finally, under APDRP, nine States have shown a cash loss reduction of Rs 5254.60 crore over their loss levels of 2001–02. However, the progress is small and AT&C losses continue to remain high in most States.

OTHER NEW MAJOR INITIATIVES IN THE TENTH PLAN

Guidelines Formulated for Merchant Plants/Coal Linkages

10.37 Guidelines were formulated on Merchant Power Plants with an aim to restructure the electricity industry on 3 November 2006. Under this policy, coal blocks/coal linkage will be provided to the successful bidders in setting up thermal power stations.

Guidelines for Procurement of Electricity

10.38 In compliance with Section 63 of the Electricity Act 2003, the Central Government has notified guidelines for procurement of power by Distribution Licensees through competitive bidding. Further, the Central Government has also issued the standard bid documents for long-term procurement of power from projects having specified site and location.

Launch of Ultra-mega Power Projects (UMPPs)

10.39 The Electricity Act 2003 requires competitive tariff-based bidding from independent power producers. To initiate the process and to realize the benefits of international competitive bidding and economies of scale, a scheme was launched for development of coal-based UMPPs with a capacity of 4000 MW or above through tariff-based competitive bidding. The projects will include development of power projects as well as associated coal mines in respect of pithead sites and imported coal sourcing in respect of coastal sites. These projects will be awarded to developers on BOO basis. The bidding process has been completed in respect of two projects, that is, Sasan in Madhya Pradesh and Mundra in Gujarat and the projects allotted to Reliance Energy and Tata Power, respectively. The process is underway in respect of Krishnapattanam in Andhra Pradesh.

Guidelines Issued for Encouraging Competition in Development of Transmission Projects

10.40 The Central Government has also notified guidelines for encouraging competition in development of transmission projects through tariff-based bidding.

Capacity Addition

10.41 The all-India installed generating capacity of utilities at the beginning of the Tenth Plan was 104917.50 MW. This included 26261.22 MW of hydro, 74428.82 MW of thermal, 2720.00 MW of nuclear power, and 1507.50 MW of wind energy.

10.42 The capacity addition target for the Tenth Plan was 41109.84 MW. Against this, a capacity addition of 21080.24 MW was actually achieved during the Plan period. The sector-wise, mode-wise summaries of the Tenth Plan capacity addition target and achievement are given in Table 10.7.

10.43 It may be noted that the above capacity includes 1210.6 MW thermal-based capacity (Central: 500 MW, State: 538 MW, and private: 172.60 MW) which was not included in the original Plan target. Despite these additional projects, the Tenth Plan performance has been disappointing.

10.44 The cumulative capacity at the end of the Tenth Plan was 132329.21 MW, including 7760.60 MW renewable sources of energy, the details of which are given in Table 10.8.

Transmission and Distribution (T&D) Facilities

10.45 The major portion of the HVDC, 765 kV and 400 kV transmission network planned to be set up during the Tenth Plan, was in the Central sector, while that of the 220 kV network was in the State sector. Most of the targeted addition achieved was inadequate as neither the targeted generation nor the projected demand was realized. A summary of the Tenth Plan transmission achievement up to 31 March 2007 is given in Table 10.9.

Transmission and Distribution (T&D) Losses/AT&C Losses

10.46 T&D losses in India continue to be among the highest in the world and are the main concern in the development of power sector. The reported all-India average T&D losses increased from 19.8% in 1992–93 to 33.98% at the beginning of the Tenth Plan. There is a wide variation in the losses reported by different States. T&D losses for the country as a whole are estimated to be in the range of 35%–45%.

10.47 As T&D losses figures did not capture the gap between the billing and the collection, the concept of AT&C loss was introduced in 2001–02 to capture the

TABLE 10.7
Installed Capacity Addition during the Tenth Plan

Type	Target				Achievement			
	Central Sector	State Sector	Private Sector	Total	Central Sector	State Sector	Private Sector	Total
Hydro	7842.00	5381.20	1170.00	14393.20	4495.00	2691.00	700.00	7886.00
Thermal	12790.00	6675.64	5951.00	25416.64	6590.00	3553.64	1970.60	12114.24
Nuclear	1300.00	0.00	0.00	1300.00	1080.00	0.00	0.00	1080.00
Total	21932.00	12056.84	7121.00	41109.84	12165.00	6244.64	2670.60	21080.24

Source: Central Electricity Authority (CEA).

TABLE 10.8
All-India Cumulative Generating Capacity

(MW)

	Hydro	Thermal	Nuclear	Total
Centre	7562.00	33658.99	3900.00	45120.99
State/UTs	25785.62	43334.33	0.00	69119.95
Private	1306.15	9021.52	0.00	10327.67
Total	34653.77	86014.84	3900.00	124568.61#

Note: # excludes the capacity of 7760.60 MW from renewable energy sources (State: 975.65 MW and private: 6784.95 MW).
Source: CEA.

TABLE 10.9
Cumulative Achievements of Transmission Lines at the End of the Tenth Plan

Transmission System Type/Voltage Class	Unit	At the End of Ninth Plan (March 2002)	Addition during Tenth Plan	At the End of Tenth Plan (March 2007)
		Transmission Lines		
(i) 765 kV	ckm	971	733	1704
(ii) HVDC + 500kV Bi-pole	ckm	3138	2734	5872
(iii) 400 kV	ckm	49378	26344	75722
(iv) 230/220kV	ckm	96993	117636	114629
(v) HVDC 200 kV Mono-pole	ckm	162	0	162
Total of (i), (ii), (iii), (iv), and (v)	ckm	150642	47447	198089
		Sub-stations		
(i) 765 kV	MVA	0	2000	2000
(ii) 400 kV	MVA	60380	32562	92942
(iii) 230/220 kV	MVA	116363	40134	156497
Total of (i), (ii), and (iii)	MVA	176743	74696	251439
		HVDC		
(i) Bi-pole link capacity	MW	3000	2000	5000
(ii) Back-to-back capacity	MW	2000	1000	3000
(iii) Mono-pole link capacity	MW	200	0	200
Total of (i), (ii), and (iii)	MW	5200	3000	8200

Source: CEA.

total performance of the utility. The AT&C losses are presently in the range of 18% to 62% in various States. The average AT&C loss in the country is about 40%. There is wide variation of losses among the States and variation among the distribution companies within the States. The major portion of losses is due to theft and pilferage, which is estimated at about Rs 20000 crore annually as per the *Economic Survey 2006–07*. More than 75%–80% of the total technical loss and almost the entire commercial loss occur at the distribution stage.

Programme for Central Assistance under APDRP

10.48 To encourage distribution reforms, the APDRP was launched in March 2003 consisting of an investment financing component and an incentive component for improved performance. Under the investment component, projects worth Rs 17033.58 crore had been sanctioned. All of these projects were designed to reduce the AT&C losses through strengthening of the sub-transmission and distribution system. While the total investment needs for projects in special category States were to be met by the GoI, the non-special category States were required to fund 75% of the approved project outlay through counterpart funding arranged by the State Governments. A broad summary of the investment component is given in Table 10.10.

TABLE 10.10
Summary of Investment Component of APDRP (as on 31 August 2007) (at Current Price)

(Rs Crore)

S. No.	Category of States	Project Outlay	Revised APDRP Component to be Funded by GoI	Amount Actually Released by GoI	Counterpart Funds Provided by States	Total Utilization (Actual Investment)
1.	Non-special	13668.28	5567.26	5094.32	4750.97	9232.01
2.	Special	3365.30	3152.81	2292.49	62.95	1830.41
Grand Total		17033.58	8720.07	7386.83	4813.92	11062.42

Source: MoP.

10.49 APDRP was promoted with the promise of bringing down AT&C losses to 15% over five years. Actual performance has not come anywhere close to the targeted level. Table 10.11 summarizes the performance of SEBs. The scope for further tariff increase is limited since tariffs for paying customers are already among the highest in the world and it may make sense for them to opt out for captive generation.

TABLE 10.11
Viability of State Utilities not Improving

(Rs Crore)

	2001–02 (Actual)	2002–03 (Actual)	2003–04 (Actual)	2004–05 (Actual)	2005–06 (Provi.)
Energy sold/energy available (%)	66.02	67.46	67.47	68.75	69.58
Revenue from sale of electricity (Rs crore)	68135	76640	85942	91738	100000
Cost of electricity sold (Rs crore)	98541	102247	110553	118975	128853
Loss on sale of electricity (Rs crore)	30407	25607	24611	27237	28853
Average cost of supply (paise/kWh)	374.57	351.72 (–6.10%)	353.80 (–5.54%)	357.35 (–4.60%)	366.96 (–2.03%)
Average tariff (paise/kWh)	258.99	263.63 (1.79%)	275.04 (6.20%)	275.55 (6.39%)	284.79 (9.96%)
Gap between the cost of supply and tariff (paise)	115.58	88.09	78.76	81.80	82.17

Note: 1. Financial Performance of 20 major States excluding Delhi and Orissa—as reported.
2. Figure in brackets are growth rates over 2001–02.
3. Approved tariffs hikes exceed average tariff increases estimated above.

Source: Power utilities of various States.

10.50 The reported AT&C loss of Rs 28853 crore for 20 major States is an underestimate. SEB accounts conceal more than they reveal—because of unaccounted ghost billing, manipulated consumer mix, and recording of sales and expenditure on accrual and cash basis, respectively. Further, audit comments have also not been incorporated. As per the Auditor's comments, Gujarat SEB's losses for 2002–03 have increased from Rs 476 crore to Rs 985 crore. Similar results for Uttar Pradesh could not be confirmed as for Uttar Pradesh State Electricity Board even cash balances remain un-reconciled. Actual AT&C losses are estimated to exceed Rs 40000 crore.

10.51 The performance varies across States. Haryana and Andhra Pradesh have shown considerable improvement in this regard. However, Haryana started with a very low ratio (energy billed/energy available) in 2001–02, but later its performance deteriorated considerably in 2006–07. Some States such as Rajasthan, Uttar Pradesh, Bihar, Gujarat, and Kerala have shown significant worsening between 2001–02 and 2005–06. However, Gujarat has shown improvement in 2006–07. Given absence of a baseline, lack of consistency in reporting and fluctuating performances, it may be difficult to state whether the improvement, if any, is of a permanent in nature.

10.52 Evaluation studies have shown what is wrong with APDRP:

- It was an investment driven programme without any outcome accountability.
- The project reports were ill-prepared. They replicated the same type of investments without a full buy-in by the host utility.
- There was no baseline data established on the distribution losses or on billing/collection efficiency. This makes it difficult to determine what has been achieved.
- Unrealistic targets were set and the scheme did not provide incentive for SEB staff to co-operate.

10.53 The APDRP needs to be restructured in order to obtain better results.

Plan Expenditure during the Tenth Plan

10.54 The Plan expenditure for Centre, State, and union territories on the basis of actual for 2002–03, 2003–04, 2004–05, revised estimates (RE) for 2005–06, and approved outlay for 2006–07 (Table 10.12) reveal the following.

TABLE 10.12
Outlay/Expenditure—Centre, State and UTs

(Rs Crore)

Sector	Tenth Plan Approved Outlay	2002–03 (Actual)	2003–04 (Actual)	2004–05 (Actual)	2005–06 (Actual)	2006–07 (RE)	Tenth Plan Likely Expenditure	% Utilization
States and UTs	93225.71	17102.58	17836.89	17035.28	17330.07	19371.57	88676.39	95.12
	(93225.71)	(16462.20)	(16541.68)	(15137.09)	(14742.72)	(15580.77)	(78464.46)	(84.17)
Central Sector	177050.64	10993.42	14327.50	17039.96	21045.93	27271.04	90677.85	51.22
	(177050.64)	(10581.79)	(13287.12)	(15141.25)	(17903.81)	(21934.40)	(78848.37)	(44.53)
All	270276.35	28096.00	32164.39	34075.24	38376.00	46642.61	179354.24	66.36
	(270276.35)	(27043.99)	(29828.80)	(30278.34)	(32646.53)	(37515.17)	(157312.82)	(58.20)

Note: Figures in the bracket are at 2001–02 price.
Source: Planning Commission.

10.55 The shortfall in fund utilization in the Central sector is on account of the following:

- During the first two years, there was a delay in according investment approval for various projects such as Teesta Low Dam-III and IV, Sewa-II, Omkareshwar, Subansari Lower, Parbati-III, Purulia PSP (Pump Storage Project), Chamera HEP-III (Hydro Electric Project), Uri-II, Kishanganga, Tipaimukh, Turial HEP, Tuivai HEP, Lower Kopali HEP, Ranganadi Stage II, Kameng, Tripura Gas, etc.
- In case of NTPC, an outlay of about Rs 3000 crore was included as GBS to be utilized if need be. However, it was decided to fund the projects from its internal resources and in addition gas projects such as Kawas and Gandhar could not take off.

10.56 In the State sector the major shortfalls were in the States of Gujarat, Himachal Pradesh, Maharashtra, Orissa, Punjab, Tamil Nadu, Uttar Pradesh, and Uttarakhand.

ELEVENTH PLAN PROGRAMMES

GENERATION

Capacity Additions

10.57 The gross electricity requirement by the end of the Eleventh Plan projected by the Working Group on power is 1038 Billion Unit (BU) and peak demand estimation is 151000 MW whereas the EC on Integrated Energy Policy has projected the gross electricity requirement of 1097 BU and peak demand of 158000 MW. To fulfil the estimated electricity demand requirement, the Working Group recommended the capacity addition programme initially of 78530 MW and updated at 78577 MW during the Eleventh Plan (Table 10.13). The mode-wise capacity addition is depicted in Table 10.14.

10.58 The public sector will continue to play a dominant role during the Eleventh Plan while progress along the reform path helps to clear the roadblock for greater private participation in the medium to long term.

TABLE 10.13
Status of Capacity Addition during the Eleventh Plan

(in MW)

		Central	State	Private	Total
1.	Projects commissioned (as on 18 October 2007)	1360	1350	250	2960
2.	Projects under construction	28765	16342	7378	52485
3.	New Projects	9740	10260	3132	23132
	Total	39865	27952	10760	78577

Note: At the time of going to press on 8 May 2008, 9573 MW were commissioned, 62717 MW are under construction and 6410 MW are likely to come up.
Source: CEA/Planning Commission.

TABLE 10.14
Sector-wise, Mode-wise Capacity Addition during the Eleventh Plan

(in MW)

	Source	Central	State	Private	Total
1.	Hydro	9685	3605	3263	16553
2.	Thermal	26800	24347	7497	58644
3.	Nuclear	3380	0	0	3380
	Total	39865	27952	10760	78577

Note: At the time of going to press on 8 May 2008, the mix of thermal/hydro has undergone some changes.
Source: CEA/Planning Commission.

10.59 The proposed capacity addition is three and a half times of that achieved in the Tenth Plan and in that sense is very ambitious. Effective implementation is also contingent upon fuel linkages being firmed up and early start of work on new projects. For the new projects, particularly in the Central sector, it is essential to simplify and streamline procedures for input linkages, techno-economic clearance, and investment clearance. On the basis of this, the cumulative generation capacity in the country by the end of 2011–12 will be as given in Table 10.15.

Hydro Power Development

10.60 The share of hydro capacity in the total generating capacity of the country has declined from 34% at the end of the Sixth Plan to 25% at the end of the Ninth Plan. The present share of hydro capacity of 26% is envisaged to be about 23% by the end of the Eleventh Plan if the targeted Eleventh Plan capacity addition programme is achieved.

10.61 A 50000 MW hydro initiative was launched in 2003 for accelerated development of hydro in the country and Preliminary Feasibility Reports of 162 projects totaling to 48000 MW were prepared. Out of this, 77 projects with total capacity of about 37000 MW, for which first-year tariff is expected to be less than Rs 2.50 per unit, were selected for execution. In the Eleventh Plan, a capacity addition of about 16553 MW has been earmarked keeping in view the present preparedness of these projects. Projects totaling to a capacity of 30000 MW have been identified for the Twelfth Plan on which necessary preparations have to be made from now onwards to ensure their commissioning during the Twelfth Plan. Thus, the effect of 50000 MW initiatives would be visible in the Twelfth Plan period.

10.62 Geological uncertainty, contract management, resettlement and rehabilitation, delay in land acquisition and infrastructure development have been the main reasons for time and cost over-runs in hydro projects. In order to avoid delays in project implementation, the following steps need to be taken before the zero date of the project implementation:

- Bankable DPR, based on a detailed survey, should be prepared to avoid geological uncertainty.
- Contract monitoring, as distinct from project monitoring, should be emphasized.
- Land acquisition and infrastructure development should be settled and completed before the start of the project.

10.63 Further, the following steps need to be taken in order to accelerate the pace of hydro development:

- Preparation of a DPR based on economic viability to be expedited.
- Streamline clearances for pursuing priority projects.
- Simplify approval procedures.
- Facilitate the early financial closure of projects.

TABLE 10.15
Generating Capacity Anticipated at the End of the Eleventh Plan

(in MW)

	Hydro	Thermal	Nuclear	Wind and Renewables	Total
Installed capacity as on 31 March 2007	34653.77	86014.84	3900.00	7760.60	132329.21
Addition during Eleventh Plan	16553.00	58644.00	3380.00	14000.00	92577.00
Total capacity anticipated as on 31 March 2012	51206.77	144658.84	7280.00	21760.60	224906.21

Source: Planning Commission.

- Priority to be given to projects for which concurrence has already been issued by the CEA.
- High priority to be accorded to smaller capacity Run of the River-type hydro projects having gestation period less than five years.
- Basin-wise optimization studies for all the major river basins should be carried out.
- Competitive bidding other than tariff-based competitive bidding could also be considered for hydro projects since there are formidable construction risks in hydro power construction due to geological uncertainties and other factors.

Nuclear Power

10.64 Atomic energy is an important source of electric power which has environmental advantages and is also likely to be economical in the longer run. At present, nuclear energy installed capacity is 3900 MW_e which is 3.1% of total installed capacity. The PLF of Nuclear Power Corporation of India Limited (NPCIL) stations increased from 60% in 1995–96 to 82% in 2000–01 but it has decreased to 57% in 2006–07. Constraint in nuclear fuel availability is the main reason for lower PLF. NPCIL made major strides in cutting costs and construction periods for nuclear power projects in the Tenth Plan. The lower construction period and improved contracting and contract management have resulted in reduction in the capital cost per MW_e.

10.65 The Kudankulam project (2 × 1000 MW_e) is being set up, based on light water reactor technology, and NPCIL has initiated pre-project activities for its expansion with another two units of 1000 MW_e. Further, the design of 700 MW_e indigenous PHWRs has been undertaken by NPCIL to enhance the pace of first stage capacity addition programme. Pre-project activities of four such units have been initiated.

10.66 Having successfully completed the R&D phase of the FBR technology, the DAE has engaged the Indira Gandhi Centre for Atomic Research (IGCAR) for the design, development, construction, and operation of the country's first 500 MW_e liquid-sodium-cooled FBR. The government has set up a new company, Bharatiya Nabhikiya Vidyut Nigam Limited, in September 2003 to implement the first project based on the FBR technology. The first 500 MW_e prototype FBR is likely to be commissioned in the Eleventh Plan. The FBR technology is critical for developing the second stage of India's nuclear power programmes. Without developing the wide-scale use of FBR technology, India would find it difficult to go beyond 10000 MW_e nuclear capacity based on known indigenous uranium resources. About 20000 MW_e nuclear power programme is critical to developing the thorium-based third stage of India's nuclear power programme. Use of FBR technology would enable indigenous uranium resources to support it. The BARC is also engaged in R&D activities to develop advanced heavy water reactors of 300 MW_e capacity that would provide an alternative route to the thorium-based third stage of India's nuclear power programme.

10.67 The Eleventh Plan power programme includes 3380 MW_e of nuclear power plants. The GoI is making efforts to import nuclear fuel from abroad which is expected to improve the supply of nuclear fuel for nuclear power plants. It is also expected that the execution of nuclear projects will also be opened up to enable participation by other PSUs and private sector. The effect of this is likely to be visible in the Twelfth Plan period. NPCIL has indicated a capacity addition of about 11000 MW during the Twelfth Plan.

Merchant Power Plants

10.68 A merchant power plant does not have long-term Power Purchase Agreement for sale of its power and is generally developed on the balance sheet of developers. The GoI has reserved coal block with reserves of 3.2 billion tonnes of coal for allotment by Screening Committee of Ministry of Coal (MoC) for merchant and captive plants. About 10000 MW capacity is expected to be developed through this initiative. This capacity has not been taken into account while working out the capacity requirement over the Eleventh Plan period as it is not likely to materialize before the Twelfth Plan.

Captive Power Generation

10.69 Large number of captive plants including co-generation power plants of varied type and sizes exist in the country which are either utilized in process industry or used for in-house power consumption. A number of industries have set up their own captive plants so as to get reliable and quality power. The installed capacity of captive power plants has increased from 588 MW in 1950 to 24680 MW in March 2007. The annual generation from captive power plants at the end of the Tenth Plan is likely to be about 78 billion units. Captive plants including co-generation power plants could, therefore, play a supplementary role in meeting the country's power demand. It is envisaged that during the Eleventh Plan period about 12000 MW capacity power plants would be added to the system which will take care of the demand of the industry and also supply surplus power to the grid.

Private Sector Participation (Box 10.3)

10.70 New initiatives in power sector development such as UMPPs, Merchant Power Plants, and Captive Power Plants are expected to trigger the capacity addition in private sector during ensuring Five Year Plans.

Box 10.3
Private Sector Participation

The policy of inducting private investment into the power sector, initiated in 1991, was expected to result in the addition of 17588 MW of power capacity in the Ninth Plan. The actual achievement was 5061 MW, a mere 29% of the target. Further, during the Tenth Plan capacity addition target in private sector was 7121 MW against which actual capacity addition was 2670.60 MW which is merely 37.50%, while the achievement ratio for Central and State sectors were higher at 55.47% and 51.79%, respectively. The main impediments have been:

- The chronic financial weakness of SEBs.
- Unviable tariffs to IPPs, due to factors such as high cost of liquid fuels, risk factors involved, slow growth in demand for future power below the expected levels, etc.
- The absence of enabling regulatory, legislative, and market environment.
- The lack of recognition of the fact that the distribution segment would need to be made efficient and bankable before private investment and competition emerges in generation.

Fuel Requirements

10.71 The requirement of various fuels for the thermal plants by the terminal year of the Eleventh Plan (2011–12) considering a capacity addition of about 58644 MW, based on normative generation parameters such as PLF and specific fuel consumption, is summarized in the Table 10.16.

TABLE 10.16
Fuel Requirement during 2011–12

Fuel	Requirement	Availability
Coal	545 mt	482 mt
Lignite	33 mt	33 mt
Gas/LNG	89 MMSCMD	36 MMSCMD

Source: Working Group Report on Power.

10.72 However, total coal availability for power sector from domestic sources is expected to be 482 million tonnes per annum by 2011–12. There is need for augmenting availability of domestic coal for the power sector or import coal to bridge the gap between requirement and domestic supply. Further, 89 MMSCMD (million standard cubic metres per day) of gas requirement has been projected in 2011–12. At present, the availability of gas is of the order of 40 MMSCMD which is not sufficient to meet the requirement of even existing plants. Additional gas supply is expected from the K–G basin finds during the Eleventh Plan.

TRANSMISSION

Perspective Transmission System

10.73 The transmission system facilities had earlier been planned on regional basis with provision of inter-regional link to transfer regional surplus power arising out of diversity in demand. The generation resources in the country are unevenly located, the hydro in the northern and North Eastern States and coal being mainly in the eastern part of the country. Development of strong national grid has become a necessity to ensure reliable supply of power to all. A national grid can exploit the diversity of peak demand across regions, reduce it to the required peak capacity as well as facilitate better use of national hydro power capacity. The planning and operation of the transmission system has thus shifted from the regional level to the national level.

Transmission Capacity Requirement

10.74 The focus of transmission system development programme for the Eleventh Plan is to provide adequate inter-regional and intra-regional transmission capacity so as to consolidate and strengthen the national grid network towards a strong all-India grid. The inter-regional power exchange requirement has been assessed from possible scenarios of regional surpluses and deficits for the peak and off-peak conditions of winter, summer, and monsoon months. The projections are based on programme of generation and anticipated demand aim at estimating the transmission requirement at the inter-regional level. Grid expansion plan based on this projection would be able to cater to the needs of various feasible operating scenarios and also provide required margins to support market-oriented power exchanges.

Development of National Grid

10.75 It is envisaged to add new inter-regional capacities of 20700 MW at 220 kV and above during the Eleventh Plan period. This would increase the total inter-regional transmission capacity of national power grid at 220 kV and above from 14100 MW (by the end of the Tenth Plan) to 37750 MW by 2011–12. The plan for national power grid and the schemes have been identified. NER, Sikkim, and Bhutan have vast untapped hydro potential which is planned for development during the Eleventh Plan and beyond. The requirement of transmission system for evacuation of the NER hydro power has been estimated corresponding to the capacity of hydro projects which may be feasible to develop in the next 20 years. This generation is estimated to be about 35000 MW in the NER, about 8000 MW in Sikkim, and about 15000 MW in Bhutan. Taking local development at accelerated pace resulting in demand within the NER, Sikkim, and Bhutan to be in the range of 10000–12000 MW (presently it is about 1500 MW), the transmission requirement through the chicken neck works out to be of the order of 45000 MW. The total requirement including additional circuits for meeting the contingencies and reliability needs would work out to seven or eight HVDC bi-pole lines of 800 kV and four or five double-circuit lines of 400 kV—a total of 12 high-capacity transmission corridors passing through the chicken neck. For this, Right of Width requirement would be about 1.5 km in width considering the minimum distance between adjacent towers to be such that fall of any tower does not affect the adjoining line. The first 800 kV HVDC bi-pole line has been planned from a pooling sub-station at Biswanath Chariyali in the NER upto Agra in the northern region. This is being programmed for commissioning matching with Subansiri Lower HEP in 2011–12.

Transmission Capacity for Trading/Margins

10.76 The method adopted for evolving the national transmission system expansion plan provides sufficient transmission capacities which would have inherent margins for trading transactions. Transmission system implemented on the basis of the expansion plan evolved in this manner would enable trading across the regional boundaries towards optimal utilization of generation resources in the country for ultimate benefit of the consumer.

Distribution

10.77 Distribution is the key segment of the electricity supply chain. The distribution sector caters to the rural and urban areas. Rural distribution segment is characterized by wide dispersal of network over large areas with long lines, low demand density, high cost of supply, low paying capacity of the people, large number of subsidized customers, unmetered flat rate supply to farmers, non-metering due to high cost and practical difficulties, low load and low rate of load growth. Urban distribution is characterized by high consumer density and higher rate of growth of load. Both segments are distinct with different problems and issues. The biggest challenge of the power sector is the high T&D losses. A combination of technical and non-technical factors is contributing to high T&D losses. Lack of consumer awareness, political interference, and inefficient use of electricity is further aggravating the problem. In urban areas too, the distribution system suffers from a large number of unauthorized connections and power theft.

10.78 The sub-transmission and distribution system were the thrust areas during the Tenth Plan. The performance of APDRP scheme has not been up to the mark in the Tenth Plan period and needs to be restructured in the Eleventh Plan period as distribution is the key element for improving the overall performance of the power sector. For APDRP restructuring, following actions are suggested to be taken during the Eleventh Plan:

- All distribution companies should target a reduction of 3% per annum of their AT&C losses in next five years. High loss making feeders need to be franchised by distribution companies.
- Setting up of peaking power plants should be encouraged to overcome peaking shortages as the additional power cost of supply from such a plant could then be passed on to the consumer who opt for uninterruptible/reliable supply.
- Introducing bifurcation of feeders for agricultural users with unmetered power supply, automated metering of all distribution transformers, and GIS mapping of all consumers.
- Preparation of baseline data in respect of energy flow for each distribution transformer within three months of completing the above.
- Incentive for staff linked to specific measures of improvement.
- Web-based transparency of performance of each distribution transformer level including names of the staff responsible.
- Independent external audit to track and monitor outliers.
- Funds initially to be given as loan which may be converted to grant based on achievement of specific milestones on outcomes of investments.

10.79 The Working Group of the Eleventh Plan has assessed a total investment requirement of this sector as more than Rs 2 lakh crore. A major investment of this size is beyond the capacity of State utilities. It is therefore planned to set up a National Electricity Fund (NEF) to cater to the requirement of these companies. State utilities could prepare their distribution investment plans along with supportive measures including appointment of franchises, high voltage distribution supply, fast track courts to punish persons guilty of theft of electricity, use of covered cables in areas prone to theft of electricity, installation of metres, and a monitoring system with complete audit of electricity generated and received by the company. The APDRP funds could be used to provide grant (25%) for utilities, the balance being the loan from the NEF and for North Eastern States this could be (90%) grant.

Rajiv Gandhi Grameen Vidyutikaran Yojana (RGGVY)

10.80 The GoI launched RGGVY in April 2005 to provide electricity access to all rural households and extend free connections to all BPL households (estimated at 2.3 crore) by 2009. RGGVY subsidizes the capital cost by 90% through GoI grants. The approved capital cost estimate for RGGVY is Rs 16000 crore with a subsidy component of Rs 14750 crore. The physical targets included electrification of 125000 un-electrified villages by creating rural electricity distribution backbone and village electrification infrastructure and last mile service connectivity to 10% households in the village at a rate of Rs 6.50 lakh per village. The target to give free connections to 2.34 crore BPL households was also included in the above estimates. Further, the estimates covered intensification works in already electrified villages at a rate of Rs one lakh per village for 4.62 lakh villages.

10.81 While approval was accorded to Phase-I of the scheme of Rural Electricity Infrastructure and Household Electrification, which was later renamed as RGGVY by CCEA in December 2004, it was decided that implementation of Phase-I of the scheme in the Tenth Plan will have a provision of Rs 5000 crore as subsidy under the Plan Budget of the MoP for the remaining two years of the Tenth Plan, namely, 2005–06 and 2006–07. It was also decided that prior commitment of the States will be obtained, before grant of subsidy, for (i) deployment of franchisees for the management of rural distribution in projects financed under the scheme and (ii) the provision of the requisite revenue subsidies to the State utilities by the State Government as required under the Electricity Act 2003. CCEA also decided that the scheme is to be subject to concurrent evaluation and a view on modifications required for implementation during the Eleventh Plan may be taken after a comprehensive review towards the end of the Tenth Plan.

10.82 The target set by the MoP was electrification of 10000 villages in 2005–06 and the achievement reported was 9819 villages during the same period. In addition, intensification works were carried out in 350 already electrified villages. Against the total subsidy amount of Rs 1100 crore provided for 2005–06, an amount of Rs 1031.067 crore was released to the States. The total amount of funds released for RGGVY in 2005–06 was Rs 1616.24 crore which includes loans provided by Rural Electrification Corporation Ltd (REC) to meet the capital cost over and above the subsidy amount released for the scheme. The MoP had also reported that a total of 34003 households (including 16815 BPL households) were provided electricity access. The implementation of RGGVY in 2005–06 was mainly in the States of Bihar, Karnataka, Rajasthan, Uttar Pradesh, Uttarakhand, and West Bengal. However, the achievement of villages electrified in accordance with the revised definition of village electrification (requiring a mandatory coverage of at least 10% of the households to be electrified in a village declared as electrified) is yet to be verified and reported by the MoP.

10.83 The MoP set a target to electrify 40000 un-electrified villages under RGGVY in 2006–07. An amount of Rs 3000 crore was provided in the budget of the MoP to meet the subsidy requirements of RGGVY during the year. As on 31 March 2007, the MoP had reported a cumulative achievement of electrification of 50402 villages during 2005–06 and 2006–07, which includes 11177 electrified villages where intensive electrification had been carried out. In other words, the number of un-electrified villages electrified during 2006–07 is limited to 28706 only, that is 72.64% of the set target of 40000 villages. The intensification works had been carried out in 11177 villages. In respect of electricity access provided to households, the cumulative achievement was 731527 households (including 672588 BPL households). During 2006–07, a total of 697524 households (including 655773 BPL households) were provided with electricity access. The total funds released for RGGVY during the Tenth Plan were Rs 5475.15 crore which includes 10% of the loan component over and above the Central subsidy provided at 90%.

RGGVY in the Eleventh Plan

10.84 An amount of Rs 3983 crore has been provided in the MoP budget for 2007–08 to meet capital subsidy under RGGVY. The MoP has set a target to electrify 40000 un-electrified villages during 2007–08. Meanwhile RGGVY for the Eleventh Plan has been approved by the Cabinet at the cost of Rs 28000 crore. A GoM has been appointed to look into enhancing the effectiveness of the scheme implementation.

10.85 The Rural Electrification component under the Bharat Nirman Programme envisages electrification of all 125000 un-electrified villages and 2.3 crore households (out of total 7.8 crore un-electrified households in the country) by 2009. Thus the Rural Electrification component under Bharat Nirman Programme is the sub-set of RGGVY. The time frame for these two programmes coincides.

R&D in Power Sector

10.86 With the twin cries of depletion of energy resources and environmental pollution, it has become more crucial to develop efficient and clean power plants and their delivery system. These plants should be capable of effective utilization of resources such as coal, NG, and other sources of energy. Thus, in order to meet India-centric requirements, various sectors related to the field of energy have been identified for segregating different research avenues. The depletion of fuel resources has resulted into the need of exploring renewable power generation. Similarly, the application of distributed power generation may be useful for electrification of remotely located un-electrified villages. Apart from this, application of new technologies in the field of generation, transmission, and distribution also needs to be given utmost emphasis.

Policy Issues

The following are the policy issues:

- Technology advancements and R&D have so far not been properly addressed. Major organizations such as NTPC, NHPC, Power Grid Corporation of India Ltd (POWERGRID) on the generation side and Bharat Heavy Electricals Ltd (BHEL), Asea Brown Boveri Ltd (ABB), and Siemens on the manufacturing side must enhance substantially their budget allocations for R&D. The utilities should aim at least about 1% of their profit to be utilized for R&D activities and the manufacturing organizations should consider 3%–4% to be provided for technology development.

- Ultra Super Critical boiler technology, IGCC technology, and oxy-fuel technology are well researched abroad but have to be developed for Indian coal. NTPC, the major Indian Central Sector utility should have its R&D centre strengthened to expedite the work started during the Tenth Plan on IGCC. This project may be given top priority.
- There is a need to work with specialized S&T laboratories under CSIR and other space and nuclear establishments to develop material technology for advanced boilers, fuel cells, solar power, battery, and super conducting material application in power sector.
- The projects of national interest have to be taken upon collaborative research route. In future capital fund support for R&D should be reduced and utilities and industries should collaborate to fund R&D projects.
- R&D import should be exempted from custom duty to encourage indigenous R&D.
- A High Power Committee in R&D should monitor R&D projects and regulate funds. This will avoid duplication and ensure competitive R&D.

Human Resource Development and Capacity Building

10.87 Human resource development and capacity building in the present power scenario demands a very comprehensive and pragmatic approach to attract, utilize, develop, and conserve valuable human resources. Training, re-training, and career prospects are some of the important elements of human resource development. The reforms in the power sector have led to change in the role of senior engineers from a purely government-controlled technical management to business management in a corporatized framework.

10.88 Technically trained manpower comprising skilled engineers, supervisors, artisans, and managers is required in every sphere of the power supply industry. Due to the introduction of more sophisticated technology and automation, the Man/MW ratio is declining over the years. The overall Man/MW ratio in power sector which was 9.42 at the end of the Ninth Plan is expected to go down to 7.00 at the end of the Tenth Plan and it is expected to be 5.82 at the end of the Eleventh Plan. This indicates the increasing importance of each individual, the man behind the machine. Therefore, the human resource development/training needs of technical, non-technical, and supporting staff should be given importance keeping in view the National Training Policy for the power sector.

10.89 It is estimated that during the Eleventh Plan, the availability of infrastructure for training is about 0.77 lakh man-months per year against the requirement of 3.40 lakh man-months per year. This shows that there is a deficit of about 77%. In spite of such a situation of lack of availability of required infrastructure, quite often a number of training institutes remain underutilized. Therefore, there is need to network various training and academic institutions such as National Power Training Institute, Indian Institute of Management (IIMs), Administrative Staff College of India and other reputed institutions for providing training to power sector personnel.

Legislative and Policy Issues

10.90 The Electricity Act 2003 has put in place a liberal and progressive framework for the development of electricity sector in the country. Its main objectives are promoting competition, protecting interest of consumers, supply of electricity to all areas, rationalization of electricity tariff, and ensuring transparent policies regarding subsidies.

10.91 The National Electricity Policy and the Tariff Policy have been notified under the provisions of the Act. The National Electricity Policy aims at providing access to electricity to all in the next five years by overcoming energy and peaking shortages and having adequate spinning reserves by the year 2012 for fully meeting the demand and supply of reliable and quality power of specific standards in an efficient manner and at reasonable rates. The Tariff Policy aims at ensuring financial viability of the sector and promoting transparency, consistency, and predictability in regulatory approaches. It also aims at promoting competition and efficiency in operation and meeting quality of supply. Further, the Integrated Energy Policy aimed at promoting overall development of the sector has been announced. The Electricity Tariff Policy based bidding is mandatory for all plants from January 2006 excepting for public sector plants which are required to do so by 2011.

10.92 The legal provisions of the Electricity Act 2003, National Electricity Policy, Tariff Policy, and the Integrated Energy Policy provide an appropriate legislative and policy framework for the development of the power sector. The provisions of these policies must be implemented within the stipulated time in order to make power available at affordable cost to all by 2012. The major issues to be addressed in this regard during the Eleventh Plan are as follows.

Issues Related to Capacity Building

The issues related to capacity building are the following:

- There is a need to streamline and standardize the procedure to shorten the time cycle for obtaining environmental/forest clearance for power projects.
- The captive coal blocks development should be done in advance to match with commissioning schedule of power projects.
- The number of agencies having authorization to undertake exploration of coal blocks also needs to be increased.
- State governments should take suitable policy measures to make captive generation more attractive.
- To encourage R&M of old power plants, CERC should set up benchmarks for capital expenditure on R&M.

Issues Related to Promotion of Open Access and Trading

The following are the issues related to promotion of open access and trading:

- There is a requirement of having an enabling policy framework for merchant power plants which could be in the size of up to 1000 MW so that adequate power is available for open access.
- To provide transmission corridors for merchant power plants, adequate redundancy should be built at the stage of transmission planning.
- A rational transmission tariff framework is essential for facilitating optimum network use, promoting power trade, and facilitating open access.

Issues Related to Control Cost of Bulk Power

The issues related to control cost of bulk power are the following:

- Coal blocks should be offered on the basis of competitive tariff-based bidding as part of the integrated coal mine cum power project to reduce the fuel cost as major part of the cost of bulk power is fuel cost.
- The price of domestic natural gas and its allocation should be independently regulated on a cost plus basis including reasonable return till the time domestic supply exceeds demand by fertilizer and stranded power plants after which it should be market determined. An exception needs to be made for hydro plants that involve significant geological uncertainties.
- Various taxes and initiatives on generation, transmission, and distribution projects should be identical to remove distortions.
- Taxes on fuels should not distort economic fuel choices.

Issues Related to Improvement in Distribution Segment

The issues related to improvement in distribution segment are as follows:

- An National Electricity Fund be set up and supportive measures taken to bring major improvement in the distribution system.
- There is a need to restructure the APDRP to make it sustainable for better results.
- To reduce distribution losses and improve quality of supply to the consumers. The larger investments would be required for upgradation of distribution networks and a special drive would be necessary for identifying high loss areas and controlling commercial losses in such areas.
- AT&C loss reduction of 3% every year in next five years should be targeted by all States.

- Setting up of peaking power stations should be encouraged by time of day tariff for both producers and consumers to overcome peaking shortages as the additional power cost of supply from such a station could then be passed on to the consumers who opt for uninterrupted/reliable supply.

PLAN OUTLAYS

10.93 A public sector tentative outlay for the Eleventh Plan is Rs 554766 crore at constant price. This consists of Rs 343387 crore for the Central sector and Rs 211379 crore for the State sector. The proposed outlay for Central sector includes Rs 313722 crore IEBR requirement of PSUs (Rs 278781 crore for PSUs under the MoP, Rs 12218 crore for Power projects of Neyveli Lignite Corporation (NLC), and Rs 22723 crore for power projects of Atomic Energy). It also includes Rs 29665 crore budgetary support (Rs 26924 crore for programmes of the MoP and Rs 2741 crore for power related programmes of DAE). The State sector investments include borrowing amount of Rs 25000 crore for the APDRP scheme initially as loan to the SPUs by Central PSUs of the MoP. In addition, investment would have to be made to meet the gap, particularly in the T&D systems for which a group of ministers has been set up.

PETROLEUM AND NATURAL GAS SECTOR

ISSUES AND CHALLENGES

10.94 Currently, India's per capita consumption of petroleum products is about one-fifth of world's average per capita consumption. The share of hydrocarbons in the commercial energy is about 45% out of which the share of oil is 36% and that of natural gas is around 9%. In India, the indigenous production of crude oil has not been increasing in tandem with the consumption/demand of petroleum products. Considering the global trend of shift in energy mix from oil to gas, the share of gas in consumption pattern is also likely to increase gradually. India's current import of crude oil is more than 70% of its total requirements and the share is expected to increase in the near future. The impact of high oil prices in the international market and stagnant domestic oil supply has led to accelerated efforts on domestic exploration, venturing into overseas equity oil and gas and LNG imports as measures for ensuring energy security. The hydrocarbon industry has been passing through very turbulent and challenging phases for the last few years.

10.95 The challenges before the country are:

- Maximizing supply of crude oil and gas at the least possible cost as part of energy security by getting as much as possible from known reserves, encouraging exploration for new finds, and getting equity oil abroad.
- Developing suitable gas market through exploration for finding new gas fields, rapid development of existing fields, creating a pipeline network for distribution and competitiveness.
- Creating conditions for competitive markets of petroleum products and regulating it to ensure that fair competition protects interests of all stakeholders.
- Rationalizing subsidies for kerosene and domestic LPG whose burden has increased dramatically. Effective delivery and targeting of subsidies are critical to reduce the burden.
- Ensuring large investment for creating marketing and associated infrastructure such as ports, storage, pipelines, etc.

10.96 Various policies and programmes have been pursued in the past for the petroleum and natural gas sector. A brief review of these is given below.

REVIEW OF THE TENTH PLAN

10.97 A brief review of the thrust areas identified during the Tenth Plan is given below.

Oil Security

- Under six rounds of NELP, 162 blocks have been awarded. A total of 37 discoveries have been made so far and development plans for their exploitation are under progress. In addition, 26 blocks have been awarded for exploitation of CBM and 6 TCF (trillion cubic feet) of gas reserves have been established so far.
- A number of Improved Oil Recovery (IOR) and Enhanced Oil Recovery (EOR) schemes were implemented to enhance the indigenous production of crude oil.

- Oil and gas PSUs were encouraged to pursue equity oil and gas opportunities overseas. OVL (ONGC Videsh Ltd), OIL, IOC (Indian Oil Corporation), and GAIL are actively involved in acquiring overseas exploration and production assets. Against the acquisition target of 10.14 million tonnes of oil and oil equivalent of gas (O&OEG) during the Tenth Plan period, OVL achievement was 22.24 million tonnes of O&OEG from its overseas activities.
- About 5 million tonnes strategic crude oil storage is under construction at three locations.
- Biofuels Policy initiatives for blending of petrol with ethanol and biodiesel with diesel were taken up.

Infrastructure Development

- Refining capacity at the beginning of the Tenth Plan was 118.37 million tonnes per annum which increased to 148.97 million tonnes per annum in the terminal year of the Tenth Plan.
- Private sector was allowed to market transportation fuels, namely, motor spirit, high-speed diesel, and ATF. However, the desired competition could not be achieved due to unprecedented increase in crude oil prices in the international market which led to the government intervention for moderating the prices of petroleum products.

Efficiency Improvement

- A number of energy efficiency projects were implemented to reduce energy consumption in various refineries.
- Petroleum Conservation and Research Association and other organizations have taken up a number of programmes on conservation of petroleum products in transport, industry, agriculture, and household sectors. However, the savings of petroleum products due to conservation and efficiency improvement measures have yet to be quantified.

Environment and Quality Improvement

- Road map was prepared for achieving product quality norms based on the Auto Fuel Policy Report. Diesel Hydro Desulphurization projects were implemented in the refineries.
- Introduction of Bharat Stage II petrol throughout the country was achieved by 1 April 2005. Introduction of Bharat Stage II diesel in a phased manner was completed in various States. EURO III petrol and diesel were introduced in 11 major cities.

Reforms

- Petroleum and Natural Gas Regulatory Board Bill was passed and the Board has now been constituted.
- Dismantling of administered price mechanism (APM) regime was initiated w.e.f. 1 April 2002. However, the envisaged competition in the marketing of petroleum products could not be achieved. The GoI currently exercises control by declaring price caps. As a practical matter, full competition at refinery gate and retail level within the declared price caps should be allowed. Such competition will lead to lower prices and, over a period, lead to limiting/eliminating the government support on automotive fuels. If such price caps entail any compensation to National Oil Companies (NOCs) through pricing of crude oil or otherwise then such benefit should be made available evenly to both public and private sector players. The ultimate objective should be to remove government intervention in pricing of all petroleum products and provide targeted subsidies directly to the intended beneficiaries. Such subsidies should be funded through the National Budget. Full competition at the refinery gate and retail level would lead to trade parity prices.
- The phasing out of subsidies on domestic LPG and PDS kerosene envisaged during the Tenth Plan was not achieved.

10.98 The physical and financial performances of the petroleum and natural gas are given in Tables 10.17 and 10.18.

Exploration and Development

10.99 Under NELP, so far 162 exploration blocks have been awarded, covering an area of less than 40% of the Indian sedimentary basins. Out of the above 162 blocks, 115 blocks were awarded during the Tenth Plan.

10.100 Under the CBM policy, contracts with PSUs/private companies for 23 blocks in three rounds of bidding were signed. In addition, three blocks—two blocks to ONGC–CIL consortium and one block to

TABLE 10.17
Physical Programmes—Petroleum and Natural Gas

Programme	Ninth Plan Actual	Tenth Plan Target	2002–03 Actual	2003–04 Actual	2004–05 Actual	2005–06 Actual	2006–07 (Prov.) Actual	Achievement 2002–07	% of Target
Demand/consumption (million tonnes)	100.43#	120.4#	104.2	107.75	111.63	111.92	119.85	119.85#	99.5
Reserve accretion (Mtoe)	795.13	785–914	329.47	348.32	337.15	222.95	387.53	1652.92	178–207
Crude oil production (million tonnes)	162.99	169.38	33.04	33.37	33.98	32.19	33.98	166.56	98.3
Natural gas production (bcm)	140.92	177.48	31.39	31.96	31.76	32.20	31.55	158.86	89.5
			Net Import						
Crude oil	–	–	81.99	90.43	95.86	99.41	111.50	–	–
Petroleum products	–	–	–13.06	–6.72	–9.38	–9.38	–15.77	–	–
Refining capacity (million tonnes) as on 1 April	118.37	138–155#	118.37	127.37	127.37	132.47	148.97	148.97#	–

Note: # Figures for the terminal year of the Tenth Plan.
Source: Ministry of Petroleum and Natural Gas.

TABLE 10.18
Outlays/Expenditure—Petroleum and Natural Gas

(Rs Crore)

Tenth Plan Approved Outlay	2002–03 (Actual)	2003–04 (Actual)	2004–05 (Actual)	2005–06 (Actual)	2006–07 (Actual) (Prov.)	Likely Achievement 2002–07	% Utilization
96041.19 (119409.99)	15805.67 (18915.35)	16625.99 (19169.83)	20981.19 (23178.51)	251414.57 (26879.50)	29175.23 (29175.23)	108002.65 (117318.43)	112.45 (98.25)

Note: Figures in the bracket are at 2006–07 price.
Source: Planning Commission

Great Eastern Energy Corporation Ltd—were awarded on nomination basis.

Financial Performance

10.101 An outlay of Rs 96041.19 crore was approved for the Tenth Plan for oil and gas PSUs against which the actual expenditure was Rs 108002.65 crore at current price. At constant 2006–07 price the expenditure was 98.25% of the approved outlay.

Thrust Areas in the Eleventh Plan

10.102 The policy issues that need to be addressed in the petroleum and natural gas sector relate to oil and gas security, pricing of petroleum products, pricing of domestically produced natural gas and its allocation to the power and fertilizer industry, ensuring competition and open access in the pipeline transportation and distribution grid, and conservation of petroleum products and natural gas.

Oil and Gas Security

Enhanced Exploration and Development

10.103 The Eleventh Plan envisages bringing more and more acreage under exploration especially those in the frontier areas/basins, adoption of state-of-the-art Exploration and Production (E&P) technology, faster development of discovered reserves, development of marginal fields, and continuation of IOR/EOR schemes. These efforts would lead to a projected total crude oil production of 206.76 million tonnes against the actual production of 166.56 million tonnes during the Tenth Plan. Similarly, the projected gas production will be 255.76 bcm against the Tenth Plan production of 159.06 bcm. In addition, CBM blocks would be awarded during the Eleventh Plan in Madhya Pradesh, Jharkhand, Gujarat, Tamil Nadu, and Arunachal Pradesh. During the Eleventh Plan, the CBM production is projected to be around 3.78 bcm.

Acquisition of Equity Oil and Gas Abroad

10.104 Considering the continuing gap between the demand and indigenous production of crude oil and natural gas and low crude oil reserves replenishment, NOCs and private companies are being encouraged to venture abroad. The various strategic options in this regard are: focus on ventures with producing property in the short term; purchase of equity share of companies as a part of reserves portfolio management; focus on exploration acreages in short to medium term, and promoting upstream sector services.

Strategic Crude Oil Storage

10.105 The government has taken in principle decision to construct 15 million tonnes of strategic storage in various phases. In the first phase, a project for creating a strategic storage of 5.0 million tonnes for crude oil is under implementation at three locations, viz., 1 million tonne at Visakhapatnam, 1.5 million tonnes at Mangalore, and 2.5 million tonnes at Padur, a site near Mangalore. This storage will be over and above the existing storage capacity for crude oil and petroleum products at the various refineries and would act as emergency response in case of short-term supply disruption. The project is anticipated to be completed during the Eleventh Plan.

Development of Alternate Fuels

Coal Bed Methane

10.106 A total of 26 CBM blocks have already been offered in the three rounds of bidding. These fields are under development stage and production of CBM is expected in the Eleventh Plan. The bidding rounds will be continued in the Eleventh Plan and it is planned to offer CBM blocks in Assam, Arunachal Pradesh, Orissa, Jharkhand, Madhya Pradesh, Gujarat, and Tamil Nadu.

Gas Hydrates

10.107 National Gas Hydrates Programme was started in 1997. Till now, a large number of seismic surveys have been conducted. K–G basin, Mahanadi basin, and Konkan and Kerala basins have been identified as potential areas. The production of gas from the gas hydrates is one of the biggest challenges facing the energy sector and technology is still to be established in this area. Pilot test production is planned to be carried out in India by 2009–10.

Underground Coal Gasification (UCG)

10.108 ONGC and GAIL have been exploring the possibilities of exploiting the gas through UCG process. The techno-economic feasibility and commercial exploitation is proposed to be carried out during the Eleventh Plan. ONGC has planned to produce 2.7 MMSCMD of gas through UCG process and envisages producing 2.99 bcm of UCG gas during the Eleventh Plan.

Coal to Liquid

10.109 OIL has carried out pre-feasibility studies on Catalytic Two-Stage Liquefaction Technology and Direct Liquefaction Technologies in order to select the best suitable technology for the North East coal for liquification. The feasibility study on the selected technology will be carried out during the Eleventh Plan. A joint task force between OIL and CIL has been constructed by MOP&NG to confirm availability and assured supply of coal in Assam, Arunachal Pradesh, and Meghalaya for a commercial plant.

Biofuels

10.110 After stabilization of 5% ethanol blending petrol sales, the content of ethanol in petrol would be considered for increasing up to 10% by the middle of the Eleventh Plan, subject to ethanol availability and commercial viability of blending. Depending upon the bio-diesel production and availability, the entire country may be progressively covered with sale of 5% bio-diesel blended diesel by the end of the Eleventh Plan.

Oil Shale

10.111 In India, shale formation is exposed to the surface in the region of Belt of Schuppen falling in Assam, Arunachal Pradesh, and Nagaland. The oil shale reserves are estimated at about 100 billion barrels. However, the production of shale oil requires large amount of energy and water. Environment and monetary cost have so far made production of oil from oil shale uneconomical.

REFORMS

Petroleum Product Pricing

10.112 With the dismantling of APM for petroleum products w.e.f. 1 April 2002, it was envisaged that the price of petroleum products would be moved from APM to market-determined pricing mechanism. An import parity pricing mechanism was followed by the oil industry which was subsequently modified to a trade parity pricing as an approximation to competitive market prices. Full price competition at the refinery gate and retail level needs to be adopted to enhance competition in the sector.

Phasing Out Subsidies on PDS Kerosene and Domestic LPG

10.113 For kerosene, it is proposed to provide direct subsidies to the consumers, particularly those below the poverty line. A system of smart card for supply of kerosene to BPL families would be introduced. With the smart card, kerosene may be bought from any shop at market price. In case of domestic cooking gas also, it is proposed to phase out subsidy gradually with the introduction of smart cards for domestic LPG which would help in preventing diversion of domestic LPG to the commercial sector.

Unified State Taxes and Removal of Tax Anomalies

10.114 There is a need to amalgamate the individual State markets into one nation-wide market with unified State taxes. Therefore, there is need to remove State tax anomaly, provide level playing field to domestic production vis-à-vis direct import, and introduce a uniform VAT which provides full set-off for local levies such as octroi and entry-tax at the State level.

ENVIRONMENTAL AND QUALITY MANAGEMENT

10.115 Efforts would be made to improve the Health Safety and Environment (HSE) management so as to provide occupationally healthier work force, reduced accident rates, cleaner and greener product with reduced emissions and effluents. The following measures would be implemented in the exploration and production sector during the Eleventh Plan period:

- Establishing environment management system for all oil and gas field installations and drilling rigs based on international standards to ensure improvements towards reducing discharges and emissions to internationally acceptable levels.
- Eco-rating of major installations and compulsory environmental audits.
- Pro-active measures to prevent marine pollution and to effectively combat oil spills.
- Benchmarking at par with international oil majors with respect to environmental practices.

10.116 On the basis of the assessment of the impact of Bharat Stage-II norms in the entire country and EURO III equivalent norms in identified cities, EURO IV equivalent norms in identified cities and EURO III equivalent norms in the entire country would be introduced w.e.f. 1 April 2010.

INFRASTRUCTURE DEVELOPMENT

Marketing Infrastructure

10.117 In view of the proposed increase in refining capacity during the Eleventh Plan, a large investment would be required for creating marketing and associated infrastructure such as ports, storage, pipelines, and terminals.

Manpower Planning

10.118 The rapid development of the oil and gas sector in the last few years has led to acute shortage of skilled manpower. Therefore, high degree of collaboration between the industry and academia, expanding training programmes to address emerging skill shortages, would be a major thrust area for planning sustained availability of knowledge workers in the petroleum and natural gas sector.

Servicing of E&P Activities in India

10.119 E&P service providers play a key role in enabling success for E&P operators. The accelerated growth of E&P activities has led to multifold growth in demand of technology and oilfield services worldwide. Therefore, availability of services in India is becoming constrained and expensive. Hence, there is a need to facilitate the growth of E&P service industry.

PHYSICAL PROGRAMMES

DEMAND/CONSUMPTION OF PETROLEUM PRODUCTS

10.120 The demand of petroleum products in the terminal year of the Eleventh Plan (2011–12) is projected at 131.77 million tonnes to 141.79 million tonnes against the anticipated consumption of 119.85 million tonnes in 2006–07, indicating a CAGR of 1.91% to 3.42% during the Eleventh Plan. The actual growth may be lower if the prevailing high oil prices continue during the Eleventh Plan resulting in policies encouraging energy efficiencies.

DEMAND OF NATURAL GAS

10.121 About 70% of the natural gas is currently being consumed in the fertilizer and power sectors. As per the Working Group on Petroleum and Natural Gas, the demand for natural gas in the terminal year of the Eleventh Plan is expected to increase up to 279.43 MMSCMD out of which 126.57 MMSCMD has been assumed for power sector and 76.26 MMSCMD for fertilizer sector. However, as per the MoP projections, the demand of natural gas for power sector would be only 89 MMSCMD. The lower projected demand of natural gas by the MoP is taking into account the prevailing market price and availability of APM gas. Taking into account the lower demand for natural gas by the MoP, the total demand of natural gas in the terminal year of the Plan would be 241.86 MMSCMD. However, materialization of this demand would depend upon the price of natural gas.

HYDROCARBON RESERVE ACCRETION

10.122 The anticipated reserve accretion during the Tenth Plan was 1652.92 million tonnes, excluding Pvt/Joint Venture Company (JVC) share, against the target of 785–914 million tonnes. The projected indicative hydrocarbon in-place reserves during the Eleventh Plan are of 2129.44 million tonnes.

CRUDE OIL AND NATURAL GAS PRODUCTION

10.123 The targets for production of crude oil and natural gas are given Tables 10.19 and 10.20, respectively.

10.124 It may be seen from above that against the projected demand of 241.86 MMSCMD in the terminal year of the Eleventh Plan, the production will be only 173.23 MMSCMD. The additional requirement would have to be met through the import of natural gas.

TABLE 10.19
Crude Oil Production

(Million Tonnes)

Organization	2007–08	2008–09	2009–10	2010–11	2011–12	Total
ONGC	27.16	28.00	29.00	28.53	27.37	140.06
OIL	3.50	3.55	3.73	3.91	4.30	18.99
Pvt/JVC	10.57	10.78	9.76	8.75	7.85	47.71
Total	41.23	42.33	42.49	41.19	39.51	206.76

Source: Working Group Report on Petroleum and Natural Gas.

TABLE 10.20
Natural Gas Production

(bcm)

Organization	2007–08	2008–09	2009–10	2010–11	2011–12	Total
ONGC	22.10	22.53	22.77	22.99	22.00	112.39
OIL	3.13	3.21	3.25	3.28	3.56	16.43
Pvt/JVC	8.55	22.55	29.41	28.77	37.61	126.45
Total	33.78	48.29	55.43	55.03	63.23	255.76
Total (MMSCMD)	92.20	132.30	151.86	150.79	173.23	700.38

Source: Working Group Report on Petroleum and Natural Gas.

LNG Supply during the Eleventh Plan

10.125 Currently 5 million tonnes per annum of LNG is being imported at Dahej terminal. The Hazira terminal of Shell with capacity of 2.5 million tonnes per annum is operational but is yet to stabilize its operation. LNG supply is projected to reach a level of 23.75 million tonnes per annum by the year 2011–12. A detailed break-up of LNG supply during the Eleventh Plan is given in Table 10.21.

10.126 The projected crude oil and gas production from the NOCs overseas ventures is given in Tables 10.19, 10.20, and 10.22 .

Refining Capacity

10.127 The refining capacity is projected to go up to 240.96 million tonnes per annum in the terminal year of the Eleventh Plan as against 148.97 million tonnes per annum in the beginning of the Plan. This addition to the refining capacity during the Eleventh Plan period would be 91.99 million tonnes per annum. This addition includes 38.5 million tonnes per annum (Essar—3.5 million tonnes per annum; Reliance—29 million tonnes per annum; and Nagarjun—6 million tonnes per annum) from the private sector. Against the 240.96 million tonnes per annum of the projected refining capacity, the demand for products would be ranging between 132 million tonnes during the terminal year of the Eleventh Plan. Thus, the country would be in surplus of the refining capacity by almost 108 million tonnes. In view of the above, the setting of new capacity needs to be reviewed.

Research and Development (R&D)

10.128 India is spending around Rs 200–250 crore per annum on R&D efforts in the hydrocarbon sector having an annual turnover only of oil PSUs of around Rs 4 lakh crore. This is substantially lower compared to the research expenditure in developed countries that spend about 1% of the turnover towards R&D. A mission-oriented approach on co-operative basis needs to be adopted for developing technologies pertaining to exploration and exploitation of gas hydrates, UCG, conversion of coal to liquid (CTL), development of

TABLE 10.21
LNG Supply Projections during the Eleventh Plan

LNG Supply Source	2007–08	2008–09	2009–10	2010–11	2011–12
Dahej	5.00	5.00	7.5	10.00	10.00
Hazira	2.50	2.50	2.50	2.50	2.50
Dabhol	1.20	2.10	5.00	5.00	5.00
Kochi	–	–	–	2.50	5.00
Mangalore	–	–	–	–	1.25
Total LNG Supply (million tonnes per annum)	8.70	9.60	15.00	20.00	23.75
Total LNG Supply (MMSCMD)	30.45	33.60	52.50	70.00	83.12

Assumptions:
1. Hazira expansion to 5.0 million tonnes per annum is not considered in the Eleventh Plan.
2. Mangalore terminal is expected to be partially commissioned in 2011–12.
Source: Working Group Report on Petroleum and Natural Gas.

TABLE 10.22
Projected Crude Oil and Natural Gas Production from Overseas

		2007–08	2008–09	2009–10	2010–11	2011–12	Total
Crude oil production	OIL	0.25	0.5	1.0	1.53	1.6	4.88
(million tonnes)	OVL	7.02	6.53	5.97	5.76	5.35	30.63
	Total	7.27	7.03	6.97	7.29	6.95	35.51
Natural gas production (bcm)	OVL	1.75	1.82	1.93	1.97	2.2	9.67

Source: Working Group Report on Petroleum and Natural Gas.

shale oil, biofuels and hydrogen, etc. Presently, most of the funding comes from the government or the public sector. Under the present scenario the private sector is playing a significant role in the growth of the petroleum industry. Therefore, funding of R&D programmes from the private sector should also be encouraged.

PLAN OUTLAYS

10.129 A public sector tentative outlay for the Eleventh Plan is Rs 213514.59 crore at current price. This consists of Rs 150932.49 crore for exploration and production and Rs 62582.10 crore for refining and marketing sector. The PSU-wise outlays are given in Table 10.23.

10.130 In addition, during the Eleventh Plan, the government has decided to set up Rajiv Gandhi Institute of Petroleum Technology, an institute to cater to the education and training requirements of all segments of petroleum and natural gas industry. The total estimated cost of the institute is estimated to be Rs 695.58 crore, out of which Rs 285 crore is proposed to be met through the budgetary support.

TABLE 10.23
Public Sector Outlays for the Eleventh Plan

(Rs Crore)

PSUs	Eleventh Plan Outlay
A. Exploration and Production	
ONGC-OVL	45332.87
ONGC	75983.77
OIL	13439.02
GAIL	10326.83
IOC	2982.00
HPCL	2000.00
BPCL	868.00
Subtotal (A)	150932.49
B. Refining and Marketing	
HPCL	8714.00
BPCL, incl. KRL	11344.80
CPCL	3275.00
BRPL	1444.53
IOC	28567.75
IBP	0.00
NRL	593.00
MRPL	8643.02
Subtotal (B)	62582.10
Total petroleum and natural gas sector	213514.59

Source: Ministry of Petroleum and Natural Gas.

COAL SECTOR

ISSUES AND CHALLENGES

10.131 Coal provides 25.1% of global primary energy needs against 34.3% from oil, 20.9% from gas, 6.5% from nuclear, 2.2% from hydro, and 11% from renewable. The contribution of coal in the world's electricity generation is around 40%. Coal accounts for over 50% of India's commercial energy consumption and about 78% of domestic coal production is dedicated to power generation. The global hard coal consumption in 2005 was 4990 million tonnes. China is the largest producer of coal (2226 million tonnes) followed by the US (951 million tonnes) and India (398 million tonnes). The major coal exporters are Australia (231 million tonnes), Indonesia (108 million tonnes), Russia (76 million tonnes), South Africa (73 million tonnes), and China (72 million tonnes). The major coal importing countries are Japan (178 million tonnes), Republic of Korea (77 million tonnes), Chinese Taipei (61 million tonnes), UK (44 million tonnes), and Germany (38 million tonnes).

10.132 The growth in demand of coal in the Eleventh Plan is pegged at more than 9% per annum for enabling the power sector to attain the anticipated growth. The coal producing companies may not be able to jump from the present growth rate of less than 6% to more than 9% within a year, but there is need for aligning strategies so that the projected coal production from coal PSUs as well as captive coal mines materializes by the end of the Eleventh Plan. Under the Coal Mines (Nationalization) Act 1973, coal can be mined by public sector companies as well as designated captive users, which are steel, cement, and power at present, for their own use. An increase in the number of producers can help reach the targeted production. At the same time we will need to import more coal, which needs to be facilitated. Further, it is necessary to take required steps for addressing the need for matching the growth of infrastructure with the proposed growth in coal production. The desired expansion of the rail network and rolling stock for moving the projected quantities of coal from mines to load centres would need large investments. Coal movement should also be economical; therefore the railway freight rate for movement of coal needs to be rationalized.

A high freight rate increases coal price at a distance and distorts choice of fuels, reduces competitiveness, and results in mislocation of industries.

10.133 A competitive coal market is required for economic efficiency. Since for power plants, the major users of coal, coal cost is a pass through cost, price discovery mechanism is a challenge. We need to streamline the process of e-auction of non-coking coal and sell at least 20% of the non-coking coal production through this process for effective discovery of market price of coal.

10.134 An independent coal regulator is required to oversee the price discovery mechanism, regulate upstream allotment, and exploit available coal blocks to yield coal, coal bed methane, mine mouth methane, CTL, and for in situ coal gasification so that India, with the third largest reserves of coal in the world, becomes a long-term player in the highly liquid international market for coal. In order to deliver, coal companies must ensure that productivity of men and machines is at par with international standards. The cost of coal movement can also be reduced by washing and beneficiating coal as Indian coal has a high ash content. A change in the coal pricing system, where price of coal is fully variable based on its gross calorific value (GCV) rather than the current practice of grading coal by using wide ranges of useful heat values (UHV), is also called for.

10.135 The extractable coal reserves in the country will run out in about 45 years if domestic coal production continues to grow at 5% per year. However only about 45% of the potential coal bearing area has currently been covered by regional exploration and detailed drilling. Rapid increase of coal production requires accelerated exploration, augmentation of drilling capacity and capacity to assess coal reserves, and preparing geological reports.

REVIEW OF THE TENTH PLAN

Coal Demand and Production

10.136 Demand for coal in the terminal year of the Tenth Plan was projected at 460.50 million tonnes comprising 37.21 million tonnes of coking coal and 423.29 million tonnes of non-coking or thermal coal. Demand from the power sector (utilities) touched 297.37 million tonnes. The CAGR of the demand was 5.66% against 5.74% envisaged at the time of formulation of the Plan and 3% actually achieved during the Ninth Plan.

10.137 To meet the surge in the demand of coal, Emergency Coal Production Plan of CIL was approved to raise the production by advancing the production schedule in 12 existing mines/ongoing projects and by taking up four new projects with a likely capital investment of Rs 2085.05 crore. Outsourcing of coal and overburden removal activities in these projects was proposed. Though the earmarked projects did not yield additional production during the Tenth Plan, they set the pace of implementation of new projects.

10.138 Production of coal in 2006–07 touched 430.54 million tonnes against the target of 430.10 million tonnes. While there were delays in taking up new projects during the Tenth Plan, augmentation of coal production was made possible by increasing the production from existing mines and acceleration in activities to reduce production build up period of ongoing projects. CAGR of production during the Tenth Plan period was 5.6% against 4.46% envisaged at the time of formulation of the Plan and 2.5% actually achieved in the Ninth Plan. Growth in CIL's production during the Tenth Plan was 5.28%. The output of captive mines increased at a higher rate.

Demand Supply Management

10.139 It is pointed out that the demand and production numbers are not weighted for quality of coal and differences in coal quality can also impact the demand realized. Finally, use of washed coal in power generation or the use of Corex technology in the steel sector is also not well accounted in establishing the demand numbers. The physical gap of 45 million tonnes between the demand and supply in the terminal year (2006–07) of the Tenth Five Year Plan was met through import of 45 million tonnes of coal (coking coal, 22 million tonnes; thermal coal, 23 million tonnes) as envisaged. Though the import of thermal coal by the power sector helped its planned generation programme, it resulted in reduced domestic off-take, resulting in additional stock build-up at pit heads.

Lignite Consumption and Production

10.140 Demand of lignite in the terminal year (2006–07) of the Tenth Plan was projected as 57.79 million tonnes (Tamil Nadu, 35.86 million tonnes; Gujarat, 16.27 million tonnes; Rajasthan, 5.65 million tonnes) but the materialization was about 30.63 million tonnes (Tamil Nadu, 20.51 million tonnes; Gujarat, 9.65 million tonnes; Rajasthan, 0.47 million tonnes) showing a CAGR of 4.93%. Linked to 16.36 BU of Gross Power Generation, the demand for NLC in 2006–07 was projected as 21.50 million tonnes. Consequent upon the downward revision of Gross Power Generation target to 15.71 BU, the demand for lignite was lowered by 1.09 million tonnes and kept at 20.41 million tonnes. NLC produced 19.38 million tonnes of lignite and generated 14.85 BU of gross power.

Coal and Lignite Inventories (Reserves)

10.141 As on 1 January 2007, the national coal inventory stood at 255 billion tonnes, out of which 97.92 billion tonnes are in the proved category. The inventory of lignite resources stood at 38.27 billion tonnes, as on 1 April 2006, with 4.5 billion tonnes in the proved category. Table 10.24 gives accretion of coal reserves over the years.

Central Sector Plan Schemes

PROMOTIONAL EXPLORATION

10.142 An outlay of Rs 275.80 crore was provided during the Tenth Plan for plan scheme of 'Regional/Promotional Drilling' for drilling 6 lakh metres, comprising 3.3 lakh metres for coal covering 43 blocks and 2.7 lakh metres for lignite covering 13 blocks; and for other exploratory services including creation of coal/lignite database and CBM studies. Project-based approach was adopted for this plan scheme and 121 projects were sanctioned for implementation. Against the projection, 6.288 lakh metres (91%) of drilling was achieved during the Tenth Plan establishing 19.78 billion tonnes of coal resource and 17.53 billion tonnes of lignite resource.

DETAILED DRILLING IN NON-CIL BLOCKS

10.143 The blocks outside the purview of CIL were proposed to be explored in detail for reducing the time lag between offering the blocks to potential entrepreneurs and start of mining operations by them through the scheme of 'Detailed Drilling in Non-CIL Blocks' with budgetary support. The cost of exploration was to be recovered from the recipients of these blocks. This scheme continued from the Ninth Plan and an outlay of Rs 70.66 crore (Rs 57.86 crore for drilling and Rs 12.80 crore for other exploratory services) was provided during the Tenth Plan for drilling 2.13 lakh metre to bring 3.65 billion tonnes of resources under the proved category. Revised cost estimate of this Plan Scheme was approved in March 2006 where physical target was revised to 2.83 lakh metre of drilling with an outlay of Rs 93.84 crore. Against the projections, drilling of 2.84 lakh metre was achieved during the Tenth Plan, establishing 7.06 billion tonnes of coal resource as proved.

SCIENCE AND TECHNOLOGY (R&D)

10.144 Despite the thrust laid on coal science and technology (S&T) programme, the continuing scheme since 1975, the progress has not been satisfactory both

Table 10.24
Accretion of Coal Reserves over the Years

(In Million Tonnes)

Coal Reserves as on	Proved Category	Accretion in Proved Category	Inferred Category	Indicated Category	Total Reserve	Reserve Accretion
1 January 2002	87320	–	109377	37417	234114	–
1 January 2003	90085	2765	112613	38050	240748	6634
1 January 2004	91631	1546	116174	37888	245693	4945
1 January 2005	92960	1329	117090	37797	247847	2154
1 January 2006	95866	2906	119769	37666	253301	5454
1 January 2007	97920	2054	118992	38260	255172	1871

Source: Coal Directory of India.

in terms of taking up of new projects and utilizing the outlays provided to various ongoing projects. The cumulative expenditure during the Tenth Plan under this scheme was Rs 50.94 crore.

ENVIRONMENTAL MEASURES AND SUBSIDENCE CONTROL (EMSC)

10.145 The Ninth Plan scheme, namely, 'Rehabilitation, Control of Fire, and Subsidence in Jharia and Raniganj Coalfields' was merged in this Tenth Plan scheme. The purpose of the scheme is to improve the environmental conditions in old mined out areas, particularly, Jharia and Raniganj coalfields, through implementation of a number of projects for mitigating the damages that occurred due to unscientific mining carried out prior to nationalization of coal mines. Against an outlay of Rs 163.00 crore provided under this scheme, the cumulative expenditure in the Tenth Plan is Rs 52.57 crore. The progress of implementation has not been satisfactory due to constraints of land acquisition, agitation/frequent interruption by local people, non-finalization of site of rehabilitation by local authorities, some technical problems, etc.

INFORMATION TECHNOLOGY

10.146 The government had mandated all the ministries to formulate a plan scheme with an outlay of about 2% of the total Plan outlay in the field of information technology in order to give a boost to e-governance. Accordingly, the MoC spent Rs 4.21 crore in the Tenth Plan for improving infrastructure needed for e-governance.

COAL CONTROLLER ORGANIZATION (CCO)

10.147 CCO under Collection of Statistics Act 1953 and Rules 1959 undertakes the activity of collection of coal and lignite related data and publishes 'coal statistics' annually using an outlay of Rs 0.22 crore. The Tenth Plan expenditure under this scheme was Rs 0.93 crore.

CONSERVATION AND SAFETY IN COAL MINES AND DEVELOPMENT OF TRANSPORT AND INFRASTRUCTURE IN COAL MINES

10.148 On the directions of the Ministry of Finance, MoC in the year 2005–06 had proposed two plan schemes with an outlay of Rs 117 crore and Rs 135.79 crore, respectively. Activities under these schemes are funded as reimbursement of a portion of the stowing excise duty, which is statutorily levied as per the Coal Mines (Conservation and Development) Act 1974 and deposited in the government treasury account. Prior to 2005–06, the expenditure incurred in these schemes was shown under the non-Plan head. In spite of the fact that the Planning Commission insisted on treating activities under these schemes as non-Plan activities, matter could not be resolved with the Ministry of Finance. A token provision of Rs 0.01 crore in each of these schemes was provided in last two years of the Tenth Plan period.

Productivity of Coal and Lignite PSUs

EQUIPMENT PRODUCTIVITY

10.149 The Heavy Earth Moving Machinery (HEMM) productivity has improved significantly in the Tenth Plan. In Coal India Ltd (CIL), the increase in productivity of shovels was by 124%, dumpers by 15%, drills by 25%, and dozers by 14% over the achievements of the Ninth Plan whereas the productivity of draglines remained constant. In the case of Singareni Collieries Company Ltd (SCCL), the improvements in the productivity are to the tune of 18% in draglines, 21% in shovels, 50% in dumpers, and 6% in the performance of dozers. System capacity utilization in most of the coal companies is consistently indicated as more than 100%. However, the percentage utilization of machinery (except dragline machine) in open-cast mines remained below the standard norms of Central Mine Planning and Design Institute.

MANPOWER PRODUCTIVITY

10.150 The overall productivity in terms of the output per man-shift (OMS) has increased from 2.45 tonnes in the beginning of the Tenth Plan to 3.54 tonnes in 2006–07 in CIL and from 1.88 tonnes to 2.32 tonnes in SCCL. In NLC, the OMS has increased from 8.84 tonnes in the beginning of the Plan to 10.16 tonnes in 2006–07. Many activities have been outsourced by different coal companies during the Tenth Plan but its effect on manpower productivity has not been captured while assessing manpower productivity of respective coal companies.

Coal Movement

10.151 The Tenth Plan identified certain critical rail links in potential coalfields and the railways have taken up most of these for implementation. It was also envisaged to strengthen the infrastructure such as port capacity and backward rail linkages for higher coal imports. The movement of raw coal and coal products by rail from CIL and SCCL increased from 199.74 million tonnes (63.7% of the total coal off-take) in 2001–02 to 217.20 million tonnes (53.4% of the total coal off-take) in 2006–07. The component of merry go round movement has increased from 74.62 million tonnes (23.8% of the total coal off-take) in the beginning of the Tenth Plan to 96.35 million tonnes (23.9% of the total off-take) in the terminal year. The movement of coal by road in the beginning of the Plan was 51.35 million tonnes (16.4% of the total coal off-take) and has increased to 94.32 million tonnes (22.5% of the total coal off-take) in 2006–07. Coastal shipment (inland) of coal increased from 16.10 million tonnes in 2001–02 to 17.47 million tonnes in 2006–07.

Initiatives on Clean Coal Technologies

10.152 Higher thermal efficiency and better environmental performance are apparent benefits of Circulatory Fluidized Bed Combustion, Integrated Gas Combined Cycle (IGCC), and super-critical boiler. High ash Indian coal and high sulphur lignite have been found to be good for these technologies. Initiatives were taken in the Tenth Plan for improving efficiency of energy conversion of Pulverized Coal Combustion (PCC) boilers by giving thrust on adoption of super critical and ultra super critical technologies.

10.153 Coal India Ltd, SCCL, and NLC entered into MoU with ONGC for developing UCG technology. ONGC, in turn, tied up with Skochinsky Institute of Technology, Moscow for technical assistance. NLC took up an R&D project for gasification of lignite seams in Rajasthan but the project remained non-starter as technical consultant or adviser could not be found even after two rounds of global bid. Finally, NLC chose to enter into MoU with ONGC for consultancy in the project. A joint venture between GAIL and CIL proposed for surface gasification of coal is under active consideration.

10.154 Interaction between CIL and OIL has taken place on the business initiatives of Coal Liquefaction project by way of creating a 'Joint Task Force'. The project for converting coal from North Eastern Coalfields (NEC) to liquid would cost Rs 12600 crore including Rs 3500 crore for producing 3.5 million tonnes of coal.

10.155 A demonstration Coal Bed Methane project is under implementation with financial support from the Global Environment Facility and UNDP. Several CBM blocks have also been awarded to private companies for exploration and production during three rounds of bidding. Apart from this, exploration works on two blocks were awarded to two PSUs on nomination basis. Commercial production of CBM is expected in the beginning of the Eleventh Plan.

Safety and Welfare

10.156 Implementation of safe practices in all operations by the coal companies lowered number of serious and fatal accidents in mines. However, the number of casualty was inflated during the Plan period due to five disasters involving more than 10 deaths. The practice of monitoring mine safety through Worker's Participation in Safety in association with Internal Safety Organization of coal companies, risk assessment techniques, and safety audits was strengthened.

10.157 The wages of workmen in the CIL and SCCL were revised in 2005. In addition to enhancement in the quantum of fringe benefits and allowances, the minimum wage was increased to Rs 238.63 per day. There were substantial improvements in respect of welfare amenities such as housing satisfaction, water supply, education facilities, health care, etc.

10.158 The coal companies are committed to bear the social responsibilities in medical services, education, water supply, housing, co-operatives and banking, ecology and environment, and community development for their employees. In addition to this, community development activities were also undertaken by different coal companies of Coal India Ltd. During the Tenth Plan, CIL spent an amount of about Rs 85 crore on various community development projects.

Revival of Loss Making Companies

10.159 Three subsidiary companies of CIL, namely Eastern Coalfields Limited (ECL), Bharat Coking Coal Limited (BCCL), and Central Coalfields Limited (CCL), were loss making at the terminal year of the Ninth Plan period (2001–02). During the Ninth Plan period, efforts were made with little success to turn these companies around. Eventually, during the Tenth Plan these companies were referred to BIFR for devising strategy/measures for their revival/rehabilitation. One of the companies, CCL managed to come out of BIFR in the year 2005–06. Increased production and higher revenue earned by sale of coal through e-auction made it possible for BCCL to show profits for the first time since nationalization. CCEA approved the BIFR sanctioned rehabilitation scheme for ECL for making the net worth of the company positive by 2009–10.

Expenditure Pattern

10.160 The cumulative expenditure in the Tenth Plan in form of investment by PSUs (funded through IEBR) was Rs 9574.49 crore (at 2001–02 price) against a provision of Rs 30556.48 crore which is 31.33% of the total outlay provided. Investments in CIL, SCCL, and NLC are 44%, 60%, and 33% of the outlay proposed during the Tenth Plan, respectively (see Table 10.25). Poor performance has been attributed to the late start of projects. Outsourcing of mining activities in many projects also brought down the requirement of capital investment as envisaged earlier.

Policy Reforms

- Pending the passage of the Coal Mines Nationalization (Amendment) Bill 2000, many policy initiatives such as permitting captive block holders to sell incidental coal surpluses during development and operation of the block to CIL or directly to currently linked end users, allowing group-captive mines, etc. were taken to increase the number of players in coal mining by making more coal available for allocation to different private and public companies for captive consumption and the State Governments for commercial mining. Initiative was taken to amend

TABLE 10.25
Company-wise/Scheme-wise Expenditure during the Tenth Plan

(Rs Crore)

Company/Scheme	2002–03	2003–04	2004–05	2005–06	2006–07	Tenth Plan	
	Actual	Actual	Actual	Actual	Actual	Original	Achieved#
(A) PSUs under MoC (IEBR)							
CIL	1147.54	1072.82	1055.90	1370.68	1674.10	14310.00	6321.04
SCCL	134.27	151.55	244.24	360.85	371.82	2113.00	1262.74
NLC	418.55	146.56	194.61	322.99	908.00	14133.48	1990.71
Total IEBR	1700.36	1370.94	1494.75	2054.52	2953.92	30556.48	9574.49
(B) Central Sector Plan Schemes (GBS)							
R&D (S&T)	6.74	9.11	11.32	12.54	4.85	100.00	44.55
Regional exploration	16.84	33.57	38.21	41.23	32.32	275.80	162.17
Detailed drilling–Non-CIL block	12.06	13.97	19.99	19.36	16.95	70.66	82.34
Environmental measures and subsidence control	12.63	0.00	4.31	21.46	6.46	163.00	44.87
Conservation and safety in coal mines	0	0	0	56.24	145.45	0	201.69
Development of transportation infrastructure in coalfield areas	0	0	0	42.54	11.16	0	53.69
Others (including VRS* and North East component)	115.39	16.80	94.05	1.01	24.79	425.06	252.05
Total GBS	163.66	73.45	167.88	194.38	242.00	1034.52	841.36
Total MoC	1864.02	1444.38	1662.63	2248.90	3195.92	31591.00	10415.85

Note: # At constant price (2001–02); * GBS was provided for implementing Voluntary Retirement Scheme (VRS) in the Tenth Plan but expenditure under this scheme occurred only in 2002–03 and 2004–05.
Source: MoC.

existing provisions of Mines and Minerals (Development and Regulation) Act (MMDR Act) 1957 to facilitate offering of coal blocks to potential entrepreneurs through competitive bidding.

- Coal has been removed from the list of essential commodities under the Essential Commodities Act 1956.
- System of e-auctioning of coal open to both consumers and traders was introduced.
- Existing system of calculation of the royalty on coal and lignite on the tonnage basis was revised to hybrid formula-based system comprising fixed part (tonnage basis) and variable part (ad valorem basis).
- Coal gasification and coal liquefaction has been notified as end-use under the Coal Mines (Nationalization) Act 1973 for the purpose of allocation of captive coal blocks.

THE ELEVENTH PLAN

COAL DEMAND AND PRODUCTION

10.161 Coal demand is projected to reach 731.10 million tonnes by the end of the Eleventh Plan. Cumulative Annual Growth Rate in coal demand during the Eleventh Plan is projected at 9.7%. The sector-wise break up of the requirement is shown in Figure 10.1 and Annexure 10.1.

10.162 Coal production is envisaged to reach 680 million tonnes in the terminal year of the Eleventh Plan. The incremental production is envisaged to be 247.50 million tonnes as against 104.71 million tonnes added in the Tenth Plan. CIL is expected to add 156.70 million tonnes, SCCL 3.30 million tonnes, and captive blocks 86.53 million tonnes. CIL envisages taking up 114 projects with an ultimate capacity of 230 million tonnes (to contribute 70 million tonnes in 2011–12) and SCCL 38 projects with an ultimate capacity of 55.40 million tonnes (to contribute about 8 million tonnes in 2011–12). Cumulative Annual Growth Rate in coal production during the Eleventh Plan is projected at 9.47% (Annexure 10.2).

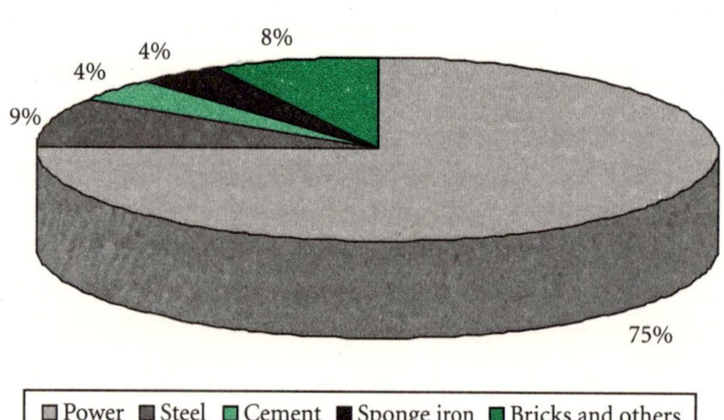

Source: Working Group Report on Coal and Lignite.

FIGURE 10.1: Estimated Sector-wise Demand for Coal in 2011–12

DEMAND SUPPLY MANAGEMENT

10.163 In overall terms, the physical gap between the projected demand of 731.10 million tonnes and the projected domestic availability of 680 million tonnes works out to 51.10 million tonnes in 2011–12. This comprises 40.85 million tonnes of coking coal and 10.25 million tonnes of thermal coal. This requirement would need to be met from imports. In case production from captive blocks does not come as envisaged, the quantity of imports would be higher.

10.164 Given the fact that captive mines will take seven or eight years to ramp to full production, the end-use projects would either have to be delayed or some interim supply arrangements would have to be made. Since coal import for inland sites is not a viable option, coal PSUs would need to provide coal to those power plants that have been allotted captive mines till their captive mines achieve full production.

10.165 Coking coal production during the Eleventh Plan is projected to grow by 9.1% from the current level hovering between 17–18 million tonnes to 27.65 million tonnes in spite of the fact that no new resource of coking coal has been found.

LIGNITE DEMAND AND PRODUCTION

10.166 The Eleventh Plan envisages a lignite demand of 55.59 million tonnes (Tamil Nadu, 23.59 million tonnes; Gujarat, 23.73 million tonnes; Rajasthan, 8.27 million tonnes) in 2011–12. The additional lignite-based power-generation capacity in the Eleventh Plan is envisaged as 2225 MW. Lignite demand from NLC in 2011–12 has been projected to be 27.04 million tonnes implying CAGR of 6.89%. Lignite-based power generation by NLC during the Eleventh Plan is expected to reach 26077 Million Unit (MU) implying CAGR of 11.91%. The lignite production is projected to reach 54.96 million tonnes (Tamil Nadu, 24.23 million tonnes; Gujarat, 22.26 million tonnes, Rajasthan, 8.47 million tonnes). NLC is expected to meet this level of demand growth.

Central Sector Plan Schemes

10.167 Exploration activities undertaken under two plans schemes of the Tenth Plan namely regional/promotional exploration and detailed drilling in non-CIL blocks need to be carried forward in the Eleventh Plan for enhancing the pace of exploration in coal and lignite. Jharia–Raniganj Action Plan has been proposed in the Eleventh Plan to recover remaining coal before it gets burnt or become uneconomic due to sterilization. Existing EMSC scheme is proposed to continue with the objective of implementing the action plan. Existing S&T scheme is also proposed to continue in the Eleventh Plan.

Regional/Promotional Exploration

10.168 An outlay of Rs 383.50 crore has been proposed by the MoC for undertaking exploration activities under this scheme. A projection of 4.0 lakh metre of drilling in coal and 3.5 lakh metre in lignite has been envisaged to establish about 20 billion tonnes of coal and 4.06 billion tonnes of lignite resources. This excludes the programme for regional exploration by GSI where 1.94 lakh metre of drilling in coal and 0.10 lakh metre of drilling in lignite has been projected.

Detailed Exploration in Non-CIL Blocks

10.169 About 10 lakh metre of drilling has been proposed to be undertaken in 32 non-CIL blocks during the Eleventh Plan targeting 10.75 billion tonnes of resources to be brought under proved category. Major part of the exploration activity would be outsourced by CMPDI. The total fund requirement for detailed exploration in non-CIL blocks scheme during the Eleventh Plan has been estimated at Rs 893.89 crore.

Environmental Measures and Subsidence Control

10.170 The issue of land subsidence and fire in old mined out areas of Raniganj coalfields of West Bengal and Jharia coalfields of Jharkhand has been under consideration of the government for quite some time. A scheme was formulated for mitigating adverse impacts of fire and subsidence problems caused due to unscientific mining activities by erstwhile owners before nationalization. However, the scheme did not yield desired results during previous Plan periods.

10.171 The Jharia–Raniganj Action Plan would be taken up for implementation during the Eleventh Plan under this scheme. The Action Plan proposes to deal with fires, rehabilitation of the uncontrollable subsidence prone inhabited areas, and diversion of railway lines/roads within the command area of BCCL and ECL. Total outlay proposed for the Action Plan is Rs 8638.87 crore spread over a 10-year period. The annual outgo for implementing the proposal would be of the order of Rs 860 crore as per the tentative cost estimates furnished above. It is proposed to fund Rs 350 crore per annum through accrual of cess by additional cess of Rs 6.50 per tonne under Coal Conservation and Development Act (CCDA) already being charged on all type of coal produced in the country, Rs 200 crore per annum through internal resources of CIL, and the remaining Rs 310 crore per annum through budgetary support. As accruals from cess are considered revenue to the government, the net budgetary support needed for the scheme would be Rs 660 crore per annum staring from the second year of the Eleventh Plan.

Science and Technology (S&T)

10.172 The main thrust areas in this scheme are promotion of clean coal technologies including coal beneficiation, in situ coal gasification, carbon capture and sequestration, coal bed methane/coal mine methane/abandoned mine methane, coal gasification, coal to oil, etc. Research efforts for industry-oriented projects would be promoted. Areas such as extraction of steep and thick coal seams, open-cast bench slope stability, strata control, etc. would be given special attention. An outlay of Rs 100 crore has been proposed for the implementation of this scheme.

Conservation and Safety in Coal Mines and Development of Transport Infrastructure in Coalfield Areas

10.173 Line entries were maintained under these schemes till the matter of treating them as non-Plan schemes are settled with the Ministry of Finance. Planning Commission had not agreed with the proposal of the MoC for treating these schemes as Plan schemes as activities under these schemes are funded as reimbursement of a portion of the stowing excise duty, which is statutorily levied as per the CCDA and deposited in the government treasury account. The Ministry of Finance, now, is of the view that these schemes should be treated as Plan schemes for better monitoring. As the source of funding of these schemes is through the dedicated Subsidence Excise Duty collected under CCDA, funding would not be a problem.

Initiatives in Information and Communication Technology

10.174 In order to improve efficacy of the project monitoring system and e-governance, the thrust areas that have been identified for introduction of ICT in the Eleventh Five Year Plan are computerization of various business functions up to project level; coal and lignite resource information system; resource depletion information system; Integrated CoalNet Application Software; GPS-based truck despatch system; GIS for mapping, spatial concepts, and time/space operations technology; integrated safety, production and environment monitoring and control in underground mines; centralized mail/messaging system; employee welfare. The estimated expenditure in this scheme is Rs 10 crore in the Eleventh Plan.

Benchmarking of Productivity

10.175 The Eleventh Plan envisages achieving a productivity level of 5.54 tonnes per person shift in CIL and 2.67 tonnes in SCCL in the terminal year of the Plan. Thrust would be given on improvement of operational efficiency of the coal mining companies by establishing benchmarks for different mining operations/equipments and manpower productivity comparable with international standards and measures. The productivity norms of different HEMM benchmarked earlier for both availability and utilization in different coal companies would be revisited so that these are comparable with the international standards.

Strategies for Coal Movement

10.176 In the terminal year of the Eleventh Plan (2011–12) it is proposed to move 348 million tonnes of raw coal and products from CIL using railway network which is about 50% more than the rail movement in 2006–07. As against a Four Wheeler Wagon (FWW) requirement of 25300 per day by the end of the Tenth Plan, the Eleventh Plan envisages 36728 FWW per day in 2011–12 which is about 45% increase from the current level. It is proposed to augment rail movement of coal through independent freight corridors, matching wagon volume and matching unloading facilities at power stations, etc. Power stations will have to equip themselves for handling multiple types of wagons.

10.177 The port infrastructure needs to be strengthened in order to facilitate rise in imports as well as coastal shipment. About 110 million tonnes of coal is required to be handled at the end of the Eleventh Plan including coastal shipment implying a port capacity of about 120–130 million tonnes by 2011–12.

10.178 To ease out the load on rail infrastructure, it is equally important to develop alternative modes of transportation of coal through inland waterways and coastal movement.

Initiatives on Clean Coal Technologies

10.179 Coal fired power generation would continue to occupy center-stage of India's energy scenario. Hence, it is desirable to have continuing improvements in its environmental performance, thermal efficiency, and thereby economics. Diffusion of new high-efficiency technologies in the field of energy conversion can lead to reduction in energy intensity of the economy. The process of producing energy has a significant impact on the environment, hence pollution abatement processes also form an important part of the development in this regard. A number of technologies have emerged for improving thermal efficiency and environmental performance. Different initiatives in this field are termed as clean coal technology, which include pre-combustion processes, combustion processes, and alternative use such as gasification of coal, coal bed methane, in situ coal gasification, etc. Different clean coal technologies do not compete with each other and have distinctive advantages.

10.180 Coal beneficiation is one of the prime clean coal technologies. The effect of coal washing and thereby ensuring a more consistent fuel supply to conventional PCC boilers may improve their efficiency by around 1%.

10.181 High ash Indian coal needs clean coal technology for improving thermal efficiency of energy conversion processes and finally environmental performances. Use of washed coal ensures consistency of coal qualities and results in boiler performance improvement by allowing the unit and auxiliaries to operate near the design (optimum efficiency) points. The projected capacity increase in the country warrants introduction of higher capacity units (in the range of 800–1000 MW) where it is desirable to use washed coal for limiting the size/number of unit and auxiliaries within the conventionally available sizes.

10.182 The use of washed thermal coal has been on the rise during the Tenth Five Year Plan from 17.12 million tonnes in 2002–03 to 55.24 million tonnes in 2006–07. It is estimated that 243 million tonnes per annum of thermal coal is required to be washed by the end of the Eleventh Plan and accordingly about 140 million tonnes of additional thermal coal washing capacity would be created. The perfect growth in coal washing may be realized if the Planning Commission's suggestion to price coal on a fully variable GCV is implemented. Such a pricing methodology will provide the right incentive to both the producer and the consumer of coal to improve quality. However, enhancing washing capacity would increase demand for raw coal, unless the fines are used productively.

10.183 First 100 MW IGCC demonstration project will be taken up by a consortium of NTPC and BHEL with part funding from the GoI.

10.184 Underground coal and lignite gasification technology utilize fuel in different form and can be beneficial when used for inaccessible resources. CBM extraction enhances energy security by tapping an additional source of fuel which would otherwise have gone waste. CBM in association with CO_2 sequestration enhances methane recovery while reducing green house gas. Coal liquefaction involved conversion of coal into oil through gasification requiring surface gasifier. CIL and NLC in association with ONGC would work towards making the technology successful.

10.185 CBM and CTL have been covered under petroleum and natural gas sector.

Mining Technology, Safety, and Welfare

10.186 Safety in coal mines is governed by the Mines Act 1952 and the rules and regulations framed hereunder. The Directorate General of Mines Safety (DGMS), under the Ministry of Labour and Employment has been empowered to enforce the statutes relating to mine safety. There is a Standing Committee on Safety in Coal Mines which is chaired by Minister in Charge of Coal. The strategies for action includes introduction of the concept of self-regulation, development of legislation, planning and technology, emergency response and disaster management, human resource development, and R&D effort including identification of areas of application of information technology in safety.

R&D in Coal Sector

10.187 R&D in coal sector is carried out under four broad areas, namely, production, productivity, and safety; coal beneficiation; coal utilization; and environment and ecology. In addition to initiatives in clean coal technologies, efforts should be made to undertake industry-oriented R&D projects which may include areas such as extraction of steep and thick coal seams, open-cast bench slope stability, strata control, etc.

Investment Needs and Financing Pattern

10.188 The proposed public sector investment for the Eleventh Plan for supporting their production plans is Rs 35774 crore (CIL, Rs 17390 crore; SCCL, Rs 3340 crore; NLC, Rs 15044 crore including Rs 176.00 crore for the ongoing projects – NLC Mines Rs 2993 crore; NLC Power Rs 12051 crore). The outlay proposed for coal PSUs for the Eleventh Plan is about 117% more than the Tenth Plan outlay of Rs 30556.48 crore.

10.189 Against the estimated IEBR availability of Rs 69926.77 crore (CIL, Rs 51542.55 crore; SCCL, Rs 3340.30 crore; NLC, Rs 15043.92 crore), the proposed plan outlay of PSUs is Rs 35774 crore (at constant price). While the resource position of SCCL and NLC is just sufficient to meet the plan outlay, there is a huge surplus in the resource position of Coal India Ltd and CIL has to consider productive investment of the surplus resources through feasible diversification plans.

10.190 The proposed outlay for departmental schemes to be supported through domestic budgetary support including North East component is Rs 6667.76 crore (at constant price) comprising promotional exploration, Rs 383.50 crore; detailed drilling in non-CIL blocks, Rs 893.39 crore; R&D, Rs 100.00 crore; EMSC/Jharia Action Plan, Rs 3614.07 crore; schemes under CCDA, Rs 1665.60 crore (Rs 692.95 crore for stowing and protective works and Rs. 972.65 crore for road and rail infrastructure); publication of coal statistics Rs 1.2 crore; and Rs 10 crore for e-governance. The Jharia–Raniganj Action Plan under EMSC scheme is proposed to be financed partly through the IEBR of Coal India Ltd (Rs 800 crore) and the rest Rs 1400 crore through the CCDA fund and Rs 1200 crore through budgetary support. Accordingly, the MoC would need Rs 5867.76 crore of domestic budgetary support for implementing above Plan schemes. This includes Rs 3065.72 crore coming from the accrued fund of Subsidence Excised Duty being collected under the CCDA at the rate of Rs 10 per tonne of all types of coal sold.

10.191 Thus the total plan outlay proposed for MoC for the Eleventh Five Year Plan is Rs 42442 crore (at constant price) which is 134% more than the Tenth Plan outlay of Rs 31591 crore.

Policy Reforms

10.192 Policy interventions required in the Eleventh Plan for:

- Restructuring CIL for optimizing their operations.
- Improvement in productivity of the sector by establishing benchmarks for different operations equipments comparable with international standards.
- Ensuring sale of at least 20% of coal production through e-auctions open to both consumers and traders.
- Promoting additional thermal coal imports under long-term supply contracts. Such coal imports could feed coastal power plants.
- Changing grading and pricing of non-coking coal from the existing UHV to the international practice of pricing coal based on GCV.
- Replacing coal linkages with fuel supply agreements.
- Promoting in situ coal gasification and tapping of coal bed methane/coal mine methane.
- Rationalization of rail freight rates for coal transport.
- Extending infrastructure status to the coal industry. Lower duties on capital goods imported for coal mines.
- Instituting an independent regulatory mechanism for the coal sector.
- Amending the provisions of Contract Labour (Regulation and Abolition) Act 1970 which prohibit employment of contract labour in mining activities. This will facilitate offloading of certain activities in coal mining for improved economics of operations.
- Promoting underground mining operations for extraction of deep seated deposits.
- Augmenting domestic coking coal supplies by opening up new mines and coal washeries.
- Augmenting port infrastructure capacity to facilitate envisaged rise in import.
- Exploration for CBM and detailed drilling in non-NLC lignite blocks should be included in existing Plan schemes.
- Institutional framework for maintenance of database on coal and lignite resource (net of depletion) is required which will have access to the geological data in respect of all coal/lignite blocks (whether held by public or private).
- Identifying forest areas as 'Yes' and 'No' zones for exploration, for saving energy in exploration in the area which can never be mined.
- Involving reputed domestic and international agencies in coal/lignite exploration.
- Concerted efforts for addressing the issues related to decommissioning of mines/mine closure after exhaustion of reserves are required to be made.
- Need for developing mechanism for management of occupational safety and health of coal miners and persons living in the vicinity of coal mining areas.

- Need for evolving appropriate corporate social responsibility for fulfilling the aspirations of population living in and around coalfield areas and to promote environmentally sustainable mining practices.
- Recruitment and skill upgradation of mining engineers and other professionals required for operation and statutory purposes in the coal/lignite mines need to be stressed upon. It is necessary to strengthen internal safety organization of respective coal producing companies and introduce safety audit of mines by independent auditors. Infrastructure including human resource for rescue and emergency response systems also needs reinforcement.
- Coal mining should be opened to private players without the restriction of captive use which requires passage of the Coal Mines (Nationalization) Bill 2000.
- Introduction of competitive bidding process in allocation of coal blocks by making suitable amendments in the MMDR Act. This would not only ensure optimal allocation of precious resources, but would also attract more serious players into coal sector.
- Need for a suitable Resettlement and Rehabilitation Policy which is acceptable to all concerned that is, State Governments, project-affected people (PAP), and coal and lignite producing companies.
- In order to gain confidence of the PAP, coal and lignite producing companies should return the restored/reclaimed land to PAP for appropriate use after mining operations have ceased in the area.
- Establishing standards for undertaking Energy Efficient and Conservation Programmes in all critical operations in the value chain starting from exploration to utilization and mechanisms for independent monitoring and verification of achieved energy savings and cost effectiveness of such programmes.

ENERGY EFFICIENCY AND DEMAND SIDE MANAGEMENT (DSM) PROGRAMMES

10.193 Energy conservation is a multi-faceted approach with the involvement of supply side, demand side, and also T&D system. The success of the energy conservation programme depends upon the aspects such as pricing of different fuels and electricity for different categories of consumers, awareness among the users to appreciate the necessity of energy conservation, an effective institutional arrangement to coordinate energy conservation programmes, and other aspects that include mobilizing financial resources to fund energy conservation programmes. It is worthwhile to give necessary importance for energy conservation programmes in view of the fact that it is economical and wise to invest in energy conservation adequately in order to avoid creation of equivalent new capacities for generation with significant level of investment.

10.194 In India, DSM measures have a key role in eliminating power shortages to a considerable extent. The demand for electricity fluctuates within a 24-hour cycle as well as between seasons. This has important implication in planning generating capacities. In a developing country like India, where per capita availability of energy is very low, need-based demand for energy can be unlimited. But, supply side is limited by insufficiency of investible resources and the demand side by lack of purchasing power. In such a situation, it is clear that a capacity to provide additional energy is always likely to lag behind the rising demand, unless consumption of energy is also economized.

10.195 The basic problem in power generation and supply is the maintenance of the frequency of the grid and the power factor of the loads at stipulated levels. The low-frequency conditions lead to instability of the interconnected grid and thereby causing frequent tripping. Sometimes this results in cascade tripping leading to total black out. It is essential that frequency is maintained between 49.8–50.2 Hz for effective grid management as well as maximization of useful life of thermal/nuclear generating plants. At present, the situation is managed by resorting to emergency manual load shedding by switching off various feeders. However, these are only temporary measures adopted to meet exigencies, arising from time to time, without attempting any strategy to influence the basic pattern of load curves.

BARRIERS IN IMPLEMENTING DSM

10.196 One of the basic reasons for energy inefficiency in India is energy pricing. Electricity rates, kept deliberately low for a large block of consumption, do not send correct signals to consumers to alter their consumption behaviour. A typical case relates to the low agricultural tariffs (subsidies are as high as 80%–90% in most States) that have resulted in gross misuse of both electricity and groundwater. Low tariffs for domestic consumers also do not offer any incentive to encourage efficient use of energy. There is therefore an urgent need to look into the issue of pricing and efficient operation and management of the SEBs. Other innovative pricing options, which have proved successful in managing electricity demand in several developed and developing countries such as time-of-day tariffs, interruptible tariffs, and seasonal tariffs should be initiated by the utilities on an experimental basis.

10.197 The other important constraint in the implementation of Demand side Management (DSM) programme is the information gap. Indian consumers are not fully aware of the opportunities available for improving energy efficiency.

ENERGY-EFFICIENCY PROGRAMMES IN THE ELEVENTH PLAN

10.198 In the Eleventh Five Year Plan, Bureau of Energy Efficiency (BEE) will be strengthened as a nodal organization at the national level and will be empowered to provide direction to the energy conservation programmes in the States. An 'Energy Conservation Information Centre' will be set up within BEE to collate energy use data and analyse energy consumption trends and monitor energy conservation achievements in the country. Supporting organizational set-up will also be strengthened in the State designated agencies (SDAs) in various States and UTs. For this, a matching grant support from Central Government restricted to the contribution made by the respective States/UTs governments is proposed to establish State Energy Conservation Fund as mandated under EC Act. In the Eleventh Five Year Plan, BEE will focus energy conservation programmes in the following targeted sectors.

TARGETED SECTORS

Industrial Sector (Energy Intensive Industries)

10.199 BEE will develop 15 industry-specific energy efficiency manuals/guides for the following sectors: aluminium, fertilizers, iron and steel, cement, pulp and paper, chlor alkali, sugar, textile, chemicals, railways, port trust, transport sector (industries and services), petrochemical and petroleum refineries, thermal power stations and hydel power stations, electricity transmission companies and distribution companies. The manuals will cover specific energy consumption norms as required to be established under the EC Act, energy efficient processes and technologies, best practices, case studies, etc. Follow up activities will be undertaken in the States by SDAs and manuals will be disseminated to all the concerned units in the industries.

Small and Medium Enterprises (SMEs)

10.200 SDAs in consultation with BEE will initiate diagnostic studies in 25 SME clusters in the country, including four to five priority clusters in the NER, and develop cluster-specific energy-efficiency manuals/booklets and other documents to enhance energy conservation in SMEs.

Commercial Buildings and Establishments

10.201 BEE will prepare building specific energy-efficiency manuals covering specific energy consumption norms, energy-efficient technologies, best practices, etc. As a follow up, SDAs would initiate energy audits and their implementation in 10 government buildings in each State and one or two buildings at UT level. BEE will also assist SDAs in the establishment and promulgation of energy conservation building codes (ECBC) in the States, and facilitate SDAs to adapt ECBC.

Residential/Domestic Sector

10.202 BEE will enhance its ongoing energy labeling programme to include 10 other appliances, –namely, air conditioners, ceiling fans, agricultural pump-sets, electric motors (general purpose), Compact Fluorescent Lamps, Flurescent Tube Light (FTL)–61 cm, television sets, microwave ovens, set top boxes, DVD players, and desktop monitors. To facilitate this consumer awareness will also be enhanced nation wide.

Street Lighting and Municipal Water Pumping

10.203 To promote energy efficiency in municipal areas in various States, SDAs in association with State utilities will initiate pilot energy conservation projects in selected municipal water pumping systems and street lighting to provide basis for designing State-level programmes.

Agriculture Sector

10.204 In the Eleventh Plan, SDAs will disseminate information on successful projects implemented in some States, launch awareness campaigns in all regional languages in print and electronic media, and initiate development of State-level programmes along with utilities.

Transport Sector

10.205 SDAs with assistance of concerned institutions/agencies will conduct diagnostic studies to establish the status of energy consumption and conservation in the sector. BEE will also set up labeling and/or norms for specific fuel consumption for a few automobile and transport categories (services/public transport). BEE in association with SDAs will facilitate State utilities to pursue DSM options by focusing on orientation workshops for awareness building, setting up of DSM cells in utilities to conceive and implement DSM programs, support load research and studies to rationalize the tariff structures, and initiation of DSM programmes, especially in the residential, agricultural pumping and municipal water works, and street lighting sectors.

10.206 Policy research on legislative amendments, policy interventions including fiscal and non-fiscal measures are planned to be undertaken in the Eleventh Plan.

Proposed Target of Energy Savings by the End of the Eleventh Plan

10.207 It is proposed to set a target of 5% of the anticipated energy consumption level in the beginning of the Eleventh Plan as energy savings to be achieved at the end of the Eleventh Plan. Financial provision for the same has been made in the outlay of power sector.

Conservation and Efficiency Improvement

Demand Side Management

10.208 Road transportation consumes about one-third of the total consumption of the petroleum products in India. There is a need to reduce this consumption by shifting goods and passenger traffic from roads to rails, improving the road infrastructure, streamlining of traffic signals, mandating fuel efficiency levels in transport vehicles, and developing hybrid electric vehicles (EVs).

Conservation of Petroleum Products

10.209 The major focus would be towards efficient use of petroleum products, minimizing the waste of energy sources, development of efficient equipments and their commercialization, educating and motivating the people towards conservation techniques and practices. There is a need to establish a system approach to quantify the conservation potential.

Benchmarking of Hydrocarbon Sector

10.210 To make the hydrocarbon sector globally competitive, the oil and gas industry needs to benchmark their operations against the best in the world and should upgrade their technology for improving the efficiency.

NEW AND RENEWABLE ENERGY SECTOR

Issues and Challenges

10.211 From a longer term perspective of the growing threat of climate change and keeping in mind the need to maximally develop domestic supply options as well as the need to diversify energy sources, renewables remain important to India's energy sector. Solar power could be important for attaining energy independence as well as a green house gas-free energy system in the long run. However, based on present technology with a concerted push and a 40-fold increase in their contribution to primary energy, renewables excluding hydroelectricity may account for only 5%–6% of India's energy mix by 2031–32. While this figure appears small, the distributed nature of renewables can provide many socio-economic benefits.

10.212 While there were renewable energy programmes taken up in the past to address the above challenges, the impact of these programmes were rather marginal. The lack of institutional support at the grassroots, poor focus on training and maintenance aspects, lack of awareness among rural community, subsidies acting as barrier in cost reduction, etc., were found to be the bottlenecks for the programmes not achieving desired results. The actual benefit of the subsidies did not reach the beneficiaries but only acted as barriers in attempts for cost reduction and efficiency improvement of the renewable energy devices and gadgets.

10.213 A renewable energy source may be environment-friendly. It may be locally available thereby making it possible to supply energy earlier than in a centralized system. Grid-connected renewables could improve the quality of supply and provide system benefits by generating energy at the ends of the grid where otherwise supply would have been lax. Further, renewables may provide employment and livelihood to the poor. Hence, subsidies to renewables may be justifiable; however, they should be linked to outcomes and given for a well-defined period.

10.214 A majority of India's people especially in rural areas use traditional fuels such as dung, agricultural wastes, and firewood for cooking food. These fuels cause indoor pollution. The 1999–2000 NSS 55th Round revealed that for 86% of rural households the primary source of cooking energy was firewood and chips or dung cake. In urban areas too more than 20% households relied mainly on firewood and chips. Only 5% of the households in rural areas and 44% households in urban areas used LPG. Kerosene is used by 22% of urban households and only 2.7% of rural households for cooking. Other primary source of cooking energy used by urban and rural household covers coke and charcoal, biogas, electricity, and other fuels. The situation in rural areas calls for provision of sustainable and clean energy supplies. In this context the role of renewable energy sources such as biogas, improved cook stoves, solar energy, and biomass based systems to meet the basic needs of cooking, lighting, and water heating is important.

10.215 The total quantities of traditional fuels used to meet the basic energy needs are substantial. Table 10.26 gives the data on household energy use. The biomass-based fuels dominate particularly in rural areas.

10.216 Use of traditional fuels for cooking with the attendant pollution and the cost of gathering them impose a heavy burden on people particularly women and girls. The need to gather fuels may deprive the girl child from schooling. Use of such fuels, overtime, increases the risks of eye infections and respiratory diseases. Lack of access to clean and convenient energy impacts the health of women and the girl child more adversely as they spend more time indoors and are primarily responsible for cooking. Women's micro-enterprises (an important factor in household income, as well as in women's welfare and empowerment) are heat-intensive (food processing), labour-intensive, and/or light-intensive (home industries with work in evenings). The lack of adequate energy supplies—and other co-ordinated support—affects women's ability to use these micro-enterprises profitably and safely. Furthermore, women often face additional barriers in making best use of available opportunities and obtaining improved energy services. There are social and practical constraints related to ownership and control over productive resources—women are typically excluded/marginalized from decision-making and

TABLE 10.26
Household Energy Consumption in India (July 1999–June 2000)

Fuel Type	Physical Units			Mtoe		
	Rural	Urban	Total	Rural	Urban	Total
Fire wood and chips (million tonnes)	158.87	18.08	176.95	71.49	8.13	79.62
Electricity (BkWh)	40.76	57.26	98.02	3.51	4.92	8.43
Dung cake (million tonnes)	132.95	8.03	140.98	27.92	1.69	29.61
Kerosene (million litre)	7.38	4.51	11.89	6.25	3.82	10.07
Coal (million tonnes)	1.20	1.54	2.74	0.49	0.63	1.12
LPG (million tonnes)	1.25	4.43	5.68	1.41	5.00	6.41

Source: Derived from NSS 55th Round (July 1999–June 2000) data, NSSO, Ministry of Statistics and Programme Implementation, GoI.

suffer barriers related to illiteracy, lack of exposure to information and training. It is estimated that in rural north India 30 billion hours are spent annually in gathering fuel-wood and other traditional fuels. The economic burden of traditional biomass-based fuels, time to gather fuels, time lost in sickness, and cost of medicines is estimated to be some Rs 300 billion. An energy policy responsive to social welfare must address this fact.

10.217 National surveys have indicated that for 86% of rural households, the primary source of cooking energy was firewood and chips or dung cake. The efficiency of fuel use is of vital importance for the users of these traditional fuels. The inefficient methods of using such fuels result in low thermal efficiency and high emission products. The traditional cooking methods produce very high concentration of air pollutants such as total suspended particulates, carbon monoxide, formaldehyde, etc. This is the major cause of indoor air pollution in the rural areas. Indoor air pollution makes the women and children who spend sufficiently long time in kitchens suffer from bronchial asthma, bronchitis, TB, and chest infection. Risk from all respiratory diseases and eye diseases increases with length of use of traditional fuels. The collection of traditional fuels results in drudgery of women and children since they have to walk long distances to collect such fuels. Moreover, the time spent for this purpose is significantly long, depriving them of their additional income which they would have earned during that time. Further, deforestation and environmental degradation also results in the long run. Collection of traditional fuels is at zero private cost but at tremendous social cost. Supply of clean cooking fuels for rural households would go a long way in addressing the social aspects associated with use of traditional fuels discussed above.

10.218 The Ministry of New and Renewable Energy (MNRE) is responsible for programmes covering renewable energy sources. The mission of the MNRE is as follows:

- Reduce dependence on oil imports through development and deployment of alternate fuels (hydrogen, biofuels, and synthetic fuels) and their applications to contribute towards bridging the gap between domestic oil supply and demand and thereby improve energy security.
- Increase the share of clean power by promoting renewable electricity to supplement fossil fuel based electricity generation.
- Enlarge energy availability and improve access to meet needs for clean energy for cooking, heating, motive power and captive generation in rural, urban, industrial, and commercial sectors.
- Encourage convenient, safe, and reliable new and renewable energy supply options to be cost-competitive.

10.219 MNRE programmes include (i) grid connected and stand-alone power generation from small hydro, wind, solar, biomass, and industrial/urban wastes; (ii) rural energy programmes such as electrification of remote villages, biogas, and improved chulhas for cooking; (iii) solar energy applications such as thermal water heaters, solar photovoltaic applications for lighting and water pumping; and (iv) integrated rural energy programme (IREP). Research, development, and demonstration programmes in new technologies such as geo-thermal, hydrogen energy, fuel cells, alternative fuels for surface transport, etc., are also undertaken by MNRE. Indian Renewable Energy Development Agency (IREDA), a financial institution under the administrative control of MNRE, supports the renewable energy programmes by providing concessional funds. By the end of the Tenth Plan (as on 31 March 2007) the contribution of power generation from renewables had reached 10406.69 MW representing about 8.1% of total installed generating capacity. Of this, wind power accounted for 7092 MW followed by small hydro at 1975.60 MW and biomass (including co-generation) at 1158.63 MW. The estimated medium-term potential and achievement as on 31 March 2007 have been given in Table 10.27.

10.220 The progress in grid interactive renewable power at a glance is given in Table 10.28.

10.221 Table 10.29 gives the typical capital cost per megawatt and cost of electricity generated per kWh through different renewable energy sources.

TABLE 10.27
Estimated Medium-term (2032) Potential and Cumulative Achievements as on 31 March 2007

S. No.	Sources/Systems	Estimated Potential	Units	Cumulative Achievements
I.	Power from Renewables			
	A. Grid interactive renewable power			
	1. Bio power (agro residues and plantations)	16881*	MW	524.80
	2. Wind power	45195**	MW	7092.00
	3. Small hydro power (up to 25 MW)	15000	MW	1975.60
	4. Co-generation (bagasse)	5000	MW	615.83
	5. Waste to energy	7000	MW	43.45
	Subtotal (in MW)	133000	MW	10251.68
	B. CHP/distributed renewable power			
	6. Solar power	50000***	MW	2.92
	7 Biomass/co-generation (non-bagasse)		MW	45.80
	8. Biomass gasifier	–	MW	86.53#
	9. Energy recovery from waste	–	MW	19.76 MW
	Subtotal	50000	MW	155.01
	Total (A+B)	183000	MW	10406.69
	10. Remote village electrification	–	Nos	2821/830 (villages/hamlets)
II.	Decentralized Energy Systems			
	11. Family type biogas plants	120	Lakh Nos	38.90
	12. Solar photovoltaic programme	20	MW/sq km	
	(i) Solar street lighting system	–	Nos	61321
	(ii) Home lighting system	–	Nos	313859
	(iii) Solar lantern	–	Nos	565658
	(iv) Solar power plants	–	kWp	1870.00
	13. Solar thermal programme	–		
	(i) Solar water heating systems	140	Million sq m collector area	1.90
	(ii) Solar cookers	–	Lakh Nos	6.03
	14. Wind pumps	–	Nos	1180
	15. Aero-generator/hybrid systems	–	kW	608.27
	16. Solar photovoltaic pumps	–	Nos	7068

Note: # Progress upto 15 March 2007.

* Although potential is based on surplus agro-residues, in practice biomass power generation units prefer to use fuel-wood for techno-economic reasons. A potential of 45000 MW from around 20 MH of wastelands assumed to be yielding 10MT/ha/annum of woody biomass having 4000 k-cal/kg with system efficiency of 30% and 75% PLF has not been taken into account. In order to realize this potential a major inter-Ministerial initiative involving, among others, Environment and Forests, Agriculture, Rural Development, and Panchayat Raj would be required. Further, a Biomass atlas is under preparation which is expected to more accurately assess State-wise renewable energy potential from agro-residues.

** Potential based on areas having wind power density (wpd) greater than 200 W/m^2 assuming land availability in potential areas @ 1% and requirement of wind farms @ 12 ha/MW, all of which may not be technically feasible or economically viable for grid interactive wind power. This economically viable potential could get enhanced with higher level of land availability than what has been assumed. Areas having lower wpds might be suitable for off-grid applications. Further, preliminary surveys do not at this juncture suggest a sizeable grid interactive off-shore wind power potential.

*** Potential for solar power is dependent on future developments that might make solar technology cost-competitive for grid interactive power generation applications. However, insolation in the country varies between 4–7 kWh/m^2/day.

MW = megawatt; kW = kilowatt; kWp = kilowatt peak; sq m = square metre; sq km = square kilometre; CHP = combined heat and power.

Source: MNRE, GoI.

TABLE 10.28
Progress in Grid Interactive Renewable Power

(In MW)

Resource	By the End of the Ninth Plan	Tenth Plan Addition	Eleventh Plan#	By the End of Eleventh Plan
Wind power	1667	5415	10500	17582
Small hydro	1438	520	1400	3358
Bio-power	368	750	2100	3218
Solar power	2	1	50*	53
Total	3475	6686	14050	24211

Note: # Anticipated in the Eleventh Plan.
* Dependent on future developments to make solar technology cost competitive for grid interactive power generation.
Source: MNRE.

TABLE 10.29
Capital Costs and the Typical Cost of Generated Electricity from the Renewable Options

S. No.	Source	Capital Cost (Crore of Rs per MW)	Estimated Cost of Generation per Unit (Rs per kWh)
1.	Small hydro-power#	5.00–6.00	1.50–2.50
2.	Wind power	4.00–5.00	2.00–3.00
3.	Biomass power	4.00	2.50–3.50
4.	Bagasse co-generation	3.5	2.50–3.00
5.	Biomass gasifier	1.94	2.50–3.50
6.	Solar photovoltaic	26.5	15.00–20.00
7.	Energy from waste	2.50–10.0	2.50–7.50

Note: # Up to 25 MW station capacity is covered under small hydro power.
Source: IEPR, 2006.

REVIEW OF THE TENTH PLAN

10.222 The approved outlay for the Tenth Plan for New and Renewable Energy Programmes was Rs 7167 crore comprising Rs 4000 crore as GBS and Rs 3167 crore of IEBR. The likely expenditure at the end of the Tenth Plan is Rs 4000 crore.

10.223 While the overall target has been achieved there are shortfalls in some programmes especially in solar thermal power. During the Tenth Plan wind power capacity of 5415 MW has been created achieving 3.61 times of the set target (Table 10.30).

10.224 In addition to the programmes of power generation other programmes relating to rural energy, urban applications, and R&D programmes have been implemented during the Tenth Plan. Around 5000 remote villages/hamlets have been provided with electricity from renewable energy sources mainly through solar energy. Village Energy Security Projects are under implementation in 100 villages. Around 5

TABLE 10.30
Power Generation through Grid Interactive Renewable Power

Source	Tenth Plan	
	Target (MW)	Actual (MW)
Wind	1500	5415
Small hydro	600	520
Biomass power and biomass	700	750
gasification	50	
Waste to energy	80	25
Solar photovoltaic	5	1
Solar thermal power	140	0
Total	3075	6711

Source: MNRE.

lakh biogas plants have been installed. In the programmes catering to the requirement of urban areas under the solar water heaters progranm-mes 12.5 lakh sq m collector areas of water heating systems have been installed. R&D activities have been carried out especially in the area of alternative fuel for transport including hydrogen energy.

ELEVENTH PLAN PROGRAMME

10.225 The various programmes of the MNRE for the Eleventh Plan have been drawn up in the light of recommendations made by Planning Commission and those made in IEPR. The five programmes proposed are:

- Grid Interactive and Distributed Renewable Power.
- Renewable Energy for Rural Applications.
- Renewable Energy for Urban, Industrial, and Commercial Applications.
- Research, Design, and Development for New and Renewable Energy.
- Information, publicity and extension, international relations, HRD and training, equity support to IREDA and spill-over liabilities.

10.226 Proposed outlay of Rs 10460 crore (at constant price) includes GBS of Rs 3537 crore. The physical targets and the financial outlays proposed by MNRE for the above programmes are given in Table 10.31 and 10.32.

TABLE 10.31
Financial Outlays Proposed for the Eleventh Plan

(Rs Crore)

Grid Interactive and Distributed Renewable Power		3925.00
Grid interactive renewable power	1800.00	
Off-grid/distributed renewable power	2100.00	
Performance testing	25.00	
Renewable energy for rural applications		2250.00
Renewable energy for urban, industrial, and commercial applications		685.00
Research, design, and development		1500.00
Programmes to support information, publicity and extension, international relations, HRD and training, equity for IREDA, and spill-over liabilities		2100.00
Plan Outlay		10460.00

Source: Working Group on New and Renewable Energy.

TABLE 10.32
Physical Targets Proposed for the Eleventh Plan

Programme Component	Physical Target for Eleventh Plan (in MW)
Wind power	10500
Small hydro power	1400
Biomass power	1200
Co-generation	500
Urban waste to energy	200
Industrial waste to energy	200
Total	14000
Off-grid renewable power	
Wind/hybrid power	950
Small hydro power	
Bio power	
Solar power (grid/off-grid)	50
Total	1000
For remote villages/hamlets	
Remote village lighting	9000 villages/hamlets
Village energy security test projects	1000 villages
Common component for cooking/ supplementary motive power	10000 villages/hamlets
For all villages	
Solar thermal systems—flat plate—concentrating	15 lakh sq m 1 lakh sq m
Family type biogas plants	20 lakh plants
Total	
Solar thermal systems/devices	
Water heating @Rs 1550/m^2	9.50 million sq m
Drying @Rs 1250/m^2	0. 25 million sq m
Other (steam generation) @Rs 2500/m^2	0. 25 million sq m –
Instl./prog. support @Rs 200/m^2)	10 nos
Municipal corporations—incentive	
Energy-efficient buildings	50 lakh sq m floor area
Akshay Urja Shops	2000 nos
Cities with RPOs	100 nos
Total	

Note: RPOs = Regional Project Offices.
Source: Working Group on New and Renewable Energy.

POLICY APPROACH

10.227 Capital subsidies that encourage investment without ensuring outcomes would be phased out. Incentives provided for grid connected power from renewable sources would be linked to generation and not to power capacities created. Thus power regulators will be asked to create alternative incentive structures such as mandated feed-in laws or differential tariffs for grid interactive power.

10.228 Alternatively grid interactive renewable power will be promoted by mandating a renewable portfolio standard for all power distribution companies and providing a subsidy for each unit of renewable electricity purchased. The utilities would be free to meet their requirement by purchasing certificates from other utilities that may have a surplus of renewable electricity in their portfolios. Many State Electricity Regulators have stipulated RPS as required by the Electricity Act 2003.

10.229 To eliminate subsidy for other renewable system for rural, urban, industrial, and commercial applications, instead a large prize may be offered to one who sells a lakh or a million units first (for outputs sold directly to households), for example, solar water heaters, biogas plants, solar lighting systems, etc. This will promote competition, innovation, and consumer requirement oriented development.

10.230 To facilitate biofuels that require action by many different actors such as producer, processor, distributor, and consumers, a well-defined policy that provides incentives and leads to a competitive industry is needed. Also the policy has to be incentive compatible for all actors in the chain. With these in mind, the national biofuel policy has to be finalized.

10.231 To increase availability of finance for new and renewable energy, IREDA is to be restructured by broad basing its equity structure. IREDA needs low cost funds. It should be permitted to issue Capital Gains Bonds similar to those issued by REC and NHAI to the tune of Rs 300–400 crore per year during the Eleventh Plan. IREDA's role in financing renewable energy program-mes is to be enhanced.

R&D in the Energy Sector

10.232 R&D in energy sector is critical to augment our resources, meet our long-term needs, promote efficiency, attain energy independence, enhance our energy security, and ensure harmony with the environment. Energy R&D has not kept pace with the development of the energy sector in the country. There is a need to substantially augment the resources for energy R&D and to allocate these resources strategically.

10.233 The report of the EC on Integrated Energy Policy has recommended setting up of a National Energy Fund (NEF [R&D]) for supporting studies on a regular basis in a number of institutions. The studies should be commissioned by NEF (R&D) from experienced and qualified individuals. The important areas are research and analysis for energy policy leading to outlining of technology road maps; energy policy modelling; launching of technology missions for developing near-commercial technologies and rolling out new technologies in a time bound manner; coordinated R&D in all stages of the innovation chain, etc. It is further recommended that each company in the field of energy should be mandated to spend at least 0.4% of its turnover on R&D.

10.234 Keeping the need in mind, a separate working group on R&D for the energy sector was set up for the formulation of the Eleventh Five Year Plan which supported the creation of NEF (R&D). In addition to the projected needs of Atomic Energy Commission and some R&D activities already being undertaken by individual energy ministries, the Working Group has identified areas which need support through NEF (R&D) in the Eleventh Plan (Table 10.33). The NEF (R&D) would be governed by an independent board with representatives from Department of Science and Technology, Planning Commission, and energy ministries. The government would finance the fund directly and through fiscal incentives. The fund would be used for supporting inter-institutional and inter-ministerial/inter-departmental research and for setting-up of Centres of Excellence in Universities/National Laboratories/Mission-oriented Agencies in the areas of identified energy technology.

10.235 Technology missions are the most appropriate mechanism, particularly when it requires coordinated action in a number of different areas, involving different ministries/departments, industry, academia, India's R&D infrastructure of laboratories and research institutions, and the private sector. The following National Technology Missions may be taken up in the Eleventh Plan. The list however excludes the

TABLE 10.33
Proposed R&D Initiatives in the Eleventh Plan

(in Rs Crore)

S. No.	Items	Amount Projected
1.	Development and production of new material	100.00
2.	R&D in biofuels	200.00
3.	Combustion research initiative	200.00
4.	Energy R&D in Indian railways	45.00
5.	Hydrogen as a source of clean energy	350.00
6.	Advanced coal technologies	
	(i) Setting up of first 100 MWe IGCC demonstration plant	350.00
	(ii) In situ coal gasification of coal and lignite	30.00
	(iii) Coal to oil conversion	200.00
	(iv) Coal bed methane	35.00
	(v) Carbon capture and storage (incl. climate change issues)	125.00
7.	Ultra super critical technologies	30.00
8.	Energy storage systems	400.00
9.	Futuristic energy sources	
	(i) Gas hydrates	350.00
	(ii) Oil shale	15.00
10.	Energy efficiency	205.00
11.	Technologically important crystals—facility to manufacture polysilicon for production of single crystals of silicon	1200.00
12.	Light-emitting diodes (LEDs)—a viable alternative to fluorescent lighting	1000
13.	EVs and hybrid electric vehicles—viable alternate propulsion systems	175
	Grand Total	5310.00

Source: Working Group on Energy R&D.

initiative likely to be taken up by the Atomic Energy Commission.

- In situ coal gasification.
- IGCC.
- Carbon capture and sequestration.
- Bio-energy.
- Solar energy/technologically important crystals.
- Increased/enhanced oil and gas recovery and recovery of hydrocarbons from abandoned and isolated fields.
- Fuel-efficient vehicles. The automotive industry should be asked to achieve higher fuel efficiency standards.
- Combustion research initiatives.
- Development and production of new materials.

ANNEXURE 10.1
Coal Demand/Supply—Sector-wise Break-up

(Million Tonnes)

	Sector		2001–02 (Actual)	2002–03 (Actual)	2003–04 (Actual)	2004–05 (Actual)	2005–06 (Actual)	2006–07 (Prov.)	2007–08 (BE)	2011–12 (Proj.)
I.	Coking Coal									
1.	Steel and cokeries (indigenous)		18.73	17.66	16.68	17.51	16.99	17.51	18.00	27.65
2.	Coking coal import		11.11	12.95	12.99	16.93	17.11	22.00	20.00	40.85
	Subtotal		29.84	30.61	29.67	34.43	34.10	39.51	38.00	68.50
II.	Non Coking Coal									
3.	Power (utilities)	RC	249.23	255.47	268.21	285.55	299.76	307.03	330.00	483.00
		MID	(1.86)	(1.71)	(1.44)	(1.48)	(1.48)			
4.	Power (captive)	RC	19.22	19.55	18.19	27.10	26.58	24.65	33.60	57.06
		MID	(1.36)	(1.53)	(1.74)	(1.71)	(1.71)			
5.	Cement (incl. CPPs)		15.22	16.37	16.64	18.33	18.71	18.92	26.80	31.90
6.	Sponge iron/CDI		4.40	6.17	7.59	10.99	14.73	13.07	15.10	28.96
7.	BRK/others/export/SSF/	RC	33.58	35.19	40.62	32.39	39.64	60.33	49.00	61.58
	NLW coke/loco/colly.cons	MID	(0.28)	(0.01)	(0.00)	(0.00)	(0.00)			
	Subtotal	RC	321.65	332.74	351.24	374.35	399.41	424.00	454.50	662.50
		MID	(3.50)	(3.25)	(3.18)	(3.19)	(3.19)			
	Total raw coal		351.49	363.35	380.91	408.79	433.51	463.51	492.50	731.00
	Middling		(3.50)	(3.25)	(3.18)	(3.19)	(3.19)			

Note: colly.cons = Colliery consumption.

Source: Coal Directory of India/Planning Commission.

ANNEXURE 10.2
Company-wise Coal Production Programme

(Million Tonnes)

Company	Ninth Plan	Tenth Plan					Eleventh Plan					Twelfth Plan
	2001–02 (Actual)	2002–03 (Actual)	2003–04 (Actual)	2004–05 (Actual)	2005–06 (Actual) (Prov.)	2006–07 (Actual)	2007–08 (Target/BE)	2008–09 (Proj.)	2009–10 (Proj.)	2010–11 (Proj.)	2011–12 (Proj.)	2016–17 (Proj.)
ECL	28.55	27.18	28.00	27.25	31.11	30.47	33.41	39.76	43.74	45.08	46.00	48.00
BCCL	25.25	24.15	22.68	22.31	23.31	24.20	25.20	26.50	27.50	28.50	30.00	35.00
CCL	33.81	36.98	37.33	37.39	40.51	41.35	44.00	47.00	55.00	65.00	78.00	115.00
NCL	42.46	45.10	47.03	49.95	51.52	52.16	58.00	60.50	65.00	68.00	70.00	80.50
WCL	37.01	37.82	39.53	41.41	43.20	43.21	42.40	42.95	43.65	44.50	45.00	45.00
SECL	64.12	66.60	71.01	78.55	83.02	88.50	91.50	93.65	101.10	106.30	111.00	140.00
MCL	47.81	52.23	60.05	66.08	69.60	80.00	88.00	99.00	111.00	122.00	137.00	197.00
NEC	0.64	0.63	0.73	0.63	1.10	1.05	2.00	2.00	2.50	3.00	3.50	3.50
CIL—Total	279.65	290.69	306.36	323.58	343.39	360.93	384.51	411.36	449.49	482.38	520.50	664.00
SCCL	30.81	33.16	33.85	35.30	36.14	37.71	38.04	38.30	39.00	40.00	40.80	45.00
Other Public Sector#	2.07	1.54	1.64	1.90	1.81	1.77	1.92	2.02	2.32	2.52	2.52	2.52
Private—TISCO	5.64	5.92	6.14	6.37	6.52	7.00	6.50	6.50	6.50	6.50	6.50	6.50
Captive Mining*	4.46	5.51	7.61	10.11	13.59	17.54	23.93	36.22	47.09	73.00	104.08	331.38
Meghalaya	5.02	4.41	5.44	5.35	5.57	5.57	5.60	5.60	5.60	5.60	5.60	5.60
All-India	327.64	341.23	361.04	382.62	407.01	430.52	460.50	500.00	550.00	610.00	680.00	1055.00

Note: # includes IISCO, DVC, JSMDCL, and JKML; * includes Bengal Emta, JSPL, Hindalco, Monnet, ICML, Castron, and BLA Industries.

Source: Coal Directory of India/Working Group Report on Coal and Lignite.

ANNEXURE 10.3
Calorific Values, Units and Conversion Factors

Calorific Value of Various Fuels

S. No.	Name of Fuel	Unit	Calorific Value (kilocalories)
1.	Biogas	m^3	4713
2.	Kerosene	kg	10638
3.	Firewood	kg	4500
4.	Cowdung cakes	kg	2100
5.	Coal	kg	4000
6.	Lignite	kg	2865
7.	Charcoal	kg	6930
8.	Soft coke	kg	6292
9.	Oil	kg	10000
10.	LPG	kg	11300
11.	Furnace oil	kg	9041
12.	Coal gas	m^3	4004
13.	Natural gas	m^3	9000
14.	Electricity	kWh	860

Conversion Factors

1 kilocalorie	3.96832 btu, 4186.8 joules
1 kilowatt hour	3412.14 btu, 3.6×10^6 joules
1 btu	0.252 kilo cal, 1.055 kilo joules
1 US Gallon	0.833 Imperial Gallon, 0.134 cft, 0.00378 cum
1 Imperial Gallon	1.2009 US Gallon, 0.1605 cft, 0.0045 cum
1 Cubic Metres	264.172 US Gallons, 219.969 Imperial Gallons, 35.3147 cft,
1 Cubic Feet	7.4805 US Gallons, 6.2288 Imperial Gallons, 0.0283 cum
1 BkWh hydro or wind electricity	0.086 Mtoe#
1 BkWh nuclear electricity	0.261 Mtoe
1 million tonne of coal	0.41 Mtoe
1 million tonne of lignite	0.2865 Mtoe
1 billion cubic meter of gas	0.9 Mtoe
1 million tonne of LNG	1.23 Mtoe
1 million tonne of fuel wood	0.45 Mtoe
1 million tonne of dung cake	0.21 Mtoe

Note: # Mtoe conversion factors are as per International Energy Agency (IEA) Practice.

Abbreviations

Unit	Name	Unit	Name
bcm	Billion Cubic Metre	MMBtu	Million British Thermal Unit
BkWh	Billion Kilowatt Hours	MMSCMD	Million Standard Cubic Meters per Day
Bt	Billion Tonne	Mt	Million Tonnes
btu	British Thermal Unit		
GW_e	Gigawatt Electrical	Mtoe	Million Tonne of Oil Equivalent
GW-Yr	Gigawatt Year	MVA	Million Volt Amperes
kcal	Kilocalorie	MW	Megawatt
kWh	Kilowatt Hour	MW_e	Megawatt Electrical
TCF	Trillion Cubic Feet		

11

Urban Infrastructure, Housing, Basic Services and Poverty Alleviation

OVERVIEW

URBAN SCENARIO IN THE GLOBAL CONTEXT

11.1 Urbanization is a key indicator of economic development and should be seen as a positive factor for overall development. Also, as an economy grows, its towns and cities expand in size and volume and the contribution of the urban sector to the national economy increases. For instance, the contribution of urban sector to India's GDP has increased from 29% in 1950–51 to 47% in 1980–81. The urban sector presently contributes about 62%–63% of the GDP and this is expected to increase to 75% by 2021 (see Box 11.1).

Box 11.1
Vision

Indian cities will be the locus and engine of economic growth over the next two decades, and the realization of an ambitious goal of 9%–10% growth in GDP depends fundamentally on making Indian cities much more livable, inclusive, bankable, and competitive.

11.2 The trends of urbanization in India in the recent decades indicate the following key features:

- The degree of urbanization in India is one of the lowest in the world. With about 27.8% of the total population living in the urban areas, India is less urbanized compared to many countries of Asia, viz., China (32%), Indonesia (37%), Japan (78%), South Korea (83%), and Pakistan (35%).
- There is a continued concentration of the urban population in large cities and existing city agglomerations (Class I cities with population over one lakh) account for 68.9% of the urban population and this proportion has been growing. The growth of rural settlements which are acquiring urban characteristic is very slow and there is reluctance on the part of the States to notify the rural settlements as a town.
- There are large variations in the spatial patterns of urbanization across the States and cities.
- The pattern of population concentration in large cities reflects spatial polarization of the employment opportunities.

11.3 This phenomenon has led to tremendous pressure on civic infrastructure systems, water supply, sewerage and drainage, uncollected solid waste, parks and open spaces, transport, etc. It has also led to deterioration in the quality of city environments. In several cities, the problems of traffic congestion, pollution, poverty, inadequate housing, crime, and social unrest are assuming alarming proportions.

11.4 The number of urban agglomerations and towns has increased from 3768 in 1991 to 5161 in 2001. Further, this urbanization is characterized by incomplete devolution of functions to the elected bodies, lack of adequate financial resources, unwillingness to progress towards municipal autonomy, adherence to outdated methods in property taxation, hesitation in levy of user charges, unsatisfactory role of parastatals in the provision of water supply and sanitation services. Also, the governance requirements under the 74th Constitution Amendment Act (CAA) in respect of the District Planning Committees and Metropolitan Planning Committees (MPCs) have not been met in a number of States.

11.5 The extent and magnitude of the urban population calls for extra efforts by city planners and managers to cope up with the ever-growing strain on the urban infrastructure. Special attention is needed for management and governance of urban areas which are at present fragmented between different State-level agencies and urban local bodies (ULBs), with lack of co-ordination.

11.6 The policymakers need to focus on new ways to achieve the results and on different benchmarks that capture efficiency, effectiveness, quality, and sustainability in governance, service delivery, intergovernmental municipal finances, and social development. Some of the strategic interventions are summarized in Box 11.2.

National Urbanization Policy

11.7 The time is ripe to formulate a long-term National Urbanization Policy indicating the emerging pattern of urbanization and measures to channelize future urban growth in an equitable and sustainable manner. It should encompass the changing economic scenario, reform agenda of Jawaharlal Nehru National Urban Renewal Mission (JNNURM), and the role of ULBs in the era of globalization. The objectives of balanced and sustainable development are to be achieved by reducing spatial disparities.

Regional Development Plans

11.8 The regional development plans at the State level need to be formulated as a broad policy and vision document for the development of urban and rural growth centres in an integrated manner.

Role of Government as a Facilitator

11.9 The GoI should play the role of a facilitator as is being done through JNNURM and various other reform initiatives such as property tax reforms, municipal accounting reforms, model municipal law, guidelines on private sector participation, etc. It should also come up with a policy framework for regulators in the urban sector. The State Governments should play a similar role to facilitate the ULBs in order to provide an enabling environment for the ULBs to function as effective units of self-governance at the local level. Urban poverty alleviation, slum up gradation, and basic services to the urban poor will continue to remain as functions belonging to the public domain. These functions are redistributive in nature and are best handled through redistributive taxes at the control of Central and State Governments. Thus, Central–State–ULB partnerships will be necessary as potentially effective ways to address the emerging issues of urban development.

Private Sector Participation

11.10 Private sector participation in the water supply and sanitation sector could not make significant progress till now. There is substantial need and potential for the same in the Eleventh Plan. However, without aiming at the full cost recovery, private sector participation cannot be a successful proposition.

Box 11.2
Strategy of Urban Development

- Strengthening urban local bodies through capacity building and better financial management.
- Increasing the efficiency and productivity of cities by deregulation and development of land.
- Dismantling public sector monopoly over urban infrastructure and creating conducive atmosphere for the private sector to invest.
- Establishing autonomous regulatory framework to oversee the functioning of the public and private sector.
- Reducing incidence of poverty.
- Using technology and innovation in a big way.

THE CONSTRAINTS

11.11 The transformation of the Indian cities faces several structural constraints. Foremost, the current urban development model starves cities of financing. Also, weak or outdated urban management practices—inappropriate planning systems, unsustainable service delivery models, and lack of focus on the urban poor—negate the benefits of agglomeration economies in Indian cities by distorting land and housing markets, rendering cities non-creditworthy, and leaving them with expensive yet poorly functioning urban services.

11.12 The current urban management techniques are also out-moded. The Master Plan concept—as currently practised in India—is not widely used elsewhere. Besides, it is not well suited to rapidly growing cities and multi-jurisdiction urban agglomerations. The Master Plan concept has also not been useful in addressing India's large and widely spread slums. By locking-in the supply of buildable land and space, the Master Plan, inter alia, inhibits the development of housing markets and contributes to the proliferation of slums. Therefore, there is an urgent need to develop new management and service delivery approaches across the board.

REVIEW OF SCHEMES OF THE TENTH PLAN

JAWAHARLAL NEHRU NATIONAL URBAN RENEWAL MISSION (JNNURM)

11.13 Consistent with the policies of the present government, the Prime Minister of India launched JNNURM on 3 December 2005 to give focused attention to integrated development of urban infrastructure and services in select 63 cities with emphasis on provision of basic services to the urban poor, including housing, water supply, sanitation, road network, urban transport, development of inner (old) city areas, etc. A provision of Rs 50000 crore has been made as reform-linked Central assistance over the Mission period of seven years beginning from 2005–06. The provision of Central assistance is linked to the implementation of certain mandatory as well as optional reforms at the State and ULB/parastatal levels during the Mission period. Against the allocation of Rs 4900 crore for 2006–07, an amount of Rs 3906 crore was released. In 2007–08, an amount of Rs 5500 crore has been allocated. Subsequently, additional Rs 500 crore was allocated in 'Plan B'.

11.14 In its initial period, the Mission has focused on finding good urban infrastructure investments that can ultimately be undertaken on a self-sustaining basis. Now that this search process has been put in place, a more systematic perspective needs to be adopted. It has to be realized that the ability to tap India's increasingly sophisticated financial markets will remain severely circumscribed till the local bodies become credible and accountable.

URBAN REFORM INCENTIVE FUND (URIF)

11.15 The Tenth Plan underlined the need for broad-based reforms to overcome the impediments of urban growth and stipulated that conformity to the reform agenda through the URIF will be made obligatory for the Central assistance. URIF called upon the States to repeal the Urban Land (Ceilings and Regulation) Act 1976, reform Rent Control Acts, strengthen property tax system, reduce stamp duty, introduce double entry accounting system, and revise user charges to cover operations and maintenance costs. An allocation of Rs 300 crore was made under URIF for allocation to different States for implementing the reform agenda. The scheme was later subsumed in JNNURM.

MEGA CITY

11.16 A CSS for infrastructure development in the mega cities was introduced in 1993–94 to cover a wide range of projects on water supply and sewerage, roads and bridges, city transport, solid waste management, etc. The Central share released during Tenth Plan amounts to Rs 908.69 crore (anticipated expenditure) against an allocation of Rs 1050 crore. The scheme has since been subsumed in JNNURM.

INTEGRATED DEVELOPMENT OF SMALL AND MEDIUM TOWNS (IDSMT)

11.17 IDSMT was launched in 1979–80 to improve the economic and physical infrastructure and to provide essential facilities and services in small and medium towns. Since inception, upto 31 March 2007, a total of 1854 towns, out of 5092 small and medium towns (2001 Census), were covered under the scheme. Out of an approved outlay of Rs 1304.65 crore for the

Tenth Plan, the anticipated expenditure is Rs 566.43 crore (43.4%). As the performance of the scheme was not satisfactory, an evaluation was carried out in 2002 which showed that the scheme suffered from (i) lack of capacity for implementation, (ii) non-availability of matching States share, and (iii) non-availability of unencumbered land for the projects. The scheme has since been subsumed in JNNURM as Urban Infrastructure Development Scheme for Small and Medium Towns (UIDSSMT).

ACCELERATED URBAN WATER SUPPLY PROGRAMME (AUWSP)

11.18 AUWSP was launched in March 1994 to provide safe and adequate water supply to towns having population less than 20000 (as per 1991 Census), to improve environment and quality of life, and to bring about better socio-economic conditions to sustain the economy. Since its inception, 1244 towns have been covered and 639 projects have been completed at an estimated cost of Rs 1822.38 crore, including Central funds of Rs 828.06 crore. Against the approved outlay of Rs 900 crore for the Tenth Plan, an expenditure of Rs 406.50 crore was incurred which is about 45.2%. Concurrent evaluation of the scheme was made in November 2003 for 62 towns in 24 States. Major recommendations of the study included handing over of the scheme to ULBs, timely release of State funds, periodic review of tariff, and training to field engineers for effective implementation. The scheme has since been subsumed under JNNURM. However, for completion of ongoing projects, Rs 32.50 crore has been provided for 2007–08.

PILOT PROJECT ON SOLID WASTE MANAGEMENT NEAR AIRPORT IN FEW SELECTED CITIES

11.19 A Central sector scheme on solid waste management in 10 selected air field towns was approved in 2003 as 100% grant from the GoI towards capital cost and was to be completed in three years. Subsequent to the completion of the project, the scheme was to be handed over to the concerned ULBs for day-to-day O&M. While eight projects, viz., Sirsa, Jodhpur, Pune, Gwalior, Tezpur, Adampur, Dindigul, and Ambala are being executed by National Building Construction Corporation (NBCC), projects for Hindon and Bareilly are being executed by Uttar Pradesh Jal Nigam. The approved cost of the project is Rs 99.34 crore. The projects are under various stages of execution.

NEW INITIATIVES FOR THE ELEVENTH PLAN

POOLED FINANCE DEVELOPMENT FUND (PFDF)

11.20 The government had approved on 29 September 2006 a proposal for setting up of a PFDF to provide credit enhancement to the ULBs to access market borrowings based on their credit worthiness through State-level Pooled Finance mechanism. The broad objectives of PFDF are:

- Facilitate implementation of bankable urban infrastructure projects through appropriate capacity-building measures and financial structuring of projects.
- Facilitate the ULBs to access capital and financial markets for investment in critical urban infrastructure by providing credit enhancement grants to State-pooled Finance Entities for accessing capital markets through Pooled Financing Bonds on behalf of one or more identified ULBs for investment in the urban infrastructure projects.
- Reduce the cost of borrowing to local bodies with appropriate credit enhancement measures and through restructuring of existing costly debts.
- Facilitate development of Municipal Bond Market.

11.21 All State/UT governments have been requested to take necessary preparatory action for operationalization of the scheme to avail benefit from this financial year. In this connection, to sensitize the State Governments and all stakeholders for implementation of the scheme in a time-bound manner, a National Workshop was organized in Chennai on 20 November 2006 and the scheme was formally launched. During 2006–07, Rs 50.00 crore has been provided for the scheme. An amount of Rs 100 crore has been provided to the Ministry of Urban Development for 2007–08 for PFDF. For the Eleventh Plan period, a provision of Rs 2500 crore has been made.

NATIONAL URBAN INFRASTRUCTURE FUND (NUIF)

11.22 The NUIF is proposed to be set up as a trust to provide source of funding for bankable projects/ schemes pertaining to the ULBs. The commercial banks are hesitant to lend to ULBs due to apparent lack of capacity of the ULBs to meet their debt service obligations on the one hand and lack of expertise amongst financial institutions to lend for viable urban infrastructure projects on the other. NUIF will serve as an SPV that will create necessary comfort level amongst financial institutions with respect to repayments by avoiding direct exposure of commercial banks to the ULBs. The process of consultation for setting up of NUIF is presently in the advanced stage.

Development of Satellite Cities/Counter Magnet Cities

11.23 Metros and mega cities, which have become the centre of trade and commerce, have to cope with their own problems along with unabated in-migration from small and medium towns and vast rural hinterland. These have to be planned beyond the municipal limits and due importance may be given to integrated transport and communication. The other settlements located in the vicinity of the mother city are to be developed as satellite/counter magnets to reduce and to redistribute the population and population influx. To cope with the above problem, the government has proposed a new scheme for development of satellite towns/counter magnet cities. This will help in the development of metropolitan regions. Token provision for the scheme has been made in the Budget of the Ministry of Urban Development for 2007–08.

E-Governance in Municipalities

11.24 The key objectives of the Mission are to introduce e-governance in the municipalities to provide single window services to the citizens, to increase efficiency and productivity of the ULBs, to provide timely and reliable management information, etc.

11.25 The scheme envisages to cover all ULBs in Class I cities (423 in total having population of one lakh or more) during 2007–08 to 2011–12. A total of 35 cities with million plus population are proposed to be covered as part of JNNURM. However, a new CSS Scheme for other cities and towns other than 35 cities would wait for the present till the implementation is watched in 35 cities as a part of JNNURM. Eight services relating to birth and death certificates, property tax, building plan approval, health programme, solid waste management, accounting system, etc., will be covered under the programme.

JNNURM—An Instrument of Change

11.26 Cities and towns have a vital role in India's socio-economic transformation. The cities in India are serving as a nodal point for innovation and are playing a vital role in the Global Market. Most cities and towns are severely stressed in terms of infrastructure and service availability. In 2001, 50.3% of the urban households had no piped water within their premises and 44% of them were devoid of sanitation facilities. About 25.7% of country's urban population continues to be below the poverty line in 2004–05. According to the 2001 Census, 14.12% of the urban population lives in slums with a significant proportion of it without access to basic services.

Overview of the Mission

11.27 JNNURM rests on the postulate that cities make a meaningful contribution to India's economic growth and poverty reduction. This programme seeks to fulfil the Millennium Development Goals, and is envisaged to operate in a Mission mode by facilitating investments in the urban sector. It seeks to incentivize policy and institutional reforms, leading to sustainable socio-economic growth, service delivery, and improved governance in the Mission cities. It also aims at developing appropriate enabling frameworks to enhance the creditworthiness of the municipal bodies and integrate the poor with the service delivery systems.

Strategy of the Mission

11.28 The Mission seeks to achieve the objective of integrated development of cities, for which the cities are required to formulate a City Development Plan (CDP), bringing out long-term vision for the cities and support their efforts through funding of project proposals. A CDP is anchored on the goal of JNNURM in creating economically productive, efficient, equitable, and responsive cities. The essential requirement of the Mission is implementation of urban reforms, within the Mission period. On the basis of the satisfactory completion of the above tasks, funding support is provided in the form of ACA, ranging from 35% to 90% of the project cost, based on the city category. The Mission also aims to leverage and incorporate private sector efficiencies in development, management, implementation, and financing of projects, through PPP arrangements, wherever appropriate.

Expected Outcomes of JNNURM

- Financially sustainable cities for improved governance and service delivery.
- Universal access to basic services in urban areas.
- Transparency and accountability in governance.
- Adoption of modern transparent budgeting, accounting, and financial management systems.

11.29 There is an increased application of e-governance in service delivery and internal operations.

Operational Issues Linked to JNNURM Process

11.30 Sustaining momentum of the Mission by continuous engagement with all cities and at the same time ensuring wider ownership has been a major challenge while operationalizing the Mission.

11.31 The capacity of city-level agencies to absorb the investment support and delivery on reforms is a critical bottleneck. The Mission needs to calibrate and pace its capacity-building efforts in a manner so as to ensure that all Mission cities are able to reap the benefits of the programme and meet its stated goals and objectives.

11.32 Projects hitherto being implemented by city-level agencies have been very small in size compared to those being taken up under JNNURM. The overall institutional capacity and more specifically the project implementation capacity is clearly inadequate to deal with such large projects. This calls for immediate lateral expansion of human resources with appropriate skills, backed up by good project management systems. There is also a shortfall in the contracting capacity in the private sector. Large/organized sector players in infrastructure industry have not yet seriously looked at municipal infrastructure because of uncertainty in enabling environment. The project sizes have been small, with overdependence on the government funding. Poor credibility of implementing agencies is also one of the concerned areas.

11.33 Successful implementation of reforms within the committed timeframe is critical to the success of the Mission. The challenge is to facilitate the cities to internalize the reforms. Simultaneously, the process of reporting and monitoring progress of reforms needs to be sustained throughout the Mission period. The experience of implementation of JNNURM shows that the following issues need to be addressed:

- Need for adequate attention to the priority sectors, viz., water supply, sewerage, sanitation, storm water drainage, etc., in the CDPs prepared under JNNURM. Undue focus is presently given to on-road projects and flyovers.
- Need for focus on recovery of O&M costs and possibility of involving private sector through the PPP mode in the CDPs.
- Need for synergy between the Ministries of Urban Development and HUPA in the implementation of JNNURM. Both the ministries need to work in close co-ordination and synergy.
- Need to ensure improvement in urban governance so that the ULBs/parastatal agencies become financially sound. The Central and State agencies must ensure timely implementation of the agenda of reforms.
- Need to strengthen monitoring mechanism and ensuring that milestones for reforms are achieved during the project period and not extended to the Mission period.

11.34 As the programme is in the third year of implementation, the programme needs to be evaluated by an independent agency so as to take timely appropriate remedial measures.

Measures to Strengthen JNNURM Processes

11.35 Several workshops and seminars have been organized at regional and State level, apart from day-to-day interactions to speed up the participation of low performing States in the Mission.

11.36 The government is organizing a series of workshops/seminars with the objective of dissemination of the Mission objectives among the elected representatives and municipal functionaries. These fora have been instrumental in enhancing citizen involvement and improving technical capacities for project preparation and implementation by the ULBs/other city-level agencies, in various cities and States. To enhance community participation in the planning process and in various aspects of implementing JNNURM, the sub-Mission on urban infrastructure and governance has created a Community Participation Fund. This is to enable the citizens to develop a sense of ownership on community assets and take on responsibilities for community-based projects. To improve community participation in the implementation of the Mission, a Technical Advisory Group has been set up at the national level, which is to be further supported by similar structures at the State and city levels.

11.37 The Mission is in the process of preparing a framework for capacity-building and up-scaling of all related activities in order to bridge the capacity gap in implementation of projects and reforms. It is proposing to conduct a rapid training programme for municipal functionaries in key areas such as governance and reforms, DPR preparation, and project preparation. For fulfilling the long-term requirement of human resource challenges in the ULBs, the government is in the process of establishing a network of regional institutions across the country, which will address training and capacity-building needs for the States, cities, and other related institutions.

11.38 Strengthening communication channels to facilitate institutionalization and internalization of reforms is a key to the success of the Mission. The government has also appointed independent agencies for monitoring the implementation of the reforms. A quarterly progress reporting system for the cities and States has been instituted under the Mission. Apart from this, an MIS has been developed for monitoring projects and reforms.

11.39 To address the issues of credibility and financial sustainability of the ULBs, Municipal Finance Improvement Programme has been launched. A Task Force constituted under the programme has recommended measures to synergize all financial resources at city level and improve environment to access finance. As a part of the recommendation, all the ULBs under JNNURM are being rated on the basis of their financial capacities and credit worthiness.

11.40 In order to strengthen the UIDSSMT, State Governments have been advised to get the CDP prepared for the cities covered under UIDSSMT as a Vision Document. State-level Nodal Agencies (SLNAs) should develop in-house capacity to advise and guide the ULBs in preparing viable DPRs. The State Governments should ensure adequate budgetary provisions in their Budget to meet State/ULBs' share as stipulated in the guidelines. For monitoring and implementation of the project and reforms at the local level, a Project Implementation and Monitoring Cell may be established within the respective ULBs. SLNAs may prepare a panel of consultants by following a transparent procedure for preparation of DPRs.

Preparation and Dissemination of Best Practice Documents

11.41 The best practices under the Mission are being disseminated through the websites, workshops, and seminars. Apart from this, the government has launched an initiative called Peer Experience and Reflective Learning (PEARL) to facilitate networking among JNNURM cities to encourage cross learning and knowledge sharing. The cities have organized themselves in various groups/networks having similar socio-economic profile. The city networks have selected a Knowledge Manager for the respective groups to anchor partnerships within and outside the networks for exchange of best practices in urban governance and reforms.

Issues for Future Actions

- Rapid economic growth will inevitably lead to an increase in urbanization as the cities provide large economies of agglomeration for individual activity. The biggest constraint on rapid growth in the years ahead will be the inadequacy of urban infrastructure and its poor quality compared with global scenario. We have to strive for equity and inclusiveness in urban infrastructure so as to ensure that the city-wide infrastructure systems get linked with service networks in slums and low income settlements.

- The main challenge would be to bring about planned urbanization for the country and creation of new growth centres around existing small and medium towns.
- Urban reforms may be made essential for eligibility for assistance under all Urban Infrastructure Developments Schemes.
- Safe drinking water supply and sanitation facilities are basic needs and are crucial for achieving the goal of 'Health for All'.
- JNNURM has the potential to transform infrastructure and improve the civic amenities in selected cities greatly. It, therefore, needs to be implemented with vigour.

DETAILS OF SCHEMES/PROGRAMMES FOR THE ELEVENTH PLAN

NATIONAL CAPITAL REGION PLANNING BOARD (NCRPB)

11.42 The key rationale for constituting an NCRPB in 1985 was to reduce the rate of in-migration into the National Capital as well as to develop the region at a level comparable to the best in the world. Keeping in view with its objectives, the Board has prepared regional plans, 2001 and 2021, along with complementary functional plans related to the key elements of infrastructure.

11.43 In order to implement major thrust areas of the regional plans, the Board is also arranging for and overseeing the financing of selected development projects in NCR through Central grants and contribution from the Government of National Capital Territory of Delhi, by recycling loan repayments and internal accruals. To supplement its resources, the Board has also raised resources from the capital market in the form of bonds in the past.

11.44 The Government of Delhi in its Plan document has desired that NCRPB should contribute significantly in the development process of Delhi by initiating a number of inter-state projects in the NCR in the areas of power generation, water supply, sanitation, etc. The projects identified for being financed during the Eleventh Plan involve a total cost of Rs 15000 crore. Some of these projects will be taken up in collaboration with other stakeholders. Out of the total projected cost of projects, it is expected that the loan component will be above Rs 11000 crore.

NATIONAL URBAN INFORMATION SYSTEM (NUIS)

11.45 The major objective of the NUIS is to establish a comprehensive information system in the ULBs for planning, management, and decentralized governance in the context of implementation of the 74th CAA. The following activities have been undertaken:

- Mapping at 1:10000 scale from satellite images, 1:2000 scale from aerial photos, and 1:1000 scale utility mapping for 24 towns being taken up by Survey of India.
- Establishment of NUIS cells in State nodal agencies.
- Setting up of National Urban Databank and Indicator in each State nodal agency.
- Capacity building among town planners for use of modern automated methods.

11.46 So far, implementation of NUIS scheme has been slow and, therefore, all stakeholders of the scheme need to speed up the implementation of the scheme. States and UTs need to release their share for purchase of hardware and software for the NUIS cells in State nodal agencies and ULBs. The capacity building component under NUIS scheme has trained 160 personnel. A total of 22 programmes are proposed to be conducted to train 440 officers during 2007–08. An outlay of Rs 24 crore and Rs 9 crore has been allocated in the Annual Plan 2006–07 and 2007–08 respectively.

COMMONWEALTH GAMES

11.47 Delhi Development Authority has been assigned the task of development of Games Village, Competition Venues for sports events, viz., Table Tennis, Badminton, Squash, Billiards, Snookers, etc. for the forthcoming Commonwealth Games, 2010. To develop requisite facility at sports complexes in Delhi, a provision of Rs 80 crore has been made to the Ministry of Urban Development for 2007–08.

URBAN BASIC SERVICES

STATUS OF URBAN BASIC SERVICES

11.48 The quality of water and its distribution are areas that require special attention in the Eleventh Plan. Table 11.1 gives the status of city/town-wise access to drinking water. Sewerage facilities are almost absent in a large number of unauthorized and resettlement colonies and slum and squatter settlements. At certain places, cost incurred by the poor to fetch water is much higher than for valid connection holders. Waste water and sewage treatment and its reuse for non-potable purposes and industries are also limited and need attention. Moreover, cattle menace, open defecation, dumping of solid wastes along roadsides, open dumping of medical and hazardous wastes, etc., are commonly sighted (see Box 11.3 below). Concerted efforts are required to fill these gaps and make cities clean, healthy, and livable.

TABLE 11.1
City/Town-wise Average Access to Drinking Water

City/Towns (Population)	Average Access to Drinking Water (%)
Class I cities (100000 and above)	73
Class II cities (50000–99999)	63
Class III cities (20000–49999)	61
Other cities/towns (<20000)	58

Source: Ministry of Urban Development, GoI.

URBAN WATER SUPPLY

11.49 To achieve 100% coverage of population with urban water supply by the end of the Eleventh Five Year Plan, the following steps need to be taken:

- To bring out State Ground Water Legislation based on the Model Ground Water Legislation brought out by the CGWB.
- Keeping in view the NWP, the States should formulate State Water Policy to meet drinking water needs.
- Under JNNURM, special attention should be given to cities and towns which are affected by water contamination due to presence of chemicals such as iron

Box 11.3
Status of Urban Services

Water Supply

- As per 54th round of NSS, 70% of urban households reported being served by tap and 21% by tubewell or hand pump.
- 66% of urban households reported having their principal source of water within their premises while 32% had it within 0.2 km.
- 41% had sole access to their principal source of drinking water and 59% were sharing a public source.

Sewerage

- 54th round of NSS reported 26% of households having no latrines, 35% using septic tank, and 22% using sewerage system.
- In urban areas sewerage connections varied from 48% to 70%.
- According to Central Pollution Control Board, the waste water generated in 300 Class I cities is about 15800 million litres per day while the treatment facilities exist for hardly 3750 million litres per day.

Solid Waste

- It is estimated that about 115000 metric tonnes of municipal solid waste is generated daily in the country.
- Per capita waste generation in cities varies between 0.2–0.6 kg per day and it is increasing by 1.3% per annum. With the growth of urban population, the increase in solid waste is estimated at 5%.
- The solid waste generated by the million plus cities varies from 1200 metric tpd in cities like Ahmedabad and Pune to a maximum of 5000–5500 metric tpd in cities like Delhi and Mumbai.
- The per capita solid waste generation varies from 300 gm in Bangalore to 500–550 gm in Mumbai and Delhi.
- Out of total waste generated in the million plus cities, hardly 30% is treated before disposal.

and fluoride. Water Quality Testing Laboratories may be set up in all cities and towns and existing labs be strengthened to check water-borne diseases.
- Suitable strategy should be evolved by the States/ ULBs for meeting O&M costs. Metering of water may be made mandatory for generating sufficient revenues. Telescopic water tariff/user charges should be formulated and levied to discourage excessive use of water.
- Need to check the leakages and unaccounted water, particularly in cities where it is as high as 50%. Such losses should be minimized or eliminated through intensive leak detection and rectification programme.
- The State Governments/ULBs should take up reform measures under JNNURM for water and energy audit, reuse and recycling, levy of realistic user charges, efficient water use and its equitable distribution, rain water harvesting, commercial accounting systems, consumer orientation, cost recovery, artificial recharge of groundwater, etc.
- To meet the requirement of funds, efforts should be made to step up the quantum of funds through institutional financing, foreign direct investment, assistance from bilateral and multi-lateral agencies, newly launched Pooled Finance Development Scheme, tax-free municipal bonds, PPPs, Member of Parliament Local Area Development Programme (MPLAD) funds, etc.

Management of Municipal Solid Waste

11.50 On an average, the collection efficiency of solid waste ranges between 70% and 90% in metro cities, whereas in several smaller cities it is below 50%. The ULBs spend Rs 500–1500 per tonne on solid waste collection, transportation, treatment, and disposal. During the Eleventh Five Year Plan, emphasis would be laid on scientific and safe disposal of waste. Waste recycle, reuse, resource recovery, adoption of advanced technological measures for effective and economical disposal will have to be followed vigorously.

11.51 Private parties have shown encouraging response and they need to be increasingly involved. With the application of modern technology, the waste can be converted into profitable products such as organic pellets, construction material, etc. To deal with the solid waste management the States should encourage the PPP mode projects.

11.52 With rapid industrialization, growth of services sector, and rise in incomes, the rate of waste generation has gone up manifold. The following steps need to be taken for its management:

- Cities and towns should be provided with appropriate solid waste management facilities with emphasis on use of low-energy consuming technologies for processing and treatment of municipal solid waste.
- Compulsory production of compost from solid waste and application of this organic manure in agriculture and horticulture to improve soil fertility.
- Implementation of the recommendations of Report of the Inter-Ministerial Task Force on the 'Integrated Plant Nutrient Management Using City Compost' in managing the city garbage in a sustainable manner.
- Segregation and storage of waste, door-to-door collection, and transportation along with appropriate plant design should be enforced as per Municipal Solid Waste Management and Handling Rules, 2000. NGOs should be encouraged to provide organizational support and identity to the ragpickers, who play an important role in recycling of the waste.
- Adequate land should be earmarked/allotted at the planning stage itself for setting up of sanitary land fills, compost plants, and other processing units including provision for future expansion.

Sewerage, Low-cost Sanitation, Storm Water Drainage

11.53 About 63% of the urban population has access to sewerage and sanitation facilities as on 31 March 2004. This includes both underground as well as sanitation through septic tanks. The access to underground sewerage facilities is very low, that is below 30% in many States, viz., Rajasthan, Orissa, Chhattisgarh, Madhya Pradesh, Andhra Pradesh, and West Bengal. According to the MTA of the Tenth Five Year Plan, nearly 46% of urban households have water toilets, but only 36% of the urban households are connected to the public sewerage system.

11.54 Underground network of sewerage has developed to a considerable extent in urbanized States where cities have developed in a planned manner, viz., Delhi, Chandigarh, Greater Noida, etc. However, within the cities, large number of unauthorized colonies, resettlement colonies, slums, and squatter settlements are often deprived of underground sewerage facilities.

11.55 To achieve 100% population coverage for sewerage, sewage treatment, and low-cost sanitation facilities in urban areas during the Eleventh Plan, the following steps need to be taken:

- Install more plants to treat, recycle, and reuse sewage.
- Industrial and commercial establishments must reuse and recycle treated sewage to reduce fresh water demand.
- The ULBs should amend their by-laws to make it mandatory for all residents to connect their toilets to the existing sewerage system.
- Fringe areas of cities and colonies of economically weaker sections and slum dwellers should be covered with low-cost sanitation facilities, either on individual household basis or community basis with 'pay and use system' with adequate maintenance arrangements. Necessary penal clause should be enforced effectively to stop open defecation practice as well as indiscriminate throwing of garbage/litter in public places.
- Targeted subsidy may be given to urban poor for taking water supply/sewerage house service connections, metering, and construction of toilets.
- Comprehensive storm water drainage system should be developed in all cities and towns in order to avoid water logging during monsoon.

Investment Needs for Urban Water Supply and Sanitation, Sewerage, Drainage, and Solid Waste Management Sectors during the Eleventh Five Year Plan

11.56 The total fund requirement for the implementation of the Eleventh Five Year Plan schemes in respect of urban water supply, sewerage and sanitation, drainage, and solid waste management is estimated as given in Table 11.2.

Availability of Funds

11.57 To improve the infrastructure relating to water supply and sanitation in the urban centres, the government is assisting the ULBs and the State Governments through various schemes and special Central assistance (SCA). Under JNNURM, water supply and sanitation have been accorded highest priority among the eligible components and almost 40% of the outlay would be spent on water supply and sanitation sector leaving a gap of Rs 89237 crore.

TABLE 11.2
Funds Requirement—Urban Basic Services

(Rs in Crore)

S. No.	Sub-Sector	Estimated Amount
1.	Urban water supply	53666
2.	Urban sewerage and sewage treatment	53168
3.	Urban drainage	20173
4.	Solid waste management	2212
5.	MIS	8
6.	R&D and PHE training	10
	Total	129237

Source: Ministry of Urban Development, GoI.

For bridging the gap, the following possible sources are identified. Table 11.3 gives the proposed flow of funds.

TABLE 11.3
Proposed Flow of Funds

Source of Funding	Amount (in Rs Crore)
Central sector outlay	70000*
State sector outlay	35000
Institutional financing	10000
Assistance from external support agencies	10000
FDI and private sector	4237
Total	129237

Note: * The actual allocation provided for JNNURM is Rs 50000 crore during 2005–12 out of which the amount available for Urban Water Supply, Sewerage, Solid Waste Management is expected to be in the range of Rs 15000 crore. The shortfall will need to be met by other sources of finance if the objective of covering 100% population with Water Supply and Sanitation facilities is to be met during the Eleventh Plan.
Source: Ministry of Urban Development, GoI.

Central Sector Outlay

11.58 The Central sector outlay may be stepped up from the present Rs 50000 crore to around Rs 70000 crore under the ongoing Central programme of JNNURM so that great thrust could be given to water supply and sanitation sector in the urban areas.

State Sector Outlay

- Likewise, the State sector outlay which stood at Rs 18749 crore during the Tenth Plan may be stepped up to around Rs 35000 crore.

Institutional Financing

- Funds may be mobilized through national financial institutions such as LIC, HUDCO, IL&FS, etc., to the tune of Rs 10000 crore.

Additional Assistance from External Support Agencies (ESA)

- Funds may be mobilized from external funding agencies viz. World Bank, JBIC, ADB, and other agencies to the tune of about Rs 10000 crore.

FDI and Private Sector

- In addition, foreign direct investment and private sector funds up to Rs 4237 crore may be mobilized to support the sector's activities.

Provision of Basic Services to the Urban Poor at their Workplace

11.59 In all stages of planning, formulation, and execution of water and sanitation projects, poor and disadvantaged sections of society and SC/ST population should be included and their needs accorded top priority. The programmes of other Central Ministries such as SC/ST Plans and Tribal Welfare Plan may be suitably dovetailed with JNNURM. CDPs should give special attention to the problems and needs of these vulnerable sections of society.

Urban Poverty Alleviation and Slum Development

11.60 The percentage of BPL population in the urban areas in India has declined from 32.3% in 1993–94 to 25.7% in 2004–05 (based on uniform recall period). The NSSO 61st Round shows that urban poverty has registered a decline in percentage terms; however, it has increased in absolute terms by 4.4 million persons. The fact is that the number of urban poor is rising continuously since 1973–74 as per the uniform recall period. A comparison of poverty estimates based on uniform recall period and mixed recall period is given in Tables 11.4 and 11.5, respectively. The number of persons below poverty line in the urban and rural areas is given in Table 11.6.

11.61 The incidence of urban poverty as well as number of the urban poor has increased in Orissa and Rajasthan over the 1993–94 to 2004–05 period. In contrast, both the incidence of urban poverty and the number of the urban poor have declined

TABLE 11.4
Comparison of Poverty Estimates Based on Uniform Recall Period

(Percentage of the Total Population)

	1993–94	2004–05
Rural	37.3	28.3
Urban	32.4	25.7
Total	36.0	27.5

Source: Planning Commission.

TABLE 11.5
Comparison of Poverty Estimates Based on Mixed Recall Period

(Percentage of the Total Population)

	1999–2000	2004–05
Rural	27.1	21.8
Urban	23.64	21.7
Total	26.1	21.8

Source: Planning Commission.

TABLE 11.6
Number of Persons below Poverty Line in Urban and Rural Areas

(Lakh)

Year	Urban	Rural	Total
Mixed Recall Period			
1973–74	600.46	2612.90	3213.36
1977–78	646.48	2642.47	3288.95
1983	709.40	2519.57	3228.97
1987–88	751.69	2318.79	3070.49
1999–2000	670.07	1932.43	2602.50
2004–05	682.00	1702.99	2384.99
Uniform Recall Period			
1973–74	600.46	2612.90	3213.36
1977–78	646.48	2642.47	3288.95
1983	709.40	2519.57	3228.97
1987–88	751.69	2318.79	3070.49
1999–2000	763.37	2440.31	3203.68
2004–05	807.96	2209.24	3017.20

Source: Planning Commission.

in the States of Gujarat, Kerala, Punjab, Tamil Nadu, and West Bengal during the same period. In other States, there has been a decline in the incidence of poverty but not in their total number (Boxes 11.4, 11.5, 11.6).

11.62 A large number of workers engaged in the urban economy as self-employed in the informal sector, regular low wage/salaried workers, and casual workers fall in the category of the urban poor. They play a role in wealth creation, development of infrastructure, and providing a quality of life to the urbanites. However, they have themselves been denied shelter, basic urban amenities, healthy urban environment, and a dignified life.

Box 11.4
Objectives for Urban Poverty Alleviation

The Eleventh Plan has the following objectives for the urban poor:

- To provide them affordable shelter and decent living and working conditions.
- To make adequate provision of land for the poor in the Master Plan itself.
- To help in developing self-employment enterprises and job creation for the wage employment earners.
- To protect the economic interest and safety of women and other vulnerable sections of our society.

Box 11.5
Slums

Slums are housing clusters having insufficient facilities of hygiene, toilet, drinking water, sanitation, etc.

Box 11.6
Integrated Slum Development

Some of the measures that are required to be pursued and strengthened further for integrated slum development are:

- Creating and updating database on slums.
- City-wise perspective and integrated slum development plans.
- Augmenting and facilitating access to services for slum dwellers.
- Granting tenure security to slum dwellers.
- Insitu upgradation and resettlement options for slum improvement.
- Using land as a resource for housing and shelter development for slum dwellers.

11.63 In recent decades, the gap between the urban rich and poor has widened considerably. The Eleventh Plan aspires to empower the persons engaged in the informal sector living in urban areas by providing training to them to have better skills, higher productivity, and higher incomes on the one hand and a greater voice in decision-making by implementing the 74th CAA on the other hand. In this manner, an effort would be made during the Eleventh Plan to focus the spotlight on 'inclusive growth' in the urban areas.

SLUMS AND SLUM REHABILITATION

11.64 As per estimates, the slum population in 2001 was 61.82 million out of which the reported slum population in the 640 towns and cities having population of 50000 and above is 42.58 million. The total urban population of thcsc 640 towns is 184.35 million. Data pertaining to slum population, as per the 2001 Census and the availability of housing and other basic amenities to them, are given in Tables 11.12 and 11.13.

Housing for Slum Dwellers

11.65 Registrar General of India has for the first time collected slum data in the 2001 Census for cities having urban population of 50000 and more. Box 11.7 provides the gist of slum population data in the country.

Box 11.7
Spread of Slums

- 640 towns spread over 26 States/UTs have reported existence of slums.
- 42.6 million people consisting of 8.2 million households reside in slums of these towns.
- It is a coincidence that both Census of India in 2001 and NSSO in 2002 found that every seventh person in urban India is a slum dweller.

REVIEW OF SCHEMES

11.66 A number of social housing schemes for poor—as indicated in the Table 11.7—have been undertaken by the GoI over the last two decades:

TABLE 11.7
Social Housing Schemes

S.No.	Name of the Scheme	Started in
1.	Indira Awas Yojana	1990
2.	EWS Housing Scheme for beedi workers and *hamals*	1991
3.	National Slum Development Programme	1996
4.	A two million Housing Programme for EWS/LIG	1998
5.	PM Gramin Awas Yojana	2000
6.	Valmiki Ambedkar Awas Yojana (VAMBAY)	2001
7.	JNNURM (BSUP and IHSDP)	2005

Source: Ministry of Housing and Urban Poverty Alleviation (MoHUPA), GoI.

11.67 These and other policy frameworks and subsequent development of programmes and schemes have yielded fairly positive results in the area of housing and human settlements. There has been a quantum jump in the supply of serviced land, habitable shelter, and related infrastructure, as detailed in the Box 11.8.

11.68 Effective measures are needed to stop the mushrooming of new slums. Providing affordable urban services to slum dwellers and granting them tenure rights will be the focus of the Eleventh Plan. State governments have to ensure that the ULBs earmark a part of their budget for the urban poor. Urban poverty cells have already been created at district level. Their functioning has to be made effective. A National Slum Policy needs to be formulated so as to evolve a holistic approach towards slum improvement.

11.69 To promote integrated city development and to enable the people living in slums to gain access to basic services, a number of schemes and programmes have been launched from time to time, for example Environmental Improvement of Urban Slums, National Slum Development Programme (NSDP), Integrated Low Cost Sanitation Scheme (ILCS), etc.

PROGRAMMES AND SCHEMES OF URBAN POVERTY ALLEVIATION IN THE ELEVENTH PLAN

SWARNA JAYANTI SHAHRI ROZGAR YOJANA (SJSRY)

11.70 This CSS, launched in 1997, was meant to provide gainful employment to the urban unemployed/under-unemployed (below the urban poverty line) through:

- encouraging setting up of self-employment ventures;
- provision of wage employment.

11.71 It relied on creation of suitable community structures and delivery of inputs through the ULBs. In the Tenth Plan, there was a target of assisting four lakh urban poor in setting up individual/group micro enterprises and imparting skill training to five lakh urban poor.

11.72 Under self-employment component of SJSRY, 891679 beneficiaries have been assisted by now and 934649 persons were provided various types of skill

Box 11.8
Housing Construction and Ownership

- Under the Valmiki Ambedkar Awas Yojana (VAMBAY) of the GoI, a subsidy of Rs 932.56 crore has been released for construction of 459728 dwelling units and 65580 toilet seats since the inception of the scheme up to 2005–06.
- Under the NSDP, a total amount of Rs 3089.64 crore has been released to the States/UTs covering 436.28 lakh urban poor since inception of the scheme up to 2005–06.
- The period 1991 to 2001 witnessed a net addition of 19.52 million dwelling units in the urban housing stock, amounting to average annual construction of 1.95 million houses.
- The share of ownership housing in urban areas has increased from 63% in 1991 to 67% in 2001 (Census 2001).
- It is important to note that households having one-room accommodation declined significantly in urban areas from 39.55% to 35.1% during the period 1991–2001. This is a result of upward shift of accommodation and accelerated supply of housing stock.

trainings. So far, 52701 Development of Women and Children in Urban Areas (DWCUA) groups have been formed and 198314 women beneficiaries have been assisted under this scheme for setting up of group enterprises. A total of 177508 Thrift and Credit Societies (T&CS) have also been formed under SJSRY. The number of beneficiaries covered under the Community Structure Component of SJSRY is 337.40 lakh and the number of man-days of work generated under the wage employment component of SJSRY is 583.06 lakh.

11.73 A comprehensive evaluation of SJSRY scheme on an all-India basis was carried out in 2005–06 by Human Settlement and Management Institute. The main findings of the evaluation are: (i) the pro-gramme is working well in some of the States; (ii) most of the beneficiaries of training are below 30 years; (iii) women groups market their products by themselves except in the eastern and North Eastern States; (iv) the formation of DWCUA groups has had a positive impact on women; (v) T&CS are very active in promoting small savings and resolving disputes; (vi) non-achievement of physical targets in some States is due to inadequate skill training, wrong choice of projects, lack of publicity, etc. (see Box 11.9).

11.74 SJSRY is being revised in terms of the following features:

Self-employment Component

- The self-employment component of the scheme will be made more market driven in terms of market surveys which will assist micro entrepreneurs to locate niche segments where there is potential demand for their products and services.
- Clusters of micro production units will be developed in keeping with the factors of localization pertaining to traditional skills and in terms of towns renowned for given products.
- Appropriate or intermediate technology inputs will be used to strengthen the technological base of selected clusters in terms of common facilities centres providing critical machinery/equipment required for common use as well as ensuring supply of quality raw materials at reasonable prices. These common facilities centres would be run by associations of micro entrepreneurs themselves related to the selected economic activity.
- High-quality Small Enterprise Advisory Services will be provided to the micro entrepreneurs.
- Resource institutions will be selected all over the country for providing upgraded technical skills combined with certification.
- Self-employment efforts will be buttressed by encouraging T&CS at the community level.
- Micro entrepreneurs will be encouraged to develop trade-based organizations.
- The mission approach of the 'Kudumbshree' model of Kerala and other best practices in different parts of the country will be adopted for suitable application under SJSRY.
- Design and development services from IITs and other institutions will be sought for development of mobile vending outlets.
- An integrated approach will be adopted with special attention to backward and forward linkages under the aegis of a designated Institute and a specific Task Force.

Box 11.9
New Focus in SJSRY

In its present form, the scheme has not succeeded in providing effective employment opportunities to the urban poor. It is now proposed to bring new focus into the scheme in keeping with the fact that urban areas have developed new skill requirements. Towards this end, 43 new trades have been identified in which it is proposed to build capacity by:

- Skill development—PPP mode.
- SHGs.
- Self-employment skills plus facilitation of credit for setting up self-employment.

11.75 Wage-employment Component

- High-quality training for proficiency in technical services will be organized with leading institutions preparing detailed training modules for specific trades.
- Training in a wide variety of trades such as construction, beauty and skincare, hair styling, hospitality, tourist guides, security, transport, and secretarial trades will be encouraged along with placement services.

- Special emphasis will be laid on construction of community assets in low-income neighbourhoods with strong involvement and participation of local communities.

11.76 Structural and Organizational Component

- Strengthening the delivery mechanism by improving the competency level and outreach of the Programme Management Units at the State level and Programme Implementation Agencies (PIAs) at the ULB level.
- There is need to earmark 25% of the budget for the urban poor in municipal budgets.
- There is need for convergence of services to the urban poor with special reference to health, education, and social security.
- The National Building Organization (NBO) needs to be strengthened for providing statistical and monitoring inputs for effective implementation of the revised SJSRY.
- Suitable networking with the UNDP-funded National Strategy for the Urban Poor Project as well as UN and other multilateral/bilateral projects is required for focused thrust on capacity building and innovative and experimental pilot projects.

11.77 Given the fact that 25.7% of the urban population as per uniform recall period lives below the poverty line, a concerted effort need be made during the Eleventh Plan for creation of at least 30 million additional jobs in the urban areas. The outlay for alleviation of urban poverty during the Eleventh Plan needs to be suitably enhanced. The revised SJSRY will be market-led combined with an integrated provision of backward and forward linkages.

11.78 The Ministry of HUPA also proposes to launch a scheme for the 'Skill Training for Employment Promotion amongst the Urban Poor' during the Eleventh Five Year Plan as a part of the National Skill Development Mission specially targeting the urban poor in the development of their skills to enable them access market-based employment opportunities or undertake self-employment to improve their living conditions and overcome poverty. This will make available skilled and semi-skilled manpower needed by the industry and service sectors in response to changing global, national, and local imperatives and opportunities. This will lead to reduction in unemployment rate among the urban poor, especially women, and will enhance their productivity and real wages making the economic growth inclusive.

11.79 Urban Statistics for HR Assessment Scheme

Aims at the development and maintenance of a national database, MIS, and knowledge repository on urban poverty, slums, housing, construction, and other urbanization-related statistics. Its key objective is to support the government with an information base and knowledge inputs for planning, policy-making, project design, formulation, implementation, monitoring, assessment, and evaluation, particularly in the context of programmes relating to urban poverty, slums, and housing. The scheme was earlier known as MIS on Housing Data, Research and Survey.

11.80 Future Approach/Strategies

- There is need to address the issue of urban poverty alleviation in a systematic, scientific, and time-bound manner by adopting the Mission approach as is being done in Kerala through the 'Kudumbshree' model. The approach has to be target-oriented with specific focus on primary issues such as skill upgradation, entrepreneurship development, wage employment, etc.
- Skill development has to be correlated to the demands of industry and service sector in and around the city. For this purpose, periodic labour market surveys have to be carried out in collaboration with the private sector by professionally competent organizations/NGOs so as to devise appropriate training modules for building skills in the relevant disciplines, where the demand exists or is projected. This exercise is likely to lead to a pool of human capital which can be appropriately utilized in the contemporary labour market.
- The 74th CAA envisages that the functions of urban poverty alleviation and improvement of slums and their upgradation, including the provisioning of urban basic amenities to the poor, are among the key functions of the municipalities. Therefore, the ULBs have to compulsorily make appropriate

provisions in their budget. ULBs have to follow a convergence approach in formulating service delivery to the urban poor by optimum utilization of both financial and manpower resources available in various Central and State sector schemes and programmes.

- Any urban poverty alleviation programme without adequate manpower equipped with the capability, capacity, and sensitivity to effectively implement such social sector programmes will not succeed. Therefore, it is absolutely necessary for Urban Poverty Alleviation Cells at the ULB/district/State level to have trained and dedicated manpower.
- City-specific urban poverty reduction plans need to be prepared by the ULBs and fund release has to be demand driven.
- Although the urban poor is the most vulnerable section of society, the delivery of health services is almost negligible to them. Therefore, there is need to work out a comprehensive health and accident insurance plan/scheme for the entire urban poor as a special package to resolve their health-related issues. There is also need to develop a social security network for this most vulnerable section, specially the single women, widows, aged, disabled, weaker, and minority sections.

URBAN HOUSING

11.81 Role of Housing: Housing, besides being a very basic requirement for the urban settlers, also holds the key to accelerate the pace of development. Status of housing stock and basic amenities are provided in Table 11.13. Investments in housing, like any other industry, have a multiplier effect on income and employment. It is estimated that the overall employment generation in the economy due to additional investment in the housing/construction sector is eight times of the direct employment (IIM-Ahmedabad Study 2005). Construction sector employment is growing at the rate of 7% per annum. Housing provides opportunities for home-based economic activities. Housing also has a direct impact on the steel and cement, marble/ceramic tiles, electrical wiring, PVC pipes, and various types of fittings industry, which make a significant contribution to the national economy. Contribution of the housing industry to the GDP is summarized in the Box 11.10.

Box 11.10
Housing Stock

- Less than one-third of India's people live in cities and towns.
- These areas generate over two-thirds of the country's GDP and account for 90% of government revenues.
- As per CSO estimates, housing sector's contribution to GDP in the year 2003–04 was 4.5% (3.13% for urban areas) at current price.
- Housing stock in 2001 was 50.95 million (for 55.8 million urban households).

11.82 The National Urban Housing and Habitat Policy provides the basic framework for achieving the objective of 'shelter for all'. The policy was evolved in 1998 with the long-term goal of eradicating houselessness, improving the housing conditions of the inadequately housed, and providing a minimum level of basic services and amenities to all. It was formulated to address the issues of sustainable development, infrastructure development, and for strong PPPs for shelter delivery with the objective of creating surpluses in housing stock and facilitating construction of two million dwelling units each year in pursuance of the National Agenda for Governance. However, the housing sector has witnessed several changes since then. The 1998 National Housing Policy has been replaced by a National Habitat and Housing Policy, 2007 with land and the development of civic amenities to make land habitable as its two critical elements.

11.83 In order to improve the quality of life in urban areas, it is of critical significance that the housing stock is improved through urban renewal, in situ slum improvement, and development of new housing stock in existing cities as well as new townships.

Magnitude of Housing Need

11.84 Considerable efforts were made during the Tenth Plan to enlarge the resource base and initiate innovative institutional mechanisms to augment housing delivery in urban areas. Focused efforts were also initiated to cover the poor and vulnerable groups of society to enable them to access basic shelter related services. Fiscal concessions coupled with legislative measures were also initiated to encourage increased investments in housing by individuals and corporates. However, despite many policy measures and initiatives, the coverage of urban poor with these intended benefits has not been achieved to the desired extent. Pressure on urban land has also been increasing due to market forces supported by upward trend in economic growth (see Box 11.11 below).

Box 11.11
Housing Shortage and Requirement

- According to the report of the Technical Group on estimation of housing shortage constituted in the context of formulation of the Eleventh Five-Year Plan, housing shortage is estimated to be around 24.71 million. About 99% of such households are from EWS and low income groups (LIG).
- During the Eleventh Plan period, total housing requirement, including the backlog, is estimated at 26.53 million.

Land Availability, Land Tenure, and Land Reforms

11.85 Access to land and legal security of tenure are strategic prerequisites for the provision of adequate shelter for all and for the development of sustainable human settlements affecting both urban and rural areas. The present policy of the Central Government lays stress on an enabling approach. It is for the State Governments to bring in the required institutional reforms and legislative measures to augment housing both by State agencies and the private sector.

11.86 While recognizing the existence of different national laws and/or systems of land tenure, governments at the appropriate levels, including local authorities, have to strive to remove all possible obstacles that may hamper equitable access to land and ensure that equal rights of women and men related to land and property are protected under the law. The failure to adopt, at all levels, appropriate rural and urban land policies and land management practices remains a primary cause of inequity and poverty. Urban planning tools including master planning, zoning, and regulations are not enough to make land available in pace with the rapid urbanization, resulting in insufficient land supply and increase in land prices. It is important to have flexible land policy wherein conversion from one use to another is cost effective and efficient. Computerization of land records and data and e-governance should also constitute important elements of the urban land policy.

National Land Policy

11.87 We have to evolve a National Land Policy which will allow both public and private developers to legally purchase land for conversion into urban habitats and townships through transparent rules and regulations. Inadequate availability of serviced land in the urban areas is a major constraining factor in taking up housing projects for the poor.

11.88 In the process of spatially delimiting the specific areas of urban extensions of existing towns and the areas for new townships, care needs to be taken that as far as possible, prime agricultural land is not utilized but more emphasis is laid on using degraded land for urbanization. Even today, the country is importing certain basic food items from time to time. Further, each State/UT which acquires land must put into place *a suitable resettlement and rehabilitation policy* for the displaced rural families while developing urban extensions or new townships.

11.89 Care also needs to be taken that rivers and their flood plains, other water bodies, and natural drainage systems are not disturbed during the process of urbanization. Moreover, it is also essential to enhance the green lungs of cities as well as develop green belts around urban settlements with a view to stemming indiscriminate urban sprawl. Cities and towns should invariably be surrounded by a rural hinterland so that the ecology of the sub-region is preserved. Access to micro finance has a direct correlation with the land title. Therefore, the State Governments need to facilitate security of land tenure for the urban poor. The title has to be mortgagable to access credit.

Investment Required

11.90 For estimating the investment requirements for the Eleventh Plan, the Working Group on Urban Housing made different assumptions on unit cost of construction of houses in million plus cities and other urban areas (see Box 11.12 below).

11.91 During the Eleventh Five Year Plan, integrated efforts have to be made by the Central and State/UT governments to create an integrated and holistic approach on human settlements which adequately address issues of land, finance, legal, and regulatory framework, technology support, and PPP. However, it has to be understood that there can be no one solution and various options and initiatives would be needed based on national and local priorities.

Housing Market

11.92 The government has to create an enabling framework for a well-functioning housing market. Flexible instruments for the regulation of housing markets, including the rental market, taking into account the special needs of vulnerable groups need to be developed.

Housing Finance

11.93 With the introduction of reforms in the banking sector, considerable improvement has been made in enlarging access to finance for housing by individual families and also through co-operatives as well as private developers. In this context, it is pertinent to note that the RBI requires commercial banks to lend 3% of the incremental deposits of the commercial banks to be deployed to priority sector lending including financing housing by individuals and others including co-operatives and private sector. Besides, RBI also reckons investments made by banks in the bonds issued by HUDCO under priority sector lending. Box 11.3 provides some details of financing of housing loans.

Box 11.12
Investment Requirement

The total investment requirement for meeting the housing requirement would be of the order of Rs 361318.10 crore consisting of Rs 147195 crore required for mitigating housing shortage at the beginning of the Eleventh Plan and Rs 214123.10 crore for new additions to be made during the Eleventh Plan period (this includes pucca, upgradation of semi-pucca, and kutcha housing units).

11.94 HUDCO's housing portfolio covers a wide range of target groups spread all over the country both in urban and rural areas. During the Eleventh Plan period, HUDCO proposes to extend a large quantum of assistance for supporting the housing and urban development requirements both in urban and rural areas. The proposals envisage a total sanction of Rs 74596 crore during the Eleventh Plan period for both its housing and urban development programmes. Of this, an amount of Rs 14919 crore has been tentatively identified for its housing operations.

Flow of Funds for Housing

11.95 In view of the current economic and monetary scenario, it is expected that the housing finance disbursals by banks, HFCs, and co-operative sector institutions would grow at a rate of about 15% per annum during the Eleventh Plan period. Taking this into account, it is estimated that the flow of credit disbursal from these institutions would be about Rs 7.75 lakh crore (gross flow of funds) during 2007–12. These projected fund flow figures include

Box 11.13
Financing of Housing Loans

- Most of the clients of Housing Finance Institutions/banks under retail home loans belong to MIG/HIG categories and housing loan finance still remains unaffordable in a large way to the EWS/LIG sections.
- Only 0.2% of housing loans extended by HFCs are of value less than Rs 50000 and about 7% of housing loans is of value between Rs 50000–100000.
- More than 73% of housing loans extended by HFCs is of value exceeding Rs 3 lakh and about 93% of value exceeding Rs 1 lakh.
- The fastest growing housing value bracket is between Rs 10 lakh to Rs 25 lakh.
- This highlights the need to evolve a system or a scheme for financing housing loans on a large scale for the lower income groups whose affordability for housing loans falls in the range below Rs 3 lakh, as over 90% of the housing shortage is on account of EWS/LIG.

multiple counting and resale of properties, in the sense that cross-funding/bulk borrowing is involved among the various institutions. It is, therefore, assumed that the net flow of funds to the housing sector from formal sector institutions would be 50% of the gross flow of funds for construction of new houses. This comes to approximately Rs 2.90 lakh crore, which is 80% of the total investment requirements for urban housing for the Eleventh Plan.

RESOURCE MOBILIZATION

11.96 Some corrective measures including legislative and regulatory, outreach related, and those related to expansion of housing finance would be required to promote larger flow of funds to accelerate supply of housing to a cross-section of households.

11.97 Liquidity of housing finance with particular reference to EWS, low-income group, and middle-income group households has to be improved so that financial institutions are in a position to supply the requisite funds. Development of Secondary Mortgage Market is important in this regard. Recognizing the role of securitization as a source of funding, initiatives for developing the secondary mortgage market have already been taken by the NHB. The government needs to also provide a conducive and supportive fiscal and regulatory framework for banks and other participants to actively engage in Residential Mortgage Backed Securitization transactions.

ROLE OF PRIVATE SECTOR AND FDI

11.98 The Eleventh Plan focuses on clearing the backlog in housing and infrastructure assets including up-gradation activities. Institutions such as National Real Estate Development Council (NARDCO) and the Confederation of Real Estate Developers Association of India are playing an important role in regulating the activities of private developers by accrediting them and also by rating such institutions based on their experience and capacities. The GoI has permitted 100% FDI for development of townships including construction of development projects, subject to minimum capitalization, minimum land/built up area, etc. However, to encourage larger inflow of FDI, there is need to minimize the procedural delays in sanctions and approval of projects.

ROLE OF CO-OPERATIVES

11.99 The co-operative housing movement has received support over consecutive Five Year Plans and a strong institutional framework is getting evolved within the co-operative movement. The performance of housing co-operatives is highly influenced by the quantum of funds available to them. During the first three years of the Tenth Five Year Plan, that is, 2002–03, 2003–04, and 2004–05, the Apex Co-operative Housing Federations could raise an amount of Rs 1774.43 crore from various funding agencies such as LIC, NHB, HUDCO, Commercial and Co-operative Bank, and other sources.

11.100 Community-linked Finance Facility (CLIFF) which is a financial mechanism that facilitates access to capital by organizations of the urban poor is now in its third year of operation in India. As of December 2004, CLIFF capital funds had supported 10 community-led development projects; eight housing developments, providing safe, secure, and affordable shelter with secure tenure for 2816 households; and two sanitation projects designed to benefit over 200000 families living in slums in Mumbai and Pune, both in the State of Maharashtra.

RENTAL HOUSING

11.101 One of the major constraints in the development of housing is the rent control legislation in many States. Rental housing in the urban areas needs to be promoted through enabling legislative and administrative measures to serve a wide cross-section of population in need of housing during their stay in cities. Model Rent Control Act needs to be advocated extensively by the States with suitable variations to suit the local requirements. The State Governments need to encourage public housing institutions, corporate bodies, educational institutions, and private sector agencies, through fiscal incentives and soft loans, to take up rental housing for specific groups under their coverage and focus.

HOUSING TECHNOLOGY

11.102 The BMTPC was established in 1980 with the objective of promoting cost-effective, environment-friendly, energy-efficient, and disaster-resistant technologies and building materials for sustainable habitat development. Around 39 technologies relating to innovative building materials have been developed and licensed to private entrepreneurs for commercial production. About 12 technologies are in various stages of development. A recently developed technology pertains to *bamboo mat corrugated sheets* for roofing and is a substitute for asbestos or iron corrugated sheets. Further, the Council has successfully completed 252 demonstration houses under Valmiki Ambedkar Awas Yojana (VAMBAY) at Bangalore using cost-effective technologies. The Council has also completed 100 demonstration houses at Dehradun (Uttarakhand) and 70 demonstration houses at Nagpur (Maharashtra) under VAMBAY. The construction of 270 demonstration houses at Bilaspur (Chhattisgarh), Trichy (Tamil Nadu), and Kodulu (Karnataka) are under progress.

11.103 The efforts made by BMTPC through an integrated approach involving simultaneous action for standardization, grading awareness, promotion through governmental recognition in terms of policy support and fiscal incentives have certainly enhanced acceptability and have demonstrated the efficacy of an integrated system of technology transfer. Use of alternative materials such as fly ash, bricks, blocks, and simple prefab systems for slabs/roofing needs to be further encouraged. Flexibility should be extended to building and construction material standards.

11.104 A major achievement of BMTPC has been the preparation of Vulnerability Atlas of India for formulating disaster mitigation plans and establishing techno-legal raging in disaster-prone areas. This Atlas has been revised in digitized format with latest data. As an extension of the Vulnerability Atlas, it has brought out the Landslide Hazard Zonation Atlas of India. BMTPC has also formulated guidelines for construction of safer and durable houses to withstand earthquake/cyclone. During the Eleventh Plan, BMTPC proposes to focus on up-scaling and modernization of home-grown production technologies, economy and efficiency in housing/building construction projects, use of bamboo in housing and building construction and vulnerability reduction, risk assessment, and disaster resistance construction. Besides, it will take steps for improving the design and layout of EWS/LIG houses. The total requirement of funds for BMTPC for this purpose is estimated at Rs 55.19 crore.

11.105 The Hindustan Prefab Limited (HPL) was set up as the Hindustan Housing Factory Limited in 1953 and was given the status of a PSU in 1955. The company was re-titled as HPL in 1978. The objective of HPL is to develop cost-effective prefabricated building components. HPL is currently in the process of restructuring and modernizing its operations vis-à-vis prefabricated building components. It is expected that the company will continue this focus in the Eleventh Plan, while at the same time, moving into the areas of on-site supervision, project management services, turnkey construction projects, preparation of DPRs of housing and infrastructure projects, project appraisal, and training in construction trades.

Policy Measures and Strategy for Addressing the Problems of Slums

11.106 JNNURM is the single largest initiative ever launched by the GoI to address the problems of urban housing, infrastructure, and basic services to the poor in 63 cities and towns in a holistic manner. JNNURM comprises two broad segments, namely (i) the Sub-Mission on Urban Infrastructure and Governance and (ii) the Sub-Mission on Basic Services to the Urban Poor (BSUP) covering 63 identified cities. The non-Mission cities and towns are covered under the UIDSSMT and Integrated Housing and Slum Development Programme (IHSDP). The MoHUPA is the nodal ministry for BSUP and IHSDP programmes which cater to housing and basic amenities to urban poor, especially slum dwellers. These schemes/programmes will, in addition to improved housing, also cater to other basic services such as sanitation, water supply, sewerage, solid waste disposal, etc.

11.107 Interest subsidy scheme for housing the urban poor has been proposed during the Eleventh Plan so as to provide an interest subsidy of 5% per annum, for a period of five years only, to commercial lenders for lending to EWS/LIG segments of the urban areas. Interest subsidy is expected to leverage markets funds to flow into housing for poor. The scheme is expected to add 15 lakh houses to the housing stock during the Eleventh Plan.

Integrated Low-cost Sanitation Scheme

11.108 The low-cost sanitation scheme operating during the Tenth Plan, with the objective of liberating manual scavengers from the obnoxious and age old practice of manual carrying of night soil, is in the process of being revised. The current scheme involves subsidy of 45% for the EWS beneficiaries and 25% for the LIG beneficiaries for construction of two-pit pour flush units up to the plinth level. The under revised scheme subsidy for the super structure beyond the plinth level is also provided. The upper ceiling cost will be Rs 10000 to enable construction of a complete unit of two-pit pour flush latrine with super structure. Suitable additionality in cost for constructing a two-pit pour flush latrine in hilly areas would be provided. In this manner, the ILCS will be more comprehensive, and is expected to complete the process of liberation from manual scavenging in the country.

URBAN PLANNING AND MANAGEMENT

11.109 The United Nations has projected that between 2000 and 2030, India's urban population will increase from 282 million to 590 million (assuming moderate 2.5% compound annual growth rate). Looking forward, one facet of India's urban planning challenge is to accommodate an additional 10 million urban dwellers per year, provide them with adequate public services and infrastructure, create opportunities for economic development, and ensure that urbanization is environmentally sustainable.

EMERGING ISSUES IN URBAN PLANNING AND MANAGEMENT

11.110 The 74th CAA 1992 is a historic piece of legislation that provides for a democratic and participatory planning process so as to incorporate the needs of the people, particularly poor and socially disadvantaged groups, in the planning process. The Act stipulates the setting up of District Planning Committees and MPCs for integration of spatial and economic development as well as rural and urban planning, while keeping the needs of environmental conservation in view.

11.111 State governments need to take concrete steps to constitute and functionalize the MPCs and District Planning Committees. In this regard, Urban Development and Plan Formulation and Implementation Guidelines brought out by the Ministry of Urban Development are relevant which have, in fact, duly incorporated the provisions of the 74th CAA.

THRUST AREAS OF THE ELEVENTH PLAN

11.112 In order to make the urban planning and development process sustainable, it would be appropriate to interlink the planning framework comprising national-level spatial strategies, regional-level strategy plans, metropolitan regional strategy plans, and city- and ward-level land use and development plans.

11.113 For an effective urban planning system, there is need to have inter-related plans at three levels, namely, perspective/structure plans (20–25 years), short-term integrated infrastructure development Plans (five years) co-terminus with the National Five Year Plans, and plans of specific projects and schemes.

11.114 The national spatial strategy should incorporate policies for industrial location and development, employment generation, human settlement pattern, and structure and infrastructure development, both for rural and urban areas. The State spatial plans should be prepared by taking into account demographic and economic potentials, broad land use configurations, infrastructure requirements, and project implementation schedules including mechanism for the PPPs.

11.115 Each district should prepare a District Development Plan that integrates the plans for its constituent urban and rural areas as well as the sectoral allocations for various schemes under the purview of existing district agencies.

11.116 The Metropolitan Development Plan should be prepared on the basis of plans prepared by Municipalities and Panchayats under the metropolitan area and in the context of overall objectives and priorities set by the Central and State Governments.

11.117 The legal and institutional framework should provide the municipalities with adequate infrastructure and manpower to undertake the preparation of these plans. Further, the process of preparation of development plans should be facilitated by developing urban and regional information system and providing access to remotely sensed data, aerial photographs, GIS, setting up MIS cells to build database at national and State level, etc. Evolving suitable mechanism for strong database for all cities/towns with regard to coverage of urban population with water supply, sewerage, drainage, and solid waste management facilities is most essential in the wake of the large number of infrastructure projects that are being considered by different States.

Public Health Engineering (PHE) Training Programme

11.118 The scope of PHE training programme needs to be widened so as to provide requisite training for increasing the skills and expertise of all personnel involved in the water supply and sanitation sector. The infrastructure being developed by various ULBs/State departments for drinking water supply, sewerage, sanitation, drainage, sewage waste management under JNNURM would require more qualified and trained manpower for better planning, designing, implementation, and O&M of water supply and sanitation schemes.

Role and Involvement of External Support Agencies

11.119 Technical and financial assistance from external support agencies such as WHO, UNDP, World Bank, ADB, and bilateral agencies needs to be explored on a case to case basis. It is also essential that the external donor agencies cut short their processing/decision-making time to less than a year, so that projects planned under JNNURM are able to get financial and technical support of the external donor agency without hampering the progress of project implementation.

Linking of Budget Provisions of Ministry of Urban Development and Ministry of DoNER meant for North Eastern States and Sikkim with JNNURM

11.120 The 10% lump sum pool of resources of Ministry of Urban Development and Non-Lapsable Central Pool of Resources (NLCPR) under Ministry of DoNER meant for North Eastern States and Sikkim provide funding for creation of urban infrastructure including water supply, sewerage, drainage, and solid waste management on the same pattern of funding as that of JNNURM, that is 90:10 basis. These programmes need to be integrated with JNNURM to avoid duplicity in projects by different ministries and adherence to projects based on City Development Plans.

Role of IT in Efficient Governance and in Provision and Management of Urban Services

11.121 With the use of modern technology there have been perceptible changes in urban governance. The advent of digital technology coupled with the availability of various modes of fast communication such as Internet, intranet, cellular phones, and menu-based software has revolutionized the concept of governance. There has also been a change in the outlook of administrators and policy makers in adopting latest technology, and go for paperless work and make governance more citizen-friendly. E-governance encompasses the strategic and systematic use of modern ICT by the government to improve the efficiency, transparency, and accountability in its functioning and interface with citizens.

MUNICIPAL GOVERNANCE AND REFORMS

The Constitution (Seventy-fourth Amendment) Act (CAA)

11.122 The Act has ensured decentralization and successfully created a set up of democratic institutions of self-government. However, despite 15 years of enactment, most of the States are yet to implement its several provisions. While the CAA envisions decentralization of functions, finances, and functionaries to enable the ULBs to function as 'institutions of self-government', in reality, fiscal and administrative decentralization have lagged behind political decentralization. The amended Municipal Acts do not specifically assign functions and financial powers to the ULBs, including town planning. To achieve the twin objectives of ambitious growth paired with inclusive growth, the country needs to functionalize the institutional framework that fosters livable, bankable, and competitive cities.

Involvement of Community and Elected Representatives in Decision-making and Implementation

11.123 The CAA has empowered elected representatives and the community leaders with decision-making powers through institutional frameworks such as Ward Committees, MPCs, and District Planning Committees. Now from a 'top-down' approach, the emphasis has thus shifted to the 'bottom-up' approach.

Skill Upgradation and Capacity Building of the ULBs

11.124 Lack of skilled manpower to undertake various additional tasks entrusted to the ULBs is a cause of concern. Many of the ULBs have only one or two engineers for preparing projects and almost no town planner for preparing City Development Plan and Project Reports. During the Eleventh Plan, emphasis would be laid on the capacity building of the functionaries of the ULBs. There is a need to set up an apex agency to co-ordinate the activities of all national- and State-level training institutions. The Administrative Reforms Commission has proposed the creation of three to five year 'urban governance capacity building programmes' to be initiated by the Central and State Governments. Deficiencies of the ULBs need to be addressed through various capacity building program-mes under JNNURM and other CSS.

Independent Regulatory Institutions

11.125 An independent regulatory institution with professional urban managers is needed at the State level to ensure that the ULBs operate with autonomy but within the framework decided by the independent regulatory institution. It can decide parameters such as framing minimum and maximum limits for various types of local taxes, fees, user charges, administrative expenditure, etc. Setting up the regulatory institution can go a long way in improving the performance of local bodies in delivery of civic services to people.

Preparation of Operating Manual for ULBs

11.126 The independent regulatory institution for the ULBs can be entrusted with the responsibility of preparing operating manuals relating to various services being provided by the ULBs. The operating manuals can definitely improve the quality of assets that are being created by the ULBs. To ensure quality control and uniformity, the manual may lay down standards for all materials that are used for creation of assets. Operating manuals need not only be for engineering aspects but can cover the whole gamut of services in which the ULBs are involved.

Municipal Finance

11.127 Municipalities have neither the responsibility nor the autonomy of fiscal powers for delivering the urban services expected from them. There is a mismatch between ULB revenue capacities and their financial requirement.

11.128 The Ministries of Urban Development and Housing and Urban Poverty Alleviation have estimated a huge resource gap of Rs 76896 crore for all States during the period 2005–10 for O&M of various civic services in urban areas (Twelfth Finance Commission, TFC report). To fill this huge gap, our strategy revolves around stricter guidelines, policy prescriptions, and stress on local revenue enhancement efforts by the ULBs. It will certainly achieve financial viability at the ULB level. Further, ULBs need to take steps for broad-basing the revenue from own sources through improving the collection of existing revenue sources, reforms in property tax, levy of new taxes and charges, enhanced cost recovery for utility charges and fees, improved information, registration, billing and collection systems of taxes and charges, reducing administrative expenses, etc. Innovative methods of service delivery and involvement of private sector will improve the financial position of municipalities.

Evolve Alternative Ways to Augment Municipal Resources

11.129 The following steps need to be initiated for augmenting revenue generation by the ULBs:

Land as a Resource

- Land is a good resource to generate revenue for the local bodies and should be explored by the ULBs to the extent possible.

New Levies

- New levies/cess should be levied to augment revenue resources such as drainage fee, parking fee, hoarding fees, vacant land tax, development impact fee, etc.

Pooled Financing

- New thrusts for mobilizing urban infrastructure finance, a State-level Pooled Financing Mechanism is working successfully in Tamil Nadu, with the financial assistance from the United States Agency for International Development (USAID). The Central Government has set up a PFDF with the objective to facilitate development of bankable urban infrastructure projects through appropriate capacity building measures and financial structuring. An amount of Rs 100 crore has been provided to the Ministry of Urban Development for 2007–08 for PFDF.

Secondary Markets

- The ULBs will have to be made credible and accountable institutions so as to tap India's increasingly sophisticated financial markets including secondary markets.

Accessing Capital Markets

- To ensure sound local government credit markets, the government will have to evolve effective financial institutions and instruments for financial market regulations and supervision. The ULBs' credit worthiness would be enhanced on a stand-alone basis so that the supply of bankable projects could be increased.

ROLE OF FINANCIAL INTERMEDIATION FOR LOCAL GOVERNMENTS

Municipal Development Funds

11.130 Around the world, more than 60 countries have established financial intermediaries. For example, in Brazil, individual States often have established their own municipal development funds. Both the World Bank and the ADB have announced that they intend to rely more heavily on municipal development funds as a key part of their strategy to help finance local investment needs in Asia. The goal is not merely to give municipalities access to credit, but to do so in a manner that increases the efficiency of local investment and reinforce financial sector reforms in the rest of the economy.

Municipal Bond Markets

11.131 The advantages of using municipal bonds to finance urban infrastructure are increasingly evident in India. The Indian Bond Market is becoming vibrant. Ahmedabad Municipal Corporation issued a first historical Municipal Bond in Asia to raise Rs 100 crore from the capital market for part financing a water supply project. An illustrative list of ULBs/parastatals, which have been granted permission to issue Municipal Bonds, is given Table 11.8.

TABLE 11.8

Urban Local Bodies/Parastatals which have been Granted Permission for Issue of Tax-Free Bonds

S. No.	Name	Year	Amount (Rs in Crore)
1.	Ahmedabad Municipal Corporation	2001	100.00
2.	Hyderabad Municipal Corporation	2002	82.50
3.	Nasik Municipal Corporation	2003	50.00
4.	Visakhapatnam Municipal Corporation	2003	50.00
5.	Hyderabad Metropolitan Water Supply and Sewerage Board	2003	50.00
6.	Ahmedabad Municipal Corporation	2004	58.00
7.	Chennai Metropolitan Water Supply and Sewerage Board	2004	42.00
8.	Karnataka Water and Sanitation Pooled Fund Trust	2004	100.00
9.	Chennai Metropolitan Water Supply and Sewerage Board	2005	50.00
10.	Chennai Corporation	2005	44.80
11.	Ahmedabad Municipal Corporation	2005	100.00

Source: Ministry of Urban Development, GoI.

Budgetary Support

11.132 The TFC has recommended a sum of Rs 5000 crore for the municipalities to be provided as grants-in-aid to augment the consolidated fund of the States for the years 2005–10 to be distributed with inter se shares.

Cost Efficiency and Productive Use of Resources

11.133 Projects being carried out by contractors have to be carefully supervised to ensure quality and timely completion. Cost over-runs in projects due to delay caused by contractors need to be penalized by incorporating the penalty clause in the contract itself.

Thrust of the Eleventh Five Year Plan towards Municipal Finances

11.134 India's urban areas will need to compete nationally and internationally for investments and human resources. Most of the ULBs are technically and financially ill-equipped to meet the ever-growing demand for urban services, so the capacity building exercises have to be accorded priority. The Eleventh Plan strategy would be to create a conducive environment for efficient tax administration, increasing use of non-tax sources, efficient pricing of services, PPPs in provision and maintenance of urban services, adopting alternative sources of finance including access to capital markets, involvement of community and private sector in raising revenue. The States need to ensure rating of municipalities for facilitating access to capital markets.

URBAN TRANSPORT

Urbanization Trends and Travel Needs

11.135 Urbanization has lead to corresponding increase in demand for transportation. The growth in transport infrastructure has not kept pace with the increased demand and the share of public transport vehicles has declined. The problem of congestion and its consequences are posing a severe threat to sustainability of the urban areas. Confederation of Indian Industry (CII) survey 2003 of the urban population in southern India showed that 58% of those interviewed were dissatisfied with public transport services. It also showed that 65% were willing to pay higher public transport fares for comfortable travel. The situation in other parts of the country is similar.

11.136 Managing urban expansion is a critical element towards achieving the goals set by the National Urban Transport Policy. The National Urban Transport Policy, 2006 focuses on the need to 'Move people—Not vehicles', by encouraging public transport and use of non-motorized modes. The policy suggests involvement of private sector, innovative financing mechanisms to enhance efficiency, reduction in travel demand by encouraging a better integration of and use and transport planning.

11.137 As per 2001 Census, there are 35 cities with million plus population. Except for Mumbai, Kolkata, and Delhi, none of the mega cities have a Mass Rapid Transit System (MRTS). The Delhi Metro Project is progressing as per schedule and Phase-I is fully operational. Other metropolitan cities are also in the process of preparing DPRs for a metro-rail system.

Suggestions for Urban Transport Planning for the Eleventh Plan Period

- All cities need to prepare a comprehensive mobility plan which includes a Master Plan for non-motorized transport taking into account projected growth in the next ten years.
- Proposals for preparation of DPR should be preceded by professional evaluation by technology neutral agencies.
- A comprehensive program of capacity building should be implemented.
- All cities should formulate a realistic 'hawker/vendor policy'.
- Cities may prepare a plan for traffic calming to reduce emissions and road accident rates.
- All million plus cities may prepare plans to introduce/upgrade existing bus services as also introduce BRT systems on selected arterials during the Eleventh Plan period.
- All cities may have a parking policy. State governments need to amend building by-laws so that adequate parking space is made available for all residents/users. FAR norms may be modified. Multi-level parking complexes may be made mandatory in mega cities. All cities may upgrade taxi and three-wheeler fleets.

Specific Interventions Required for Enhancing Mobility Needs in Towns

- Improvement in the quality and maintenance of roads and provision of pedestrian pavements and cycle tracks.
- De-congestion of crowded areas.
- Developing transport corridors to enable orderly flow of public transport.
- Creation of parking spaces for para-transit and other vehicles.
- Facilities for public bus services, pedestrian subways, and larger parking facilities.
- Mobility needs of 40 lakh plus population cities would generally need mass transit systems with medium to high capacity with a larger network of feeder systems.

Actions Required for the Development of Integrated City Transport as per NUTP

Land-use interventions

- Encourage 'Transit Oriented Development' with high density areas.
- Either develop all new/satellite townships/SEZ along the defined major transport corridors or integrate them with mass transit system in the Master Plan itself.
- Allow land use changes from time to time, including for public/government use.
- Discourage sprawl through introduction of vacant land tax and levy of 'Transport Impact Fee' on developments in the periphery.

Transportation Interventions

- Promote non-motorized vehicles by creating facilities for safe use.
- Promote public transit systems that are cost effective and able to meet the demand levels optimally. Encourage investments in premium bus systems.
- Develop ring roads and city bypass roads as well as rail line bypasses.
- Develop freight transport terminals outside city limits.
- Shift inter-state bus terminals from the city centre to the peripheries.

Institutional/Regulatory Interventions

- Modify the enabling legislations.
- Establish fare policies and a fare regulator.
- Implement fiscal measures that encourage use of public transport.

Scheme for Preparation of DPRs and Conduct of Traffic and Transportation Studies

11.138 Under this scheme, support is provided by the government for the preparation of DPRs and in the conduct of comprehensive traffic and transportation studies to the extent of 40% of the cost. Although the scheme has resulted in many such studies being carried out, yet these have not subsequently translated into a meaningful set of projects. Table 11.9 below shows that the outlays and expenditure under the scheme have not been satisfactory during the Ninth and Tenth Plan periods. In line with the National Urban Transport Policy, the scheme is being revised to raise the GoI grant.

11.139 A Task Force has been set up to suggest institutional mechanism for better coordination in policy formulation, planning, and regulation of traffic and transportation project in all million plus cities.

Integration of Land Use and Transport Planning

11.140 Corridor development may be encouraged for inter-city movement of goods and services while deliberate attempt may be made to discourage

TABLE 11.9
Outlay and Expenditure

(Rs in Crore)

Item	Ninth Plan		Tenth Plan	
	Outlay	Expenditure	Outlay	Expenditure
Urban transport planning	24.76	3.33	91.00	12.59

Source: Ministry of Urban Development, GoI.

ribbon development, multi-modal corridors, and SEZs in close proximity to city areas need to be developed.

Pedestrianization and Non-motorized Transport (NMT)

11.141 Special consideration needs to be given to designing pedestrian and cyclist facilities along the road and at intersections and the needs of the physically challenged persons need to be taken care of. The entire road network including footpaths, road crossings, service roads, carriageways, medians, bus stops, terminals, mass transit stations, parking facilities, etc. may be considered as per disabled-friendly design principles.

Integration of Transport System

11.142 The benefits of common ticketing to the operators are reduced transactions and lower recurring costs. Despite these advantages, the system of common ticketing has not picked up in India. A necessary condition for common ticketing across operators is the creation of a mechanism that allows a fair share of the revenues earned from such common tickets. If there is only a single service provider, sharing of revenue will not be a problem while with multiple providers this is a complex task. Indore model of public transport could be replicated in other cities.

Appropriate/Cleaner Technologies for Public Transport

11.143 Vehicular emission is directly related to the fuel used, the technology employed, and the driving technique. Improvement in fuel quality can be achieved through removal/reduction of emission related constituents in the fuels such as sulphur in diesel and sulphur, lead, benzene, and other aromatics in petrol. Further reduction of emissions can be obtained through improved engine technology and exhaust treatment systems. Vehicles manufactured before First Mass Emission Norms introduced in 1991 would require to be replaced.

Role of Intelligent Transport Systems

11.144 ITS encompasses a broad range of wireless and wire line communications-based information and electronics technologies. When integrated into the transportation system's infrastructure, these technologies relieve congestion, improve safety, and enhance productivity. Applied effectively, ITS and Services can save lives, time, and money as well as reduce threats to our environment and create new business opportunities.

11.145 A large investment of Rs 38000 crore has been identified for the introduction of modern buses in the country during the Eleventh Plan. The government aims to replace all the existing urban buses with 'truck chassis body' with low floor/semi low floor ultra modern buses on PPP basis. Table 11.10 provides the financial requirement during the Eleventh Plan.

11.146 The financial requirement to cater to the growing demand in the Eleventh Plan would be Rs 132590 crore as summarized in Table 11.11.

Box 11.14
Best Practices in Public Transport

1. Indore Model

   Indore city in Madhya Pradesh has evolved a PPP model for operation of city bus services. In this model, the investment on the rolling stock is planned through private participation. The source of revenue for the private operator is from fare collection and from advertisements.
2. Revival of public transport in Bangalore

   Bangalore Metropolitan Transport Corporation (BMTC) was created in 1997 by separating Bangalore depots of the troubled Karnataka Road Transport Corporation from the mother company. It carried out a thorough internal restructuring, introduced cost and service monitoring, and sub-contracted some services to private operators on a gross-cost based scheme. In the span of two to three years, BMTC improved its services and fleet/staff productivity, and became profit making.

TABLE 11.10
Funds Requirement

Cities (Population in Lakh)	Total No. of Towns	% of Towns Proposed for Eleventh Plan	Average Requirement	Rs in Crore
1–5	370	50	40	7400
5–10	39	50	400	7800
10–40	28	100	930	26040
> 40	7	100	3000	21000
MRTS	8	100		32000
Modern buses				38000
Capacity building and transport planning				350
Total				132590

Source: Ministry of Urban Development, GoI.

TABLE 11.11
Sources of Funding

Source	Funding (in Rs crore)
*JNNURM (GoI) including UIDSSMT	15500
*Non-JNNURM (Budgetary Support)	4400
VGF	6000
Resourced from States/ULBs	19500
Loan from financial institutions	61190
Participation by private promoters	26000
Total	132590

Note: * The actual allocation provided for JNNURM is Rs 50000 crore during 2005–12 out of which the amount available for urban transport is expected to be in the range of Rs 10000 crore. As regards non-JNNURM, budgetary support is Rs 3055 crore. The shortfall will need to be met by other sources of finance.

Source: Ministry of Urban Development, GoI.

TABLE 11.12
Slum Population—Census 2001

Slum population 1991 (TCPO estimates)	46.26 million
Slum population 2001 (TCPO estimates)	61.82 million
No. of towns reporting slums in Census 2001	640#
Reported slum population in 640 towns, 2001	42.58 million
Population of towns/cities reporting slums, 2001	184.35 million
Share of slum population to population of towns/cities reporting slums, 2001	23.1%

Note: # Towns with population of 50000 or more.

11.147 The total outlay for the Eleventh Plan for Ministry of Urban Development is Rs 24600 crore at 2006–07 price (Rs 26041 crore at current price) which includes Rs 11001 crore of GBS at 2006–07 price (Rs 12443 crore at current price). Likewise, the total outlay for the Eleventh Plan for Ministry of Housing and Urban Poverty Alleviation is Rs 43480 crore at 2006–07 price (Rs 50958 crore at current price) which includes Rs 3260 crore of GBS at 2006–07 price (Rs 3687 crore at current price).

TABLE 11.13
Population, Housing and Basic Amenities

Total population of India, 2001	1028.6 million
Urban population, 2001	286.1 million
% share urban, 2001	27.8%
Total urban housing stock, 2001	52.0 million
Pucca houses	79.16%
Semi-pucca houses	15.58%
Kutcha houses	5.27%
Household with Tenure Status, Urban, 2001	
Owned	66.8%
Rented	28.5%
Others	4.7%
Households having Access to, Urban, 2001	
Safe drinking water	90.01%
Electricity	87.59%
Toilet	73.72%
Drainage	77.86%
Kitchen within the house	75.96%
LPG for cooking	47.96%
Electricity for cooking	0.31%
Biogas for cooking	0.37%

Source: MoHUPA, GoI.

12

Communications and Information Technology

12.1 TELECOMMUNICATIONS

OVERVIEW

12.1.1 The development of world-class telecommunication infrastructure is the key to rapid economic and social development of the country. Driven by various policy initiatives, which include New Telecom Policy (NTP)-1994 and later the NTP-1999, the Indian telecom sector witnessed a complete transformation in the last decade. During this period, it has achieved phenomenal growth and is poised to take a quantum leap. For bringing further accelerated growth along with modernization in line with the trends in other developed countries, the telecommunication sector demands initiation of further policy measures and induction of state-of-the-art technologies.

PRESENT STATUS OF TELECOM NETWORKS

12.1.2 The telecom services network has expanded from about 84000 connections (fixed line) at the time of independence to about 206.83 million working connections as on March 2007 (which in turn consists of 40.77 million fixed telephone lines and 166.05 million mobile phones). Thus India's present 206 million robust telephone network, including mobile phones, is one of the largest in the world and second largest among the emerging economies (after China) with a wide range of services such as basic, cellular, Internet, paging, Very Small Aperture Terminal (VSAT), etc. The status of the present telecom network is as shown in Table 12.1.1.

12.1.3 The National Internet Exchange of India has been set up by the Department of Information Technology (DIT) to ensure that Internet traffic, originating and destined for India, is routed within India. This is expected to substantially bring down the cost of Internet usage. This will also enable more efficient use of international bandwidth and saving of foreign exchange. It will further improve the quality of services for the customers by being able to avoid multiple international hops and thus lowering delays. All these in turn will lead to the popularization of '.in' domain name and expansion of Internet.

TABLE 12.1.1
Telecom Network Status in India as on March 2007

Number of telephone connections	206.83 million
Number of telephone exchanges	38338
Switching capacity (Public)	88.82 million (PSU)
VPTs	564610
Rural phones (Fixed + CDMA)	22655691
Wireless (CDMA & GSM) subscribers	166.05 million
Internet connections	9.21 million
Broadband subscribers	2.28 million
Optical fibre route length (Public)	519155 route km
Microwave route length (BSNL)	64506.64 km

Source: DoT.

12.1.4 The government has taken several steps to encourage participation of private players to create a competitive environment in the sector. Consequently, the private sector is now playing an important role in expansion of the telecom sector. The number of private sector licensees in telecommunications as shown in Table 12.1.2 also confirms this.

TELECOM DEVELOPMENT—INTERNATIONAL COMPARISON

12.1.5 Telecommunication has grown very rapidly in India. However, viewed in the context of global growth pattern and indicators, it needs to achieve more in terms of teledensity as compared to other countries. There is a positive corelation between the teledensity and the GDP of a country as the growth in the telecommunication sector has linkages to the growth of other sectors of the economy. The status of teledensity along with other indicators such as per capita GDP, Internet users, etc., at international level is given in the Table 12.1.3.

TABLE 12.1.2
Private Sector Participation (as on 31 March 2006)
(Registrations/Licenses Issues)

Purpose/Area	No. of Licenses/ LOIs/Registration
Unified Access/Cellular Mobiles	78
Basic Services	2
National Long Distance	4
Infrastructure Provider-I	105
International Long Distance	5
Internet Service	399
Voice Mail and Audiotext Service	15
Public Mobile Radio Trunk Service	37
VSAT Service	11

Source: Working Group Report for Eleventh Plan on Telecommunications Sector, DoT.

REVIEW OF THE TENTH PLAN

Growth during the Tenth Plan Period

12.1.6 The telecom sector has shown tremendous growth during the Tenth Plan period. It has also undergone a substantial change in terms of mobile versus fixed phones and public versus private participation. The Tenth Plan had envisaged a teledensity of 9.91% by March 2007. In order to achieve this target, about 65.0 million additional connections were needed to be provided during the Tenth Plan. However, during 2002–07, the total telephone connections increased by 161.86 million as on 31 March 2007, thereby achieving a teledensity of 18.31% by March 2007 and exceeding the Tenth Plan target by 149%. With the opening of the telecom sector to the private operators, their share in the number of subscribers has significantly increased, which is evident from the Table 12.1.4.

TABLE 12.1.3
Status of Telecom Indicators in Some Countries as on December 2005

Country	Population (Million)	GDP (per capita) US$ 2004	Telephones ('000)	Teledensity (%)	Internet Users ('000)
US	298.21	36273	360347	122.71	185000
UK	59.67	26369	94791	158.51	37600
Australia	20.16	25436	29880	148.25	14190
Brazil	186.41	3338	107987	59.78	22000
Mexico	107.03	6328	66974	62.58	18622
Sri Lanka	20.74	1031	4606	22.20	280
Korea (Rep)	48.29	14136	62087	128.56	33010
Japan	128.08	31324	153525	119.86	64160
Indonesia	222.87	1156	59682	26.79	16000
China	1315.84	1268	743861	56.53	111000
Pakistan	153.96	614	18049	11.72	10500
India#	111.59	634	142092	12.74	60000
World	6728.08	5944	3309379	49.45	964272

Note: #As on 31 March 2006.
Source: International Telecommunication Union.

TABLE 12.1.4
Expansion of Telecom Network—Public and Private Operators and Fixed and Mobile (PSUs and Private Operators) during the Tenth Plan Period (2002–07)

Year Ending 31 March	Public (in million)	Private (in million)	Fixed Lines (in million)	Wireless (in million)	Total Phones	Teledensity (%)			Rural Phones (in million)	Urban Phones (in million)
						Rural	Urban	Total		
2002	38.17	6.80	38.29	6.68	44.97	1.21	12.20	4.29	9.04	35.96
2003	43.18	11.45	41.33	13.30	54.63	1.49	14.32	5.11	11.41	43.22
2004	46.48	30.05	40.92	35.61	76.53	1.57	20.74	7.02	12.27	64.26
2005	52.08	46.29	41.42	56.95	98.37	1.73	26.88	8.95	13.57	84.80
2006	61.07	81.00	40.22	101.85	142.07	1.86	39.45	12.74	14.77	127.30
2007	71.39	135.44	40.78	166.05	206.83	2.83	55.94	18.31	22.66	184.17

Source: DoT.

Recognizing that the telecom sector is one of the prime movers of the economy, the regulatory and policy initiatives taken by the government during the Tenth Plan have been directed towards establishing a world-class telecommunications infrastructure in the country. This has led to a positive result in the sector and major objectives envisaged in the Tenth Plan were achieved to a great extent. Affordable and effective communication services could be offered as the tariff declined substantially due to intense competition among the operators.

12.1.7 During the Tenth Plan period, the Internet subscribers grew from 3.64 million in 2002–03 to 9.21 million in 2006–07. The broadband subscribers base stood at only 2.28 million connections (2006–07) from 1.8 lakh connections in 2004–05. One of the factors for such a low broadband subscriber base could be the pricing structure.

12.1.8 The number of telephones has increased from 44.97 million as on 31 March 2002 to 206.83 million as on 31 March 2007, exhibiting a CAGR of around 35.68%. The number of mobile phone/wireless subscribers increased from 6.68 million as on 31 March 2002 to 166.05 million as on 31 March 2007, exhibiting a CAGR of 90.15%. The number of Internet subscribers grew at 23%, while the broadband subscribers grew from a meager 0.18 million during the year 2004–05 to 2.28 million during the year 2006–07.

MOBILE VERSUS FIXED TELEPHONES

12.1.9 The preference for use of wireless phones has also been predominant in the sector. This is confirmed from the rising share of wireless phones, which increased from 14.85% (6.68 million telephones) in March 2002 to 80.28% (166.05 million telephones) in March 2007.

TREND IN TELEDENSITY

12.1.10 Teledensity in the country is steadily increasing from 4.29% as on 31 March 2002 to 18.31% as on 31 March 2007. However, there is a wide gap between urban teledensity (55.94%) and rural teledensity (2.83%). In fact, the rural telephony has not kept pace with the impressive growth in the urban connectivity.

RURAL TELEPHONY

12.1.11 Apart from the 14.77 million fixed and wireless in local loop (WLL) connections provided in the rural areas, 564610 VPTs have also been provided. Thus, 90% of the villages in India have been covered by the VPTs. In addition, more than 2 lakh public call offices (PCOs) are also providing community access in the rural areas. Mobile Gramin Sanchar Sewak Scheme—a mobile PCO service—is also being provided at the doorstep of villagers. At present, 2772 GSSs are covering 12043 villages. Further, in order to provide Internet services, *Sanchar Dhabas* (Internet kiosks) have been provided in more than 3500 block headquarters out of the total 6337 blocks in the country.

12.1.12 The telecom network in the rural areas also expanded during the Tenth Plan (2002–07). The number of phones in the rural area has increased from 9.01 million in March 2002 to 22.66 million by March 2007. The rural teledensity increased from 1.21% in

March 2002 to 2.83% in March 2007. The bulk of the investment in rural telecom has been made by the public sector operator, viz., BSNL. The private operators have provided only 12665 VPTs by the end of March 2006.

REDUCTION IN TARIFF CHANGES

12.1.13 The Indian telecommunication sector has witnessed major changes in the tariff structure. The Telecommunication Tariff Order 1999, issued by Telecom Regulatory Authority of India (TRAI), started the process of tariff rebalancing with a view to bringing them closer to the costs. Further, increased competition in the telecom sector has also resulted in a substantial fall in the tariffs.

PERFORMANCE OF TELECOM EQUIPMENT MANUFACTURING SECTOR

12.1.14 Steady growth has been observed in the telecom equipment manufacturing sector during the Tenth Five Year Plan period, as may be seen from Table 12.1.5.

TABLE 12.1.5
Performance of Telecom Equipment Manufacturing Sector during Tenth Plan

(Rs Crore)

Year	Production	Export
2002–03	14400	402
2003–04	14000	250
2004–05	16090	400
2005–06	17833	1500

Source: Working Group Report for Eleventh Plan on Telecommunications sector, DoT.

12.1.15 Some of the major policy initiatives introduced in the telecom sector during the Tenth Plan period for giving a boost to the sector are as follows:

- National long distance (NLD) service was opened to operators w.e.f. 13 August 2002.
- National Frequency Allocation Policy 2002 was evolved.
- The monopoly of Videsh Sanchar Nigam Limited (VSNL) in International long distance (ILD) terminated on 31 March 2002.
- National Internet Backbone covering all States has been commissioned.
- Instruction issued to all State Governments to provide expeditious approval for right of way.
- Guidelines for Unified Access Service License regime were issued on 11 November 2003.
- Calling Party Pays (CPP) regime was implemented w.e.f. 1 May 2003, under which landline telephone users were to pay airtime charges apart from normal charges if the call was made to a cellular phone.
- Indian Telegraph Act was amended for establishment of USOF. Non-lapsable USOF was created on April 2002.
- Interconnection Usage Charge regime was introduced.
- Several directives/regulations have been issued by TRAI regarding different telecom services, their tariffs, quality and Internet services, which have contributed positively towards the growth of telecommunication sector.
- Internet Service Providers (ISPs) allowed setting up submarine cable landing stations for international gateways for Internet.
- Radio frequency (RF) spectrum management has been modernized and automated to efficiently address dynamic needs of the liberalized user.
- Broadband policy was announced on 14 October 2004.
- ISPs have been permitted to use underground copper cables for establishing last mile linkages.
- FDI ceiling has been raised to 74% for various telecom services.
- The operation of automated spectrum management was commenced in January 2005.
- Access service provider can provide Internet telephony, Internet services, and broadband services. They can use the network of NLD/ILD service.
- Prior experience in telecom sector is no more a pre-requisite for grant of telecom service licenses.
- Annual license fee for NLD, ILD, Infrastructure Providers, VSAT Commercial, and ISP has been reduced to 6% of Adjusted Gross Revenue (AGR) with effect from 1 January 2006.
- Internet Protocol based Virtual Private Network service is permitted to ISPs.
- Delicensing has been done of 2.40–2.4835 GHz frequency band for indoor and outdoor use and 5.15–5.13 GHZ frequency band for indoor use.

12.1.16 In addition to the above, certain exemptions/concessions have been given on the customs duty for important equipments as well as components, besides excise duty exemptions for benefit under indirect taxes.

Investments during the Tenth Plan

12.1.17 During this period, the public sector operators, viz., BSNL and MTNL, as well as the private operators made major investments in cellular mobile segment. While PSUs account for 71.39 million connections (both fixed and mobile) as on March 2007, the private operators account for 135.44 million lines. More than 97% of the private sector lines are in the wireless category. The total estimated investments by the public sector operators during the Tenth Plan were Rs 39467.21 crore.

BROAD OBJECTIVES AND THRUST AREAS IN TELECOM SECTOR DURING THE ELEVENTH PLAN

12.1.18 Keeping in view the targets for the telecom sector, the Eleventh Plan has been formulated accordingly. Basically, the approach will be towards achieving faster, broader, and inclusive growth. Further, keeping in view the digital divide, special attention will be paid to enhance the rural connectivity. The broad objectives for the telecom sector during the Eleventh Plan period (2007–12) will be as follows:

- To reach a telecom subscriber base of 600 million.
- To provide 200 million rural telephone connections by 2012, that is to reach a rural teledensity of 25%.
- To provide telephone connection on demand across the country at an affordable price.
- To reach a target of 20 million broadband connections and 40 million Internet connections by 2010 as envisaged in Broadband Policy 2004.
- To provide broadband connection on demand across the country by 2012.
- To provide Third Generation (3G) services in all cities/towns with more than 1 lakh population.
- To facilitate introduction of mobile TV.
- To provide broadband connectivity to every secondary school (SS), health centre, GP on demand in two years.
- To make India a hub for telecom equipment manufacturing by facilitating establishment of telecom specific SEZs.

12.1.19 Establishing centres of excellence in premier educational institutions and other reputed organizations in the country in PPP mode. The centres can focus on emerging areas such as Next Generation Networks (NGN), Wireless Broadband, Telecom Network Security, etc. Special intervention is required to connect rural areas for providing voice and data connectivity.

Targets in Telecom Sector during the Eleventh Five Year Plan

12.1.20 In consonance with the above objectives, the broad targets identified by the DoT for the Eleventh Plan period are given in the following paragraphs.

12.1.21 Network Expansion and Rural Telephony

- One telephone per three rural households by 2007 (about 50 million rural connections).
- One phone per two rural households by 2010 (about 100 million rural connections).
- 200 million rural connections by 2012 (i.e. a rural teledensity of 25%).
- For rural telephony network expansion the strategies will be to provide individual access: (i) through market forces for viable areas and (ii) USOF for non-viable areas.
- For providing public access in rural areas, USOF will be provided for (i) VPTs; and (ii) Rural Community Phones (RCPs).
- For rural telephony the infrastructure will be shared at least amongst three service providers.
- To support for development of general telecom infrastructure in rural areas, initially pilot projects would be undertaken for the same.

12.1.22 Broadband Coverage

- Broadband coverage for all secondary and higher secondary schools is stipulated by 2007.
- Broadband coverage for all public health care centres is stipulated by 2007.
- Broadband coverage for all GPs is stipulated by 2010.
- Linkage is to be provided between block headquarters and nearest exchange for completing State-wide area networks (SWANs) connectivity.

- Existing infrastructure of rural exchanges and OFC will be used.
- Wireless technology will be deployed.

12.1.23 Manufacturing and R&D

- Making India a hub for telecom manufacturing by facilitating more and more telecom specific SEZs.
- Providing platform for export promotion of telephone equipment and services by setting up Export Promotion Council.
- Promoting R&D in key and emerging technologies appropriate for the country as well as in the area of telecom network security.

12.1.24 The DoT has proposed to take up the following programmes/initiatives during the Eleventh Five Year Plan period:

- Identify and make available adequate spectrum for both expansion of network and introduction of new value-added services.
- Setting up of Telecom Testing and Security Certification Centre (TETC).
- Setting up of Centre for Communication Security Research and Monitoring.
- Setting up of NGN Laboratory.
- Undersea cabling between Mainland and Andaman & Nicobar (A&N) Islands.
- Modernization of Radio Spectrum Monitoring Capabilities.
- Promote induction of new technologies at Indian Telephone Industries.
- Setting up of Telecom Export Promotion Forum/ Council for promotion of export of telecom services.

Projection of Investment in Telecom Sector for the Eleventh Plan

12.1.25 The public sector investment in the telecommunication sector (through BSNL and MTNL) would be mainly funded through IEBR to the tune of Rs 80753.00 crore at 2006–07 price and Rs 89581.56 crore at current price (including Rs 337.47 crore by C-DOT as internal resources) over the Eleventh Plan period. It is assumed that the private investment in this sector will also grow substantially. The total investment in the telecommunication sector during the Eleventh Plan period is projected at about Rs 231000 crore.

Key Constraints and Challenges

12.1.26 Some of the major constraints and challenges being faced by the Indian telecom sector are:

- RF spectrum being a limited resource, with competing and increasing demands, there is a need to have optimal and efficient use with greater sharing of this resource by all stakeholders. Therefore, effective RF spectrum planning has to be carried out for short term, medium term, and long term, taking into account the emerging new technologies.
- Although a teledensity of 18.31% has been achieved, there exists a wide gap between urban teledensity (55.94%) and rural teledensity (2.83%). Considering the fact that 70% of the population lives in rural areas in India, the real challenge will be to connect rural India.
- As voice-based connectivity (telephony) alone may not be the best economically viable option. Therefore, the connectivity should predominantly be data based having killer applications to make it sustainable on which voice services can also be provided.
- For an effective roll out the rural broadband connectivity would also need support through the USOF.
- To accelerate broadband connectivity, equipments need to be made available at an affordable price. In addition, local content in local languages need to be developed.
- The transformation of traditional public telecommunications networks into Internet Protocol (IP) based NGN will require significant technical, human, as well as financial resources. Further activities relating to migration to Internet Protocol version-6 will have to be given priority, in order to spread Internet much faster.
- Communication network needs to be adequately protected for which necessary network security related initiatives need to be put in place.
- The slow growth of telecom manufacturing sector is an area of major concern. The NTP 1999 sought to promote exports of telecom equipments and services. But till date export of telecom equipment remains minimal. Most of the state-of-the-art telecom equipment including mobile phones are imported from abroad. There is thus an immense potential for indigenous manufacturing in India.

Policy Issues

12.1.27 In order to achieve the targets laid down in telecom sector for the Eleventh Five Year Plan, proper and conducive policy initiatives need to be introduced by the government in its various sub-sectors, such as Rural Network Expansion, Broadband and Internet, Telecom Equipment Manufacturing, Telecom R&D, etc. The broad policy initiatives envisaged in this regard may be as follows:

- It is absolutely essential to carry out appropriate re-farming of the RF spectrum keeping in view the needs of various sectors. Further, some amount of spectrum may have to be kept reserved for deploying new services including rural broadband, 3G, Voice over Internet Protocol (VoIP), etc. While allocating spectrum the international practices should be kept in view, so that India can take advantage of the economies of scale. Bringing in a regime of unified licensing could also be considered for most efficient utilization of the allotted spectrum.
- It is essential to promote sharing of infrastructure by the service providers and incentivizing such sharing so that overall costs can be kept down. This is also expected to accelerate the pace of rural penetration of the telecom networks.
- Special attention needs to be paid to the most backward and remote areas such as, the North East, J&K, tribal belts, and island authorities. Cost may not be a consideration, while providing connectivity to these areas.
- Suitable policy initiatives need to be introduced for promoting telecom equipment manufacturing in the country. Further, there should be a co-ordinated approach to promote PPPs for R&D activities in telecom equipment. In addition, initiatives such as formation of common product certification to International Standards and Testing Facility for Global Accreditation, setting up of Mega Fabrication Units (FAB) facility for the manufacture of Integrated Circuits (IC), Development of Hardware Manufacturing Cluster Parks (HMCPs), etc., also need to be taken up to make India a telecom equipment manufacture hub.
- Adequate and availability of international and national bandwidth at low cost also need to be ensured through appropriate technologies and policy interventions.

Special Issues in Successful Roll Out of Rural Telephony and Broadband

12.1.28 As has been observed that in spite of substantial achievements in telecom sector during the Tenth Plan period, the rural teledensity continues to be very low as compared to the present national average of 18.31%. The mobile telephony costs are one-fifth of the fixed line costs. The low penetration of cellular mobile services in the rural areas so far can be attributed to inadequate infrastructure, in the form of towers and power supply, as well as lower revenue potential. However, with mobile tariffs falling, there is a likelihood of huge demand for mobile telephones in rural areas. But for successful rural roll out of mobile telephones, unless there is adequate coverage of towers and other related infrastructure, the demand cannot be met.

12.1.29 The government has introduced a scheme for expansion of rural mobile infrastructure through creation of shared passive infrastructure under USOF. Moreover, rural telecom expansion needs to be facilitated through setting up of triple play networks (viz. 3G networks) to deliver multiple services (i.e., voice, data, and video) at viable prices and bridge the information divide in rural areas. Through such networks, a single operator would be able to deliver various services to subscribers on a single medium.

12.1.30 Thus, for the successful roll out of telephones and broadband in the rural areas the following aspects should be considered by the policy makers and other stakeholders on priority basis: (i) proper infrastructure for access to telecom network; (ii) suitable access devices; and (iii) proper and adequate content. Ultimately, for any service to be useful, it should have value for the consumer. Therefore, the rural service should have adequate and relevant content. Each category of consumers has different needs and assigns different value to the various content and services being offered. Therefore solutions regarding content and services for high-end consumers, the middle class in cities and towns, the mass market, and rural users need to be considered separately. As such, there will be a need to develop large numbers of content providers, particularly RCPs including local language content providers, for which proper training courses may be designed and implemented through various existing institutions. Further, proper policy initiatives should be put in place to regulate the content effectively as per existing standards.

New Initiatives in Telecommunication Sector

12.1.31 It has been seen that broadband/bandwidth penetration has a multiplier effect on the economy. Experience in other countries has shown that broadband penetration has a positive correlation with the national income.

12.1.32 Bandwidth is an essential ingredient for carrying signals in today's information-based economy. It is a fact that despite nearly 850000 route km of OFC infrastructure, the geographical availability of the bandwidth remains poor in as much as the rural and remote areas which constitute bulk of the nation and continue to suffer from poor availability and expensive bandwidth. Many countries are putting in place national strategies for broadband promotion. In India, with the liberalization of telecom sector, broadband access has been driven largely by the private sector. The government has set a target for 20 million broadband and 40 million internet users (connections) by 2010. For this to happen, the PC penetration has to be substantially increased by way of suitable policy interventions both fiscal and non-fiscal.

12.1.33 India is poised with many interventions such as e-governance, rural connectivity, and e-education leading to creation of the bandwidth capacity which is also likely to increase the penetration of personal computers (PC), Internet, and broadband users. The bandwidth requirements would be in excess of 10 terabits per second (Tbps), of which at least 2000 gigabits per second (Gbps) (2 Tbps) would be the international bandwidth requirements. Keeping in view such a large bandwidth requirement there is a need to put in place appropriate policy initiatives such as:

- Pricing Policy: India is a highly price-sensitive market. If the price is right then the acceptance of a service or goods is very high, and the telecommunications market has amply proven this fact. Bandwidth, if looked at as a commodity, needs to be priced rightly for bringing in the desired off-take. Reselling of bandwidth for domestic usage should be allowed which is one of the best ways to create competition and roll out of infrastructure.
- Fiscal Policies: The following aspects need to be considered:
  - Encourage availability of low-cost access devices.
  - Decrease duties on items used in broadband networks and equalize duties on inputs for domestically manufactured goods with those on finished imports.
  - Provide appropriate tax structure to enable growth, without having to forego significant revenue.
- Co-ordination between PSUs: BSNL should be encouraged to co-ordinate with the consortium of PSUs—POWERTEL, GAILTEL, and RAILTEL—to identify clearly the additional villages that could be provided broadband connectivity by utilizing the latter's network due to the nature of coverage provided by their network. Suitable financial incentives should be worked out by the USO Administrator to facilitate this programme.

Introduction of New Value-added Services

- Over the last decade, television landscape has undergone a sea change. Now, Internet Protocol Television (IPTV) has arrived, which uses point-to-point connection as compared to broadcast connection and uses multi-casting techniques to give broadcasting effect. Since it is a point-to-point connection similar to the normal voice and data connections, it leads to converged provisioning of voice, video, and data—referred to as triple play—through a single medium. IPTV can be provided by cable TV service operators as well as telephony service operators. In fact, IPTV is widely regarded as the killer application for broadband particularly in the rural areas. This would also help in making the Common Service Centres (CSCs) more viable.
- Mobile TV is yet another technology which permits integration of mobility with TV viewing. Since the hand-held device used for mobile TV reception can also be used for normal voice and data communication, this technology represents a four-way convergence referred to as quadruple play. The use of

services such as 3G for video transmission should bring in mobile TV in the normal course. However, the alternative approach promises great advantages since it uses broadcast technology for video reception at a frequency other than the one used for voice and data applications, such as the FM radio on handsets.

- On the regulatory and pricing front, there will be a need for the down-linking guidelines to be modified to permit broadcasters/content providers to provide their content to IPTV and mobile TV service providers also. The technology enables the service providers to add their own content also on these platforms. Therefore, there will also be a need for regulatory mechanism to regulate the content on the IPTV and mobile TV.

The Path Ahead

12.1.34 In order to ensure further accelerated development in the telecom sector during the Eleventh Five Year Plan, the following aspects will have to be considered:

- The overall focus of the Eleventh Five Year Plan, in respect of telecom, would be on evolving a strategy for the development of world-class infrastructure for supporting accelerated growth of all sectors, bridging the digital divide, an optimum utilization of spectrum, focus on policy recommendations for promotion of private sector investment including FDI, and to take suitable initiatives for improving the performance of telecom equipment manufacturing sector.
- Availability of local content and applications is an important constituent for overall growth of Internet and broadband services. For achieving these goals following major steps may have to be undertaken: (i) facilitation for creation of multimedia and video content in the country; (ii) devising proper incentive for development of regional and local language content; (iii) thrust to the development of content and application for e-governance, e-education, e-health.
- Effective promotion and diversified use of shared rural broadband infrastructure to provide new opportunities, augment income, promote overall development in the areas of tele-education, telemedicine, and e-governance.
- Online retail in a broadband environment may be promoted. The role of other facilitators such as electricity authorities, Department of IT of various State Governments, department of local self-governments, Panchayats, Department of Agriculture, Department of Health and Family Welfare, Department of Education, needs to be properly co-ordinated, so that these departments/organizations/agencies can carry forward the advantages of broadband services to users particularly in rural areas.

12.1.35 The GBS for the Eleventh Five Year Plan of the DoT has been tentatively fixed at Rs 1549 crore at 2006–07 constant price (Rs 1752 crore at current price) and Rs 79204 crore of IEBR at 2006–07 price (Rs 89582 crore at current price).

12.2 INFORMATION TECHNOLOGY

OVERVIEW

12.2.1 Information Technology has contributed tremendously to the progress of our country and provided great leadership to Indian enterprise and creativity in the past decade. Breakthroughs in technology and innovative applications have brought vast benefits to various sectors and sub-sectors of the economy of the country. The entire gamut of IT-related services—including software and services, data and business processing services, and IT-enabled services—have emerged as a large knowledge-based sector of our economy. The industry has not only come into its own, both in terms of investment and employment, but is also having a positive knock-on effect on other manufacturing and services sectors. It is contributing to increased productivity and competitiveness across a wide range of activities. We have a dynamic entrepreneurial class that has gained confidence in its ability to compete, with skilled professionals and excellent management capability. Today, a majority of the companies in India have already aligned their internal processes and practices to international standards.

REVIEW OF THE TENTH PLAN

IT Software (Domestic Segment)

12.2.2 The domestic IT market in India was valued at approximately Rs 54000 crore in 2006. This segment has grown at a CAGR of 19.7% over the past six years.

Policy Reforms Introduced and New Initiatives

12.2.3 Some of the major policy initiatives introduced as well as other programmatic initiatives taken by the Central and various State Governments in the IT sector during the Tenth Plan period are given in Boxes 12.2.1 and 12.2.2.

National Informatics Centre (NIC)

12.2.4 NIC is a nodal S&T organization providing e-governance network and technical support to the Central Government, State Governments, UTs, and about 600 district administrations in the country. It has been facilitating the process of e-governance in the country for the last 30 years.

IT Hardware Manufacturing

12.2.5 Hardware manufacturing has been recognized as one of the engines for economic growth and creation of wealth. India's manufacturing competitiveness is because of the factors such as low-cost labour and the talent pool of three million graduates passing out of universities every year. Also, the raw material is one of the richest sources of our country. The electronics production and electronics export of various sectors of IT hardware and software in the Tenth Five Year Plan are given in Annexures 12.2.1 and 12.2.2. The overall annual growth in electronics hardware production was 15%–16%. The exports constituted about 16% of the total production.

Human Resource Development in IT

12.2.6 India has been developing as a major hub in knowledge creation in IT and electronics in the global arena. The number of professionals employed in this sector had grown to 1.28 million by 2005–06.

Nanotechnology

12.2.7 Nanotechnology is widely regarded as the next technological revolution. It has attracted the attention of scientists, researchers, and technologists all over the world and is likely to have a profound effect on almost

Box 12.2.1
Major Government Initiatives

- NeGP: The NeGP unveiled by the government covers 27 MMPs and 8 support components which are to be implemented at Central, State, and local government levels, at an estimated cost of Rs 23000 crore.
- SWANs: The scheme envisages establishment of SWANs across the country in all 29 States and 6 UTs from State headquarters up to the block level with a minimum bandwidth capacity of 2 Mbps, at a total cost of Rs 3334 crore.
- Community Information Centres (CICs): CICs numbering 487 in the North Eastern States, 135 in Jammu and Kashmir, 41 in A&N Islands, and 30 in Lakshadweep Islands have been established at a total cost of Rs 305 crore and are providing e-governance services and training to the local populace effectively.
- Common Service Centres (CSCs): The scheme envisages establishment of more than 100000 CSCs across the country at a total cost of Rs 5742 crore. The CSCs will be established in a honeycomb pattern covering all the 600000 villages in the country for delivery of content and services such as e-governance, education, entertainment, telemedicine, agriculture, etc.
- Project Relating to Spatial Data Infrastructure for Multi-Layered GIS for Planning: Starting with village as a unit, multi-layered databases would be developed in stand-alone GIS, distributed GIS, and web-based network-centric GIS environments to demonstrate the benefits of GIS at various levels of planning and decision making.
- Computer-aided Digital Mapping Project for Six Cities—Ahmedabad, Bangalore, Chennai, Hyderabad, Kolkata, and Mumbai: The benefits of the project include better services to citizens at large and better preparedness for disaster management. This project involves preparation of digital maps along with the digital mapping of utilities such as water, sewage, electricity, roads, communications, gas, pipelines, etc.
- Semiconductor Industry/FAB: The time is ripe to make India a preferred destination for the manufacture of semiconductors and associated devices. The government has issued a notification in March 2007 relating to the Special Incentive Package for setting up of semiconductor fabrication and other micro and nanotechnology manufacture industries in India.

Box 12.2.2
Indicative List of Successful Initiatives in the States

Project	Initiative of Government of
Computerization of the Registration Department: CARD, HIMRIS, STAR, PRENA, SCORE, SARITA, KAVERI, TRIS, DASTAVAZ, ORCHID, PRISM	AP, Himachal Pradesh, TN, UP, Bihar, Maharashtra, Karnataka, Tripura , Delhi, Sikkim, Punjab
Computerization of Transport Department: SARATHI AND VAHAN	About 500 RTOs/DTOs in various States
Computerization of district administration and Citizen Centric Services: PRAGATI, AKSHAYA, LOKVANI, NAIDISHA, SUWIDHA	Assam, Meghalaya, Kerala, UP, Haryana, Punjab
Back-end PRI Solutions: INFOGRAM, e-gram, e-Panchayat, Asthi, Panchlekha, etc. (village Panchayat)	Goa, Gujarat, AP, Karnataka, MP, etc.
Computerization of Land Records: BHOOMI, TAMILNILAM, BHULEKH, DHARITRI, BHUMI, APNAKHATA, BHUYAN, DEVBHUMI, HIMBHOOMI	Karnataka, TN, MP, Assam, WB, Rajasthan, Chhattisgarh, Uttrakhand, Manipur, Haryana
HALRIS (Integration of property registration and land records administration)	Haryana
NREGSoft (Online Monitoring of NREGS)	All States
Computerization of Treasuries: e-KOSH, Koshvahini	Rajasthan, Chhattisgarh, Maharashtra, UP, Manipur, Haryana, Kerala, Himachal Pradesh
e-Municipality	Maharashtra
Monitoring of Construction of Permanent Shelters for Earthquake and Tsunami Victims	A&N Islands
Employment Exchange	Lakshadweep, Gujarat
Common Integrated Police Application	Around 1800 police stations across States
e-Courts (court orders, cause list, e-filing in Supreme Court)	Supreme Court, 21 High Courts; being extended to 13000 subordinate courts in States
Passport System	Passport offices in States
VAT (Value-added Tax Computerization)	WB, Sikkim, Haryana
AGMARKNET	2800 Agricultural *Mandis* in various States
National Panchayat Portal	Portals of all PRIs across the States
PRIASoft (PRI accounting software)	Orissa, MP, etc.
RuralBazar (Web store to promote marketing of Rural Products)	TN, Goa, Tripura, etc.
RuralSoft (Information systems for Poverty Alleviation Schemes)	UP, Orissa, AP, etc.
Rural Water Supply & Sanitation/PHED Computerization	Arunachal Pradesh, UP, MP, AP, Rajasthan, TN, etc.—20 States
Open e-NRICH (Community Software Solution Framework and Content Management System)	Kerala, North Eastern States, Bihar, etc.
e-post	Post Offices in States
Instant Money Order	Post Offices in States
COIN (Co-operative Bank Information Network)	Bihar
CONFONET-Computerization and Networking of Consumer Forums	All States
Integrated Information System for food grains management	All States

all industry sectors and application areas. India started R&D funding in the area of nanotechnology during the Tenth Plan and projects relating to nano-electronics with a total outlay of about Rs 127 crore have been initiated.

VISION AND STRATEGY FOR THE ELEVENTH FIVE YEAR PLAN

12.2.8 The Eleventh Plan Vision for the Information Technology sector envisages newer technology development, entrepreneurship, and innovation. Building on the existing strengths and base in the software sector, we need to address the shortage of trained human resource, bridging the digital divide, and strengthening the IT hardware manufacturing base in the country so that India emerges as a regional hub for hardware manufacturing and exports. Our software industry needs to move up in the value chain from services to product development and create IPR.

12.2.9 Appropriate strategies encompassing fiscal and non-fiscal initiatives would need to be introduced in a co-ordinated manner to enable India to become world leader in IT software and services including ITES and become a regional hub for IT and electronics hardware manufacturing. Taking advantage of the demographic dividend, we need to create a bank of highly trained manpower not only to meet the domestic requirement but also for the rest of the world.

Policy Issues, Programme Reforms, and New Initiatives in the Eleventh Plan

12.2.10 The Eleventh Plan objective of faster and inclusive growth calls for many new initiatives, namely, creation of integrated modern townships across the country for IT industries, formulation of proactive IT-electronics hardware manufacturing policy, development of trained manpower to meet the requirement of the industries on a continuous basis, and promoting R&D in few selected niche areas wherein we have the ability to become global leaders. Another important area which needs acceleration is the NeGp for providing all government services to the common man in his locality through common service delivery outlets and ensuring efficiency, transparency, and reliability of such services at affordable costs to realize the basic needs of the common man. Issues of re-engineering and management of change are of paramount importance in comparison to technical issues associated with e-governance.

12.2.11 The demand for hardware is expected to grow at a rate of 30%, as against 18% at present. This would be fuelled by the aspirations of the younger generation and the large middle class with increasing disposable incomes in India. By the year 2010, the hardware market is expected to be of the order of US$ 85 billion. If the hardware production continues to grow at the present growth rate, there would be a large gap between demand and supply, which will have to be met through imports. In this scenario, we will approach a situation wherein foreign exchange outgo on account of import of hardware could be more than the foreign exchange earned by the country through export of software and services. In addition, this sector has the potential of generating large employment opportunities. Keeping this in view, electronics/IT hardware manufacturing has been identified as a thrust area. Major policy intervention on priority basis is required to promote the growth of Electronics/IT Hardware Manufacturing Industry so as to meet the growing demand.

12.2.12 Semiconductor Manufacturing Industry: With increasing demand for domestic electronic goods and the availability of a pool of talented engineers, India is fast creating a footprint in the semiconductor area. The Indian semiconductor industry is currently dominated by players engaged in chip designing activities. India must compete aggressively by adopting a coherent strategy for building up a semiconductor fabrication facility. The electronic goods manufacturers would create a substantial demand for IC in the country. The fabrication facility would help reap benefits for the nanotechnology industries in the coming years. FAB would cater not only to the domestic market, but the country would also be able to reach out to the global semiconductor market in specific product categories. A special incentive package has been announced for setting up of semiconductor fabrication and other micro-technology and nanotechnology manufacturing industries in India which is expected to fuel further growth of semiconductor manufacturing in India.

SETTING-UP OF INTEGRATED MODERN TOWNSHIPS FOR SUNRISE INDUSTRIES INCLUDING IT AND BPO

12.2.13 IT industry lends itself for easy mobility, and with the large number of educational institutions coming up across the country, there is a need to move the IT-ITES/BPO industries to tier-2 and tier-3 cities for promoting inclusive growth. In addition, it is also important to create 'Information Technology Investment Regions' for setting-up Integrated Modern Townships for Sunrise Industries including IT/ITES/electronic hardware in the country.

CYBER SECURITY

12.2.14 As IT infrastructure is increasingly becoming a substratum of all economic activities, the operational stability and security of critical information infrastructure has become vital for economic security of the country. This calls for concerted efforts from the government, the industry as well as the service providers to secure their IT infrastructure. Following organizations are presently dealing with the cyber security issues in the country.

INDIAN COMPUTER EMERGENCY RESPONSE TEAM (CERT-IN)

- CERT-In is a functional organization with the objective of securing Indian cyber space. It provides incident prevention and response services as well as security and quality management services, and creates awareness on security issues through dissemination of information on its website and operates 24 × 7 Incident Response Help Desk. Its activities comprise handling of security incidents, issuing of e-security alerts, publishing of advisories, vulnerability notes; and security guidelines, tracking of Indian website defacements, etc.

GOVERNMENT DEPARTMENTS SECURITY

- NIC, the e-governance support organization for government departments, has been taking various security measures for providing secure IT environment. These include data centre security, user systems security, security polices and procedure, and regular security audits for compliance checking. The data centre security comprises network firewall, intrusion prevention systems, application firewalls, Secure Sockets Layer (SSL)/Virtual Private Network (VPN) security, etc. The application security audit is conducted on any new application before it can be hosted. Besides, antivirus and software patch management is ensured for the servers and desktop systems all over National Informatics Centre Network (NICNET). Continuous security monitoring of network is done.

REGIONAL CYBER SECURITY RESEARCH CENTRE (RCSRC)

- NASSCOM in association with Chandigarh Administration has established an RCSRC to deal with all cyber security issues in collaboration with the IT industry. The Centre will aid and advise organizations in cyber security policy enforcements, conduct of security audits and incident handling. It will also provide various IT organizations and the police department, consultancy for design of secure networks, including deployment of security administration software such as intrusion detection, management of security software, and vulnerability checking, protection against port scanners, password crackers, and other issues.

HIGH PERFORMANCE COMPUTING

12.2.15 High performance and grid computing is the next generation of computing facilities which would be widely used in a number of areas such as solving newer class of mathematical problems of various complexities, high energy physics, nuclear physics, climate science, structural biology, enzyme catalysis, genomics, bioinformatics, etc. The objective of grid application is to share the computational power across the grid by the members for enhanced service delivery and enable fast data access. There is a need for developing high-speed backbone connecting the computers on the grid, development of application software, and capacity building through R&D and training of required human resources.

TECHNOLOGY DEVELOPMENT IN INDIAN LANGUAGES

12.2.16 India is a multilingual country. There is, therefore, a need to provide user-friendly and cost-effective tools, applications, and content that enable access to ICT infrastructure in Indian languages. The issues relating to linguistic data resource, content creation, language processing tools, and such technologies as optical character recognition, text-to-speech, speech recognition, cross-lingual information retrieval, and machine translation in multilingual environment are being addressed. To make available the fruits of IT development to the common man, fonts and software tools for some of the Indian languages such as Hindi, Tamil, Telugu, Assamese, Kannada, Malayalam, Marathi, Oriya, Punjabi, and Urdu have been released in public domains. There is need for developing similar software tools and fonts for other languages in the coming years.

DIGITAL LIBRARY OF INDIA

12.2.17 Digital library offers many advantages over the traditional libraries. Having no physical boundaries and space constraints, the digital libraries are available round the clock with multiple accesses at multiple locations in a most cost-effective way.

12.2.18 The Digital Library of India, hosted by the Indian Institute of Science, Bangalore, provides free access to many books in English and Indian languages and has digitized more than 2.97 lakh books containing a total of approximately 80.7 million pages till September 2007. Similarly, other digital libraries, which are mostly accessible to their own members, have been in existence at many locations in India as well as in many other countries. Therefore, the main initiative, in addition to digitization and preservation of data available in physical form, should be the integration of all the digital libraries all over the world so that all significant literary, artistic, and scientific works of mankind will be made available in every corner of the world for the education, study, and appreciation of our generation as well as that of all our future generations.

OPEN TECHNOLOGY CENTRE (OTC)

12.2.19 To facilitate use of open technologies in e-governance and strategic applications and services, OTC has been set up at Chennai. It has provided DSpace, an open-source archival solution, for archival of speeches, video, and audio speeches of Members of Rajya Sabha. It has enabled to archive documents of speeches in Urdu and Hindi in addition to English.

LIBRARY AUTOMATION

12.2.20 e-Granthalaya has been developed by NIC as standardized and robust library automation software. Already implemented in about 1000 libraries, it is going to be rolled out to a large number of libraries in the country.

CREATION OF A NATIONAL KNOWLEDGE NETWORK

12.2.21 A National Knowledge Network can go a long way in bringing India in the forefront of education, S&T, innovation, etc. National Research and Education Networks are driving the pace of collaboration, innovation, and discovery amongst scientists. Some of the major initiatives required in this direction include:

- Creation of a suitable mechanism for setting up and operating a National Knowledge Network.
- Connecting all major R&D establishments, Central institutions, universities, colleges, and libraries by using a dynamically configurable national multigigabit backbone network.
- Empowering campuses through wireless network.
- Having a Central Data Centre with 30 terabyte storage, capable of expanding to petabyte storage in future.
- Create a National educational portal which could host free educational content for e-learning.

SCHOOL CONNECTIVITY

12.2.22 Education infrastructure needs to be strengthened and upgraded. In the first phase, broadband access needs to be provided to every school. There are 108000 government and government-aided schools in India. All these schools need to be put on the network progressively.

INCREASING EFFICIENCY OF E-GOVERNANCE INVESTMENTS

12.2.23 The following initiatives would need to be taken up for accelerating the National e-governance programme:

- Encourage the Central and State Governments to procure e-governance services.
- Fast replication of already successful e-governance programmes.

- Make digital signatures mandatory for e-commerce, e-government, and e-banking initiatives.
- Identify and develop 'Killer Applications'—Online auctions, e-voting, home banking, etc.
- Speedy and effective implementation of various MMPs under the NEGP.
- Promotion of technologies such as Digital Subscriber Lines (xDSL), Wireless Fidelity (WiFi), and Worldwide Inter-operability for Microwave Access (WiMAX) for providing the last mile connectivity to the places where copper wiring is not possible.
- Technologies such as Broadband on Power Lines should also be explored.

THRUST AREAS FOR R&D IN IT SECTOR IN THE ELEVENTH PLAN

12.2.24 R&D in identified thrust areas is one of the major functions of the DIT. This support has helped in building infrastructure and competencies at a large number of academic and research institutions, and has produced the required manpower to take up R&D in the industry besides development of various products and packages. Some of the major thrust areas for R&D in the Eleventh Plan include: ubiquitous computing, RFI, high performance computing, grid computing, high performance networking, bio-informatics, open source software, software engineering, web technologies, and electronics— nanotechnology, photonics, microelectronics, industrial electronics, automation electronics, embedded systems, and electronics material development program.

CONVERGENCE OF BIO-INFO-NANO TECHNOLOGIES AND COGNITIVE SCIENCE

12.2.25 Information technology and communication technology have already converged leading to ICT. Information technology combined with bio-technology has led to bio-informatics. Now, nanotechnology is knocking at our doors. It is the field of the future that will replace microelectronics and many other fields with tremendous application potential in the areas of medicine, electronics, material science, etc. Convergence of bio-nano-info technologies can lead to the development of nano-robots. Likewise, a new revolution is also expected to be ushered in by the convergence of bio-info-nano technologies with the cognitive science in the coming years.

ICT Measurement for Knowledge Economy

12.2.26 The GoI has set up the National Statistical Commission with a wide ranging mandate to serve as a nodal and empowered body for all core statistical activities in the country and to evolve, monitor, and enforce statistical priorities and standards and to ensure statistical co-ordination among the different agencies involved. The Commission was formally constituted in July 2006.

12.2.27 This has enhanced the need for credible and timely data on ICT. The ultimate aim of collecting ICT statistics and indicators is to inform policy makers about the impact of ICT on the economy and the society. For this to be possible, data need to be collected not only on the ICT industry but also on how ICT is used by people, business, and the public administration. Therefore, there is a need to shift the emphasis a bit from measurement of the ICT industry to measuring the use of ICT across the economy in the Eleventh Plan.

12.2.28 In order to address this emerging need in the Eleventh Plan following course of action may be considered:

- Conduct model surveys of ICT usage by households, individuals, and businesses, including e-commerce and e-business.
- Study impact of ICT: What does ICT do for the economy?
- Pursue international co-operation and the partnership on measuring ICT for development.

Constraints and Challenges

12.2.29 Some of the key constraints and challenges being faced by the IT and hardware manufacturing sector in the country are as follows:

SMALL SIZE/SCALE OF OPERATIONS

- The size and scale of operation of most manufacturing plants are very small compared to the global market leaders. This leads to poor economies of scales for manufacturing as well as for sourcing. Lower capacities translate to higher per unit overheads. Even though the cost of labour in India is low, it fails to offset the adverse impact of poor economies of scale.

HIGH RATE OF TECHNOLOGICAL OBSOLESCENCE

- Due to the changes in technology, newer methods get introduced, calling for modern processes and equipment, which give a competitive advantage in terms of cost, speed, and quality. Yet, Indian companies find it unviable to upgrade before the investments in earlier equipment are recovered.

UNIFICATION OF MANUFACTURING

- With rapid convergence of consumer electronics, IT, and telecom and fast introduction of newer products in the market, new vistas for the manufacture of accessories to support the new gadgets are emerging. Therefore, unification of product categories has to be attempted for manufacturing.
- There appears to be lack of credible and timely data on ICT usage (e-Stat) and its impact on the economy.

The Path Ahead

12.2.30 The future of IT industry in India looks extremely positive. The government aims to start many new initiatives in this Eleventh Five Year Plan and strengthen the already running schemes. Some of the important initiatives in addition to those enumerated above that would help in reaching the goal of faster and inclusive growth are as follows:

- Encourage the adoption of e-procurement model in all government procurements.
- Encourage State Governments to initiate major citizen-centric mission projects under NeGP, preferably in the PPP mode.
- Promote electronics/IT hardware manufacturing industry as it is one of the thrust areas of the GoI.
- Policy needs to be put in place to set up HMCPs in private sector or public sector or PPP and to co-locate the inter-dependent units in the same complex.
- Policy need to be drafted to address the different issues related to the National Digital Library.
- Operationalize the Unique Identification Project to create a core database (using the most reliable pre-existing digitized database) which is then regularly updated and is easily accessible to and used by all departments for identification of residents in the country for various purposes.
- Initiate MMPs and projects for developing quality human resource which is industry ready.
- Initiate programmes for development of quality faculty.

12.2.31 The GBS for the Eleventh Five Year Plan of the DIT has been tentatively fixed at Rs 11048 crore at 2006–07 constant price and Rs 12496 crore at current price.

12.3 INDIA POST

OVERVIEW

12.3.1 Post office is the only institution in the country which touches every person's life. A prompt and efficient postal system is very important for the development of a country. On one hand it provides personal services to the people, and on the other it also provides service to businesses which is crucial for the growth of the economy. The importance of Postal Services becomes all the more important when a USO Fund is created by the government.

12.3.2 With the emergence of private sector as a player in the areas of courier service and express service and with the development of information technology applications in every field, the posts stand to face competition. The basic profile of the sector is given in Box 12.3.1.

REVIEW OF THE TENTH PLAN

12.3.3 The Tenth Plan basically aimed at making the postal services self-sufficient. The major objectives envisaged for the Tenth Plan were (i) provision of universal postal services at affordable prices, (ii) ensuring quality of services at par with international standards, (iii) modernization, and (iv) process re-engineering with a view to achieving better administrative efficiency, financial management, and satisfaction. The technology upgradation component constituted nearly 80% of the Tenth Plan outlay. The policy of opening of post offices was reviewed and it was decided that in order to rationalize the postal network, new post offices should be set up only through the redeployment of staff or relocation of the existing post offices.

Box 12.3.1
Basic Profile of the Postal Sector

- Except for courier services, postal operations are still a government monopoly.
- Postal services in India have been highly subsidized as part of the government policy.
- Indian postal system is the largest in the world in terms of number of post offices/outlets numbering about 1.55 lakh, out of which nearly 90% post offices are in rural areas and remaining 10% post offices are in urban areas. In addition, 5405 Panchayat Sanchar Sewa Kendras are also providing basic postal facilities in rural areas.
- India Post is presently being served by as many as 5.4 lakh employees including 2.47 lakh departmental and 2.93 lakh extra-departmental employees to run its operations all over the country.
- The total expenditure in percentage of receipts for Posts was 123% in India as compared to 101% in the UK and 102% in the US.

Targets and Performance of the Tenth Plan

12.3.4 As against a target of opening of 450 extra-departmental post offices, the department has been able to open 440 extra-departmental post offices. As regards the opening of Postal Sanchar Seva Kendras against a target set for 2400, the achievement has been 2371. The department has also been able to achieve fully its target of opening 45 post offices. As many as 8263 post offices were computerized against a target of 7700 post offices. In addition, 19 postal accounts offices were computerized as against a target of 22. All the 245 administrative post offices have also been computerized. There has been 100% achievement in computerization of 48 head record offices.

12.3.5 In the area of modernization, as against a target of 811, as many as 822 post offices have been modernized. The department has been able to modernize 338 speed post centres as against a target of 350. Modernization has also been done of mail motor depots as per the target. The department has set up 290 postal finance marts (PFMs) as against a target of 300.

12.3.6 In the field of philately upgradation, the department has performed well. Human resource development, which is the crucial element for supporting the whole process of modernization and induction of technology, has also been taken up by the department. As many as 303769 persons from different cadres were trained in their respective fields as against a target of 315700 persons. The department also established the National Data Centre that would help them in providing various services across their network similar to anywhere banking.

Vision and Strategy for the Eleventh Five Year Plan

12.3.7 The vision statement of India Post reaffirms its social commitment and its focus on technology induction, entrepreneurial management, and achieving financial self-sufficiency. Taking into consideration the internal and external opportunities and challenges, the Eleventh Plan would focus on an all-round development of the DoP with a number of policy initiatives and building a brand image. The department would also aim to effectively utilize its network and reach for providing value-added services by developing appropriate linkages with various agencies/organizations.

Key Constraints and Challenges

12.3.8 Owing to increasing competition and availability of other means of affordable communication including telephone, Internet, etc., India Post needs to become commercially viable by increasing revenue, while fulfilling the rising expectations of the customers through adoption of competitive and customer-friendly business strategies. This calls for an urgent need to redefine and reposition the department in the changed scenario. There is a need to improve quality of services and adapting them to the needs of the rapidly evolving and increasingly technology driven world. Besides, India Post also needs to focus its efforts on non-core activities based on information technology by leveraging its network and the last mile reach through partnerships.

12.3.9 The domestic postal market faces a number of opportunities and threats:

COMMUNICATION MARKET

- Electronics alternatives as well as organized and ad hoc couriers are both competing with India Post.

LOGISTICS MARKET

- National and international players are entering the logistics and express markets for providing better value-added services aimed at business customers.

MASS MEDIA MARKET

- Opportunities exist to develop direct mail and target the growing middle class community with targeted marketing.

RETAIL AND FINANCIAL MARKET

- With its extensive network, India Post is well placed to partner with banks, insurance companies, and other financial service providers for extending financial services to the rural and hitherto unreached population.

Policy Issues for the Eleventh Five Year Plan

12.3.10 Taking into consideration the internal and external opportunities and challenges, the Eleventh Five Year Plan would focus on an all-round development and repositioning of the DoP. A few but important policy issues for the Eleventh Five Year Plan are mentioned below:

- Reorganize the DoP around the emerging technological and market realities and expand into newer business potential areas such as Global Business, Financial Services, Retail, Rural Business, etc.
- Widespread induction of technology aimed at computerizing and networking of all post offices using Central server-based system. Induction of other state-of-art processing systems including mail processing systems so as to provide service on par with global industry standards.
- Greater focus on human resource development with the objective of transformation of the human resource of the department into a technology-savvy, business-oriented workforce led by world-class managers.
- Transforming Postal Life Insurance into a commercial business entity making its own investment decisions and competing on a level playing field with other insurance entities, while conforming to requirements of Insurance Regulatory and Development Authority (IRDA) norms.
- Adoption of PPP model for development of postal estates by setting up a SPV for their commercial exploitation and revenue generation.
- Utilizing the widespread network and reach of India Post to act as an interface for the Central and State Governments with beneficiaries for delivery of various social sector schemes, and also for trade, business, and banking sectors.
- A new division is to be created to specifically target rural postal network with a view to utilizing the rural network and delivery strengths for revenue generation and extension of services/amenities to the rural areas.

SCHEMES/PROGRAMMES TO BE IMPLEMENTED IN THE ELEVENTH FIVE YEAR PLAN

Network

12.3.11 The programme for the expansion of the postal network will be carried out in the Eleventh Five Year Plan, keeping in view the requirement of the customers, USO, accessibility, standards, and business potential through adoption of alternate/innovative means of providing access to the postal network, such as opening of franchisee outlets through induction of latest technology, apart from opening of new post offices.

12.3.12 There is an urgent need to utilize this unparalleled network to support various retail services through tie-ups with the Central and State Governments and private organizations and also support e-governance initiatives of the Central and State Governments. Post offices can function as retail outlets and as an interface between the customer and the governments, both Central and State, particularly in rural areas for the social sector schemes.

Mail Operations

12.3.13 Mail operations, viz., collection, transmission, and delivery would require focus. There is need to resort to automation in mail handling at the important centres where substantial amount of load is there. Mail operations require prompt and efficient multimodal transport system, which could be met by hiring/leasing of fast moving transport system, conveyors, transport for delivery and pick up of postal articles and wet-leasing of freighter air craft, etc. Mechanization of runner lines in rural areas is also needed for faster movement of mail in these areas.

12.3.14 There is a need to introduce and streamline proper track and trace systems for all the varieties of articles such as parcels, registered items, money orders, etc. Mail Business Centres (MBCs) are being set up as front line business wing of India Post offering one-stop solutions for varied mailing needs of the customers. MBCs will act as integrated mail business hub, undertaking the task of collection, processing, and delivery of mails. A total of 300 MBCs are proposed to be opened during the current Plan. MBCs will fulfil the objective of improvement in quality of service, reduction in cost of operations, and growth in mail business. The establishment of parcel post as a major strategic business unit of India Post has also been envisaged in the Eleventh Plan, as this business is expected to become a major source of revenue. Major parcel hubs will be provided with automatic parcel sorting systems, RFI systems, hydraulic pallet trucks, fork lifts, taper rollers, and other parcel handling equipments. It is also proposed to develop and establish a commercial system for parcel post for providing end-to-end solutions, covering booking, tracking, billing, and customer information system.

12.3.15 The objective during the Eleventh Five Year Plan is to work towards making India Post a major player in the logistics and supply chain management arena by providing distribution channels, inventory management, packaging services, warehousing, transportation, and time-definite distribution programmes. It is proposed to establish logistics centres in metro cities and major business towns and a logistics centre for international operations. India Post also needs to enter the international parcel and logistics business and function as the logistics partner for providing event-specific services for trade fairs, Commonwealth games, and State-sponsored events.

12.3.16 It is proposed to offer e-commerce solutions through tie-ups with suppliers which will provide various products to the customers to be delivered through posts. International mail segment has become highly competitive with the emergence of private operators in the sector and cross border posting of mails. Therefore, the Offices of Exchange in India, that is Airmail Offices, International Express Mail Service, and Foreign Post Offices at Delhi, Mumbai, Kolkata, Chennai, and Kochi, which process the international mail, would require capacity augmentation for high speed processing of mails and security during the Eleventh Plan in order to meet the challenges of competitive market.

FINANCIAL SERVICES

Postal Finance Marts (PFMs)

12.3.17 PFMs are one-stop shops for financial services such as mutual funds and other financial instruments. The PFMs would help in creating a distinct identity and branding of postal financial outlets, which can serve as a front end for the tie-ups with financial institutions and banks for vending their retail services. The success of these marts will depend on the kind of results they produce for the customers, which in turn will depend upon the expertise of the financial adviser.

Banking

12.3.18 Post office saving bank is the single largest source of revenue for the department. It has been able to make a business of Rs 3500 crore as on 30 June 2007 With a customer base of 17.5 crore account holders, a branch network double the size of all the banks in the country put together, and with a diverse product range, the Post Office Savings Bank is the largest retail banking network in the country. This network and the depth of reach should be utilized to implement the 'Sampoorna Dak Khana Bachat Yojana Gram' Scheme.

12.3.19 Since any time anywhere banking, is the need of the hour, it is proposed to switch over computerization programme of Savings Bank and allied functions from local area network in individual post offices to central server-based technology. For this, investment on technology infrastructure, hardware and software requirements, and networking would be needed. This also includes tele-banking, ATM, etc. Post office can also have tie-ups with existing banks for providing services to the customers.

Money Transfer

12.3.20 Instant money-order (iMO) service was initiated during the Tenth Plan. There is a need to expand this service and extend its scope to interface the iMO with international payment gateways. We are tying up with other countries having large population of Indian origin through bilateral/multilateral agreements for International Financial Service. The existing money-order services will be progressively replaced by an electronic, IT-based money-order service which will offer many new service features and differential tariff structure.

Insurance

12.3.21 Transforming Postal Life Insurance into a commercial business entity making its own investment decisions and competing on level playing field with other insurance entities, while conforming to requirements of IRDA norms is essential. In this direction, investment would be required for customization of products, improvement of after sale service, and modernization of customer interaction points. Funds would also be required for hardware and software support. There is also a need to develop internal expertise for fund management to enable investment of Post Office Life Insurance Fund/Rural Post Office Life Insurance Fund as per the investment pattern of IRDA.

Philately

12.3.22 The focus on philately would continue to have its place during the Eleventh Five Year Plan as well. The following initiatives would need to be undertaken for promotion, product innovation, and quality/technology induction.

- Initiate online trading of philatelic items through the internet-based trading portals such as e-Bay, etc.
- Introduce new products like personalized stamps which have been very successful abroad.
- Introduce new postal stamps based on the different themes of national importance with emphasis on using postal stamps as medium of advertisement to generate additional revenue.

Global Business Division

12.3.23 A Global Business Division has been set up in India Post to capitalize on the liberalized economy and also to exploit the business opportunities by opening of the postal sector as a result of WTO/GATT agreements. The Global Business Division would provide a single window solution for international business requirements of its customers. The Global Business Division projects India Post as a strategic partner for value addition to international business in mail, express, logistics, and remittance sectors. Besides this, the Global Business Division would provide an avenue for tapping new markets around the world for India Post.

SUPPORT SYSTEMS

Technology Induction

12.3.24 It is proposed to undertake an extensive technology induction/upgradation programme during the Eleventh Five Year Plan with a view to achieving the goal of financial self-sufficiency for the department. During the Tenth Five Year Plan the department has been able to computerize about 8263 large departmental post offices. Now in the Eleventh Five Year Plan efforts would be made to computerize and network 17878 departmental post offices for providing effective and satisfactory service to its customers. In addition, 64000 selected branch post offices located in block/*tehsil* headquarters or in remote areas also will be computerized. Further, remaining administrative offices (up to sub-divisional level) including Postal Directorate, PSD/CSDs, Civil Wing offices, etc. will also be taken up for computerization. The proposed networking would enable the department to start various online services, viz., any time, any-where savings bank and other financial services, improve delivery thereby getting additional revenue. Networked hand-held digital devices could be developed to be carried by postmen/postal staff to enable not only delivery of articles and intimation of their status in real time, but also for booking of articles and offering other services such as accepting deposits, bill payment, other e-enabled services, etc. The same device could also be used to create franchise network.

Human Resource Management

12.3.25 The objective is a greater focus on human resource development with the objective of transformation of the human resource into a technology-savvy, business-oriented workforce led by world-class managers. Behavioural training is also essential to enable effective customer interaction. This would require restructuring of the Postal Staff College India (PSCI) and the postal training center network. It is also envisaged to evaluate the role of PSCI from a training institution to a nodal training policy institute with international linkages.

Marketing, Research, and Development

12.3.26 For the wide range of activities planned to augment business and garner additional revenue, it is necessary to have a professional marketing, research, and product development organization to support the implementation of the plans. This plan scheme envisages setting up of marketing, research, and product development centre after carrying out feasibility study. The programme proposed to be implemented includes the development of a National Address Management System which will add to the professional strength of the department and creation of a brand identity for India Post.

Estate Management

12.3.27 In order to fulfil the USO for providing easy access to postal services, construction of buildings is essential to provide the vital infrastructure for efficient postal operations, while simultaneously focusing on revenue generation from estates in commercial locations. The strategy for construction would be to construct buildings in identified highly commercial locations in PPP mode through an SPV set up for this purpose. The existing programme for construction of buildings with government funding would also be continued on plots with low commercial value.

12.3.28 Departmental buildings in remote and inaccessible areas are proposed to be provided with solar panels for easy access to power using environment-friendly technology. Attention is also proposed to be given to improvement of the working environment and ergonomics and branding of operative offices, with particular emphasis on post offices.

Material Management

12.3.29 Setting up of an efficient material management system through upgradation of technology and provision of required equipment facilities is essential, since the Postal Store Depots and post offices handle a very large volume of stationery, including forms for use in operative offices and equipment which is essential for the smooth functioning of the postal system.

SUPPLY OF EQUIPMENTS

12.3.30 All the necessary and the other modern equipments for packing, unpacking, binding, moving, stapling, cash counting, etc. would need to be procured and supplied in time.

QUALITY

12.3.31 There is a need to develop an R&D centre under marketing and to encourage development of indigenous franking machines, mail processing equipment, vending machines, etc.

PROCESS IMPROVEMENT

12.3.32 It also proposed to set up call centres all over the country based on Interactive Voice Response System, starting initially with eight locations.

THE PATH AHEAD

12.3.33 The Eleventh Five Year Plan would endeavour to transform India Post into a modern, efficient, and self-sufficient organization responsive to market conditions and fully utilizing its potential for service and revenue generation, while maintaining its commitment to deliver on its USO. To achieve this, the major initiatives/action points envisaged for the Eleventh Five Year Plan are the following:

- Preparing an action plan for restructuring the DoP in order to reaffirm its vision statement on its social commitment to the people of our country.
- Focus on utilizing the unparalleled network of the DoP to support e-governance initiatives of the Central and State Governments and as a retail outlet/interface between the customer and the governments both at Centre and State, particularly in rural areas.
- Focus on providing technological support for an extensive computerization of the network using integrated software and central–server technology.
- With a view to further reducing the deficit, the DoP

needs to define its USO, introduce suitable legislative amendments in the IPO Act 1898, and set-up a regulatory mechanism for the postal sector to ensure a level playing field.

- Transforming Postal Life Insurance into a commercial business entity making its own investment decisions and competing on level playing field with other insurance entities, while conforming to requirements of IRDA norms.
- Action plan needs to be put in place for postal estates management.
- Action plan needs to be prepared to set up and maintain MBCs as frontline business wing of India Post offering one-stop solutions for varied mailing needs of the customers.
- Action plan needs to be prepared to set up and maintain prompt and efficient multi-modal transport system incorporating wet-leasing of aircraft, road transport, etc.
- Action plan needs to be prepared to set up and maintain a grid of automated mail processing centres for various hubs in the country to support the mail sorting processes.
- Make efforts to expand the Plan programme for setting up PFMs.
- Focus on human resource management, particularly training, to support the delivery of services to customers, induction of new technology, specializing in banking and insurance sectors.
- Develop a professional organization to support marketing, research, and product development initiatives to various services offered by the department.
- For all-round development of Ladhakh, Andaman and Nicobar Islands, and Lakshadweep Island, SCPs would be made operative particularly for opening branch offices, construction of buildings, and other needs.
- Focus on special needs of the North East circle as per the comprehensive sub-plan which includes mail operations, banking and money transfer, computerization and training as well as construction of buildings.

12.3.34 The GBS for the Eleventh Five Year Plan of the DoP has been tentatively fixed at Rs 3536 crore at 2006–07 constant price and Rs 4000 crore at current price.

[1] The figures in bracket refer to CAGR.

12.4 INFORMATION AND BROADCASTING

OVERVIEW

12.4.1 One of the sectors which has consistently outperformed the GDP growth year after year is the Entertainment and Media Services Sector which is expected to grow at a CAGR of 18% till 2010 and beyond during the Eleventh Plan period. This sector comprises television (CAGR, 22%),[1] films (16%), radio (28%), music (4%), print media (13%), live entertainment (16%), out-of-home advertisement (17%), and Internet advertising (43%). Its existing as well as annual turnover and its CAGR are given in Table 12.4.1.

12.4.2 It is one sector which responds to extraordinary GDP growth with a multiplier. When incomes rise, more resources get spent on leisure. The contribution of each media sub-sector to the overall revenues as in 2006 and as projected for 2011 clearly brings out growing preponderance of electronic media over print media as depicted in Figures 12.4.1(a) and (b).

12.4.3 Growth in infrastructure, technology, and institutional support in the information and broadcasting (I&B) sector was in consonance with overall national development perspective. Film, information, and broadcasting sectors of the economy have achieved formidable strength. The share of I&B sector in total employment, income, and investment has gone up significantly. Issues in the national scenario of this sector revolved around foreign investment, regulation, intellectual property rights, content enrichment, restructuring of Prasar Bharati, digitalization and maintaining archives of the entire spectrum of I&B media unit.

REVIEW OF THE TENTH PLAN

Information Sector

12.4.4 During the Tenth Plan, information sector of the Ministry of I&B focused on the following:

- Directorate of Advertisement and Visual Publicity, with its function of providing multi-media publicity to government's development programmes and

TABLE 12.4.1
Annual Growth of Indian Entertainment and Media Industry

(Rs Million)

	2004	2005	2006E	2007F	2008F	2009F	2010F	2011F	CAGR
Television	128700	158000	191200	219900	266000	331000	431000	519000	
Annual growth		23%	21%	15%	21%	24%	30%	20%	22%
Filmed entertainment	59900	68100	84500	96800	112000	126450	146000	175000	
Annual growth		14%	24%	15%	16%	13%	15%	20%	16%
Radio	2400	3200	5000	6500	8500	11000	14000	17000	
Annual growth		33%	56%	30%	31%	29%	27%	21%	28%
Music	6700	7000	7200	7400	7500	7600	8000	8700	
Annual growth		4%	3%	3%	1%	1%	5%	9%	4%
Live entertainment	7000	8000	9000	11000	13000	16000	18000	19000	
Annual growth		14%	13%	22%	18%	23%	13%	6%	16%
Entertainment industry#	204700	244300	296900	341600	407000	492050	617000	738700	
Annual growth		19%	22%	15%	19%	21%	25%	20%	
Print media	87800	109500	127900	144000	162200	182300	206500	232000	
Annual growth		25%	17%	13%	12%	13%	12%	13%	13%
OOH advertisement	8500	9000	10000	12500	14500	16500	19000	21500	
Annual growth		6%	11%	25%	16%	14%	15%	13%	17%
Internet advertising	600	1000	1600	2700	4200	6000	8200	9500	
Annual growth		67%	60%	69%	56%	43%	37%	16%	43%
Total entertainment and media industry#	301600	363800	436400	500800	587900	696850	850700	1001700	
Annual growth rate (%)		21%	20%	15%	17%	19%	22%	18%	18%

Note: # The figures taken above include only the legitimate revenues in each segment. Revenues from the Animation and Gaming segments have not been included in the industry size as these are traditionally included in the Indian IT and Software Revenues; E = Estimates; F = Forecasted

Source: Industry estimates and PwC analysis/Federation of Indian Chambers of Commerce and Industry (FICCI): Indian Entertainment and Media Industry, March 2007.

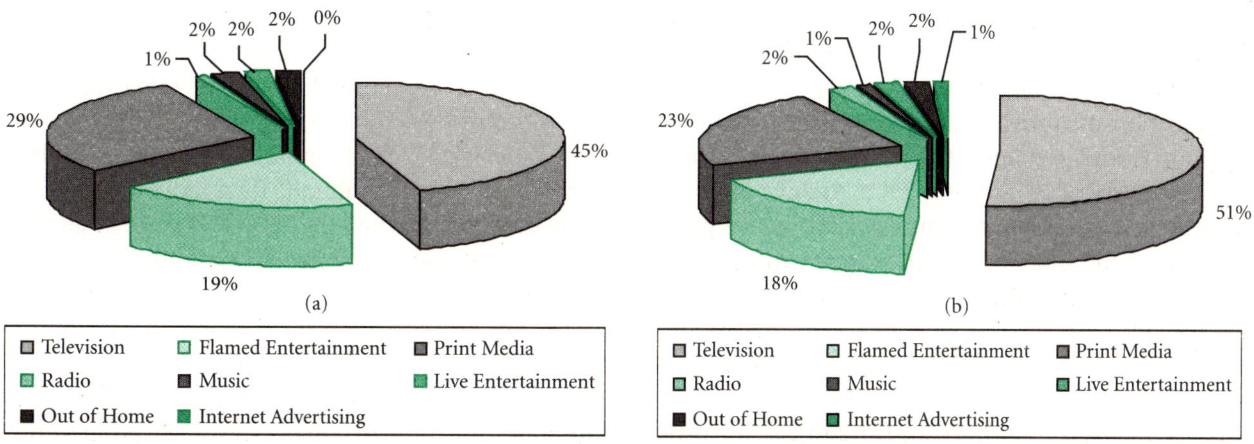

Source: Industry estimates and PWC analysis/FICCI: Indian Entertainment and Media Industry, March 2007.

FIGURE 12.4.1: Indian Entertainment and Media industry—Status and Projections

policies in various fields, and achievement in these areas, focused on the need for technological upgradation of its communication equipments and modernization of its programme designs.

- Song and Drama Division (SDD)—being related to publicity, education, and entertainment through the traditional media of folk music, dance, theatre, and puppetry—targeted at extensive use of traditional media for communication and modernizing its facilities for programme and designs.

- Directorate of Field Publicity (DFP) set goals for increasing its coverage, computerization of regional offices, creation of local software for effective communication, and streaming of its feedback mechanism.
- Some of the major policy initiatives taken include:
  - Indian editions of foreign scientific, technical, and specialty magazines, periodicals, and journals were allowed.
  - Foreign investment up to 100% in publishing companies publishing specialty magazines was allowed.
  - 26% foreign equity in Indian firms publishing newspapers and news and current affairs periodicals should be allowed.
- New Advertisement Policy came into effect from 1 January 2006. Audio-Visual Advertisement Policy was also approved by the government on 8 November 2006 and guidelines were also issued for empanelment of Audio and Video Producers on 21 June 2006.

Film Sector

12.4.5 The main objectives of the film sector were to produce, collect, display good quality films, children's films, documentaries, short films, animation films for internal and external publicity, and capacity building in film producing, directing, acting, editing, etc. Certification of films for exhibition is a continuous regulatory work pertaining to this sector. Maintenance and enforcement of National Film Archive of India and of the Archives of the Films Division enables preservation of the film wealth for posterity. It acts as a facilitator for the industry to organize film festivals and provide marketing support including import and export of films. Indian films are important tools for cultural diplomacy. The I&B Ministry participates in various international fairs and organizes festivals in collaboration with Indian Embassies abroad. Although the Indian film industry produces over a 1000 films a year, it has a negligible share in the global film industry revenues. Therefore, it requires a strong policy support to achieve a place of prominence in the world market. Piracy menace had been a major cause of loss of revenue to film industry. The activities of the film institutes, such as Satyajit Ray Film and Television Institute (SRFTI), Kolkata; Film and Television Institute of India (FTII), Pune; and IIMC were focused on modernization of training infrastructure and improvement in quality of training. IIMC has introduced TV journalism in its curriculum in response to growing demand for this discipline from the student community.

Broadcasting Sector

12.4.6 The broadcasting sector has already achieved major milestones on its growth journey, beginning with All-India Radio (AIR) and Doordarshan (DD). The scale of its operation, technological up-datedness, and timeliness in the move towards excellence in content and transmission make it a vibrant sector. Radio broadcasting infrastructure consists of 229 AIR analogue terrestrial radio Medium Wave and Short Wave stations, 264 analogue private terrestrial stations, and one private satellite radio, that is, World Space. The television broadcasting setup consists of 1398 analogue terrestrial transmitters and 4 digital transmitters in public sector, 6000 Multi-System Operators, and 65000 Local Cable Operators in private sector, 3 digital DTH satellite television operators in public and private sector.

12.4.7 Out of 210 million houses, by 2001 Census figure, television has reached 108 million, with cable and satellite in 68 million homes. The DTH subscription is around 5.6 million (DD DTH share 4.0 million, and private DTH 1.6 million). Similarly, number of radio sets was 132 million. Total radio coverage by population has reached 99.13%. There are in all 229 AIR channels and 42 private FM stations.

12.4.8 The creation of excellent content has become a vital need for survival of public service broadcaster to achieve its three-some objective of entertainment, education, and information in every single programme produced. During the Tenth Five Year Plan, first time high-quality content creation gathered serious attention to provide public service broadcaster a competitive edge vis-à-vis rapidly flourishing private broadcasting firms and rising broadcasting standards. In response to this, an alternative mechanism for creating rich content was devised by providing funds to institutions and individuals, known for professional excellence and high standards.

12.4.9 DD completed the J&K Special Package Phase I, and North East Package Phase I. This has enhanced coverage of television in these areas. The national channel coverage, both terrestrial as well as satellite, has reached a 90.7% population. News channel coverage has reached 48% of the population. DD also started the nation-wide DTH Ku band telecasting through 35 TV and 20 AIR Audio channels free of cost.

12.4.10 There were significant shortfalls during the Tenth Plan period both in terms of extending coverage and enhancing digitalization. Broadcasting in High Definition Television (HDTV) and interactive multimedia TV services have not yet started. The Conditional Access System (CAS) is being implemented in four metros only. As regards radio broadcasting, Digital Radio Mondiale (DRM) transmission has not yet started, and FM services did not reach the Tenth Plan target of 60% coverage. Internet radio broadcasting also did not take off as envisaged. The Tenth Plan strategy of content creation through alternative mechanism of funding did not go beyond signing an MoU between the Prasar Bharati and Public Service Broadcasting Trust.

VISION AND STRATEGY IN THE ELEVENTH FIVE YEAR PLAN

12.4.11 The growth potential of various media units needs to be harnessed fully to place broadcasting economy on a high growth path during the Eleventh Five Year Plan. The media units have an immense role to play in education, entertainment, and information dissemination. For a sustained growth in these areas, appropriate content, technology, and policy initiatives have to be evolved. Competitiveness and cost-effectiveness comes on the wings of appropriate technology and compatible manpower in all segments. In rapidly changing information and broadcasting sector, adopting new technologies and conceiving new technological solutions are crucial. PPP is the one of the most plausible solution for funding new technological interventions and bringing in competitiveness.

12.4.12 The Public Service Broadcaster in India, namely, the Prasar Bharati, enjoyed monopoly in broadcasting till recently. There was near absence of private sector broadcasters. Now in the liberalized information and broadcasting sector with global and domestic private players, public service broad-casting no more plays that dominant role in reach and technology. This new reality required government to assume simultaneously the role of facilitator and promoter of the information and broadcasting sector.

POLICY ISSUES, PROGRAMME REFORMS, AND NEW INITIATIVES IN THE ELEVENTH FIVE YEAR PLAN

12.4.13 Information

- In recognition of the importance of traditional media units, emphasis should be on the use of IT-enabled applications and other technological advancement for increasing their reach.
- There is a need for promoting partnership with the private sector in the field of traditional media units for bridging the information gap.
- The issues pertaining to Intellectual Property Rights in the information sector need to be addressed.
- Press and Registration of Books Act 1867 needs to be revisited to make it in tune with contemporary needs.
- Modernization of SDD's infrastructure in view of its importance needs to be emphasized.
- Redefining the objectives of the DFP and repositioning its network to reach remote, inaccessible, and strategic areas for effective reach and publicity.
- Strengthening the organizational set up of the Registrar of Newspaper for India (RNI) in North East and Central Zones.
- Completion of National Media Centre, a project of Press Information Bureau.
- Transformation of the IIMC into a global school in journalism.

12.4.14 Films

- Formulation of a National Digital Policy for entertainment sector.
- Revamping of Cinematograph Act of 1952 to address the emerging technologies and new challenges.
- Need to encourage film tourism for targeting the opportunities in global film sector.
- Building up a Centre of Excellence for animation, gaming, and special effects through PPP mode projects.

- Transforming FTII and SRFTI into global film and television schools.
- Encouraging the industry in creating new markets abroad and developing existing markets by supporting participation in film markets and festivals.

12.4.15 Broadcasting Content

- Public Service Broadcasting should focus on developmental programmes of the government and bringing in social awareness.
- Reorganization of Prasar Bharati.
- With the re-emergence of radio as a medium of profound reach and impact, especially FM radio, AIR needs to forge partnerships with private FM players to expand and effectively utilize this medium.
- Establish an International Channel through PPP.
- Facilitating emergence of India as an important source for high-quality animation-based content.

12.4.16 Expansion of Transmission Network, Digitalization, and Mobile Media

- The DTH market has matured and the arrival of IPTV and mobile broadcasting is imminent and need to be nurtured.
- With the convergence of technologies and availability of single gadgets with multiple applications, there are issues relating to policies, standardization of infrastructure, practices, and convergence which will need to be dealt with. One issue dominating the mind of telecom companies entering the area of IPTV is whether this will be regulated by Telecom FDI norms or Broadcasting FDI norms. A Joint Group of Ministry of Information and Broadcasting (MoI&B) and Department of Telecom has recommended that IPTV be governed as per licenses issued by Ministry of Communication and IT. Recommendations of the Joint Group are under consideration of the government.
- Digitization of content, phasing out analogue broadcasting, and creating an enabling environment for promotion of audio/video on demand.
- Digital archiving of films acquired by National Films archives and produced by Films Division.
- Introduction of HDTV Broadcasting and removal of barriers for spread of Digital Terrestrial Transmission (DTT), DTH, IPTV, and Mobile Broadcasting.
- Articulation of an effective IPR protection regime for film, music, and home-video.
- FM coverage to be enhanced from 35% to 45% by using DRM+ compatible transmitters.
- Border areas, rural areas, and semi-urban areas to be accorded priority for FM coverage.
- No further expansion of DD terrestrial network. However, emphasis should be on digitization. Very Low Power Transmission to go out of service on completion of their life. Border and uncovered areas to be covered through technologies like DTH.
- Private players' entry in the DD transmission network for providing mobile solutions and terrestrial transmission should be preferred through PPP route.

12.4.17 Miscellaneous Broadcasting Initiatives

- Mobile media solutions on a fast track basis should be implemented to provide variety in entertainment platforms.
- Digital transmission to be encouraged through Headend in the Sky.
- Common Regulator for Information, Communication, and Entertainment (ICE) Sector. The earlier initiative to create a 'Convergence Commission' with a 'carriage bureau' and a 'content bureau' needs to be revisited. In the context of the general movement of technology in the direction of convergence, that is (i) convergence of network platforms (viz., broadcast, satellite, cable, telecom) carrying similar kinds of services and (ii) merging of consumer devices such as telephones, televisions, PCs, all capable of triple-play, is a pointer that increasingly all carriage networks and devices will be able to carry all kinds of contents. It, therefore, makes sense to have a single regulator. At least this issue of a single regulator for telecom and broadcasting sectors deserves to be revisited.
- Early setting up of a Broadcast Regulator for resolution of legal and regulatory issues.
- Committee on ICE in its report on Going Digital recommended a stepwise migration path from the present analogue broadcasting economy to the digital one.

THE PATH AHEAD

12.4.18 The Eleventh Five Year Plan would aim at transforming the information and broadcasting sector, as well as the media and entertainment sector, into a modern, efficient, and responsive entity. To achieve this objective, in addition to putting in place necessary policy interventions, the barriers to investment in entertainment and media industry, which is spearheaded by the private sector, need to be effectively addressed. These include:

- Lack of uniformity in media policy for foreign investment FDI limits vary in different sectors—DTH (49%), cable (49%), and content (26%) for news on television and print; 100% for non-news in TV and print; 20% in radio; and 100% in film industry. This needs harmonization. In addition, there is a need to rationalize tax-treatment of foreign companies.
- Cross-media ownership: While policy enunciation imposes an obligation to observe cross-media ownership rules on media companies, these rules have not been formalized so far. As a result of this print and electronic media integration is taking place, which could result in emergence of media behemoths acquiring a mind-share disproportionate to what is permissible in a competitive market environment. Some boundary limits need to be laid down and this issue that needs to be revisited for the sake of long-term health of the industry.

12.4.19 There is need for incentivizing the consumer and equipment manufacturers for successful roll out of CAS and DTH across the country and timelines need to be fixed so that all the stakeholders could put their acts together.

12.4.20 Digitization of satellite transmission, production centres/studios, and terrestrial transmission needs to be undertaken in a mission mode along with introduction of HDTV, IPTV, mobile TV, and other value-added services. For the entire broadcasting sector 'Going Digital' and 'Farming out Excess Bandwidth' need to be taken up expediently to ensure switching over to digital transmission by 2015 and optimal use of scarce bandwidth.

12.4.21 The GBS for the Eleventh Five Year Plan of the MoI&B has been tentatively fixed at Rs 4809 crore at 2006–07 constant price and Rs 5439 crore at current price.

12.4.22 The progress of the plan outlays/expenditure during the Tenth Five Year Plan and the Eleventh Plan outlays of the communication and information technology sector as a whole are given at Annexure 12.4.1.

ANNEXURE 12.2.1
Performance of IT Hardware and Software during the Tenth Five Year Plan

Electronics Production (Financial Year) (Rs Crore)

Item	2001–02	2002–03	2003–04	2004–05	2005–06	2006–07#
1. Consumer electronics	12700	13800	15200	16800	18000	20000
2. Industrial electronics	4500	5550	6100	8300	8800	10400
3. Computers	3550	4250	6800	8800	10800	12800
4 Communication and broadcast equipment	4500	4800	5350	4800	7000	9500
5. Strategic electronics	1800	2500	2750	3000	3200	4500
6. Components	5700	6600	7600	8800	8800	8800
Subtotal	32750	37500	43800	50500	56600	66000
7. Software for exports	36500	46100	58240	80180	104100	141800
8. Domestic software	10874	13400	16250	21740	29600	37800
Total	80124	97000	118290	152420	190300	245600

Note: # Estimated.

Source: DIT Annual Report 2006–07.

ANNEXURE 12.2.2
Performance of Export Segment of IT Hardware and Software during the Tenth Five Year Plan

Electronics Export (Financial Year) (Rs Crore)

Item	2001–02	2002–03	2003–04	2004–05	2005–06	2006–07#*
1. Consumer electronics	700	750	825	1150	2000	
2. Industrial electronics	950	1400	1515	1500	2300	
3. Computers	1800	550	1440	1200	1025	
4. Communication and broadcast equipment	150	500	165	350	500	
5. Components	2200	2400	3755	3800	3800	
Subtotal	5800	5600	7700	8000	9625	11500
6. Computer software	36500	46100	58240	80180	104100	141800
Total	42300	51700	65940	88180	113725	153300

Note: # Estimated.

Source: DIT Annual Report 2006–07.

ANNEXURE 12.4.1
Progress of the Plan Expenditure of Communication and Information Sector

(Rs Crore)

S. No.	Communication and Information Sector	Tenth Plan (2002–07) Outlay	Annual Plan (2002–03)		Annual Plan (2003–04)		Annual Plan (2004–05)		Annual Plan (2005–06)		Annual Plan (2006–07)		Tenth Plan (2002–07)		Eleventh Plan (2007–12) Projected GBS (At Current Price)
			BE	Actual	BE	Actual	BE	Actual	BE	Actual	BE	RE	Total BE	Anticipated Expenditure	
1	2	3	4	5	6	7	8	9	10	11	12	13	14	15	16
1.	Department of Telecommunication#	80607.44	19277.79	11610.43	14955.00	7423.14	11660.00	6707.67	11801.01	8000.25	19509.31	17468.22	77203.11	51209.71	1752.00 (89581.56)
2.	Department of Information Technology#	5492.00	593.58	465.07	577.45	494.63	889.27	644.85	1087.56	879.85	1268.27	1273.27	4444.13	3757.67	12496.00 (2163.18)
3.	Department of Posts	1350.00	50.00	45.91	150.00	63.00	200.00	142.16	354.00	301.11	419.00	419.00	1173.00	874.51	4000.00
4.	Ministry of Information and Broadcasting	5130.00	878.00	693.20	890.00	524.23	955.00	421.24	1120.00	859.42	538.00	310.13	4381.00	2808.22	5439.00
	Grand Total	92579.44	20799.37	12814.61	16572.45	8505.00	13704.27	7915.92	14362.57	10040.63	21734.58	19470.62	87201.24	58650.11	23687.00 (91744.74)

Note: # includes IEBR; figures in parenthesis indicate projected IEBR.
Source: Documents of 'Annual Plan' and 'Demand for Grants' of DIT, DoP, DoT and Mo I&B.

Appendix

APPENDIX
Projected GBS for the Eleventh Plan

S. No.		Schemes/Programmes	Eleventh Plan Projections (Rs Crore) at 2006–07 Price	at Current Price	ZBB Remarks
1	2	3	4	5	6
1		**Department of Agriculture and Co-operation**			Subject to further ZBB exercise
	A	Centrally Sponsored Schemes			
	1	National Food Security Mission	4317.31	4883.00	
	2	Technology Mission on Cotton (TMC)	397.87	450.00	
	3	Enhancing Sustainability of Dryland Rainfed Farming Systems (to be merged with Rainfed Area Dev. Prog.)	0.00	0.00	
	4	Integrated Scheme of Oilseeds, Pulses, Oilpalm, and Maize (ISOPOM)	1326.23	1500.00	
	5	Technology Mission on Horticulture for NER including Sikkim, Uttarrkhand, HP, and J&K	1326.23	1500.00	
	6	Micro Irrigation	3006.11	3400.00	
	7	National Bamboo Techonology and Trade Mission	353.66	400.00	
	8	National Horticulture Mission	7788.48	8809.00	
	9	Support to State Extension Programmes for Extension Reforms	1768.30	2000.00	
	10	Rainfed Area Development Programmes (New)	3094.53	3500.00	
	11	Macro Management of Agriculture (MMA) Scheme	4862.83	5500.00	
	13	Others	0.00		
		Subtotal A	28241.54	31942.00	
	B	Central Sector Schemes			
	1	Agriculture Census	70.73	80.00	
	2	Improvement of Agricultural Statistics	132.62	150.00	
	3	Jute Technology Mission—Mini Mission II	35.37	40.00	
	4	National Oilseeds and Vegetable Oils Development Board (NOVOD) including Tree Borne Oilseeds and Biodiesel (Jetropha Plantation)	61.89	70.00	
	5	National Horticulture Board (including Cold Chain)	558.78	632.00	
	6	Coconut Development Board including Technology Mission on Coconut	176.83	200.00	
	7	Central Institute of Horticulture, Nagaland	22.10	25.00	
	8	Strengthening of Central Fertilizer Quality Control & Training Institute & Regional Fertilizer Control Laboratories	22.10	25.00	
	8a	National Project on Promotion of Balanced Use of Fertilizers	397.87	450.00	
	9	National Project on Promotion of Organic Farming	101.68	115.00	

(Appendix contd.)

(Appendix contd.)

1	2	3	4	5	6
	10	Scheme for Implementation of Protection of Plant Varieties and Farmers' Rights' Act 2001	106.10	120.00	
	11	Restructuring/Loan to National Seed Corporation and State Farm Corporation of India (NSC & SFCI)	33.60	38.00	
	12	Development and Strengthening of Infrastructure Facilities for Production and Distribution of Quality Seeds	397.87	450.00	
	13	Strengthening and Modernization of Pest Management in Country	79.57	90.00	
	14	National Scheme on Integrated Pest Management (New Scheme)	88.42	100.00	
	15	Strengthening and Modernization of Plant Quarantine Facilities in India	70.73	80.00	
	16	Monitoring of Pesticide Residues at National Level	48.63	55.00	
	17	Post Harvest Technology and Management (New Scheme)	35.37	40.00	
	18	Watershed Development Council	0.00		
	19	National Rainfed Area Authority (New Scheme)	15.91	18.00	
	20	Investment in Debenture of State Land Development Banks (SLDBs)	353.66	400.00	
	21	National Agricultural Insurance Scheme (NAIS)	3094.53	3500.00	
	22	Co-operative Education and Training	132.62	150.00	
	23	Assistance to NCDC for Development of Co-operatives	282.93	320.00	
	24	Extension Support to Central Institutes/Directorate of Extension (DOE)	61.89	70.00	
	25	Agri-Clinics/Agri-Business Centres	132.62	150.00	
	26	Mass Media Support to Agriculture Extension	397.87	450.00	
	27	Studies in Agricultural Economic Policy & Development	132.62	150.00	
	28	Forecasting and Remote Sensing Application in Crop Husbandry	0.00		
	29	Forecasting Agricultural Output using Space, Agro-Meteorology, and Land Based Observation (FASAL)	44.21	50.00	
	30	Marketing Research Surveys and Information Network (MRIN)	13.26	15.00	
	31	Strengthening Agmark Grading and Export Quality Controls	5.30	6.00	
	32	Development of Market Infrastructure, Grading, and Standardization	335.98	380.00	
	33	Gramin Bhandran Yojana	353.66	400.00	
	34	Small Farmers' Agri Business Consortium (SFAC)	106.10	120.00	
	35	Strengthening/Promoting Agricultural Information System + DAC IT apparatus	309.45	350.00	
	36	Capacity Building to Enhance Competitiveness of Indian Agriculture and Registration of Organic Products Aboard	4.42	5.00	
	37	Natural Disaster Management	0.00	0.00	
	38	Secretariat Economic Service	4.42	5.00	
	39	National Commission on Farmers	0.00	0.00	
	40	Promotion and Strengthening of Agricultural Mechanization through Training, Testing, and Demonstration	31.83	36.00	

(Appendix contd.)

(Appendix contd.)

1	2	3	4	5	6
	41	All India Soil and Land Use Survey	39.79	45.00	
	42	Grant-in-aid to National Institute of Agricultural Marketing (NIAM)	13.26	15.00	
	43	Restrutured Scheme for Institutions (including the schemes mentioned at S. No. 21, 23, 40, 41)	0.00	0.00	
		Subtotal B	8306.60	9395.00	
		Subtotal (A+B)	36548.13	41337.00	
	C	State Plan Scheme			
	1	Control of Shifting Cultivation (Watershed Development in Shifting Cultivation Area in NE States)	212.20	240.00	
	2	Rashtriya Krishi Vikas Yojana	22103.77	25000.00	
		Subtotal C	22312.41	25240.00	
		Grand Total (A+B+C)	58860.55	66577.00	
2		**Department of Animal Husbandry, Dairying, and Fisheries (DAHD&F)**			
	I	ANIMAL HUSBANDRY	3645.35	4123.00	
	A	Centrally Sponsored Schemes			
	1	National Project for Livestock Development**	1211.29	1370.00	
	2	Project for Feed and Fodder	125.02	141.40	
	3	Livestock Insurance	45.09	51.00	
	4	National Livestock Disease Control Programme (NLDCP)	1149.40	1300.00	
	5	Livestock Extension & Delivery Services*$	13.26	15.00	
		Total CSS (A&H)	2256.71	2552.40	
	B	Central Sector Schemes			
	1	Livestock Census	397.87	450.00	
	2	Integrated Sample Survey	70.73	80.00	
	3	Central Cattle Development Organization	92.84	105.00	
	4	Central Sheep Breeding Farm	11.49	13.00	
	5	Central Fodder Development Organization	70.73	80.00	
	6	Central Poultry Development Organization	44.21	50.00	

Notes: **Project for Cattle & Buffalo Breeding, Poultry Development (Assistance to State Poultry/Duck Farms, Rural Backyard Development, Establishment of Poultry Estates), Project for Slaughter Houses and CU Plants, Establishment/Modernization of rural slaughter houses, including mobile slaughter plants (New Scheme)*, Utilization of Fallen Animals (New Scheme)*, Consevation of Threatened Livestock Breeds.

*$ Support for Private Veterinary Clinics and AI Centres, Strengthening Livestock Extension System.

(Appendix contd.)

1	2	3	4	5	6
	7	Directorate of Animal Health	81.87	92.60	
	8	Small Ruminant Development	176.83	200.00	
	9	Piggery Development	132.62	150.00	
	10	Salvaging and Rearing of Male Buffalo Calves	265.25	300.00	
	11	Food Safety and Traceability	44.21	50.00	
		Total CS (A&H)	1388.65	1570.60	
	II	DAIRY DEVELOPMENT	689.64	780.00	
	A	Centrally Sponsored Schemes			
	1	Dairy Development Projects*#	198.94	225.01	
	B	Central Sector Schemes	0.00	0.00	
	1	Assistance to Co-operatives	44.21	50.00	
	2	Delhi Milk Scheme	4.42	5.00	
	3	Venture Capital Fund*^	442.08	500.00	
		Total CS (DD)	490.70	555.00	
	III	FISHERIES	2454.40	2776.00	
	A	Centrally Sponsored Schemes			
	1	Development of Inland Fisheries & Aquaculture (including new components)	265.25	300.00	
	2	Development of Marine Fisheries, Infrastructure, & Post Harvest Operations (including new components)	309.45	350.00	
	3	National Scheme of Welfare of Fishermen, Fisheries Training, and Extension (including new components)	159.15	180.00	
		Total CSS (Fisheries)	733.85	830.00	
	B	Central Sector Schemes			
	1	Strengthening of Database & Information Networking for Fisheries & Animal Husbandry	22.10	25.00	
	2	Assistance to Fisheries Institutes (CIFNET, CICEF, IFP, & FSI)	328.02	371.00	
	3	National Fisheries Development Board	1370.43	1550.00	
		Total CS (Fisheries)	1720.56	1946.00	

Note: *# Project for Dairy Development (DAHD for Non-potential districts), National Dairy Plan (By Consortium in 325 Milk Potential Districts).
*^ Dairy Venture Capital Fund, Poultry Venture Capital Fund.

(Appendix contd.)

1	2	3	4	5	6
	IV	SECRETARIAT & ECONOMIC SERVICES	30.95	35.00	
	V	SPECIAL PACKAGE FOR 31 SUICIDE PRONE DISTRICTS OF ANDHRA PRADESH, KARNATAKA, KERALA, & MAHARASHTRA	300.61	340.00	
		Total Centrally Sponsored Schemes	3490.10	3947.40	
		Total Central Sector Schemes	3630.85	4106.60	
		Total	7120.95	8054.00	
	VI	EXTERNALLY AIDED PROJECTS (EAP)			
		Control & Containment of Avian Influenza—EAP	106.10	120.00	
3		**Department of Agriculture Research and Education (DARE)**			
	1	Assistance to Research Institutes in Crop Sciences	1679.96	1900.08	
	2	Assistance to Research Institutes in Horticulture	621.18	702.57	
	3	Assistance to Research Institutes in Natural Resources Management (Soil and Water Nutrition)	645.54	730.12	
	4	Assistance to Research Institutes in Agricultural Engineering	231.82	262.20	
	5	Assistance to Research Institutes in Animal Science	858.50	970.99	
	6	Assistance to Research Institutes in Fisheries	310.25	350.90	
	7	Assistance to Research Institutes in Agri. Econ. & Statistics	23.03	26.05	
	8	Assistance to Research Institutes in Agri. Extension (included Rs 500 crore for new KVKs)	1989.34	2250.00	
	9	Assistance to Research Institutes in Agriculture Education + Centre of Excellence—support to SAUs	2785.96	3151.00	
	10	Assistance to Research Institutes in DARE + CAU, Manipur	671.31	759.27	
	11	MIS/ICAR Hq. including IPR Management	105.95	119.83	
	12	National Fund for Basic and Strategic Research	111.40	126.00	
	13	National Agricultural Innovation Project (WB Project)	963.72	1089.99	
	14	Indo-US Knowledge Initiative	44.21	50.00	
	15	New Initiatives	88.42	100.00	
		Total	11130.57	12589.00	
4		**Department of Atomic Energy**			
		Central Sector Schemes			
		Research & Development (R&D) Sector			
	1	AERB	17.97	20.33	

(Appendix contd.)

1	2	3	4	5	6
	2	AMD	329.63	372.82	
	3	BARC	3232.45	3656.00	
	4	RRCAT	557.15	630.15	
	5	DAE Projects	65.61	74.21	
	6	DCS&EM	166.37	188.17	
	7	Grant-in-aid Support to Research and Education	2314.05	2617.26	
	8	IGCAR	596.05	674.15	
	9	IPR	404.06	457.00	
	10	International Thermo Nuclear Experimental Reactor	1317.05	1489.62	
	11	TMC	198.05	224.00	
	12	VECC	527.22	596.30	
		Industries Sector			
	1	BARC	2846.97	3220.00	
	2	BRIT	36.25	41.00	
	3	DAE Project	207.78	235.00	
	4	ECIL	0.00	0.00	
	5	HWB	442.08	500.00	
	6	IGCAR	751.53	850.00	
	7	NFC	530.49	600.00	
		Minerals Sector			
	1	AMD	150.31	170.00	
	2	DAE Projects	0.00	0.00	
	3	UCIL	1131.71	1280.00	
	4	IREL	0.00	0.00	
		Power Sector			
	1	BARC	265.25	300.00	
	2	IGCAR	17.68	20.00	
	3	DAE Projects	30.06	34.00	
	4	NPCIL			
		(i) Investment	0.00	0.00	
		(ii) Russian Credit	2212.14	2502.00	
	5	KKNP	201.59	228.00	
	6	BHAVINI	1768.30	2000.00	
		Grand Total	22529.93	22980.00	

(Appendix contd.)

1	2	3	4	5	6
5		**Department of AYUSH**			
	A	Central Sector Schemes			
	1	Systems Strengthening	249.99	282.75	
		(i) Strengthening of Department of AYUSH	41.56	47.00	
		(ii) Statutory Institutions	2.61	2.95	
		(iii) Hospitals and Dispensaries	143.94	162.80	
		(iv) Strengthening of Pharmacopeial Laboratories	22.10	25.00	
		(v) Information, Education, and Communication	22.10	25.00	
		(vi) AYUSH & Public Health	17.68	20.00	
	2	Educational Institutions	363.10	410.68	
	3	R&D including Medicinal Plants	636.21	719.57	
		(i) Research Councils	317.85	359.50	
		(ii) Medicinal Plants	318.36	360.07	
	4	HRD (Training Programme/Fellowship/Exposure Visit/Upgradation of Skills etc.)	26.52	30.00	
	5	Cataloguing, Digitization of Manuscripts and AYUSH IT Network	35.37	40.00	
	6	International Co-operation	35.37	40.00	
	7	Development of AYUSH Industry	446.50	505.00	
	8	Funding of NGOs Engaged in Local Health Traditions/Midwifery Practices etc., under AYUSH.	22.10	25.00	
		Total A	1815.16	2053.00	
	B	Centrally Sponsored Schemes			
	1	Promotion of AYUSH	1237.81	1400.00	
		(i) Development of Institutions	486.28	550.00	
		(ii) Hospitals and Dispensaries (under NRHM)	552.59	625.00	
		(iii) Drugs Quality Control	198.93	225.00	
		New Initiatives	473.02	535.00	
	2	Public–Private Partnership for Setting up of Specialty Clinics/IPDs	44.21	50.00	
	3	Medicinal Plants Processing Zones	428.81	485.00	
		Total B	1710.83	1935.00	
		Grand Total (A+B)	3525.99	3988.00	

(Appendix contd.)

1	2	3	4	5	6
6		**Department of Biotechnology**			
	1	Human Resource Development	221.04	250.00	(1) SC/ST and gender budgeting should not be universal and S&T department should be particularly exempted from it. (2) DBT should draw up a crash programme for pulses and oilseeds in consultation with Ministry of Agriculture for improving their productivity in the country. (3) DBT needs to have a close interaction with the ICAR to avoid duplication and insure synergy and also accelerate transfer of technologies to the farmers. (4) Efforts should be made to create CoEs within the existing institutions and creation of new institutions may be taken up only in areas in which nucleating facilities do not exist. (5) DBT may prioritize its activities, do careful annual physical and financial phasing so that most important programme could be fully provided in the Eleventh Plan.
	2	Programmes for Promotion of Excellence and Innovation	309.45	350.00	
	3	Biotech Facilities	221.04	250.00	
	4	Bioinformatics	110.52	125.00	
	5	R&D	1382.81	1564.00	
	6	Grand Challenge Programmes	353.66	400.00	
	7	International Co-operation	88.42	100.00	
	8	Biotechnology for Societal Development	88.42	100.00	
	9	Support to Autonomous R&D institutions	2210.38	2500.00	
		I&M Sector	663.11	750.00	
	1	Assistance for Technology Incubators, Pilot Projects, Biotechnology Parks and Biotech Development Fund			
	2	PPP (Small Business Innovative Research Initiative, SBIRI; Biotechnology Industry Partnership Programme, BIPP; Establishment of Biotechnology Industrial Research Assistance Council, BIRAC			
		Total	5648.84	6389.00	
7		**Department of Chemicals & Petrochemicals**			
		Ongoing Schemes			
	1	Support of Existing PSUs on Project Basis (i) Hindustan Organics Chemicals Limited (HOCL) (ii) Hindustan Insecticides Limited (HIL) (iii) Indian Drug and Pharmaceuticals Limited (IDPL) (iv) Bengal Chemicals and Pharmaceuticals Limited (BCPL) (v) Hindustan Antibiotics Limited (HAL) (vi) KAPL/RDPL	318.29	360.00	Routine AMRs for PSUs should be on non-Plan or IEBR side. Outlays proposed for individual PSUs be merged into one scheme under the name 'Project Based Support to PSUs'. Future support to PSUs would be project based and on commercial justification.
	2	Support to Autonomous Bodies on Project Basis (i) Central Institute of Plastics Engineering and Technology (CIPET) (ii) National Institute of Pharmaceutical Education and Research (NIPER) (iii) Institute of Pesticides Formulation Technology (IPFT) (iv) National Pharmaceutical Pricing Authority (NPPA)	169.76	192.00	Further funding depnds on in-depth evaluation by independent agency. Instead of outlay to each institution, there would be one scheme of Project Based Support to Autonomous Institutions.

(Appendix contd.)

1	2	3	4	5	6
	3	Assam Gas Cracker Project	176.83	200.00	
	4	Chemical Promotion & Development Scheme (CPDS)—restructured as Pharma & Chemical Promotion & Development Scheme (PCPDS)	13.26	15.00	This scheme has been merged with Pharma Export Promotion Scheme under S. No. 12 and restructured as Pharma & Chemical Promotion & Development Scheme.
	5	Chemical Weapons Convention (CWC)			
	6	IT/Secretariat	3.54	4.00	
			0.88	1.00	
		New Schemes			
	7	New Scheme of CIPET	61.89	70.00	This scheme be clubbed with provision for autonomous institution in S. No. 2 subject to evaluation of autonomous institute.
	8	Other New Schemes of Petrochemicals	44.21	50.00	Specific schemes to be identified and further provision only after receiving specific proposal.
	9	New Scheme of NIPER, Mohali	61.01	69.00	This scheme be clubbed with provision for autonomous institution in S. No. 2 subject to evaluation.
	10	New NIPER-like Institutes	454.45	514.00	
	11	Interest Subsidy for Scheduled M Compliance	300.61	340.00	
	12	Pharma Export Promotion Scheme			
		(i) PPP Schemes for Drug Banks			These scheme should be in the domain of M/o Health instead of DCPC.
		(ii) PPP Schemes for Cancer Medicines			
	13	Strengthening of NPPA	53.05	60.00	
	14	Creation of IPR Facilitation Centre at Pharmaeaxcil	4.42	5.00	
	15	ERP, R&D Parks	4.42	5.00	
	16	Critical Assistance for WHO pre-qualification for Pharma PSUs/R&D	66.31	75.00	
		Apex Body for Re-positioning of Pharma PSUs	0.00	0.00	No need for such body.
		Grand Total	1732.94	1960.00	
8		**Ministry of Civil Aviation**			
	1	Airports Authority of India	1301.27	1471.68	
	2	Indira Gandhi Rashtriya Uran Akademi	113.06	127.87	Revision in funding pattern for airport projects in NER. Funds should directly flow to MoCA instead of being routed through NEC. Modernization of Kolkata Airport through IR of AAI.
	3	Directorate General of Civil Aviation	128.43	145.25	
	4	Aero Club of India	72.68	82.20	
	5	Bureau of Civil Aviation Security	64.55	73.00	
		Grand Total	1680.00	1900.00	

(Appendix contd.)

(Appendix contd.)

1	2	3	4	5	6
9		Ministry of Coal			
	1	R&D	75.35	85.24	All the ongoing schemes be evaluated through professional agency and findings be used for restructuring/weeding of the same.
	2	Regional Exploration	164.02	185.54	
	3	Detailed Drilling in Non-CIL Blocks	472.94	535.00	
	4	Environment Measures & Subsidence Control	155.34	175.72	It could be done in a PPP mode.
	5	Conservation & Safety in Coal Mines	170.67	193.06	
	6	Development of Transportation Infrastructure in Coal fields	277.63	314.06	
	7	Coal Controller Organization	1.22	1.38	
	8	Information Technology	8.84	10.00	
		Grand Total	1326.00	1500.00	
10		Ministry of Culture			
	A	Central Sector Schemes			
	1	Modernization & Computerization	4.42	5.00	Dropping or Restructuring for 2008–09 is subject to evaluation.
	2	Promotion & Dissemination	689.64	780.00	
	3	Archaeology	548.17	620.00	Dropping or Restructuring for 2008–09 is subject to evaluation; to be merged together under 'Scheme for Archaeology, Archives, & Museums' in consultation with M/o Culture.
	4	Archives & Records	61.89	70.00	
	5	Museums	540.98	611.86	
	6	Anthropology & Ethnology	46.09	52.13	
	7	Public Libraries	416.07	470.59	
	8	IGNCA	90.80	102.70	
	9	Inst. of Buddhist & Tibetan Studies	50.69	57.33	Dropping or Restructuring for 2008–09 is subject to evaluation.
	10	Memorials	114.94	130.00	
	11	Activities for NER	347.47	393.00	
	12	Building Project of Subordinate Offices	204.68	231.50	
		Grand Total	3115.84	3524.11	
11		Department Of Commerce			
	A	Central Sector Schemes			
	1	National Export Insurance Account (NEIA)	884.15	1000.00	ECGC, NEIA, MAI should be evaluated in-depth through independent agencies before further GBS is provided. Subsidies should form part of non-Plan expenditure.
	2	Investment in ECGC	707.32	800.00	
	3	Export Promotion, Quality Control, and Inspection			All schemes with more than Rs 50 crore outlay be evaluated and findings incorporated.
		(i) Export Inspection Council (EIC)	44.21	50.00	Project based support should be given to EIC.
		(ii) Market Access Initiatives	486.28	550.00	

(Appendix contd.)

(Appendix contd.)

1	2	3	4	5	6
	4	R&D Institutes			
		(i) Indian Institute of Foreign Trade (IIFT)	35.37	40.00	One composite scheme as 'Project Based Support to Autonomous Institutions' for all autonomous institutions (IIFT, IIP, IIPM, FDDI, Centre for WTO Studies). All the autonomous institutions to be evaluated in-depth through independent agencies before futher GBS is provided.
		(ii) Indian Institute of Packaging (IIP)	26.52	30.00	
		(iii) Footwear Design and Development Institute (FDDI)	88.42	100.00	
		(iv) Center for WTO Studies	17.68	20.00	
		(v) Indian Institute of Plantation Management (IIPM)	0.44	0.50	
	5	Modernization and Upgradation			
		(i) Secretariat—Economic Services	15.03	17.00	
		(ii) DGFT	22.10	25.00	
		(iii) DGCIS	15.03	17.00	
		(iv) Computerization DGS&D	20.34	23.00	
		Agricultural Sector			
	6	APEDA	637.03	720.50	Schemes of APEDA/MPEDA should be restructured in a way not to duplicate the efforts of M/o Agriculture, Food Processing, and Health.
	7	MPEDA	397.87	450.00	Concrete Action Plan to be submitted before providing enhanced allocation.
	8	Cashew Export Promotion Council	0.00	0.00	GBS allocation depends on approval by competent authority.
	9	Tea Board	707.32	800.00	Plantation Boards should focus on export-oriented production in synergy with M/o Agriculture.
	10	Coffee Board	530.49	600.00	
	11	Rubber Board	512.81	580.00	
	12	Spices Board	265.25	300.00	
		Total A	5413.65	6123.00	
	B	Centrally Sponsored Scheme			
		Industry & Mineral Sector			
	13	ASIDE	3353.58	3793.00	
		Total B	3353.58	3793.00	
		Grand Total (A+B)	8767.23	9916.00	
12		**Department of Consumer Affairs**			
		Central Sector Schemes			
	1	Consumer Awareness	361.62	409.00	
	2	Consumer Protection (Confonet, integrated project NCDRC, NCPA, State Consumer Helpline)	162.95	184.30	

(Appendix contd.)

(Appendix contd.)

1	2	3	4	5	6
	3	Consumer Education and Training, HRD/Capacity Building	13.26	15.00	
	4	Forward Market Commission	83.29	94.20	
	5	Weights & Measures	165.34	187.00	To be merged with scheme at S. No. 6 (National Test House) from 2008–09. Existing schemes and new initiatives concerning standards, conformity assessment, and testing activities/programmes would be merged into one single scheme under the name 'Measures for Standards & Testing'.
	6	National Test House	77.81	88.00	Further funding would be in project mode and subject to in-depth evaluation.
	7	National System for Standardization, Database, Assessment, and Quality Campaign including Bureau of Indian Standards	83.99	95.00	Further funding would be in project mode and subject to in-depth evaluation.
	8	Gold Hallmarking	9.28	10.50	
		Grand Total	957.54	1083.00	
13		**Ministry of Corporate Affairs**			
	1	Indian Institute of Corporate affairs	186.56	211.00	
		Grand Total	186.56	211.00	
14		**Department Of Drinking Water**			
		Centrally Sponsored Schemes			
	1	Rural Drinking Water	34915.52	39490.47	
	2	Central Rural Sanitation Campaign	6910.22	7815.66	
		Grand Total	41825.75	47306.13	
15		**Ministry of Development of North East Region (DoNER)**			
	1	NEDFI	339.61	384.43	Impact assessment of the activities be carried out for NEDFI.
	2	Advocacy	36.32	41.11	Evaluation of the scheme for continuation in the next year.
	3	Capacity Building	69.70	78.90	Evaluation of the scheme indicating numbers targeted and achievement for further funding.
	4	Development of Inland Water Transport in the NE	1.32	1.49	The scheme be transferred to D/o Shipping as CS.
	5	Development of Cities/Roads (EAP)	0.06	0.06	NEUDP be transferred to MoUD. For NESRDP, state share be provided throgh NLCPR route.
		Grand Total	447.00	506.00	
16		**Department of Expenditure**			
	1	Central Plan scheme for funding 15 Seats to a high level Professional Course covering basic elements of MBA (Finance) for the Officers of	4.42	5.00	(1) Training scheme would target officers of all States/UTs and Central govt. (2) Training capacity to be increased from 15 to

(Appendix contd.)

1	2	3	4	5	6
		North Eastern/Special Category States/BIMARU States dealing with Accounts & Finance Matters to be offered by the National Institute of Financial Management (NIFM) Society			100 (80 for States and 20 for Central). (3) Deptt. of Expenditure with NIFM to work out additional infrastructure requirement (4) Evaluation and feedback mechanism to be instituted at once. At least 3 Finance Secretaries of the States and Adviser (FR) Planning Commission to be included in NIFM Board. (5) Deptt. of Expenditure in consultation with CGA would formulate a scheme, in the project mode, for modification of accounting system for effective monitoring of entire range of Plan Schemes implemented by Central and State Governments.
		Grand Total	4.42	5.00	
17		**Ministry of Environment & Forest**			
	A	Central Sector Scheme			
	I	ENVIRONMENT	960.19	1086.00	
	1	Environmental Monitoring and Governance	190.98	216.00	
	2	Pollution Abatement	207.78	235.00	
	3	R&D for Conservation & Development	265.25	300.00	
	4	Environment Information, Education, & Awareness	216.62	245.00	
	5	International Co-operation Activities	70.73	80.00	
	6	National Coastal Management Programme (EAP)	8.84	10.00	
	II	FORESTRY & WILDLIFE	1043.30	1180.00	
	7	Grants-in-aid to F&WL Institutions	397.87	450.00	
	8	Capacity Building in Forestry Sector	97.26	110.00	
	9	Strengthening Forestry Divisions	88.42	100.00	
	10	Strengthening of Wildlife Divisions	132.62	150.00	
	11	National Afforestation & Eco-development Board (NAEB)	221.04	250.00	
	12	Animal Welfare	106.10	120.00	
		Total A	2003.49	2266.00	
	B	Centrally Sponsored Schemes			
	I	ENVIRONMENT	530.50	600.01	
	1	Conservation of Natural Resources and Ecosystems	530.49	600.00	
	2	Environmental Management in Heritage, Pilgrimage, and Tourist Centres Including Taj Protection	0.01	0.01	

1	2	3	4	5	6
	II	RIVER AND LAKE CONSERVATION	1856.72	2100.00	
	3	National River Conservation Plan (NRCP)	1856.72	2100.00	
	III	FORESTRY & WILDLIFE	3655.07	4133.99	
	4	Gregarious Flowering of Muli (*Melacanna baccifera*) Bamboos	32.71	37.00	
	5	Intensification of Forest Management (former Integrated Forest Protection Scheme)	530.49	600.00	
	6	Integrated Development of Wild Life Habitats	707.32	800.00	
	7	Project Tiger	543.75	615.00	
	8	Project Elephant	72.49	81.99	
	9	National Afforestation Programme	1768.30	2000.00	
		New Scheme in CSS	795.74	900.00	
	10	Social Forestry with Communities (Panchayat Van Yojana)	795.74	900.00	
		Total B	6838.02	7734.00	
		Grand Total (A+B)	8841.51	10000.00	
18		**Department of Economic Affairs**			
	A	Central Sector Schemes			
	1	Assistance for Infrastructure Development—VGF	196.28	222.00	
	2	Contribution for Railways Safety Works against Additional Levies on Motor Spirit and High Speed Diesel (Cess to Railways) (i) Central Road Fund—MH 3054 (ii) Umbrella Support Project under CCF II—MH 2075 (iii) National Equity Fund (NEF) Scheme—MH 2885 (iv) Additional Budgetary Support to NABARD for Water Harvesting Scheme—MH 2416	3749.68	4241.00	
		Total A	3945.96	4463.00	
19		**Department of School Education & Literacy**			
	A	Central Sector Schemes			
	I	ELEMENTARY EDUCATION			
	1	Bal Bhavan	30.95	35.00	
	2	NCTE	4.42	5.00	

(*Appendix contd.*)

1	2	3	4	5	6
	II	ADULT EDUCATION			
	3	Directorate of Adult Education	44.21	50.00	
	4	NLMA	17.68	20.00	To be evaluated.
	5	Grants to NGOs			
		(i) SRC	176.83	200.00	
		(ii) Field Innovative Projects (Support to NGO + SRC + NIAE + Pop. Edn)	64.54	73.00	
		(iii) Jan Shikshan Sansthan (+ Skill Development Mission Rs 140)	353.66	400.00	
	6	Projects for Removal of Illiteracy	884.15	1000.00	
	7	Support to NER	23.87	27.00	
	8	Adult Education Studies by University Department of Adult Education	26.52	30.00	
	III	SECONDARY EDUCATION			
	9	NCERT	224.57	254.00	To be evaluated.
	10	National Open School	88.42	100.00	To be evaluated. The admission, transfer procedures, and other guidelines, utilization of funds for transparency should be on the website.
	11	Navodya Vidyalayas	4067.09	4600.00	
	12	Kendriya Vidayalas	1326.23	1500.00	
	13	Central Tibetan School Admn (CTSA)	36.25	41.00	
	14	Joint Indo-Mongolian School at Mongolia	4.42	5.00	
		Total A	7373.82	8340.00	
	B	Centrally Sponsored Schemes			
		Elementary Education			
	1	Sarva Shiksha Abhiyan (SSA)	62774.69	71000.00	To be evaluated on priority.
	2	DPEP	114.94	130.00	
	3	Mid-day Meal	42439.23	48000.00	To be evaluated on priority.
	4	Teacher Education	3536.60	4000.00	
	5	Mahila Samakhya	185.67	210.00	
		New Scheme			
	6	Pre Primary Schooling (1 year)	1768.30	2000.00	To be launched in 2008–09.
	7	Revamped Lifelong Education and Awareness Programme (LEAP) (TLC + PLP + CEP)	3359.77	3800.00	
	8	Literacy Programmes for 35+ age group illiterates	353.66	400.00	

(*Appendix contd.*)

1	2	3	4	5	6
		Secondary Education			
	9	SUCCESS			
		(i) Infrastructure Support for Secondary Schools			
		(a) 15000 UPS upgraded to SS @ 60 lakh per School (75:25)	5968.02	6750.00	
		(b) Strengthening of existing 44000 SS @ Rs 40 lakh per school (75:25)	10167.73	11500.00	
		(ii) ICT in Schools	5304.90	6000.00	Universalization of ICT in schools & institutions on a single portal.
		(iii) Girl Child Incentive	1326.23	1500.00	
		(iv) IEDSS	884.15	1000.00	
		(v) In service training to teachers @ Rs1000/teacher/annum for 17 lakh	1768.30	2000.00	
		(vi) Support for Science Labs and Library @ Rs 4 lakh/Lab—25000 Schools	769.21	870.00	
		(vii) New Model Schools (6000)	884.15	1000.00	
		(viii) Vocational Education	11272.92	12750.00	To be launched in 2008–09.
	10	Upgrading 2000 KGBVs (Residential Schools/Hostels)	1768.30	2000.00	
	11	OSC Merit/National Means cum Merit Scholarship	1485.37	1680.00	
		Total B	156132.16	176590.00	
		Grand Total (A+B)	163505.98	184930.00	
20		**Ministry of External Affairs**			
		Central Sector Schemes			
	1	Tala Power Project	44.21	50.00	Complition in 2007–08.
	2	Dungsum Cement Project	274.09	310.00	MEA's total commitment is Rs 300 Crore for plant.
	3	Punatsangchu Hydroelectric Project (for DPR-07–08)	1.47	1.66	
	4	Pul-e-Khumri Project in Afghanistan	265.25	300.00	
		New Schemes			
	1	Kaladan Multi-modal Transit Transport Project—Myanmar	265.25	300.00	Project is absolutely unviable and EFC has made a number of observations which need to be rectified.
	2	Punatsangchu-I Hydroelectric Project	1060.98	1200.00	
	3	Pre-Construction Activities for Punatsangchu-I Hydroelectric Project	11.27	12.75	
	4	Integrated Development of Selected Border Checkposts (5)	70.73	80.00	Either MEA or MHA should build the checkposts to avoid duplication/overlapping and be completed in 3 years instead of 5 years. A meeting be held with MHA and MEA to sort out this aspect.
	5	Development of Road Infrastructure in the Terai Region of Nepal	61.89	70.00	
	6	Naumure Hydel Project in Nepal	145.00	164.00	
		Cross Border Raillink between India and Nepal	0.00	0.00	

(*Appendix contd.*)

(Appendix contd.)

1	2	3	4	5	6
		New Schemes—from 2008–09	0.00	0.00	
		Construction of Embankment on Kamla River	0.00	0.00	
		5600 MW Pancheshwar Multipurpose Project (MPP)	0.00	0.00	Projects under consideration for Eleventh Plan Estimates not available yet.
		330 MW Sun Koshi Sapta Koshi Multipurpose Project	0.00	0.00	
		10800 MW Karnali Chisapani Multipurpose Project	0.00	0.00	
		Grand Total	2200.13	2488.41	
21		**Department of Earth Sciences**			
	1	Polar Science	241.37	273.00	Polar and Ocean Science Programme (New Merged Scheme).
	2	Polymetallic Nodules (PMN) Programme	282.04	319.00	Ocean Resource Suveys (New Merged Scheme).
	3	Ocean Observation and Information System (OOIS)	88.42	100.00	Information and Advisory Services (New Merged Scheme).
	4	Marine Research and Technology Development (MRTD)	284.70	322.00	Technology Development/Demonstration Programmes (New Merged Scheme).
	5	Delineation of the Outer Limits of Continental Shelf	5.30	6.00	
	6	Coastal Research Vessels and Other Research vessels	68.96	78.00	Research Vessels/Platforms (New Merged Scheme).
	7	National Institute of Ocean Technology (NIOT)	239.60	271.00	Technology Development/Demonstration Programmes (New Merged Scheme).
	8	Information Technology	17.68	20.00	Information and Advisory Services (New Merged Scheme).
	9	Comprehensive Topography Surveys	45.98	52.00	
	10	Gas Hydrates	49.51	56.00	Ocean Resource Suveys (New Merged Scheme).
	11	Acquisition of Research Vessel 'Sagar Nidhi'	154.73	175.00	Research Vessels/Platforms (New Merged Scheme).
	12	Data Buoy Programme/Integrated Sustain Ocean Observation	50.40	57.00	Information and Advisory Services (New Merged Scheme).
	13	Tsunami & Storm Surge Warning System	87.53	99.00	Information and Advisory Services (New Merged Scheme).
	14	National Centre for Antarctic and Ocean Research (NCAOR)	59.24	67.00	Polar and Ocean Science Programme (New Merged Scheme).
	15	Indian National Centre for Ocean Information Services (INCOIS)	100.79	114.00	Information and Advisory Services (New Merged Scheme).
	16	Seafront facilities	92.84	105.00	
	17	National Centre for Medium Range Weather Forecast (NCMRWF)	61.01	69.00	Atmospheric Science Programme (New Merged Scheme).
	18	Indian Institute of Tropical Meteorology (IITM)	211.31	239.00	
	19	Indian Meteorological Department (IMD)			Meteorological Services (New Merged Scheme).
		(i) Space Meteorology	44.21	50.00	
		(ii) Agro Met Advisory Services	38.90	44.00	
		(iii) Seismic Hazard and Risk Evaluation	329.79	373.00	
		(iv) Operation & Maintenance	83.11	94.00	
		(v) Aviation Meteorology	130.85	148.00	
		(vi) Modernization of IMD (Communication, Observation, Cyclone warning, Forecasting, Aviation Services, Instrumentation, Infrastructural Development)	2219.22	2510.00	

(Appendix contd.)

(Appendix contd.)

1	2	3	4	5	6
	20	Development of Manned Submersible	83.99	95.00	Technology Development/Demonstration Programmes (New Merged Scheme).
	21	Multichannel Seismic System onboard ORV Sagar Kanya	62.77	71.00	
	22	Expeditions to the Arctic Region	40.67	46.00	Polar and Ocean Science Programme (New Merged Scheme)
	23	Desalination Plant	115.82	131.00	Technology Development/Demonstration Programmes (New Merged Scheme).
	24	National Oceanarium	88.42	100.00	
	25	Demonstration of Shoreline Protection Measures	30.95	35.00	Technology Development/Demonstration Programmes (New Merged Scheme).
	26	Integrated Ocean Drilling Prog. & Geotechnoic Studies (IODP)	53.93	61.00	Polar and Ocean Science Programme (New Merged Scheme)
	27	Ice-Class Research Vessel	389.03	440.00	Research Vessels/Platforms (New Merged Scheme).
	28	Headquarters Building	44.21	50.00	
	29	Multi-hazards Early Warning Support System	17.68	20.00	
	30	Centre for Climate Change	142.35	161.00	
	31	Dedicated Weather Channel & Commonwealth Games	75.15	85.00	
	32	NIOT Extension Centre West Bengal	28.29	32.00	
	33	R&D in Earth & Atmopsheric Sciences	31.83	36.00	
		Grand Total	6192.59	7004.00	
22		**Department of Fertilizers**			
		Central Sector Schemes			
	1	Revival of Sick CPSEs	537.00	607.36	(1) Regarding the conversion of FO/LSHS based plants to gas besed, D/o Fertilizer would explore various possibilities including setting up of large ammonia unit at Panipat (2) Revival of CPSEs will depend upon proper and bankable study and timely submission of DPRs.
	2	Capital Subsidy for Conversion of 4 Existing FO/LSHS Plants to NG/LNG	782.58	885.12	
		Grand Total	1319.58	1492.48	
23		**Department of Food & Public Distribution**			
	1	Construction of Godowns by Food Corporation of India etc.	147.26	166.56	PFPD would propose a new modified scheme for creating storage capacity for the Eleventh Plan.
	2	Integrated Information System for Foodgrains Management (IISFM)	180.47	204.12	Evaluation, Monitoring, & Research for food grain management & strengthening of PDS.
	3	Strengthening of PDS	129.94	146.96	
	4	NSI, Kanpur	10.83	12.25	Govt. should support its modernization which should be funded through PPP.
	5	Consultancies, Training, and Research	23.10	26.13	Various schemes of training, evaluation, and consultancy may be merged under a single scheme—'Training, Evaluation, and Consultancy'.

(Appendix contd.)

1	2	3	4	5	6
		Training, Research, Monitoring, and Concurrent Evaluation (06–07)	0.00	0.00	
		Research, Development, and Modernization of Labs of VVO&F (operational in 2006–07)	0.00	0.00	DFPD to submit a DPR for modernization of the laboratory of Directorate of VVO & Fats.
		Technical Studies & Consultancies (06–07)	0.00	0.00	
	6	Village Grain Bank	122.00	137.98	Evaluation should be done and further funding to be based on this evaluation.
		Computerization of PDS Operations	0.00	0.00	DPR should be prepared. A National Portal of DFPD should provide in modules, all information online & on real-time basis for PDS, FPS, FCI Godowns, Warehouses, and Ministry itself.
		Grand Total	613.60	694.00	
24		Ministry of Food Processing Industries			
	1	Scheme for Infrastructure Development	2310.29	2613.00	
	2	Scheme for Technology Upgradation/Establishment/Modernization of Food Processing	530.49	600.00	
	3	Scheme for Upgradation of Quality of Street Food	157.38	178.00	
	4	Scheme for Quality Assurance, Codex Standards, and R&D	221.04	250.00	
	5	Scheme for Human Resource Development	57.47	65.00	
	6	Scheme for Stregthening of Institution	287.35	325.00	
		Grand Total	3564.01	4031.00	
25		Department of Health & Family Welfare			
	A	Central Sector Scheme			
	1	National Rural Health Mission	2481.81	2807.00	
	2	Oversight Committee	1615.34	1827.00	
	3	Strengthening of the Institutes for Control of Communicable Diseases	469.69	531.23	
	4	Strengthening of Hospitals and Dispensaries	1027.68	1162.34	
	5	Strengthening of the Institutes for Medical Education, Training, and Research	5876.98	6647.03	Department of Health Research to get from this.
	6	System Strengthening including Emergency Medical Relief/Disaster Management	978.38	1106.58	
	7	Pradhan Mantri Swasthya Suraksha Yojana	3496.82	3955.00	PPP to be encouraged in facilitating tertiary health care.

(Appendix contd.)

1	2	3	4	5	6
		New Initiatives under CS	6151.32	6957.32	
	8	Forward Linkages to NRHM in NE*	795.74*	900*	
	9	National Centre for Disease Control	397.87	450.00	Redevelopment of NICD as World Class 'National Centre for Disease Control'.
	10	Advisory Board for Standards	19.45	22.00	
	11	Programme for Blood and Blood Products	397.87	450.00	
	12	Redevelopment of Hospitals/Institutions	5336.13	6035.32	
		Total A	22098.02	24993.50	
	B	Centrally Sponsored Schemes			
	1	NRHM	76630.22	86671.00	Salary component to be transferred to Non-Plan. Time bound financial and physical targets to be fixed.
	2	National AIDS Control Programme including STD Control	5064.41	5728.00	Composite lab facility for all diseases and PPP should be encouraged.
	3	(i) National Cancer Control Programme	2121.96	2400.00	The Programme for Control of Cancer and Tobacco can be taken as two components. Convergence with communicable disease programme should be attempted.
		(ii) Tobacco Control	417.25	471.92	
	4	National Mental Health Programme	884.15	1000.00	
	5	Assistance to States for Drug & PFA Control	229.88	260.00	
	6	Assistance to States for Capacity Building in Trauma Care	648.04	732.95	
		New initiatives under CSS	12280.52	13889.63	
	7	e-Health (including Telemedicine)	161.80	183.00	
	8	National Programme for Prevention and Control of Diabetes, Cardiovascular Disease, and Stroke	1468.13	1660.50	
	9	Health Care of Older Persons	353.66	400.00	
	10	District Hospitals	2457.94	2780.00	
	11	Human Resources for Health#	3536.60	4000.00	

Note: * Through earmarked 10% allocation for NE—to come from different schemes.
#Additional requirement for Oversight Committee can be covered under this.

(Appendix contd.)

(Appendix contd.)

1	2	3	4	5	6
	12	Health Insurance based National Urban Health Mission	3974.26	4495.00	Not launched in 2007–08. It may be taken up for Eleventh Plan.
	13	Pilot Projects:			
		(i) Sports Medicine	79.57	90.00	A few pilot projects would be taken up which will be eventually, depending on the success and experience gained, upscaled and put under NRHM/NUHM.
		(ii) Deafness	88.42	100.00	
		(iii) Leptospirosis Control	3.96	4.48	
		(iv) Control of Human Rabies	7.65	8.65	
		(v) Medical Rehabilitation	44.21	50.00	
		(vi) Oral Health	22.10	25.00	
		(vii) Fluorosis	60.12	68.00	
		(viii) Organ Transplant	22.10	25.00	
		Total B	21646.21	111153.50	
		Grand Total (A+B)	120374.45	136147.00	
26		**Department of Heavy Industry**			
	1	(i) National Automative Testing and R&D Infrastructure Project (NATRIP) and (ii) FID	1149.40	1300.00	NATRIP & FID, Secretariat expenditure of DHI would continue in the Eleventh Plan.
	2	Restructuring of PSEs under DHI (lumpsum provision for pending proposals)			CPSEs/Autonomous Institutes other than CPSEs which are yet to be considered for restructuring be brought under one
	3	Project based Support to CPSEs/Autonomous Institutes	2147.87	2429.30	composite scheme namely 'Project Based Support to CPSEs/ Autonomous Institutes' for meeting budgetary support for approved restructuring,approved schemes, and project based scheme.
	4	Modernization fund for Capital Goods Sector	265.25	300.00	Experience of similar parks under other Ministries needs to be considered in this case.
	5	Additions Modifications and Replacements (AMR)	44.21	50.00	Crucial Balancing Investment should be dropped. AMR to continue in Eleventh Plan. Some component such as professional & special services, other administrative expenses and advertisement and publicity be merged as 'Professional &
	6	Professional and Special Services	8.84	10.00	Special Services as One Single Scheme'.
	7	Secretariat Expenditure (Computerization)	3.27	3.70	The project should be supported fully through IEBR of CPSUs.
		Coal Gasification Demonstration Project			
		Grand Total	3618.83	4093.00	
27		**Ministry of Home Affairs**			
	1	Police Housing	2210.38	2500.00	Police infrastructure scheme should be on non-Plan side and sufficient justification for taking up some component under Plan budget.
	2	Critical Infrastructure in Extremist Affected Areas	442.08	500.00	

(Appendix contd.)

(Appendix contd.)

1	2	3	4	5	6
		Police Education & Training			
	3	Police Education & Training	66.31	75.00	Functions like Research, Education, and Training be treated as one continuum for all such institutions. A comprehensive project for upgradation of capacities in existing training institutions be prepared not only for Delhi but also for other states. Expansion of communication infrastructure should be a part of crime reporting/detection system. All activities wth financial implications be categorized as Plan and non-Plan. All police buildings should be modern, functional, eco friendly, IT-friendlly and approvals subject to their being so.
	4	BPR&D	132.62	150.00	
	5	Strengthening of North Eastern Police Academy (NEPA)	44.21	50.00	
	6	Upgradation of NPA into NPU	1.77	2.00	
	7	Modernization of Delhi Police	424.39	480.00	
		Scheme of Forensic Science			
	8	Directorate of Forensic Science—CFSLs & GEQD	265.25	300.00	All institutions & major ongoing schemes to be evaluated in-depth through professional agencies on priority. Schemes to be designed and implemented in project mode with well defined outcomes and targets. DPRs to be prepared for every scheme/project. Project preparation and implementation should be separated. Whole crime detection and forensic system be evaluated by an IIM for major increase in funding. One composite scheme as Modernization of Forensic Science Applications for better design and implementation. Nomenclature and nature of schemes for Eleventh Plan need to be rationalized.
	9	Directorate of CFSL—CFSL (CBI), New Delhi	7.07	8.00	
	10	National Institute of Criminology and Forensic Sciences (NICFS)	13.26	15.00	
	11	Crime and Criminal Tracking Network and Systems	1768.30	2000.00	
	12	NCRB	8.84	10.00	
	13	Official Language	35.37	40.00	There should be no overlap of schemes of Department of OL with that of schems of HRD. Focus should be on few major areas and rest should be subjected to ZBB.
		Registrar General of India			Schemes of RGI to be reorganized in to few composite schemes.
	14	Improvement in Vital Statistics System & Other Schemes	132.62	150.00	
	15	National Population Register	265.25	300.00	
	16	NE Division	4.42	5.00	New innovative scheme for this division and proposed objective should be pursued by DoNER.

(Appendix contd.)

1	2	3	4	5	6
		Human Rights Division			
	17	Construction of Manav Adhikar Bhavan	4.42	5.00	
	18	Complaints Handling Management System	8.84	10.00	The cost of MAB and its phasing need to be reviewed. CHMS to be supported on submission of DPR.
		National Disaster Management			Functions of NDMA & M/o Earth Sciences needs to be synergized and integrated.
	19	Strengthening of Fire and Emergency Services	176.83	200.00	
	20	All Other Disaster Management Schemes/Projects (Development of Advance Warning Systems, Capacity Building, Protocol for Disasters, National Portal on Disasters, etc.)	88.42	100.00	
	21	Revamping of Civil Defence	88.42	100.00	
		Grand Total	6189.05	7000.00	
28		Department of Industrial Policy and Promotion			
		Central Sector Scheme			
	1	Transport Subsidy scheme	0.88	1.00	Further allocation would be subject to an in-depth evaluation.
	2	IC&JV and Asia Enterprise in India & Undertaking Investment Promotion Activities	85.76	97.00	Merge IC&JV with Investment Promotion Activities and e-Biz pilot project should be a part of this scheme.
	3	D/o Explosives	10.61	12.00	All autonomous institutions and major schemes (annual outlay over Rs 50 cr) would be evaluated before further GBS disbursal.
	4	Modernization and Strengthening of Patent Office (Revenue)	282.93	320.00	
	5	Project Based Support to Autonomous Institutions	493.36	558.00	
		(i) CMTI			Venturing into nanotechnolgy application be done by D/o S&T and DIPP need not duplicate this.
		(ii) CPPRI (iii) Quality Council of India(QCI) (iv) National Institute of Design (NID)			Instead of providing outlay to each autonomous body, an integrated scheme of Project Based Support to Autonomous Institutions be put in place. In-depth evaluation by independent agency to justify continuation of budgetary support.
		(v) NCCBM (vi) IRMRA (vii) NPC (viii) NMCC			
	6	Indian Leather Development Programme (ILDP)	1149.40	1300.00	Detailed analysis of the expenditure to be provided before enhancing the outlays.
	7	Salt Commissioner (for NMAY)	4.42	5.00	NMAY to be merged with IAY as per the fesibility of operation.

(Appendix contd.)

1	2	3	4	5	6
	8	Industrial Infrastructure Upgradation Scheme (IIUS)			New version of IIUS under the name 'IIUS for NE States only'. Rapid assessment of the scheme for ensuring appropriate regional spread.
	9	Technology Upgradation (New Initiative)*	928.36	1050.00	Sufficient justification to be provided for this new scheme.
	10	Delhi Mumbai Industrial Corridor Development Corporation	291.77	330.00	
		Total	3247.49	3673.00	
		Centrally Sponsored Scheme			
	11	NEIP Package (including Integrated Infrastructure Development Scheme)	265.25	300.00	Close scrutiny of Regional Developemnt Scheme.
	12	Package for (Other than North East) Special Category States	176.83	200.00	
	13	Growth Centre Scheme (other than NE)	8.84	10.00	
		Total	450.92	510.00	
		Grand Total (A+B)	3698.40	4183.00	
29		**Department of Information & Technology**			
	A	Central Sector Schemes			
	I	R&D PROGRAMME			
	1	SAMEER	130.85	148.00	
	2	Microelectronics and Nanotech Dev. Prog.	221.04	250.00	
	3	Technology Dev. Council (Including IPR)	309.45	350.00	
	4	Convergence, Comm., and Strategic Electronics	176.83	200.00	
	5	Components, Material and Photonics Dev. Prog.	88.42	100.00	
	6	C-DAC	795.74	900.00	
	7	Electronics in Health and Telemedicine	88.42	100.00	
	8	Technology Dev. for Indian Languages	88.42	100.00	
	9	IT for Masses (Gender, SC/ST)	137.93	156.00	
	10	Media Lab. In Asia	265.25	300.00	
		R&D Subtotal	2302.33	2604.00	
	II	INFRASTRUCTURE DEVELOPMENT			
	1	STQC	291.77	330.00	
	2	STPI/EHTP	39.79	45.00	
	3	Digital DNA Park	8.84	10.00	
	4	Electronic Governance	4413.68	4992.00	

Note: * Not yet decided

(Appendix contd.)

(Appendix contd.)

1	2	3	4	5	6
	5	Cyber Security including Cert-in IT Act	530.49	600.00	
	6	ERNET	8.84	10.00	
	7	Promotion of Electronics/IT Hardware Manufacturing	972.57	1100.00	
		Infrastructure Subtotal	6265.98	7087.00	
	III	HUMAN RESOURCE DEVELOPMENT			
	1	DOEACC	8.84	10.00	
	2	Manpower Development	296.19	335.00	
	3	Facilitation of Setting up of Integrated Townships	53.05	60.00	
		HRD Subtotal	358.08	405.00	
	IV	OTHERS			
	4	Others—Headquarter (Secretariat & Bld.)	88.42	100.00	
	5	NIC	2033.55	2300.00	
		HRD Subtotal	2121.96	2400.00	
		Grand Total	11048.35	12496.00	
30		**Ministry of Information & Broadcasting**			
	A	Information	277.63	314.00	
	1	PIB	74.23	83.95	
	2	Publications Division	2.20	2.49	
	3	DAVP	50.35	56.95	
	4	IIMC	38.93	44.03	
	5	Photo Division	2.92	3.30	
	6	DFP	6.01	6.80	
	7	Song & Drama Division	19.81	22.40	
	8	RRTD	6.63	7.50	
	9	RNI	1.36	1.54	
	10	Main Secretariat Scheme (Information Wing)	75.19	85.04	
	B	Film	397.88	450.00	
	1	Films Division	62.64	70.85	
	2	NFAI	26.53	30.00	
	3	Directorate of Film Festivals	4.42	5.00	
	4	CFSI	18.36	20.77	
	5	CBFC	11.05	12.50	
	6	NFDC	40.88	46.23	

(Appendix contd.)

(Appendix contd.)

1	2	3	4	5	6
	7	FTII	84.27	95.31	
	8	SRFTI	53.05	60.00	
	9	Main Secretariat Scheme (Film Wing)	61.01	69.00	
	C	Broadcasting	4133.49	4675.00	
	1	AIR (Including Expansion of FM Services)	1430.59	1618.00	
	2	Doordarshan	2680.80	3032.00	
	3	Main Secretariat Scheme (Broadcasting Wing)	22.10	25.00	
		Grand Total (A+B+C)	4809.00	5439.00	
31		**Department of Justice**			
	A	Central Sector Schemes			
	1	Domestic Resources for 'Indian Administration of Justice' Project in Collaboration with the ADB (EAP) (New Scheme)	3.60	4.07	
	2	Admn. of Justice India Project (ADB) (New Scheme)	1.45	1.64	
		Total A	5.05	5.71	
	B	Centrally Sponsored Schemes			
	1	Computerization of District and Subordinate Courts	654.80	740.60	
	2	Capacity building and Infrastructure facilities for Judiciary (i) To UTs without Legislature (ii) To State Governments (iii) To UTs with Legislature	619.86	701.08	
	3	Study of Justice Reforms & Assessment Status (New Scheme)	20.00	22.62	
		Total B	1294.66	1464.30	
		Grand Total (A+B)	1299.71	1470.01	
32		**Ministry of Labour & Employment**			
	A	Central Sector Schemes			
	I	DGE&T (EMPLOYMENT)	29.53	33.40	
	1	Construction of Office Building, Staff Quarters, and Skill Training Institutes	19.45	22.00	
	2	Continuation and Setting up of New Vocational Rehabilitation Centres for Handicapped persons including Skill Training Workshops and Rural Rehabilitation Extension Centres.	5.66	6.40	

(Appendix contd.)

1	2	3	4	5	6
	3	Welfare of SC/ST Job Seekers through Coaching, Guidance, and Vocational Trg. and Intro. of New Courses in Existing CGCs & Estt of New CGCs in States not Covered so far	4.42	5.00	
	II	DGE&T (TRAINING)	102.52	115.95	
	4	National Instructional Media Institute, Chennai	12.11	13.70	
	5	Upgradation of Apprenticeship Training	9.73	11.00	
	6	Diversification, Upgradation, and Expansion of Training to Women	15.47	17.50	
	7	Foremen Trg Inst. at Jamshedpur & Bangalore	5.30	6.00	
	8	Model Industrial Training Institutes (MITIs)	8.84	10.00	
	9	Diversification, Upgradation, and Expansion of Advanced/Central Trg. Inst. and Intro. of Hi-tech Trg.	22.10	25.00	
	10	Strengthening of Trainers' Skills and MIS	4.64	5.25	
	11	Upgradation of Training Infrastructure in DGE&T Institutes including CSTARI	7.96	9.00	
	12	Project Impl. And Trade Testing in DGE&T HQ	3.09	3.50	
	13	Building equipment & Establishment for RVTIs (Calcutta, Hissar, Allahabad, Indore, Bubhaneswar, Vadodara, Jaipur, and Tura)	13.26	15.00	
	III	INDUSTRIAL RELATIONS	41.38	46.80	
	14	Strengthening of Adjudication Machinery & Holding Lok Adalats	11.32	12.80	Two schemes (i) Strengthening of Adjudication Machinery and (ii) Holding of Lok Adalats in the CGIT-cum-Labour Courts as an Alternative Grievance Redressal Mechanism have been merged under it.
	15	Machinery for Better Conciliation and Upgradation of Office Infrastructure at CLC's and RLC's	28.29	32.00	Two schemes (i) Upgradation of Office Infrastructure at CLC(C) & RLC(C), ND, and (ii) Machinery for better conciliation and preventive mediation and more effective enforcement of labour laws have been merged under it.
	16	Improvement and Strengthening of Training Wing of Central Labour Service Officers	1.77	2.00	
	IV	CENTRAL BOARD FOR WORKERS' EDUCATION (CBWE)	44.21	50.00	
	17	Central Board for Workers' Education (CBWE)	44.21	50.00	
	V	CHILD LABOUR	579.16	655.05	
	18	Child Labour Cell	0.04	0.05	To be transferred to Non-Plan.
	19	National Child Labour Project (including Grants-in-aid to Voluntary Agencies)	552.59	625.00	

(*Appendix contd.*)

(Appendix contd.)

1	2	3	4	5	6
	20	Indo-American CLP (INDUS) with matching US grant	26.52	30.00	
	VI	WOMEN LABOUR	2.40	2.71	
	21	Women Cell	0.01	0.01	To be transferred to Non-Plan.
	22	Grants-in-Aid to Voluntary Agencies	2.39	2.70	
	VII	LABOUR BUREAU	38.02	43.00	
	23	Consumer Price Index for Industrial Workers 2001 Series and Rural Labour Enquiry	7.07	8.00	To be merged together under 'Labour Statistics'.
	24	Labour Statistics	13.26	15.00	Emerged after merging (i) Socio-economic Surveys of different segments of Labour, (ii) Collection of Labour Statistics under the Annual Survey of Industries (Extension to Sample Sector), (iii) Occupational Wage Survey (Sixth) Round, (iv) Modernization of Machine Tabulation Unit, and (v) Rural Labour Enquiry including CPI for Agricultural & Rural Labour.
	25	Improvement in the Labour and Employment Statistical System	17.68	20.00	
	VIII	DIRECTOR GENERAL OF MINES SAFETY (DGMS)	34.35	38.85	
	26	Mine Accident Analysis and Modernization of Information Database (MAMID)	10.61	12.00	Schemes (i) Study of Mine Accidents (SOMA) and Development of Information System and (ii) Modernization of Survey capabilities in DGMS through Digitization of mines plan and automated survey system (MSC) and Modernization of Information database relating to Mines Management have been merged.
	27	Strengthening of Core Functions of DGMS (SOCFOD)	14.68	16.60	Schemes (i) Augmentation of Science & Techonology Capabilities, Mine Rescue Services, and Human Resource Development (S&T) and (ii) Strengthening of Machinery for Conduct of Statutory Examinations (SSEX) have been merged together.
	28	Improving Efficiency by Providing Infrastructural Facilities in DGMS (PIF)	9.06	10.25	
	IX	DIRECTOR GENERAL, FACTORY ADVICE SERVICE, AND LABOUR INSTITUTE (DGFASLI)	22.10	25.00	
	29	Establishment of a New Regional Labour Institute	8.84	10.00	
	30	Strengthening of DGFASLI Organization and Occupational Safety and Health in Factories, Ports, and Docks	13.26	15.00	

(Appendix contd.)

(Appendix contd.)

1	2	3	4	5	6
	X	NATIONAL LABOUR INSTITUTE (NLI)	22.10	25.00	
	31	National Labour Institute	22.10	25.00	
		Other Schemes	10.17	11.50	
	32	Scheme on Information Technology	8.84	10.00	
	33	Grants-in-aid to Research/Academic Institutions & Non-governmental Voluntary Organizations for Undertaking Research in Labour Related Subjects	1.33	1.50	
		New Scheme under CS	4.43	5.01	
	34	Skill Development (Mission Mode)	4.43	5.01	
		Total A	930.37	1052.27	
	B	Centrally Sponsored Schemes			
	I	DGE&T (TRAINING)	117.00	132.33	
	1	Establishment of New ITIs in NE States, Sikkim and Strengthening and Modernization of ITIs in the State of J&K.	55.11	62.33	
	2	Upgradation of 100 ITIs into Centres of Excellence.	61.89	70.00	
	3	Testing & Certification of Skills for Workers in the Informal Sector			To be dropped as activities are taken under Skill Development Initiatives.
	II	DGLW	13.26	15.00	
	4	Rehabilitation of Bonded Labour	13.26	15.00	
		New Schemes under CSS	1149.40	1300.00	
	III	DGE&T (TRAINING)	574.70	650.00	
	5	Skill Development Initiative through PPP	486.28	550.00	
	6	Externally Aided Project for Reforms & Improvement in Vocational Training Services Rendered by Central & State Governments	88.42	100.00	
	IV	DGLW	574.70	650.00	
	7	Social Security for Unorganized Sector Workers	265.25	300.00	
	8	Health Insurance for Unorganized Sector Workers	309.45	350.00	
		Total B	1279.66	1447.33	
		Grand Total (A+B)	2210.02	2499.60	

(Appendix contd.)

(Appendix contd.)

1	2	3	4	5	6
33		Department of Land Resources			
	A	Central Sector Schemes			
	1	Professional Support, Capacity Building, M&E, IEC & Related Activities, TDET, Implementation/Monitoring of National Rehabilitation Policy etc.	428.25	484.36	(1) Comprehensive & result oriented master plan be prepared for better watershed management. (2) Computerization of Land Records, Strengthening of Revenue Machinery, and Updating of Land Records, Comprehensive Modernization of Land Records be integrated under the head 'National Programme for Comprehensive Land Resource Management'. (3) M&E, Capacity-building and Professional Support be merged in one Integrated programme—'Monitoring and Capacity Building'. (4) In-depth evaluation of ongoing programme to be done through independent agency on top priority.
	2	Others	39.67	44.87	
		Total A	467.92	529.23	
	B	Centrally Sponsored Schemes			
	1	Integrated Watershed Development Programme (i) DPAP, (ii) DDP, (iii) IWDP	15359.46	17372.00	
	2	National Programme for Comprehensive Resource Management (i) CLR, (ii) SRA & ULR, (iii) CMLR	513.69	581.00	
	3	Biofuels	403.17	456.00	Biodiesel Programme to be merged with IWMP.
	4	EAP	461.24	521.67	
		Total B	16737.57	18930.67	
		Grand Total (A+B)	17205.49	19459.90	
34		Ministry of Mines			
	1	MECL	44.19	50.00	
	2	GSI	901.58	1020.00	
	3	IBM	79.55	90.00	
	4	S&T	17.68	20.00	
		Grand Total	1043.00	1180.00	
35		Ministry of Minority Affairs			
	A	Central Sector Schemes			
	1	Grant-in-aid to Maulana Azad Education Foundation	442.08	500.00	
	2	National Minorities Development & Finance Corporation (NMDFC)	442.08	500.00	Scheme 'Additional Equity Contribution to NMDFC for Development of Wakfs' has been merged with Grant-in-aid to NMDFC.
	3	Free Coaching & Allied Scheme for Minorities	39.79	45.00	
	4	Research/Studies, Monitoring, and Evaluation of Development Schemes for Minorities including Publicity	30.95	35.00	

(Appendix contd.)

1	2	3	4	5	6
		New Schemes in CS			
	5	Grant-in-aid to State Channelizing Agency	17.68	20.00	
		Total A	972.57	1100.00	
	B	Centrally Sponsored Schemes			
	1	Merit-cum-Means Scholarship for Professional and Technical Courses	530.49	600.00	
		New Schemes in CSS			
	2	Pre-Matric Scholarships for Minorities	1237.81	1400.00	
	3	Post-Matric Scholarships for Minorities	1016.77	1150.00	
	4	Multi Sectoral Development Programme for Minorities in Selected Minority Concentration Districts	2431.41	2750.00	
		Total B	5216.49	5900.00	
		Grand Total (A+B)	6189.05	7000.00	
36		**Ministry of Micro, Small, and Medium Enterprises**			
	A	Micro, Small, and Medium Enterprises			
	1	Quality of Technology Support Institutions and Programmes (Tool Room), (CLCSS, ISO)	1374.85	1555	Enhanced allocation for existing tool rooms and for setting up new tool rooms.
	2	Promotional Services Institutions and Programmes	306.80	347	
	3	MSME Clusters Development Programmes and MSME Growth Poles	583.54	660	
	4	Credit Support Programme (Credit Guarantee, Micro Finance, Women Enterprise Promotion, SC, SP, PSP, Minority Component)	919.52	1040	
	5	Market Development Assistance	42.44	48	
	6	Upgradation of Data base	88.42	100	
		Subtotal of DC (MSME)	3315.56	3750	
		National Small Industries Corporation			
	7	Marketing Assistance Schemes	53.93	61	
	8	Performance and Credit Rating Scheme	46.86	53	
	9	Incubator/SEs Establishment Programme	17.68	20	
		Subtotal of (NSIC)	118.48	134	
		Other Schemes			
	10	Survey, Studies, and Policies Research	3.09	3.5	
	11	Promotion and Hand Holding of Micro and Small Enterprises	61.01	69	

1	2	3	4	5	6
	12	Training Institutions	22.99	26	All autonomous bodies/institutions should be evaluated and findings to be incorporated. All training centres/institutes will be supported for revamping of existing courses and introduction of new courses as per industry requirement. Support to existing training centres/institutes for upgradation of infrastructure and setting of new centres/institutes.
	13	International Cooperations	8.84	10	
	14	National Commission on Enterprises in the Unorganized Sector	6.63	7.5	
		Subtotal of Other Schemes	102.56	116	
		Total of MSME	3536.60	4000	
	B	Agro and Rural Industries			
		Khadi & Village Industries Commission (KVIC)			
		(i) Khadi			
	1	Khadi Grant (including MDA of Rs 10.00 crore for Khadi)	761.13	860.86	
	2	Khadi R&D, Scheme for Enhancing Productivity & Competitiveness of Khadi Industries and Artisans and Khadi Interest Subsidy and Loan	110.52	125	
		Subtotal of Khadi	871.65	985.86	
		(ii) Village Industries			
	3	Village Industries—Grant, Loan, Interest Subsidy, HRD, Marketing	327.68	370.62	
	4	Restructured Rural Employment Generation Programme (REGP)*	2873.49	3250	
	5	Setting up of Mahatma Gandhi Institute for Rural Industrialization (MGIRI), Wardha	14.44	16.33	
	6	Workshed-cum-Housing Scheme for Khadi Weavers	83.99	95	
	7	Package for Developing Infrastructure for Khadi Institutions and including Nursing Fund for Weak Institutions	44.21	50	
	8	Scheme for Enhancing Productivity of Khadi Industries	79.57	90	
		Subtotal of Village Industries	3423.39	3871.95	
		Total of KVIC	4295.04	4857.81	
		Coir Board			
	9	Research & Development and Rejuvenation, Modernization, and Technology Upgradation for Coir Industry	125.55	142	

Note: * PMRY and REGP will be merged into a new scheme called Prime Minister's Employment Generation Programme (PMEGP) once it is approved by the competent authority.

(*Appendix contd.*)

1	2	3	4	5	6
	10	Training, Extension, Quality Improvement, Mahila Coir Yojana, and Welfare Measures	124.14	140.41	
		Total of Coir Board	249.69	282.41	
		Prime Minister's Rozgar Yojana (PMRY)*			
	11	Subsidy for PMRY and EDP	2024.70	2290	
		SFURTI			
	12	Scheme of Fund for Regeneration of Traditional Industries (SFURTI)	61.70	69.78	
		Total of A&RI	6631.13	7500	
		Grand Total of MSME	10167.73	11500	
37		**Ministry of New & Renewable Energy**			
	1	Grid Interactive Power and Distributed Renewable Power	442.08	500.00	Bifurcation of establishment including salary component into Plan and non-Plan from next year under various schemes. Independent evaluation of major schemes with emphasis on small hydro power in NE, wind power & biomass/cogeneration. Enhanced funding depends on evaluation & incorporation of findings.
	2	Renewable Energy for Rural Aplications	1105.19	1250.00	
	3	Renewable Energy for Urban, Industrial, and Commercial Applications	442.08	500.00	
	4	R&D	1060.98	1200.00	Three technical institutions uder umbrella programme on R&D. Project based support to R&D institutions. R&D should be on top priority with higher allocation. GBS should be for R&D and not for subsidies.
	5	Supporting Programmes (Awareness Generation, International Relation, HRD & Training, M&E, IREDA, Support to State Govt. & Industry)	397.87	450.00	Schemes relating to International Co-operation, HRD, Training & Seminars to be retained under Plan head.
	6	Spill over liabilities of Tenth Plan (IREP)	88.42	100.00	
		Grand Total	3536.60	4000.00	
38		**Department of Public Enterprises**			
	1	Retraining & Redeployment of rationalized workers of CPSUs	42.00	47.50	Survey of present/intended activity status of VRS optees for last two year for restructuring/reorienting the scheme. Revival packages should be on commercial viability. Cleaning balance sheet will not serve the purpose and manpower rationalization is important.

1	2	3	4	5	6
		New Scheme (08–09)	5.75	6.50	
	2	Research Development and Consultancy			
		(i) Support to IPE, Hyderabad			For annual survey of SLPEs on regular basis, these two schemes proposed for Eleventh Plan.
		(ii) Annual Survey on SLPEs by IPE			
		(iii) Contribution to Corpus Fund of NFCG			A new scheme as Research Development & Consultancy has been undertaken to initiate new activities by DPE.
		(iv) Thematic Consultancy & Studies			
		(v) Seminars, Workshops etc., on Generic Issues of CPSEs			
		Grand Total	47.74	54.00	
39		**Ministry of Personnel, Public Grievances, and Pensions**			
		Central Sector Schemes			
	1	Training for all-Support for Training Activities & Capacity Building for Project Appraisal	59.68	67.50	(1) Need to upgrade ATIs especially in lagging States like Bihar and UP after in-depth evaluation. DoPT to formulate a new CSS for strengthening State ATIs, in consultation with the State Governments. (2) The amount spent in 06–07 on Domestic Funded Foreign Training is much higher than domestic training under the scheme 'Training for All'. This needs to be rationalized. (3) EAP schemes would be consolidated and made wide spread. (4) LBSNAA needed to be upgraded to a centre of global excellence for global quality 'Mid Career Training Programme for IAS and other Apex Civil Services'. (5) Each Plan schemes of DoPT need evaluation. (6) 'e-Procurement' to be universalized in a time bound manner. (7) DoPT would submit a Plan Scheme for strengthening of State Vigilance Departments (8) The Scheme 'Public Library' implemented by the Departmrnt of Culture, may be transferred to Ministry of Human Resource Development. D/o ARPG would submit a note on setting up of public libraries network in the rural areas.
	2	Domestic Funding of Foreign Training	60.30	68.20	
	3	Grant to IIPA	8.84	10.00	
	4	Augmentation of Training facilities in ISTM	3.82	4.32	
	5	UNDP—(i) Strengthening of STIs, (ii) Citizen's Access to Information, (iii) Capacity Building for Access to Information	31.03	35.10	
	6	DFID Project for Capacity Building for Poverty Reduction (Training Component)	30.95	35.00	
	7	Improvement of Infrastructure & Upgradation of Essential Facilities at LBSNAA	0.00	0.00	
		(i) Upgradation of LBSNAA to a Centre of Excellence	95.49	108.00	
		(ii) Setting up of National Centre for Good Governance	38.02	43.00	
	8	Plan Schemes for Administrative Reforms	62.60	70.80	
	9	Setting up of Administrative Reforms Commission	14.32	16.20	
	10	Plan Scheme of CBI	0.00	0.00	
		(i) Modernization of Training Centre of CBI	4.77	5.40	
		(ii) Construction of CBI HQ Office building	52.52	59.40	
		(iii) CBI e-goverance	3.34	3.78	
	11	Plan Scheme of CIC	0.00	0.00	
		(i) Other Plan Schemes of CIC	7.16	8.10	
		(ii) New Sch. Construction of CIC Office Building	16.36	18.50	
	12	Pensioners' Portal	2.39	2.70	
		Grand Total	491.59	556.00	

1	2	3	4	5	6
40		Department of Posts			
	1	Access to Postal network	48.73	55.11	
	2	Mail Operations	416.33	470.88	
	3	Banking and Money Transfer Operations	125.99	142.50	
	4	Insurance Operations	30.95	35.00	This business needs to be expanded. Adequate initial Plan funding could be provided subject to operations being corporatized.
	5	Philately Operations	13.26	15.00	
	6	Estate management	112.12	126.81	
	7	IT Induction—Postal Operations	2387.21	2700.00	
	8	Material Management	44.21	50.00	
	9	Human Resource Management	88.81	100.45	Training programmes need to be strengthened and training facilities expanded for ensuring training for all, particularly on best practices.
	10	Marketing, Research and Product Development	263.37	297.88	
	11	Quality Management	5.63	6.37	
		Grand Total	3536.60	4000.00	
41		Ministry of Power			
	1	NHPC	0.88	1.00	No GBS for NHPC except Rs 1 crore provided during 2007–08.
	2	THDC	263.44	297.96	
	3	SJVN	291.77	330.00	
	4	NEEPCO	1821.26	2059.90	
	5	MoP (Others)			
		(i) Central Electricity Authority	115.91	131.10	
		(ii) National Power Training Institute	49.41	55.89	
		(iii) Central Power Research Institute	110.52	125.00	
		(iv) Interest Subsidy for REC-RGGVY	23432.64	26503.00	RGGVY to continue in Eleventh Plan with more focus and regular flow of funds.
		(v) Consultancy Charges & Enabling Activities for APDRP-II Project	383.72	434.00	APDRP-support to programme with 100% loan funding and depending on performance, it would be converted into grant. No GBS for APDRP-II as the amount will be raised by CPSUs (PFC & REC). APDRP to continue in Eleventh Plan with some restructuring.
		(vi) Comprehensive Award Scheme for Power Sector	1.14	1.29	
		(vii) Future Generation Project	44.21	50.00	
		(viii) BEE	149.31	168.87	
		(ix) Energy Conservation			To be merged with BEE as both are serving similar purpose.

(Appendix contd.)

1	2	3	4	5	6
		(x) Computerization & Office Equipment	4.33	4.90	Bifurcation of establishment including salary component into Plan and non-Plan from next year. Some of these components of MoP (other) may be weeded out in 2008–09 as the activities under Plan budget is over.
		(xi) Funds for Evaluation Studies & Consultancy			
		(xii) Setting up of Joint SERC			
		(xiii) Assistance for Capacity Building			
		(xiv) Scheme for Equity Gap Funding	255.52	289.00	
		Grand Total	26924.08	30451.91	
42		**Ministry of Panchayati Raj**			
	A	Central Sector Schemes			
	1	Panchayat Empowerment and Accountability Incentive Scheme	101.68	115.00	
	2	Management Cell	6.19	7.00	To be transferred to non-Plan from 2008–09.
	3	Contribution to International Organization	0.09	0.10	This can be reconstructed into non-Plan.
	4	Allocation for NER and Sikkim	77.47	87.62	
	5	External Assistance under Projects Assisted by UN Agencies	38.02	43.00	
		Total A	223.44	252.72	
	B	Centrally Sponsored Schemes			
	1	Rashtriya Gram Swaraj Yojana including Media Publicity and Advocacy	551.40	623.65	Media Publicity & Advocacy has been merged with RGSY.
		Total B	551.40	623.65	
		Grand Total (A+B)	774.84	876.37	
43		**Ministry of Planning**			
		Central Sector Schemes			
	A	Planning			
	1	Tsunami Rehabilitation Programme	14.35	16.23	
	2	Renovation & Alteration	21.53	24.35	
	3	Information Technology	4.78	5.41	
	4	Economic Advisory Council to Prime Minister	9.57	10.82	
	5	National Knowledge Commission	14.35	16.23	
	6	50th Year Initiative for Planning	57.41	64.93	
	7	Strengthening Evaluation Capacity in Government	124.39	140.69	
	8	Other General Economic Services	0.00	0.00	
		(i) Grant-in-aid to IAMR for Taking up Studies on Topics of Current Interest to Planning Commission.	14.35	16.23	
		(ii) Grant-in-aid to Universities & Research Institutions for Training, Research, Institutional Development etc.	9.57	10.82	
		(iii) Expertise for Planning Process (Payments for Professionals etc.)	4.78	5.41	

(Appendix contd.)

(Appendix contd.)

1	2	3	4	5	6
		(iv) UNDP Assistance for Capacity Building for State Human Development Reports	90.90	102.81	
		(v) UNDP Assistance for Rural Decentralization and Participatory Planning for Poverty Reduction	28.71	32.47	
		(vi) Other Expenditure (Modernization and IT etc.)	35.88	40.58	
		Total A	430.58	487.00	
	B	Energy R&D	2210.38	2500.00	
	C	Skill Development	20158.63	22800.00	
		Total (A+B+C)	22799.59	25787.00	
44		**Ministry of Petroleum & Natural Gas**			
		Rajiv Gandhi Institute of Petroleum Technology	174.18	197.00	
		Total	174.18	197.00	
45		**Ministry of Rural Development**			
		Central Sector Schemes			
	1	Assistance to CAPART	221.04	250.00	Establishment charges to be transferred to non-Plan and indepth evaluation of the organization.
	2	Grants to National Institute of Rural Development	92.84	105.00	Establishment charges to be transferred to non-Plan and indepth evaluation of the organization.
	3	Management Support to RD Programmes and Strengthening of District Planning Process in lieu of Programmes	486.28	550.00	Training under MoRD & MoPR to be integrated.
	4	EGOM on SC Welfare-Model Villages			Yet to be approved.
		Total A	800.16	905.00	
		Centrally Sponsored Schemes			
	1	NREGS	88415.06	100000.00	To be continued.
	2	Rural Housing/IAY	23767.92	26882.21	To be continued.
	3	PMGSY	38240.46	43251.07	To be continued.
	4	SGRY	4951.24	5600.00	To be phased out.
	5	SGSY	15740.53	17803.00	To be continued.
	6	DRDA Administration	187.44	212.00	To be dropped during 2007–08. To be transferred to non-Plan side under State Government.
	7	Provision for Urban Amenities in Rural Areas (PURA)	247.56	280.00	
		Total B	171550.22	194028.28	
		Grand Total (A+B)	172350.38	194933.28	

(Appendix contd.)

1	2	3	4	5	6
46		Department of Road Transport & Highways			
	A	Central Sector Schemes			
	1	Externally Aided Projects—NHAI	4454	5037.57	
		(i) Grant to NHAI	3563.2	4030.06	
		(ii) Loan to NHAI	890.8	1007.51	
	2	NH (Original) including Machinery & Equipment and Travel Expenses	16500	18662	
	3	Works under BRDB	2500	2827.55	
	4	Strategic Roads under BRDB	500	565.51	
	5	NHAI (Investment)	36238	40985.95	
	6	Special Accelerated Road Development Programme for NE	9562	10814.83	
	7	Kaladan Multi Modal Project	315.65	357.01	
	8	Rail-cum-Road Bridge at Ganga, Munger	392	443.36	
	9	Rail-cum-Road Bridge at Bogibeel, Assam	700	791.71	
	10	Other Charges & IT			
	11	R&D and Training			
	12	Charged Expenditure	200	226.2	
		Subtotal A	71361.65	80711.69	
	B	Road Transport			
	13	Road Safety$ (Model Driving Training School dropped w.e.f. 2007–08)	363.3	448	
	14	National Database Network	113.5	127	
	15	Inspection & Maintenance Centre, Strengthening of Public Transport, Creation of National Road Safety Board	523.2	556	
		Subtotal B	1000	1131	
		Total (A+B)	72361.65	81842.69	
	C	Centrally Sponsored Scheme			
	16	E&I from CRF#			
		(i) States			
		(ii) UTs	1168.35	1321.43	
		Subtotal C	1168.35	1321.43	
		Total (A+B+C)	73530.00	83164.12	

Note: $ This also includes past liabilities for 'Model Driving Training Schools'.
Includes Rs 140.85 crore for Harichandanpur-Naranpur (Rs 159.30 crore at current price) & Rs 127.50 crore (Rs 144.21 crore at current price) for Mug[illegible]al Road.

1	2	3	4	5	6
47		**Ministry of Railways**			
	1	New Lines	11493.96	13000.00	Priority would be DFC, High Density Corridors of national importance & Development of rail network in NE. GBS should be given against specific projects only and as per national priorities.
	2	Gauge Conversion	3095.00	3500.00	
	3	Traffic Facilities	1655.13	1872.00	
	4	Computerization	618.91	700.00	
	5	Bridge Works	119.36	135.00	
	6	Signalling & Telecom	2033.55	2300.00	
	7	Electrification Projects (for Tracks)	2608.24	2950.00	
	8	Other Electrical Works (Contribution towards JV with NTPC)	1679.89	1900.00	
	9	Workshops incldg. Production Units	3094.53	3500.00	
	10	Staff Quarters*	190.09	215.00	
	11	Staff Amenities	132.62	150.00	
	12	Other Specified Works*	300.00	340.00	
	13	Metropolitan Transport Project	1282.02	1450.00	
	14	Rolling Stock	4451.70	5035.00	
	15	Machinery & Plant	574.70	650.00	
	16	Investment in PSUs	5304.90	6000.00	
	17	Inventories	1878.82	2125.00	
		Total GBS for M/o Railway	40513.41	45822.00	
	18	Road Safety—LC/ROB (CESS) (Under Department of Economic Affairs)	3749.68	4241.00	
		Grand Total	44263.09	50063.00	
48		**Department of Scientific & Industrial Research (DSIR) Including CSIR**			
		CSIR			
	1	National Laboratories	5658.56	6400.00	Prioritization:—(1) Refocus outlays according to Plan objective & priorities. (2) Clear prioritization, annual financial and physical phasing, and earmarking a percentage of outlay for each scheme be done to refocus the outlays. (3) Establishment expenditure should be identified for transfer to non-Plan. Evaluation:—(1) In-depth evaluation of all ongoing schemes/programmes involving substantial outlays so that if need be, the schemes coulld be restructured/redesigned accordingly. (2) In-depth evaluation of organizational structure, management practices and functioning of all institutions should also be done for refocussing efforts in a highly competitive scientific world.
	2	National S&T Human Resource Development	707.32	800.00	
	3	Intellectual Property & Technology Development	212.20	240.00	
	4	R&D Management Support	141.46	160.00	
	5	New Millenium Indian Technology Leadership Initiative	618.91	700.00	

Note: *M/o Railways should use Plan GBS for National Projects rather than for Staff Quarters and Other specified works.

(Appendix contd.)

1	2	3	4	5	6
	6	Setting up of Institute of Translational Research	88.42	100.00	
		Total CSIR	7426.87	8400.00	
		DSIR			
	1	Technology Promotion, Development, and Utilization	358.08	405.00	Prioritization:—(1) Refocus outlays according to Plan objective & priorities. (2) Clear prioritization, annual financial and physical phasing, and earmarking a percentage of outlay for each scheme be done to refocus the outlays. (3) Establishment expenditure should be identified for transfer to non-Plan. Evaluation:—(1) In-depth evaluation of all ongoing schemes/programmes involving substantial outlays so that if need be, the schemes coulld be restructured/redesigned accordingly. (2) In-depth evaluation of organizational structure, management practices and functioning of all institutions should also be done for refocussing efforts in a highly competitive scientific world.
	2	Central Electronics Limited	44.21	50.00	
	3	National Research and Development	88.42	100.00	
	4	Consultancy Development Centre	8.84	10.00	
	5	DSIR Building & Infrastructure	30.95	35.00	
		Total DSIR	530.49	600.00	
		Grand Total (CSIR + DSIR)	7957.36	9000.00	
49		**Department of Higher Education**			
	A	Central Sector Schemes			
	I	ONGOING SCHEMES			
	1	University and Higher Education (including OSC)	12492.78	14129.70	
	2	Distance Learning	582.96	659.35	
	3	Rashtriya Sanskrit Sansthan	154.73	175.00	
	4	Book Promotion	61.89	70.00	
	5	Planning & Administration	69.06	78.11	
	6	Technical Education (including OSC)	11391.07	12883.63	
		New Schemes			
	1	IGNOU—Skill Dev. Mission (Vocational Education and Training)	44.21	50.00	
	2	New 210 Community Colleges (NGOs) Skill Dev. Mission	88.42	100.00	
	3	Inter Universities Research Institute for Policy & Evaluation (UGC)	88.42	100.00	
	4	Expansion and upgradation of 200 State Engineering Insitutions	804.58	910.00	
	5	Upgrading 7 technical institutions	618.91	700.00	
	6	2 IISERs (Pune & Kolkata)	707.32	800.00	

(Appendix contd.)

(*Appendix contd.*)

1	2	3	4	5	6
	7	Setting up of 2 New SPAs	212.20	240.00	
	8	Establishing 50 Centres for Training and Research in Frontier Areas	132.62	150.00	
	9	Faculty Development (AICTE)	839.94	950.00	
	II	SPECIAL PLAN FOR HIGHER EDUCATION			
	1	16 New Central Universities in uncovered States	1768.30	2000.00	
	2	5 Medical and Engineering Colleges in New CU	884.15	1000.00	
	3	14 World Class Central Universities (WCCU)	2475.62	2800.00	
	4	5 Medical and Engineering Colleges in WCCU	1503.06	1700.00	
	5	Setting up of 370 Degree Colleges	691.41	782.00	
	6	Incentivizing States for Expansion, Inclusion, and Excellence	5481.73	6200.00	
	7	Supporting uncovered State Universities (150) and Colleges (6000)	6189.05	7000.00	
	8	Addl. Assistance to already covered Universities (160)/colleges (5500)	2652.45	3000.00	
	9	Strengthening Science-based Higher Education & Research in Universities.	1060.98	1200.00	
	10	National Education Mission through ICT (including OSC)	4420.75	5000.00	
	III	TECHNICAL EDUCATION			
	1	Expansion of National level/Advanced Institutes:			
		(i) Setting up of 8 New IITs	1768.30	2000.00	
		(ii) Setting up of 20 New NITs	442.08	500.00	
		(iii) Setting up of 20 New IIITs	831.10	940.00	
		(iv) Setting up of 3 IISERs (Mohali, TVN, Bhopal)	795.74	900.00	
		(v) Setting up of 7 New IIMs	583.54	660.00	
	2	Increase of fellowship amounts for MTech Students	884.15	1000.00	
	IV	SKILL DEVELOPMENT THROUGH VOCATIONAL TRAINING			
	3	580 New Community Polytechnics	512.81	580.00	
	4	Support to Engineering Colleges for Diploma Courses	884.15	1000.00	
	5	Women's Hostel in 500 Polytechnics	442.08	500.00	
	V	OTHERS			
	1	Increase Research Fellowship for NET Qualified and non-NET Qualified PhD Students	2033.55	2300.00	
	2	Educational Loan Interest Subsidy	3536.60	4000.00	
	3	Scholarship for 2% of the Total Students	884.15	1000.00	
	4	Construction of Girls' Hostels	884.15	1000.00	

(*Appendix contd.*)

(*Appendix contd.*)

1	2	3	4	5	6
	5	Reduction of Regional Imbalances/Social Gaps & Promotion of Inclusiveness			
		(i) Higher Education	1892.97	2141.00	
		(ii) Technical Education	884.15	1000.00	
		Total A	72676.11	82198.79	
	B	Centrally Sponsored Schemes			
	1	Setting up of new Polytechnics & Strengthening of Existing Polytechnics			
		(i) Establishment of New Polytechnics in unserved Districts, Establishment of 300 Polytechnics in PPP and 400 in Private Sector	1167.08	1320.00	
		(ii) Strengtheing of 400 Polytechnics	884.15	1000.00	
	2	Area Intensive & Madarsa Modernization Programme	308.57	349.00	
	3	Appointment of Language Teachers	66.31	75.00	
		Total B	2426.11	2744.00	
		Total (A+B)	75102.22	84942.79	
50		**Department of Shipping**			
	1	DG (Shipping)	58.35	66.00	Further allocation depends on in-depth evaluation of all on-going schemes by professional agencies. Scheme of maritime development-professional services involving Rs 0.27 crore for 2007–08 should go to non-Plan.
	2	Indian Maritime University	265.25	300.00	
	3	DG (Light house and Light ships)	132.62	150.00	
	4	IWT Sector	543.75	615.00	Allocation for three new national waterways should be limited to development and should not include maintenance.
	5	Ship Building and Repairs	150.31	170.00	
	6	Major Ports (KoPT, MbPT, JNPT, ChPT, CoPT, VPT, KPT, MoPT, PPT, NMPT, TPT, EPL)	1818.68	2056.98	All 12 individual schemes for major ports be merged into one composite scheme as 'Investment in Infrastructure Development in Major Ports' and allocation to individual ports should be project based. GBS requirement of Rs 100 crore for VGF for infrastructure development under PPP projects be provided in case it could not be made available out of DoEA budget.
	7	ALHW	235.51	266.37	
	8	Others*	1260.49	1425.65	Post Tsunami Works requires close monitoring by DoS. Survey Vessels should be transferred to M/o Defence.
		Grand Total	4464.96	5050.00	

Note: *Includes Post-Tsunami Works, Development of Deep Sea Ports, Survey Vessels, R&D, Sethusamudram Project, Assistance to Minor Ports, and Web-based EDI.

(*Appendix contd.*)

1	2	3	4	5	6
51		**Ministry of Social Justice & Empowerment**			
	A	Central Sector Schemes			
	I	BACKWARD CLASSES SECTOR (SCs & OBC)			
	1	Special Central Assistance (SCA) to Special Component Plan (SCP)	2714.09	3069.71	
	2	National Finance Development Corporations for Weaker Sections	381.07	431.00	
	3	GIA to NGOs for SCs, OBCs & Research & Training	221.04	250.00	To be merged with 'GIA for Research, Training, Information, and Miscellaneous' and to be rechristened as 'GIA for Research, Training, Information, and Miscellaneous'.
	4	Rajiv Gandhi National Fellowship for SCs	508.17	574.75	
	5	Top Class Education for SCs	180.81	204.50	
	6	Dr. B.R. Ambedkar Foundation	5.53	6.25	
	7	Self-Employment Scheme for Rehabilitation of Manual Scavengers	309.45	350.00	
		New Schemes under CS			
	8	National Overseas Scholarships Scheme for SCs.	110.52	125.00	
	II	SOCIAL WELFARE			
	9	Scheme for Funding to National Institutes	317.41	359.00	
	10	Artificial Limbs Manufacturing Corporation, Kanpur (ALIMCO)	10.61	12.00	
	11	Scheme of Assistance to Disabled Person for Purchasing/Fitting of Aids & Appliances	442.08	500.00	
	12	Scheme to Promote Voluntary Action for Persons with Disabilities (Deen Dayal Disabled Rehabilitation Scheme)	442.08	500.00	
	13	Implementation of the Persons with Disabilities (PWD) Act, 1995.	22.10	25.00	
	14	Assistance to Voluntary Organizations for providing Social Defence Services including Prevention of Alcoholism & Drug Abuse	243.14	275.00	
	15	Assistance to Voluntary Organizations for Programmes related to Aged			To be merged together as 'Assistance to Panchayati Raj Institutions/Voluntary Organizations/Self Help Group for Programmes related to Aged' and construction of old age home can be taken as one component of it.
	16	Assistance to Panchayati Raj Institutions/Voluntary Organizations/ SHGs for construction of Old Age Homes/Multi Services Centres for Older Persons	181.25	205.00	
	17	Grant-in-aid for Research, Training, Information and Miscellaneous	66.31	75.00	To be merged with GIA to NGO for SCs, OBCs, & Research & Training and rechristened as 'GIA for Research, Training, Information and Miscellaneous'.
		Total A	6155.65	6962.21	

(Appendix contd.)

1	2	3	4	5	6
	B	Centrally Sponsored Schemes			
	1	Post-Matric Scholarships & Book Banks for SC students	3609.10	4082.00	
	2	Pre-Matric Scholarship for Children of those Families Engaged in Unclean Occupation	176.83	200.00	
	3	Hostels for SC and OBC	512.81	580.00	
	4	Scheduled Caste Development Corporation (SCDCs)	77.81	88.00	
	5	National Handicapped Finance and Development Corporation (NHFDC)	27.23	30.80	
	6	Coaching and Allied Scheme for SCs/OBCs & other Weaker Sections	101.68	115.00	
	7	Upgradation of Merit of SC Students	8.84	10.00	
	8	Implementation of PCR Act,1955 & the SC/ST(POA) Act,1989	8.84	10.00	To be transferred to States.
	9	Merit based Scholarships for OBC	853.21	965.00	
		(i) Post-Matric Scholarship for OBCs	618.91	700.00	
		(ii) Pre-Matric Scholarship for OBCs	234.30	265.00	
	10	Setting up of Residential Schools for SCs for Pursuing Studying in Class VI to XII			
		Total B	5376.34	6080.80	
		Grand Total (A+B)	11531.99	13043.01	
52		Ministry of Statistics and Programme Implementation			
	A	Central Sector Schemes			
	1	India Statistical Strenthening Project (Modernization of Statistical System of India)	79.57	90.00	
	2	Addition/Alteration and Modernization of Office Building	0.35	0.40	May be transferred to non-Plan.
	3	Capacity Development of CSO	59.48	67.27	To be merged with scheme at S. No. 4, i.e., Capacity Development of NSSO and renamed as 'Capacity Development' having different components.
	4	Improvement of National Accounts Statistics			
	5	Development of Social, Environment, and Price Statistics			
	6	Improvement of Informal Sector Statistics			
	7	Capacity Development of NSSO	216.62	245.00	
	8	Strengthening of Field Operations of NSSO	0.00	0.00	
	9	Strengthening of Data Processing Capacity of NSSO	0.00	0.00	
	10	Strengthening of Survey Design and Research Capabilities of NSSO	0.00	0.00	
	11	Grants-in-aid to States for Carrying Out NSS Survey Work in NER	0.00	0.00	
	12	Strengthening of Data Processing, Storage, and Dissemination of Computer Centre	9.40	10.63	To be renamed as 'Strengthening of Computer Centre'.
	13	Grants-in-aid to Indian Statistical Institute, Kolkata	79.57	90.00	

(Appendix contd.)

(Appendix contd.)

1	2	3	4	5	6
	14	Institutional Development and Capacity Building for Project Planning, Implementation, Monitoring, and Performance Management of Infrastructure in Public Sector	8.84	10.00	To be renamed as 'Monitoring & Evaluation and Information, Education, and Communication'.
	15	Institutional Development and Capacity Building (PI Wing)			Ministry to expeditiously conduct in-depth and independent evaluation of its schemes and institutions and use findings for restructuring/reorientation of the same and Plan funding in 2008–09 for these scheme would depend on this.
	16	Institutional Development and Capacity Building (Statistics Wing)			
	17	Fifth Economic Census	69.85	79.00	
	18	Basic Statistics			
		Total A	523.68	592.30	
	B	Centrally Sponsored Schemes			
	1	Basic Statistics for Local Level Development MPLADS	6.81	7.70	
		Total B	6.81	7.70	
		Grand Total (A+B)	530.49	600.00	
53		Ministry of Steel			
	1	Hindustan Steelworks Construction Ltd (for AMR)	30.95	35.00	AMR is for a manufacturing unit and not for a servicing unit. HSCL is a servicing unit.
	2	MECON Ltd (for Approved Restructuring Package)	55.70	63.00	CPSEs should meet their AMR requirement from internal resources (IR) and only project based support would be provided. Restructuring package should be on commercial viability.
	3	Bird Group of Companies	0.88	1.00	
	4	Scheme for Promotion of Research & Development in Iron and Steel Sector	104.33	118.00	
		Grand Total	191.86	217.00	
54		Department of Science & Technology			
	1	Research & Development Support	2829.28	3200.00	
	2	Technology Development Programme	265.25	300.00	
	3	S&T Programme For Socio-economic Development	353.66	400.00	
	4	International Co-operation	221.04	250.00	
	5	State Science & Technology Programme	88.42	100.00	
	6	Modernization of Mapping Professional Bodies (SOI & NATMO)	176.83	200.00	
	7	Autonomous Institutions & Professional Bodies	2046.81	2315.00	
	8	Vocational Employment Generation	2.65	3.00	
	9	Technology For Bamboo Products (Mission Mode Project)	70.73	80.00	
	10	Synergy Projects (O/O Principal Scientific Adviser)	30.95	35.00	
	11	Information Technology	13.26	15.00	
	12	National Training Programme For Scientists/Technologist Working with GoI	26.52	30.00	

(Appendix contd.)

1	2	3	4	5	6
	13	Drugs & Pharmaceuticals Research	442.08	500.00	
	14	National Mission For Nano-Science & Nanotechnology	884.15	1000.00	
	15	Science & Engineering Research Board*			
	16	Scholarships For Science In Higher Education (Oversight Committee Recommendation)	1326.23	1500.00	
	17	Water Technology Initiative	44.21	50.00	
	18	INSPIRE	663.11	750.00	
	19	Innovation Clusters	44.21	50.00	
	20	Security Technology Initiative	44.21	50.00	
	21	Mega Facilities For Basic Research	176.83	200.00	
		Grand Total	9750.41	11028.00	
55		**Department of Space**			
	1	Launch Vehicle Missions			
		(i) GSLV MKI	17.68	20.00	
		(ii) GSLV Operational	1998.18	2260.00	
		(iii) Cryogenic Upper Stage Project (CUSP)	4.42	5.00	
		(iv) GSLV MK III Development	1198.91	1356.00	
		(v) GSLV MK III Operational	499.55	565.00	
		(vi) PSLV-C	1628.61	1842.00	
		Subtotal 1	5347.34	6048.00	
	2	Earth Observation Mission			
		(i) Oceansat-2 & 3	199.82	226.00	
		(ii) Radar Imaging Satellite	150.31	170.00	
		(iii) Resourcesat-2 & 3	199.82	226.00	
		(iv) GEO HR Imager	274.97	311.00	
		(v) Cartosat-3	299.73	339.00	
		(vi) Altika-Argoes	99.91	113.00	
		(vii) Technology Experiment Satellites	299.73	339.00	
		(viii) Disaster Management Satellite (DM-SAR)	299.73	339.00	
		(ix) E O Followon Satellites	299.73	339.00	
		Subtotal 2	2123.73	2402.00	
	3	Space Science Mission			
		(i) Chandrayan-1 & 2	449.15	508.00	
		(ii) Megha Trpiques	60.12	68.00	
		(iii) Astrosat 1 & 2	199.82	226.00	
		(iv) Advanced Planetary Missions	299.73	339.00	
		(v) Small Satellites for Atmospheric Research & Astronomy	199.82	226.00	
		Subtotal 3	1208.63	1367.00	

Note: *Included in S. No. 1.

(*Appendix contd.*)

1	2	3	4	5	6
	4	INSAT Satellites			
		(i) INSAT-3 satellite	53.05	60.00	
		(ii) GSAT-4	26.52	30.00	
		(iii) GSAT-5/INSAT-4D	70.73	80.00	
		(iv) GSAT-6/INSAT-4E	176.83	200.00	A clear prioritization, annual financial and physical phasing and earmarking a percentage of the total outlay for each scheme be done so as to refocus the outlays according to the Plan objectives and priorities and use available resources in the most judicious and economically efficient manner, rather than spreading it thin and not achieving the main objectives Other decisions:—(i) DOS would undertake in-depth evaluation and impact assessment study of its ongoing plans/programmes. (ii) For developing application oriented programmes, more concerted efforts are needed to strengthen the organic linkage with the related ministries and State Governments. (iii) Application of Space Sciences needs to be upscaled in the States and DOS would prepare a comprehensive action plan for the Eleventh Plan. (iv)Concerted efforts to be made for integration of indigenous development of satellites, launch vehicles, and associated ground segments. (v) utilization of EDUSAT to be maximized and modernized. (vi) A presentation to be made by DOS on full application of remote sensing in agriculture and urban planning in the presence of concerned stakeholders. (vii) The Disaster Management Initiatives, prepared by the Disaster Management Authority need to be integrated with DOS programmes.
		(v) GSAT-8/INSAT-4G	599.45	678.00	
		(vi) INSAT-4CR	49.51	56.00	
		(vii) INSAT-4/GSAT Satellites (GSAT-9 to GSAT-14)	1498.64	1695.00	
		(viii) Advanced Communication Technology Satellites	804.58	910.00	
		(ix) INSAT Capacity Augmentation (Short Term)	99.91	113.00	
		(x) INSAT/GSAT Followon Satellites	199.82	226.00	
		Subtotal 4	3579.04	4048.00	
	5	Satellite Navigation	2397.82	2712.00	
	6	Advanced Launch Vehicle Development	0.00	0.00	
		(i) Semi Cryogenic Engine/Stage Development	499.55	565.00	
		(ii) Human Space Flight	1591.47	1800.00	
		(iii) Space capsure Recovery experiment-SRE	79.57	90.00	
		(iv) Reusable Launch Vehicle Technologies	199.82	226.00	
		Subtotal 5	2370.41	2681.00	
	7	Major Space Applications and Space Science Research			
		(i) Remote sensing application (inc. NNRMS, NR CENSUS, RSAM, NRSA, NESAC etc.)	649.85	735.00	
		(ii) Disaster Management Support	199.82	226.00	
		(iii) SATCOM Application Programme	299.73	339.00	
		(iv) Space Science & Environment (inc. PRL, NARL)	599.45	678.00	
		Subtotal 6	1748.85	1978.00	
	8	Information Technology Related Applications			
		(i) National Natural Resources Database	35.37	40.00	
		(ii) Village Resource Centres	249.33	282.00	
		(iii) EDUSAT IT Network	141.46	160.00	
		(iv) Telemedicine Network	88.42	100.00	
		Subtotal 7	514.58	582.00	
	9	R&D, Technology, and Process Development			
		(i) Technology Development Programme/R&D/Small Satellites/ Development of Semiconductor Technology	799.27	904.00	
		(ii) Development of Space Material & Component & Advance Actions	799.27	904.00	
		(iii) Sponsored Research	99.91	113.00	
		Subtotal 8	1698.45	1921.00	

1	2	3	4	5	6
	10	Infrastructure/Auxilliary Facilities/Capacity Building for Space Programme			
		(i) Indian Institute of Space Science & Technology/HRD	399.64	452.00	
		(ii) Technical Facilities Replacement/Augmenation	1998.18	2260.00	
		(iii) Industry Interface and Productionization	299.73	339.00	
		(iv) International Co-operation Programme	22.10	25.00	
		(v) Technical & Auxiliary Facilities Support	2997.27	3390.00	
		(vi) General Civil Works & Housing	599.45	678.00	
		Subtotal 9	6316.37	7144.00	
		Grand Total	27305.22	30883.00	
56		**Department of Telecommunications**			
	1	Indian Telephone Industry (ITI)—Residual Commitment towards sanctioned revival	93.60	105.87	ITI to prepare bankable business plan for Eleventh Plan proposal through a professional agency. ITI to explore possibility for selling some real estate assets to meet its revival needs.
	2	Wireless Monitoring Organization (WMO)	110.00	124.42	
	3	Wireless Planning & Co-ordination (WPC) Wing	11.40	12.89	
	4	Telecom Regulatory Authority of India (TRAI)	15.00	16.97	
	5	Telecom Disputes Settlement & Appellate Tribunal (TDSAT)	8.00	9.05	
	6	Telecom Engineering Centre (TEC)	50.00	56.55	
	7	Centre for Development of Telematics (C-DOT) and Telecom Security Certification Centre (TETC)	655.01	740.84	TETC has been made part of C-DOT.
	8	Undersea Cabling between Mainland and Andaman & Nicobar (A&N) Islands (UMA&N)	181.00	204.72	
	9	Technical assistance in Telecom Sector (TAT)	25.00	28.28	TAT should be renamed suitably to reflect its function.
	10	Optical Fibre Cable Network for Defense Services	400.01	452.42	
		Grand Total	1549.03	1752.00	
57		**Ministry of Textiles**			
	A	Central Sector Schemes			
	1	Handlooms	1211.48	1370.45	All the schemes have been merged into 5 major components of this sector.
	2	Handicrafts	861.97	975.07	
	3	Sericulture	417.72	472.54	Only 4 major schemes would be under operation in this sector. The Catalytic Development Programme would be implemented as CSS.
	4	Powerlooms	101.46	114.78	
	5	Wool Development Board	59.37	67.16	
		Total VSE	2652.00	3000.00	

(Appendix contd.)

1	2	3	4	5	6
	1	NIFT	44.21	50.00	Provision for Rai Bareili centre upto 2008–09 and beyond would be restricted to one centre only.
	2	R&D including TRAs	8.84	10.00	
	3	Technology Upgradation Fund (TUFS)	7073.21	8000.00	TUFS might continue up to 31.03.09 and commitments have to be calibrated to avoid any spillover liability. It could be considered for 2008–09 and subsequently only after in depth evaluation.
	4	Scheme for Integrated Textile Park	1768.30	2000.00	Rapid assessment study through an independent agency of at least 5–6 park before further disbursal of GBS.
	5	Jute Technology Mission	314.76	356.00	
	6	Export Promotion Studies	4.42	5.00	Further funding is subject to independent and in-depth evaluation of institutions/schemes.
	7	SVPITM—Coimbatore	11.49	13.00	
	8	Brand Promotion (New Scheme from 07–08)			Regarding new scheme, due procedure has to be followed as prescribed by Planning Commission and D/o Expenditure.
	9	Foreign Promotin Scheme FDI CELL (New Scheme from 07–08)	202.47	229.00	FDI Cell could be merged with Export Promotion Studies at S. No. 6.
	10	Textilpolis (New Scheme from 07–08)			It would be appropriate to have one composite scheme for Textilpolis & Fashion Hub.
	11	Fashion Hub (New Scheme from 07–08)			
	12	Common Compliance Code (New Scheme from 07–08)			
	13	HRD (New Scheme from 07–08)			
	14	Textile engineering (New Scheme from 07–08)			MoT to formulate the scheme in consultation with DHI.
	15	Technical Textiles (New Scheme from 07–08)	84.88	96.00	
		Total A	12164.58	13759.00	
	B	Centrally Sponsored Schemes			
	16	Cotton Technology Mission	213.08	241.00	
		Total B	213.08	241.00	
		Grand Total (A+B)	12377.66	14000.00	
58		**Ministry of Tourism**			
		Central Sector Schemes			
	1	Externally Aided Projects			
		(i) Buddhist Centres	32.71	37.00	
		(ii) UNDP Endogenous Projects	1.77	2.00	
	2	Assistance to IHMs/FCIs/etc.	437.65	495.00	
	3	Capacity Building for Service Providers	83.99	95.00	

(Appendix contd.)

1	2	3	4	5	6
	4	Overseas Promotion & Publicity including Market Development Assistance	892.99	1010.00	(1) Ministry would restructure its scheme of Assistance to Central Agencies for Tourism Infrastructure Development. (2) In-depth evaluation of Domestic and Overseas Promotion and Publicity should be done on priority and findings incorporated for more effective campaign. (3) The scheme of Large Revenue Generating Project and Incentive to accommodation infrastructure are not justified since the private sector should create these as commercial ventures. (4) Scheme of Capacity Building for Service Providers to be restructured to include NGOs for conducting the programmes. The scheme is to train persons engaged in tourism services. (5) The scheme Infrastructure Development for Destinations and Circuits is justified only in PPP mode. (6) MoT would create an interactive tourist portal for both domestic and international tourists.
	5	Domestic Promotion & Publicity including Hospitality	376.65	426.00	
	6	Incentives to Accommodation Infrastructure	207.78	235.00	
	7	Construction of Buildings for IISM at Gulmarg, Kashmir (J&K Package)	11.49	13.00	
	8	Computerization & Information Technology	106.98	121.00	
	9	Market Research including 20 Years Perspective Plan	25.64	29.00	
	10	Assistance for Large Revenue Generating Projects	176.83	200.00	
	11	Creation of Lead Bank Hotels	12.38	14.00	
	12	Equity Contribution to ITDC (Equity up to 07–08 only)	64.54	73.00	
	13	Assitance to Central Agencies for Tourism Infrastructure Development	22.10	25.00	
		Total A	2453.52	2775.00	
		Centrally Sponsored Schemes			
	1	Product/Infrastructure Development for Destinations and Circuits	2105.16	2381.00	
		Total B	2105.16	2381.00	
		Grand Total (A+B)	4558.68	5156.00	
59		**Ministry of Tribal Affairs**			
		Central Sector Schemes			
	1	Grant-in-aid to NGOs for Coaching ST Students for Competitive Exams	265.25	300.00	
	2	Vocational Training Centres in Tribal Areas	88.03	99.56	
	3	Educational Complexes in Low Literacy Pockets	264.18	298.79	
	4	Investment in TRIFED and Price support	61.53	69.59	
	5	Grant-in-aid to STDCs for MFP Village Grain Banks	153.84	174.00	
	6	Development of Primitive Tribal Groups (PTGs)	592.38	670.00	
	7	Support to National ST Finance & Development Corporation and GIA to State ST Dev. & Finance Corporations	229.88	260.00	
	8	Construction of Adivasi Bhavan in New Delhi			
	9	Fellowship programme for ST students	139.17	157.41	
		(i) Rajiv Gandhi Fellowship	132.62	150.00	
		(ii) National Overseas Scholarships Scheme (New Scheme)	6.55	7.41	
		New Schemes under CS			
	10	National Institute of Tribal Affairs (NITA)			Yet to be approved.
	11	Scheme of Institute of Excellence/Top Class Education	65.25	73.80	
		Total A	1859.50	2103.15	

(*Appendix contd.*)

(Appendix contd.)

1	2	3	4	5	6
	B	Centrally Sponsored Schemes			
	1	Scheme of PMS, Book Banks, and Upgradation of Merit of ST Students	1322.95	1496.29	
	2	Scheme of Hostels for ST Students	241.34	272.96	
	3	Ashram Schools in TSP Areas	130.50	147.60	This scheme should be evaluated and should be merged with 'Educational Complexes in Low Literacy Pockets'.
	4	Research & Mass Education, Tribal Festivals, and Others	78.35	88.62	
		Total B	1773.14	2005.47	
		Grand Total (A+B)	3632.64	4108.62	
60		**Ministry of Urban Development**			
	A	Central Sector Schemes			
	1	Contribution to NCR Planning Board	795.74	900.00	
	2	Research, Development, and Capacity Building and Upgradation of Institutions + UNDP Programme + CPWD training	110.52	125.00	
	3	Global Environment Facility	4.42	5.00	
	4	National Mission Mode Project on e-Governance	515.46	583.00	
	5	Urban Transport Planning and Capacity Building	134.39	152.00	
	6	Urban Transport under Metro Head	1856.72	2100.00	
	7	Passthrough Assistance from JBIC	1063.63	1203.00	
	8	Equity to HUDCO for Urban Infrastructure and Water Supply	0.00		
	9	Computerization	8.84	10.00	
	10	Pilot Project on Solid Waste Management near Airport in few Selected Cities	17.68	20.00	To be completed during 2007–08.
	11	General Pool Accommodation (Residential)	1564.95	1770.00	
	12	General Pool Accommodation (Non-residential)	972.57	1100.00	
	13	Modernization of CPWD/Computerization	44.21	50.00	
	14	CPWD Training Institute	23.87	27.00	
	15	NE Lumpsum Provision	707.32	800.00	
	16	Commonwealth Games/Games Village	287.35	325.00	
	17	National Urban Infrastrudture Fund	0.88	1.00	
	18	Assisance for ULBs Capacity Building from UNDP	26.52	30.00	
	19	City Challenge Fund			
	20	Pooled Finance Development Fund	2210.38	2500.00	
	21	National Urban Information System	7.96	9.00	To be completed during 2007–08.
	22	Adminstrative Expenses for JNNURM	176.83	200.00	

(Appendix contd.)

(Appendix contd.)

1	2	3	4	5	6
		New Schemes			
	23	Urban Infrastructure Dev. in Satellite Cities/Counter-Magnet Cities (Non-NCR)	442.08	500.00	
		Total A	10972.31	12410.00	
	B	Centrally Sponsored Schemes			
	1	Mega City Scheme			
	2	IDSMT (Including CUISS)			Subsumed under JNNURM.
	3	AUWSP	28.73	32.50	To be completed during 2007–08.
		Total B	28.73	32.50	
		Grand Total (A+B)	11001.04	12442.50	
61		**Ministry of Housing and Urban Poverty Alleviation**			
		Central Sector Schemes			
	A	BMTPC	31.83	36.00	
	1	Grant to NCHF	2.65	3.00	
	2	UNDP Assistance for National Strategy for Urban Poor	4.42	5.00	
	3	NE Lumpsum Provision	176.83	200.00	
	4	Computerization	4.42	5.00	
	5	Building Centres Scheme	4.42	5.00	
	6	Administrative Expenses for JNNURM	61.89	70.00	
	7	MIS on Housing, Data, Research & Survey	30.95	35.00	
	8	HUDCO Equity for Housing			
		Total A	317.41	359.00	
	B	Centrally Sponsored Schemes			
	1	Integrated Low Cost sanitation	176.83	200.00	
	2	SJSRY	1547.26	1750.00	
	3	Interest Subsidy Scheme for Housing to Urban Poor	1218.36	1378.00	
		Total B	2942.45	3328.00	
		Grand Total (A+B)	3259.86	3687.00	
62		**Ministry of Water Resources**			
		Central Sector Schemes			
	1	Development of Water Resource Management System	154.73	175.00	
	2	Hydrology Project	159.15	180.00	
	3	Groundwater Management and Regulation	349.24	395.00	

(Appendix contd.)

(Appendix contd.)

1	2	3	4	5	6
	4	Investigation for WR Development Scheme	194.51	220.00	
	5	Research And Development	260.82	295.00	
	6	National Water Academy	13.26	15.00	
	7	Rajiv Gandhi National Institute of Training and Research	22.10	25.00	
	8	Information, Education, and Communication (New Scheme)	44.21	50.00	
	9	Pagladiya Dam Project	486.28	550.00	
	10	Farakka Barrage Project	145.88	165.00	MOWR would prepare and continuously update water availability and quality maps in consultation with the MoE&F and share the same with all stakeholders.
	11	Dam Safety Studies And Planning	44.21	50.00	
	12	River Basin Organization/Authority (New Scheme)	8.84	10.00	
	13	Flood Forecasting	110.52	125.00	
	14	River Management Activities and Works related to Border Areas	787.78	891.00	
	15	Infrastructure Development	88.42	100.00	
		Total A	2869.95	3246.00	
		Grand Total	2869.95	3246.00	
63		**Department of Women and Child Development**			
	A	Central Sector Schemes			
	I	CHILD DEVELOPMENT	645.43	730.00	
	1	Rajeev Gandhi National Creche Scheme for Children of Working Mothers	486.28	550.00	To be revamped and converted to Centrally Sponsored Scheme.
	2	National Commission for Protection of Child Rights (NCPCR)	30.95	35.00	All GIA schemes to be merged under one heading and institute/organization under CS can be taken as component.
	3	NIPCCD	30.95	35.00	Its function and acheivement to be evaluated by independent agency. All GIA schemes to be merged under one heading and institute/organization under CS can be taken as component.
	4	Conditional Cash Transfer Scheme for the Girl Child with Insurance Cover (New Scheme)	70.73	80.00	
	5	Comprehensive Scheme on Combating Trafficking of Women & Children (New Scheme)	26.52	30.00	
	II	WOMEN EMPOWERMENT	637.47	721.00	
	6	Hostel for Working Women	66.31	75.00	Operation and maintainance cost to be met through user charges.
	7	STEP	88.42	100.00	To be converted to Centrally Sponsored Scheme and merged with Swayamsidha.
	8	NCW	22.10	25.00	Its function and acheivement to be evaluated by independent agency. All GIA schemes to be merged under one heading and institute/organization under CS can be taken as component.

(Appendix contd.)

(Appendix contd.)

1	2	3	4	5	6
	9	RMK	95.49	108.00	To be integrated with Swayamsidha.
	10	Swadhar	95.49	108.00	
	11	GIA to CSWB	229.88	260.00	Its function and acheivement to be evaluated by independent agency. All GIA schemes to be merged under one heading and institute/organization under CS can be taken as component.
	12	Scheme for Relief and Rehabilitation of Victims of Rape (New Scheme)	22.10	25.00	
	13	Gender Budgeting (New Scheme)	17.68	20.00	
		Other Grants-in-aid	145.88	165.00	
	14	GIA to Research, Publication, and Monitoring	13.26	15.00	
	15	Inovative Work on Women & Children	17.68	20.00	All GIA schemes to be merged together.
	16	Information, Mass Edu., and Publication	66.31	75.00	
	17	Information Technology	4.42	5.00	To be merged under 'Information, Education, and Communication'.
	18	Nutrition Education (FNB)	44.21	50.00	Its function and acheivement to be evaluated by independent agency. All GIA schemes to be merged under one heading and institute/organisation under CS can be taken as component.
		Total A	1428.79	1616.00	
	B	Centrally Sponsored Schemes			
	I	CHILD DEVELOPMENT	46394.92	52474.00	
	1	Integrated Child Development Services (ICDS) including Training			
		(i) Restructured ICDS	37487.99	42400.00	
		(ii) Conditional Maternity Benefit for Pregnant and Lactating Mothers	7957.36	9000.00	
	2	National Nutrition Mission (NNM)	0.88	1.00	
	3	Integrated Child Protection Scheme (ICPS)	948.69	1073.00	
	II	WOMEN'S EMPOWERMENT	543.75	615.00	
	4	Integrated Women's Empowerment Programme (Swayamsiddha)	442.08	500.00	STEP to be merged with Swayamsidha.
	5	Priyadarshini Scheme	83.99	95.00	
	6	Scheme for Leadership Development of Minority Women (New Scheme)	17.68	20.00	
	III	SCHEMES TRANSFERRED FROM THE MINISTRY OF SOCIAL JUSTICE & EMPOWERMENT	53.05	60.00	
	7	Scheme for the Welfare of Working Children in need of Care & Protection	8.84	10.00	To be integrated with ICPS.
	8	Integrated Scheme for Street Children	13.26	15.00	To be merged with ICPS.

(Appendix contd.)

1	2	3	4	5	6
	9	Shishu Greh Scheme	4.42	5.00	
	10	Scheme for Prevention and Control of Juvenile Social Maladjustment	22.10	25.00	
	11	Central Adoption Resource Agency (CARA)	4.42	5.00	
		Total B	46991.72	53149.00	
		Grand Total (A+B)	48420.51	54765.00	
64		Ministry of Youth and Sports Affairs			
	A	Youth Affairs			
	1	National Service Scheme—a CSS	375.76	425.00	
	2	Nehru Yuva Kendra Sangathan (NYKS)	397.87	450.00	
	3	Rajeev Gandhi National Institute of Youth Dev.	35.37	40.00	
	4	Youth Hostels	10.61	12.00	To be discontinued after completion of ongoing projects.
	5	Volunters' Scheme			
		(i) National Service Volunteer Scheme (NSVS)	69.85	79.00	
		(ii) Rashtriya Sadbhavana Yojana (RSY)	42.44	48.00	To be merged with Nehru Yuva Kendra Sangathan.
	6	Fin. Assist. for Prom. of Adolescents & Youth Development			
		(i) Promotion of Youth Activities & Trg.	30.95	35.00	
		(ii) Promotion of National Integration	70.73	80.00	To be merged together under 'National Programme for Youth & Adolescent's Development'.
		(iii) Dev. & Empowerment of Adolescents	123.78	140.00	
		(iv) Promotion of adventure	17.68	20.00	
	7	Promotion of Scouting & Guiding	13.26	15.00	
	8	International Co-operation	17.68	20.00	
		Total A	1205.98	1364.00	
	B	Sports & Physical Education			
	10	GIA to Institutions	979.64	1108.00	
		(i) Sports Authority of India	928.36	1050.00	
		(ii) Laxmi Bai National Institute of Phy. Edn. (LNIPE)	48.63	55.00	
		(iii) National Physical Fitness Prog. (under LNIPE)	2.65	3.00	
	11	Panchayat Yuva Krida aur Khel Abhiyan (Incl. existing Rural Sports Prog.)	1326.23	1500.00	
	12	Assistance to National Sports Federations	327.14	370.00	
	13	Incentives to Sports Persons and for Promotion of Sports Trg. Acivities	141.46	160.00	
	14	Prom. of Sports among Persons with Disability	30.95	35.00	
	15	Anti-Doping (Incl. WADA contribution)	17.68	20.00	
	16	Mega/Multi-Sporting Event	2.65	3.00	
	17	Commonwealth Games—2010 (Incl. GYG-2008, Pune)	1096.35	1240.00	
	18	Other New Initiatives	176.83	200.00	
		Total B	4098.92	4636.00	
		Grand Total (A+B)	5304.90	6000.00	